Chaplain
R. Prescott. Laundrie
Sea View Hosp
Staten Island 14
N.Y.

THE BOOK OF SAINTS

THE MACMILLAN COMPANY
NEW YORK · BOSTON · CHICAGO · DALLAS
ATLANTA · SAN FRANCISCO
MACMILLAN AND CO., Limited
LONDON · BOMBAY · CALCUTTA · MADRAS
MELBOURNE
THE MACMILLAN COMPANY
OF CANADA, Limited
TORONTO

THE
BOOK OF SAINTS

A DICTIONARY OF
SERVANTS OF GOD CANONIZED BY
THE CATHOLIC CHURCH:
EXTRACTED FROM
THE ROMAN & OTHER MARTYROLOGIES

Compiled by
THE BENEDICTINE MONKS OF
ST. AUGUSTINE'S ABBEY, RAMSGATE

FOURTH EDITION
Revised and Enlarged
WITH A CALENDAR OF SAINTS

NEW YORK
THE MACMILLAN COMPANY
1947

𝔑𝔦𝔥𝔦𝔩 𝔒𝔟𝔰𝔱𝔞𝔱

HADRIANUS TAYLOR, O.S.B.
Abbas.

𝔍𝔪𝔭𝔯𝔦𝔪𝔞𝔱𝔲𝔯

HUBERTUS GIBNEY, VIC. GEN.
Southwarci.

die 29a Aprilis 1947.

PREFACE TO THE FIRST EDITION

MENTION of the Saints of the Catholic Church very frequently occurs both in general reading and as having given their names to churches, towns, villages and topographical features. The object of this compilation is to enable the personage referred to readily to be identified. Nothing more is attempted in this volume. Of a certain number of the Saints detailed Lives have been published in English. Of many more full accounts in other languages, particularly in French and Italian, are easily accessible. Again, there are several good and reliable Series of Lives of the more prominent Saints. The best known of these to English-speaking people is Alban Butler's *Lives of the Saints*, an eighteenth century work which has been many times reprinted. In no language, however, does there exist any exhaustive work of the kind; nor in the nature of things can there be. The nearest approach thereto we have is the Latin "Acta Sanctorum" of the Bollandists, a body of Jesuit Fathers gathered together in Belgium for the special purpose of carefully sifting and reproducing all documents bearing historically on the life and *cultus* after death of each individual Saint. Of their work, begun in the seventeenth century by a certain Father Bolland, nearly seventy huge folio volumes have appeared. It is still far from complete, and on account of the results of modern historical research in many places needs development and extensive revision. Moreover, of no small number of canonized Saints no record at all now remains. We have to be content with proof that in bygone times they were popularly honoured as Saints, and by the Church formally recognized as such. Nor is it even possible to estimate the number of God's servants whom the Church has at one place or another venerated as Saints. In the first Ages of Christianity canonization was effected in each country by the joint act of one or more Bishops and their people. Of this act they left as a rule sufficient testimony by dedicating a church in honour of the new Saint, whose name it thenceforth bore, and by instituting an annual festival in his honour. From about the eleventh century the procedure began to be systemized and centralized, with the result that canonizing is now reserved exclusively to the Holy See. The legislation of Pope Alexander III in the twelfth century and of Urban VIII in the seventeenth has firmly established this principle.

The present process of canonization is exceedingly complex. It consists in the first place of a thorough investigation into all the particulars that can be ascertained of the life and death of the alleged Saint, all facts connected with whose career, both public and private, together with all his utterances and writings, are tested in every way. He must be shown to have been God-fearing, pious, just in his dealings, patient, self-denying, charitable, and so on, far above the average of ordinary good men. In this, as in all subsequent stages of the procedure, every witness is examined under oath and in the presence of a trained

Church lawyer, who is obliged to urge all the objections he can think of, and who is at liberty not only to cross-examine the witnesses put forward but to call any number of others he pleases in order to rebut their testimony. Supposing the judgment of the Court of First Instance to be favourable, the case goes for retrial to a higher tribunal. In these proceedings not only are witnesses called to testify to individual facts, but particular stress is put upon the popular verdict concerning the alleged Saint, that is, upon the repute in which he was held by those who may have had dealings with him or had opportunities of forming an opinion about him. Depositions of all kinds must be gathered together with as little delay as possible, and duly sworn to; but in order to guard against mere enthusiasm playing any part in the matter, at one stage of the proceedings a surcease of at least ten years is enjoined.

The above official enquiry into the conduct in life and virtues of the deceased Christian for whom the supreme honour of canonization is claimed is deemed unnecessary only in the case of a Martyr, that is, of one of the Faithful who has deliberately laid down his life rather than deny Christ. In his case it has to be fully proved that he was put to death on account of his religion, and not because he was guilty of some political or other crime, true or only alleged.

Canonization is the official recognition by the Church of the fact that one of her children has won his place in Heaven; and since Almighty God alone can make known this fact to mankind every canonization essentially depends on proof that miracles have been wrought in witness thereto. It must be shown that because of the alleged Saint the laws of Nature have by Almighty God in some particular instances been overruled. This, from the circumstances of the happening, may well bear testimony to the fact, otherwise unascertainable, that a servant of God deceased is already among those who in the glory of Heaven are yet mindful of their fellow-creatures on earth, and are interceding with God on their behalf. Among the miracles required for a canonization are such wonders as the giving sight to the blind, hearing to the deaf, instantaneous healing of the sick, raising of the dead to life, the very wonders wrought by Christ and His disciples in proof of the truth of the revelation they announced to mankind. Clear proof of at least four miracles is required as a condition of canonization. It must be shown in each case that the fact alleged as miraculous has really taken place, that it cannot be explained away or attributed to any natural cause, and that the miracle directly followed upon an appeal made to Almighty God through His servant departed this life. All possible objections are freely urged and have to be fully answered. In cases of alleged miraculous healing of the sick competent medical experts are called in and all theories advanced by them patiently discussed. It cannot be wondered at that a great number of alleged miracles, perhaps the major part, are rejected, the limits of the powers of Nature being so little known to us and so great allowance having to be made for the play of imagination, and for what there may be of truth in processes of purely natural "Faith-healing."

Usually, the procedure in causes of canonization takes many years to complete; for there are numerous hearings and rehearings to be allowed for. A first stage is that of "Beatification," which is reached on proof of extraordinary holiness of life and of two miracles. In modern procedure this is rarely reached within fifty years of the death of the Saint. At Beatification, permission is given for local veneration. For Canonization proper, proof of two more miracles wrought since Beatification is demanded. The Servant of God is then enrolled in the Canon of Saints, his or her name being inserted in the Roman Martyrology or official catalogue of Saints proposed to the veneration of the Universal Church.

The Roman Martyrology contains about five thousand entries; but in the case of the Martyrs of the first centuries of Christianity, they often appear in groups, the name of only the leaders of each band of heroes being registered. It is impossible to reckon up the number of holy men and women reputed and locally honoured as Saints in various places during the many ages which preceded the formulating the minute rules for the Process of Canonization which have obtained for the last few centuries. In many instances the claims of those commonly and from early times styled Saints have in modern times been officially enquired into with the result that their *cultus* has been sanctioned; in others, as, for example, that of the famous Christian writer, Clement of Alexandria, who flourished and died about A.D. 216, the claim has been disallowed. This does not mean that the Church condemns or repudiates the individual; but only that She has no proof that he was a Saint in the strict sense of the word.

But there are many hundreds of "Saints" whose claims to that title rest on the traditional veneration accorded them from ancient times, and witnessed to in many cases by the dedication of churches in their honour, but of the legitimacy of whose canonization, from dearth of documents or for other reason, no proof is now extant. These remain with that recognition only which was given them by the ancient Bishops and peoples, their contemporaries, but with a strict prohibition of any extension of their *cultus*.

Although the scope of this book of reference only admits of the cataloguing of Saints of some prominence, an endeavour has been made to include, in addition to the Saints of the Roman Martyrology, all others generally known, at least by name, especially those who have given place-names to towns or villages in the British Isles.

Liturgically, Saints are classified as Apostles, Martyrs, Bishops or Confessors (Saints who were neither Bishops nor Martyrs); similarly female Saints are Martyrs, Virgins, Widows, Penitents, etc. These designations have been added (as far as needful) in every instance.

In regard to the more ancient Saints, considerable difficulty is often occasioned by the varying spelling of the Saint's name. Certain names indeed are at first sight all but unrecognisable. St. Olaus or Olave corrupted into Tooley, and St. Vedast written Foster, are examples.

Again, the early converts to Christianity often changed their names on receiving Baptism. Saul of Tarsus, our St. Paul, at once occurs to the mind. The new names assumed were ordinarily Greek or Latin nouns significant of some virtue or quality. Hence, the countless SS. Eusebius, Victor, Justus, Probus, etc. Later too, when Christianity spread among the then Barbarians of Northern and Western Europe, for Teutonic and Celtic appellations Latin forms were frequently substituted. Thus the Anglo-Saxon Winfried is the famous St. Boniface, Apostle of Germany.

From confusion of names have arisen difficulties and uncertainties in distinguishing the early Saints, when more or less contemporaries, the one from the other, and frequent mistakes made by Mediæval biographers. We find at times a single happening attributed by one writer to one Saint and by another writer to another Saint of the same or similar name; and on the other hand a personage with two names is at times presented to us as two distinct individuals. But in the accounts we have of Saints who have lived within the last thousand years these errors scarcely occur, and the official or approved Lives of Saints of the Middle Ages and of modern times may be taken as substantially accurate.

As the present compilation aims at no more than the stretching of the historical framework of a Saint's life, the sifting of the details elaborated by the chroniclers of the old legends does not occur. Similarly, it has not been deemed necessary specially to particularize the miracles which in every case have borne witness to the holy man or woman's right to a place in a catalogue of Saints. In the main (as stated above) these miracles are of the kind performed by our Blessed Lord and his Apostles. Their occurrence from time to time was foretold by Him: "They shall cast out devils. They shall speak with new tongues. They shall take up serpents; and if they shall drink any deadly thing, it shall not hurt them. They shall lay their hands on the sick and they shall recover" (Mark xvi. 17, 18). Or again, the supernatural power abides in their earthly remains: "They cast the body into the sepulchre of Eliseus. And when it had touched the bones of Eliseus, the man came to life and stood upon his feet" (4 Kings xiii. 21). Wonders like to this last take place in the twentieth century, even as they did in past ages; and they justify the veneration which the Catholic Church teaches her children to be due to the relics of God's Saints.

In the Lives of the Saints, fulfilments of Christ's prophecy are frequently recorded either as effected by the Saint himself in life or as occurring after his death in response to a call upon him for help.

Lastly, in going over one by one the names of Saints specially and publicly venerated as such by the Church of God on earth, it must never be forgotten that they form but a small proportion of the "great multitude which no man can number of all nations and tribes and peoples and tongues, standing before the throne and in sight of the Lamb, clothed with white robes and palms in their hands" (Apoc. vii. 9). We rely on the intercession of all the Blessed in Heaven, for "the prayers of all are offered, upon the golden Altar which is before the throne of God" (Apoc. viii. 3).

NOTE TO THIRD EDITION

In the second edition the opportunity was taken to add a Supplement containing the names of Saints who had been canonized or beatified since the original publication of this book, and these were printed at the front of the book.

In the present edition this Supplement has been placed at the end of the book and footnotes have been added in the body of the book to all the Saints whose names appear in the Supplement.

In addition a Calendar of all the Saints appearing in this volume has been compiled and appears at the end of the volume; it is believed that this will be greatly appreciated by all who use the volume and by many who have hitherto not found it necessary to have such a work to their hands.

January 1934.

FURTHER NECESSARY OBSERVATIONS
FOR THE FOURTH EDITION

The BOOK OF SAINTS first appeared in 1921. It was a pioneer work and it certainly filled a gap in English hagiological literature. The fact that it was several times reprinted proves that it achieved success, and the demand for this new edition shows that a considerable public still finds it useful.

Since 1921, however, several similar dictionaries, some of which are evidently indebted to the BOOK OF SAINTS, even to the extent of embodying verbatim transcriptions therefrom, have been put on the market, as the reader may see from the bibliographical list given below. These later works have inevitably rendered our BOOK OF SAINTS more or less out of date. For this reason and also in view of a number of valuable suggestions and corrections made by reviewers of former editions, we put it to the publishers, when they asked us to prepare this fourth edition, that, in fairness to our readers and to ourselves, a re-casting of the whole work was imperative. This we now offer to the public. A few observations on this new BOOK OF SAINTS are, however, necessary for a proper appreciation of its scope, and we therefore beg the reader not to skim the following pages.

The original BOOK OF SAINTS was conceived, planned, directed and in part written by a very great scholar, namely, the Right Rev. Dom Thomas Bergh (d. 1924), monk of Ramsgate and Abbot Visitor of the English Province of the Benedictine Subiaco Congregation. Our description of him as a great scholar is fully deserved. He wrote copiously and published much, but except for a few articles contributed to the *Catholic Encyclopaedia* or similar publications in which the author's name had, as a matter of policy, to be signed, his work was, from a lifelong habit of self-effacement, given to the public anonymously. Thus he was the unnamed editor of the first manual English Missal with complete Latin text ever published in England (Desclée, 1910). He also is the anonymous helper referred to in the preface to Adrian Fortescue's standard work on the *Ceremonies of the Roman Rite* (Burns and Oates, 1918). He sometimes engaged in literary controversy, for instance in *The Tablet* with Father Thurston, S.J., on the ancient rites of the Eucharist, but on these occasions he invariably made use of a *nom de plume*. He found a specially useful outlet for his scholarly gifts as diocesan Censor of books, an office which he discharged for some twenty-five years. In this capacity he was able to give much valuable advice to other writers, as the correspondence preserved in our archives amply testifies.

We mention these facts first in order to give honour to whom honour is due, and also to show that the BOOK OF SAINTS was not just the work of good, pious monks, better fitted for prayer than for critical scholarship. It was the work of a scholar of recognized standing. Abbot Bergh was helped in the compilation of the book by other monks of the community, two especially. His policy was to leave intact the entries contributed by the others, correcting only here and there when he deemed it necessary. For this reason the work is somewhat uneven. Another point that needs mentioning is Abbot Bergh's bent of mind. Although, as we have stated, he was a scholar of high standing in matters biblical, theological and hagiological, his outlook was definitely conservative. This explains his unwillingness to discard ancient legends especially if sanctioned by liturgical use. He would certainly never have approved of the ruthlessly iconoclastic methods of some modern writers. This explains some of the well-founded criticism levelled at his work.

The BOOK OF SAINTS which we now offer to the public has been compiled on a different method and from a different angle. One of the Fathers of this community of Ramsgate has re-written the whole book, entry by entry. It has then been revised and checked by two other Fathers. All three have kept before their minds the most recent findings of hagiological research. They do not always agree with these findings, but in most cases they let the reader know when the data given in the book are uncertain or debatable.

The book remains anonymous. We are only too happy to follow the example set us by its original compiler. Moreover, by doing so, we are acting, even in a small work like this, according to the best Benedictine traditions.

Some further observations as to the aim and use of the book as now revised seem to be called for. As regards its aim, we must first of all repeat here the words written by Abbot Bergh in the original preface: "The present compilation aims at no more than the stretching of the historical framework of a saint's life." The saints, however, included in this new edition are considerably more numerous than those included by Abbot Bergh. The additions comprise not only those saints who have been canonized or beatified or whose cult has been officially recognized by the Holy See since 1921, but also a great number of others omitted in the first edition. The expansion of this latter category is due to our adoption of a more liberal criterion in judging claims to recognized sainthood, and also to our desire to include, within reasonable limits, every holy person whose memory is venerated, or whose feast is celebrated, as that of a saint in a particular country or diocese or religious order.

It is of course beyond human power to achieve absolute completeness. This is especially the case where there are a number of saints of the same name, belonging to the same country, and presenting similar — usually very jejune — biographical data: this phenomenon is common among Irish saints, e.g., Bracan, Brendan, Conall, Conan, etc. The most plausible hypothesis in such cases is that one individual saint, by being venerated in different localities, has achieved a kind of multiple personality, whence it has now become impossible to say to which particular place he originally belonged. Possibly, in other instances, two or three saints of the same or similar name have been blended into one by popular piety. Irish hagiology — and the same applies to Welsh and Cornish — still stands in need of methodical research. May we respectfully bring this need to the notice of our learned Benedictine confrères at Glenstal?

We may also note here that the present volume, although aiming at accuracy, is not, except in the case of most of the Benedictine saints, a work of original research. The compilers have for the most part adopted what they consider to be the sanest conclusions of modern critical hagiography.

To facilitate the use of this book we will now outline briefly the method followed in its compilation. The entries are drawn up on the following plan. We give

(i) The name of each saint in alphabetical order. If there are several saints of the same name, we follow the order of their respective feast days in the calendar. The spelling of proper names, whether of saints or of places, has created some difficulty. In the case of a great number of saints' names the spellings are so various that it would require too much space to enter each form under a separate heading.[1] For certain names in common use at the present time (e.g., James, John, Paul, Peter) we have in each case inserted a special entry giving its different forms in modern European languages. For the spelling of place names the *Encyclopaedia Britannica* usually, but not invariably, has been followed.

(ii) The saint's surname or his distinctive appellation, if any; for instance: James *Kisai*, James *of Tarantaise*, James *the Almsgiver*.

(iii) The saint's hagiological rank, viz., *Saint* (St) or *Blessed* (Bl).

(iv) The liturgical group to which the saint belongs, e.g. *Martyr* (M), *Confessor* (C), etc. *Confessor* (C), however, has often been omitted as understood, as also *Monk*, *Nun*, when that is obvious from the entry itself.

(v) The religious order, if any, to which the saint belonged.

(vi) The present state of the saint's cult, that is, whether the name of the saint is included in the Roman Martyrology (R.M.), whether the cult has been approved — *Approved Cult* (A.C.), or whether it is an unofficial *Popular Cult* (P.C.). By *Approved Cult* (A.C.) we mean that there is positive historical evidence of a saint having been venerated as such, even if, as in many instances among the Cornish and Welsh saints, that evidence rests solely on ancient church dedications and there is no other official recognition by the Church, such as an approved liturgical office. *Popular Cult* (P.C.) is affixed to the names of those saints who are invariably styled so, or are given the title of *Blessed*, or are usually referred to as *Saint* or *Blessed* in ancient writers, but whose veneration has never been accompanied by any recognized external sign of cult.

(vii) The date of the saint's feast. Note that feast days of saints, especially of those not included in the Roman Martyrology, often vary from diocese to diocese or from one religious order to another. In these cases we sometimes give more than one date, but we usually confine ourselves to the date of death, which is the normal day for celebrating a saint's feast.

(viii) The year of the saint's death, whether definite, e.g., *d. 890* or approximate: *d.c.* (*circiter:* about) *890*. Failing this, we give the century, or if even this is unverifiable, we put an interrogation mark (?). When possible, as in the case of the more recent saints, two figures are given, that of their birth and that of their death, e.g. 1810–1890.

---

[1] We would recommend *Baptismal Names* by Joseph L. Weidenham, S. T. L., Washington, 1919, as a very useful reference book, particularly for variant forms of saints' names.

(ix) The text of each entry gives only the chief features of the saint's career. Legendary matter is not altogether excluded, but, when admitted, some warning is usually given. To write of St. Catherine of Alexandria without mention of the wheel, or of St. Laurence of Rome ignoring the gridiron, would probably be more confusing than useful, even though scholars question the historicity of the episodes in which these instruments figure.

In the case of some early martyrs whose names are listed in the martyrologies in the genitive, it is hardly possible, in the absence of other evidence, to determine the sex of the saint. Thus, for example, *Passio S. Zenaidis* might refer to a holy man named Zenaides or to a woman named Zenais.

Finally, (x) each entry ends with an abbreviated bibliography in italics, referring the reader to the bibliographical list following these observations. The authors cited will usually serve to corroborate or check the information given in the text. In a few instances they are cited because they disagree with it, to forewarn the critics that the present compilers are already acquainted with the contrary opinions. They are, however, chiefly intended as a help to those readers who want to get more abundant information. This is a completely new feature of the book, and we trust that its value as a work of reference will be thereby greatly increased. We trust also that, in spite of the difference in our point of view, our revered Abbot Bergh, whose memory is still held in benediction amongst us, would approve and bless this re-writing of his original BOOK OF SAINTS.

In conclusion we would record our gratitude to Miss Marguerite Selby for undertaking the onerous task of typing out the manuscript. Without her co-operation the preparation of this work would, owing to the war, have been indefinitely delayed.

LIST OF WORKS, WITH THEIR RESPECTIVE ABBREVIATIONS, REFERRED TO IN THIS VOLUME

A. A. S. — *Acta Apostolicae Sedis.* Rome, 1909-1939. The official review, inaugurated under Pope Pius X, reproducing all the documents issued by the Holy See, among which are to be found those decreeing the beatification and canonization of saints or recognizing their ancient cult, and usually giving an account of their lives.

All. Hist. per. — *P. Allard. Histoire des Persécutions.* 5 vol., Paris, 1892. Though somewhat antiquated, it is still very useful.

Anal. Bolland. — *Analecta Bollandiana.* A series of 40 volumes, begun in 1882 and published at Brussels by the Bollandist Fathers, S.J., to supplement their monumental *Acts of the Saints.*

Arnold-Forster. — *Studies in Church Dedications or England's Patron Saints.* By Frances Arnold-Forster. 3 vol. London, 1899.

Att. — *A Dictionary of the Saints. Being also an Index to the revised edition of Alban Butler's "Lives of the Saints."* Compiled by Donald Attwater. London, 1938. The most consistently critical of all the dictionaries known to us.

Baring-Gould — *Lives of the British Saints,* by Rev. S. Baring-Gould, M.A. 16 vol., London, 1897.

Baronius — *Card. Baronii Annales Ecclesiastici.* Edited by Mansi, Lucca, 1738-1759.

Baud. — *Dictionnaire d' Hagiographie mis à jour à l'aide des travaux les plus récents,* par Dom J. Baudot, O.S.B. (Monk of Farnborough). Paris, 1925. Too conservative.

Bolland. — *Acta Sanctorum quotquot toto orbe coluntur, etc., edita primum a P. Joh. Bollando, S.J., deinde a Sociis Bollandianis.* Antwerp 1643 deinde Brusselis usque ad nostra tempora. One of the largest quarries from which hagiographers draw their information.

Butler-Thurston — *Lives of the Saints.* Butler's work re-edited, revised and copiously supplemented by Herbert Thurston, S.J. 12 vol., London, 1926-1938.

Camm — *Lives of the English Martyrs: First Series.* Edited by Dom Bede Camm, O.S.B. 2 vol., London, 1904-1905.

Chev. — *Répertoire des Sources Historiques du Moyen Age,* par Ulisse Chévalier. *Bio-bibliographie.* 2 vol., Paris, 1907. A mine of information, especially as regards chronology.

Chron. Einsiedeln. — *Chronicon Einsiedelnse,* Einsiedeln, 1900.

Colgan — *Joannes Colganus. Acta Sanctorum veteris et majoris Scotiae seu Hiberniae.* Louvain, 1645.

Dict. Baudrill. — *Dictionnaire d' Histoire et de Géographie ecclésiastiques.* Edited by Card. Baudrillart. Paris, 1922 sqq. In course of publication.

Duch. Fast. Episc. — *Mgr. L. Duchesne. Fastes épiscopaux de l'ancienne Gaule.* 3 vol. 2nd. edition, Paris, 1907-1915.

Eulog. Cord. Memor. — *Eulogius Cordubensis (Sanctus). Memoria Martyrum Cordubensium.* Madrid, 1850.

Gams — *Series Episcoporum Ecclesiae Catholicae, quotquot innotuerunt a Beato Petro Apostolo. A multis adjutus edidit P. Pius Bonifacius Gams, O.S.B.* 2nd. edition, Leipzig, 1931. Meticulously accurate.

H. L. — *Heiligen-Lexicon, oder Lebensgeschichte alter Heiligen.* Von Dr. J. E. Stadler. Augsburg, 1861.

Holw. — *A Biographical Dictionary of the Saints. With an Introduction on Hagiology.* By the Right Rev. F. G. Holweck, Domestic Prelate to His Holiness Pope Pius XI. St. Louis-London, 1924. Most comprehensive but not very accurate or reliable.

Il Faggio Vall. — *Il Faggio Vallombrosano.* A Monthly edited by the Vallombrosan Fathers of the abbey of la Sma. Trinità in Florence. In the years 1928-1932 there appeared therein a series of short Lives of Vallombrosan Saints.

Lob. — *Dom Lobineau, O.S.B. Les Vies des Saints de Bretagne.* 2nd. edition by A. Tresvaux. 4 vol., Paris, 1836-1837.

Mab. — *Acta Sanctorum Ordinis S. Benedicti in saeculorum classes distributa et notis illustrata. Saec. I-VI in 9 vol. Ediderunt (Lucas d'Achery) J. Mabillon et Theodoricus Ruinart.* Paris 1668-1701. 2nd. edition, Venice, 1733-1740. A monumental pioneer work of critical research: it has by no means yet been superseded, either by the Bollandists or by other later compilations.

Martyrol. Cister. — *Kalendarium Cisterciense seu Martyrologium Sacri Ordinis Cisterciensis, a Sacra Rituum Congregatione approbatum.* Westmalle, 1921.

Menzies — *The Saints in Italy.* A Book of Reference to the Saints in Italian Art and Dedication, by Lucy Menzies. London, 1924.

Men. Cist. — *Menologium Cisterciense notationibus illustratum a P. Joan. Chrys. Henriquez, S.O. Cist.* Antwerp, 1630 *in folio.* A medley of spurious and uncritical legends, with here and there a few reliable pages.

Newdigate — *Our Martyrs. A Chronological List of those who died for the Faith in England and Wales in the 16th and 17th centuries.* With notes by C. A. Newdigate, S.J. London, C.T.S. Very accurate and very useful.

O' Hanlon — *Lives of the Irish Saints, compiled from Calendars, Martyrologies and various sources by John O' Hanlon.* Dublin, 1875 sqq. Lacks critical discrimination.

P.G. and P.L. — *Patrologiae Cursus completus, curante J. P. Migne:*
1. *Patrologia Graeca (P.G.) 161 tomi, usque ad saec. XV.* Paris, 1857-1866.
2. *Patrologia Latina (P.L.) 221 tomi, usque ad Innocentium III.* Paris, 1844-1864.
3. *Tomi 218-221, Indices.*

P. Or. — *Patrologia Orientalis, by R. Graffin and F. Nau.* Paris, 1903 sqq.

P. B. — *Les Petits Bollandistes. Vies des Saints de l'Ancien et du Nouveau Testament, etc. par Mgr. Paul Guérin.* 17 vol. 1st. vol. ed. Paris, 1865.

P. de U. — *Año. Cristiano, por Fr. Justo Pérez de Urbel, O.S.B., monje de Silos.* 5 vol. Madrid, 1933-1935. Without pretensions to be a critical work, it is nevertheless most reliable, especially in those monographs devoted to the Spanish saints. It is a work of great literary charm.

Prop. Camald. — *Proprium Camaldulensium.*

Prop. Cist. — *Proprium Cistercensium.*

Prop. O.F.M. — *Proprium Ordinis Fratrum Minorum.*

Prop. O. P. — *Proprium Ordinis Praedicatorum.*

Prop. S. J. — *Proprium Societatis Jesu.*
These abbreviations are used to indicate that the proper Calendar—*Ordo recitandi divinum Officium*—of one or other of the above-mentioned Orders has been consulted and that the saint in connexion with whom it is cited is liturgically honoured in that particular Order.

R. M.— *Martyrologium Romanum* (Roman Martyrology). The edition used in this volume is that of Rome of the year 1930.

Ram (de) — *P. F. X. de Ram. Hagiographie Nationale: Vies des Saints . . . qui ont vécu dans les anciennes provinces belges.* 2 vol. Louvain, 1864-1867.

Rév. Bénéd. — A review of high critical standing, first appearing in 1884 and edited by the Benedictine monks of Maredsous in Belgium. Its original title, *Le Messager des Fidèles,* was changed in 1890 to the present one of *Révue Bénédictine.*

Ricci — *Mille Santi nell'Arte. Raccolti da Elisa Ricci. Prefazione da Conrado Ricci.* 700 illustrations. Milan 1931. Very useful, particularly for the study of the different emblems of saints used in religious art.

Vitae Patrum — *Rufinus, Vitae Patrum.* The well known work of Rufinus on the Fathers of the desert.

Ruinart — *Acta Martyrum sincera a P. Th. Ruinart (O.S.B.) opera et studio collecta.* Ratisbon, 1859. The work of a Benedictine Maurist, still a classic of its kind.

Stanton — *Menology of England and Wales.* Compiled by order of the Cardinal Archbishop and the Bishops of the province of Westminster. By R. Stanton (Oratorian). London, 1887.

Zimm. — *P. Alfons M. Zimmermann, O.S.B., Monch der abtei Metten. Kalendarium Benedictinum. Die Heiligen und Seligen des Benediktinerordens und seine Zweige.* 3 vol., Metten, 1933-1935. The latest work on the saints who professed the Benedictine Rule.

ABBREVIATIONS

(i) Chronological

a. — *ante*, i.e., before.
c. — *circiter* (or *circa*), i.e., about.
d. — died.
p. — *post*, i.e., after.
cent. — century.

(ii) Canonical

A.C. — Approved Cult.
Bl, BB — Blessed.
P.C. — Popular Cult.
St, SS — Saint, saints.

(iii) Liturgical

Ab. — Abbot.
Abs. — Abbess.
Bp, Bps— Bishop, -s.
C, Cc — Confessor, -s.
Card — Cardinal.
Comp. — Companions.
Dr — Doctor of the Church.
H, HH — Hermit, -s.
Mk — Monk.
M, MM — Martyr, -s.
N — Nun.
V, VV — Virgin, -s.
W — Widow.

(iv) Religious Orders

Barn. — Barnabites.
Bridg. — Bridgettines.
C.M. — *Congregationis Missionis* (Vincentians, Paulists).
C.P. — *Congregationis Passionis* (Passionist Fathers).

C.SS.R. — *Congregationis Sanctissimi Redemptoris.* (Redemptorists)
Orat. — Oratorians.
O.C. — Carmelites.
O.C.D. — Discalced Carmelites.
O. Cart. — Carthusians.
O.F.M. — *Ordinis Fratrum Minorum.* (Franciscans)
O.F.M. Cap.— Capuchins.
O. Merc. — Mercedarians.
O. Minim. — Minims.
O.P. — *Ordinis Praedicatorum.* (Dominicans)
O. Praem. — Praemonstratensians.
O.S.A. — Augustinians.
O.S.A. Erem. — Augustinian Hermits.
O.S. Bas — Basilians.
O.S.B.— Benedictines.
O.S.B. Cam. — (Benedictine) Camaldolese.
O.S.B. Cel. — (Benedictine) Celestines.
O.S.B. Cist. — (Benedictine) Cistercians.
O.S.B. Hum. — (Benedictine) Humiliati.
O.S.B. Oliv. — (Benedictine) Olivetans.
O.S.B. Silv. — (Benedictine) Silvestrines.
O.S.B. Vall. — (Benedictine) Vallombrosans.
O.S.B. Virgil. — (Benedictine) Montevirginians.
O.S. Trin. — Trinitarians.
O.S. Ursulae — Ursulines.
S.J. — Jesuits.
Tert. — Tertiary.

A

AARON (St) Ab. **A.C. June 22**
d. p.552. A Briton who crossed into
Armorica (Brittany) and lived as a hermit
in the island of Cesambre, now St Malo.
Eventually he was joined by a group of
disciples and became their abbot. Among
the disciples was St Malo, who arrived from
Wales about the middle of the 6th cent.
Cf. J. Loth. SS. Breton. — Baud. — Holw.

AARON (St) 1st High Priest R.M. July 1
15th cent. B.C. Great grandson of Levi,
son of Jacob, and the first of the Jewish
High Priests, to which office he was appointed by God Himself. He was the
elder brother of Moses, the Hebrew Lawgiver, with whom he shared the leadership
of the people of Israel. Like Moses he
never entered the Land of Promise, but
died on Mt Hor, on the borders of Edom.
In art he is represented with a rod in
flower, a censer and a Jewish mitre.
*Cf. Book of Exodus. — Baud. — Holw. —
Bolland.*

AARON (St) M. **R.M. July 1**
See Julius and Aaron (Aakon).

AARON (Bl) Abp. O.S.B. **P.C. Oct. 9**
d. 15 May 1059. He was the first abbot
(1040) of the Benedictine monastery of
Tyniec in Poland. In 1046 he became the
first archbishop of Cracow. According to
the Polish legend he had been a monk of
Cluny under St Odilo.
Cf. Gams — Zimm.

ABACHUM (St) M **R.M. Jan. 19**
See Marius, Martha, etc.

ABB (St) V. Abs. **A.C. Aug. 25**
Otherwise Ebba, q.v.

ABBAN (St) Ab. **A.C. March 16**
5th cent. An Irish saint, contemporary
with St Patrick and nephew of St Ibar.
Founder of Kill-Abban Abbey in Leinster.
*Cf. Colgan, AA. SS. Hibern. I, 624 —
Baud. — Holw.*

ABBAN (St) Ab. **A.C. Oct. 27**
6th cent. Nephew of St Kevin; founder
of many monasteries, mostly in S. Ireland.
His name is especially connected with that
of Magh-Armuidhe, now Adamstown, in
Wexford. The lives of this saint, of the
foregoing St Abban, and of sundry others
of the same name are hopelessly confused.
Cf. ib. — Baud. — Holw.

ABBO (St) Bp. **A.C. Sept. 19**
Otherwise Goeric, q.v.

ABBO (St) Ab. M. O.S.B. **A.C. Nov. 13**
c. 945-1004. Born near Orleans, he took
the habit at Fleury (St Benoît-sur-Loire)
and was reputed one of the greatest
scholars of his age. He was invited by
St Oswald of Worcester to take charge of
the abbey school of Ramsey in Huntingdonshire, where he stayed for two years.
He was then appointed abbot of Fleury
(988), where he introduced the Cluniac
observance. He was often called in as
mediator between the king of France and
the Holy See. He was martyred at La
Réole in Gascony by monks whom he had
set out to reform.
*Cf. Bolland. — Att. — Baud. — Holw. —
Zimm.*

ABBO (St) Bp. O.S.B. **P.C. Dec. 3**
d. c. 860. Monk and abbot of the monastery of St Germain at Auxerre. In 857
he was chosen bishop of the same city, but
resigned in 859 and died shortly after.
*Cf. Duch. Fast. Episc. II, 451 — Bolland.
Bib. hag. Lat. 1898 — Baud. — Holw. —
Zimm. — Gams.*

ABBRICI (Bl)
See Magdalen Abbrici.

ABDAS (St) M. **R.M. May 16**
Otherwise Audas, q.v.

ABDECHALAS (St) M. **R.M. Apr. 21**
See Simeon and Comp.

ABDIAS (ABDIS, OBADIAH) (St)
Prophet. **R.M. Nov. 19**
9th cent. B.C. The name means Servant
of the Lord. He is the fourth of the
twelve minor prophets. Some identify
him with Ahab's steward (3 Kings XVIII,
3). His prophecy is contained in a single
chapter of twenty-five verses. He foretells the destruction of Edom. The R.M.
locates his memory at "Samaria in Palestine."
Cf. Baud. — Holw.

ABDIESUS (HEBEDJESUS) (St) M.
                                    R.M. Apr. 22
4th cent.   He was one of the vast multitude of Persians, named and unnamed,
martyred under King Shapur (Sapor) II.
This persecution lasted from A.D. 341 to
A.D. 380. Abdiesus is styled a deacon in
the R.M., and is probably not to be identified with another martyr of the same
name who was bishop of Cashcar.
Cf. Bolland. — Baud. — Holw.

ABDON and SENNEN (SS) MM.
                                    R.M. July 30
3rd or 4th cent.   Persian nobles, brought
to Rome as captives, who devoted themselves to the service of the imprisoned
Christians and to burying the bodies of
the martyrs. Some authorities place
their martyrdom in the reign of Decius,
others in that of Diocletian. They are
still annually commemorated by the Roman Church on July 30.
Cf. All. Hist. pers. II 312 — Baud. —
Att. — Holw.

ABEL (St) Patriarch.   **A.C. Jan. 2**
The second son of Adam, killed by his
brother Cain. He is invoked in the litany
for the dying, and there is a reference to
his sacrifice in the Canon of the Mass.
Cf. Book of Genesis

ABEL, THOMAS (Bl)   **A.C. July 30**
See Thomas Abel.

ABEL (St) Abp. O.S.B.   **P.C. Aug. 5**
d. c.751.   English, or Irish, in origin, he
accompanied St Boniface to the Continent.
He was chosen archbishop of Reims, his
election being ratified by the council of
Soissons (744) and by Pope St Zachary,
but he could not take possession of his see,
which was occupied by the intruder Milo.
He retired to Lobbes, where he became
abbot and died.
Cf. Duch. Fast. Episc. III 86 — Gams —
Chev. — Baud. — Holw.

ABELLON (Bl) O.P.   **A.C. May 15**
See Andrew Abellon.

ABERCIUS (St) Bp.   **R.M. Oct. 22**
d. c.167.   Bishop of Hierapolis in Phrygia,
in which see he is stated to have succeeded
the famous Papias. Imprisoned for his
zeal against paganism, he was set free and
died in peace at Hierapolis. His epitaph,

composed by himself and discovered in
1882, is now in the Lateran Museum. It
sheds vivid light on several points of
Christian doctrine, e.g., baptism, the
eucharist, the Roman primacy. Its authenticity is beyond doubt.
Cf. Att. — Baud. — Holw.

ABIBAS (ABIBO) (St) C.   **R.M. Aug. 3**
1st cent.   Second son of Gamaliel (Acts V
34, XXII 3), at whose feet St Paul had sat.
Like his father he became a Christian.
He lived till his eightieth year. In 415
his remains were found at Capergamela,
near Jerusalem, together with those of
SS Stephen, Gamaliel and Nicodemus.
Cf. Baud. Holw.

ABIBUS (St) M.   **R.M. Nov. 15**
d. 322.   A deacon of Edessa in Syria,
martyred by burning under the emperor
Licinius, and buried with his friends
SS Gurias and Samonas.
Cf. P.B. Baud. — Holw.

ABILIUS (St) Bp.   **R.M. Feb. 22**
d. c.98.   Third bishop, in succession to
SS Mark and Anianus, of Alexandria in
Egypt, to which see he was appointed c.84.
Cf. Baud. — Holw.

ABLEBERT (St) Bp.   **A.C. Jan. 15**
Otherwise Emebert, q.v.

ABRA (St) V.   **A.C. Dec.12**
c. 342 — c. 360.   Daughter of St Hilary
of Poitiers, born to him before he was
raised to the episcopate. Following his
advice she consecrated herself to God as a
nun, but died in her eighteenth year. Her
feast is kept at Poitiers.
Cf. de Cheryé, SS du Poitou, p. 367 —
Baud. — Holw. — Chev.

ABRAHAM (ABRAAMIOS) (St) Bp. M.
                                    A.C. Feb. 5
d. c. 344-48.   Bishop of Arbela in Assyria.
He was put to death in the village of
Telman under Shapur II of Persia.
Cf. Baud. — Holw.

ABRAHAM (ABRAAMES) (St) Bp.
                                    A.C. Feb. 14
d. c.422.   A hermit in Syria, who succeeded in converting a village in the
Lebanon by borrowing money to pay its
taxes. Eventually he became bishop of
Harran (Charres) in Mesopotamia. He

had a great influence on Theodosius the Younger and his court. He died at Constantinople while on a visit to the emperor. *Cf. Att. — Baud. — Holw.*

ABRAHAM (St) C.　　**R.M. March 16**
d. c.366. Surnamed Kidunaia, from the name of his parish at Beth-Kiduna. Flying from a wealthy home and a promising marriage, he lived as a hermit in a desert near Edessa. At the entreaty of his bishop he was ordained and appointed to the town of Beth-Kiduna, which he completely converted to Christianity. His life was written by St Ephraem, who was his personal friend and admirer. The episodes connected with his niece Mary are now considered spurious. *Cf. Att. — Baud. — Holw.*

ABRAHAM (St) Ab.　　**R.M. June 15**
d. c.480. Born on the banks of the Euphrates, he journeyed to Egypt, where he fell among thieves, who held him captive five years. He succeeded in escaping and boarded a ship bound for Gaul. He settled near Clermont in Auvergne as a solitary. Eventually he was given charge as abbot of the monastery of St Cyriacus (St Cyrgues) and was ordained priest. His protection is invoked against fever. *Cf. Bolland. — Baud. — Holw.*

ABRAHAM (St) Patriarch　**R.M. Oct. 9**
20th cent. B.C. The Father of all believers and progenitor of the Hebrew nation. Born at Ur in Chaldea, Abram, whom God renamed Abraham — the father of many, migrated at God's command to Canaan, the land which God had promised him. Here he lived a pastoral and nomad life. In his Seed — Christ, the Messiah — all nations have been blessed, in accordance with the covenant which God made with him. He died at the age of one hundred and seventy-five. *Cf. Book of Genesis.*

ABRAHAM (St) H.　　**A.C. Oct. 27**
d. 367. Surnamed "the Poor" or "the Child." Born at Menuf in Egypt, he became a disciple of St Pachomius. After twenty-three years he retired to a cave, where he spent seventeen years. His cult is widespread among the Copts. *Cf. Pat. Or. I 377 — Baud. — Holw.*

ABRAHAM (St) Abp.　　**A.C. Oct. 28**
6th cent. Built the monastery of the Abrahamites by the Golden Gate at Constantinople and the monastery of the Byzantines near Jerusalem. Eventually he became archbishop of Ephesus. He was a writer on ecclesiastical subjects. *Cf. Pargoire, R.Q.H. — Baud.*

ABRAHAM (St) Bp.　　**A.C. Dec. 6**
474-c.558. Born at Emesa in Syria, while still very young he was chosen abbot of a monastery at Kratia in Bithynia. Later he was made bishop of the same place. Twice he secretly fled in search of quiet: the second time he found a refuge in a Palestinian monastery, where he died. *Cf. Att. — Baud.*

ABRAHAMITE MONKS (SS) MM.
　　　　　　　R.M. July 8
Between 830 and 840. This group of monks belonged to the monastery founded by St. Abraham of Ephesus (q.v., Oct. 28) at Constantinople. They were put to death under the emperor Theophilus for their brave defence of the cult of images. *Cf. Baud. — Holw.*

ABRAN (St)　　　　**A.C. May 8**
See Gibrian

ABROSIMUS (St) M.　　**A.C. Apr. 22**
d. 341. His name is also spelt Abrosima. A Persian priest stoned to death with many of his flock under King Shapur II. The Greeks keep his feast on Nov. 10. *Cf. Baud. — Holw.*

ABSALE (ABSALON) (St) M.
　　　　　　　R.M. March 2
See Lucius, Absalon and Lorgius.

ABUDIMUS (ABUDEMIUS) (St) M.
　　　　　　　R.M. July 15
4th cent. A native of the island of Tenedos in the Aegean, who was martyred under Diocletian. *Cf. Bolland. — Baud. — Holw.*

ABUNDANTIUS (St) M.　R.M. March 1
See Leo, Donatus, etc.

ABUNDANTIUS (St) M.　R.M. Sept. 16
See Abundius, Abundantius, etc.

ABUNDIUS (St) M.　　**R.M. Feb. 27**
See Alexander, Abundius, etc.

ABUNDIUS (St) Bp.　　**R.M. Apr. 2**
d. 469. A Greek priest who became

bishop of Como in N. Italy. He was an able theologian and was entrusted by St Leo the Great with a mission to the emperor Theodosius the Younger, which resulted in the calling of the Council of Chalcedon (451), at which Abundius presided as the pope's legate. St Abundius is represented in art either with a hart or raising a dead child to life.
Cf. Bolland. — Att. — Baud. — Ricci.

ABUNDIUS (St) C.   R.M. Apr. 14
d. c.564. Sacristan (mansionarius) of St Peter's, Rome. St Gregory the Great makes mention of his humble but divinely favoured life. His feast is kept as a double major at St Peter's.
Cf. Bolland. — Baud. — Holw.

ABUNDIUS (St) M.   R.M. July 11
d. 854. Parish priest of Ananelos, a village in the mountains near Cordova in Spain. He entertained no thought of martyrdom, but suddenly found himself drawn into the conflict. He valiantly confessed Christ before the tribunal of the Moorish Caliph of Cordova, was beheaded and his body thrown to the dogs.
Cf. Eulog. Cord. memor. — Bolland. — Baud. — Holw. — P. de U.

ABUNDIUS (St) M.   R.M. Aug. 26
See Irenaeus and Abundius.

ABUNDIUS, ABUNDANTIUS, MARCIAN and JOHN (SS) MM.
R.M. Sept. 16
d. c.303. Their *laus* in the R.M. reads as follows: "At Rome on the Flaminian Way, the memory of the holy martyrs Abundius, priest, and Abundantius, his deacon, whom the emperor Diocletian ordered to be beheaded ten miles from the city, together with Marcian, a senator, and John, his son, whom Abundius had raised from the dead." Their *Acta*, however, are by no means trustworthy.
Cf. Bolland. — Baud. — Holw. — Att.

ABUNDIUS (St) M.   R.M. Dec. 10
See Carpophorus and Abundius.

ABUNDIUS (St) M.   R.M. Dec. 14
See Justus and Abundius.

ACACIUS
Note. The following variant spellings of this and all the following entries under the same name should be noted: — ACHATIUS, ACHACIUS, ACATHIUS, ACHATHIUS, ACHATES, and even, more rarely, AGATIUS, AGATHIUS.

ACACIUS (St) Bp.   A.C. March 31
d. c.251. Surnamed by the Greeks Agathangelos (the Good Angel) and the Wonder-worker. He was a bishop in Hither Asia, and, under the Decian persecution, he is said so to have impressed his judges by his defence of Christianity that he was set free. He is held in great veneration in the East.
Cf. Ruinart — Att. — Baud. — Holw.

ACACIUS (St) Bp.   R.M. Apr. 9
d. p.421. Bishop of Amida (Diarbekir) in Mesopotamia, and distinguished for his charity to the Persian prisoners, for whose ransom he melted down and sold the sacred vessels of his church. This won for him the friendship of King Bahram V (Varannes) of Persia, who is said to have forthwith ceased to persecute his Christian subjects.
Cf. Baud. — Holw.

ACACIUS (St) M.   R.M. Apr. 28
See Patrick, Acacius, etc.

ACACIUS (St) M.   R.M. May 8
d. c.303. A Cappadocian centurion in the Roman army stationed in Thrace, who was tortured and beheaded at Byzantium under Diocletian. Constantine the Great built a church in his honour. He is the S. Agario venerated at Squillace in Calabria and the San Acato of Avila and Cuenca in Spain.
Cf. Bolland. — Chev. — Att. — Baud. — Holw.

ACACIUS (St) M.   June 22
The story of a martyrdom of St Acacius and ten thousand Roman soldiers under his command on Mt Ararat, which had great vogue in the later Middle Ages, is now discarded as pure romance.
Cf. Anal. Bolland. Oct. 1894.

ACACIUS (St) M.   R.M. July 28
d. c.310. A martyr at Miletus under the emperor Licinius.
Cf. Bolland. — Ruinart — Baud. — Holw.

ACACIUS (St) M.   R.M. Nov. 27
See Hirenarchus, Acacius, etc.

ACCA (St) Bp. O.S.B. A.C. Oct. 20
c. 660-742. A Northumbrian disciple of
St Bosa of York and of St Wilfrid, and a
constant companion of the latter in his
journeys in England, Italy and Frisia.
St Wilfrid appointed him abbot of St
Andrew's at Hexham. In 709 Acca succeeded Wilfrid as bishop of the same place.
For a time he was exiled from his see.
St Bede was his great friend and dedicated
several works to him. Acca is described
by Bede as "great in the sight of God and
man," and he was certainly one of the
most learned Anglo-Saxon prelates of his
day.
*Cf. Mab. — Att. — Baud. — Holw. —
Zimm.*

ACCURSIUS (St) M. O.F.M.
R.M. Jan. 16
See Berardus, Peter, etc.

ACEPSIMAS (St) Bp. M. R.M. Apr. 22
d. 10 Oct. 376. An octogenarian bishop
of Hnaita in W. Persia, who was racked
and flogged to death under Shapur II.
The Acts of his martyrdom are quite
genuine.
Cf. Ruinart — Bolland — Baud.

ACEPSIMAS (St) H. A.C. Nov. 3
5th cent. A hermit who lived for sixty
years in a cave near Cyrrhus in Syria in
the time of Theodosius I. He died shortly
after his ordination to the priesthood.
*Cf. Baud. — Holw. — also P.G. t.82 col.
1413.*

ACESTES (St) M. A.C. July 2.
1st cent. According to the legend he was
one of the three soldiers who led St Paul
to execution: having been converted by
him, they were beheaded after him.
Cf. Holw.

ACHACIUS, or ACHATIUS (*several***)**
See under Acacius.

ACHARD (St) Ab. O.S.B. R.M. Sept. 15
Otherwise Aichardus, q.v.

ACHARIUS (St) Bp. A.C. Nov. 27
d. 640. Monk of Luxeuil under St Eustace. In 621 he was chosen bishop of
Noyon-Tournai, and as such fostered the
missionary efforts of St Amandus of
Maestricht and obtained from King
Dagobert I the erection of the see of

Térouanne, in which he placed his friend
St Omer.
Cf. Mab. — Baud. — Holw. — Zimm.

ACHE and ACHEUL (SS) MM.
A.C. May 1
Otherwise Acius and Aceolus, q.v.

**ACHERIC and WILLIAM (SS) Mks.
O.S.B.** P.C. Nov. 3
d. after 860. Hermits, and afterwards
monks in a monastery founded by Bi-
dulph, archdeacon of Metz, in the Vosges
mountains in the diocese of Strassburg.
Cf. Baud. — Holw. — Zimm.

ACHILLAS and AMOES (SS) HH.
A.C. Jan. 17
4th cent. Achillas, in Latin Achilleus, is
mentioned by Rufinus. He is venerated
by the Greeks at the beginning of Lent,
together with Amoes. They both lived
as solitaries in Egypt and are called in the
Greek liturgy "the flowers of the desert."
*Cf. Rufinus, Vitae PP. in P.L. t.65 col.
123 — Baud. — Holw.*

ACHILLAS (St) Bp. R.M. Nov. 7
d. 313. Successor to St Peter the martyr
in the see of Alexandria. He raised to the
priesthood the man who afterwards became world-famous as the heresiarch
Arius. St Athanasius extols the virtues
of St Achillas, who was maligned by the
party of Meletius on account of the purity
of his doctrine.
Cf. Baud. — Holw.

ACHILLES (St) Bp. A.C. May 15
d. c.330. In Latin Achillius. Metropolitan of Larissa in Thessaly. He is supposed to have assisted at the 1st Council
of Nicaea. Since 978 his relics have been
venerated at Presba (Achilli) in Bulgaria.
Cf. Baud. — Holw.

ACHILLEUS (St) M. R.M. Apr. 23
See Felix, Fortunatus and Achilleus.

ACHILLEUS (St) M. R.M. May 12
See Nereus, Achilleus, etc.

ACINDYNUS (St) M. R.M. Apr. 20
See Victor, Zoticus, etc.

**ACINDYNUS, PEGASIUS, APHTHON-
IUS, ELPIDEPHORUS and ANEMPO-
DISTUS (SS) MM.** R.M. Nov. 2
d. 345. Persian Christians, priests and

clerics, who suffered for the Faith under Shapur II.
Cf. Bolland. — Baud. — Holw.

ACISCLUS and VICTORIA (SS) MM.
                                    R.M. Nov. 17
d. 304. Brother and sister, natives of Cordova in Spain, who suffered martyrdom probably under Diocletian. Their home was turned into a church. They are the principal patron saints of Cordova and are greatly venerated throughout Spain and S. France.
Cf. Eul. Cord. mem. P.L. t. 115 col 805 — Baud. — Holw. — P. de U.

ACIUS (ACHE) and ACEOLUS (ACHEUL) MM.   **A.C. May 1**
d. c.303. The former a deacon, the latter a subdeacon, martyred near Amiens under Diocletian. Their cult is widespread in the diocese of Amiens. Their *Acta*, however, are not trustworthy.
Cf. Baud. — Holw.

ACTINEA and GRAECINA (SS) VV. MM.
                                    A.C. June 16
4th cent. The former was beheaded at Volterra in Etruria in the persecution of Diocletian. In 1140 her remains, together with those of Graecina, were found in the Camaldolese church of SS. Justus and Clement.
Cf. Dict. Baudrill. I 415 — Baud. — Holw.

ACUTIUS (St) M.   R.M. Sept. 19
See Januarius, Festus, etc.

ACYLLINUS (St) M.   R.M. July 17
See Scillitan Martyrs.

ADAL-, AETHEL-, AL-, ADRE-, AU-, EDIL-, ETHEL-,
Note. All these prefixes to names of Teutonic origin are more or less interchangeable. Thus, Etheldreda, Ediltrudis, Audrey, are one and the same personage. That which appears the more usual manner of spelling a saint's name in English has, as a rule, been followed here.

ADA (St) Abs.   A.C. Dec. 4
End of 7th cent. Niece of St Engebert, bishop of Mans. She was a nun at Soissons and was appointed abbess of Saint-Julien-des-Prés at Mans. Her name has the variants: Adenette, Adna, Adnette, Adrechildis.

ADALAR (ADALHER) (St) M. O.S.B.
                                    R.M. June 5
d. 755. Monk-priest and companion of St Boniface, with whom he was martyred at Dokkum in Frisia.
Cf. Mab. — Bolland. — Holw. — Zimm.

ADALARD (St) Ab. O.S.B.   A.C. Jan. 2
c. 751-827. His name is also written Adalhard, Adelhard, Adalardus, Adelardus, Alard. Grandson of Charles Martel, monk and abbot of ·Corbie in France, and one of Charlemagne's chief advisers. The ups and downs of his political career belong to general history. Throughout he remained a great abbot. He founded the abbey of Corbie (Corvey) in Saxony.
Cf. Mab. — Bolland. — Att. — Holw. — Zimm.

ADALARD (Bl) Mk. O.S.B. P.C. July 15
d. c.824. Surnamed the younger. Monk of Corbie under the abbot St Adalard. Died in his twentieth year.
Cf. Chev. — Zimm.

ADALBALD (St) M.   A.C. Feb. 2
d. 625. Surnamed "D'Ostrevant." Born in Flanders, a son or grandson of St Gertrude of Hamage. He served at the court of Dagobert I and married a Gascon lady named Rictrude, who is also venerated as a saint, as also were their four children, Maurontius, Clotsindis, Eusebia and Adalsindis. Adalbald was slain by some relatives of his wife who disapproved of the match, and was thereafter venerated as a martyr.
Cf. Bolland. — Att. — Baud. — Holw.

ADALBERO (Bl) Bp.   P.C. Jan. 1
d. 1128. A brother of Godfrey Le Barbu, count of Louvain. Successively canon of Metz and bishop of Liége, where he founded the abbey of Saint-Gilles.
Cf. P.B. — de Ram. — Baud. — Holw.

ADALBERO (Bl) Bp. O.S.B. P.C. Apr. 28
d. 909. He belonged to the family of the counts of Dillingen, and was uncle to St Ulric. Monk (850) and afterwards abbot of Ellwangen, abbot-restorer of Lorsch and bishop of Augsburg (after 887). Chief adviser of the emperor Arnulph, tutor to his son Louis and regent of the Empire during the latter's childhood. He was well versed in science and the arts, chiefly as a musician.
Cf. H.L. — Chev. — Holw.

ADALBERO (St or Bl) Bp. A.C. Oct. 6
1045-1090. Son of Count Arnold of Lambach. A student at Paris with St Altmann of Passau. Eventually he became bishop of Würzburg and sided with Gregory VII against Henry IV. On this account he was driven from his see (1085) and retired to the Benedictine abbey of Lambach in Austria, to the foundation of which he had largely contributed. It was there that he died. Cult approved in 1883.
Cf. Dict. Baudrill. — Baud. — Holw. — P. de U.

ADALBERO (Bl) Bp. P.C. Dec. 15
d. 1005. Of the family of the dukes of Lorraine. Educated at the Benedictine abbey of Gorze, he became bishop of Verdun, but was transferred in the same year (984) to Metz. He was zealous in spreading the Cluniac observance by founding monasteries and churches.
Cf. P.B. — Baud. — Holw.

ADALBERT (St) Abp. M. O.S.B.
R.M. Apr. 23
956-997. In Czech Voitech. Born in Bohemia and educated by St Adalbert of Magdeburg. He was consecrated bishop of Prague (983), but disheartened at the result of his labours, he went to Rome and became a Benedictine at the abbey of SS Boniface and Alexius on the Aventine. Twice he returned to his former mission, and twice he had to abandon it. However, on each occasion he preached instead in Poland, Prussia, Hungary and even Russia, with signal success; hence he is styled the Apostle of the Slavs. He was martyred by the Prussians near Danzig. .
Cf. Mab. — Bolland. — Att. — Dict. Baudrill. — Zimm.

ADALBERT (St) Abp. O.S.B.
A.C. June 20
d. 981. Monk of St Maximin of Trèves, he was chosen by the emperor Otto III to evangelize Russia. Arrived there in 961, all his companions were killed, and he himself escaped with difficulty. He was then appointed abbot of Weissenburg, and in 968 first archbishop of Magdeburg with jurisdiction over the Wends. He did much to encourage learning, especially as abbot of Weissenburg.
Cf. H.D. — Att. — Holw. — Zimm.

ADALBERT (St) Mk. R.M. June 25
d. c.740. A Northumbrian by birth who became a monk of Rathmelgisi and accompanied St Willibrord as one of his deacons to Friesland. He laboured especially round Egmont, of which abbey he was the patron saint.
Cf. Mab. — Bolland. — Att. — Holw.

ADALBERT (Bl) Mk. O.S.B.
P.C. Nov. 23
d. p. 1045. Monk of Cassoria — Cassauria, Pescara — in the Abruzzi, under Abbot St Guido. He retired to Mt Caramanico near Chieti, where he founded the abbey of St Nicholas.
Cf. Mab. — Chev. — Holw. — Zimm.

ADALGIS (ADELGIS, ALGIS) (St)
Priest H. A.C. June 2
d. c.686. An Irish monk, disciple of St Fursey. He evangelized the country around Arras and Laon. In the forest of Thiérarche in Picardy he founded a small monastery, around which afterwards grew up the village of Saint-Algis.
Cf. Mab. — Baud. — Holw. — Dict. Baudrill. — Zimm.

ADALGIS (St) Bp. A.C. Oct. 7
c. 850. Bishop of Novara c. 830-c. 850. An important churchman under the emperor Lothair. Venerated at Novara, where he is buried in the church of San Gaudenzio.
Cf. Chev. — Dict. Baudrill. — Baud.

ADALGOTT (St) Bp. O.S.B.Cist.
A.C. Oct. 3
d. 1165. Professed as a monk under St Bernard at Clairvaux. In 1150 he became abbot of the Black Benedictines at Dissentis and bishop of Chur, where he founded a hospital for the poor and proved himself an excellent pastor.
Cf. Dict. Baudrill. — Baud. — Holw.

ADALGOTT (Bl) Ab. O.S.B.
A.C. Oct. 26
d. 1031. Monk of Einsiedeln and from 1012 abbot of Dissentis, both of which abbeys are in Switzerland.
Cf. Chron. Einsiedeln. I 70 — Baud. — Holw.

ADALSINDIS (St) Abs. A.C. May 3
c. 680. Sister of St Waldalenus, abbot-founder of Bèze. She became abbess of a

convent near Bèze under the supervision of her brother.

Cf. Dict. Baudrill. — Baud.

ADALSINDIS (St) N. O.S.B.

P.C. Dec. 25

c. 715. One of the daughters of SS Adalbald and Rictrudis, who took the veil at Hamay-les-Marchiennes, in the diocese of Arras, under her own sister St Eusebia.

Cf. Mab. — de Ram. Biog. Belg. — Baud.

ADAM (St) Ab. O.S.B.   A.C. May 16

d. p. 1212. Born at Fermo. First hermit, and then monk and abbot, of San Sabino on Mt Vissiano, near Fermo. His relics are enshrined in the cathedral of Fermo, where his feast is kept.

Cf. Bolland. — Chev. — Holw.

ADAM (Bl) Mk. O.S.B.Cist.

P.C. Dec. 22

d. c.1210. Priest and sacristan in the Cistercian abbey of Loccum in Saxony. Remarkable, like most Cistercian saints, for his devotion to our Lady.

Cf. Dict. Baudrill. — Att. — Baud.

ADAM and EVE (SS)   A.C. Dec. 24

First parents of the human race. Adam died aged nine hundred and thirty years. Their feast is given different dates in the martyrologies: Jan. 18-23, March 24, April 24, Dec. 19, Dec. 24. The last date is the most common.

Cf. Book of Genesis. — Baud. — Holw.

ADAMNAN (St) Mk. O.S.B.

A.C. Jan. 31

d. c.680. An Irish pilgrim who became a monk at Coldingham, near Berwick, under the abbess St Ebba. Cult confirmed by Leo XIII in 1898.

Cf. Dict. Baudrill. — Att. — Zimm. — Baud.

ADAMNAN (St) Ab.   A.C. Sept. 23

c. 630-704. Surnamed McRonan. Called also Adam, Aunan, Eunan. An Irish saint who became abbot of Iona (679) and zealously advocated the Roman observance of Easter, which however his own abbey did not adopt. He is best remembered for his life of St Columba, a most important hagiographical document.

Cf. Dict. Baudrill. — Att. — Holw. — Baud.

ADAUCTUS (St) M.   R.M. Aug. 30

See Felix and Adauctus.

ADAUCTUS and CALLISTHENE (SS) M, V.   A.C. Oct. 4

c. 312 and p. These two saints were Ephesians, father and daughter. The former suffered under Maximinus Daza c. 312. Callisthene escaped martydom and devoted herself to works of charity till her death at Ephesus.

Cf. Dict. Baudrill. — Baud.

ADAUCUS (ADAUCTUS) (St) M.

R.M. Feb. 7

d. 304. An Italian who held the office of finance minister at the imperial court of Diocletian in Phrygia. The emperor sacrificed him on discovering his religion. A large nun.ber of Christians were martyred with him, their town being burnt over their heads.

Cf. Dict. Baudrill. — Att. — Baud. — Holw.

ADDAI and MARI (SS) Bps.

A.C. Aug. 5

2nd cent. They are styled "Our Holy Apostles" alike by Syrians and Persians. Addai was probably a missionary bishop at Edessa in the second century. Of Mari nothing trustworthy is known.

Cf. Att. — Holw.

ADEGRIN (ADALGRIN, ALDEGRIN) (St) Mk. O.S.B.   P.C. June 4

d. 939. A knight who joined St Odo, the future abbot of Cluny, at Baume, and shortly after embraced the eremitical life near the same abbey.

Cf. P.B. — Dict. Baudrill. — Baud. — Chev.

ADELA (St) W.   P.C. Feb. 24

c.1062-1137. Youngest daughter of William the Conqueror. In 1080 she married Stephen of Blois, played a great part in political affairs, and generously endowed abbeys and churches.

Cf. Dict. Baudrill. — Baud. — Chev.

ADELA (St) W. O.S.B.   P.C. Sept. 8

d. 1071. Wife of Count Baldwin IV of Flanders, who, in her widowhood, received the habit from Pope Alexander II (1067) and retired to the Benedictine convent of Messines, near Ypres, where she died.

Cf. Baud.

ADELA (St) W. Abs. O.S.B.
P.C. Dec. 24
d. c.730. Daughter of Dagobert II, king of the Franks. In her widowhood she founded and became first abbess of Pfalzel (Palatiolum) near Trèves.
Cf. Dict. Baudrill. — Att. — Baud. — Holw.

ADELAIDE (St) Abs. O.S.B.
A.C. Feb. 5
d. c.1015. Abbess of Bellich (Willich) near Bonn, and of Our Lady of the Capitol at Cologne. Both were Benedictine convents founded by her father.
Cf. Dict. Baudrill. — Att. — Baud. — P. de U.

ADELAIDE (ALEYDIS) (St) V. O.S.B. Cist.
A.C. June 15
d. 1250. A young nun of the Cistercian convent of La Cambre who was visited with many physical afflictions. She became blind, contracted leprosy, and was struck with paralysis. She had to be segregated from her community. She offered up her sufferings for the souls in purgatory and had visions of their being set free through her intercession. Her life was written by a contemporary. Cult confirmed in 1907.
Cf. Att. — Dict. Baudrill. — Baud.

ADELAIDE (St) W. Empress.
A.C. Dec. 16
c. 930-999. Daughter of the king of Burgundy, she was married (947) to Lothair II of Italy, on whose death she was treated with great brutality by Berengarius of Ivrea. She was rescued by the emperor Otto the Great, who married her. Again left a widow (973), she was ill-treated by her son and daughter-in-law. In her old age she became the regent of the Empire. Throughout her life she received strong support from the abbots of Cluny, with whom she was on terms of close friendship. Before her death she retired to a convent.
Cf. Dict. Baudrill. — Att. — Baud. — Holw.

ADELBERT (several)
Otherwise Adalbert, q.v.

ADELELMUS (Fr. ALEAUME, Sp. LESMES) (St) Ab. O.S.B. A.C. Jan. 30
d. c.1100. Born at Laudun, Poitou. He became a soldier. On his return from a pilgrimage to Rome he met at Issoire St Robert, founder of Chaise-Dieu, and joined his community. He seems to have been abbot there for a time. In 1079 he was called to Burgos, Old Castile, by Queen Constance of Burgundy, wife of Alphonsus VI of Castile. Adelelmus received from the king a church and a hospital by the gates of Burgos, where the great abbey of St John (now the church of St Lesmes) was founded with the saint as first abbot.
Cf. Mab. — Bolland. — Dict. Baudrill.— P. de U. — Zimm.

ADELELMUS (St) H. P.C. Apr. 27
d. 1152. Born in Flanders, he became eventually a disciple of St Bernard of Tiron, and afterwards founder of the monastery of Etival-en-Charnie.
Cf. Dict. Baudrill. — Baud. — Zimm.

ADELELMUS (ADELHELM) (Bl) Ab. O.S.B. P.C. Feb. 25
d. 1131. A monk of St Blasien in the Black Forest, he was sent to found the monastery of Engelberg in Switzerland, of which he became prior and subsequently abbot. Little more is known of his life.
Cf. Baud. — Chev. — Holw. — Zimm.

ADELGOTT
Otherwise Adalgott, q.v.

ADELHEIDIS (Bl) V. O.S.B.Cist.
P.C. Dec. 27
d. 1273. Of the family of Thöningen. She sanctified herself as a recluse under the obedience of the Cistercian abbey of Tennenbach.
Cf. Chron. Cist. — Zimm.

ADELIN, ADELINUS
Otherwise Hadelin, Hadelinus, q.v.

ADELINA (Bl) V. O.S.B.Cist.
P.C. Aug. 28
c. 1170. Daughter of Bl Guy, brother of St Bernard of Clairvaux. She was educated at Juilly and became a nun, and afterwards abbess, of the Cistercian convent of Poulangy, diocese of Langres.
Cf. Dict. Baudrill. — Baud. — Holw. — Zimm.

ADELINA (St) V. O.S.B. A.C. Oct. 20
d. 1125. Granddaughter of William the

Conqueror and sister of St Vitalis of Savigny. She became abbess of La Blanche at Moriton (les Dames Blanches de Mortain) in Normandy, founded by her brother.
Cf. Baud. — Holw. — Zimm.

ADELINDIS (Bl) W. O.S.B. P.C. Aug. 28
d. c.930. In her widowhood she founded and eventually became a nun — and perhaps abbess — of Buchau, on the Federsee in Wurtemburg.
Cf. Dict. Baudrill. — Chev. — Baud. — Holw. — Zimm.

ADELOGA (HADELOGA) (St) V. O.S.B.
A.C. Feb. 2
d. c.745. A Frankish princess who was the foundress and first abbess of the great Benedictine nunnery of Kitzingen in Franconia.
Cf. P.B. — Baud. — Holw. — Zimm.

ADELPHUS (St) Bp.   R.M. Aug. 29
5th cent. The R.M. has: "At Metz in France the memory of St Adelphus, bishop and confessor." Nothing more is known about him. His cult at Metz from early times is indisputable. The solemn translation of his relics to Neuweiler in Alsace in the ninth century was the occasion of great popular rejoicings.
Cf. Dict. Baudrill. — Chev. — Baud.

ADELPHUS (St) Ab. O.S.B.
A.C. Sept. 11
d. c.670. Grandson of St Romaricus, and his successor (653) as abbot of Remiremont. He died at Luxeuil.
Cf. Dict. Baudrill. — Chev. — Baud. — Holw.

ADELTRUDIS (St) Abs. O.S.B.
A.C. Feb. 25
Otherwise Aldetrudis, q.v.

ADEODATUS
Saints of this name are better known as Deusdedit or Dieudonné.

ADERALD (St) C.   A.C. Oct. 20
d. 1004. Archdeacon of Troyes. He led a pilgrimage to Palestine, and on his return "with much booty in the shape of holy relics" he built for their reception the Benedictine abbey of St Sepulchre at Samblières.
Cf. Baud. — P.B. — Holw.

ADHERITUS (ABDERITUS, ADERY)
(St) Bp.   R.M. Sept. 27
d. 2nd or 3rd cent. A Greek by birth, successor of St Apollinaris in the see of Ravenna. Since the early Middle Ages his body has been enshrined in the Benedictine basilica of Classe near Ravenna.
Cf. Dict. Baudrill. — Baud. — Holw.

ADILIA
Otherwise Adela, Odilia or Othilia, q.v.

ADJUTOR (AYUTRE) (St) H. O.S.B.
A.C. Apr. 30
d. 1131. A Norman knight, lord of Vernon-sur-Seine, who fought in the Crusades and on his return became a monk at Tiron. He afterwards led the life of a recluse at Vernon-sur-Seine, where he died.
Cf. Dict. Baudrill.—Baud.—Holw.—Chev.

ADJUTOR (St) C.   R.M. Sept. 1
See Priscus, Castrensis, etc.

ADJUTOR (St) M.   R.M. Dec. 18
See Victurus, Victor, etc.

ADJUTUS (St) M. O.F.M. R.M. Jan. 16
See Berardus, Peter, etc.

ADJUTUS (St) Ab.   R.M. Dec. 19
Otherwise Avitus (or Avy), q.v.

ADO (St) Bp. O.S.B.   R.M. Dec. 16
799-875. Born in Burgundy and educated under Lupus Servatus at Ferrières, he was professed as a Benedictine at Ferrières, but the abbot of Prüm, near Trèves, succeeded in enlisting his services as headmaster of the monastic school at Prüm. After some years the jealousy of certain monks drove him from Prüm, and he travelled to Rome. On his return to France he stayed for a while at Lyons and in 859 was made bishop of Vienne. He proved an altogether admirable prelate. He is best remembered, however, as the compiler of the martyrology which bears his name and of other minor writings which unfortunately "were responsible for the perpetuation of a number of baseless and misleading statements." (Att.)
Cf. Dict. Baudrill. — Baud. — Att. — Holw. — P. de U. — Zimm.

ADOLPH (St) Ab. (or Bp.) O.S.B.
A.C. June 17
See Botulph and Adulph.

ADOLPHUS (St) Bp. O.S.B.Cist.
A.C. Feb. 11
c. 1185-1224. Born in Westphalia, of the family of the counts of Tecklenburg, he became a canon of Cologne, but resigned to become a Cistercian at Camp on the Rhine. In 1216 he was nominated bishop of Osnabrück, where he became known as "the almoner of the poor." He died on June 30.
Cf. Dict. Baudrill. — Baud. — Holw. — P. de U. — Zimm. — Att.

ADOLPHUS LUDIGO-MKASA (Bl) M.
A.C. June 3
See Uganda (Martyrs of).

ADOLPHUS and JOHN (SS) MM.
R.M. Sept. 27
d. c.850. Two brothers, born at Seville of a Moorish father and a Christian mother, who were martyred at Cordova under Abderraman II.
Cf. Dict. Baudrill. — Baud. — Holw. — P. de U.

ADRIA (St) M.   **R.M. Dec. 2**
See Eusebius, Marcellus, etc.

ADRIAN
Note. This name is in certain cases also spelt with an initial H.

ADRIAN (St) Ab. O.S.B.   **A.C. Jan. 9**
d. 710. An African by birth, he became abbot of Nerida, not far from Naples. Pope Vitalian chose him to be archbishop of Canterbury, but he declined the office and recommended instead St Theodore of Tarsus, with whom he came to England as assistant and adviser. He became abbot of SS Peter and Paul, afterwards St Augustine's, Canterbury, where he supervised a flourishing school. He was eminent for his learning as well as his sanctity. His cultus revived in 1091, when his body was discovered.
Cf. Richard Whyford's English Martyrology (pub. 1525) — Bolland. — Mab. — Baud. — Stanton — Zimm. — Att.

ADRIAN (St) M.   **R.M. March 1**
See Hermes and Adrian.

ADRIAN and Comp. (SS) MM.
A.C. March 4
d. c.875. Adrian was a missionary bishop on the isle of May in the Firth of Forth,

who was martyred by the Danes together with some fellow missionaries who were monks. The saint's connexion with Hungary seems to be a myth.
Cf. Att. — Holw.

ADRIAN and EUBULUS (SS) MM.
R.M. March 5 and 7
d. 308. Both were martyred at Caesarea in Palestine when they came to visit the Christians there — Adrian on March 5 and Eubulus two days later.
Cf. Dict. Baudrill. — Baud. — Att.

ADRIAN (St) M.   **A.C. March 19**
d. c.668. A disciple of St Landoald. He was murdered by robbers while begging alms for his community near Maestricht, and afterwards locally venerated as a martyr.
Cf. Holw.

ADRIAN III (St) Pope   **R.M. July 8**
d. 885. He became pope in 884, and almost at once set out to take part in the diet of Worms, intending to ask for help against the Saracens. He died on his way, near Modena, and was buried at Nonantola. Cult confirmed in 1892.
Cf. Dict. Baudrill. — Att. — Baud. — Holw.

ADRIAN BEANUS (St) M. O.Praem.
R.M. July 9
See Gorkum (Martyrs of).

ADRIAN FORTESCUE (Bl) M.
A.C. July 9
1476-1539. Born at Punsbourne in Hertfordshire, he was first cousin to Anne Boleyn. In 1499 he married Anne Stonor. He was a knight of St John and most faithful in the discharge of his duties. He refused the oath of supremacy, and was for this reason beheaded on Tower Hill by order of Henry VIII. Beatified by Leo XIII in 1895.
Cf. Att. — Baud. — Holw. — Stanton.

ADRIAN (St) M.   **R.M. Aug. 26**
? The R.M. describes this saint as a martyr of Nicomedia. It is not quite clear whether he should be identified with the St Adrian venerated on Sept. 8.
Cf. Dict. Baudrill. — Baud. — Att.

ADRIAN and NATALIA (SS) M., W.
R.M. Sept. 8
d. c.304. Adrian, a pagan officer at the

imperial court at Nicomedia, befriended
the Christian prisoners and was himself
cast into prison, where he and his fellow-
prisoners were tended by his wife Natalia.
All the prisoners were martyred on March
4. Natalia survived to transfer her husband's relics to Argyropolis, where she
died. In later times the relics were translated to Rome, Sept. 8 being the date of
this translation. St Adrian is the patron
of soldiers and butchers.
*Cf. Dict. Baudrill. — Att. — Baud. —
Holw.*

ADRIAN (Bl) M. O.P.   A.C. Dec. 21
13th cent. Adrian, a Friar Preacher, and
twenty-seven companions were put to
death by the Mohammedans in Dalmatia.
Cf. Baud.

ADRIO, VICTOR and BASILLA (SS)
MM.   R.M. May 17
? Martyrs of Alexandria, whether at the
hands of pagans or Arians is not known.
Cf. Dict. Baudrill. — Baud. — Holw.

ADULPHUS
Otherwise Adolphus or Adolph, q.v.

ADVENTOR (St) M.   R.M. Nov. 20
See Octavius, Solutor and Adventor.

AE
Note. Names of saints beginning with
this diphthong are frequently spelt with
A or E only as the initial letter. Thus for
Aelphege we have also Alphege (Alphage)
and Elphege.

AEDAN (St) Bp.   A.C. Jan. 31
d. 632. Among many variants of the
name the following are the commonest:
Aidan, Aedhan, Edan. He is also called
Maidhoc, Maodhog, Mogue, and, in
Brittany, Dé. A disciple of St David of
Wales who, on his return to Ireland, be-
came bishop of Ferns.
Cf. Holw.

AEDESIUS (St) M.   R.M. Apr. 8
d. c.306. His *laus* in the R.M. is as
follows: "At Alexandria, the memory of
St Aedesius, martyr, a brother of blessed
Apphian, who, under Maximian Galerius
the emperor, openly withstood an impious
judge because he handed over to pimps
virgins consecrated to God. He was laid
hold of by the soldiery, afflicted with most

cruel punishments, and drowned in the sea
for the Lord Christ."
Cf. Bolland. — Holw.

AEDH MacBRICC (St) Bp.
**   A.C. Nov. 10**
6th cent. The name is also spelt Aod and
Aedsind, and it is Latinized as Aidus. He
was a disciple of St Ithlathan at Rathlihen
in Offaly, and is said to have founded
churches at Rathugh and other places in
his native Meath, where he held the office
of bishop.
Cf. Att. — Holw.

AEDH, AEDHAN
Note. Holweck lists eighteen more Irish
saints of the name of Aedh, and twenty
under Aedhan, but the historical data are
hopelessly confused.

AEGIDIUS
One of the most popular saint's names in
the Middle Ages. In Italian: Egidio;
in French: Gilles; in Spanish and Portuguese: Gil; in English: Giles, q.v.

AELGIFU (St) W. O.S.B.   A.C. May 18
Otherwise Elgiva, q.v.

AELPHLEAH, AELPHEGE (St) Bp.
Otherwise Elphege, q.v.

AELRED (St) Ab. O.S.B.Cist
**   A.C. Jan. 12**
1109-1167. Born in the north of England,
Aelred became master of the household of
King David of Scotland. In 1133 he
joined the Cistercian community of Rievaulx in Yorkshire. Soon he was made
abbot, first of Revesby, then of Rievaulx
itself. Austere with himself, he was, we
are told, remarkably gentle with his
monks, of whom he dismissed not one in
seventeen years. His ascetical treatises,
especially that *On Spiritual Friendship,*
are full of charm. He was canonized by
the General Chapter of Cîteaux in 1250.
*Cf. Dict. Baudrill. — Att. — Baud. —
P. de U. — Zimm.*

**AEMILIAN — AEMILIANA — AEMILIO
— AEMILIUS**
Otherwise Emilian — Emiliana — Emilio
— Emilius, q.v.

AENGUS (OENGUS, OENGOBA) (St)
Bp.   A.C. March 11
d. c.830. Known as "the Culdee." He

is said to have been first a monk of Clone-nagh and then of Tallacht Hill. He is best remembered as the composer of a celebrated metrical hymn to the saints, called Felire (Festilogium, metrical mar-tyrology). Though he was famous in his day, no early account of him is extant and he is not commemorated liturgically in any Irish diocese. From Tallacht Hill he returned to Clonenagh, where he be-came abbot and bishop.
Cf. Att. (whom we have followed closely in the above notice) — Dict. Baudrill. — Holw.

AESCHILUS (St) Bp. M.   A.C. June 13
Otherwise Eskill, q.v.

AETHELGIFU
Otherwise Ethelgiva or Elgiva, q.v.

AETHELHARD (St) Bp.   A.C. May 12
Otherwise Ethelhard, q.v.

AETHERIUS (several)
Otherwise Etherius, q.v.

AETIUS (St) M.   R.M. March 10
See Forty Armenian Martyrs.

AFAN (St) Bp.   A.C. Nov. 16
6th cent. A Welsh saint of the Cunedda family, by some supposed to have been a bishop. He has given its title to the church of Llanafan (Brecknock).
Cf. Holw.

AFFROSA (St) V.M.   R.M. Jan. 4
Otherwise Dafrosa (or Daphrosa), q.v.

AFRA (St) V.M.   R.M. May 24
? A martyr of Brescia, connected by legend with SS Faustinus and Jovita. The rest of the legend is untrustworthy.
Cf. Dict. Baudrill. — Att. — Baud.

AFRA (St) V.M.   R.M. Aug. 5
d. c.304. A martyr who suffered at Augs-burg, probably under Diocletian. She was venerated there from early times, and the great Benedictine abbey of that city was dedicated to her. The story of her being a converted harlot from Cyprus is worthless.
Cf. Dict. Baudrill. — Att. — Baud. — Holw. — Ruinart.

AFRICA (Martyrs of) (SS)
By Africa here is meant only North West-ern Africa, or *Africa Latina*. North

Eastern Africa goes under the heading Egypt or Ethiopia. The following anony-mous groups of martyrs are mentioned in the Roman Martyrology:

R.M. Jan. 6
d. c.210. A number of Christians of either sex burnt at the stake under Septimius Severus.

R.M. Feb. 11
d. c.303. Martyrs known as the "Guard-ians of the Holy Scriptures." They chose to die rather than to deliver the sacred books to be burnt. They suffered under Diocletian. St Augustine mentions especially those of Numidia.

R.M. Apr. 5
d. 459. A large group martyred on Easter Sunday while assisting at Mass, under Genseric, the Arian king of the Vandals. The lector, who was at the moment inton-ing the Alleluja, had his throat pierced by an arrow.

R.M. Apr. 9
? A group of Christians martyred at Masyla (Martyres Massylitani). St Augustine and Prudentius sang their praises.

R.M. Oct. 16
? Two hundred and twenty Christians were put to death on this day, where, when and how is not known.

R.M. Oct. 30
? A group of Christians, numbering be-tween one (and) two hundred, massacred in one of the early persecutions. No other details are available.

R.M. Dec. 16
d. 482. A great number of women butch-ered under Hunneric, Arian king of the Vandals.

AFRICANUS (St) M.   R.M. Apr. 10
See Terentius, Africanus, etc.

AFRICUS (St) C.   A.C. Nov. 16
7th cent. A saint of Comminges in S. France, celebrated for his zeal for ortho-doxy. His shrine was destroyed by the Calvinists, but his cultus still endures. Tradition makes him bishop of that city, but his name is not mentioned in the French Episcopologia.
Cf. P. de U.

AGABIUS (St) Bp.   R.M. Aug. 4
c. 250. An early bishop of Verona.
Cf. Dict. Baudrill. — Gams — Bolland. — Baud.

14 THE BOOK OF SAINTS

AGABUS (St) C. R.M. Feb. 13
1st cent. A prophet twice mentioned in
the Acts of the Apostles. (XI 28; XXI
10-12.) A Carmelite legend has led to his
being usually represented in art robed in
the Carmelite habit and holding the model
of a church.
Cf. Att. — Baud. — Holw.

AGAMUND (St) M. O.S.B. A.C. Apr. 9
See Theodore and Comp.

AGANUS (St) Ab. O.S.B. P.C. Feb. 16
c. 1050-1100. An abbot of St Gabriel's
at Airola in Campania, diocese of St
Agatha dei Goti.
Cf. Holw. — Zimm.

AGAPE (St) M. R.M. Jan. 25
See Donatus, Sabinus, etc.
Note. The genitive case Agapis in the
R.M. may designate a saint of either sex.

AGAPE (St) V.M. R.M. Feb. 15
c. 273. A martyred maiden especially
venerated at Terni in Umbria, where a
church was dedicated under her title as
early as the 6th cent. She was a contemporary of St Valentine, bishop of the
same place.
*Cf. Dict. Baudrill. — Att. — Baud. —
Holw.*

AGAPE, CHIONIA and IRENE (SS)
VV. MM. R.M. Apr. 3
d. 304. Three sisters who were burnt alive
with several companions under Diocletian
at Salonika. All suffered on April 3 except
Irene, who was exposed in a brothel and
put to death later.
*Cf. Ruinart — Dict. Baudrill. — Att. —
Baud.*

AGAPE (St) V. M. R.M. Aug. 1
Otherwise Charity, q.v.

AGAPE (St) V. M. R.M. Dec. 28
See Indes, Domna, etc.

AGAPITUS (St) Bp. R.M. March 16
4th cent. Bishop of Ravenna.
Cf. Baud. — Holw. — Gams.

AGAPITUS (St) Bp. R.M. March 24
3rd cent. Bishop of Synnada in Phrygia.
Cf. Baud.

AGAPITUS (St) M. R.M. Aug. 6
See Xystus and Comp.

AGAPITUS (St) M. R.M. Aug. 18
d. c.274. A boy of fifteen who bravely
confessed Christ and was martyred at
Palestrina, near Rome. He is the patron
saint of Palestrina, where as early as the
5th cent. a church was dedicated to him by
Pope Felix III (483-492).
*Cf. Dict. Baudrill. — Baud. — Att. —
Holw.*

AGAPITUS (St) M. R.M. Sept. 20
See Eustace, Theopistus, etc.

AGAPITUS I (St) Pope.
R.M. Sept. 20 (and Apr. 22)
d. 536. A Roman by birth and archdeacon of the Roman Church, he was
elected pope in May 535 and died at Constantinople on April 22, 536. As pope he
showed great strength of character in deposing the Monophysite patriarch of Constantinople. His body was taken back to
Rome on Sept. 20, on which date he is
commemorated a second time in the R.M.
In common with many other Italian
saints of the same period he owes his cult
to the devotion of St Gregory the Great.
*Cf. Dict. Baudrill. — Bolland. — Att. —
Baud.*

AGAPITUS (St) M. R.M. Nov. 20
See Bassus, Dionysius, etc.

AGAPIUS (St) M. R.M. March 24
See Timolaus, Dionysius, etc.

AGAPIUS (St) M. R.M. Apr. 28
See Aphrodisius, Caralippus, etc.

AGAPIUS and Comp. (SS) MM.
R.M. Apr. 29
c. 259. The Spanish saints Agapius and
Secundinus, bishops or priests, were banished to Cirta, Numidia, in the persecution under Valerian. There they suffered
martyrdom together with Emilian, a soldier, Tertulla and Antonia, virgins, and a
certain woman with her twin children.
*Cf. Ruinart — Dict. Baudrill. — Baud. —
P. de U.*

AGAPIUS (St) M. R.M. Aug. 19
See Timothy, Thecla and Agapius.
St. Agapius is also commemorated sepa-
rately on Nov. 20, q.v.

AGAPIUS (St) M. R.M. Aug. 21
See Bassa, Theogonius, etc.

AGAPIUS (or AGAPITUS) (St) Bp.
R.M. Sept. 10
d. c.420. Bishop of Novara in Piedmont
from c. 400 to c. 420. Successor to St
Gaudentius, "whose footsteps he fol-
lowed."
Cf. Gams — Bolland. — Dict. Baudrill. —
Baud. (Agabius).

AGAPIUS (St) M. **R.M. Nov. 2**
See Carterius, Styriacus, etc.

AGAPIUS (St) M. **R.M. Nov. 20**
d. c.306. Martyred at Caesarea in Palestine under Diocletian. He was thrice
imprisoned for the Faith. Again arrested, he was chained to a murderer and
taken to the amphitheatre to be thrown to
the wild beasts. His companion was
pardoned, and liberty was also offered to
Agapius if he would renounce Christ. He
refused, and a bear was let loose upon him
which almost mauled him to death. He
was taken back to prison and on the following day weighted with heavy stones
and cast into the sea. He is also commemorated on Aug. 19.
Cf. Ruinart — Bolland. — Dict. Baudrill.

AGATHA (St) V.M. **R.M. Feb. 5**
d. c.250. Born either at Catania or
Palermo in Sicily, she suffered martyrdom
at Catania. According to the *legenda*, she
was handed over to a prostitute and her
breasts were cut off. St Peter cured her of
this mutilation while she was in prison,
where she subsequently died. Her cult
spread throughout the Church. To this
day her name is to be found in the litany
of the saints, in the canon of the Mass, and
in all the martyrologies, Greek and Latin.
In art she is represented holding a pair of
pincers or bearing her breasts on a platter:
later these were mistaken for loaves,
whence arose the custom of blessing bread
on a dish on St Agatha's day. The miracles by which she has preserved Catania
from successive eruptions of Mt Etna are
well accredited. She is the patroness of
wet-nurses, bell-founders and jewellers.
Cf. Ruinart — Bolland. — Dict. Baudrill.
— Att. — Baud. — P. de U. — Holw.

AGATHA (St) W. **P.C. Feb. 5**
d. 1024. Wife of Paul, count of Carinthia.
A model of devotion to her domestic duties
and of patience under the brutal ill-
treatment of her jealous husband, whom

she converted. She is highly venerated in
Carinthia.
Cf. Baud. — Holw.

AGATHA LIN (Bl) V.M. **A.C. Feb. 18**
1817-1858. A Chinese school-teacher,
born at Ma-Tchang and beheaded for the
Faith at Mao-ken on Jan. 28. She was
beatified on May 2, 1909.
Cf. Holw.

AGATHA (St) V. O.S.B. **A.C. Dec. 12**
d. c.790. Nun of Wimborne, disciple of
St Lioba, with whom she crossed over to
Germany to help St Boniface in his mis-
sionary labours.
Cf. Dict. Baudrill. — Holw.

AGATHANGELUS (St) M.
R.M. Jan. 23
d. c.309. Agathangelus was converted
and baptized by St Clement, bishop of
Ancyra, while the latter was a prisoner in
Rome. He followed the bishop to the
East, and both were martyred at Ancyra.
Their *Acta* are most romantic, but un-
fortunately spurious.
Cf. Dict. Baudrill. — Baud. — Holw.

AGATHANGELUS and CASSIAN (BB)
MM. O.F.M.Cap. **A.C. Aug. 7**
d. 1638. Agathangelus of Vendôme —
his baptismal name was Francis Noury —
became a Capuchin friar at Vendôme and
eventually was sent to Egypt (1633) to
work for the reconciliation of the dissident
Coptic Christians. There he joined his
fellow-Capuchin, Fr Cassian of Nantes.
Their mission failed and they passed on
into Abyssinia. They were at once re-
ported to King Fasilidas by a German Protestant and stoned to death on entering
the country. They were beatified in 1904.
Cf. Att. — Baud.

AGATHIUS (St) M. **R.M. May 8**
Otherwise Acacius, q.v.

AGATHO (St) Pope. **R.M. Jan. 10**
d. 681. Pope from June 27, 678, to
Jan. 10, 681. He was a Sicilian of Palermo
and probably a monk, whether Benedictine or Basilian is not certain. As pope
he convened the 6th oecumenical council
held at Constantinople in 680 against the
Monothelites. He restored St Wilfrid to
the see of York.
Cf. Dict. Baudrill.—Att.—Baud.— Holw.

AGATHO (St) M.   **R.M. Feb. 14**
See Cyrion, Bassian, etc.

AGATHO and TRIPHINA (SS) MM.
           R.M. July 5
d. ? 306. Sicilian martyrs about whom nothing further is known. There is doubt even as to the sex of the latter saint.
Cf. Dict. Baudrill. — Baud.

AGATHO (St) Ab.   **A.C. Oct. 21**
4th cent. Hermit and abbot in Egypt. Often quoted in the *Lives of the Fathers of the Desert.*
Cf. Dict. Baudrill. — Baud. — Holw.

AGATHO (St) M.   **R.M. Dec. 7**
d. 250. This Agatho has been identified with St Besas, whom the R.M. mentions on Feb. 27 together with SS Julian and Ennus, q.v.
Cf. Quentin, O.S.B., Martyrol. hist. du M. A: 619, 658 — Baud. — Att.

AGATHOCLIA (or AGATHOLICA) (St) V. M.   **R.M. Sept. 17**
? The *laus* of the R.M. is as follows: "On the same day the birthday of St Agathoclia, the handmaid of a certain infidel woman, who for a long time afflicted her with stripes and other torments to make her deny Christ. She was at last taken before the judge and treated with even greater cruelty, and as she persisted in the confession of the Faith, her tongue was cut out and she was cast into the fire." It is probable that she was a Greek, but at a later period she was said to have been a Spaniard, perhaps because she was the patron saint of Mequinenza in Aragon.
Cf. Baud. — Holw.

AGATHODORUS (St) Bp. M.
           R.M. March 4
See Basil, Eugene, etc.

AGATHODORUS (St) M.   **R.M. Apr. 13**
See Carpus, Papylus, etc.

AGATHONICA (St) V. M.   **R.M. Apr. 13**
See Carpus, Papylus, etc.

AGATHONICA (St) V. M.   **R.M. Aug. 10**
See Bassa, Paula and Agathonica.

AGATHONICUS, ZOTICUS and Comp. (SS) MM.   **R.M. Aug. 22**
d. end of 3rd cent. Agathonicus, a patrician, was put to death in the neighbour-hood of Constantinople under Maximian Herculius. Zoticus, a philosopher of Bithynia, and several of his disciples were martyred about the same time. A magnificent basilica was built in their honour at Byzantium.
Cf. Dict. Baudrill. — An. Bol. II 99 V. 396 — Holw.

AGATHOPEDES (AGATHOPUS) and THEODULUS (SS) MM.   **R.M. Apr. 4**
d. 303. Agathopedes, a deacon, and Theodulus, a young reader, of the church of Thessalonica were martyred by drowning under Maximinian Herculius for refusing to give up the sacred books.
Cf. Dict. Baudrill. — Att. — Baud.

AGATHOPEDES (AGATHOPUS) (St) C.   **R.M. Apr. 25**
See Philo and Agathopedes.

AGATHOPUS (St) M.   **R.M. Dec. 23**
See Theodulus, Saturninus, etc.

AGERANUS (AYRAN, AYRMAN) (St) M. O.S.B.   **P.C. May 21**
d. 888. Ageranus was a monk of Bèze in the Côte d'Or. When the Normans invaded Burgundy (886-889) most of the monks escaped, but Ageranus remained with four other monks — Genesius, Berard, Sifrard and Rodron — the boy Adalaric and the priest Ansuinus. All were massacred by the invaders.
Cf. Chev. — Dict. Baudrill. — Baud.

AGERICUS (AGUY, AIRY) (St) Ab. O.S.B.   **P.C. Apr. 11**
d. c.680. A disciple of St Eligius (Eloi) who became abbot of St Martin's at Tours.
Cf. Chev. — Baud. — Zimm. — Holw.

AGERICUS (AGUY, AIRY) (St) Bp.
           R.M. Dec. 1
c. 521-591. Successor of St Desiderius in the see of Verdun (554). He was greatly admired by his contemporaries SS Gregory of Tours and Venantius Fortunatus. He was buried in his own home, which was turned into a church. Around it was built in 1037 the Benedictine abbey of Saint-Airy.
Cf. Gams — Dict. Baudrill. — Att. — Baud. (Airy).

AGGAEUS (St) M.   **R.M. Jan. 4**
See Hermes, Aggaeus and Caius.

AGGAEUS (AGGEUS, HAGGAI) (St)
Prophet. **R.M. July 4**
d. c.516 B.C. The tenth of the Minor
Prophets. He belongs to the period after
the exile, and the purpose of his divine
message was to forward the rebuilding of
the Temple of Jerusalem.
Cf. His prophecy and commentaries.

AGIA (AIA, AUSTEGILDIS, AYE) (St)
N. O.S.B. **A.C. Apr. 18**
d. c.714. Wife of St Hydulphus of Hainault. Both desiring to become religious,
she entered the nunnery of Mons (Cas-
trilocus), while he joined the monks of
Lobbes. She is especially venerated by
the Beguines of Belgium.
Cf. Mab. — Baud. — Chev.

AGIA (AIA, AYE) (St) **W.** **A.C. Sept. 1**
6th cent. Mother of St Lupus of Sens.
Cf. Holw.

AGILBERT (AGLIBERT) (St) **Bp. O.S.B.**
P.C. Oct. 11
d. c.685. A Frankish monk of Jouarre
under the abbot Ado. He studied scripture in France and then crossed over to
England and preached in Wessex. He was
invited to remain as bishop of the West
Saxons, and as such he came in contact
with St Wilfrid. The two saints were
leaders of the "Roman party" in the synod
of Whitby. When King Coinwalch grew
impatient of the presence in his realm of a
foreign bishop, Agilbert returned to France
and was made bishop of Paris in 668. He
was buried at Jouarre.
*Cf. Mab. — Chev. — Gams — Att. —
Zimm.*

**AGILBERTA (AGUILBERTA, GIL-
BERTA)** (St) **Abs. O.S.B.** **A.C. Aug. 10**
d. c.680. Second abbess of Jouarre,
elected about the year 660 She was a
relative of St Ebrigisil, of St Ado, founder
of Jouarre, and of St Agilbert, bishop of
Paris.
Cf. Dict. Baudrill. — Baud. — Holw.

AGILEUS (St) **M.** **R.M. Oct. 15**
d. c.300. An African Christian who
suffered martyrdom at Carthage. His
relics were afterwards translated to Rome.
He was held in great veneration in the
Latin Church, especially in Africa. We
have a sermon of St Augustine's in the
martyr's honour.
Cf. Bolland. — Baud. — Holw.

AGILO (Bl) **Ab. O.S.B.** **P.C. Aug. 27**
d. 957. Monk of St Aper at Toul. He
was invited by St Gerard of Brogne to
restore monastic discipline at Sithin
(Saint-Bertin).
Cf. Mab. — P.B. — Zimm.

AGILULPH (St) **M. Abp. O.S.B.**
A.C. July 9
d. p.720. Monk and abbot of Stavelot-
Malmédy and archbishop of Cologne.
His martyrdom was the result of the zeal-
ous discharge of his ministry, and, it
seems, with the connivance of Charles
Martel.
*Cf. Mab. — Chev. — Holw. — Baud. —
Zimm.*

AGILUS (St) **Ab.** **A.C. Aug. 30**
c. 580-650. A young Frankish nobleman
who became a monk under St Columbanus
at Luxeuil. He remained at Luxeuil
under the founder's successor, St Eustace,
but eventually departed to evangelize
Bavaria. On his return to France he became abbot of Rebais, near Paris. He is
known also as Aile, Ail, Aisle, Ayeul,
Ely.
Cf. Dict. Baudrill. — Baud. — Holw.

AGLIBERT (St) **M.** **R.M. June 24**
See Agoard, Aglibert, etc.

AGNELLUS of PISA (Bl) **C. O.F.M.**
A.C. March 13
1194-1236. Born at Pisa, Agnellus was
received by St Francis himself among the
Friars Minor and sent by him to open a
house at Paris. He was later appointed
by Francis the first Provincial of the Order
in England. Agnellus arrived at Dover
in 1224 and founded houses at Canterbury
and Oxford. He worked also for some
time in London. At Oxford he established
a school which became famous, and at Oxford he died. Cult confirmed in 1892.
Cf. Att. — Holw. — Dict. Baudrill.

AGNELLUS (St) **Ab. O.S.B. R.M. Dec. 14**
d. c.596. Hermit and afterwards abbot
of San Gaudioso near Naples. He is one
of the patron saints of the city and, the
R.M. adds, "was often seen to free the besieged city from its foes by the banner of
the cross."
Cf. Mab. — Chev. — Baud. — Zimm.

AGNES (St) **V. M.** **R.M. Jan. 21**
d. c.304. A Roman maiden, aged twelve

or thirteen years, who was martyred under Diocletian and buried beside the Via Nomentana, where a basilica in her honour has stood since the time of Constantine the Great. St Ambrose, St Damasus and Prudentius sang her praises. Her name occurs in the canon of the Mass, and as a special patroness of chastity she is one of the most popular of saints. Unfortunately the details of her *Acta* are not trustworthy. In art she is usually represented with a lamb.
Cf. Ruinart — Bolland — Att. — Baud. — Dict. Baudrill.

AGNES OF BENIGAMIN (Bl) V. O.S.A.
Disc.   **A.C. Jan. 22**
d. 1696. A nun of the discalced Augustinians of the convent of Benigamin in the archdiocese of Valencia, Spain. Beatified in 1888.
Cf. Holw.

AGNES DE (Bl) M.   **A.C. Feb. 18**
d. July 12, 1841. Born of Christian parents at Bai-den in W. Tonkin, she died in prison for the Faith at Nam-dinh. Beatified in 1909.
Cf. Holw.

AGNES of BOHEMIA (Bl) V. Poor Clare
                             A.C. March 2
1200-1282. Born at Prague, daughter of the king of Bohemia, she was educated by the Cistercian nuns of Trebnitz and betrothed to several princes in turn. She refused to marry, and, with the help of Pope Gregory IX, became a Poor Clare in a foundation of her own at Prague, to which St Clare sent five nuns from Assisi. Agnes remained here till her death, forty-six years later.
Cf. Dict. Baudrill. — Att. — Holw.

AGNES of MONTEPULCIANO (St) V.
O.P.   **R.M. Apr. 20**
1268-1317. Born near Montepulciano in Tuscany, she entered the convent *del Sacco* at the age of nine. At fourteen she was given charge of the temporalities, and at fifteen she was made first abbess of the convent at Procena. After some seventeen years she was asked to return to Montepulciano to take charge of a new house of Dominican nuns. Here she spent the remainder of her life. Canonized by Benedict XIII in 1726.
Cf. Dict. Baudrill. — Att. — Holw. — Baud.

AGNES of POITIERS (St) Abs.
                             A.C. May 13
d. 588. Chosen by St Radegund to be abbess of the nunnery of Holy Cross at Poitiers, Agnes adopted the Rule of St Caesarius, handed to her by the holy bishop himself. She is best known as the friend of the poet St Venantius Fortunatus.
Cf. Dict. Baudrill. — Baud. — Holw.

AGNES of VENOSA (Bl) V. O.S.B.Mont.
                             P.C. Sept. 1
d. c.1144. Said to have been one of the dancing girls sent to tempt St William of Vercelli. She repented and joined the Monteverginian nuns at Venosa, where she became abbess.
Cf. Zimm.

AGNES of BAGNO (Bl) V. O.S.B.Cam.
                             A.C. Sept. 4
d. c.1105. A Camaldolese nun at Santa Lucia, near Bagno di Romagna in Tuscany. Her cult was confirmed in 1823. Her relics are enshrined in the village church of Pereto.
Cf. Zimm.

AGNES TAQUEA (Bl) M.   A.C. Sept. 10
d. 1662. Wife of Bl Cosmas Taquea. A native Japanese woman beheaded at Nagasaki. She and her husband belong to the group of fifty-one Christians who were martyred on the same day with Bl Charles Spinola, S.J., q.v. Beatified in 1867.
Cf. Holw.

AGNES of BAVARIA (Bl) V.
                             P.C. Nov. 11
d. 1532. Daughter of Louis IV, duke of Bavaria, she was educated by the Poor Clares of St James at Munich, where she died aged seven.
Cf. Baud. — Dict. Baudrill.

AGNES of ASSISI (St) V. Abs. Poor Clare.
                             A.C. Nov. 16
1198-1253. Younger sister of St Clare, whom she followed, aged sixteen, to the Benedictine convent of Panso, near Assisi, and then to San Damiano. She became the first abbess of Monticelli at Florence, opened houses at Padua, Venice and Mantua, and returned to San Damiano, where she died three months after her sister. Cult confirmed by Benedict XIV.
Cf. Dict. Baudrill. — Baud. — Holw. — Att.

AGNES TSAO-KOUY (Bl) W. M.
A.C. Nov. 24
d. Feb. 25, 1856. A young Chinese widow who served the missionaries as catechist. She was killed by "cage torture" at Kwang-si. Beatified in 1900.
Cf. Holw.

AGOARD, AGLIBERT and others (SS) MM. R.M. June 24
5th to 7th cent. The R.M. has the legend: "In the neighbourhood of Paris, in the village of Creteil, the passion of the holy martyrs Agoard and Aglibert, and numberless others of both sexes." The Bollandists fix the date of their martyrdom between the 1st and the 3rd centuries, but in all probability it took place between the 5th and the 7th.
Cf. Bolland.— Baud. — Dict. Baudrill.

AGOBARD (St) Bp. A.C. June 6
c. 769-840. A native of Spain, he escaped in his youth from the invading Saracens and joined the clergy of Lyons in France. He became archbishop of that city in 813. He played a prominent part in both the ecclesiastical and the political affairs of his time. But his greatest work was done as a theologian, chiefly in the field of liturgy, and he has left many important writings.
Cf. Dict. Baudrill. — Baud. — P. de U.

AGOFREDUS (St) Ab. O.S.B.
A.C. June 21
d. 738. Brother of St Leofridus (Leffroi) and his successor as abbot of Holy Cross (La-Croix-Saint-Leuffroi), a Benedictine abbey in the diocese of Evreux, Normandy. He became abbot in 738.
Cf. Holw.

AGRECIUS (AGRITIUS) (St) Bp.
R.M. Jan. 13
d. c.333. Bishop of Trèves and predecessor in that see of St Maximinus. He took part in the council of Arles (314). He is connected with the legend of the Holy Coat of Trèves, said to be the seamless garment of our Lord.
Cf. Dict. Baudrill. — Att. — Baud.

AGRICOLA (St) Bp. A.C. Feb. 5
d. 420. He is listed as the eleventh bishop of Tongres in a catalogue of the 10th century transcribed from the ancient diptychs.
Cf. Dict. Baudrill. — P.B. — Baud.

AGRICOLA (St) Bp. A.C. Feb. 26
d. c.594. Said to have been bishop of Nevers between 570 and 594.
Cf. Dict. Baudrill. — Duch. Fast. Episc. — Baud. — Gams.

AGRICOLA (St) Bp. R.M. March 17
d. 580. In French Arègle or Agrèle. Bishop of Châlon-sur-Saône. His contemporary St Gregory of Tours enlarges upon the austerity of his life.
Cf. Duch. Fast. Episc. t. 1.— Dict. Baudrill. — Att. — Baud.

AGRICOLA (or AGRICOLUS) (St) Bp.
A.C. Sept. 2
c. 630-700. Son of St Magnus, bishop of Avignon. At the age of sixteen he was professed a monk at Lérins, where he remained sixteen years. His father called him to Avignon and made him his coadjutor, and in 660 he became bishop of the city. He built a church in Avignon to be served by the monks of Lérins and also a convent for Benedictine nuns. By his blessing he put an end to an invasion of storks. All the above particulars are based on documents dating only from the 15th century, and only since 1647 has Agricola been the patron saint of Avignon.
Cf. Dict. Baudrill. — Att. — Baud.

AGRICOLA (St) M. R.M. Nov. 4
See Vitalis and Agricola.

AGRICOLA (St) M. R.M. Dec. 3
? A martyr in Pannonia, details of whose life have not come down to us, but whose name appears in all the ancient registers.
Cf. Baud.

AGRICOLA (St) M. R.M. Dec. 16
See Valentine, Concordius, etc.

AGRIPPINA (St) V. M. R.M. June 23
d. c.262. A Roman maiden who was martyred, it is surmised, under Valerian. She is especially venerated by the Sicilians and by the Greeks, both claiming to have her relics, the former at Mineo, the latter at Constantinople.
Cf. Dict. Baudrill. — Att. — Baud.

AGRIPPINUS (St) Bp. A.C. Jan. 30
d. c.180. The ninth bishop of Alexandria after St Mark.
Cf. Dict. Baudrill. — Baud. — Holw.

AGRIPPINUS (St) Bp.   P.C. June 17
d. 615. Bishop of Como in N. Italy.
There are well-founded doubts about his
claim to the title of saint.
Cf. Gams — Dict. Baudrill. — Baud.

AGRIPPINUS (St) Bp.   A.C. July 9
d. 538. Bishop of Autun, who ordained
St Germanus of Paris to the deaconate and
the priesthood.
*Cf. Gams — Duch. Fast. Episc. — Dict.
Baudrill.*

AGRIPPINUS (ARPINO) (St) Bp.
R.M. Nov. 9
2nd or 3rd cent. Bishop of Naples, where
he has been greatly venerated from time
immemorial. His relics are enshrined
under the high altar of the cathedral of
Naples with the bodies of SS Eutychius
and Acutius, companions of St Januarius.
*Cf. Gams — Dict. Baudrill. — Baud. —
Holw.*

AGRITIUS (St) Bp.   R.M. Jan. 13
Otherwise Agrecius, q.v.

AGUY
An abbreviated popular form of the names
Agericus and Agritius, q.v.

AIA (St) W.   A.C. Sept. 1
Otherwise Agia, q.v.

AIBERT (AYBERT) (St) H. O.S.B.
A.C. Apr. 7
c. 1060-1140. Born at Espain, near
Tournai, he became a monk at the abbey
of St Crespin, where for twenty-three
years he was provost and cellarer; then
he retired to live as a recluse. His devotion to the Holy Sacrifice took the form
of saying two masses daily, one for the
living and one for the dead.
*Cf. Chev. — Dict. Baudrill. — Holw. —
P.B.*

AICHARDUS (AICARD, ACHARD) (St)
Ab. O.S.B.   R.M. Sept. 15
d. c.687. Born at Poitiers, the son of an
officer at the court of Clotaire II. He was
educated at the abbey of St Hilaire at
Poitiers and early in life was professed as
a monk of Ansion in Poitou. Here he
spent thirty-nine years; afterwards he
became abbot of St Benedict's at Quinçay,
near Poitiers. Finally he succeeded St
Philibert at Jumièges, where he ruled close
on a thousand monks.
Cf. Mab. — Att. — Baud. — Holw.

AICHARDUS (Bl) Mk. O.S.B. Cist.
P.C. Sept. 15
d. c.1170. Entered Clairvaux (c. 1124)
and made his profession in the hands of St
Bernard, who sent him to several foundations. Having returned to Clairvaux he
was made novice-master by St Bernard
himself.
Cf. Baud. — Butler-Thurston (Sept. 15)

AID (St) Ab.   A.C. Apr. 11
? An abbot of Achard-Finglas in Co.
Carlow, possibly one and the same with
St Aed or Maedhogh of Clonmore.
Cf. O' Hanlon.

AIDAN (or MAEDOC) (St) Bp.
A.C. Jan. 31
d. 626. The first bishop of Ferns in Co.
Wexford, Eire, where he founded and
ruled a monastery as well. In his youth
he had come under the influence of St
David in Wales. The miracles which he is
said to have wrought seem very strange to
modern readers.
Cf. Att. — Holw.

AIDAN (AEDAN) (St) Bp. ˉR.M. Aug. 31
d. 651. An Irish monk of Iona who, at
the request of St Oswald king of Northumbria, was sent to evangelize N. England. He fixed his see at Lindisfarne
(Holy Island) where he ruled as abbot and
bishop, his diocese reaching from the
Forth to the Humber. His apostolate,
furthered by numberless miracles, was
most fruitful, as is witnessed by the writings of St Bede. He died at Bamborough.
In art he is represented sometimes with a
stag near him, suggested by a legend that
by his prayer he once rendered invisible a
deer pursued by huntsmen.
*Cf. Mab. — Dict. Baudrill. — Baud. —
Holw. — Att.*

AIDAN (St) Bp.   A.C. Oct. 20
d. 768. An Irish bishop in Mayo.
Cf. O'Hanlon.

AIGNAN (AGNAN) (St) Bp.
R.M. Nov. 17
Otherwise Anianus, q.v.

**AIGULPHUS (AYOUL, AIEUL, AOUT,
HOU) (St) Bp.   A.C. May 22**
d. p.835. After an excellent education he
chose to live as a recluse. However,
about the year 812 he was against his will

placed in the see of Bourges, which he governed till his death.
Cf. Dict. Baudrill. — Baud. — P.B. — Gams.

AIGULPHUS (AYOU, AYOUL) (St) Ab. M. O.S.B. R.M. Sept. 3
c. 630-676. Born at Blois, at the age of twenty he entered Fleury, then in its first fervour of Benedictine observance. He was sent first to Montecassino to rescue the relics of St Benedict, and then (c. 670) as abbot to Lérins to introduce the Benedictine Rule. Some malcontents — laymen, it appears — opposed him and caused him to be taken, with four of his monks, to an island near Corsica where they were done to death.
Cf. Mab. — Dict. Baudrill. — Att. — Zimm. — Chev. — Baud.

AILBE (ALBEUS, AILBHE) (St) Bp. A.C. Sept. 12
We transcribe Donald Attwater's excellent summary: "A commemoration of the feast of St Ailbe (*Albeus*) is made throughout Ireland, but his recorded life is a confusion of valueless legends and contradictory traditions. He is venerated as the first bishop at Emly, in the early sixth century, and is reputed as author of a monastic rule."

AILRED (St) Ab. O.S.B. Cist. A.C. Jan. 12
Otherwise Aelred, q.v.

AIMARD (Bl) Ab. O.S.B. A.C. Oct. 5
Otherwise Aymard, q.v.

AIMÉ (AMÉ) (St) Ab. O.S.B. R.M. Sept. 13
Otherwise Amatus, q.v.

AIMO (AIMONIUS) (St) Mk. P.C. Feb. 13
d. c.790. Founder of the nunnery of St Victor at Meda in the archdiocese of Milan.
Cf. Mab. — Bolland. — Chev. — Holw.

AIMO (AYMO, HAIMO) (St) Mk. O.S.B. A.C. Apr. 30
d. 1173. Born in the diocese of Rennes, Aimo joined the community of Savigny in Normandy. Suspected of being a leper, he offered to serve two religious who were actually lepers. Afterwards he was admitted to profession, and ordained priest and appointed to various offices. He had many severe trials and was favoured with mystical experiences.
Cf. Baud. — Chev. — P. de U. — Holw.

AIMO TAPARELLI (Bl) C. O.P. A.C. Aug. 18
1395-1495. A native of Savigliano in Piedmont and a member of the family of the counts of Lagnasco. He became a Dominican, and was appointed chaplain to Bl Duke Amadeus of Savoy and inquisitor general for Lombardy and Liguria. He died a centenarian. Cult confirmed in 1856.
Cf. Att. — Baud. — Holw.

AIRALDUS (AYRALDUS) Bp. O. Cart. A.C. Jan. 2
d. 1160. Carthusian prior of Portes, in the diocese of Belley, and, from 1132 to 1156, bishop of St John of Maurienne in Savoy.
Cf. Gams — Att. — Holw. — Baud.

AIRY (St) Bp. R.M. Dec. 1
Otherwise Agericus, q.v.

AISLE (AILEU) (St) Ab. A.C. Aug. 30
Otherwise Agilus, q.v.

AITHALAS (St) M. R.M. Apr. 22
4th cent. One of the band of Persian martyrs whose leader was St Abdiesus, q.v.

AIZAN and SAZAN (SS) MM. A.C. Oct. 1
d. c.400. Two brothers, petty chieftains in Abyssinia, very zealous in spreading the gospel in their own country. They were great friends of St Athanasius.
Cf. Holw.

AJOU (AJON) (St) Ab. M. O.S.B. R.M. Sept. 3
Otherwise Aigulphus, q.v.

AJUTRE (St) H. O.S.B. A.C. Apr. 30
Otherwise Adjutor, q.v.

ALACOQUE, MARGARET MARY (St) V. R.M. Oct. 17
See Margaret Mary Alacoque.

ALACRINUS (Bl) Bp. O.S.B. Cist. P.C. Jan. 5
d. 1216. Cistercian prior of Casamari, diocese of Veroli, he was sent as papal

legate to Germany under Popes Innocent III and Honorius III.
Cf. Chev. — Holw. — Zimm.

ALADIUS (St) Bp.　　　**A.C. Oct. 1**
Otherwise Albaud, q.v.

ALANUS (St) Ab. O.S.B. Cist.
　　　　　　　　　　　　P.C. June 28
Otherwise Almus, q.v.

ALANUS (Bl) H. O.S.B.　　**A.C. July 18**
d. 1311. An Austrian monk who in the jubilee year of 1300 journeyed to Rome and afterwards joined the Italian community of Sassovivo. In 1311 he became a recluse.
Cf. Zimm.

ALANUS de RUPE (ALAIN de la ROCHE) (Bl) C. O.P.　　**P.C. Sept. 8**
c. 1428-1475. A native of Brittany, he became a Dominican at Dinan, diocese of St Malo and was stationed at the Dominican houses of Paris, Lille, Ghent, and Zwoll, where he died. He is famous for his zeal in spreading the devotion of the Holy Rosary. Cult not yet officially confirmed.
Cf. Baud. — Dict. Baudrill.

ALANUS (St) Ab. O.S.B.　　**A.C. Nov. 25**
7th cent. Abbot-founder of Lavaur in Gascony.
Cf. Zimm. — Holw.

ALANUS and ALORUS (SS) Bps.
　　　　　　　　　　　　A.C. Oct. 26
5th cent. Two bishops of Quimper in Brittany, concerning whom no reliable particulars have come down to us, except the fact of the popular and liturgical cult given to them from early ages.
Cf. Baud. — Holw.

ALARICUS (ADALRICUS, ADALRAI) (Bl) H. O.S.B.　　**A.C. Sept. 29**
d. 975. Son of Duke Burkhard II of Swabia. Educated, and then a monk, at Einsiedeln in Switzerland. Eventually he became a recluse on the small island of Uffnau, on the lake of Zurich.
Cf. Bolland. — Chev. — Baud. — Zimm. — Holw.

ALBAN BARTHOLOMEW ROE (Bl) M. O.S.B.　　**A.C. Jan. 21**
d. 1642. A Suffolk man of Protestant parentage, who was educated at Cam-

bridge and became a Catholic at Douai and a Benedictine under the name of Alban at Dieuleward (now Ampleforth) in 1612. He laboured in the English mission from 1615 to 1642 and was martyred for his priesthood at Tyburn.
Cf. Camm — Zimm. — Att.

ALBAN (St) M.　　　**R.M. June 21**
d. c.400. A Greek priest of Naxos who, sent into exile by the Arians, preached the gospel in parts of Germany about Mainz. Here he was again attacked by the Arians and put to death. The Benedictine abbey at Mainz, dedicated in his honour, has preserved his memory.
Cf. Dict. Baudrill. — Baud. — Holw.

ALBAN (St) M.　　　**R.M. June 22**
3rd or 4th cent. Venerated as the protomartyr of Britain. He was a citizen of Verulam converted by a persecuted priest whom he sheltered in his house. He was executed on Holmhurst Hill. On that spot King Offa erected the Benedictine abbey of St Alban's by which name Verulam has since been known.
Cf. Att. — Holw. — Baud. — Dict. Baudrill.

ALBAUD (ALADIUS) (St) Bp.
　　　　　　　　　　　　A.C. Oct. 1
d. c.520. Bishop of Toul. He built the church of St Aper (Epvre), his predecessor in the see, which was at a later period the abbey church of the Benedictine monastery of Saint-Aper.
Cf. Dict. Baudrill. — Baud.

ALBERIC (St) Ab. O.S.B. Cist.
　　　　　　　　　　　　A.C. Jan. 26
d. 1109. One of the three founders of the Cistercians. He was first a hermit at Collan, near Châtillon-sur-Seine; then he followed St Robert to Molesmes (1075) and was prior there and afterwards accompanied him to Cîteaux (1093) where he was again prior and succeeded St Robert as abbot in 1100. The old Cistercian martyrology adds: "He had a filial devotion to our Lady, from whom he received the white cowl."
Cf. Dict. Baudrill. — Att. — Baud. — Zimm.

ALBERIC (St) H. O.S.B. Cam.
　　　　　　　　　　　　A.C. Aug. 29
d. c.1050. A Camaldolese monk who lived

as a recluse at Ocri in the diocese of Sartena. His relics are enshrined in the Camaldolese church of S. Anastasio, diocese of Montefeltro.
Cf. Zimm. — Dict. Baudrill. — Baud. — Holw. — Bolland.

ALBERIC (St) Ab. O.S.B. P.C. Oct. 28
d. 779. Abbot of Stavelot-Malmédy. His feast is kept together with that of four other abbots of the same monastery.
Cf. Zimm. — Holw.

ALBERIC (St) Bp. O.S.B. A.C. Nov. 14
d. 784 (Aug. 21). Nephew of St Gregory of Utrecht, he became cathedral prior, and on his uncle's death in 775, bishop of St Martin's at Utrecht. He was a highly educated man, a great friend of Alcuin. His apostolate among the pagan Teutons was exceedingly fruitful.
Cf. Dict. Baudrill. — Zimm. — Baud. — Holw.

ALBERIC (Bl) Mk. O.S.B. A.C. Dec. 24
10th cent. Monk of Gladbach. Others call him Albert, and give him the title of saint.
Cf. Zimm. — Baud. (Albert) — Holw.

ALBERT of CASHEL (St) Bp.
A.C. Jan. 8
7th cent. Patron saint of Cashel in Ireland. According to the — rather unreliable — account of his life, he was an Englishman who laboured in Ireland and afterwards evangelized Bavaria, went to Jerusalem and on his return died and was interred at Ratisbon.
Cf. Att. — Holw.

ALBERT (St) King A.C. Feb. 24
Otherwise Ethelbert, q.v.

ALBERT of MONTECORVINO (St) Bp.
A.C. Apr. 5
d. 1127. Of Norman origin, Albert settled with his parents at Montecorvino and became bishop there. In his old age, he lost his sight and was given a coadjutor who treated him with amazing indignity and cruelty. The saint went through this trial with heroic patience.
Cf. Att. — Baud. — Holw.

ALBERT of BERGAMO (Bl) Tert. O.P.
A.C. May 11
d. 1279. Also called "Albert the Farmer." He was a peasant farmer who helped the poor and destitute. For his generosity he was persecuted by his shrewish wife and jealous relatives. He was a native of Ogna near Bergamo, but later lived at Cremona and died there. He was a Dominican tertiary. Cult approved in 1748.
Cf. Att. — Baud.

ALBERT of BOLOGNA (Bl) Ab. O.S.B.
Vall. A.C. May 20
d. 1245. Born at Bologna, a member of the Parisi family. He became a monk at, and eventually abbot of a Vallombrosan abbey near Bologna, which afterwards was called S. Alberto.
Cf. Baud. — Dict. Baudrill. — Holw. — Bolland. — 11 Faggio Vallombrosano. An. XV. N.1. — Chev.

ALBERT (ARIBERT) of COMO (St) Bp.
O.S.B. A.C. June 3
d. c.1092. A hermit at Rho, and afterwards monk and abbot of San Carpofero. He died bishop of Como.
Cf. Zimm.

ALBERT QUADRELLI (St) Bp.
A.C. July 4
d. 1179. Born at Rivolta d'Adda in the diocese of Cremona, he was parish priest of his native town for twenty-five years and in 1168 was chosen bishop of Lodi.
Cf. Gams — Dict. Baudrill. — Baud.

ALBERT of GENOA (St) C. O.S.B. Cist.
A.C. July 8
d. 1239. Albert, or Lambert, was born at Genoa and was professed as a lay-brother of the Cistercian abbey of Sestri da Ponente, near that city. Eventually he lived as a hermit near the abbey. His cult is very popular.
Cf. Bolland. — Chev. — Zimm. — Dict. Baudrill. — Baud.

ALBERT of VALLOMBROSA (Bl) Mk.
O.S.B. Vall. A.C. Aug. 1
Late 11th cent. A monk of Vallombrosa under St John Gualbert. Cult approved in 1600.
Cf. Holw.

ALBERT of TRAPANI (St) C. O.C.
R.M. Aug. 7
d. 1306. A native of Trapani in Sicily, he entered very young the Carmelite monastery of his native town situated on Mt

Trapani. After his ordination, he was stationed at the Carmelite house of Messina, where he devoted himself with marvellous success to the conversion of the Jews. Cult confirmed in 1453.
Cf. Dict. Baudrill. — Att. — Holw.

ALBERT (St) Ab. O.S.B.   **A.C. Sept. 5**
d. 1073. Abbot-founder of Butrio, in the diocese of Tortona.
Cf. Zimm.

ALBERT of PONTIDA (Bl) Ab. O.S.B.
A.C. Sept. 5
d. 1095 (May 1). A soldier of Bergamo, who was severely wounded and vowed, if he were cured, to become a religious. He first went as a pilgrim to Compostella and afterwards founded the Benedictine abbey of Pontida, near Bergamo, dedicated to St James, and placed it under the obedience of St Hugh of Cluny. His relics were enshrined at Santa Maria Maggiore of Bergamo, and in 1928 were brought back to Pontida.
Cf. Bolland. — Zimm. — Holw. — Baud. — Dict. Baudrill.

ALBERT of JERUSALEM (St) Bp. M.
A.C. Sept. 25
c. 1149-1214. An Italian canon regular who became successively prior general of his Institute, bishop of Bobbio, bishop of Vercelli, and in 1205, under Pope Innocent III, patriarch of Jerusalem. He is best known as co-founder of the Carmelite Friars, for whom, at the request of St Brocard, he wrote a rule. He was assassinated by an evil-liver whom he had rebuked, and has since been venerated as a martyr.
Cf. Dict. Baudrill. — Att. — Holw. — Baud.

ALBERT of SASSOFERRATO (Bl) C. O.S.B.   **A.C. Oct. 25**
d. 1330 (Aug. 7). A monk of Santa Croce di Tripozzo before the Camaldolese had taken possession of that house. Cult confirmed in 1837.
Cf. Chev. — Dict. Baudrill. — Proprium in Camaldolese Martyrology.

ALBERT the GREAT (St) Bp. Dr. O.P.
R.M. Nov. 15
1206-1280. A Swabian by descent, Albert was sent to the university of Padua where he joined the Dominicans. Appointed lector of theology, he taught at Cologne and Paris. Here St Thomas Aquinas was his disciple, and Albert was the first to recognize Thomas's genius and to foretell the future work of his pupil. Albert became provincial of his Order in Germany and, in 1260, accepted under obedience the see of Ratisbon. He resigned two years later and retired to Cologne, where he spent the rest of his life teaching and writing. Albert was the chief pioneer in the application of the Aristotelian system to theology. His printed works fill thirty-eight quarto volumes and deal with all branches of learning. For this reason he is called "the Great" and *"Doctor Universalis."* He was beatified in 1622 and was equivalently canonized by being declared a Doctor of the Church in 1931.
Cf. Dict. Baudrill. — Att. — Baud.

ALBERT of LOUVAIN (St) Bp. M.
R.M. Nov. 21
c. 1166-1192. Born at Mont César in Louvain and chosen bishop of Liége in 1191. His election was opposed by the emperor Henry VI who favoured another candidate. St Albert appealed to Pope Celestine III, who decided in his favour, and Albert was consecrated at Reims on Sept. 29, 1192, but he was murdered by three German knights only two months afterwards (Nov. 24). Cult confirmed in 1613.
Cf. Dict. Baudrill. — Att. — Baud.

ALBERT of HAIGERLOCK (Bl) Mk. O.S.B.   **A.C. Nov. 26**
d. 1311. Of the family of the counts of Haigerlock in Hohenzollern. He was a monk of Oberaltaich in Bavaria from 1261 to 1311, where he sanctified himself in the offices of prior and parish priest.
Cf. Zimm. — Chev. — Holw.

ALBERT of SASSOVIVO (Bl) Ab. O.S.B.
P.C. Dec. 10
d. p.1102. A son of Count Walter (Gualterio), the benefactor who gave to St Mainardus the site to found the abbey of the Holy Cross at Sassovivo. Bl. Albert became a monk there, and eventually third abbot of the monastery.
Cf. Zimm.

ALBERT (St) Bp.   **R.M. Dec. 13**
Otherwise Autbert, q.v.

ALBERT of GAMBRON (St) Ab. O.S.B.
A.C. Dec. 29
7th cent. A courtier who became a hermit and afterwards the abbot-founder of the small abbey of Gambron-sur-l'Authion, where the Rules of St Benedict and St Columbanus were observed simultaneously.
Cf. Mab. — Bolland. — Chev. — Zimm. — Dict. Baudrill.

ALBERTA (St) V.M. A.C. March 11
d. c.286. One of the first victims of the persecution under Diocletian. She suffered at Agen in company with St Faith and others of the same city.
Cf. Baud. — Holw.

ALBERTINUS (St) C. O.S.B.
A.C. Aug. 31
d. 1294. A monk of the monastery of the Holy Cross of Fonteavellana — head house of a Benedictine congregation which in 1570 was united with the Camaldolese. He was elected prior general of his congregation and succeeded in making peace between the bishop and the people of Gubbio. Cult confirmed by Pius VI.
Cf. Zimm. — Dict. Baudrill. — Chev. — Bolland. — Proprium of the Camaldolese — Baud.

ALBEUS (St) Bp. A.C. Sept. 12
Otherwise Ailbe, q.v.

ALBINA (St) V.M. R.M. Dec. 16
d. 250. A young Christian maiden who suffered at Caesarea under Decius. The R.M. mentions Formiae, now Mola di Gaeta in the Campagna, as the place of her death, and her relics have certainly from time immemorial been enshrined at Gaeta near Naples. The Greeks maintain that her body was miraculously translated after martyrdom.
Cf. Baud. — Dict. Baudrill.

ALBINUS (ALBUINUS) (St) Bp.
R.M. Feb. 5
See Genuinus and Albinus.

ALBINUS (AUBIN) (St) Bp.
R.M. March 1
d. c.554. A native of Vannes. Monk and abbot of Tincillac, between Angers and Saumur, and then bishop of Angers (c. 529–c. 554). He took a prominent part in the third council of Orleans (538). The abbey

of Saint-Aubin at Angers was erected in his memory. Saint-Aubin de Moeslain (Haute Marne) is to this day a popular place of pilgrimage.
Cf. Dict. Baudrill. — Mab. — Zimm. — Baud.

ALBINUS (St) Bp. O.S.B. A.C. Sept. 5
Otherwise Alvitus, q.v.

ALBINUS (AUBIN, ALPIN) (St) Bp.
R.M. Sept. 15
d. c.390. The successor of St Justus in the see of Lyons between 380 and 390. He is said to have built the church of St Stephen and to have chosen it for his cathedral.
Cf. Gams — Baud.

ALBINUS (ALBUINUS) (St) Bp. O.S.B.
A.C. Oct. 26
d. p.760. An Anglo-Saxon monk, whose native name was Witta, but who latinized it as Albinus when setting out as a fellow-worker with St Boniface in the conversion of Germany. In 741 he was consecrated bishop of Buraburg in Hesse.
Cf. Zimm. — Gams.

ALBURGA (St) W.N. O.S.B.
A.C. Dec. 25
d. c.800. Sister to King Egbert of Wessex and wife of Wulstan of Wiltshire. She founded Wilton abbey, near Salisbury, whither she retired and took the veil in her widowhood.
Cf. Mab. — Baud. — Zimm.

ALCMUND (ALCHMUND) (St) M.
A.C. March 19
d. c.800. Prince of the royal house of Northumbria, who after many years of exile among the Picts of Scotland met his death in Shropshire in circumstances which led to his being venerated as a martyr, first at Lilleshall and then at Derby.
Cf. Dict. Baudrill. — Att. — Baud.

ALCMUND (St) Bp. O.S.B. A.C. Sept. 7
d. 781. The seventh bishop of Hexham.
Cf. Att. — Dict. Baudrill. — Baud. — Holw. — Zimm. — Mab.

ALCOBER (JOHN) (Bl) O.P.
A.C. May 27
See Peter Sanz and Comp.

ALCUIN (FLACCUS ALBINUS) (Bl) Ab. O.S.B. P.C. May 19
d. 804. A native of York, who was edu-

cated at the monastic cathedral of that city and became a monk there. Eventually he was ordained deacon and appointed headmaster of his old school. He travelled to Italy to obtain the *pallium* for his bishop and at Parma met Charlemagne who forthwith enlisted his services in the cause of education. The monk became, in fact, the "minister of education" of the Frankish Empire and founded and directed the school (*schola palatina*) where Charlemagne himself became a pupil. In his old age Alcuin was given, among others, the abbey of St Martin of Tours, where he presided as abbot and restored the monastic observance with the help of St Benedict of Aniane. He was a very prolific writer, chiefly on theology and liturgy. Many martyrologies list his name as a *beatus*.
Cf. Dict. Baudrill. — Zimm. — Mab. — Baud. —Chev. — P. de U.

ALDA (ALDOBRANDESCA) (Bl) W. O.S.B. Hum. A.C. Apr. 26
1249-1309. A Sienese maiden who married a very pious husband and lived with him in conjugal continency. Upon the death of her husband Alda joined the third order of the Humiliati and devoted her life to almsdeeds and mortification. She is greatly honoured at Siena. Variants of her name are Aude, Blanca and Bruna.
Cf. Att. — Dict. Baudrill. — Baud. — Holw.

ALDATE (ELDATE) (St) C. A.C. Feb. 4
5th cent. A Briton who lived in W. England and became celebrated for his patriotism in stirring up his fellow-countrymen to resist the heathen invaders of the land. In some legends he is given as bishop of Gloucester. Many churches bear his name as their titular saint, but trustworthy data of his life are lacking.
Cf. Holw.

ALDEBRANDUS (HILDEBRAND) (St) Bp. A.C. May 1
1119-1219. Born at Sorrivoli, diocese of Cesena, he became provost of Rimini, where he was known for his brave, outspoken stand against all licentiousness: once indeed he had to flee for his life on account of his frank preaching. In 1170 he became bishop of Fossombrone of which town he is now the principal patron saint.
Cf. Att. — Baud. — Gams — Holw.

ALDEGUND (St) V. Abs. O.S.B. R.M. Jan. 30
630-634. Sister of St Waudon, abbess of Mons. She became the foundress and first abbess of Maubeuge. She died from cancer of the breast, and, we are told, "in an ecstasy of serene joy."
Cf. Att. — Dict. Baudrill. — Baud. — Holw.

ALDEMAR (St) Ab. O.S.B. A.C. March 24
d. c.1080. Surnamed "the Wise." Born at Capua, he was educated at Montecassino, where also he was professed. He was sent as a director to St Laurence's nunnery at Capua; but he was so much talked about on account of his miracles that he was recalled to Montecassino. Eventually Aldemar became the founder of Bocchignano abbey in the Abruzzi, the first of several houses which he founded and ruled with much success. He was a great lover of animals.
Cf. Mab. — Bolland. — Chev. — Zimm. — Baud. — Att.

ALDERICUS (ALDRIC, AUDRY) (St) Bp. A.C. Jan. 7
d. 856. Chaplain to the emperor Louis the Pious, and bishop of Le Mans (832). He excelled alike as a saintly prelate and as an able administrator of public affairs. Some of his works are still extant.
Cf. Dict. Baudrill. — Att. — Baud.

ALDERICUS (ALDRIC, AUDRI) (St) Bp. O.S.B. A.C. Oct. 10
790-841. Born in the Gatinais, he became a Benedictine at Ferrières. The archbishop of Sens attached him to the clergy of the archdiocese. Then he was summoned to the palace as "master and chancellor" (*magister et cancellarius*). Lastly he was raised to the archbishopric of Sens (828). He was a zealous fosterer of ecclesiastical studies.
Cf. Dict. Baudrill. — Baud. — Holw. — Chev.

ALDETRUDIS (ADELTRUDIS) (St) V. Abs. O.S.B. A.C. Feb. 25
d. c.696. Daughter of SS Vincent-Maldegarius and Waudon, and a niece of St Aldegund of Maubeuge, she was confided to her aunt's care at this nunnery, of which she became second abbess.
Cf. Baud. — Zimm. — P. de U.

ALDHELM (ADHELM ALDELMUS)
(St) Bp. O.S.B. **R.M. May 25**
639-709. A native of Wessex who became
a monk at Malmesbury. He was educated partly at Malmesbury and partly
under St Adrian at Canterbury. He was
given charge of the school at Malmesbury
and in 675 was made abbot. Lastly in
705 he was named first bishop of Sherborne. Aldhelm was the first Anglo-
Saxon to attain distinction as a scholar and
a Latin poet. His love of books is one of
the most attractive traits of his character.
He has been described as the first English
librarian.
*Cf. Att. — Baud. — Mab. — P. de U. —
Zimm.*

ALDO (Bl) O.S.B. **A.C. March 31**
d. late 8th cent. Count of Ostrevant, he
became a monk at Hasnon abbey in Belgium, which had been founded by his
brother John. Aldo was chosen second
abbot.
Cf. Baud. — Holw.

ALEMAN **A.C. Sept. 16**
See Louis Aleman.

ALENA (St) V.M. **A.C. June 24**
d. c.640. Born of pagan parents near
Brussels, Alena was baptized without their
knowledge. She was put to death while
secretly journeying to hear Mass.
Cf. Baud. — Holw.

ALETH (Bl) W. **P.C. Apr. 4**
d. 1105. Wife of Tecolin and mother of
several saintly children, the most famous
of whom is St Bernard of Clairvaux. In
1110 her relics were interred in the Benedictine abbey of St Benignus at Dijon and
in 1250 they were transferred to Clairvaux.
Cf. Baud. — Dict. Baudrill.

ALEXANDER (St) Bp. M. R.M. Jan. 11
d. c.250. A native of Fermo, near Ancona,
who became bishop of his native city, and
was martyred under Decius. His relics
are enshrined in the cathedral.
Cf. Gams — Holw.

ALEXANDER AKIMETES (St) Ab.
A.C. Jan. 15
d. 430. A Greek who became a monk in
Syria and eventually founded a *laura* by
the Euphrates, where he soon had some
four hundred monks under his rule. He

was a somewhat restless archimandrite,
fond of new places and faces. He is best
known as the founder of the "sleepless"
(*akoimetoi*) monks who sang the divine
office in relays without intermission day
and night. One of these houses he established at Constantinople.
Cf. Baud. — Dict. Baudrill. — Att.

ALEXANDER (St) M. **R.M. Jan. 30**
3rd cent. The R.M. describes him as a
martyr under Decius "glorious for his venerable age and his repeated confession."
On account of this description some writers
have identified him with St Alexander of
Jerusalem (see March 18).
Cf. Baud. — Holw.

ALEXANDER (St) M. **R.M. Feb. 9**
? A martyr of Rome who was accompanied in his confession and death by thirty-
eight others. On this same day the R.M.
mentions another St Alexander, martyred
at Seli in Cyprus together with St
Ammonius. See under Ammonius.
Cf. Baud. — Bolland.

ALEXANDER of LUGO (Bl) M. O.P.
A.C. Feb. 10
d. 1645. A Spanish Dominican martyred
by the Turks.
Cf. Prop. O.P.

ALEXANDER (St) M. **R.M. Feb. 18**
See Maximus, Claudius, etc.

ALEXANDER of ADRUMETUM (St) M.
(R.M.) Feb. 21
See Verulus, etc.

ALEXANDER of ALEXANDRIA (St) Bp.
R.M. Feb. 26
c. 250-326. Patriarch of Alexandria, who,
as such, convicted of heresy and condemned Arius, one of his own clergy, and
on the other hand realized the great gifts
of Athanasius, whom he made his deacon
and favoured with his confidence. Both
the patriarch and his deacon assisted at
the council of Nicea (325) where Arius was
again condemned. Alexander died shortly
after his return to Alexandria.
*Cf. Att. — Baud. — Dict. Baudrill. —
Bolland.*

ALEXANDER, ABUNDIUS, ANTIGO-
NUS, and FORTUNATUS (SS) MM.
R.M. Feb. 27
? A group of martyrs who suffered either

in Rome or in Thessaly, when and how is not known.
Cf. Baud. — Holw. — Bolland.

ALEXANDER (St) M.   R.M. March 10
See Caius and Alexander.

ALEXANDER and THEODORE (SS) MM.   R.M. March 17
? Besides the fact that their names are mentioned both in the Hieronymian and in the Roman Martyrologies, nothing certain can be stated about these two martyrs.
Cf. Baud. — Bolland.

ALEXANDER of JERUSALEM (St) Bp. M.   R.M. March 18
d. 251. A fellow-student with Origen at Alexandria, he became bishop of his native city in Cappadocia and was imprisoned for the Faith under Severus. On his release he journeyed to Jerusalem where he was made coadjutor to the bishop of the holy city — the first recorded example of an episcopal translation and coadjutorship. Here he received Origen, now an exile, and founded for him a library and a school. Alexander died in chains at Caesarea in Palestine under Decius.
Cf. Att. — Baud. — Dict. Baudrill.

ALEXANDER (SS) MM. R.M. March 24
Two martyrs of the same name included in the group Timolaus, Dionysius, etc. q.v.

ALEXANDER (St) M.   R.M. March 27
3rd cent. A soldier, described in the R.M. as having suffered as a Christian in Pannonia under Maximian Herculius. It seems that he should be identified with the anonymous martyr of Thrace of May 13.
Cf. R.M.

ALEXANDER (St) M.   R.M. March 28
See Priscus, Malchus, etc.

ALEXANDER RAWLINS (Bl) Priest, M.   A.C. Apr. 7
d. 1595. A secular priest born in Gloucestershire (?) educated at Reims and ordained in 1590. He was captured while labouring in the York mission and martyred for his priesthood. Beatified in 1929.
Cf. Att. — Newdigate.

ALEXANDER and Comp. (SS) MM.   R.M. Apr. 24
d. 177. A Greek by birth and the friend and companion of St Epipodius of Lyons. He was arrested, tortured and then crucified. Thirty-four others suffered at the same time.
Cf. Ruinart-Bolland. — Baud.

ALEXANDER, EVENTIUS and THEODULUS (SS) MM.   R.M. May 3
d. c.113. Three Roman martyrs buried on the Via Nomentana. The R.M. erroneously identifies the Alexander of this group with Pope St Alexander I.
Cf. Duch. Lib. Pont. — Att. — Dict. Baudrill.

ALEXANDER I (St) Pope   R.M. May 3
Pope from c. 107 to c. 113. See the preceding notice.

ALEXANDER and ANTONINA (ANTONIA) V. (SS) MM.   R.M. May 3
d. 313. The *laus* of the R.M. is as follows: "At Constantinople the birthday of the martyrs SS Alexander, the soldier, and Antonina, a virgin. In the persecution of Maximian she was condemned to the stews by Festus the Governor. But she was secretly delivered by Alexander, who changed garments with her and remained there in her place. She was afterwards commanded to be tortured with him; and both were together cast into the flames, with their hands cut off, and were crowned after ending a mighty contest."

ALEXANDER (Bl) Mk O.S.B. Cist.   P.C. May 3
c. 1180-1229. Born in Scotland a descendant of Scottish kings, he entered as a lay-brother the Cistercian abbey of Foigny (Fusciniacum), diocese of Laon.
Cf. Bolland. (I maji) — Chev. — Zimm. — P. de U. — Holw.

ALEXANDER VINCIOLI (Bl) Bp.   A.C. May 3
d. 1363. Born at Perugia, he joined the Franciscans. Pope John XXII chose him as his penitentiary and named him bishop of Nocera in Umbria. St Alexander died at Sassoferrato.
Cf. Baud. — Dict. Baudrill.

ALEXANDER (St) M.   R.M. May 20
See Thalelaeus, Asterius, etc.

ALEXANDER (St) M.   R.M. May 29
See Sisinius, Martyrius and Alexander.

ALEXANDER (St) M.   **R.M. June 2**
See Photinus (Pothinus), Sanctus, etc.

ALEXANDER (St) Bp.   **R.M. June 4**
8th cent. A bishop of Verona, of whom
nothing further is known.
Cf. Gams — Baud.

ALEXANDER (St) Bp. M.   **R.M. June 6**
d. 590. Bishop of Fiesole in Tuscany, a
brave defender of the Church against the
kings of Lombardy. His opponents way-
laid him and drowned him in the R.
Reno, near Bologna.
Cf. Dict. Baudrill. — Baud. — Bolland.

ALEXANDER of NOYON (St) M.
                     R.M. June 6
See Amantius, Alexander, etc.

ALEXANDER (St) M.   **R.M. July 9**
See Patermuthius, Copras and Alexander.

ALEXANDER (St) M.   **R.M. July 10**
One of the Seven Holy Brothers, q.v.

ALEXANDER (St) M.   **R.M. July 21**
See Victor, Alexander, etc.

ALEXANDER (St) M.   **R.M. Aug. 1**
See Leontius, Attius, etc.

ALEXANDER (St) Bp. M. R.M. Aug. 11
d. 250. Surnamed Carbonarius (charcoal-
burner) from the trade he followed before
being appointed bishop of Comana in
Pontus on the recommendation of St
Gregory Thaumaturgus. He was burnt
at the stake.
Cf. Att. — Dict. Baudrill. — Baud.

ALEXANDER (St) M.   **R.M. Aug. 26**
d. 297. Tribune in the Theban Legion
(see Maurice, etc.) who, being condemned
to death, made his escape from the prison
at Milan, but was recaptured near Bergamo and there beheaded.
Cf. Baud. — Holw.

ALEXANDER (St) Bp.   **R.M. Aug. 28**
d. 340. Patriarch of Constantinople from
317 to 340, i.e. during the period of the
struggle of the church against Arianism.
He assisted at the first council of Nicea
(325) and took a firm stand against Arius.
Indeed, the R.M. adds "by the power of
his (Alexander's) prayers Arius, condemned by the judgment of God, brake in

the midst and his bowels poured out."
He died "a glorious old man" after fifteen
years of labour.
Cf. Dict. Baudrill. — Att. — Bolland.

ALEXANDER (St) M.   **R.M. Sept. 9**
See Hyacinth, Alexander and Tiburtius.

ALEXANDER (St) Bp. M. R.M. Sept. 21
2nd cent. A bishop in the neighbourhood
of Rome. His miracles attracted the
attention of the people and he was arrested and martyred on the Claudian Way,
some twenty miles from Rome. St Damascus translated his relics and enshrined
them in one of the Roman churches.
Cf. Baud. — Holw. — Bolland.

ALEXANDER (St) M.   **R.M. Sept. 28**
See Mark, Alphius, etc.

ALEXANDER (St) M.   **(R.M.) Oct. 5**
3rd cent. One of the "innumerable multitude" put to death at Tréves by the
prefect Rictiovarus during the persecution of Diocletian.
Cf. Dict. Baudrill. — Baud.

ALEXANDER SAULI (St) Bp.
                     R.M. Oct. 11
1534-1593. A native of Milan who joined
the Barnabites in 1550. Ordained priest,
he became a zealous preacher and confessor and was for many years director of
St Charles Borromeo. He was elected
general of his Congregation, and, in 1569,
bishop of the Corsican diocese of Aleria
which he completely reformed during his
20 years rule. In 1592 Pope Gregory XIV
commanded him to accept the transfer to
Pavia, where he died the following year in
the course of his first pastoral visitation.
Beatified in 1741-2 and canonized in 1904.
Cf. Att. — Baud. — Dict. Baudrill.

ALEXANDER (St) M.   **R.M. Oct. 17**
See Victor, Alexander and Marianus.

ALEXANDER, HERACLIUS and Comp.
(SS) MM.   **R.M. Oct. 22**
? Alexander, a bishop, made by his
preaching such an impression on the multitude that many, both Jews and pagans,
became Christians. He was arrested and
tortured, and such was his constancy that
Heraclius, one of the soldiers of the guard,
was at once converted. Others followed
his example. All were put to death to-

gether with St Alexander. Neither place nor year is recorded.
Cf. Baud. — Holw. — Bolland.

ALEXANDER (St) M.   R.M. Nov. 9
4th cent. A martyr of Salonica under Maximian Herculius.

ALEXANDER (St) M.   R.M. Nov. 24
d. 361. A martyr at Corinth under Julian the Apostate.

ALEXANDER BRIANT (Bl) Priest M. S.J.   A.C. Dec. 1
d. 1581. A secular priest, who was admitted into the Society of Jesus in prison, cruelly tortured to make him disclose the whereabouts of Father Parsons S.J. and martyred at Tyburn together with BB. Ralph Sherwin and Edmund Campion S.J. for complicity in a fictitious plot. He was only 25 years of age. Beatified in 1886.
Cf. Camm — Att. — Baud.

ALEXANDER (St) M.   R.M. Dec. 12
See Epimachus and Alexander.

ALEXANDRA, CLAUDIA, EUPHRASIA, MATRONA, JULIANA, EUPHREMIA, THEODOSIA, DERPHUTA and a Sister of DERPHUTA (SS) MM.
R.M. March 20
d. c.300. Christian women, natives of Amisus in Paphlagonia, burnt to death under Diocletian.
Cf. Dict. Baudrill. — Baud. — Holw.

ALEXANDRA (St) V.M.   R.M. May 18
See Theodotus, Thecusa, etc.

ALEXANDRIA (Martyrs of)
The R.M. makes mention of the following anonymous groups of martyrs put to death for Christ at Alexandria in Egypt:

R.M. Jan. 28
d. 356. A great number of Catholics were ordered to be put to death by an Arian officer while they were in church assisting at the Holy Sacrifice offered by St Athanasius. St Athanasius himself was able to escape.

R.M. Feb. 28
d. 261. The *laus* of the R.M. concerning this group of martyrs reads as follows: "At Alexandria . . . the commemoration of

the holy priests, deacons, and many others who, in the time of the emperor Valerian, when a most deadly pestilence was raging, freely met their death whilst ministering to the sick; whom the religious faith of pious persons is wont to honour as martyrs."

R.M. March 17
d. 390. During the reign of the emperor Theodosius, a heathen mob of worshippers of Seramis massacred a multitude of Christians who refused to join in the sacrifices to the pagan idol. Theodosius had the temple of Seramis destroyed and a Christian church built on its site.

R.M. March 21
d. 342. The R.M. reads: "At Alexandria, the commemoration of the holy martyrs who were slain on Good Friday under the emperor Constantius and Philagrius the Prefect, when the Arians and heathens rushed into the churches." This happened after St Athanasius had been deposed and expelled for the second time.

R.M. May 13
d. 372. A great number of Catholics of both sexes were put to death or exiled from Alexandria when, for the fifth time, St Athanasius had been driven from his flock under the Arian emperor Valens. The R.M. makes special mention of those massacred in the church of Theonas.

R.M. Aug. 10
d. 260-267. The R.M. has this *laus*: "At Alexandria the commemoration of the holy martyrs who in the persecution of Valerian, under Emilian the Governor, were long tormented with various and sharp tortures, and obtained the crown of martyrdom by divers kinds of deaths."
St Dionysius of Alexandria has left a graphic account of them all.

ALEXANDRINA di LETTO (Bl) Abs Poor Clare   P.C. Apr. 3
1385-1458. Born at Sulmona, she joined the Poor Clares when fifteen years of age and after some twenty-three years founded a convent of her order at Foligno of which she became first abbess. Here she initiated a new Franciscan reform, which was blessed and encouraged by Pope Martin V.
Cf. Baud.

ALEXIUS FALCONIERI (St) C.
R.M. Feb. 12 and 17
One of the Seven Holy Founders of the Servite Order, q.v.

ALEXIUS (Bl) M. O.P. A.C. June 1
d. 1614. A Japanese catechist and novice of the Dominican missionaries in Japan. He was burnt alive on the day of the great martyrdom, Sept. 10, at Nagasaki. Beatified in 1867.
Cf. Holw.

ALEXIUS DELGADO (Bl) M. S.J.
A.C. July 15
1556-1570. A native of Elvas in Portugal, he became a Jesuit novice, and was only fourteen years old when he was killed by Calvinist French pirates near Palma on his way to the W. Indies with a group of Jesuits under the leadership of Bl. Ignatius d'Azevedo, q.v. Beatified in 1854.
Cf. Baud. — Holw.

ALEXIUS (ALEXIS) (St) C.
R.M. July 17
d. early 5th cent. A saint originally distinguished with the anonymous title of "the man of God," at a later period he was named Alexis or in Latin Alexius. The legend of his life came from the East and spread throughout the West in the 10th century, when the Greek monks were given the Benedictine abbey of St Boniface on the Aventine, which they renamed SS Boniface and Alexius. The *laus* of the R.M. sums up the legend somewhat as follows: Alexius the son of a Roman senator, in order to serve God in humility, on his wedding day fled from his parental home disguised as a beggar. He set sail for Edessa where after seventeen years an image of our Lady proclaimed him "the man of God." Alexius fled again and eventually returned to Rome and for another seventeen years lived unrecognized as a beggar in his own home. After his death a mysterious voice again proclaimed him "the man of God." This attractive legend made St Alexius one of the most popular of "popular saints." However, only this seems certain: that the saint lived, and died and was buried at Edessa.
Cf. Dict. Baudrill. — Baud. — Holw. — Att.

ALEXIUS NACAMURA (Bl) M.
A.C. Nov. 27
1619. A Japanese layman, born in Figen, of the royal family of Firando. Beheaded with ten companions at Nagasaki. Beatified in 1867.
Cf. Holw.

ALEYDIS (St) V. A.C. June 15
Otherwise Adelaide, q.v.

ALFANUS (ALPHANUS) (St) Bp. O.S.B.
P.C. Oct. 9
d. 1085. A monk of Montecassino, who was consecrated at Rome archbishop of Salerno in 1058. It was he who assisted Pope St Gregory VII on his deathbed.
Cf. Gams — Chev.

ALFERIUS, (ALPHERIUS, ADALFERICUS) (St) Ab. O.S.B. A.C. Apr. 12
930-1050. A Norman by origin, he was born at Salerno and belonged to the family of Pappacarbone. Sent as an ambassador to France, he fell ill at the abbey of Chiusa, and on his recovery betook himself to Cluny and was professed under St Odilo. The duke of Salerno asked for his return, and Alferius settled at Mt. Fenestra, near Salerno, and there founded the abbey of La Cava, under the Cluniac observance. Soon the abbey counted its affiliated houses by hundreds and became a potent civilizing influence in S. Italy. Cult confirmed in 1893.
Cf. Dict. Baudrill. — Zimm.— Att. — Baud. — Mab.

ALFONSO
Note. This is the modern spelling of Alphonsus in Spanish, Portuguese and Italian; the French spell it Alphonse. The old Spanish spelling is Alonso, and the Portuguese Alonzo. All are derivatives of the original Spanish name Ildephonsus or Aldephonsus. See Alphonsus.

ALFRED (St) Bp. O.S.B. A.C. Aug. 15
Otherwise Altfrid, q.v.

ALFREDA (ELFREDA, ETHELFREDA) (St) V. O.S.B. A.C. Aug. 2
Otherwise Etheldritha, q.v.

ALFRICK (St) Bp. O.S.B. A.C. Nov. 16
d. 1005. Monk and abbot of Abingdon, and afterwards, successively, bishop of Wilton (990) and archbishop of Canterbury (995) He governed the church very

ably in the critical times of the Danish invasion of Kent.
Cf. Chev. — Holw. — Stanton — Gams.

ALFWOLD (St) Bp. O.S.B.
A.C. March 26
d. 1058. A monk of Winchester who was chosen bishop of Sherborne in 1045. He was known for his great devotion to SS Cuthbert and Swithun, whose cult he propagated.
Cf. Gams — Stanton — Att. — Zimm.

ALGERIC (St) Bp. R.M. Dec. 1
Otherwise Agericus, q.v.

ALICE (St) V. A.C. Feb. 5
Otherwise Adelhlid or Adelaide, q.v.

ALICE RICH (Bl) V. O.S.B.
P.C. Aug. 24
c. 1270. Sister of St Edmund, archbishop of Canterbury. She joined the Benedictine nuns of Catesby, and became their prioress.
Cf. Baud.

ALIPIUS (ALYPIUS) (St) Bp.
R.M. Aug. 15
d. c.430. Disciple and lifelong friend of St Augustine. They were baptized together at Milan on Easter Eve, 387. Upon their return to Africa they spent some time in solitude as religious. St Alipius then visited Palestine. About the year 393 he became bishop of Tagaste and was St Augustine's chief assistant in all his public work.
Cf. Att. — Holw.

ALIPRANDUS (or LEUPRANDUS) (St) Ab. O.S.B. A.C. July 24
8th cent. An abbot of the monastery of St. Augustine in Ciel d'Oro (*in coelo aureo*) at Pavia. He was related to the royal family of the Lombards.
Cf. Chev. — Zimm. — Baud.

ALKELD (or ATHILDA) (St) V.
P.C. March 27
? 10th cent. Two Yorkshire churches are dedicated to this saint, of whom nothing else is known, except that an ancient painting represents her being strangled by Danish pirates.
Cf. Stanton.

ALKMUND (St) M. A.C. March 19
Otherwise Alcmund, q.v.

ALLAN (ALLEN) (St) C. A.C. Jan. 12
Otherwise Elian, q.v.

ALLEAUME (ALEAUME) (St) Ab.
A.C. Jan. 30
The French form of Adelelmus, q.v.

ALLOYNE (St) C. R.M. Oct. 1
Otherwise Bavo, q.v.

ALLUCIO (St) C. A.C. Oct. 23
d. 1134. Born in the diocese of Pescia in Tuscany, Allucio started life as a herdsman. Eventually his fellow citizens entrusted him with the direction of an almshouse at Val di Nievole, near Pescia, and he became in fact the second founder of that charity. He had some followers who were named the Brethren of St Allucio. Cult confirmed by Pius IX.
Cf. Att. — Baud.

ALLYRE (St) Bp. R.M. July 7
Otherwise Illidius, q.v.

ALMACHIUS (or TELEMACHUS), (St) H.M. R.M. Jan. 1
d. c.400. A hermit who came to Rome from the East, and publicly protested against the gladiatorial combats in the Roman amphitheatre. He was seized and cut to pieces by order of the prefect Alipius. As a consequence, the emperor Honorius is said to have abolished such spectacles.
Cf. Att. — Baud. — Dict. Baudrill.

ALMEDHA (ELED, ELEVETHA) (St) V.M. A.C. Aug. 1
9th cent. A descendant of King Brychan of Brecknock. The tradition is that she suffered martyrdom on a hill near Brecknock.
Cf. Baud. — Dict. Baudrill.

ALMIRUS (ALMER, ALMIRE) (St) Ab.
P.C. Sept. 11
d. c.560. A native of Auvergne, he was educated at Menat, where he met SS Avitus and Carileph. With them he went to Maine. After a short stay at Micy, St Almirus lived as a hermit at Gréez-sur-Roc, where he died.
Cf. Baud. — Dict. Baudrill. — P.B. — Holw.

ALMUS (ALME, or ALANUS) (St) Ab. O.S.B. Cist. P.C. June 28
d. 1270. Cistercian monk of Melrose who

became the first abbot of the Scottish monastery of Balmerino, founded in 1229 by Ermengardis, widow of William I of Scotland.
Cf. Chev. — Baud. — Dict. Baudrill.

ALNOTH (St) M. A.C. Nov. 25
d. c.700. A cowherd attached to St Werburg's monastery at Weedon (Northants). Later he lived as a hermit at Stowe, near Bugbrooke. He was put to death by robbers and venerated as a martyr.
Cf. Att.

ALODIA (St) V.M. R.M. Oct. 22
See Nunilo and Alodia.

ALONSO or ALONZO
Otherwise Alphonsus, q.v.

ALORUS (St) Bp. A.C. Oct. 26
See Alanus and Alorus.

ALOYSIUS, or LUDOVICUS
Note. These are two Latin forms of the French Louis, radically identical with Chlodovicus and Clovis. The modern languages have usually derived variants from both forms: thus in Italian: Luigi, Lodovico; in Spanish: Luis, Ludovico; in Portuguese: Luiz, Ludovico; in Catalan: Lluis, Ludovic; in German: Aloys, Ludwig; in English: Lewis (Aloysius), Ludovic.

ALOYSIUS RABATA (Bl) C. O.C.
A.C. May 11
c. 1430-1490. A Sicilian friar of the Carmelite monastery of Randazzo. He died from the effects of a blow on the head from an assailant whom he refused to bring to justice. Cult confirmed by Gregory XVI.
Cf. Att. — Baud. — Holw.

ALOYSIUS GONZAGA (St) C. S.J.
R.M. June 21
1568-1591. Born in the castle of Castiglione in Lombardy, he served as a page at the courts of Tuscany, Mantua and Spain, and, in his eighteenth year entered the Society of Jesus, after having overcome the opposition of his family. Within six years he fell sick while nursing the plague-stricken and died. He was beatified in 1605 and canonized in 1726. Benedict XIII declared him special protector of young students and Pius XI proclaimed

him patron of Christian Youth. Oversentimental biographies and cheap art have rather damaged his attractive personality.
Cf. Att. — Baud. — Holw. — Bolland.

ALPAIS (Bl) V. A.C. Nov. 3
d. 1211. Born in the small village of Cudot, diocese of Sens, of a peasant family, she helped her parents in the fields until, still very young she became bed-ridden with leprosy. For a long time her only food was the Eucharist. Her patience and gentleness made a great impression on her contemporaries. Cult confirmed by Pius IX in 1874.
Cf. Att. — Baud. — Dict. Baudrill.

ALPHAEUS (St) C. A.C. May 26
1st cent. Mentioned in Matt. X 3 as the father of St James the Less. The Greek liturgy commemorates him on this day. The apocryphal books have embellished his life, but they deserve no credence.
Cf. Holw.

ALPHAEUS and ZACHAEUS (SS) MM.
R.M. Nov. 17
d. 303. Alphaeus was a reader and exorcist at Caesarea in Palestine, and Zachaeus, his cousin, a deacon at Gadara beyond the Jordan. They were beheaded at Caesarea under Diocletian.
Cf. Att. — Dict. Baudrill. — Ruinart.

ALPHAGE or ALPHEGE (St) Bp. M.
O.S.B. R.M. Apr. 19
Otherwise Elphege, q.v.

ALPHANUS (St) Bp. O.S.B. P.C. Oct. 9

Otherwise Alfanus, q.v.

ALPHERIUS (St) Ab. O.S.B.
A.C. Apr. 12
Otherwise Alferius, q.v.

ALPHIUS, PHILADELPHUS and CYRINUS (SS) MM. R.M. May 10
d. 251. Sicilian saints, said to have been brothers. They appear to have suffered under Decius. They are held in great veneration in Sicily (chiefly at Lentini, of which town they are patron saints) and also among the Greeks.
Cf. Dict. Baudrill. — Att. — Baud. — Holw.

ALPHIUS (St) M.   **R.M. Sept. 28**
See Mark, Alphius, etc.

ALPHONSUS of ASTORGA (St) Bp.
O.S.B.   **A.C. Jan. 26**
9th cent. A bishop of Astorga who retired and became a monk at the abbey of St Stephen de Ribas de Sil, in Spanish Galicia.
Cf. Dict. Baudrill. — Baud. — Holw.

ALPHONSUS de ROJAS (Bl) C. O.F.M.
A.C March 21
d. 1617. Successively professor at Salamanca, tutor to a young duke, canon of Coria and a Franciscan friar. His feast at Coria is kept on March 26.
Cf. P. de U. — Baud.

ALPHONSUS NAVARRETE (Bl) M. O.P.
A.C. June 1
d. 1617. Born at Valladolid, he entered the Dominican Order and worked first as a missionary in the Philippine Islands, whence, in 1611, he was sent to Japan where he was appointed provincial vicar. He converted, we are told, many thousands to Christianity. He was beheaded on the isle of Tacaxima. Beatified in 1867.
Cf. Dict. Baudrill. — Att. — Baud. — Holw.

ALPHONSUS de MENA (Bl) M. O.P.
A.C. June 1
d. 1622 (Sept. 10). Born at Logroño, in Spain, he became a Friar Preacher at Salamanca. He was a nephew of Bl. Peter Navarrete, whom he accompanied to Japan. Here he was burnt alive at Nagasaki with the group led by Bl Charles Spinola, S.J. Beatified in 1867.
Cf. Baud. — Holw.

ALPHONSUS de VAENA (Bl) M. S.J.
A.C. July 15
d. 1570. Born at Toledo, he entered the Society of Jesus as a coadjutor. He belonged to the band of Jesuit martyrs led by Bl. Ignatius d'Azevedo. Beatified in 1854.
Cf. Baud. — Holw.

ALPHONSUS PACHECO (Bl) M. S.J.
A.C. July 25
1550-1583. Born at Minayá in Catalonia, he joined the Jesuits in 1566 and was sent to Goa, where he was ordained priest.

After a very laborious apostolate among the Goanese he was killed with Bl. Rudolph Acquaviva at Salsette, near Goa. Beatified in 1893.
Cf. Holw.

ALPHONSUS MARY LIGUORI (St) Bp.
Dr. Founder C.SS.R.   **R.M. Aug. 2**
1696-1787. Born near Naples of a distinguished family, he became a barrister, but soon abandoned this promising career and became a priest in 1726. He joined a society of priests engaged in catechizing the peasants of the country districts, and this led him to the foundation of the congregation of the Most Holy Redeemer, which, after many great trials, was approved in 1749. In 1762 an order of the pope forced the saint to accept the bishopric of Sant' Agata de' Goti, which he held until 1775, when he was compelled to resign through ill-health. He returned to live with the members of his own congregation which was then a prey to schism and external opposition. Throughout all these years as a priest, bishop and religious he produced a steady output of ascetical, theological and historical works, as well as much religious verse which he set to music, being always mindful of the vow he had made to God, never to lose a moment of time in idleness. The Church, besides declaring him a Doctor (1871), has proclaimed him a sure guide in moral theology. Beatified in 1816 and canonized in 1839.
Cf. Bolland. — Att. — Baud. — Holw.

ALPHONSUS de OROZCO (Bl) C. O.S.A.
A.C. Sept. 19
1500-1591. Born at Oropesa in Castile, he studied at the university of Salamanca, where as an undergraduate he was drawn to the Augustinian Hermits by the sermons of St Thomas of Villanova. After his profession Bl Alphonsus became preacher at the court of Philip II of Spain. He was a prolific writer and his works are reckoned among the classics of Spanish literature. Beatified in 1882.
Cf. Att. — Baud. — Dict. Baudrill. — Holw.

ALPHONSUS RODRIGUEZ (St) C. S.J.
R.M. Oct. 31
1531-1617. Born at Segovia in Spain, he became a merchant and married, but lost his wife and children, and at the age of

forty-four was received into the Society of Jesus as coadjutor and sent to Palma in Majorca. From 1580 to 1604 he was doorkeeper of the college of Montesión. In this office he edified the whole island. Beatified in 1825 and canonized in 1888. *Cf. Att. — Dict. Baudrill. — Holw. — Baud. — P. de U.*

ALPINIAN (St) C. R.M. June 30
See Martial, Alpinian and Austriclinian.

ALRADUS (Bl) Mk, O.S.B. Cist.
P.C. Nov. 11
d. c.1250. A lay-brother of the Cistercian abbey of Isenhagen.
Cf. Zimm.

ALRICK (St) C. A.C. June 30
11th cent. An English hermit associated with St Godric, who assisted him at his death.
Cf. Baud. — Stanton. — Holw.

ALTFRID (St) Bp. O.S.B. P.C. Aug. 15
d. 874. Monk and headmaster of the school at the abbey of Corvey in Saxony. In 851 he became bishop of Hildesheim. He was known throughout the Frankish empire as a fosterer of peace and goodwill, a champion of his Benedictine brethren, an upholder of the ecclesiastical canons, and a devout client of our Lady.
Cf. Zimm. — Dict. Baudrill. — Gams — Baud.

ALTHEUS (St) C. A.C. Dec. 26
Otherwise Tathai, q.v.

ALTHRYDA (ALFRIDA, ETHELDRY-THA) (St) V. O.S.B. A.C. Aug. 2
Otherwise Etheldritha, q.v.

ALTIGIANUS and HILARINUS (SS) MM. O.S.B. P.C. Aug. 23
d. 731. Two monks killed by the Saracens at Saint-Seine, diocese of Langres, Côte d'Or.
Cf. Bolland. — Chev. — Dict. Baudrill. — Baud.

ALTINUS (ATTINUS) (St) Bp. M.
A.C. Oct. 19
1st or 4th cent. An alleged disciple of our Lord, founder of the churches of Orleans and Chartres. Others state that he was a martyr of the 4th century.
Cf. Duch. Fast. Episc. — Gams—Dict. Baudrill. — Baud.

ALTMAN (St or Bl) Bp. A.C. Aug. 8
c. 1020-1091. Born in Westphalia, he studied at Paris, became a canon regular, chaplain to the emperor Henry III and finally bishop of Passau in 1065. He upheld the authority of St Gregory VII against Henry IV and was driven from his see, but he continued to exercise great influence throughout the Germanies. He was buried at the Benedictine abbey of Gottweig in Austria, which he had founded. Cult confirmed by Leo XIII.
Cf. Att. — Baud. — Holw.

ALTO (St) Ab. O.S.B. A.C. Feb. 9
d. c.760. A monk, probably Irish, who crossed over into Germany (c.743) and settled as a hermit in a wood near Augsburg. King Pepin made him a grant of that place, and there the saint founded an abbey, since called Altomünster (Alto's monastery). St Boniface dedicated its church in 750.
Cf. Mab. — Chev. — Zimm. — Att.

ALUINUS (St) Bp. O.S.B. A.C. Sept. 5
Otherwise Alvitus, q.v.

ALVAREZ BARTHOLOMEW (Bl) M. S.J. A.C. Jan. 12
See John Gaspard Cratz, etc.

ALVAREZ, EMMANUEL (Bl) M. S.J.
A.C. July 15

ALVAREZ, FRANCIS (Bl) M. S.J.

ALVAREZ, GASPAR (Bl) M. S.J.
Three Jesuit martyrs belonging to the group of Bl. Ignatius d'Azevedo, q.v.

ALVARO (ALVAREZ) of CORDOVA (Bl) C. O.P. A.C. Feb. 9
d. c.1430. He became a Dominican at Cordova in 1368 and worked with great success in Andalusia and Italy. He was chosen by the queen-mother of Spain, Catherine, daughter of John of Gaunt, as her adviser and as tutor of her son John II. Bl. Alvaro opposed the Avignon pope Peter de Luna. His priory near Cordova became a centre of learning and piety. Cult confirmed in 1741.
Cf. Att. — Baud. — Dict. Baudrill. — P. de U.

ALVARO GARCIA (Bl) M. A.C. June 11
See Peter Rodriguez and Comp.

ALVITUS (AVITUS, ALUINUS, ALBINUS) (St) Bp. O.S.B.   A.C. Sept. 5
d. c.1063. He was born in Spanish Galicia and belonged to the family of Rudesind, the great abbot-bishop of Mondoñedo. St Alvitus became a Benedictine at Sahagún (Cluniac observance) and in 1057 was appointed bishop of León by King Ferdinand I. He transferred the relics of St Isidore from Seville to León.
Cf. P. de U. — Gams — Holw.

AMABILIS (St) V.   P.C. July 11
d. c.634. According to tradition she was a daughter of an Anglo-Saxon king. She became a nun of Saint-Amand at Rouen.
Cf. Baud. — Dict. Baudrill. — Holw. — P.B.

AMABILIS (St) C.   A.C. Nov. 1
d. 475. It seems that he was precentor of the cathedral at Clermont and afterwards parish priest of Tiom in Auvergne. He is invoked as a protector against fire and snakes.
Cf. Dict. Baudrill. — Baud. — Holw. — P.B.

AMADEUS of CLERMONT (Bl) C. O.S.B. Cist.   S.C. Jan. 14
d. c.1150. Lord of Hauterives (Drôme), he left the world with 16 of his vassals (c.1119) and entered the Cistercian abbey of Bonnevaux. Later he spent some time at Cluny to attend to the education of his son Bl. Amadeus of Lausanne. He founded four monasteries: Léoncel, Mazan, Montperoux and Tamis. Returned to Bonnevaux where he died.
Cf. Dict. Baudrill. — Baud. — See, however, Zimm., who denies that there ever was a cult.

AMADEUS (Bl) Bp. O.S.B. Cist.   A.C. Jan. 28
c. 1110-1159. Son of (Bl) Amadeus of Clermont, he was educated at Cluny and afterwards served in the court of the emperor Henry V. In 1125 he became a monk at Clairvaux under St Bernard, by whom he was sent in 1139 to govern as abbot the abbey of Hautecombe in Savoy which had adopted the Cistercian observance. In 1144 the pope put him under obedience to accept the bishopric of Lausanne. During the last years of his life he was also co-regent of Savoy and chancellor of Burgundy. Cult approved in 1910. The Cistercians usually call him saint.
Cf. Zimm. — Att. — Baud. — Chev. — Gams.

AMADEUS IX of SAVOY (Bl) C.   A.C. March 30
1435-1472. Born at Thonon, son of the duke of Savoy, he began to rule in 1455. He suffered from epilepsy, but nevertheless governed in such a way as to endear himself to all his subjects, until compelled to resign in favour of his wife. He was proclaimed a saint immediately after his death, but was beatified only in 1677. He is an ancestor of the royal house of Savoy, which has chosen him for its patron.
Cf. Dict. Baudrill. — Att. — Baud. — Holw.

AMADEUS of PORTUGAL (Bl) C. O.F.M.   P.C. Aug. 10
c. 1420-1482. The elder brother of Bl Beatrice da Silva. Born in Portugal, after a short period of married life, he joined the Hieronymites in 1442 and some ten years later the Franciscans of Ubeda in Lombardy as a lay-brother. The superiors, however, presented him for Holy Orders and after his ordination in 1459 he set out to reform the observance of the Friars Minor at Marignano, near Milan. The reform spread and led to the branch of the "Amadeists." After a stay in Rome, as the confessor of the pope, he died at Milan.
Cf. Att. — Dict. Baudrill. — Baud.

AMADOR, AMADOUR (several)
Otherwise Amator, q.v.

AMAETHLU (MAETHLU) (St) C.   A.C. Dec. 22
6th cent. A Welsh saint who has left his name to Llanfaethlu, a church founded by him in Anglesey.
Cf. Holw.

AMANDUS (St) Bp.   R. M. Feb. 6
c. 676. Born near Nantes, he lived for fifteen years as a solitary at Bourges. At the age of thirty-three he journeyed to Rome and received from the pope his commission as a missionary bishop. As such he preached in Flanders, to the Slavs in Carinthia and the Basques in Navarre. He founded many monasteries in all these places, of which the best known is Elnon,

where he retired in his old age and died a nonagenarian. In art he is represented carrying a church in his hand.
Cf. Att. — Baud. — Dict. Baudrill. — Bolland.

AMANDUS (St) Bp. R.M. June 18
d. c.431. Successor of St Delphinus as bishop of Bordeaux (c. 404). He is chiefly known from the works of St Paulinus of Nola, whom St Amandus converted and prepared for baptism.
Cf. Dict. Baudrill. — Baud. — Att. — Gams.

AMANDUS and ANSELM (SS) Abbots O.S.B. A.C. Nov. 18
Amandus d. 708: Anselm later in the 8th cent. St Amandus succeeded St Aigulphus as abbot of Lérins in 676 and ruled the monastery with a firm hand. St Anselm, another abbot of Lérins, lived later in the 8th century.
Cf. Zimm. — Holw. — Chev.

AMANDUS or AMANTIUS (AMATIUS)
Note. There are a number of saints of this name, belonging to the 4th, 5th, 6th and 7th centuries, of whom only the bare fact of their existence is known. Among these, the following are likely identifications: (1) Amandus, abbot-founder of Moissac, d. 644, feast Feb. 6. (2) Abbot-founder of Nantua, 7th cent, feast id. (3) Count of Grisalba, near Bergamo, d. April 6th, 515, feast Apr. 6th. (4) Abbot-founder of Saint-Amand-de-Boixe, feast May 22. (5) A Scottish hermit at Beaumont, diocese of Reims, 6th cent, feast June 16. (6) Abbot-founder of Saint-Amand de Coly (Dordogne), diocese of Limoges, 6th cent, feast June 25. (7) A hermit in a solitude at the meeting of the rivers Glanne and Vienne, diocese of Limoges, 5th cent, feast Oct. 16. (8) The first bishop of Strassburg, d. 346, feast Oct. 26. (9) A bishop of Worms, 4th cent, feast id. (10) A bishop of Rodez (otherwise Amantius) 4th cent. He is mentioned in the R.M. on Nov. 4. (11) A bishop of Avignon, id. (12) A bishop of Rennes, 4th cent, feast Nov. 13.
Cf. Duch. Fast. Episc. — Dict. Baudrill. — Baud. — Zimm. — Gams — locis respectivis.

AMANTIUS (St) M. R.M. Feb. 10
See Zoticus, Irenaeus, etc.

AMANTIUS (St) C. R.M. March 19
See Landoaldus and Amantius.

AMANTIUS (St) Bp. R.M. Apr. 8
d. 440. Successor of St Providus in the see of Como. He is still held in great veneration in his diocese.
Cf. Baud. — Bolland.

AMANTIUS, ALEXANDER, and Comp. (SS) MM. R.M. June 6
? Said to have been four brothers, priests. Amantius is given as bishop of Noyon, who evangelized Cannes, diocese of Carcassonne, where he was martyred with the other three.
Cf. Dict. Baudrill. — Baud. — see, however, Holw.

AMANTIUS (St) M. R.M. June 10
See Getulius, Cerealis, etc.

AMANTIUS (St) C. R.M. Sept. 26
d. c.600. A priest of Città di Castello (*Tiphernum*) near Perugia, who was personally known to St Gregory the Great and held in great veneration by the holy pontiff. He is the patron saint of Città di Castello.
Cf. Holw.

AMARAND (St) Bp. O.S.B. A.C. Nov. 7
d. p.700. Abbot of Moissac, who became bishop of Albi sometime between 689 and 722.
Cf. Gams — Chev.

AMARANTHUS (St) M. R.M. Nov. 7
3rd cent. A martyr venerated at Albi in S. France. The fact of his martyrdom is attested by St Gregory of Tours. Other data are lacking.
Cf. Dict. Baudrill. — Baud.

AMARINUS (St) M. Ab. O.S.B. R.M. Jan. 25
d. 676. Abbot of a monastery in the Vosges. Companion in martyrdom of St Praejectus (St Priest), bishop of Clermont. The valley of Saint-Amaria in Alsace is named after him.
Cf. Butler-Thurston (Jan. 25) — Zimm. — Holw. — P.B.

AMASIUS (St) Bp. A.C. Jan. 23
d. 356. A Greek, driven from the East by the Arians, who became second bishop

of Teano in 346. His cult is still flourishing in several dioceses of central Italy.
Cf. Gams — Holw.

AMASWINTHUS (St) Ab.   A.C. Dec. 22
d. 982. Monk and abbot for forty-two years of a monastery at Silva de Málaga in Andalusia.
Cf. Chev. — Zimm. — Holw.

AMATA (St) V. Poor Clare P.C. Feb. 20
d. c.1250. A niece of St Clare of Assisi, healed by her aunt of a disease and thereby converted to the life of the cloister. Her name is in the Franciscan martyrologies.
Cf. Holw.

AMATA (Bl) V. O.P.   P.C. June 10
d. 1270. A Dominican nun of San Sisto in Rome. A co-foundress of the convent of St Agnes at Valle di Pietro, Bologna.
Cf. Holw.

AMATOR (AMADOR) (St) C.
                                A.C. March 27
? A Portuguese hermit, of the diocese of Guarda, to whom several churches are dedicated in his country. He has often been confused with St Amator of Rocamadour (see below, Aug. 20).
Cf. Anal. Bolland. 1909. t. 28, p. 5 — Dict. Baudrill.

AMATOR, PETER and LOUIS (SS) MM.
                                R.M. Apr. 30
d. 855. Amator was born at Martos, near Cordova, in which latter city he studied and was ordained priest. He, together with a monk, Peter by name, and a lay-man called Louis was put to death by the Saracens for having publicly confessed Christ.
Cf. Dict. Baudrill. — Baud. — Holw.

AMATOR (AMATRE, AMADOUR) (St)
Bp.   R.M. May 1
d. 418. Bishop of Auxerre. He had been married to a holy woman venerated locally as St Martha. St Amator ordained as a priest his successor St Germanus, who has left us the biography of his predecessor.
Cf. Dict. Baudrill. — Gams — Baud. — Holw.

AMATOR (AMADOUR) (St) C.
                                A.C. Aug. 20
? Supposed to have been the first Christian to live a hermit's life in Gaul. He is

also said to have been the founder of the shrine of our Lady of Rocamadour, still a favourite place of pilgrimage. He is honoured in Quercy and the Limousin. At a much later date he was identified with the publican Zacchaeus of the gospel.
Cf. Dict. Baudrill. — Att. — Baud. — Holw.

AMATOR (St) Bp.   R.M. Nov. 26
3rd cent. Bishop of Autun. There is nothing further known for certain about him.
Cf. Dict. Baudrill. — Baud. — Holw.

AMATUS RONCONI (Bl) Mk. O.S.B.
                                A.C. May 8
d. 1292. Born near Rimini, after having four times made the pilgrimage to Compostella, he became a lay-brother at the abbey of San Giuliano near his native town.
Cf. Zimm. — Dict. Baudrill. — Baud.

AMATUS (St) Bp. O.S.B.   R.M. Aug. 31
d. 1093 or 1193. There is conflicting evidence about the actual date of St Amatus's life. The proven facts seem to be that he was born at Nusco, became a priest and a Benedictine, either at Fontigliano or at Montevergine, and lastly bishop of Nusco.
Cf. Chev. — Gams — Baud. — Holw.

**AMATUS (AMAT, AMÉ, AIMÉ, AMA-
DO) (St) Ab. O.S.B.   R.M. Sept. 13**
c.567–c.630. Born at Grenoble, he entered as a boy the abbey of St Maurice of Agaune in Switzerland where he lived as a monk hermit for over thirty years. St Eustace induced him to migrate to Luxeuil. Here he turned the heart of St Romaricus to God, and when this nobleman founded the abbey of Habendum (Remiremont: Romarici mons) in 620, under the Benedictine Rule, St Amatus was made its first abbot. Here he lived until his death.
Cf. Butler-Thurston (Sept. 13) Att. — Zimm. — Baud.

AMATUS (St) Bp. O.S.B.   R.M. Sept. 13
d. 690. Abbot of Agaune, he became the tenth bishop of Sion in Valais — *Sedunensis*, not *Senonensis* (Sens). As a result of a false accusation, he was banished to the abbey of Péronne, and then to that of Breuil, diocese of Arras, where he lived as one of the monks, and where he died.
Cf. Baud. — Att. — Holw.

AMBICUS, VICTOR and JULIUS (SS) MM. R.M. Dec. 3
4th cent Christians martyred at Nicomedia under Diocletian, whose imperial residence was in that city.
Cf. Baud. — Holw.

AMBROSE FERNANDEZ (Bl) M. S.J. A.C. March 14
1551-1620. Born at Sisto in Portugal, he went to Japan to seek his fortune, which he found in 1577 by entering the Society of Jesus as a lay-brother. He died in the horrible prison of Suzota (Omura) of apoplexy, aged sixty-nine. Beatified in 1867.
Cf. Holw.

AMBROSE (St) C. A.C. March 17
d. c.250. A rich nobleman of Alexandria, who befriended and helped Origen financially. He suffered imprisonment for the Faith under Maximinus, but was released and died a confessor.
Cf. Baud. — Dict. Baudrill.

AMBROSE SANSEDONI (Bl) C. O.P. R.M. March 20
1220-1287. Born at Siena, he joined the Dominicans in 1237 and was a fellow student of St Thomas Aquinas under St Albert the Great. He excelled as a preacher, and in the performance of this office he travelled through Germany, France and Italy. He was also Master of the Sacred Palace. His death was hastened by the vehemence of his preaching. In art he is represented as holding in his hand a model of his native city. Cult confirmed in 1413 and 1622.
Cf. Rizzi — Att. — Dict. Baudrill. — Baud.

AMBROSE KIBUKA (Bl) M. A.C. June 3
d. 1886. Page to King Mwanga of Uganda; he was baptized on Nov. 17, 1885, and burnt alive the following year. Beatified in 1920.
Cf. Baud. — Holw.

AMBROSE AUTPERTUS (St) Ab. O.S.B. A.C. July 19
d. c.778. Born in Gaul, he was Charlemagne's tutor at the court of Pepin the Short. He went to Italy as the king's envoy and visited the Benedictine abbey of St Vincent by the river Volturno, in the duchy of Benevento, and forthwith entered there as a monk. Eventually he became abbot. He was an able exegete and his works were considered as authoritative as those written by the greatest of the Latin Fathers. In fact, though not in title, he is one of the Doctors of the Church.
Cf. Att. — Dict. Baudrill. — Chev. — Baud. — Mab.

AMBROSE (St) M. R.M. Aug. 16
d. c.303. A centurion put to death under Diocletian at Ferentino in central Italy. His *Acta* are preserved only in a MS. of the 14th century.
Cf. Dict. Baudrill. — Baud. — Holw.

AMBROSE PICCOLOMINI and PATRICK de' PATRIZI (BB) Mks O.S.B. Oliv. P.C. Aug. 21
d. ? 1347. With Bl Bernard Tolomei they were co-founders of Montoliveto Maggiore, near Siena. They are always called *Beati* by the Olivetans.
Cf. P. Lugano, L'Italia Benedettina, Rome, 1929.

AMBROSE (St) Bp. A.C. Aug. 28
d. p.475. A bishop of Saintes, whose episcopate lasted for about fourteen years. He is mentioned in the life of his successor St Bibianus and is honoured together with him in the diocese of La Rochelle.
Cf. Duch. Fast. Episc. — Gams — Dict. Baudrill. — Baud.

AMBROSE (St) Bp. A.C. Sept. 3
d. c.455. Bishop of Sens, of whom nothing else is known.
Cf. Gams — Dict. Baudrill. — Baud. — Holw.

AMBROSE EDWARD BARLOW (Bl) M. O.S.B. A.C. Sept. 10
d. 1641. Baptized a Catholic, he was educated a Protestant, but was reconverted to the Faith and studied for the priesthood at Douai and Valladolid. In 1615 he was professed a monk at St Gregory's, Douai, now Downside; but he asked to be affiliated to the Spanish abbey of Celanova; and the community granted his petition. He was sent to the English mission in his native Lancashire, where he laboured for twenty-four years. Four times he was imprisoned and released, the fifth time he was executed at Lancaster for his priesthood. Beatified in 1929.
Cf. Att. — Camm — Newdigate.

AMBROSE (St) Bp. R.M. Oct. 16
d. c.752. The thirteenth bishop of
Cahors. Eventually he resigned and
lived as a recluse. After a pilgrimage to
Rome he died at Ernotrum (now Saint-
Ambroise-sur-Arnon), in Berry.
*Cf. Gams — Duch. Fast. Episc. — Dict.
Baudrill. — Baud.*

AMBROSE (St) Ab. R.M. Nov. 2
523 and 582. There were two abbots of
this name of the abbey of Agaune, St
Moritz, Switzerland. The former, who
had formerly been abbot of Ste Barbe, near
Lyons, is the one commemorated by the
R.M.; the latter died in 582.
Cf. Dict. Baudrill. — Baud. — Holw.

AMBROSE TRAVERSARI (Bl) Ab.
O.S.B. Cam. P.C. Nov. 20
1376-1439. Born at Portico, near Florence, he studied under the Greek humanist Chrysoloras at Venice, and became a
typical "all round" Renaissance scholar.
In 1400 he joined the Camaldolese at
Santa Maria degli Angeli, at Florence;
here he continued his studies, wrote much,
chiefly in Greek, and collected a large library. He was the soul of the Council of
Florence for the reunion of the Greeks.
In 1431 he became abbot-general. He was
both a great churchman and a great
scholar.
*Cf. Zimm. — Att. — Baud. — Chev. —
Dict. Baudrill.*

AMBROSE (St) Bp. Dr. R.M. Dec. 7
c.340-397. Born in Gaul, where his
father, who belonged to the Roman nobility, was praetorian prefect. Still very
young, Ambrose became a barrister at
Rome and before his thirty-fifth year was
appointed governor of Liguria and Aemilia
with his headquarters at Milan. The
whole province was rent by the Arian controversy. When in 374 the bishop of
Milan died, Ambrose, as governor, went to
the cathedral to ensure peace and order in
the new election, with the result that he
himself, though a catechumen, was elected
by acclamation, after a child has been suddenly heard to cry out "Ambrose for
bishop." Ambrose's objections were overruled and he was consecrated on Dec. 7,
374 (the day on which his feast is now
kept). He proved to be one of the greatest and most beloved bishops of all time.
He excelled as an administrator, as a writ-

er, as a protector of the poor, as the "hammer of Arianism." He was prompt and
outspoken in withstanding the tyranny of
the emperors. His courage in reproving
Theodosius the Great was a noble example
of Christian heroism. He died on Good
Friday, April 4, 397, hardly fifty years
of age. He is one of the four great Latin
Fathers and Doctors.
Cf. Chev. — Att. — and all hagiographies.

AMÉ, AIMÉ (St)
Otherwise Amatus, q.v.

AMELBERGA
Note. Variant forms of this name are:
Amalberga, Amalburga, Amalia, Amelia.

AMELBERGA (St) V. O.S.B.
R.M. July 10
d. c.772. She was a nun of Münsterbilsen
in Flanders, receiving the veil from St
Willibrord. Her relics were transferred
to the abbey church of St Peter at Ghent
in 1073.
*Cf. Dict. Baudrill. — Att. — Anal. Bol-
land. 1912, t. 31, p. 401.*

AMELBERGA (St) W. O.S.B.
A.C. July 10
d. 690. Born in Brabant, she was a niece,
or sister, of Bl Pepin of Landen. She was
married to Count Witger and mother of
SS Gudula, Emebert, etc. When Witger
became a Benedictine monk at Lobbes,
she too joined the nunnery of Maubeuge
under the same rule. Often confused with
the preceding.
Cf. Att. — Baud. — Dict. Baudrill.

AMELBERGA (St) Abs. O.S.B.
A.C. Nov. 21
d. p.900. Abbess of Susteren. She educated in her convent two daughters of the
king of Lorraine.
Cf. Zimm. — Dict. Baudrill. — Baud.

AMICUS and AMELIUS (SS) MM.
A.C. Oct. 12
d. 773. French knights who took part in
Charlemagne's campaign against the
Lombards in Upper Italy, where they were
killed, or fell in battle, and have been ven-
erated as martyrs ever since at Mortara in
Lombardy.
*Cf. Dict. Baudrill. — Baud. — Holw. —
P.B.*

AMICUS (St) Mk. O.S.B. A.C. Nov. 2
d. c.1045. Born near Camerino, he became a secular priest, then a hermit and finally a monk of St Peter's at Fonteavellana, founded by St Dominic of Sora in 1025 (not that governed by St Peter Damian). St Peter's was at that time a daughter-house of Montecassino, and for this reason St Amicus is often called a monk of Montecassino, and was held in special veneration at that abbey.
Cf. Zimm. — Att. — Chev. — Dict. Baudrill. — Baud.

AMICUS (St) Ab. O.S.B. A.C. Nov. 2
Early 11th cent. Abbot of Rambara.
Cf. Zimm.

AMIDAEUS (AMIDEI AMADIO) (St) C. O.S.M. R.M. Feb. 12 (Apr. 18)
One of the Seven Holy Founders of the Servite Order, q.v.

AMMIA (St) Matron R.M. Aug. 31
See Theodotus, Rufina and Ammia.

AMMIANUS (St) M. R.M. Sept. 4
See Theodore, Oceanus, etc.

AMMON, EMILIAN, LASSA and Comp. (SS) MM. A.C. Feb. 9
? A band of forty-four Christians martyred at Membressa in Africa.
Cf. Dict. Baudrill. — Baud.

AMMON and Comp. (SS) MM.
R.M. Sept. 1
d. c.322. Ammon, a deacon, was put to death under Licinius at Heraclea in Thrace, together with forty young women, his converts. The executioner killed St Ammon by placing a red-hot helmet on his head. Both the Greeks and the Latins commemorate their passion.
Cf. Dict. Baudrill. — Baud. — Att.

AMMON, THEOPHILUS, NEOTERIUS and Comp. (SS) MM. R.M. Sept. 8
? These three, together with twenty-two more Christians, suffered at Alexandria. The Bollandists give the names of all, but no other data are known.
Cf. Bolland. — Dict. Baudrill. — Baud.

AMMON the GREAT (St) Ab.
A.C. Oct. 4
d. c.350. Of a wealthy Egyptian family, Ammon married, and for eighteen years he and his wife lived as brother and sister.

Then by mutual agreement they embraced the religious life. Ammon retired to the Nitrian desert and eventually had under his charge from four to five thousand monks or hermits. In his later years Ammon ate only once every three or four days. He is one of the earliest and greatest hermit-monks.
Cf. Dict. Baudrill. — Att. — Baud.

AMMON, ZENO, PTOLEMY, INGEN, and THEOPHILUS (SS) MM.
R.M. Dec. 20
d. 249. The first four were soldiers. They, together with Theophilus, were present when a Christian on trial at Alexandria showed signs of wavering. They forthwith encouraged him and were beheaded on that account.
Cf. Att. — Baud.

AMMONARIA, MERCURIA, DIONYSIA, and a second AMMONARIA (SS) MM. R.M. Dec. 12
c.250. A band of holy women of Alexandria martyred under Decius. Mercuria is described as an aged woman, Dionysia as the mother of many children and the two Ammonarias as young girls.
Cf. Baud. — Dict. Baudrill.

AMMONIUS (St) M. R.M. Jan. 18
See Moseus and Ammonius.

AMMONIUS and ALEXANDER (SS) MM. R.M. Feb. 9
? Two Christians martyred at Soli in Cyprus.

AMMONIUS (St) M. R.M. Feb. 12
See Modestus and Ammonius.

AMMONIUS (St) M. R.M. Feb. 14
See Dionysius and Ammonius.

AMMONIUS (St) M. R.M. March 26
See Theodore, Irenaeus, etc.

AMMONIUS (St) M. R.M. Nov. 26
See Faustus, Didius, etc.

AMNICHAD (AMNUCHAD) (Bl) H. O.S.B. A.C. Jan. 30
d. 1043. Born either in Ireland or in Scotland, he travelled to Germany and became first a monk, and then a recluse, at Fulda.
Cf. Chev. — Baud. — Dict. Baudrill. — Holw.

AMO (AMON) (St) Bp. A.C. Oct. 23
4th cent. Second known bishop of Toul, the successor of St Mansuetus in that see.
Cf. Gams — Baud. — Dict. Baudrill.

AMOR (AMOUR) (St) M. A.C. Aug. 9
? Venerated in the Franche-Comté together with St Viator. Their relics are enshrined at Saint-Amour, in Burgundy.
Cf. Baud. — Dict. Baudrill. — Holw. — P.B.

AMOR (AMATOR, AMOUR) (St) Ab. O.S.B. A.C. Aug. 17
d. c.767. Companion of St Pirminius in the evangelization of Germany. Abbot-founder of Amorbach in Franconia.
Cf. Chev. — Baud. — Dict. Baudrill. — Holw. — Zimm.

AMOR (AMOUR) of AQUITAINE (St) H. A.C. Oct. 8
9th cent. Born in Aquitaine, he lived as a recluse at Maestricht. Eventually he founded Münsterbilsen nunnery, in the diocese of Liége. He has been wrongly identified with St Amor, founder of Amorbach.
Cf. P.B. — Baud. — Dict. Baudrill. — Holw.

AMOS (St) Prophet. R.M. March 31
8th cent. B.C. One of the minor prophets, a shepherd of Tekoah (Koa) near Bethlehem, who aptly describes himself as "a herdsman plucking wild figs" (VII 13). He was — the R.M. says — "transfixed with an iron bar through the temples." He was buried in his native place.
Cf. Baud.

AMPELIUS (St) M. R.M. Feb. 11
See Saturninus, Dativus, etc.

AMPELIUS (St) Bp. A.C. July 7
d. c.672. Bishop of Milan during the Lombard period. He wielded a great influence for good among the invading Lombards.
Cf. Dict. Baudrill. — Baud. — Holw. — Gams.

AMPELUS and CAIUS (SS) MM. R.M. Nov. 20
d. c.302. They are presumed to have been Sicilians, martyred at Messina under Diocletian. Actually nothing is known about them.
Cf. Dict. Baudrill. — Baud. — Holw.

AMPHIANUS (APPIAN, APIAN) (St) M. R.M. Apr. 2
d. c.305. A young Christian of Lycia, Asia Minor, who entered the governor's house when the latter was on the point of offering sacrifices to idols and boldly reproached him for his crime of idolatry. He was forthwith arrested and most cruelly tortured to death.
Cf. Baud. — Holw.

AMPHIBALUS (St) M. A.C. June 24
d. c.304. The supposed fellow-martyr of St Alban of Verulam. In the original *Acta* it is only said that St Alban put on the priest's cloak (amphibalus) and was arrested *instead* of the priest who had taken refuge in his house — not *with* the priest. Geoffrey of Monmouth took the word *amphibalus* to be the name of the priest.
Cf. Dict. Baudrill. — Baud. — Holw.

AMPHILOCHIUS (St) M. R.M. March 27
See Philetus, Lydia, etc.

AMPHILOCHIUS (St) Bp. R.M. Nov. 23
d. c.400. Fellow-student of St Basil under Libanius, a successful lawyer at Constantinople, a hermit, and finally one of the group of Cappadocian bishops, friends of St Basil, appointed by the latter to counteract Arianism in Cappadocia. Amphilochius was appointed to the see of Iconium. He opposed the Macedonian heretics, against whom he wrote a work on the Holy Ghost highly commended by St Jerome. He presided at the synod of Sidon which condemned the Messalians, who asserted that prayer is the only means of salvation.
Cf. Att. — Baud. — Dict. Baudrill.

AMPHION (St) Bp. R.M. June 12
d. p.325. The R.M. describes him as "an excellent confessor in the time of Galerius Maximian." He was then bishop of Epiphania in Cilicia. During the Arian troubles he was elected by the Catholic party to Nicomedia. Amphion was one of the "illustrious confessors" who attended the council of Nicea. St Athanasius approved of his writings.
Cf. Dict. Baudrill. — Baud. — Holw.

AMPLIATUS, URBAN and NARCISSUS (SS) MM. R.M. Oct. 31
1st cent. St Paul mentions these three

saints in Romans XVI. 8 sqq: "Salute
Ampliatus, most beloved by me in the
Lord. Salute Urban our helper in Jesus
Christ. Salute them that are of Narcis-
sus's household who are in the Lord."
Later, chiefly Greek, traditions have made
Ampliatus a bishop, and all three disciples
of our Lord, and preachers of the gospel
with St Andrew in the Balkan countries.
The R.M. adds "they were slain by Jews
and Gentiles."
Cf. Dict. Baudrill. — Baud.

AMULWINUS (AMOLVINUS) (St) Ab.
Bp. O.S.B.   A.C. Feb. 7
d. c.750. He was an abbot-bishop
(chorepiscopus) of Lobbes, successor of
St Erminus (d. 737).
Cf. Zimm. — Dict. Baudrill. — Baud.

AMUNIA (St) W. O.S.B.   A.C. March 11
d. c.1069. The mother of St Aurea (Oria),
whom she joined in her widowhood as a
recluse under the obedience of the abbot of
San Millán de la Cogolla, in La Rioja,
Spain.
Cf. Zimm.

ANACHARIUS (AUNACHARIUS, AU-
NACHAIRE, AUNAIRE.) (St) Bp.
R.M. Sept. 25
d. 604. Born near Orleans and educated
at the court of King Guntram of Burgundy, he became bishop of Auxerre in
561. He ordered the Litany of the Saints
to be sung daily in the chief centres of
population by rotation and enforced the
recitation of the Divine Office in all
churches of the diocese.
Cf. Chev. — Gams — Baud. — Holw.

ANACLETUS (ANENCLETUS) (St)
Pope, M.   R.M. July 13
1st cent. One of the earliest popes, he is
now regarded as identical with St Cletus,
q.v.

ANANIAS (St) M.   R.M. Jan. 25
1st cent. The disciple at Damascus who
baptized St Paul (Acts IX), and who,
according to tradition, evangelized Damascus, Eleutheropolis and other places,
and was ultimately martyred.
Cf. Dict. Baudrill. — Baud. — Holw.

ANANIAS and Comp. (SS) MM.
A.C. Feb. 25
d. c.298. A martyr-priest of Phoenicia

under Diocletian. Thrown into prison, he
converted his gaoler and seven soldiers of
the guard. All were put to death together.
Cf. Baud. — Dict. Baudrill. — Holw.

ANANIAS (St) M.   R.M. Apr. 21
See Simeon, Abdechalas, etc.

ANANIAS (St) M.   R.M. Dec. 1
? A layman, martyred at Arbela, either
the Persian or the Assyrian (Erbel) town of
that name.
Cf. Baud. — Holw.

ANANIAS, AZARIAS and MISAEL (SS)
R.M. Dec. 16
7th cent. B.C. Named otherwise Sidrach,
Misach and Abdenago (A.V. Shadrach,
Meshach, Abed-nego). The three children cast into the fiery furnace by order of
the king Nebuchadnezzar (Dan. III).
The R.M. adds: "whose bodies are buried near Babylon in a certain cave."

ANASTASIA the PATRICIAN (St) V.H.
A.C. March 10
6th cent. Her life is counted by many as
a pious legend, the first of many similar
historiettes. She belonged to the nobility
of Byzantium, and found favour in the
eyes of the emperor Justinian, thus excit-
ing the empress's jealousy. Anastasia
escaped first to a nunnery near Alexandria,
and after the empress's death, when the
emperor instituted a search for her, she
disguised herself in male attire and lived
in Scythia as a monk-hermit for twenty-
eight years. The Greeks keep her feast
on March 10.
Cf. Att. — Dict. Baudrill. — Holw.

ANASTASIA (St) M.   R.M. Apr. 15
See Basilissa and Anastasia.

ANASTASIA and CYRIL (SS) MM.
R.M. Oct. 28
d. ? 253. All that we know concerning
these two saints is given in the R.M.:
"At Rome, the passion of SS Anastasia the
Elder, the Virgin, and Cyril, Martyrs.
The former was bound with chains in
Valerian's persecution under the Prefect
Probus, tortured . . . her breasts cut off,
her nails torn out, her teeth broken, her
hands and feet cut off, and being beheaded
. . . she passed to her Spouse; Cyril, who
offered her water when she begged thereof,

received martyrdom for his reward." Unfortunately the whole *passio* is a fictitious composition and it is doubtful that the saints ever existed.
Cf. Dict. Baudrill. — Baud. — Att.

ANASTASIA (St) M.　　　**R.M. Dec. 25**
d. c.? 304. She is one of the best known martyrs on account of her being commemorated in the second Mass of Christmas and mentioned in the Canon of the Mass and in the Litany of the Saints. She suffered at Sirmium in Dalmatia, her relics were translated to Constantinople and her cult spread to Rome under the influence of Byzantine officials who dwelt in the aristocratic quarters by the Forum where there is a basilica dedicated in her honour, the ancient *titulus Anastasiae.* The *Acta* of her martyrdom are worthless.
Cf. Dict. Baudrill. — Holw. — Att.

ANASTASIUS (St) Bp.　　　**A.C. Jan. 7**
d. 977. Archbishop of Sens from 968 to 977, he began the building of the cathedral, and greatly favoured the monks of Saint-Pierre-le-Vif, in whose church he was buried.
Cf. Gams. Dict. Baudrill. — Baud.

ANASTASIUS (St) M.　　　**R.M. Jan. 9**
See Julian and Comp.

ANASTASIUS (St) Ab. O.S.B.
　　　　　　　　　　　R.M. Jan. 11
d. c.570. A notary of the Roman church, who became monk and abbot of Suppentonia (Castel Sant' Elia), diocese of Nepi, near Mt Soracte. St Gregory the Great narrates that, at the summons of an angel, St Anastasius and his monks died in quick succession.
Cf. Baud. — Dict. Baudrill. — Holw.

ANASTASIUS the PERSIAN (St) M.
　　　　　　　　　　　R.M. Jan. 22
d. 628. A Persian monk of Jerusalem, arrested at Caesarea, tortured and taken to the Persian king in Assyria, who ordered his execution. His head was brought to Rome and enshrined in a church dedicated to him and St Vincent, the Spanish martyr. Hence, his wide-spread cult in the West.
Cf. Att. — Baud. — Holw. — Dict. Baudrill.

ANASTASIUS (St) M.　　　**A.C. March 20**
d. c.797. The archimandrite (superior) of

the *laura* of St Sabas, at Jerusalem. The *laura* (a cluster of hermitages) was attacked by robbers and all its monks massacred with the archimandrite at their head. The Greeks keep their feast on the anniversary of their death.
Cf. Dict. Baudrill. — Baud.

ANASTASIUS the SINAITE (St) C.
　　　　　　　　　　　? R.M. Apr. 21
d. c.678. A Palestinian hermit, who eventually fixed his abode on Mt. Sinai, hence his surname "the Sinaite." He took part in all the Christological controversies of his time, in Syria, in Egypt, and elsewhere. He has left ascetical and theological writings of considerable value.
Cf. Baud. — Holw.

ANASTASIUS I (St) Patriarch.
　　　　　　　　　　　? R.M. Apr. 21
d. 599. Often confused with his namesake "the Sinaite." He was patriarch of Antioch and a resolute opponent of the imperial politico-theological rule. For this reason he was threatened with deposition by Justinian, and actually banished from his see for twenty-three years by Justin II. He was restored to Antioch by St Gregory the Great and the emperor Maurice.
Cf. Att. — Dict. Baudrill. — Holw. — Baud.

ANASTASIUS and Comp. (SS) MM.
　　　　　　　　　　　R.M. May 11
d. 251. Anastasius, a tribune in the army of the emperor Decius, was converted to Christianity on witnessing the courage of the martyrs whom in his capacity as tribune he was torturing to death. A few days after his conversion he was arrested and beheaded with all his family and servants. Their relics are venerated at Camerino in central Italy.
Cf. Baud. — Dict. Baudrill. — Holw.

ANASTASIUS (St) C.　　　**A.C. May 11**
? The patron saint of the city of Lérida in Spanish Catalonia. He is probably to be identified with one of the many *Anastasii* martyrs listed here, although the people of Lérida assert that their Anastasius was a native of that city.
Cf. Holw. — P. de U.

ANASTASIUS (St) Bp.　　　**R.M. May 20**
d. 610. Bishop of Brescia in Lombardy. He greatly contributed to the conversion of

the Lombards from Arianism.   St Charles
Borromeo solemnly translated his relics
in 1604.
Cf. Dict. Baudrill. — Gams — Holw.

ANASTASIUS (St) Bp.   R.M. May 30
d. 680.   A convert from Arianism, who
became bishop of Pavia in Lombardy 668-
680.   He is commonly called Anastasius
II, to distinguish him from one of his
predecessors in the see.
Cf. Baud. — Dict. Baudrill. — Holw.

ANASTASIUS, FELIX and DIGNA (SS)
MM. O.S.B.   R.M. June 14
d. 853.   Anastasius was a deacon of the
church of St Acisclus at Cordova, who
became a monk of the double abbey of
Tábanos, near the same city.   Felix was
born at Alcalá (Complutum) of a Berber
family, was professed a monk in Asturias
but joined the community of Tábanos,
being desirous of martyrdom.   Digna
belonged to the nunnery of the double
abbey.   The three were among the first
to confess Christ at Cordova, and were
beheaded by order of the Caliph.
Cf. P. de U. — Baud. — Dict. Baudrill.

ANASTASIUS (St) M.   R.M. June 29
See Marcellus and Anastasius.

ANASTASIUS (SS) Cc.   R.M. Aug. 13
See Maximus etc.

ANASTASIUS (St) Bp.   R.M. Aug. 17
d. ? 553.   Bishop of Terni at the time of
the invasion of Totila.   Said to have
come from Syria and to have been a hermit
near Perugia.   The Bollandists state that
there has been a confusion between a hermit martyr and a bishop of Terni.   St
Anastasius the bishop did not find a place
in the R.M. until 1518.
Cf. Bolland. — Dict. Baudrill. — Holw.

ANASTASIUS CORNICULARIUS (St)
M.   R.M. Aug. 21
d. 274.   A military tribune (*cornicularius*,
sub-officer) converted to Christ on behold-
ing the courage of the young St Agapitus.
This happened at Salone, twelve miles
from Palestrina, near Rome.   The R.M.,
however, gives Salona in Dalmatia, as the
place of martyrdom.   The story itself is a
duplication of that of St Anastasius of
Camerino (May 11) and, as regards its
location in Dalmatia, of that of St Anas-

tasius the Fuller (see below, Sept. 7).
All is very confused.
Cf. Att. — Dict. Baudrill. — Baud. —
Holw.

ANASTASIUS the Fuller (St) M.
R.M. Sept. 7
d. 304.   A fuller of Aquileia, not far from
Venice.   He crossed into Dalmatia and
continued to ply his trade at Salona and
to profess his religion openly, painting a
conspicuous cross on his door.   He was
seized and drowned.   He is now commonly identified with the Anastasius of
August 21.
Cf. Att. — Baud. — Anal. Bolland 1897,
t. 16. p. 488.

ANASTASIUS, PLACID, GENESIUS and
Comp. (SS) MM.   R.M. Oct. 11
? The R.M. has this entry: "The passion
of SS Anastasius, a priest, Placid, Genesius,
and their companions."   And this is all
we know about them.
Cf. Baud. — Dict. Baudrill. — Holw.

ANASTASIUS of CLUNY (St) Mk. O.S.B.
A.C. Oct. 16
c.1020-1085.   A native of Venice and a
man of considerable substance and learning, he became a monk of Mont-Saint-
Michel in Normandy, but left the abbey,
being dissatisfied with the abbot, who was
accused of simony.   In 1066 St Hugh of
Cluny made his acquaintance and invited
him to join Cluny.   After about seven
years Gregory VII ordered him to go to
Spain to preach to the Moors.   He did so,
but after another seven years returned to
Cluny; then he lived for a time as a recluse near Toulouse.   Recalled again to
Cluny, he died on the way.
Cf. Att. — Dict. Baudrill. — Baud. —
Chev. — Holw.

ANASTASIUS (or ASTERICUS, ASTRI-
CUS, ASCRICK) (St) Bp. O.S.B.
A.C. Nov. 12
d. c.1030.   A native of Bohemia, he became a monk of SS Boniface and Alexius
at Rome, and accompanied St Adalbert to
the Bohemian mission.   He became the
first abbot of Brevnov, but had to flee to
Hungary, where again he was appointed
the first abbot of Pannonhalma, recently
founded by King Stephen.   Anastasius
was the king's ambassador, sent to negotiate the recognition of the new Hungarian

kingdom by the pope. St Stephen was crowned king by Anastasius, who died archbishop of Esztergom.
Cf. Zimm. — Att. — Mab. — Chev. — Baud.

ANASTASIUS II (St) Pope
? P.C. Nov. 19
d. 498. He was pope for only two years: 496-498. On account of his conciliatory attitude towards the Acacian schism of Constantinople he was maligned by the intransigents. As a result his memory remained under a cloud for centuries, and this led Dante to give the saintly pontiff a place in hell (Inferno, XI, 4). The pope's name is found with the title of Saint in many calendars on Sept. 8.
Cf. Baud. — Dict. Baudrill. — Holw.

ANASTASIUS (St) M.   R.M. Dec. 5
? The *laus* of the R.M. is as follows: "The passion of St Anastasius the martyr, who in his ardent desire for martyrdom gave himself up, of his own accord, to the persecutors." Nothing else is known about him.
Cf. Baud. — Holw.

ANASTASIUS (St) M.   R.M. Dec. 19
See Cyriacus, Paulillus, etc.

ANASTASIUS I (St) Pope R.M. Dec. 19
d. 401. The R.M. has this *laus:* "At Rome, the death of Pope St Anastasius I, a man of extreme poverty and apostolic solicitude. St Jerome in his writings saith that Rome did not deserve to possess him for long . . ." The saintly pope is given similar praises by SS Augustine and Paulinus of Nola. He stopped the spread of the errors attributed to Origen.
Cf. Att. — Dict. Baudrill. — Baud. (Apr. 27).

ANASTASIUS II the YOUNGER (St) Patriarch, M.   R.M. Dec. 21
d. 609. In 599 he succeeded St Anastasius I in the see of Antioch. During his episcopate there took place at Antioch a rising of the Syrian Jews against the tyranny of the emperor Phocas, and Anastasius was murdered by the mob and was looked on as a martyr.
Cf. Att. — Dict. Baudrill. — Holw. — Baud.

ANATHALON (St) Bp.   R.M. Sept. 24
1st cent. The oldest catalogues give him as the first bishop of Milan, sent there by St Barnabas whose disciple he was. As first bishop of Milan he evangelized the surrounding district, including Brescia, where he died.
Cf. Bolland. — Gams — Dict. Baudrill. — Baud. — Holw.

ANATOLE KIRIGGWAJJO (Bl) M.
A.C. June 3
d. 1886. One of the young pages of King Mwanga of Uganda. Martyred together with several others. Beatified in 1920. See Uganda (Martyrs of).
Cf. Baud.

ANATOLIA and AUDAX (SS) MM.
R.M. July 9
d. c.250. There are two *legenda* connected with these martyrs, who suffered under Decius. The martyrology of St Jerome makes Anatolia a Roman maiden, denounced with her sister Victoria, by their rejected lovers. They were confined to a prison near Rieti, here their miracles converted Audax, one of the guards. The R.M., however, does not mention Victoria, and places the scene of the martyrdom at Thora, in the diocese of Rieti, not far from the small village now called Sant' Anatolia. Otherwise the two stories agree.
Cf. Dict. Baudrill. — Holw. — Baud.

ANATOLIUS (St) Bp.   A.C. Feb. 3
9th cent. A Scottish bishop who went as a pilgrim to Rome and settled as a hermit at Salins in the Jura, where at a later date a church was built in his honour.
Cf. Dict. Baudrill. — Holw. — Baud.

ANATOLIUS (St) Bp.   A.C. Feb. 7
? A supposed bishop of Cahors whose relics were venerated at the abbey of Saint-Mihiel, diocese of Verdun. The whole account of his life bristles with inaccuracies.
Cf. Dict. Baudrill. — Baud. — Holw.

ANATOLIUS (St) M.   R.M. March 20
See Photina, Joseph, etc.

ANATOLIUS (St) Bp.   R.M. July 3
d. c.283. Head of the Aristotelian school at Alexandria, his native city. He excelled as a philosopher and a mathematician. About the year 269 he was chosen bishop of Laodicea. St Jerome commends his works.
Cf. Att. — Baud. — Dict. Baudrill.

ANATOLIUS (St) Bp. A.C. July 3
d. 458. Patriarch of Constantinople from
449 to 458. The Bollandists have vindicated his claims to sanctity. His feast is
kept by the Byzantine Catholics.
Cf. Att.

ANATOLIUS (St) M. R.M. Nov. 20
See Eustace, Thespesius and Anatolius.

ANCINA, JUVENAL de (Bl) A.C. Aug. 31
See Juvenal de Ancina.

ANDÉOL (St) Bp. R.M. Oct. 15
Otherwise Antiochus, q.v.

ANDEOLUS (St) M. R.M. May 1
d. 208. A subdeacon of Smyrna sent to
France by St Polycarp. He is said to have
been martyred near Viviers on the Rhône.
Cf. Att. — Dict. Baudrill. — Baud.

**ANDOCHIUS, THYRSUS and FELIX
(SS) MM.** R.M. Sept. 24
2nd cent. Andochius, a priest, and Thyrsus, a deacon of Smyrna, sent to Gaul by
St Polycarp. They established themselves at Autun where they converted
their host, a rich merchant, by name Felix.
All three were martyred together. Their
cult was wide-spread throughout Gaul.
Cf. Dict. Baudrill. — Baud. — Bolland.

ANDREW (St) ? Bp. ? M. ? Jan. 13
d. ? 235. The supposed twelfth bishop of
Trèves, whom some chroniclers make also
a martyr.
*Cf. Baud. — Holw. — See, however, Gams,
who does not even list his name.*

ANDREW of PESCHIERA (Bl) C. O.P.
A.C. Jan. 19
d. 1485. Called "the Apostle of the
Valtellina." He was born at Peschiera
on the southern shore of Lake Garda, diocese of Verona. At the age of fifteen he
became a Friar Preacher at Brescia, studied at San Marco in Florence, and afterwards for forty-five years carried out a
most successful apostolate in the Vatellina
district on the borders of Switzerland and
Italy.
*Cf. Dict. Baudrill. — Att. — Baud. —
Holw.*

ANDREW CORSINI (St) Bp. O.C.
R.M. Feb. 4
1302-1373. Born in Florence of the illustrious Corsini family. After wasting his
early years in dissipation, he joined the
Carmelites in 1318, and embarked on a
life of the most austere penance. He
studied in Paris and at Avignon, was made
prior at Florence. As bishop he continued
his extraordinary life of penance, was a
father of the poor, and mediator between
the quarrelsome Italian states of that time.
He died on Jan. 6.
*Cf. Att. — Bolland. — Dict. Baudrill. —
Baud.*

ANDREW of ELNONE (Bl) Ab. O.S.B.
A.C. Feb. 6
d. c.690. Monk and disciple of St Amandus at Elnone, whom he succeeded as
abbot. His relics were "raised" together
with those of St Amandus in 694.
Cf. Chev. — Baud. — Holw.

ANDREW and APONIUS (SS) MM.
A.C. Feb. 10
1st cent. Martyred at Bethlehem, it is
said, during the persecution mentioned
in Acts XII, in which St James the Great
was put to death.
Cf. Baud.

ANDREW CONTI (Bl) C. O.F.M.
A.C. Feb. 15
d. 1302 (Feb. 1). Andrew of the counts of
Segni, or Andrew of Anagni, as he is called
from his birthplace, was a nephew of Pope
Alexander IV. He became a Franciscan
lay-brother and remained in that position
although offered a cardinal's hat by Pope
Boniface VIII. He was equipollently
beatified in 1724.
*Cf. Att. — Dict. Baudrill. — Baud. —
Holw.*

ANDREW NAM-THUNG (Bl) M.
A.C. Feb. 18
c.1790-1855. A native catechist of
Cochin-China and mayor of his village.
He died on the way to exile at Mi-Tho, E.
Cochin-China. Beatified in 1909.
Cf. Holw.

ANDREW of FLORENCE (St) Bp.
R.M. Feb. 26
d. c.407. The successor — according to
Gams, the predecessor — of St Zenobius
in the see of Florence. Gams lists a
second Andrew as a successor — with an
interrogation mark.
Cf. Gams — Holw. — Baud.

ANDREW of STRUMI (Bl) Ab. O.S.B. Vall. A.C. March 10
d. 1097. Surnamed "the Ligurian." Born at Parma, he was the disciple and chief supporter of the deacon St Arialdo in the campaign against simony at Milan. After his master's martyrdom Andrew became a Vallombrosan monk. Eventually he was made abbot of San Fedele at Strumi on the Arno. He excelled as a peacemaker between Florence and Arezzo. He is also the biographer of SS John Gualbert and Arialdo.
Cf. Zimm. — P. de U. — Baud. — Chev. — Dict. Baudrill. — Att. — Holw.

ANDREW de' GALLERANI (Bl) C. A.C. March 19
d. 1251. He was a distinguished Sienese soldier, who accidentally killed a man whom he had heard blaspheming. Exiled from Siena, he led a life of extraordinary penance and charity until he was allowed to return to his native city, where he founded the Brothers of Mercy.
Cf. Dict. Baudrill. — Att. — Baud.

ANDREW of MONTEREALE (Bl) C. O.S.A. A.C. Apr. 12
1397-1480. Born at Mascioni, diocese of Rieti, at the age of fourteen he became an Augustinian hermit at Montereale. Ordained priest, he preached and laboured for fifty years throughout Italy and France, disciplining himself by severe fasts. He was for a time provincial of his order in Umbria. Cult confirmed in 1764.
Cf. Baud. — Dict. Baudrill. — Holw. — Att.

ANDREW HIBERNON (Bl) C. O.F.M. A.C. Apr. 18
1534-1602. Born at Alcantarilla, near Murcia, in Spain, of noble but poor parents, he worked in order to help his sister financially, but was robbed of his savings and, disillusioned, joined the Conventual Franciscans as a lay-brother. In 1537 he passed over, at Elche, to the Alcantarine Reform. He converted many Moors by his frank simplicity. He died while helping to introduce the reform at Gandia. Beatified in 1791.
Cf. P. de U. — Att. — Dict. Baudrill. — Baud. — Holw.

ANDREW FOURNET (St) C. A.C. May 13
1752-1834. Born at Maillé, near Poitiers.

After several false starts, he was ordained and appointed parish priest of his native town, which he served unremittingly, even at the risk of his life, during the French Revolution. In 1807 he, with Elizabeth des Anges, founded the Congregation of the Daughters of the Cross for nursing and teaching. Beatified in 1926 and canonized in 1933.
Cf. Att.

ANDREW (St) M. R.M. May 15
See Peter, Andrew, etc.

ANDREW ABELLON (Bl) C. O.P. A.C. May 15
1375-1450. A Dominican friar, prior of the royal monastery of St Mary Magdalen at Saint-Maximin, in France. Cult confirmed in 1902.
Cf. Att. (May 17) — Baud. — Holw. — Dict. Baudrill.

ANDREW BOBOLA (St) M. S.J. A.C. May 23
1592-1657 (May 16). Called by the schismatics Duszochwat (robber of souls). He was a Pole, who joined the Society of Jesus at Vilna in 1611 and spent his whole life reconciling dissident Orthodox with the Holy See. For this reason he was cruelly tormented and partially flayed alive and finally put to death by a gang of Cossacks at Janov, near Pinsk. Beatified in 1853, canonized in 1938.
Cf. Att. — Dict. Baudrill. — Baud. — Holw.

ANDREW FRANCHI (Bl) Bp. O.P. A.C. May 30
1335-1401. Of the family dei Franchi Boccagni. He was born at Pistoia, where he took the Dominican habit and eventually (1378) was chosen bishop. One year before his death he resigned and retired to his old friary. Cult confirmed in 1921.
Cf. Att. — Holw. — Gams.

ANDREW TOCUAN (Bl) M. A.C. June 1
d. 1619 (Nov. 18). A Japanese layman, born at Nagasaki, he was a member of the confraternity of the Holy Rosary, and was burnt alive, together with Bl Leonard, because he had sheltered the missionaries. Beatified in 1867.
Cf. Holw.

ANDREW TSHOCHINDA (Bl) M.
A.C. June 1
d. 1617 (Oct. 1). A Japanese layman and member of the confraternity of the Holy Rosary. Martyred at Nagasaki for having given shelter to the Dominican missionaries. Beatified in 1867.
Cf. Holw.

ANDREW CACCIOLI (Bl) C. O.F.M.
A.C. June 3
d. 1254 (or 1264). Born at Spello, near Assisi, he was ordained priest and was possessed of considerable wealth. He gave it all to charity and became one of the first seventy-two followers of St Francis. He favoured a strict interpretation of the Franciscan Rule, against the innovations of Brother Elias, and was for this reason persecuted and imprisoned. He died at Spello, where he had founded a friary. Cult confirmed by Clement XII.
Cf. Att. — Dict. Baudrill. — Baud. — Holw.

ANDREW KAGWA (Bl) M.
A.C. June 3
d. 1886. A native of Uganda and a page of King Mwanga; later a military officer. Baptized in 1881, he was condemned to death for the Faith, and after his right arm had been severed from his body he was beheaded in 1886. Beatified in 1920.
Cf. Holw. — Baud.

ANDREW of CRETE (St) Bp.
A.C. July 4
c.660-740. Surnamed also "of Jerusalem." He was born at Damascus, became a monk of Mar Saba and then of the Holy Sepulchre at Jerusalem, a deacon of St Sophia at Constantinople, and finally archbishop of Gortyna in Crete. He excelled as a writer of homilies and panegyrics of saints; he is also considered to be the initiator of the *Kanon* of the Byzantine Liturgy.
Cf. Dict. Baudrill. — Baud. — Att.

ANDREW WOUTERS (St) M.
R.M. July 9
d. 1572. One of the martyrs of Gorkum (*q.v.*). He was a secular priest at Heinot near Dortrecht in Holland. He led a scandalous life, but when the Calvinists tried to compel him to renounce the Catholic faith, he expiated his past by a brave confession, was imprisoned at Briel with the other martyrs and hanged with them. Beatified in 1675, canonized in 1867.
Cf. Holw. — Baud.

ANDREW of RINN (Bl) M.
A.C. July 12
1459-1462. A boy, aged three, alleged to have been put to death by Jews out of hatred of Christ at Rinn, near Innsbruck. The facts are doubtful. Benedict XIV allowed the continuation of the local *cultus* but refused to proceed to Andrew's canonization.
Cf. Att. — Dict. Baudrill. — Baud.

ANDREW and BENEDICT (SS) MM. O.S.B. (Cam)
A.C. July 17
d. c.1020. Born in Poland, Andrew together with his disciple Benedict, lived as a hermit in Moravia, whence they passed over to Hungary and joined the Benedictines at Zobor Abbey. They were killed by marauders and venerated as martyrs.
Cf. Dict. Baudrill. — Baud. — Holw. — Chev.

ANDREW the TRIBUNE and Comp. (SS) MM.
R.M. Aug. 19
d. c.303. An officer in the army of Maximian Galerius, who took part in an expedition against the Persians. Accused with a number of his comrades of being a Christian, he and they were expelled from the army and took refuge in the Taurus mountains in Cilicia, but were tracked and put to death.
Cf. Att. — Dict. Baudrill. — Baud. — Holw.

ANDREW of TUSCANY (St) Ab. O.S.B.
A.C. Aug. 22
d. c.880. An Irish or Scottish pilgrim to Rome, who settled at Fiesole and became the abbot-restorer of San Martino in Mensula. These seem to be the only trustworthy facts in his life, which has come down to us largely embellished with fiction.
Cf. Zimm. — Att. — Dict. Baudrill. — Baud. — Holw.

ANDREW (St) M.
R.M. Aug. 29
See Hypatius and Andrew.

ANDREW DOTTI (Bl) C. O.S.M.
A.C. Sept. 3
1256-1315 (Aug. 31). Born at Borgo San Sepolcro, Italy, from being a military

captain he followed St Philip Benizi into the Servite Order and accompanied him on his preaching expeditions. He retired to the solitude of Montevecchio, where he died. Cult confirmed in 1806.
Cf. Att. — Dict. Baudrill. — Baud. — Holw.

ANDREW, JOHN, PETER, and ANTONY (SS) MM. R.M. Sept. 23
d. c.900. According to the Greek Menology these saints were deported from Syracuse to Africa by the Saracens, at that time masters of Sicily. They were there subjected to savage tortures and put to death.
Cf. Baud. — Holw.

ANDREW CHAKICHI (Bl) M.
A.C. Oct. 2
d. 1622. A Japanese boy, aged eight, son of Louis and Lucia Chakichi and brother of Francis. The four were beheaded at Nagasaki. The four were also beatified together in 1867.
Cf. Holw.

ANDREW the CALABYTE (St) M.
R.M. Oct. 20
d. 766. A native of Crete, and a monk there, who went to Constantinople and openly denounced the emperor Constantine Copronymus for heresy on account of the latter's edict against the veneration of images. The emperor ordered the brave monk to be put to the torture and finally abandoned him to the mob, who led him through the streets in derision and stabbed him to death.
Cf. Att. — Dict. Baudrill. — Baud.

ANDREW of BAUDIMENT (Bl) Ab.
O.S.B. Cist. P.C. Nov. 10 (Apr. 29)
d. 1142. A Cistercian monk of Pontigny, he became the abbot-founder of Chablis (*Caroli-loci*).
Cf. Dict. Baudrill. — Baud. — Zimm.

ANDREW AVELLINO (St) C. Theatine.
R.M. Nov. 10
1521-1608. Born near Naples and christened Lancelot. Ordained priest, he was at first an ecclesiastical lawyer and as such was entrusted with the reform of a certain nunnery, being nearly killed in the enterprise. He then joined the Theatine Clerks Regular and took the name of Andrew. He worked with great success, chiefly in Lombardy where he became a personal friend and advisor of St Charles Borromeo. He died at Naples, in his eightieth year, at the foot of the altar when beginning Mass. Beatified in 1624 and canonized in 1712.
Cf. Att. — Baud. — Dict. Baudrill. — Holw.

ANDREW TRONG (Bl) M.
A.C. Nov. 18
1817-1835. A native soldier of Cochin-China attached to the Society of Foreign Missions of Paris. He was arrested with other Christians in 1834. His mother assisted at his execution and received his falling head into her lap. Beatified in 1906.
Cf. Holw.

ANDREW (St) M. R.M. Nov. 28
See Stephen the Younger, etc.

ANDREW the APOSTLE (St) M.
R.M. Nov. 30
1st cent. A native of Bethsaida in Galilee, elder brother of St Peter and like him a fisherman. He was a disciple of St John the Baptist and the first to be called to Christ's apostleship. He is said to have evangelized Asia Minor and Greece and to have been crucified at Patras in Achaia. The *Acta* of his martyrdom seem to date from the 4th century. His alleged relics, stolen from Constantinople in 1210, rest now at Amalfi in S. Italy. St Andrew is the patron saint of Scotland, Russia and Greece; his name occurs in the Canon of the Mass and in the embolism of the Lord's prayer. His emblem in art is the traditional cross of his martyrdom — shaped like an X.
Cf. Att. — Dict. Baudrill. — Holw. — Baud.

ANDREW of ANTIOCH (Bl) C. O.S.A.
A.C. Nov. 30
1268-1348. A descendant of Robert Guiscard, he was born at Antioch of Norman parents. He joined the Canons Regular of the Holy Sepulchre at Jerusalem and was sent into Europe to collect funds for the Eastern houses of his order. In this quest he died at Annecy (March 27).
Cf. Dict. Baudrill. — Baud. — Holw. — Att. — P.B.

ANDREW DUNG (Bl) M. A.C. Dec. 26
1785-1839. A native of Tonkin. Arrested with Bl Peter Thi, both were beheaded on Dec. 26. Beatified in 1900.
Cf. Holw.

ANDRONICUS and JUNIAS (SS) MM.
A.C. May 17
1st cent. A disciple of St Paul, who makes mention of him in Romans XVI, 7: "Salute Andronicus and Junias, my kinsmen and fellow-prisoners, who are of note among the Apostles, who also were in Christ before me." This is all we know about them. The Greeks celebrate their feast on May 17; their names have been dropped from the R.M.
Cf. Dict. Baudrill. — Baud. — Holw.

ANDRONICUS and ATHANASIA (SS)
HH. R.M. Oct. 9
5th cent. Husband and wife, citizens of Antioch in Syria, where the former was a silversmith or banker. On the death of their two children they agreed to separate and live as hermits in Egypt. Years later they met and occupied adjoining cells, Andronicus not recognizing his wife until after her death. They are particularly venerated in Egypt and Ethiopia.
Cf. Att. — Baud. — Holw.

ANDRONICUS (St) M. R.M. Oct. 11
See Tharacus, Probus and Andronicus.

ANECTUS (St) M. R.M. March 10
See Codratus, Dionysius, etc.

ANECTUS (ANICETUS) (St) M.
R.M. June 27
d. 303. Nothing really is known about him. Baronius, who wrote the *laus* for the R.M., places him at Caesarea in Palestine under Diocletian, but remarks that the Greek *Acta* are very vague.
Cf. Dict. Baudrill. — Baud. — Holw.

ANEMPODISTUS (St) M. R.M. Nov. 2
See Acindynus, Pegasius, etc.

ANESIUS (St) M. R.M. March 31
See Theodulus, Anesius, etc.

ANEURIN (or GILDAS) and GWINOC
(SS) CC. A.C. Oct. 26
6th cent. Welsh monks, father and son. The latter has left some Celtic poems of a certain literary value.
Cf. Baud. (under Gwinoc).

ANGADRESIMA (ANGADRISMA, ANGADREME) (St) Abs. O.S.B.
A.C. Oct. 14
d. c.695. Cousin to St Lambert of Lyons, monk of Fontenelle. She herself received the veil at the hands of St Ouen. Eventually she became abbess of the Benedictine nunnery of Oroër-des-Vierges, near Beauvais.
Cf. Att. — Baud. — Dict. Baudrill. — Holw.

ANGELA of FOLIGNO (Bl) W. Tert.
O.F.M. A.C. Jan. 4
1248-1309. Born at Foligno of good family, she led a worldly self-indulgent life in the married state, until her conversion, when she became a Franciscan tertiary. After the death of her husband and children she gave herself up completely to God and to penance and became the leader of a large group of tertiaries, men and women. At the request of her confessor, Friar Arnold, she dictated to him an account of her visions and ecstasies in which she reveals herself as one of the greatest of mystics. Cult confirmed in 1693.
Cf. Att. — Dict. Baudrill. — Baud. — Holw.

ANGELA de' MERICI (St) V. Foundress.
R.M. May 31
1474-1540 (Jan. 24). Born at Desenzano on Lake Garda, diocese of Verona, she devoted herself to the education of girls, and the care of sick women. She was joined by several companions, and this led to the foundation of the Institute of St Ursula in 1535, the first specifically teaching order of women established in the Church. Canonized in 1807.
Cf. Att.—Baud.—Dict. Baudrill.—Holw.

ANGELELMUS (St or Bl) Bp. O.S.B?
P.C. July 7
d. 828. He is said to have been abbot of SS Gervase and Protase at Auxerre. He was bishop there from c. 813 to 828.
Cf. Gams — Zimm. — Holw.

ANGELICO (Bl) C. O.P. P.C. March 18
1387-1455. His baptismal name was John. Born at Mugello near Florence, he became a Dominican in 1407 at Fiesole. He resided for a time at San Marco in Florence, which he decorated with his wonderful paintings and died at the Dominican friary of La Minerva at Rome.

He is one of the best known and admired religious painters of all times. He is usually called *il Beato Angelico*, although he has never been beatified or given a public cult.
Cf. E. Ricci. Mille Santi nell'arte. Milano, 1931. — Baud.

ANGELINA of MARSCIANO (Bl) W. Tert. O.F.M.　　　　A.C. July 15
1377-1435. Born at Montegiove in Umbria, she married in her fifteenth year and was left a widow at seventeen. She was inspired to found a convent of regular tertiaries of St Francis at Foligno. It was finished in 1397, and before her death there were a hundred and thirty-five such houses under her direction as superior general. Cult confirmed in 1825.
Cf. Att. — Baud. — Dict. Baudrill.

ANGELUS
Note. This is the Latin form of a name which is very common in Latin countries: Angelo in Italian; Ange in French; Angel in Spanish; Anjo in Portuguese.

ANGELUS of FURCI (Bl) C. O.S.A.
　　　　　　　　　　　　A.C. Feb. 6
1246-1327. Born at Furci in the Abruzzi, diocese of Chieti, he joined the Augustinians at an early age, studied in Paris where he became lector of theology, and on his return to Italy spent the rest of his life as professor of theology at Naples. Without giving up his teaching he became for a time provincial of his order and refused several bishoprics. Cult confirmed in 1888.
Cf. Att. — Baud. — Holw.

ANGELUS of GUALDO (Bl) C. O.S.B. Cam.　　　　　　A.C. Feb. 14
c. 1265-1325 (Jan. 25). A native of Gualdo (Valido), diocese of Nocera, on the borders of Umbria. In his youth he travelled barefoot from Italy to Compostella. He was professed a Camaldolese lay-brother and for forty years lived as a hermit walled up in his cell. All his life he was distinguished for his extreme simplicity, innocence and gentleness. Cult confirmed in 1825.
Cf. Att. — Baud. — Dict. Baudrill. — Holw. — Zimm. — Prop. Cam.

ANGELUS of BORGO SAN SEPOLCRO (Bl) C. O.S.A.　　　A.C. Feb. 15
d. c.1306. A native of Borgo San Sepol-

cro in Umbria, and a scion of the family of Scarpetti. He entered the order of Augustinian Friars and became a fellow-student of St Nicholas of Tolentino. It is said that Bl Angelus worked in England and founded several friaries there. He was famed as a wonder-worker: once, it was narrated, he asked pardon for a man condemned to death and was refused this request, but after the man's execution he raised him to life again. Cult approved in 1921.
Cf. Att. — Dict. Baudrill. — Holw.

ANGELUS PORTASOLE (Bl) Bp. O.P.
　　　　　　　　　　　　P.C. Feb. 22
c. 1296-1334. A native of Perugia, he was elected bishop of Iglesias, in Sardinia, in 1330. He died at Ischia.
Cf. Holw. — Gams (without any hagiological title).

ANGELUS CARLETTI, or, of CHIVASSO (Bl) C. O.F.M.　　　A.C. Apr. 12
d. 1495. Born at Chivasso, diocese of Ivrea, near Turin, he studied law at Bologna and practised at Monferrato. Elected a senator, he left all to become a Friar Minor at Genoa. In the order he filled important offices; preached among the Saracens and the Waldensians and against usurious money-lenders; wrote a book of "Moral Cases" (the *Summa Angelica*), and effected many conversions. Cult approved by Benedict XIII.
Cf. Att. — Baud. — Dict. Baudrill. — Holw.

ANGELUS of JERUSALEM (St) M. O.C.
　　　　　　　　　　　　R.M. May 5
1145-1220. Born in Jerusalem of convert Jewish parents. He was one of the early friar-hermits of Mt Carmel (1203). Commissioned to obtain the approval of Honorius III for the Rule written by St Albert for the use of the new friars, he journeyed to Rome and shortly after went to preach in Sicily, where he was killed by a man whose crimes he had denounced.
Cf. Att. — Baud. — Dict. Baudrill.

ANGELUS of MASSACCIO (Bl) M. O.S.B. Cam.　　　　　A.C. May 8
d. 1458. A Camaldolese monk of Santa Maria di Serra in the Marches of Ancona. He was put to death by the heretics, called Fraticelli or Bertolani, on account of his

vehement preaching in defence of the Catholic faith.
Cf. Zimm. — Chev. — Prop. Cam. — Holw. — Baud.

ANGELUS AGOSTINI MAZZINGHI (Bl) C. O.C. A.C. Aug. 16
1377-1438. Born at Florence, a member of the Agostini family, he was professed a Carmelite in his native city. After his ordination he was professor of theology, prior at Frascati and Florence, and provincial. He died in retirement, revered by all as a model religious. Cult approved in 1761.
Cf. Att.—Dict. Baudrill.—Baud.— Holw.

ANGELUS of ACQUAPAGANA (Bl) C. O.S.B. Cam. A.C. Aug. 19
1271-1313. A Camaldolese lay-brother of the monastery of San Salvatore at Acquapagana, diocese of Camerino. A model of patience throughout a lingering attack of consumption. He died kneeling. Cult approved in 1815.
Cf. Chev. — Zimm. — Prop. Cam. — Holw. — Baud.

ANGELUS of FOLIGNO (Bl) C. O.S.A. A.C. Aug. 27
1226-1312. Born at Foligno, at the age of twenty he became an Augustinian Friar, and like Bl Angelus of Borgo San Sepolcro, he was linked in friendship with St Nicholas of Tolentino. He founded three houses of the order in Umbria. Cult confirmed in 1891.
Cf. Att.—Dict. Baudrill.—Baud.— Holw.

ANGELUS ORSUCCI (Bl) M. O.P. A.C. Sept. 10
1573-1622. A native of Lucca, in Italy, he became a Dominican there and passed over to Valencia in Spain to finish his studies. Eventually he went to the missions of the order in the Philippine Islands and Japan. Here he was arrested and for four years languished in the horrible prison of Omura until he was burnt alive at Nagasaki. Beatified in 1867.
Cf. Dict. Baudrill. — Holw. — Baud.

ANGELUS (St) M. R.M. Oct. 10
See Daniel, Samuel, etc.

ANGELUS of ACRI (Bl) C. O.F.M. Cap. A.C. Oct. 30
1669-1739. Born at Acri, diocese of Bisignano, in Calabria. Twice he attempted unsuccessfully to become a religious, the third time, after a tempestuous novitiate, he was professed as a Capuchin. His public life as a preacher was again quite unsuccessful in the beginning and "tempestuously successful" afterwards. Beatified in 1825.
Cf. Dict. Baudrill.—Att.—Holw.—Baud.

ANGELUS SINESIUS (Bl) Ab. O.S.B. P.C. Nov. 27
d. c.1386. Born at Catania, he joined the Benedictines at the abbey of San Nicolo del' Arena and eventually was chosen abbot of San Martino della Scala at Palermo, whence he influenced all the Sicilian Benedictine abbeys in restoring monastic observance.
Cf. Zimm. — Chev. — Holw.

ANGILBERT (St) Ab. O.S.B. A.C. Feb. 18
c. 740-814. Nicknamed "Homer" at the court of Charlemagne, because he was a fluent verse-writer. His early life was worldly, if not dissipated. He excelled, however, as a minister and filled several important offices — secretary to the emperor, privy councillor, etc. As a reward Charlemagne gave him the abbey of St Riquier (Centula) and Angilbert became a model abbot. He introduced the continuous chanting of the office, using his three hundred monks and one hundred boys in relays, enriched the library and completed the buildings. He died twenty-two days after his friend the emperor. He has always been venerated with a public cult.
Cf. Zimm. — Att. — Chev. — Baud. — Dict. Baudrill. — Mab. — P. de U.

ANGLINUS (St) Ab. O.S.B. A.C. Oct. 28
d. c.768. The tenth abbot of Stavelot-Malmédy, in the province of Liége, Belgium.
Cf. Zimm. — Baud. — Dict. Baudrill. — Chev.

ANGUS of KELD (St) A.C. March 11
Otherwise Aengus, q.v.

ANIANUS (St) Bp. R.M. Apr. 25
1st cent. "A man well pleasing to God." Disciple and immediate successor of St Mark in the see of Alexandria. He is said to have been a shoemaker.
Cf. Att. — Baud.

ANIANUS (St) M.   **R.M. Nov. 10**
See Demetrius, Anianus, etc.

ANIANUS (AIGNAN) (St) Bp.
             R.M. Nov. 17
d. 453. Fifth bishop of Orleans. He is
best known in history as the prelate who
organized the defence of his episcopal city
at the time of the invasion of the Huns
under Attila and interviewed the latter on
his approach to Orleans, thus saving the
city.
*Cf. Duch. Fast. Episc. — Gams — Dict.
Baudrill. — Baud.*

ANIANUS (AGNAN)(St) Bp.   **A.C. Dec. 7**
5th cent. Fifth bishop of Chartres. We
know nothing else about him.
*Cf. Duch. Fast. Episc. — Dict. Baudrill. —
Gams — Baud.*

ANICETUS (St) Pope M.   **R.M. Apr. 17**
d. 160. A Syrian by descent, he was pope
from about 152 till 160. During his
pontificate St Polycarp of Smyrna visited
Rome to settle with the pope the question
of the date of Easter. Anicetus took a
firm stand against the Gnostics. It does
not seem that he died a martyr, although
he is venerated as such.
Cf. Dict. Baudrill. — Baud. — Att.

**ANICLETUS, PHOTINUS and Comp
(SS) MM.**   **R.M. Aug. 12**
c. 305. Martyrs of Nicomedia under Diocletian. Anicetus and Photinus were
closely related by blood.
Cf. Dict. Baudrill. — Baud.

ANNA the PROPHETESS (St) W.
              R.M. Sept. 1
1st cent. "Daughter of Phanuel, of the
tribe of Asher; she was far advanced in
years, and lived with her husband seven
years from her virginity. And she was a
widow until four score and four years;
who departed not from the temple by fast-
ings and prayers serving night and day.
Now she at the same hour (of our Lord's
being brought to the temple) coming in,
confessed to the Lord; and spoke of Him
to all that looked for the redemption of
Israel." (Luke II, 36-38). The Greeks
keep her feast on Feb. 3.

ANNAM (Martyrs of) BB.
          A.C. July 11 and Nov. 19
1820-1841 and 1745-1861. Two groups

of martyrs who suffered in Indo-China
between the dates given above. They
were beatified respectively in 1900 and
1906. Each martyr is listed under his
own name.
Cf. Att.

ANNE LINE (Bl) M.   **A.C. Feb. 27**
d. 1601. A gentlewoman, née Higham,
born at Dunmow in Essex. A convert,
she was hanged at Tyburn for harbouring
priests. Beatified in 1929.
Cf. Camm — Newdigate.

**ANNE of St BARTHOLOMEW (Bl) V.
O.C.D.**   **A.C. June 7**
1549-1626. Anne García was born at
Almendral, diocese of Avila, Spain, the
daughter of poor shepherds. A shepherdess herself in her early years, she was
the first to join St Teresa's reform at Avila
as a lay-sister. Eventually she became St
Teresa's secretary and companion in her
foundations throughout Spain. In 1606
she was sent to establish the reform in
France, was promoted to the choir, and
appointed prioress at Pontoise and Tours.
She was the foundress of the convent at
Antwerp, primarily intended for English
refugees. She has left some delightful
religious verse. Beatified in 1917.
Cf. Att. — Baud. — Dict. Baudrill.

ANNE MARY TAIGI (Bl) Matron
              A.C. June 9
1769-1837. Born at Siena, daughter of a
druggist named Giannetti, whose business
failed, she was brought to Rome and
worked for a time as a domestic servant.
In 1790 she married Dominic Taigi, a
butler of the Chigi family in Rome, and
lived the normal life of a married woman of
the working class. In the discharge of
these humble duties and in the bringing up
of her seven children she attained a high
degree of holiness. Endowed with the
gift of prophecy, she read thoughts and
described distant events. Her home became the rendezvous of cardinals and
other dignitaries who sought her counsel.
Beatified in 1920.
*Cf. Att. — Dict. Baudrill. — Holw. —
Baud.*

**ANNE PELRAS and ANNE MARY
THOURET (BB.) VV. MM. O.C.**
              A.C. July 17
See Carmelites of Compiègne.

ANNE (St) V.H.   **A.C. July 23**
c.840-c.918. Called also Susanna. A maiden of Constantinople who, while in her first youth, was left an orphan with a large fortune and was importuned to marry by unsuitable suitors. She refused, spent her money in the service of the poor, and finally lived half a century as a solitary on the Leucadian promontory of Epirus.
Cf. Dict. Baudrill. — Att. — Baud.

ANNE (St) Mother of Our Lady.
     R.M. July 26
1st cent. The gospels do not mention the names of our Lady's parents. Tradition gives them as Joachim and Anne (Hannah — "Grace"). St Anne's *cultus* already appears in the 6th century in some of the Eastern liturgies and in the eighth in the West, but it did not become general till the 14th century was well advanced. St Anne is usually represented as teaching her little daughter to read the Bible.
Cf. Att. — Baud. — Holw. — Ricci.

ANNE MARY ERRAUX and ANNE JOSEPH LEROUX (BB) VV. MM. O.S. Ursulae.   **A.C. Oct. 23**
See Ursulines of Valenciennes.

ANNE or EUPHEMIANUS (St) W. H.
     A.C. Oct. 29
d. 820. Born at Constantinople, a maiden of good family, she was married against her will but, after the death of her husband, under the name of Euphemianus and in male attire, became a monk at an abbey on Mt. Olympus. Here she made rapid progress in virtue, and was asked to take charge of an abbey built by the patriarch of Constantinople. She declined, and died instead in a small out-of-the-way monastery. The Greeks keep her feast.
Cf. Baud. — Dict. Baudrill.

ANNEMUNDUS (St) Bp. M.
     A.C. Sept. 28
d. 657. Called in French either Annemond or Chamond, and by St Bede, in error, Dalphinus. He was archbishop of Lyons and friend and patron of the young St Wilfrid of York, to whom he gave shelter for three years in his diocese. St Wilfrid was present when Annemundus was murdered at Châlon-sur-Saône by order of Ebroin.
Cf. Att. — Baud.

ANNO (HANNO, ANNON) (St) Bp.
     A.C. May 13
d. 780. A native of Verona, who became bishop there and is remembered chiefly in connection with the translation of the relics of SS Firminus and Rusticus.
Cf. Baud. — Gams — Dict. Baudrill.

ANNON (St) Bp.   **R.M. Dec. 4**
c.1010-1075. Son of a poor knight, he eventually became archbishop-elector of Cologne (1056) in spite of the hostility of his flock who thought him insufficiently well-born for their see. After a crowded career, full of political events, in which he took a great, and often leading, albeit not uniformly edifying part, he retired to the Benedictine abbey of Siegburg, which he had founded, and spent there the last twelve months of his life in rigorous penance.
Cf. Att. — Baud. — Dict. Baudrill.

ANNOBERT (ALNOBERT) (St) Bp. O.S.B.   **A.C. May 16**
d. p.689. Monk of Almenêches, who was raised to the see of Séez about the year 685.
Cf. Gams — Zimm. — Baud.

ANONYMOUS
Note. By counting up the number of saints listed anonymously in the R.M. under such headings as *companions, many, a great number, twenty, seventy, one hundred, etc.*, we reach the approximate figure of 36,000.

ANSANUS (St) M.   **R.M. Dec. 1**
c.304. A scion of the Anician family of Rome, he became a Christian when twelve years old. His own father accused him to the authorities, but the boy contrived to escape, and converted so many pagans, first at Bagnorea and then at Siena, that he was called "the Baptizer." He was at last arrested and beheaded.
Cf. Att. — Dict. Baudrill. — Baud.

ANSBALD (St) Ab. O.S.B.   **A.C. July 12**
d. 886. Born in Luxemburg of the counts of Querry, he became a monk of Prüm, and afterwards abbot of Saint-Hubert in the Ardennes, and finally of Prüm in 860. In 882 his abbey was burnt down by the Normans, and he succeeded in restoring it with the help of Charles the Fat.
Cf. Mab. — Chev. — Baud. — Holw. — and Butler-Thurston (March 8: -Humphrey).

ANSBERT (St) Bp. O.S.B. R.M. Feb. 9
d. c.700. From being chancellor at the
court of Clotaire III he became a monk
at Fontenelle under St Wandrille. He
was chosen the third abbot and in 683 was
promoted to the see of Rouen. Pepin of
Heristal banished him to the monastery of
Hautmont on the Sambre, where he died.
*Cf. Dict. Baudrill. — Att. — Chev. —
Baud. — Zimm.*

ANSCHAR (ANSGAR, SCHARIES) (St)
Bp. O.S.B. R.M. Feb. 3
801-865. Born near Amiens, he was received as a boy by the Benedictines of Old
Corbie in Picardy, and educated there
under St Abelard as abbot and St Paschasius Radbert as headmaster. After
his monastic profession he was transferred
to New Corbie in Saxony, whence he was
taken by King Harold of Denmark to
evangelize the heathen Danes. For thirteen years he worked there as first archbishop of Hamburg and legate of the Holy
See; his mission extended to Sweden,
Norway and N. Germany. The success
achieved by his personal efforts was unfortunately not lasting and most of those
northern churches relapsed into paganism.
*Cf. Att. — Baud. — Dict. Baudrill. —
Holw. — Zimm.*

ANSEGISUS (St) Ab. O.S.B.
A.C. July 20
c. 770-833. Monk of Fontenelle at
eighteen, he was soon chosen by Charlemagne to be the restorer of several abbeys,
and he ruled successively those of St
Sixtus at Reims, St Meuge near Châlons,
St Germer at Flaix, Luxeuil and Fontenelle. He excelled as a canonist, and
wrote a collection of capitularies, which
became the official law-book of the Empire. "His life," writes Father Thurston,
"is a characteristic example of Benedictine
work for Christianity and civilization such
as went on throughout the Dark Ages of
Europe," typical of that "all-roundness
which characterized most of them."
Cf. Butler-Thurston (July 20)

ANSELM (St) Ab. O.S.B. A.C. March 3
d. 830. Brother-in-Law of the Lombard
king Aistulph, and duke of Friuli, Anselm
founded the abbey of Fanano, near Modena, and a second at Nonantola, which
he dedicated to our Lady and St Benedict.
To both he attached sundry hospitals and

hostels. He himself became a Benedictine and abbot of Nonantola and soon had
one thousand monks under him. King
Desiderius banished him to Montecassino, but after seven years he was restored
to Nonantola by Charlemagne, and there
he died.
*Cf. Zimm. — Att. — Chev. — Baud. —
Mab.*

ANSELM of LUCCA (St) Bp. O.S.B.
R.M. March 18
1036-1086. Born at Mantua. His uncle
Pope Alexander II, nominated him bishop
of Lucca; but Anselm refused to accept
investiture at his hands and withdrew to
the Cluniac abbey of Polirone where he
was professed as a Benedictine. Gregory
VII recalled him to Lucca and the saint
obeyed. He tried to reform the canons,
who raised a revolt, and Anselm again
withdrew. He was the spiritual director
of the Countess Matilda. A man of great
learning, he excelled as a canonist. He
was Gregory VII's staunch supporter. He
Before his death at Mantua he became
apostolic legate in Lombardy.
*Cf. Att. — Dict. Baudrill. — Baud. —
Holw.*

ANSELM (St) Abp. Dr. O.S.B.
R.M. Apr. 21
c.1033-1109. Born at Aosta in Piedmont,
he left Italy in his youth and became a
Benedictine at Bec in Normandy under Bl
Herluin as abbot and Bl Lanfranc as prior
and teacher. He succeeded to each of
these offices at Bec and was finally appointed, after Bl Lanfranc, to the see of
Canterbury in 1093. For his resistance to
King William Rufus's encroachments on
ecclesiastical rights he was exiled to the
Continent. In 1098 he assisted at the
council of Bari, and, at the pope's request,
resolved the theological doubts of the
Italo-Greek bishops. On Rufus's death
Anselm returned to Canterbury, at the invitation of the new king Henry I, whom,
however, he had also to oppose on the
question of investitures. Hence a second
exile, terminating in a triumphal return
(1106). In spite of his somewhat stormy
career, Anselm was one of the gentlest of
saints. He stands out also in Church History as the link between St Augustine of
Hippo and St Thomas Aquinas, and is
known as the Father of Scholasticism. He
was officially declared a Doctor of the

Church in 1720. His life was written by his own secretary, the monk Eadmer of Christ Church, Canterbury.
Cf. Mab. — Bolland. — Att. — Baud. — Zimm.

ANSELM (St) Ab. O.S.B. P.C. Nov. 18
c.750. Abbot of Lérins. Mentioned in most menologies together with St Amand of Lérins.
Cf. Zimm. — Holw.

ANSFRIDUS (St) Bp. O.S.B. A.C. May 3
d. 1010. Count of Brabant and a knight in the service of the emperors Otto III and Henry II. In 992 he built the convent of Thorn for his daughter and wife, being himself desirous of becoming a monk. He was appointed instead archbishop of Utrecht. As such, he founded the Benedictine abbey of Hohorst (Heiligenberg) and, when stricken with blindness, he retired there and realized his ambition of taking monastic vows. There too he ended his days.
Cf. Zimm. — Mab. — Att. — Baud.

ANSGAR (St) Bp. O.S.B. R.M. Feb. 3
Otherwise Anschar q.v.

ANSILIO (St) Mk. O.S.B. A.C. Oct. 11
d. late 7th cent. A monk whose relics were enshrined at the Benedictine abbey of Lagny, diocese of Meaux.
Cf. Zimm. — Dict. Baudrill. — Baud.

ANSOVINUS (St) Bp. R.M. March 13
d. 840. A native of Camerino in Italy, who from being a hermit at Castel Raimondo, near Torcello, was raised to the episcopal see of his native town. He accepted the office on condition that he should be exempt from the service of recruiting soldiers, then imposed upon most bishops in their capacity of feudal lords.
Cf. Att. — Baud. — Dict. Baudrill.

ANSTRUDIS (AUSTRUDE, AUSTRU) (St) V. O.S.B. A.C. Oct. 17
d. 688. Daughter of SS Blandinus and Salaberga, the founders of the nunnery of St John the Baptist at Laon. Mother and daughter were successively the first two abbesses. She had to suffer much at the hands of Ebroin, the mayor of the palace and oppressor of all the saints of that period.
Cf. Att. — Chev. — Holw. — P.B.

ANSUERUS and Comp. (SS) MM. O.S.B. A.C. July 17
d. p. 1066. He belonged to the nobility of Sleswig and was a monk and abbot of the Benedictine monastery of St Georgenberg, near Ratzeburg in Denmark, whence he and his monks evangelized that country. Ansuerus and twenty-eight of his community were stoned to death in the antichristian reaction which took place among the Wends after the emperor Henry III's death.
Cf. Butler-Thurston (St Gotteschalc, June 7) — Baud. — Chev. — Holw.

ANSURIUS (ADURI, ASURIUS, ISAURI) (St) Bp. O.S.B. A.C. Jan. 26
d. 925. He was bishop of Orense in Spanish Galicia and helped in the foundation of the Benedictine abbey of Ribas de Sil. He was elected to the see in 915, and in 922 he resigned and became a monk at the above-mentioned monastery. After his death he was venerated there, together with seven other bishops who had followed his example.
Cf. Zimm. — Gams — P. de U. — Baud. — Dict. Baudrill.

ANTHELMUS (St) Bp. O.Cart. R.M. June 26
1105-1178. A Savoyard nobleman who, ordained priest early in life, went on a chance visit to the Charterhouse of Portes and stayed there as a monk. In 1169 he was chosen prior of the Grande Chartreuse, and it is owing to his efforts that the Carthusians, from being more or less a branch of Benedictine Monachism, became definitely a new religious order. In 1163 he accepted the bishopric of Belley under obedience to the pope, and so much did he endear himself to the people that, after his death, the city was called for a time Anthelmopolis. He was sent to England to try to bring about a reconciliation between King Henry II and St Thomas Becket. To the end of his life his heart was in his beloved Charterhouse which he revisited on every possible occasion.
Cf. Att. — Baud. — Dict. Baudrill.

ANTHEROS (St) Pope. R.M. Jan. 3
d. 236. A Greek who was pope only a few weeks. It is not quite certain whether he died a martyr, as his name is not mentioned in the *Depositio Martyrum*. He

was buried in the catacomb of St Callistus. A large fragment of his epitaph has been recovered.
Cf. Dict. Baudrill. — Att. — Baud.

ANTHES (St) M. R.M. Aug. 28
See Fortunatus, Caius, and Anthes.

ANTHIA (St) M. R.M. Apr. 18
See Eleutherius and Anthia.

ANTHIMUS (St) Bp. M. R.M. Apr. 27
d. 303. Bishop of Nicomedia where he was beheaded for the Faith under Diocletian. His death was followed by a wholesale slaughter of the Christian communities of the district.
Cf. Baud. — Dict. Baudrill. — Att. — Holw.

ANTHIMUS (St) M. R.M. May 11
d. 303. A priest at Rome, who is said to have converted the pagan husband, a prefect, of the Christian matron Lucina, well known for her charity to her imprisoned fellow-Christians. The martyr, thrown into the Tiber but miraculously rescued by an angel, was afterwards recaptured and beheaded.
Cf. Dict. Baudrill. — Baud.

ANTHIMUS (St) M. R.M. Sept. 27
d. c.303. Mentioned in the legendary *Acta* as a companion martyr of SS Cosmas and Damian, q.v.

ANTHOLIAN (ANATOLIANUS) (St) M.
R.M. Feb. 6
c.267. Mentioned by St Gregory of Tours as one of the martyrs of Auvergne under Valerian and Gallienus. Other fellow-sufferers were SS Cassius, M ximus, Limininus and Victorinus.
Cf. Dict. Baudrill. — Baud. — Holw.

ANTHOLIN (St) Ab. R.M. Jan. 17
Otherwise Antony, q.v.

ANTHONIUS (St) M. R.M. May 11
Otherwise Anthimus, q.v.

ANTHONY
Note. From the Greek Anthonios and the Latin Anthonius or Antonius. The usual modern forms are: in Italian and Portuguese: Antonio; in Spanish: Antonio or Anton; in Catalan: Antoni; in French: Antoine; in German: Anton; in English: Antony, q.v.

ANTHUSA (St) V. R.M. July 27
8th cent. First a recluse, and then abbess of a nunnery near Constantinople. Known for her open veneration of the images of saints. For this reason she had to appear before the emperor Constantine Copronymus, by whose orders she was put to the torture. The empress, however, befriended Anthusa, who lived to an advanced age.
Cf. Dict. Baudrill. — Baud. — Holw.

ANTHUSA the ELDER (St) M.
R.M. Aug. 22
See Athanasius, Anthusa, etc.

ANTHUSA (St) V.M. R.M. Aug. 27
? Called St Anthusa the Younger, to distinguish her from St Anthusa of Seleucia (Aug. 22). She was probably a Persian and suffered in that country. She is said to have been sewn up in a sack and drowned in a well.
Cf. Dict. Baudrill. — Baud. — Holw.

ANTIDIUS (ANTEL, ANTIBLE, TUDE) (St) Bp. M. R.M. June 17
d. c.265. Disciple and successor of St Froninus in the see of Besançon. He was put to death by a horde of Vandals at a place called Ruffey.
Cf. Dict. Baudrill. — Gams — Baud.

ANTIGONUS (St) M. R.M. Feb. 27
See Alexander, Abundius, etc.

ANTIMUS (St) Ab. O.S.B. A.C. Jan. 28
8th cent. He was, it seems, one of the first abbots of Brantôme, an abbey founded by Charlemagne in 769 and destroyed by the Normans in 817.
Cf. Baud. — Chev. — P. de U.

ANTINOGENES (St) M. R.M. July 24
See Victor, Stercatius and Antinogenes.

ANTIOCH in SYRIA (Martyrs of) (SS)
The following anonymous groups of martyrs put to death at Antioch in Syria are given in the R.M.:
R.M. March 11
c.300. "Many holy martyrs . . . under Maximian set upon red hot gridirons and condemned not to death but continued torture," while others were afflicted with other cruel torments.
R.M. Nov. 6
d. 637. "Ten holy martyrs, who are said

to have suffered at the hands of the Saracens," i.e., after their seizure of Antioch. Some records put their number at forty or more.

R.M. Dec. 24
d. 250. Forty Christian maidens put to death under Decius.

ANTIOCHUS (St) M.   R.M. May 21
See Nicostratus and Antiochus.

ANTIOCHUS and CYRIACUS (SS) MM.
R.M. July 15
3rd cent. The R.M. has this *laus:* "At Sebaste the passion of St Antiochus the physician who was beheaded under the governor Hadrian; and when milk flowed forth from the severed head in place of blood, Cyriacus, the executioner, was converted to Christ, and himself also suffered martyrdom."

ANTIOCHUS (ANDEOL) (St) Bp.
R.M. Oct. 15
5th cent. When St Justus, bishop of Lyons, joined the solitaries in Egypt, the priest Antiochus was sent to seek him out and induce him to return to his see. The priest's efforts were in vain, and on his own return to Lyons he was himself chosen bishop.
Cf. Dict. Baudrill. — Baud.

ANTIOCHUS (St) M.   R.M. Dec. 13
d. c.110. A martyr of Solta (Sulci), a small island near Sardinia, under the emperor Hadrian. The island is now also known as the *Isola di Sant' Antioco.*
Cf. Dict. Baudrill. — Baud. — Holw.

ANTIPAS (St) Bp. M.   R.M. Apr. 11
d. c.90. The bishop of Pergamus in Asia Minor mentioned in the Apocalypse (II, 13) as the "faithful witness." He was martyred under Domitian by being thrown into a red-hot brazen bull.
Cf. Baud. — Holw.

ANTOINETTE
French diminutive form of the names Antonia, Antonina, q.v.

ANTOINETTE ROUSSEL (Bl) V. O.C.D.
A.C. July 17
See Carmelites of Compiègne.

ANTONIA of FLORENCE (Bl) W. O.F.M.
A.C. Feb. 28
1400-1472. Born in Florence, she was

left a widow in early life and joined the Franciscan tertiaries. Later she was chosen superioress at Aquila, where she adopted the original rule of the Poor Clares. She contracted a painful disease, which afflicted her for fifteen years, and she was sorely tried by the misconduct of her only son, but these and other trials she bore bravely under the guidance of St John Capistran. Cult confirmed in 1847.
Cf. Att. — Dict. Baudrill. — Baud.

ANTONIA (St) V.M.   R.M. Apr. 29
See Agapius and Comp.

ANTONIA (or ANTONINA) V.M.
R.M. June 12 (March 1 and May 4)
d. ? 304. There are no verifiable data about this martyr. She seems to be triplicated in the R.M., March 1 and May 4, and is claimed by three different places called Cea. Very likely she suffered at Nicomedia.
Cf. Att. — Baud. — Holw.

ANTONIA of BRESCIA (Bl) V. O.P.
P.C. Oct. 27
1407-1507. Having entered as a young girl at the Dominican convent of Brescia, she was, at the age of sixty-six, chosen prioress of St Catherine's Convent at Ferrara, which she ruled justly but rigorously. She was deposed and underwent other trials, always with much patience and humility.
Cf. Dict. Baudrill. — Baud. — Holw.

ANTONINA (St) V.M.   R.M. May 3
See Alexander and Antonina.

ANTONINUS of SORRENTO (St) Ab.
O.S.B.   R.M. Feb. 14
d. 830. A Benedictine monk in one of the daughter houses of Montecassino. Forced to leave his monastery by the wars raging in the country, he became a hermit, until he was invited by the people of Sorrento to live among them. He did so as abbot of St Agrippinus. He is now venerated as the patron saint of the town.
Cf. Att. — Chev. — Dict. Baudrill. — Zimm.

ANTONINUS (St) M.   R.M. Apr. 20
See Victor, Zoticus, etc.

ANTONINUS (St) Bp. O.P.
R.M. May 10
1389-1459 (May 2). A Florentine of the

Pierozzi family, he joined the Friars Preachers at Fiesole, and while still very young was made prior of the Minerva at Rome. In 1436 he founded San Marco at Florence, and in 1446 he was against his will appointed archbishop of that city. He was the "people's prelate" and "the protector of the poor." He also distinguished himself as a writer on moral theology and international law. Canonized in 1523.
Cf. Att. — Baud. — Holw. — Dict. Baudrill.

ANTONINUS (St) M.   R.M. July 6
See Lucy, Antoninus, etc.

ANTONINUS (St) M.   R.M. July 29
See Lucilla, Flora, etc.

ANTONINUS (St) M.   R.M. Aug. 22
d. 186. One of the public executioners in Rome under Commodus. While awaiting the result of the trial of SS Eusebius and companions, he saw a vision of angels and, proclaiming himself a Christian, was himself beheaded.
Cf. Holw.

ANTONINUS (St) M.   R.M. Sept. 2
? It is not certain whether the Pamia mentioned in the R.M. is a town named Apomea in Syria or Pamiers in France. In both places there are traditions connected with a martyr named Antoninus.
Cf. Bolland. — Dict. Baudrill. — Att. — Baud.

ANTONINUS (St) M.   R.M. Sept. 3
See Aristaeus and Antoninus.

ANTONINUS (St) M.   R.M. Sept. 30
3rd cent. A soldier of the Theban Legion, martyred on the banks of the Trebbia, near Piacenza, in Italy. His blood, kept in a phial, is said to have the same miraculous properties as that of St Januarius.
Cf. Baud. — Holw.

ANTONINUS (St) M.   R.M. Oct. 25
See Marcellinus, Claudius, etc.

ANTONINUS (St) Bp.   R.M. Oct. 31
d. 660. Surnamed Fontana. He was archbishop of Milan for one year. In 1581 St Charles Borromeo enshrined his relics beneath a magnificent altar in the church of St Simplician.
Cf. Dict. Baudrill. — Holw. — Baud. — Gams.

ANTONINUS, ZEBINAS, GERMANUS and ENNATHA (SS) MM.
                              R.M. Nov. 13
d. 297. Martyrs under Galerius at Caesarea in Palestine. St Ennatha, a virgin, was burnt alive; her male fellow-sufferers were beheaded.
Cf. Dict. Baudrill. — Baud. — Holw.

ANTONY (St) M.   R.M. Jan. 9
See Julian, Basilissa, etc.

ANTONY (St) Ab.   R.M. Jan. 17
251-356. The patriarch of all monks. Born at Coma in Upper Egypt, at the age of twenty he gave away his property, which was considerable, to the poor and lived as a hermit near his native place. About the year 305 he established a community at Fayum and another shortly after at Pispir. Thus he was the first to establish the religious life as we know it to-day, by gathering together large groups of hermits into loose communities. Soon he became famous throughout Egypt and beyond, and was in great demand as an advisor by people of every rank. He was a personal friend of St Athanasius and his staunch supporter against the Arians, whom he arraigned as heretics in a public sermon preached at Alexandria at the invitation of Athanasius, when he was ninety years old. Athanasius himself became St Antony's biographer. St Antony died in his hermitage on Mt Kolzim, near the Red Sea. In art he is frequently shown with a T-shaped cross and a pig. The latter, perhaps originally the symbol of evil, became associated with a privilege of the Hospital Brothers of St Antony founded in the 17th cent. St Antony's fire was apparently an epidemic form of erysipelas against which the saint's intercession was invoked.
Cf. Chev. — Holw. — Baud.

ANTONY, MERULUS and JOHN (SS)
Mks. O.S.B.   R.M. Jan. 17
6th cent. Three monks of St Andrew's on the Coelian Hill, Rome. St Gregory the Great, who was their abbot, has left us an account of their virtues and miraculous power.
Cf. Zimm. — P. de U. — Baud. — Mab.

ANTONY FATATI (Bl) Bp.
                              A.C. Jan. 19
c.1410-1484 (Jan. 9). Born at Ancona, he

held successively the office of Arch-priest of Ancona, vicar-general of Siena, canon of the Vatican at Rome, bishop of Teramo and bishop of Ancona. His feast is celebrated in all these places. Cult approved by Pius VI.
Cf. Gams — Holw.

ANTONY of AMANDOLA (Bl) C. O.S.A.
A.C. Jan. 28
c.1355-1450. A native of Amandola in the Marches of Ancona, he joined the Augustinian Hermits and followed in the footsteps of St Nicholas of Tolentino, with whom he was on terms of friendship. His cult was confirmed in 1759, and he is honoured chiefly at Ancona.
Cf. Att. — Dict. Baudrill. — Baud. — Holw.

ANTONY MANZONI (or MANZI) (Bl) C. P.C. Feb. 1
c.1237-1267. Surnamed "the Pilgrim." Born at Padua of a wealthy family, he gave all his patrimony to the poor and spent the rest of his life living on alms and tramping his way to Loreto, Rome, Compostella and Palestine. On account of his wandering habits, his relatives, especially his two sisters who were nuns, looked on him with marked disfavour.
Cf. Dict. Baudrill. — Att. — Baud. — Holw.

ANTONY DEYNAN (St) M.
R.M. Feb. 5
d. 1597. Born at Nagasaki of Japanese parents, he was an altar boy (thirteen years old) and a tertiary of St Francis, when he was crucified for the Faith at his native town. Beatified in 1627, canonized in 1862. (See Japan, Martyrs of.)
Cf. Baud. — Holw.

ANTONY of STRONCONE (Bl) C. O.F.M. A.C. Feb. 7
1391-1461. Antony dei Vici became a Franciscan lay-brother in his twelfth year. Notwithstanding his humble status, he was chosen to assist Bl Thomas of Florence in an important mission on behalf of the Holy See. Afterwards he retired to the friary of the Carceri, near Assisi, where he lived for forty years, combating the heresy of the Fraticelli and practising rigorous penance. Cult confirmed in 1687.
Cf. Att. — Dict. Baudrill. — Holw.

ANTONY CAULEAS (St) Bp.
R.M. Feb. 12
829-901. Born near Constantinople, he became monk and then abbot of a monastery of that city. Eventually he became patriarch, the second after Photius, the effects of whose schism he laboured to remove.
Cf. Att. — Baud. — Holw. — Dict. Baudrill.

ANTONY of SAXONY, GREGORY of TRAGURIO, NICHOLAS of HUNGARY, THOMAS of FOLIGNO, and LADISLAUS of HUNGARY (BB) MM. O.F.M. P.C. Feb. 12
d. 1369. Franciscan friars put to death for the Faith by King Bazarath at the village of Widdin (in modern Yugoslavia) and in the presence of the heretic monk by whom they had been arrested.
Cf. Baud.

ANTONY (St) M. R.M. Feb. 14
See Bassus, Antony and Protolicus.

ANTONY (St) Mk. O.S.B. A.C. March 9
10th cent. A monk of Luxeuil, who became a recluse at Froidemont, in Franche-Comté.
Cf. Baud. — Holw. — P.B.

ANTONY of MILAN (Bl) M. O.S.B. P.C. March 15
See Monaldus of Ancona, etc.

ANTONY FUSTER (Bl) C. O.P. P.C. Apr. 5
14th cent. A disciple of St Vincent Ferrer, he was called "the Angel of Peace." He is highly honoured at Vich in Catalonia.
Cf. Holw. — P.B.

ANTONY PAVONI (Bl) M. O.P. A.C. Apr. 9
1326-1374. Born at Savigliano, he joined the Dominicans and became their prior in his native town, and finally inquisitor-general for Liguria and Piedmont. On Low Sunday, 1374, he preached a vigorous sermon against heresy at Brichera, and on leaving the church was killed by heretics. Cult confirmed in 1856.
Cf. Dict. Baudrill. — Baud. — Holw. — Att.

ANTONY NEYROT (Bl) M. O.P. A.C. Apr. 10
d. 1460. A native of Rivoli, diocese of

Turin, in Piedmont, he was professed a Friar Preacher. He was captured by Moorish pirates and carried off to Tunis, where he apostatized to Islam and married. After a few months he repented, put on the Dominican habit, publicly confessed Christ, and was stoned to death. Cult approved by Clement XIII.
Cf. Att.—Dict. Baudrill.— Holw.—Baud.

ANTONY, JOHN and EUSTACE (SS) MM.   A.C. Apr. 14
d. 1342. Officials of the court of the grand duke of Lithuania, at Vilna. Ant ny and John, who were brothers, were crucified for having refused to eat meat on an abstinence day. Eustace became a Christian on witnessing their heroic fortitude, and was himself martyred for the Faith. They are the patron saints of Vilna.
Cf. Baud. — Holw.

ANTONY de' PATRIZZI (Bl) C. O.S.A.   A.C. Apr. 27
d. 1311. Born at Siena, Antony became a Hermit Friar of St Augustine at the friary of Monticiano, of which he eventually became superior. Cult confirmed in 1804.
Cf. Att. — Baud. — Holw. — Dict. Baudrill.

ANTONY (St) Ab. O.S.B.   A.C. May 4
6th cent. A supposed disciple of St Benedict and companion of St Maurus on his mission to France. He was the abbot-founder of Saint-Julian at Tours. He is surnamed "du Rocher" because he ended his days as a recluse on a spot called le Rocher. The story of St Maurus's mission to France is now discarded by all historians, with the exception of a few of French nationality.
Cf. Dict. Baudrill.— Holw.—Baud.—Chev.

ANTONY MIDDLETON (Bl) M.   A.C. May 6
d. 1590. Born at Middleton Tyas, Yorks, he was educated at Reims for the secular clergy. He was hanged, drawn and quartered at Clerkenwell, London, for his priesthood. Beatified in 1929.
Cf. Newdigate — Camm — Att.

ANTONY MARY GIANELLI (Bl) Bp.   A.C. June 7
1789-1846. Born at Cerreto near Genoa, he was ordained priest in 1812 and, after twelve years spent as a devoted parish

priest, was consecrated bishop of Bobbio in 1838. As a parish priest he organized a congregation of missioners and another of teaching sisters. Beatified in 1925.
Cf. Att.

ANTONY of PADUA (St) C. Dr. O.F.M.   R.M. June 13
1195-1231. A native of Lisbon and christened Ferdinand, he joined the Canons Regular at an early age, but a few years later (1212) passed over to the recently founded Friars Minor at Coimbra. Bent on martyrdom he sailed for Africa, but illness and storm brought him to Italy, where under the guidance of St Francis, he began his career as a preacher— "the hammer of heretics" — and as a wonder-worker. He died at Padua and was canonized by Gregory IX in the following year. "He is one of the most 'popular' saints of the Church, with a great reputation for retrieving lost belongings of careless people." (Att.) In art he is usually represented bearing the Child Jesus in his arms and holding a lily.
Cf. Att. — Ricci — Baud. — Bolland. — Chev. — Dict. Baudrill.

ANTONY MARY ZACCARIA (St) C. Founder Barn.   R.M. July 5
1502-1539. Born at Cremona he studied medicine, but changed his mind and became a secular priest. His zeal, moulded on that of St Paul, knew no bounds. In 1530 he founded the congregation of clerks regular under the patronage of St Paul, called Barnabites from their headquarters at the church of St Barnabas at Milan. It was approved in 1533. He died as a result of his unceasing apostolic toil. Canonized in 1897.
Cf. Att. — Baud. — Holw.

ANTONY VAN HORNAER and ANTONY VAN WERDEN (SS) MM.   R.M. July 9
See Gorkum (Martyrs of).

ANTONY FRANCISCO (Bl) M. S.J.   A.C. July 15
d. 1538. Born at Coimbra in Portugal. After his profession as a Jesuit in 1570, he was sent to India, and after his ordination he took charge of the mission of Arlin on the peninsula of Salsette, near Goa. He was martyred with Bl Rudolph Acquaviva, q.v.
Cf. Holw.

ANTONY CORREA, ANTONY FER-NANDEZ and ANTONY SUAREZ (BB) MM. S.J. A.C. July 15
d. 1570. Three Jesuits — companions of Bl Ignatius d' Azevedo, q.v.

ANTONY TURRIANI (or TURRIANO, of TORRE) (Bl) C. O.S.A. A.C. July 24
d. 1694. Born at Milan, he studied medicine at Padua and practised at Milan. Then he became an Augustinian Friar Hermit. After several apostolic journeys, including three years at Compostella in Spain, he died at Aquila in the kingdom of Naples. Cult confirmed in 1759.
Cf. Dict. Baudrill. — Baud. — Holw.

ANTONY della CHIESA (Bl) C. O.P. A.C. July 28
1394-1459 (Jan. 22). Born at San Germano, near Vercelli, in Piedmont, he belonged to the family of the Marquis della Chiesa. He became a Dominican and ruled, as prior, the friaries of Como, Savona, Florence and Bologna, sharing in the apostolic labours of St Bernardino of Siena. Cult confirmed in 1819. Bl Antony was a collateral ancestor of Pope Benedict XV.
Cf. Att. — Dict. Baudrill. — Baud. — Holw.

ANTONY DICH (Bl) M. A.C. Aug. 12
d. 1838. A wealthy native farmer of Tonkin, attached to the Foreign Missions of Paris. He was beheaded for sheltering a priest. Beatified in 1900.
Cf. Holw.

ANTONY PRIMALDI and Comp. (BB) MM. A.C. Aug. 14
d. 1480. An aged artisan, eminent for his piety, of the city of Otranto in Italy. When the Turks raided that city in 1480, they gave the inhabitants the choice between death and apostasy. Antony became the leader and spokesman of eight hundred citizens, all men who chose death for Christ, and were accordingly hacked to pieces. Cult approved in 1771.
Cf. Att. — Holw. — Dict. Baudrill. — Baud.

ANTONY of ST FRANCIS (Bl) M. A.C. Aug. 17
d. 1627. He belonged to the group of martyrs under the Bl Apollinaris Franco (Sept. 10) q.v.

ANTONY DSHMANANDA (Bl) M. A.C. Aug. 19
d. 1622. A Japanese sailor on board the ship of Bl Joachim Firaiama. He was beheaded at Nagasaki. Beatified in 1867.
Cf. Holw.

ANTONY IXIDA and Comp. (BB) MM. A.C. Sept. 3
d. 1632. A Japanese Jesuit, famed for his learning and eloquence, who with five Franciscan and Augustinian friars was tortured for thirty-three days, by the application of scalding water, in a vain effort to make them apostatize. Finally they were burnt alive at Nagasaki. Beatified in 1867.
Cf. Holw.—Dict. Baudrill.—Baud.—Att.

ANTONY of ST BONAVENTURE (Bl) M. O.F.M. A.C. Sept. 8
1588-1628. A native of Tuy in Galicia, Spain, he studied at Salamanca, became a Franciscan, and was appointed to the mission of Manila in the Philippines. Here he was ordained priest and crossed over to Japan, where it is on record that he reconciled over 2,700 apostates. He was burnt alive at Nagasaki. Beatified in 1867.
Cf. Holw.

ANTONY of ST DOMINIC (Bl) M. Sept. 8
d. 1628. A Japanese youth of twenty years, tertiary of St Dominic, companion of Bl Dominic Castellet. He was beheaded at Nagasaki. Beatified in 1867.
Cf. Holw.

ANTONY KIUN (Bl) M. S.J. A.C. Sept. 10
1572-1622. A native of the province of Mikata in Japan, he was received into the Society of Jesus at Omura, and burnt alive at Nagasaki. Beatified in 1867.
Cf. Holw.

ANTONY of COREA (Bl) M. A.C. Sept. 10
d. 1622. Born in Corea, catechist under the Jesuit Fathers in Japan, he was beheaded at Nagasaki. Beatified in 1867.
Cf. Holw.

ANTONY SANGA (Bl) M. A.C. Sept. 10
d. 1622. A Japanese catechist beheaded with Bl Charles Spinola, q.v.
Cf. Holw.

ANTONY VOM (Bl) M. **A.C. Sept. 10**
d. 1622. Son of Bl Clement Vom. Beheaded at Nagasaki with his father. Beatified in 1867.
Cf. Holw.

ANTONY (St) M. **R.M. Sept. 23**
See Andrew, John, etc.

ANTONY MARY CLARET (Bl) Bp. Founder. **A.C. Oct. 24**
d. 1870. Born at Vich in Catalonia, he started life as a weaver, but soon became a student for the secular priesthood. He was ordained in 1835 and devoted himself to missionary work among the people, helped by a group of priests, whom he formed into the Institute of "Missionary Sons of the Immaculate Heart of Mary" — Claretians. Bl Antony was raised to the see of Santiago de Cuba, and in 1856 was made confessor to Queen Isabella II and was exiled with her in 1868. Both in Cuba and in Spain he encountered the hostility of the Spanish liberal (i.e., anticlerical) politicians. He had the gifts of prophecy and miracles. Beatified in 1934.
Cf. Att.

ANTONY (St) M. **R.M. Nov. 7**
See Melasippus, Antony and Carina.

ANTONY BALDINUCCI (Bl) C. S.J. **A.C. Nov. 7**
1665-1717. Born at Florence, he became a Jesuit in 1681. He worked as a missionary chiefly in the Colli Albani near Rome, adopting very unconventional methods of preaching and calling people to penance. Beatified in 1893.
Cf. Holw. — Att. — Baud.

ANTONY QUINH-NAM (Bl) M. **A.C. Nov. 24**
d. 1840 (July 10). A native priest and physician of Cochin-China, who became attached to the Foreign Missions of Paris. He was imprisoned for the Faith in 1838, and martyred two years later. Beatified in 1900.
Cf. Holw.

ANTONY KIMURA (Bl) M. A.C. Nov. 27
1595-1619. A Japanese of the royal family of Firando, aged twenty-three, a relative of Bl Leonard Kimura. He was beheaded with ten companions at Nagasaki. Beatified in 1867.
Cf. Holw.

ANTONY BONFADINI (Bl) C. O.F.M. **A.C. Dec. 1**
1400-1482. Born at Ferrara, he joined the Franciscan Friars of the Observance and was sent to the mission of the Holy Land. He died at Cotignola, diocese of Faenza. Cult confirmed in 1901.
Cf. Holw. — Att. — Dict. Baudrill. — Baud.

ANTONY GRASSI (Bl) C. Orat. **A.C. Dec. 13**
d. c.1672. Priest of the Oratory at Fermo in the Italian Marches, and its superior from 1635 until his death. In 1621 he was struck by lightning, but this only seemed to increase his marked serenity of manner. He had the gift of reading consciences and excelled as a director of souls. Beatified in 1900.
Cf. Holw. — Att.

ANTONY (St) M. **R.M. Dec. 15**
See Irenaeus, Antony, etc.

ANTONY of LÉRINS (St) H. **R.M. Dec. 28**
d. c.520. Born in Lower Pannonia, he served God as a recluse in several places north of the Alps until he found rest for the last two years of his life as a monk at Lérins.
Cf. Att. — Baud. — Dict. Baudrill.

ANYSIA (St) M. **R.M. Dec. 30**
d. 304. A maiden of Salonika, put to death by a soldier when she resisted an attempt to drag her to a pagan sacrifice.
Cf. Att. — Baud. — Dict. Baudrill.

ANYSIUS (St) Bp. **R.M. Dec. 30**
d. c.407. The successor of St Ascolus in the see of Salonika. He was a friend of St Ambrose, Vicar Apostolic of Pope Damasus in Illyria, and loyal defender of St John Chrysostom.
Cf. Att. — Dict. Baudrill.

AOUT (St) C. **R.M. Oct. 7**
Otherwise Augustus, q.v.

APELLES (APELLIUS), LUCIUS (LUKE) and CLEMENT (SS) MM.
R.M. Apr. 22 and Sept. 10
1st cent. Apelles and Lucius are described by the R.M. as "from among the first disciples of Christ." They are usually identified with the "Apelles, approved

in Christ" and "Lucius, my kinsman" mentioned by St Paul (Rom. XVI, 10, 21). These names are duplicated in the R.M., in the second entry (Sept. 10) a third name Clement being added. Tradition adds that St Apelles was bishop of Smyrna, and Lucius bishop of Laodicea.
Cf. Baud. — Holw.

APHRAATES (St) H. R.M. Apr. 7
4th cent. A Persian hermit who settled at Edessa in Mesopotamia, and later on removed to Antioch in Syria, where he valiantly opposed Arianism during the reign of Valens. Some authors have endeavoured to identify him with the famous "Aphraates the Syrian," the ecclesiastical writer.
Cf. Att. — Baud. — Dict. Baudrill.

APHRODISIUS (St) M. R.M. March 14
See Peter and Aphrodisius.

APHRODISIUS, CARALIPPUS, AGAPITUS, and EUSEBIUS (SS) MM.
R.M. Apr. 28
1st cent. A French legend, now universally rejected, makes this Aphrodisius an Egyptian who sheltered the Holy Family during their flight into Egypt. After the Ascension he attached himself first to St Peter, then to St Paul, whom he followed from Rome to Spain and by whom he was left in Languedoc to evangelize that country. Here he was martyred with the other three mentioned above.
Cf. Dict. Baudrill. — Baud.

APHRODISIUS and Comp. (SS) MM.
R.M. Apr. 30
? An Egyptian priest put to death at Alexandria with a group of some thirty of his flock.
Cf. however, Holw.

APHTHONIUS (St) S. R.M. Nov. 2
See Acindynus, Pegasius, etc.

APIAN
Otherwise Amphianus, Apphianus, Appianus, Appian, Apphian. Here we adopt the spelling Appian, q.v.

APODEMUS (St) M. R.M. Apr. 16
One of the martyrs of Saragossa, q.v.

APOLLINARIS SYNCLETICA (St) V.
R.M. Jan. 5
c.450. The heroine of a religious romance who disguised herself in boy's clothes and lived undiscovered in an Egyptian hermitage as a disciple of one of the Saints Macarius.
Cf. Att. — Baud. — Dict. Baudrill.

APOLLINARIS the APOLOGIST (St) Bp.
R.M. Jan. 8
d. c.180. Claudius Apollinaris, a bishop of Hierapolis in Phrygia, is now only known from the Apologia for the Christian Faith which he dedicated to Marcus Aurelius towards the middle of the second century.
Cf. Att. — Baud.

APOLLINARIS (St) M. R.M. June 21
See Cyriacus and Apollinaris.

APOLLINARIS (St) Bp. M.
R.M. July 23
? 1st cent. He is usually described as a disciple of St Peter. He certainly was the first bishop of Ravenna and was repeatedly put to the torture for the Faith and died of its effects. The exact date is not known. His shrine at the Benedictine abbey of Classe at Ravenna became famous throughout Christendom.
Cf. Dict. Baudrill. — Baud. — Att.

APOLLINARIS and TIMOTHY (SS) MM. R.M. Aug. 23
3rd cent. Apollinaris was the executioner in the gaol at Reims, who became a Christian on witnessing the fortitude of St Timothy under repeated torture. Both were beheaded for Christ and their tomb became famous in that district.
Cf. Baud. — Holw.

APOLLINARIS SIDONIUS (St) Bp.
A.C. Aug. 23
See Sidonius Apollinaris.

APOLLINARIS FRANCO and Comp. (BB) MM. O.F.M. A.C. Sept. 10
d. 1622. Born at Aquilar del Campo in Old Castile, he studied law at Salamanca, and entered the Franciscan Order of the Observance, and eventually was sent to Japan (1614) as commissary general of the missions of his order there. He was arrested in 1617 and detained in the horrible prison of Omura until he was burnt alive on Sept. 10. From 1617 to 1628, seventeen other Franciscan friars, all Spanish, and twenty-two lay tertiaries — mostly

native Japanese — were cruelly tortured and martyred for refusing to apostatize. All were beatified with the other groups of Japanese martyrs in 1867. Each receives a separate notice in this dictionary.
Cf. Dict. Baudrill. — Baud. — Holw. — Att.

APOLLINARIS (AIPLONAY) (St) Bp.
R.M. Oct. 5
d. c.520. Elder brother of St Avitus of Vienne, he became bishop of Valence, where he died after a glorious and indefatigable apostolate. He is the patron saint of the diocese.
Cf. Duch. Fast. Episc. — Dict. Baudrill. — Gams — Att. — Baud. — Bolland.

APOLLINARIS (Bl or St) Ab. O.S.B.
P.C. Nov. 27
d. 828. The fourteenth abbot of Montecassino, he governed the archabbey for eleven years. He has always been greatly venerated at Montecassino.
Cf. Mab. — Chev. — Zimm. — Baud. — Holw.

APOLLINE (St) V.M.   **R.M. Feb. 9**
Otherwise Apollonia, q.v.

APOLLO (St) Ab.   **A.C. Jan. 25**
c.316-c.395. An Egyptian hermit who, after forty years of solitude, became the abbot of over five hundred monks, near Heliopolis. Once only he left the desert, in order to rebuke Julian the Apostate.
Cf. Att. — Baud. — Holw.

APOLLO, ISACIUS and CROTATES (CODRATUS) (SS) MM.   **R.M. Apr. 21**
d. c.302. Three servants at the palace of Alexandra, wife of Diocletian. Crotates was beheaded for the Faith, the other two were left to die of hunger in prison.
Cf. Baud. — Holw.

APOLLONIA (APOLLINE) (St) V.M.
R.M. Feb. 9
d. 249. An aged deaconess of Alexandria, martyred under Decius. Her teeth were broken with pincers, and for this reason she is invoked against toothache and is represented in art holding a tooth in pincers. Finally she was led to a kindled pyre to be burnt alive unless she renounced Christ, and "of her own accord leaped into the pyre, being kindled within

by the greater fire of the Holy Ghost." (R.M.).
Cf. Bolland. — Ruinart — Baud. — Dict. Baudrill.

APOLLONIUS (St) M.   **R.M. Feb. 14**
See Proculus, Ephebus and Apollonius.

APOLLONIUS (St) M.   **R.M. March 8**
See Philemon and Apollonius.

APOLLONIUS and LEONTIUS (or LEONTINUS) Bps. MM.   **R.M. March 19**
? Neither the see nor the date of martyrdom of these two bishops is known. Their names, however, already occur in the martyrology of St Jerome. The Portuguese have claimed them for their see of Braga, and this seems the most likely solution.
Cf. Baud. — Bolland.

APOLLONIUS (St) M.   **R.M. Apr. 10**
? Martyred at Alexandria under Decius.
Cf. Baud. — Bolland.

APOLLONIUS the APOLOGIST (St) M.
R.M. Apr. 18
d. c.190. A Roman senator, denounced as a Christian by one of his own slaves and condemned to be beheaded. His eloquent defence of the Faith (*apologia*) delivered before the Senate at his trial is one of the most priceless documents of Christian antiquity. It was discovered in an Armenian text in 1874.
Cf. Att. — Baud. — Dict. Baudrill.

APOLLONIUS (St) M.   **R.M. June 5**
See Marcian, Nicanor, etc.

APOLLONIUS (St) Bp.   **R.M. July 7**
? A bishop of Brescia in Lombardy. He is mentioned in the acts of SS Faustinus and Jovita which, however, cannot be relied upon. His relics are enshrined in the cathedral of Brescia.
Cf. Baud. — Bolland. — Dict. Baudrill.

APOLLONIUS (St) Bp.   **A.C. July 8**
d. p. 326. Bishop of Benevento. He went into hiding during the last persecution under Diocletian.
Cf. Gams — Dict. Baudrill. — Baud.

APOLLONIUS (St) M.   **R.M. July 10**
d. early 4th cent. A native of Sardis in

Lydia, Asia Minor, he was scourged and crucified at Iconium.
Cf. Baud.

APOLLONIUS and EUGENE (SS) MM.
R.M. July 23
? Roman martyrs, the former was pierced with arrows at the stake, the latter was beheaded.
Cf. Baud. — Bolland.

APPHIA (St) M. R.M. Nov. 22
See Philemon and Apphia.

APPIAN (St) Mk. O.S.B. A.C. Nov. 6
d. c.800. Born in Liguria, he became a Benedictine at the abbey of St Peter of Ciel d'Oro (*in caelo aureo*) at Pavia. Eventually he became a recluse at Commacchio on the shores of the Adriatic, and evangelized that country.
Cf. Mab. — Chev. — Bolland. (March 4)— *Zimm. — Baud.*

APPIAN and Comp. (SS) MM.
R.M. Dec. 30
See Mansuetus, Severus, etc.

APRONIA (EVRONIE) (St) V.
A.C. July 15
5th and 6th cent. Born near Trèves. Sister of St Aprus (Evre), bishop of Toul, at whose hands she received the veil. She died at Troyes.
Cf. Baud. — Dict. Baudrill.

APRONIAN (St) M. R.M. Feb. 2
d. c.304. A Roman executioner who was converted to Christianity when taking the martyr St Sisinnius before the tribunal, and was himself thereupon put to death.
Cf. Dict. Baudrill. — Baud. — Holw.

APRUS (APER, APRE, EPVRE, EVRE) (St) Bp. R.M. Sept. 15
d. 507. Born near Trèves, he became a very able and just lawyer. He gave up this profession to be ordained priest, and in time was chosen bishop of Toul, which see he governed for seven years. Some authorities reject the tradition of his having been a lawyer.
Cf. Gams — Duch. Fast. Episc. — Bolland.

APULEIUS (St) M. R.M. Oct. 7
See Marcellus and Apuleius.

AQUILA (St) M. R.M. Jan. 23
See Severianus and Aquila.

AQUILA (St) M. R.M. March 23
See Domitius, Pelagia, etc.

AQUILA (St) M. R.M. May 20
d. 311. An Egyptian, torn to pieces with iron combs under Maximinus Daza. The prefect Arianus, who had ordered this torture, subsequently became a Christian and a martyr in the same persecution.
Cf. Baud. — Bolland.

AQUILA and PRISCILLA (SS)
R.M. July 8
1st cent. Husband and wife, belonging to the Jewish diaspora, who worked as tentmakers at Rome, whence they were banished with all other Jews under Claudius. They settled at Corinth, where they received St Paul into their house (Acts XVIII, 3). Under Nero they returned to Rome and St Paul sends greetings to them as follows: "Salute Prisca and Aquila my helpers in Christ, who have for my life laid down their own necks" (Rom. XVI, 3-4). There is a tradition in Rome that they were martyred there.
Cf. Att. — Baud.

AQUILA (St) M. R.M. Aug. 1
See Cyril, Aquila, etc.

AQUILINA (St) V.M. R.M. June 13
d. 293. A young girl — said to have been no more than twelve years old — who was tortured and beheaded at Byblus in Syria. The account of her passion is not trustworthy.
Cf. Att. — Baud. — Dict. Baudrill.

AQUILINA (St) M. R.M. July 24
See Nicetas and Aquilina.

AQUILINUS, GEMINUS, EUGENE, MARCIAN, QUINTUS, THEODOTUS and TRYPHON (SS) MM. R.M. Jan. 4
c.484. A band of martyrs put to death in Africa under the Arian Hunneric, king of the Vandals. Their acts are now lost, but it seems that Ven. Bede had access to them in the eighth century.
Cf. Dict. Baudrill. — Bolland.— Baud.

AQUILINUS (St) M. R.M. Jan. 29
d. 650. A Bavarian by birth, who flying

from the prospect of high ecclesiastical preferment at Cologne, Paris and Pavia, came to Milan and spent himself in preaching against Arianism. On this account he was assassinated by the Arians. His relics are venerated at Milan.
Cf. Dict. Baudrill. — Baud.

AQUILINUS, GEMINUS, GELASIUS, MAGNUS and DONATUS (SS) MM.
R.M. Feb. 4
3rd cent. Martyrs at Fossombrone in central Italy at the close of the 3rd century. No details survive.
Cf. Dict. Baudrill. — Holw. — Baud.

AQUILINUS and VICTORIAN (SS) MM.
R.M. May 16
? Martyrs in the Province of Isauria, in Asia Minor and, as such, registered by Ven. Bede in his martyrology. Nothing else is known about them.
Cf. Bolland. — Baud.

AQUILINUS (St) M. R.M. May 17
See Heradius, Paul, etc.

AQUILINUS (St) Bp. R.M. Oct. 19
c.620-695. A native of Bayeux, he spent forty years in the service of Clovis II. On his return from the war against the Visigoths, he and his wife agreed to give themselves up to works of charity. They retired to Evreux, and Aquilinus was soon made bishop of that city. He managed, however, to live more as a hermit than a prelate.
Cf. Dict. Baudrill. — Baud. — Holw.

ARABIA (Martyrs of) R.M. Feb. 22
By the term Arabia is here understood, conformably to the usage of the period, the countries, mainly desert, east of the Jordan, and, again, the mountainous districts south of the Dead Sea. The R.M. has this entry: "In Arabia, the memory of many holy martyrs, who were cruelly slain under the emperor Galerius Maximian."

ARABIA (St) M. R.M. March 13
See Theusetas, Horres, etc.

ARATOR, FORTUNATUS, FELIX, SILVIUS and VITALIS (SS) MM.
R.M. Apr. 21
? St Arator was a priest of Alexandria in Egypt, put to death with the other Christians named above, in one of the earlier persecutions. No particulars are now extant.
Cf. Baud. — Holw.

ARATOR (St) Bp. A.C. Sept. 6
d. c.460. The fourth bishop of Verdun.
Cf. Duch. Fast. Episc. — Baud. — Gams (without any hagiological title).

ARBOGAST (St) Bp. R.M. July 21
d. c.678. Born in Aquitaine, not as has been maintained in Ireland or Scotland. He was living as a recluse in Alsace when King Dagobert II forced on him the see of Strasburg, which he ruled with great humility and wisdom. At his own request he was interred in the place set apart for the burial of criminals. A church was soon built over his tomb. In art he is represented as walking dry-shod over a river.
Cf. Att. — Duch. Fast. Episc. — Gams — Baud.

ARCADIUS (St) M. R.M. Jan. 12
d. c.302. A prominent citizen of Caesarea in Mauretania (near Algiers) who under Maximianus Herculius was slowly and barbarously mutilated until he died under the torture.
Cf. Att. — Baud. — Holw.

ARCADIUS (St) Bp. M. R.M. March 4
See Basil, Eugene, etc.

ARCADIUS, PASCHASIUS, PROBUS, EUTYCHIAN and PAULILLUS (SS) MM.
R.M. Nov. 13
d. 437. All of these were Spaniards, exiled to Africa by the Vandal Arian King Genseric, where they became the protomartyrs of the Vandal persecution. Paulillus was only a boy, the little brother of SS Paschasius and Eutychian. "As he could not be turned from the Catholic Faith he was long beaten with rods, and condemned to the basest servitude" (R.M.).
Cf. Att. — Baud. — Ruinart — Bolland.

ARCANUS (St) Ab. O.S.B. A.C. Sept. 1
See Giles and Arcanus.

ARCHANGELA GIRLANI (Bl) V. O.C.
A.C. Feb. 13
1461-1494. A native of Trino, in the Monferrato, Italy, she became a Carmelite

at Parmo and, at the request of the Gonzagas, was sent to found a new Carmel at Mantua. She was its first prioress, a living pattern of perfection. Cult confirmed in 1864.
Cf. Att. — Baud. — Holw.

ARCHANGELUS CANETULI (Bl) C. O.S.A. A.C. Apr. 16
d. 1513. Born at Bologna, he became an Augustinian canon regular, conspicuous for his gifts, natural and supernatural. He died as archbishop-elect of Florence.
Cf. Holw. — Att. — Baud.

ARCHANGELUS of CALAFATIMI (Bl) C. O.F.M. A.C. July 30
d. 1460. Born at Calafatimi in Sicily, he was a hermit at the time when Pope Martin V suppressed the Sicilian hermitages. He then joined the Franciscans of the Observance and was a great promoter of this new branch throughout Sicily. Cult confirmed in 1836.
Cf. Att. — Holw. — Baud.

ARCHELAIS, THECLA and SUSANNA (SS) VV. MM. A.C. Jan. 18
d. 293. Three Christian maidens of the Romagna who retired to Nola in the Campagna in order to escape death; but there too they were accused of being Christians, tortured, taken to Salerno and beheaded.
Cf. Holw.

ARCHELAUS, CYRIL and PHOTIUS (SS) MM. R.M. March 4
Nothing is known about these martyrs.

ARCHELAUS (St) M. R.M. Aug. 23
See Quiriacus, Maximus, etc.

ARCHELAUS (St) Bp. R.M. Dec. 26
d. c.278. Bishop of Kashkar in Mesopotamia. He seems to have been a formidable opponent of Manicheism during his life, but the writings against these heretics attributed to him are not his work.
Cf. Att. — Baud. — Holw.

ARCHIPPUS (St) R.M. March 20
1st cent. St Paul calls him "my fellow-soldier" (Philem. 2) and mentions him also in his epistle to the Colossians (IV, 17). Tradition, basing itself on St Paul's words, has made Archippus the first bishop of Colossae.
Cf. Baud. — Holw.

ARCONTIUS (St) Bp. M. A.C. Feb. 5
8th (or 11th) cent. Bishop of Viviers, killed by a mob for having upheld the rights of his church.
Cf. Duch. Fast. Episc. — Baud. — See, however, Gams.

ARCONTIUS (St) M. R.M. Sept. 5
See Quinctius, Arcontius and Donatus.

ARDALION (St) M. R.M. Apr. 14
d. c.300. An actor who suddenly proclaimed himself a Christian while engaged in ridiculing Christianity on the stage. He was roasted alive in the public square.
Cf. Baud. — Att. — Holw.

ARDANUS (ARDAING, ARDAGNE, ARDAGNUS, ARDAN) (St) Ab. O.S.B. A.C. Feb. 11
d. 1058. The thirteenth abbot of the Benedictine monastery of Tournus, now in the diocese of Autun. He restored the monastic buildings and was a father to the people during the famine of 1030-1033.
Cf. Mab.—Chev.—Baud.—P.B.—Holw.

ARDO (St) Ab. O.S.B. A.C. March 7
d. 843. A native of Languedoc, he changed his baptismal name of Smaragdus on entering the abbey of Aniane under its first abbot St Benedict. He became director of the schools attached to the abbey, St Benedict's travelling companion and secretary — and eventually also his biographer — and his successor at Aniane when St Benedict went to reside at Aix-la-Chapelle. His cult was well established at Aniane at an early date.
Cf. Mab. — Chev. — Att. — Baud. — P. de U. — Zimm.

ARDUINUS (ARDWYNE, ARDOIN) (St) A.C. July 28
7th cent. With his fellow-countrymen from England, SS Gerard, Fulk and Bernard, he died of a pestilence in Italy while on a pilgrimage to Rome. St Arduinus is venerated as the patron saint of the town of Ceprano.
Cf. Holw. — Baud.

ARDUINUS (St) H. O.S.B. A.C. Aug. 15
d. 1009. A priest of Rimini who lived first as a hermit and ended by becoming a monk at San Gaudenzio. Mabillon counts him among the Benedictine saints.
Cf. Mab. — Zimm. — Baud.

AREDIUS (YRIEIX, YRIEZ) (St) Ab.
A.C. Aug. 25
d. 591. Born at Limoges, after a period of service at the court of the Frankish kings, he became the abbot-founder of the abbey of Atane in the Limousin, which later on was called after him, as was also the village of Saint-Yrieux which grew up around the abbey. Other variants are: Yriel, Ysary, Ysère, Yséry.
Cf. Baud. (Yriez)— Holw.—Chev.—Zimm.

AREGLOE, AREGLE Bp. R.M. March 17
Otherwise Agricola, q.v.

ARESIUS, ROGATIUS and Comp. MM.
R.M. June 10
? A band of seventeen African martyrs, particulars concerning whom have been lost. Some martyrologies class them with the Roman martyrs, Basilides and others, commemorated on the same day.

ARETAS and Comp. (SS) MM.
R.M. Oct. 1
? According to the R.M. St Aretas suffered at Rome with five hundred and four others. The first to mention this number was Usuardus. Some try to identify this group with that mentioned on Oct. 24. See Nagran (Martyrs of).

ARETAS (St) M.   **R.M. Oct. 24**
See Nagran (Martyrs of).

ARETIUS (ARECIUS, AREGIUS) and DACIAN (SS) MM.   **R.M. June 4**
? Roman martyrs who were buried in the catacombs on the Appian Way.

ARGARIARGA (St) V.   **A.C. Sept. 9**
Otherwise Osmanna, q.v.

ARGEUS, NARCISSUS and MARCEL-LINUS (SS) MM.   **R.M. Jan. 2**
d. 320. Three brothers enrolled as soldiers in the army of the emperor Licinius who suffered martyrdom at Tomi in Pontus, on the Black Sea. Marcellinus was only "a boy enrolled as a recruit, who, on refusing to perform military service, was first flogged most cruelly, then kept long in prison, and lastly thrown into the sea." His brothers were beheaded.
Cf. Holw. — Baud.

ARGYMIRUS (St) M. Mk.
R.M. June 28
d. 858. A native of Cabra, near Cordova, who held high official position among the Mohammedans of that city. He was deprived of his office on account of his Christian faith and became a monk. Shortly after he openly denounced Mohammed and confessed Christ and was beheaded.
Cf. P. de U. — Baud. — Holw.

ARIADNE (St) M.   **R.M. Sept. 17**
d. c.130. A Christian woman slave of a Phrygian prince, who, after being flogged for refusing to join in the heathen rites celebrated on the anniversary of her master's birthday, took refuge in a chasm in the rock which miraculously opened before her and closed on her entering, thus affording her a tomb and the crown of martyrdom.
Cf. Holw. — Baud.

ARIALDUS (St) M.   **A.C. June 27**
d. 1066. A deacon of Milan, who distinguished himself for his zeal against the rampant simony of his time, chiefly at Milan. For this reason he was first excommunicated and, after much persecution, killed by the party of the simoniac archbishop of Milan. Cult approved in 1904.
Cf.   Baud. — Holw. — Anal.   Bolland.
XXII, 113.

ARIANUS, THEOTICUS and Comp. (SS) MM.   **R.M. March 8**
c. 311. Arianus, governor of Thebes, in Egypt, with Theoticus and three others was converted to Christianity on witnessing at Alexandria the martyrdom of SS Apollonius and Philemon. The judge ordered them to be drowned in the sea. There is a legend that their bodies were brought ashore by dolphins.
Cf. Baud. — Holw.

ARILDA (St) V.M.   **A.C. Oct. 30**
? A maiden of Gloucestershire who met her death in defence of her chastity. The church at Oldbury-on-the-Hill is dedicated to her.
Cf. Baring-Gould.

ARISTAEUS and ANTONINUS (SS) MM.   **R.M. Sept. 3**
? Aristaeus is said to have been bishop of Capua, but modern research inclines rather to identify him with the Egyptian martyr Aristaeus, venerated by the

Greeks on Sept. 3. Similarly the child-martyr, Antoninus, seems to be a duplicate of St Antoninus of Apamea, commemorated in the R.M. on Sept. 2. At Capua there is no record of either saint.
Cf. Baud. — Holw. — Bolland.

ARISTARCHUS (St) Bp. M.
R.M. Aug. 4
1st cent. A native of Salonika and a companion of St Paul in his travels (Acts XX, 4; XXVII, 2). He was arrested with the apostle at Ephesus, and shared his imprisonment. He is described as "his fellow-worker" (Philem. 24). Tradition makes him the first bishop of Salonika and adds that he was beheaded in Rome with St Paul.
Cf. Holw. — Baud.

ARISTIDES (St) **R.M. Aug. 31**
d. c.123. An Athenian philosopher, famous for his *Apologia* for Christianity, which he presented to the emperor Hadrian. The text, long lost, has now been recovered in Syriac, Armenian and Greek.
Cf. Baud. — Holw. — Bardenhewer.

ARISTION (St) M. **R.M. Feb. 22**
1st cent. One of the seventy-two disciples of our Lord. He preached in Cyprus and died there a martyr, at Salamis. Others assert that he was martyred at Alexandria.
Cf. Baud. — Holw.

ARISTOBULUS (St) M. R.M. March 15
1st cent. One of the seventy-two disciples of our Lord. Perhaps he is the Aristobulus mentioned by St Paul (Rom. XVI, 11). He has been identified with Zebedee, the father of SS James and John, and Britain has been allotted to him as the place of his labours and martyrdom — all without the slightest foundation.
Cf. Holw. — Baud.

ARISTON, CRESCENTIAN, EUTYCHIAN, URBAN, VITALIS, JUSTUS, FELICISSIMUS, FELIX, MARCIA, and SYMPHOROSA (SS) MM. R.M. July 2
d. c.285. A band of martyrs put to death in the Campagna, S. Italy, under Diocletian. Nothing more is known about them.

ARISTONICUS (St) M. **R.M. Apr. 19**
See Hermogenes, Caius, etc.

ARMAGILLUS (ARMEL) (St) C.
A.C. Aug. 16
d. c.570. Born in S. Wales, a cousin of St Samson. A Cornish church was dedicated to him — St Erme. He crossed over to Brittany and founded Saint-Armel-des-Boscheaux and Plou-Ermel (Ploermel). Like all the Celtic names of that period, Armel has taken countless variants. Here are a few: Ermel, Erme, Ermin, Arthmael, Armail, Arzel, Armahel, Hermel, Thiarmail. In Latin it is translated as Armagillus.
Cf. Att. — Baud. — Holw.

ARMAND (St) C. **A.C. Jan. 23**
Otherwise Ormond, q.v.

ARMEL (St) C. **A.C. Aug. 16**
Otherwise Armagillus, q.v.

ARMENTARIUS (St) Bp. **A.C. Jan. 30**
d. p. 451. First bishop of Antibes in Provence. An old church is dedicated in his name at Draguignan.
Cf. Gams — Duch. Fast. Episc. — Baud.

ARMENTARIUS (St) Bp. **R.M. Jan. 30**
d. c.711. Bishop of Pavia. During his episcopate the see of Pavia was withdrawn from the jurisdiction of the metropolitan see of Milan and directly attached to the Roman Church.
Cf. Gams — Baud. — Holw. — Bolland.

ARMOGASTES and Comp. (SS) MM.
R.M. March 29
d. p. 460. In the former editions of the R.M. the reading was as follows: "Armogastes the Count, Masculas, Archinimus (or Archimimus) and Saturus," etc. In the latest edition however, we read: "Armogastes the Count, Masculas, the chief-actor (*archimimus*) and Saturus . . ." Even so, it is not quite certain whether we should not read: "Armogastes, the officer, the President of the theatre at Mascula, and Saturus; or Armogastes . . . a native of Mascula." Armogastes and Saturus, high officers at the palace, suffered in Africa during the Arian persecution under the Vandal king, Genseric. First they were tortured, then sent to labour in the mines, then condemned to slavery as cowherds near Carthage. They were not put to death "lest the Romans should venerate them as martyrs." Thus Victor of Vita, the contemporary writer

who has preserved for us their *Acta*.
They are, however, venerated as martyrs.
*Cf. Att. — Baud. — Holw. — Ruinart. —
Bolland.*

ARMON (St) Bp.   R.M. July 31
Otherwise Germanus of Auxerre, q.v.

**ARNOLD (ARNALD, ARNAUD) (Bl) Ab.
M. O.S.B.   A.C. March 14**
d. 1254. Born at Padua of the noble family de'Cattanei, he became a Benedictine
at St Justina, Padua, and eventually its
abbot. The tyrant Ezzelino da Romano,
after persecuting him for a long time, imprisoned him at Asolo and loaded him
with chains. He bore it all patiently for
eight years and died in prison at the age
of seventy.
*Cf. Zimm. — Att. — Chev. — Bolland. —
P. de U. — Baud.*

ARNOLD (St) C.   A.C. July 8
d. c.800. A Greek by birth, attached to
the court of Charlemagne. He was famed
for his charity to the poor. He has left
his name to the village, Arnold-Villiers
(Arnoldsweiler) near Julich.
Cf. Holw. — H.L.

ARNOLD (Bl) Ab. O.S.B.   A.C. Nov. 30
d. 1155. A Benedictine of the abbey of St
Nicasius at Reims, who became abbot
of Gemblours.
Cf. Zimm.

**ARNULF (ARNULPHUS, ARNULPH,
ARNOUL) (Bl) Mk. O.S.B. Cist.
                               A.C. June 30**
d. 1228. Surnamed "Cornibout" or "of
Villers." He was born at Brussels, and
after a pleasure-loving youth, he became a
lay-brother at the Cistercian abbey of
Villers in Brabant, where he atoned for his
past by long years of prayer and penance.
He attained to a high degr e of mystical
prayer.
*Cf. Zimm. — Att. — P. de U. — Baud. —
Holw.*

ARNULF (St) Bp. M.   A.C. July 1
d. 1160. Archbishop of Mainz from 1153.
He was murdered by his own diocesans
and is venerated as a martyr.
Cf. Baud.

ARNULF (St) Bp.   R.M. July 18
d. 640. A courtier of high standing in the

palace of the Austrasian kings, he determined to become a monk at Lérins. His
wife took the veil and Arnulf was just on
the point of retiring to Lérins when he
was made bishop of Metz (c.610). A few
years before his death he resigned and
retired to a hermitage near the abbey of
Remiremont.
Cf. Att. — Baud. — Bolland.

ARNULF (St) Bp. O.S.B.   R.M. Aug. 15
c. 1040-1087. Born in Flanders, after
some years in the armies of Robert and
Henry I, kings of France, he became a
Benedictine at the abbey of St Medardus
at Soissons. After his profession he lived
as a recluse under the abbot's obedience.
In 1082 he was obliged to accept the
bishopric of Soissons. Some time after he
resigned and founded the abbey of Ouden-
bourg in Flanders, where he died.
Cf. Att. — Baud. — Holw. — Bolland.

ARNULF (St) H.   A.C. Aug. 22
9th cent. The relics of this saint were
venerated at Arnulphsbury, or Eynesbury,
in Huntingdonshire. He has been described as an English hermit of that district, but he is probably a duplicate of
St Arnulf of Metz.
Cf. Baud. — Holw.

ARNULF (St) Bp. O.S.B.   A.C. Sept. 19
d. 1070. Born at Vendôme, he became a
Benedictine at the abbey of Holy Trinity
in his native city. In 1063 Pope Alexander II consecrated him bishop of Gap.
As such he restored the cathedral of his
episcopal city. He is the principal patron
saint of Gap.
*Cf. Gams — Eaud. — Holw. — Chev. —
Mab. — Bolland. — Zimm.*

ARNULF (St) M. O.S.B.   A.C. Oct. 31
d. c.840. A monk of Novalese, in Piedmont, who was put to death by the Saracens.
Cf. Zimm. — Holw.

ARNULF (St) Bp.   A.C. Nov. 15
d. 871. Bishop of Toul from 847 to 871.
He was a firm and outspoken opponent of
the divorce of King Lothair.
Cf. Duch. Fast. Episc. — Gams — Baud.

**ARONTIUS (ORONTIUS) (St) M.
                   R.M. Aug. 27 and Sept. 1**
See Honoratus and Comp. (Sept. 1).

ARPINUS (St) Bp. R.M. Nov. 9
Otherwise Agrippinus, q.v.

ARSACIUS (URSACIUS) (St) C.
R.M. Aug. 16
d. 358. A Persian soldier in the Roman army, who on his conversion retired to live as a recluse in a high tower overlooking Nicomedia. He forewarned its inhabitants of the impending destruction of their city by the great earthquake of 358. Some survivors found refuge in the tower, where Arsacius had already died in the attitude of prayer.
Cf. Att. — Baud. — Bolland.

ARSENIUS (St) Bp. A.C. Jan. 19
d. 959. A native of Constantinople of Jewish descent, he became the first bishop of Corfu, of which he is now venerated as the principal patron.
Cf. Baud. — Holw.

ARSENIUS the GREAT (St) H.
R.M. July 19
d. c.449. Surnamed also "the Roman" and "the deacon," being actually a Roman deacon. He was summoned by Theodosius the Great to Constantinople to become the tutor of Arcadius and Honorius, the emperor's sons (c.383). After ten years in that thankless office (c.393) he abandoned the court and retired to the desert of Skete as a hermit. A hermit he remained for the rest of his life, living in various places in Egypt and ever "weeping over the feebleness of Arcadius and the foolishness of Honorius." He breathed his last at the rock of Troë, near Memphis.
Cf. Att. — Baud. — Holw. — Bolland.

ARSENIUS (St) M. O.S.B. A.C. Aug. 30
See Pelagius, Arsenius and Sylvanus.

ARSENIUS (St) M. R.M. Dec. 14
See Heron, Arsenius, etc.

ARTALDUS (ARTHAUD, ARTAUD) (Bl)
Bp. O.Cart. A.C. Oct. 7
1101-1206. Served at the court of Amadeus III of Saxony, and then became a Carthusian at Portes (1120). In 1140 he founded the charterhouse of Arvières-en-Valromey in Saxony. He was an octogenarian when he was appointed bishop of Belley (1188) but resigned after two years

(1190) and returned to Valromey where he died. Cult approved in 1834.
Cf. Att. — Baud. — Holw.

ARTEMAS (St) M. A.C. Jan. 25
? Said to have been a boy of Pozzuoli (Puteoli) who was stabbed to death with iron pens by his pagan school-fellows. It seems, however, that the whole story is a pious romance.
Cf. Att. — Baud. — Holw.

ARTEMAS (St) Bp. A.C. Oct. 30
1st cent. One of St Paul's disciples, he is mentioned by the apostle in his letter to Titus (III, 12). A later tradition has made of him a bishop of Lystra. He is venerated by the Greeks.
Cf. Baud. — Holw.

ARTEMIUS (ARTHEMIUS) (St) Bp.
A.C. Jan. 24
d. 396. An imperial legate who, on his way to Spain, fell sick in Gaul and settled at Clermont, in Auvergne, where eventually he became bishop.
Cf. Duch. Fast. Episc. — Gams — Baud.— Att.

ARTEMIUS (St) Bp. A.C. Apr. 28
d. 609. A native of Sens where he became bishop. He admitted to public penance a Spaniard, named Baldus (in modern French Bond), whom he trained to be a great saint.
Cf. Duch. Fast. Episc. — Baud. — Holw.

ARTEMIUS, CANDIDA and PAULINA (SS) MM. R.M. June 6
d. 302. Artemius, gaoler of one of the Roman prisons, with his wife Candida and daughter Paulina, was converted to Christ by St Peter the exorcist and baptized by St Marcellinus. Artemius was beheaded, and his wife and daughter buried alive under a pile of stones.
Cf. Baud. — Holw. — Bolland.

ARTEMIUS (St) M. R.M. Oct. 20
d. 363. An officer of high rank under Constantine the Great. A pronounced Arian, he was made by Constantius prefect of Egypt and, as such, persecuted St Athanasius and harassed the Catholics, nor is there any record of his having renounced Arianism. He was beheaded as a Christian under Julian the Apostate.

He is called by the Greeks the Megalo-martyr.
Cf. Att. — Baud. — Holw.

ARTEMON (St) M. R.M. Oct. 8
d. c.305. A priest of Laodicea (in Phrygia) burnt to death under Diocletian.
Cf. Baud. — Holw.

ARTHELAIS (St) V. A.C. March 3
6th cent. One of the patron saints of Benevento, whither she is said to have fled from Constantinople to escape the attentions of the emperor Justinian.
Cf. Att. — Baud. — Holw.

ARTHEN (St)
? This saint seems untraceable. He appears to be one and the same with the St Arvan or Aroan who has left his name at St Arvans and Cwmcarvan in Monmouthshire. Stanton's Menology, following Challoner, identifies St Arvan with Maruanus, a companion of SS Banca (or Breaca) and Sennen (6th cent.) .

ARWALD (SS) MM. A.C. Apr. 22
d. 686. Two brothers, sons of Arwald, a prince in the Isle of Wight, whose proper names are lost. They were put to death by soldiers of King Ceadwalla, then a pagan, on the day after their baptism.
Cf. Baud. — Holw.

ASAPH (St) Bp. R.M. May 1
d. c.600. One of St Kentigern's monks in N. Wales. He succeeded St Kentigern as abbot and bishop, leaving his own name to the see. Moreover, he founded Llanasa in N.E. Flintshire. Many of his kinsfolk — Deiniol, Tysilo, etc. — are also venerated as saints.
Cf. Att. — Holw. — Baud. — Bolland.

ASCLAS (St) M. R.M. Jan. 23
d. c.287. Martyred under Diocletian by being thrown into the Nile at Antinoe.
Cf. Baud. — Att. — Holw. — Bolland.

ASCLEPIADES (St) Bp. M.
R.M. Oct. 18
d. 217. St Serapion's successor in the see of Antioch, from 211 to 217. He is usually given the title of martyr, probably on account of all that he underwent during the persecution of Severus.
Cf. Baud. — Holw.

ASCLEPIODOTUS (ASCLEPIADORUS) (St) M. R.M. Sept. 15
See Maximus, Theodore and Asclepiodotus.

ASELLA (St) V. R.M. Dec. 6
d. c.406. St Jerome, who became her panegyrist, calls her "a flower of the Lord," and tells us that this Roman maiden took the veil at the age of ten, and retired to a small cubicle at twelve, where she lived for long years until she became "the mother of many virgins." Palladius visited her in Rome, where she had her community.
Cf. Baud. — Holw.

ASICUS (ASCICUS, or TASSACH) (St) Bp. A.C. Apr. 27
d. c.490. One of the earliest disciples of St Patrick, by whom he was placed at the head of the monastery and diocese of Elphin, of which he is now venerated as the patron saint. He excelled as a copper-smith, and some remarkable specimens of his handiwork yet remain.
Cf. Holw. — Att.

ASPASIUS (St) Bp. A.C. Jan. 2
d. c.560. A bishop of Eauze—now Auch—who took part in the councils of Orleans, 533, 541 and 549, besides holding a provincial council at Eauze in 551. He is honoured in the diocese of Meaux, and especially at Melun.
Cf. Baud. — Gams — Duch. Fast. Episc.—Att.

ASPREN (ASPRONAS) (St) Bp.
R.M. Aug. 3
1st cent. The tradition, dating from time immemorial, concerning this saint is recorded by the R.M. as follows: "At Naples in Campania, the birthday of St Aspren the bishop, who was cured of infirmity by St Peter the Apostle, and afterwards baptized and ordained bishop of that city."
Cf. Gams.

ASTERIA (HESTERIA) (St) V.M.
R.M. Aug. 10
d. c.307. A martyr venerated from time immemorial at Bergamo in Lombardy, where she was beheaded under Diocletian. She was a sister of St Grata, and both were associated in the burial of St Alexander

(Aug. 26), a martyred soldier of the Theban Legion.
Cf. Baud. — Holw.

ASTERICUS (ASTRICUS) (St) Bp. O.S.B.   **A.C. Nov. 12**
Otherwise Anastasius, q.v.

ASTERIUS (St) M.   **R.M. March 3**
See Marinus and Asterius.

ASTERIUS (St) M.   **R.M. May 20**
See Thalelaeus, Asterius, etc.

ASTERIUS (St) Bp.   **R.M. June 10**
d. p. 362. Formerly an Arian who, after his conversion, became bishop of Petra in Arabia, and earned the hatred of the heretics by publishing the story of their intrigues at the council of Sardica (347). Banished to Libya by Constantius, but recalled by Julian the Apostate, he was present at the council of Alexandria in 362, and was chosen to be the bearer of the letter from the council to the Church of Antioch. He died shortly after.
Cf. Holw.

ASTERIUS (St) M.   **R.M. Aug. 23**
See Claudius, Asterius, etc.

ASTERIUS (St) M.   **R.M. Oct. 21**
d. c.223. A Roman priest under Pope St Callistus, whose body he secretly buried. For this reason he himself was cast into the Tiber at Ostia by order of the emperor Alexander. The Christians recovered his body and buried it at Ostia, where it is now enshrined in the cathedral.
Cf. Baud. — Holw.

ASTERIUS (St) Bp.   **A.C. Oct. 30**
d. c.400. Bishop of Amasea in Pontus, Asia Minor. He was renowned as a preacher: twenty-one of his sermons are still extant.
Cf. Att. — Baud. — Gams.

ASTIUS (St) Bp. M.   **R.M. July 7**
See Peregrinus, Lucian, etc.

ASYNCRITUS (St) Bp.   **R.M. Apr. 8**
See Herodion, Asyncritus and Phlegon.

ATHAN (St)
Place-name near Pontypridd. No record.

ATHANASIA (St) W.   **R.M. Aug. 14**
d. 860. Born in the island of Aegina of an ancient Greek family. Her first husband died fighting against the Saracens; her second husband, with her consent, left her to become a monk. She turned her house into a convent, and eventually numerous disciples gathered around her whom she ruled as an abbess. The seven years before her death she spent in a cell at Constantinople as adviser of the empress Theodora.
Cf. Att. — Baud. — Holw.

ATHANASIA (St) H.   **R.M. Oct. 9**
See Andronicus and Athanasia.

ATHANASIUS (St)   **R.M. Jan. 3**
See Zosimus and Athanasius.

ATHANASIUS (St) Bp.   **A.C. Jan. 26**
? He is honoured at Sorrento in S. Italy as one of its bishops and patron saints. Nothing is known about him. Perhaps he is to be identified with St Athanasius of Naples (July 15).
Cf. Baud. — Holw. — Gams.

ATHANASIUS (St) Bp.   **A.C. Jan. 31**
d. c.885. A native of Catania in Sicily. During the invasion of the Saracens he fled to Patras in Peloponnesus, became a Basilian monk, and eventually also bishop of Modon.
Cf. Holw. — Baud.

ATHANASIUS (St) Ab.   **A.C. Feb. 22**
d. c.818. Born at Constantinople, he became abbot of the Paulo-Petrian monastery, near Nicomedia. He had to suffer much at the hands of the Iconoclast emperor, Leo the Armenian.
Cf. Holw. — Baud.

ATHANASIUS (St) Bp. Dr. R.M. May 2
c.297-373. History has given him the titles, amply deserved, of "Father of Orthodoxy," "Pillar of the Church," and "Champion of Christ's Divinity." A native of Alexandria, he began his public career when, still a deacon, he denounced Arius as a heretic. He accompanied his bishop to the council of Nicaea, and on his return to Alexandria (328) was made patriarch of that city, which he governed for over forty years. His life-work was the defeat of Arianism and the vindication of the deity of Christ. For this cause he was five times exiled from his see: 335-338 to Trèves; 341-346 to Rome; 356-362 to

the desert; 362-363 and a second time during four months of 363 again to the desert. Through it all he managed to guide his flock, and to write for them most illuminating treatises on Catholic dogma. One of his most attractive characteristics was his unfailing humour, which often proved a deadly weapon against his adversaries. He is revered in the universal Church as one of the four great Greek Doctors, and in the East as one of the three Holy Hierarchs. He is the pioneer of scientific theology.
Cf. Chev. — Att. — Holw.

ATHANASIUS BADZEKUKETTA (Bl) M.   A.C. June 3
d. 1886 (May 17). A page to King Mwanga of Uganda. He was baptized in 1885 and martyred by the king's soldiers in the following year.
Cf. Holw. — Baud.

ATHANASIUS (St) M.   R.M. July 5
d. 452. A deacon of Jerusalem. He denounced the heretic Theodosius, who had supplanted the Catholic St Juvenal in the see of Jerusalem. For this act he was seized by the soldiery and beheaded.
Cf. Baud. — Holw.

ATHANASIUS the ATHONITE (St) Ab.   A.C. July 5
c.920-1003. Born at Trebizond, he embraced the monastic life in Bithynia, whence he migrated to Mt Athos. Here he founded a laura (961), which became the first nucleus of what has ever since been a wholly monastic republic. When he died he ruled as abbot-general over some sixty communities of hermits and monks living on Mt Athos. Shortly after the founder's death the monks became schismatics.
Cf. Att. — Baud. — Bolland. — Holw.

ATHANASIUS (St) Bp.   R.M. July 15
d. 872. Son of the duke of Naples, he was made bishop of that city at the age of eighteen. After he had ruled it for twenty years he began to suffer from the exactions of relatives, in whose hands rested the civil authority of Naples. Imprisoned, and then exiled, he died at Veroli and was buried at Montecassino, whence his body was transferred to Naples.
Cf. Att. — Baud. — Holw. — Bolland.

ATHANASIUS, ANTHUSA and Comp. (SS) MM.   R.M. Aug. 22
d. c.257. Athanasius was bishop of Tarsus in Cilicia. Anthusa, a noble lady of Seleucia, was baptized by him together with two of her slaves, Charisius and Neophytus. The three men were martyred under Valerian; Anthusa survived twenty-three years.
Cf. Baud. — Bolland. — Holw.

ATHEIM (St) Bp. O.S.B.   P.C. Jan. 8
d. 923. Paternal uncle of St Dunstan. A monk, and then abbot, of Glastonbury, he was appointed first bishop of Wells in Somerset, and in 914 transferred to the see of Canterbury.
Cf. Gams — Stanton — Zimm. — Holw. — Baud.

ATHENODORUS (St) Bp. M.   R.M. Oct. 18
d. c.269. A native of Neo-Caesarea in Cappadocia and a brother of St Gregory the Wonder-Worker. After their conversion the two brothers studied under Origen at Caesarea and then became bishops, Athenodorus of an unnamed see in Pontus. He suffered martyrdom under Aurelian.
Cf. Bolland. — Baud. — Holw.

ATHENODORUS (St) M.   R.M. Nov. 11
d. c.304. A martyr of Mesopotamia under Diocletian, who, according to the R.M. "was tormented with fire and tried with other punishments . . . at length he was condemned to capital punishment, but when the executioner fell to the ground, and none other dared smite him with the sword, he fell asleep in the Lord in prayer."
Cf. Holw.

ATHENOGENES (St) Bp. M.   R.M. Jan. 18, July 16
? On Jan. 18 the R.M. has: "In Pontus, the birthday of St Athenogenes, an aged theologian, who, when about to consummate his martyrdom by fire, sang a hymn of joy, which he left in writing to his disciples." The martyr is to be identified, it seems, with the bishop who suffered at Sebaste in Armenia with ten disciples, under Diocletian (R.M. July 16). The hymn referred to above, is, according to St Basil, the beautiful *Phos hilaron*, feature

of the vespers service in the Byzantine liturgy.
Cf. Att. — Baud.

ATHEUS (St) C. **A.C. Dec. 26**
Otherwise Tathai, q.v.

ATHILDA (St) V.M. **A.C. March 27**
Otherwise Alkeld, q.v.

ATTALA (ATTALUS) (St) Ab. O.S.B.
A.C. Apr. 3
d. c.800. A Benedictine monk and abbot of a monastery at Taormina in Sicily.
Cf. Zimm. — Chev. — Bolland. (Apr. 1). — P. de U.

ATTALAS (St) Ab. **R.M. March 10**
d. 627. Born in Burgundy, he was professed a monk at Lérins, whence he passed over to Luxeuil under St Columbanus, whom he followed to Bobbio in N. Italy, helping him in the foundation of the abbey and succeeding him as abbot (615). It was during his abbacy that most of the monks stood out against the severity of the Columbanian Rule.
Cf. Mab. — Bolland. — Holw. — Baud.

ATTALIA (ATTALA) (St) Abs. O.S.B.
A.C. Dec. 3
c. 697-741. A niece of St Ottilia. She became a Benedictine nun and abbess of St Stephen's nunnery at Strasburg.
Cf. Mab. — Chev. — Zimm. — Baud.

ATTALUS (St) M. **R.M. June 2**
See Pothinus (Photinus), Vetius, etc.

ATTALUS (St) M. **R.M. Dec. 31**
See Stephen, Pontian, etc.

ATTICUS (St) Bp. **A.C. Jan. 8**
d. 425 (Oct. 10). A convert from heresy, he opposed St John Chrysostom and was intruded as bishop of Constantinople during the latter's second banishment. However, he repented of his opposition and submitted to Pope Innocent's ruling. Afterwards he lived as an eminently virtuous prelate.
Cf. Att. — Bolland.

ATTICUS (St) M. **R.M. Nov. 6**
? The R.M. has: "In Phrygia St Atticus, Martyr." Nothing else is known about him.

ATTILANUS (St) Bp. O.S.B. R.M. Oct. 5
c. 939-1009. A native of Tarazona, near Saragossa, he became a Benedictine at Moreruela under St Froilan, who chose him as prior of the abbey. The two sees of Leon and Zamora becoming vacant, Froilan was appointed to the former and Attilanus to the latter, and they were consecrated together on Whit-Sunday, 990. St Attilanus was canonized in 1089.
Cf. Mab. — P. de U. — Zimm. — Baud. — Att.

ATTIUS (St) M. **R.M. Aug. 1**
See Leontius, Attius, etc.

ATTO (ATTHO) (St) Bp. O.S.B. Vall.
R.M. May 22
d. 1153. Born at Badajoz in Spain — some Italian writers claim him for Florence in Italy. He became a Benedictine at Vallombrosa, and eventually abbot-general of the congregation and bishop of Pistoia. He wrote the lives of St John Gualbert and of St Bernard of Parma and a work on Compostella in Spain.
Cf. Mab. — Chev. — Zimm. — Baud.

ATTO (St) Bp. O.S.B. **A.C. June 1**
d. c.1044. Benedictine monk at Oña, in Old Castile, under St Enneco. Afterwards bishop of Oca-Valpuesta.
Cf. Zimm. — Gams.

ATTO (St) Ab. O.S.B. **A.C. Nov. 19**
d.p. 1010. First abbot of Tordino, near Teramo, a house founded by Montecassino in 1004.
Cf. Zimm.

ATTRACTA (ATHRACHT) (St) V.
A.C. Aug. 11
? 5th cent. She seems to have been a contemporary of St Patrick. She certainly was a recluse, first at Killaraght, on Lough Gara, and then at Drum, near Boyle. Both places eventually grew into nunneries under her direction. She is venerated throughout Ireland.
Cf. Att. — Holw. — Baud.

AUBERT (several)
Otherwise Autbert, q.v.

AUBIERGE (St) V. **R.M. July 7**
Otherwise Ethelburga, q.v.

AUBIN (AUBYN) (St) Bp. **R.M. March 1**
Otherwise Albinus, q.v.

AUCEJAS and LUCEIA (SS) MM.
R.M. June 25
See Lucy and Companions.

AUCTUS, TAURION and THESSALON-ICA (SS) MM. **R.M. Nov. 7**
? Martyrs at Amphipolis in Macedonia. Nothing else is known of them.

AUDACTUS (ADAUCTUS) (St) M.
R.M. Oct. 24
See Felix, Audactus, etc.

AUDAS (or ABDAS) (St) Bp. M.
R. M. May 16
d. 420. A Persian bishop, martyred together with seven priests, nine deacons and seven virgins. Their death marked the beginning of a widespread persecution of Christians throughout the kingdom.
Cf. Baud. (Abdas) — Holw. — Bolland.

AUDAX (St) M. **R.M. July 9**
See Anatolia and Audax.

AUDIFAX (St) M. **R.M. Jan. 19**
See Marius, Martha, etc.

AUDOENUS (St) Bp. **R.M. Aug. 24**
Otherwise Ouen, q.v.

AUDOMARUS (St) Bp. **R.M. Sept. 9**
Otherwise Omer, q.v.

AUDREY (AWDREY) (St) V.
V.
R.M. June 23
Otherwise Etheldreda, q.v.

AUGULUS (AUGURIUS, AULE) (St) Bp.
M. **R.M. Feb. 7**
d. c.303. His name appears in the martyrology of St Jerome as a bishop. Others describe him as a martyr put to death in London under Diocletian. French writers usually identify him with St Aule of Normandy.
Cf. Baud. — Holw.

AUGURIUS (St) M. **R.M. Jan. 21**
See Fructuosus, Augurius and Eulogius.

AUGUSTA (St) V.M. **A.C. March 27**
? Daughter of the Teuton duke of Friuli. Her conversion to Christianity so enraged her father that he killed her with his own hand. She has been venerated from time immemorial at Serravalle, near Treviso, in N. Italy.
Cf. Baud. — Holw.

AUGUSTALIS (AUTAL) (St) Bp.
R.M. Sept. 7
? c. 450. A bishop in Gaul, probably at Arles.
Cf. Gams — Baud. — Duch. Fast. Episc.

AUGUSTINE SCHÖFFLER (Bl) M.
A.C. May 1
1822-1851. Born at Mittelbronn in Lorraine, he joined the Paris Society of Foreign Missions and was sent to Annam where he was beheaded for the Faith. Beatified in 1900.
Cf. Att. — Baud. — Holw.

AUGUSTINE WEBSTER (Bl) M.O.Cart.
A.C. May 4
d. 1535. Prior of the Charterhouse of Axholme, England; he was arrested at the London Charterhouse and executed at Tyburn.
Cf. Baud. — Holw.

AUGUSTINE of NICOMEDIA (St) M.
R.M. May 7
See Flavius, Augustus and Augustine.

AUGUSTINE NOVELLO (Bl) C. O.S.A.
A.C. May 19
d. 1309. Born at Taormina, in Sicily, the scion of a noble Spanish family settled in the island, he was called in baptism Matthew. After taking his doctorate in law at Bologna, he was appointed chancellor to King Manfred of Sicily. Left for dead on the battlefield at Benevento, after his recovery he joined the Augustinian friars as a lay-brother with the new name of Augustine Novello. His gifts were soon discovered and he was commanded to receive priest's orders. Eventually he became prior-general of the Order, confessor to the pope, and legate. Cult confirmed in 1759.
Cf. Att. — Baud. — Holw.

AUGUSTINE OF CANTERBURY (St)
Bp. O.S.B. **R.M. May 26 (28)**
d. 604. He shares with St Gregory the Great the title of Apostle of the English. He was prior of St Andrew's on the Caelian Hill when he was sent by Pope Gregory the Great with a band of forty companions to evangelize England. The missionaries landed at Ebbsfleet near Ramsgate, Thanet, in 597. Soon Augustine had converted the king of Kent with thousands of his subjects to the Faith. He was conse-

crated bishop at Arles (597) and established his see at Canterbury. He was not so successful in his relations with the Celtic missionaries. He died shortly after St Gregory the Great.
Cf. Att. — Mab. — Zimm. — Baud.

AUGUSTINE FANGI (Bl) C. O.P.
A.C. July 22
d. 1493. He was born at Biella, where he joined the Dominicans. After a crowded apostolic life and great bodily sufferings he died at Venice. Cult approved in 1872.
Cf. Baud. — Holw. — Att.

AUGUSTINE GAZOTICH (Bl) Bp. O.P.
A.C. Aug. 3
1262-1323. A native of Trau in Dalmatia, he became a Friar Preacher at the age of twenty. Eventually he was sent to preach among the Slavs and Hungarians and in 1303 was chosen bishop of Zagreb in Croatia. Later he was translated to Lucera (Nocera) in Italy. His characteristic was gentleness, and he had the gift of healing. Beatified by Clement XI.
Cf. Baud. — Att. — Holw.

AUGUSTINE of HIPPO (St) Bp. Dr.
Founder.   R.M. Aug. 28 (see also
Feb. 28, Apr. 2, May 4)
Nov. 13, 354 — Aug. 28, 430. A native of Tagaste in N. Africa. In spite of his early training by his mother St Monica, he spent his youth in vice, and all but became a Manichaean. A professor of rhetoric by profession, he taught successively at Tagaste, Carthage, Rome (383) and Milan (384-386). Under the influence of St Ambrose, of St Paul's epistles and of some neoplatonist writings, he saw the light and was baptized at thirty-two by St Ambrose at Easter, 387. The same year he left for Africa, his mother dying at Ostia. From 388 to 391, he lived a sort of monastic life with a few friends near Tagaste. In 391 he was ordained priest at Hippo and three years later coadjutor-bishop of the same city. From this time on he devoted all his energy and extraordinary intellectual gifts to the defence of Christian faith and morals and to the refutation of heresy and schism, thus opposing Manichaeans, Priscillianists, Donatists, Pelagians and Semipelagians, and Arian Vandals. He is the Doctor of Grace and the Oracle of the Western Church. His leading ideas and principles on religious life are still followed by numerous canons, friars, hermits and nuns. He is one of the most prolific, and certainly the most influential, of all the doctors. His two works, the *Confessions* and the *City of God*, are reckoned among the world's classics. In his life he is a miracle of divine grace, since even the child of his sin, Adeodatus, is now venerated as a saint. His relics were first translated to Sardinia, and thence to Pavia, where they are enshrined in the basilica of St Peter.
Cf. Chev. — Holw. — Att.

AUGUSTINE AMBROSE CHEVREAUX (Bl) M. O.S.B.
A.C. Sept. 2
d. 1792. The last superior-general of the French Benedictine congregation of St Maur — the Maurists. He was imprisoned with a numerous band of ecclesiastics at the Carmelite monastery of Paris (*Les Carmes*) and put to death in the general massacre of Sept. 2. Beatified in 1931.
Cf. P. de U. — Zimm.

AUGUSTINE, SANCTIAN and BEATA (SS) MM.
A.C. Sept. 6
d. 273. Three Spanish Christians, who fled to Gaul in time of persecution and were martyred near Sens, where they are still venerated.
Cf. Baud. — Holw.

AUGUSTINE OTA (Bl) M. S.J.
A.C. Sept. 25
1622 (Aug. 10). A native of Firando, Japan, who helped the missionaries as a catechist, was imprisoned at Iki, received into the Society of Jesus in prison, and beheaded at Iki. Beatified in 1867.
Cf. Holw.

AUGUSTINE and PAULINUS (SS) Mks. O.S.B.
A.C. Nov. 5
6th cent. According to the Cassinese tradition, they were monks sent by St Benedict to the foundation of Terracina.
Cf. Zimm. — Mab.

AUGUSTINE MOI (Bl) M. A.C. Dec. 18
d. 1839. A poor day-labourer in Tonkin, a Dominican tertiary, he was beheaded because he refused to trample on a crucifix. Beatified in 1900.
Cf. Holw.

AUGUSTUS CHAPDELAINE (Bl) M.
　　　　　　　　　　A.C. Feb. 27
1814-1856. Born in France, the ninth
child of a peasant. After his ordination
to the priesthood, he served as a curate,
and then went to China to work as a missionary priest in the apostolic vicariate of
Kwang-si. He was put to death with every refinement of cruelty. Beatified in
1900.
Cf. Att. — Holw.

AUGUSTUS (St) M.　　　R.M. May 7
See Flavius, Augustus, and Augustine.

AUGUSTUS (St) C.　　　R.M. Sept. 1
See Priscus, Castrensis, etc.

AUGUSTUS (St) C.　　　R.M. Oct. 7
6th cent. An abbot of Bourges in France,
friend of St Germanus of Paris. He is
chiefly notable for having discovered the
body of St Ursinus, apostle of that district.
Cf. Baud. — Holw.

AULAIRE (St) V.M.　　　R.M. Feb. 12
Otherwise Eulalia of Barcelona, q.v.

AULD (St) Bp.　　　　　　Feb. 4
Otherwise Aldate, q.v.

AUNAIRE (St) Bp.　　　R.M. Sept. 25
Otherwise Anacharius, q.v.

AUREA (ORIA) (St) V. O.S.B.
　　　　　　　　　　A.C. March 11
d. c.1069. An anchoress, attached to the
Benedictine abbey of San Millan de la
Cogolla in the old kingdom of Navarre,
Upper Ebro, Spain. She lived under
obedience of the abbot and was directed
by St Dominic of Silos. She died at the
age of twenty-seven.
*Cf. Zimm. — P. de U. — Chev. — Att. —
Baud.*

AUREA (AURA) (St) W.M. R.M. July 19
d. 856. Born at Cordova, daughter of
infidel parents, in her widowhood she became a Christian and a nun at Cuteclara,
where she remained for more than twenty
years. She was then denounced as a
Christian by her own family and beheaded.
Cf. P. de U. — Baud. — Holw.

AUREA (St) V.M.　　　R.M. Aug. 24
d. c.260. The Acts of St Aurea's martyrdom are full of conflicting statements.

The clear facts seem to be that she was a
devout Roman lady who helped the imprisoned Christians, and that she was
thrown into the sea at Ostia under the
emperor Claudius.
Cf. Baud. — Bolland.

AUREA (St) Abs.　　　R.M. Oct. 4
d. 666. A Syrian lady, placed by St
Eligius at the head of the nunnery of St
Martial at Paris (633). She governed the
community thirty-three years and died of
the plague, together with one hundred
and sixty of her nuns.
Cf. Baud. — Holw.

AUREA (St) Abs.　　　A.C. Oct. 6
8th cent. A young girl of Amiens who
retired to Boves and eventually became
the abbess of a numerous community.
Cf. Baud. — Holw. — P.B.

AURELIA and NEOMISIA (SS) VV.
　　　　　　　　　　R.M. Sept. 25
? Born in Asia, they visited Palestine and
Rome. At Capua they were maltreated
by the Saracens (?) but escaped under
cover of a thunderstorm. They took
shelter at Macerata, near Anagni, where
they died.
Cf. Baud. — Holw.

AURELIA (St) V. O.S.B. R.M. Oct. 15
d. 1027. A French princess who spent
fifty-five years as a recluse at Strasburg
under the obedience of a Benedictine
abbey. Her name has been associated
with that of St Wolfgang.
Cf. Zimm. — Baud. — Holw.

AURELIA (St) M.　　　R.M. Dec. 2
See Eusebius, Marcellus, etc.

AURELIAN (St) Bp.　　　A.C. May 10
(1st or) 3rd cent. Disciple of St Martial
of Limoges, and eventually bishop of that
city.
Cf. Gams — Duch. Fast. Episc. — Baud.

AURELIAN (St) Bp.　　　R.M. June 16
d. c.550. Raised to the see of Arles in
546, he was appointed papal legate in
Gaul by Pope Vigilius. He founded two
monasteries, one for monks and one for
nuns, and drew up for each a monastic
rule, based on that of St Caesarius.
*Cf. Baud. — Duch. Fast. Episc. — Gams—
Mab.*

AURELIAN (St) Bp. O.S.B. A.C. July 4
d. 895. Monk and abbot of Ainay and
afterwards archbishop of Lyons.
Cf. Mab. — Duch. Fast. Episc. — Baud.

AURELIUS (St) Bp. A.C. July 20
d. 429. Bishop of Carthage, metropolitan, friend and fellow-worker of St Augustine of Hippo. He was among the first
to detect and oppose Pelagianism. He
was forced by the violence of his adversaries to invoke the civil power against
them, much against his own will.
Cf. Att. — Baud. — Holw.

AURELIUS of CORDOVA (St) M.
R.M. July 27
See George, Felix, etc., and the transla-
tion of their relics to Paris, in the R.M.
Oct. 20.

AURELIUS and PUBLIUS (SS) Bps.
MM. R.M. Nov. 12
2nd cent. Two bishops who wrote against
the Montanists or Cata-Phrygians. They
were martyred, probably in Asia, according to others in N. Africa.
Cf. Baud. — Holw. — Bolland.

AUREUS, JUSTINA and Comp. (SS)
MM. R.M. June 16
? During an invasion of the Huns, St
Aureus, bishop of Mainz, was driven from
his see and was followed by his sister, Justina, and others. On their return, while
the bishop was celebrating Mass, he and
the others were murdered in the church.
Cf. Baud. — Holw.

AUSONIUS (St) Bp. M. A.C. May 22
1st (or 3rd) cent. Supposed to have been
a disciple of St Martial of Limoges, and
first bishop of Angoulême.
*Cf. Duch. Fast. Episc. — Baud. — Holw.
— Gams.*

AUSPICIUS (St) Bp. R.M. July 8
d. c.130. Said to have been the fourth
bishop of Trèves and successor of St
Maternus (c.130). It seems, however,
that he should be identified with a first-
century bishop of Toul of the same name.
Cf. Baud.

AUSPICIUS (St) Bp. A.C. July 8
d. c.475. According to Sidonius Apollinaris, he was bishop of Toul. He was
buried at Saint-Mansuy.
Cf. Gams — Duch. Fast. Episc. — Baud.

AUSTELL (St) C. A.C. June 28
6th cent. A disciple of St Mewan or
Mevan of Cornwall. He lived probably
in the district where a place-name preserves his memory. Some modern writers
conjecture that Austell (Hawystill) is a
woman saint, one of the daughters of the
famous Brychan of Wales, who has perhaps left her name to Aust of Awst in
Gloucestershire.
Cf. Baring-Gould.

AUSTIN (St)
Otherwise Augustine (especially St Augustine of Canterbury).

AUSTINDUS (St) Bp. O.S.B.
A.C. Sept. 25
d. 1068. A native of Bordeaux, he became a monk and then abbot of Saint-
Orens, at Auch, where he introduced the
Cluniac observance. In 1041 he was
elected archbishop of Auch and proved a
brave upholder of the rights of his church
against simoniacal customs.
*Cf. Chev. — Baud. — Anal. Bolland. XV,
439.*

AUSTREBERTA (EUSTREBERTA) (St)
V. Abs. O.S.B. R.M. Feb. 10
630-704. Born near Thérouanne, in Artois, daughter of St Framechildis and the
count palatine Badefrid. She received
the veil at the hands of St Omer in the
nunnery of Abbeville (Port-sur-Somme) of
which she became abbess. As abbess she
governed Pavilly in Normandy and proved
a most successful ruler.
Cf. Mab. — Chev. — Att. — Baud.

AUSTREGILDIS (St) W. A.C. Sept. 1
Otherwise Agia, q.v.

AUSTREGISILUS (AOUSTRILLE, OU-
TRILLE) (St) Bp. R.M. May 20
551-624. Born at Bourges, he was edu-
cated as a courtier, but preferred the life
of a monk and entered the abbey of Saint-
Nizier at Lyons, where he became abbot.
In 612 he was elected bishop of Bourges.
He has always been honoured as a saint.
Cf. Bolland. — Chev. — Att. — Baud.

AUSTREMONIUS (STREMOINE) (St)
Bp. R.M. Nov. 1
(1st or) 3rd cent. One of the seven missionaries sent from Rome to evangelize

Gaul. He preached in Auvergne and was the first bishop of Clermont-Ferrand.
Cf. Baud. — Att. — Anal. Bolland. XIII, 33.

AUSTRICLINIAN (St) C. R.M. June 30
(1st or) 3rd cent. A fellow-worker of St Aurelian under St Martial of Limoges.
Cf. Baud. — Holw.

AUSTRUDE (St) V. A.C. Oct. 17
Otherwise Anstrudis, q.v.

AUTBERT (St) Mk. O.S.B. A.C. Feb. 1
d. 1129. A Benedictine monk of Lande-venec in Brittany, who became chaplain to the nuns of St Sulpice, near Reims. He is honoured liturgically at Reims.
Cf. Baud. — Chev. — Holw.

AUTBERT (St) Bp. A.C. Sept. 10
d. p. 709. A bishop of Avranches, famous because he founded the abbey-church and monastery of Mont-St-Michel *in periculo maris* on the Normandy coast.
Cf. Att. — Baud. — Holw.

AUTBERT (St) Bp. R.M. Dec. 13
d. c.669. Bishop of Cambrai-Arras. As such he was a great fosterer of monastic life and the founder of monasteries, among others, of the great abbey of St Vedastus (Saint Vaast) at Arras. He does not seem, however, to have been a monk him-self. Under him Hainault and Flanders became a vast monastic colony.
Cf. Att. — Baud. — Chev. — Gams — Zimm.

AUTBODUS (St) C. A.C. Nov. 20
d. 690. An Irish missionary who preached in Artois, Hainault, and Picardy, and died as a hermit near Laon.
Cf. Baud. — Zimm.

AUTEL (St) Bp. R.M. Sept. 7
Otherwise Augustalis, q.v.

AUTHAIRE (OYE) (St) C. A.C. Apr. 24
7th cent. A courtier at the palace of King Dagobert I of France, and father of St Ouen of Rouen. He is the patron saint of the village La-Ferté-sous-Jouarre, where he usually resided.
Cf. Baud. — Holw.

AUTHBERTUS (AUDBERT, AUBERT, ALBERT) (*several*)
Otherwise Autbert, q.v.

AUTONOMUS (St) Bp. M.
R.M. Sept. 12
d. c.300. Said by the Greeks to have been an Italian bishop, who, to escape the fury of the persecution under Diocletian, fled into Bithynia in Asia Minor, where he made many converts and afterwards was martyred.
Cf. Baud. — Bolland.

AUTOR (ADINCTOR, AUTEUR) (St) Bp.
A.C. Aug. 9
5th cent. The thirteenth bishop of Metz. In 830 his relics were translated to the abbey of Marmoutiers.
Cf. Duch. Fast. Episc. — Gams — Baud.

AUXANUS (St) Bp. R.M. Sept. 3
d. 568. Known in Milan as Sant' Ansano. He was bishop of that city, where he has always been held in great veneration.
Cf. Baud. — Holw.

AUXENTIUS (St) H. R.M. Feb. 14
d. c.470. Born in Syria, of Persian par-ents, he served as a soldier in the guards of the emperor Theodosius the Younger. Later he retired to live as a hermit in Bithynia. He was accused of heresy at the council of Chalcedon, but most suc-cessfully vindicated his orthodoxy.
Cf. Att. — Baud. — Holw.

AUXENTIUS (St) M. R.M. Dec. 13
See Eustratius, Auxentius, etc.

AUXENTIUS (St) Bp. R.M. Dec. 18
d. p. 321. A soldier in the army of the emperor Licinius, he had to suffer for re-fusing to take part in idolatrous practices. However, he survived the persecution and became a priest and lastly bishop of Mopsuestia in Cilicia.
Cf. Baud. — Holw.

AUXIBIUS (St) Bp. R.M. Feb. 19
1st cent. Said to have been baptized by St Mark and consecrated by St Paul as first bishop of Soli in Cyprus.
Cf. Baud. — Holw.

AUXILIUS (St) M. R.M. Nov. 27
See Basileus, Auxilius and Saturninus.

AUXILIUS, ISSERNINUS and SECUN-DINUS (SS) Bps. A.C. Dec. 6
5th cent. Fellow-workers under St Pat-rick in the evangelization of Ireland. The

decree signed by the four, reminding the Irish clergy that appeals from the judgment of Armagh may be made to Rome, is still extant.
Cf. Holw.

AVA (or AVIA) (St) Abs. O.S.B.
A.C. Apr. 29
d. p. 845. A niece of King Pepin, in her childhood and youth she was blind, but was cured miraculously by St Rainfredis. She entered a nunnery at Dinart in Hainault, where she became abbess.
Cf. Zimm. — Baud. — Holw.

AVENTINUS of CHARTRES (St) Bp.
A.C. Feb. 4
d. c.520. Bishop of Chartres, in which office he succeeded his brother St Solemnis.
Cf. Duch. Fast. Episc. — Gams — Att.

AVENTINUS of TROYES (St) H.
R.M. Feb. 4
c. 538. Born in central France, he acted as almoner to St Lupus, bishop of Troyes, until he retired to live as a hermit. The spot where he thus lived is now called Saint-Aventin.
Cf. Baud. — Holw.

AVENTINUS (St) M. **A.C. June 7**
d. 732. Born at Bagnères in the Pyrenees, he became a recluse in the valley of Larboush, where the Saracens discovered him, and put him to death.
Cf. Baud. — Holw.

AVERTANUS (St) C. O.C. A.C. Feb. 25
d. 1380. A native of Limoges, where he was professed as a Carmelite lay-brother. He died outside Lucca while on a pilgrimage to Palestine.
Cf. Att. — Baud. — Holw.

AVITUS (St) M. **R.M. Jan. 27**
? The R.M. mentions a martyr of this name in Africa, who is probably to be identified with the St Avitus, venerated in the Canary Islands as their apostle and first bishop.
Cf. Gams — Baud. — Holw.

AVITUS of VIENNE (St) Bp.
R.M. Feb. 5
d. c.519. Born in Auvergne and brother to St Apollinaris, bishop of Valence. Their father St Isychius, a Roman senator, had been bishop of Vienne. Avitus suc-

ceeded him. As a bishop he commanded the respect of his flock, as also of the pagan Franks and Arian Burgundians. It was he who converted the Burgundian king Sigismund. St Avitus was also an elegant writer.
Cf. Att. — Duch. Fast. Episc. — Baud. — Holw.

AVITUS II of CLERMONT (St) Bp.
A.C. Feb. 21
d. 689. Bishop of Clermont in Auvergne from 676 to 689. He was succeeded by his younger brother, St Bonitus (St Bont).
Cf. Duch. Fast. Episc. — Baud.

AVITUS (AVY) (St) Ab. **R.M. June 17**
d. c.530. First a monk of Menat in Auvergne, then abbot of Micy, near Orleans, finally a hermit in the French province of Perche, where he was forced by numerous followers to build, and govern, a new monastery.
Cf. Mab. — Baud. — Att.

AVITUS I of CLERMONT (St) Bp.
A.C. Aug. 21
d. c.600. Eighteenth bishop of Clermont, contemporary of St Gregory of Tours, whom he ordained deacon.
Cf. Duch. Fast. Episc. — Baud.

AVITUS (or ADJUTUS) (St) Ab.
R.M. Dec. 19
? The R.M. calls him Adjutus. It seems that he was an abbot of Micy, near Orleans. If so, there must have been two of the same name, and almost contemporaries, in the same abbey (see Avitus, June 17).
Cf. Mab. — Baud. — Anal. Bolland. T. XXIV. pp. 14-84.

AYBERT (St) H. O.S.B. **A.C. Apr. 7**
d. 1140. Born in the diocese of Tournai he was a recluse almost from childhood; then he entered the Benedictine abbey of Crépin, and was its provost and cellarer for twenty-five years. Another twenty-two years he spent as a recluse under the obedience of the abbey. He is famous for his practice of reciting the Hail Mary fifty times in succession.
Cf. Att. — Baud.

AYE (St) **A.C. Apr. 18 or Sept. 1**
Otherwise Agia, q.v.

AYMARD (Bl) Ab. O.S.B. A.C. Oct. 5
d. 965. He succeeded St Odo in the
abbacy of Cluny (942); but, after about
ten years he became blind and resigned
his office to St Majolus, giving to all during the rest of his life an example of wonderful resignation. Many writers call
him saint.
Cf. Mab. — Zimm. — P. de U. — Baud.

AZADAMES and AZADES (SS) MM.
R.M. Apr. 22
d. 341-342. The former a deacon, the
latter an officer of high standing at the
court of the Persian king, Shapur II.
They were martyred together with Abdiesus and others.
Cf. Baud. — Holw.

AZARIAH (AZARIAS) (St) R.M. Dec. 16
6th cent. B.C. One of the three youths
cast into the fiery furnace at Babylon by
order of Nebuchadnezzar. The Babylon-
ian officials gave him the name of Abed-
nego.
Cf. Book of Daniel ch. I-III.

AZAS and Comp. (SS) MM.
R.M. Nov. 19
d. c.304. About one hundred and fifty
Christian soldiers martyred in Isauria,
Asia Minor, under Diocletian.
Cf. Baud. — Holw.

B

**BABILAS (BABYLAS), URBAN, PRILI-
DIAN and EPOLONIUS (SS) MM.**
R.M. Jan. 24
d. c.250. Babilas was bishop of Antioch,
the most celebrated occupant of that see
after St. Ignatius. The other three were
his pupils. Babilas died in chains awaiting execution under Decius; the three
youths were put to death.
Cf. Att. — Baud. — Dict. Baudrill.

BABILLA (St) V.M. R.M. May 20
Otherwise Basilla, q.v.

BABOLENUS (St) Ab. A.C. June 26
d. c.677. Monk of Luxeuil under St
Columbanus, and afterwards first abbot
of St Peter, later St Maur-des-Fossés, near
Paris. He was helped by St Fursey in the
erection of many churches and hospitals in
the diocese of Paris.
Cf. Zimm. — Mab. — Chev. — Baud.

BABOLENUS (St) Ab. O.S.B.
A.C. Aug. 31
d. c.640. Fourth abbot of Bobbio in
Italy, where he introduced the Benedictine
Rule in place of that of St Columbanus.
Cf. Chev. — Holw.

BACCHUS (St) M. R.M. Oct. 7
See Sergius and Bacchus.

BADARN (PADARN) (several)
Otherwise Paternus, q.v.

BADEMUS (St) M. A.C. Apr. 10
c.380. A native of Persia, founder and
abbot of a monastery near Beth-Lapat in
his own country. He suffered martyrdom
under Shapur II.
Cf. Baud. — Att. — Holw.

BADILO (St) Ab. O.S.B. A.C. Oct. 8
d. c.870. A Benedictine monk of Vezelay
(Yonne), who became abbot of Leuze
(*Lutsa*) in Hainault.
Cf. Zimm. — Chev. — Holw. — Baud.

BADULFUS (BADOUR, BADOLF) (St)
Ab. O.S.B. A.C. Aug. 19
d. c.850. Monk and abbot of Ainay,
Lyons. The new *Proprium* of Lyons has
a commemoration on Aug. 19.
Cf. Baud. — Chev. — Holw. — Zimm.

BAGLAN (SS)
? There are two Welsh saints of this name,
both attributed to the fifth century, but
beyond the fact of there being existing
churches dedicated to their honour, and a
mention in an ancient litany, nothing is
known of them.
Cf. Holw.

BAIN (BAINUS, BAGNUS) (St) Bp.
O.S.B. A.C. June 20
d. c.710. Monk of Fontenelle under St
Wandrille. In 685 he was raised to the
see of Thérouanne, which then included
Calais. After twelve years he resigned
and went back to Fontenelle, and three
years later became its abbot. Towards
the end of his life he had to govern, in addition, the abbey of Fleury which Pepin
had just restored. He is the principal
patron saint of Calais.
*Cf. Att. — Baud. — Chev. — Mab. —
Holw.*

BAISIL (St)
? Patron of a church in the Llandaff diocese. There is no record of such a saint in Welsh hagiology. It may be that *Baisil* is only a misspelling of some other appellative.

BAITHIN (St) Ab.   **A.C. June 9**
d. c.598. Also called Comin or Cominus, and described as first cousin to St Columbkille, whom he succeeded as abbot of Iona. He is said to have died on the anniversary of the death of St Columba.
Cf. O' Hanlon.

BAJULUS (St) M.   **R.M. Dec. 20**
See Liberatus and Bajulus.

BALBINA (St) V.M.   **R.M. March 31**
d. c.130. The R.M. has this *laus:* "At Rome, the birthday of St. Balbina the Virgin, daughter of blessed Quirinus the martyr; she was baptized by Pope Alexander, and chose Christ as her Spouse in her virginity; after completing the course of this world she was buried on the Appian Way near her father." Later on, her relics were enshrined in the church dedicated in her name on the Aventine. Modern writers query the truth of all the above statements, admitting merely that there was a Roman virgin of this name.
Cf. Att. — Baud. — Holw. — Dict. Baudrill.

BALDA (St) Abs. O.S.B.   **P.C. Dec. 9**
d. late 7th cent. Third abbess of Jouarre in the diocese of Meaux. Her relics were enshrined in the abbey church of Nesle-la-Reposte, diocese of Troyes.
Cf. Zimm. — Chev. — Baud. — Holw.

BALDEGUNDIS (St) Abs.   **P.C. Feb. 10**
c.580. Abbess of Sainte-Croix, Poitiers, one of the most ancient of French nunneries.
Cf. Chev. — Zimm.

BALDERIC (BAUDRY) (St) Ab.
    A.C. Oct. 16
7th cent. He and his sister, St Bova, were children of Sigebert I, king of Austrasia. Eventually he became the abbot-founder of Montfaucon in Champagne as well as the founder and protector of a nunnery at Reims where his sister took the veil.
Cf. Zimm. — Baud. — Holw.

BALDOMERUS (or GALMIER) (St) Mk.
    R.M. Feb. 27
d. c.650. By trade a locksmith at Lyons, later in life he retired to the monastery of St Justus under Abbot Viventius, and was ordained sub-deacon. He is the patron saint of locksmiths, and is represented in art carrying pincers and blacksmith's tools.
Cf. Ricci — Att. — Holw. — Baud.

BALDRED (St) Bp.   **A.C. March 6**
d. 756. A Scottish bishop alleged to have been the successor of St Kentigern or Mungo at Glasgow, and to have ended his life as a hermit on the coast of the Firth of Forth. Some identify him with St Balther, the hermit of Tinningham.
Cf. Baud. — Holw.

BALDUS (St) H.   **A.C. Oct. 29**
Otherwise Baud, Baudin, or Bond. See Bond.

BALDWIN (St) Ab. O.S.B. Cist.
    A.C. July 15
d. 1140. An Italian, who became a monk of Clairvaux under St Bernard and one of the most beloved disciples of the holy founder. He was sent back to Italy as abbot of San Pastore in the diocese of Rieti. He is the principal patron saint of Rieti.
Cf. Zimm. — Prop. Cist. — P. de U. Chev.

BALDWIN (BALDUINUS, BAUDOIN) (St) M.   **A.C. Oct. 16**
d. c.680. Son of St Salaberga and brother of St Anstrude, abbess at Laon. He was archdeacon at Laon, and was murdered in circumstances which have led to his being honoured as a martyr.
Cf. Att. — Holw. — Baud.

BALIN (BALANUS, BALLOIN) (St)
    A.C. Sept. 3
7th cent. Said to have been the brother of St Gerald (March 13) and one of the four sons of an Anglo-Saxon king. He and his brothers, after accompanying St Colman of Lindisfarne to Iona, retired into Connaught in Ireland and settled at Tecksaxon, "the house of the Saxons," in the diocese of Tuam.
Cf. Holw.

BALSAMUS (Bl) Ab. O.S.B. A.C. Nov. 24
d. 1232. Tenth abbot of Cava, which he

governed from 1208 to 1232. He is described by John of Capua, as "the gem of the priesthood and the crown of prelates." Cult approved in 1928.
Cf. Zimm. — P. de U. — Holw.

BALTHASAR (St)   **A.C. Jan. 6**
One of the Magi, q.v.

BALTHASAR de TORRES (Bl) M. S.J.
A.C. June 20
1563-1626. Born at Granada, he became a Jesuit (1579), was sent to India (1586), taught theology at Goa and Macao, and passed over to Japan (1606) where he remained during the terrible persecution which broke out soon after. He was burnt alive at Nagasaki. Beatified in 1867.
Cf. Holw.

BALTHASAR of CHIAVARI (Bl) C.
O.F.M.   **A.C. Oct. 17**
d. 1492. A Friar Minor and fellow preacher with Bl Bernardino of Feltre. He is venerated in the diocese of Pavia. Cult confirmed in 1930.
Cf. Att.

BALTHER (BALDRED, BALREDUS)
(St) Mk. O.S.B.   **A. C. March 6**
d. 756. A monk-priest of Lindisfarne, who became an anchorite at Tinningham on the Scottish border, where he lived on Bass Rock, near Berwick, almost surrounded by the sea. His relics were enshrined at Durham, with those of St Bilfrid, the anchorite.
Cf. Att. — Zimm. — Holw. — Baud.

BANDARIDUS (BANDERIK, BANDERY) (St) Bp.   **A.C. Aug. 9**
d. 566. Bishop of Soissons from 540 to 566 and founder of Crépin abbey. He was banished by Clotaire I and worked for seven years, without making himself known, as a gardener in an English abbey. At length Clotaire discovered his place of refuge and recalled him to his see. He was buried in the abbey he had founded.
Cf. Baud. — Holw.

BANKA (St) V.   **A.C. Oct. 27**
Otherwise Breaca, q.v.

BAPTIST or BAPTISTA (*several*)
See under John Baptist.

BARACHISIUS (St) M.   R.M. March 29
See Jonas and Barachisius.

BARADATES (St) H.   **A.C. Feb. 22**
d. c.460. Theodoret in his *Philotheus* gives a glowing account of this Syrian solitary, whom he calls "the admirable Baradates." The emperor Leo I of Constantinople wrote to consult Baradates regarding the council of Chalcedon.
Cf. Baud. — Holw.— Att.

BARAT, MAGDALEN (St) R.M. May 25
See Magdalen-Sophie Barat.

BARBARA (St) V.M.   **R.M. Dec. 4**
? One of the most popular saints of the Calendar. According to the extant legend, first told by Metaphrastes in the tenth century, she was shut up in a tower by her father, who himself killed her for being a Christian, whereupon he was struck dead by lightning. According to the R.M. this happened at Nicomedia under Maximinus Thrax. But the whole legend is obviously spurious, and some doubt whether she ever existed. She is the patron saint of firework makers, artillerymen, architects, founders, stonemasons, grave-diggers, fortifications, magazines, and a protectress against lightning, fire, sudden death and impenitence. In art she is usually represented holding a tower and with the palm of martyrdom.
Cf. Ricci — Att. — P. de U.—Baud. — Holw.

BARBASYMAS (BARBASCEMIN) and
Comp. (SS) MM.   **A.C. June 14**
d. 346. Bishop of Seleucia-Ctesiphon in Persia. Under Shapur II he was incarcerated for eleven months with sixteen companions in an infected prison. After being tortured, they were all put to death.
Cf. Baud. — Att. — Holw.

BARBATIAN (St) C.   **R.M. Dec. 31**
5th cent. A priest of Antioch who came to Rome and there attracted the attention of the empress Placidia Augusta. She induced him to fix his residence at Ravenna, near the imperial court, where she built for him a monastery. By his prudent advice he rendered signal services to the state.
Cf. Baud. — Holw.

BARBATUS (BARBAS) (St) Bp.
R.M. Feb. 19
c. 612-632. A native of Benevento where, as a priest and later as a bishop (663), he rendered signal services to his native

town, especially when it was besieged by the emperor Constans II of Byzantium. He assisted at the sixth general council, held at Constantinople, at which the Monothelites were condemned. *Cf. Att. — Holw. — Baud.*

BARBE (St) V.M. R.M. Dec. 4
The French for Barbara, q.v.

BARBEA (St) M. R.M. Jan. 29
See Sarbelius and Barbea.

BARDO (St) Bp. O.S.B. A.C. June 10
982-1053. Born at Oppershofen and educated at Fulda, where he received the Benedictine habit and became a dean. In 1029 he was chosen abbot of Werden on the Ruhr, in 1031 abbot of Hersfeld, and in the same year archbishop of Mainz. He was for a time the Chancellor and Grand Almoner of the Empire. He was noted for his love of the poor, the destitute, and of animals. He was also noted for his austerities, which Pope St Leo IX considered too severe and advised him to relax. *Cf. Att. — Holw. — Baud. — Mab. — Zimm.*

BARDOMIAN, EUCARPUS and Comp. (SS) MM. R.M. Sept. 25
? Twenty-eight martyrs of Asia Minor in one of the early persecutions.

BARHADBESCIABAS (St) M.
A.C. July 20
d. 355. A deacon of Arbela in Persia beheaded under Shapur II. *Cf. Att. — Baud.*

BARLAAM (St) M. R.M. Nov. 19
d. c.304. A martyr of Caesarea in Cappadocia under Diocletian. His memory has been preserved in one of St Basil's homilies, preached in his honour. *Cf. Att. — Baud. — Holw.*

BARLAAM and JOSAPHAT (SS)
R.M. Nov. 27
? These two supposed saints are the protagonists of a Christian version of a Buddhist romance. The present Greek text dates from the 7th century and was popularized by St John Damascene. By a piece of great good fortune the entire text of the apology for Christianity of Aristides, the Athenian, was embodied in the romance and has thus come down to us. *Cf. Att. — Holw. — Baud.*

BARNABAS (St) Apostle M.
R.M. June 11
1st cent. A native of Cyprus and one of the seventy-two disciples. He is one of the most attractive characters of the New Testament, and the early chapters of the Acts of the Apostles are full of his name and deeds. It was he who "introduced" St Paul to the Apostles and thus to the Church. He was not one of the twelve, but has always been honoured as an apostle. An old tradition has it that he died a martyr in Cyprus. His name is in the Canon of the Mass. *Cf. Att. — Baud. — Holw.*

BARNARD (St) Bp. O.S.B. A.C. Jan. 23
777-841. Born in the Lyonnais, he was educated at the court of Charlemagne. He restored the abbey of Ambronay and became a monk therein and finally abbot. In 810 he was raised to the see of Vienne, and became one of the most influential prelates of his age. As archbishop he founded the abbey of Romans (c. 837) where he was buried. Cult as a saint approved in 1907. *Cf. Att. — Holw. — Baud. — Mab. — Zimm.*

BARNOCH (St) C. A.C. Sept. 27
Otherwise Barrog. q.v.

BARONTIUS and DESIDERIUS (SS) Mks. O.S.B. R. M. March 25
c. 725. Barontius was a gentleman of Berry who became a monk at Lonrey, diocese of Bourges. As a result of a vision he asked permission to become a hermit, set out for Italy, and established himself in the district of Pistoia. There he lived a most austere life with another monk, Desiderius, by name, who is also honoured as a saint. *Cf. Mab. — Chev. — Att. — Baud. — Holw.*

BARR (FINBAR, BARROCUS) (St) Bp.
A.C. Sept. 25
6th cent. A native of Connaught, who founded, and presided over, a monastic school at Lough Eire, thus originating the city of Cork, of which he became first bishop. He died at Cloyne. *Cf. Holw. — Baud.*

BARRFOIN (BAIRRFHIONN BARRIN-DUS) (St)   **A.C. May 21**
6th cent. Said to have had charge of the church founded by St Columbkille at Drum Cullen Offaly, and afterwards to have lived at Killbarron, near Bally-shannon, in Donegal. It is added that he reached America on one of his missions by sea, and informed St Brendan the Navigator of his discovery. By some he is said to have been a bishop. The details of his life are very vague.
Cf. Holw.

BARROG (BARRWG, BARNOCH) (St) H.   **A.C. Sept. 27**
7th cent. A disciple of the great Welsh St Cadoc, he has left his name (often spelled Barruc or Barnoch) to Barry Island, off the coast of Glamorgan, where he lived as a hermit.
Cf. Baud. — Holw.

BARSABAS and Comp. (SS) MM.   **A.C. Oct. 20**
d. c.342. A Persian abbot and his eleven monks put to death under Shapur II near the ruins of Persepolis.
Cf. Baud. — Holw.

BARSABAS (St) M.   **R.M. Dec. 11**
d. c.342. A Persian abbot, who, with several of his monks, suffered under Shapur II. Some identify him with St Barsabas of Oct. 20, others with St Simon Barasbae, commemorated on Apr. 21.
Cf. Baud. — Holw. — Att.

BARSANUPHIUS (St) H.   **R.M. Apr. 11**
d. c.540. An anchorite near Gaza, in Palestine, greatly venerated among the Greeks, who keep his feast on Feb. 6. A village near Sipontum (present-day Manfredonia) in S. Italy claims to possess his relics.
Cf. Baud. — Holw. — Att.

BARSES (BARSO, BARSAS) (St) Bp.   **R.M. Jan. 30**
d. c.379. A bishop of Edessa in Syria, banished to W. Egypt on the frontiers of Libya by the Arian emperor Valens. He died in exile.
Cf. Baud. — Holw.

BARSENORIUS (St) Ab. O.S.B.   **A.C. Sept. 13**
7th cent. Successor of St Leutfridus

(Leufroy) as abbot of La-Croix-Saint-Leuffroi, in the diocese of Evreux. His relics are at Fécamp.
Cf. Chev. — Baud. — Holw. —Zimm.

BARSIMAEUS (BARSAMJA) (St) Bp. M.   **R.M. Jan. 30**
c. 114. According to the R.M., a bishop of Edessa, who, after converting many to the Faith, suffered under Trajan. The story, however, of his martyrdom is now rejected.
Cf. Att. — Baud. — Holw.

BARTHOLOMAEA BAGNESI (Bl) V. O.P.   **A.C. May 27**
1511-1577. Born at Florence, she became a Dominican nun in 1544, and until her death was afflicted with many and varied sufferings, including diabolical obsessions. Cult approved by Pius VII.
Cf. Holw.

BARTHOLOMAEA CAPITANIO (Bl) V. Foundress   **A.C. July 26**
1807-1833. Together with the Ven. Vincenza Gerna she founded the Congregation of the Italian Sisters of Charity. She was a prolific writer on spiritual subjects.
Cf. Att.

BARTHOLOMEW ALVAREZ (Bl) M. S.J.   **A.C. Jan. 12**
d. 1737. A Portuguese, born near Braganza, who joined the Jesuits at Coimbra in 1723. He was sent to Tonkin, where he was arrested in March, 1736, and beheaded the following year.
Cf. Baud. — Holw.

BARTHOLOMEW ALBAN ROE (Bl) M. O.S.B.   **A.C. Jan. 21**
See Alban Bartholomew Roe.

BARTHOLOMEW AIUTAMICRISTO (Bl) H. O.S.B. Cam.   **A.C. Jan. 28**
d. 1224. He received the surname Aiutamicristo ("Christ help me") because this ejaculation was always on his lips. He was born at Pisa, and became a Camaldole lay-brother at the monastery of San Frediano in his native city. Cult approved in 1857.
Cf. Chev. — Zimm. — Baud. — Holw.

BARTHOLOMEW of CERVERE (Bl) M. O.P.   **A.C. Apr. 21**
1420-1466. Born at Savigliano in Pied-

mont. He taught theology at Turin and afterwards was appointed inquisitor in Piedmont. For his zeal in exercising his office he was killed by heretics at Cervere, diocese of Fossano. Cult approved by Pius IX.
Cf. Att. — Holw. — Baud.

BARTHOLOMEW PUCCI-FRANCES-CHI (Bl) C. O.F.M. A.C. May 23
d. 1330 (May 6). A wealthy married layman of Montepulciano, who, with his wife's consent, became a Franciscan friar, and is usually described as having become "a fool for Christ's sake." Cult confirmed in 1880.
Cf. Att. — Holw.

BARTHOLOMEW of DURHAM (St) H. O.S.B. A.C. June 24
d. c.1193. A native of Whitby who, after being ordained a priest in Norway, became a Benedictine at Durham, and was subsequently given leave by the abbot to lead an eremitical life on Farne Island, in the cell consecrated of old by St Cuthbert. There he spent forty-two years and there he died.
Cf. Att. — Baud. — Chev. — Zimm. — P. de U.

BARTHOLOMEW de VIR (Bl) Bp. O.S.B. Cist. P.C. June 26
d. 1157. As bishop of Laon (1113-1151) he helped St Norbert in the foundation of Prémontré. In 1121 he built the Cistercian abbey of Foigny, where he became a monk in 1151.
Cf. Zimm.

BARTHOLOMEW LAUREL (Bl) M. O.F.M. A.C. Aug. 17
d. 1627. Born at Mexico City, he became a Franciscan lay-brother and in 1609 was sent to Manila, where he studied medicine. In 1622 he crossed over to Japan and a few years later was burnt alive at Nagasaki.
Cf. Holw. — Baud.

BARTHOLOMEW MONFIORE (Bl) M. A.C. Aug. 19
d. 1622. A Japanese sailor in the ship of Bl Joachim Firaiama. He was beheaded at Nagasaki. Beatified in 1867.
Cf. Holw.

BARTHOLOMEW (St) Apostle M. R.M. Aug. 24
1st cent. One of the Twelve, he is usually

identified with Nathanael (John I). He is said to have preached in Asia Minor, N.W. India and Greater Armenia, and to have been flayed alive. His relics are enshrined in Rome on the island in the Tiber called after him, Isola di San Bartolomeo.
Cf. Att. — Baud. — Bolland.

BARTHOLOMEW GUTIERREZ (Bl) M. O.S.A. A.C. Sept. 3
1530-1632. A native of Mexico, he joined the Augustinian Friars (1596), was ordained at Puebla and sent to Manila in 1606. In 1612 he went to Japan as prior of Ukusi. He worked most zealously, though his life was in continual danger. At last, in 1629 he was betrayed, imprisoned for three years at Omura, and burnt alive at Nagasaki. Beatified in 1867.
Cf. Holw.

BARTHOLOMEW XIKIEMON (Bl) M. A.C. Sept. 10
d. 1622. A Japanese layman, beheaded at Nagasaki He belongs to the group of Bl Charles Spinola, q.v.
Cf. Holw. — Baud.

BARTHOLOMEW of BRAGANZA (Bl) Bp. O.P. A.C. Oct. 23
c. 1200-1271. Born at Vicenza, he received the Dominican habit at the hands of St Dominic himself at Padua. In 1233 he founded a sort of military order — the *Fratres Gaudentes* — for the preservation of public order. In 1252 he was sent to Cyprus as bishop of Nimesia, whence he was translated to Vicenza (1256). Cult approved in 1793.
Cf. Att. — Baud. — Holw.

BARTHOLOMEW of MARMOUTIER (Bl) Bp. O.S.B. A.C. Nov. 11
d. 1067. Abbot of Marmoutier, and archbishop of Tours from 1052 to 1067. He was a tireless worker in the face of many difficulties. He strove unavailingly to bring back Berengarius to the Catholic Faith.
Cf. Chev. — Baud. — Holw. — P.B.

BARTHOLOMEW of ROSSANO (St) Ab. R.M. Nov. 11
d. 1065. Of Greek extraction, he was born at Rossano, in Calabria. He followed St Nilus to the foundation of Grotta-ferrata, at Frascati, near Rome, under St Basil's

Rule and in the Greek rite. St Bartholomew is rightly considered its second founder. He excelled as a composer of Greek hymns. It was he who persuaded Pope Benedict IX to reform his life and do penance at Grotta-ferrata.
Cf. Att. — Baud. — Holw.

BARTHOLOMEW XEKI (Bl) M.
A.C. Nov. 27
d. 1619. A Japanese layman of the royal family of Firando, beheaded at Nagasaki. Beatified 1867.
Cf. Holw.

BARTHOLOMEW FANTI (Bl) C. O.C.
A.C. Dec. 5
1443-1495. Born at Mantua, where he joined the Carmelites. He was the instructor of St John Baptist Spagnuolo, and was famous as a preacher and director of souls as well as for his gift of healing. Cult confirmed in 1909.
Cf. Holw. — Att. — Baud.

BARTHOLOMEW (BARTOLO) BUON-PEDONI (Bl) C. A.C. Dec. 14
d. 1300. Born near San Geminiano, in Italy, he was first a lay-servant at the Benedictine abbey of San Vito, at Pisa. Later he became a Franciscan tertiary. When he was thirty years of age the bishop of Volterra ordained him priest, and he served the village of Peccioli, near Volterra. The last twenty years of his life he spent as a leper ministering to his fellow-sufferers with infinite patience. Cult confirmed in 1910.
Cf. Att. — Baud. — Holw.

BARULA (St) M. R.M. Nov. 18
See Romanus and Barula.

BARYPSABAS (St) M. A.C. Sept. 10
1st cent. A hermit from the East who suffered martyrdom in Dalmatia. A Greek legend has it that Barypsebas had carried to Rome a vessel containing some of the Precious Blood which flowed from the side of our Lord on the Cross.
Cf. Baud. — Holw.

BASIL (St) Bp. A.C. Jan. 1
d. 521. A priest of Arles who became second bishop of Aix, in Provence.
Cf. Duch. Fast. Episc. — Gams — Baud.— P.B.

BASIL and PROCOPIUS (SS) CC.
R.M. Feb. 27
d. c.750. Two courageous defenders of the veneration of images against the emperor Leo the Isaurian.
Cf. Baud. — Holw.

BASIL, EUGENE, AGATHODORUS, ELPIDIUS, AETHERIUS, CAPITON, EPHREM, NESTOR and ARCADIUS (SS) Bps. MM. R.M. March 4
4th cent. Missionary bishops: the first seven preached in the Crimea and S. Russia; the last two in Cyprus. All are honoured by the Greeks, on March 7, as martyrs.
Cf. Baud. — Bolland. — Holw.

BASIL (St) Bp. R.M. March 6
d. 335. Consecrated bishop of Bologna by Pope St Sylvester, he ruled his diocese for twenty years, 315-335.
Cf. Gams — Baud. — Holw. — Bolland.

BASIL of ANCYRA (St) M.
R.M. March 22
d. 362. A priest of Ancyra in Galatia, who distinguished himself as a staunch upholder of orthodoxy against Arianism. Under Julian the Apostate he was thrown to the wild beasts in the arena at Caesarea in Palestine.
Cf. Holw. — Att. — Baud. — Bolland.

BASIL the YOUNGER (St) H.
A.C. March 26
d. 952. An anchorite near Constantinople who was seized as a spy and put to the torture by the imperial officers. He lived to be a centenarian.
Cf. Att. — Baud. — Holw.

BASIL and EMMELIA (SS)
R.M. May 30
d. c.370. Parents of SS Basil the Great, Gregory of Nyssa, Peter of Sebaste and Macrina the Younger. They were exiled under Galerius Maximinus, but returned after the peace of the Church to their native city of Caesarea in Cappadocia. St Basil was educated by his mother St Macrina the Elder.
Cf. Baud. — Holw.

BASIL the GREAT (St) Bp. Dr.
R.M. June 14 (and Jan. 1)
329-379 (Jan. 1). Born at Caesarea in Cappadocia. His parents, his paternal

grandparents, his two brothers and one sister, are all honoured as saints. After his studies at Constantinople and Athens, Basil visited the monastic colonies of Egypt, Palestine and Syria, and founded one himself on the river Iris, in Pontus, for which he wrote his Rules, still the standard works of their kind in the East. In 370 he was made metropolitan of Caesarea, and at once entered upon his brave fight for orthodoxy against Arians and Macedonians, who had the support of the imperial authorities at Byzantium. Nothing daunted, Basil saved the whole of Cappadocia for the Catholic faith. For this purpose he spent himself in preaching and writing doctrinal works, in both of which activities he excelled as much as in the administration of his diocese. His work on the Holy Ghost is still unsurpassed in Catholic theology. He edited also the Eucharistic Liturgy which bears his name. In the East Basil is the first of the three Holy Hierarchs, in the West one of the four Greek Doctors.
Cf. Att. — Baud.

BASIL (St) M.   **R.M. Nov. 28**
See Stephen, Basil, etc.

BASILEUS (St) M.   **R.M. March 2**
See Jovinus and Basileus.

BASILEUS (St) Bp. M.   **R.M. Apr. 26**
d. 319. Bishop of Amasea in Pontus, martyred by drowning in the sea under Licinius. The R.M. adds that one of his disciples, by name Elpidiphorus, instructed by an angel, recovered the body and gave it Christian burial.
Cf. Baud. — Holw.

BASILEUS (St) M.   **R.M. May 23**
See Epitacius and Basileus.

BASILEUS, AUXILIUS and SATURNINUS (SS) MM.   **R.M. Nov. 27**
? Basileus, a bishop of an unknown see, was put to death at Antioch in Syria together with Auxilius and Saturninus. Nothing further is known about them.
Cf. Baud. — Holw.

BASILIAN (St) M.   **R.M. Dec. 18**
See Theotimus and Basilian.

BASILIDES, TRIPOS, MANDAL and Comp. (SS) MM.   **R.M. June 10**
270-275. A group of twenty-three Christians martyred at Rome on the Aurelian Way, under Aurelian. Probably to be identified with the next group (June 12).
Cf. Att. — Baud. — Holw. — Bolland.

BASILIDES, CYRINUS, NABOR and NAZARIUS (SS) MM.   **R.M. June 12**
? The R.M. has this *laus:* "At Rome on the Aurelian Way, the birthday of the holy martyrs Basilides, Cyrinus, Nabor, and Nazarius, soldiers who were cast into prison in the persecution of Diocletian and Maximian, under the prefect Aurelius for the confession of the Christian name, scourged with scorpions and beheaded." It seems, however, more likely that this group is the result of confusion of names in the martyrologies: Basilides is probably the Roman martyr of June 10: Cyrinus (or Quirinus) the martyr of June 4; Nabor and Nazarius, two Milanese martyrs, of whom nothing can be ascertained.
Cf. Att. — Baud. — Holw.

BASILIDES (St) M.   **R.M. June 30**
d. 205. A soldier of the guard of the prefect of Egypt, told off to execute St Potamiana, whom he defended from the insults of the mob. He was rewarded with the gift of faith, for which he was martyred shortly after under Septimius Severus.
Cf. Baud. — Bolland. — Holw.

BASILIDES and Comp. (SS) MM.   **R.M. Dec. 23**
See Theodulus, Saturninus, etc.

BASILISCUS (BASILICUS) (St) M.   **R.M. March 3**
See Cleonicus, Eutropius and Basiliscus.

BASILISCUS (St) M.   **R.M. May 22**
d. 312. Bishop of Comana in Pontus, Asia Minor. He was beheaded under Maximin the Thracian and his body thrown into a river near Nicomedia. It was recovered and translated to Comana. This was the martyr who appeared to St John Chrysostom on the eve of the holy doctor's death.
Cf. Baud. — Holw. — Bolland.

BASILISSA (St) V.M.   **R.M. Jan. 9**
See Julian, Basilissa, etc.

BASILISSA (St) M.   **R.M. March 22**
See Callinica and Basilissa.

BASILISSA and ANASTASIA (SS) MM.
                              R.M. Apr. 15
d. c.68 Noble Roman ladies, disciples of
the Apostles Peter and Paul, whose bodies
they buried. They were martyred themselves under Nero. Some modern writers
have cast doubts on their very existence.
Cf. Att. — Baud. — Bolland. — Holw.

BASILISSA (St) V.M.   R.M. Sept. 3
d. c.303. The R.M. has her full story:
"At Nicomedia, the passion of St Basilissa
virgin and martyr; though she was only
nine years of age, yet by the power of God,
she overcame scourges, fire and the beasts
under the governor Alexander, in the persecution of the emperor Diocletian; by
this she converted the governor to the
faith of Christ, and at length she gave up
her spirit to God, while she was at prayer
outside the city."

BASILISSA (St) Abs. O.S.B. P.C. Dec. 5
d. c.780. A Benedictine abbess at the
nunnery of Oehren (*Horreum*) in the
diocese of Trèves.
*Cf. Chev. — Baud. — Holw. — See, how-
ever, Zimm.*

BASILLA (St) M.   R.M. May 17
See Adrio, Victor and Basilla.

BASILLA (St) V.M.   R.M. May 20
d. 304. A Roman maiden, betrothed to a
pagan patrician, whom she refused to
marry on becoming a Christian. Forced
to choose between her bridegroom and
death, she at once chose the latter and was
accordingly martyred for Christ. This
summary of her *Acta* shows that they con-
form to a type common in hagiological
literature.
Cf. Att. — Baud. — Holw. — Bolland.

BASILLA (St) V.   R.M. Aug. 29
? A holy woman, who, according to the
R.M., died at Smyrna. Other martyrolo-
gies, instead of Smyrna, have Sirmium in
Pannonia (now Mitrovica).
Cf. Baud. — Holw.

BASINUS (St) Bp. O.S.B. A.C. March 4
d. c.705. Monk and abbot of the Benedictine monastery of St Maximin at
Trèves, he succeeded St Numerian as
bishop of the city. In this capacity he
greatly helped the English missionaries,
notably St Willibrord. He died at St

Maximin, whither he had again retired in
his old age.
*Cf. Att. — Chev. — Baud. — Holw. —
Gams.*

BASOLUS (BASLE) (St) H.
                              R.M. Nov. 26
c.555-c.620. A native of Limoges, he
became a monk at Verzy, near Reims, and
then a hermit, living for forty years in a
cell on the top of a hill overlooking the city.
He was celebrated as a wonder-worker.
Cf. Att. — Chev. — Baud. — Mab.

BASSA (St) M.   R.M. March 6
See Victor, Victorinus, etc.

**BASSA, PAULA and AGATHONICA (SS)
VV. MM.   R.M. Aug. 10**
? Three Christian maidens registered in
the accepted lists as having been martyred
at Carthage.
Cf. Baud. — Bolland.

**BASSA, THEOGONIUS, AGAPIUS and
FIDELIS (SS) MM.   R.M. Aug. 21**
d. 304. Bassa, wife of a pagan priest, was
martyred with her three sons at Edessa in
Syria under Diocletian. Like the mother
of the Maccabees, she chose to suffer last
in order to encourage her children in their
agony.
Cf. Baud. — Bolland. — Holw.

BASSIAN (St) Bp.   R.M. Jan. 19
d. 413. A Sicilian by birth, he became
bishop of Lodi in Lombardy. He was held
in high esteem by his friend St Ambrose of
Milan, with whom he attended the council
of Aquileia (381) and whom he assisted at
his death (390).
Cf. Baud. — Holw. — Bolland. — Gams.

BASSIAN (St) M.   R.M. Feb. 14
See Cyrion, Bassian, etc.

BASSIAN (St) M.   R.M. Dec. 9
See Peter, Successus, etc.

**BASSUS, ANTONY and PROTOLICUS
(SS) MM.   R.M. Feb. 14**
? A group of martyrs who were cast into
the sea at Alexandria in Egypt. Some
ancient accounts add nine fellow-sufferers
to this group.
Cf. Baud. — Bolland. — Holw.

BASSUS (St) M.   R.M. May 11
See Maximus, Bassus and Fabius.

BASSUS, DIONYSIUS, AGAPITUS and **Comp. (SS) MM.** R.M. Nov. 20
? A band of forty-three Christians put to death at Heraclea in Thrace.
Cf. Baud. — Holw.

BASSUS (St) Bp. M. R.M. Dec. 5
d. c.257. Bishop of Nice in Gaul. He was martyred under Decius by having his body transfixed with two huge nails.
Cf. Baud. — Holw.

BATHILDIS (St) Queen, O.S.B.
R.M. Jan. 30
d. 680. An English girl sold as a slave to the mayor of the palace of the kingdom of Neustria. King Clovis II married her in 649, and she became the mother of three future kings. After her husband's death she was for eight years regent of France (656-664). When Clotaire III came of age, she entered the nunnery of Chelles, which she had founded, and lived there as a simple nun. Her biography was written by a contemporary.
Cf. Att. — Chev. — Mab. — Baud. — Holw. — Zimm.

BAUDACARIUS (St) Mk. O.S.B.
A.C. Dec. 21
d. 650. Monk of Bobbio, in N. Italy. His relics were solemnly translated in 1483.
Cf. Zimm. — Chev.

BAUDELIUS (St) M. R.M. May 20
2nd (or 3rd) cent. A native of Orleans, a married man, who worked zealously in the cause of Christianity. He was martyred at Nîmes. His cult spread throughout France and N. Spain: there are some four hundred churches dedicated in his honour.
Cf. Baud. — Att. — Holw.

BAUDRY (St) C. A.C. Oct. 16
Otherwise Balderic, q.v.

BAVO (St) H. O.S.B. R.M. Oct. 1
c.589-654. Born in Brabant, in the district of Liége, in his early years he led a very irregular life. Left a widower, he was converted by a sermon of St Amandus and entered upon a course of canonical penance. Next he founded the abbey of St Peter on his estate at Ghent (later called St Bavo's), and became a monk under St Amandus. Finally he lived as a recluse in the forest of Malmédun, and in a cell by St Peter's.
Cf. Mab. — Zimm. — Chev. — Baud. — Att.

BAYA and MAURA (SS) VV. A.C. Nov. 2
10th cent. Recluses in Scotland, St Baya being the instructress of St Maura, and the latter in her turn the abbess of a community which attached itself to her. Some authors identify St Baya with St Begha or Bee.
Cf. Holw. — Baring-Gould.

BEAN (St) Bp. A.C. Oct. 26
d. p. 1012. Bishop of Mortlach in Banff, from which see he was later transferred to Aberdeen.
Cf. Baud. — Att.

BEAN (St) Bp. R.M. Dec. 16
? Bishop of Leinster in Ireland.
Cf. Baud. — Att.

BRANDAN (BREANDAN) (St) Ab.
A.C. Jan. 11
5th cent. An Irishman who crossed into Britain and had to suffer much there at the hands of the Pelagians. He took refuge in a monastery of Gaul, of which he eventually became abbot.
Cf. Baud.

BEATA (St) M. R.M. March 8
See Cyril, Rogatus, etc.

BEATRIX II of ESTE (Bl) N. O.S.B.
A.C. Jan. 18
d. 1262. A niece of Bl Beatrix I of Este (see May 10). Being bereft of her husband (or fiancé) at an early age, she founded, in the teeth of much opposition, the Benedictine convent of St Antony at Ferrara and became a nun there. Cult confirmed in 1774.
Cf. Att. — Zimm.— P. de U. — Baud. — Chev.

BEATRIX of LENS (Bl) N. O.S.B. Cist.
A.C. Jan. 19
d. p. 1216. Born at Lens, in the diocese of Arras. She founded the Cistercian monastery of Epinlieu near Mons, and became a nun there.
Cf. Chev. — Baud. — Holw.

BEATRIX d'ORNACIEUX (Bl) N.O. Cart.
A.C. Feb. 13
d. 1309 (Nov. 25). A Carthusian nun

of Parménie, and one of the foundresses of the Esmue nunnery of the same order. For many years she had remarkable mystical experiences as well as diabolical persecutions. Cult confirmed in 1869. *Cf. Att. — Baud. — Holw.*

BEATRIX I of ESTE (Bl) V.N. O.S.B.
　　　　　　　　　　A.C. May 10
1206-1226. Daughter of the Marchese Azzo d'Este, she was left an orphan at the age of six. When she was fourteen she secretly left her home, and, against the wishes of her relatives, became a Benedictine nun at Solarola, near Padua. Shortly afterwards she was transferred to Gemmola, where she died a victim of loving self-immolation. Cult confirmed in 1763. *Cf. Att.— Baud. — Holw. — Chev.*

BEATRIX (St) M.　　　**R.M. July 29**
See Simplicius, Faustinus and Beatrix

BEATRIX (Bl) N. O.S.B. Cist.
　　　　　　　　　　P.C. July 26
d. 1268. Cisterian nun of Valfleury, who became prioress of Our Lady of Nazareth, near Lier, in Brabant. Cult not yet officially approved.
Cf. Chev. — Holw. — P.B.

BEATRIX (BRITES) da SILVA (Bl) Abs.
O.S.B. Cist.　　　　　**A.C. Aug. 18**
1424-1490. Born in Portugal, a daughter of the count of Viana. At the age of twenty she accompanied Princess Isabel of Portugal to the Spanish court, where, however, she did not long remain. Eventually she entered the Cistercian nunnery of St Dominic of Silos at Toledo. Later she founded the Congregation of the Immaculate Conception (Conceptionists) under the Benedictine Rule. After Bl Beatrix's death Cardinal Cisneros gave them the rule of St Clare. Cult confirmed in 1926.
Cf. P. de U. — Zimm. — Att. — Acta Ap. Sedis 1926, pp. 496-499.

BEATUS (St) Mk.　　　**A.C. Feb. 19**
d. 789. A native of Asturias, in Spain, monk and priest of Liébana, famous for his firm stand against Helipandus, archbishop of Toledo and the other Adoptionists. He travelled to the council of Frankfort, to denounce the heresy, and his adversaries denounced him as "a vagabond

mountaineer." When the Adoptionists were condemned, the saint retired to the monastery of Valcavado, where he wrote his celebrated commentary on the Apocalypse.
Cf. Att. — P. de U. — Mab. — Chev. — Baud.

BEATUS (St) Bp.　　　**A.C. March 8**
Otherwise Beoadh, q.v.

BEATUS (St) H.　　　**R.M. May 9**
? An early hermit, venerated as the apostle of Switzerland. His hermitage was at the place now called Beatenberg, above the lake of Thun.
Cf. Att. — Holw.

BECAN (BEGAN) (St) Ab.　**A.C. Apr. 5**
6th cent. One of the "twelve Apostles of Ireland." He was connected by blood with St Columbkille. He founded a monastery at Kill-Beggan, Westmeath, which centuries later became a Cistercian abbey. He also gave its name to the church and parish of Imleach-Becain, Meath.
Cf. Baud. — O' Hanlon.

BECAN (St) H.　　　**A.C. May 26**
6th cent. An Irish hermit in the time of St Columbkille. He lived in the neighbourhood of Cork.
Cf. Baud. — Holw.

BECHE, JOHN (Bl) M.　　**A.C. Dec. 1**
See John Beche.

BEDE the YOUNGER (St) Mk. O.S.B.
　　　　　　　　　　A.C. Apr. 10
d. 883. One of the chief officials at the court of Charles the Bald of France, who became a Benedictine at the abbey of Gavello, near Rovigo, in N. Italy. He refused several bishoprics. His relics were translated to Subiaco in the 19th cent.
Cf. Holw. — Baud. — Chev.

BEDE the VENERABLE (St) Dr. O.S.B.
　　　　　　　　　　R.M. May 27
673-735. Born at Wearmouth, he was offered as a child to the double abbey of SS Peter and Paul at Wearmouth-Jarrow, was professed there under the founder St Benedict Biscop, and there he spent his whole life, "always writing, always praying, always reading, always teaching." He was ordained priest by St John of

Beverley, and it was owing to this dignity, then rather rare among monks, that he was styled Venerable, the title by which priests were usually addressed at that time, much as now-a-days they are called reverend. The Bible was his principal study, and then history. His *Ecclesiastical History of the English People* has earned for him the title of Father of English History. He is the type of the Benedictine scholar of all periods, and has been declared Doctor of the Church. He died on Ascension Eve, and his dying words were *Gloria Patri et Filio et Spiritui Sancto.*
Cf. Mab. — Chev. — Att. — Baud. — Zimm. — P. de U.

BEE (St) V.   **A.C. Oct. 31**
Otherwise Begh or Bega, q.v.

BEGA (BEGH, BEE) (St) V.
                                  A.C. Oct. 31
d. 681. An Irish maiden who founded a nunnery on the promontory of St Bee's Head, in Cumberland, which still perpetuates her memory, as does also the name of the village, Kilbees, in Scotland. Two other saints of the same name are mentioned by hagiographers, a nun in Yorkshire and an abbess at Kilbees.
Cf. Att. — Holw. — Zimm.

BEGGA (St) W. Abs. O.S.B.
                                  R.M. Dec. 17
d. 698. Daughter of Bl Pepin of Landen and of St Ida, and sister of two other saints. She married Angisilus (Ansegis), son of St Arnulf of Metz, and of their union was born Pepin of Heristal, the founder of the Carolingian dynasty. After her husband's death St Begga founded a nunnery at Andenne on the Meuse, which she governed as abbess.
Cf. Att. — Chev. — Baud. — Holw.

BELINA (St) V.M.   **A.C. Feb. 19**
d. 1135. A peasant girl of the district of Troyes (France), who died in defence of her chastity, threatened by the feudal lord of the territory. Canonized in 1203.
Cf. Baud. — Holw. — P.B.

BELLATANUS and SAVINUS' (BB) HH.
O.S.B. Cam.   **A.C. May 19**
? Camaldolese hermits of Montacuto in the neighbourhood of Perugia.
Cf. Zimm.

BELLINUS (St) Bp. M.   R.M. Nov. 26
d. 1151. A bishop of Padua who suffered death in the faithful discharge of pastoral duties, and was canonized three centuries later by Pope Eugene IV.
Cf. Baud. — Holw.

BENEDICT
Note. In Latin Benedictus; in Italian: Benedetto; in French: Benoît; in Spanish: Benito; in Portuguese: Bento; in Catalan: Benet (accent on the second syllable); in German: Benedikt; in English: Benet and Benedict.

BENEDICT BISCOP (St) Ab. O.S.B.
                                  R.M. Jan. 12
628-690. A Northumbrian by birth, Biscop Baducing made two pilgrimages to Rome early in life, and after the second became a monk at Lérins. After a third journey to Rome he returned to England and founded the abbey of Wearmouth and Jarrow (674-682). Twice more he visited Rome, whence he brought the precentor of the Vatican to train the English monks in the Roman ways. He was the spiritual father of the Venerable Bede.
Cf. Mab. — Chev. — Zimm. — Att. — P. de U.

BENEDICT RICASOLI (Bl) H. O.S.B.
Vall.   **A.C. Jan. 20**
d. 1107. Born at Coltiboni, in the diocese of Fiesole. He entered the monastery founded by his parents for the monks of Vallombrosa on a mountain near Coltiboni. Later he became a hermit in a cell near by. Cult confirmed in 1907.
Cf. Chev. — Att. — Zimm. — P. de U. — Baud.

BENEDICT of ANIANE (St) Ab. O.S.B.
                                  A.C. Feb. 11
751-821. A Visigoth, by name Witiza, born in Languedoc, he served as a cupbearer at the court of Pepin and Charlemagne. In 774 he became a monk at Saint-Seine, near Dijon, and was appointed cellarer. In 782 he founded an abbey on his native estate, in Languedoc, by the brook Aniane. The emperor ordered him to undertake the oversight of all the abbeys of Languedoc, Provence and Gascony, and eventually also the reform of all the French and German houses. As a kind of model abbey St Benedict, with the emperor's active help, founded the

abbey of Cornelimünster, near Aix-la-Chapelle. It was at Aix-la-Chapelle that he presided over a meeting of all the abbots of the empire (817) — a turning point in Benedictine history. St Benedict has been rightly styled "the second founder of the Benedictines" and "the second St Benedict."
Cf. Att.—Zimm.—Baud.—P. de U. Chev.

BENEDICT REVELLI (St) Bp. O.S.B.
A.C. Feb. 12
c.900. He is said to have been a Benedictine monk of Santa Maria dei Fonti, and then a hermit on the island of Gallinaria, in the Gulf of Genoa. In 870 he was chosen Bishop of Albenga towards the western end of the Ligurian riviera. His cult, as a saint was confirmed by Pope Gregory XVI
Cf. Baud. — Holw.

BENEDICT of CAGLIARI (St) Bp. O.S.B.
A.C. Feb. 17
d. p. 1112. Monk of the monastery attached to the basilica of St Saturninus, at Cagliari, in Sardinia. He was bishop of Dolia, also in Sardinia, from 1107 to 1112. In his old age he resigned and returned to his abbey, where he died shortly after.
Cf. Zimm. — Gams. — P. de U.

BENEDICT CRISPUS of MILAN (St) Bp.
R.M. March 11
d. 725. Archbishop of Milan, he governed his see for forty-five years. He composed the epitaph for the tomb of Ceadwaller, king of Wessex, buried in St Peter's Rome.
Cf. Baud. — Holw. — Att.

BENEDICT (St) Ab. Founder
R.M. March 21
c.480-c.550. Born in the district of Norcia, in Umbria, central Italy, he was sent to Rome for his studies; but fled from the moral dangers which beset him and joined (c.500) a sort of community of ecclesiastical students at Affile. Shortly after he retired to a cave near Subiaco — now the Sacro Speco — to live as a hermit. Here his sanctity was soon discovered and many disciples flocked to him; for these he built a *laura*, composed of twelve small monasteries, himself retaining the command over all. About the year 530 he left Subiaco for Montecassino, where on the road to Naples he founded the great arch-abbey and where he lived till his death, famous as a wonder-worker. Here,

too, he promulgated his Rule, which is justly considered one of the most potent factors in building up the civilization of Christian Europe. Eventually it became the norm for all western monks, and was simply called "The Holy Rule," "the Papal Rule," "the Roman Rule" of monks. The little we know of St Benedict's own personality shows him to us as a strong but lovable character. He died standing erect in prayer before the altar. He has been called "the Father of Western Europe," "the Patriarch of Labour" and "the Father of Peace." His large spiritual family still carries on an intense apostolate of prayer and work in the service of Christ and His Church. In art St Benedict is usually represented holding either the book of the Holy Rule or a broken cup with a serpent and a raven at his feet — allusions to episodes of his life.
Cf. Mab. — Chev. — Zimm. — Ricci — Att. — P. de U. — Baud. — Holw.

BENEDICT of CAMPANIA (St) H.
R.M. March 23
d. c.550. A contemporary of St Benedict of Montecassino, and a hermit in the Campagna, who was delivered by a miracle from death by burning at the hands of Totila the Goth.
Cf. Att. — Baud. — Holw. — Bolland.

BENEDICT the MOOR (St) C. O.F.M.
R. M. Apr. 4
1526-1589. Called in Italian "il Moro" — "the Black." He was in fact born of Negro parents, serfs near Messina in Sicily. He first became a hermit and then joined the Friars Minor of the Observance at Palermo as a lay-brother. Nevertheless, he was appointed guardian and novice-master of the friary and he excelled in both offices. His heart, however, was in the kitchen, whither he returned in his old age. Beatified in 1743 and canonized in 1807.
Cf. Att. — Baud. — Holw.

BENEDICT (BÉNÉZET) the BRIDGE-BUILDER (St) C.
A.C. Apr. 14
d. 1184. A shepherd boy of Avignon who, as the result of a vision, asked the blessing and help of the bishop of the city to build a bridge at a dangerous ford over the Rhône. A series of miracles accompanied the carrying out of the work.
Cf. Att. — Baud. — Holw.

BENEDICT JOSEPH LABRE (St) C.
R.M. Apr. 16
1748-1783. A native of Anettes, then in
the diocese of Boulogne-sur-Mer. He
came of a family of shopkeepers in easy
circumstances, and was educated by an
uncle, a priest. He tried without success
to join the Trappists. Then he found his
vocation as a pilgrim-beggar, tramping
from shrine to shrine throughout Europe,
living on alms, and spending long hours
before the Blessed Sacrament. He died in
Rome during Holy Week. He was beatified in 1860 and canonized in 1883.
Cf. Baud. — Att. — Holw.

BENEDICT of URBINO (Bl) C. O.F.M.
Cap. **A.C. Apr. 30**
1560-1625. Born at Urbino, of the family
de' Passionei, he was a lawyer at Urbino
before he joined the Capuchin friars at
Fano (1584). He was the companion of
St Laurence of Brindisi, whom he followed
to Austria and Bohemia. He died at the
monastery of Fossombrone. Beatified in
1867.
Cf. Att. — Baud. — Holw.

BENEDICT II (St) Pope **R.M. May 8**
d. 685. A Roman by birth, he was chosen
pope in 683, but his enthronement was delayed a year awaiting the arrival of the
confirmation from Constantinople. He
governed the Church eleven months.
Cf. Att. — Baud. — Holw.

BENEDICT XI (Bl) Pope, O.P.
R.M. July 7
1240-1304. A native of Treviso, Nicholas
Boccasini, as he was called in baptism,
joined the Dominicans and became their
ninth master-general. Eventually he was
created cardinal-bishop of Ostia and papal
legate. He was elected pope in 1303. He
continued to the end his religious observances and penances. Beatified in 1736.
Cf. Att. — Baud. — Holw.

BENEDICT d' ALIGNAN (Bl) Bp. O. F.M.
P.C. July 8
d. 1268. A Benedictine abbot who was
chosen bishop of Marseilles. He made a
pilgrimage to the Holy Land, and on his
return resigned the bishopric and joined
the Friars Minor.
Cf. Holw. — P.B.

BENEDICT (St) Bp. **A.C. July 15**
d. c.820. Bishop of Angers in the reign of
Louis the Pious.
Cf. Duch. Fast. Episc. — Gams — Baud.

BENEDICT de CASTRO (Bl)M. S.J.
A.C. July 15
d. 1570. A native of Chacim, diocese of
Miranda in Portugal. He belonged to the
group of Jesuit martyrs under the leader-
ship of Bl Ignatius Azevedo, q.v., killed by
Calvinistic pirates.
Cf. Holw.

BENEDICT of MACERAC (St) Ab.
A.C. Oct. 22
d. 845. A Greek abbot who fled from
Petras and settled at Macerac, in the diocese of Nantes. His relics were later
transferred to the abbey of Redon.
Cf. Zimm. — Baud. — Holw.

BENEDICT of SEBASTE (St) Bp.
R.M. Oct. 23
d. c.654. An alleged bishop of Sebaste in
Samaria, who had to escape to Gaul dur-
ing the persecution of Julian the Apostate.
He built a hermitage near Poitiers which
later became the abbey of St Benedict of
Quincay. Not all the above details, how-
ever, are above suspicion.
Cf. Bolland. — Holw. — Baud.

BENEDICT, JOHN, MATTHEW, ISAAC
and CHRISTINUS (CHRISTIAN) (SS)
MM. O.S.B. **R.M. Nov. 12**
d. 1005. Italian Benedictines who followed St Adalbert of Prague to the mission among the Slavs, and were massacred
by robbers at their monastery near Gnesen
(May 11). They were canonized by
Julius II.
Cf. Att. — Zimm. — P. de U. — Baud. —
(See also Proprium Camald.)

BENEDICT de PONTE (Bl) C. O.P.
P.C. Nov. 22
13th cent. Dominican missionary among
the Tartars. He died immediately after
preaching a sermon.
Cf. Baud.

BENEDICTA (St) V.M. **R.M. Jan. 4**
See Priscus, Priscillian and Benedicta.

BENEDICTA (St) V. **R.M. May 6**
6th cent. A nun of the convent founded
in Rome by St Galla, of whom St Gregory

the Great narrates that her death was foretold to her by St Peter in a vision.
Cf. Baud. — Holw. — Bolland.

BENEDICTA (St) V. M.?   R.M. June 29
? The R.M. styles her simply "a virgin in the territory of Sens." Later legends add that she was a sister of SS Augustine and Sanctian, all three natives of Spain, and that they passed into France and were martyred under Aurelian.
Cf. Baud. — Holw. — P.B.

BENEDICTA and CAECILIA (SS) Abs. O.S.B.   P.C. Aug. 17
10th cent. These two daughters of the king of Lorraine became nuns and successive abbesses of Susteren in the Rhineland.
Cf. Chev. — Baud. — Holw. — Bolland.

BENEDICTA (St) V. M.   R.M. Oct. 8
? The R.M. has only this *laus*: "In the country of Laon (the birthday) of St Benedicta, Virgin and Martyr." Further details, added by later writers, are conflicting.
Cf. Baud. — Holw. — P.B.

**BENEDICTINE MARTYRS (BB)
                              A.C. Dec. 1**
See Richard Whiting, Hugh Faringdon and John Beche.

BÉNÉZET (St) C.   A.C. Apr. 14
See Benedict the Bridge-Builder.

BENIGNUS (St) M.   R.M. Feb. 13
d. c.303. A priest of Todi in Umbria, put to death under Diocletian.
Cf. Baud. — Holw. — Ruinart.

**BENIGNUS (St) Ab. O.S.B.
                          A.C. March 20**
d. 725. Monk and abbot of Fontenelle, he was exiled from the abbey and retired to Flay where the monks asked him to be their abbot. He returned to Fontenelle, retaining the government of Flay, and died shortly after.
Cf. Mab. — Chev. — Baud.

BENIGNUS (St) M.   R.M. Apr. 3
See Evagrius and Benignus.

**BENIGNUS (St) Mk. O.S.B. Cist.
                           P.C. June 20**
13th cent. Cistercian monk at Breslau,

in Silesia, martyred by the Tartars with many other members of his abbey. The Cistercian menologies commemorate him on June 20.
Cf. Chev. — Baud.

BENIGNUS (St) Bp. M.   R.M. June 28
6th cent. This bishop is mentioned in a decretal of Pope Pelagius II as desirous of resigning his see. He appears to have retired to Utrecht; at any rate the R.M. places him there, and his relics were there rediscovered in 996.
Cf. Baud. — Holw.

BENIGNUS VISDOMINI (Bl) Ab. O.S.B. Vall.   A.C. July 17
d. 1236. A Florentine priest, who fell into sin, repented and entered the abbey of Vallombrosa. He became abbot-general but, always conscious of his past guilt, resigned and died as a hermit.
Cf. Chev. — P. de U. — Baud. — Zimm.

**BENIGNUS (St) Mk. O.S.B.
                          A.C. July 21**
See John and Benignus.

BENIGNUS (St) M.   R.M. Nov. 1
3rd cent. A martyr venerated at Dijon from early times, over whose tomb there was erected the magnificent abbey church — now cathedral — of St Benignus. His alleged connection with St Polycarp of Smyrna is rejected by most modern writers.
Cf. Att. — Baud. — Holw.

**BENIGNUS (BENEN) (St) Bp.
                           A.C. Nov. 9**
d. c.466. "Benen, son of Sessenen, St Patrick's Psalmsinger." A favourite disciple of St Patrick, whom he succeeded as chief bishop of the Irish church. He preached, it is said, chiefly in Clare and Kerry and founded a monastery at Drumlease. His connection with Glastonbury has no historical foundation.
Cf. Att. — Holw.

BENIGNUS (St) Bp.   R.M. Nov. 20
d. c.477. Archbishop of Milan, during whose pontificate the Heruli, under Odoacer, occupied the city.
Cf. Baud. — Holw.

BENILDIS (St) M.   R.M. June 15
d. 853. A woman of Cordova, who was so

moved by the fortitude displayed by St Athanasius, a Spanish priest, during his martyrdom at the hands of the Moors, that she braved death at the stake on the following day. Her ashes were thrown into the Guadalquivir.
Cf. P. de U. — Baud. — Holw.

BENINCASA (Bl) Ab. O.S.B.
A.C. Jan. 10
d. 1194. Eighth abbot of La Cava, near Salerno, from 1171 to 1194. It was during his abbacy that a hundred monks were sent from Cava to staff the new monastery of Monreale recently founded by the king of Sicily in that island. Beatified in 1928.
Cf. Chev. — Baud. — Holw.

BENINCASA (Bl) C. O.S.M. A.C. May 11
1376-1426. A native of Florence, who joined the Servites at Montepulciano. He spent his whole life as a hermit, first at Montagnata, near Siena, and then in the almost inaccessible cave of Montechiello. Cult confirmed in 1829.
Cf. Att. — Baud. — Holw.

BENJAMIN (St) M. R.M. March 31
c. 421. A Persian deacon who, having been imprisoned for the Faith, and refusing as a condition of his release to cease preaching Christianity, was tortured to death under Isdegerdes.
Cf. Baud. — Att. — Holw

BENNO (St) Bp. R.M. June 16
1010-1106. Born at Hildesheim and educated at the abbey of St Michael in his native city. He became canon of Gozlar, chaplain to the emperor Henry III and finally bishop of Meissen. He is one of the protagonists in the quarrel between Pope Gregory VII and Henry IV. He upheld the former but not at all times with equal zeal. In later years he preached to the Wends. His canonization in 1525 roused Luther to fury.
Cf. Att. — Zimm. — Baud. (twice: Beunon and Bennon.)

BENNO (Bl) Bp. O.S.B. A.C. July 12
d. 1088. A Swabian, he was educated and professed as a Benedictine at Reichenau, where he was taught by Bl Herman the Cripple. He himself became the headmaster at Gozlar in Hanover, and finally of the cathedral school of Hildesheim. He was also the official architect to Henry III. He was archbishop of Osnabrück (1067) and as such always upheld the pope's cause. He founded Iburg abbey where he retired to die.
Cf. Att. — Holw.

BENNO (Bl) Bp. O.S.B. A.C. Aug. 3
d. 940. A Swabian, canon of Strasburg, he became a hermit on Mt Etzel, in Switzerland, St Meinrad's former hermitage, whose shrine of our Lady Bl Benno restored. He lived there with a few disciples, thus becoming the founder of the abbey of Einsiedeln, which still exists. In 927 he was called to the see of Metz. Striving to remedy abuses, he was attacked and blinded by those whom he had rebuked. He resigned and returned to Einsiedeln, which had already grown into a numerous community.
Cf. Att. — Baud. — Holw.

BENTIVOGLIO de BONIS (Bl) C. O.F.M.
A.C. Jan. 2
d. 1232 (Dec. 25). Born at San Severino, in the Italian Marches, he was one of St Francis's earliest disciples, and as such he is mentioned in the *Fioretti*. Cult confirmed by Pius IX.
Cf. Att. — Holw.

BENVENUTA BOJANI (Bl) V. Tert. O.P. A.C. Oct. 30
d. 1292. The seventh of seven daughters, christened by her parents Benvenuta, although they had asked for a son. Having become a Dominican tertiary at an early age, she spent her whole life at her home in Cividale, N. Italy, busy with her domestic duties, praying, and working miracles. Cult approved in 1763.
Cf. Att. — Holw. — Baud.

BENVENUTUS SCOTIVOLI (St) Bp. O.F.M. R.M. March 22
d. 1282. Born at Ancona, he studied law at Bologna, where he was a fellow-student of St Sylvester. Soon he was appointed archdeacon of Ancona, and finally bishop of Osimo. Before his consecration he professed the Franciscan Rule and donned the Franciscan habit. Canonized by Martin IV.
Cf. Att. — Holw. — Baud.

BENVENUTUS of RECANATI (Bl) C. O.F.M. A.C. May 21
d. 1289. Born at Recanati, near Loreto,

of the Mareni family. He joined the Friars Minor as a lay-brother and was mostly employed in the kitchen, where he was constantly favoured with ecstasies and visions. Cult confirmed by Pius VII. *Cf. Att. — Baud. — Holw.*

BENVENUTUS of GUBBIO (Bl) C. **O.F.M.** A.C. June 27
d. 1232. An uncouth soldier, he was received into the Franciscan order by St Francis himself. At his own request the new friar was allowed to tend lepers, a task which he carried out with the utmost charity. Cult authorized by Gregory IX. *Cf. Att. — Baud. — Holw.*

BEOADH (BEATUS) (St) Bp. A.C. March 8
d. between 518 and 525. Aeodh (Aidus), an Irish saint, acquired the prefix *Bo* on account of the greatness of his virtues, and was appointed bishop of Ardcarne (Roscommon). The "Bell of St Beoadh," a beautiful work of art, was long in veneration as a relic of the saint. *Cf. Baud. — O'Hanlon.*

BEOC (BEANUS, DABEOC, MOBEOC) (St) Ab. A.C. Jan. 1
5th (or 6th) cent. By race he was a Cambro-Briton. He crossed over from Wales to Ireland and founded a monastery on an island in Lough Derg, Donegal. *Cf. Holw. — O'Hanlon.*

BEOCCA, ETHOR and Comp. (SS) MM. **O.S.B.** A.C. Apr. 10
d. c.870. The Danes, in their continuous raids on England, singled out the Anglo-Saxon abbeys as the special object of their ferocity. Thus at Chertsey Abbey in Surrey, they put to death SS Beocca, abbot, Ethor, monk-priest, and some ninety monks; at Peterborough, they killed St Hedda, abbot, and others of his community; at Thorney Abbey, St Torthred and others. All were justly venerated as martyrs. *Cf. Att. — Stanton. — Baud. — Holw.*

BERACH (BARACHIAS, BERACHIUS) (St) Ab. A.C. Feb. 15
6th cent. From his birth he was placed under the care of his uncle, St Freoch, and St Patrick predicted his future sanctity. He afterwards became St Kevin's disciple, and founded an abbey at Clusin-

Coirpte, in Connaught. He is the patron saint of Kilbarry, County Dublin. *Cf. Baud. — Holw.*

BERARDUS, PETER, OTTO, ACCURSIUS and ADJUTUS (SS) MM. O.F.M. R.M. Jan. 16
d. 1220. Sent by St Francis to evangelize the Mohammedans of the West, these friars travelled from Italy to Aragon, then to Coimbra in Portugal, to Seville and finally to Morocco, where they were beheaded. Berardus, Peter and Otto were priests, Adjutus and Accursius laybrothers. Canonized in 1481. *Cf. Att. — Holw. — Baud.*

BERARIUS (St) Bp. A.C. Oct. 17
d. c.680. Bishop of Le Mans. During his episcopate St Scholastica's relics were translated from Montecassino to Le Mans. *Cf. Duch. Fast. Episc. — Gams — Baud.— Holw. — P.B.*

BERCHAM (St) Bp. A.C. Apr. 6
Otherwise Berthanc, q.v.

BERCHARIUS (St) Ab. M. O.S.B. R.M. Oct. 16
d. 696. Monk of Luxeuil and first abbot of Hautvilliers, which had been founded by St Nivard, bishop of Reims. St Bercharius himself founded two new houses, Moutier-en-Der for monks, and Puelle-moutier for nuns. He went on pilgrimage to Rome and Palestine and on his return settled at Moutier-en-Der. A young monk, whom he had corrected, fatally stabbed him by night. Bercharius died, forgiving his murderer, and is venerated as a martyr. *Cf. Att. — Baud. — Chev. — Holw.*

BERCTHUN (BERTIN) (St) Ab. O.S.B. A.C. Sept. 24
d. 733. A disciple of St John of Beverley and by him appointed first abbot of Beverley, where he died *Cf. Stanton — Holw.*

BERCTUALD (St) Ab. O.S.B. A.C. Jan. 9
Otherwise Brithwald, q.v.

BERE, RICHARD (Bl) M. A.C. May 4
See Carthusian Martyrs.

BEREGISUS (St) C. A.C. Oct. 2
d. p. 725. A priest, confessor of Pepin

of Heristal, with whose help he founded the abbey of Saint-Hubert, in the Ardennes. It is not certain if he was himself a monk, although some writers call him abbot.

Cf. Chev. — Zimm. — Baud.

BERENCARDUS (BERENGER) (St) C. O.S.B. A.C. May 26

d. 1293. Born near Toulouse, he became a Benedictine at the abbey of St Papoul in Languedoc. After his ordination he filled the offices of novice-master, almoner and master of works (*operarius*) of the abbey. He was noted for his kind charity and patience.

Cf. Zimm. — Chev. — Baud. — Holw. — P.B.

BERENGARIUS (Bl) Ab. O.S.B. A.C. Oct. 29

d. 1108. First abbot of the Benedictine abbey of Formbach in Bavaria (1094-1108.)

Cf. Zimm. — Chev.

BERENICE (St) M. A.C. Oct. 4

See Domnina, Berenice and Prosdoce.

BERLINDA (BERLINDIS, BELLAUDE) (St) V. O.S.B. A.C. Feb. 3

d. 702. A niece of St Amandus, she became a Benedictine nun of St Mary's convent, at Mooriel, near Alost, in Belgium, and afterwards a recluse at Meerbeke.

Cf. Mab. — Att. — Baud.

BERNARDETTE (BERNARDETTA, BERNARDA) (St) V. A.C. Apr. 16

1844-1879. Born at Lourdes, Bernardette Soubirous was the daughter of a miller in very poor circumstances. When she was fourteen years of age, she was favoured with a series of apparitions of our Lady, who chose the uneducated peasant girl to reveal to the world the healing shrine at Lourdes. In 1866 she joined the Institute of the Sisters of Notre Dame at Nevers, where her one desire was to remain hidden and forgotten by the world. Canonized in 1933.

Cf. A.A. S.

BERNARD of CORLEONE (Bl) C. O.F.M. Cap. A.C. Jan. 19

1605-1667. Born at Corleone in Sicily, Philip Latini, a shoemaker by trade, was reckoned "the best swordsman of Sicily."

After an assault on the police, he took sanctuary in the church of the Capuchin friars at Palermo, was there and then converted and joined them as a lay-brother (1632) and henceforth became "a prodigy of austerity" till his death. Beatified in 1768.

Cf. Holw. — Att. — Baud.

BERNARD of LIPPE (Bl) Bp. O.S.B. Cist. P.C. Jan. 23

d. 1217. Count of Lippe in Westphalia. He professed the Cistercian Rule and was made abbot of Dünemunde, and later bishop of Semgallen in Kurland.

Cf. Holw.

BERNARD SCAMMACCA (Bl) C. O.P. A.C. Feb. 16

d. 1486. A native of Catania, he belonged to a wealthy family, and in his youth gave himself up to riotous living until, made wiser by a serious illness, he changed his ways and joined the Friars Preachers. As a friar he atoned by a life of continuous penance for his former evil courses. Cult approved in 1825.

Cf. Att. — Holw. — Baud.

BERNARD of CARINOLA (St) Bp. R.M. March 12

d. 1109. A native of Capua, he was appointed bishop of Forum Claudii in 1087 by Pope Victor III. He transferred the see (1100) to Carinola. Both cities belong to the Italian province of *Terra di Lavoro*. St Bernard died in extreme old age. He is now the principal patron saint of Carinola.

Cf. Holw. — Baud. — Att.

BERNARD of THIRON (or of ABBE-VILLE) (St) Ab. O.S.B. A.C. Apr. 14

1046-1117. Born near Abbeville, Bernard professed the Benedictine Rule at St Cyprian's, Poitiers, and later was appointed prior of St Sabinus. After some twenty years in this office he retired as a recluse to Craon. He was next made abbot of St Cyprian's, but soon retired again to the forest of Thiron in Picardy, where he founded the Congregation of that name, of which the main feature was hard manual labour. The Congregation spread rapidly throughout France, England and Scotland. Cult as a saint confirmed in 1861.

Cf. Zimm. — P. de U. — Baud. — Att.

BERNARD the PENITENT (Bl) Mk.
O.S.B. A.C. Apr. 19
d. 1182. A native of Provence who, owing to some horrible crime which he had committed, was sentenced by the bishop of Maguelone to seven years public penance. He performed this penance loaded with seven heavy iron bands, which he dragged from shrine to shrine — Compostella, Rome, Palestine — until he came to the abbey of St Bertin (Sithin), where he first lived as a hermit and then ventured to ask the monks to receive him in their community. The monks welcomed him with open arms, for they already regarded him as a saint. He died in the Benedictine habit. *Cf. Holw. — Att. — P. de U. — Zimm. — Chev. — Baud.*

BERNARD of MENTHON (St) C. O.S.A.
R.M. May 28
d. c.1081. For forty years he served the bishop of Aosta as vicar-general of the diocese, visiting every mountain and valley in the Alps, and taking particular care of travellers. For this purpose he established two hospices on the great and little passes which bear his name, placing them under Augustinian canons regular. Pius XI named him patron saint of mountaineers. *Cf. Att.*

BERNARD, MARY and GRACIA (GRACE) (SS) MM. O.S.B. Cist
A.C. June 1
d. c.1180. Children of Almanzor, the Mohammedan caliph of Lérida in Catalonia. Their Moorish names were respectively Achmed, Zoraida and Zaida. Achmed was converted to Christianity and became a Cistercian monk at Poblet (Populetum) near Tarragona, under the name of Bernard. He in his turn converted his two sisters, who were in some way affiliated to the Cistercian Order. As a result of their endeavour to convert their brother Almanzor, they were handed over by him to the executioners and martyred *in odium fidei.* They are the patron saints of Alcira, in Valencia, Spain. *Cf. P. de U. — Prop. Cist. — Holw. — Baud.*

BERNARD of BADEN (Bl) C.
A.C. July 15
1428-1458. Margrave of Baden, he renounced the rights of his title in favour of his brother and offered himself to several European courts to organize a crusade against the Turks. He died without having attained his object. Cult confirmed in 1481 and again in 1769. *Cf. Att. — Baud.*

BERNARD of RODEZ (de RUTHENIS) (Bl) Card. O.S.B. A.C. July 19
d. 1079. Abbot of St Victor at Marseilles (1064). A fast friend of SS Gregory VII, Hugh of Cluny and William of Hirschau, he zealously fostered the Cluniac observance. He was made cardinal and sent as papal legate to Germany (1077) and Spain (1078). *Cf. Zimm. — Chev. — (see also Holw. — Baud. — P.L.)*

BERNARD DUE (Bl) M. A.C. Aug. 1
1755-1838. A native of Tonkin, he helped the missionary priests for over fifty years and finally voluntarily shared their prison and was beheaded for his constancy. Beatified 1900. *Cf. Holw.*

BERNARD of CLAIRVAUX (St) Ab. Dr.
O.S.B. Cist. R.M. Aug. 20
1091-1153. Born near Dijon, at the age of twenty-two he joined (1113) the recently founded struggling abbey of Cîteaux, after having persuaded thirty other young noblemen to follow him thither. Scarcely had he finished his novitiate when he was sent as abbot-founder to Clairvaux (1115) and as such became the real founder of the Cistercians. During his lifetime he established sixty-eight Cistercian houses, was the adviser of popes, kings and councils, the preacher of the second crusade (which, however, was a failure), the arbiter of Europe, who, as has been said, "carried the 12th century on his shoulders." In the theological field, he confuted Abelard, wrote profusely on the love of God, commented for his monks on the *Song of Songs,* sent a noble treatise, *De consideratione,* to his former monk, Pope Eugene III, and produced many other works. He was declared a doctor in 1830 and is known as the *Doctor Mellifluus* ("the Honeysweet Doctor"). In art he is often represented with three mitres on a book or at his feet, in allusion to his having refused three bishoprics. *Cf. Mab. — Bolland. — Zimm. — Att. — Chev*

BERNARD of VALDEIGLESIAS (St)
Mk. O.S.B.   A.C. Aug. 20
d. p. 1155. A monk of Valdeiglesias in
Spanish Galicia. He is the patron saint
of Candelada.
Cf. Zimm. — Chev.

BERNARD TOLOMEO (Bl) Founder,
O.S.B. Oliv.   R.M. Aug. 21
1272-1348. Born at Siena, he was educated by his uncle, a Dominican friar. He
studied law, and filled several municipal
offices, including that of *podestà* (mayor).
In 1313 he withdrew to a place ten miles
from the city and there he became the
founder of the abbey and Congregation of
Montoliveto. He was summoned to
Avignon to give an account of this new
foundation, and received papal approval
(1324). After years spent in wonderful
deeds of charity, he died of the pestilence
whilst nursing the sick, together with some
eighty of his monks. Cult officially approved in 1644. Among the Olivetans he
is usually given the title of Saint.
Cf. Att. — Zimm. — Chev. — Baud. — P.
de U. — Holw.

BERNARD of OFFIDA (Bl) C. O.F.M.
Cap.   A.C. Aug. 22
1604-1694. An Italian peasant, born at
Appignano, diocese of Ascoli-Piceno. He
took his vows as a Capuchin lay-brother
at Offida and here, and at the friary of
Fermo, he became famous for his wisdom
and miracles.
Cf. Att. — Baud. — Holw.

BERNARD of ARCE (St) C.
                             R.M. Oct. 14
9th cent. Either an Englishman or a
Frenchman, who undertook a pilgrimage
to the Holy Land and Rome and then lived
as a recluse at Arpino in the Campagna.
His relics are enshrined at Rocca d'Arce.
Cf. Baud. — Holw.

BERNARD of BAGNOREA (or of Castro)
(St) Bp.   A.C. Oct. 20
d. p. 800. A native of Bagnorea, he was
chosen bishop of Vulcia in Tuscany,
whence he transferred the see to Ischia di
Castro.
Cf. Holw.

BERNARD CALVO (St) Bp. O.S.B. Cist.
                             A.C. Oct. 24
d. 1243. A native of Manso Calvo, in
Catalonia, he became a Cistercian and
eventually the first abbot of Santas Creus,
near Tarragona. In 1233 he was chosen
bishop of Vich.
Cf. P. de U. — Zimm. — Prop. Cist. —
Gams — Chev. — Holw.

BERNARD de la TOUR (Bl) C. O.Cart.
                             P.C. Oct. 30
d. 1258. A Carthusian monk of Portes,
diocese of Belley, who became the thirteenth superior general of the Order.
Cf. Holw. — Baud. — P.B.

BERNARD of HILDESHEIM (St) Bp.
                             R.M. Nov. 20
Otherwise Bernward, q.v.

BERNARD of TOULOUSE (Bl) M. O.P.
                             P.C. Dec. 3
d. 1320. A Dominican friar, who in his
campaign against the Albigenses was
seized by them, put to torture and sawn in
two.
Cf. Holw. — Baud. — P.B.

BERNARD degli UBERTI (St) Bp.
O.S.B. Vall.   R.M. Dec. 4
d. 1133. A native of Florence, he was
professed a monk at Vallombrosa. He
was appointed successively abbot of San
Salvi, general of Vallombrosa, cardinal
(1097), papal legate and finally bishop of
Parma (1106), at that time the storm-
centre of the anti-pope's supporters.
Twice he was exiled, but he proved a most
successful prelate.
Cf. Att. — Baud. — Chev. — Prop. Vall.

BERNARD (or BERARD) PALEARA (St)
Bp. O.S.B.   A.C. Dec. 19
d. 1122. A monk of Montecassino, chosen
bishop of Teramo in 1115. He is venerated as the principal patron saint of
Teramo.
Cf. Gams — Chev. — Holw.

BERNARDINUS of SIENA (St) C. O.F.M.
                             R.M. May 20
1380-1444. Born on Sept. 8 at Massa
Maritima near Siena, of the family
degl'Albizzeschi. He took the Franciscan
habit (Sept. 8, 1402), and was ordained
priest (Sept. 8, 1404) and, having preached
his first sermon (Sept. 8, 1417), his career
as a preacher ended only with his life. He
was accounted the foremost Italian
missioner of the 15th century. He was

particularly eloquent when preaching on the Holy Name of Jesus, devotion to which he spread far and wide. He was also responsible for the revival of discipline among the Franciscans, and from 1438 to 1442 he was vicar-general of the order. Canonized in 1450. In art he is represented holding to his breast the monogram of the Sacred Name — IHS.
Cf. Att. — Holw. — Baud.

BERNARDINUS REALINI (Bl) C. S.J.
A.C. July 3
1530-1616. A native of Modena, he became a lawyer, but when aged thirty-four joined the Society of Jesus. He worked for ten years at Naples and was then appointed rector of the college at Lecce, where he died. Beatified by Leo XIII.
Cf. Holw. — Baud. — Att.

BERNARDINUS of FELTRE (Bl) C. O.F.M.   **A.C. Sept. 28**
c.1439-1494. A native of Feltre, his baptismal name was Martin Tomitani. He took his vows as a Franciscan and was first employed as a teacher in various houses of the order, but developed before long into a tempestuous preacher, the terror of all evil-doers, but especially of usurers. To protect the people against these he suggested the establishment of *monti di pietà*, of which he organized over thirty in various Italian cities. Beatified in 1728.
Cf. Att. — Baud. — Holw.

BERNARDINUS of FOSSA (Bl) C. O.F.M.   **A.C. Nov. 27**
d. 1503. Bernardino Amici was born at Fossa, diocese of Aquila in central Italy. In 1445 he received the Franciscan habit, and after filling successfully several offices in the order, he embarked on a career of mission-preaching throughout Italy, Dalmatia and Bosnia, being still engaged in this apostolate when he died at Aquila.
Cf. Att.— Holw. — Baud.

BERNO (St) Ab. O.S.B.   **A.C. Jan. 13**
d. 927. A native of Burgundy and a monk of St Martin, Autun. He was abbot restorer of Baume-les-Messieurs, where he gave the habit to St Odo in 909, and the abbot-founder of Gigny, Bourg-Dieu, Massay and finally of Cluny (910), which he governed till 926. In that year he resigned and was succeeded by St Odo.

History, whether sacred or profane, has done less than justice to St Berno for his great work for the Church and for civilization.
Cf. Att. — Chev. — Baud. — Zimm. — P. de U.

BERNOLD (Bl) Mk. O.S.B. A.C. Nov. 25.
d. c.1050. A monk-priest of Ottobeuren in Bavaria, renowned as a wonder-worker, especially after his death.
Cf. Zimm. — Chev. — Holw.

BERNWARD (BERWARD) (St) Bp. O.S.B.   **R.M. Nov. 20**
d. 1022. Bernward is one of the most attractive figures of medieval Germany — a German St Dunstan. He excelled as an architect, painter, sculptor, decorator and metal-smith. He was also the tutor of the emperor Otto III. In 993 he was made bishop of Hildesheim. He died "after having assumed the habit of St Benedict." (See Butler-Thurston). Canonized in 1193.
Cf. Att. — P. de U. — Chev. — Zimm. — Mab.

BERONIGUS, PELAGIA and Comp. (SS) MM.   **R.M. Oct. 19**
? A group of fifty-one Christians put to death at Antioch in Syria in one of the early persecutions.
Cf. Baud. — Holw.

BERTELLIN (St) C.   **A.C. Sept. 9**
Otherwise Bettelin, q.v.

BERTHA (Bl) Abs. O.S.B. Vall.
A.C. March 24
d. 1163. Born in Florence, a member of the Alberti family (she is often wrongly called de'Bardi). She became a nun at the Vallombrosan convent of St Felicitas at Florence, whence Bl Qualdo Galli, the general of the Vallombrosans, sent her to Cavriglia in the Valdardo, as abbess. She died ten years later on Easter Sunday.
Cf. Att. — Baud. — Holw. — Chev.

BERTHA (St) M.   **A.C. May 1**
d. p. 680. Abbess-foundress of Avenay, diocese of Châlons-sur-Marne. She was perfidiously put to death and is venerated as a martyr.
Cf. Zimm. — Baud. — Chev. — Holw.

BERTHA (St) A.C. May 15
See Rupert and Bertha.

BERTHA (St) W. O.S.B. A.C. July 4
d. c.725. A lady of high station, who
after her husband's death entered the
nunnery of Blangy, in Artois, which she
had founded, and became its abbess.
Cf. Att. — Chev. — Baud. — Holw.

BERTHA of MARBAIS (Bl) W. O.S.B.
Cist. P.C. July 18
d. 1247. A near relative of the count of
Flanders, she married the chatelain of
Molembais. Left a widow, she became a
Cistercian at Ayvrières. Her family
founded the nunnery of Marquette,
whither she was sent as abbess. She has
a liturgical cult in the diocese of Namur.
Cf. Baud. — Holw. — Chev.

BERTHALDUS (BERTAUD) (St) H.
A.C. June 16
d. c.540. A hermit in the Ardennes who
was ordained priest by St Remigius.
Cf. Att. — Baud.

BERTHANC (BERCHAN) (St) Bp.
A.C. Apr. 6
d. c.840. A Scottish saint, who is said to
have been a monk of Iona and later bishop
of Kirkwall in the Orkneys. He seems to
have died in Ireland, and his tomb was
shown at Inishmore in Galway Bay.
Hence perhaps his surname of Fer-da-
Leithe (the man of two parts or countries).
Cf. Holw. — O'Hanlon.

BERTHARIUS (St) Ab. M. O.S.B.
A.C. Oct. 22
d. c.884. A scion of the royal house of
France, he was professed at Montecassino
and chosen as its abbot in 856. While
kneeling in prayer he was martyred, with
several of his monks, by a band of invading
Saracens. He is the author of homilies,
poems, etc. One of the altars of Montecassino is consecrated in his name.
Cf. Zimm. — P. de U. — Chev. — Baud.

BERTHOALD (St) Bp. A.C. Oct. 13
7th cent. Fifth bishop of Cambrai Arras.
Cf. Duch. Fast. Episc. — Baud.

BERTHOLD (St) C. O.C. A.C. March 29
d. c.1195. A Frenchman and a brilliant
student at the university of Paris, he set
out for Palestine as a crusader. There he

joined the group of hermits who dwelt on
Mt Carmel and eventually was appointed
by this brother Aymeric, Latin patriarch
of Antioch, their first superior general.
For all practical purposes he may be considered the founder of the Carmelite order.
Cf. Att. — Baud. — Holw.

BERTHOLD of SCHEDA (Bl) C. O.
Praem. P.C. July 13
d. c.1214. Founder of the Premonstraten-
sian abbey of Frodenburg (Vrundeberg).
He was a brother of Bl Menrich of Lübeck.
Cf. Baud. — Holw.

BERTHOLD of GARSTEN (Bl) Ab.
O.S.B. A.C. July 27
1090-1142. Born on the shores of the lake
of Constance, Berthold belonged to the
family of the counts of Bogen. After a
short period of married life he was left a
widower at the age of thirty and at once
joined the Benedictines of Blasien in the
Black Forest. He became their prior, and
then prior of Gottweig in Austria and
abbot of Garsten in Styria, where he
founded a hospice for the poor. He enjoyed a great reputation as a confessor.
Cf. Att. — Baud. — Holw. — Chev.

BERTHOLD (BERTOLDO) (St) C.
O.S.B. A.C. Oct. 21
d. 1111. An Anglo-Saxon by descent, his
parents having fled from England at the
Norman Conquest, Berthold was born at
Parma. He spent his whole life as a lay-
brother in the service of the nuns of St
Alexander in that city.
Cf. Zimm. — Chev. — P. de U. — Baud.

BERTHOLD (Bl) Ab. O.S.B.
P.C. Nov. 3
d. 1197. A monk of Engelberg in Switzerland, who excelled as a transcriber of
books. He became the third abbot of the
monastery (1178). His memory is liturgically celebrated at Einsiedeln and Engelberg.
Cf. Holw. — Chev.

BERTILIA (St) V. A.C. Jan. 3
d. c.705. A noble maiden who together
with her husband took a vow of perpetual
continence, and on the death of the latter
lived as a recluse near a church she had
founded at Maroeuil (Marolles) in Flanders.
Cf. Att. — Baud. — Holw.

BERTILLA (St) V. O.S.B.   A.C. Nov. 5
d. c.705. A nun at Jouarre, near Meaux,
where she held the offices of infirmarian,
headmistress of the convent school and
prioress. When St Bathildis restored the
nunnery of Chelles, St Bertilla was made
its first abbess and she governed it for
half a century. Great numbers flocked to
her convent, including many Anglo-Saxon
girls.
Cf. Att. — Mab. — Chev. — Baud.

BERTILO (Bl) M. O.S.B. A.C. March 26
d. c.878-888. Abbot of St Benignus, at
Dijon. The Normans sacked his abbey
and massacred him and several of his community at the foot of the altar.
Cf. Mab. — Chev. — Holw.

**BERTINUS the YOUNGER (Bl) C.
O.S.B.   A.C. May 2**
d. c.699. Monk of Sithin under its
founder, St Bertin the Great.
Cf. Zimm.

BERTINUS (St) Ab. O.S.B. R.M. Sept. 5
d. c.709. Born near Constance, he became
a monk at Luxeuil under St Walbert, who
had introduced there the Benedictine
Rule. He was sent to help St Omer,
bishop of Thérouanne, by whom he was
made abbot of Sithin (afterwards called
St Bertin). Under his government the
community increased in a remarkable
manner, and he was obliged to establish
several new houses. He is one of the
greatest of Benedictine abbots.
*Cf. Mab. — Chev. — Baud. — Zimm. —
Att. — Holw.*

BERTOARA (St) Abs.   A.C. Dec. 4
d. p. 614. Abbess of Notre-Dame-de-
Sales, in Bourges (612-614) under the
Columbanian Rule.
Cf. Baud. — Zimm. — Holw.

BERTRAM (St) C.   A.C. Sept. 9
Otherwise Bettelin, q.v.

**BERTRAND (BERTRAM, BERTRAN,
EBERTRAM) (St) Ab. O.S.B. A.C. Jan. 24**
7th cent. One of St Bertinus's disciples,
and one of St Omer's helpers in the
evangelization of N. France and Flanders.
At a later date he was made abbot of Saint-
Quentin.
Cf. Chev. — Baud. — Holw. — P.B.

BERTRAND (St) Bp. M.   A.C. June 6
1260-1350. Born near Cahors, he became
dean of the cathedral chapter of Angoulême, from which position he was
raised to the patriarchate of Aquileia.
He met his death in defence of the rights
of his church. Cult approved by Benedict
XIV.
Cf. Baud. — Holw.

**BERTRAND (BERTICHRAMNUS) (St)
Bp.   A.C. June 30**
d. 623. A native of Autun, he was educated by St Germanus at Paris, and
appointed archdeacon of that city and
some time later bishop of Le Mans. He
took a great interest in agriculture and
wine-growing. He was especially noted
for his benefactions to the poor.
*Cf. Att. — Baud. — Holw. — Duch. Fast
Episc.*

**BERTRAND of GARRIGUE (Bl) C. O.P.
                            A.C. Sept. 6**
d. 1230. A native of Garrigue, diocese of
Nîmes. He was already a secular priest
when he became a disciple of St Dominic
and helped him in his first foundation at
Paris. He was the constant companion of
the holy founder until his appointment as
provincial of the Dominicans in Provence.
Cult confirmed by Leo XIII.
Cf. Att. — Holw. — Baud.

**BERTRAND of COMMINGES (St) Bp.
                            A.C. Oct. 16**
d. 1123. The most celebrated of the
bishops of Comminges (now included in
the diocese of Toulouse), he may be considered as the second founder of his episcopal city. He was its pastor for fifty
years — energetic, fearless, enterprising,
zealous. Canonized by Alexander III.
Cf. Att. — Baud. — Holw.

**BERTRAND of GRANDSELVE (Bl) Ab.
O.S.B. Cist.   A.C. Oct. 23**
d. 1149 (July 11). Cistercian abbot of
Grandselve for twenty years. He was
often favoured with heavenly visions.
*Cf. Chev. — Baud. — Holw. — (Butler-
Thurston, Oct. p. 16)*

BERTUIN (St) Bp. O.S.B.   A.C. Nov. 11
d. c.698. An Anglo-Saxon monk of the
small abbey of Othelle. He was consecrated a missionary bishop, left for Rome
where he spent two years, and finally be-

came the abbot-founder of the abbey of Malonne, in the territory of Namur, henceforward the centre of his missionary labours.
Cf. Zimm. — Holw. — Baud.

BERTULFUS (BERTHULPH) (St) Ab. O.S.B. A.C. Feb. 5
d. 705. Born in Pannonia, a pagan, he migrated to Flanders, where he became a Christian and a priest. Count Wambert entrusted to him the administration of his estate, and gave him the land of Renty. Here the saint founded an abbey whither he retired after his benefactor's death.
Cf. Att. — Baud. — Holw.

BERTULFUS (St) Ab. A.C. Aug. 19
d. 640. Of Frankish origin, he entered the abbey of Luxeuil and was professed there under St Eustace. Then he migrated to Bobbio, where he was chosen abbot on St Attalas's death (637). As abbot of Bobbio he is best remembered for having obtained from Pope Honorius I the exemption of his abbey from episcopal jurisdiction, the first case recorded in history.
Cf. Att. — Chev. — P. de U. — Baud. — Zimm.

BESAS (St) M. R.M. Feb. 27
See Julian, Eunus and Besas.

BESSARION (St) H. R.M. June 17
d. c.400. One of the fathers of the Egyptian desert, greatly venerated among the Greeks, who keep his feast on June 6.
Cf. Baud. — Holw.

BETTELIN (BETHLIN, BETHELM) (St) H. O.S.B. A.C. Sept. 9
8th cent. Disciple of St Guthlac of Croyland. After the death of his master, Bettelin and his companions lived at Croyland under Kenulphus, first abbot of the monastery founded there by King Ethelbald of Mercia. A saint of the name of Bettelin was patron of the town of Stafford.
Cf. Att. — Baud. — Holw.

BETTO (St) Bp. O.S.B. P.C. Feb. 24
d. 918. A Benedictine monk of the abbey of Sainte-Colombe, at Sens, who became bishop of Auxerre in 889.
Cf. Gams — Baud. — Chev.

BEUNO (St) Ab. A.C. Apr. 21
d. c.630. A Welshman by birth, he was the founder of several monasteries; but his name is chiefly connected with that of Clynnog in Carnarvonshire. His memory has been revived in modern times by the Jesuit establishment of St Beuno's College, in N. Wales.
Cf. Att. — Baud. — Holw.

BEUVE (St) V. O.S.B. A.C. Apr. 24
Otherwise Bova, q.v.

BIANOR and SYLVANUS (SS) MM. R.M. July 10
4th cent. Martyrs beheaded in Pisidia, in Asia Minor. Their extant Greek Acts are untrustworthy.
Cf. Holw. — Baud.

BIBIANA (VIBIANA, VIVIAN) (St) V.M. R.M. Dec. 2
? A virgin martyred at Rome. This is all that is certain about her. Her *acta* are a medieval romance, much read and admired throughout Europe, and especially in Germany and Spain, as witness the great number of churches dedicated in her honour.
Cf. Att. — Baud. — Holw.

BIBLIG (PEBLIG) (St) A.C. July 3
Otherwise Byblig, q.v.

BIBLIS (or BIBLIDES) (St) M. R.M. June 2
One of the martyrs of Lyons. See Pothinus (Photinus) and Comp.

BICOR (St) M. R.M. Apr. 22
See Persia (Martyrs of).

BIEUZY (St) M. A.C. Nov. 24
7th cent. A native of Britain who followed St Gildas to Brittany. We have no particulars of his life or of the martyrdom which closed it.
Cf. Baud. — Duch. Fast. Episc. (Vannes).

BILFRID (BILLFRITH) (St) H. O.S.B. A.C. March 6
d. c.758. A monk-hermit of Lindisfarne and an expert goldsmith, who bound in gold the Lindisfarne copy of the Gospels, written and illuminated by bishop Eaddfrid. In life and in death he was the centre of great popular veneration.
Cf. Zimm. — Baud. — Holw.

BILHILD (St) W. O.S.B.   A.C. Nov. 27
c.630-c.710. Born near Würzburg, Bilhild married the duke of Thuringia.
After the death of her husband, she became the abbess-foundress of the nunnery
of Altenmünster in Mainz.
*Cf. Zimm. — Chev. — P. de U. — Baud.
— Holw.*

BIRGITTA (St) W.   R.M. Oct. 8
Otherwise Brigid of Sweden, q.v.

BIRILLUS (St) Bp.   R.M. March 21
d. c.90. Said to have been consecrated
first bishop of Catania in Sicily by St Peter
the Apostle, with whom he had travelled
from Antioch. He died in extreme old age.
Cf. Baud. — Holw. — Gams.

BIRINUS (St) Bp.   R.M. Dec. 3
d. c.650. A Roman missionary priest
commonly said to have been a monk, who
offered himself for the foreign missions and
was sent by Pope St Honorius to Britain.
He was consecrated bishop at Genoa and
on his arrival in England converted
Cynegils, king of the West Saxons, and
was given Dorchester in Oxfordshire for
his see. He is known as the "Apostle of
Wessex."
Cf. Gams — Att. — Chev. — Holw.

**BIRNSTAN (BIRRSTAN, BRYNSTAN)
(St) Bp. O.S.B.   A.C. Nov. 4**
d. c.934. Successor of St Frithestan in
the see of Winchester and a disciple of
St Grimbald. He was noted for his devotion to the holy souls in Purgatory.
Cf. Baud. — Holw. — Stanton.

BITEUS (St) C.   A.C. July 22
Otherwise Movean, q.v.

**BITHEUS and GENOCUS (SS) CC.
A.C. Apr. 18**
6th cent. Two British monks who accompanied St Finnian of Clonard to
Ireland, and there attained a great reputation for sanctity.
Cf. Holw.

BLAAN (St) Bp.   A.C. Aug. 10
Otherwise Blane, q.v.

BLADUS (St) Bp.   A.C. July 3
? According to tradition, one of the early
bishops of the Isle of Man.
Cf. Holw.

BLAESILLA (St) W.   A.C. Jan. 22
d. 383. Daughter of St Paula and a disciple of St Jerome. In her widowhood she
consecrated herself to God. She died in
Rome aged twenty.
Cf. Att.

**BLAISE (BLASIUS, BLASE) (St) Bp. M.
R.M. Feb. 3**
d. c.316. According to his legendary acts,
which became widely known in W.
Europe at the time of the crusades, Blaise
was a physician who became bishop of
Sebaste in Armenia, where he was martyred. One of his miracles was the saving
of the life of a boy who had half swallowed
a fish-bone which could not be extricated;
hence the rite of the *Blessing of St Blaise*,
incorporated in the Roman Ritual, against
affections of the throat. His feast is observed with much solemnity throughout
the East, as was also the case, in ancient
times, in the West. The popularity of the
saint may be inferred from the variants of
his name: Biagio in Italian; Blas in
Spanish; Blaise in French; Blaz in Portuguese; Blasien in German. He is the
patron saint of physicians, wool-combers
and wax-chandlers.
Cf. Att. — Baud. — Holw.

**BLAISE of AUVERGNE (Bl) C. O.P.
A.C. Apr. 5**
14th cent. A disciple of St Vincent
Ferrer, and like him an impassioned Do-
minican preacher.
Cf. Baud. — Holw.

**BLAISE and DEMETRIUS (SS) MM.
R.M. Nov. 29**
? Martyrs of Veroli in central Italy.
Their connection with St Mary Salome is
discarded by most writers.
Cf. Baud. — Holw

**BLAITHMAIC (BLATHMAC, BLAITH-
MALE) (St) M.   A.C. Jan. 15**
d. c.823. An Irish abbot, who, desirous of
martyrdom, crossed over to England, then
a prey to heathen Danes. He was murdered by the Danes on the altar steps of
the abbey church at Iona. Walafrid
Strabo narrates his life in verse.
Cf. Baud. — Holw. — Mab.

BLANCA W.   A.C. Apr. 26
Otherwise Alda, q.v.

BLANCHE (*several*)
Otherwise Gwen, q.v.

BLANDA (St) M.   R.M. May 10
See Calepodius, Palmutius, etc.

BLANDINA (St) M.   R.M. June 2
See Photinus (Pothinus) and Comp.

BLANE (**BLAAN, BLAIN**) (St) Bp.
     A.C. Aug. 10
6th cent. A Scottish bishop, disciple of
SS Comgall and Canice in Ireland, who
flourished in the 6th century, and was
buried at the place now called Dunblane.
There has been such controversy over the
actual dates of his life; but the above
summary is now commonly agreed upon
by scholars.
Cf. Att. — Holw. — Bolland.

BLATH (**FLORA**) (St) V.   A.C. Jan. 29
d. 523. In the Irish martyrologies several
saints are registered under the name
Blath (latinized Flora). The one best
remembered was a lay-sister, the cook in
St Brigid's nunnery at Kildare, where she
earned a great reputation for sanctity.
Cf. Holw. — O'Hanlon.

BLEDRWS (St)
? There is a church in Cardiganshire
named after St Bledrws, but it has not
been found possible to identify the saint.

BLEIDDAN (**BLEWDIAN**) (St) Bp.
     R.M. July 29
Otherwise Lupus of Troyes, q.v.

BLENWYDD (St)
? The dedication of a chapel to this saint
in the Isle of Anglesey is all that perpetuates his memory.
Cf. Holw.

BLIDULF (**BLADULPH**) (St) Mk.
     A.C. Jan. 2
d. c.630. A monk of Bobbio, who courageously denounced the heresy of the
Lombard king Ariovald.
Cf. Zimm. — Chev. — Baud.

BLINLIVET (**BLEVILEGUETUS**) (St)
Bp.   A.C. Nov. 7
9th cent. The twenty-fifth bishop of
Vannes in Brittany. Before his death he
resigned and became a monk at Quimperlé.
Cf. Baud.

BLITHARIUS (**BLIER**) (St) C.
     A.C. June 11
7th cent. A native of Scotland, who
passed over into France with St Fursey,
and settled at Seganne in Champagne,
where he is still held in great veneration.
Cf. Baud. — Holw. — P.B.

BLITMUND (St) Ab.   A.C. Jan. 3
d. 650. Monk of Bobbio under St Attalas.
He followed St Walaricus (St Valéry) to
France, where they founded the abbey of
Leucone (later on called Saint-Valéry;
now the village of the same name). St
Blitmund survived his master and ruled
the abbey as its second abbot.
Cf. Baud. — Zimm. — Chev.

BOADIN (St) H. O.S.B.   A.C. Jan. 11
? An Irishman who passed over to France
and became a Benedictine monk there.
Cf. Baud.

BOBINUS (St) Bp. O.S.B.   A.C. Jan. 31
d. c.766. A native of Aquitaine, monk
of Moutier-la-Celle, which was enriched
by his benefactions when he became bishop
of Troyes (760).
*Cf. Zimm. — Duch. Fast. Episc. —
Gams — Baud.*

BOBO (**BEUVON**) (St) H.   A.C. May 22
d. c.985. A knight of Provence, who
fought bravely against the invading
Saracens and then retired as a hermit to
lead a life of penance. He died at Pavia
in Lombardy while on a pilgrimage to
Rome.
Cf. Att. — Baud.

BODAGISIL (St) Ab.   A.C. Dec. 18
d. 588. A Frankish courtier, who later
became the founder and first abbot of an
abbey on the banks of the Meuse. St
Venantius Fortunatus and St Gregory of
Tours are loud in his praises.
Cf. Baud. — Holw.

BODFAN (**BOBOUAN**) (St)   A.C. June 2
7th cent. The patron saint of Abern in
Carnarvon. The only extant tradition
about him is that the great inundation
that formed Beaumaris Bay impelled him,
with his father and other relations, to em-
brace the religious life.
Cf. Baring-Gould.

BODO (St) Bp. O.S.B.   A.C. Sept. 11
d. p. 670. A native of Toul, brother to
St Salaberga. He married, but by mutual
consent both he and his wife became religious. He entered an abbey at Laon,
which, however, he was forced to leave in
order to become bishop of Toul. He
founded Etival, Bon-Moutier, and Affon-
ville abbeys.
Cf. Baud. — Holw. — Gams.

BOETHARIUS (St) Bp.   A.C. Aug. 2
7th cent. Chaplain of King Clotaire II,
and afterwards bishop of Chartres (c.595).
Cf. Baud. — Duch. Fast. Episc. — Gams.

BOETHIAN (St) M. O.S.B. A.C. May 22
7th cent. A disciple of St Fursey and an
Irishman by birth. He built the monastery of Pierrepont, near Laon, in France,
and was eventually murdered by those
whom he had felt bound to rebuke. His
shrine is still a place of pilgrimage.
Cf. Baud. — Holw. — P.B.

BOETHIUS (Bl) C.   A.C. Oct. 23
See Severinus Boethius.

BOGUMILUS (i.e. THEOPHILUS) (St)
Bp. O.S.B. Cam.   A.C. June 10
d. 1182. A native of Dobrow, a little
Polish town on the Wartha. After his
studies at the university of Paris he was
appointed parish priest of Dobrow, and
then archbishop of Gnesen. As such he
founded the Cistercian abbey of Coronowa.
In spite of his wisdom and zeal his clergy
paid little heed to his admonitions. He
resigned in 1172 and became a Camaldolese monk at Uniejow. Cult approved
in 1925.
Cf. Att. — Baud. — Chev. — Holw.

BOISIL (St) Ab.   A.C. Feb. 23
Otherwise Boswell, q.v.

BOLCAN (OLCAN) (St) Bp.
**   A.C. Feb. 20**
d. c.480. Baptized by St Patrick and
sent by him to study in Gaul, Bolcan was
subsequently by the same saint consecrated bishop of Derkan in N. Ireland.
His school there was one of the best
equipped in the island. Another St Bolcan is venerated in the diocese of Elphin.
He is known as St Olcan of Kilmoyle.
Cf. Baud. — Holw. — Baring-Gould (Olcan) — *O'Hanlon.*

BOLONIA (St) V.M.   A.C. Oct. 16
d. 362. A maiden of fifteen who was
martyred under Julian the Apostate, and
who has left her name to the village of
Saint Boulogne in the Haute Marne.
Cf. Baud. — Holw.

BONA (St) V.   A.C. Apr. 24
Otherwise Bova, q.v.

BONAJUNCTA (St) C.
**   R.M. Aug. 31 and Feb. 12**
One of the Seven Founders of the Servite
Order, q.v.

BONANNUS (Bl) C. O.S.B. Cel.
**   A.C. Jan. 1**
d. c.1320. A Benedictine of the Celestine
Congregation, monk of the monastery of
St Laurence in the Abruzzi.
Cf. Zimm.

BONAVENTURE of MEACO (Bl) M.
Tert. O.F.M.   A.C. Feb. 5
d. 1597. A native of Meaco in Japan,
this saint became a Franciscan tertiary
and helped the Franciscan missionaries as
a catechist. He was crucified at Nagasaki. Beatified in 1862.
Cf. Holw.

BONAVENTURE TORNIELLI (Bl) C.
O.S.M.   A.C. March 31
d. 1491. Born at Forlì, he became a
Servite in 1448. At the order of the pope
he preached continually throughout the
papal states and S. Italy. He was for
some years vicar-general of the Servites.
Cult confirmed in 1911.
Cf. Holw. — Baud. — Att.

BONAVENTURE BADUARIO of PERA-
GA (Bl) C. O.S.A. Erem.   P.C. June 10
1332-1386. A native of Peraga, near
Padua, where he was professed as an
Augustinian hermit. After having been
general of the Order he was created cardi-
nal-priest of St Caecilia — the first of the
Order to attain that honour. He was
killed in Rome by an arrow, probably in
retaliation for his defence of the rights of
the Church.
Cf. Att. — Holw. — Baud.

BONAVENTURE (St) Bp. Dr. O.F.M.
**   R.M. July 14**
1221-1274. Born at Bagnorea, near Vi-

terbo. His baptismal name was John. The name Bonaventure (good fortune) was given to him by St Francis of Assisi, who cured him miraculously when he was a small child, and exclaimed: *O buona ventura!* At the age of twenty he became a Franciscan, and at thirty-six minister-general of the Order. He was nominated archbishop of York, but refused the honour. Finally in 1273 he was created cardinal bishop of Albano. He died during the general council of Lyons. A disciple of Alexander of Hales and a friend and admirer of St Thomas Aquinas, Bonaventure is known as the "Seraphic Doctor," and was officially given the title of Doctor of the Church by Sixtus V. Besides theological and philosophical works, St Bonaventure has left us sundry ascetical treatises, and a touchingly beautiful life of St Francis of Assisi written with the aim of promoting unity among the Friars Minor. Canonized in 1482. *Cf. Att. — Baud. — Holw.*

BONAVENTURE GRAU (Bl) C. O.F.M.
A.C. Sept. 11
1620-1684. Born at Riudoms, near Barcelona, left a widower after a short period of married life, he joined the Friars Minor at Escornalbou. To escape notoriety for his mystical gits he went to Rome where he was made doorkeeper at St Isidore. He founded several retreat-convents in the Roman province of his order. His advice was sought by popes and cardinals. Cult approved in 1906.
Cf. Holw. — Baud.

BONAVENTURE of POTENZA (Bl) C. O.F.M.   **A.C. Oct. 26**
1651-1711. A native of Potenza in the Napolitano. He entered the Franciscan order at Nocera and spent his life as a missioner in S. Italy, chiefly at Amalfi, and as a novice master. He died in an ecstasy singing psalms.
Cf. Baud. — Holw. — Att.

BONAVENTURE BUONACCORSI (Bl) C. O.S.M.   **A.C. Dec. 14**
d. 1313. A native of Pistoja in Tuscany and the leader of the Ghibellines there, he was converted in 1276 by St Philip Benizi, who was acting as a peace-maker between the parties. He followed St Philip into the Servite Order and as a Servite friar went about preaching peace. The people

called him "il Beato" even during his lifetime. Cult approved in 1822.
Cf. Att. — Holw. — Baud.

BONAVENTURE TOLOMEI (Bl) C. O.P.   **P.C. Dec. 27**
d. 1348. Born at Siena in Tuscany. As a child he was favoured with divine charismata, but in early manhood he abandoned himself for four years to a life of impurity and sacrilege. He repented, visited on foot all the celebrated shrines and subsequently entered the Dominican order. He died while tending the plague-stricken in Siena.
Cf. Baud.

BONAVITA (Bl) C. Tert. O.F.M.   **P.C. March 1**
d. 1375. A blacksmith of Lugo, near Ravenna. He was a Franciscan tertiary, wholly devoted to prayer and good works.
Cf. Att. — Holw. — Baud.

BOND (BALDUS) (St) H.   A.C. Oct. 29
7th cent. A penitent hermit venerated at Sens in France.
Cf. Baud. — Holw.

BONET (BONT) (St) Bp.   R.M. Jan. 15
Otherwise Bonitus, q.v.

BONFILIUS MONALDI (St)
R.M. Jan. 1 and Feb. 12
One of the Seven Founders of the Servite Order, q.v.

BONFILIUS (St) Bp. O.S.B.
A.C. Sept. 27
1040-1125. A native of Osimo in Piceno, he became a monk, and then abbot, of the monastery of Our Lady, at Storace. In 1078 he was made bishop of Foligno: but in 1096, after a pilgrimage to the Holy Land, he resigned and retired to the abbey of Santa Maria della Fara, diocese of Cingoli, where he died.
Cf. Gams — Chev. — Baud. — Holw.

BONIFACE of LAUSANNE (St) Bp.
A.C. Feb. 19
d. 1265. Born in Brussels and educated by nuns of La Cambre (Camera S. Mariae), near his native city. He then studied at Paris, where he taught dogma, afterwards transferring his chair to the university of Cologne. About the year 1230 he was made bishop of Lausanne,

but owing to the impossibility of reaching an understanding with several of his clergy, he resigned (1239) and henceforth lived at La Cambre as chaplain to the nuns. The Cistercians claim him for their order.
Cf. Gams — Chev. — Baud. — Zimm. — Att.

BONIFACE of SAVOY (Bl) Bp. O.Cart.
A.C. March 13
d. 1270. A member of the ducal house of Savoy, who became a Carthusian monk (and prior) and then bishop of Valence, and finally archbishop of Canterbury (1241). Besides his fame as a saint, the fact that he was uncle to Henry III's wife explains the appointment, which, however, proved very unpopular in England. He died in Savoy and was buried at Haute-combe. Cult confirmed in 1830.
Cf. Att. — Holw. — Baud. — Gams.

BONIFACE (St) Bp.   A.C. March 14
d. c.630. A bishop, very likely a Roman by birth, who evangelized the Picts and Scots, one of the chief features of his mission being the introducing of the Roman discipline and observance, as opposed to the Celtic usages. He is said to have founded a very great number of churches.
Cf. Att. — Baud. — Holw.

BONIFACE of VALPERGA (Bl) Bp.
P.C. Apr. 25
d. 1243. Monk of the Benedictine abbey of Fruttuaria, who was chosen prior of the Augustinian canons regular of St Ursus at Aosta (1212) and finally bishop of Aosta (1219-1243).
Cf. Zimm.

BONIFACE IV (St) Pope.   R.M. May 8
d. 615. Born at Valeria in the Abruzzi, he became, according to a tradition which cannot, however, be substantiated, a Benedictine monk of St Sebastian, in Rome. He was pope from 608 to 615 and is best remembered for his dedication of the Pantheon to our Lady and all the saints. St Columbanus addressed to him a famous — or notorious — letter.
Cf. Att. — Baud. — Chev.

BONIFACE of TARSUS (St) M.
R.M. May 14
d. c.307. A martyr beheaded at Tarsus in Cilicia, whither, his fictitious acts add, he had gone from Rome to recover the bodies of certain martyrs. His own relics are enshrined in the church of SS Alexius and Boniface on the Aventine.
Cf. Att. — Baud. — Holw.

BONIFACE (St) Bp.   R.M. May 14
6th cent. Bishop of Ferentino in Tuscany at the time of the emperor Justin. He is commemorated by St Gregory the Great.
Cf. Baud. — Holw. — Gams.

BONIFACE (Bl) Mk. O.S.B. Cist.
P.C. June 4
d. c.1280. Monk and prior of the great Cistercian abbey of Villers in Brabant.
Cf. Zimm.

BONIFACE (St) Bp. M. O.S.B.
R.M. June 5
680-755. An Anglo-Saxon, whose baptismal name was Winfrid, born at Crediton in Devon. At the age of five he entered a monastery at Exeter, there to become a Benedictine monk. He was transferred to Nutshulling, diocese of Winchester, where he became head of the abbey school and was ordained priest in 710. In 716 he set out for Germany on his first missionary expedition, which proved a failure. In 718 he left England again, this time for Rome, to get the pope's blessing on his enterprise, and forthwith evangelized Bavaria, Hesse, Friesland, Thuringia and Franconia. In 723 Gregory II consecrated him regionary bishop with full jurisdiction over the Germanies. In 731 he was made by the pope metropolitan beyond the Rhine, in 738 papal legate, and in 747 archbishop of Mainz. A few years before his death he founded the abbey of Fulda (where his body now rests) as the focus of German missionary activities. Before this he had already established a great number of abbeys and nunneries, with attached schools, and to staff them he had invited bands of monks and nuns from England. He was martyred in his old age, with fifty-two companions at Dokkum. He was responsible for the organization of the Frankish church. Always on the best of terms with the Carolingians, he became their mentor and support. He is rightly styled the Apostle of Germany. Among

the apostles of all time he stands on a par with St Paul and St Francis Xavier.
Cf. Chev. — Gams — Zimm. — P. de U.— Att.

BONIFACE (St) M. O.S.B.
R.M. June 19
Otherwise Bruno of Querfurt, q.v.

BONIFACE (St) M. R.M. Aug. 17
See Liberatus, Boniface, etc.

BONIFACE and THECLA (SS) MM.
R.M. Aug. 30
d. c.250. Husband and wife put to death with twelve children at Hadrumetum in Africa during the persecution of Decius. There is much difficulty in reconciling all the details of their acts. Some writers assert that the twelve children are those commemorated in the Liturgy on Sept. 1.
Cf. Baud. — Holw.

BONIFACE I (St) Pope. R.M. Sept. 4
d. 423. A Roman priest who was elected pope in 418. He was opposed by the anti-pope Eulalius and later on was troubled by the ever-recurring claims of the Patriarch of Constantinople. Gently but firmly he defended the rights of the Roman see. St Augustine dedicated to him several treatises against Pelagianism.
Cf. Att. — Baud. — Holw.

BONIFACE (St) M. R.M. Oct. 5
Said to be the name of one of the martyrs who suffered with St Palmatius, q.v.

BONIFACE (St) M. R.M. Dec. 6
See Dionysia, Dativa, etc.

BONIFACE (St) M. R.M. Dec. 29
See Callistus, Felix and Boniface.

BONITUS (St) Bp. O.S.B. R.M. Jan. 15
623-c.710. A native of Auvergne who became successively chancellor to King Sigebert III, governor of Provence, and bishop of Clermont in Auvergne. After ten years as bishop, he resigned, owing to a scruple of conscience, and retired to the Benedictine abbey of Manlieu, where he became a monk and died in extreme old age.
Cf. Mab. — Att. — Holw. — Baud. — Gams.

BONITUS (St) Ab. O.S.B. A.C. July 7
d. c.582. Fourth successor of St Benedict

as abbot of Montecassino. During his abbacy the Lombards under Zoto of Benevento plundered and destroyed the arch-abbey (c.581). The monks saved themselves by flight and were housed in the Lateran in Rome. Bonitus died shortly after.
Cf. Holw.

BONIZELLA (Bl) W. P.C. May 6
d. 1300. The wife of Naddo Piccolomini of Siena. In her widowhood she devoted herself and all her wealth to the service of the poor in the district of Belvederio.
Cf. Att. — Baud.

BONONIUS (St) Ab. O.S.B. Cam.
R.M. Aug. 30
d. 1026. A native of Bologna and a Benedictine monk of St Stephen's in the same city. He became a disciple of St Romuald, by whom he was sent to preach the gospel in Egypt and Syria. On his return he was made abbot of Locedio in Piedmont.
Cf. Mab. — Zimm. — P. de U. — Baud.— Chev. — Prop. Camald. — Holw.

BONOSA (St) M. R.M. July 15
See Eutropius, Zosima and Bonosa.

BONOSUS and MAXIMIAN (SS) MM.
R.M. Aug. 21
d. 362. Two officers of the Herculean Cohort at Antioch, under Julian the Apostate. They were tortured and beheaded for refusing to change Constantine's Christian banner — the *labarum* — for a new idolatrous standard.
Cf. Att. — Baud. — Holw.

BONUS, FAUSTUS, MAURUS and Comp.
(SS) MM. R.M. Aug. 1
d. 257. Bonus, a priest, with Faustus, Maurus and nine companions, was martyred at Rome under Valerian.
Cf. Baud. — Holw.

BORIS and GLEB (SS) MM.
A.C. July 24
See Romanus and David.

BOSA (St) Bp. O.S.B. A.C. March 9
d. 686. Monk of Whitby under St Hilda, he was consecrated bishop of York by St Theodore (678) when the titular of that see, St Wilfrid, was in exile. St Bede praises St Bosa in the following words:

"a man beloved by God . . . of most unusual merit and sanctity."
Cf. Att. — Baud. — Stanton — Chev.

BOSWELL (BOISIL) (St) Ab.
                              A.C. Feb. 23
d. c.664. Abbot of Melrose. He counted SS Cuthbert and Egbert among his monks. Both had a great admiration for him, as had also St Bede. His favourite reading was the Gospel of St John.
Cf. Att. — Baud. — Zimm.

BOTULPH and ADULPH (SS) CC. O.S.B.
                              A.C. June 17
d. c.680. Brothers, sons of noble Saxon parents. They were educated, and received the Benedictine habit, in Belgian Gaul. Adulph is said to have been raised to the episcopate. Botulph returned to England and became one of the foremost missionaries of the 7th century. He founded an abbey at Ikanhoe, formerly thought to be near Boston in Lincolnshire, but now generally supposed to be Iken in Suffolk. More than seventy English churches were dedicated to St Botulph, including four at the gates of the city of London.
Cf. Att. — Mab. — Baud. — Holw.

BOTWID (St) M.   **A.C. July 28**
d. 1100. A Swede, converted to the Faith in England, who became an apostle in his own country. He was murdered by a Finnish slave whom he thought he had converted and whom he had set free.
Cf. Att. — Baud. — Holw.

BOVA and DODA (SS) VV. O.S.B.
                              R.M. Apr. 24
d. c.680. St Bova was a sister, and St Doda a niece, of St Baldericus (Baudry), the founder of Montfaucon and of the nunnery of our Lady at Reims. He appointed Bova first abbess of this convent and she was succeeded by Doda.
Cf. Att. — Holw. — Baud.

BRADAN and ORORA (CRORA) (SS)
                              A.C. Oct. 20
? Two saints venerated in the Isle of Man. In the church of St Bradan, Kirk-Braddan, near Douglas, Mark, the bishop of Sodor, held a synod in 1291. In a map of the 16th century, reference is made to the churches of SS Patrick and Crora.
Cf. Holw. — O'Hanlon.

BRANNOCK (St) Ab.   **A.C. Jan. 7**
6th cent. A saint who appears to have migrated from S. Wales into Devon, and to have founded a monastery at Braunton, near Barnstaple. The traditions concerning him are very untrustworthy. See also Brynach.
Cf. Holw.

BRANWALLADER (St) Bp. A.C. Jan. 19
? 6th cent. Said to have been a bishop in Jersey. King Athelstan, who founded Milton Abbey in Dorset, had this saint's relics translated there in 935.
Cf. Holw.

BRAULIO (St) Bp.   **R.M. March 26**
d. 646. A native of Saragossa and a monk of St Engratia's monastery in that city, whence he was sent to Seville to study under St Isidore. He was ordained priest by his own brother, John, whom he succeeded as archbishop of Saragossa. He was a ready writer and excelled chiefly as a hagiographer. He is one of the patron saints of Aragon.
Cf. Att. — P. de U. — Dict. Baudrill. — Chev. — Gams — Baud.

BREACA (St) V.   **A.C. June 4**
5th-6th cent. A disciple of St Brigid who is said to have gone from Ireland to Cornwall (c.460) with several companions and to have landed on the eastern bank of the river Hayle. Variants of her name are: Breague, Branca, Banka, etc.
Cf. Holw. — Baud. — Baring-Gould — O'Hanlon.

BREGWIN (St) Bp. O.S.B. A.C. Aug. 26
d. 765. The twelfth archbishop of Canterbury (761-765). His life was written by Eadmer. Letters of his to St Lullus of Mainz are still extant.
Cf. Baud. — Stanton — Gams — Chev.

BRENACH (St) H.   **A.C. Apr. 7**
Otherwise Brynach, q.v.

BRENDAN the VOYAGER (St) Ab.
                              R.M. May 16
c.435-c.583. One of the three most famous saints of Ireland. He was born on Fenit peninsular, Kerry, and educated for five years under St Ita, becoming afterwards a disciple of St Finnian at Clonard and of St Gildas at Llancarfan in Wales. He was a great founder of monasteries, the

chief of which was Clonfert. To his monks he gave a Rule of remarkable austerity. He is best known in history for his voyages, in which, it is said, he reached the American continent. Though they can scarcely be admitted as historical facts, they have nevertheless had some influence on history, since legends of St Brendan's journey to discover the Isles of the Blessed were popular throughout Europe. St Brendan is most fittingly venerated as the patron saint of sailors.
Cf. Holw. — Att. — Baud.

BRENDAN of BIRR (St) Ab. A.C. Nov. 29
d. c.562. A contemporary of St Brendan the Voyager, and his fellow-disciple under St Finnian at Clonfert. His abbey of Birr was somewhere near Parsonstown in Offaly. He was the great friend and advisor of St Columba, who in a vision saw the soul of St Brendan carried by angels to heaven at the moment of his death.
Cf. Holw. — Baud.

BRETANNION (St) Bp.   R.M. Jan. 25
d. c.380. Bishop of Tomi in Scythia on the Black Sea, near the mouth of the Danube. The Arian emperor, Valens, exiled him for his brave defence of Christ's divinity, but was compelled by popular discontent to recall him.
Cf. Baud. — Holw.

BRIACH (St) Ab.   A.C. Dec. 17
d. c.627. An Irishman who became a monk in Wales under St Tudwall, whom he accompanied to Brittany. He built a monastery at Guingamp. He died at Bourbiac.
Cf. Baud. — Holw.

BRIANT, ALEXANDER   A.C. Dec. 1
See Alexander Briant.

BRIAVEL (BREVILE) (St) H.
A.C. June 17
? The name of this saint (possibly a variant of Ebrulfus) is perpetuated as that of the patron saint of the parish of St Briavels in the Forest of Dean in Gloucestershire; but no record of his life is extant.
Cf. Stanton.

BRICE (BRITIUS, BRIXIUS) (St) Bp.
R.M. Nov. 13
d. 444. A disciple of St Martin of Tours,

but, unlike his master, a proud, ambitious and even licentious cleric. Nevertheless, he was chosen to be St Martin's successor at Tours, and during twenty years he continued to be a very unsatisfactory ecclesiastic, being for this reason eventually driven from his see. He went to Rome, repented, and was reinstated at Tours, and such was his change of manners that his flock proclaimed him a saint immediately after his death. His cult spread throughout N. Europe.
Cf. Att. — Baud. — Holw.

BRICTIUS (St) Bp.   R.M. July 9
d. c.312. Bishop of Martola near Spoleto in Umbria, imprisoned for the Faith under Diocletian. He escaped death, and died a confessor under Constantine.
Cf. Baud. — Holw.

BRIDGET (*several*)
Otherwise Brigid, q.v.

BRIEUC (BRIOCUS, BRIOC) (St) Bp.
A.C. May 1
c.420-c.510. Born in Cardiganshire, he was educated in France by St Germanus of Auxerre. He laboured very successfully first in his native land, and then in Brittany, where he founded two abbeys, one near Tréguier, and the other where the town of St Brieuc now stands. He is greatly venerated in Cornwall.
Cf. Att. — Baud. — Holw.

BRIGID (BRIGA) (St) V.   A.C. Jan. 21
6th cent. Known as St Brigid of Kilbride and venerated in the diocese of Lismore. It is recorded that her famous namesake of Kildare visited her more than once at Kilbride.
Cf. Holw. — O'Hanlon.

BRIGID (BRIDGET, BRIDE, FFRAID)
(St) V. Foundress.   R.M. Feb. 1
c.450-c.525. Surnamed "the Mary of the Gael." Born at Faughart, near Dundalk, she took the veil in her youth and eventually founded the nunnery of Kildare, the first to be erected on Irish soil, thus becoming the spiritual mother of all Irish nuns. Around her name there have been formed hundreds of legends, which could be fittingly described as "the Little Flowers of St Brigid," the key-note of them all being mercy and pity for the poor. In art St Brigid is represented holding a cross,

with a flame over her head, and sometimes with a cow near her, since she is reputed to be the protectress of those engaged in dairy work.
Cf. Att. — Holw. — Baud.

BRIGID (St) V.   A.C. Feb. 1
9th cent. Alleged sister of St Andrew, abbot of St Donatus at Fiesole in Tuscany. It is said that she was carried by angels to her brother's deathbed. She died as a recluse in the Apennines. Most modern writers discard all this as pure fiction.
Cf. Holw.

BRIGID and MAURA (SS) A.C. July 13
5th cent. Venerated as two daughters of a Scottish chieftain, said to have been martyred in Picardy while on a pilgrimage to Rome. They are most probably to be identified with SS Britta and Maura mentioned by St Gregory of Tours, and with SS Baya and Maura, whose names are listed in the ancient Scottish calendars.
Cf. Baud. — Holw.

BRIGID of SWEDEN (BRIDGET, BIR-GITTA) (St) W. Foundress   R.M. Oct. 8
1304-1373. Born of a noble Swedish family, Brigid married, before she was fifteen, a Swedish prince, with whom she lived happily for twenty-eight years, and to whom she bore eight children. She proved to be the ideal busy, home-loving wife. In her widowhood she founded the monastery of Wadstena (1344), thus instituting the Order of the Most Holy Saviour, known as "the Bridgettines." She is also famous for the visions and revelations with which she was favoured by God, and which she recorded in writing. She died in Rome on her return from Jerusalem (July 23) and was canonized twenty years later (1391). In art she is represented clothed in the religious habit of her Order, bearing a pilgrim's staff, holding a heart marked with a cross and with our Saviour near her.
Cf. Att. — Baud. — Holw.

BRINSTAN (St) Bp.   A.C. Nov. 4
Otherwise Birnstan, q.v.

BRIOC, BRIOCUS (St) Bp.   A.C. May 1
Otherwise Brieuc, q.v.

BRITHWALD (BRIHTWALD, BERTH-WALD, BERCTUALD) (St) Bp. O.S.B.   A.C. Jan. 9
d. 731. An Anglo-Saxon, educated prob-ably at Canterbury; afterwards monk and abbot of Reculver in Kent. He was elected archbishop of Canterbury in 692 and governed that see for thirty-seven years.
Cf. Mab. — Zimm. — Att. — Baud. — Holw.

BRITHWOLD (St) Bp. O.S.B.   A.C. Jan. 22
d. 1045. A monk of Glastonbury. He was chosen bishop of Ramsbury (1005), whence he removed the see to Old Sarum. He was a great benefactor of Malmesbury and Glastonbury, where he was buried.
Cf. Mab. — Chev. — Att. — Zimm. — Holw. — Baud.

BRITO (BRITONIUS) (St) Bp.   A.C. May 5
d. 386. Bishop of Trèves. A stout opponent of the Priscillian heretics, whom he nevertheless always refused to hand over for punishment by the state.
Cf. Att.

BRITWIN (BRITHWIN, BRITHUN) (St) Ab. O.S.B.   A.C. May 15
d. c.733. Abbot of Beverley. He received his great friend and patron, St John of Beverley, into his monastery, after the latter had resigned the bishopric of York.
Cf. Holw. — Chev. — Baud.

BRIXIUS (St) Bp.   R.M. Nov. 13
Otherwise Brice, q.v.

BROCARD (St) C. O.C.   A.C. Sept. 2
d. 1231. St Berthold's successor as prior of the Frankish hermits of Mt Carmel. At his request St Albert, patriarch of Jerusalem, drew up for them the rule under which they developed in the West into the Order of Mt Carmel. He was highly respected by the Mohammedans.
Cf. Att. — Holw. — Baud.

BRON (St) Bp.   A.C. June 8
d. c.511. A disciple of St Patrick, consecrated bishop of Cassel-Irra, near the town of Sligo.
Cf. O'Hanlon.

BRONACH (BROMANA) (St) V.   A.C. Apr. 2
? Called the Virgin of Glen-Seichis and registered in the martyrologies of Tallaght and Donegal. Glen-Seichis is the old name of Kilbrony or Kilbronach, in Co.

Down, which takes its present appellation from her.

Cf. Holw. — O'Hanlon.

BRONISLAVA (Bl) V. O.Praem.
A.C. Aug. 30

d. 1259. A cousin of St Hyacinth of Poland. She was a professed Premonstratensian nun in Poland, but died a recluse. Cult confirmed in 1839.

Cf. Att. — Holw.

BROTHEN and GWENDOLEN (SS)
A.C. Oct. 18

? 6th cent. Welsh saints, of whom nothing is known but the names and the fact that they were given a public cult in Wales. St Brothen is still the patron saint of Llanbrothen in Merionethshire. Dolwyddelen and Llanwyddelan in Montgomeryshire suggest a St Gwendolen; this and similar names are diminutives of Gwen (white) and are equivalent to our Blanche and its allied forms.

Cf. Baring-Gould.

BRUNO and Comp. (SS) MM. A.C. Feb. 2

d. 880. Bruno was a duke in command of an army of the Christian king, Louis III, which was surprised by pagan Northmen at Ebsdorf in Saxony. Besides the duke many others were slain in the battle, or were afterwards put to death. They have been venerated as martyrs.

Cf. Holw.

BRUNO (St) Bp. R.M. May 27

d. 1045. Appointed bishop of Würzburg in 1033 and best remembered as the fosterer of church-building throughout the diocese, on which work he spent all his private fortune. While he was dining with the emperor Henry III at Bosenburg on the Danube, a gallery gave way, killing the saintly bishop on the spot.

Cf. Att. — Baud. — Holw.

BRUNO SERONKUMA (Bl) M.
A.C. June 3

d. 1885. A soldier of King Mwanga of Uganda. He was baptized on Nov. 18, 1885, and burnt alive a few weeks later. Beatified in 1912.

Cf. Holw.

BRUNO-BONIFACE (St) M. O.S.B. Cam.
R.M. June 19 and Oct. 15

d. 1009. Born at Querfurt, and educated at the cathedral-school of Magdeburg. He accompanied Otto III to Italy (996) and there he received the Camaldolese habit from St Romuald, by whom he was eventually sent to evangelize Prussia and Russia. He was martyred with eighteen companions (Feb. 14). Note that St Boniface of the R.M. on June 19 and St Bruno on Oct. 15 are one and the same person. Bruno was the baptismal, and Boniface the monastic, name of the saint.

Cf. All. — Baud. — Holw. — Zimm. — Mab. — P. de U. — Chev.

BRUNO of SEGNI (St) Bp. O.S.B.
R.M. July 18

1049-1123. Born at Solero (Asti) in Piedmont, he studied in the monastery of St Perpetuus at Asti, and at Bologna. He first became known as the opponent of Berengarius. In 1079 Gregory VII made him bishop of Segni; but he left the see and became a monk, and then abbot, of Montecassino. The pope, however, although allowing him to become a monk, had not definitely accepted his resignation of the see, and eventually Bruno had to return to it. Among other offices held by the saint were those of librarian of the Holy Roman See and cardinal legate. He was a profound theologian, and his work on the Holy Eucharist is still very useful. Canonized in 1183.

Cf. Zimm. — Baud. — P. de U. — Att. — Gams.

BRUNO (St) Founder. R.M. Oct. 6

1030-1101. Born at Cologne, he studied at Reims and Paris, and became chancellor of the diocese of Reims. In 1084 he retired with six companions to La Grande Chartreuse, near Grenoble, and there he founded his order, or rather a monastery of monk-hermits, under the Benedictine rule, which at a later period grew into the Carthusian Institute. Bl Urban II, who had been St Bruno's student at Reims, called the saint to Rome, to be a papal counsellor. Even here, though never fully released from the pope's service, St Bruno managed to establish another Charterhouse at La Torre in Calabria, whither he was allowed to retire. He refused the see of Reggio. St Bruno excelled as a biblical exegete, writing on the psalms and on St Paul's epistles.

Cf. Att. — Baud. — Holw. — Bolland.

BRUNO (St) Bp.   **A.C. Oct. 11**
c.925-965. Called "the Great," a title
which nowadays would seem rather to
belong to the founder of the Carthusians.
This Bruno was the youngest son of the
emperor, Henry the Fowler, and St Matilda. From childhood, we are told, he
was devoted to learning; Prudentius was
his bedside book. In 953 he was made
bishop of Cologne, being already com-
mendatory abbot of Lorsch and Corvey.
As archbishop his political influence was
a factor in the consolidation of the German
States.
Cf. Att. — Baud. — Holw.

BRUNO (Bl) C. O.S.B.   **A.C. Dec. 24**
d. c.1050. A Benedictine lay-brother of
the abbey of Ottobeuren in Bavaria.
Cf. Zimm.

BRYNACH (BERNACH, BERNACUS)
(St) C.   **A.C. Apr. 7**
? 5th cent. An Irishman who settled in
Wales, where he built a cell and a church
at a place called Carn-Englyi (Mountain
of Angels), overhanging the Nevern
(Pembrokeshire). Some authors identify
him with St Brannock of Braunton.
Cf. Stanton (Brenach) — Baring-Gould.

BRYNOTH (St) Bp.   **A.C. May 9**
d. 1317 (Feb. 6). A Swede, bishop of
Scara in W. Gothland. Canonized in 1498.
Cf. Baud. — Holw.

BUDOC (BUDEAUX)(St) Bp. A.C. Dec. 9
? 7th cent. A Breton, educated in Ireland, where he became abbot of Youghal.
Returning afterwards to Brittany, he succeeded SS Samson and Maglorius in the
see of Dol. He has given his name to
several places in Devon and Cornwall.
Cf. Att. — Baud. — Holw.

BUITHE (BUITE, BOETHIUS) (St) C.
          A.C. Dec. 7
d. 521. A Scot, who spent some years in
Italy and elsewhere on the continent and,
returning to Scotland, evangelized the
Picts. From him it seems that Carbuddo
(Castrum Butthi) takes its name.
Cf. Baud. — Holw.

BULGARIA (Martyrs of) (SS)
          R.M. July 23
9th cent. During the war between the
Greek emperor, Nicephorus, and the Bul-

gars, not as yet Christians, many Catholics, besides those slain in battle, were put
to death on account of their Faith. There
is much uncertainty as to the exact circumstances, but they have always been
reckoned as martyrs.
Cf. Baud. — Holw.

BURCHARD (Bl) Ab. O.S.B. Cist.
          P.C. Apr. 19
d. 1164. A favourite monk and disciple
of St Bernard at Clairvaux. He was
appointed successively abbot of Balerne
(1136) and of Bellevaux (c.1157).
Cf. Chev. — Baud. — P. de U. — Holw.

BURCHARD (Bl) Ab. O.S.B. A.C. June 25
d. 1122. Monk of the Benedictine abbey
of St Michael at Bamberg, and first abbot
of Mallersdorf in Bavaria.
Cf. Zimm.

BURCHARD (Bl) Bp. O.S.B. A.C. Aug. 20
d. 1026. A native of Hesse who, after
studying at Coblentz, became a monk at
Lobbes. In 1006 he was compelled by the
emperor Otto to accept the bishopric of
Worms. He is famous as a compiler of
canons and decretals.
*Cf. P. de U. — Zimm. — Gams — Baud.
— Holw.*

BURCHARD (St) Bp. O.S.B.
          R.M. Oct. 14
d. c.754. An English priest and monk
who joined the German mission under St
Boniface (c.732). He was consecrated
first bishop of Würzburg (Herbipolis), and
founded there several Benedictine abbeys,
of which the most important was St
Andrew's, afterwards called after him.
About the year 753 he resigned his bishopric to a monk of Fritzlar and spent the
remaining months of his life in monastic
retirement.
Cf. Att. — Baud. — Holw.

BURGINUS and GUIIMINUS (BB) Mks.
O.S.B.   **P.C. Nov. 18**
d. p. 1065. Two Benedictine monks who
were among the pioneers of the priory of
Thouacé in Anjou, founded by St Florentius.
Cf. Zimm.

BURGUNDOFARA (or FARA) (St) Abs.
O.S.B.   **R.M. Apr. 3 and Dec. 7**
d.657. Blessed by St Columbanus in her

infancy, Burgundofara early developed a religious vocation in spite of the fierce opposition of her father, a noble Frankish courtier. In the end he had to give way and founded for her the nunnery of Brige (Brie) or *Evoriacum* — later called Faremoutiers, i.e. Fara's Monastery — over which she ruled for thirty-seven years. Many English nun-saints were trained under her.
Cf. Mab. — Bolland. — Att. — Baud. — Zimm.

BURIANA (St) V.   A.C. June 4
6th cent. An Irishwoman who lived as a recluse in Cornwall. The place-name St Buryan, opposite the Scilly Islands, perpetuates her memory.
Cf. Baud. — Holw.

BYBLIG (BIBLIG, PEBLIG, PIBLIG, PUBLICIUS)   A.C. July 3
? 5th cent. A holy man connected with Carnarvon and honoured with a cult in parts of Wales, of whom, however, nothing certain is known.
Cf. Holw. — Baring-Gould (Peblig).

C

CADELL (St)   ?
7th cent. A Welsh saint, giving its name to Llangadell in Glamorgan.
Cf. Holw.

CADFAN (St) Ab.   A.C. Nov. 1
d. early 6th cent. A native of Brittany, who came over to Wales and founded several monasteries. His name is chiefly associated with those of Towyn in Merionethshire and Bardsey Island (Ynys Enlli).
Cf. Att. — Holw. — Baud.

CADFARCH (St)   A.C. Oct. 24
6th cent. A Welsh saint, disciple of St Illtyd, and member of a family of saints. He is said to have founded churches at Penegoes and Abererch.
Cf. Holw.

CADOC (DOCUS, CATHMAEL, CADVAEL) (St) Bp. M.   A.C. Jan. 24
d. c.580. A Welsh monk, founder of the great monastery of Llancarfan not far from Cardiff, which became a veritable house of saints. Accompanied by St Gildas, St Cadoc later continued his religious life on an island off the coast of Vannes in Brittany. He returned to Britain and is said to have taken spiritual charge of the Britons, his compatriots, in the Eastern counties, during their last struggle with the conquering Saxons, by whom he was martyred near Weedon (Benevenna).
Cf. Att. — Holw. — Baud.

CADOG (GADOGA) (St)   ?
5th cent. The titular saint of Llangadock in Carmarthen, not to be confused with the later St Cadoc or Docus.
Cf. Isaac Taylor: Words and Places, p. 313 n.

CADROE (CADROEL) (St) Ab. O.S.B.
     A.C. March 6
d. 976. The son of a Scottish prince, he was sent to Ireland to be educated at Armagh. He came to England and is said to have saved London from destruction by fire. Then he passed over to France and took the Benedictine habit at Fleury. Shortly after he was made abbot of the new foundation of Waulsort on the Meuse and finally called to Metz to restore St Clement's.
Cf. Mab. — Chev. — Baud. — Zimm. — Att.

CADWALLADOR (St) King.
     A.C. Nov. 12 (Oct. 9)
d. c.682. A chieftain in Wales of the ancient British race, not to be confused with the Anglo-Saxon St Ceadwalla.
Cf. Stanton — Baring-Gould.

CAECILIA, CAECILIANUS, CAELESTINE.
Otherwise often written Cecilia, Cecilanus, Celestine, and sometimes Coelestine.

CAECILIA (Bl) V. O.P.   A.C. June 9
See Diana, Caecilia and Amata — the first Dominican nuns.

CAECILIA (St) Abs. O.S.B. P.C. Aug. 17
See Benedicta and Caecilia.

CAECILIA (St) V.M.   R.M. Nov. 22
2nd-3rd cent. One of the most famous of martyred Roman maidens. Having suffered for Christ, she was buried in the cemetery of St Callistus. Her name is in the Canon of the Mass. At about the

same time there suffered at Rome SS Valerian and Tiburtius who were buried in the cemetery of Praetextatus. What connection they had with St Caecilia, it is difficult now to ascertain. The relics of all three rest at present beneath the high altar of the basilica of St Caecilia in Trastevere. All this is certain, and certain too it is that as early as the 4th century St Caecilia was already celebrated as one of the greatest Roman martyrs. The acts, however, which we now possess cannot be admitted as history. St Caecilia is the patron saint of musicians. In art she is represented playing the organ or the harp.
Cf. Ruinart — Baud. — Holw. — Att.

CAECILIA of FERRARA (Bl) V. O.P.
P.C. Dec. 19
d. 1511. Married to a very virtuous husband, they separated by mutual consent to become religious, and she joined the Dominican nuns at Ferrara.
Cf. Baud. — Holw.

CAECILIAN (St) M. R.M. Apr. 16
See Saragossa (Martyrs of).

CAECILIAN (St) C. R.M. June 3
Otherwise Caecilius, q.v.

CAECILIUS (St) Bp. R.M. May 15
See Torquatus, Ctesiphon, etc.

CAECILIUS (CAECILIAN) (St) C.
R.M. June 3
3rd cent. A priest of Carthage, who, according to the R.M., brought St Cyprian to the faith of Christ. St Cyprian never ceased to revere Caecilius's name, adding it to his own, and on Caecilius's death taking charge of his wife and children.
Cf. Baud. — Att. — Holw.

CAEDMON (St) Mk. O.S.B.
A.C. Feb. 11
d. c. 680 A Northumbrian, attached first as a farm-servant and then as a lay-brother to the community of Whitby under St Hilda. He was the first of the Anglo-Saxons to write in verse.
Cf. Zimm. — Chev. — Baud. — Holw. — P. de U. — Mab.

CAELIAN (St) M. R.M. Dec. 15
See Faustinus, Lucius, etc.

CAELLAINN (CAOILFIONN) (St) V.
A.C. Feb. 3
? 6th cent. An Irish saint listed in the Martyrology of Donegal. A church in Roscommon perpetuates her memory.
Cf. O' Hanlon.

CAEREALIS, PUPULUS, CAIUS and SERAPION (SS) MM. R.M. Feb. 28
? Martyrs at Alexandria in Egypt. Some ancient MSS read Cerulus or Celerius for Caerealis.
Cf. Baud. — Holw.

CAEREALIS (St) M. R.M. June 10
See Getulius, Caerealis, etc.

CAEREALIS and SALLUSTIA (SS) MM.
R.M. Sept. 14
d. 251. Caerealis, a soldier, and his wife Sallustia were instructed in the Faith by Pope St Cornelius, and martyred at Rome under Decius.
Cf. Holw. — Baud.

CAESAREA (St) V. A.C. May 15
? An Italian maiden, who in defence of her virtue took refuge in a cave, near Otranto, S. Italy, and lived therein as a recluse. This cave is now a place of popular pilgrimage.
Cf. Baud. — Holw.

CAESAREUS (St) M. R.M. Apr. 20
See Victor, Zoticus, etc.

CAESARIA (St) V. A.C. Jan. 12
d. c.530. Sister of St Caesarius of Arles, and abbess of the great nunnery founded by her brother in that city. According to the testimony of her contemporaries, Gregory of Tours and Venantius Fortunatus, she was a person of outstanding gifts.
Cf. Baud. — Att. — Holw.

CAESARIUS (St) C. A.C. Jan. 29
1st cent. Deacon of Angoulême under its first bishop St Ausonius.
Cf. Baud. — Holw.

CAESARIUS of NAZIANZUS (St) C.
R.M. Feb. 25
d. 369. Brother of St Gregory Nazianzen and physician at the imperial court of Byzantium, even under Julian the Apostate, who endeavoured unsuccessfully to drag Caesarius back to paganism. The

saint, however, remained a catechumen nearly all his life, and was baptized only after a narrow escape from death in an earthquake at Nicea in Bithynia. We owe all these details to the funeral oration delivered by his brother Gregory.
Cf. Att. — Baud.

CAESARIUS of ARLES (St) Bp.
R.M. Aug. 27
470-542. A native of Châlon-sur-Saône, at the age of twenty he became a monk at Lérins, and at the age of thirty (500) was chosen bishop of Arles. A great churchman, he presided over several councils, notably over that of Orange (529) which condemned Semi-pelagianism. He founded the great nunnery afterwards called by his name at Arles, for which he drew up a monastic rule and of which his sister St Caesaria became abbess. He was zealous for decorum in liturgical worship. He excelled as a preacher, and his homilies may still be read with much profit. His people looked upon him as their leader even in social and political affairs, and he always proved worthy of their trust. During the distress caused by the siege of Arles in 508 he sold the treasures of his church to relieve the poor. He is said to have been the first archbishop in Western Europe to receive the *pallium* from the pope.
Cf. Att. — Baud. — Holw. — Bolland.

CAESARIUS and JULIAN (SS) MM.
R.M. Nov. 1
? The former was an African deacon, the latter a priest. Both were martyred at Terracina, and their names appear in the earliest martyrologies. The church of St Caesarius on the Appian Way in Rome, now a title of one of the cardinal deacons, is dedicated to St Caesarius the African.
Cf. Att. — Holw. — Baud.

CAESARIUS, DACIUS and Comp. (SS) MM.
R.M. Nov. 1
? A group of seven martyrs who suffered at Damascus.
Cf. Baud. — Holw.

CAESARIUS (St) Bp. • A.C. Nov. 1
d. p. 627. The nineteenth or the twenty-second bishop of Clermont.
Cf. Gams — Duch. Fast. Episc. — Baud.

CAESARIUS (St) M. R.M. Nov. 3
See Germanus, Theophilus, etc.

CAESARIUS (St) M. R.M. Dec. 28
d. 309. Father of a notorious Arian, Eudoxius by name, his own past life had not been above reproach; but he atoned for it all by his heroic death at the stake at Arabissus in Armenia, under Galerius Maximian.
Cf. Baud. — Holw.

CAESIDIUS and Comp. (SS) MM.
R.M. Aug. 31
3rd cent. Said to have been the son of St Rufinus, bishop and martyr. He was himself a priest and was martyred, with a group of Christians, on the shores of Lake Fucino, sixty miles E. of Rome.
Cf. Holw. — Baud.

CAGNOALD (St) Bp. A.C. Sept. 6
d. c.635. Brother of St Faro and St Burgundofara. He became a monk at Luxeuil under St Columbanus, and afterwards the sixth bishop of Laon.
Cf. Gams — Chev. — Duch. Fast. Episc. — Baud.

CAIAN (St) A.C. Sept. 25
5th cent. A son or grandson of King Brychan of Brecknock. His church at Tregaian in Anglesey perpetuates his memory.
Cf. Stanton.

CAIDOC and FRICOR (ADRIAN) (SS) HH. A.C. Apr. 1
7th cent. Two Irishmen who evangelized the country of the Morini in N. France. St Ricarius, the future founder of Centula (Saint-Riquier), was one of their converts. Their relics are still venerated at the parish church of Saint-Riquier, diocese of Amiens.
Cf. Baud. — Mab. — Holw.

CAILLIN (St) Bp. A.C. Nov. 13
7th cent. Associated with St Aedan (Maidhoc) of Ferns. It is narrated of him that he turned certain unbelieving Druids into stone.

CAIMIN (CAMMIN) of INNISKELTRA (St) Ab. A.C. March 24 or 25
d. 653. An Irish recluse who had led a life of great austerity on an island in Lough Derg, to which his reputation for sanctity attracted many disciples. Later in life he founded a monastery and church on the island of the Seven Churches. He

was a fellow-worker with St Sennen. A
fragment of the Psalter of St Caimin,
copied with his own hand, still exists.
Cf. O'Hanlon — Holw. — Baud.

CAIRLON (CAORLAN) (St) Bp.
A.C. March 24
6th cent. An Irish abbot, said to have
died and to have been restored to life by
St Dageus. Afterwards, when St Cairlon
had been made archbishop of Cashel, St
Dageus placed himself and his monks
under his rule.
Cf. Holw. — O'Hanlon.

CAIRNECH (St) A.C. May 16
Otherwise Carantac, q.v.

CAIUS (St) M. R.M. Jan. 4
See Hermes, Aggaeus and Caius.

CAIUS FRANCIS (St) M. Tert. O.F.M.
R.M. Feb. 5
d. 1597. A Japanese soldier, recently baptized and received as a Franciscan tertiary, who insisted on being arrested with the
friars. He was crucified with twenty-five
companions at Nagasaki. Beatified 1627,
canonized in 1862.
Cf. Holw.

CAIUS (St) M. R.M. Feb. 28
See Caerealis, Pupulus, etc.

CAIUS and Comp. (SS) MM.
R.M. March 4
d. 254-259. Caius, an officer of the imperial palace, was with twenty-seven
(some MSS have thirty-seven) other Christians thrown into the sea. The place is not
recorded.
Cf. Baud. — Holw.

CAIUS and ALEXANDER (SS) MM.
R.M. March 10
d. c.172. Two Christians martyred at
Apamea in Phrygia under Marcus Aurelius. They had previously distinguished
themselves as firm opponents of the
Montanists.
Cf. Baud. — Holw.

CAIUS and CREMENTIUS (SS) MM.
R.M. Apr. 16
d. 304. Martyrs at Saragossa in Spain in
the persecution under Diocletian.

CAIUS of MELITENE (St) M.
R.M. Apr. 19
See Hermogenes, Caius, etc.

CAIUS (St) Pope, M. R.M. Apr. 22
d. c.296. Nothing reliable is known about
the life or death of this pope. He is said
to have been a Dalmatian, a relative of
Diocletian and the pope who recognized
officially the six orders preceding the
priesthood.
Cf. Att. — Baud. — Holw.

CAIUS XEYMON (Bl) M. Tert. O.P.
A.C. June 1
d. 627. A Japanese born of Christian
parents on the isle of Amakusa. He became a Dominican tertiary and helped the
friars in their missionary work. He was
burnt alive at Nagasaki (Aug. 17). Beatified in 1867.
Cf. Holw.

CAIUS and LEO (SS) MM.
R.M. June 30
? Martyrs either in Africa or in Rome.
Caius was a priest and Leo a subdeacon.

CAIUS of SALERNO (St) M. R.M. Aug. 28
See Fortunatus, Caius and Anthes.

CAIUS of MILAN (St) Bp. R.M. Sept. 27
1st cent. He is said to have been the successor of St Barnabas the Apostle in the
see of Milan, which he governed for
twenty-four years. He is also said to have
baptized the martyr St Vitalis and his sons
SS Gervase and Protase. St Charles Borromeo enshrined his relics in the church of
St Francis at Milan (1571).
Cf. Bolland.

CAIUS (St) M. R.M. Oct. 3
See Dionysius, Faustus, etc.

CAIUS of CORINTH R.M. Oct. 4
See Crispus and Caius.

**CAIUS, FAUSTUS, EUSEBIUS, CHAER
EMON, LUCIUS and Comp. (SS) MM.**
R.M. Oct. 4
3rd cent. Victims at Alexandria of the
persecution under Valerian (257). Caius
and Faustus are probably the saints of
those names commemorated with St
Dionysius of Alexandria, their bishop, on
Oct. 3. Eusebius, a deacon, survived to
become bishop of Laodicea, and died in
269. Chaeremon, who had already
suffered under Decius, was sent into exile.
Of Lucius nothing certain is known.
Cf. Baud. — Bolland. — Holw.

CAIUS (St) M. R.M. Oct. 21
See Dasius and Comp.

CAIUS of COREA (Bl) M. A.C. Nov. 15
d. 1624. A native of Corea, he was taken to Japan as a prisoner of war, where he was baptized and attached himself to the Jesuit missionaries as a catechist. He was burnt alive at Nagasaki. Beatified in 1867.
Cf. Holw.

CAIUS (St) M. R.M. Nov. 20
See Ampelus and Caius.

CAJETAN (GAETANO) (St) Founder.
R.M. Aug. 7
1480-1547. Born at Vicenza, in Lombardy, a scion of the family of the counts of Thienna (Tiene). He renounced the dignities offered him in Rome in order to devote his life to the service of the sick and the poor at Vicenza. Later, with Peter Caraffa (afterwards Pope Paul IV), he founded the congregation of clerks regularly called *Theatines*, from Theate (Chieti), in the Abruzzi, where Caraffa was bishop. The institute, characterized by absolute trust in divine providence, played a part in the counter-Reformation. St Cajetan died at Naples; he was canonized in 1671.
Cf. Att. — Baud. — Holw. — P. de U.

CALAIS (St) Ab. A.C. July 1
Otherwise Carilefus, q.v.

CALANICUS (St) M. R.M. Dec. 17
See Florian, Calanicus, etc.

CALEPODIUS, PALMATIUS, SIMPLICIUS, FELIX, BLANDA and Comp. (SS) MM. R.M. May 10
d. 222-232. A number of Roman martyrs who suffered under Alexander Severus, during the pontificate of Callistus I. Calepodius, a priest, was the first to suffer; he has given its name to a Roman catacomb. St Palmatius, of consular rank, died with his wife and children and forty-two of his household. St Simplicius, a senator, was martyred with sixty-five of his family and dependents. SS Felix and Blanda were husband and wife. All were victims of an outburst of fury on the part of the heathen mob.
Cf. Att. — Holw. — Baud.

CALETRICUS (St) Bp. A.C. Sept. 4
529-c.580. Born at Chartres he became bishop of that city after the death of St Lubinus (c.557).
Cf. Gams — Baud. — Duch. Fast. Episc.

CALIMERIUS (St) Bp. M. R.M. July 31
d. c.190. A Greek, educated in Rome by Pope St Telesphorus, he became bishop of Milan. He was the apostle of the valley of the Po. Under the emperor Commodus he was martyred by being cast headlong into a deep well. He is buried under the high altar of his church at Milan.
Cf. Holw. — Baud.

CALIMERIUS of MONTECHIERO (Bl) C. O.P. P.C. Nov. 28
d. 1521. A Friar Preacher who spent his life preaching throughout Italy. When a nonagenarian and unable to climb into the pulpit he persuaded others to lift him into it in order that he might preach.
Cf. Baud.

CALIXTUS (several)
Otherwise Callistus, q.v.

CALLINICA and BASILISSA (SS) MM.
R.M. March 22
d. 250. Rich ladies of Galatia in Asia Minor, who spent their fortune in succouring the Christians imprisoned for their faith. Both were martyred on that account.
Cf. Baud. — Holw.

CALLINICIUS (St) M. R.M. July 29
? 3rd cent. A native of Gangra, the chief town of Paphlagonia in Asia Minor. He was burnt to death. Metaphrastes gives full details of his martyrdom, and he is held in high esteem in the Eastern Churches.
Cf. Baud. — Holw.

CALLINICUS (St) M. R.M. Jan. 28
See Thyrsus, Leucius and Callinicus.

CALLIOPE (St) M. R.M. June 8
d. ?250. An Eastern martyr, beheaded for Christ. Neither the place nor the exact date of her martyrdom is known. Her acts are untrustworthy.
Cf. Holw. — Baud.

CALLIOPIUS (St) M. R.M. Apr. 7
d. c.303. A martyr, who, under Diocle-

tian, was crucified head downwards at Pompeiopolis in Cilicia.
Cf. Baud. — Holw.

CALLISTA (St) M. R.M. Sept. 2
See Evodius, Hermogenes and Callista.

CALLISTHENE (St) V. A.C. Oct. 4
See Adauctus and Callisthene.

CALLISTRATUS and Comp. (SS) MM.
R.M. Sept. 26
d. c.300. A body of fifty African soldiers put to death at Constantinople under Diocletian. They were sewn up in sacks and cast into the sea.
Cf. Baud. — Holw.

CALLISTUS, CHARISIUS and Comp. (SS) MM. R.M. Apr. 16
? Nine Christians of Corinth, martyred by being thrown into the sea.
Cf. Baud. — Holw.

CALLISTUS (St) Bp. M. R.M. Aug. 14
d. 528. Bishop of Todi in central Italy, distinguished for his zeal in repressing Arianism. He was put to death by the servants of some noblemen of evil life whom he had reproved. He is honoured as a martyr.
Cf. Baud. — Holw.

CALLISTUS I (St) Pope M. R.M. Oct. 14
d. c.222. A Christian slave of Rome, of outstanding natural gifts, who was made deacon by Pope St Zephyrinus, whom he succeeded as pope (217). For his lenient attitude towards repentant sinners he incurred the wrath of the rigorists — notably St Hippolytus, Tertullian and Novatian. He condemned Sabellianism and other heresies. As deacon he had superintended the Christian cemetery on the Appian Way, which is still known by his name. He was probably martyred.
Cf. Att. — Holw. — Baud.

CALLISTUS (St) M. A.C. Oct. 15
d. 1003. A native of Huesca, in Aragon, who, together with St Mercurialis, passed over to France and died there fighting against the Saracens. They are still venerated in the diocese of Tarbes.
Cf. Baud.

CALLISTUS, FELIX and BONIFACE (SS) MM. R.M. Dec. 29
? Roman martyrs, whose names are listed in all the Western martyrologies, but about whom nothing is known.

CALLIXTUS, CALIXTUS (*several*)
Otherwise Callistus, q.v.

CALMINIUS (CALMILIUS) (St) H.
A.C. Aug. 19
d. c.690. A hermit in Gaul who founded the abbeys of Villars (Calminiacum, Saint-Chaffe), and Mauzac, near Riom.

CALOCERUS (St) Bp. R.M. Feb. 11
d. c.130. A disciple of St Apollinaris, whom he succeeded in the see of Ravenna.
Cf. Baud. — Holw. — Gams.

CALOCERUS (St) M. R.M. Apr. 18
? Nothing reliable is known about this martyr. His acts, which belong to a much later period, connect him with SS Faustinus and Jovita, and make him an officer of the emperor Hadrian at Brescia in Lombardy.
Cf. Att. — Baud. — Holw.

CALOCERUS and PARTHENIUS (SS) MM. R.M. May 19
d. 250. Two brothers, eunuchs in the palace of Tryphonia, wife of the emperor Decius. They were martyred at Rome in the Decian persecution.
Cf. Att. — Holw. — Baud.

CALOGERUS the ANCHORET (St) M.
R.M. June 18
d. c.486. A Greek who received the monastic habit at the hands of the pope at Rome, and lived for thirty-five years as a recluse near Girgenti in Sicily, after having evangelized the isles of Lipari.
Cf. Baud. — Holw.

CALOGERUS (St) Ab. A.C. June 18
See Gregory, Demetrius and Calogerus.

CALUPAN (St) H. A.C. March 3
d. 575. Monk of Meallet in Auvergne, and afterwards a recluse in a neighbouring cave.
Cf. Baud. — Holw.

CAMELIAN (St) Bp. A.C. July 28
d. c.525. Successor of St Lupus in the see of Troyes (478-c.525).
Cf. Duch. Fast. Episc. — Gams — Baud.

CAMERINUS (St) M. R.M. Aug. 21
See Luxorius, Cisellus and Camerinus.

CAMILLA (St) V. A.C. March 3
d. c.437. A native of Civitavecchia who
became a disciple of St Germanus of
Auxerre at Ravenna and accompanied his
corpse to Auxerre. She settled near that
place as a recluse and died there.
Cf. Holw. — Baud.

CAMILLA GENTILI (Bl) V. A.C. May 18
d. 1486. A maiden of holy life who is
venerated in the church of the Dominican
friars at San Severino. Cult approved in
1841.
Cf. Holw. — Baud.

CAMILLA VARANI (Bl) Abs. Poor Clare.
A.C. May 31
d. 1527. Abbess of a convent founded by
her father at Camerino, in Italy. Cult
confirmed in 1843.
Cf. Holw.

CAMILLUS de LELLIS (St) Founder.
R.M. July 18
1550-1614. A native of the Abruzzi in
central Italy, who after some years of
soldiering, tried to join the Capuchins,
but had to leave them on account of a
disease of the feet, which proved incura-
ble. Ultimately he found his vocation in
the service of the sick, for whom he founded
the nursing congregation of the Ministers
of the Sick, approved in 1591. Before
this, St Camillus had been ordained priest
by Thomas Goldwell of St Asaph, the last
English bishop of the old hierarchy.
Canonized in 1746, and declared by Leo
XIII patron saint of the sick and of their
nurses.
Cf. Att. — Baud. — Holw.

CAMILLUS CONSTANZI (Bl) M. S.J.
A.C. Oct. 12
1572-1622. An Italian Jesuit and a missionary in Japan, who was banished from
that country as a Christian, but returned
and was burnt to death over a slow fire at
Firando (Sept. 15). Beatified in 1867.
Cf. Att. — Baud. — Holw.

CAMIN of INNISKELTRA (St) Ab.
A.C. March 24 or 25
Otherwise Caimin, q.v.

CAMPANIA (Martyrs of) (SS)
R.M. March 2
6th cent. Christians put to death by the
Lombards. They numbered several hun-

dreds (the R.M. mentions eighty). As to
their claim to the title of martyrs, we have
the testimony of St Gregory the Great,
their contemporary.
Cf. Holw.

CAMPION, EDMUND (Bl) M. S.J.
A.C. Dec. 1
See Edmund Campion, S.J.

CANDIDA (St) W. A.C. Jan. 27
d. c.798. Mother of St Emerius, the
founder of the abbey of St Stephen of
Bañoles. She died as a recluse near the
monastery, in the diocese of Gerona,
Spain.
Cf. Baud. — Holw.

CANDIDA (St) M. R.M. June 6
See Artemius, Candida and Paulina.

CANDIDA (St) V.M. R.M. Aug. 29
? One of a group of martyrs who suffered
on the Ostian Way, outside the gates of
Rome. In the 9th century Pope St
Paschal I enshrined her relics in the church
of St Praxedes.
Cf. Baud. — Holw. — Bolland.

CANDIDA the ELDER (St) V.M.
R.M. Sept. 4
d. c.78. An aged woman who is said to
have welcomed St Peter when passing
through Naples on his way to Rome and
to have been miraculously cured by him
of a malady. In her turn she converted
St Aspren, who became the first bishop
of Naples.
Cf. Baud. — Holw. — Bolland.

CANDIDA the YOUNGER (St)
R.M. Sept. 10
d. ? 586. A married woman of Naples,
who sanctified herself by fulfilling perfectly
her duties as a wife and as a mother. The
R.M. describes her as "famous for her
miracles."
Cf. Baud. — Holw. — Bolland.

CANDIDA (St) V.M. R.M. Sept. 20
d. c.300. A martyred maiden of Carthage
under Maximian Herculius. The date of
her martyrdom is contested; see the Bollandists on this controversy.
Cf. Bolland. — Holw. — Baud.

CANDIDA (St) M. R.M. Dec. 1
See Lucius, Rogatus, etc.

CANDIDUS of ROME (St) M.
R.M. Feb. 2
See Fortunatus, Felician, etc.

CANDIDUS (St) M.   R.M. March 10
One of the Forty Armenian Martyrs, q.v.

**CANDIDUS, PIPERION and Comp. (SS)
MM.   R.M. March 11**
d. c.254-259. Twenty-two African martyrs who suffered either at Carthage or at Alexandria, most probably under Valerian and Gallienus. Particulars are lost.
Cf. Bolland. — Holw. — Baud.

CANDIDUS (St) M.   R.M. Sept. 22
See Theban Legion.

CANDIDUS (St) M.   R.M. Oct. 3
? A Roman martyr, buried on the Esquiline Hill, in the place called *"ad Ursum Pileatum."*
Cf. Bolland. — Baud. — Holw.

CANDIDUS (St) M.   R.M. Dec. 15
See Faustinus, Lucius, etc.

CANDRES (St) Bp.   A.C. Dec. 1
5th cent. A regionary bishop who evangelized the territory of Maestricht. He is still liturgically commemorated in the diocese of Rouen.
Cf. Baud. — Rev. Bénéd., VIII, 176.

CANICE (CANICUS, CAINNECH, KENNY, KENNETH) (St) Ab.   R.M. Oct. 11
c.515-599. Born in N. Ireland, he was trained to the monastic life under St Finnian of Clonard, and St Cadoc in Wales. Then he went to Glasnevin. He founded the monastery of Aghaboe and perhaps of Kilkenny, and later preached in Scotland under St Columba and was the first to build a church in the place now known as St Andrews. He has always been very popular in Ireland; the city of Kilkenny is named after him.
Cf. Att. — Holw. — O' Hanlon.

CANION (St) C.   R.M. Sept. 1
See Priscus, Castrensis, etc.

CANNATUS (St) Bp.   A.C. Oct. 15
5th cent. Bishop of Marseilles after St Honoratus.
Cf. Baud. — Holw. — Duch. Fast. Episc.

**CANNERA (CAINDER, KINNERA) (St)
V.   A.C Jan. 28**
d. c.530. An Irish maiden who lived as a recluse near Bantry. She died after visiting St Senan and receiving Holy Communion at his hands. She was buried on St Senan's island of Inniscathy.
Cf. Holw. — O' Hanlon.

CANOG (CYNOG) M.   A.C. Oct. 7
d. c.492. Eldest son of King Brychan of Brecknock. He met his death as a result of an inroad of barbarians at Merthyr-Cynog. Several churches in Wales were dedicated to him. In Brittany he is known as St Cenneur.
Cf. Stanton — Baring-Gould.

**CANTIAN and CANTIANILLA (SS)
MM.   R.M. May 31**
See Cantius, Cantian, etc.

**CANTIDIUS, CANTIDIAN and SOBEL
(SS) MM.   R.M. Aug. 5**
? Egyptian martyrs of whom nothing is known except the fact of their martyrdom.

**CANTIUS, CANTIAN, CANTIANILLA
and PROTUS (SS) MM.   R.M. May 31**
d. c.304. Two brothers and their sister, said to have belonged to the Roman family of the Anicii. They were martyred at Aquileia, whither they had retired, together with their tutor, Protus by name, under Diocletian. We have still a panegyric preached in their honour by St Maximus of Turin.
Cf. Att. — Baud. — Holw.

CANUTE (KNUD) LAVARD (St) M.
R.M. Jan. 7
d. 1133. A nephew of St Canute, king of Denmark, with whom he is sometimes confused. He was duke of Schleswig, and his life was spent mostly in war against the viking pirates. He was slain as a result of a conspiracy of the Danes, headed by a kinsman of his, pretender to the throne. Canonized in 1171 and venerated as a martyr.
Cf. Att. — Holw. — Baud.

CANUTE (KNUD) (St) King, M.
R.M. Jan. 19
d. 1086. Natural son of Sweyn III, king of Denmark, and great-nephew of Canute, king of England, he succeeded to the Danish throne as Canute IV. He displayed a

warlike zeal for the spreading of the gospel in Denmark itself, Courland, Livonia and elsewhere. He was prevented by treachery from helping the Anglo-Saxons against their Norman conquerors. Though well liked by his people, he was ki led in a church by a party of malcontents, headed by his brother Olaf (July 10). As this crime was prompted by opposition to the laws he had enacted to enforce the payment of tithes, he was considered a martyr and as such was canonized by the Holy See, at the request of Eric III, king of Denmark, in 1101.
Cf. Att. — Baud. — Holw.

CAPITO (St) Bp. M.   R.M. March 4
See Basil, Eugene, etc.

CAPITO (St) M.   R.M. July 24
See Meneus and Capito.

CAPITOLINA and EROTHEIS (SS) MM.   R.M. Oct. 27
d. 304. A Cappadocian lady and her hand-maid, martyred under Diocletian.
Cf. Baud. — Holw.

CAPPADOCIA (Martyrs of) (SS) R.M. May 23
d. 303. A group of martyrs, put to death in Cappadocia, under Galerius, after having suffered exquisite tortures.
Cf. Baud. — Holw.

CAPRASIUS (St) Ab.   R.M. June 1
d. c.430. A native of Gaul, he retired to the island of Lérins to live as a hermit. Thither he was followed by SS Honoratus and Venantius, and together they went to the East to visit the monastic colonies there. Venantius died in Greece; the other two returned to Lérins, where St Honoratus founded the famous abbey, and on his being appointed bishop of Arles, he was succeeded by Caprasius as abbot.
Cf. Att. — Baud. — Mab. — Bolland.

CAPRASIUS (St) M.   R.M. Oct. 20
d. 303. A native of Agen in S. France, who, owing to fear, concealed himself during the persecution of Diocletian; but on hearing of the courage of St Faith at the stake, he came forth and boldly confessed his religion. He was forthwith beheaded.
Cf. Baud. — Att. — Holw.

CARADOC (St) Ab.   A.C. Apr. 13
d. 1124. A Welshman, harpist at the court of King Rhys of S. Wales, who became a monk at Llandaff, and eventually lived as a hermit in different places — on Barry Island, at St Issels, etc. — in S. Wales. He had much to suffer during the English invasion under Henry I. He was buried with great honour in the cathedral of St David's.
Cf. Att. — Baud. — Holw.

CARALIPPUS (St) M.   R.M. Apr. 28
See Aphrodisius, Caralippus, etc.

CARANTAC (CARANTOG, CAIRNACH, CARNATH) (St)   A.C. May 16
5th cent. A Welsh prince who laboured under St Patrick in the evangelization of Ireland.
Cf. Baud. — Holw.

CARANTOCK (St) Ab.   A.C. May 16
6th cent. A Welsh abbot, founder of the church of Llangranog. He is associated with Crantock in Cornwall and Carhampton in Somerset. He is also highly venerated in Brittany. Some writers identify him with St Carantac.
Cf. Att.

CARANUS (St) Bp.   A.C. Dec. 24
7th cent. A saint commemorated in the Aberdeen breviary. He belonged to E. Scotland.

CARAUNUS (CERAUNUS, CHERON) (St) M.   R.M. May 28
5th cent. A Christian of Roman descent, he preached the gospel in Gaul, and was killed by robbers near Chartres. A church and monastery were built over his tomb.
Cf. Holw. — Baud. — P.B.

CARILEFUS (CARILEPHUS, CARILEFF, CALAIS) (St) Ab.   A.C. July 1
d. c.536. A French monk, friend and companion of St Avitus. He was the abbot-founder of the abbey of Anisole in Maine. His cult is found chiefly at Blois.
Cf. Att. — Baud. — Holw. — Mab.

CARINA (St) M.   R.M. Nov. 7
See Melasippus, Antony and Carina.

CARISSIMA (St) V.   A.C. Sept. 7
5th cent. A native of Albi, in France. She retired to a forest near the city, then to the nunnery of Viants (Vious). She is liturgically commemorated at Albi.
Cf. Baud. — Holw. — P.B.

CARITAS (St) V.M. R.M. Aug. 1
Otherwise Charity. See Faith, Hope and
Charity.

CARLOMAN (Bl) Mk. O.S.B.
A.C. Aug. 17
707-755. Eldest son of Charles Martel,
brother of Pepin the Short. On his
father's death he became king of Austrasia. As such, he promoted the foundation of the abbeys of Fulda, Lobbes,
Stavelot, etc., helped St Boniface in the
evangelization of the Germanies, and endeavoured to remedy the injustice done by
Charles Martel with regard to ecclesiastical property. On St Boniface's advice
he left the kingdom to his brother, received
the Benedictine habit at the hands of Pope
St Zachary and was a monk first on Mt
Soracte and then at Montecassino, where
he was employed in the kitchen and as the
shepherd of the abbey. Sent by the pope
to make peace between Pepin and the
Lombards, he died in a monastery at
Vienne. He has an altar dedicated to him
at Montecassino.

*Cf. Mab. — Zimm. — P. de U. — Chev. —
Baud. — Holw.*

**CARMELITE NUNS of COMPIÈGNE
(BB) MM.** A.C. July 17
d. 1794. Sixteen nuns of the Carmel of
Compiègne, guillotined in Paris during the
French Revolution. They went to the
scaffold singing the *Salve Regina.* Beatified in 1906. Each is given a separate
notice in this book.
Cf. Baud.

CARMES (Martyrs des) (BB)
A.C. Sept. 2
See September (Martyrs of)

CARNATH or CARNECH (St) Ab.
A.C. May 16
Otherwise Carantac, q.v.

CARON (St) ? Bp. A.C. March 5
? The title saint of Tregaron in Cardigan-
shire. Nothing is known about him.
Cf. Baring-Gould.

**CARPONIUS, EVARISTUS and PRIS-
CIAN (SS) MM.** R.M. Oct. 14
d. c.304. Three brothers who, with their
sister St Fortunata, were among the
Christians martyred under Diocletian at

Caesarea in Palestine. Their relics were
translated to Naples.
Cf. Holw. — Baud.

**CARPOPHORUS, EXANTHUS, CAS-
SIUS, SEVERINUS, SECUNDUS and
LICINIUS (SS) MM.** R.M. Aug. 7
d. c.295. Christian soldiers who were put
to death at Como in N. Italy, under
Maximian Herculius.
Cf. Bolland. — Baud. — Holw.

CARPOPHORUS (St) M. R.M. Aug. 27
See Rufus and Carpophorus.

CARPOPHORUS (St) M. R.M. Nov. 8
See Four Crowned Martyrs.

**CARPOPHORUS and ABUNDIUS (SS)
MM.** R.M. Dec. 10
d. 290-300. A priest and his deacon who
suffered under Diocletian. Rome, Spoleto and Seville have been given as the
place of their martyrdom.
Cf. Baud. — Holw.

**CARPUS, PAPYLUS, AGATHONICA,
AGATHADORUS and Comp. (SS) MM.**
R.M. Apr. 13
d. 150 (or 250). Carpus was the bishop of
Thyatira, Papylus, his deacon, Agathonica, the latter's sister, and Agathodorus, their servant. They were martyred with many others at Pergamos in
the time of Marcus Aurelius or of Decius.
Cf. Att. — Baud. — Bolland. — Holw.

CARPUS (St) R.M. Oct. 13
1st cent. The Carpus of Troas on the
Hellespont with whom St Paul (II Tim. IV,
13) says "he had left his cloak." Nothing
more is known about him. Some Greek
writers make him a bishop.
Cf. Holw. — Baud.

CARTERIUS (St) M. A.C. Jan. 8
d. 304. A priest of Caesarea in Cappadocia, who suffered under Diocletian. He
is venerated by the Grecks.
Cf. Baud. — Holw.

**CARTERIUS, STYRIACUS, TOBIAS,
EUDOXIUS, AGAPIUS and Comp. (SS)
MM.** R.M. Nov. 2
d. c.315. Ten Christian soldiers in the
army of the emperor Licinius, burnt at the
stake at Sebaste in Armenia.
Cf. Baud. — Holw.

CARTHAGE the ELDER (St) Bp.
A.C. March 5
d. c.540. The successor of St Kieran in the see of Ossory. He is said to have been the son or grandson of King Aengus.
Cf. Holw. — O' Hanlon.

CARTHAGE (CARTHACH MOCHUDA) the YOUNGER (St) Bp. A.C. May 14
d. c.637. Born in Kerry, he founded (c.590) an abbey at Rathin in Westmeath, of which he was abbot-bishop, and for which he wrote a monastic rule in verse. Shortly before his death (c.635) he and his community were expelled. He led his monks to the banks of the Blackwater and there established the monastery-school of Lismore. Cult confirmed in 1903.
Cf. Att. — Holw. — O' Hanlon.

CARTHUSIAN MARTYRS (BB)
A.C. May 4
1535-1540. Eighteen monks of the Carthusian Order in England, put to death for their allegiance to the Holy See under Henry VIII. Beatified in 1886. Each is given a separate notice in this book.
Cf. Att. — Holw.

CASDOE (St) M. R.M. Sept. 29
See Dadas, Casdoe and Gabdelas.

CASILDA (St) V. A.C. Apr. 9
d. c.1050. A native of Toledo and said to have been of Moorish parentage. She became a Christian and led the life of an anchoress near Briviesca in the province of Burgos. She is greatly venerated throughout Spain, chiefly in the provinces of Burgos and Toledo.
Cf. P. de U. — Att. — Holw.

CASIMIR of POLAND (St) C.
R.M. March 4
1458-1483. The second son of King Casimir IV of Poland. His father wished him to seize the crown of Hungary which was offered to him by a powerful party among the Hungarians: but the prince refused to employ force and was imprisoned by his father for three months. The remainder of his life he devoted to prayer and study. He died of consumption in 1483. He is the patron saint of Poland and Lithuania.
Cf. Att. — Holw. — Baud.

CASPAR (GASPAR) (St) A.C. Jan. 8
One of the Magi, q.v.

CASPAR SADAMAZU (Bl) M. S.J.
A.C. June 20
d. 1626. A native of Omura in Japan, he was received into the Society of Jesus at Bungo 1582. He acted as secretary to several provincials, the last being Bl Francis Pacheco, with whom he was buried alive at Nagasaki. Beatified in 1867.
Cf. Holw.

CASPAR de BONO (Bl) C. Minim.
A.C. July 14
1530-1604. A native of Valencia in Spain, he became a silk merchant, then a trooper and finally a Minim friar. After his ordination in 1561 he was twice appointed corrector provincial of the Spanish province of Minims. Beatified in 1786.
Cf. Att. — Holw. — Baud.

CASPAR ALVAREZ (Bl) M. S.J.
A.C. July 15
d. 1570. Born at Oporto in Portugal, he became a Jesuit lay-brother, and was one of a band of martyrs who suffered with Bl Ignatius de Azevedo. Beatified in 1854.
Cf. Holw.

CASPAR and MARY VAZ (BB) MM.
A.C. Aug. 17
d. 1627. Husband and wife, natives of Japan and tertiaries of St Francis, martyred at Nagasaki. Caspar was burnt alive and his wife beheaded. Beatified in 1867.
Cf. Holw.

CASPAR COTENDA (Bl) M.
A.C. Sept. 11
d. 1622. A Japanese belonging to the royal family of Firando. He was martyred at Nagasaki. Beatified in 1867.
Cf. Holw.

CASPAR FISOGIRO (Bl) M. A.C. Oct. 1
d. 1617. A Japanese Christian, member of the Confraternity of the Holy Rosary. He was beheaded at Nagasaki for having befriended Bl Alfonsus Navarrete, O.P. Beatified in 1867.
Cf. Holw. — Baud.

CASPAR del BUFALO (Bl) Founder.
A.C. Dec. 28
1786-1837. A native of Rome, who studied for the priesthood at the Roman College, and was ordained in 1808. He was exiled to Corsica for refusing to swear

allegiance to Napoleon. On his return in 1814 he founded at Giano, diocese of Spoleto, the first house of the Missioners of the Most Precious Blood for mission work at home. After much opposition it received the approval of the Holy See, but by that time Caspar was already dead. Beatified in 1904.
Cf. Att. — Holw.

CASSIA (St) M. R.M. July 20
See Sabinus, Julian, etc.

CASSIAN (St) M. R.M. March 26
See Peter, Marcian, etc.

CASSIAN (St) Ab. A.C. July 23
Otherwise John Cassian, q.v.

CASSIAN of AUTUN (St) Bp.
R.M. Aug. 5
d. c.350. Probably an Egyptian by birth. Coming to Autun in France he attached himself to the bishop St Reticius, whom he eventually succeeded in the see.
Cf. Baud. — Duch. Fast. Episc. — Holw.

CASSIAN VAZ LÓPEZ-NETO (Bl) O.F.M. Cap. A.C. Aug. 7
1607-1638. Born at Nantes in France but of Spanish descent, he took the Capuchin habit at Angers, and was sent to Egypt to preach to the Copts, together with Bl Agathangelus, q.v. He was stoned to death on entering Abyssinia. Beatified in 1904.
Cf. Holw. — Baud.

CASSIAN of BENEVENTO (St) Bp.
A.C. Aug. 12
d. c.340. Bishop of Benevento in S. Italy. His relics are enshrined in the church of St Mary in the same city.
Cf. Baud. — Holw.

CASSIAN of IMOLA (St) M.
R.M. Aug. 13
? The *laus* of the R.M. reads as follows: "The birthday of holy Cassian the martyr. When he refused to worship idols, the persecutor summoned certain boys whose hatred Cassian had incurred by acting as their schoolmaster, and afforded them the opportunity of killing him. As their efforts were puny, so was his suffering bitter above the ordinary and his death protracted."
Cf. also Att. — Holw. — Bolland.

CASSIAN of TODI (St) Bp. M.
R.M. Aug. 13
4th cent. A convert of St Pontian, bishop of Todi, in Central Italy, and his successor in that see. He was martyred under Maximian Herculeus. Unfortunately his acts have been confused with those of the more famous St Cassian of Imola, venerated on the same day.
Cf. Baud. — Holw.

CASSIAN (St) M. R.M. Dec. 1
See Lucius, Rogatus, etc.

CASSIAN (St) M. R.M. Dec. 3
d. 298. During the trial of St Marcellus (October 30) at Tangier under Diocletian, Cassian, as the *exceptor* (official shorthand-writer or recorder) of the court, was taking down the *acta* of the proceedings. Indignant at the injustice done to the martyr, he threw down his pen and declared himself a Christian. He was arrested and a few weeks later he too suffered martyrdom. His acts are quite authentic; he is also mentioned in one of the hymns of Prudentius.
Cf. Ruinart — Att. — Holw. — Baud.

CASSIUS, VICTORINUS, MAXIMUS and Comp. (SS) MM. R.M. May 15
d. 260. A group of martyrs of Clermont in Auvergne, who suffered at the hands of Chrocas, chief of the invading Teutonic barbarians.
Cf. Baud. — Holw.

CASSIUS of NARNI (St) Bp.
R.M. June 29
d. 558. Bishop of Narni from 537 to 558. St Gregory the Great has left on record the virtues of this holy prelate.
Cf. Att. — Baud. — Holw.

CASSIUS (St) M. R.M. Aug. 7
See Carpophorus, Exanthus, etc.

CASSIUS, FLORENTIUS and Comp. (SS) MM. R.M. Oct. 10
d. 303. Christians put to death by the emperor Maximian Herculeus at Bonn in Germany.
Cf. Holw. — Baud.

CASTOR and DOROTHEUS (SS) MM.
R.M. March 28
? Two martyrs who suffered at Tarsus in Cilicia in one of the early persecutions.
Cf. Baud. — Holw.

CASTOR and STEPHEN (SS) MM.
R.M. Apr. 27
? Two martyrs who suffered at Tarsus in Cilicia in one of the early persecutions. Some writers identify them with the preceding pair.
Cf. Holw. — Baud. — Bolland.

CASTOR (St) Bp. A.C. Sept. 2
d. c.420. A native of Nîmes, who married a wife and settled at Marseilles. After a short time they separated by mutual consent and both became religious. Castor founded the monastery of Manauque, and shortly after was chosen bishop of Apt. St John Cassian wrote the *De Institutis Coenobiorum* at Castor's request.
Cf. Att. — Baud. — Holw. — Duch. Fast. Episc.

CASTOR, VICTOR, and ROGATIANUS (SS) MM. R.M. Dec. 28
? African martyrs of whom the names only are known.

CASTORA GABRIELLI (Bl) W.
P.C. June 14
d. 1391. A Franciscan tertiary, wife and widow of Santuccio Sanfonerio, a lawyer at Sant' Angelo in Vado in Umbria. She sanctified herself by the daily practice of the domestic virtues.
Cf. Att. — Holw.

CASTORIUS (St) M.
R.M. July 7 and Nov. 8
See Claudius, Nicostratus, etc., and Four Crowned Martyrs.

CASTRENSIS (St) Bp. R.M. Feb. 11
5th cent. One of the Catholic bishops banished from Africa by the Arian Vandals. He continued to exercise his episcopal office at Capua in S. Italy. Most likely he is to be identified with the Capuan bishop St Priscus (R.M. Sept. 1) Castrensis, that is, formerly bishop of Castra, in N. Africa.
Cf. Baud. — Holw. — Bolland.

CASTRENSIS (St) Bp. R.M. Sept. 1
See Priscus, Castrensis, etc.

CASTRITIAN (St) Bp. R.M. Dec. 1
d. 137. The predecesser of St Calimerius in the see of Milan. He governed that see for forty-two years.
Cf. Baud. — Holw.

CASTULUS (St) M. R.M. Jan. 12
See Zoticus, Rogatus, etc.

CASTULUS (St) M. R.M. Feb. 15
See Saturninus, Castulus, etc.

CASTULUS (St) M. R.M. March 26
d. 288. An officer of the palace in Rome of the emperor Diocletian. For having sheltered some of his fellow Christians he was put to the torture and buried alive. A cemetery was named after his burial place on the Via Labicana.
Cf. Att. — Holw. — Baud.

CASTULUS and EUPREPIS (SS) MM.
R.M. Nov. 30
? Roman martyrs of whom nothing is known.

CASTUS and AEMILIUS (SS) MM.
R.M. May 22
d. c.250. Two African martyrs, who suffered under Decius. They at first gave way under torture, but repented, and on being seized a second time, were burned to death. Their contemporary, St Cyprian, and also St Augustine are loud in their praise of these two martyrs.
Cf. Att. — Baud. — Ruinart.

CASTUS and SECUNDINUS (SS) Bps.
R.M. July 1
c.305. Two saints much venerated in S. Italy. The martyrologies register them as of Sinuessa (Mondragone) near Caserta.
Cf. Baud. — Holw.

CASTUS (St) M. R.M. Sept. 4
See Magnus, Castus and Maximus.

CASTUS (St) M. R.M. Oct. 6
See Marcellus, Castus, etc.

CATALDUS (St) Bp. R.M. May 10
7th cent. Born in Munster, Ireland, he was first a pupil, and then the headmaster, of the monastic school of Lismore. On his return from a pilgrimage to the Holy Land, he was chosen bishop of their city by the people of Taranto, in S. Italy. He is the titular of the cathedral of Taranto and the principal patron saint of the diocese.
Cf. Att. — Baud. — Holw.

CATELLUS (St) Bp. A.C. Jan. 19
9th cent. Bishop of Castellamare, south

of Naples. He was an intimate friend of St Antoninus, O.S.B. He is venerated as the principal saint of the city and diocese of Castellamare.
Cf. Holw. — Gams.

CATHALDUS (CATHAL) (St) Bp.
R.M. May 10
Otherwise Cataldus, q.v.

CATHAN (CATAN, CADAN) (St) Bp.
A.C. May 17
6th or 7th cent. He seems to have been bishop in the Isle of Bute, often called after him Kil-Cathan. His tomb is shown at Tamlacht near Londonderry, but the Scots contend that he rests in the Isle of Bute. Possibly there were two saints of the same name.
Cf. Holw. — Baring–Gould — O' Hanlon.

CATHERINE dei RICCI (St) V. O.P.
R.M. Feb. 2
1522-1590. Born at Florence, she became in 1535 a regular tertiary of St Dominic, and eventually filled the offices of novice-mistress and prioress. She was famous for her ecstasies in which she beheld and enacted the scenes of our Lord's passion. It is narrated that she met in vision St Philip Neri, still alive in Rome. Three future popes were among the thousands who flocked to her convent to ask her prayers. Canonized in 1746.
Cf. Att. — Holw. — Baud.

CATHERINE of BOLOGNA (St) V. Poor Clare.
R.M. March 9
1413-1463. Born at Bologna, she was a maid of honour to Margaret d'Este. Eventually she took the veil of the Augustinian nuns at Ferra, who afterwards became Poor Clares. Catherine was appointed novice-mistress and then abbess of a daughter convent of Poor Clares at Bologna. Here she spent her life praying for sinners, favoured by God with amazing visions, and committing to writing her mystical experiences. Canonized in 1712.
Cf. Att. — Baud. — Holw.

CATHERINE of SWEDEN (St) Bridg.
R.M. March 24
1331-1381. Born in Sweden, the fourth child of St Brigid, she married Eggard Lydersson, a life-long invalid, with whom she lived in continency, and whom she tended with great devotion. After his death, Catherine followed her mother to Palestine and Rome, and on St Brigid's death returned to Sweden and became abbess of Wadstena. In 1375-1380 she was again in Rome, obtaining the approval of the Salvatorian Order and promoting the canonization of her own mother. Cult confirmed in 1474.
Cf. Att. — Holw. — Baud.

CATHERINE TOMAS (St) V. O.S.A.
A.C. Apr. 1
1533-1574. Born on the island of Majorca. She joined the canonesses regular of St Augustine at Palma and there she spent her whole life, subject to a great number of strange phenomena and mystical experiences; during the last years of her life she was continually in ecstasy. Canonized in 1930.
Cf. Att. — Baud. — Holw.

CATHERINE of PALLANZA (Bl) V. O.S.A.
A.C. Apr. 6
c.1437-1478. A native of Pallanza, diocese of Novara. At fourteen years of age she began to live the life of a recluse in the mountain district above Varese, near Milan. Disciples gathered round her and she gathered them into a community under the rule of St Augustine. Cult confirmed in 1769.
Cf. Att. — Baud. — Holw.

CATHERINE of SIENA (St) V. Tert. O.P.
R.M. Apr. 30
1347-1380. Born at Siena in Tuscany, the twenty-fifth child of a wool-dyer, Catherine Benincasa received the habit of the third order of St Dominic at the age of sixteen, continuing, however, to live at home. Soon her sanctity attracted a number of persons, clerical and lay, round her — the Caterinati — of whom she was a sort of leader. She worked among the poor of Siena and was most active and successful in the conversion of hardened sinners. She had especially at heart the unity and welfare of the Church and was instrumental in persuading Pope Gregory IX to abandon Avignon and return to Rome. She tried to heal the great schism of the West, rallying all Italy around Pope Urban VI. In 1378 she was summoned by the pope to Rome and there died, fighting still in the cause of the true pope. She has left over four hundred letters and a Dialogue which is one of the most remark-

able mystical works of all time. Canonized in 1461 and declared patron saint of Italy in 1939.
Cf. Att. — Holw. — Baud.

CATHERINE of PARC-AUX-DAMES (Bl)
V. O.S.B. Cist. **P.C. May 4**
13th cent. A daughter of Jewish parents of Louvain, her name was Rachel. The chaplain of the duke of Brabant was a frequent visitor to her home, and the little Rachel was an eager listener when he would defend the Catholic religion against the attacks of her Jewish father. When she was twelve years old, she secretly left her home, received baptism and joined the Cistercian nuns at Parc-aux-Dames, near Louvain, where she lived till her death.
Cf. Att. — Baud. — Holw.

CATHERINE of CARDONA (Bl) V.
P.C. May 21
1519-1577. Born at Naples of a noble Spanish family, she lived for a time at the court of Philip II of Spain; then she retired to live as a recluse near Roda in S. Spain. She remained there for twenty years until she was received into a Carmelite convent, where, however, she continued to live as an anchoress. St Teresa speaks very highly of her.
Cf. Baud. — P. de U.

CATHERINE TANACA (Bl) M.
A.C. July 12
d. 1626. Wife of Bl John Tanaca. Both were beheaded at Nagasaki, Japan. Beatified in 1867.
Cf. Holw. — P.B.

CATHERINE SOIRON (Bl) V. M.
A.C. July 17
d. 1794. She, and her sister Teresa, were the door-keepers (*tourières*) for the Carmelite nuns at Compiègne and were guillotined with them at Paris. They were not in vows. Beatified in 1904.
Cf. Holw. — Baud.

CATHERINE MATTEI (Bl) V. Tert. O.P.
A.C. Sept. 4
d. 1547. Born at Racconigi in the diocese of Cuneo, daughter of a poor working man. She took the Dominican habit of the third order and tried faithfully to imitate her namesake of Siena. She too is said to have been favoured with signal mystical experiences. Cult confirmed in 1810.
Cf. Att. — Holw. — Baud.

CATHERINE (Bl) M. **A.C. Sept. 10**
d. 1622. A Japanese widow. She was beheaded at Nagasaki together with Bl Charles Spinola and his fifty-one companions. Beatified in 1867.
Cf. Holw. — Baud.

CATHERINE of GENOA (St) W.
R.M. Sept. 15
1477-1510. Born in Genoa, of the noble Fieschi family, she married Julian Adorno when she was sixteen. She led a life of active charity, devoting herself to the service of others both at home and in the hospitals and poor quarters of the city. At first her work was made exceedingly difficult by the attitude of her profligate husband, whom she succeeded in converting to better ways. She wrote a treatise on Purgatory and a Dialogue between the soul and the body — two outstanding documents of Christian mysticism. Canonized in 1737.
Cf. Att. — Holw. — Baud.

CATHERINE of ALEXANDRIA (St)
V.M. **R.M. Nov. 25**
d. c.310. A maiden martyred at Alexandria under Maximinus Daza. The legend adds that she argued with fifty pagan philosophers before she was put to death by means of an engine fitted with a spiked wheel. She overcame them all, and on this account she is considered the patroness of philosophers. Her alleged relics have been enshrined for the last thousand years in the Orthodox monastery of Mt. Sinai. In art she is represented with the spiked wheel of her martyrdom, or arguing with the pagan philosophers.
Cf. Ricci. — Att. — Holw. — Baud.

CATHERINE LABOURÉ (Bl) V.
A.C. Dec. 31
1806-1875. Born in the Côte d'Or, daughter of a yeoman farmer, she became a Sister of Charity of St Vincent de Paul in 1830, and spent her whole life much as the ordinary Sister of Charity spends it, except for a series of visions with which she was favoured by God. The first "miraculous medal" was struck as the result of one of these visions. She died in the convent of Enghien-Reuilly and was beatified in 1933.
Cf. Att.

CATHOLDUS, ANNO and DIETHAR-DUS (BB) Mks. O.S.B.   A.C. Sept. 29
d. late 8th cent. Three Benedictine monks who preached the gospel in the diocese of Eichstätt. Catholdus was a monk of Herrieden (built in 790).
Cf. Zimm.

CATULINUS (CATHOLINUS), JANU-ARIUS, FLORENTIUS, JULIA and JUS-TA (SS) MM.   R.M. July 15
? Carthaginian martyrs. Their bodies were enshrined in the basilica of Fausta at Carthage. Of St Catulinus, a deacon, we have a panegyric preached by St Augustine. Nothing else is known about them.
Cf. Holw. — Baud.

CATUS (St) M.   R.M. Jan. 19
See Paul, Gerontius, etc.

CAWRDAF (St)   A.C. Dec. 5
6th cent. The son and successor of Caradog, chieftain of Brecknock and Hereford. He ended life as a monk under St Illtyd.
Cf. Holw. — Baring-Gould.

CE
Note. In many names this syllable is often written Cae, or Che, or Ke, or Kae, etc.

CEADDA (St) Bp.   R.M. March 2
Otherwise Chad, q.v.

**CEADWALLA (CADWALLA) (St) King.
A.C. Apr. 20**
d. 689. King of Wessex, who, while yet a pagan, showed himself not less cruel and crafty than other conquerors of his race and time. He was converted by St Wilfrid and journeyed to Rome, where he was baptized by Pope St Sergius and died while yet wearing the white robe of the neophytes. There is no evidence of an ancient cult.
Cf. Att. — Holw. — Baud.

**CEALLACH (KELLACH) (St) Bp.
A.C. May 1**
6th cent. A disciple of St Kieran of Clonmacnoise, who became bishop of Killala but ended his life as a hermit, by some accounts as a martyr. There are several other saints of the same name.
Cf. Holw. — O' Hanlon.

**CEARAN (CIARAN) (St) Ab.
A.C. June 14**
d. 870. An Irish abbot of Bellach-Duin,

now Castle-Keerant, Co. Meath, surnamed The Devout.
Cf. O' Hanlon.

CECILIA, CECILY
Otherwise Caecilia, q.v.

CEDD (St) Bp. O.S.B.   A.C. Jan. 7
d. 664 (Oct. 26). Brother of St Chad of Lichfield. He was a monk of Lindisfarne who evangelized the midlands of England and afterwards was made bishop of the East Saxons. He founded the abbeys of Tilbury and of Lastingham. At the synod of Whitby he abandoned the Celtic for the Roman observances. In his old age he retired to his own foundation at Lastingham in Yorkshire to die under monastic obedience.
Cf. Att. — Holw. — Baud. — Chev.

CEITHO (St)   A.C. Nov. 1
6th cent. One of five brothers, saints of the great Welsh family of Cunedda. A church at Pumpsant was dedicated to the five brothers. That at Llangeith, in Cardiganshire, was founded by St Ceitho.
Cf. Holw. — Baring-Gould.

CELE-CHRIST (St) Bp.   A.C. March 3
d. c.728. St Cele-Christ, otherwise *Christicola* (worshipper of Christ), for many years led an eremitical life but ultimately was forced to accept a bishopric in Leinster.
Cf. O' Hanlon — Bolland.

CELERINA (St) M.   R.M. Feb. 3
See Laurentinus, Ignatius and Celerina.

CELERINUS (St) M.   R.M. Feb. 3
d. p. 250. An African who, without shedding his blood, earned the title of martyr on account of the sufferings he endured under Decius during a visit to Rome. Set at liberty, he returned to Carthage where he was ordained deacon by St Cyprian. A church was dedicated in his name at Carthage.
Cf. Holw. — Baud.

CELESTINE (St) M.   R.M. May 2
See Saturninus, Neopolus, etc.

CELESTINE V (St) Pope   R.M. May 19
Otherwise Peter Celestine, q.v.

CELESTINE I (St) Pope.   R.M. July 27
d. 432 (Aug. 1). Born in Campania, he

joined the Roman clergy and succeeded St Boniface I as pope (422). Three great events stand out in his pontificate: he supported the campaign of St Germanus of Auxerre against Pelagius; he sent Palladius to preach in Ireland shortly before St Patrick's mission there; and he condemned Nestorianism, presiding, through his legates, over the council of Ephesus (431).
Cf. Att. — Baud. — Holw.

CELLACH (CEILACH, KEILACH—latinized as CELSUS).
Note. Colgan enumerates no less than thirty-three Celtic saints named Cellach. Most of them, however, are evidently the same person.

CELLACH (CEILACH, KEILACH) (St) Bp. A.C. Apr. 1
9th cent. Archbishop of Armagh, possibly before his consecration abbot of Iona and founder of the abbey of Kells.
Cf. O' Hanlon.

CELLACH (in the R.M.: CELSUS) (St) Bp. R.M. Apr. 1
d. 1129. Cellach McAedh, a native of Ireland, seems to have been a Benedictine of Glastonbury. He certainly was for a time at Oxford, and in 1106 was consecrated archbishop of Armagh. He proved to be a great prelate, restorer of ecclesiastical discipline throughout the island. When dying he sent his pastoral staff to St Malachy, then bishop of Connor, who in fact became his successor.
Cf. Gams — Chev. — Baud. — Holw.

CELLOCH (St) Ab. A.C. March 26
Otherwise Mochelloc, q.v.

CELSUS (several)
Otherwise Cellach, q.v.

CELSUS of ANTIOCH (St) M. R.M. Jan. 9
See Julian, Basilissa, etc.

CELSUS (St) M. R.M. July 28 and May 10
See Nazarius and Celsus.

CELSUS and CLEMENT (SS) MM. R.M. Nov. 21
? Roman martyrs of whom the names only have come down to us.

CENSURIUS (St) Bp. R.M. June 10
d. 486. The successor of St Germanus in the see of Auxerre. He governed that see from 448 to 486. He was buried in the church of St Germanus, which he himself had built.
Cf. Gams — Baud. — Holw.

CENTOLLA and HELEN (SS) MM. R.M. Aug. 13
d. ? c.304. Two Spanish maidens who suffered martyrdom near Burgos.
Cf. Holw. — Baud. — P. de U.

CEOLFRID (GEOFFREY) (St) Ab. O.S.B. A.C. Sept. 25
642-716. A Northumbrian who became a monk at Gilling in Yorkshire, whence he migrated to Ripon, where St Benedict's Rule was observed. After a visit to Canterbury, he became novice-master at Ripon, but later migrated to Wearmouth, at St Benet Biscop's invitation (672). Eventually he became abbot of Wearmouth-Jarrow, which he governed for twenty-six years. He was a great abbot and deserves a special recognition for the help he gave to St Bede, who was one of his monks. In 716 he resigned and died at Langres in Champagne on his way to Rome.
Cf. Att. — Zimm. — Mab. — Chev. — Baud.

CEOLLACH (St) Bp. A.C. Oct. 6
? 7th cent. An Irish prelate who for a short time governed as bishop the diocese of the Mercians or Mid-Angles. Thence he retired to Iona but returned to die in his native country.
Cf. Holw.

CEOLWULPH (St) King, Mk. O.S.B. A.C. Jan. 15
d. 764. King of Northumbria, fosterer of learning and of the monastic life. To him St Bede dedicated his Ecclesiastical History. He ended his days as a monk at Lindisfarne.
Cf. Att. — Zimm. — Mab. — Baud. — Holw.

CERA (CIAR, CYRA, CIOR, CEARA) (St) V. A.C. Jan. 5
7th cent. An Irish abbess, a native of Tipperary, who governed two nunneries, one at Kilkeary and the other at Tech Telle, now Tehelly.
Cf. O' Hanlon.

CERATIUS (CÉRASE) (St) Bp.
A.C. June 6
d. c.455. Bishop of Grenoble in France.
Cult confirmed in 1903.
Cf. Duch. Fast. Episc. — Gams — Att. — Baud.

CERAUNUS (CERAN) (St) Bp.
A.C. Sept. 27
d. p. 614. Bishop of Paris. His relics
were formerly enshrined in the church of
St Geneviève.
Cf. Gams — Duch. Fast. Episc. — Baud.— Holw.

CERBONIUS (St) Bp. R.M. Oct. 10
d. c.580. One of the African bishops
driven from their sees by the Arian Vandals. He settled at Piombino (*Popu-
lonium*) in Tuscany and is said to have become a bishop there.
Cf. Att. — Gams — Baud. — Holw.

CERBONIUS (St) Bp. R.M. Oct. 10
d. ? c. 400. Bishop of Verona in Italy, of
whom nothing is known.

CERNEUF (St) M. A.C. Feb. 23
Otherwise Serenus, q.v.

CESLAS (Bl) C. O.P. A.C. July 17
d. 1242. A native of Poland, who received the habit of the Friars Preachers
together with St Hyacinth, from the hands
of St Dominic himself. He acted as
spiritual director to the duchess St Hed-
wige of Poland. The successful resistance
of the people of Breslau in Silesia to the
Mongols in their great invasion of 1240, is
attributed to the prayers of the saint.
Cf. Att. — Baud. — Holw.

CETTIN (CETHAGH) (St) Bp.
A.C. June 16
5th cent. A disciple of St Patrick, consecrated bishop to assist him in his apostolic work. Some authorities distinguish
Cethagh from Cettin.
Cf. O'Hanlon.

CEWYDD (St) A.C. July 1
6th cent. A Welsh saint who flourished in
Anglesey.
Cf. Baring-Gould.

CH
Note. Saints' names beginning with Ch,
should also be looked for under Ca, Co, or

K, the spelling being frequently very
uncertain and variable.

CHAD (CEADDA) (St) Bp.
R.M. March 2
d. 673. Brother of St Cedd. Educated
at Lindisfarne under St Aidan, and in Ireland. On returning to England, he was
made abbot of Lastingham, where at that
time, i.e., before the synod of Whitby,
St Columba's Rule was strictly observed.
During one of St Wilfrid's absences in
France, St Chad was made archbishop of
York, but was removed by St Theodore of
Canterbury. St Chad readily withdrew,
and St Theodore arranged for him to exercise his episcopate in Mercia. The saint
fixed his residence at Lichfield and there he
died shortly after.
Cf. Att. — Baud. — Holw.

CHAEREMON (St) M. R.M. Oct. 4
See Caius, Faustus, etc.

CHAEREMON and Comp. (SS) MM.
R.M. Dec. 22
d. p. 250. Bishop of Nilopolis in Egypt.
He was already a very old man when the
Decian persecution broke out. He was
forced to flee to the mountainous district
of the Arabian desert with several companions, and they were never seen again.
Cf. Att. — Baud. — Holw.

CHAFFRE (St) Ab. O.S.B. A.C. Oct. 19
Otherwise Theofrid, q.v.

**CHAINOALDUS (CHAGNOALD, CAG-
NOU) (St) Bp.** A.C. Sept. 6
d. 633. Brother of St Faro and of St
Fara. A disciple of St Columbanus,
whom he accompanied to Bobbio and
helped in the foundation of the abbey
there. Afterwards he became bishop of
Laon.
Cf. Att. — Zimm. — Baud. — Gams.

CHALCEDON (Martyrs of) (SS)
R.M. Sept. 24
d. 304. A band of forty-nine martyrs who
suffered at Chalcedon under Diocletian.
They seem to have been the choir of
singers of the church of Chalcedon.
Cf. Holw. — Baud.

CHAMOND (ANNEMOND) (St) Bp. M.
A.C. Sept. 28
d. 657. A courtier in the palace of King

Clovis II who became archbishop of Lyons. The arch-tyrant Ebroin, mayor of the palace, caused the saint to be assassinated. St Wilfrid of York took part in the ceremony of the enshrining of the relics of the martyr.
Cf. Baud. — Mab. — Duch. Fast. Episc.

CHARALAMPIAS and Comp. (SS) MM.
A.C. Feb. 18
d. 203. Martyrs of Magnesia in Asia Minor in the persecution under Septimius Severus. St Charalampias was a priest. With him suffered two soldiers and three women.
Cf. Baud.

CHARISIUS (St) M. R.M. Apr. 16
See Callistus, Charisius, etc.

CHARITINA (St) V.M. R.M. Oct. 5
d. c.304. A Christian maiden who breathed forth her soul in the torture chamber. She suffered under Diocletian and probably at Amisus on the Black Sea.
Cf. Holw. — Baud.

CHARITON (St) M. R.M. Sept. 3
See Zeno and Chariton.

CHARITY (St) V.M. R.M. Aug. 1
Otherwise Caritas or Agape. See Faith, Hope, and Charity.

CHARLEMAGNE (Bl) Emperor.
A.C. Jan. 28
742-814. Son of Pepin the Short. King of the Franks in 768, on Christmas Day of the year 800, he was crowned first Holy Roman Emperor by Pope St Leo III. Popular devotion to Bl Charlemagne took root chiefly at the time of the great quarrel between the pope and Frederick Barbarossa; in France it was made compulsory by the state in 1475. Benedict XIV confirmed, or allowed, the title of Blessed given to the emperor. His feast is observed still in several German dioceses.
Cf. Att. — Holw. — Baud.

CHARLES BORROMEO (St) C. Bp.
R.M. Nov. 4
1538-1584. Son of Count Gilbert Borromeo by a Medici mother. His uncle Pope Pius IV appointed him archbishop of Milan and cardinal when he was aged only twenty-two. He did not receive priestly or episcopal orders until the year 1563. He was the most imposing and influential figure of the counter-reformation in Italy. He was a model bishop — zealous, selfless, prodigal even of his life. An attempt was made on his life by evildoers. Canonized in 1610.
Cf. Att. — Holw. — Baud.

CHARLES LUANGA (Bl) M. A.C. June 3
d. 1886. A servant of King Mwanga of Uganda. He was baptized in Nov. 1885. and burnt alive the following June at Namuyongo. Beatified in 1912.
Cf. Holw.

CHARLES SPINOLA (Bl) M. S.J.
A.C. Sept. 11
d. 1622. Though born at Prague he belonged to the Italian noble house of Spinola. He became a Jesuit in 1584 and in 1594 was sent to the missions of Japan. He worked there until 1618 when he was arrested and kept in prison for four years. He was then burnt to death with twenty-four companions. Each of them is given separate notice in this book. Beatified in 1867.
Cf. Holw. — Att. — Baud.

CHARLES of BLOIS (Bl) C.
A.C. Sept. 29
1316-1364. Nephew of Philip VI of France. He married Joan of Brittany in 1341 and claimed her dukedom against John de Montfort. This led to the war in which he was engaged for the rest of his life, except for nine years spent as a prisoner in the Tower of London. He fell in battle in 1364. Cult confirmed in 1904.
Cf. Baud. — Att.

CHARLES of SEZZE (Bl) C. O.F.M.
A.C. Jan. 6
d. 1670. A native of Sezze in the Roman Campagna. He professed the Franciscan rule as a lay-brother at Rome. His was a life of great mystical experiences, and it is narrated that his heart was pierced by a ray of light proceeding from the Sacred Host, which left a visible wound. Beatified in 1882.
Cf. Holw. — Att. — Baud.

CHARLES of SAYN (Bl) Ab. O.S.B. Cist.
A.C. Jan. 29
d. 1212. A soldier who became a Cistercian at Hemmerode (1185). In 1189 he was chosen prior of Heisterbach and in

1197 abbot of Villers in Brabant. In 1209 he resigned and returned to Hemmerode to prepare for death. He has always been venerated as a *beatus*, at any rate by the Cistercians.
Cf. Holw. — Baud.

CHARLES the GOOD (Bl) M.
A.C. March 2
d. 1127. Son of St Canute of Denmark. He fought in the second Crusade and on his return succeeded Robert II as count of Flanders. His rule was a continuous defence of the poor against the profiteers of his time, both clerical and lay. He was called "the Good" by popular acclamation and was done to death in the church of St Donatian at Bruges as a result of a conspiracy of the rich people whom he had offended. Cult confirmed in 1883.
Cf. Att. — Holw. — Baud.

CHEF (St) Ab.
A.C. Oct. 29
Otherwise Theodore, q.v.

CHELEDONIUS (St) M. R.M. March 3
See Hemiterius and Cheledonius.

CHELIDONIA (St) V. O.S.B.
R.M. Oct. 13
d. 1152. Born at Ciculum in the Abruzzi, she early fled into the mountains above Tivoli, near Subiaco, where she dwelt as a recluse in a cave, now called Morra Ferogna. From Cuno, cardinal of Frascati, she received the Benedictine habit in the abbey church of St Scholastica at Subiaco, but continued to live as a recluse under the obedience of the abbot. Her body now reposes in the church of St Scholastica. She is one of the patron saints of Subiaco.
Cf. Holw. — Baud.

CHELY (St) Bp.
R.M. Oct. 25
Otherwise Hilary of Mende, q.v.

CHERON (St) M.
R.M. May 28
Otherwise Caraunus, q.v.

CHERUBINUS TESTA of AVIGLIANA (Bl) C. O.S.A.
A.C. Dec. 17
1449-1479. An Augustinian friar-hermit of Avigliana in Piedmont. Cult approved by Pius IX.
Cf. Holw.

CHILIAN (St) Bp. M.
R.M. July 8
See Kilian, Colman and Totnan.

CHILLIEN (KILLIAN, CHILIANUS) (St)
A.C. Nov. 13
7th cent. An Irishman, kinsman of St Fiacre, who became a missionary in Artois. His body was enshrined at Aubigny, near Arras.
Cf. Baud.

CHIONIA (St) V.M.
R.M. Apr. 3
See Agape and Chionia.

CHL
Note. Names so beginning are often spelt Cl or Kl.

CHR
Note. Names so beginning are often spelt Cr.

CHRISTETA (St) M.
R.M. Oct. 27
See Vincent, Sabina and Christeta.

CHRISTIAN (Bl) Ab. O.S.B. Cist.
A.C. March 18
d. 1186. His Celtic name was Giolla Croist O'Conarchy. An Irish priest, who professed the Cistercian Rule at Clairvaux under St Bernard and eventually was sent back to Ireland (1142) to introduce the Cistercians there. He was in fact the abbot-founder of Mellifont Abbey. It is said that he became bishop of Lismore and papal legate in Ireland.
Cf. Att. — Baud. — Holw. — Zimm. — Chev.

CHRISTIAN (Bl) C.
P.C. Apr. 7
? A priest of Douai, whose relics are in the church of St Albinus.
Cf. Baud. — Holw. — P.B.

CHRISTIAN (St) Bp.
A.C. June 12
d. 1138. Croistan O'Morgair, brother of St Malachy of Armagh. He was made bishop of Clogher (1126) and obtained several privileges from the Holy See for his diocese.
Cf. Holw. — O'Hanlon.

CHRISTIAN (CHRISTINUS) (St) M.
O.S.B.
R.M. Nov. 12
See Benedict, John, etc.

CHRISTIAN (Bl) Bp.
A.C. Nov. 22
d. c.873. Thirty-seventh bishop of Auxerre.
Cf. Baud. — Duch. Fast. Episc. — Gams.

CHRISTIAN (Bl) C. O.P. P.C. Dec. 1
13th cent. One of the first disciples of St Dominic, whom he helped in the foundation of the friary at Perugia.
Cf. Baud.

CHRISTIAN (Bl) Bp. O.S.B. Cist.
P.C. Dec. 4
d. 1245. A Cistercian monk, probably belonging to the great abbey of Oliva, near Danzig. He went to Prussia as a missionary (1207), and was nominated bishop in 1215. He was instrumental in introducing the Teutonic Knights there. His efforts to convert Prussia were only partially successful.
Cf. Holw.

CHRISTIANA of the CROSS (Bl) V.
A.C. Jan. 10
Otherwise Oringa, q.v.

CHRISTIANA (St) V. A.C. July 24
7th cent. Said to have been the daughter of an Anglo-Saxon king. She crossed over to Flanders where she lived until her death. She is the patron saint of Termonde in Belgium.
Cf. Baud. — Holw.

CHRISTIANA (St) V. R.M. Dec. 15
Otherwise Nino, q.v.

CHRISTICOLA (St) Bp. A.C. March 3
Otherwise Cele-Christ, q.v.

CHRISTINA CICCARELLI (Bl) V. O.S.A.
A.C. Jan. 18
1481-1543. A native of Luco in the Abruzzi and a nun and prioress of the Augustinian hermits, who died at Aquila. Cult confirmed in 1841.
Cf. Att. — Baud. — Holw.

CHRISTINA of SPOLETO (Bl) Penitent.
A.C. Feb. 13
1435-1458. Christina Camozzi was born near Lake Lugano, the daughter of a physician. After a few years spent in frivolity she embraced a life of extreme bodily mortifications. She died at Spoleto aged twenty-three. Cult confirmed in 1834.
Cf. Att. — Baud. — Holw.

CHRISTINA (St) V.M. R. M. March 13
? A Persian maiden who was scourged to death.
Cf. Baud. — Holw.

CHRISTINA (St) V.M. R.M. July 24
? A maiden, perhaps a native of Rome, who was put to death near the Lake of Bolsena in Tuscany. Her legendary acts have been confused with those of a St Christina of Tyre, whose very existence, however, is very doubtful.
Cf. Att. — Holw. — Baud.

CHRISTINA the ASTONISHING (*Mirabilis*) (Bl) V. P.C. July 24
1150-1224. Born near Liége. In 1182, after a cataleptic fit, she was the subject of a life-long series of most astonishing experiences, recorded by a contemporary Dominican. She died in the convent of St Catherine at Trond. Cult never officially confirmed.
Cf. Att. — Holw. — Baud.

CHRISTINA of STOMMELN (Bl) V.
A.C. Nov. 6
1242-1312. Christina Bruzo, or Bruso, was born at Stommeln, near Cologne. Like her namesake of Belgium, she too could be styled "the Astonishing," since her life is a continuous record of most extraordinary phenomena which indeed tax the faith of the reader. They were recorded by a contemporary Friar Preacher. Cult confirmed in 1908.
Cf. Att. — Holw. — Baud.

CHRISTINA (St) V. O.S.B. A.C. Dec. 26
d. 1160. Nun and recluse of Markgate under the obedience of the abbot of St Alban's. Her spiritual director was Bl Roger of St Alban's.
Cf. Zimm.

CHRISTINUS (St) M. O.S.B.
R.M. Nov. 12
See Benedict, John, etc.

CHRISTOPHER
Note. The Latin Christophorus means the Christ-Bearer. It was one of the most popular names during the Middle Ages. Its variants are numerous: Cristoforo, Christophe, Cristobal, Tobal, Cristobalón, Kester, Kitt, etc.

CHRISTOPHER of MILAN (Bl) C. O.P.
A.C. March 1
d. 1484. A Friar Preacher who, true to his profession, preached with extraordinary success throughout Liguria and the Milanese. At Taggia, as a result of his

preaching, the people built a friary and the saint was made its first prior. He died there. Cult confirmed in 1875.
Cf. Att. — Baud. — Holw.

CHRISTOPHER BALES (Bl) M.
A.C. March 4
d. 1590. Born at Coniscliffe, Durham. He was educated at Rome and Reims and ordained priest at Douai (1587). In 1588 he crossed over to England and two years later was seized, condemned for his priesthood, and hanged drawn and quartered in Fleet Street, London. Beatified in 1929.
Cf. Att. — Newdigate.

CHRISTOPHER MACASSOLI (Bl) C. O.F.M. **A.C. March 11**
d. 1485. Born at Milan, he joined the Franciscans and eventually founded a friary at Vigevano, in the province of Milan, where thousands sought his help and advice. Cult confirmed in 1890.
Cf. Att. — Holw. — Baud.

CHRISTOPHER (St) M. R.M. July 25
? The R.M. makes him a martyr of Lycia under Decius, but beyond the fact of his martyrdom, nothing is known about him. Many legends, however, some of them very beautiful but others unbelievable and absurd, have grown up around his name. The most graceful is that of his carrying an unknown child across a ford, and being borne down by its weight, despite his own gigantic stature and great strength: the child was Christ, carrying in His hand the weight of the whole world. This episode has led to the usual representation of the saint in art. He is one of the Fourteen Holy Helpers.
Cf. Att. — Holw. — Baud. — Bolland.

CHRISTOPHER (St) M. R.M. Aug. 20
See Leovigildus and Christopher.

CHRISTOPHER of GUARDIA (St) M.
A.C. Sept. 25
d. c.1490. A boy of Guardia, near Toledo, in Spain, who at the age of three years was stolen by Jews at Toledo and crucified at Guardia, under Ferdinand and Isabella. His cult was officially confirmed, with the title of saint, by Pius VII in 1805. He is the principal patron saint of Guardia.
Cf. Holw. — Baud.

CHRISTOPHER BUXTON (Bl) M.
A.C. Oct. 1
d. 1588. Born at Tideswell in Derbyshire, educated at Reims and Rome, and ordained priest in 1586. Two years later he was hanged, drawn and quartered for his priesthood at Canterbury. Beatified in 1929.
Cf. Newdigate.

CHRISTOPHER of ROMAGNOLA (Bl) C. O.F.M. **A.C. Oct. 31**
c.1172-1272. A parish priest in the diocese of Cesena, who resigned his office, and joined St Francis of Assisi. He was sent to establish the Order in Gascony, where he died at Cahors. Cult approved in 1905.
Cf. Att. — Holw.

CHRISTOPHER (Bl) M. P.C. Nov. 12
d. c.1500. A Portuguese knight of the Order of Christ (under the Cistercian Rule), who was beheaded for the Faith by the Mohammedan prince of Ceylon.
Cf. Zimm.

CHRODEGANG (St) Bp. A.C. March 6
d. 766. A near relative of Pepin, he became the chief minister to Charles Martel and ultimately bishop of Metz (742). He is best known for the rule he wrote for the secular clerks whom he gathered together in chapters of canons with common life. He also introduced the Roman liturgy and chant into his diocese and thus into N. Europe.
Cf. Att. — Baud. — Gams.

CHROMATIUS (St) C. A.C. Aug. 11
3rd cent. Said to have been prefect of Rome and father of St Tiburtius the martyr.
Cf. Att. — Holw. — Baud.

CHROMATIUS (St) Bp. R.M. Dec. 2
d. c.406. Bishop of Aquileia, near Venice, from 387 to 406. St Jerome styles him "a most learned and most holy man," and dedicated to him several of his works. Chromatius was also a friend of St John Chrysostom and of Rufinus. We still possess part of his commentary on St Matthew.
Cf. Att. — Baud. — Holw.

CHRONAN (St) Ab. A.C. Apr. 28
Otherwise Cronan, q.v.

CHRONIDAS (St) M.   R.M. March 27
See Philetus, Lydia, etc.

CHRYSANTHUS and DARIA (SS) MM.
R.M. Oct. 25
d. 283. Chrysanthus, an Egyptian, with
his wife Daria, a Greek, were distinguished
in Rome for their zealous profession and
practice of the Christian religion. This
led to their martyrdom under Numerian
and Carinus.
Cf. Att. — Baud. — Holw.

CHRYSOGONUS (St) M. R.M. Nov. 24
d. c.304. A martyr who suffered at
Aquileia. His name occurs in the Canon
of the Roman Mass. His association with
the martyr St Anastasia of Sirmium is
now generally rejected.
Cf. Att. — Holw. — Baud.

CHRYSOLIUS (St) Bp. M.   A.C. Feb. 7
4th cent. An Armenian who evangelized
N.E. Gaul, where, it is said, he was consecrated bishop. He had left Armenia during the persecution of Diocletian, but won
the crown of martyrdom in Flanders.
His relics are venerated at Bruges.
Cf. Baud. — Holw.

CHRYSOLOGUS (St) Bp.   R.M. Dec. 2
See Peter Chrysologus.

CHRYSOPHORUS (St) M. R.M. Apr. 20
See Victor, Zoticus, etc.

CHRYSOSTOM (St) Bp. Dr.
R.M. Jan. 27
See John Chrysostom.

CHRYSOTELUS (St) M.   R.M. Apr. 22
See Parmenius, Helimenas, etc.

CHUNIALD and GISLAR (SS) CC.
A.C. Sept. 24
7th cent. Missionaries, probably of Irish
or Scottish origin, who evangelized S.
Germany and Austria, under the leadership of St Rupert of Salzburg.
Cf. Holw. — Baud.

CIAN (St) C.   A.C. Dec. 11
6th cent. A Welsh saint who ended his
life as a hermit in Carnarvonshire. He is
sometimes described as a servant of St
Peris.
Cf. Baring-Gould.

CIANAN (St) Bp.   A.C. Nov. 24
Otherwise Kenan, q.v.

CIARAN (St) Bp.   A.C. March 5
Otherwise Kieran, q.v.

CIARAN (St) Ab.   R.M. Sept. 9
Otherwise Kieran, q.v.

CICELY (St) V.M.   R.M. Nov. 22
Otherwise Caecilia, q.v.

CICCO of PESARO (Bl) C. Tert. O.F.M.
A.C. Aug. 4
d. 1350. A native of Pesaro, and a tertiary of St Francis, who led the life of a
recluse near Pesaro. Cult confirmed by
Pius IX.
Cf. Holw. — Baud.

CILINIA (St) Matron.   R.M. Oct. 21
d. p. 458. Mother of St Principius,
bishop of Soissons, and of St Remigius,
bishop of Reims. She died at Laon.
Cf. Holw. — Baud.

CILLENE (St) Ab.   A.C. July 3
d. c.752. An Irish monk who migrated
to Iona and was there elected abbot in 726.
Cf. Holw.

CINDEUS (St) M.   R.M. July 11
d. c.300. A priest of Pamphylia in Asia
Minor who was burnt at the stake under
Diocletian.
Cf. Holw. — Baud.

CINNIA (St) V.   A.C. Feb. 1
5th cent. A princess of Ulster converted
by St Patrick, who also gave her the veil.
Cf. Holw.

CISELLUS (St) M.   R.M. Aug. 21
See Luxorius, Cisellus and Camerinus.

CISSA (St) H. O.S.B.   A.C. Sept. 23
Late 7th cent. Monk-recluse in North-
umbria, most probably at Lindisfarne.
Cf. Zimm.

CIWA (St) V.   A.C. Feb. 8
Otherwise Kigwe, q.v.

CLAIR (St) M.   A.C. Nov. 4
The French spelling of Clarus, q.v.

CLARE AGOLANTI of RIMINI (Bl) W.
Tert. O.F.M.   A.C. Feb. 10
1282-1346. She belonged to the nobility

of Rimini and was twice married. During her married life she wasted her time in sinful dissipations. On the execution of her father and brother, as a result of civil disturbances, she completely changed her life. She became a Franciscan tertiary and founded a nunnery, but never became a nun herself. She practised rigorous penances, some of which were considered extravagant even by her contemporaries. Cult sanctioned in 1784.
Cf. Att. — Baud. — Holw.

CLARE GAMBACORTA (Bl) W. O.P.
A.C. Apr. 17

1362-1419. Daughter of the head of the state at Pisa. Being left a widow at fifteen, she wished to become a Poor Clare. Her father strongly opposed this at first, but eventually relented and built for her a nunnery where she introduced the strict Dominican observance. As a superior she was continually beset by financial troubles.
Cf. Att. — Baud. — Holw.

CLARE of ASSISI (St) V. Foundress
R.M. Aug. 12

c. 1193-1253. Born at Assisi. At the age of eighteen she was irresistibly drawn to the ideal of Christian poverty preached by St Francis. She ran away from home and took the veil from St Francis himself, who provided a refuge for her with the Benedictine nuns of San Paolo and finally at San Damiano, where the first convent of Poor Clares was established under her guidance. She governed it for forty years, and popes, cardinals and bishops came to consult her. She was indeed as much instrumental in the rapid spreading of the Franciscan movement as St Francis himself. She was canonized two years after her death. In art she is usually represented with a monstrance in her hand in memory of her having in this attitude miraculously saved her convent from assault.
Cf. Att. — Baud. — Holw.

CLARE of MONTEFALCO (St) V. O.S.A.
R.M. Aug. 17

c. 1268-1308. Surnamed Clare of the Cross. She was a native of Montefalco, in the diocese of Spoleto. She joined a convent of Franciscan tertiaries, who in 1290 exchanged their rule for that of the Augustinian hermits, and she became their abbess. Her distinctive devotion was the Passion of Christ: a cross was found depicted on the flesh of her heart after her death. Canonized in 1881.
Cf. Att. — Holw. — Baud.

CLARE XAMADA (Bl) M.   A.C. Sept. 10
d. 1622. A Japanese matron, wife of Bl Dominic Xamada. Both were beheaded at Nagasaki, in Japan.
Cf. Holw.

CLARITUS (CHIARITO) VOGLIA (Bl) C.
P.C. May 25

d. 1348. A Florentine, who in 1342 founded a convent of Augustinian nuns at Florence. His wife became a nun there, and he remained in the convent as a manservant till his death.
Cf. Att. — Holw.

CLARENTIUS (St) Bp.   R.M. Apr. 26
d. c.620. The successor of St Etherius in the see of Vienne.
Cf. Baud. — Duch. Fast. Episc. — Gams.

CLARUS (St) Ab. O.S.B.   A.C. Jan. 1
d. c.660. A monk of the abbey of St Ferreol, who was chosen abbot of the monastery of St Marcellus at Vienne in Dauphiny. He was the spiritual director of the convent of St Blandina, where his own mother had taken the veil. Cult approved in 1907.
Cf. Att. — Baud. — Holw. — Mab. — Zimm. — Chev.

CLARUS (St) H. O.S.B.   A.C. Feb. 1
d. c.1048. A monk of Seligenstadt, in the diocese of Mainz. He lived for thirty years as a recluse, given to great austerities. His motto was: "Christ and Him crucified."
Cf. Bolland. (Jan. 1) — Mab. — Baud. — Chev. — Holw.

CLARUS (St) Bp. M.   A.C. June 1
? A regionary bishop, said to have been sent from Rome to preach the gospel in Aquitaine, where he was martyred. He is not to be confused with St Clarus, bishop of Nantes (Oct. 10).
Cf. Holw. — Baud. — P.B.

CLARUS (St) Bp.   A.C. Oct. 10
? Bishop of Nantes. Some writers make him a disciple of St Peter and the first apostle of Armorica (Brittany). Others

postpone his apostolate till the third century.
*Cf. Holw. — Baud. — Duch. Fast. Episc.
— Gams.*

CLARUS (St) M. O.S.B. R.M. Nov. 4
d. c.875. He is described as a native of
Rochester, who crossed over to France,
where he was first a monk and then a hermit in the diocese of Rouen. He was
murdered at the instigation of a woman
whose advances he had rejected. The
village Saint-Clair-sur-Epte is named
after him.
Cf. Att. — Baud. — Holw. — Zimm.

CLARUS (St) H. R.M. Nov. 8
d. 397. Born at Tours in France, he
joined the community of Marmoutier
under St Martin. He was ordained priest
and henceforth lived as a hermit near the
same abbey.
Cf. Baud. — Holw.

CLASSICUS (St) M. R.M. Feb. 18
See Lucius, Sylvanus, etc.

CLATEUS (St) Bp. R.M. June 4
d. c.64. One of the earliest bishops of
Brescia, who suffered martyrdom under
Nero.
Cf. Holw. — Baud. — Gams.

CLAUD or CLAUDE (*several*)
Otherwise Claudius, q.v.

CLAUDIA (St) M. R.M. March 20
See Alexandra, Claudia, etc.

CLAUDIA (St) V.M. R.M. May 18
See Theodotus, Thecusa, etc.

CLAUDIA (St) W. A.C. Aug. 7
1st cent. A woman mentioned by St Paul
in his second letter to Timothy (IV, 21).
A much later, and rather improbable,
tradition asserts that she was a Briton,
the wife of Aulus Pudens, a senator, and
the mother of SS Praxedes and Pudentiana.
Cf. Att. — Baud. — Holw.

CLAUDIAN (St) M. R.M. Feb. 25
See Victorinus, Victor, etc.

CLAUDIAN (St) M. R.M. Feb. 26
See Papias, Diodorus, etc.

CLAUDIAN (St) M. R.M. March 6
See Victor, Victorinus, etc.

CLAUDIUS (CLAUDE) de la COLOMBIÈRE (Bl) C. S.J. A.C. Feb. 15
1641-1682. Born near Grenoble, he became a Jesuit in 1659 at Avignon. While
superior of the Jesuits at Paray-le-Monial
he was the spiritual director of St Margaret Mary Alacoque and was instrumental in spreading devotion to the Sacred
Heart. Sent to England in 1676 as chaplain to the Duchess of York, he was
arrested and banished for alleged complicity in the imaginary "Popish Plot."
Beatified in 1929.
Cf. Att.

CLAUDIUS (St) M. R.M. Feb. 18
See Maximus, Claudius, etc.

CLAUDIUS (St) M. R.M. June 3
See Lucillian, Claudius, etc.

**CLAUDIUS of BESANÇON (St) Bp.
O.S.B.** R.M. June 6
d. c.699. A native of Franche-Comté, he
was trained to bear arms, but decided to
be a priest and eventually was appointed
canon of Besançon. He next became a
monk, and abbot, of Condat Abbey, in
the Jura mountains, where he introduced,
or enforced, the rule of St Benedict. In
685 he was chosen bishop of Besançon but
retained the direction of the abbey, to
which he retired again before his death.
The abbey was afterwards known as
Saint-Claude.
Cf. Mab. — Zimm. — Chev. — Att.

CLAUDIUS, NICOSTRATUS, CASTORIUS, VICTORINUS and SYMPHORIAN (SS) MM. R.M. July 7
d. c.288. Described in the very untrustworthy Acts of St Sebastian as having
suffered martyrdom at the same time as
that saint. They are very likely identical
with the group of saints honoured on
Nov. 8 with the Four Crowned Martyrs.
Cf. Holw. — Baud. — Bolland.

**CLAUDIUS, JUSTUS, JUCUNDINUS
and Comp (SS) MM.** R.M. July 21
d. 273. A group of eight martyrs who
suffered with St Julia at Troyes in Gaul,
under Aurelian. Their bodies were enshrined in the Benedictine nunnery of
Jouarre, near Meaux.
Cf. Baud. — Holw.

**CLAUDIUS, ASTERIUS, NEON, DON-
VINA and THEONILLA (SS) MM.**
R.M. Aug. 23
d. 303. The first three were brothers who
were accused to the magistrate of Aegea in
Cilicia by their step-mother, who hoped
to inherit their estate. Donvina (Domnina) and Theonilla, the former a maiden,
the latter an aged widow, were on trial as
Christians at the same time. The men
were crucified; the women scourged to
death.
Cf. Att. — Baud. — Bolland. — Ruinart.

CLAUDIUS (St) M.   R.M. Oct. 25
See Marcellinus, Claudius, etc.

**CLAUDIUS, LUPERCUS and VICTOR-
IUS (SS) MM.**   R.M. Oct. 30
d. c.300. Three brothers, sons of the
centurion, St Marcellus. They were
martyred at León in Spain under Diocletian. They are the titular saints of St
Claudius in Galicia, one of the earliest
Benedictine abbeys in Spain.
Cf. P. de U. Baud. — Holw.

**CLAUDIUS, NICOSTRATUS and Comp·
(SS) MM.**   R.M. Nov. 8
These saints belong to the group of the
Four Crowned Martyrs, q.v.

**CLAUDIUS, HILARIA, JASON, MAUR-
US (MARIS) and Comp. (SS) MM.**
R.M. Dec. 3
d. ? 283. This group of martyrs, con-
sisting of Claudius, a military tribune,
Hilaria his wife, their two sons, and sev-
enty soldiers, belong to the larger group
figuring in the legendary acts of SS
Chrysanthus and Daria.
Cf. Att. — Baud. — Holw.

**CLAUDIUS, CRISPIN, MAGINA, JOHN
and STEPHEN (SS) MM.**   R.M. Dec. 3
? African martyrs, of whom nothing is
known.

CLEAR (CLEER) (St) Bp.   A.C. Oct. 10
Otherwise Clarus, or it may be Clether,
q.v.

CLEDOG (CLYDOG, CLEODICUS) (St)
A.C. Oct. 23
Otherwise Clether, q.v.

CLEDWYN (CLYDWYN) (St) C.
A.C. Nov. 1
5th cent. Patron saint of Llangledwyn

in Carmarthenshire. Alleged to have
been the eldest son of King Brychan, and
to have succeeded him as ruler of part
of his dominions.
Cf. Baring-Gould.

CLEMENT (St) Bp. M.   R.M. Jan. 23
d. 303. Bishop of Ancyra in Galatia,
martyred under Diocletian.
Cf. Att. — Baud. — Holw.

CLEMENT (St) Ab. O.S.B.
A.C. March 5
c. 800. Abbot of Santa Lucia, in Syracuse, the oldest Benedictine monastery
in Sicily.
Cf. Zimm.

**CLEMENT MARY HOFBAUER (St) C.
C.SS.R.**   R.M. March 15
1751-1820. A Slav, born in Moravia,
whose real name was John Dvorak. He
was the son of a grazier, and he himself
started life as a baker and then became a
hermit. While on a pilgrimage to Rome
he received the habit officially as a recluse
at the hands of the bishop of Tivoli, the
future pope Pius VII, who changed John's
name into that of Clement Mary. In
1783 he joined the recently founded Redemptorists at Rome and four years later
was sent to Warsaw to establish the first
house of the congregation beyond the
Alps. There the untiring zeal of the Redemptorists met with signal success,
though the development of the institute
was retarded by the Napoleonic wars.
Clement spent the last twelve years of his
life at Vienna, firmly planting the Re-
demptorist institute in German lands,
whence it spread to Belgium, Ireland,
England and the British Empire. Canonized in 1909.
Cf. Att. — Baud. — Holw.

CLEMENT of St. ELPIDIO (Bl) C. O.S.A.
A.C. Apr. 8
d. 1291. A native of Osimo and a hermit
friar of St Augustine. In 1270 he was
chosen General of the Order and as such
he drew up its constitutions, which were
approved in 1287. For this reason he is
considered the second founder of the
order. Cult approved in 1572.
Cf. Att. — Baud. — Holw.

CLEMENT (St) M.   A.C. June 27
d. c.298. A martyr of Cordova, in Spain,

under Diocletian. He belongs to the group led by St Zoilus, q.v.
Cf. Baud.

CLEMENT of OKHRIDA (St) C.
A.C. July 17
See Seven Apostles of Bulgaria.

CLEMENT (St) M. R.M. Sept. 10
See Apelles, Lucius and Clement.

CLEMENT VOM (Bl) M. A.C. Sept. 10
d. 1622. A Japanese layman, martyred at Nagasaki. He belongs to the group of Bl Charles Spinola, q.v.
Cf. Holw.

CLEMENT KINGEMON (Bl) M.
A.C. Nov. 1
d. 1622. A native of Arima in Japan. He was the servant of Bl Paul Navarro, whose life he wrote. He was burnt alive with his master at Ximabarra. Beatified in 1867.
Cf. Holw.

CLEMENT (St) M. R.M. Nov. 21
See Celsus and Clement.

CLEMENT I (St) Pope, M. R.M. Nov. 23
d. c.100. The third successor of St Peter in the see of Rome, he governed the Church for about ten years. In his capacity as pope, he wrote to the church of Corinth to settle some disputes there; the letter is one of the most important documents of the sub-apostolic age. He is venerated as a martyr, but his martyrdom cannot be proved, much less the legends attached to it. He is mentioned in the Canon of the Mass.
Cf. Att. — Holw.

CLEMENT (St) Bp. A.C. Nov. 23
? The first bishop of Metz, sent directly from Rome to evangelize that district of Roman Gaul.
Cf. Duch. Fast. Episc. — Baud. — Holw.

CLEMENT of ALEXANDRIA (St) C.
P.C. Dec. 4
d. c.217. Titus Flavius Clemens succeeded Panthenus as the head of the catechetical school of Alexandria, where he had Origen as one of his pupils. He has left numerous writings. His name was listed in the R.M. up to 1751.
Cf. Holw.

CLEMENTIA (Bl) N. O.S.B.
P.C. March 21
d. 1176. Daughter of Adolph, count of Hohenburg. A model wife, she became in her widowhood a nun at Oehren, Trèves.
Cf. Chev. — Zimm. — Baud.

CLEMENTINUS, THEODOTUS and PHILOMENUS (SS) MM. R.M. Nov. 14
? Martyrs of Heraclea in Thrace. Nothing else is known about them.

CLEOMENES (LEOMENES) (St) M.
R.M. Dec. 23
See Theodulus, Saturninus, etc.

CLEONICUS, EUTROPIUS and BASILISCUS (SS) MM. R.M. March 3
d. c.298. These saints belong to a group of martyrs put to death in the province of Pontus on the Black Sea, under Diocletian. Most of the group — some forty to fifty — seem to have been soldiers in the imperial army; several, however, were crucified, the punishment reserved for slaves.
Cf. Baud. — Holw.

CLEOPATRA (St) W. A.C. Oct. 19
d. 319. A widow of Palestine who succeeded in securing the body of St Varus, martyred under Diocletian, and enshrined it at her home at Derâ'a in Syria. On the day of the dedication of the church her twelve-year-old son died, and he and St Varus appeared in a vision to comfort her.
Cf. Att. — Baud. — Holw.

CLEOPHAS (St) M. R.M. Sept. 25
1st cent. One of the two disciples whom Christ met on the way to Emmaus (Luke XXIV). The R.M. states that he was murdered by the Jews in the house in which he entertained our Lord on that first Easter day. He is sometimes identified, without any real grounds, with Clopas or Alpheus, the father of St James the Less (Matt. X, 3). Hegesippus adds that he was a brother of St Joseph.
Cf. Holw. — Baud.

CLERUS (St) M. R.M. Jan. 7
d. c.300. A Syrian deacon, martyred at Antioch.

CLETHER (CLEER, CLYDOG, SCLE-DOG, Latinized: CLITANUS or CLEOD-IUS) (St)   **A.C. Oct. 23**
d. c.520. One of the saints descended from King Brychan of Brecknock, or at least of his clan. Several dedications of churches — for instance, St Cleer, near Liskeard — perpetuate his memory. Another Clether, or Cledog, is commemorated on Aug. 19. He is alleged to have died a martyr in Herefordshire.
Cf. Holw. — Baring-Gould.

CLETUS (or ANACLETUS) (St) Pope, M.
          R.M. Apr. 26 (July 13)
d. c.91. The second successor of St Peter. He was probably martyred under Domitian. His name is in the Canon of the Mass.
Cf. Att. — Holw. — Baud.

CLICERIUS (St) Bp.   R.M. Sept. 20
d. c.438. Bishop of Milan, of whom no record is extant.

CLINIUS (St) Ab. O.S.B.
          R.M. March 30
? A Greek and a Benedictine of Montecassino, who was made superior of the daughter-house of St Peter, near Pontecorvo, where his relics are venerated.
Cf. Holw. — Baud.

CLODOALDUS (French: CLOUD) (St) Ab.   R.M. Sept. 7
d. c.560. Grandson of King Clovis and of St Clotilde. When his two brothers were murdered he was taken to safety in Provence. Afterwards he became a priest, a recluse, and the abbot-founder of Nogent-sur-Seine, near Versailles, now called after him Saint-Cloud.
Cf. Att. — Holw. — Baud.

CLODULPHUS (French: CLOU) (St) Bp.   R.M. June 8
605-696. Son of St Arnulfus, bishop of Metz. He too became bishop of Metz, succeeding his father in 656 and ruling over his diocese for forty years.
Cf. Duch. Fast. Episc. — Gams — Baud.— Att.

CLOTILDE (St) Queen.   R.M. June 3
c. 474-545. Born at Lyons, daughter of Chilperic, king of Burgundy, she married Clovis, king of the Salian Franks, and was the means of leading her husband to em-brace Christianity (496). She had much to suffer on account of the quarrels between her three sons. In old age she retired to Tours, where she died by St Martin's tomb.
Cf. Att. — Baud. — Holw.

CLOTILDE PAILLOT (Bl) M.
          A.C. Oct. 23
1739-1794. Born at Bavay, professed as an Ursuline in 1756, superior of the house of Valenciennes. She was guillotined at Valenciennes. She belongs to the group of the Ursuline martyrs beatified in 1920, q.v.
Cf. Baud.

CLOTSINDIS (CLOTSEND) (St) Abs. O.S.B.   A.C. June 30
d. c.700. Daughter of St Adalbald and of St Rictrude, later the abbess-foundress of Marchiennes in Flanders. She was educated at Marchiennes by her own mother, the abbess-foundress, whom she succeeded as second abbess (688).
Cf. Baud. — Chev.

CLOU (St) Bp.   R.M. June 8
Otherwise Clodulphus, q.v.

CLOUD (St) Ab.   R.M. Sept. 7
Otherwise Clodoaldus, q.v.

CLYDOG (St)   A.C. Oct. 23
Otherwise Clether, q.v.

CLYTANUS (CLITANUS) (St)
          A.C. Oct. 23
Otherwise Clether, q.v.

COCCA (CUCCA, CUACH) (St) V.
          A.C. June 6
? Patroness of Kilcock on the borders of Cos. Meath and Kildare.
Cf. O' Hanlon.

COCHA (COECHA) (St) V. A.C. June 29
6th cent. Said to have cared for St Kieran of Saighir in his infancy. She was afterwards abbess of Ross-Benchuir.
Cf. O' Hanlon.

CODRATUS (CHUADRATUS), DI-ONYSIUS, CYPRIAN, ANECTUS, PAUL and CRESCENS (SS) MM.
          R.M. March 10
d. c.258. Greek martyrs, beheaded at Corinth, under Valerian. Previously to

this, Codratus, then a child, appears to have been driven into the woods to escape from the persecution under Decius (250).
Cf. Att. — Baud. — Holw.

CODRATUS (St) M. R.M. March 26
Otherwise Quadratus, q.v.

COELESTINE (St) Pope. R.M. May 19
See Peter Celestine.

COEMGEN (St) Ab. A.C. June 3
Otherwise Kevin, q.v.

COGITOSUS (St) A.C. Apr. 18
? 8th cent. He appears to have been a monk of Kildare. If the tradition representing him as the author of the life of St Brigid be trustworthy, we are indebted to him for much interesting information regarding that saint and her times.
Cf. Holw. — O'Hanlon.

COINTHA (QUINTA) (St) M.
R.M. Feb. 8
d. 249. An Egyptian lady — some say a young maiden — martyred under Decius. She was fastened to the tail of a horse, and dragged by her feet through the streets of Alexandria till she died.
Cf. Holw. — Baud.

COLAN (St) May 21
The Cornish form of the name of the Welsh St Collen, or Gollen, q.v.

COLETTE (St) V. R.M. March 6
1381-1447. Nicolette Boilet was born at Corbie, in Picardy, a carpenter's daughter. She tried her religious vocation with the Beguines and the Benedictines, but failed. Next she became a recluse at Corbie, and finally she found her vocation in reviving the Franciscan spirit among the Poor Clares. Her plan was blessed by Peter de Luna, at that time acknowledged as pope in France. She was made superioress of the whole order, and her reform spread throughout France, Savoy, Germany and Flanders, many convents being restored and seventeen new ones founded by her. She helped St Vincent Ferrer in the work of healing the papal schism. She died at Ghent, and was canonized in 1807.
Cf. Att. — Baud. — Holw.

COLGAN (St) Ab. A.C. Feb. 20
d. c.796. Surnamed "the Wise" and "the Chief Scribe of the Scots." Abbot of Clonmacnoise, in Offaly. He was a great friend of Bl Alcuin.
Cf. Holw. — Baud.

COLMAN — in Latin: COLMANUS
Note. Probably the most popular baptismal name in the early Irish church. There are ninety-six saints of this name in the martyrology of Donegal, two hundred and nine in the Book of Leinster and many others. Holweck lists seventy-one; several, however, are evidently duplicates.
Cf. Att. — Baud. — Holw.

COLMAN of LISMORE (St) Bp.
A.C. Jan. 23
d. c.702. Abbot-bishop of the monastery of Lismore, in the government of which he succeeded St Hierlug (Zailug) in 698. Under his rule the fame of Lismore reached its peak.
Cf. Baud. — Holw.

COLMAN of LINDISFARNE (St) Bp.
A.C. Feb. 18
d. 676. A native of Connaught and a monk of Iona, he was chosen third abbot-bishop of Lindisfarne. His reluctance to accept the Roman traditions prescribed for England at the synod of Whitby (664) led him to withdraw with his monks to Ireland. Here he founded a monastery on Innisboffin Island, but later was compelled to establish another (Mayo of the Saxons) on the mainland for his English monks as they were not on good terms with their Irish brethren.
Cf. Att. — Baud. — Holw.

COLMAN of ARMAGH (St) C.
A.C. March 5
5th cent. A disciple of St Patrick. He died during the lifetime of his master, by whom he was buried at Armagh.
Cf. Baud. — O'Hanlon.

COLMAN MAC UALAOIGHSE (St) Ab.
A.C. May 15
6th cent. Named also Columbanus. He was a disciple of St Columba and of St Fintan of Clonenagh. He founded, and governed, a monastery at Oughaval.
Cf. Holw. — Baud. — O'Hanlon.

COLMAN of DROMORE (St) Bp.
A.C. June 7
6th cent. A native of Argyll who settled

in Ireland and became the abbot-founder and bishop of Dromore in Co. Down. He is said to have been the teacher of St Finnian of Clonard. Cult approved in 1903.
Cf. Att. — Holw. — Baud. — O' Hanlon.

COLMAN Mc ROI (St) Ab. A.C. June 16
6th cent. A deacon, disciple of St Columbkill, and himself abbot-founder of a monastery at Reachrain, now Lambay Island, Dublin.
Cf. Holw. — Baud. — O' Hanlon.

COLMAN (COLOMANNUS) (St) M.
R.M. July 8
See Kilian and Comp.

COLMAN ELO (St) Ab.   A.C. Sept. 26
d. c.610. A nephew of St Columba and the abbot-founder of monasteries at Lynally (Land-Elo, Lin-Alli) and at Muckamore. He is credited with the authorship of the Alphabet of Devotion.
Cf. Att. — Baud. — Holw. — O' Hanlon.

COLMAN of STOCKERAU (St) M.
R.M. Oct. 13
d. 1012. An Irish, or Scottish, pilgrim, who passing through Austria, on his way to the Holy Land, was seized as a spy, racked and hanged with a couple of malefactors, at Stockerau, near Vienna. Miracles were wrought by his dead body, and he was venerated as a saint. He is honoured as one of the patron saints of Austria.
Cf. Holw. — Baud. — O' Hanlon.

COLMAN of KILROOT (St) Bp.
A.C. Oct. 17
6th cent. A disciple of St Ailbe of Emly, and abbot-bishop of Kilroot, near Carrickfergus.
Cf. Baud. — Holw.

COLMAN OF SENBOTH–FOLA (St) Ab.   A.C. Oct. 27
d. c.632. An Irish abbot of Senboth-Fola, in the diocese of Ferns, and associated with St Maidoc, bishop of that see.
Cf. Baud.

COLMAN of KILMACDUAGH (St) Bp.
A.C. Oct. 29
d. 632. A son of the Irish chieftain Duac. He was first a recluse at Arranmore and at Burren in Co. Clare; then he founded the monastery of Kilmacduagh i.e. the church

of the son of Duac, and governed it as abbot-bishop. Cult approved in 1903.
Cf. Att. — Holw. — Baud.

COLMAN of CLOYNE (St) Bp.
A.C. Nov. 24
522-c.600. Born in Cork, a poet and a royal bard at the court of Cashel. In middle age he was baptized by St Brendan, embraced the monastic life, was ordained priest and preached in Limerick and Cork. Finally he founded the church of Cloyne and was consecrated its first bishop. Cult approved in 1903.
Cf. Att. — Holw. — Baud.

COLMAN of GLENDALOUGH (St) Ab.
A.C. Dec. 12
d. 659. An abbot of Glendalough, mentioned in the Irish calendars.
Cf. Baud. — Holw.

COLMOC (MACHOLMOC) (St) Bp.
A.C. June 7
Otherwise Colman of Dromore, q.v.

COLUMBA (COLUM, COLM, COLUMBKILL, COLUMCILLE, COLUMBUS, COMBS) (St) Ab.   R.M. June 9
c.521-597. The most famous of the saints of Scotland. He was a native of Garton, in Co. Donegal, studied at Moville and Clonard, embraced the monastic life at Glasnevin, was ordained priest, and forthwith embarked upon his life's work of founding monasteries and churches, first in Ireland, and after 563 in Scotland. On Whitsun eve of that year he landed with twelve companions on the island of Iona (Holy Island) where he established the greatest and most celebrated of his monasteries, which became thenceforward the most potent factor in the conversion of Picts, Scots, and the Northern English. The description given of him by his biographer and successor Adamnan, is famous: "He had the face of an angel; he was of an excellent nature, polished in speech, holy in deed, great in counsel . . . loving unto all."
Cf. Att. — Baud. — Mab. — Bolland. — Chev.

COLUMBA (St) Ab.   A.C. Dec. 12
d. 548. A native of Leinster and disciple of St Finnian. He governed the monastery of Tyrdaglas in Munster.
Cf. Holw.

**COLUMBA of RIETI (Bl) V. Tert. O.P.
A.C. May 20**
1467-1501. Angelella Guardagnoli was
born at Rieti in Umbria. She became a
Dominican of the third order at Perugia
and won the confidence of all in that city,
so that even the magistrates would ask her
advice. She is said to have been ruthlessly persecuted by Lucrezia Borgia.
Beatified in 1627.
Cf. Att. — Holw. — Baud.

COLUMBA (St) V.M.   R.M. Sept. 17
d. 853. A native of Cordova and a nun at
Tábanos, whence she was driven by the
Moorish persecution of 852. She took
refuge at Cordova, where at a later date,
being called upon to deny Christ, she
openly reviled Mohammed and thereupon
was beheaded.
Cf. Att. — P. de U. — Baud. — Holw.

COLUMBA (St) V. M.   A.C. Nov. 13
? Said to have been a Christian maiden
put to death by a heathen king of Cornwall. She is the patron saint of two parishes in Cornwall.
Cf. Holw. — Baring-Gould.

**COLUMBA of SENS (St) V.M.
R.M. Dec. 31**
d. 273. A Spanish girl who abandoned her
country in order to avoid being denounced
as a Christian. She went to France with
other Spanish Christians and all were put
to death near Meaux, under Aurelian.
Her shrine was at Sens, and she was
formerly venerated throughout France.
Cf. Att. — Baud. — Holw.

COLUMBANUS (St) H.   A.C. Feb. 2
d. 959. An Irish recluse whose hermitage
was near the church of Saint-Bavo at
Ghent.
Cf. Chev. — Baud.

COLUMBANUS (St) Ab.   R.M. Nov. 21
c.545-615. A native of Leinster and a
monk of Bangor. In 580 he left Ireland
with a band of monks and worked first in
England, then in Brittany and finally in
the Vosges district where he founded the
great abbey at Luxeuil which he governed
for twenty-five years. His outspoken
protest against the disorders of the Frankish court led to his exile. He ended his
days in N. Italy, in the abbey of Bobbio
which he founded shortly before his death.

His somewhat intemperate defence of the
Celtic, as opposed to some of the Roman
observances and the austerity of his rule,
make him a rather forbidding personality;
but on the other hand, through the numerous abbeys, founded by himself and by
his disciples, especially after they had become Benedictine, he exerted a determin-
ing and lasting influence on the civilization
of Western Europe.
*Cf. Att. — Baud. — Holw. — Mab. —
Zimm.*

**COLUMBANUS JUNIOR (St) M.
A.C. Nov. 21**
d. p.616. A disciple of St Columbanus
and a monk at Luxeuil.
Cf. Zimm.

**COLUMBINUS (St) Ab. O.S.B.
A.C. Sept. 13**
d. c.680. Successor of St Deicola as
abbot of Lure.
Cf. Zimm.

COLUMBUS (Bl) C. O.P.   P.C. Nov. 8
d. 1229. Dominican prior of Toulouse
and Montpellier. He died while preaching at Fréjus. His relics are in the cathedral of Fréjus.
Cf. Holw. — P.B.

COMBS (St) Ab.   R.M. June 9
A corrupt form of the name Columbkill or
Columba, q.v.

**COMGALL (COMGALLUS) (St) Ab.
A.C. May 10**
c.516-601. Born in Ulster, he became a
monk under St Fintan and eventually the
abbot-founder of Bangor (Ben-Chor)
where he was teacher of St Columbanus
and the band of monks who evangelized
Central Europe. He wrote a rather severe rule for his monks. It seems that
he lived some time in Wales, Cornwall
and Scotland.
Cf. Att. — Mab. — Baud. — Holw.

COMGAN (St) Ab.   A.C. Oct. 13
8th cent. An Irish prince, brother of St
Kentigern, who embraced the monastic
life in Scotland. His feast is kept in the
diocese of Aberdeen.
Cf. Att. — Baud. — Holw.

COMINUS (St)
There are several saints of this name, and

they have been confused by hagiographers.
The following are the most important:

A.C. May 1
A martyr of Catania in Sicily.

A.C. June 3
A companion of St Photinus (Pothinus),
martyr of Lyons.

A.C. June 12
An Irish abbot, patron saint of Ardcavan.
See also Baithin (June 9).
Cf. Baud. — Holw.

**COMPANIUS (COMPAGNO, COM-
PANY) (Bl) Ab. O.S.B. Cam.**
A.C. Oct. 8
12th cent. First abbot of the Camaldo-
lese abbey of our Lady of Porzia in Italy.
Cf. P. de U.

CONALD (St) C.   A.C. Sept. 24
Otherwise Chuniald, q.v.

CONALL (COEL, CONALD) (St) Ab.
A.C. May 22
7th cent. Abbot of the monastery of
Inniscoel, Donegal, where there is a holy
well called after him.
Cf. Holw. — Baud. — O' Hanlon.

CONAN (St) Bp.   A.C. Jan. 26
d. ?c.648. A native of Ireland and a
monk of Iona, said to have been a bishop
in the Isle of Man.
Cf. Att. — Holw. — O' Hanlon.

CONCESSA (St) M.   R.M. Apr. 8
? A martyr anciently venerated at Carthage.

CONCESSUS (St) M.   R.M. Apr. 9
See Demetrius and Comp.

CONCORDIA (St) V.M.   R.M. Aug. 13
See Hippolytus and Concordia.

CONCORDIUS (St) M.   R.M. Jan. 1
d. 175. A subdeacon put to death at
Spoleto, central Italy, under Marcus
Aurelius.
Cf. Att. — Baud. — Holw.

CONCORDIUS (St) M.   R.M. June 23
See John and Concordius.

CONCORDIUS (St) M.   R.M. Sept. 2
See Zeno, Concordius and Theodore.

CONCORDIUS (St) M.   R.M. Dec. 16
See Valentine, Concordius, etc.

**CONDEDUS (CONDÉ, CONDÈDE) H.
O.S.B.   A.C. Oct. 21**
d. c.690. An Englishman who became a
hermit at Fontaine-de-Saint-Valéry, on
the Somme, France. There he heard of
the abbey of Fontenelle and asked to be
received into the community (c.673).
After some years as a monk he obtained
leave to preach, while residing as a recluse
on an island in the Seine, near Caudebec.
*Cf. Att. — Baud. — Holw. — Chev. —
Zimm.*

CONGAN (St) Ab.   A.C. Oct. 13
Otherwise Comgan, q.v.

CONINDRUS (St) Bp.   A.C. Dec. 28
See Romulus and Conindrus.

CONLETH (St) Bp.   A.C. May 3
d. c.519. An Irish recluse at Old Connell
on the Liffey. St Brigid came to know
him and made him the spiritual director
of her nuns at Kildare. Eventually he
became the first bishop of this place. He
was a metal-worker and very skilled as a
copyist and illuminator.
Cf. Att. — Baud. — Holw. — O' Hanlon.

CONNAT (COMNATAN) (St) V.
A.C. Jan. 1
d. c.590. Abbess of St Brigid's convent
in Kildare.
Cf. Holw. — O' Hanlon.

**CONOGAN (GWEN — latinized into AL-
BINUS) (St) Bp.   A.C. Oct. 16**
d. 460. The successor of St Corentin in
the see of Quimper, in Brittany. His
memory is still held in great veneration.
Cf. Holw. — Baud.

CONON (St) M.   R.M. Feb. 26
See Papias, Diodorus, etc.

CONON (St) M.   R.M. March 6
d. 250. A Christian from Nazareth in
Galilee who worked as a poor gardener at
Mandona (Carmel), in Pamphylia, mar-
tyred under Decius.
Cf. Holw. — Baud.

CONON (St) Ab.   A.C. March 28
d. 1236. A Basilian monk and abbot of
the Greek monastery of Nesi in Sicily.
Cf. Att. — Holw. — Baud.

CONON, Father and Son (SS) MM.
R.M. May 29
d. 275. Both were martyred at Iconium in Asia Minor under Aurelian. The boy was only twelve years of age. They were roasted before a slow fire and then racked to death.
Cf. Holw. — Baud. — Ruinart.

CONRAD of MONDSEE (Bl) Ab. M. O.S.B. P.C. Jan. 16
d. 1145. Conrad Bosinlother was born near Trèves and became a Benedictine at Siegburg. In 1127 he was appointed abbot of Mondsee (*Lunaelacensis*) in Upper Austria. His firmness in reclaiming the alienated possessions of the abbey led some nobles to murder him at Oberwang near Mondsee. From the time of his death he was publicly venerated at his abbey as a martyr.
Cf. Holw.

CONRAD of BAVARIA (Bl) O.S.B. Cist.
A.C. Feb. 15
1105-1154. Son of Henry the Black, duke of Bavaria. While a student at Cologne he was drawn to the monastic life by St Bernard, who professed him at Clairvaux. After some years he was granted permission to visit the Holy Land and on his return journey he died near Molfetta in Apulia. Cult approved in 1832.
Cf. Zimm. — Baud. — Att. — P. de U. — Chev.

CONRAD of PIACENZA (St) C. Tert. O.F.M. A.C. Feb. 19
1290-1354. A nobleman of Piacenza who once when out hunting caused a great conflagration, for which a poor man was unjustly accused and condemned to death. Conrad confessed his guilt and forfeited all his fortune to make restitution. After this he and his wife decided to become religious: she was professed as a Poor Clare, he joined the third order of St Francis as a hermit. To avoid publicity he betook himself after a time to Sicily and there passed the last thirty years of his life as a recluse. Cult approved, with the title of Saint, by Paul III.
Cf. Att. — Baud. — Holw.

CONRAD of HILDESHEIM (Bl) C. O.F.M. A.C. Apr. 14
c.1190-? An Italian by birth and one of the first followers of St Francis, by whom he was sent to establish the order in N. Germany. He did so at Hildesheim, where his *cultus* survived till the Reformation.
Cf. Holw.

CONRAD MILIANI of ASCOLI (Bl) C. O.F.M. A.C. Apr. 19
1234-1289. A native of Ascoli Piceno, he joined the Franciscans together with Jerome Masci, afterwards Pope Nicholas IV, whose future elevation he foretold. Conrad was sent to evangelize Libya in N. Africa, whence he was recalled to act as advisor of Jerome Masci, when the latter became a cardinal.
Cf. Att. — Baud. — Holw.

CONRAD of PARZHAM (St) C. O.F.M. Cap. A.C. Apr. 21
1818-1894. Born of poor parents at Parzham near Passau in Bavaria, he joined the Capuchins as a lay-brother at the age of thirty-one and spent more than forty years as doorkeeper at his friary. He was endowed with the gift of prophecy and the power to read hearts. Beatified in 1930 and canonized in 1934.
Cf. Att.

CONRAD of SELDENBÜREN (Bl) M. O.S.B. A.C. May 2
d. 1126. A scion of the royal house of Seldenbüren and founder of the Swiss abbey of Engelberg in Unterwalden where he was professed as a Benedictine lay-brother. He was sent to Zurich to defend the rights of his abbey and was murdered there by his opponents. He is venerated as a martyr.
Cf. Att. — Holw. — Baud.

CONRAD (CUNO) of TRÈVES (St) Bp. M. A.C. June 1
d. 1066. Of the noble family of Pfullingen in Swabia. His uncle, St Anno, archbishop of Cologne, appointed him bishop of Trèves, in defiance of the right of election of the Trèves chapter. Conrad was seized on his way to Trèves and cast from the battlements of the castle of Uerzig. He is venerated as a martyr.
Cf. Att. — Holw. — Baud.

CONRAD of HESSEN (Bl) Ab. O.S.B. Cist. P.C. June 1
13th cent. Cistercian abbot of Haina in Hessen.
Cf. Zimm.

CONRAD of OTTOBEUREN (Bl) Ab. O.S.B.			**P.C. July 27**
d. 1227. Abbot of Ottobeuren Abbey in Bavaria from 1193 till his death. He is described as a "lover of the brethren and of the poor."
Cf. Zimm.

CONRAD NANTWIN (Bl) M.
			A.C. Aug. 10
d. 1268. Unjustly burnt at the stake at Wolfrathshausen, near Munich. His cult was approved by Boniface VIII, and a church is dedicated to him.
Cf. Holw.

CONRAD of ZÄHRINGEN (Bl) Card. O.S.B. Cist.			**P.C. Sept. 30**
d. 1227. A member of the family of the counts of Seyne. In early life he was made a canon of St Lambert's, Liége; then he passed over to the Cistercians at Villiers in Brabant. Subsequently he became successively abbot of Villiers (1209), of Clairvaux (1214), of Cîteaux (1217), cardinal-bishop of Porto and Santa Rufina (1219) and papal legate in Languedoc (1224-1226). He died at Bari. The Cistercians have always given him the title of Saint.
Cf. Gams — Chev. — Holw. — Baud.

CONRAD of FRISACH (Bl) C. O.P.
			P.C. Nov. 25
d. 1239. A doctor at the university of Bologna whom St Dominic received into the Order and sent to Germany. He died at Magdeburg singing the Psalm, *Cantate Domino canticum novum.*
Cf. Holw.

CONRAD of HEISTERBACH (Bl) C. O.S.B. Cist.			**P.C. Nov. 25**
d. c.1200. A soldier and a minister to the margraves of Thuringia until his fiftieth year, and then a Cistercian at Heisterbach. Cult not yet officially approved.
Cf. Holw.

CONRAD of CONSTANCE (St) Bp.
			R.M. Nov. 26
d. 975. Bishop of Constance in Switzerland from 934 till his death. Three times he made the pilgrimage to the Holy Land, and in an age when most prelates were continually involved in secular politics, he succeeded in attending exclusively to ecclesiastical interests. Canonized in 1123.
Cf. Att. — Baud. — Holw.

CONRAD of OFFIDA (Bl) C. O.F.M.
			A.C. Dec. 14
c.1241-1306. A native of Offida, diocese of Ascoli Piceno. When fourteen years of age he joined the Franciscans and throughout his life as a Minorite, he favoured the "spiritual" and eremitical tendencies in the order. He died at Bastia in Umbria while preaching a sermon. Cult confirmed in 1817.
Cf. Att. — Holw. — Baud.

CONRADIN of BRESCIA (Bl) C. O.P.
			P.C. Nov. 1
d. 1429. Born at Bornato, in the diocese of Brescia, he was professed a Friar Preacher at Padua (1413) and was chosen prior of Bologna. Here he was twice imprisoned for defending the pope.
Cf. Baud. — Holw.

CONRAN (St) Bp.			**Feb. 14**
The legend of a holy bishop of the Orkney Islands so named lacks all historical foundation.
Cf. Att. — Baud. — Holw.

CONSORTIA (St) V.		**R.M. June 22**
d. ? 570. Said to have been the foundress of a convent generously endowed by King Clotaire out of gratitude for her having miraculously healed his dying daughter. She was venerated at Cluny, but nothing certain is known about her.
Cf. Holw. — Baud. — Baronius.

CONSTABILIS (St) Ab. O.S.B.
			A.C. Feb. 17
1060-1124. A native of Lucania, he became a Benedictine under St Leo at the abbey of Cava near Salerno, and in 1122 was chosen its fourth abbot. He built the town of Castelabbate, where he is now venerated as the principal patron saint. Canonized in 1893.
Cf. Mab. — Chev. — Baud. — Holw.

CONSTANCE (St) M.		**R.M. Sept. 19**
See Felix and Constance.

CONSTANT (St) M.		**A.C. Nov. 18**
d. 777. An Irish priest-hermit at Lough Erne who died under circumstances which led to his being venerated as a martyr.
Cf. Holw.

CONSTANTIAN (St) Ab.   A.C. Dec. 1
d. 570. A native of Auvergne, monk at
Micy (Orleans) and abbot-founder of
Javron abbey.
Cf. Baud. — Holw.

CONSTANTINE (St) M. R.M. March 11
? A martyr of Carthage whose Acts have
been lost.

CONSTANTINE (St) M.   A.C. March 11
d. 576. Said to have been a king of Cornwall, who after a career of vice and greed,
led a penitent's life in Wales and Ireland,
whence he went as a missionary to Scotland. There he was put to death by
pirates. There is little serious historical
foundation for this story.
*Cf. Att. — Baud. — Holw. — Baring —
Gould.*

CONSTANTINE (St) King, M. A.C. Apr. 2
d. 874. Constantine II, king of Scotland,
was slain in a battle against heathen invaders of his country and was henceforth
locally honoured as a martyr. He was
buried at Iona.
Cf. Holw.

CONSTANTINE (St) Bp.   R.M. Apr. 12
d. 529. The first bishop of Gap in France,
about whom nothing else is known.
*Cf. Att. — Duch. Fast. Episc. — Baud. —
Holw.*

CONSTANTINE (St) Bp.   A.C. June 15
d. c.706. Said to have been a monk under
St Philibert at Jumièges, and then bishop
of Beauvais.
Cf. Holw. — Baud. — Zimm.

CONSTANTINE (St) Ab. O.S.B.
A.C. July 21
d. c.560. Disciple and first successor of
St Benedict at Montecassino.
Cf. Mab. — Chev. — Holw.

CONSTANTINE (St) M.   R.M. July 27
One of the Seven Sleepers, q.v.

CONSTANTINOPLE (Martyrs of):
Three anonymous groups of martyrs put
to death at Constantinople are commemorated in the R.M., viz. —
R.M. Feb. 8
d. 485. The community of monks of St
Dius martyred at the time of the Acacian
schism for their fidelity to the Holy See.

R.M. March 30
d. 351-359. A great number of people who
suffered under the Arian emperor Constantius.
R.M. July 8
d. 832. The Abrahamite monks, put to
death under the iconoclast emperor
Theophilus.

CONSTANTIUS and Comp. (SS) MM.
R.M. Jan. 29
d.170. Constantius, first bishop of
Perugia, was put to death with numerous
Christians of his flock, under Marcus
Aurelius. The Acts of these martyrs are
far from trustworthy.
Cf. Holw. — Baud.

CONSTANTIUS of FABRIANO (Bl)
C. O.P.   A.C. Feb. 25
d.1481. Constantius Bernocchi was
born at Fabriano in the Marches of An-
cona and at the age of fifteen entered the
Dominican Order. He had as masters Bl
Conradin and St Antoninus. Appointed
prior of the friary of San Marco at Flor-
ence, he achieved there a complete reform.
He was renowned for his gift of prophecy.
Beatified in 1811.
Cf. Att. — Baud. — Holw.

CONSTANTIUS (St) M.   R.M. Aug. 26
See Simplicius and Constantius.

CONSTANTIUS (St) Bp.   R.M. Sept. 1
d. c.520. Bishop of Aquino. He is mentioned with great honour by St Gregory
the Great in his Dialogues.
Cf. Baud. — Holw.

CONSTANTIUS (St) C.   R.M. Sept. 23
6th cent. Sacristan of the ancient church
of St Stephen at Ancona. He is still
greatly venerated in that city.
Cf. Holw. — Att.

CONSTANTIUS (St) C.   R.M. Nov. 30
5th cent. A priest of Rome who strongly
opposed the Pelagians, at whose hands he
had much to endure.
Cf. Holw. — Baud.

CONSTANTIUS (St) M.   R.M. Dec. 12
See Maxentius, Constantius, etc.

CONTARDO of ESTE (St) C. A.C. Apr. 16
d. 1249. Surnamed "the Pilgrim." He
belonged to the Este family of Ferrara.

He set out on a pilgrimage to Compostella, but died at Broni, diocese of Tortona, in extreme poverty.
Cf. Att. — Holw. — Baud.

CONTESTUS (St) Bp.   **A.C. Jan. 19**
d. c.510.   Bishop of Bayeux in Normandy from 480 till his death.
Cf. Duch. Fast. Episc. — Gams — Baud.— Holw.

CONUS (St) Mk. O.S.B.   **A.C. June 3**
d. c.1200.   Benedictine monk of Cardossa in Lucania.   His relics were enshrined in the neighbouring village of Diano (1261), the saint's native place.
Cf. Zimm. — Chev. — Holw. — Bolland. (*Bibl. hag. lat. 1899, p. 293.*)

CONVOYON (St) Ab. O.S.B.   **A.C. Jan. 5**
d. 868.   A Breton by birth, he became successively deacon of Vannes, recluse, monk at Glanfeuil, and lastly abbot-founder of the great Benedictine monastery of St Saviour (831) near Redon, in Brittany. He was driven from his abbey by the Norsemen and died in exile.   Cult confirmed, with the title of saint, in 1866.
Cf. Att. — Zimm. — Chev. — Baud. — Holw.

CONWALL (CONVAL) (St) C.
A.C. Sept. 28
d. c.630.   An Irish priest, disciple of St Kentigern, who preached and died in Scotland.
Cf. Baud. — Holw.

COPRES (St) M.   **R.M. July 9**
See Patermuthius, Copres, etc.

CORBICAN (St) C.   **A.C. June 26**
8th cent.   An Irish recluse in the Low Countries who spent part of his day helping and instructing the peasants.
Cf. Holw. — Baud.

CORBINIAN (St) Bp.   **R.M. Sept. 8**
670-730.   A Frank who spent fourteen years as a hermit and then went to Rome, where Pope Gregory II consecrated him bishop and sent him to evangelize Germany.   Corbinian fixed his residence at Freising in Bavaria.   His last years were made very trying by Duke Grimoald, whose incestuous marriage the saint had denounced.
Cf. Att. — Holw. — Baud.

CORBMAC (St) Ab.   **A.C. June 21**
6th cent.   A disciple of St Columbkill, placed by him over the monastery he had founded at Durrow.
Cf. Holw.

CORDULA (St) V.M.   **R.M. Oct. 22**
d. c.453.   An apocryphal saint who belongs to the legendary group of St Ursula and her eleven thousand virgins.

COREA (Martyrs of)   **A.C. Sept. 2.**
d. 1839.   Laurence Imbert, titular bishop of Capsa and vicar apostolic of Corea, two other priests of the Paris Foreign Missions and seventy-six Corean lay-people, gave their lives for Christ during the persecution of 1839.   Beatified in 1925.
Cf. Att.

COREBUS (St) M.   **R.M. Apr. 18**
c.117-138.   A prefect of Messina in Sicily converted to Christ by St Eleutherius and martyred under the emperor Hadrian.   It seems, however, that the whole narrative is only a legend.
Cf. Holw. — Baud.

CORENTINUS (CURY) (St) Bp.
A.C. Dec. 12
d. c.490.   The first bishop of Cornouaille, now Quimper, in Brittany.   He had been a recluse at Plomodiern.   His cult spread throughout S. W. England, where he was known as St Cury.
Cf. Att. — Baud. — Holw.

CORFU (Martyrs of)   **R.M. Apr. 29**
1st cent.   Known as "the Seven Holy Thieves."   Seven criminals converted to Christ, it is said, by St Jason, a disciple of our Lord (Acts XVII, 5).   Their names are given as Saturninus, Inischolus, Faustian, Januarius, Massalius, Euphrasius, and Mannonius.   They were martyred in the island of Corfu.
Cf. Holw.

CORMAC (St) Bp.   **A.C. Sept. 14**
d. 908.   Probably the first bishop of Cashel.   He is likewise known as king of Munster and was slain in battle.   The "Psalter of Cashel" compiled by him is still extant.
Cf. Holw. — O'Hanlon.

CORMAC (St) Ab.   **A.C. Dec. 12**
6th cent.   An Irish abbot, friend of St Columba.
Cf. Holw.

CORNELIA (St) M.   R.M. March 31
See Theodulus, Anesius, etc.

CORNELIUS (St) Bp.   R.M. Feb. 2
1st cent. The centurion of the Italic
cohort, baptized at Caesarea in Palestine
by the apostle St Peter (Acts X).
Tradition makes him the first bishop of
Caesarea; and as such he is described in
the R.M.
Cf. Baud. — Holw.

CORNELIUS (St) Bp. O.S.A. A.C. June 4
c.1120-1176. Cornelius MacConchail-
leadh, an Irishman by birth, joined the
Augustinian canons regular at Armagh in
1140, was chosen abbot there in 1151, and
finally became archbishop of that city in
1174. He died at Chambéry in Savoy on
his return from a pilgrimage to Rome and
is still held in great veneration there.
Cf. Holw. — Baud. — O'Hanlon.

CORNELIUS (St) M. O.F.M.
                         R.M. July 9
d. 1572. Born at Dorestat near Utrecht,
he took the Franciscan habit at Gorkum,
Holland, and was hanged by Calvinists at
Briel with eighteen companions. (See
Gorkum Martyrs.)
Cf. Holw. — Att. — Baud.

CORNELIUS (St) Pope M. R.M. Sept. 16
d. 253. A Roman priest raised to the
papal throne after an interregnum of
fourteen months. He was opposed by
Novatian, the first anti-pope. Cornelius
had at once to attend to the condemnation
of Novatian's rigoristic principles on the
readmission of those Christians who had
fallen away during the persecution. Cornelius's pontificate is an excellent illus-
tration of how the papal authority was
recognized everywhere by the faithful.
He died in the persecution of Gallus.
Shortly before his death he had been banished to Centumcellae (Civita Vecchia).
His name is mentioned in the Canon of
the Mass.
Cf. Att. — Baud. — Holw.

CORNELIUS (St) M.   R.M. Dec. 31
See Stephen, Pontian, etc.

CORONA (Bl) V. O.S.B.   A.C. Apr. 24
? A Benedictine nun of the convent of
Elche, near Valencia in Spain.
Cf. Prop. diocesis Valent.

CORONA (St) M.   R.M. May 14
See Victor and Corona.

COSMAS TACHEGIA (ZAQUIRA) (St)
M. Tert. O.F.M.   R.M. Feb. 5
d. 1597. A Japanese Franciscan tertiary,
who served the Franciscan missionaries as
interpreter. He was crucified with St
Peter Baptist and twenty-four companions
at Nagasaki. Beatified in 1627; canonized in 1862.
Cf. Holw.

COSMAS TAQUEA (Bl) M.   A.C. June 1
d. 1619 (Nov. 18). A layman, native of
Corea, taken to Japan as a prisoner of war.
There he became a member of the Confra-
ternity of the Rosary and gave shelter to
Bl John of St Dominic. He was in con-
sequence burnt alive. Beatified in 1867.
Cf. Holw.

COSMAS (St) Bp. M.   A.C. Sept. 10
d. 1160. Born at Palermo in Sicily, he
was appointed bishop of Aphrodisia and
consecrated by Eugene III. The Saracens
captured his episcopal city and he died as
a consequence of maltreatment at their
hands. Cult approved by Leo XIII.
Cf. Holw.

COSMAS and DAMIAN (SS) MM.
                         R.M. Sept. 27
d. c.303. Twin Arab brothers, physicians
by profession, who were martyred at
Aegea in Cilicia, under Diocletian.
They practised their profession without
taking payment from their patients, and
on this account they are surnamed in the
East Anargyroi (the moneyless ones).
Their relics were brought to Rome, whence
their cult spread throughout the West.
They are mentioned in the Canon of the
Roman Mass.
Cf. Att. — Baud. — Holw.

COSMO di CARBOGNANO (Bl)
                         A.C. Nov. 5
Otherwise Gomidas, q.v.

COTTAM (THOMAS) (Bl) M.
                         A.C. May 30
See Thomas Cottam.

COTTIDUS, EUGENE and Comp. (SS)
MM.   R.M. Sept. 6
? Cappadocian martyrs, whose Acta have
not come down to us. St Cottidus is
described as a deacon.

COTTOLENGO (JOSEPH-BENEDICT) (St)   A.C. Apr. 29
See Joseph-Benedict Cottolengo.

CRATON and Comp. (SS) MM.
R.M. Feb. 15
d. c.273. Craton, a philosopher and professor of rhetoric, was converted to Christ by St Valentine, bishop of Terni. He was martyred in Rome shortly after, together with his wife, children, and many of his household.
Cf. Holw. — Bolland. — Baud.

CREDAN (St) Ab. O.S.B.   A.C. Aug. 19
d.c.780. Eighth abbot of Evesham in the time of King Offa of Mercia.
Cf. Holw. — Stanton.

CREMENTIUS (St) M.   R.M. Apr. 16
See Caius and Crementius.

CRESCENS (St) M.   R.M. March 10
See Codratus, Dionysius, etc.

CRESCENS (St) M.   R.M. Apr. 15
?¹ A martyr of Myra in Lycia, Asia Minor, who perished at the stake.
Cf. Baud. — Holw.

CRESCENS, DIOSCORIDES, PAUL and HELLADIUS (SS) MM.   R.M. May 28
d. c.244. Roman Christians who were burnt to death. Helladius does not seem to have belonged to this group.
Cf. Holw.

CRESCENS (St) Bp. M.
R.M. June 27 and Dec. 29
2nd cent. The disciple of St Paul mentioned by him (II Tim. IV, 10) as having gone into Galatia. He is stated to have been appointed bishop of the Galatians. Tradition tells us of his apostolate in France and also that he founded the see of Mainz in Gaul. The R.M. adds that he returned to the east and was martyred under Trajan. It is certain that the Crescens who was first bishop of Vienne and the Crescens who worked at Mainz are not the disciple of St Paul, even if they did really exist.
Cf. Holw.

CRESCENS (St) M.   R.M. July 18
See Symphorosa and Comp.

CRESCENS (St) M.   R.M. Oct. 1
See Priscus, Crescens and Evagrius.

CRESCENS (St) Bp.   R.M. Nov. 28
See Valerian, Urban, etc.

CRESCENTIA HÖSS (Bl) V. Tert. O.F.M.   A.C. Apr. 5
1682-1744. Born at Kaufbeuren in Bavaria. In 1703, at the request of the Protestant mayor of the town, she was admitted to the convent of the Franciscan regular tertiaries, but the nuns neglected and even persecuted her because she had entered without a dowry. Her holiness, however, overcame their hostility, and eventually she was made novice-mistress, and superioress. Beatified in 1900.
Cf. Att. — Holw. — Baud.

CRESCENTIA (St) V.M.   R.M. June 15
See Vitus, Modestus and Crescentia.

CRESCENTIAN (St) M.   R.M. May 31
d. c.130. A martyr who suffered at Sassari, in Sardinia, at the same time as SS Gabinus and Crispulus, in the reign of the emperor Hadrian. He is still held in great veneration there.
Cf. Holw. — Baud.

CRESCENTIAN (St) M.   R.M. June 1
d. c.287. A soldier beheaded at Saldo, near Città di Castello (Tiphernum) in Italy. His historical existence is doubtful.
Cf. Att. — Holw. — Baud.

CRESCENTIAN (St) M.   R.M. July 2
See Ariston, Crescentian, etc.

CRESCENTIAN (St) M.   R.M. Aug. 12
See Hilaria, Digna, etc.

CRESCENTIAN, VICTOR, ROSULA, and GENERALIS (SS) MM.   R.M. Sept. 14
d. c.258. African martyrs, alleged to have suffered at the same time and place as St Cyprian.

CRESCENTIAN (St) M.   R.M. Nov. 24
d. 309. A martyr who suffered at Rome in company with SS Cyriacus, Largus and Smaragdus, expiring on the rack in their presence under Maxentius.
Cf. Holw. — Baud.

CRESCENTIAN (St) Bp.   R.M. Nov. 28
See Valerian, Urban, etc.

CRESCENTIANA (St) M.   R.M. May 5
5th cent. Beyond the fact that as early

as the time of Pope Symmachus (498-514) a church in Rome was dedicated to her, nothing is known of this martyr.

CRESCENTION (St) M. R.M. Sept. 17
See Narcissus and Crescention.

CRESCENTIUS (St) C. R.M. Apr. 19
d. c.396. A subdeacon of Florence, a disciple of St Zenobius and of St Ambrose.
Cf. Att. — Baud. — Holw.

CRESCENTIUS (St) M. R.M. Sept. 14
d. c.300. A boy, only eleven years of age, the son of St Euthymius, who, in the persecution of Diocletian, was brought from Perugia to Rome, bravely confessed Christ under torture, and was beheaded.
Cf. Baud. — Holw.

CRESCENTIUS (St) M. R.M. Dec. 12
See Maxentius, Constantine, etc.

CRESCENTIUS (St) Bp. R.M. Dec. 29
Otherwise Crescens (June 27) q.v.

CRESCENTIUS (St) M. R.M. Dec. 29
See Dominic, Victor, etc.

CRESCONIUS (St) Bp. M. R.M. Nov. 28
See Valerian, Urban, etc.

CRETE (Martyrs of) Dec. 23
For this group of ten martyrs, who suffered in Crete, see Theodulus and Comp.

CREWENNA (St) Feb. 1
5th cent. This saint accompanied St Breaca from Ireland to Cornwall. There is no record of him beyond the place-name Crowan near St Erth.
Cf. Baring-Gould.

CRISPIN (St) Bp. R.M. Jan. 7
Two bishops of this name, both saints, governed the see of Pavia in Lombardy: one in the first half of the third century occupied the see for thirty-five years, the second was bishop during the reign of Pope St Leo the Great and in 451 subscribed the acts of the council of Milan.
Cf. Holw. — Baud.

CRISPIN of VITERBO (Bl) C. O.F.M. Cap. A.C. May 23
1668-1750. A native of Viterbo, who joined the Capuchins as a lay-brother and was employed as a cook in the friaries of Viterbo, Tolfa, Rome and Albano. He loved to call himself "the little beast of burden of the Capuchins." Beatified in 1806.
Cf. Att. — Baud. — Holw.

CRISPIN and CRISPINIAN (SS) MM. R.M. Oct. 25
d. c.287. Two brothers, shoemakers by trade, who were beheaded at Soissons in France under Diocletian. They were held in great popular veneration throughout the Middle Ages (see in this connection Shakespeare's Henry V, Act. IV, Scene 2) and are still recognized as the patron saints of shoemakers.
Cf. Holw. — Att. — Baud. — Ricci.

CRISPIN (St) Bp. M. R.M. Nov. 19
4th cent. Bishop of Ecija (*Astiagis*) in Andalusia, beheaded under Maximian Herculius. He is honoured with a special office in the Mozarabic breviary.
Cf. Holw. — Baud.

CRISPIN (St) M. R.M. Dec. 3
See Claudius, Crispin, etc.

CRISPIN (St) M. R.M. Dec. 5
See Julius, Potamia, etc.

CRISPINA (St) V.M. R.M. Dec. 5
d. 304. A wealthy matron of Thebeste in Numidia. She was tortured, forced to undergo the most shameful indignities and ultimately beheaded. We have still a glowing panegyric preached by St Augustine in her honour.
Cf. Att. — Baud. — Holw.

CRISPULUS (St) M. R.M. May 30
See Gabinus and Crispulus.

CRISPULUS and RESTITUTUS (SS) MM. R.M. June 10
1st cent. Martyrs believed to have suffered under Nero, and probably in Rome. Baronius, however, following Rhabanus Maurus, assigns them to Spain. No account of them is extant.
Cf. Holw. — Baud.

CRISPUS (St) M. R.M. Aug. 18
See John and Crispus.

CRISPUS and CAIUS (SS) MM. R.M. Oct. 4
1st cent. Saints of the apostolic age, the

only two whom St Paul baptized at Corinth (I Cor 1, 14). Crispus was ruler of the synagogue in that city (Acts XVIII, 8). Caius in all likelihood is the same person whom the Apostle styles "my host" (Rom XVI, 23), and also the "dearly beloved Gaius (Caius)" to whom St John addressed his third epistle. According to traditions, both became bishops: the former of the island of Aegina, the latter of Thessalonica.
Cf. Holw. — Baud.

CRISTIOLUS (St)   A.C. Nov. 3
7th cent. A Welsh saint, brother of St Sulian and founder of churches in Pembrokeshire and Anglesey.
Cf. Holw. — Baring-Gould.

CROIDAN, MEDAN and DEGAN (SS)
A.C. June 4
6th cent. Three disciples of St Petroc, q.v.

CRONAN BEG (St) Bp.   A.C. Jan. 7
7th cent. A bishop of ancient Aendrum, Co. Down, mentioned in connection with the paschal controversy in 640.
Cf. O'Hanlon.

CRONAN the WISE (St) Bp. A.C. Feb. 9
? 8th cent. Surnamed "the wise" on account of his ability in systematizing Irish canon law. He is probably identical with St Ronan, bishop of Lismore.
Cf. Holw. — Baud.

CRONAN of ROSCREA (St) Ab.
A.C. Apr. 28
d. c.626. Born in Munster, founder of several religious houses in various parts of Ireland, chief among them being that of Roscrea.
Cf. Att. — Holw. — Baud.

CRONAN (St)   A.C. June 3
d. 617. Surnamed "the Tanner." A disciple of St Kevin.
Cf. Holw.

CRONIDES (St) M.   R.M. March 27
See Philetus, Lydia, etc.

CRONION (St) M.
R.M. Feb. 27 and Oct. 30
See Julian, Cronion, etc.

CROTATES (St) M.   R.M. Apr. 21
See Apollo, Isacius, etc.

CROYLAND (Martyrs of) (SS) O.S.B.
A.C. Apr. 9
See Theodore and Comp.

CRUMMINE (St) Bp.   A.C. June 28
5th cent. A disciple of St Patrick, placed by him over the church of Leccuine (Lackan) Co. Westmeath.
Cf. Holw.

CTESIPHON (St) Bp.   R.M. May 15
See Torquatus, Ctesiphon, etc.

CUAN (St) Ab.   A.C. Jan. 1
6th cent. An Irish abbot, called Mochua or Moncan, who founded many churches and monasteries, and who lived to close upon his hundredth year.
Cf. Bolland. — O'Hanlon.

CUARAN (CURVINUS, CRONAN) (St) Bp.   A.C. Feb. 9
d. p. 700. An Irish bishop, surnamed like several others, "the Wise," who concealed his dignity in order to become a simple monk at Iona, where, however he was recognized by St Columba
Cf. Baud. — Holw.

CUBY (CYBY) (St) Bp.   A.C. Nov. 8
6th cent. A Cornish saint, a cousin of St David of Wales. Consecrated bishop, he settled with ten disciples near Tregony, but later passed some time in Ireland. Ultimately he came to Wales and founded a monastery near Holyhead. He is the patron saint of Llangibbi (Monmouth) and of Llangybi (Carnarvon).
Cf. Baring-Gould.

CUCUPHAS (CUCUFATE, CUGAT, GUINEFORT, QOQOFAS) (St) M.
R.M. July 25
d. 304. A son of noble parents of Punic descent resident at Scillis in Africa. He crossed over to Spain and was martyred near Barcelona at the place where some centuries later arose the Benedictine abbey of St Cugat del Valles. He is one of the most celebrated of the Spanish martyrs. Prudentius composed some exquisite stanzas in his honour. Part of his relics were venerated at Paris.
Cf. Att. — Baud. — Holw.

CULMATIUS (St) M.   R.M. June 19
See Gaudentius and Culmatius.

CUMGAR (CUNGAR, CYNGAR) (St) C.
A.C. Nov. 2
6th (or 8th) cent. A native of Devon, founder of monasteries at Budgworth, Congresbury (Somerset) and at Llangonys (Glamorgan). He is to be identified with St Docuinus, or Doguinus. This seems to be the name which was later corrupted into Oue and Kew. St Cumgar was buried at Congresbury, to which town he has given his name.
Cf. Baring-Gould — Stanton.

CUMINE the WHITE (St) Ab.
A.C. Feb. 24 or Oct. 6
d. 669. An abbot of Iona of Irish descent, who wrote a life of St Columba.
Cf. Holw. — O' Hanlon — Bolland.

CUMMIAN (CUMIAN, CUMMIN) (St) Bp. O.S.B. A.C. June 9
1st half 8th cent. An Irish bishop who in his wanderings through Italy visited Bobbio and remained there as a monk. By this time Bobbio was already a Benedictine abbey; Cummian himself was an ardent advocate of the Roman observances.
Cf. Zimm. — Mab. — Holw. — Baud.

CUMMIAN FADA (St) Ab. A.C. Nov. 12
d. 662. An Irish monk who had charge of the monastic school at Clonfert and became the abbot-founder of the monastery at Kilcummin, where he strenuously defended the Roman computation of Easter against his Celtic brethren.
Cf. Att. — Baud. — Holw.

CUNCOLIM (Martyrs of) A.C. July 27
See Rudolph Acquaviva and Comp.

CUNEGUND (St) V. O.S.B.
R.M. March 3
d. 1039. Wife of Henry II, Holy Roman Emperor, with whom she lived in conjugal virginity and is, for this reason, venerated as a virgin. She founded the Benedictine nunnery of Kaufungen, which she entered on the first anniversary of her husband's death (1024) and where she earnestly endeavoured to forget her past dignity. Canonized in 1200.
Cf. Att. — Zimm. — Baud. — Chev.

CUNEGUND (Bl) V. O.S.B. A.C. May 4
d. p. 1052. A Benedictine nun of the convent of Niedermunster in Ratisbon.
Cf. Zimm.

CUNEGUND (Bl) V. A.C. July 24
Otherwise Kinga, q.v.

CUNERA (St) V. A.C. June 12
? A saint venerated more particularly in Germany, but said to have been of British birth. The traditions relating to her are most untrustworthy.
Cf. Holw. — Baud.

CUNIBERT (St) Ab. O.S.B. A.C. Sept. 16
d. c.680. Successor of St Humbert as abbot of Maroilles, in the diocese of Cambrai.
Cf. Baud. — Holw.

CUNIBERT (St) Bp. R.M. Nov. 12
d. c.633. A Frankish courtier who became successively archdeacon of Trèves and archbishop of Cologne. He filled the office of chief minister during the minority of King Sigebert of Austrasia. He was an untiring builder of churches and monasteries.
Cf. Holw. — Att. — Baud.

CURCODOMUS (St) C. R.M. May 4
3rd cent. A Roman deacon, sent by the pope to attend St Peregrinus, first bishop of Auxerre, on his mission into Gaul.
Cf. Holw.

CURÉ d'ARS (St) C. R.M. Aug. 9
See John Baptist Vianney.

CURIG (St) Bp. A.C. June 16
6th cent. Stated to have been bishop of Llanbadarn in Wales, in which country several churches are dedicated in his honour. There is, however, great difficulty in distinguishing him from other saints bearing similar names.
Cf. Baring-Gould.

CURITAN (St) Bp. A.C. March 14
Otherwise Boniface, q.v.

CURONOTUS (St) Bp. M. R.M. Sept. 12
d. c.258. A bishop of Iconium in Lycaonia, Asia Minor, martyred under Valerian.
Cf. Holw. — Baud.

CURY (St) Bp. A.C. Dec. 12
Otherwise Corentinus, q.v.

CUTHBERT (St) Bp. O.S.B.
R.M. March 20
d. 687. A Briton who in his youth

tended his father's sheep until he embraced the monastic life at Melrose. When Ripon abbey was founded he was sent there as guest-master, then he became prior of Melrose. Finally, after the council of Whitby, he was asked to go to Lindisfarne, now under the new Benedictine observance, and was made prior of the abbey. In March, 685, he was consecrated abbot-bishop of Lindisfarne by St Theodore at York. St Cuthbert is one of the most famous of English saints and combines in his person the best traits of both the Celtic and the Roman type of monachism. He was moreover the wonder-worker of England, and his shrine at Durham was one of the most frequented in the Middle Ages: it was already an ancient shrine before St Thomas of Canterbury was born.
Cf. Zimm. — Att. — Holw. — Baud. — Mab. — Chev.

CUTHBERT (St) Bp. O.S.B.   P.C. Oct. 26
d. 758. A monk of Lyminge in Kent who became bishop of Hereford (c.736) and archbishop of Canterbury (c.740). He is best remembered as one of the English correspondents of St Boniface.
Cf. Holw. — Chev. — Butler-Thurston (Oct. p. 244).

CUTHBERT MAYNE (Bl) M.
A.C. Nov. 29
1544-1577. Born near Barnstaple in Devonshire, he was educated as a Protestant, but he was converted to Catholicism while an undergraduate at St John's, Oxford. He was ordained at Douai and sent to the English mission (c.1575). He laboured in Cornwall, but before a year had elapsed was captured and condemned for the crime of saying Mass. He was executed at Launceston. Beatified in 1886, he is the protomartyr of the English seminaries.
Cf. Att. — Baud. — Holw.

CUTHBURGA (St) Abs. O.S.B.
A.C. Aug. 31
d. c.725. Sister to King Ina of Wessex. She married Aldfrid of Northumbria (688) who allowed her to enter as a nun at Barking under St Hildelitha. Some time after 705 she founded, with her sister St Queenburga, Wimborne abbey in Dorset, which she governed as abbess. From this nunnery came forth the band of missionary nuns who helped in the evangelization of Germany.
Cf. Att. — Zimm. — Chev. — Holw. — Mab.

CUTHMAN (St) H.   A.C. Feb. 8
9th cent. A south of England saint who lived a holy life as a shepherd near Steyning in Sussex. The old church of that place was dedicated in his honour.
Cf. Stanton — Holw. — Baud.

CUTIAS (St) M.   R.M. Feb. 18
See Maximus, Claudius, etc.

CYBAR (St) Ab.   R.M. July 1
Otherwise Eparchius, q.v.

CYBY (St) Bp.   A.C. Nov. 8
Otherwise Cuby, q.v.

CYNDEYRN (St) Bp.   A.C. Jan. 14
Otherwise Kentigern, q.v.

CYNFARCH (St)   A.C. Sept. 8
Otherwise Kingsmark, q.v.

CYNFRAN (St) C.   A.C. Nov. 11
5th cent. A Welsh saint, one of the sons of the chieftain Brychan of Brecknock and founder of a church in Carnarvonshire. There is also a St Cynfran's well.
Cf. Holw. — Baring-Gould.

CYNIHILL (St) C.   A.C. March 2
7th cent. A brother of SS Chad and Cedd who also laboured in the evangelization of the Anglo-Saxons.
Cf. Stanton.

CYNIDR (KENEDRUS) (St) Ab.
A.C. Apr. 27
Otherwise Enoder, q.v.

CYNLLO (St)   A.C. July 17
5th cent. A Welsh saint, in whose honour several churches are dedicated.
Cf. Baring-Gould.

CYNOG (St) M.   A.C. Oct. 7
Otherwise Canog, q.v.

CYNWL (St) H.   A.C. Apr. 30
6th cent. The brother of St Deiniol, first bishop of Bangor. He lived an austere life in N. Wales, and after his death churches were dedicated in his honour.
Cf. Holw. — Baring-Gould.

CYPRIAN (St) M.   R.M. March 10
See Codratus, Dionysius, etc.

CYPRIAN (St) Bp.   A.C. Apr. 21
d. 582. Bishop of Brescia in Lombardy.
His relics are enshrined in the church of
San Pietro in Oliveto at Brescia.
Cf. Holw. — Baud.

CYPRIAN (St) M.   R.M. July 11
See Savinus and Cyprian.

CYPRIAN (St) Bp. M.   R.M. Sept. 16
c.210-258. Thascius Caecilius Cyprianus
was born in Proconsular Africa, became a
lawyer, was converted to Christianity and
was consecrated bishop of Carthage
(c.249). It is as a bishop that he played a
most important part in the history of the
Western Church. As such he produced
numerous treatises on various theological
subjects, one of the most important being
De Unitate, and wrote numerous letters.
He is in fact, like Tertullian, a pioneer of
Latin Christian literature. He is a witness to the belief of the faithful in the
necessary oneness of the Church founded
on the Rock of Peter. He seconded Pope
St Cornelius's teaching on the reconciliation of fallen Christians. He erred, however, on the doctrine of the validity of
baptism conferred by heretics. Nevertheless, the Roman Church has always been
grateful to his memory and mentions his
name in the Canon of the Mass. Cyprian
went into hiding during the persecution of
Decius, but was arrested and beheaded
under the first edict of Valerian. The
Acts of his martyrdom are of great charm
and interest.
Cf. Att. — Ruinart. — Ricci — Holw.

**CYPRIAN and JUSTINA (SS) MM.
R.M. Sept. 26**
The legend is that Cyprian, a pagan
necromancer and astrologer, was converted
to Christianity by the virgin Justina whom
he had tried to lead astray. In the persecution under Diocletian they were both
arrested and beheaded at Nicomedia.
There is no evidence whatever to justify
the belief that these two persons ever
existed. The story is merely a moral
fable.
Cf. Att.

CYPRIAN (St) Bp.   A.C. Oct. 3
6th cent. Monk of St Victor at Mar-

seilles, and bishop of Toulon (516). He
was a staunch opponent of Semi-Pelagianism. He has left us the life of his master
St Caesarius of Arles.
Cf. Baud. — Holw. — Duch. Fast. Episc.

CYPRIAN (St) M.   R.M. Oct. 12
See Felix and Cyprian.

CYPRIAN (St) Ab.   R.M. Dec. 9
d. 586. A monk of Périgueux, France,
who ended his life as a hermit on the banks
of the Dordogne. St Gregory of Tours
has left an account of St Cyprian's life and
miracles.
Cf. Baud. — Holw.

CYR (St) M.   R.M. June 16
Otherwise Quiricus, q.v.

CYRA (St)   R.M. Aug. 3
See Marana and Cyra.

**CYRENIA and JULIANA (SS) MM.
R.M. Nov. 1**
d. 306. Two Christian women burnt to
death at Tarsus in Asia Minor under Diocletian.
Cf. Holw. — Baud.

CYRIA (St) M.   R.M. June 5
See Zenais, Cyria, etc.

CYRIACA, CYRIACUS, etc.
Note. These names, common to many
saints, are often found written Quiriacus,
Quiriaca, etc. Sometimes they are replaced by their equivalent Latin forms
Dominicus, Dominica, etc. Less frequently, the spelling Kyriacus, Kiriacus,
etc., is met with.

CYRIACA (St) M.   R.M. March 20
See Photina, Joseph, etc.

**CYRIACA and Comp. (SS) VV. MM.
R.M. May 19**
d. 307. Six Christian maidens who per-
ished at the stake at Nicomedia under
Maximinian Galerius.
Cf. Holw. — Baud.

**CYRIACA (DOMINICA) (St) M.
R.M. Aug. 21**
d. 249. A wealthy Roman widow, who
sheltered the persecuted Christians and
to whose house St Laurence, the deacon
and martyr, was accustomed to repair to

distribute his alms. She was scourged to death for her charity. The Roman Church of St Mary in *Dominica* perpetuates her name.
Cf. Holw. — Baud.

CYRIACUS (St) M. **R.M. Jan. 31**
See Tarcisius, Zoticus, etc.

CYRIACUS (St) M. **R.M. Feb. 8**
See Paul, Lucius and Cyriacus.

CYRIACUS and Comp. (SS) MM.
R.M. Apr. 7
? Eleven Christians, martyred at Nicomedia in Asia Minor.
Cf. Baud. — Holw.

CYRIACUS (St) M. **R.M. May 2**
See Exuperius, Zoe, etc.

CYRIACUS (QUIRIACUS) (St) M. Bp.
R.M. May 4
? Most probably a bishop of Ancona in Italy, who while making his pilgrimage to the Holy Land, was martyred under Julian the Apostate. Others assert that he was a bishop of Jerusalem put to death under Hadrian.
Cf. Baud. — Holw.

CYRIACUS (St) M. **R.M. June 5**
See Florentius, Julian, etc.

CYRIACUS and JULITTA (SS) MM.
R.M. June 16
Otherwise Quiricus and Julitta, q.v.

CYRIACUS and PAULA (St) MM.
R.M. June 18
d. 305. Two Christians, stoned to death at Málaga in Spain under Diocletian. St Paula is registered as a virgin-martyr.
Cf. P. de U. — Baud. — Holw.

CYRIACUS (St) M. **R.M. June 20**
See Paul and Cyriacus.

CYRIACUS and APOLLINARIS (SS) MM. **R.M. June 21**
? African martyrs, registered in the Martyrologies, but whose Acts have been lost.

CYRIACUS (St) M. **R.M. June 24**
See Orentius, Heros, etc.

CYRIACUS (St) M. **R.M. July 15**
See Antiochus and Cyriacus.

CYRIACUS, LARGUS, SMARAGDUS and Comp. (SS) MM.
R.M. Aug. 8 and March 16
d. 304. A group of twenty-three martyrs who suffered in Rome under Diocletian. At their head was St Cyriacus, a deacon, who at a later period gave his name to a church, now the seat of a cardinal deacon.
Cf. Att. — Baud. — Holw.

CYRIACUS (St) H. **A.C. Sept. 29**
d. 556. Hermit and abbot in Palestine. He died in the *laura* of St Sabas. His life was written by St Cyril of Scythopolis.
Cf. Baud. — Holw.

CYRIACUS (St) Bp. **A.C. Oct. 27**
d. 606. Administrator, and afterwards patriarch, of Constantinople. The Greeks commemorate him on Oct. 29.
Cf. Baud. — Holw.

CYRIACUS, PAULILLUS, SECUNDUS, ANASTASIUS, SINDIMIUS and Comp. (SS) MM. **R.M. Dec. 19**
d. 303. A group of Christians, martyred at Nicomedia under Diocletian. No other particulars are extant.
Cf. Holw. — Baud.

CYRIL of ALEXANDRIA (St) Bp. Dr.
R.M. Feb. 9
c.376-444. A native of Alexandria who became patriarch of that city in 412. His name in history is famous as the untiring opponent of Nestorianism, which he denounced to Pope St Celestine I. The pope appointed him to preside at the council of Ephesus in 431, at which Nestorius was definitely condemned. Stressing the truth of Christ's divinity, St Cyril sometimes seems to favour Monophysitism, and this is the reason why Monophysite Copts, Syrians and Ethiopians venerate him as their chief teacher. He was declared Doctor of the Church by Leo XIII.
Cf. Att. — Baud. — Holw.

CYRIL (St) M. **R.M. March 4**
See Archelaus and Cyril.

CYRIL of CONSTANTINOPLE (St) C. O.C. **A.C. March 6**
d. 1235. Prior-general of the Carmelites in Palestine. Curiously enough some writers have confused him with his namesakes of Jerusalem and of Alexandria.
Cf. Att. — Baud. — Holw.

CYRIL, ROGATUS, FELIX, another ROGATUS, BEATA, HERENIA, FELICITAS, URBAN, SYLVANUS, and MAMILLUS (SS) MM. R.M. March 8
? African martyrs — Cyril is described as a bishop — registered in all the ancient lists, but of whom nothing is known.
Cf. Baud. — Holw.

CYRIL of JERUSALEM (St) Bp. Dr.
R.M. March 18
c.315-387. Born near Jerusalem, he became a priest in 345, and patriarch of the city from 350 till his death. Seventeen years of his patriarchate he spent in exile. His name is forever connected with his work as a catechist: his instructions on Christian doctrine, addressed to the catechumens before baptism are gems of theological literature. He was declared Doctor of the Church by Leo XIII. The myth that he ever sided with the Arians is now universally rejected.
Cf. Att. — Baud. — Holw.

CYRIL (St) M. R.M. March 20
See Paul, Cyril, etc.

CYRIL (St) M. R.M. March 29
d. c.362. A deacon of Heliopolis in the Lebanon, who suffered under Julian the Apostate.
Cf. Att. — Baud. — Holw.

CYRIL (St) Bp. A.C. May 19
5th cent. A bishop of Trèves, whose relics were enshrined in the abbey church St Matthias in that city.
Cf. Baud. — Gams — Holw.

CYRIL (St) M. A.C. May 29
d. ? 251. A boy of Caesarea in Cappadocia, who embraced Christianity without his father's knowledge. He was turned out of his home, arrested and put to death.
Cf. Att. — Baud. — Holw.

CYRIL and METHODIUS (SS) CC.
R.M. July 7
d. 869 and 885. Two brothers who are venerated as the "Apostles of the Slavs." Cyril, or Constantine, was a secular priest and Methodius a monk in a Greek monastery. In 863 they began to evangelize Moravia. They met with opposition there and came to Rome to ask the apostolic blessing on their work. Cyril now became a monk at SS Boniface and Alexius on the Aventine, and died shortly after.

Methodius was consecrated bishop and returned to preach in Moravia and Pannonia with permission to celebrate the liturgy in Slavonic. This concession turned the German bishops against his work, and they even put him in prison. His apostolate, however, met with signal success. He translated most of the Bible into Slavonic.
Cf. Att. — Holw. — Baud.

CYRIL (St) Bp. M. R.M. July 9
d. 250. An aged bishop of Gortyna in Crete, tortured and beheaded under Decius.
Cf. Baud. — Holw.

CYRIL (St) Bp. R.M. July 22
d. c.300. The successor of Timaeus (280) in the patriarchate of Antioch. He had much to endure in the persecution of Diocletian, but appears to have died in peace.
Cf. Baud. — Holw.

CYRIL, AQUILA, PETER, DOMITIAN, RUFUS, and MENANDER (SS) MM.
R.M. Aug. 1
? Martyrs of one of the early centuries, listed in the Martyrologies as of Philadelphia in Arabia.
Cf. Holw. — Baud.

CYRIL (St) M. R.M. Oct. 2
See Primus, Cyril and Secundarius.

CYRIL (St) M. R.M. Oct. 28
See Anastasia and Cyril.

CYRILLA (St) M. R.M. July 5
d. c.300. An aged widow of Cyrene, condemned to death, but who appears to have expired in the torture chamber. Several other martyrs suffered at the same time.
Cf. Holw. — Baud.

CYRILLA (St) V.M. R.M. Oct. 28
d. 268-270. The daughter of St Tryphonia and a sharer in the good works of that saintly Roman widow. She was put to death under the emperor Claudius II.
Cf. Holw. — Baud.

CYRINUS, PRIMUS, and THEOGENES (SS) MM. R.M. Jan. 3
d. 320. Soldiers in the imperial army who were martyred at Cyzicus on the Hellespont under the emperor Licinius.
Cf. Holw. — Baud.

CYRINUS (St) M.   **R.M. May 10**
See Alphius, Philadelphus and Cyrinus.

CYRINUS (St) M.   **R.M. June 12**
See Basilides, Cyrinus, etc.

CYRINUS (St) M.   **R.M. Oct. 25**
3rd cent. A Roman martyr under Diocletian of whom mention is made in the Acts of St Marcellinus, pope and martyr. *Cf. Holw. — Baud.*

CYRION, BASSIAN, AGATHO and MOSES (SS) MM.   **R.M. Feb. 14**
? A group of martyrs of Alexandria, listed together because all perished at the stake. Cyrion was a priest, Bassian a lector, Agatho an exorcist, and Moses a layman. *Cf. Baud. — Holw.*

CYRION and CANDIDUS (SS) MM.   **R.M. March 9**
The two most conspicuous among the Forty Armenian Martyrs, q.v.

CYRUS and JOHN (SS) MM.   **R.M. Jan. 31**
d. c.303. Two physicians of Alexandria who went to Canopus to assist a woman and her three daughters who were being persecuted as Christians. All were martyred together. *Cf. Att. — Baud. — Holw.*

CYRUS of CARTHAGE (St) Bp.   **R.M. July 14**
? St Possidius, the biographer of St Augustine, speaks of a sermon delivered by the latter on the feast of St Cyrus. Probably he meant St Cyprian.

CYTHINUS (St) M.   **R.M. July 17**
One of the Scillitan Martyrs, q.v.

D

DABEOC (St) Ab.   **A.C. Jan. 1**
Otherwise Beoc, q.v.

DABIUS (DAVIUS) (St) C.   **A.C. July 22**
? An Irish priest who worked in Scotland, where he is the titular of several churches. He may be identical with St Movean or Biteus, disciple of St Patrick. *Cf. Holw.*

DACIAN (DATIANUS) (St) M.   **R.M. June 4**
See Aretius and Dacian.

DACIUS (St) M.   **R.M. Nov. 1**
See Caesarius, Dacius, etc.

DADAS (St) M.   **R.M. Apr. 13**
See Maximus, Quinctilian and Dadas.

DADAS (DIDAS), CASDOE, and GAB-DELAS (SS) MM.   **R.M. Sept. 29**
c.310-368. Dadas, a noble Persian, Casdoe, his wife, and Gabdelas, probably their son, were of the number of the many martyrs who suffered under Shapur (Sapor) II, to whom Dadas was kinsman. *Cf. Holw. — Baud.*

DAFROSA (AFFROSA) (St) M.   **R.M. Jan. 4**
? According to the untrustworthy Acts of St Bibiana, St Dafrosa, her mother, was exiled, and beheaded, under Julian the Apostate. *Cf. Bolland. — Baud. — Holw.*

DAGAEUS (St) Bp.   **A.C. Aug. 18**
d. c.560. An Irish bishop at Iniskin near Dundalk. He ministered at the deathbed of St Mochteus. *Cf. Holw. — Baud.*

DAGAN (St) M.   **A.C. Aug. 27**
Otherwise Decuman, q.v.

DAGOBERT II (St) King M.   **P.C. Dec. 23**
d. 679. Son of St Sigebert III, and king of Austrasia. He was exiled to a monastery in 656, recalled in 675 and murdered by order of Ebroin, mayor of the palace. His death has been traditionally regarded as a martyrdom. *Cf. Att. — Holw. — Baud.*

DALLAN FORGAILL (of CLUAIN DALLAIN) (St) M.   **A.C. Jan. 29**
d. 598. A kinsman of St Edan of Ferns, born in Connaught, and a great scholar. Through his application to study he became blind. He is best remembered for his poem in honour of St Columba, called *Ambra Choluim Kille*. He was murdered at Inis-coel by pirates. *Cf. Holw. — Baud. — O'Hanlon.*

DALMATIUS MONER (Bl) C. O.P.   **A.C. Sept. 26**
1291-1341. Born near Gerona, in Spain, he joined the Friars Preachers. His life among them was uneventful as regards

dignities and offices, which he constantly refused, but was a living pattern of fidelity to the rule. Cult confirmed in 1721.
Cf. Baud. — Holw. — Att.

DALMATIUS (St) Bp.   **A.C. Nov. 13**
d. 580. Bishop of Rodez, in France, from 524 to 580. He had much to suffer at the hands of the Arian Visigoth King Amalric.
Cf. Baud. — Holw.

DALMATIUS (St) Bp. M.   **R.M. Dec. 5**
d. 304. Born at Monza of pagan parents he preached, after his conversion, in Gaul and N. Italy until his election to the see of Pavia. He was martyred under Maximian Herculius within a year of his election.
Cf. Holw. — Baud.

DAMASCUS (Martyrs of) (BB) MM.
    A.C. July 10
See Emmanuel Ruiz and Comp.

DAMASUS (St) Pope.   **R.M. Dec. 11**
d. 384. A Spaniard by descent, but probably born in Rome, he served as deacon the Spanish church of St Laurence in that city. He was chosen pope in 366 and during his pontificate he greatly increased the prestige of the Roman See. He successfully opposed the Arians and Apollinarians; commissioned his great friend St Jerome to correct the Latin Bible; developed the Roman liturgy; and restored many sacred buildings and the tombs of the martyrs, composing inscriptions for them which have become famous. St Jerome styles him "an incomparable man."
Cf. Att. — Holw. — Baud.

DAMHNADE (St) V.   **A.C. June 13**
? An Irish virgin greatly venerated in Cavan, Fermanagh, etc. Colgan identifies her with St Dympna, the martyr of Gheel in Belgium. Nothing certain is known of her life or date.
Cf. Holw. — O'Hanlon.

DAMIAN (SS) MM.   **R.M. Feb. 12**
? The Bollandists distinguish two saints of this name under the date Feb. 12: one a soldier, martyred in Africa, probably at Alexandria; the other a Roman martyr whose relics were found in the catacombs of St Callistus and sent to Salamanca in Spain. Other particulars are lacking.
Cf. Baud. — Holw.

DAMIAN, PETER (St) Bp. Dr.
    R.M. Feb. 23
See Peter Damian.

DAMIAN (St) Bp.   **R.M. Apr. 12**
d. 710. Bishop of Pavia in Lombardy, elected to that office in 680. He vigorously opposed the Monothelites, and acted successfully as peacemaker between the Emperor of Byzantium and the Lombards.
Cf. Holw. — Baud. — Bolland.

DAMIAN (St) M.   **R.M. May 26**
Otherwise Dyfan, q.v.

DAMIAN VAZ (Bl) M.   **A.C. June 11**
d. 1242. A Portuguese knight of St John, put to death by the Moors at Tavira, Algarbes, Portugal (see Peter Rodriguez).
Cf. Holw.

DAMIAN YAMIKI (Bl) M. A.C. Sept. 10
d. 1622. A Japanese layman, beheaded at Nagasaki. He belongs to the group of Bl Charles Spinola, q.v.
Cf. Holw.

DAMIAN (St) M.   **R.M. Sept. 27**
See Cosmas and Damian.

DAMIAN dei FULCHERI (Bl) C. O.P.
    A.C. Oct. 26
d. 1484. A native of Finale (*Finarium*) near Savona, in Liguria, he took the Dominican habit at Savona, and preached in nearly all the cities of Italy. He died at Reggio d' Emilia. Cult approved in 1848.
Cf. Holw. — Att. — Baud.

DANIEL (St) M.   **R.M. Jan. 3**
d. 168. A deacon, said to have been of Jewish extraction, who aided St Prosdocimus, first bishop of Padua, in his apostolate in N.E. Italy. He was martyred in 168. His body was discovered many centuries later and solemnly enshrined Jan. 3, 1064.
Cf. Holw. — Baud.

DANIEL (Bl) Ab. O.S.B. Cist.
    P.C. Jan. 20
d. 1232. The third abbot of the Cistercian monastery of Cambron, in Hainault.
Cf. Baud. — Holw.

DANIEL (St) M.   **R.M. Feb. 16**
See Elias, Jeremias, etc.

DANIEL and VERDA (SS) MM.
A.C. Feb. 21
d. 344. Persian martyrs, greatly honoured in the East, who suffered under King Shapur II.
Cf. Bolland. — Holw. — Baud.

DANIEL (St) H. O.S.B. Cam.
A.C. March 31
d. 1411. A German merchant who through travelling to Venice on business came to know the Camaldolese monks of Murano. He lived a hermit's life under their direction and rule, but in his own house, and was wont to spend long periods with them. He was killed by robbers in his cell.
Cf. Holw. — Baud. — Chev.

DANIEL (St) M.
A.C. Apr. 29
9th cent. A hermit-martyr, the titular of the abbey-church of the Benedictine nuns at Gerona in Spain. According to the legend, which defies all historical verification, he was a native of Asia Minor, and flourished in the times of Charlemagne.
Cf. Baud.

DANIEL (St) M.
R.M. July 10
See Leontius, Mauritius, etc.

DANIEL (St) Prophet.
R.M. July 21
5th cent. B.C. One of the four great prophets of the O.T. His 'ife belongs to the Jewish, rather than to the Christian calendar. The R.M. mentions Babylon as the place of his death. His relics are said to have been translated first to Alexandria and then to Venice.
Cf. Holw. — Baud.

DANIEL (St) Bp.
A.C. Sept. 11
d. 545. Consecrated first bishop of Bangor by St Dyfrig. The Cathedral of Bangor and other churches are dedicated in his name.
Cf. Holw. — Baud.

DANIEL, SAMUEL, ANGELUS (ANGELUCCIO), DOMNUS, LEO, NICHOLAS and HUGOLINUS (SS) MM. O.F.M.
R.M. Oct. 13
d. 1221. This band of Franciscan missionaries was sent by St Francis himself to preach the gospel to the Moors in Morocco. The leader of the band was Brother Daniel, provincial of Calabria. On their arrival at Ceuta the friars were first treated as madmen, but on their refusal to apostatize to Islam, they were beheaded, having been in the country less than three weeks. Canonized in 1516.
Cf. Att. — Baud. — Holw.

DANIEL the STYLITE (St)
R.M. Dec. 11
d. 493. After St Simon the Elder, the greatest and best known of the pillar-saints. He was a monk near Samosata, on the Upper Euphrates. When travelling with his abbot he came to know of St Simon Stylites, who lived on the top of a pillar near Antioch. He forthwith determined to follow the same way of life at a spot near Constantinople. Here the emperor Leo I built for him a series of pillars, and here too he was ordained priest by St Gennadius. From the top of his pillar he became the oracle of the whole city. He lived on his pillar for thirty years, during which time he came down only once from it in order to rebuke the usurping emperor Basiliscus for supporting the Monophysites.
Cf. Att. — Baud. — Holw.

DANIEL (Bl) C. O.S.B. Cist.
P.C. Dec. 26
Late 12th cent. Monk and cellarer of the great Cistercian abbey of Villiers in Brabant. He is listed as a *beatus* in the Cistercian catalogues.
Cf. Baud. — Holw. — Chev. — Zimm.

DARERCA (St) W.
A.C. March 22
? 5th cent. St Patrick's sister. Her name, derived from the Irish *Diar-Sheare*, means constant and firm love. She is reputed to have left fifteen sons, some ten of whom became bishops.
Cf. Holw. — Baud.

DARIA (St) M.
R.M. Oct. 25
See Chrysanthus and Daria.

DARIUS, ZOSIMUS, PAUL and SECUNDUS (SS) MM.
R.M. Dec. 19
? A group of martyrs who suffered at Nicaea, of whom nothing else is known.

DARLUGDACH (DARDULACHA, DERLUGDACH) (St) V.
A.C. Feb. 1
d. c.524. Successor of St Brigid and second abbess of Kildare.
Cf. O'Hanlon — Baring-Gould.

DASIUS, ZOTICUS, CAIUS and Comp. (SS) MM. R.M. Oct. 21
d. c.303. A group of fifteen soldiers who suffered martyrdom at Nicomedia under Diocletian.
Cf. Bolland. — Baud. — Holw.

DASIUS (St) M. R.M. Nov. 20
d. c.303. A Roman soldier who refused to take part in the heathen orgies of the Saturnalia, and was for this reason martyred at Dorostorum in Mysia, Asia Minor.
Cf. Att. — Baud. — Holw.

DATHUS (DATUS) (St) Bp. R.M. July 3
d. 190. Bishop of Ravenna. His election was due to the miraculous appearance of a dove hovering over his head. He governed his see during the reign of the emperor Commodus.
Cf. Baud. — Holw.

DATIUS (St) Bp. R.M. Jan. 14
d. 552. Bishop of Milan, being elected to that see some time after 530. His whole diocese was overrun by the Arian Ostrogoths, and he had to flee to Constantinople, where he spent the rest of his life. Here he defended Pope Vigilius in the dispute about the "Three Chapters."
Cf. Att. — Baud. — Holw.

DATIUS, REATRUS (RESTIUS) and Comp., and DATIUS (DATIVUS), JULIAN, VINCENT and 27 Comp. (SS) MM. R.M. Jan. 27
? Two groups of African martyrs; the second group suffered under the Arian Vandals.

DATIVA (St) M. R.M. Dec. 6
See Dionysia, Dativa, etc.

DATIVUS (St) M. R.M. Feb. 11
See Saturninus, Dativus, etc.

DATIVUS (St) Bp. M. R.M. Sept. 10
See Nemesian, Felix, etc.

DAVID (St) Bp. A.C. March 1
5th-6th cent. Born in S. Wales and educated by St Paulinus, the disciple of St Germanus of Auxerre. He founded a monastery at Mynyw (Menevia) in the far west of Pembrokeshire and is honoured as the first bishop in those parts. The place is now called St Davids. The monks followed an exceedingly austere rule and their monastery became a veritable nursery of saints. The biography of St David, as handed down to us, is full of anachronisms. He is the principal patron saint of Wales.
Cf. Att. — Baud. — Holw. — Bolland.

DAVID (St) H. R.M. June 26
? 5th cent. Said to have been a native of Mesopotamia who settled in a solitary place outside Thessalonica, where he served God for seventy years. His relics were translated to Pavia in 1054.
Cf. Holw. — Baud.

DAVID GONSON (Bl) M. A.C. July 12
d. 1541. Son of Vice-Admiral Gonson (or Gunston), and a knight of St John. He was hanged, drawn and quartered at Southwark. Beatified in 1929.
Cf. Newdigate.

DAVID of SWEDEN (St) Bp. O.S.B. A.C. July 15
d.c. 1080. Tradition makes him an English Benedictine, who had a passionate desire to give his life to Christ by martyrdom. When he heard of the death of St Sigfrid's three nephews he offered himself to the saint and was sent to Sinenga. Eventually he founded a Benedictine abbey, afterwards called Monkentorp, which he governed as abbot. He is said to have been the first bishop of Västeräss.
Cf. Att. — Holw. — Baud. — Gams.

DAVID (GLEB) (St) C. A.C. July 24
See Romanus and David.

DAVID LEWIS (Bl) M. S.J. A.C. Aug. 27
1616-1679. David Lewis (*alias* Charles Baker) was born in Monmouthshire and educated at Abergavenny. He was converted to the Faith, studied for the priesthood at Rome and became a Jesuit in 1645. He worked in S. Wales for thirty-one years. He was martyred for his priesthood at Usk. Beatified in 1929.
Cf. Newdigate. — Att.

DAVID of HIMMERODE (Bl) Ab. O.S.B. Cist. A.C. Dec. 11
d. 1179. A native of Florence, who took the Cistercian habit at Clairvaux under St Bernard (1131). In 1134 he was sent to Germany as abbot-founder of Himmerode, in the diocese of Trèves. Cult approved by Rome.
Cf. Holw.

DAVID (St) King and Prophet.
　　　　　　　　　　R.M. Dec. 29
10th cent. B.C.　David "the beloved" and "the man after God's own heart." He is one of the types of Christ in the O.T., and indeed one of the most lovable characters in history. His story is fully told in Kings (Samuel) Bks. I and II and in Paralipomenon (or Chronicles). The Greeks keep his feast, together with all other saints who were ancestors of our Lord, on Dec. 19.
Cf. Holw. — Baud.

DAVINUS (St) C.　　? R.M. June 3
d. 1051.　A native of Armenia who set out on a pilgrimage to Rome and Compostella. On his way he stopped at Lucca, where he succumbed to a fatal malady and was venerated as a saint.
Cf. Att. — Baud. — Holw.

DAVY (JOHN) (Bl) M.　　A.C. May 4
See Carthusian Martyrs.

DAY (DYE) (St) Ab.　? R.M. Jan. 18
? This saint, otherwise unknown, to whom a Cornish church is dedicated, may possibly be St Deicola, abbot, q.v.

DÉ (St) Bp.　　　　A.C. Jan. 31
Breton form of the name of St Aedan or Edan of Ferns, q.v.

DECLAN (St) Bp.　　A.C. July 24
5th cent.　A disciple of St Colman who became a bishop in the district of Ardmore.
Cf. Att. — Holw. — Baud.

DECOROSUS (St) Bp.　R.M. Feb. 15
d. 695.　For thirty years bishop of Capua, St Decorosus was one of the prelates who assisted at the council of Rome under Pope St Agatho (680).
Cf. Baud. — Holw.

DECUMAN (DAGAN) (St) M.
　　　　　　　　　　A.C. Aug. 27
d. 716.　A Welsh saint who lived as a recluse in Somersetshire, where he was murdered.
Cf. Holw.

DEEL (DEILLE) (St) Ab.　R.M. Jan. 18
Otherwise Deicola (Dichul), q.v.

DEGADH (St)　　　　A.C. Aug. 18
Otherwise Dagaeus, q.v.

DEGENHARD (Bl) H. O.S.B.
　　　　　　　　　　P.C. Sept. 3
d. 1374.　A native of Bavaria and a monk of Niederaltaich. After some years in the abbey he retired to live as a recluse under BB Otto and Hermann, also Benedictine monks of Niederaltaich, in their cell at Frauenau, in the Bavarian Forest, and afterwards at Breitenau on the Danube.
Cf. Zimm. — Holw. — Baud.

**DEICOLA (DEICOLUS, DESLE, DICHUL, DEEL, DELLE, DEILLE, etc.)
(St) Ab.　　　　　R.M. Jan. 18**
d. c.625.　A monk of Bangor who followed St Columbanus to Burgundy, where he helped in the foundation of Luxeuil. When St Columbanus left France, he stayed behind and founded the abbey of Lure (Lutra) in the Vosges.
Cf. Zimm. — Att. — Baud. — Holw.

DEIFER (St) Ab.　　A.C. March 7
6th cent.　A Welsh saint, abbot-founder of Bodfari in Flintshire.
Cf. Holw.

DEINIOL (St)　　　A.C. Sept. 11
Welsh form of the name Daniel, q.v.

DELPHINA (Bl) V. Tert. O.F.M.
　　　　　　　　　　A.C. Dec. 9
1283-1358.　Born at Château-Puy-Michel in Languedoc, she became the wife of St Elzear, and is said to have been a member of the third order of St Francis. After her husband's death she lived in retirement at the court of Naples. Cult approved by Urban VIII.
Cf. Att. — Baud. — Holw.

DELPHINUS (St) Bp.　R.M. Dec. 24
d. 404.　Bishop of Bordeaux. He is best remembered as having been instrumental in the conversion of St Paulinus of Nola, and as an untiring opponent of the Priscillianists.
Cf. Att. — Duch. Fast. Episc. — Baud.

DEMETRIA (St) V. M.　R.M. June 21
d. 363.　An alleged sister of St Bibiana and daughter of SS Flavian and Dafrosa, q.v.

DEMETRIAN (St) Bp.　A.C. Nov. 6
d. c.912.　A native of Cyprus who became monk and *hegoumenos* of St Antony's and finally bishop of Khytri, both in his native

island. He is one of the most venerated of Cypriote saints.
Cf. Att. — Baud. — Holw.

DEMETRIUS, CONCESSUS, HILARY and Comp. (SS) MM. R.M. Apr. 9
? A group composed of martyrs from different localities, but about whom no particulars are extant.
Cf. Holw. — Baud.

DEMETRIUS (St) M. R.M. Aug. 14
? A martyr of whose death neither the place nor circumstances can be verified. The R.M., however, describes him as an African martyr.
Cf. Baud. — Holw.

DEMETRIUS (DIMITRI) (St) M. R.M. Oct. 8
Early 4th cent. Surnamed by the Greeks "the Megalomartyr," he is, after St George, the most famous military martyr of the East. His military career, however, is a legend. He was probably a deacon who suffered at Sirmium in Dalmatia, under Diocletian, though the centre of his cult was at Salonika, where a magnificent basilica was erected in his name. He is mentioned to this day in the preparation of the Byzantine liturgy.
Cf. Att. — Holw. — Baud.

DEMETRIUS (St) Bp. A.C. Oct. 9
d. 231. The twelfth patriarch of Alexandria, during whose episcopate the catechetical school of that city attained its highest fame. He was a close friend of Origen, whom later he had to banish from the diocese for being uncanonically ordained.
Cf. Att. — Holw.

DEMETRIUS, ANIANUS, EUSTOSIUS and Comp. (SS) MM. R.M. Nov. 10
? A band of twenty-three martyrs registered as having suffered at Antioch in Syria. St Demetrius is described as a bishop and St Anianus as his deacon.
Cf. Holw. — Baud.

DEMETRIUS and HONORIUS (SS) MM. R.M. Nov. 21
? Old Roman manuscripts describe these saints as martyrs who suffered at Ostia at the mouth of the Tiber.
Cf. Baud. — Holw.

DEMETRIUS (St) M. R.M. Nov. 29
See Blaise and Demetrius.

DEMETRIUS, HONORATUS and FLORUS (SS) MM. R.M. Dec. 22
? These martyrs are stated to have suffered at Ostia at the mouth of the Tiber. They probably are to be identified with SS Demetrius and Honorius of Nov. 21.

DEMOCRITUS, SECUNDUS and DIONYSIUS (SS) MM. R.M. July 31
? Martyrs, some say of Phrygia, some of Africa. Nothing really is known about them.

DENIS, DENNIS, DENYS (*several*)
French forms of the name Dionysius, q.v.

DENISE (*several*)
French form of the name Dionysia, q.v.

DENTLIN (DENTELIN, DENAIN) (St) C. A.C. March 16
7th cent. The little son of St Vincent of Soignies and of St Waltrude, and brother of SS Landric, Adeltrude and Madelberta. He was only seven years old when he died. A church in the duchy of Cleves is dedicated in his honour.
Cf. Holw. — Baud.

DEOCHAR (THEUTGER or GOTTLIEB) (St) Ab. O.S.B. A.C. June 7
d. 847. A hermit in the wilds of Franconia, for whom Charlemagne founded the abbey of Herriedon under the Benedictine rule, Deochar becoming its first abbot. In 802 he was appointed *missus regius*. In 819 he took part in the translation of St Boniface's relics to Fulda.
Cf. Att. — Zimm. — Holw. — Baud.

DEODATUS (St) Mk. O.S.B. A.C. Feb. 3
8th cent. A monk of Lagny in the archdiocese of Paris.
Cf. Chev.

DEODATUS (St) Ab. A.C. Apr. 24
d. c.525. A hermit, or abbot, in the neighbourhood of Blois. At a later period the town of Saint-Dié grew up round his cell (or monastery).
Cf. Att. — Baud. — Zimm.

DEODATUS (DIÉ, DIDIER, DIEUDONNÉ, ADÉODAT) (St) Bp. O.S.B. A.C. June 19
d. p. 680. A bishop (of Nevers?) who

founded (c.660) and was abbot of the monastery of Vallis-Galilaea (Val-de-Galilée — Jointures Abbey).
Cf. Zimm. — Att. — Baud. — Chev.

DEODATUS (St) Bp.   A.C. June 19
d. 679. Bishop of Nevers in 655 and then a solitary in the Vosges. Later he was abbot-founder of Ebersheimmünster, near Strasburg. He is often confused with St Deodatus of Vallis-Galilaea.
Cf. Zimm. — Baud. — Att.

DEODATUS (St) Bp.   A.C. June 27
d. 473. Deacon to St Paulinus, bishop of Nola, and his successor in that see. His relics were brought to Benevento in 839.
Cf. Menzies — Baud. — Holw.

DEODATUS (St) M. (or C.)
A.C. Sept. 27
? A saint of Sora (central Italy) whose relics were enshrined in the cathedral of Sora in 1621.
Cf. Menzies — Baud. — Holw.

DEOGRATIAS (St) Bp.   R.M. March 22
d. 457. Consecrated bishop of Carthage, in 456, fourteen years after the death of his predecessor, St Quodvultdeus, who had been driven into exile by the Arian Vandals. The Vandal king, Genseric, having brought many Italian captives to Carthage, St Deogratias sold all that he or his church possessed, even the sacred vessels, to ransom them. He was bishop only one year.
Cf. Att. — Baud. — Holw.

DERFEL - GADARN (St)   ?
6th cent. A Welsh saint, a soldier and afterwards a solitary at Llanderfel in Merionethshire. He was greatly venerated by the Catholic Welsh.
Cf. Baring-Gould.

DERPHUTA (St) M.   R.M. March 20
See Alexandra, Claudia, etc.

DERUVIANUS (St) M.
A.C. May 14 (R.M. May 26)
Otherwise Dyfan, q.v.

DERWA (St) M.   A.C. ?
The patron saint of Menadarva (Merthyr-Dava, i.e. the Martyr Derwa) near Camborne in Cornwall. Nothing is known about this saint. Probably he is no other

than St Dyfan (Damian or Deruvianus), one of the missionaries sent to Britain in the second century by Pope St Eleutherius.
Cf. Holw.

DESIDERATUS (DÉSIRÉ) (St) Bp.
A.C. Feb. 10 and 11
6th cent. Successor of St Avitus as bishop of Clermont in Auvergne.
Cf. Duch. Fast. Episc. — Chev. — Gams — Baud.

DESIDERATUS (St) H.   A.C. Apr. 30
d. c.569. A French solitary who lived at Gourdon, near Châlon-sur-Saône.
Cf. Baud. — Chev. — Holw.

DESIDERATUS (St) Bp.   A.C. May 8
6th cent. Successor of St Arcadius in the bishopric of Bourges.
Cf. Duch. Fast. Episc. — Gams — Baud. — Chev.

DESIDERATUS (St) Mk. O.S.B.
A.C. Dec. 18
d. c.700. Son of St Waneng, the founder of Fécamp abbey, he became a monk of Fontenelle. His relics were enshrined at Ghent.
Cf. Baud. — Holw. — P.B.

DESIDERIUS (DIDIER) (Bl) Bp.
P.C. Jan. 20
d. 1194. The thirty-third bishop of Thérouanne and founder of the Cistercian abbey of Blandecques (Blandyke) near Saint-Omer. He is usually styled a saint and is claimed by the Cistercians as one of their own. Cult not yet officially confirmed.
Cf. Att. — Baud. — Holw.

DESIDERIUS (St) Bp. M.
R.M. Feb. 11 and May 23
d. 668. A native of Autun, educated at Vienne, where he became archdeacon and then bishop. He was persecuted by Queen Brunhildis, who was also instrumental in securing his murder at the place now called Saint-Didier-sur-Chalaronne. See also May 23, below.
Cf. Att. — Baud. — Gams — Duch. Fast. Episc.

DESIDERIUS (St) M.   R.M. March 25
See Barontius and Desiderius.

DESIDERIUS (St) Bp. M. R.M. May 23
? Said to have been a native of Genoa who eventually preached in and became bishop of Langres in France. He was killed at the time of a barbarian invasion while pleading for his people. However, the traditions concerning him are so conflicting that it is now believed that there were two or more of the same name connected with Langres. See also Feb. 11 above.
Cf. Baud. — Duch. Fast. Episc.

DESIDERIUS (St) Pope, O.S.B.
R.M. Sept. 16
Otherwise Victor III, q.v.

DESIDERIUS (St) M. R.M. Sept. 19
See Januarius and Comp.

DESIDERIUS (St) Mk. O.S.B.
A.C. Oct. 19
d. c.705. A monk of Lonrey, and a disciple of St Sigiran, who became a recluse at La Brenne (*Ruriacus*) in the diocese of Bourges, France.
Cf. Zimm. — Baud. — Holw. — P.B.

DESIDERIUS (St) Bp. A.C. Oct. 27
d. c.625. The successor of St Aunarius (Aunaire) in the bishopric of Auxerre. He has often been confused with St Desiderius of Vienne (Feb. 11).
Cf. Duch. Fast. Episc. — Baud. — Holw.

DESIDERIUS (St) Bp. A.C. Nov. 15
d. 655. The successor of his own brother St Rusticus as bishop of Cahors (630-655).
Cf. Duch. Fast. Episc. — Gams — Baud.— Att.

DEUSDEDIT (St) Bp. O.S.B. A.C. Jan. 14
d. 664. An Anglo-Saxon, Frithona by name. He was the first of his race to occupy the primatial see of Canterbury as the successor of St Honorius. He died a victim to the great pestilence.
Cf. Att. — Baud. — Zimm. — Stanton.

DEUSDEDIT (St) C. R.M. Aug. 10
6th cent. A poor shoemaker in Rome, contemporary of St Gregory the Great, of whom the latter relates that he gave away to the poor every Saturday all that he earned at his trade during the week.
Cf. Menzies — Baud. — Holw.

DEUSDEDIT (St) Ab. M. O.S.B.
R.M. Oct. 9
d. 836. Monk of Montecassino, chosen

abbot about the year 830. He was especially noted for his generous almsgiving. To extort money from him the tyrant, Sicard of Benevento, ill-treated and imprisoned him. He died in prison of hunger and misery. He is venerated as a martyr.
Cf. Zimm. — P. de U. — Baud. — Chev. — Holw.

DEUSDEDIT (ADEODATUS I) (St) Pope
R.M. Nov. 8
d. 618. A Roman by birth, he became pope in 615. During his pontificate a pestilence raged in Rome and he worked untiringly for the plague-stricken. In all ancient Benedictine menologies he is called a Benedictine monk, but there is no certain evidence for it.
Cf. Att. — Baud. — Holw. — Menzies.

DEUSDEDIT of BRESCIA (St) Bp.
R.M. Dec. 10
d. c.700. A bishop of Brescia who played a leading part in the councils convened against the Monothelite heretics.
Cf. Menzies — Baud. — Holw.

DEVEREUX (St) Bp. A.C. Nov. 13
Otherwise Dubritius, q.v.

DEVINICUS (DENICK, TEAVNECK)
(St) Bp. A.C. Nov. 13
6th cent. A native of N. Scotland who in his old age associated himself with the missionary work of SS Columba and Machar and evangelized Caithness. He is reputed to have been a bishop.
Cf. Holw.

DEVOTA (St) V.M. A.C. Jan. 27
d. 303. A maiden of Corsica who expired on the rack in the persecution of Diocletian. Her relics are at Monaco on the Riviera di Ponente. She is the patron saint of both Corsica and Monaco.
Cf. Holw. — Baud.

DEWI (St) Bp. A.C. March 1
Otherwise David of Wales, q.v.

DEYNIOLEN (St) A.C. Nov. 22
d. 621. Also known as St Deiniol the Younger. He was abbot of Bangor at the time of the slaughter of his monks and the destruction of their monastery by King Ethelfrid of Northumbria (616). The saint appears to have escaped the massacre.
Cf. Baring-Gould.

DIACONUS (St) M.   R.M. March 14
6th cent. So described on account of his
office of deacon, which he held in the
church of the Marsi in central Italy. St
Gregory narrates of him that together
with two monks he was put to death by
the Lombards.
Cf. Baud. — Holw.

**DIANA, CAECILIA and AMIATA (BB)
VV. O.P.   A.C. June 9**
13th cent. The three first members of
the first house of Dominican nuns at
Bologna. Diana, of the ancient family of
the Carbonesi, was a native of Bologna.
After a very worldly youth she embraced
religion against the wish of her family;
she died in 1236. The other two later became nuns of the Roman convent of San
Sisto. Beatified in 1891.
Cf. Att. — Holw. — Baud. — Menzies.

**DIARMIS (DIERMIT, DERMOT) (St)
Ab.   A.C. Jan. 18**
6th cent. The spiritual director and
teacher of St Kiernan of Clonmacnois and
later abbot-founder of a monastery on
Innis-Clotran Island.
Cf. Holw.

DICHU (St)   A.C. Apr. 29
5th cent. The first convert made by St
Patrick in Ulster. He was originally a
swineherd. After his conversion, we are
told, he continued to the end faithful to
Christ and St Patrick.
Cf. Holw.

DICHUL (St) Ab.   R.M. Jan. 18
Otherwise Deicola, q.v.

DICTINUS (St) Bp.   A.C. July 24
d. 420. An adherent of Priscillianism, he
was converted by St Ambrose and re-
canted his errors at the council of Toledo
(400). Soon after he was raised to the
bishopric of Astorga in Spain.
Cf. Holw.

**DIDACUS (DIEGO) de AZEVEDO (Bl)
Bp. O.S.B. Cist.   P.C. Feb. 6**
d. 1207 (Dec. 30). Provost of the cathedral of Osma, in Old Castile, where he obtained a canonry for St Dominic Guzmán.
In 1201 he became bishop of Osma. He
was sent to Rome by King Alphonsus of
Castile and took St Dominic as a companion on his journey: this was the occa-

sion of the founding of the Dominican
Order. Didacus became a Cistercian in
order to join the crusade against the
Albigenses. He has always been styled a
beatus, or a saint, by the Cistercians.
Cf. Holw.

**DIDACUS CARVALHO (Bl) M. S.J.
A.C. Feb. 25**
1578-1624. Born at Coimbra in Portugal,
he joined the Jesuits in 1594. He was
sent to India in 1600, where he was ordained priest. In 1609 he migrated to
Japan. Here he worked untiringly until
1623, when he was arrested with a number
of his flock and carried off to Sendai,
suffering many indignities on the way.
The story of their martyrdom is a miracle
of endurance. Beatified in 1867.
Cf. Att. — Baud. — Holw.

**DIDACUS (DIEGO, DIAZ) (Bl) C.
O.F.M. Cap.   A.C. March 24**
1743-1801. A native of Cádiz, he joined
the Capuchins at Seville in 1759, and
after his ordination to the priesthood began to preach throughout Spain, but
chiefly in Andalusia, of which province he
is called "the Apostle." Most of his time
which remained over from preaching he
spent in the confessional. Beatified in
1894.
Cf. Att. — Baud. — Holw.

**DIDACUS PEREZ (Bl) M. S.J.
A.C. July 15**
d. 1570. A Jesuit novice who formed one
of the band of missionaries led by Bl
Ignatius Azevedo, whose martyrdom he
shared.
Cf. Holw. —- Baud.

**DIDACUS (DIEGO, DIAZ) (St) C. O.F.M.
R.M. Nov. 12 (and 13)**
c.1400-1463. Born of poor parents in the
diocese of Seville, he joined the Franciscans as a lay-brother at Arrizafa. Although remaining a lay-brother, he was
appointed, on account of his remarkable
ability and goodness, guardian of the principal friary in the Canary Islands, at
Fuerteventura (1445). Later he was recalled to Spain, and after a pilgrimage to
Rome in 1450, died at the friary of Alcalà,
in Castile. His chief devotion was to our
Lord in the Bl Sacrament. Canonized
in 1588.
Cf. Att. — Baud. — P. de U. — Menzies.

DIDIER (St) Bp. M.　　**R.M. May 23**
Otherwise Desiderius, q.v.

DIDIUS (St) M.　　**R.M. Nov. 26**
See Faustus, Didius, etc.

DIDYMUS (St) M.　　**R.M. Apr. 28**
See Theodora and Didymus.

DIDYMUS (St) M.　　**R.M. Sept. 11**
See Diodorus, Diomedes, etc.

DIÉ (St) Bp.　　**A.C. June 19**
Otherwise Deodatus, q.v.

DIEGO (*several*)
Otherwise Didacus, q.v.
Note. Diego is really a corrupt form of
the Spanish name for St James, viz.
Santiago (Sant-Iago, San Tiego, San
Diego). Only in modern times has Diego
been latinized into Didacus.

DIEMUT (DIEMUDA) (Bl) H. O.S.B.
　　A.C. March 29
d. c.1130. A nun at the Benedictine monastery of Wessobrunn in Bavaria, who was
granted leave to live as a solitary under
the obedience of the monastery. She
spent her time in copying manuscripts,
some of which are still extant.
Cf. Att. — Baud. — Holw. — Chev.

DIETRICH (St) Bp. M.　　**A.C. Feb. 2**
See Bruno and Comp.

DIEUDONNÉ (*several*)
The French form for Deusdedit or Adeodatus, q.v.

DIGAIN (St) C.　　**A.C. Nov. 21**
5th cent. A son of Constantine, king or
chieftain of Cornwall. Llangernw, Denbighshire, perpetuates his memory.
Cf. Holw.

DIGNA (St) M.　　**R.M. June 14**
See Anastasius, Felix and Digna.

DIGNA (St) V.　　**R.M. Aug. 11**
4th cent. A maiden of Todi in Umbria,
who lived as a solitary in the mountains
near her native city during the persecution
of Diocletian.
Cf. Menzies. — Baud. — Holw.

DIGNA (St) M.　　**R.M. Aug. 12**
See Hilaria, Digna, etc.

DIGNA and EMERITA (SS) VV. MM.
　　R.M. Sept. 22
d. 254-259. Roman maidens martyred
under Valerian. They expired standing
before their judges and praying. Their
relics are enshrined in the church of St
Marcellus at Rome.
Cf. Menzies — Baud. — Holw.

DIMAN (DIMAS, DIMA) (St) Bp.
　　A.C. Jan. 6
d. 658. Surnamed *Diman Dubh* (Diman
the Black). A monk under St Columba,
and afterwards abbot and bishop of
Connor. He is one of the prelates to
whom (640) the Roman church, after the
death of Pope Honorius, addressed the
epistle on the pascal controversy and on
Pelagianism.
Cf. Holw. — Baud.

DIMITRI (St) M.　　**R.M. Oct. 8**
Otherwise Demetrius, q.v.

DINGAD (St) C.　　**A.C. Nov. 1**
5th cent. A son of the chieftain Brychan
of Brecknock, who led a monastic or
eremitical life at Llandingad in Monmouthshire.
Cf. Baring-Gould.

DIOCLES (St) M.　　**R.M. May 24**
See Zoellus, Servilius, etc.

DIOCLETIUS (St) M.　　**R.M. May 11**
See Sisinius, Diocletius, etc.

DIODORUS (St) M.　　**R.M. Feb. 26**
See Papias, Diodorus, etc.

**DIODORUS and RHODOPIANUS (SS)
MM.**　　**R.M. May 3**
Early 4th cent. Two deacons martyred
under Diocletian in the province of Caria,
Asia Minor.
Cf. Bolland. — Holw. — Baud.

DIODORUS (St) M.　　**R.M. July 6**
See Lucy, Antoninus, etc.

**DIODORUS, DIOMEDES and DIDY-
MUS (SS) MM.**　　**R.M. Sept. 11**
? Martyrs of Laodicea (Kulat-el-Husn or
Ladhikijeh) in Syria.

**DIDORUS, MARIANUS and Comp. (SS)
MM.**　　**R.M. Dec. 1**
d. 283. Roman martyrs under Numerian.

They are described as being very numerous. In fact, it appears to have been a case of a Christian congregation surprised while asembled at prayer in the catacombs and disposed of by having the entrance to their subterranean oratory blocked up. *Cf. Holw. — Baud.*

DIOGENES (St) M. R.M. Apr. 6
See Timothy and Diogenes.

DIOGO (*several*)
The Portuguese form of James or Didacus, q.v. (Cf. note on Diego).

DIOMEDES (St) M. R.M. Aug. 16
d. 300. A native of Tarsus in Cilicia, by profession a physician, and a zealous propagator of Christianity. He was arrested at Nicaea in Bithynia and martyred under Diocletian. *Cf. Holw. — Baud.*

DIOMEDES, JULIAN, PHILIP, EUTYCHIAN, HESYCHIUS, LEONIDES, PHILADELPHUS, MENALIPPUS and PANTAGAPES (SS) MM.
R.M. Sept. 2
? Some perished at the stake, others were drowned, or beheaded, or crucified. Place and other circumstances unknown.

DIOMEDES (St) M. R.M. Sept. 11
See Diodorus, Diomedes, etc.

DIOMMA (St) A.C. May 12
5th cent. An Irish saint, said to have been the teacher of St Declan of Ardmore and other saints. He is now venerated as the patron saint of Kildimo, Co Limerick. *Cf. Holw.*

DION (St) M. R.M. July 6
See Lucy, Antoninus, etc.

DIONYSIA, DIONYSIUS.
Note. These Greco-Latin names became very popular in the Middle Ages under the corresponding French forms of Denise, Denis, Denys. Sydney in English is a corrupt form of St Denys.

DIONYSIA (St) M. R.M. May 15
See Peter, Andrew, etc.

DIONYSIA, DATIVA, LEONTIA, TERTIUS, AEMILIAN, BONIFACE, and Comp. (SS) MM. R.M. Dec. 6
d. 484. African martyrs under the Arian Vandal king, Hunneric. We have a quite genuine account of their martyrdom from Victor of Utica. Dionysia, a widow, perished at the stake with her little child, Majoricus, and her sister Dativa. Aemilian, a physician, and Tertius, a monk, were flayed alive. The fanatics seem to have amused themselves by devising strange kinds of death for the rest of the heroic band. *Cf. Att. — Ruinari.*

DIONYSIA (St) M. R.M. Dec. 12
See Ammonaria and Dionysia.

DIONYSIUS, AEMILIAN and SEBASTIAN (SS) MM. R.M. Feb. 8
? The R.M. describes them as Armenian monks. We know nothing about them, save their bare names.

DIONYSIUS and AMMONIUS (SS) MM. R.M. Feb. 14
? Martyrs beheaded, it seems, at Alexandria in Egypt.

DIONYSIUS of AUGSBURG (St) Bp. MM. A.C. Feb. 26
d. c.303. Venerated as first bishop of Augsburg in Germany. He is said to have been converted to Christ, baptized and later consecrated bishop by St Narcissus. He was martyred under Diocletian. *Cf. Baud. — Holw.*

DIONYSIUS FUGIXIMA (Bl) M. S.J.
A.C. March 5
d. 1622 (Nov. 1). A Japanese, born of noble parents at Aitzu, Arima, who became a Jesuit novice and worked under Bl Paul Navarro, with whom he was burnt alive at Ximabara. Beatified in 1867. *Cf. Baud. — Holw.*

DIONYSIUS (St) M. R.M. March 10
See Codratus, Dionysius, etc.

DIONYSIUS the CARTHUSIAN (Bl) C. O. Cart. P.C. March 12
d. 1471. Born at Ryckel, near Loos, in Flanders, he gained his doctorate at the university of Cologne in his twenty-second year. In 1423 he entered the Carthusian Order. He excelled as a mystical writer and on this account has been given the title of *Doctor Ecstaticus.* He is com-

memorated as a *beatus* in several martyrologies.
Cf. Baud.

DIONYSIUS (St) M. R.M. March 16
See Hilary, Tatian, etc.

DIONYSIUS (SS) MM. R.M. March 24
Two of the same name who suffered together. See Timolaus, Dionysius, etc.

DIONYSIUS of CORINTH (St) Bp.
R.M. Apr. 8
d. c.180. A bishop of Corinth who was a great leader of the Church in the second century. He is now best remembered as an ecclesiastical writer. Several of his letters to various churches are still extant: especially notewothy is that in which he records the martyrdom of SS Peter and Paul in Rome. The Greeks venerate him as a martyr (Nov. 20).
Cf. Baud. — Holw. — Att.

DIONYSIUS (St) M. R.M. Apr. 19
See Socrates and Dionysius.

DIONYSIUS (St) Bp. R.M. May 8
d. p. 193. Said to have been one of the ten missionaries sent with St Peregrinus into Gaul by Pope Sixtus I, early in the 2nd century. He succeeded St Justus in the bishopric of Vienne in Dauphiné. Some have erroneously described him as a martyr.
Cf. Baud. — Bolland. — Duch. Fast. Episc.

DIONYSIUS (St) M. R.M. May 12
d. 304. An Asiatic by birth and uncle of the youthful martyr St Pancras, to whom he acted as guardian. They came together to Rome, were converted to Christianity, and martyred under Diocletian, Dionysius dying in prison.
Cf. Baud.

DIONYSIUS of MILAN (St) Bp.
R.M. May 25
d. c.359. The successor of St Protase in the see of Milan in 351. In 355 he was banished to Cappadocia by the Arian emperor Constantius for having upheld the cause of St Athanasius. He died in exile, but St Ambrose had his remains translated to Milan.
Cf. Att. — Baud. — Holw.

DIONYSIUS (St) M. R.M. June 3
See Lucillian, Claudius, etc.

DIONYSIUS SEBUGGWAO (Bl) M.
A.C. June 3
d. 1885. A servant of King Mwanga of Uganda; he was pierced with a lance by the king — the first victim of the persecution. Beatified in 1912.
Cf. Holw. — Baud.

DIONYSIUS (St) M. R.M. July 27
One of the Seven Sleepers, q.v.

DIONYSIUS (St) M. R.M. July 31
See Democritus, Secundus and Dionysius.

DIONYSIUS and PRIVATUS (SS) MM.
R.M. Sept. 20
? Martyrs of Phrygia in Asia Minor.

DIONYSIUS, FAUSTUS, C A I U S, PETER, PAUL and Comp. (SS) MM.
R.M. Oct. 3
d. 257. A group of Christians from Alexandria in Egypt, banished to Libya under Decius (250) and again brought to trial and martyred at Alexandria under Valerian. There is much confusion as to the identity of each of these martyrs.
Cf. Baud. — Holw.

DIONYSIUS (St) Bp. M. R.M. Oct. 9
1st cent. This is Denis the Areopagite who was converted at Athens by St Paul (Acts XVII, 34). Early writers say that he became first bishop of Athens and died a martyr (c.95). Unfortunately, at a much later period he was identified with St Dionysius of Paris, and the works of an ecclesiastical writer of the 5th century — the pseudo-Dionysius — were falsely attributed to him. The confusion is still maintained in the R.M., although Pope Benedict XIV intended to remedy it by suppressing the feast altogether.
Cf. Att.

DIONYSIUS, RUSTICUS and ELEUTHERIUS (SS) MM. R.M. Oct. 9
3rd cent. According to St Gregory of Tours, Dionysius, first bishop of Paris, was born in Italy and, with six other bishops, was sent from Rome to Gaul, settled on an island in the Seine and evangelized the surrounding district. He was beheaded at Paris with the priest Rusticus and the deacon Eleutherius under Decius. Their bodies were thrown into the Seine, from

which they were rescued and buried by a Christian lady named Catulla. A small chapel was built over their tomb, around which arose the Benedictine abbey of Saint-Denis. About the 7th century this Dionysius began to be identified with St Denis the Areopagite, and this identification gained general acceptance until the 19th century. Now it has been discarded by all writers.
Cf. Att. — Holw. — Bolland.

DIONYSIUS of ALEXANDRIA (St) Bp.
        R.M. Nov. 17
d. 265. Called also Dionysius the Great. A native of Alexandria, he studied under Origen, whom he succeeded as a master of the catechetical school. In 248 he became patriarch of Alexandria, but two years later, under Decius, was banished to Libya, whence he continued to govern his diocese. He returned to Alexandria, but was again driven from it under Valerian. He was restored under Gallienus. He was a great theologian; St Athanasius styles him "the teacher of the whole Church."
Cf. Att. — Baud. — Holw.

DIONYSIUS (St) M.   **R.M. Nov. 20**
See Bassus, Dionysius, etc.

DIONYSIUS and REDEMPTUS (BB) MM. O.C.   **A.C. Nov. 29**
d. 1653. Dionysius of the Nativity (Peter Berthelot) was a French shipmaster and trader who became a Carmelite at Goa in 1635 and was ordained in 1638. This same year he was sent on an embassy to Sumatra. A Carmelite lay-brother, Redemptus of the cross (Thomas Rodriguez da Cunha), a Portuguese by birth, was given him as a companion. The embassy proved a failure, and both friars were put to death by the Sumatrans. Beatified in 1900.
Cf. Att. — Baud. — Holw.

DIONYSIUS (St) Pope   **R.M. Dec. 26**
d. 269. A Roman priest who was chosen pope in 259 and very energetically and successfully restored the Roman church after the persecution of Gallienus. He opposed Sabellius and condemned Paul of Samosata.
Cf. Att. — Baud. — Holw.

DIOSCORIDES (St) M.   **R.M. May 10**
? A martyr of Smyrna in Asia Minor.
Cf. Holw.

DIOSCORIDES (St) M.   **R.M. May 28**
See Crescens and Dioscorides.

DIOSCORUS (St) M.   **R.M. Feb. 25**
See Victorinus and Dioscorus.

DIOSCORUS (St) M.   **R.M. May 18**
d. c.305. A reader of the church of Kynopolis in Egypt. He was burnt with hot irons and he died under the torture.
Cf. Holw. — Baud.

DIOSCORUS (St) M.   **R.M. Dec. 14**
See Heron and Dioscorus.

DIOSCORUS (St) M.   **R.M. Dec. 21**
See Themistocles and Dioscorus.

DIRUVIANUS (St) M.
    A.C. May 14 (R.M. May 26)
Otherwise Dyfan, q.v.

DISIBOD (DISIBODE, DISEN) (St) Bp. O.S.B.   **A.C. Sept. 8**
d. c.700. An Irishman — a bishop ? — who passed over to the continent with several conpanions and founded a monastery on a hill in the valley of the Nahe, near Bingen, which became known as Disibodenberg or Disenberg, *Mons Disibodi*. It became famous in a later age on account of the residence there of St Hildegarde.
Cf. Mab. — Zimm. — Att.

DISMAS (St)   **R.M. March 25**
The name given by tradition to the Good Thief, q.v.

DIUMA (St) C.   **?**
7th cent. A Scottish priest sent with St Cedd to convert Mercia.

DIZIER (St) Bp. M.   **R.M. May 23**
Otherwise Desiderius, q.v.

DOCANUS or DOCCO (St) Ab.
    A.C. Nov. 7
Otherwise Cumgar (or Cungar), q.v.

DOCHOW (St)   **Feb. 15**
? The English menology mentions him on this day as a Welsh saint, but there is much uncertainty about the name. He may be St Cadoc, sometimes called Dochoe, or St Dogmael, (Docmael). A church in the diocese of St Asaph is dedicated to St Docwy or Dogway.

DOCUS (St) Bp. M.   A.C. Jan. 24
Otherwise Cadoc, q.v.

DODA (St) V. O.S.B.   R.M. Apr. 24
See Bova (Bona) and Doda.

DODO (Bl) C. H.   P.C. March 30
d. 1231. A hermit at Asch in Frisia, who
practised astonishing austerities. He is
reputed to have received the stigmata.
Cf. Att. — Baud. — Holw.

DODO (St) Ab. O.S.B.   A.C. Oct. 1
d. c.750. Born in the territory of Laon.
Placed from childhood under St Ursmarus,
he became a monk at Lobbes and eventually was made abbot of Wallers-en-Faigne.
Cf. Chev. — Baud. — Holw.

DODOLINUS (St) Bp.   A.C. Apr. 1
7th cent. Bishop of Vienne in Dauphiné,
France.
Cf. Duch. Fast. Episc. — Gams.

DOGFAN (DOEWAN) (St) M.
    A.C. July 13
5th cent. A Welshman, one of the sons of
the chieftain Brychan. He is said to have
been put to death by heathen invaders of
Pembrokeshire, where a church was built
to his memory.
Cf. Holw.

DOGMAEL (St) C.   A.C. June 14
5th-6th cent. A Welsh monk of the house
of Cunedda. He founded several cells in
Pembrokeshire, Brittany and elsewhere.
Cf. Att. — Holw.

DOMANGARD (DONARD) (St) C.
    A.C. March 24
d. c.500. The patron of Maghera, Co.
Down, who in the time of St Patrick lived
as a hermit on the mountain now called
after him Slieve-Donard.
Cf. Holw. — Baud.

DOMETIUS and Comp. (SS) MM.
    R.M. Aug. 7
Otherwise Domitius, q.v.

DOMINATOR (St) Bp.   R.M. Nov. 5
d. ? 495. The fourteenth bishop of
Brescia in Lombardy.
Cf. Menzies — Holw. — Baud.

DOMINIC
Note. Dominicus, Dominica are latinized

forms of Cyriacus (*Kuriakos*) and Cyriaca
(*Kuriake*). The Latin Dominicus has the
following derivatives in modern languages:
in Italian, Domenico; in Spanish and
Portuguese, Domingo; in French, Do-
minique; in English, Dominic.

DOMINIC of SORA (St) Ab. O.S.B.
    R.M. Jan. 22
d. 1031. Born at Foligno in Etruria, he
became a Benedictine and eventually the
abbot-founder of several monasteries —
at Scandrilia, Sora, Sangro, and elsewhere
in the old kingdom of Naples. He died at
Sora in Campania when eighty years old.
*Cf. Zimm. — P. de U. — Chev. — Baud.
— Att.*

DOMINIC JORJES (Bl) M.
    A.C. March 14
d. 1619. A Portuguese soldier, born at
Aguilar de Sousa, who settled in Japan,
where he gave shelter to Bl Charles Spinola. For this reason he was burnt alive
at Nagasaki (Nov. 18). Beatified in 1819.
Cf. Holw. — Baud.

DOMINIC TUOC (Bl) M.   A.C. Apr. 2
d. 1839. A native of Tonkin, and a priest
of the third order of Friars Preachers.
He died of his wounds in prison. Beatified
in 1900.
Cf. Holw.

**DOMINIC VERNAGALLI (Bl) Mk
O.S.B. Cam.**   A.C. Apr. 20
d. 1218. A native of Pisa who was professed a Camaldolese at the abbey of St
Michael in his native city. He founded a
hospital attached to the monastery. Cult
confirmed in 1854.
*Cf. Zimm. — Baud. — Chev. — Att. —
Holw.*

DOMINIC and GREGORY (BB) CC. O.P.
    A.C. Apr. 26
d. 1300. Two Spanish Dominicans who
preached in the villages of the Somontano,
at the foot of the Pyrenees, near Barbastro, in Aragon. They were killed near
Perarúa by the fall of a rock, under which
they had sought refuge during a thunderstorm. Their relics are enshrined at
Besians, diocese of Barbastro. Cult confirmed by Pius IX.
Cf. Att. — Baud. — Holw.

DOMINIC de la CALZADA (St) H.
R.M. May 12
d. c.1109. Born at Victoria in Biscay, he tried unsuccessfully his religious vocation at Valvanera and then became a hermit in Rioja. He devoted his days to making a road — *Calzada* (causeway) — for pilgrims on their way to Compostella. The spot where he lived, now the township of La Calzada, became a great pilgrimage shrine.
Cf. Att. — Baud. — Holw.

DOMINIC of the HOLY ROSARY (Bl) M. O.P. A.C. June 1
d. 1622. A Japanese catechist and novice of the Dominican Order. He was beheaded on the day of the great martyrdom — Sept. 10, 1622 — at Nagasaki. Beatified in 1867.
Cf. Holw.

DOMINIC of FIUNGA (Bl) M.
A.C. June 1
d. 1622 (Sept. 12). A Japanese catechist, of the third order of Friars Preachers, burnt alive at Omura with Bl Thomas Zumarraga and companions. Beatified in 1867.
Cf. Holw.

DOMINIC CASTELLET (Bl) M. O.P.
A.C. June 1
1592-1628. (Sept. 8). A native of Esparraguera, province of Barcelona. He took the Dominican habit at Barcelona and was sent to the Dominican mission of Japan, of which he was vicar provincial at the time of his martyrdom. He was burnt alive at Nagasaki. Beatified in 1867.
Cf. Baud. — Holw

DOMINIC TOMAKI (Bl) M.
A.C. June 1
d. 1628. (Sept. 8). Son of Bl John Tomaki, beheaded at the age of sixteen with his father and brothers at Nagasaki. Beatified in 1867.
Cf. Holw.

DOMINIC NIFAKI (Bl) M. A.C. June 1
d. 1628 (Sept. 8). A child, two years old, beheaded at Nagasaki with his father, Bl Louis Nifaki, and his brother Francis. Beatified in 1867.
Cf. Holw

DOMINIC XIBIOJE (Bl) M.
A.C. June 1
d. 1628 (Sept. 26). A Japanese layman, of the third order of Friars Preachers, who sheltered the missionaries. Beheaded at Nagasaki. Beatified in 1867.
Cf. Holw.

DOMINIC of COMACCHIO (Bl) Mk O.S.B. A.C. June 21
d. p. 820. A Benedictine monk of Comacchio, near Venice. According to the legend, it was he who in 820 went as a pilgrim to the Holy Land and brought the relics of St Mark from Alexandria to Venice.
Cf. Zimm.

DOMINIC HENARES (Bl) Bp. M. O.P.
A.C. June 25
d. 1838. A Spaniard by birth and a Dominican friar by profession, he became in 1803 bishop-coadjutor to Bl Ignatius Delgado, vicar apostolic of Tonkin. He was beheaded with his catechist, Bl Francis Chien, during the Annamite persecution. Beatified in 1900.
Cf. Att. — Holw.

DOMINIC FERNÁNDEZ (Bl) M. S.J.
A.C. July 15
d. 1570. A Jesuit laybrother. Born at Villa Viciosa in Portugal. A companion of Bl Ignatius de Azevedo, q.v.
Cf. Holw.

DOMINIC NICOLAUS DAT (Bl) M.
A.C. July 18
d. 1838. A native soldier in Tonkin, who was strangled during the persecution of the Christians. Beatified in 1900.
Cf. Holw.

DOMINIC DIEN (Bl) M. O.P. A.C. Aug. 1
d. 1838. A native of Tonkin, and a priest of the Dominican Order. He was executed in his sixty-seventh year. Beatified in 1900.
Cf. Holw.

DOMINIC de GUZMÁN (St) Founder O.P. R.M. Aug. 4
1170-1221. A native of Calaruega, province of Burgos, in Old Castile, and an Augustinian canon regular at the cathedral of Osma. In 1203 he accompanied his bishop, Bl Diego de Azevedo, to S. France, where the heretical sect known as the Albigenses was at that time devastating,

morally and materially, those fair provinces. Dominic began his life-long apostolate among the heretics, and in 1206 succeeded in opening a convent at Prouille for nun-converts from Albigensianism. This was the germ of his order of friars known as the Friars Preachers, whom Dominic sent everywhere to preach and teach. The order was approved in 1216 and within a few years it had spread throughout Europe. The Order of Preachers, with that founded by St Francis and known as the Friars Minor, marks the culminating point of that powerful tide of Christian asceticism which had begun with Cluny and been continued by Cîteaux. By his personal charm St Dominic won the enthusiastic affection of his followers. He likewise incurred the blind opposition of those who condemned him without coming in contact with his winning character. He died at Bologna, and was canonized in 1234.
Cf. Menzies — Att. — Baud. — Holw.

DOMINIC del VAL (St) M. A.C. Aug. 31
d. 1250. In Spain he is usually called San Dominguito — Little Dominic. He was a seven-year-old altar boy at the cathedral of Saragossa, who was kidnapped by Jews and nailed against a wall. His feast is celebrated throughout Aragon.
Cf. P. de U. — Holw.

DOMINIC of NAGASAKI (Bl) M. O.F.M.
A.C. Sept. 8
d. 1628. A Japanese catechist. He received the Franciscan habit in the prison at Omura from Bl Antony of St Bonaventure and was burnt alive at Nagasaki. Beatified in 1867.
Cf. Holw.

DOMINIC NACANO (Bl) M.
A.C. Sept. 10
d. 1622. Son of Bl Matthias Nacano. He was beheaded at Nagasaki. Beatified in 1854.
Cf. Holw.

DOMINIC XAMADA (Bl) M.
A.C. Sept. 10
d. 1622. A Japanese layman, beheaded at Nagasaki. Beatified in 1854.
Cf. Holw.

DOMINIC TRACH (Bl) M. A.C. Sept. 18
d. 1843. A native priest of Tonkin, and

a member of the Dominican third order. He was beheaded for his faith. Beatified in 1900.
Cf. Holw.

DOMINIC SPADAFORA (Bl) C. O.P.
A.C. Oct. 3
d. 1521. A native of Palermo, who, after having finished his studies at Padua, joined the Friars Preachers and spent his life in continuous preaching throughout Italy and Sicily. Cult confirmed in 1921.
Cf. Att. — Holw.

DOMINIC LORICATUS (the MAILED) (St) H. O.S.B.   R.M. Oct. 14
995-1060. Born in Umbria. By means of a bribe his father had him ordained priest in contravention of canon law, and on learning this, the saint determined to do penance for it during the rest of his life. He first became a hermit and then a Benedictine monk under St Peter Damian at Fontavellana. He is surnamed "the Mailed" because he wore for years a rough iron coat-of-mail next to his skin.
Cf. Zimm. — Mab. — Att. — Chev. — Baud.

DOMINIC DOAN (XUYEN) (Bl) M. O.P.
A.C. Oct. 26
d. 1839. A native of Tonkin, and a member of the Dominican order, beheaded with Bl Thomas Din. Beatified in 1900.
Cf. Holw.

DOMINIC UY (Bl) M.   A.C. Dec. 19
d. 1839. A native catechist of Tonkin, who belonged to the third order of St Dominic. He was hanged at the age of twenty-six. Beatified in 1900.
Cf. Holw.

DOMINIC of BRESCIA (St) Bp.
R.M. Dec. 20
d. c.612. The successor of St Anastasius in the see of Brescia. St Charles Borromeo translated and enshrined his relics.
Cf. Menzies — Holw.

DOMINIC of SILOS (St) Ab. O.S.B.
R.M. Dec. 20
c.1000-1073. Born at Cañas — then Spanish Navarre, now Rioja — he became a Benedictine at San Millán de la Cogolla. As prior of this great abbey he came into conflict with King García III of Navarre by whom he was exiled from the kingdom,

King Ferdinand I of Old Castile received him kindly and sent him as abbot to restore the old monastery of St Sebastian — now St Dominic — of Silos. The saint was most successful in this task and was responsible for a virtual rebuilding of the abbey. He was a lover of the arts, and the scriptorium of his abbey produced under his inspiration the best specimens of Spanish Christian art. The cloisters of the abbey — a gem of Romanesque architecture — stand to this day as the best monument to his enterprise. He was also renowned for rescuing Christian slaves from the Moors. He is one of the best beloved of Spanish saints. At his shrine Bl Aza de Guzmán obtained the child whom she called Dominic, after the abbot of Silos, and who became the founder of the Dominican Friars.
Cf. P. de U. — Zimm. — Chev. — Baud. — Att.

DOMINIC, VICTOR, PRIMIAN, LYBOSUS, SATURNINUS, CRESCENTIUS, SECUNDUS, and HONORATUS (SS) MM. R.M. Dec. 29
? African martyrs whose Acts have been lost.

DOMINICA (St) V.M. R.M. July 6
? Said to have been a martyr in Campania under Diocletian. Possibly she is to be identified with St Cyriaca — *Dominica*, venerated on this day in the East as a martyr at Nicomedia.
Cf. Att. — Baud. — Holw.

DOMINICA (St) M. R.M. Aug. 21
Otherwise Cyriaca, q.v.

DOMINICA ONGATA (Bl) M. A.C. Sept. 10
d. 1622. A Japanese woman, beheaded at Nagasaki. See Bl Charles Spinola.
Cf. Holw.

DOMINICAN MARTYRS (BB) A.C. Jan. 22, Nov. 1 and 7
A group of seven Dominican fathers martyred in the missions of the Far East in the years 1745, 1773 and 1861, and beatified in 1908. Each of these martyrs receives here a special notice.

DOMITIAN (St) Bp. A.C. May 7
d. c.560. Bishop of Maestricht, and apostle of the Meuse valley. His relics are venerated at Huy.
Cf. Att. — Baud. — Holw.

DOMITIAN and HADELINUS (SS) Mks O.S.B. A.C. June 15
d. c.686. Two disciples of St Landelinus at the abbey of Lobbes. They were connected also, it seems, with Crépin Abbey.
Cf. Zimm. — Baud. — Holw.

DOMITIAN (St) Ab. R.M. July 1
c.347-c.440. Born in Rome and left an orphan at an early age, he passed into Gaul and became a monk and a priest at Lérins. Later he founded the monastery of Bebron, now St Rambert de Joux. The sources, however, of St Domitian's life are very unreliable.
Cf. Baud. — Holw.

DOMITIAN (St) M. R.M. Aug. 1
See Cyril, Aquila, etc

DOMITIAN of CHÂLONS (St) Bp. R.M. Aug. 9
? The third bishop of Châlons-sur-Marne in France, in which see he succeeded his master St Donatian.
Cf. Baud. — Holw.

DOMITIAN (St) M. R.M. Dec. 28
See Eutychius and Domitian.

DOMITILLA (St) V. M. R.M. May 7
More correctly Flavia Domitilla, q.v.

DOMITIUS, PELAGIA, AQUILA, EPARCHIUS and THEODOSIA (SS) MM. R.M. March 23
d. 361. St Domitius was a Phrygian who died by the sword under Julian the Apostate, probably at Caesarea in Palestine. He is said to have publicly attacked the errors of heathenism in the circus, where the pagans were gathered for the festival games held in honour of the gods. Several others were martyred with him.
Cf. Baud. — Holw.

DOMITIUS (St) M. R.M. July 5
d. 362. A Persian, or a Phrygian monk, stoned to death under Julian the Apostate, in much the same circumstances as St Domitius of March 23.
Cf. Holw.

**DOMITIUS (DOMETIUS) and Comp.
(SS) MM.** R.M. Aug. 7
4th cent. The entry in the R.M. is: At
Nisibis in Mesopotamia St Dometius, a
Persian monk who with two of his disciples was stoned to death under Julian the
Apostate. This Domitius is probably
identical with the preceding two of March
23 and July 5.

DOMITIUS (St) C. R.M. Oct. 23
8th cent. A priest, or deacon, of the
diocese of Amiens, who retired to a solitude
and lived as an anchorite.
Cf. Baud. — Holw.

DOMNA (St) V.M. R.M. Dec. 28
See Indes, Domna, etc.

**DOMNEVA (DOMNA EVA) (St) W.
O.S.B.** A.C. Nov. 19
Otherwise Ebba or Ermenburga, q.v.

DOMNINA and Another (SS) VV. MM.
R.M. Apr. 14
? Two maidens, the name of only one of
whom is known, who were martyred at
Terni, in Umbria, at the same time, it is
said, as the bishop St Valentine.
Cf. Menzies — Holw. — Baud.

**DOMNINA, BERENICE and PROS-
DOCE (SS) MM.** A.C. Oct. 4
d. 303-310. St Domnina and her two
daughters were martyred in Syria during
the persecution of Diocletian. They are
commemorated by several contemporary
Greek writers.
Cf. Holw.

DOMNINA (St) M. R.M. Oct. 12
d. 303. A Christian woman who, after
cruel torments, died in prison at Anazarbus under the prefect Lysias.
Cf. Baud. — Holw.

DOMNINUS (St) M. R.M. March 21
See Philemon and Domninus.

**DOMNINUS, VICTOR and Comp. (SS)
MM.** R.M. March 30
? St Domninus appears to have suffered
at Thessalonica under Maximian Hercul-
ius, together with Philocalus, Achaicus and
Palotinus. He is to be identified with St
Domninus of Oct 1 (see below), on which
day he is venerated by the Greeks. St
Victor and his companions, some ten in

number, suffered elsewhere, the name of
the place being no longer known.
Cf. Baud. — Holw.

DOMNINUS (St) R.M. Apr. 20
See Marcellinus, Vincent and Domninus.

DOMNINUS (St) M. R.M. Oct. 1
The same as Domninus commemorated on
March 30, q.v.

DOMNINUS (DONNINO) (St) M.
R.M. Oct. 9
d. 304. A native of Parma, who, while
trying to escape in time of persecution,
was overtaken and beheaded on the Via
Claudia or Aemilia, a few miles out of
Parma at a place now called after him
Borgo San Donnino, where his relics are
held in great veneration.
Cf. Baud. — Holw. — Menzies.

**DOMNINUS, THEOTIMUS, PHILO-
THEUS, SYLVANUS and Comp. (SS)
MM.** R.M. Nov. 5
? St Domninus, a young physician, and
St Sylvanus, a Syrian bishop, were to-
gether condemned to work in the mines.
The former was burnt alive somewhere in
Palestine, the latter was martyred much
later. The rest seem to have suffered
under Maximian.
Cf. Baud. — Holw.

DOMNINUS (St) Bp. A.C. Nov. 5
4th cent. This St Domninus is given as
the first bishop of Grenoble in France.
Cf. Duch. Fast. Episc. — Baud.

DOMNIO and Comp. (SS) MM.
R.M. Apr. 11
? According to an old legend, Domnio,
one of the seventy-two disciples of Christ,
was sent from Rome by St Peter to evangelize Dalmatia, where he was martyred
as first bishop of Salona. A more probable version states that he was martyred
during the persecution of Diocletian.

DOMNIO (St) M. R.M. July 16
d. c.295. A martyr of Bergamo in Lombardy under Diocletian.
Cf. Holw. — Baud. — Menzies.

DOMNIO (St) C. R.M. Dec. 28
4th cent. A Roman priest, of whom his
contemporaries SS Jerome and Augustine
speak in glowing terms.
Cf. Baud. — Holw.

DOMNOC (St)   A.C. Feb. 13
Otherwise Modomnoc, q.v.

DOMNOLUS (St) Bp.   R.M. May 16
d. 581. Abbot of the monastery of St Laurence, near Paris. In 543 he was chosen bishop of Le Mans. He was the founder of many monasteries, hospitals and churches.
Cf. Baud. — Att. — Holw.

DOMNUS (St) M. O.F.M.   R.M. Oct. 13
See Daniel, Samuel, etc.

DOMNUS of VIENNE (St) Bp.
            R.M. Nov. 3
d. 527. Successor of St Desiderius the martyr in the bishopric of Vienne. He was most zealous in ransoming the captives taken in the incessant wars of that period.
Cf. Holw. — Duch. Fast. Episc. — Baud.

DONALD (DONIVALD) (St) C.
            A.C. July 15
8th cent. A holy man of Scotland who with his nine daughters — the "Nine Maidens," led the life of a religious at Ogilvy in Forfarshire.
Cf. Att. — Baud. — Holw.

DONARD (St)   A.C. March 24
Otherwise Domangard, q.v.

DONAS (St) Bp.   R.M. Oct. 14
Otherwise Donatian, q.v.

DONAT (DUNWYD) (St)   A.C. Aug. 7
The patron saint of St Donat's or Llandunwyd, Glamorgan. This from the English Menology. Nothing more is discoverable.

DONATA (St) M.   R.M. July 17
One of the Scillitan Martyrs, q.v.

DONATA, PAULINA, RUSTICA, NOMINANDA, SEROTINA, HILARIA and Comp. (SS) MM.   R.M. Dec. 31
? A band of Roman women martyred in one of the early persecutions and whose relics were enshrined in the catacombs of the Via Salaria.

DONATIAN and ROGATIAN (SS) MM.
            R.M. May 24
d. 299. Two brothers of Nantes in Brittany put to death by Rictiovarus under Diocletian.
Cf. Baud. — Holw.

DONATIAN (St) Bp.   R.M. Aug. 7
? Second bishop of Châlons-sur-Marne.
Cf. Duch. Fast. Episc. — Baud.

DONATIAN, PRAESIDIUS, MANSUETUS, GERMANUS, FUSCULUS and LAETUS (SS) MM.   R.M. Sept. 6
5th cent. Some of the more prominent among the Catholics driven from Africa into exile by Hunneric, the Arian king of the Vandals. An account of them is given by Victor of Utica in his history of that persecution. It is said that the number of exiles reached nearly five thousand in a single year.
Cf. Holw. — Baud.

DONATIAN (DONAS) (St) Bp.
            R.M. Oct. 14
d. 390. A Roman by birth and bishop of Reims from 360 to 390. His relics were translated to Bruges in the 9th century. He has been since venerated as the patron saint of Bruges.
Cf. Duch. Fast. Episc. — Baud. — Holw.

DONATILLA (St) V.M.   R.M. July 30
See Maxima, Donatilla and Secunda.

DONATUS, SABINUS and AGAPE (SS) MM.   R.M. Jan. 25
? Martyrs whose names are listed in the R.M. but of whom no record is extant.

DONATUS (St) M.   R.M. Feb. 4
See Aquilinus, Geminus, etc.

DONATUS (St) M.   R.M. Feb. 9
See Primus and Donatus.

DONATUS, SECUNDIAN, ROMULUS and Comp. (SS) MM.   R.M. Feb. 17
d. 304. A group of eighty-nine martyrs who suffered under Diocletian. They were put to death at Porto Gruaro (Concordia), not far from Venice.
Cf. Holw. — Baud.

DONATUS, JUSTUS, HERENA and Comp. (SS) MM.   R.M. Feb. 25
3rd cent. A band of fifty martyrs who suffered in Africa under Decius.

DONATUS (St) M.   R.M. March 1
See Leo, Donatus, etc.

DONATUS (St) M.   R.M. Apr. 7
See Epiphanius, Donatus, etc.

DONATUS (St) Bp. R.M. Apr. 30
d. late 4th cent. Bishop of Euraea in
Epirus (Albania). His sanctity is recorded by Sozomen and other Greek
writers.
Cf. Baud. — Holw.

DONATUS (St) M. R.M. May 21
See Polyeuctus, Victorius and Donatus.

DONATUS and HILARY (SS) MM.
R.M. Aug. 7
d. 361. St Donatus, bishop of Arezzo in
Tuscany, is commemorated liturgically
on Aug. 7. He, with the monk Hilary (or
Hilarinus), was put to death under Julian
the Apostate. Hilary was scourged to
death; Donatus was beheaded.
Cf. Att. — Baud. — Holw.

DONATUS (St) Bp. O.S.B. A.C. Aug. 7
d. a. 660. A monk of Luxeuil. Bishop
of Besançon in 624. He was a most
zealous fosterer of monasticism and
founded at Besançon the abbey of St
Paul, under the rules of SS. Benedict and
Columbanus.
Cf. Zimm. — Baud.

DONATUS (St) Mk O.S.B. A.C. Aug. 17
1179-1198. Born at Ripacandida, in the
diocese of Rapallo. He became a monk
of the Benedictine congregation of Montevergine at S. Onofrio at Petina (1194) and
here he died, only nineteen years old. He
is now the principal patron saint of
Ripacandida.
Cf. Holw. — Zimm. — Chev.

DONATUS (St) C. R.M. Aug. 19
d. c.535. A native of Orleans, who lived
as a hermit on Mt Jura near Sisteron in
Provence.
Cf. Baud. — Holw.

DONATUS of ANTIOCH (St) M.
R.M. Aug. 23
See Restitutus, Donatus, etc.

DONATUS and FELIX (SS) MM.
R.M. Sept. 1
Two of the "Twelve Holy Brothers," so-
called, q.v.

DONATUS of CAPUA (St) M.
R.M. Sept. 5
See Quinctius, Arcontius and Donatus.

DONATUS (St) M. R.M. Oct. 5
See Placid and Comp.

DONATUS of FIESOLE (St) Bp.
R.M. Oct. 22
d. 874. An Irishman who, while passing
through Tuscany on his return from a pilgrimage to Rome, was made bishop of
Fiesole near Florence. His feast is observed throughout Ireland.
Cf. Att. — Menzies. — Holw. — Baud.

DONATUS of CORFU (St) C.
R.M. Oct. 29
? All we know of this saint is that, about
the year 600, St Gregory the Great directed that his relics, brought to Corfu by
a refugee priest from Asia Minor, should
be enshrined in one of the churches of the
island.
Cf. Holw. — Baud.

DONATUS (St) M. R.M. Dec. 12
See Hermogenes, Donatus, etc.

DONATUS of ALEXANDRIA (St) M.
R.M. Dec. 30
See Mansuetus, Severus, etc.

**DONNAN (DOUNAN) and Comp. (SS)
MM.** A.C. Apr. 17
d. c.616. St Donnan was a monk of Iona
under St Columba. He eventually became the abbot-founder of a monastery
on Eigg Island in the Inner Hebrides, off
the W. coast of Scotland. He and his
fifty-two monks were massacred by
heathen raiders.
Cf. Att. — Holw.

DONVINA (St) M. R.M. Aug. 23
See Claudius, Asterius, etc.

DORBHENE (St) Ab. A.C. Oct. 28
d. 713. Abbot of Iona, descended from
a brother of St Columba. A copy of St
Adamnan's life of the latter written by
St Dorbhene is still in existence.
Cf. Holw.

DORCAS (St) W. A.C. Oct. 25
Otherwise Tabitha, q.v.

DORIS (several)
Otherwise Dorothy, q.v.

DOROTHEUS (St) M. R.M. March 28
See Castor and Dorotheus.

DOROTHEUS of TYRE (St) M.
R.M. June 5
d. c.362. A priest of Tyre, who was exiled under Diocletian. On his return he was chosen bishop of Tyre, and as such assisted at the council of Nicaea. Under Julian the Apostate he was beaten to death at Varna on the Black Sea. All the above details, however, are more or less guess-work.
Cf. Att. — Baud. — Bolland.

DOROTHEUS the ARCHIMANDRITE (St) Ab.
? P.C. June 5
d. c.640. A monk of Gaza, who became archimandrite of an unknown monastery. His writings were greatly admired by Abbot de Rancé.
Cf. Att. — Holw.

DOROTHEUS the YOUNGER (St) Ab.
A.C. June 5
11th cent. Born at Trebizond, he was first a monk at Samsun on the Black Sea and afterwards abbot-founder of a monastery at Khiliokomos nearby.
Cf. Att. — Holw.

DOROTHEUS and GORGONIUS (SS) MM.
R.M. Sept. 9
d. 303. Favourites of the emperor Diocletian and officials of his body-guard at Nicomedia. The emperor had them hanged for their faith. Eusebius of Caesarea, a contemporary, records their martyrdom.
Cf. Holw. — Baud.

DOROTHY (DORA, DOROTHEA) (St) V.M.
R.M. Feb. 6
d. c.300. A virgin-martyr of Caesarea in Cappadocia who suffered under Diocletian. Her Acta are apocryphal.
Cf. Att. — Holw. — Baud.

DOROTHY (St) V.M.
R.M. Sept. 3
See Euphemia, Dorothy, etc.

DOROTHY of MONTAU (St) W.
P.C. Oct. 30
1336-1394. A peasant girl of Montau in Prussia, who married a wealthy swordsmith Albert by name. She bore him nine children and by her gentle patience completely changed his surly disposition. After his death Dorothy lived as a recluse at Marienwerder. Though she was never canonized her cult is still to be found in Central Europe.
Cf. Att. — Holw. — Baud.

DORYMEDON (St) M.
R.M. Sept. 19
See Trophimus, Sabbatius and Dorymedon.

DOSITHEUS (St) Mk.
A.C. Feb. 23
d. c.530. A rich young man who became a Christian at Jerusalem and shortly after a monk at Gaza. His poor health prevented him from fasting, and moreover he did not work any miracles: these facts scandalized his fellow monks. His abbot, however, considered him a great saint, since he had completely given up his own will. This has been the verdict of history, which has canonized him.
Cf. Att. — Holw.

DOTTO (St) Ab.
? Apr. 9
? 6th cent. Said to have been abbot of a monastery in the Orkney Islands.
Cf. Bolland.

DOUAI (Martyrs of) (BB)
A.C. Oct. 29
More than a hundred and sixty "seminary priests" from the English College at Douai were martyred in England and Wales during the century following its foundation in 1568. Over eighty of them were beatified in 1929. Each receives here a special notice. A collective feast is kept in their honour in several English dioceses.
Cf. Newdigate.

DRAUSINUS (DRAUSIUS) (St) Bp.
A.C. March 7
d. c.576. Bishop of Soissons. A great fosterer of monastic life, he even enlisted the services of the tyrant Ebroin for the building of a convent near Soissons. For this reason he is invoked against the machinations of enemies, and St Thomas Becket is said to have visited his shrine before returning to England for the last time.
Cf. Att. — Baud.

DREUX (St) H
R.M. Apr. 16
Otherwise Drogo, q.v.

DRILLO (St) C.
A.C. June 15
Otherwise Trillo, q.v.

DRITHELM (St) H.
A.C. Aug. 17
d. c.700. A Northumbrian who, terrified

by a vision, embraced the monastic life at Melrose, where he lived a life of great austerity in a special cell near the abbey.
Cf. Att. — Baud. — Holw.

DROCTOVEUS (DROCTONIUS — in French DROTTÉ) (St) Ab.
R.M. March 10
d. c.580. A disciple of St Germanus of Paris, who became abbot of the monastery of St Symphorian at Autun and was afterwards called by his old master to Paris as first abbot of the new monastery of St Vincent and the Holy Cross — afterwards renamed Saint-Germain-des-Prés.
Cf. Mab. — Att. — Baud. — Holw.

DROGO (Bl) Mk O.S.B. A.C. Apr. 2
10th cent. After a worldly life, Drogo entered the Benedictine abbey of Fleury-sur-Loire, and afterwards migrated to that of Baume-les-Messieurs, where he was engaged in tending the flocks of the abbey.
Cf. Chev. — Zimm. — P. de U. — Holw.

DROGO (DREUX, DRUON) (St) H.
R.M. Apr. 16
d. 1186. A Fleming by birth and an orphan at twenty years of age, he disposed of all his property and served as a shepherd in France. Nine times he made the pilgrimage to Rome. Stricken with a most unsightly bodily affliction, he built himself a hut under the shadow of the church of Sebourg in Hainault, where he died aged eighty-four.
Cf. Att. — Baud. — Holw.

DROSTAN (St) Ab. A.C. July 11
d. c.610. An Irishman by birth, monk under St Columba, and first abbot of Deer in Aberdeenshire. He is venerated as one of the apostles of Scotland.
Cf. Att. — Baud. — Holw.

DRUSUS, ZOSIMUS and THEODORE (SS) MM. R.M. Dec. 14
? Christians martyred in Syria, probably at Antioch. Some MSS have Drusina for Drusus. St John Chrysostom has left a homily preached on their festival day.
Cf. Baud. — Holw.

DRUSUS (St) M. R.M. Dec. 24
See Lucian, Metrobius, etc.

DRUTHMAR (St) Ab. O.S.B.
A.C. Feb. 15
d. 1046. A Benedictine of Lorsch, who in 1014 was appointed by the emperor St Henry II abbot of Corvey in Saxony. Fervour and good observance were marks of his rule.
Cf. Zimm. — Chev. — Baud. — Holw.

DUBRICIUS (DUBRIC, DYFRIG, DEVEREUX) (St) Bp. A.C. Nov. 14
d. c.545. One of the founders of monastic life in Wales. His chief centres of monachism were at Henllan and Moccas, whence he established many other religious houses in what is now Herefordshire and Monmouthshire. He had jurisdiction over Caldey Island and appointed St Samson abbot of the monastery there, and later consecrated him bishop. A later legend makes St Dubricius archbishop of Caerleon. He died on the Isle of Bardsey.
Cf. Att. — Holw.

DUBTACH (St) Bp. A.C. Oct. 7
d. c.513. Archbishop of Armagh from 497 to c.513.
Cf. Holw.

DULA (St) V.M. R.M. March 25
? The slave of a pagan soldier at Nicomedia in Asia Minor. She suffered death at his hands in defence of her chastity.
Cf. Baud. — Holw.

DULAS (St) M. R.M. June 15
d. 300. A Christian of Zepherinum in Cilicia, martyred after having undergone the most frightful tortures.
Cf. Holw. — Baud.

DULCARDUS (St) H. A.C. Oct. 25
d. 584. Monk of Micy (Saint-Mesmin) in Orleans, and afterwards a hermit near Bourges, where now stands the village of Saint-Doulchard (Cher).
Cf. Baud. — Zimm.

DULCIDIUS (DULCET, DOUCIS) (St) Bp. A.C. Oct. 16
d. c.450. Successor of St Phoebadius in the bishopric of Agen in France.
Cf. Duch. Fast. Episc. — Gams — Baud.

DULCISSIMA (St) V.M. A.C. Sept. 16
? Nothing is really known about this saint, but from time immemorial she has been venerated at Sutri, formerly in the Papal States, as a virgin-martyr and as the principal patron saint of the town and diocese.
Cf. Menzies — Holw.

DUMHAID (St) Ab.   **A.C. May 25**
Otherwise Dunchadh, q.v.

DUNCHADH (St) Ab.   **A.C. May 25**
d. 717. Abbot of Iona in Scotland from 710 till his death. In his time the Roman customs — tonsure, date of Easter, Benedictine Rule — were finally adopted by the Celtic monks in Scotland.
Cf. Baud. — Zimm. — Holw.

DUNCHAID O'BRAOIN (St) Ab.
              A.C. Jan. 16
d. 988. Born in Westmeath, he was an anchorite near the monastery of Clonmacnoise until the year 969, when he was chosen abbot of that place. In his old age he retired to Armagh, where he died.
Cf. Holw.

DUNSTAN (St) Bp. O.S.B. R.M. May 19
c.910-988. One of the great figures in English history — abbot, archbishop, statesman, and saint. An Anglo-Saxon by origin, he was born near Glastonbury, where he was also educated and became a monk. In 943 he was made abbot, and under his rule the monastery became the greatest centre of learning in England. He himself excelled as a goldsmith, an illuminator and a musician. He was summoned to court to be a royal counsellor, but was forced into exile by King Edwy, whom he had rebuked. Dunstan now spent one year at Ghent, then a great centre of monastic restoration. He was recalled to England by King Edgar and became his chief adviser, being promoted to the see of Worcester (957) and to that of Canterbury (961). Moreover, Pope John XII appointed Dunstan his legate in England (961). He now achieved, together with SS Ethelwold of Winchester and Oswald of York, a thorough monastic and ecclesiastical reform throughout England and initiated a vigorous policy of national unification and moral restoration. Active and energetic to the very end, he died peacefully at Canterbury, in his cathedral of Christ Church.
Cf. Att. — Baud. — Holw. — Zimm. — Stanton.

DUTHAC (St) Bp.   **A.C. March 8**
d. 1065. An Irishman by birth, he became bishop of Ross in Scotland, where his memory is preserved in several place-names, e.g., Kilduthie, etc.
Cf. Att. — Baud. — Holw.

DWYNWEN (St) V.   **A.C. Jan. 25**
d. c.460. A Welsh saint of the family of Brychan of Brecknock. The maxim "nothing wins hearts like cheerfulness" is attributed to her. Churches dedicated to her are to be found in Wales and Cornwall.
Cf. Holw.

DWYNWEN (St) W.   **A.C. July 18**
Otherwise Theneva, q.v.

DYFAN (DERUVIANUS, DAMIAN) (St) M.   **A.C. May 14 (R.M. May 26)**
2nd cent. Said to have been one of the missionaries sent to the Britons by Pope St Eleutherius at the instance of King St Lucius. His church of Merthyr Dyfan shows the popular tradition that he ended his days by martyrdom.
Cf. Holw.

DYFNAN (St) C.   **A.C. Apr. 24**
5th cent. A son of the Welsh chieftain Brychan. He founded a church in Anglesey.
Cf. Holw.

DYFNOG (St) C.   **A.C. Feb. 13**
7th cent. A Welsh saint of the family of Caradog. He was formerly held in local veneration in Denbighshire.
Cf. Holw.

DYFRIG (St) Bp.   **A.C. Nov. 14**
Otherwise Dubricius, q.v.

DYMPNA (DYMPHNA) (St) V.M.
              R.M. May 15
? Popular legend makes her the daughter of an Irish chieftain who escaped to Belgium accompanied by her chaplain St Gerebernus. Their relics were discovered at Gheel, near Antwerp, in the 13th century, and since then numberless cases of insanity, epilepsy, etc., have been cured at their shrine. The asylum built at Gheel in the 13th century still stands, equipped with all up-to-date improvements. St Dympna is invoked as the patroness of lunatics.
Cf. Att. — Baud. — Holw.

E

Note. Saints' names beginning with the letter E are often found written with the diphthong AE, or OE, as the initial letter.

EADBERT (St) Bp. O.S.B. R.M. May 6
d. 698. A monk of Lindisfarne who succeeded St Cuthbert as abbot-bishop of the island. He was remarkable for his knowledge of holy scripture.
Cf. Att. — Baud. — Holw.

EADBURGA (*several*)
Otherwise Edburga, q.v.

EADFRID (St) Mk. O.S.B. A.C. Oct. 26
d. c.675. A Northumbrian monk-priest who preached in Mercia and founded, and was the first superior of, Leominister Priory.
Cf. Stanton.

EADGITH (*several*)
Otherwise Edith, q.v.

EADNOT (St) Bp. O.S.B. ? Oct. 19
d. 1016. Monk of Worcester and abbot of Ramsey. In 1006 he became bishop of Dorchester. As such he helped and seconded St Oswald of York. He died in a battle against the Danes, and is sometimes termed a martyr.
Cf. Baring-Gould — Zimm.

EADSIN (St) Bp. A.C. Oct. 28
d. 1050. Archbishop of Canterbury. He crowned St Edward the Confessor on the restoration of the Anglo-Saxon line in England. He resigned his see some years before his death.
Cf. Stanton.

EANFLEDA (St) W. O.S.B. A.C. Nov. 24
d. c.700. Daughter of King St Edwin of Northumbria and of his wife St Ethelburga of Kent, baptized as an infant by St Paulinus. She was a great benefactress of St Wilfrid. In her widowhood she became a nun at Whitby under her own daughter, St Elfleda.
Cf. Stanton — Baud. — Holw.

EANSWIDA (EANSWITH) (St) Abs O.S.B. A.C. Sept. 12
d. c.640. Granddaughter of King St Ethelbert of Kent. She was the abbess-foundress (630) of a nunnery on the coast near Folkestone. Her convent was destroyed by the Danes but re-founded for Benedictine monks in 1095. Part of it was swallowed up by the sea, and it was removed to Folkestone. Its successor is now the church of SS Mary and Eanswida.
Cf. Stanton — Att. — Zimm. — Baud. — Holw.

EASTERWINE (St) Ab. O.S.B.
A.C. March 7
Otherwise Esterwine, q.v.

EATA (St) Bp. O.S.B. A.C. Oct. 26
d. c.686. An Englishman by origin, he was educated by St Aidan in the Celtic observance at Ripon. When St Wilfrid arrived at this abbey, he left it for Melrose, where he became abbot. After the council of Whitby, however, he adopted fully the Roman observances and was made abbot of Lindisfarne. In 678 he became bishop of the Bernicians, being consecrated by St Theodore, with his see first at Lindisfarne and then at the Benedictine abbey of Hexham.
Cf. Zimm. — Att. — Stanton.

EBBA THE YOUNGER and Comp. (SS) VV. MM. O.S.B. A.C. Aug. 23
d. c.870. Abbess of the great Benedictine nunnery of Coldingham, on the Scottish border, founded two centuries earlier by St Ebba the Elder. During a Danish incursion St Ebba fearing for her virginity mutilated her face and invited her nuns to do the same. The Danes set fire to the nunnery and all the community perished in the flames.
Cf. Stanton — Chev. — Baud.

EBBA the ELDER (St) Abs. O.S.B.
A.C. Aug. 25
d. 683. Sister of SS Oswald and Oswy, kings of Northumbria. She took the veil from St Finon at Lindisfarne and founded the double monastery of Coldingham, on the coast of Berwick, of which she was first abbess. The organization of the abbey resembled that of Whitby in most points. Ebba, we are told, was personally a very holy abbess, but not a great success as an administrator.
Cf. Att. — Holw. — Zimm.

EBBO (St) Bp. O.S.B. A.C. Aug. 27
d. 740. A native of Tonnerre and a Benedictine monk of Saint-Pierre-le-Vif, at Sens. About the year 709 he was raised to the see of Sens. In 725 he saved the city when it was besieged by Saracens.
Cf. Mab. — Duch. Fast. Episc. — Gams — Chev. — Zimm. — Baud.

EBERHARD (*several*)
Note. This Teutonic name, when transliterated into other languages, is often

softened into Everhard, Everard, Evard, Erhard, Erard, etc.

EBERHARD (Bl) Mk. O.S.B. Cist.
P.C. March 20
d. c.1150. Count of Mons in Belgium. In expiation of a crime committed as a soldier, he went on pilgrimage to Rome and Compostella and finally asked to be hired as a swineherd at the Cistercian abbey of Morimond. When his identity was discovered, he was induced to continue his life of penance as a monk, and accordingly took the vows. In 1142 he founded Einberg and then Mont-Saint-George. He is officially venerated by the Cistercians. *Cf. Holw. — Baud.*

EBERHARD of SCHAFFHAUSEN (Bl) Mk. O.S.B. P.C. Apr. 7
1018-1078. Eberhard III, count of Nellenburg, was a relative of Pope St Leo IX and the emperor St Henry II. In 1050 he founded the Benedictine abbey of Schaffhausen in Switzerland — now a town — and took the habit there. *Cf. Chev. — P. de U. — Zimm. — Baud.*

EBERHARD (Bl) O. Praem. P.C. Apr. 17
d. 1178. Premonstratensian monk of Roth, later provost of Marchtal in Swabia when it was handed over to the Premonstratensians in 1166. *Cf. Att. — Holw.*

EBERHARD of SALZBURG (St) Bp. O.S.B. A.C. June 22
1085-1164 (June 11). Born at Nuremberg and educated by the monks of Michelberg at Bamberg, he obtained a canonry at Bamberg, which, however, he gave up in order to become a Benedictine at Prüfening (1125). In 1133 he was made abbot of Biburg, and in 1147 archbishop of Salzburg. He was the greatest supporter of the pope in Germany during the investiture controversy. *Cf. Att. — Baud. — Holw. — Zimm.*

EBERHARD of EINSIEDELN (Bl) Ab. O.S.B. A.C. Aug. 14
d. 958. Of the ducal family of Swabia. He was already provost of the cathedral chapter at Strasburg when, in 934, he joined his friend Bl Benno at Einsiedeln. After Bl Benno's death he was acknowledged as the first abbot of Einsiedeln. It was during his abbacy that, according to

the legend, the abbey church was consecrated by our Lord, assisted by the four evangelists, St Peter and St Gregory the Great. *Cf. Att. — Baud. — Chev.*

EBONTIUS (PONTIUS, PONCE, EBON) (St) Bp. O.S.B. P.C. Oct. 3
d. 1104. Born at Comminges, Haute Garonne, France, and a Benedictine of Sainte-Foi of Tomières, he became abbot of St Victorian (Asán), near Ainsa, in Upper Aragon, and first bishop of Barbastro after its recapture from the Moors. It is doubtful, however, whether the fact of his cultus can be proved. *Cf. P. de U. — Baud.*

EBREGESILUS (St) Bp. M.
R.M. Oct. 24
Otherwise Evergislus, q.v.

EBRULFUS (EVROULT) (St) Ab.
A.C. July 25
d. c.600. Born at Beauvais in France, he became a hermit and afterwards abbot-founder of Saint-Fuscien-aux-Bois. *Cf. Chev. — Zimm. — Baud.*

EBRULFUS (EVROULT) (St) Ab.
R.M. Dec. 29
517-596. A native of Bayeux in Normandy, he became a courtier at the palace of King Childebert I. He left the court to become a monk at the abbey of Deux Jumeaux, diocese of Bayeux, and later the abbot-founder of Ouche and of other smaller houses. *Cf. Att. — Baud. — Holw. — Chev.*

EBSDORF (Martyrs of) (SS) A.C. Feb. 2
d. 880. In the winter of 880 Duke St Bruno led the army of King Louis III against the invading Northmen. On the marshy heath of Luneburg, at Ebsdorf, in Saxony, the army was caught in ice and snow and defeated by the Northmen. Bruno, with two bishops, eleven noblemen, and many others were slain and forthwith venerated as martyrs. *Cf. Att. — Holw.*

ECCLESIUS (St) Bp. A.C. July 27
d. 532. Bishop of Ravenna from 521 till 532. He began the building of San Vitale, at Ravenna, where there is a figure of him in mosaic. *Cf. Menzies.*

ECHA (ETHA)(St) H. O.S.B. A.C. May 5
d. 767. An Anglo-Saxon priest and monk-hermit at Crayk, near York.
Cf. Zimm. — Stanton — Holw.

EDAN (St) Bp. A.C. Jan. 31
Otherwise Aedan, q.v.

EDANA (ETAOIN) (St) V. A.C. July 5
? An Irish saint, patron of parishes in W. Ireland. A famous holy well bears her name. She appears to have lived near the confluence of the rivers Boyle and Shannon. Some have thought her to be one and the same with St Modwenna, who is also commemorated on July 5.
Cf. Holw.

EDBERT (St) Bp. R.M. May 6
Otherwise Eadbert, q.v.

EDBERT (St) King, O.S.B. A.C. Aug. 20
d. 768. The successor of St Ceolwulph on the throne of Northumbria. After a properous reign of twenty years, he resigned and retired to the abbey of York, where he spent a further ten years in prayer and seclusion.
Cf. Stanton — Baud. — Holw.

EDBURGA (several)
Note. The name is spelt in many different ways: Iderberga, Edberga, Eadburga, Ideberga, Idaberga, etc.

EDBURGA of WINCHESTER (St) Abs. O.S.B. A.C. June 15
d. 960. Daughter of Edward the Elder, granddaughter of Alfred the Great, she was placed as a child in the nunnery which King Alfred's widow had founded at Winchester, of which she herself later became abbess. Her shrine at Pershore in Worcestershire was famous for its miracles.
Cf. Mab. — Att. — Chev. — Stanton.

EDBURGA of CAISTOR (St) N. O.S.B. A.C. June 20
Late 7th cent. The daughter of the pagan Penda, king of Mercia, a nun at Caistor (Domundcaster) Northamptonshire, whence her relics were transferred to Peterborough and later to Flanders.
Cf. Stanton — Baud. — Holw.

EDBURGA and EDITH (SS) Ns. O.S.B. A.C. July 16
d. c.650. Sisters, Anglo-Saxon princesses, nuns at Ailesbury.
Cf. Zimm. — Stanton — Baud.

EDBURGA of THANET (St) Abs. O.S.B. A.C. Dec. 12
d. 751. Of the royal family of Kent. A disciple of St Mildred, whom she probably succeeded as abbess of Minster-in-Thanet. She was a friend and correspondent of St Boniface, whom she helped with books, altar vestments and other gifts. She had a new church built for her convent at Minster.
Cf. Zimm. — Att. — Baud. — Chev. — Holw.

EDBURGA (St) N. O.S.B. A.C. Dec. 13
7th cent. A nun of Lyminge in Kent.
Cf. Zimm.

EDEYRN (St) H. A.C. Jan. 6
6th cent. The patron saint of a church in Brittany. The legend describes him as a Briton, associating him with King Arthur, and making him end his days as a hermit in Armorica.
Cf. Holw. — Baring-Gould.

EDGAR the PEACEFUL (St) King. P.C. July 8
d. 975. The great friend of St Dunstan, whom he took as his adviser. His reign is marked by a strong religious revival in England. Though he enjoyed a local cultus at Glastonbury, he would not now-a-days be reckoned a likely candidate for canonization.
Cf. Att. — Stanton — Holw.

EDILBURGA (St) V. R.M. July 7
Otherwise Ethelburga, q.v.

EDILTRUDIS (St) V. R.M. June 23
Otherwise Etheldreda, q.v.

EDISTIUS (St) M. R.M. Oct. 12
d. c.303. A martyr of Ravenna under Diocletian.
Cf. Holw. — Menzies.

EDITH of POLESWORTH (St) W. O.S.B. A.C. July 15
d. ?925. There is much confusion as to the identity of this St Edith. She was certainly the widow of a king of Northumbria and died as a nun — probably abbess — of Polesworth in Warwickshire.
Cf. Att. — Stanton — Holw.

EDITH (St) V. O.S.B. A.C. July 18
See Edburga and Edith.

EDITH of WILTON (St) N. O.S.B.
R.M. Sept. 16
961-984. Daughter of King Edgar and of St Wilfrida. Taken to Wilton abbey shortly after birth, she never left it, so that, in the words of the R.M. "she rather knew not this world than forsook it." She was professed before her fifteenth year, her father being present. She declined to accept the government of three abbeys, preferring to remain a simple nun at Wilton. When her father died, she was offered the throne, and refused. She died at the age of twenty-two, St Dunstan assisting her in her last illness.
Cf. Att. — Stanton — Holw.

EDMUND ARROWSMITH (Bl) M. S.J.
A.C. Aug. 28
d. 1628. Born at Haydock, near St Helen's, in Lancashire, of a recusant yeoman family. He was educated at Douai, ordained priest (1612), and sent to the English mission, where he worked from 1613 to 1628, being received into the Society of Jesus in 1623. He was hanged, drawn and quartered at Lancaster, where he exercised his apostolate. Beatified in 1929.
Cf. Att. — Newdigate.

EDMUND RICH (St) Bp. R.M. Nov. 16
1180-1242. Born at Abingdon, he studied at Oxford and Paris, and became professor of philosophy at Oxford (1219-1226), canon of Salisbury, and archbishop of Canterbury (1233). His uncompromising stand in favour of good discipline, monastic observance, and justice in high quarters, brought him into conflict with King Henry III, with several monasteries and with his own chapter. He was moreover opposed by the papal legate. In 1240 he retired to the Cistercian abbey of Pontigny, where, according to the Cistercian tradition, he lived and died in the Cistercian habit. Canonized in 1246.
Cf. Att. — Chev. — Zimm.

EDMUND (St) King M. R.M. Nov. 20
849-870. King of the East Angles from 855. In the Danish inroad of 870 he was taken prisoner and savagely done to death at Hoxne in Suffolk. He expired with the name of Jesus on his lips. His shrine gave its name to the Benedictine abbey and town of Bury St Edmund's.
Cf. Stanton — Att. — Baud. — Holw.

EDMUND CAMPION (Bl) M. S.J.
A.C. Dec. 1
c.1540-1581. "The Pope's Champion." Born in London and educated at Christ's Hospital, he was a brilliant student at Oxford. Reconciled to the Catholic Church, he passed on to Douai and then to Rome, where he joined the Jesuits. Next he worked in Bohemia, and finally, for one year, on the English mission. His extraordinary success caused him to be hunted down relentlessly. He was betrayed, racked and martyred at Tyburn.
Cf. Att. — Newdigate.

EDMUND GENINGS (Bl) M.
A.C. Dec. 10
d. 1591. Born at Lichfield, and a convert from Protestantism, he studied and was ordained priest at Reims (1590). He passed on to the English mission and was condemned to death for his priesthood the following year. He was hanged, drawn and quartered at Gray's Inn Fields, London. Beatified in 1929.
Cf. Newdigate.

EDWARD the CONFESSOR (St) King
R.M. (Jan. 5 and) Oct. 13
1004-1066. Born at Islip, near Oxford, the son of King Ethelred the Unready. He became king of England in 1042. Considerate, just, gentle and unselfish, his reign was one of peace, prosperity and good government. Some of the nobility opposed him, but the commoners were all for "good King Edward." He was much given to prayer, and hunting. In commutation of a vow to go on pilgrimage to Rome he rebuilt Westminster Abbey, where he was buried. He was canonized in 1161, and his relics solemnly enshrined on Oct. 13, 1162, on which day his feast is celebrated throughout Christendom, though the date of his death was Jan. 5.
Cf. Chev. — Att.

EDWARD WATERSON (Bl) M.
A.C. Jan. 7
d. 1593. Born in London and a convert. He studied at Reims and was ordained in 1592. The following year he was executed for his priesthood at Newcastle. Beatified in 1929.
Cf. Newdigate — Camm.

EDWARD STRANSHAM (Bl) M.
A.C. Jan. 21
d. 1586. Born at Oxford, and educated

at St John's College there. He studied for the priesthood at Douai and Reims, was ordained in 1580, and sent to the English mission in 1581. He worked in London and in Oxford. He was condemned for his priesthood and executed at Tyburn. Beatified in 1929.
Cf. Newdigate — Camm.

EDWARD the MARTYR (St) King M. R.M. March 18
d. 979. The son of Edgar the Peaceful, and king of England at the age of thirteen, after his father's death (975). In 979 he was murdered at Wareham in Dorsetshire, at the instigation of his stepmother Elfrida; and he was forthwith popularly acclaimed as a martyr.
Cf. Att. — Stanton — Holw.

EDWARD OLDCORNE (Bl) M. S.J. A.C. Apr. 7
d. 1606. A native of York, he was ordained priest at Rome and received into the Society of Jesus in 1587. He worked in the Midlands from 1588 to 1606, and was condemned to death at Worcester for alleged complicity in the Gunpowder Plot. Beatified in 1929.
Cf. Newdigate — Att.

EDWARD CATHERICK (Bl) M. A.C. Apr. 13
d. 1642. Born at Carlton, near Richmond, Yorks. He was educated at Douai and laboured as a missionary priest in England from 1635 till his death. He was executed for his priesthood at York. Beatified in 1929.
Cf. Newdigate — Camm.

EDWARD JONES (Bl) M. A.C. May 6
d. 1590. Born in the diocese of St Asaph in Wales and a convert. He studied for the priesthood at Reims, and was ordained in 1588. He was captured and executed for his priesthood in Fleet Street. Beatified in 1929.
Cf. Newdigate — Att.

EDWARD FULTHROP (Bl) M. A.C. July 4
d. 1597. A gentleman of Yorkshire executed at York for having been reconciled to the Catholic Church. Beatified in 1929.
Cf. Newdigate — Camm.

EDWARD POWELL (Bl) M. A.C. July 30
d. 1540. A Welshman who became a canon of Salisbury and a fellow of Oriel and was well known in Europe as the author of various treatises against Luther. He was chosen by Queen Catherine of Aragon as one of her counsel. After six years in prison he was hanged, drawn and quartered at Smithfield, London, for denying the king's spiritual supremacy. Beatified in 1886.
Cf. Att. — Newdigate.

EDWARD SHELLEY (Bl) M. A.C. Aug. 30
d. 1588. A gentleman of Warminghurst, Sussex, hanged at Tyburn for harbouring priests. Beatified in 1929.
Cf. Newdigate — Camm.

EDWARD BARLOW (Bl) M. O.S.B. A.C. Sept. 10
Otherwise Ambrose Edward Barlow, q.v.

EDWARD JAMES (Bl) M. A.C. Oct. 1
d. 1588. A native of Breaston, near Derby, and an undergraduate of St John's College, Oxford. After his conversion he studied at Reims and Rome. Ordained priest in 1583, he was condemned and executed at Chichester for his priesthood. Beatified in 1929.
Cf. Newdigate — Camm.

EDWARD CAMPION (Bl) M. A.C. Oct. 1
d. 1588. Born at Ludlow in Shropshire, he studied at Jesus College, Oxford. After his conversion he was trained for the priesthood at Reims and ordained in 1587. He was condemned for his priesthood and executed at Canterbury. Beatified in 1929.
Newdigate — Camm.

EDWARD COLEMAN (Bl) M. A.C. Dec. 3
d. 1678. A gentleman of Suffolk, educated at Peterhouse, Cambridge, and a convert to the Catholic Faith. He was secretary to the duchess of York, and was executed at Tyburn on a false charge of conspiring with a foreign power to restore the Catholic Church in England. He was the first victim of the "Titus Oates Plot." Beatified in 1929.
Cf. Newdigate — Camm.

EDWEN (St) V.   **A.C. Nov. 6**
7th cent. The alleged patron saint of
Llanedwen, Anglesey. She is described as
having been a daughter of King Edwin of
Northumberland.
Cf. Holw. — Baring-Gould.

EDWIN (St) King M.   **A.C. Oct. 12**
d. 633. King of Northumbria from 616.
He married as his second wife Ethelburga
of Kent and was baptized by her chaplain
St Paulinus (627). He fell in battle at
Hatfield Chase fighting against the pagan
Mercians and Welsh. Hence he was ven-
erated as a martyr.
Cf. Stanton — Holw. — Att.

EDWOLD (St) C.   **A.C. Nov. 27**
9th cent. Brother of St Edmund the
Martyr, king of East Anglia. He lived as
a recluse at Carne in Dorsetshire.
Cf. Holw. — Stanton.

EFFLAM (St) C.   **A.C. Nov. 6**
d. c.700. Son of a British prince who,
crossing to France, became abbot of a
monastery he had founded in Brittany.
Cf. Baud. — Holw. — Baring-Gould.

EGBERT (St) Mk. O.S.B. A.C. March 18
d. c.720. Monk, probably of Ripon,
where his relics were venerated from about
the year 1000.
Cf. Zimm.

EGBERT (St) Mk. O.S.B. R.M. Apr. 24
d. 729. An English monk of Lindisfarne
who migrated to Ireland and lived at
Rathelmigisi in Connaught. Here he
trained several bands of monks for the
German mission. He passed over to Iona
to induce the monks to adopt the Roman
usages. He succeeded at last: in fact on
the day of his death Easter was for the first
time celebrated at Iona according to the
Roman reckoning.
Cf. Att. — Stanton.

EGDUNUS and Comp. (SS) MM.
     R.M. March 12
d. 303. Martyrs at Nicomedia under
Diocletian. They were eight in number:
they were suspended head downwards
over a fire and suffocated by its smoke.
Cf. Holw. — Baud.

EGELNOTH (St) Bp. O.S.B. A.C. Oct. 30
d. 1038. Surnamed "the Good." Monk

of Glastonbury, and archbishop of Canterbury from 1020 till his death.
Cf. Mab. — Baud. — Holw. — Stanton.

EGELRED (St) M. O.S.B. A.C. Sept. 25
d. c.870. A monk-martyr of Croyland
Abbey, put to death with his abbot and
many others of the community by the
heathen Danes.
Cf. Baud. — Holw.

EGELWINE (St) C.   **A.C. Nov. 26**
7th cent. A prince of the house of Wessex who lived at Athelney in Somersetshire.
Cf. Stanton — Holw.

EGIDIUS (St) Ab.   **R.M. Sept. 1**
Otherwise Giles, q.v.

EGILHARD (St) M. O.S.B. P.C. May 25
d. 881. The eighth abbot of Cornelimünster, near Aix-la-Chapelle. He was
killed by the Normans at Bercheim.
Cf. Holw.

EGILO (EGILON, EIGIL) (St) Ab. O.S.B.
     A.C. June 28
d. 871. Monk of Prüm, near Trèves, and
then abbot there. As abbot he gave the
habit to St Humphrey at Prüm. In 860
the emperor Charles the Bald directed him
to restore Flavigny, in the diocese of Dijon.
Later on he founded the abbey of Corbigny, Yonne.
Cf. Butler-Thurston, in the life of St Humphrey, March 8 — Holw.

EGINO (EGON) (St) Ab. O.S.B.
     P.C. July 15
d. 1122. Born at Augsburg and received
as a child-oblate at the abbey of SS Ulric
and Afra in the same city. In the conflict
between the pope and the emperor he sided
with the former, and was for this reason
expelled by his abbot, being welcomed at
the abbey of St Blasien (Blaise). In 1106
he was recalled to Augsburg and appointed
abbot in 1109. He had to suffer much at
the hands of the simoniacal bishop Heri-
mann and to flee to Rome in 1120. On
his return home he died at Pisa in the monastery of his Camaldolese brethren.
Cf. Chev. — Holw.

EGWIN (St) Bp. O.S.B.   **A.C. Dec. 30**
d. 717. Consecrated to God in his youth,
he eventually became the third bishop of

Worcester (692) and the founder of the abbey of Evesham. Twice he made the pilgrimage to Rome; once, indeed, to appeal to the pope against some of his flock, whose enmity he had incurred for his severity against vice.
Cf. Att. — Baud. — Holw. — P. de U. — Zimm.

EGYPT (Martyrs and Confessors of) (SS) The R.M. lists two groups of anonymous martyrs and confessors of Egypt, as follows: **R.M. Jan. 5** d. 303. "In Egypt the commemoration of many holy martyrs, who were slain in the Thebaid . . . under Diocletian." **R.M. May 21** d. c.357.: "At Alexandria, the memory of the holy bishops and priests who were sent into exile by the Arians, and merited to be joined to the holy confessors."

EIGIL (AEIGILUS) (St) Ab. O.S.B. **A.C. Dec. 17** d. 822. A monk of Fulda, he became abbot in 817, succeeding Rutgar, who had been deposed by Charlemagne on account of excessive and imprudent severity. Eigil restored peace and union among the large community and had the consolation of paving the way for the abbacy of his great successor St Rhabanus Maurus.
Cf. Chev. — Baud. — P. de U. — Zimm.

EIGRAD (St) C. **A.C. June 6** 6th cent. A brother of St Sampson of York, trained by St Illtyd, and founder of a church in Anglesey.
Cf. Holw. — Baring-Gould.

EILAN (St) C. **A.C. Jan. 12** Otherwise Elian, q.v.

EINGAN (EINION, ENEON, ANIANUS) (St) H. **A.C. Feb. 9** 6th cent. A British prince who came from Cumberland into Wales and finished his days as a hermit at Llanengan near Bangor. He is said to have been a son of the chieftain Cunedda, whose family claims no less than fifty saints.
Cf. Holw. — Baring-Gould.

EINHILDIS and ROSWINDA (SS) Ns. O.S.B. **A.C. Dec. 13** 8th cent. Nuns of Hohenburg under St Odilia. St Roswinda seems to have been St Odilia's sister. St Einhildis became

abbess of Niedermünster near Hohenburg.
Cf. Zimm. — Holw.

EKBERT (EGBERT) (Bl) Ab. O.S.B. **A.C. Nov. 25** d. 1075. Monk of Gorze and afterwards abbot of Münsterschwarzach in Bavaria.
Cf. Zimm.

EKHARD (Bl) Ab. O.S.B. **A.C. June 28** d. 1084. Canon of the cathedral of Magdeburg and first abbot of Huysburg.
Cf. Zimm.

ELAETH the KING (St) **A.C. Nov. 10** 6th cent. A Briton from the North driven into Wales by the Picts. He became a monk under St Seiriol in Anglesey. Some poems of his are still extant.
Cf. Holw. — Baring-Gould.

ELAPHIUS (St) Bp. **A.C. Aug. 19** d. 580. Bishop of Châlons-sur-Marne. He died on his return home from a pilgrimage to St Eulalia's shrine at Merida, in Spain.
Cf. Duch. Fast. Episc. — Gams — Baud.— Holw.

ELDATE (ELDAD) (St) C. **A.C. Feb. 4** Otherwise Aldate, q.v.

ELDRAD (St) Ab. O.S.B. **A.C. March 13** Otherwise Heldrad, q.v.

ELEAZAR (St) M. **R.M. Aug. 1** See Machabees.

ELEAZAR (St) M. **R.M. Aug. 23** See Minervus, Eleazar, etc.

ELEAZAR (St) C. **R.M. Sept. 27** Otherwise Elzear, q.v.

ELERIUS (St) C. **A.C. Nov. 3** 6th cent. A Welsh saint, mentioned in the legends concerning St Winifred. He is supposed to have presided over a monastery in N. Wales.
Cf. Holw.

ELESBAAN (St) King **R.M. Oct. 27** d. c.555. Called by the Abyssinians Calam-Negus. He was a Christian king of Ethiopia, who successfully fought the Jewish usurper Dhu-newas, a persecutor of Christianity. After an eventful reign, during which he showed more than once

his cruel and revengeful disposition, he died as an exemplary monk at Jerusalem. It seems, however, that he always remained a Monophysite.
Cf. Att. — Holw. — Baud.

ELESMES (St) Ab. O.S.B.   A.C. Jan. 30
Otherwise Adelelmus, q.v.

ELEUCHADIUS (St) Bp.   R.M. Feb. 14
d. 112. A Greek by origin, he was converted by St Apollinaris of Ravenna, and in his absence he governed the church there, together with other priests and deacons. In 100 he was himself chosen bishop of Ravenna.
Cf. Holw. — Baud. — Gams.

ELEUSIPPUS (St) M.   R.M. Jan. 17
See Speusippus, Eleusippus, etc.

ELEUTHERIUS (St) Bp. M.
                                    R.M. Feb. 20
d. c. 310. Said to have been bishop of Byzantium and a martyr. Most writers, after the Bollandists, identify him with St Eleutherius commemorated on Aug. 4, q.v.

ELEUTHERIUS of TOURNAI (St) Bp. M.
                                    R.M. Feb. 20
d. 532. A native of Tournai, bishop of that city from 486, who evangelized the Franks then settled in and near Tournai and died from wounds inflicted by the Arian heretics of that district.
Cf. Att. — Baud. — Holw.

ELEUTHERIUS and ANTHIA (SS) MM.
                                    R.M. Apr. 18
d. 117-138. Eleutherius, a bishop of Illyria, his mother Anthia and eleven others, are said to have been martyred in Illyria under the emperor Hadrian. The whole story has been proved to be merely a pious romance of Greek origin.
Cf. Att. — Baud. — Holw.

ELEUTHERIUS (St) Pope, M.
                                    R.M. May 26
d. 189. A Greek by origin who became a deacon of the Roman Church. He succeeded St Soter as pope in 175. Very little is known about him. The story of his sending missionaries to Briton is abandoned by most modern scholars.
Cf. Att. — Baud. — Holw.

ELEUTHERIUS (St) C.   R.M. May 29
? An English pilgrim, said to have been the brother of SS Grimwald and Fulk, who died at Rocca d'Arce, near Aquino, in S. Italy. He is venerated there as principal patron saint.
Cf. Holw. — Baud. — Stanton.

ELEUTHERIUS (St) M.   R.M. Aug. 4
d. c.310. Chamberlain to the emperor Maximian Galerius at Constantinople. On becoming a Christian he retired to Bithynia, where he was arrested and beheaded.
Cf. Baud. — Holw.

ELEUTHERIUS and LEONIDES (SS) MM.   R.M. Aug. 8
? Martyrs burnt to death at Constantinople.
Cf. Baud. — Holw.

ELEUTHERIUS (St) Bp.   R.M. Aug. 16
d. 561. Bishop of Auxerre, 532-561.
Cf. Holw. — Gams.

ELEUTHERIUS (St) Ab. O.S.B.
                                    R.M. Sept. 6
d. c.590. Mentioned several times by St Gregory the Great as a well-known wonder-worker. He was abbot of St Mark at Spoleto, whence he migrated to St Gregory's own abbey in Rome, where he lived for many years as a simple monk.
Cf. Att. — Baud. — Chev. — Holw. — Zimm.

ELEUTHERIUS and Comp. (SS) MM.   R.M. Oct. 2
d. c.303. A soldier-martyr of Nicomedia under Diocletian. The story told in the R.M. is wholly untrustworthy.
Cf. Att. — Baud. — Holw.

ELEUTHERIUS (St) M.   R.M. Oct. 9
See Dionysius, Rusticus and Eleutherius.

ELEVATHA (St) V.M.   A.C. Aug. 1
Otherwise Almedha, q.v.

ELFLEDA (ETHELFLEDA, EDIL-FLEDA, ELGIVA) (St) Abs. O.S.B.   A.C. Feb. 8
d. 714. Daughter of Oswy, king of Northumbria. She was offered to God as a tiny child at the nunnery of Hartlepool under St Hilda, with whom she migrated to Whitby and whom she succeeded as

abbess there. She was one of the most influential personages of her time and was instrumental in reconciling SS Theodore and Wilfrid.
Cf. Att. — Stanton — Chev.

ELFLEDA (St) N. O.S.B. A.C. Oct. 23
d. c.936. An Anglo-Saxon princess who lived as a recluse at Glastonbury under the obedience of the abbey. She was held in great veneration by St Dunstan.
Cf. Holw. — Baud. — Chev.

ELFLEDA (St) Abs. O.S.B. A.C. Oct. 29
d. c.1000. Daughter of Earl Ethelwold, founder of Ramsey, where she became a nun and eventually abbess.
Cf. Stanton — Chev. — Holw. — Baud.

ELFERDA (St) V. O.S.B. A.C. Aug. 2
Otherwise Etheldritha, q.v.

ELFRIC (St) Bp. O.S.B. A.C. Nov. 16
Otherwise Alfrick, q.v.

ELGAR (St) H. A.C. June 14
d. c.1100. Born in Devonshire. After some years of captivity in Ireland, he settled as a hermit in the isle of Bardsey off the coast of Carnarvon.
Cf. Holw. — Stanton.

ELGIVA (St) W. O.S.B. A.C. May 18
d. 971. The mother of Kings Edwy and Edgar, and wife of King Edmund. On the death of her husband she retired to the nunnery at Shaftesbury where she ended her days.
Cf. Stanton — Holw.

ELIAN (EILAN, ALLAN) (St) H.
A.C. Jan. 13
6th cent. A Cornish or Breton saint of the family of St Ismael. He has given his name to Llanelian in Anglesey and Llanelian in Denbighshire and was titular of St Allen's church in Cornwall. His name is often confused with that of St Hilary.
Cf. Holw. — Baring-Gould.

ELIAN ap ERBIN (St) C. A.C. Jan. 13
? 5th cent. This name appears in some Welsh calendars.
Cf. Stanton.

ELIAS, JEREMIAS, ISAIAS, SAMUEL and DANIEL (SS) MM. R.M. Feb. 16
d. 309. Five Egyptians who on their return journey from visiting some of their fellow-Christians, condemned to the mines

of Cilicia, were themselves arrested at Caesarea in Palestine and beheaded. The graphic account of their martyrdom is given by Eusebius who at that time was living at Caesarea.
Cf. Att. — Holw. — Baud.

ELIAS (Bl) Ab. O.S.B. A.C. Apr. 16
d. 1042. An Irishman who became monk and abbot (1020) of the Scottish abbey of St Martin the Great at Cologne. The archbishop placed also under his care the abbey of St Pantaleon.
Cf. Zimm. — Chev.

ELIAS, PAUL and ISIDORE (SS) MM.
R.M. Apr. 17
d. 856. Elias, a priest of Cordova, was put to death by the Moors in his old age together with SS Paul and Isidore, two young men under his spiritual direction. St Eulogius, an eye-witness, has left us an account of their martyrdom.
Cf. Holw. — Baud.

ELIAS of BOURDEILLES (Bl) Bp O.F.M. P.C. July 5
1407-1484. Born in Périgord, of the family of the counts of Bourdeilles, he took the Franciscan habit at the age of ten. He was successively bishop of Périgueux (1437), archbishop of Tours (1468) and cardinal (1483), being also confessor of King Louis XI. He is best known in history for his written defence of St Joan of Arc. The process of his beatification was begun in 1526, but never finished.
Cf. Att. — Holw.

ELIAS (ELIJAH) (St) Prophet.
R.M. July 20
9th cent. B.C. The great prophet of the Old Law, the account of whose eventful life is given in III and IV Kings. His association with Mt Carmel is also to be found there. The Carmelite Order liturgically commemorates this great prophet as its principal patron saint.
Cf. Att. — Baud. — Holw.

ELIAS OF JERUSALEM (St) Bp.
R.M. July 20
See Flavian and Elias.

ELIAS (St) Bp. O.S.B. A.C. Aug. 26
d. 660. A Benedictine monk of Sicily, who died bishop of Syracuse.
Cf. Gams.

ELIAS (St) Bp. M.   **R.M. Sept. 19**
See Peleus, Nilus and Elias.

ELIGIUS (ELOI, ELOY) (St) Bp.
R.M. Dec. 1
588-660. A native of Limoges, he became a very skilful metal-smith, and was appointed master of the mint at Paris under King Clotaire II. In 640 he abandoned this office to become a priest and soon after was consecrated bishop of Noyon. He evangelized the districts round Antwerp, Ghent and Courtrai, founded Solignac Abbey and many other monasteries and convents. He was one of the most lovable of saints and most "popular" throughout the Middle Ages.
Cf. Att. — Baud.

ELINED (St) V.M.   **A.C. Aug. 1**
Otherwise Almedha, q.v. The name is also written Ellyw, and the saint is probably the one whose memory is perpetuated in the Welsh place-names of Llanelly and Llanelieu, besides perhaps the Breton Lanhelen.

ELIPHIUS (ELOFF) (St) M. R.M. Oct. 16
d. 362. An Irishman — or Scot — by birth, who suffered at Toul in France under Julian the Apostate. His relics were translated in the 10th century to Cologne.
Cf. Baud. — Holw.

ELISABETH BARTHOLOMEA PICE-NARDI (Bl) V. O.S.M.   **A.C. Feb. 20**
1428-1468. Born at Mantua in Italy. After her mother's death she joined the third young order of the Servites. Several young girls banded themselves together to live in community under her direction. Beatified in 1804.
Cf. Att. — Baud. — Holw.

ELISABETH SALVIATI (Bl) Abs. O.S.B.
Cam.   **A.C. Feb. 11**
d. 1519. Camaldolese nun and abbess of the convent of San Giovanni Evangelista at Boldrone. Pope Urban VIII allowed pictures of her with the title of *beata* underneath to be printed in Rome.
Cf. Zimm.

ELISABETH of PORTUGAL (St) Queen,
Tert. O.F.M.   **R.M. July 8**
1271-1336. Born in Aragon, Spain, Isabel was the daughter of King Peter III of that kingdom, and was married at twelve years of age to the dissolute and selfish King Denis of Portugal. She distinguished herself as a peace-maker between the kings of Portugal, Castile and Aragon. After the death of her husband she retired to a Poor Clare convent as a tertiary. She was canonized in 1625.
Cf. Att. — Baud. — Holw.

ELISABETH of SCHÖNAU (St) Abs.
O.S.B.   **R.M. June 18**
1126-1164. At the age of twelve she entered the Black Benedictine — not the Cistercian — convent of Schönau, about sixteen miles N.E. of Bonn. She was professed in 1147, and shortly after she became subject to extraordinary supernatural manifestations. In 1157 she was made abbess of Schönau. Her brother Egbert, who governed the Benedictine monks at the same place, wrote her life.
Cf. Att. — Baud. — P. de U. — Zimm.

ELISABETH (St) W.   **R.M. Nov. 5**
1st cent. The mother of St John the Baptist. All that we know about her is limited to what we find in the first chapter of St Luke's Gospel.

ELISEUS (ELISHA) (St) Prophet
R.M. June 14
8th cent. B.C. The holy man on whom fell the mantle of Elias, and who continued the work of that great prophet, as is described in IV Kings. The feast of St Eliseus is liturgically observed in the Carmelite Order, and also generally in the East.
Cf. Holw. — Baud.

ELIZABETH of HUNGARY (St) Queen,
Tert. O.F.M.   **R.M. Nov. 19**
1207-1231. Born at Presburg, the daughter of King Andrew II of Hungary and a niece of St Hedwig. At the age of fourteen she was married to Louis IV, landgrave of Thuringia, and bore him three children. Hers was a very happy married life until 1227 when her husband went to the crusade and died at Otranto. She now became a Franciscan tertiary and devoted herself to the relief of the destitute, living a life of voluntary poverty until her death at twenty-four. She was canonized three years later (1235).
Cf. Att. — Holw.

ELIZABETH the GOOD (Bl) V. Tert. O.F.M. A.C. Nov. 25
1386-1420. Born at Waldsee in Würtemberg, she lived her whole life in a small community of Franciscan tertiaries close by. She was subject to mystical experiences including the stigmata, and went for long periods without any natural food. Cult confirmed in 1766.
Cf. Att. — Holw.

ELIZABETH-ROSE (St) Abs. O.S.B. A.C. Dec. 13
d. 1130. A nun of Chelles near Paris, and afterwards abbess-foundress of the nunnery of Sainte-Marie-du-Rozoy, near Courtenay, Loiret.
Cf. Baud. — Holw.

ELLIDIUS (ILLOG) (St) C. A.C. Aug. 8
7th cent. Patron saint, it would appear, of Hirnant (Montgomery), and of a church in the Scilly Isles.
Cf. Baring-Gould.

ELLYN (St) V.M. A.C. Aug. 1
Otherwise Almedha, q.v.

ELMO (Bl) C. A.C. Apr. 15
Otherwise Peter Gonzalez, q.v. But the name Elmo usually stands for an abbreviation of that of St Erasmus (June 2).

ELOFF (ELOPHIUS) (St) M. R.M. Oct. 16
Otherwise Eliphius, q.v.

ELOI (St) Bp. R.M. Dec. 1
Otherwise Eligius, q.v.

ELOQUIUS (ELOQUE) (St) Ab. O.S.B. A.C. Dec. 3
d. p. 665. Disciple and successor of St Fursey as abbot of Lagny (Latiniacensis).
Cf. Zimm. — Chev.

ELPHEGE the ELDER (St) Bp. O.S.B. A.C. March 12
d. 951. Also surnamed "the Bald," probably on account of his monastic tonsure. From being a monk he was raised to the see of Winchester (935). He induced many to become monks, notably his young kinsman St Dunstan, whom he ordained priest. St Ethelwold too received the priesthood from St Elphege.
Cf. Att. — Stanton — Zimm. — Holw.

ELPHEGE the MARTYR (St) Bp. O.S.B. R.M. Apr. 19
954-1012. A Benedictine of Deerhurst abbey in Gloucestershire, then abbot of a monastery near Bath, he was raised to the see of Winchester in 984, and to that of Canterbury in 1006. He was greatly loved by his flock, and during the Danish invasion of 1011 he was urged to escape. He declined, and was taken prisoner and put to death at Greenwich for refusing to ransom himself with the money of the poor.
Cf. Att. — Zimm. — Stanton — Baud. — Chev.

ELPIDEPHORUS (St) M. R.M. Nov. 2
See Acindynus, Pegasius, etc.

ELPIDIUS (St) Bp. M. R.M. March 4
See Basil, Eugene, etc.

ELPIDIUS (St) M. R.M. Sept. 1
See Priscus, Castrensis, etc.

ELPIDIUS (St) Ab. R.M. Sept. 2
4th cent. A hermit in Cappadocia who lived for twenty-five years in a cave and gathered round him numerous disciples. His relics were brought to a village in the Marches of Ancona, now called Sant' Elpidio. His emblem in art is a vine in leaf in winter.
Cf. Menzies — Holw. — Baud.

ELPIDIUS (St) Bp. R.M. Sept. 2
d. 422. The successor of St Antiochus in the see of Lyons. His relics were enshrined in the church of St Justus.
Cf. Duch. Fast. Episc. — Gams — Baud.

ELPIDIUS, MARCELLUS, EUSTACHIUS, and Comp. (SS) MM. R.M. Nov. 16
d. 362. Elpidius, a dignitary at the court of the emperor Constantius, was degraded by Julian the Apostate and, with several companions, dragged at the tail of wild horses. Finally they were burnt at the stake.
Cf. Baud. — Holw.

ELPIS (St) V.M. R.M. Aug. 1
See Faith, Hope (Elpis) and Charity.

ELRIC (St) Bp. A.C. Jan. 7
Otherwise Aldericus, q.v.

ELSIAR (St) Mk. O.S.B.　　A.C. June 4
d. c.1050. A Benedictine of the abbey of
Saint-Savin in Lavedan.
Cf. Zimm. — Chev. — Holw.

ELSTAN (St) Bp. O.S.B.　　A.C. Apr. 6
d. 981. Monk of Abingdon under St
Ethelwold, celebrated as a model of blind
obedience. He succeeded St Ethelwold
both as abbot of Abingdon and bishop of
Winchester.
Cf. Att. — Stanton — Holw.

ELVAN and MYDWYN (SS)
　　　　　　　　　　　A.C. Jan. 1
2nd cent. Said to have been the two
Britons sent by King St Lucius to Pope
St Eleutherius to beg for missionaries to
be sent to Britain (see St Eleutherius,
pope).
Cf. Holw. — Baring-Gould.

ELVIS (St) C.　　　　　A.C. Feb. 22
Otherwise Elwyn, or Alleyn, or Allan, or
Elian. See below under Elwin.

ELWIN (St) C.　　　　　A.C. Feb. 22
6th cent. Said to have been one of the
holy men who accompanied St Breaca
from Ireland to Cornwall, and perhaps the
title saint of St Allen's church in that
country. But the traditions are very
perplexing.
Cf. Holw. — Baring-Gould.

ELZEAR (ELEAZARUS) (St) C.
　　　　　　　　　　R.M. Sept. 27
1285-1323. A native of Provence, where
he inherited the barony of Ansuis as well
as the county of Ariano in the kingdom of
Naples. Married to St Delphina of
Glandèves, he was the perfect type of
Christian gentleman. He went to Naples
as tutor to Prince Charles and as ambassador, and was for a time regent of the
kingdom. According to an old tradition
both he and his wife were Franciscan
tertiaries. His wife was present at his
canonization in 1369.
Cf. Att. — Baud. — Holw.

EMEBERT (ABLEBERT) (St) Bp.
　　　　　　　　　　A.C. Jan. 15
d. c.710. Said to have been a brother of
SS Rainaldes and Gudula. He was bishop
of Cambrai in Flanders.
Cf. Att. — Baud. — Holw.

EMERENTIANA (St) V. M.
　　　　　　　　　　R.M. Jan. 23
d. 304. According to legend, Emerentiana, the foster-sister of St Agnes, while
as yet only a catechumen, was discovered
by the pagan mob praying at the tomb of
the recently martyred St Agnes, and was
stoned to death. In point of fact St
Emerentiana is a Roman martyr of unknown date.
Cf. Att. — Baud. — Holw.

EMERIC (Bl) Bp.　　　　A.C. Aug. 1
d. 1318. Bishop of Aosta (1301-1318).
Cult approved in 1881.
Cf. Holw. — Baud.

EMERIC (St) C.　　　　R.M. Nov. 4
1007-1031. Son of St Stephen, the first
Christian king of Hungary. He was educated by St Gerard of Czanad and gave
promise of being a model king, but died
before inheriting the crown. He was
canonized with his father in 1083.
Cf. Att. — Baud. — Holw.

EMERITA (St) V. M.　　R.M. Sept. 22
See Digna and Emerita.

EMERITUS (St) M.　　　R.M. Feb. 11
See Saturninus and Comp.

EMERIUS (St) Ab. O.S.B.　A.C. Jan. 27
8th cent. A Frenchman by birth, he
founded, and ruled as first abbot, the
Benedictine abbey of St Stephen of
Bañoles, near Gerona, in Spanish Catalonia.
Cf. P. de U. — Chev. — Baud. — Holw.

EMETERIUS (St) M.　　R.M. March 3
Otherwise Hemiterius, q.v.

EMIDIUS (St) Bp. M.　　R.M. Aug. 5
Otherwise Emygius, q.v.

EMILAS and JEREMIAS (SS) MM.
　　　　　　　　　　R.M. Sept. 15
d. 852. Two Spanish youths, of whom the
former was a deacon, imprisoned and beheaded at Cordova under the caliph
Abderrahman.
Cf. Baud. — Holw.

EMILIAN (AEMILIO) (St) Mk. O.S.B.
　　　　　　　　　　A.C. Jan. 7
d. 767. A native of Vannes, and a monk
of Saujon, near Saintes, he died as a re-

cluse in the forest of Combes, Bordeaux.
Cf. Zimm. — Baud. — Holw. — Chev.

EMILIAN (St) M.   **R.M. Feb. 8**
See Dionysius and Aemilian.

EMILIAN (or EMINIAN) (St) Ab. O.S.B.
                              A.C. March 10
d. 675. An Irishman, who became a
monk, and then abbot, of Lagny in France.
Cf. Zimm. — Chev.

EMILIAN (St) M.   **R.M. Apr. 29**
See Agapius and Comp.

EMILIAN (St) M.   **R.M. July 18**
d. 362. A martyr of Silistria in Bulgaria
under Julian the Apostate.
Cf. Baud. — Holw.

EMILIAN (St) Bp.   **R.M. Aug. 8**
d. c.820. A bishop of Cyzicus, an island
off the southern shore of the sea of Mar-
mora. He died in exile for his firm stand
against the Iconoclasts.
Cf. Baud. — Holw.

EMILIAN (St) Bp.   **R.M. Sept. 11**
d. 520. A N. Italian hermit, who after
forty years as a recluse, was raised to the
see of Vercelli in Piedmont, where he died
a centenarian.
Cf. Baud. — Holw. — Menzies.

EMILIAN (St) C.   **R.M. Oct. 11**
? According to the R.M. he was a hermit
at Rennes in Brittany. No saint of this
name can be found in the Breton records.
Possibly he has been confused with St
Melanius, bishop of Rennes (d. 567).
Cf. Bolland. — Baud. — Holw.

EMILIAN (St) Ab.   **R.M. Nov. 12**
d. 574. A poor shepherd in La Rioja, in
the old kingdom of Spanish Navarre.
He became a hermit and eventually was
ordained priest by his bishop (of Tarazona) who put him in charge of the parish
of Berceo. The saint, however, returned
to his solitude and there gradually he
gathered round him a large number of
disciples of whom he became the abbot.
This gave rise to the great abbey of La
Cogolla, which afterwards adopted the
Benedictine Rule. On this account the
saint is described to this day in the "Spanish proper" of his office as the first Spanish Benedictine. He is a minor patron

saint of Spain, where he is known as San
Millan de la Cogolla — the cowled St
Emilian. In art he is usually represented
on horseback fighting the Moors.
*Cf. Mab. — Baud. — Chev. — Att. — P.
de U. — Zimm.*

EMILIAN (St) M.   **R.M. Dec. 6**
See Dionysia and Comp.

EMILIANA (St) V.   **R.M. Jan. 5**
6th cent. A Roman lady, and the paternal aunt of St Gregory the Great, from
whom we know of her saintly life, visions
and death.
Cf. Holw. — Baud.

EMILIANA (St) M.   **R.M. June 30**
? She is stated to have been a Roman
maiden who died a martyr.
Cf. Holw.

EMILIUS (St) M.   **R.M. May 22**
See Castus and Aemilius.

**EMILIUS, FELIX, PRIAM and LUCIAN
(SS) MM.**   **R.M. May 28**
? Churches are dedicated to these saints
in Sardinia; otherwise nothing is known
concerning them.
Cf. Chev. — Holw.

EMILIUS (St) M.   **R.M. Oct. 6**
See Marcellus, Castus, etc.

EMILY BICCHIERI (Bl) V. O.P.
                              A.C. Aug. 19
1238-1314. A native of Vercelli, who induced her father to build a convent, where
she professed the Dominican rule. She
was a great success as the first prioress of
the convent. Cult confirmed in 1769.
Cf. Att. — Baud. — Holw.

EMILY de RODAT (Bl) Foundress
                              A.C. Sept. 19
1787-1852. A native of Château Druelles,
near Rodez, in southern central France.
In 1816, under the direction of Mgr Marty,
later vicar general of Rodez, she started a
new teaching institute which has since
developed into the present-day Religious
Congregation of the Holy Family of Ville-
franche with houses throughout the world.
Beatified in 1940.

EMMA (several)
Otherwise Hemma, q.v.

EMMANUEL (*several*)

Note. A popular name in the Latin countries: Emmanuele in Italian; Manuel in Spanish, Portuguese and Catalan.

EMMANUEL (Bl) **Bp.**   **A.C. Feb. 27**
d. 1198. Bishop of Cremona (1190-1195). Some writers make him a Cistercian monk of Adwerth, in Frisia, before his episcopate; but Adwerth was only founded in 1192. In 1195 Bl Emmanuel indeed retired to Adwerth, where he died, possibly in the Cistercian habit.
Cf. Zimm. — Gams — Chev. — Baud. — Holw.

EMMANUEL (St) **M.   R.M. March 26**
See Quadratus, Theodosius and Emmanuel.

EMMANUEL RUIZ and Comp. (BB)
MM.   **A.C. July 10**
d. 1860. During the rising of the Druses against the Christians in the Lebanon, the Franciscan community of Damascus, eight in all, and three Maronite laymen, were offered the alternative of accepting Islam or death; they refused the former and were slain in their own friary. The guardian of the friary was Bl Emmanuel Ruiz, a Spaniard, and most of the other Friars were likewise Spaniards. Beatified in 1926.
Cf. Att.

EMMANUEL ÁLVAREZ (Bl) **M. S.J.**
                              A.C. July 15
d. 1570. A Jesuit lay-brother, companion of Bl Ignatius de Azevedo, q.v.

EMMANUEL FERNÁNDEZ (Bl) **M. S.J.**
                              A.C. July 15
d. 1570. A native of Celorico, diocese of Cuarda, Portugal, and a Jesuit cleric, companion of Bl Ignatius de Azevedo, q.v.

EMMANUEL PACHECO (Bl) **M. S.J.**
                              A.C. July 15
d. 1570. A native of Zeita, in Portugal, and a Jesuit novice, companion of Bl Ignatius de Azevedo, q.v.

EMMANUEL RODRÍGUEZ (Bl) **M. S.J.**
                              A.C. July 15
d. 1570. A native of Alconchel, Portugal, and a Jesuit cleric, companion of Bl Ignatius de Azevedo, q.v.

EMMANUEL PHUNG (Bl) **M.**
                              A.C. July 31
c. 1796-1859. Born at Dan-nuoc, in Cochin China, he worked as a catechist, and was for this reason garrotted near Chaudoc, in W. Cochin China. Beatified in 1909.
Cf. Holw.

EMMANUEL TRIEU (Bl) **M.**
                              A.C. Sept. 17
c. 1755-1797. Born in Cochin China of Christian parents, he joined the army, but was afterwards ordained priest at Pong-King and worked under the priests of the Foreign Missions of Paris. While visiting his mother he was arrested and beheaded. Beatified in 1900.
Cf. Holw.

EMMELIA (St) **Matron   R.M. May 30**
See Basil and Emmelia.

EMMERAMUS (HAIMHRAMM) (St)
Bp. M. O.S.B.   **R.M. Sept. 22**
d. c.690. A native of Poitiers, he migrated to Bavaria where he became abbot of a monastery at Ratisbon, and then bishop of that city. While on his way to Rome he was attacked by assassins, and died from the injuries received. His relics were enshrined in the great Benedictine abbey dedicated to his name at Ratisbon, where he is venerated as a martyr.
Cf. Att. — Zimm. — Baud.

EMYGDIUS (EMIDIUS) (St) **Bp. M.**
                              R.M. Aug. 5
d. c.303. Said to have been a Teuton who came to Rome and was sent to preach in the Marches of Ancona, of which region he was consecrated bishop. He was put to death, with three companions, at Ascoli under Diocletian.
Cf. Att. — Baud. — Menzies — Holw.

ENCRATIA (ENCRATIS, in Spanish: ENGRACIA) (St) **V.M.   R.M. Apr. 16**
d. ? 304. A Spanish maiden martyred at Saragossa, where the church now stands dedicated in her name. She is famous for "her ardour in suffering for Christ." Her martyrdom probably took place under Diocletian.
Cf. Att. — Baud. — Holw.

ENDA (ENDEUS, ENNA) (St) **Ab.**
                              A.C. March 21
d. c.590. Brother of St Fanchea and

founder of many monasteries, of which the principal was on Arranmore. SS Kleran and Brendan, among others, were his disciples.
Cf. Att. — Baud. — Holw.

ENECO (ENNECO, Spanish: IÑIGO) (St) Ab. O.S.B.   R.M. June 1
d. 1057. Born at Calatayud, and a monk of San Juan de la Peña, in Aragon, where the Cluniac observance had been just then introduced. After much entreaty, King Sancho the Great of Navarre induced him to accept the abbacy of Oña in Old Castile. Under Iñigo's rule the abbey rose to great splendour, and on his death he was much lamented by Christians, Jews and Saracens alike. Canonized in 1259.
Cf. Att. — Zimm. — P. de U.

ENGELBERT (St) Ab.   A.C. Feb. 18
Otherwise Angilbert, q.v.

ENGELBERT (St) Bp. M.   R.M. Nov. 7
1186-1225. A typical medieval prince-prelate. Early in his career he gained possession uncanonically of benefices, and thereby incurred excommunication. When this was lifted he became archbishop of Cologne (1216). In this position he was a great success: zealous for the discipline of his clergy, fosterer of monastic life and of learning. He was appointed tutor to the emperor's son, and chief minister of the empire. While defending the rights of a nunnery he was killed by hired assassins, and hence he is venerated as a martyr.
Cf. Att. — Baud. — Holw.

ENGELMUND (St) Ab. O.S.B.
A.C. June 21
d. c.739. An Englishman by birth and education, he received the Benedictine habit at a very early age, and became priest and abbot. He crossed over to Friesland, where he worked most successfully under St Willibrord, at Velsen, six miles north of Haarlem.
Cf. Zimm. — Att. — Baud. — Holw.

ENGHENEDL (St)   A.C. Sept. 30
7th cent. A Welsh saint to whom a church in Anglesey was dedicated. Nothing is now known about his life.
Cf. Baring-Gould.

ENGLAND (Martyrs of) (BB)   A.C. May 4
1535-1681. British-born Catholics, put to death by Protestants between the two dates given above. They are about six hundred in number. Fifty-four were beatified by Leo XIII in 1886, nine in 1895, and one hundred and thirty-seven by Pius XI in 1929: their common feast is held on May 4. The causes of over a hundred others are now being officially examined in Rome; there are still two hundred and eighty-four whose claim to martyrdom has not yet been considered by the Church. Each of these martyrs who has already been officially acknowledged as Saint or Blessed, receives a separate notice in this book.

ENGLATIUS (ENGLAT, TANGLEN) (St) Bp.   A.C. Nov. 3
d. 966. A Scottish saint, said by some to have been a bishop, who lived at Tarves in Aberdeenshire.
Cf. Baring-Gould.

ENGUERRAMMUS (ANGILRAM) (Bl) Ab. O.S.B.   P.C. Dec. 9
d. 1045. Of a humble family, he was educated at the abbey of Saint-Riquier (*Centula*), where eventually he became a monk and abbot (1022). By his contemporaries he was surnamed "the Wise" or "the learned Abbot." He was a very fluent Latin verse-writer.
Cf. P. de U. — Chev. — Baud.

ENNATHA (St) V.M.   R.M. Nov. 13
See Antoninus, Zebina, etc.

ENNODIUS (St) Bp.   R.M. July 17
473-521. Magnus Felix Ennodius was a Gallo-Roman by birth and a professor of rhetoric, who, after his conversion, became (c.514) bishop of Pavia in Lombardy. The pope entrusted him with two missions to Byzantium in connection with the Eutychian controversy. He is now best remembered as a Christian poet, whose writings, chiefly hymns, are full of interest.
Cf. Att. — Menzies — Holw.

ENOCH (St) V.   A.C. March 26
Otherwise Kennocha, q.v.

ENODER (or CYNIDR) (St) Ab.
A.C. Apr. 27
6th cent. A grandson of the Welsh chieftain Brychan. Llangynidr in Brecknockshire perpetuates his memory, as also possibly St Enoder or Enodoc in Cornwall.

Very likely he is to be identified with St Enodoch, q.v. In Breton he is called St Quidic.
Cf. Baring-Gould.

ENODOCH (WENEDOC) (St)
A.C. March 7
d. c.520. A Welsh saint of the Brychan race. Some writers identify him with St Enoder, q.v., others state that she was a daughter — instead of a son — of Brychan and call her St Qwendydd. The traditions are very confused.
Cf. Holw.

ENOGATUS (St) Bp.
A.C. Feb. 13
d. 631. The fifth successor of St Malo in the see of Aleth in Brittany.
Cf. Duch. Fast. Episc. — Gams — Baud.

EOBAN (St) M. O.S.B.
R.M. June 5
d. 755. A Benedictine monk-priest said to have been of Irish descent, who worked under SS Willibrord and Boniface in the German mission and shared in the latter's martyrdom.
Cf. Baud. — Holw. — Zimm.

EOCHOD (St)
A.C. Jan. 25
d. 597. One of St Columbkille's twelve companions, and chosen by him to evangelize N. Britain. He is called the apostle of the Picts of Galloway.
Cf. Holw.

EOGAN (St) Bp.
A.C. Aug. 23
Otherwise Eugene, q.v.

EPAPHRAS (St) Bp. M.
R.M. July 19
1st cent. "The most beloved fellow-servant" of St Paul (Col I, 7). He is traditionally said to have been bishop of Colossae and to have suffered martyrdom there. But beyond what we read in the New Testament (Col I, 7; IV, 12 and Philem 23) we know nothing of his life.

EPAPHRODITUS (St) Bp.
R.M. March 22
1st cent. St Paul mentions him as an apostle sent to the Philippians (Phil II, 25). Hence, St Epaphroditus is reputed first bishop of Philippi in Macedonia. Two saints of the same name are listed in ancient catalogues: one as the first bishop of Andriacia in Lycia, and another as the first bishop of Terracina in Italy. The three are said to have been among the seventy-two disciples of Christ. Very likely they are the same person, with different local veneration.

EPAGATHUS (St) M.
R.M. June 2
See Photinus (Pothinus), Sanctus, etc.

EPARCHIUS (St) Bp.
R.M. March 23
See Domitius, Pelagia, etc.

EPARCHIUS (French: CYBAR) (St) Ab.
R.M. July 1
504-581. Born duke of Périgord in France, he renounced his title to become a monk of Sessac. After his ordination to the priesthood he was "walled-up" at Angoulême (542) where he lived for the rest of his life, directing a community who established themselves in the neighbourhood for that purpose.
Cf. Att. — Baud. — Holw.

EPHEBUS (St) M.
R.M. Feb. 14
See Proculus, Ephebus and Apollonius.

EPHESUS (Martyrs of) (SS)
R.M. Jan. 12
d. c.762. Forty-two monks of a monastery at Ephesus, put to death by the emperor Constantine Copronymus for their firm stand against the Iconoclasts.
Cf. Holw.

EPHREM (St) Bp. M.
R.M. March 4
See Basil, Eugene, etc.

EPHREM the SYRIAN (St) Dr.
R.M. June 18
c.300-c.379. Surnamed also "the Deacon" and "the Harp of the Holy Ghost." He was a native of Nisibis in Mesopotamia and very likely the head of the catechetical school of that city before it was captured by the Persians. Afterwards he became a monk near Edessa and a deacon. Here he spent most of his long life writing copious commentaries on the Bible and composing hymns. He wrote the hymns in his native Syriac so that his people could make use of them and thus retain their Catholic faith and keep free from Arianism. He excelled in his Mariological hymns, which are an important contribution to Catholic dogma. In the terrible famine which raged throughout Mesopotamia a few years before St Ephrem's death the saint was the leader in organizing relief and help for the sick. He died in his monastic

cell, revered both in the East and in the West. Benedict XV officially declared him a Doctor of the Church in 1920.
Cf. Att. — Baud. — Holw.

EPHYSIUS (St) M.   R.M. Jan. 15
d. 303. A martyr said to have been put to death in Sardinia under Diocletian. He is still greatly venerated in the island.
Cf. Menzies — Att. — Baud. — Holw.

EPICHARIS (St) M.   R.M. Sept. 27
d. c.300. She is said to have been the wife of a Roman senator and to have been martyred at New Rome (Byzantium) under Diocletian.
Cf. Holw. — Baud.

EPICTETUS, JUCUNDUS, SECUNDUS, VITALIS, FELIX and Comp. (SS) MM.
R.M. Jan. 9
d. ? 250. Twelve African martyrs probably of the Decian persecution.

EPICTETUS (St) M.   R.M. Aug. 22
See Martial, Saturninus, etc.

EPIGMENIUS (St) M.   R.M. March 24
d. c.300. A Roman priest martyred under Diocletian.
Cf. Holw. — Baud.

EPIMACHUS (St) M.   R.M. May 10
d. 260. A native of Alexandria in Egypt, burnt there at the stake under Decius. He is commemorated also on Dec. 12, with his fellow-sufferer St Alexander.
Cf. Holw. — Baud.

EPIMACHUS and ALEXANDER (SS) MM.   R.M. Dec. 12
See Epimachus, above.

EPIPHANA (St) M.   R.M. July 12
? She is mentioned in the Acts of St Alphius, which are wholly unreliable. Nothing really is known about her.

EPIPHANIA (St) N. O.S.B.   A.C. Oct. 6
d. c.800. A Benedictine nun in the convent of Santa Maria della-Caccia — *Sancta Maria Venationum* — at Pavia in Lombardy. An old tradition adds that she was a daughter of King Ratchis, who himself became a monk at Montecassino.
Cf. Zimm. — Menzies — Chev. — Holw.

EPIPHANIUS (St) Bp.   R.M. Jan. 21
439-497. Born at Pavia, and elected

bishop of that city in 467. During his episcopate Odoacer destroyed Pavia, and Epiphanius was largely responsible for the rebuilding of the city. In order to ransom some of his flock who were held captive he travelled to Burgundy and so contracted the fever of which he died.
Cf. Att. — Baud. — Holw. — Menzies.

EPIPHANIUS, DONATUS, RUFINUS and Comp. (SS) MM.   R.M. Apr. 7
? Epiphanius was an African bishop, and his thirteen fellow-martyrs were members of his flock.

EPIPHANIUS of SALAMIS (St) Bp.
R.M. May 12
c.310-403. A native of Palestine, and a monk from his earliest youth. He became abbot at Eleutheropolis, where he wrote and preached against all heretics, but chiefly against Arianism in imperial circles. He was acclaimed "the oracle of Palestine." In 367 he was raised to the see of Salamis in Cyprus, where he continued his vehement defence of orthodoxy. In his old age he acted occasionally in a very headstrong way. His writings were his most important contribution to the Catholic cause.
Cf. Att. — Holw. — Baud.

EPIPODIUS and ALEXANDER (SS) MM.   R.M. Apr. 22
d. 178. Two young friends, citizens of Lyons, put to death under Marcus Aurelius.
Cf. Att. — Holw. — Baud.

EPISTEMIS (St) M.   R.M. Nov. 5
See Galation and Epistemis.

EPITACIUS and BASILEUS (SS) MM.
R.M. May 23
1st cent. The former is said to have been first bishop of Tuy in Spanish Galicia, and the latter first bishop of Braga in present-day Portugal — both in the apostolic age.
Cf. Holw. — Baud. — P. de U.

EPOLONIUS (St) M.   R.M. Jan. 24
See Babilas, Urban, etc.

EPPO (Bl) Ab. O.S.B.   A.C. June 27
d. 1143. Monk, and second abbot (1122) of Mallersdorf in Bavaria.
Cf. Zimm.

EPVRE (EURE) (St) Bp.   R.M. Sept. 15
Otherwise Aprus, q.v.

EQUITIUS (St) Ab.   R.M. Aug. 11
d. c.540.   A contemporary of St Benedict,
and the founder of a number of monasteries in the province of Valeria (a district
east of Rome).   St Gregory the Great
gives all we know about him in the first
book of his Dialogues.
Cf. Att. — Holw. — Baud.

ERASMA (St) V.M.   R.M. Sept. 3
See Euphemia, Dorothy, etc.

**ERASMUS (ELMO, ERARMO, ERMO)
(St) Bp. M.   R.M. June 2**
d. 303.   Stripped of all the later legendary
additions our knowledge of this saint is
reduced to the fact that he was a bishop of
Formiae in Campania, martyred under
Diocletian, and that his relics were transferred to Gaeta in 842.   The legend of his
"Acts" made him patron of sailors and
one of the fourteen Holy Helpers, greatly
revered throughout Europe in the Middle
Ages.
Cf. Att. — Baud. — Holw. — Menzies.

ERASMUS (St) M.   R.M. Nov. 25
? A Syrian, martyred at Antioch.   It is
probable that he is a duplicate of St
Erasmus of June 2.

ERASTUS (St) Bp. M.   R.M. July 26
1st cent.   The treasurer of the city of
Corinth (Rom XVI, 23) converted by St
Paul, and one of his helpers in the apostolate (Acts XIX, 22), especially at Corinth
(II Tim IV, 20).   The Greek tradition is
that he became bishop of Philippi Paneas
in Palestine: that of the Latins that his
see was Philippi in Macedonia and that he
was a martyr.
Cf. Baud. — Holw.

**ERBIN (ERVAN, ERBYN, ERME or
HERMES)   A.C. Jan. 13**
? 5th cent.   A Cornish saint who seems to
have been related to one of the Cornish or
Devonian chieftains.   Churches were dedicated to him in Cornwall.
Cf. Holw. — Baring-Gould.

ERBO (Bl) Ab. O.S.B.   A.C. Aug. 27
d. 1162.   A disciple of St Theoger and a
monk under him at St George's in the
Black Forest.   In 1121 he was chosen by

St Otto, bishop of Bamberg, to succeed
St Erminold in the abbacy of Prüfening,
which he governed for forty years, the
observance being that of Cluny-Hirschau.
Cf. Zimm.

ERCONGOTHA(St) V. O.S.B. A.C. July 7
d. 660.   A niece of St Ethelburga, third
abbess of Faremoutiers, and daughter of
King Ercombert of Kent and of St Sexburga.   She was a nun at Faremoutiers
under her aunt.
Cf. Att. — Holw. — Stanton — Chev.

**ERCONWALD (ERKENWALD) (St) Bp.
O.S.B.   R.M. Apr. 30**
d. c.686.   An East-Anglian of royal blood.
He retired to the kingdom of the East
Saxons where he founded two houses —
Chertsey abbey, in Surrey, for men; and
Barking nunnery, in Essex, for women.
He became the abbot of the former and
his sister St Ethelburga the abbess of the
latter.   In 675 he was chosen bishop of
London by St Theodore.
Cf. Att. — Chev. — Baud.

EREMBERT (St) Bp. O.S.B. A.C. May 14
d. c.672.   Born at Wocourt near Passy, he
became a Benedictine at Fontenelle
(c.640) and bishop of Toulouse (c.656)
which he ruled for twelve years.   In his
old age he resigned and went back to die
at Fontenelle.
Cf. Att. — Zimm. — Chev. — Baud.

**EREMBERT I (Bl) Ab. O.S.B.
A.C. Jan. 24**
d. p. 1050.   Abbot of Kremsmünster, in
Austria, to which office he was elected in
1050.
Cf. Zimm.

**EREMBERTA (St) Abs. O.S.B.
P.C. Oct. 16**
Late 7th cent.   Niece of St Wulmarus,
and first abbess of the nunnery of Wierre,
which he built for her.
Cf. Zimm.

**ERENTRUDIS (ERMENTRUDE) (St)
Abs. O.S.B.   A.C. June 30**
d. c.718.   A sister — or niece — of St
Rupert, the apostle of Salzburg.   She was
the first abbess of Nonnberg in Salzburg,
a nunnery founded for her by Rupert.
*Cf. Zimm. — Att. — Chev. — Baud. —
Holw.*

ERFYL (EURFYL) (St) V. A.C. July 5
? A British maiden, foundress of the
church of Llanerfyl, Montgomeryshire.
Cf. Holw.

ERGNAD (ERCNACTA) (St) V.
A.C. Jan. 8
5th cent. A native of Ulster who is said
to have received the veil from St Patrick.
Cf. O' Hanlon.

ERGOULE (St) V. A.C. Jan. 8
Otherwise Gudule, q.v. ,

ERHARD (St) Bp. R.M. Jan. 8
d. c.686. He is described as an Irishman,
who passed over to the Continent and
laboured as a missionary bishop in Bavaria, chiefly in and around Ratisbon. He
is said to have baptized St Odilia. His
cult has always been very flourishing at
Ratisbon.
Cf. Att. — Zimm. — Baud. — Holw.

ERIC (HENRY) (St) King, M.
R.M. May 18
d. 1160. Eric IX became king of Sweden
in 1150 and at once began to exert all his
influence to spread the gospel throughout
the country. He codified the laws of his
kingdom in the same spirit, and is for this
reason called "the Lawgiver." He also
laboured for the conversion of the heathen
Finns. He was murdered as he was leaving a church after hearing Mass.
Cf. Att. — Baud. — Holw.

ERIZZO (Bl) Ab. O.S.B. Vall. A.C. Feb. 9
d. 1094. A native of Florence, and the
first disciple of St John Gualbert. At a
later period he became the fourth general
of the Vallumbrosans. Cult confirmed in
1600.
Cf. Zimm. — Holw.

ERKEMBODEN (St) Bp. O.S.B.
A.C. Apr. 12
d. 714. A monk of Sithin at Saint-Omer,
who succeeded the founder, St Bertinus,
as abbot, and then became bishop of Thérouanne, continuing to rule the abbey.
He was bishop for twenty-six years.
Cf. Zimm. — Att. — Baud. — Chev.

ERLAFRID (St) Ab. O.S.B. A.C. Nov. 6
d. p. 830. Count of Calw in Swabia.
Founder of Hirschau Abbey, where he became a monk.
Cf. Holw. — Zimm.

ERLUPH (St) Bp. M. A.C. Feb. 10
d. 830. A Scottish missionary in Germany who later became bishop of Werden,
and was martyred by pagans.
Cf. Baud. — Holw.

ERMEL (ARMEL, ERME) (St) Ab.
A.C. Aug. 16
Otherwise Armagillus, q.v.

ERMELINDA (ERMELINDIS) (St) V.
A.C. Oct. 29
d. c.595. A Belgian recluse who lived at
Meldaert, near Tirlemont.
Cf. Zimm. — Holw. — Baud.

ERMEMBURGA (St) W. O.S.B.
A.C. Nov. 19
d. ? c.650. Otherwise known as Domna
Ebba (Lady Ebba), abbreviated into
Domneva. She was a Kentish princess
married to the king of Mercia, and the
mother of SS Mildred, Milburga and
Mildgith. In her old age she founded the
nunnery of Minster in Thanet, where the
place-name Ebbsfleet still perpetuates her
memory.
Cf. Stanton — Baud. — Holw. — Chev. ⟍

ERMENFRIDUS (St) Ab. O.S.B.
A.C. Sept. 25
d. c. 670. A courtier and then a monk at
Luxeuil under its third abbot, St Walbert.
Later he became the abbot-founder of
Cusance.
Cf. Zimm. — Mab. — Chev. — Baud.

ERMENGARDIS (Bl) W. O.S.B. Cist.
A.C. June 1
c.1067-c.1147. A native of Angers and
wife of the duke of Brittany (1092).
Before her death she received the Cistercian habit at the hands of St Bernard
(c.1130).
Cf. Chev. — Baud. — Holw.

ERMENGOL (St) Bp. R.M. Nov. 3
Otherwise Hermengaudius, q.v.

ERMENGYTHA (St) V. O.S.B.
A.C. July 30
d. c.680 A sister of St Ermenburga (Domneva). She lived under the latter's obedience as a nun at Minster in Thanet.
Cf. Holw.

**ERMENILDA (ERMENGILD) (St) W.
O.S.B. A.C. Feb. 13**
d. 703. Daughter of King Ercombert of

Kent and of St Sexburga. She married the king of Mercia and on his death joined her mother at Minster in Sheppey, eventually succeeding her as abbess. She then migrated to Ely where also she became abbess.
Cf. Stanton — Att. — Chev. — Zimm.

ERMINOLD (St) M. Ab. O.S.B.
A.C. Jan. 6
d. 1121. He was offered to God at the abbey of Hirschau as a child and educated and professed there. In 1110 he was chosen abbot of Lorsch; but fearing that this appointment might have been the result of simony he resigned and returned to Hirschau. In 1114 he was chosen the first prior of Prüfening and in 1117 its first abbot. One of the lay-brothers of the community struck him with a piece of timber and caused his death. He has always been venerated as a martyr.
Cf. Zimm. — Att. — Chev. — Baud. — Holw.

ERMINUS (St) Bp. O.S.B. R.M. Apr. 25
d. 737. Born at Laon. After his ordination to the priesthood he professed the Benedictine rule at Lobbes under St Ursmarus, who appointed him his successor both as abbot and as regionary bishop.
Cf. Mab. — Chev. — Zimm. — Att. — Baud. — Holw.

ERNAN (ERNIN) (*several*)
There are various Irish saints of this or a similar name. Perhaps the most notable among them is one described as a nephew of St Columba.
Cf. Holw.

ERNEST (St) Ab. O.S.B. P.C. Nov. 7
d. 1148. Benedictine abbot of Zwiefalten in Germany who joined the crusaders and preached in Persia and Arabia. He was taken prisoner and tortured to death at Mecca.
Cf. Zimm. — Chev. — Baud. — Holw.

ERNEY (St)
? The patron saint of a church at Landrake in Cornwall.
Cf. Stanton.

EROTHEIS (St) M. R.M. Oct. 27
See Capitolina and Erotheis.

EROTIS (EROTEIS)(St) M. R.M. Oct. 6
4th cent. A martyr who perished at the stake. The martyrdom seems to have taken place in Greece, though by some Erotis is identified with St Erotheis of Cappadocia, who suffered with St Capitolina.
Cf. Baud. — Holw.

ERTH (HERYGH, URITH) (St)
A.C. Oct. 31
6th cent. Brother of St Uny and St Ia (Ives). He crossed from Ireland to Cornwall, where a church is dedicated in his name. He has given his name also to the village of St Erth.
Cf. Holw.

ERVAN (St) A.C. May 29
Otherwise Erbyn or Erbin, q.v.

ERVAN (St) Ab. A.C. Aug. 16
Otherwise Armagillus, q.v.

ESDRAS (EZRA) (St) Prophet.
R.M. July 13
5th cent. B.C. A Jewish scribe and priest, born in Babylon during the captivity. In 459 he obtained permission to lead a group of exiles back to Jerusalem. He had the walls of the city built, and on the completion of the work concluded a solemn pact between God and the people. Two books of the Vulgate Bible bear his name (Ezra and Nehemiah in the A.V.) although he is not their author. Two others known as the third and fourth books of Esdras, are apocryphal.

ESKILL (St) Bp. M. A.C. June 12
d. c.1080. A fellow-missionary of St Sigfrid in Sweden by whom he was consecrated bishop. Both were English. St Eskill was stoned to death for protesting against a heathen festival at Strengnäss.
Cf. Att. — Chev. — Baud. — Holw.

ESTERWINE (St) Ab. O.S.B.
A.C. March 7
d. 688. A noble Northumbrian who spent his early years at court, and then entered the monastery of Wearmouth, where he was professed under his kinsman St Benedict Biscop, the founder of the abbey. He succeeded St Benet as abbot and ruled four years, dying before the founder. He was celebrated for his gentleness.
Cf. Zimm. — Att. — Baud. — Holw.

ETERNUS (St) Bp.   **A.C. July 15**
d. p. 660. The ninth bishop of Evreux in France.
Cf. Duch. Fast. Episc. — Gams — Baud.

ETHA (St) H. O.S.B.   **A.C. May 5**
Otherwise Echa, q.v.

ETHBIN (St) Ab.   **R.M. Oct. 19**
d. c.600. A Briton, educated in France by St Samson. When a deacon he retired to the abbey of Taurac (554), where he remained till the dispersion of the community through a raid by the Franks (556). He then crossed over to Ireland, and there led the life of a hermit near Kildare.
Cf. Holw.

ETHELBERT of KENT (St) King.
    R.M. Feb. 24
d. 616. Husband of Bertha, a Christian princess from France, he was reigning in Kent when St Augustine arrived in Thanet. Ethelbert protected the missionaries from the start, and received baptism on Whit-sunday, 597. Though he never tried to force his subjects into Christianity, hundreds followed his example. He was the founder of the abbeys of Christ Church, and SS Peter and Paul, Canterbury, and of St Andrew's, Rochester.
Cf. Att. — Stanton — Holw. — Baud.

ETHELBERT (St) M.   **A.C. May 20**
d. 793. King of East Anglia. He was treacherously murdered at the instigation of the wife of Offa of Mercia. He has always been venerated as a martyr.
Cf. Stanton — Att. — Baud.

ETHELBERT and ETHELRED (SS) MM.   **A.C. Oct. 17**
d. 670. Great-grandsons of St Ethelbert of Kent, cruelly put to death at Eastry near Sandwich. Their shrine was finally set up at Ramsey abbey in Huntingdonshire.
Cf. Stanton — Baud. — Holw.

ETHELBURGA (St) W. O.S.B.
    A.C. Apr. 5
d. c.647. Daughter of King St Ethelbert of Kent, she married King St Edwin of Northumbria. She went there accompanied by St Paulinus as her chaplain. After Edwin's death she returned to Kent

and founded the nunnery of Lyminge where she became a nun and abbess.
Cf. Att. — Stanton — Mab. — Zimm.

ETHELBURGA (St) Abs. O.S.B.
    R.M. July 7
d. c.664. The daughter of Anna, king of the East Angles. She became a nun at Faremoutier, in France, where she succeeded, as abbess, the foundress herself, St Fara. She is known in France as St Aubierge.
Cf. Att. — Stanton — Zimm. — Mab.

ETHELBURGA (St) Queen P.C. Sept. 8
See Ina and Ethelburga.

ETHELBURGA (St) Abs. O.S.B.
    A.C. Oct. 11
d. c.678. Sister of St Erconwald of London, who founded for her the nunnery of Barking in Essex. She was made abbess; but as she was quite inexperienced, St Hildelid was fetched from a French nunnery to train her. Eventually she governed alone and proved a great abbess.
Cf. Stanton — Att. — Zimm. — Mab.

ETHELDREDA (ETHELREDA, EDILTRUDIS, AUDREY) (St) Abs. O.S.B.
    R.M. June 23
d. 679. At one time the most popular of Anglo-Saxon women saints. A native of Suffolk, she was a sister to SS Sexburga, Ethelburga and Withburga. She took the veil at Coldingham under St Ebba and then migrated to Ely where she was chosen abbess of the double monastery.
Cf. Stanton — Att. — Baud. — Chev. — Zimm. — Mab.

ETHELDRITHA (or ETHELFREDA, ALFREDA, ALTHRYDA) (St) V. O.S.B.
    A.C. Aug. 2
d. 834. Daughter of King Offa of Mercia. She lived as a recluse on Croyland Island, in the desolate marshes of Lincolnshire.
Cf. Zimm. — Chev. — Baud.

ETHELDWITHA (EALSITHA) (St) W. O.S.B.   **A.C. July 20**
d. 903. An Anglo-Saxon princess, wife of King Alfred. After his death she retired to a nunnery which she founded at Winchester.
Cf. Stanton — Baud.

ETHELFLEDA (St) N. O.S.B.
A.C. Oct. 23
Otherwise Elfleda, q.v.

ETHELGITHA (St) Abs. O.S.B.
A.C. Aug. 22
d. c.720. Abbess of a convent in Northumbria.
Cf. Zimm.

ETHELGIVA (St) Abs. O.S.B.
A.C. Dec. 9
d. 896. Daughter of King Alfred the Great and abbess of Shaftesbury.
Cf. Stanton — Holw.

ETHELHARD (St) Bp.   A.C. May 12
d. 803. A bishop of Winchester, translated to Canterbury in 780.
Cf. Stanton — Holw.

ETHELNOTH (St) Bp.   A.C. Oct. 30
Otherwise Egelnoth, q.v.

ETHELRED (St) Ab.   A.C. Jan. 12
Otherwise Aelred, q.v.

ETHELRED (St) King, Ab. O.S.B.
A.C. May 4
d. 716. A king of Mercia, who resigned the crown to become a monk at Bardney, where he was afterwards elected abbot.
Cf. Stanton — Baud. — Holw.

ETHELWALD (OIDILWALD) (St) H.
O.S.B.   A.C. March 23
d. 699. A Monk of Ripon who succeeded St Cuthbert as a hermit on Farne Island, where he lived for twelve years. He was buried at Lindisfarne.
Cf. Att. — Stanton — Chev. — Baud.

ETHELWIN (St) Bp.   A.C. May 3
8th cent. The second bishop of Lindsey. He was a devoted friend of St Egbert, whom he accompanied to Ireland, where he died.
Cf. Stanton — Holw.

ETHELWOLD (AEDILUALD) (St) Bp.
A.C. Feb. 12
d. c.740. One of St Cuthbert's chief helpers. He was prior and then abbot of Old Melrose in Scotland and finally succeeded to the see of Lindisfarne.
Cf. Att. — Baud. — Stanton — Holw.

ETHELWOLD (St) Bp. O.S.B.
R.M. Aug. 1
d. 984. A native of Winchester. When St Dunstan became abbot of Glastonbury in 944 and restored there the Benedictine observance, Ethelwold, already a priest, took the habit and was made one of the deans. In 955 he became abbot of Abingdon and in 963 bishop of Winchester. Together with St Dunstan and St Oswald of York he was a leader in the monastic revival of that century, replacing secular canons by Benedictines, founding or restoring abbeys — Newminster, Milton Abbas, Chertsey, Peterborough, Thorney, Ely, etc. He was indeed worthy of the name given him, "The Father of Monks."
Cf.Stanton — Zimm. — Att.

ETHENIA and FIDELMIA (SS) VV.
A.C. Jan. 11
d. 433. Daughters of King Laoghaire, and among the first converts made by St Patrick. They received the veil from his hands, and the tradition is that on receiving Holy Communion from him immediately afterwards they died.
Cf. Holw.

ETHERIUS (AETHERIUS) (St) Bp. M.
R.M. March 4
See Basil, Eugene, etc.

ETHERIUS (St) Bp. C.   R.M. June"14
d. c.675. Bishop of Vienne in France.
Cf. Holw.

ETHERIUS (St) M.   R.M. June 18
d. c.303. A martyr who suffered at Nicomedia under Diocletian.
Cf. Holw.

ETHERIUS (St) Bp. C.   R.M. July 27
d. 573. Bishop of Auxerre, 563–573.
Cf. Holw.

ETHERIUS (ALERMIUS) (St) Bp. C.
A.C. Aug. 27
d. 602. The bishop of Lyons to whom St Gregory the Great recommended St Augustine when the latter was on his way to England.
Cf. Holw. — Bolland.

ETHERNAN (St) Bp.   A.C. Dec. 3
? A native of Scotland who studied in Ireland, and was there consecrated bishop.

He then went back to evangelize his country.
Cf. Holw.

ETHERNASCUS (St) Bp.   A.C. Aug. 18
Otherwise Ernan, q.v.

ETHOR (St) M.   A.C. Apr. 10
See Beocca, Ethor and Comp.

ETTO (HETTO) (St) Bp. O.S.B.
A.C. July 10
d. c.670. Said to have been a native of Ireland. He laboured as a missionary abbot-bishop in Belgium, using St Peter's Abbey at Fescan as his headquarters.
Cf. Zimm.

EUBULUS (St) M.   R.M. March 7
d. 308. Companion of St Adrian the martyr at Caesarea in Palestine, and the last to suffer there under Diocletian.
Cf. Baud. — Holw.

EUCARPIUS (St) M.   R.M. March 18
See Trophimus and Eucarpius.

EUCARPUS (St) M.   R.M. Sept. 25
See Bardomian, Eucarpus, etc.

EUCHARIUS (St) Bp.   R.M. Dec. 8
1st cent. Said to have been the first bishop of Trèves in apostolic times.
Cf. Holw. — Baud.

EUCHERIUS (St) Bp. O.S.B.
R.M. Feb. 20
d. 743. Born at Orleans, he received a good education, especially in theology, and entered the Benedictine abbey of Jumièges on the Seine, in the diocese of Rouen, about the year 714. In 721 he was raised to the see of Orleans. He opposed Charles Martel for the latter's high-handed distribution of ecclesiastical property, and was exiled to Cologne in 737. Here he became very popular, and was sent to Liége. He spent the rest of his life in the abbey of St Trond near Maestricht.
Cf. Att. — Holw. — Mab.

EUCHERIUS (St) Bp.   R.M. Nov. 16
d. 450. A Gallo-Roman by birth and the father, by his wife Galla, of two sons, who became bishops. He himself retired to Lérins in 422, while Galla took the veil. He spent his retirement in praying and writing, several of his ascetical works being

still extant. In 434 he was compelled to accept the bishopric of Lyons, where he laboured till his death.
Cf. Gams — Baud. — Holw.

EUDO (EUDON, EUDES, ODO) (St) Ab. O.S.B.   A.C. Nov. 20
d. c.760. Abbot-founder of the monastery of Cormèry-en-Velay (Charmillac, afterwards Saint-Chaffre). Before entering upon his duties as abbot he went to Lérins to be instructed in the monastic observance.
Cf. Zimm. — Chev. — Baud. — Holw.

EUDOCIA (St) M.   R.M. March 1
d. 98-117. A native of Heliopolis in Coele-Syria and a Samaritan by blood who led at first a profligate life, but was converted to Christianity and died a penitent. She was beheaded under Trajan.
Cf. Baud. — Holw.

EUDOXIUS, ZENO, MACARIUS and Comp. (SS) MM.   R.M. Sept. 5
2nd cent. A body of Christian soldiers, said to have been more than a thousand in number, martyred in Armenia under Trajan.
Cf. Baud. — Holw.

EUDOXIUS (St) M.   R.M. Nov. 2
See Carterius, Styriacus, etc.

EUFRIDUS (St) Mk. O.S.B. A.C. Oct. 11
7th cent. Monk of the diocese of Asti, venerated in the cathedral of Alba in Piedmont.
Cf. Baud. — Holw. — P.B.

EUGENDUS (OYEND) (St) Ab.
R.M. Jan. 1
d. c.510. The fourth abbot of Condat, near Geneva, called after him Saint-Oyend, but later Saint-Claude. He entered the abbey at the age of seven and lived there until his death at sixty-one.
Cf. Att. — Baud. — Holw.

EUGENE (*several*)
Note. The Latin form Eugenius is often used also in English.

EUGENE (St)   R.M. Jan. 4
See Aquilinus, Geminus, etc.

EUGENE (St) M.   R.M. Jan. 24
See Mardonius, Musonius, etc.

EUGENE (St) M.   March 4
See Basil, Eugene, etc.

EUGENE (St) M.   R.M. March 20
See Paul, Cyril, etc.

EUGENE (St) Bp. M.   R.M. May 2
See Vindemialis, Eugene and Longinus.

EUGENE I (St) Pope   R.M. June 2
d. 657. A Roman priest, who acted as
vicar for Pope St Martin I during the
latter's exile in the Chersonese. After St
Martin's death in 655, Eugene was chosen
to succeed him. Gentle and affable with
the poor, he firmly opposed the Monothelite emperor of Byzantium, who threatened to roast St Eugene alive.
Cf. Att. — Baud. — Holw. — Menzies.

EUGENE III (Bl) Pope O.S.B. Cist.
                            R.M. July 8
d. 1153. A native of Montemagno, between Lucca and Pisa, of the Pignatelli
family, he was called Peter in baptism,
Bernard in religion, and Eugene on the
papal throne. He was an official in the
ecclesiastical curia of Pisa, when he entered Clairvaux (1135) and was professed
under St Bernard. He was appointed
first abbot of Tre Fontane (St Anastasius)
near Rome, and in 1145 was chosen pope.
His pontificate was a troubled one, the
greater part of it being passed at a distance
from Rome owing to the hostility of the
citizens. St Antoninus fittingly called
him "one of the greatest and one of the
most afflicted of popes." Cult confirmed
in 1872.
Cf. Zimm. — Att. — Baud. — Holw.

**EUGENE, SALUTARIS, MURITTA and
COMP. (SS) MM.**   R.M. July 13
d. 505. Eugene was raised to the see of
Carthage in 481 and was shortly afterwards expelled by the Arian Vandals with
many of his flock, some of them young
boys who served as lectors in the church.
They were banished to the desert of Tripoli, where they had to undergo much hardship. In 488 they were allowed to return
to Carthage, but Eugene was banished
again some eight years later and died at
Albi. They are called martyrs on account
of their sufferings.
Cf. Att. — Holw.

EUGENE (St) M.   R.M. July 18
See Symphorosa and her children.

EUGENE (St) M.   R.M. July 23
See Apollonius and Eugene.

EUGENE (St) M.   R.M. July 29
See Lucilla, Flora, etc.

EUGENE (EOGHAN, OWEN) (St) Bp.
                            A.C. Aug. 23
d. 618. An Irishman who laboured as a
missionary in England and on the Continent, and then returned to his native
country, where he became first bishop of
Ardstraw in Tyrone, a see now replaced
by that of Derry.
Cf. Att. — Baud. — Holw.

EUGENE (St) M.   R.M. Sept. 6
See Cottidus, Eugene, and Comp.

EUGENE (St) M.   R.M. Sept. 25
See Paul, Tatta, etc.

EUGENE II of TOLEDO (St) Bp.
                            R.M. Nov. 13
d. 657. A Spanish Goth, born at Toledo,
where he was a cleric under St Helladius.
He became a monk of St Engracia at
Saragossa, and the archdeacon of St
Braulio there. Finally, in 646, he was
raised to the primatial see of Toledo. He
was a gifted poet and musician, and most
zealous for all that pertained to divine
worship.
*Cf. P. de U. — Zimm. — Att. — Baud. —
Holw.*

EUGENE (St) Bp. M.   R.M. Nov. 15
? A fellow-labourer of St Dionysius, archbishop of Paris, martyred, it is said, somewhere near that city. The R.M. wrongly
calls him archbishop of Toledo. His
relics were, it is said, translated to Toledo
many centuries afterwards.
Cf. Att. — Baud. — Holw. — Gams.

EUGENE (St) C.   R.M. Nov. 17
d. 422. A deacon of the church of Florence under the bishop St Zenobius. He
had been a disciple of St Ambrose at
Milan.
Cf. Menzies — Holw. — Baud.

EUGENE (St) M.   R.M. Dec. 13
See Eustratius, Auxentius, etc.

EUGENE and MACARIUS (SS) MM.
                            R.M. Dec. 20
d. 362. Two priests who were scourged,

banished into the desert of Arabia, and on their return put to the sword under Julian the Apostate.
Cf. Baud. — Holw.

EUGENE (St) Bp.   R.M. Dec. 30
? A bishop of Milan, of whose life no record remains.

EUGENIA (St) Abs. O.S.B. A.C. Sept. 16
d. 735. Daughter of Adalbert, duke of Alsace, she succeeded her aunt St Ottilia, as abbess of Hohenburg.
Cf. Chev. — Baud. — Holw. — Zimm.

EUGENIA (Bl) Abs. O.S.B. P.C. Nov. 22
d. c.1093. Abbess of the convent of SS Lucy and Agatha at Matera in S. Italy.
Cf. Zimm.

EUGENIA (St) V. M.   R.M. Dec. 25
d. ? 257. A Roman maiden, martyred under Valerian and buried in the cemetery of Apronian on the Via Latina. At a later period she was described quite groundlessly as a woman who disguised herself as a monk and who was accused of a crime she could not commit.
Cf. Att. — Baud. — Holw.

EUGENIAN (St) Bp. M.   R.M. Jan. 8
4th cent. He is stated to have been bishop of Autun in France, a staunch defender of the Catholic faith against Arianism, and a martyr.
Cf. Baud. — Holw.

EUGRAPHUS (St) M.   R.M. Dec. 10
See Mennas, Hermogenes and Eugraphus.

**EULALIA of BARCELONA (St) V. M.
R.M. Feb. 12**
d. 304. A maiden born at Barcelona, who suffered martyrdom under Diocletian. In all probability she is identical with St Eulalia of Mérida (see Dec. 10) though the Catalonians stoutly deny it. Under the names of Aulaire, Aulazie, Olalla, etc., she is greatly venerated throughout Spanish and French Catalonia.
Cf. Att. — Baud. — Holw.

EULALIA (St) V. M.   R.M. Dec. 10
d. 364. The most celebrated virgin martyr of Spain. Fortunately Prudentius wrote a long hymn describing her martyrdom, and she is likewise mentioned by St Augustine and others. She was a native

of Mérida, thirteen years of age, and was burnt at the stake in her native city under Diocletian.
Cf. Att. — Baud. — Holw.

EULAMPIA (St) V. M.   R.M. Oct. 10
See Eulampius, Eulampia and Comp.

EULAMPIUS, EULAMPIA and Comp. (SS) MM.   R.M. Oct. 10
d. 310. Two young children, brother and sister, martyred at Nicomedia under Gallienus. Their courage, it is added, led to the conversion and martyrdom of two hundred soldiers.
Cf. Att. — Baud. — Holw.

**EULOGIUS of TARRAGONA (St) M.
R.M. Jan. 21**
See Fructuosus, Augurius and Eulogius.

**EULOGIUS of CORDOVA (St) M.
R.M. March 11**
d. 859. A prominent priest of Cordova in the middle of the 9th century, when the Moorish persecution was at its height. In his youth he visited the Christian kingdoms of N. Spain, chiefly Navarre, to learn there the proper ecclesiastical and monastic observance. On his return to Cordova he encouraged the Christians of the province in their sufferings, and wrote *The Memorial of the Saints* for their benefit. He himself suffered martyrdom for having protected a girl converted from Islam.
Cf. Att. — Baud. — P. de U.

**EULOGIUS of EDESSA (St) Bp.
R.M. May 5**
d. p.381. A priest of Edessa, banished to the Thebaid for his firm stand against Arianism, and chosen bishop of his native town on his return after the death of Valens (375).
Cf. Holw. — Baud.

**EULOGIUS and Comp (SS) MM.
R.M. July 3**
d. 364-370. A group of Catholics martyred at Constantinople under the Arian emperor Valens.
Cf. Baud. — Holw.

**EULOGIUS of ALEXANDRIA (St) Bp.
R.M. Sept. 13**
d. 607. A Syrian by birth and a monk from early youth, Eulogius was chosen

patriarch of Alexandria in 579. He was a great friend of St Gregory the Great, who wrote to tell him about the new mission for the conversion of England.
Cf. Att. — Holw. — Baud.

EUMENES (St) Bp. **R.M. Sept. 18**
3rd cent. Bishop of Gortyna in Crete, who died in exile. He is one of those whom on account of their many miracles, the Greeks surname "the Wonder-Worker."
Cf. Baud. — Holw.

EUNAN (St) Bp. **A.C. Sept. 23**
8th cent. Identical with St Adamnan of Iona, q.v.
Cf. Att.

EUNICIAN (St) M. **R.M. Dec. 23**
See Theodulus, Saturninus, etc.

EUNOMIA (St) M. **R.M. Aug. 12**
See Hilarla, Digna, etc.

EUNUS (St) M.
 R.M. Feb. 27 and Oct. 30
See Julian, Cronion, etc.

EUPHEBIUS (St) Bp. **R.M. May 23**
? A bishop of Naples, about whom nothing is known.
Cf. Menzies.

EUPHEMIA (St) M. **R.M. March 20**
See Alexandra, Claudia, etc.

EUPHEMIA (Bl) Abs. O.S.B.
 P.C. June 17
d. 1180. Daughter of the count of Andechs, she became a nun and abbess of Altomünster in Bavaria.
Cf. Chev. — Holw. — Baud.

EUPHEMIA, DOROTHY, THECLA and ERASMA (SS) VV.MM. **R.M. Sept. 3**
? 1st cent. A group of maidens, martyred at Aquileia. They are venerated at Venice and at Ravenna.
Cf. Menzies — Holw. — Baud.

EUPHEMIA (St) V. M. **R.M. Sept. 16**
d. 307. A maiden said to have been burnt at the stake at Chalcedon. She is one of the most venerated of virgin-martyrs in the Greek church.
Cf. Att. — Baud. — Holw.

EUPHRASIA (St) V. **R.M. March 13**
d. c.420. Born at Constantinople and

connected by blood with the imperial family. She was brought up in a convent in Egypt, and when at a later date she was asked by the emperor to marry a senator she refused and remained in the convent for the rest of her life. We have her life written by a contemporary.
Cf. Att. — Baud. — Holw.

EUPHRASIA (St) M. **R.M. March 20**
See Alexandra, Claudia, etc.

EUPHRASIA PELLETIER (St) Foundress
 A.C. Apr. 24
1796-1868. A native of Noxmontier, in W. France, at eighteen she joined the institute of Our Lady of Charity founded by St John Eudes, and in 1829 founded at Angers the first convent of the Good Shepherd, a congregation which to-day numbers three hundred and thirty convents throughout the world and over ten thousand sisters. St Euphrasia visited London in 1844. She died at Angers in her seventy-second year, and was beatified in 1933 and canonized in 1940.

EUPHRASIA (St) V. M. **R.M. May 18**
See Theodotus, Thecusa, etc.

EUPHRASIUS (St) Bp. **R.M. Jan. 14**
? Perhaps identical with Eucrathius, a correspondent of St Cyprian; or else, a bishop martyred in Africa by the Arian Vandals.
Cf. Holw. — Baud.

EUPHRASIUS (St) Bp. M. R.M. May 15
See Torquatus, Ctesiphon, etc.

EUPHRONIUS (St) Bp. **R.M. Aug. 3**
d. p. 475. Bishop of Autun in France, friend of St Lupus of Troyes.
Cf. Gams — Duch. Fast Episc. — Baud.

EUPHRONIUS (St) Bp. **R.M. Aug. 4**
530-573. Bishop of Tours from 554 till his death. During his episcopate the city was burnt, and he worked most strenuously and successfully to rebuild it.
Cf. Duch. Fast. Episc. — Baud.

EUPHROSYNE (St) V. M. R.M. Jan. 1
? According to the legend, St Euphrosyne was a maiden of Alexandria in Egypt, who lived as a monk in a monastery there, her sex not being discovered till her death

many years later. It is only a replica of similar stories; see SS Pelagia (Oct. 8), Eugenia (Dec. 25) etc. It is doubtful whether St Euphrosyne ever existed.
Cf. Att. — Baud. — Holw.

EUPHROSYNE (St) V. M. R.M. May 7
See Flavia Domitilla, Euphrosyne and Theodora.

EUPLIUS (St) M. R.M. Aug. 12
d. 304. A deacon of Catania in Sicily who was found with a copy of the gospels in his possession, against Diocletian's edict. He was cruelly racked and martyred on this account.
Cf. Att. — Baud. — Holw. — Menzies.

EUPORUS (St) M. R.M. Dec. 23
See Theodulus, Saturninus, etc.

EUPREPIA (St) M. R.M. Aug. 12
See Hilaria, Digna, etc.

EUPREPIS (St) M. R.M. Nov. 30
See Castulus and Euprepis.

EUPREPIUS (St) Bp. R.M. Aug. 21
1st cent. The first bishop of Verona in N. Italy, sent there, according to an immemorial tradition, by St Peter himself.
Cf. Menzies — Baud. — Gams.

EUPREPIUS (St) M. R.M. Sept. 27
d. c.303. Mentioned in the legendary *Acta* as a companion martyr of SS Cosmas and Damian, q.v.

EUPSYCHIUS (St) M. R.M. Apr. 9
d. 362. A youth of Caesarea in Cappadocia, martyred under Julian the Apostate as leader of a group of Christians accused of having destroyed the temple of Fortune in that city.
Cf. Baud. — Holw.

EUPSYCHIUS (St) M. R.M. Sept. 7
d. c.130. A martyr of Caesarea in Cappodocia who suffered under Hadrian.
Cf. Holw. — Baud.

EURFYL (St) V. A.C. July 5
Otherwise Erfyl, q.v.

EURGAIN (St) V. A.C. June 30
6th cent. A daughter of the chieftain Caradog in Glamorgan, foundress of Cor-Eurgain, afterwards Llantwit. Another

St Eurgain, wife of a princeling in N. Wales, founded Llan-Eurgain in Flintshire.
Cf. Holw.

EUROSIA (OROSIA) (St) V. M. A.C. June 25
d. 714. According to the legend, she was a native of Bayonne — a more florid version makes her a native of Bohemia — who was martyred by the Saracens at Jaca in the Aragonese Pyrenees, close to the French frontier. She is to this day venerated as the patron saint of the diocese of Jaca, and her cult has spread throughout S. France and N. Italy. Leo XIII officially confirmed it in 1902. However, her very existence is doubtful.
Cf. Att. — Baud. — Menzies — Holw.

EUSEBIA (St) Abs. O.S.B. A.C. March 16
d. c.680. Eldest daughter of SS Adalbald and Rictrude, she was placed by her mother in the abbey of Hamage (Hamay) which had been founded by her grandmother St Gertrude. St Eusebia succeeded as abbess at the age of twelve. At a later period she was summoned to Marchiennes, where she was also abbess; but she finally went back to Hamage and continued to rule her nunnery in peace.
Cf. Att. — Baud. — Holw.

EUSEBIA (St) Abs. M. O.S.B. A.C. Sept. 20
d. c.731. Abbess of a nunnery at Marseilles. She, with some forty nuns of her community, was put to death by the Saracens at Saint-Cyr.
Cf. Zimm. — Chev. — Holw. — Baud.

EUSEBIA (St) V. M. R.M. Oct. 29
Late 3rd cent. A maiden of Bergamo, in Lombardy, niece of St Domnio, q.v., martyred under Maximian Herculius.
Cf. Baud. — Holw.

EUSEBIUS (St) H. A.C. Jan. 23
d. 4th cent. A Syrian hermit who lived on Mt Coryphe, near Antioch.
Cf. Att. — Baud. — Holw.

EUSEBIUS (St) M. O.S.B. A.C. Jan. 31
d. 884. An Irish pilgrim who took the Benedictine habit in the Swiss abbey of St Gall. Eventually he obtained leave to live as a recluse on Mt St Victor in the Vorarlberg. When he was denouncing

some godless peasants, one of them struck him with a scythe and killed him. Hence his veneration as a martyr.
Cf. Att. — Baud. — Holw. — Chev.

EUSEBIUS (Bl) H. O.S.B. Cam.
P.C. Feb. 10
d. 1501. A member of the Spanish nobility who was sent as ambassador to the republic of Venice. Here, he left all things to don the Camaldolese habit at San Michele, on the isle of Murano.
Cf. Chev. — Holw. — Zimm.

EUSEBIUS (St) H. **A.C. Feb. 15**
5th cent. A hermit of Aschia in Syria, venerated in the East.
Cf. Holw.

EUSEBIUS and Comp. (SS) MM.
R.M. March 5
? A group of ten martyrs who suffered in Africa.

EUSEBIUS (St) Ab. **A.C. March 5**
d. c.423. A native of Cremona and an intimate friend of St Jerome whom he followed to Rome and to the East. Here he succeeded the holy Doctor as abbot of Bethlehem, and was involved, like his friend, in bitter disputes on Origenism. The tradition that he founded the abbey of Guadalupe in Spain cannot be substantiated.
Cf. Att. — Baud. — Holw.

EUSEBIUS, NEON, LEONTIUS, LONGINUS and Comp. (SS) MM.
R.M. Apr. 24
? According to the Greek menologies, these were eight bystanders, who became Christians on witnessing the martyrdom of St George and were for this reason put to death. The legend should be studied in connection with that of St George.
Cf. Baud. — Holw.

EUSEBIUS (St) M. **R.M. Apr. 28**
See Aphrodisius, Caralippus, etc.

EUSEBIUS of SAMOSATA (St) Bp. M.
R.M. June 21
d. c.379. Bishop of Samosata in Syria from the year 361, he was a great friend of SS Basil and Gregory of Nazianzos, and a brave defender of orthodoxy against the Arians. He was for this reason banished to France, but recalled four years later.

He was killed by an Arian woman who threw a tile at his head.
Cf. Att. — Baud. — Holw.

EUSEBIUS of MILAN (St) Bp.
R.M. Aug. 12
d. 465. Probably a Greek by birth, he succeeded St Lazarus in the see of Milan and governed it for sixteen years. He helped Pope St Leo the Great to repress Eutychianism.
Cf. Baud. — Holw.

EUSEBIUS (St) M. **A.C. Aug. 14**
3rd cent. A martyr in Palestine under Maximian Herculius.
Cf. Holw.

EUSEBIUS (St) C. **R.M. Aug. 14**
d. c.357. A Roman priest, belonging to the patrician order, who founded the "parish church" called after him the *titulus Eusebii*. The Acts of Eusebius, according to which he publicly preached against Pope Liberius, are either entirely or in great part spurious.
Cf. Att. — Baud. — Holw. — Menzies.

EUSEBIUS (St) Pope. **R.M. Aug. 17**
d. 310. A Greek by birth, he was pope for a few months only, and died in exile in Sicily.
Cf. Att. — Baud. — Holw. — Menzies.

EUSEBIUS, PONTIAN, VINCENT and PEREGRINUS (SS) MM. R.M. Aug. 25
d. 192. Martyrs of Rome under Commodus. Their relics were translated to France in the 9th century.

EUSEBIUS, NESTABUS, ZENO and NESTOR (SS) MM. **R.M. Sept. 8**
d. 362. Martyrs massacred by the mob at Gaza in Palestine for having helped in the destruction of a pagan temple there.
Cf. Att. — Baud. — Holw.

EUSEBIUS (St) M. **R.M. Sept. 21**
? A martyr of Phoenicia, who appears to have given himself up voluntarily as a Christian.

EUSEBIUS of BOLOGNA (St) Bp.
R.M. Sept. 26
d. c.400 A bishop of Bologna from about the year 370. He was a great friend of St Ambrose of Milan, and an ardent opponent of Arianism. During his pontifi-

cate the relics of the martyrs SS Vitalis and Agricola were discovered.
Cf. Baud. — Holw. —Gams.

EUSEBIUS (St) M. R.M. Oct. 4
See Caius, Faustus, etc.

EUSEBIUS (St) M. R.M. Oct. 22
See Philip, Severus, etc.

EUSEBIUS (St) M. R.M. Nov. 5
See Felix and Eusebius.

EUSEBIUS, MARCELLUS, HIPPOLY-TUS, MAXIMUS, ADRIA, PAULINA, NEON, MARY, MARTANA and AURE-LIA (SS) MM. R.M. Dec. 2
d. 254-259. Roman martyrs under Valerian, Eusebius, a priest, Marcellus, his deacon, Neon and Mary were beheaded; Adria and Hippolytus scourged to death; Paulina died in the torture-chamber; and Maximus was thrown into the Tiber.
Cf. Holw. — Baud. — Ruinart.

EUSEBIUS of VERCELLI (St) Bp. M.
R.M. Dec. 16
c.283-c.370. A native of Sardinia, he joined the Roman clergy and was in 340 raised to the see of Vercelli in Piedmont. He fought Arianism with all the ardour of his Sardinian temperament, and with Dionysius of Milan and Lucifer of Cagliari was banished to the East. Before returning to Italy under Julian he visited St Athanasius at Alexandria. St Jerome wrote: "on the return of Eusebius, Italy put off her mourning." He was the first bishop who lived with his clergy under a rule, an example which was followed by St Augustine. On account of the sufferings he had to endure in his exile he is venerated as a martyr although he died in peace at Vercelli on Aug. 1.
Cf. Att. — Baud. — Holw. — Gams — Menzies.

EUSEUS (St) H. A.C. Feb. 15
14th cent. A hermit who lived and died near Serravalle in Piedmont. He is regarded as a patron of cobblers, since he plied that trade.
Cf. Att. — Baud. — Holw.

EUSIGNIUS (St) M. R.M. Aug. 5
d. 362. An old soldier of the army of Constantius Clorus who, surviving to the age of 110, refused to sacrifice to idols at the bidding of Julian the Apostate and was scourged and beheaded at Antioch in Syria.
Cf. Baud. — Holw.

EUSTACE (*several*)
Note. The Latin forms of this name, viz., Eustachius and Eustathius, are also used in English.

EUSTACE (EUSTASIUS) (St) Ab.
R.M. March 29
d. 625. A favourite disciple and monk of St Columbanus, whom he succeeded as second abbot of Luxeuil. He ruled over about six hundred monks, and during his abbacy the monastery was a veritable seminary of bishops and saints.
Cf. Baud. — Holw. — Mab. — Zimm.

EUSTACE (St) Bp. R.M. July 16
d. c.335. A native of Side in Pamphylia and a confessor during the last persecution, he was made bishop of Beroea in Syria and then transferred against his will to the patriarchal see of Antioch. He was present at the council of Nicaea, and from that time never ceased to oppose Arianism in preaching and writing. The Arians succeeded in deposing and banishing him, and he died in exile.
Cf. Att. — Baud. — Holw.

EUSTACE (EUSTATHIUS) (St) M.
R.M. July 28
? A martyr of Galatia who after torture appears to have been cast into a river.
Cf. Holw. — Baud.

EUSTACE (St) Ab. O.S.B. Cist.
P.C. Sept. 7
d. 1211. Born in the Beauvasis, he became a priest of the diocese of Beauvais. He later entered the Cistercian abbey of Flay (Saint-Germer) and was eventually its abbot. Under Pope Innocent III he was apostolic legate in England and on the continent against the Albigenses. He is greatly honoured by the Cistercians.
Cf. Baud. — Zimm. — Holw.

EUSTACE, THEOPISTES, AGAPITUS and THEOPISTUS (SS) MM.
R.M. Sept. 20
d. 118. Said to have been a Roman family of distinction — Eustace, an officer, Theopistes, his wife, and Agapitus and Theopistus, their two sons who were

martyred under Hadrian. Eustace owed his conversion to the vision of a stag with a crucifix between its antlers seen by him while hunting. Actually, however, nothing certain is known about him, or his supposed family, and their Acts are wholly untrustworthy.
Cf. Att. — Baud. — Holw. — Menzies.

EUSTACE (St) M. (or C.)   R.M. Oct. 12
? Hagiologists are in complete disagreement as to who this St Eustace was. The R.M. describes him as a priest and confessor in Syria; the Bollandists make of him an Egyptian martyr.
Cf. Baud. — Holw.

EUSTACE, THESPESIUS and ANATOLIUS (SS) MM.   R.M. Nov. 20
d. 235. Martyrs of Nicaea in Asia Minor under the emperor Maximinus the Thracian.
Cf. Baud. — Holw.

EUSTACE (St) M. Bp.   R.M. Nov. 28
See Valerian, Urban, etc.

EUSTACE WHITE (Bl) M. A.C. Dec. 10
d. 1591. Born at Louth, in Lincolnshire, he became a convert, and was educated for the priesthood at Reims and Rome. Ordained in 1588, he was condemned to death for his priesthood and executed at Tyburn.
Cf. Newdigate.

EUSTADIOLA (St) Abs. O.S.B.
A.C. June 8
d. 690. A native of Bourges who married early in life. Having been left a widow she spent all her fortune in building a nunnery in her native town — Moyen-Moutier, *Medianum monasterium* — whither she retired and became abbess.
Cf. Zimm. — Chev. — Baud. — Holw.

EUSTERIUS (St) Bp.   R.M. Oct. 19
5th cent. The fourth bishop of Salerno, of whom only the name is known.
Cf. Menzies.

EUSTOCHIA (St) V.   R.M. Sept. 28
Otherwise Eustochium, q.v.

EUSTOCHIUM CALAFATO (Bl) Poor Clare   A.C. Feb. 1
d. 1468. Daughter of the Countess Matilda of Calafato, she was born at Messina

in Sicily, where she became a Poor Clare, and eventually (1446) founded a convent of the strict observance at a place called *Monte delle Vergini — Montevergine* (Maidens' Hill). Cult confirmed in 1782.
Cf. Zimm. (Jan. 22) — Att. — Menzies — Baud.

EUSTOCHIUM of PADUA (Bl) N. O.S.B.
A.C. Feb. 13
1444-1469. The Cinderella of the Cloister. She was the daughter of a nun of Padua who had been seduced, and her baptismal name was Lucrezia Bellini. Gentle and pious, she became a nun in 1461 and for four years was subject to violent hysteria for which she was treated as one diabolically possessed: exorcized, kept in prison, fed on bread and water, or even deprived of food. When in her right mind she bore her treatment with heroic patience and humility. She died after her profession, aged twenty-six, and the name of Jesus was found cauterized on her breast. She is liturgically honoured at Padua.
Cf. Att. — Zimm. — Baud. — Menzies.

EUSTOCHIUM (St) V.   R.M. Sept. 28
d. 419. The third and best loved daughter of St Paula, the Roman matron who followed St Jerome to Palestine. She joined her mother at Bethlehem, where she collated manuscripts for St Jerome's translation of the Bible. She succeeded her mother in the direction of the nunnery at Bethlehem.
Cf. Att. — Baud. — Holw.

EUSTOCHIUM (St) V. M.   R.M. Nov. 2
d. 362. A maiden of Tarsus in Cilicia condemned to death under Julian the Apostate. She was barbarously tortured, and as a consequence died in prison, while engaged in prayer.
Cf. Baud. — Holw.

EUSTOCHIUS (St) Bp.   R.M. Sept. 19
d. 461. The successor (444) of St Brice in the see of Tours.
Cf. Att. — Baud. — Duch. Fast. Episc.

EUSTOCHIUS (St) M.   R.M. Nov. 16
See Elpidius, Marcellus, etc.

EUSTOLIA and SOPATRA (SS) VV.
R.M. Nov. 9
7th cent. It is uncertain whether both

of these virgins were daughters of the emperor Maurice of Constantinople (582-602) or only one of them. They were from the first revered as saints.
Cf. Baud. — Holw.

EUSTORGIUS (St) M. R.M. Apr. 11
d. ? 300. A priest of Nicomedia in Asia Minor, martyred, probably, under Diocletian.
Cf. Baud. — Holw.

EUSTORGIUS II (St) Bp. R.M. June 6
d. 518. A Roman priest who became bishop of Milan in 512. He spent large sums of money in ransoming many of his flock taken prisoners by the barbarians.
Cf. Menzies — Att. — Holw.

EUSTORGIUS I (St) Bp. M.
R.M. Sept. 18
d. p. 331. A Greek by birth, he was raised in 315 to the see of Milan, where he exerted all his influence against the Arians.
Cf. Menzies — Baud. — Holw.

EUSTOSIUS (St) M. R.M. Nov. 10
See Demetrius, Anianus, etc.

EUSTRATIUS, AUXENTIUS, EUGENE, MARDARIUS and ORESTES (SS) MM.
R.M. Dec. 13
d. c.302. Martyrs under Diocletian at Sebaste in Armenia. Eustratius was burnt to death in a furnace; Orestes, a soldier, roasted on a gridiron; the others were martyred in various ways.
Cf. Baud. — Holw.

EUSTREBERTA (St) V. A.C. Feb. 10
Otherwise Austreberta, q.v.

EUTHALIA (St) V. M. R.M. Aug. 27
? A virgin martyr of Lentini in Sicily. The Bollandists consider her very existence to be hardly proved.
Cf. Bolland. — Baud. — Menzies — Holw.

EUTHYMIUS the GREAT (St) Ab.
R.M. Jan. 20
378-473. An Armenian, born at Melitene. He was raised to the priesthood and charged with the supervision of all the monasteries of the district. Eventually he himself became a monk near Jerusalem, retiring afterwards to Jericho and further into the desert, where he established several *lauras*. He opposed Nestorianism and Eutychianism alike, and induced the empress Eudoxia to give up the latter. He is highly revered throughout the East.
Cf. Att. — Baud.

EUTHYMIUS of SARDIS (St) Bp. M.
R.M. March 11
d. 840. A monk who was made bishop of Sardis in Lydia and bravely opposed the Iconoclasts. He was banished by the emperor Nicephorus, and although he was several times given permission to return on condition of his becoming an Iconoclast, he always refused and remained in exile for twenty-nine years. He was eventually scourged to death.
Cf. Baud. — Holw.

EUTHYMIUS (St) M. R.M. May 5
? A deacon of Alexandria, martyred there.

EUTHYMIUS (St) C. R.M. Aug. 29
4th cent. A Roman who fled to Perugia with his wife and his child, St Crescentius, during the persecution of Diocletian. He died at Perugia and is venerated there.
Cf. Menzies — Baud. — Holw.

EUTHYMIUS the THESSALONIAN (St) Ab. A.C. Oct. 15
d. 886. Surnamed also "the New." Before his twentieth year, he became a monk at M. Olympus in Bithynia. Later he migrated to M. Athos and finally restored the monastery of St Andrew, and established a new nunnery, near Salonika. He returned to M. Athos to die.
Cf. Att.

EUTHYMIUS (St) M. R.M. Dec. 24
d. 303. A Christian of Nicomedia, foremost in encouraging his fellow-believers during the persecution of Diocletian, and a martyr himself under the same emperor.
Cf. Baud. — Holw.

EUTROPIA (St) V. M. R.M. June 15
See Lyobe, Levnis and Eutropia.

EUTROPIA (St) W. R.M. Sept. 15
5th cent. Said to have lived in Auvergne, France. She is first mentioned by Sidonius Apollinaris.
Cf. Baud. — Holw.

EUTROPIA (St) M. R.M. Oct. 30
d. ? 253. An African martyr, probably under Valerian.

EUTROPIA (St) V. M.   **R.M. Dec. 14**
See Nicasius, Eutropia, etc.

EUTROPIUS (St) M.   **R.M. Jan. 12**
d. 405. Reader of the church of Constantinople, he was martyred with St Tigrius and many others, for his loyalty to St John Chrysostom.
Cf. Att. — Baud. — Holw.

EUTROPIUS (St) M.   **R.M. March 3**
See Cleonicus, Eutropius and Basiliscus.

EUTROPIUS (St) Bp. M.   **R.M. Apr. 30**
? One of the alleged companions of St Dionysius of Paris. He is honoured as the first bishop of Saintes, and as a martyr.
Cf. Duch. Fast. Episc. — Gams — Att. — Baud.

EUTROPIUS (St) Bp.   **R.M. May 27**
d. p. 475. A native of Marseilles who succeeded St Justin in the see of Orange, in France, at a time when the diocese had been laid waste by the Visigoths.
Cf. Duch. Fast. Episc. — Att. — Baud. — Gams.

EUTROPIUS, ZOSIMA and BONOSA (SS) MM.   **R.M. July 15**
d. c.273. Martyrs of Porto, near Rome, under Aurelian.
Cf. Menzies.

EUTYCHES (St) M.   **R.M. Apr. 15**
See Maro, Eutyches and Victorinus.

EUTYCHIAN (St) M.   **R.M. July 2**
See Ariston, Crescentian, etc.

EUTYCHIAN (St) M.   **R.M. Aug. 17**
See Straton, Philip and Eutychian.

EUTYCHIAN (St) M.   **R.M. Sept. 2**
See Diomedes, Julian, etc.

EUTYCHIAN (St) M.   **R.M. Nov. 13**
See Arcadius, Paschasius, etc.

EUTYCHIAN (St) Pope M.   **R.M. Dec. 8**
d. 283. A native of Etruria or Tuscany. In 275 he succeeded St Felix I as pope. He is venerated as a martyr; but nothing certain is known about him.
Cf. Att. — Baud. — Menzies — Holw.

EUTYCHIUS (St) M.   **R.M. Feb. 4**
4th cent. A Roman martyr under Diocletian. From St Damasus's inscription on the tomb of the martyr we learn that he was left for twelve days in prison without food and then thrown into a well.
Cf. Baud. — Menzies — Holw.

EUTYCHIUS and Comp. (SS) MM.   **R.M. March 14**
d. 741. A considerable number of martyrs, put to death by the Mohammedans in Mesopotamia for refusing to deny Christ.
Cf. Att. — Baud. — Holw.

EUTYCHIUS of ALEXANDRIA and Comp. (SS) MM.   **R.M. March 26**
d. 356. Eutychius was a subdeacon of the church of Alexandria who, for his stand against Arianism, was condemned to slavery in the mines, but perished from exhaustion on the road thither. Many other Catholics were at the same time martyred for their opposition to Arius and their loyalty to St Athanasius.
Cf. Baud. — Holw.

EUTYCHIUS of CONSTANTINOPLE (St) Bp.   **A.C. Apr. 6**
d. 582. Appointed patriarch of Constantinople in 552, he opposed the emperor Justinian's interference in theological controversies. He was for this reason exiled for twelve years. He is honoured in the East.
Cf. Att. — Holw.

EUTYCHIUS (St) M.   **R.M. Apr. 15**
? A martyr of Ferentino in the Roman Campagna.

EUTYCHIUS (St) M.   **R.M. May 21**
See Timothy, Polius and Eutychius.

EUTYCHIUS and FLORENTIUS (SS) CC.   **R.M. May 23**
6th cent. Two monks who successively governed a monastery in Valcastoria, near Norcia, Italy. St Gregory the Great has left a glowing account of their virtues and miracles.
Cf. Menzies — Baud. — Holw.

EUTYCHIUS (St)   **R.M. Aug. 24**
1st cent. A Phrygian, disciple of St Paul. He is sometimes identified with the young man raised from the dead by the apostle at Troas (Acts XX) and is said to have attended St John at Patmos and to have died a martyr.
Cf. Baud. — Holw.

EUTYCHIUS (St) M. R.M. Sept. 19
See Januarius and Comp.

EUTYCHIUS, PLAUTUS and HERA-CLEAS (SS) MM. R.M. Sept. 29
? Martyrs in Thrace.

EUTYCHIUS (St) M. R.M. Oct. 5
See Placid and Comp.

EUTYCHIUS (St) M. R.M. Nov. 21
See Honorius, Eutychius and Stephen.

EUTYCHIUS (St) M. R.M. Dec. 11
4th cent. A Spanish martyr — San Oye — martyred at Mérida, or at Cádiz. Nothing certain is known about him.
Cf. Baud. — Holw.

EUTYCHIUS and DOMITIAN (SS) MM. R.M. Dec. 28
? A priest and his deacon, martyred at Ancyra, in Galatia.

EUVERT (St) Bp. R.M. Sept. 7
Otherwise Evortius, q.v.

EVA of LIÉGE (Bl) V. A.C. May 26
d. c.1266. A recluse of Liége who lived under the Cistercian rule, and who on the death of Bl Juliana of Cornillon successfully continued her work in favour of the institution of the liturgical feast of *Corpus Christi.* Cult confirmed in 1902.
Cf. Att. — Baud. — Holw.

EVAGRIUS (St) Bp. R.M. March 6
d. c.380. In 370, after the Arians had occupied the see of Constantinople for twenty years, the Catholics chose Evagrius for that see; but a few months later he was banished by the emperor Valens, and remained in exile till his death.
Cf. Att. — Baud. — Holw.

EVAGRIUS and BENIGNUS (SS) MM. R.M. Apr. 3
? Martyrs at Tomi on the Black Sea.

EVAGRIUS (St) M. R.M. Oct. 1
See Priscus, Crescens and Evagrius.

EVAGRIUS, PRISCIAN and Comp. (SS) MM. R.M. Oct. 12
? A group of martyrs, who suffered either in Rome or, more probably, in Syria.

EVAL (Uvol, Urfol) A.C. Nov. 20
6th cent. A British bishop in Cornwall, from whom a village in that county is named.
Cf. Baring-Gould.

EVAN (INAN) (St) H. A.C. Aug. 18
9th cent. A Scottish hermit in Ayrshire, where churches are still dedicated to him.
Cf. Holw. (Inan).

EVANDUS (St) Bp. A.C. ?
d. c.313. First bishop of Urbino.
Cf. Menzies.

EVANGELIST and PEREGRINUS (BB) CC. O.S.A. A.C. March 20
d. c.1250. These two saints were born at Verona, became friends at school, entered together the order of the Augustinian friars, were both endowed with similar miraculous gifts, and died within a few hours of each other. Their cult was approved in 1837.
Cf. Att. — Menzies — Baud. — Holw.

EVARISTUS (St) M. R.M. Oct. 14
See Carponius, Evaristus and Priscian.

EVARISTUS (St) Pope M. R.M. Oct. 26
d. c.107. A Hellenic Jew who was raised to the Roman see about the year 96 — thus becoming the fourth successor of St Peter. He is honoured as a martyr, though the fact of his martyrdom is not established.
Cf. Att. — Baud. — Menzies.

EVARISTUS (St) M. R.M. Dec. 23
See Theodulus, Saturninus, etc.

EVASIUS (St) Bp. M. R.M. Dec. 1
d. ? 362. Said to have been the first bishop of Asti in Piedmont, whence he was driven by the Arians, and finally to have been put to death under Julian the Apostate at Casale Monferrato. The accounts given of him are very untrustworthy.
Cf. Baud. — Holw. — Menzies.

EVASIUS (St) Bp. R.M. Dec. 2
? First bishop of Brescia.
Cf. Menzies.

EVELLIUS (St) M. R.M. May 11
d. c.66. Said to have been a counsellor of Nero, converted to Christ on witnessing

the patience of the martyrs, and martyred himself at Pisa.
Cf. Holw. — Baud. — Menzies.

EVENTIUS (St) M.   R.M. Apr. 16
See Saragossa (Martyrs of).

EVENTIUS (St) M.   R.M. May 3
See Alexander, Eventius and Theodulus.

EVERARD (several)
Otherwise Eberhard, or Erhard, q.v.

EVERARD HANSE (Bl) M.   A.C. July 30
d. 1581. A native of Northamptonshire who was educated at Cambridge and became a Protestant minister. After his conversion he was ordained priest at Reims (1581). A few months after he was martyred at Tyburn; when dying he was heard to exclaim: "O happy day!" Beatified in 1886.
Cf. Att. — Newdigate — Baud.

EVERGISLUS (EBREGESILUS) (St) Bp. M.   R.M. Oct. 24
? 5th cent. A bishop of Cologne, and a martyr at the hands of heathen robbers. Very probably he died at a much later period and not as a martyr.
Cf. Att. — Baud. — Holw.

EVERILDIS (St) Abs. O.S.B.   A.C. July 9
d. late 7th cent. This saint received the veil from St Wilfrid at York at a spot called "the Bishop's Farm," afterwards Everildsham, now Everingham, where she became abbess of a large community. Her two first companions were SS Bega and Wulfreda.
Cf. Att. — Baud. — Zimm. — Stanton.

EVERMARUS (St) M.   A.C. May 1
d. c.700. A pilgrim, murdered by robbers at Rousson, near Tongres, in Belgium.
Cf. Att. — Baud. — Holw.

EVERMOD (St) Bp.   A.C. Feb. 17
d. 1178. A Premonstratensian canon under St Norbert, who preached to the Wends, and eventually was chosen abbot of Gottesgnaden, then abbot of Magdeburg, and finally bishop of Ratzeburg.
Cf. Att. — Holw.

EVERMUND (EBREMUNDUS) (St) Ab. O.S.B.   A.C. June 10
d. c.720. A native of Bayeux and a courtier. He married and, with his wife's

consent, founded several religious houses, the chief of which was Fontenay -Louvet, in the diocese of Séez, where he became monk and abbot. His wife entered one of his foundations as a nun.
Cf. Baud. — Chev. — Holw.

EVILASIUS (St) M.   R.M. Sept. 20
See Fausta and Evilasius.

EVODIUS, HERMOGENES and CALLISTUS (SS) MM.   R.M. Apr. 25
? Three brothers, martyred at Syracuse in Sicily. Callistus is often written Callista, which spelling, if correct, would show that the third member of the trio was sister not brother, to the other two.
Cf. Baud. — Holw. — Menzies.

EVODIUS (St) Bp. M.   R.M. May 6
d. c.67. The successor of St Peter in the see of Antioch. Tradition makes him a martyr and one of the seventy-two disciples of our Lord.
Cf. Att. — Baud. — Holw.

EVODIUS (St) M.   R.M. Aug. 2
See Theodota, and her three sons.

EVODIUS (St) Bp.   R.M. Oct. 8
5th cent. A native of Rouen and bishop of that see. His relics were translated to Braine, near Soissons.
Cf. Duch. Fast. Episc. — Gams — Baud.

EVODIUS (St) Bp.   A.C. Nov. 12
d. p. 560. Bishop of Le Puy in France.
Cf. Duch. Fast. Episc. — Gams — Chev. — Baud.

EVORTIUS (St) Bp.   R.M. Sept. 7
d. c.340. A Roman cleric who became bishop of Orleans. The abbey of Saint-Euvert (St Evortius) was founded to enshrine his relics.
Cf. Duch. Fast. Episc. — Gams — Baud.

EVROUL (St) Ab.   R.M. Dec. 29
Otherwise Ebrulfus, q.v.

EWALD the FAIR and EWALD the DARK (SS) Mks. O.S.B.   R.M. Oct. 3
d. c.695. Two brothers of Northumbrian stock who became monks and priests, and followed St Willibrord to Frisia. After a short apostolate they were martyred together at Aplerbeke, near Dortmund.
Cf. Att. — Zimm. — Baud. — Chev. — Holw.

EXANTHUS (St) M. R.M. Aug. 7
See Carpophorus, Exanthus, etc.

EXPEDITUS of MELITENE (St) M.
R.M. Apr. 19
See Hermogenes, Caius, Expeditus, etc.

EXUPERANTIA (St) V. R.M. Apr. 26
? A saint whose relics are venerated at
Troyes in France. Nothing else is known
about her.

EXUPERANTIUS (St) Bp. R.M. Jan. 24
5th cent. Bishop of Cingoli near Ancona,
in Italy. He is believed to have been a
native of Africa.
Cf. Baud. — Holw. — Menzies.

EXUPERANTIUS (St) Bp. R.M. May 30
d. 418. Bishop of Ravenna from 398
to 418.
Cf. Menzies — Baud. — Att.

EXUPERANTIUS (St) M. R.M. Dec. 30
See Sabinus, Exuperantius, etc.

EXUPERIA (St) M. R.M. July 26
See Symphronius, Olympius, etc.

**EXUPERIUS (HESPERIUS), ZOE, CY-
RIACUS and THEODULUS (SS) MM.**
R.M. May 2
d. 140. A family of slaves — husband,
wife and two sons — owned by a rich
pagan of Attalia in Pamphylia. They
were martyred for refusing to take part
with their master in idolatrous rites.
Cf. Baud. — Holw.

EXUPERIUS (St) M. R.M. Sept. 22
See Maurice, Exuperius, etc.

EXUPERIUS (French: SPIRE) (St) Bp.
R.M. Sept. 28
d. 411. Bishop of Toulouse, a benefactor
and friend of St Jerome, noted for his
generosity in sending large contributions
to the poor of Palestine and Egypt.
*Cf. Att. — Duch. Fast. Episc. — Gams —
Baud.*

EXUPERIUS (St) M. R.M. Nov. 19
See Severinus, Exuperius and Felician.

EZECHIEL (St) Prophet. R.M. Apr. 10
6th cent. B.C. One of the four greater
prophets and the writer of a canonical
book of Scripture. The tradition is that

he was put to death, while in captivity in
Babylon, by one of the Jewish judges who
had turned pagan, and that he was buried
there in the tomb of Shem. His grave
was for the early Christians a place of
pilgrimage.
Cf. Holw.

F

FABIAN (St) Pope M. R.M. Jan. 20
d. 250. In 236 Fabian succeeded St
Antheros on the papal throne and reigned
fourteen years, until his martyrdom under
Decius. St Cyprian, his contemporary,
describes him as an "incomparable man"
and adds that the glory of his death cor-
responded with the purity and goodness of
his life.
Cf. Att. — Menzies — Baud. — Holw.

FABIAN (St) M. R.M. Dec. 31
See Stephen, Pontian, etc.

FABIOLA (St) W. A.C. Dec. 27
d. c.400. A Roman patrician maiden who
was married very young to a man of equal
rank but of dissolute habits, whom she
divorced. She then united herself with
another man, causing great scandal in
Rome. After the latter's death she performed public penance, and devoted her
great wealth to the care of the sick in a
hospital which she established in Rome —
the first of its kind in the West — associating herself in this work with St Pammachius. In 395 she visited her friend
St Jerome in the Holy Land, and wished to
enter the convent at Bethlehem; but was
dissuaded by St Jerome. She returned
accordingly to Rome and founded, and
superintended, a hostel for pilgrims near
the city. The veneration in which she
was held in Rome was demonstrated by
the great concourse of people at her
funeral.
Cf. Att. — Baud. — Holw.

FABIUS (St) M. R.M. May 11
See Maximus, Bassus and Fabius.

FABIUS (St) M. R.M. July 31
d. 300. A soldier beheaded at Caesarea in
Mauretania, under Diocletian, for refusing to carry a standard bearing idolatrous
emblems.
Cf. Holw. — Baud.

FABRICIAN and PHILIBERT (SS) MM.
R.M. Aug. 22
? Said to have been martyred in Spain. They are honoured at Toledo.
Cf. Holw. — Baud.

FACHANAN (St) Bp. A.C. Aug. 14
d. late 6th cent. Probably the first bishop of Ross, in Ireland. He founded the monastic school at what is now Rosscarbery, in Co Cork, and placed there St Brendan as one of the teachers. He is venerated as the patron saint of the diocese of Ross.
Cf. Att. — Holw. — Baud.

FACIOLUS (St) Mk. O.S.B. A.C. Sept. 7
d. c.950. A Benedictine monk of the abbey of St Cyprian at Poitiers.
Cf. Zimm.

FACUNDINUS (St) Bp. A.C. Aug. 28
d. c.620. Bishop of Taino in Umbria, where he is still venerated.
Cf. Menzies — Holw. — Baud.

FACUNDUS and PRIMITIVUS (SS) MM. R.M. Nov. 27
d. c.300. Born at León in Spain and beheaded by the river Cea, where the town of Sahagun now stands. At a later period the great Benedictine abbey of Sahagun, round which grew the present township of that name, was called after St Facundus (Sant'Facun-Sahagun).
Cf. Holw. — Baud. — P. de U.

FAGAN (St) A.C. Jan. 3 (R.M. May 26)
Otherwise Fugatius, q.v.

FAGILDUS (St) Ab. O.S.B. A.C. July 25
d. 1086. Benedictine abbot of the monastery of St Martin de Antealtares, at Compostella in Spain. The epitaph on his tomb ends with this line: "A saint, he left the world to live with the saints."
Cf. P. de U. (Los Monjes Españoles en la Edad Media, vol. II, p. 438).

FAILBHE the LITTLE (St) Ab.
A.C. March 10
d. 754. For seven years abbot of Iona, where he died at the age of eighty.
Cf. Holw.

FAILBHE (St) Ab. A.C. March 22
d. c.680. An immediate predecessor of St Adamnan as abbot of Iona. He was an Irishman and brother of St Finan of Rath. There are some twenty other saints of the same name commemorated in the Irish and Scottish menologies.
Cf. Baud. — Holw.

FAINA (St) M. R.M. May 18
See Theodotus, Thecusa, etc.

FAITH, HOPE and CHARITY (SS) VV. MM. R.M. Aug. 1
d. c.120. The English equivalent of the Greek Pistis, Elpis, Agape, and of the Latin Fides, Spes, Caritas. The legend is that they were three young girls, aged respectively twelve, ten and nine years, daughters of St Wisdom (Sophia, Sapientia) with whom they were martyred in Rome under Hadrian. The story seems to be a myth.
Cf. Att. — Menzies — Holw.

FAITH (FOI) (St) V. M. R.M. Oct. 6
? A Maiden of Agen in S. France, burnt to death in the same city (under Maximian Herculius?). Her shrine at the abbey of Conques was very famous during the Middle Ages. A portion of her relics was taken to Glastonbury; hence her place in the Sarum calendar and the dedication to her of several English churches.
Cf. Att. — Baud. — Holw.

FAL (FELE) (St) C. R.M. May 16
Otherwise Fidolus, q.v.

FALCO (St) Bp. A.C. Feb. 20
d. 512. Bishop of Maestricht from 495 till his death.
Cf. Baud. — Holw.

FALCO (Bl) Ab. O.S.B. A.C. June 6
d. 1146. Falco received the Benedictine habit at Cava, at the hands of St Peter, abbot of that monastery. Shortly after he was sent to rule the daughter house of St Mary at Cirzosimo, and in 1141 he succeeded Bl Simon as abbot of Cava. Cult confirmed in 1928.
Cf. Chev. — Holw.

FALCO (Bl) H. A.C. Aug. 9
d. 1440. A native of Calabria, who led a hermit's life in the Abruzzi. His shrine is to be found at Palena. Cult approved in 1893.
Cf. Menzies — Baud. — Holw.

FAMIANUS (QUARDUS) (St) H. O.S.B. Cist. A.C. Aug. 8
1090-1150. A native of Cologne, who made the pilgrimage to the Holy Land, to Rome and Compostella, and finally settled near the last named place as a hermit, living for twenty-five years at San Placido on the River Minho. When the Cistercian abbey of Osera was built in the neighbourhood he joined the community and professed the Rule. However, he obtained leave to visit the Holy Land once more and, on his return, died at Gallese in Umbria.
Cf. Chev. — Menzies — Baud. — Holw.

FANCHEA (GARBH) (St) V. A.C. Jan. 1
d. c. ? 585. A native of Clogher and sister of St Endeus (Enda). She was the abbess-foundress of a convent at Rossory in Fermanagh, and was buried at Killane.
Cf. Att. — Baud. — Holw.

FANDILAS (St) Mk. M. R.M. June 13
d. 853. An Andalusian by birth, he was a priest and abbot of the monastery of Peñamelaria, near Cordova. He was beheaded at Cordova by order of the emir Mohammed.
Cf. P. de U. — Zimm. — Chev. — Baud. — Holw.

FANTINUS (St) Ab. R.M. Aug. 30
d. p. 980. A Basilian monk of Calabria, and abbot of the Greek monastery of St Mercury. He was already an old man when his abbey was destroyed by the Saracens. He then travelled to the East, where he died.
Cf. Menzies — Att. — Baud. — Holw.

FARA (St) Abs. R.M. Apr. 3 and Dec. 7
Otherwise Burgundofara, q.v.

FARANNAN (St) Ab. A.C. Feb. 15
d. c.590. An Irish disciple of St Columba at Iona. Eventually he returned to Ireland to lead the life of a hermit at All-Farannan, now Allernan, Sligo, where he probably died.
Cf. Holw.

FARO (St) Bp. R.M. Oct. 28
d. c.675. A brother of SS Fara and Cagnoaldus. He gave up the office of chancellor which he held at the court of Dagobert I and became a monk (either at Luxeuil or at Rebais), a priest, and finally bishop of Meaux (626). In this capacity he was a great fosterer of monasticism.
Cf. Att. — Baud. — Chev. — Mab. — Zimm.

FASTRED (Bl) Ab. O.S.B. Cist. A.C. Apr. 21
d. 1163. Fastred de Cavamiez was a native of Hainault who received the Cistercian habit from St Bernard at Clairvaux. In 1148 he was dispatched with a colony of monks to be abbot-founder of Cambron, in the diocese of Cambrai. In 1157 he was transferred to the abbacy of Clairvaux and in 1162 to that of Cîteaux.
Cf. Att. — Baud. — Holw. — Chev.

FAUSTA and EVILASIUS (SS) MM. R.M. Sept. 20
d. 303. St Fausta, a girl of about thirteen, was being cruelly treated by order of Evilasius, a heathen magistrate, when, on seeing her constancy, the latter also confessed Christ. Both were martyred together at Cyzicum in Pontus under Diocletian.
Cf. Baud. — Holw.

FAUSTA (St) W. R.M. Dec. 19
3rd cent. The reputed mother of St Anastasia of Sirmium.
Cf. Menzies — Baud. — Holw.

FAUSTINA and LIBERATA (SS) VV. A.C. Jan. 18
d. c.580. Sisters who are said to have founded a Benedictine nunnery at Como. Their relics are in the cathedral at Como, and there are churches dedicated to them at Mantua and Verona.
Cf. Menzies.

FAUSTINIAN (St) Bp. R.M. Feb. 26
4th cent. Said to have been the second bishop of Bologna. He reorganized the diocese which had suffered much during the persecution of Diocletian, and lived to be a firm defender of the Faith against Arianism.
Cf. Menzies — Baud.

FAUSTINUS and JOVITA (SS) MM. R.M. Feb. 15
d. c. ? 121. Two brothers, belonging to the nobility of Brescia, in Lombardy, and zealous preachers of Christianity, who were beheaded in their native city, it is

said, under the emperor Hadrian. They are the chief patrons of the city.
Cf. Menzies — Ricci — Att. — Holw.

FAUSTINUS (St) Bp. R.M. Feb. 16
d. 381. The successor of St Ursicinus, about the year 360, in the see of Brescia, in Lombardy. He is said to have been a collateral descendant of SS Faustinus and Jovita and to have compiled their Acts.
Cf. Menzies — Baud. — Holw.

FAUSTINUS and Comp. (SS) MM.
 R.M. Feb. 17
? A supposed group of forty-five martyrs, of whom nothing whatever is known.

FAUSTINUS, TIMOTHY and VENUS-TUS (SS) MM. R.M. May 22
d. c.362. Roman martyrs under Julian the Apostate.

FAUSTINUS (St) M. R.M. June 5
See Florentius, Julian, etc.

FAUSTINUS (St) M. R.M. July 29
See Simplicius, Faustinus and Beatrix.

FAUSTINUS (St) C. R.M. July 29
4th cent. A disciple of St Felix, bishop of Martano, or Spello, near Spoleto, and his attendant at his martyrdom. St Faustinus himself suffered much for Christ before passing away peacefully at Todi in Umbria.
Cf. Menzies — Baud. — Holw.

FAUSTINUS, LUCIUS, CANDIDUS, CAELIAN, MARK, JANUARIUS and FORTUNATUS (SS) MM. R.M. Dec. 15
? African martyrs, about whom nothing is known.

FAUSTUS (St) Ab. A.C. Feb. 15
6th cent. An alleged disciple of St Benedict at Montecassino, and companion and biographer of St Maurus, according to the legendary *Vita Sancti Mauri* of Abbot Odo of Glanfeuil.
Cf. Zimm. — Baud. — Chev.

FAUSTUS and Comp. (SS) MM.
 R.M. June 24
? Twenty-four Roman martyrs, whose Acts have been lost. They are very probably to be identified with the group of Roman martyrs commemorated on June 25 (see Lucy and Comp.).

FAUSTUS (St) M. R.M. July 16
d. 250. A martyr of the Decian persecution, who, crucified and transfixed with arrows, is said to have lingered in his agony for five days.
Cf. Holw. — Baud.

FAUSTUS (St) M. R.M. Aug. 1
See Bonus, Faustus, etc.

FAUSTUS (St) M. R.M. Aug. 7
d. c.190. According to tradition, this St Faustus was a soldier martyred at Milan under Commodus.
Cf. Baud. — Holw.

FAUSTUS, MACARIUS and Comp. (SS) MM. R.M. Sept. 6
d. 250. A group of twelve martyrs, beheaded at Alexandria in Egypt under Decius.
Cf. Baud. — Holw.

FAUSTUS (St) Ab. A.C. Sept. 6
d. c.607. Abbot of the monastery of Santa Lucia, at Syracuse, where he taught Zosimus, the future bishop of Syracuse.
Cf. Menzies — Zimm. — Chev.

FAUSTUS (St) M. R.M. Sept. 8
See Timothy and Faustus.

FAUSTUS (St) Bp. A.C. Sept. 28
d. c.493. Born in Brittany, Faustus became a monk at Lérins and later the abbot (433) of that monastery. In 452, he was chosen bishop of Riez. He combated with great energy and success both Arianism and Pelagianism; though in his writings he himself is not exempt from semi-pelagianism. He was one of the most influential bishops of his time.
Cf. Duch. Fast. Episc. — Att. — Chev. — Gams.

FAUSTUS (St) M. R.M. Oct. 3
See Dionysius, Faustus, etc. This Faustus is identified by the R.M. with those of Oct. 4 and Nov. 19.

FAUSTUS (St) M. R.M. Oct. 4
See Caius, Faustus, etc.

FAUSTUS (St) M. R.M. Oct. 5
See Placid and Comp.

FAUSTUS, JANUARIUS and MARTIAL (SS) MM. R.M. Oct. 13
d. 304. Martyrs of Cordova under Dio-

cletian, Prudentius calls them "the Three Crowns of Cordova."
Cf. Att. — P. de U. — Baud. — Holw.

FAUSTUS (St) M.   **R.M. Nov. 19**
4th cent. The deacon of St Dionysius of Alexandria and his companion in exile. He survived his master and in extreme old age died a martyr under Diocletian. See Dionysius, Faustus, etc., and Caius, Faustus, etc.
Cf. Baud. — Holw.

FAUSTUS, DIDIUS, AMMONIUS, PHILEAS, HESYCHIUS, PACHOMIUS, THEODORE and Comp. (SS) MM.
R.M. Nov. 26
d. c.311. Egyptian martyrs under Maximian Galerius. It is said that their total number was six hundred and sixty. Phileas, Hesychius, Pachomius and Theodore were bishops, Faustus a priest of Alexandria.
Cf. Baud. — Holw.

FAZZIO (FATIUS, FAZIUS, FACIUS) (St) C.   **A.C. Jan. 18**
1190-1272. A native of Verona and a goldsmith. He founded a charitable society at Cremona, called the Order of the Holy Spirit. He made several pilgrimages on foot to Rome and to Compostella.
Cf. Menzies — Baud. — Holw.

FEBRONIA (St) V. M.   **R.M. June 25**
d. 304. A young nun, barbarously mutilated and finally put to death under Diocletian at Nisibis in Mesopotamia (not at Sybapolis in Syria). The legend adds many ghastly details; but there is good reason to doubt the very existence of this saint.
Cf. Att. — Holw. — Baud.

FECHIN (St) Ab.   **A.C. Jan. 20**
d. c.665. A native of Connaught, and the abbot-founder of several Irish monasteries. His name is particularly connected with that of Fobhar (Fore) in Westmeath. Ecclefechan and St Vigean's, near Arbroath in Scotland, also perpetuate his memory.
Cf. Att. — Baud. — Holw.

FEDLEMID (St) Bp.   **A.C. Aug. 9**
Otherwise Phelim, q.v.

FEIGHIN (St) Ab.   **A.C. Jan. 20**
Otherwise Fechin, q.v.

FELAN (St) Ab.   **A.C. Jan. 9**
Otherwise Foelan, q.v.

FELE (St) C.   **R.M. May 16**
Otherwise Fal or Fidolus, q.v.

FELICIA de MONTMORENCY (Bl) V. O.V.   **A.C. June 6**
1600-1666. Born at Rome of French parents, Marie Félicie des Ursins became a nun of the visitation at Autun, during the life-time of the foundress, St Jane Frances de Chantal.
Cf. Baud.

FELICIA MEDA (Bl) Poor Clare.
A.C. Oct. 5
1378-1444. A native of Milan, who joined the Poor Clares at the convent of St Ursula in that city (1400). In 1425 she was made abbess, and after fourteen years she was sent to Pesaro to establish a new house which she ruled with equal success. Cult approved in 1812.
Cf. Att. — Baud. — Holw. — Menzies.

FELICIAN (St) Bp. M.   **R.M. Jan. 24**
d. 254. A native of Foligno, who was consecrated bishop of that city by Pope St Victor I and governed his diocese for more than fifty years, meanwhile evangelizing the whole of Umbria. He was arrested under Decius, and, though already in his ninetieth year, was cruelly ill-treated and taken to Rome for martyrdom; but he died on his way thither. Eventually part of his relics were carried to Westphalia and this gave rise to his second feast, listed in the R.M. on Oct. 20.
Cf. Att. — Baud. — Holw.

FELICIAN, PHILAPPIAN and Comp. (SS) MM.   **R.M. Jan. 30**
? A band of one hundred and twenty-six African martyrs.

FELICIAN (St) M.   **R.M. Feb. 2**
See Fortunatus, Felician, etc.

FELICIAN (St) M.   **R.M. June 9**
See Primus and Felician.

FELICIAN (St) M.   **R.M. July 21**
See Victor, Alexander, etc.

FELICIAN (St) Bp. M.   **R.M. Oct. 20**
See Felician, Jan. 24.

FELICIAN (St) M.   R.M. Oct. 29
See Hyacinth, Quinctus, etc.

FELICIAN (St) M.   R.M. Nov. 11
See Valentine, Felician and Victorinus.

FELICIAN (St) M.   R.M. Nov. 19
See Severinus, Exuperius and Felician.

FELICINUS (St) Bp.   R.M. July 19
Otherwise Felix of Verona, q.v.

FELICISSIMA (St) V. M.   R.M. Aug. 12
See Gracilian and Felicissima.

FELICISSIMUS, HERACLIUS and PAULINUS (SS) MM.   R.M. May 26
d. 303. Martyrs under Diocletian. They suffered in all probability at Todi in Umbria, where their relics are still venerated.
Cf. Menzies — Baud. — Holw.

FELICISSIMUS (St) M.   R.M. July 2
See Ariston, Crescentian, etc.

FELICISSIMUS (St) M.   R.M. Aug. 6
See Sixtus, Felicissimus, etc.

FELICISSIMUS (St) M.   R.M. Oct. 26
See Rogatian and Felicissimus.

FELICISSIMUS (St) M.   R.M. Nov. 24
d. c.303. A martyr who suffered at Perugia, probably under Diocletian.
Cf. Menzies — Baud. — Holw.

FELICITAS (St) M.   R.M. March 7
See Perpetua, Felicitas, etc.

FELICITAS (St) M.   R.M. March 8
See Cyril, Rogatus, etc.

FELICITAS (St) V.   A.C. March 26
9th cent. A nun, in all probability of the Benedictine Order, who professed the Rule in a convent on the Colli Euganei, or else in that of SS Cosmas and Damian at Padua. Her relics are now at St Justina, Padua.
Cf. Zimm. — Chev. — Bolland. (Martii t. III, p. 679).

FELICITAS (St) M.   R.M. Nov. 23
d. 165. A Roman widow martyred at Rome with her sons under Marcus Antoninus. The R.M. identifies her sons with the seven brothers, commemorated

July 10 (see Seven Brothers) but modern writers incline to question this identification. This Felicitas may be the saint named in the Canon of the Mass, rather than the companion of St Perpetua, as usually supposed.
Cf. Att. — Baud. — Holw. — Menzies.

FELICULA (St) M.   R.M. Feb. 14
See Vitalis, Felicula and Zeno.

FELICULA (St) V. M.   R.M. June 13
d. c.90. A Roman maiden of the apostolic age, thought to have been the foster sister of St Petronilla. After the latter's martyrdom under Domitian she was left for a fortnight in her prison without food or drink, and then was thrown into a ditch to die. Her body was recovered by St Nicomedes.
Cf. Att. — Baud. — Menzies — Holw.

FELINUS and GRATIANUS (SS) MM.
               R.M. June 1
d. 250. Soldiers in the imperial army martyred at Perugia under Decius. Their relics were translated to Arona near Milan in 979.
Cf. Menzies — Holw. — Baud.

FELIX (*several*)
Note. This name is one of the most common in Christian Hagiology. There is scarcely a group of saints in the R.M. which does not contain one or more named Felix. In the following notices we list only the best known among them.

FELIX of BOURGES (St) Bp.
               A.C. Jan. 1
d. c.580. Bishop of Bourges in France. He took part in the council of Paris A.D. 576. He is still venerated at Bourges.
Cf. Att. — Holw. — Gams.

FELIX and JANUARIUS (SS) MM.
               R.M. Jan. 7
? Said to have suffered martyrdom at Heraclea, a name common to several ancient cities.
Cf. Holw. — Baud.

FELIX (St) M.   R.M. Jan. 9
See Epictetus, Jucundus, etc.

FELIX of NOLA (St) M.   R.M. Jan. 14
d. c.260. The son of a Romano-Syrian soldier who had settled at Nola, near

Naples, where he owned some land. Felix was ordained a priest and devoted himself to the service of his bishop, St Maximus, especially during the persecution which broke out under Decius. The bishop was martyred and his see was offered to Felix, but he preferred to continue in his life of service to the bishop and the poor. On account of his sufferings during the persecution, he is venerated as a martyr. St Paulinus, bishop of Nola at a later period, has left a glowing account of the popular veneration for St Felix.
Cf. Att. — Holw. — Menzies — Baud.

FELIX (St) C. A.C. Jan. 14
? A Roman priest, venerated also on Jan. 14, and often confused with St Felix. of Nola.
Cf. Baud. — Holw.

FELIX O'DULLANY (Bl) Bp. O.S.B. Cist.
P.C. Jan. 24
d. 1202. An Irish Cistercian monk, probably of Jerpoint, Kilkenny. In 1178 he was made bishop of Ossory residing at Aghaboe. He is venerated by the Cistercians as a *beatus.*
Cf. Holw.

FELIX, SYMPHRONIUS (SEMPRONIUS), HIPPOLYTUS and Comp. (SS) MM. R.M. Feb. 3
? A group of martyrs who suffered probably in Proconsular Africa.

FELIX of LYONS (St) Bp. R.M. Feb. 3
See Lupicinus and Felix.

FELIX of AFRICA (St) M. R.M. Feb. 11
See Saturninus, Dativus, etc.

FELIX of ADRUMETUM (St) M.
R.M. Feb. 21
See Verulus, Secundinus, etc.

FELIX of METZ (St) Bp. R.M. Feb. 21
2nd cent. Described as the third bishop of Metz, which see he is alleged to have occupied for over forty years in the sub-apostolic age.
Cf. Duch. Fast. Episc. — Baud. — Holw.

FELIX of BRESCIA (St) Bp.
R.M. Feb. 23
d. c.650. The twentieth bishop of Brescia. He governed the diocese for over forty eventful years during which he was occu-

pied in combating Lombard Arians and other heretics.
Cf. Menzies — Baud. — Holw.

FELIX (St) M. R.M. Feb. 26
See Fortunatus, Felix and Comp.

FELIX III (or II) (St) Pope.
R.M. March 1 (Nov. 1st)
d. 492. A Roman, said to have been an ancestor of St Gregory the Great. He was pope from 483 till his death. The nine years of his pontificate were occupied with controversy against Monophysitism and Eutychianism as also in remedying the evils caused in Africa by numerous apostasies during the Vandal persecution.
Cf. Menzies — Att. — Baud.

FELIX, LUCIOLUS, FORTUNATUS, MARCIA, and Comp. (SS) MM.
R.M. March 3
? A group of martyrs conjectured to have suffered in N. Africa.

FELIX of RHUYS (St) Ab. O.S.B.
A.C. March 4
d. 1038. A native of the diocese of Quimper in Brittany who became a hermit on Ouessant Island and afterwards a Benedictine at Fleury (Saint-Benoit-sur-Loire). The abbot of Fleury sent him to restore Rhuys abbey, the great Breton monastery founded by St Gildas, which had been destroyed by the Normans.
Cf. Chev. — Holw. — Zimm.

FELIX (St) M. R.M. March 8
See Cyril, Rogatus, etc.

FELIX of DUNWICH (St) Bp.
R.M. March 8
d. 648. A native of Burgundy who brought about the conversion of Sigebert, king of the East Angles, when that prince was in exile, and later was summoned by Sigebert to evangelize East Anglia. St Felix undertook the mission with the approval of St Honorius of Canterbury, and placed his episcopal see at Dunwich, now washed away by the sea. He preached with great success in Norfolk, Suffolk and Cambridgeshire, opening schools on the French model. He is the veritable apostle of the East Angles.
Cf. Att. — Holw. — Baud.

FELIX of AQUILEIA (St) M.
R.M. March 16
See Hilary, Tatian, etc.

FELIX of GERONA (St) M.
                              R.M. March 18
See Narcissus and Felix.

FELIX and Comp. (SS) MM.
                              R.M. March 23
5th cent. A group of about twenty-four
African martyrs who suffered under the
Arian Hunneric, king of the Vandals.

FELIX of MONTECASSINO (Bl) Mk.
                              A.C. March 23
d. c.1000. A Benedictine of Montecassino, who spent all his life in one of the
daughter-houses of the abbey. On account of the many miracles wrought at
his tomb the bishop of Chieti raised his
relics for veneration.
Cf. Zimm.

FELIX of TRÈVES (St) Bp.
                              R.M. March 26
d. c.400. Consecrated bishop of Trèves
by his friend, St Martin of Tours, in 386.
Owing to the fact that this took place
under the usurping emperor Maximus,
the legality of his election was questioned
by the Holy See and St Ambrose, and he
consequently resigned. Contemporary
writers, particularly St Sulpicius Severus
speak very highly of his virtues.
Cf. Att. — Holw. — Baud.

FELIX (St) M.   **R.M. March 31**
See Theodulus, Anesius, etc.

FELIX of SARAGOSSA (St) M.
                              R.M. Apr. 16
See Saragossa (Martyrs of).

FELIX of ALEXANDRIA (St) M.
                              R.M. Apr. 21
See Arator, Fortunatus, etc.

FELIX, FORTUNATUS and ACHILLEUS
(SS) MM.   **R.M. Apr. 23**
d. 212. St Felix, a priest, and his two
deacons, Fortunatus and Achilleus, were
sent by St Irenaeus of Lyons to evangelize
the district of Vienne, in France. After a
most successful apostolate they were
martyred.
Cf. Att. — Baud. — Holw.

FELIX of SEVILLE (St) M. R.M. May 2
? A deacon, martyred in all probability
at Seville where he is held in great veneration.

FELIX of ROME (St) M.   R.M. May 10
See Calepodius, Palmatius, etc.

FELIX and GENNADIUS (SS) MM.
                              R.M. May 16
? Two martyrs venerated from ancient
times in the city of Uzalis in Proconsular
Africa, where their relics were enshrined.
Cf. Holw. — Baud.

FELIX of SPOLETO (St) Bp. M.
                              R.M. May 18
d. c.304. A bishop, either of Spoleto or of
the neighbouring town of Spello (His-
pellum) in Umbria. He was martyred
under Diocletian.
Cf. Baud. — Holw. — Menzies.

FELIX of CANTALICE (St) O.F.M. Cap.
                              R.M. May 18
1513-1587. A native of Cantalice, near
Rieti, in Apulia, the child of peasant
farmers, he started life as a farm labourer,
and at the age of thirty joined the Capuchins in Rome as a lay-brother; thereafter for forty years he begged the daily
alms for his friary. He was a friend of St
Charles Borromeo, and an intimate of
St Philip Neri. He was nicknamed *Deo
Gratias* on account of his habitual use of
this ejaculation. His characteristic virtue
was spiritual joy. Canonized in 1724 —
the first Capuchin friar to attain this
honour.
Cf. Ricci — Att. — Menzies — Holw.

FELIX of ISTRIA (St) M.   R.M. May 24
See Zoëllus, Servilius, etc.

FELIX of SARDINIA (St) M.
                              R.M. May 28
See Emilius, Felix, etc.

FELIX (St) H.   **A.C. May 29**
See Votus, Felix and John.

FELIX I (St) Pope M.
                  R.M. May 30 and Dec. 30
d. 274. A Roman by birth and pope from
269 to 274. He was the first to condemn
the heresy of Paul of Samosata. He is
said to have died a martyr under Aurelian;
but this appears to be an error, due to confusion with another Felix.
Cf. Menzies — Att. — Baud. — Holw.

FELIX of NICOSIA (Bl) O.F.M. Cap.
                              A.C. June 1
1715-1787. A native of Nicosia in Sicily.

He began life as an apprentice to a shoe-maker; then he sought to become a religious, but failed several times. At last he was professed as a lay-brother, and in the course of his begging expeditions on behalf of his friary at Nicosia, reclaimed numerous sinners and helped the poor and the sick. Beatified in 1888.
Cf. Menzies — Att. — Holw.

FELIX of FRITZLAR (St) M. O.S.B.
A.C. June 5
d. c.790. A Benedictine monk of Fritzlar in Germany and a martyr probably at the hands of the heathen Saxons.
Cf. Zimm. — Chev. — Bolland. — Holw.

FELIX and FORTUNATUS (SS) MM.
R.M. June 11
d. 296. Two brothers, born at Vicenza in N. Italy, who suffered under Diocletian at Aquileia.
Cf. Att. — Menzies — Baud. — Holw.

FELIX of CORDOVA (St) M.
R.M. June 14
See Anastasius, Felix and Digna.

FELIX and MAURUS (SS) CC.
A.C. June 16
6th cent. Natives of Palestine, father and son, who after a pilgrimage to Rome settled at a place now called San Felice near Narni, in central Italy.
Cf. Menzies — Baud. — Holw.

FELIX of APOLLONIA (St) M.
R.M. June 17
See Isaurus, Innocent, etc.

FELIX of SUTRI (St) M. R.M. June 23
d. 257. A priest of Sutri in Tuscany, scourged to death under the emperors Valerian and Gallienus.
Cf. Holw. — Baud.

FELIX of CÎTEAUX (Bl) Mk. O.S.B. Cist.
P.C. June 23
d. 1113. A Cistercian monk, listed in the menologies of the order as a *beatus*.
Cf. Holw.

FELIX (St) M. R.M. July 2
See Ariston, Crescentian, etc.

FELIX of NANTES (St) Bp. A.C. July 7
d. 584. A great bishop who ruled over the see of Nantes for about thirty-three years.

He died on Jan. 8; July 7 is the anniversary of the translation of his relics.
Cf. Duch. Fast. Episc. — Baud. — Chev.— Att. — Holw.

FELIX (St) M. R.M. July 10
One of the Seven Brothers, MM, q.v.

FELIX (St) M. R.M. July 10
See Januarius, Marinus, etc.

FELIX of MILAN (St) M. R.M. July 12
See Nabor and Felix.

FELIX of COMO (St) Bp. R.M. July 14
d. c.390. Said to have been the first bishop of Como. He was an intimate friend of St Ambrose.
Cf. Menzies — Baud. — Holw.

FELIX of PAVIA (St) Bp. M.
R.M. July 15
? A martyr, of whom nothing is known. Some identify him with St Felix of Spoleto (May 18).
Cf. Baud. — Holw.

FELIX (St) M. R.M. July 17
One of the Scillitan Martyrs, q.v.

FELIX (FELICINUS) of VERONA (St) Bp. R. M. July 19
? A bishop of Verona, venerated from ancient times as a saint.
Cf. Menzies — Baud. — Holw.

FELIX of MANFREDONIA (St) M.
R.M. July 25
See Florentius and Felix.

FELIX of CORDOVA (St) M.
R.M. July 27
See George, Felix and Liliosa.

FELIX, JULIA and JUCUNDA (SS) MM.
R.M. July 27
? The R.M. erroneously assigns these martyrs to Nola. As to St Felix the reference would simply be the date of the consecration of St Felix, bishop of Nola (see Nov. 15). SS Jucunda and Julia are in older MSS assigned to Nicomedia in Asia Minor.
Cf. Baud. — Holw.

FELIX II (St) Pope M. R.M. July 29
d. 365. The accounts of the life of this Felix are very conflicting: he does not

seem to have been either a pope or a martyr. He certainly was intruded into the see of Rome in the year 355, when Pope Liberius was exiled by the Arian emperor Constantius. The reasons why he was listed in the R.M. are still heatedly debated.
Cf. Att. — Menzies — Baud. — Holw.

FELIX of GERONA (St) M. R.M. Aug. 1
d. 303. A Spanish martyr, who suffered at Gerona, in N. E. Spain, under Diocletian. Some verses were dedicated to him by Prudentius.
Cf. Holw. — Baud.

FELIX (FEDLIMID) (St) Bp.
                                    A.C. Aug. 9
Otherwise Phelin, q.v.

FELIX of PORTO (St) M. R.M. Aug. 22
See Martial, Saturinus, etc.

FELIX of PISTOIA (St) H. R.M. Aug. 26
9th cent. A hermit of Pistoia in Tuscany, venerated as a saint, about whom, however, almost nothing is known.
Cf. Menzies — Holw. — Baud.

FELIX (St) M.
                R.M. Aug. 28 and Sept. 1
See Septiminus, Januarius and Felix, a group among the Twelve Holy Brothers.

FELIX and ADAUCTUS (SS) MM.
                                    R.M. Aug. 30
d. c.304. Martyrs beheaded in Rome under Diocletian. St Felix was a priest; as he was being led to execution, a bystander confessed Christ and was put to death with St Felix. Because this second martyr's name was not known, he was called *Adauctus*, i.e., the one added.
Cf. Baud. — Menzies — Holw.

FELIX and AUGEBERT (SS) MM.
                                    A.C. Sept. 6
7th cent. Two English slaves sold in France, and ransomed by St Gregory the Great, who directed that they should be received and educated in a monastery with a view to their becoming missionaries in their native country. Felix was ordained priest, and Augebert deacon; but unfortunately they were killed by pagans in Champagne before they could undertake their mission.
Cf. Baud. — P.B. — Holw.

FELIX and another FELIX (SS) Bps. MM. R.M. Sept. 10
See Nemesian, Felix, etc.

FELIX and REGULA (SS) MM.
                                    A.C. Sept. 11
3rd cent. Brother and sister who at the time of the martyrdom of St Maurice under Maximian Herculius, took refuge in Switzerland, where they were eventually found and martyred near Zurich.
Cf. Holw. — Baud.

FELIX and CONSTANTIA (SS) MM.
                                    R.M. Sept. 19
1st cent. Martyrs under Nero, at Nocera, between Naples and Salerno.
Cf. Menzies — Holw. — Baud.

FELIX III (IV) (St) Pope. R.M. Sept. 22
d. 530. Less accurately Felix IV. (See above, St Felix II, July 29.) His pontificate lasted from 526 till 530 and his best remembered deed as pope was the building of the church of SS Cosmas and Damian. He was greatly loved in Rome for his simplicity and generosity to the poor.
Cf. Menzies — Att. — Baud. — Holw.

FELIX of AUTUN (St) M. R.M. Sept. 24
See Andochius, Thyrsus and Felix.

FELIX and CYPRIAN (SS) MM. Bps.
                                    R.M. Oct. 12
d. c.484. Two African bishops, leaders of a great multitude of Catholics — the number of four thousand nine hundred and sixty-six is usually given by historians — driven out to starvation and death in the Sahara desert by the Arian Vandal king Hunneric. We have the account of their sufferings from Victor of Utica, a contemporary writer.
Cf. Att. — Holw. — Baud.

FELIX (AFRICANUS), AUDACTUS (ADAUCTUS), JANUARIUS, FORTUNATUS and SEPTIMIUS (SS) MM.
                                    R.M. Oct. 24
d. 303. Felix was a bishop of Thibiuca in Africa who refused to deliver up the sacred books, and was for this reason put to death. He was one of the first victims of Diocletian's persecution. The accounts we have of the other martyrs mentioned with him are not trustworthy.
Cf. Att. — Holw. — Baud.

FELIX and EUSEBIUS (SS) MM.
R.M. Nov. 5
? 1st cent. Alleged martyrs of Terracina an Italian city between Rome and Naples.

FELIX of THYNISSA (St) M.
R.M. Nov. 6
? An African martyr who suffered at Thynissa, near Hippona (Bona). He was found dead in prison the day before he was to be executed. St Augustine preached a sermon on the martyr's feast day.
Cf. Holw. — Baud.

FELIX of FONDI (St) Mk. O.S.B.
R.M. Nov. 6
6th cent. A monk of a Benedictine house at Fondi in S. Italy — a contemporary of St Gregory the Great, by whom he was greatly revered.
Cf. Zimm. — Holw. — Baud.

FELIX of NOLA (St) Bp. M. R.M. Nov. 15
d. 287. Said to have been the first bishop of Nola, near Naples, and to have been put to death for Christ with thirty companions.
Cf. Holw. — Baud.

FELIX of VALOIS (St) C. R.M. Nov. 20
1127-1212. We first meet him as a hermit in a forest near Meaux. Eventually — some writers say he was already seventy years old — he, with St John of Matha, organized the Trinitarians in France, a religious order founded for the purpose of ransoming captives from the Moors. He is called "of Valois" because he lived for a time in that province.
Cf. Menzies — Att. — Baud. — Holw.

FELIX (St) Bp.
R.M. Nov. 28
See Valerian, Urban, etc.

FELIX of BOLOGNA (St) Bp.
R.M. Dec. 4
d. 429. A deacon of the church of Milan under St Ambrose, and afterwards the fifth bishop of Bologna.
Cf. Menzies — Holw. — Baud.

FELIX (St) M.
R.M. Dec. 5
See Julius, Potamia, etc.

FELIX of ROME (St) M. R.M. Dec. 29
See Callistus, Felix and Boniface.

FEOCK (St) V.
A.C. Feb. 2
? A saint otherwise unknown, whose name is perpetuated by a church dedication in Cornwall. Possibly she was an immigrant from Ireland. Some have it that Feock is only a variant of the name of St Fiacca the friend of St Patrick; others identify St Feock with St Vougas of Brittany.
Cf. Holw.

FERDINAND III (St) King. R.M. May 30
1198-1252. King of Castile in 1217, and of Leon in 1230. For twenty-seven years he was engaged in an almost uninterrupted crusade against the Mohammedans in Spain, from whom he recaptured Cordova (1236), Murcia, Jaen, Cadiz, and finally Seville (1249). He was a wise ruler, and was wont to say that he "feared more the curse of one old woman than the whole army of the Moors." He was the founder of the university of Salamanca and of the cathedral of Burgos. By his second wife he was the father of Eleanor, wife of Edward I of England. Canonized in 1671.
Cf. Att. — Baud. — P. de U. — Chev.

FERDINAND of ST JOSEPH AYALA (Bl) M. O.S.A. A.C. June 1
1575-1617. Born at Ballesteros, diocese of Toledo, Spain, he took the Augustinian habit at Mentilla, and in 1603 was sent to Mexico, and thence to Japan (1605) as vicar provincial. He worked at Ozaka with great success until his capture and execution at Omura. Beatified in 1867.
Cf. Holw.

FERDINAND of PORTUGAL (Bl) M.
A.C. June 5
1402-1443. Surnamed "the Constant" or "the Standard-bearer" (El Abanderado), son of King John I of Portugal, he was born at Santarem, and his leanings towards the religious life led him to become the Master General of the military order of Aviz, an order dependent on Cîteaux. In this capacity he led an expedition against the Moors in Africa, but was defeated at Tangier and given up as a hostage. He was imprisoned at Arzilla and remained a prisoner, with never a word of complaint, for five years, finally dying there of neglect. Cult approved in 1470.
Cf. Att. — Zimm.

FERDINAND of ARAGON (St) Bp.
A.C. June 27
13th cent. Related to the royal family of Aragon, then the rulers of the Two Sicilies, he became the fifth bishop of Cajazzo, in

that kingdom. His relics are now venerated at Cornello, in Sicily.
Cf. Att. — Holw.

FERDINAND SANCHEZ (Bl) M. S.J.
A.C. July 15
d. 1570. Born in Castile, and a Jesuit novice, he suffered martyrdom under the leadership of Bl Ignatius de Azevedo, q.v.
Cf. Holw.

FEREDARIUS (St) Ab. A.C. May 18
d. p. 863. An Irishman by birth, chosen abbot of Iona in 863. During his abbacy the relics of St Columba were removed to Ireland, for fear of the Danes.
Cf. Holw. — Baud.

FERONA (St) Ab. A.C. March 2
d. 637. Surnamed "the White," a kinsman and disciple of St Columba and his successor as abbot of Iona.
Cf. Holw.

FERGUS (FERGUSTUS, FERGUISIUS) (St) Bp. A.C. March 30
6th cent. A bishop of Downpatrick; but the traditions concerning him are vague in the extreme, and he may possibly be identified with St Fergus of Scotland (Nov. 18).
Cf. Holw.

FERGUS (St) Bp. A.C. Nov. 18
d. p. 721. An Irish bishop who preached in Perthshire, Caithness, Buchan and Forfarshire. He signed the Acts of the Roman council of A.D. 721, describing himself as a Pict. In the Aberdeen breviary he is called Fergustian.
Cf. Att. — Baud. — Holw.

FERNANDO (several)
The Spanish and Portuguese form of Ferdinand, q.v.

FERRAN (several).
The old Castilian and Catalan form of Ferdinand, q.v.

FERREOLUS (St) Bp. A.C. Jan. 4
d. 581. A native of Narbonne, who became bishop of Uzès. He devoted himself in particular to converting the Jews of his diocese, and is said to have got into trouble on that account. He was the founder of a monastery, for which he wrote a monastic rule.
Cf. Att. — Baud. — Holw. — Chev.

FERREOLUS (FERGÉOL) (Bl) Bp. M.
A.C. Jan. 16
d. c.670. Said to have been bishop of Grenoble in France. Cult confirmed in 1907.
Cf. Duch. Fast. Episc. — Chev. — Gams — Att. — Baud.

FERREOLUS and FERRUTIO (SS) MM.
R.M. June 16
d. c.212. Ferreolus, a priest, and Ferrutio, a deacon, are said to have been brothers and natives of Asia Minor. They were sent by St Irenaeus of Lyons to evangelize the country round Besançon, where they worked for thirty years and then were martyred.
Cf. Att. — Baud. — Holw.

FERREOLUS (St) M. R.M. Sept. 18
d. 304. An officer of the imperial army, martyred at Vienne in Gaul, under Diocletian.
Cf. Baud. — Holw.

FERREOLUS (St) Bp. A.C. Sept. 18
d. c.591. Fifth bishop of Limoges in France. He is mentioned with great veneration by St Gregory of Tours.
Cf. Baud. — Duch. Fast. Episc.

FERRUTIO (St) M. R.M. June 16
See Ferreolus and Ferrutio.

FERRUTIUS (St) M. R.M. Oct. 28
? A Roman soldier stationed at Mainz in Germany, who demanded his discharge from the army rather than take part in idolatrous worship. He was cast into prison, where he died of ill-treatment and hunger.
Cf. Holw. — Baud.

FESTUS (St) M. R.M. June 24
Otherwise Faustus, q.v.

FESTUS (St) M. R.M. Sept. 19
See Januarius and Comp.

FESTUS (St) M. R.M. Dec. 21
See John and Festus.

FIACE (FIECH) (St) Bp. A.C. Oct. 12
5th cent. An Irish bishop, friend and disciple of St Patrick, in whose honour he wrote a hymn which is still extant.
Cf. Baud. — Holw.

FIACHAN (FIANCHNE) (St) C.
                                    A.C. Apr. 29
7th cent. A native of Munster in Ireland, a monk at Lismore, and disciple of St Carthage the Younger.
Cf. Holw.

FIACRE (FIACRIUS, FIAKER, FÈVRE) (St) Ab.   R.M. Aug. 30
d. c.670. A hermit at Kilfiachra in Ireland, who crossed over to Gaul and was given land for a hermitage by St Faro of Meaux. Here he lived for the rest of his life, attracting many disciples for whom he built the abbey of Breuil. St Fiacre's shrine is still a place of pilgrimage. It is situated in the modern department of Seine-et-Marne and the township still bears his name. As patron of gardeners, he is often represented carrying a shovel.
Cf. Att. — Holw. — Baud. — Chev.

FIBITIUS (St) Bp.   R.M. Nov. 5
d. c.500. Abbot of a monastery at Trèves, and the 21st bishop of that city.
Cf. Baud. — Holw. — Duch. Fast. Episc. — Gams.

FIDELIS (St) Bp.   A.C. Feb. 7
d. c.570. An Eastern by origin, he travelled to Spain with some merchants, and settled at Mérida, where he was trained by St Paul, bishop of the city, whom he succeeded in that office.
Cf. P. de U. — Baud. — Holw. — Gams.

FIDELIS (St) M.   R.M. March 23
? An African martyr. Some writers place him in the same group of African martyrs as St Felix and his twenty companions (March 23).
Cf. Baud. — Holw.

FIDELIS of SIGMARINGEN (St) M.
O.F.M. Cap.   R.M. Apr. 24
1577-1622. Mark Rey, born at Sigmaringen, in S. Germany, practised as a lawyer, and came to be known as the "advocate of the poor." In 1612 he joined the Capuchins, receiving the new name of Fidelis, and after his ordination the newly founded Roman Congregation of Propaganda sent him as a missionary to the Swiss Protestants in the Grisons. Incensed at his success, the Calvinists raised the peasants against him by inventing the story that he was a political agent of the Austrian emperor. He was stabbed to death near Gruch.
Cf. Menzies — Att. — Ricci — Holw.

FIDELIS of EDESSA (St) M.
                                    R.M. Aug. 21
See Bassa, Theogonius, etc.

FIDELIS of COMO (St) M.
                                    R.M. Oct. 28
d. c.304. A soldier martyred in Lombardy under Maximian Herculius. His body was translated by St Charles Borromeo to Milan, but some of his relics are venerated at Como.
Cf. Menzies — Att. — Baud. — Holw.

FIDELMIA (St) V.   A.C. Jan. 11
See Ethenea and Fidelmia.

FIDENTIAN (St) M.   R.M. Nov. 15
See Secundus, Fidentian and Varicus.

FIDENTIUS and TERENTIUS (SS) MM.
                                    R.M. Sept. 27
? The relics of these martyrs were discovered in the 12th century at Todi in central Italy, where they are venerated. Nothing else is known about them. The legend of their martyrdom is quite untrustworthy.
Cf. Menzies — Baud. — Holw.

FIDENTIUS (St) Bp.   R.M. Nov. 16
2nd cent. Some make this saint a confessor, others a martyr, Baronius a bishop. Tradition assigns him to Padua and to the second century. All this is mere surmise and nothing is known about him.
Cf. Menzies — Holw. — Baud.

FIDES (St) V.M.   R.M. Aug. 1
Otherwise Faith, q.v.

FIDHARLEUS (St) Ab.   A.C. Oct. 1
d. 762. An Irish saint, the restorer of Rathin Abbey.
Cf. Holw.

FIDLEMINUS (St) Bp.   A.C. Aug. 9
Otherwise Phelim, q.v.

FIDOLUS (French: PHAL) (St) Ab.
                                    R.M. May 16
d. c.540. The son of a Roman official in Auvergne, France. Taken prisoner by the soldiers of Clovis and sold into slavery, he was ransomed by Aventinus, abbot of Aumont, near Troyes. At a later period Fidolus was himself abbot of the abbey, which was afterwards called Saint-Phal.
Cf. Att. — Baud. — Holw.

**FIDWETEN (FIVETEIN, FIDIVI-
TANUS) (St) Mk. O.S.B.   A.C. Dec. 11**
d. c.888. A Benedictine monk, disciple of
St Convoyon at the abbey of Redon, in
Brittany.
Cf. Chev. — Baud. — Holw.

FIECH (St) Bp.   A.C. Oct. 12
Otherwise Fiace, q.v.

FILLAN (St) Ab.   A.C. Jan. 9
Otherwise Foelan, q.v.

FINA (St) V.   A.C. March 12
Otherwise Seraphina, q.v.

FINAN (St) Bp.   A.C. Feb. 17
d. 661. An Irish monk of Iona, who succeeded St Aidan in the government of the
Northumbrian church. Attended by St
Cedd and other fellow-missionaries he
evangelized parts of southern England.
Cf. Holw. — Baud.

FINAN (FINNIAN) (St) Ab. A.C. Apr. 7
6th cent. A native of Munster and a disciple of St Brendan, at whose wish he
founded and governed a monastery at
Kinnitty in Offaly of which place he is
patron.
Cf. Baud. — Holw.

FINBAR (St) Ab.   A.C. July 4
6th cent. An Irish abbot of Innis-
Doimhle, Wexford.
Cf. Holw.

**FINBARR (FION-BHARR, i.e. White
Head) (St) Bp.   A.C. Sept. 25**
Otherwise Barr, q.v.

**FINDAN (or FINTAN) (St) H. O.S.B.
                         A.C. Nov. 15**
d. 879. A native of Leinster in Ireland
who was carried off as a slave to the Orkneys by Norse raiders, but managed to
escape to Scotland. He then undertook a
pilgrimage to Rome, and became a Benedictine at the abbey of Farfa in Sabina.
Thence he migrated to the abbey of Rheinau in Switzerland, where he was allowed
to live as a recluse for twenty-two years.
*Cf. Att. — Zimm. — Chev. — Holw. —
Baud.*

FINDBARR (St) Bp.   A.C. Sept. 10
Otherwise Finian, q.v.

**FINGAR (GWINNEAR), PHIALA and
COMP. (SS) MM.   A.C. Dec. 14**
5th cent. Fingar and Phiala, brother
and sister, left their native Ireland and
crossed over to Cornwall, but they were
put to death at Hayle near Penzance by
a pagan chief. Their attendants shared
their crown.
Cf. Holw. — Baud.

FINIAN LOBHAR (St) Ab.
**   A.C. March 16**
d. ? c.560. A disciple of St Columba, by
whom he is said to have been made abbot
of Swords near Dublin. He is surnamed
"the Leper," on account of a skin disease
from which he suffered. The records of
his life are most conflicting.
Cf. Att. — Holw. — Baud.

FINIAN (FINDBARR, WINNIN) (St) Bp.
**   A.C. Sept. 10**
d. c.575. Born near Stangford Lough,
he became a monk in Scotland, and was
ordained in Rome. On his return to Ireland he brought with him biblical manuscripts which led to the famous incident of
the Psalter of St Columba. He was the
founder and first abbot-bishop of the monastery of Moville in Co Down. Wrongly
identified with St Frigidian of Lucca.
Cf. Att. — Holw. — Baud.

FINIAN (FINTAN MUNNU) (St) Ab.
**   A.C. Oct. 21**
d. c.635. A disciple of St Columba at
Iona, and at a later period the abbot-
founder of the monastery of Taghmon in
Co Wexford. In Scotland he is called
St Mundus.
Cf. Att. — Holw. — Baud.

FINIAN of CLONARD (St) Bp.
**   A.C. Dec. 12**
d. c.552. Born at Myshall in Co Carlow,
early in life he became a monk in Wales,
and after a long sojourn there returned to
Ireland and founded a great number of
churches, monasteries and schools. Clonard was the greatest, and it was here that
Finian had as pupils the so-called Twelve
Apostles of Ireland, among whom was St
Columba. Finian indeed became known
as the "Teacher of the Irish Saints,"
Clonard was the greatest school of its
period, renowned chiefly for its biblical
studies.
Cf. Att. — Baud. — Holw. — Chev.

FINLUGH (FINLAG) (St) Ab.
A.C. Jan. 3
6th cent. A brother of St Fintan (Jan. 3) who crossed to Scotland, where it is thought that he became one of St Columba's disciples. Returning to Ireland he was made abbot of a monastery established by St Columba in Co Derry.
Cf. Holw.

FINTAN (St) Ab.
A.C. Jan. 3
6th cent. A disciple of St Comgall at Bangor. He is honoured as the patron saint of Doon in Limerick. His holy well is still venerated there.
Cf. Holw. — Baud.

FINTAN (St) Ab.
R.M. Feb. 17
d. 603. A disciple of St Columba, he led the life of a hermit at Clonenagh in Leix. Soon numerous disciples attached themselves to him, and he became their abbot. Such was the austerity of the life led at Clonenagh that neighbouring monasteries protested.
Cf. Att. — Baud. — Holw.

FINTAN (St) H. O.S.B.
A.C. Nov. 15
Otherwise Findan, q.v.

FIONNCHU (St) Ab.
A.C. Nov. 28
6th cent. The successor of St Comgall in the abbey of Bangor.

FIRMATUS (St) M.
R.M. Oct. 5
See Placid and Comp.

FIRMATUS and FLAVIANA (SS) MM.
R.M. Oct. 5
? Firmatus, a deacon, and Flaviana, a virgin, are venerated on Oct. 5 at Auxerre in France. Their names appear already in St Jerome's martyrology, as venerated in France long before the supposed martyrdom of St Placid and his companions (q.v.).
Cf. Holw. — Baud.

FIRMIAN (FERMANUS, FIRMINUS) (St) Ab. O.S.B.
A.C. March 11
d. c.1020. A Benedictine abbot of the monastery of San Sabino Piceno, near Fermo, in the Marches of Ancona.
Cf. Mab. — Chev. — Bolland. — (Martii t. 2, p. 96) — Holw. — Baud.

FIRMINA (St) V. M.
R.M. Nov. 24
d. c.303. A Roman maiden tortured to death at Amelia (Ameria) in Umbria, under Diocletian.
Cf. Holw. — Baud.

FIRMINUS (St) Bp.
A.C. Jan. 19
? Third bishop of Gabales (Gévaudan), Mende, in France.
Cf. Duch. Fast. Episc. — Gams — Baud.

FIRMINUS (St) Ab.
R.M. March 11
? Baronius evidently confused this Firminus a supposed abbot at Amiens, with St Firmianus, or Firminus, abbot in the Marches of Ancona (see above, March 11). No abbot-saint, of the name of Firminus, has ever been venerated at Amiens.

FIRMINUS (St) Bp.
A.C. March 29
6th cent Bishop of Viviers, in France.
Cf. Duch. Fast. Episc. — Baud.

FIRMINUS of ARMENIA (St) M.
R.M. June 24
See Orentius, Heros, etc.

FIRMINUS of METZ (St) Bp.
R.M. Aug. 18
d. 496. Greek, or Italian, by origin, he ruled the see of Metz for eight years.
Cf. Duch. Fast. Episc. — Gams — Baud.

FIRMINUS of AMIENS (I and II) (SS) Bps.
R.M. A.C. Sept. 1 and Sept. 25
2nd-3rd cent. Two bishops of the name Firminus are venerated at Amiens: one on Sept. 1, said to have been the third prelate of that city, and another on Sept. 25, the supposed first bishop of Amiens. The latter is described as a native of Pampeluna in Spanish Navarre and a convert of St Saturninus, bishop of Toulouse. The former, viz. the third bishop of Amiens, is alleged to have been the son of one of the converts of St Firminus, the first bishop of that city. Some writers consider them to have been one and the same person.
Cf. Att. — Baud. — Holw. — Duch. Fast. Episc.

FIRMINUS of UZÈS (St) Bp.
R.M. Oct. 11
d. 553. A native of Narbonne in S. France, he was educated by his uncle the bishop of Uzès, whom he succeeded as bishop at the age of twenty-two. He died at the age of thirty-seven.
Cf. Holw. — Baud. — Duch. Fast. Episc.

FIRMINUS (St) Bp. A.C. Dec. 5
d. 6th cent. The seventh bishop of
Verdun.
Cf. Baud. — Duch. Fast. Episc.

FIRMUS of ROME (St) M. R.M. Feb. 2
See Fortunatus, Felician, etc.

FIRMUS (St) M. R.M. March 11
See Gorgonius and Firmus.

FIRMUS (St) M. R.M. June 1
d. c.290. An Eastern martyr who suffered
under Maximian.
Cf. Holw. — Baud.

FIRMUS (St) M. R.M. June 24
See Orentius, Heros, etc.

FIRMUS of TAGASTE (St) Bp.
R.M. July 31
? Of him St Augustine writes that he was
firm by name but *firmer* yet by faith.
Put to the torture, he endured the most
frightful sufferings rather than betray the
hiding-place of one of his flock. This
notice of St Augustine led Baronius to
insert St Firmus's name in the R.M.
Cf. Baud. — Holw.

FIRMUS and RUSTICUS (SS) MM.
R.M. Aug. 9
d. c.290. Two kinsmen, prominent citizens of Bergamo in Lombardy, who
suffered at Verona under Maximian.
Cf. Holw. — Baud.

FISHER, JOHN (St) Bp. M. A.C. July 9
See John Fisher.

FLANNAN (St) Bp. A.C. Dec. 18
7th cent. An Irish monk consecrated
bishop by Pope John IV. He was the
first bishop of Killaloe and worked also in
the Hebrides and elsewhere, and in spite
of all this toil, he managed, we are told, to
recite daily the entire Psalter.
Cf. Att. — Baud. — Holw.

**FLAVIA DOMITILLA, EUPHROSYNA
and THEODORA (SS) VV. MM.**
R.M. May 7
2nd cent. Flavia Domitilla was a great-
niece of the emperors Domitian and Titus,
and also of St Flavius Clemens. She became a Christian, and on refusing to
marry a pagan, was banished from Rome,
and eventually martyred with her foster

sisters, Euphrosyna and Theodora, at
Terracina. The Roman liturgy associates
her name with those of SS Nereus and
Achilles, who were buried in the cemetery of Domitilla in the Via Ardeatina.
Probably there were two Roman ladies
named Flavia Domitilla and both martyrs — the one described above and her
own niece by marriage.
Cf. Att. — Baud. — Holw. — Menzies.

FLAVIA (St) V. M. R.M. Oct. 5
See Placid and Comp.

FLAVIAN (St) M. R.M. Jan. 28
d. c.304. A deputy-prefect of Rome who
suffered martyrdom at Civita Vecchia,
under Diocletian.
Cf. Holw. — Baud.

**FLAVIAN of CONSTANTINOPLE (St)
Bp. M.** R.M. Feb. 18
d. 449. Appointed patriarch of Constantinople in 447. He refused to give the
customary bribe on his accession to the
see, and it was not long before he was
compelled to denounce the heresy of
Eutyches, a favourite of the imperial
court. Pope Leo the Great approved his
condemnation of Eutychianism by sending him the famous "Dogmatic Letter."
At "the Robber Synod" of Ephesus in
499, Flavian appealed to the pope, whereupon he was exiled and maltreated, dying
shortly after of his injuries. The Council
of Chalcedon (451) proclaimed him a
saint and a martyr.
Cf. Att. — Baud. — Holw.

FLAVIAN (St) M. R.M. Feb. 24
See Montanus, Lucius, etc.

FLAVIAN and ELIAS (SS) Bps.
R.M. July 20
d. (respectively) 512 and 518. St Flavian
was patriarch of Antioch, and St Elias
patriarch of Jerusalem. Both were exiled by the Monophysite emperor Anastasius (491-518) for strenuously upholding
the decrees of the council of Chalcedon.
This is the reason for their joint commemoration in the R.M.
Cf. Att. — Baud. — Holw.

**FLAVIAN (FLAVINIAN, FLAVIUS) of
AUTUN (St) Bp.** R.M. Aug. 23
7th cent. The 21st bishop of Autun in
France.
Cf. Duch. Fast. Episc. — Baud.

FLAVIAN (St) M.   **R.M. Dec. 22**
d. 362. Said to have been an ex-prefect of Rome, branded on the forehead as a slave and exiled to the small village of Acquapendente in Tuscany by order of Julian the Apostate. At Acquapendente he died while in prayer.
Cf. Menzies — Holw. — Baud.

FLAVIANA of AUXERRE (St) V. M.
    R.M. Oct. 5
See Firmatus and Flaviana.

FLAVIUS AUGUSTUS and AUGUSTINE (SS) MM.   **R.M. May 7**
d. c.300. Flavius, bishop of Nicomedia, and his two brothers, were martyred in that city under Diocletian.
Cf. Baud. — Holw.

FLAVIUS CLEMENS (St) M.
    R.M. June 22
d. c.96. Brother of the emperor Vespasian and uncle of Titus and Domitian, whose niece, Flavia Domitilla, he married. In the year 95 he held the consular office together with Domitian. The following year Domitian had him beheaded as a Christian.
Cf. Att. — Baud. — Holw.

FLAVIUS of AUTUN (St) Bp.
    R.M. Aug. 23
Otherwise Flavian, q.v.

FLOCELLUS (St) M.   **R.M. Sept. 17**
2nd cent. A youth martyred at Autun in France under the emperor Marcus Aurelius (161-180). After having been put to the torture he was flung, half-dead, to the wild beasts in the amphitheatre.
Cf. Baud. — Holw.

FLORA (St) V.   **A.C. Jan. 29**
Otherwise Blath, q.v.

FLORA of BEAULIEU (Bl) V.
    A.C. June 11
d. 1347. Born in Auvergne, Flora, at the age of fourteen, entered the order of Hospitallers of St John of Jerusalem at Beaulieu, near Rocamadour. Her spiritual trials and the physico-mystical phenomena which accompanied them make her life of absorbing interest.
Cf. Att. — Holw. — Baud.

FLORA (St) V. M.   **R.M. July 29**
See Lucilla, Flora, etc.

FLORA and MARY (SS) VV. MM.
    R.M. Nov. 24
d. 856. Two Christian maidens of Cordova, in Spain, who gave themselves up to the Moors, and were beheaded by order of Abderrahman II.
Cf. Att. — Baud. — Holw. — P. de U.

FLORENCE (*several*)
Otherwise Florentina, Florentia or Florentius, q.v.

FLORENTIA (FLORENCE) (St) M.
    R.M. Nov. 10
See Tiberius, Modestus and Florentia.

FLORENTIAN (St) Bp.   **R.M. Nov. 28**
See Valerian, Urban, etc.

FLORENTINA (FLORENCE) (St) Abs.
    R.M. June 20
d. c.636. A native of Carthagena in Spain, and the only sister of SS Leander, Fulgentius and Isidore. Losing her parents at an early age, she was placed under the guardianship of St Leander. She retired to a convent for which St Leander wrote a rule. Eventually she governed it as abbess.
Cf. P. de U. — Zimm. — Baud. — Chev.

FLORENTINUS and HILARY (SS) MM.
    R.M. Sept. 27
? Two French solitaries, put to death in Gaul by some invading barbarians. Several places have been suggested as the place of their martyrdom. Pseudun, now Sémont in the diocese of Autun; Sion in the Valais; Suint, in Charollais; and Simond in the diocese of Dijon.
Cf. Baud. — Holw. (Florentius).

FLORENTINUS of TRÈVES (St) Bp.
    R.M. Oct. 16
4th cent. The successor of St Severianus in the see of Trèves. There is much controversy about him and about his reputed predecessor St Severinus.
Cf. Holw. — Baud.

FLORENTIUS of VIENNE (St) Bp. M.
    R.M. Jan. 3
d. p. 374. Eighth bishop of Vienne in France. There is another Florentius, also bishop of Vienne, said to have been martyred c.275.
Cf. Baud. — Duch. Fast. Episc. — Att.

FLORENTIUS of SEVILLE (St)
R.M. Feb. 23
d. c.485. A saint much venerated in Seville and its neighbourhood.
Cf. Holw. — Baud. — P. de U.

FLORENTIUS of OSIMO (St) M.
R.M. May 11
See Sisinius, Diocletius and Florentius.

FLORENTIUS of NURSIA (St) Mk.
R.M. May 23
See Eutychius and Florentius.

FLORENTIUS, JULIAN, CYRIACUS, MARCELLINUS and FAUSTINUS (SS) MM.
R.M. June 5
d. 250. These martyrs suffered under Decius, being beheaded at Perugia in central Italy.
Cf. Baud. — Holw.

FLORENTIUS of CARTHAGE (St) M.
R.M. July 15
See Catulinus, Januarius, etc.

FLORENTIUS and FELIX (SS) MM.
R.M. July 25.
d. 235. Two soldiers of the Roman imperial army put to death under Maximinius the Thracian, at Furcona, an ancient town near Aquila in S. Italy. They belong to the group of eighty-three soldiers commemorated on July 24.
Cf. Baud. — Holw.

FLORENTIUS (St) C.   R.M. Sept. 22
5th cent. A Bavarian by birth and a disciple of St Martin of Tours, by whom he was ordained priest and sent to evangelize Poitou. He eventually retired as a hermit to Mt Glonne in Anjou, where he was followed by numerous disciples. He built for them the monastery afterwards known as Saint-Florent-le-Vieux. Here he died in extreme old age.
Cf. Baud. — Holw.

FLORENTIUS (St) M.   R.M. Oct. 10
See Cassius, Florentius, etc.

FLORENTIUS (St) M.   R.M. Oct. 13
d. 312. A martyr of Thessalonica, who died at the stake, under the emperor Maximinus Daza.
Cf. Baud. — Holw.

FLORENTIUS of ORANGE (St) Bp.
R.M. Oct. 17
d. c.526. The eighth bishop of Orange in S. France.
Cf. Baud. — Holw. — Duch. Fast. Episc.

FLORENTIUS (St) M.   R.M. Oct. 27
3rd cent. A martyr who suffered at Trois-Châteaux in Burgundy.
Cf. Holw. — Baud.

FLORENTIUS of STRASBURG (St) Bp.
R.M. Nov. 7
d. c.693. An Irishman by birth, he left his country for Alsace and settled in the wilds of Haselac, where he built a monastery. About the year 678 he was raised to the see of Strasburg, where he founded another monastery — St Thomas's — chiefly for his own countrymen.
Cf. Att. — Baud. — Zimm. — Holw.

FLORENTIUS of CARRACEDO (St) Ab.
O.S.B.   A.C. Dec. 10
d. 1156. Abbot of the Black Benedictine monastery of Carracedo, in the Bierzo Mountains, province of Leon, Spain. He was greatly revered by King Alphonsus VII of Leon. After the saint's death the abbey adopted the Cistercian observance. St Florentius is still greatly venerated in his native province.
Cf. Zimm. — Martyrol. Cist.

FLORENTIUS (FLANN) (St) Ab.
A.C. Dec. 15
7th cent. An abbot of Bangor in Ireland.
Cf. Baud.

FLORIAN (St) M.   R.M. May 4
d. 304. A high Roman officer (princeps officiorum) in Noricum, now Upper Austria, who was drowned in the R. Enns (Anisus), near Lorch, under Diocletian. He is the patron of Upper Austria and Poland.
Cf. Holw. — Baud. — Att.

FLORIAN, CALANICUS and Comp. (SS) MM.   R.M. Dec. 17
d. c.637. A band of sixty martyrs, slain by the Mohammedan invaders at Eleutheropoli (Belt Jibrin) in Palestine.
Cf. Holw. — Baud.

FLORIBERT (St) Bp.   A.C. Apr. 27
d. 746. Bishop of Liége, described as "vehement in correcting." He has been

confused with St Floribert, abbot of Ghent.
Cf. Att. — Baud.

**FLORIBERT (FLORBERT) (St) Ab.
O.S.B.**   **A.C. Nov. 1**
d. c.660. Appointed by St Amadus
abbot of the new monasteries of Ghent
Mont-Blandin and Saint-Bavon.
Cf. Zimm. — Chev. — Holw.

FLORIUS of NICOMEDIA (St) M.
                                R.M. Oct. 26
See Lucian, Florius, etc.

**FLORUS, LAURUS, PROCULUS and
MAXIMUS (SS) MM.**   **R.M. Aug. 18**
2nd cent. A Greek tradition, which is
called in question by some writers, described Florus and Laurus as twin
brothers, stone masons by trade, and
Proculus and Maximus as their employ-
ers. They handed over a temple on which
they had been working to Christian worship, and as a punishment were drowned
in a well. This is said to have happened
in Illyria.
Cf. Att. — Baud. — Holw.

**FLORUS (French: FLOUR) of LODÈVE
(St) Bp.**   **A.C. Nov. 3**
d. 389. First bishop of Lodève in Languedoc. He has given his name to the
town where his relics are enshrined.
Cf. Duch. Fast. Episc. — Baud. — Holw.

FLORUS (St) M.   **R.M. Dec. 22**
See Demetrius, Honoratus and Florus.

FLOS (St) M.   **R.M. Dec. 31**
See Stephen, Pontian, etc.

FLOSCULUS (French: FLOU) (St) Bp.
                                 R.M. Feb. 2
d. p. 480. Bishop of Orleans, a contemporary of Sidonius Apollinaris.
Cf. Duch. Fast. — Episc. — Baud. — Holw.

FLOUR (St) Bp.   **A.C. Nov. 3**
Otherwise Florus of Lodève, q.v.

FLOU (St) Bp.   **R.M. Feb. 2**
Otherwise Flosculus, q.v.

FOELLAN (FOILAN, FILLAN) (St) C.
                                 A.C. Jan. 9
8th cent. A native of Ireland, who accompanied his mother, St Kentigerna,
and his kinsman, St Comgan, to Scotland,

where he became a missionary monk. The
place where he died is now called Strath-
fillan.
Cf. Holw.

FOILA (FAILE) (St) V.   A.C. March 3
6th cent. Said to have been the sister of
St Colgan. The two were patrons of the
parishes of Kil-Faile (Kileely) and Kil-
Colgan, in Galway. Kil-Faile has been a
noted place of pilgrimage.
Cf. Holw.

FOILLAN (St) Ab. O.S.B.   A.C. Oct. 31
d. c.655. Brother of SS Fursey and Ultan.
They left Ireland, their native country,
and worked in E. Anglia. St Foillan became the abbot of Burghcastle, near
Yarmouth, but when this monastery was
destroyed by the Mercians, he crossed
over to Belgium. Bl Ita of Nivelles
gave him some land at Fosses, where he
founded the abbey of that name. He was
the religious leader of Nivelles and evangelized Brabant. He was killed by robbers
and is venerated as a martyr.
Cf. Att. — Baud. — Holw.

FORANNAN (St) Bp. O.S.B.
                                  A.C. Apr. 30
d. 982. An Irish bishop who left his native country and arriving at the abbey of
Waulsort on the Meuse joined the community as a monk and in 962 became its
abbot. He spent some time at Gorze to
study the monastic observance established
there by St John, in order to introduce it
at Waulsort, which he did most successfully.
Cf. Att. — Holw. — Baud.

FORT (St) Bp. M.   A.C. May 16
? 1st cent. Venerated as the first bishop
of Bordeaux and as a martyr.
Cf. Baud. — Holw.

FORTCHERN (St) C.   A.C. Feb. 17
? 6th cent. Said to have been the second
bishop of Trim in Ireland. Others make
him a convert and disciple of St Patrick
in the 5th cent.
Cf. Holw.

FORTIS GABRIELLI (Bl) H. O.S.B.
                                  A.C. May 13
d. 1040. A native of Gubbio in Umbria,
and a hermit in the mountains near
Scheggia, under the guidance of Bl
Ludolph, founder of Fontavellana. Later

he entered that monastery and was professed there as a monk-hermit. Cult approved in 1756.
Cf. Martyrol. Camald. — *Holw.* — *Chev.* — *Zimm.* — *Baud.*

FORTUNATA (St) V. M.   R.M. Oct. 14
d. 303. A maiden martyred at Caesarea in Palestine under Diocletian. Her relics have been venerated at Naples since the 8th cent. The legend adds that her three brothers, SS Evaristus, Carponius and Priscian, suffered with her.
Cf. Baud. — *Holw.*

FORTUNATUS of SMYRNA (St) M.
R.M. Jan. 9
See Vitalis, Revocatus and Fortunatus.

FORTUNATUS, FELICIAN, FIRMUS and CANDIDUS (SS) MM. R.M. Feb. 2
? Roman martyrs who suffered, it is said, with many others.

FORTUNATUS (St) M.   R.M. Feb. 21
See Verulus, Secundinus, etc.

FORTUNATUS, FELIX and Comp. (SS) MM.   R.M. Feb. 26
? A group of twenty-nine martyrs of whom nothing is known.

FORTUNATUS (St) M.   R.M. Feb. 27
See Alexander, Abundius, etc.

FORTUNATUS (St) M.   R.M. March 3
See Felix, Luciolus, etc.

FORTUNATUS and MARCIAN (SS) MM.   R.M. Apr. 17
? Martyrs, perhaps of Antioch in Syria, but more probably of some town in Africa.

FORTUNATUS of ALEXANDRIA (St) M.
R.M. Apr. 21
See Arator, Fortunatus, etc.

FORTUNATUS of VALENCE (St) M.
R.M. Apr. 23
See Felix, Fortunatus and Achilleus.

FORTUNATUS (St) C.   R.M. June 1
d. c.400. A parish priest at a place near Spoleto, in Umbria, conspicuous for his charity to the poor.
Cf. Holw. — *Baud.*

FORTUNATUS of AQUILEIA (St) M.
R.M. June 11
See Felix and Fortunatus.

FORTUNATUS and LUCIAN (SS) MM.
R.M. June 13
? African martyrs, whose Acts have been lost. Most martyrologies register six or more other names.

FORTUNATUS the PHILOSOPHER (St)
A.C. June 18
d. c.569. An Italian bishop driven from his see in N. Italy by the Lombards. He was much esteemed by St Germanus of Paris. He must not be confused with the better known St Venantius Fortunatus, his contemporary in France.
Cf. Holw. — *Baud.*

FORTUNATUS (St) M.   R.M. July 12
See Hermagoras and Fortunatus.

FORTUNATUS (St) M.
R.M. Aug. 27 and Sept. 1
See Honoratus and Comp. (Sept. 1), and the Twelve Holy Brothers.

FORTUNATUS, CAIUS and ANTHES (SS) MM.   R.M. Aug. 28
d. 303. Martyred near Salerno under Diocletian. Their relics were enshrined at Salerno in 940, and since then they have been held in great popular veneration.
Cf. Holw. — *Baud.*

FORTUNATUS of TODI (St) Bp.
R.M. Oct. 14
d. 537. A bishop of Todi, who saved the city from being sacked by Totila the Goth.
Cf. Baud. — *Holw.*

FORTUNATUS (St) M.   R.M. Oct. 15
d. ? 537. A Roman martyr.

FORTUNATUS (St) M.   R.M. Oct. 24
See Felix, Audactus, etc.

FORTUNATUS, VENANTIUS (St) Bp.
A.C. Dec. 14
See Venantius Fortunatus.

FORTUNATUS (St) M.   R.M. Dec. 15
See Faustinus, Lucius, etc.

FORTY ARMENIAN MARTYRS (SS)
R.M. March 10
d. 320. Forty soldiers put to death by the emperor Licinius at Sebaste (Sivas) in Lesser Armenia. They were exposed naked on the ice of a frozen lake, a warm

bath being on the bank as a temptation to apostatize. One fell, but his place was taken by one of the guards who was converted by the heroism of the rest. On the morrow all were dead, save the youngest among them. His brave mother carried her child after the corpses of the rest until he too expired in her arms, and then laid his body by their side. Many ecclesiastical writers of that period speak of this group of martyrs—SS. Basil, Gregory of Nyssa, Gaudentius of Brescia, Sozomen, etc. They are still greatly venerated in the East.

Cf. Att. — Baud. — Holw.

FOSTER (St) Bp.   **R.M. Feb. 6**
The old English form of the name Vedastus or Waast. See Vedastus.

FOUR CROWNED MARTYRS, The (SS)
         R.M. Nov. 8
There are two groups of martyrs called the Four Holy Crowned Ones — *Sancti Quatuor Coronati*: one group suffered at Albano c.305, viz, Severus, Severianus, Carpophorus and Victorinus; the other group met their death in Pannonia about the same time: Claudius, Nicostratus, Symphorian and Castorius, to whom a fifth named Simplicius is added. In both cases their names were at first unknown; hence the collective title by which they are generally referred to.

Cf. Att. — Baud. — Holw.

FOURTEEN HOLY HELPERS, The, (SS)   **A.C. Aug. 8**
A collective feast is celebrated in several places, chiefly in Germany, in honour of fourteen saints, each of whom is believed to grant a special form of help. The usual fourteen are: Achatius, Barbara, Blaise, Catherine, Christopher, Cyriacus, Dionysius, Erasmus, Eustace, George, Margaret, Pantaleon, Vitus — all martyrs — and Giles. See their respective notices for the reason for their particular veneration as helpers.

FRAGAN and GWEN (BLANCHE) (SS)
         A.C. July 5
5th cent. Refugees from Britain in the troublous times consequent upon the departure of the Romans, and parents of SS Wenwaloc, Jacut and Guithern. Churches in Brittany are dedicated to each of them.

Cf. Holw.

FRANCA VISALTA (St) O.S.B. Cist.
         A.C. Apr. 26
1170-1218. A native of Piacenza in Italy. At the age of seven she was offered to God in the Benedictine convent of St Syrus. She was professed at fourteen and soon, though very young, made abbess. She seems to have been over severe, and she was in fact deposed. After some years she was transferred to the recently founded Cistercian nunnery of Pittoli, which she also governed and where she died. Cult confirmed, with the title of Saint, by Gregory X.

Cf. Att. — Baud. — Menzies — Chev. — Holw.

FRANCES of ROME (St) W. O.S.B.
         R.M. March 9
1384-1440. A native of Rome, she married in 1396 Lorenzo de Ponziani, with whom she lived for forty years, succeeding during all this time in never once annoying him. Her life was a model of fidelity and devotedness to her domestic duties; she patiently bore many severe trials, among them being the death of her children, her husband's banishment and the confiscation of their estates. In 1433 she founded the community of Benedictine Oblates of Tor de' Specci, but it was not until 1436, after the death of her husband, that she could join it. Her biography, with many particulars of visions and revelations, of her devotion to her angel guardian, whom she often saw walking by her side and guiding her, was written by John Matteotti, who had been her confessor during the last ten years of her life. Canonized in 1608.

Cf. Att. — Zimm. — Baud. — Holw.

FRANCES LANEL (Bl) M. A.C. June 26
1745-1794. A native of Eu, diocese of Rouen, she became a Sister of Charity at Rouen, and was later stationed at Cambrai and Arras. She, with three other sisters, was guillotined at Cambrai. Beatified in 1920.

Cf. Baud.

FRANCES de CROISSY and FRANCES BRIDEAU (BB) MM. O.C. A.C. July 17
d. 1794. Frances de Croissy was born at Paris in 1745 and was professed a Carmelite nun at Compiègne in 1764. She was prioress from 1779 to 1787 and at the time of her death was novice-mistress. Frances

Brideau was born at Belfort in 1752 and professed at Compiègne in 1771. She was the sub-prioress. Both were guillotined at Paris with the rest of the community in 1794. Beatified in 1906.
Cf. Baud.

FRANCES BIZZOCCA (Bl) M.
A.C. Aug. 17

d. 1627. A Japanese, the wife of Bl Leo, she belonged to the third order of Friars Preachers. She was condemned to death for sheltering missionaries in her house, and was burnt alive at Nagasaki. Beatified in 1867.
Cf. Holw.

FRANCES d'AMBOISE (Bl) O.C.
A.C. Nov. 4

1427-1485. Reared at the court of Brittany, Frances became the wife of Duke Peter of Brittany, and spent her life in endeavouring to please and pacify her jealous husband — no light task — and in charitable works. She was a great benefactress of the Carmelite Bl John Soreth, and herself became a Carmelite in her widowhood (1470) at the convent which she had founded at Nantes. Beatified in 1863.
Cf. Att. — Baud. — Holw.

FRANCES XAVIER CABRINI (Bl)
Foundress.   A.C. Dec. 22

1850-1917. Born at Sant' Angelo Lodigiano in Lombardy, the thirteenth child of Augustine and Stella Cabrini. In 1874 she was asked by the parish priest to teach in an orphanage at Codogno, diocese of Lodi. In 1877 the orphanage became the mother-house of a new institute, founded by Mother Frances under the title of Missionary Sisters of the Sacred Heart. She made her own profession at the hands of the bishop of Lodi, who in 1880 officially approved the new congregation as a diocesan institute. Mother Cabrini's dream was to send her sisters to China, but on the advice of Pope Leo XIII she dispatched them instead to the United States. In 1889 she herself accompanied the first batch of missionary sisters to New York, and from that time almost every year she crossed the sea at the head of new bands of missionaries. During her life-time she founded as many as sixty-seven religious houses — schools, orphanages, hospitals, etc. — in N. and S. America, Italy, Spain, England, etc.

She died in one of the American foundations, Columbus Hospital, Chicago. She had become an American citizen. Beatified in 1938.

FRANCIS FERDINAND de CAPILLAS (Bl) M. O.P.   A. C. Jan. 15

1606-1648. A native of Vacherim de Campos in Old Castile, Francis joined the Dominicans at Valladolid and in 1641 was sent to the Spanish missions of the Philippines, whence the following year he set out for Fo-Kien in China. He laboured there with great success, but political and religious troubles arose in the province, and Francis was executed as a spy. Beatified in 1909, and proclaimed the Protomartyr of China.
Cf. Att. — Baud. — Holw.

FRANCIS GIL (Bl) M. O.P.
A.C. Jan. 22

1702-1744. A native of Tortosa, Spain, he became a Friar Preacher at Barcelona and was sent to the Philippines. Thence he went to Tonkin, where after long apostolic labours, he was imprisoned for several years and beheaded at Checo. Beatified in 1906.
Cf. Holw. — Baud.

FRANCIS of SALES (St) Bp. Dr. Founder.
R.M. Jan. 29

1567-1622. Born near Annecy, in Savoy, the eldest son of the Seigneur de Nouvelles. He read for the Law at Paris and Padua, but abandoned his legal studies and became a priest in 1593. At once he set out for his apostolate among the Calvinists of the Chablais, where he is said to have made within two years over eight thousand converts. In 1599 he was chosen coadjutor to the bishop of Geneva, whom he succeeded in 1602. Two years later he met St Jane Frances of Chantal, with whom he founded the Order of the Visitation. He was indefatigable in the discharge of his office as a bishop: organized conferences for the clergy, directed them to teach catechism in simple words, insisted on unadorned straightforward preaching, established a seminary at Annecy which he visited regularly. He excelled as an ascetical writer, and his treatise *Introduction to the Devout Life* will always remain a classic. His people loved him and styled him "The Gentle Christ of Geneva." Canonized in 1665;

declared a Doctor of the Church in 1877, and patron saint of journalists in 1923.
Cf. Att. — Baud. — Holw.

FRANCIS XAVIER BIANCHI (Bl) Barn.
A.C. Jan. 31
1743-1815. A native of Arpino in Italy who became a Barnabite clerk regular and was ordained priest in 1767 — in the teeth of opposition from his family. Owing to overwork and to his austere life, he ruined his health and lost the use of his legs. It is related that in 1805, when Vesuvius was in eruption, he had himself carried to the spot and at his blessing the lava ceased to flow. Beatified in 1893.
Cf. Att. — Baud. — Holw. — Menzies.

FRANCIS BLANCO (St) M. O.F.M.
R.M. Feb. 5
d. 1597. A native of Monterey, in Spanish Galicia. He studied at Salamanca, and was professed as a Franciscan at Villalpando. He first laboured at Churubusco in Mexico, and in 1594 reached Japan from Manila. He was crucified at Nagasaki. Canonized in 1862.
Cf. Holw.

FRANCIS of ST MICHAEL (St) M. O.F.M.
R.M. Feb. 5
d. 1597. Born at Parilla, near Valladolid. He became a Franciscan lay-brother and in 1593 accompanied St Peter the Baptist from Manila to Japan. He was arrested with him at Verela (1596) and crucified. Canonized in 1862.
Cf. Holw.

FRANCIS of NAGASAKI (St) M.
R.M. Feb. 5
d. 1597. A Japanese physician, and a member of the third order of St Francis. He served the missionaries as a catechist and was for this reason crucified at Nagasaki. Canonized in 1862.
Cf. Holw.

FRANCIS REGIS CLET (Bl) M. C.M.
A.C. Feb. 17
1748-1820. Born at Grenoble, he joined the Lazarists and was sent to China as a missionary in 1791. Here he laboured for thirty years, in the face of incredible difficulties, and at last, in his seventy-second year, was cruelly tortured and strangled near Hankow. Beatified in 1900.
Cf. Att. — Baud. — Holw.

FRANCIS de PAOLA (St) Founder.
R.M. Apr. 2
1416-1507. Born at Paola in Calabria. At the age of fourteen he settled as a hermit on the sea coast near Paola. Many disciples followed him and eventually their community at Paola grew into the new order of Minim Friars — *Minimi*, i.e., the least of all friars. The order was approved by Sixtus IV in 1474. It was this same pope who directed St Francis to travel to France (1482) in order to assist, at Plessis-les-Tours, the dying King Louis XI. At the request of that king's successors Francis remained in France for the rest of his life and died at Plessis. Canonized in 1519.
Cf. Att. — Baud. — Menzies — Holw.

FRANCIS PAGE (Bl) M. S.J.
A.C. Apr. 20
d. 1602. Born at Antwerp, he belonged to an English Protestant family of Harrowon-the-Hill. He was reconciled to the Church, educated at Douai, ordained in 1600, sent to the English mission, captured, received in prison into the Society of Jesus and executed for his priesthood at Tyburn. Beatified in 1929.
Cf. Newdigate — Att.

FRANCIS VENIMBENE of FABRIANO (Bl) C. O.F.M.
A.C. Apr. 22
1251-1322. Born at Fabriano, the son of a physician. He joined the Franciscans in 1267 and was a disciple of St Bonaventure. He founded the first Franciscan library.
Cf. Holw. — Baud.

FRANCIS COLMENARIO (Bl) C.
A.C. Apr. 24
d. 1590. A Spanish missionary priest who evangelized the West Indies. He preached also in Guatemala.
Cf. P. de U.

FRANCIS DICKENSON (Bl) M.
A.C. Apr. 30
d. 1590. A native of Yorkshire and a convert, he was educated for the priesthood at Reims, ordained in 1589 and sent to the English mission, where the following year he was hanged, drawn and quartered for his priesthood at Rochester. Beatified in 1929.
Cf. Newdigate — Att.

FRANCIS JEROME (de GERONIMO) (St) C. S.J.   R.M. May 11

1642-1716. Born near Taranto in S. Italy, and ordained priest in 1666, he entered the Society of Jesus in 1670. From this time on he spent his whole life preaching throughout S. Italy, where his sermons were attended by huge congregations. Canonized in 1839.
Cf. Att. — Menzies — Baud. — Holw.

FRANCIS PATRIZZI (Bl) C. O.S.M.   A.C. May 12

d. 1328. A native of Siena, he was converted by a sermon of the Servite friar, Bl Ambrose Sansedoni, and was himself received into the Servite Order by St Philip Benizi. He was favoured by God with the special grace of reconciling enemies. He died at Siena. Cult approved in 1743.
Cf. Att. — Baud. — Holw.

FRANCIS RONCI (Bl) C. O.S.B. Cel.   A.C. June 4

1223-1294. Born at Abri in S. Italy, he was one of the first disciples of St Peter Celestine, and his companions at the hermitages of Orfente and Morrone. In 1285 he became prior of Santo Spirito and Majella and the first General of the Congregation until 1294. It seems probable that he was created Cardinal by St Peter in Sept. 1294; he died the following month.
Cf. Zimm.

FRANCIS CARACCIOLO (St) C.   R.M. June 4

1563-1608. A scion of the noble Neapolitan family of Caracciolo, he was born in the Abruzzi and during his early years was afflicted with a disease akin to leprosy, of which he was cured on deciding to become a priest. He did so, and in 1588 founded with John Augustine Adorno the order of Minor Clerks Regular, with perpetual adoration of the H. Eucharist as one of its main duties. Francis was the first General of the Order and spent his life in governing it and in preaching. Canonized in 1807.
Cf. Att. — Menzies — Baud.

FRANCIS PACHECO and Comp. (Bl) MM. S.J.   A.C. June 20

1566-1626. A native of Ponte da Lima in Portugal. In 1586 he became a Jesuit and was sent to Macao (1592) where he was ordained priest. He laboured at Macao and in Japan and held the office of rector, provincial, vicar general and administrator of the diocese. He was burnt alive at Nagasaki, together with two other Jesuits from Europe, a Japanese Jesuit, four Japanese laymen and a Korean. All were beatified in 1867.
Cf. Att. — Holw. — Baud.

FRANCIS CHIEN (Bl) M.   A.C. June 25

d. 1838. A Chinese catechist, arrested with Bl Dominic Henares and beheaded at Annam. Beatified in 1900.
Cf. Holw.

FRANCIS ROD (St) M. O.F.M.   R.M. July 9

d. 1572. Born at Brussels, he took the Franciscan habit at Gorkum, Holland. Shortly after his ordination he was hanged by the Calvinists at Briel.
Cf. Holw.

FRANCIS SOLANO (St) C. O.F.M.   R.M. July 14

1549-1610. A native of Andalusia in Spain. He professed the Franciscan Rule among the Observants (1569) and after twenty years of apostolic activities in Spain, he was sent to Peru (1589). Here and elsewhere in S. America he laboured for another twenty years until his death at Lima. Canonized in 1726.
Cf. Att. — Baud. — Holw. — P. de U.

FRANCIS ALVAREZ (Bl) M. S.J.   A.C. July 15

d. 1570. A native of Covilhao in Portugal, who became a Jesuit lay-brother. He was martyred with Bl Ignatius de Azevedo, q.v.
Cf. Holw. — Att.

FRANCIS ARANHA (Bl) M. S.J.   A.C. July 15

d. 1583. A native of Braga in Portugal who came to Goa with his uncle, and there joined the Society of Jesus (1571) as a coadjutor. He served the mission on the islet of Salsette, where he was martyred with Bl Rudolph Acquaviva, q.v.
Cf. Holw.

FRANCIS MAGALLANES (Bl) M. S.J.   A.C. July 15

d. 1570. A native of Alcázar do Sal, in Portugal, who became a Jesuit cleric and

shared the martyrdom of Bl Ignatius de Azevedo and companions, q.v.
Cf. Att. — Holw.

FRANCIS PEREZ GODOY (Bl) M. S.J.
A.C. July 15
d. 1570. A native of Torrijos, diocese of Toledo, in Spain. He was a Jesuit novice and a companion in martyrdom of Bl Ignatius de Azevedo, q.v.
Cf. Holw. — Att. — Baud.

FRANCIS (CEOCO) of PESARO (St)
Tert. O.F.M. A.C. Aug. 13
d. 1530. An early Franciscan tertiary who lived with others in community. Cult confirmed in 1859.
Cf. Att. — Baud. — Holw.

FRANCIS CULIOYE (Bl) M.
A.C. Aug. 17
d. 1627. A Japanese tertiary of St Francis, burnt alive at Nagasaki for having sheltered missionaries. Beatified in 1867.
Cf. Holw. — Baud.

FRANCIS CUROBIOYE (Bl) M.
A.C. Aug. 17
d. 1627. A native Japanese Christian, and a Dominican tertiary, burnt alive at Nagasaki. Beatified in 1867.
Cf. Holw. — Baud.

FRANCIS of ST MARY (Bl) M. O.F.M.
A.C. Aug. 17
d. 1627. Born at La Mancha, Spain. After his profession and ordination, he was sent to the Philippines (1605) and then to Japan (1622) during the persecution, and was forthwith arrested and finally burnt alive at Nagasaki. Beatified in 1867.
Cf. Holw.

FRANCIS of JESUS ORTEGA (Bl) M. O.S.A.
A.C. Sept. 3
d. 1632. A native of Villamediana in Spain. In 1614 he took the habit of the Hermits of St Augustine at Valladolid. In 1622 he was sent to Mexico, and thence with Bl Vincent Carvalho, to Manila, and in 1623 to Japan. He was burnt alive at Nagasaki. Beatified in 1867.
Cf. Holw.

FRANCIS NIFAKI (Bl) M. A.C. Sept. 8
d. 1628. A native boy of five years of age, beheaded at Nagasaki with his father, Bl

Louis Nifaki, and his brother Dominic. Beatified in 1867.
Cf. Holw.

FRANCIS de MORALES (Bl) M. O.P.
A.C. Sept. 10
d. 1622. A native of Madrid who became a Dominican and worked for twenty years in the Japanese mission of Satzuma. In 1608 he returned to Fuximi, and in 1614 to Nagasaki where he was burnt alive with Bl Charles Spinola and companions. Beatified in 1867.
Cf. Baud. — Holw.

FRANCIS TAQUEA (Bl) M.
A.C. Sept. 11
d. 1622. A Japanese boy of twelve years of age, a son of Bl Thomas Taquea, beheaded with Bl Caspar Cotenda at Nagasaki. Beatified in 1867.
Cf. Holw. — Baud.

FRANCIS of ST BONAVENTURE (Bl) M. O.F.M.
A.C. Sept. 12
d. 1622. Born in Musaxi, Quanto, Japan. A native catechist who worked under Bl Apollinaris Franco. He was burnt alive at Omura. Beatified in 1867.
Cf. Holw. — Baud.

FRANCIS of CALDEROLA (Bl) C. O.F.M.
A.C. Sept. 13
d. 1407. A native of Calderola, diocese of Camerino. He embraced the Franciscan rule and was a very successful preacher, with the special gift for reconciling enemies. He died at Colfana. Cult approved by Gregory XVI.
Cf. Att. — Baud. — Holw.

FRANCIS of CAMPOROSSO (Bl) C. O.F.M. Cap.
A.C. Sept. 16
1804-1866. An Italian peasant born near Ventimiglia, who became a lay-brother in the Capuchin friary of the Immaculate Virgin at Genoa. He spent forty years there and died while nursing cholera victims. Beatified in 1929.
Cf. Att.

FRANCIS de POSADAS (Bl) C. O.P.
A.C. Sept. 20
1644-1713. Born at Cordova in Spain, he took the Dominican habit at Aracoeli in 1663, and spent the rest of his life giving missions throughout S.W. Spain. He died at Aracoeli. Beatified in 1818.
Cf. Att. — Baud. — Holw.

FRANCIS JACCARD (Bl) M.
                              A.C. Sept. 21

1799-1838. Born at Onnion in Savoy. He entered the Seminary for Foreign Missions in Paris and was sent to Cochin-China in 1826. He was strangled in Annam. Beatified in 1900.
Cf. Baud. — Holw.

FRANCIS CHAKICHI (Bl) M. A.C. Oct. 2

d. 1622. A Japanese boy of four years of age, son of BB. Louis and Lucy Chakichi. He was beheaded with his mother and his brother Andrew (their father was burnt at the stake) at Nagasaki. Beatified in 1867.
Cf. Holw. — Baud.

FRANCIS of ASSISI (St) Founder.
                                R.M. Oct. 4

1181-1226. "The Poor Little Man" — *il Poverello* — one of the best known and loved of saints. A native of Assisi in Umbria, the son of a merchant. In his youth he loved pleasure, until a series of providential happenings led him, in 1209, to found the order of Friars Minor, characterized by a loving, joyous worship of the Sacred Humanity of Christ, and by a profession of poverty which was both individual and collective. The appeal of the new order to that generation may be gauged from the fact that at the General Chapter of 1219 five thousand friars were present. This same year Francis sailed for Palestine and tried to evangelize the Mohammedans, but this mission was a failure. Meanwhile, the new order was passing through a period of painful internal difficulties. Francis returned to Italy, sent friars into all western European countries, with instructions to establish themselves preferably in university centres. His rule was approved by Innocent III, and his life and message received a direct sanction from Christ in 1224, when on September 14 Francis received the stigmata of the Passion on Mt Alvernia. He died still in deacon's orders and was canonized two years after his death.
Cf. Chev.

FRANCIS TITEIMANS C. O.F.M. Cap.
                                A.C. Oct. 4

d. 1537. A student of Louvain who joined the Capuchins and ended his days tending the sick in the hospital of St James in Rome.
Cf. P. de U. — Baud.

FRANCIS TRUNG (Bl) M.   A.C. Oct. 6

1825-1858. A native of Cochin-China and a corporal in the army there. Born at Phan-xa, beheaded in An-hoa. Beatified in 1909.
Cf. Holw.

FRANCIS BORGIA (St) C. S.J.
                                R.M. Oct. 10

1510-1572. Born at Gandia, near Valencia, in Spain, of the noble family of de Borja. He was reared at the court of Charles V, married very young, and up to the time of his wife's death (1546) devoted himself to the discharge of his duties at the emperor's court and on his own estates as duke of Gandia. In 1546 he left all and joined the Society of Jesus. As General of the Society, he was one of the greatest instruments of Divine Providence in the counter-reformation. Under him the Society spread throughout Europe and the foreign missions. Austere with himself, Francis was the typical saint of the Spanish nobility — courteous, refined, kind, humble and generous, yet most determined and enterprising. He died at Ferrara, while travelling on an embassy from Pope St Pius V, his great friend, to the kings of France and Spain. Canonized in 1671.
Cf. Att. — Baud. — Holw.

FRANCIS ISIDORE GAGELIN (Bl) M.
                                A.C. Oct. 17

1799-1833. A native of Montperreux, diocese of Besançon. He belonged to the Society of Foreign Missions of Paris, and was sent to Cochin-China in 1822, where on his arrival he was ordained priest. He worked zealously until the persecution broke out, when he gave himself up to the Mandarin of Bongson and was strangled. Beatified in 1900.
Cf. Holw.

FRANCIS DIAZ (Bl) M. O.P.
                                A.C. Oct. 20

d. 1648. A Spanish Dominican missionary in Fo-Kien, China. He was strangled in prison with Bl Francis Serrano at Fotshen. Beatified in 1893.
Cf. Holw.

FRANCIS SERRANO (Bl) M. O.P.
                                A.C. Oct. 20

d. 1648. Born in Spain and sent as a missionary to China, to the province of Fo-Kien. He was arrested with Bl Peter

Sanz (1646). Whilst in prison at Fo-tshen he was elected titular bishop of Tipasa. He was strangled with three other Dominicans. Beatified in 1893. *Cf. Holw.*

FRANCIS NÉRON (Bl) M. A.C. Nov. 3
See Peter-Francis Néron.

FRANCIS XAVIER CAN (Bl) M.
A.C. Nov. 20
d. 1837. Born at Sou-Mieng, in W. Ton-kin, he was attached to the fathers of the Foreign Missions of Paris. He was strangled in prison. Beatified in 1900. *Cf. Holw. — Baud.*

FRANCIS XAVIER (St) C. S.J.
R.M. Dec. 3
1506-1552. Born at the family castle of Javier, in Spanish Navarre, Francis in-herited the best characteristics of his race — generosity, love of culture and ad-venture. He was studying with distinc-tion at the university of Paris when he met St Ignatius Loyola, and in 1534 they took their first religious vows at Montmartre. In obedience to St Ignatius's order, Fran-cis set out on his first journey to the far east in 1540, landing at Goa in 1542. He visited India, Ceylon, Malaya, Japan, and other East Indian islands, dreaming all the time of his longed-for apostolate in China. The difficulties he met with in his missionary labours were well-nigh insur-mountable: they proceeded chiefly from the politically-minded European traders. However, he was favoured with such ex-traordinary graces from heaven, that his mission proved from the start a signal success: it is reckoned that in Japan alone, some forty years afterwards, there were 400,000 Christians. Indeed, Francis Xa-vier is perhaps the greatest individual missionary the Church has produced since St. Paul. Francis died at Sancian, when about to enter China. Canonized in 1602, and proclaimed by Pius X patron of all foreign missions. *Cf. Holw.*

FRANCIS GALVEZ (Bl) M. O.F.M.
A.C. Dec. 4
1567-1623. A native of Utiel in New Cas-tile. He joined the Friars Minor at Valencia (1591), went to Manila (1609) and thence to Japan (1612). During the persecution he returned to Manila (1614); at Macao he blackened his face in order to be able to enter Japan anew (1618). He preached with great courage, and finally was burnt alive at Yeddo. Beatified in 1867. *Cf. Att. — Holw. — Baud.*

FRANCIS XAVIER MAU (Bl) M.
A.C. Dec. 19
d. 1839. A native catechist of Tonkin, strangled in prison. Beatified in 1900. *Cf. Holw. — Baud.*

FRANCO (FRANCUS) (St) H. O.S.B.
A.C. June 5
d. c.1275. A native of Castel Regni, near Asserigo, in the Abruzzi. He be-came a Benedictine at the monastery of Colimento, and after twenty years as a cenobite, spent the last fifteen years of his life as a hermit near Asserigo. *Cf. Zimm. — Holw.*

FRANCO LIPPI (Bl) C. O.C.
A.C. Dec. 11
d. 1291. A native of Grotto, near Siena. Early in life he fell in with evil companions and became their leader. A fugitive from justice, he joined a band of *condottieri* and excelled them all in crime until about his fiftieth year. Then he became blind, re-pented, went on a pilgrimage to Compos-tella, received back his sight, was absolved by Gregory X, and admitted to the Car-melite Order as a lay-brother. He was already over sixty-five, but managed to earn the title of Saint by his fervour in his new life. *Menzies — Holw.*

FRANCOVEUS (FRANCHY) (St) Mk.
A.C. May 16
7th cent. Monk of St Martin de la Bre-tonnière, he had to suffer much from the jealousy of his fellow-monks. The mon-astery being destroyed, he lived as a her-mit in the Nivernais. *Cf. Bolland. — Holw. — Chev.*

FRATERNUS (St) Bp. M. R.M. Sept. 29
d. c.450. Bishop of Auxerre in France. Tradition makes him also a martyr. *Cf. Baud. — Holw. — Duch. Fast. Episc.*

FREDEGAND (FREGAUT) (St) Ab. O.S.B. A.C. July 17
d. c.740. Said to have been an Irish com-panion of St Foillan. Monk and abbot of Kerkelodor, near Antwerp. It seems

probable that he was a fellow-worker with St Willibrord.
Cf. Zimm. — Holw.

FREDERICK (FRIDERICUS) (Bl) Mk. O.S.B. A.C. Jan. 6
d. 1020. Son of Geoffrey *le Barbu*, count of Verdun. In 997 he handed over his patrimony to the bishop of Verdun, set out for Palestine, and on his return was admitted to the Benedictine abbey of St Vanne. His friend Bl Richard, abbot of St Vanne, was transferred to the abbey of St Vedast at Arras, and Bl Frederick followed him as prior.
Cf. Zimm. — Baud. — Holw.

FREDERICK (Bl) Ab. O. Praem.
A.C. March 3
d. 1175. The abbot-founder of the Premonstratensian abbey of Mariengarten.
Cf. Holw. — Baud.

FREDERICK (Bl) Ab. O.S.B.
A.C. May 7
d. c.1070. A native of Swabia and a monk of Einsiedeln in Switzerland, he was sent with twelve monks to restore discipline in the abbey of Hirschau (1066). He was calumniated by evil-minded monks and deposed by the Count of Calw, owner of Hirschau, in 1069. He retired to Ebersberg where he died.
Cf. Zimm. — Chev. — Butler-Thurston (July 4, in the life of Bl William of Hirschau).

FREDERICK (St) Bp. A.C. May 27
d. 1121. Chosen bishop of Liége in 1119 in the room of the deposed simoniacal prelate Alexander. He was an excellent bishop, but had to suffer much, and in the end, it is said, was poisoned by Alexander's supporter the count of Louvain.
Cf. Baud. — Holw. — Att.

FREDERICK (FRIDRICH) (St) Bp. M.
R.M. July 18
d. 838. Grandson of Radbod, king of the Frisians. In 820 he was appointed bishop of Utrecht and devoted himself especially to combating the evil custom of incestuous marriages, for which reason he was murdered in church at Maestricht.
Cf. Att. — Holw. — Baud.

FREDERICK of RATISBON (Bl) O.S.A.
A.C. Nov. 29
d. 1329. Born at Ratisbon of poor par-ents. He was received as a lay-brother into the order of Augustinian Hermits at Ratisbon and was employed there as carpenter and wood-chopper. Cult approved in 1909.
Cf. Att. — Baud. — Holw.

FREDIANO (FRIGIDANUS, FRIGDIANUS) (St) Bp. R.M. March 18
d. 588. An Irishman who went on pilgrimage to Rome and settled in Italy as a hermit on Monte Pisano. Eventually he was elected bishop of Lucca and formed the clergy of the city into a community of canons regular. He rebuilt the cathedral after it had been burnt by the Lombards. He is greatly venerated at Lucca.
Cf. Menzies — Ricci — Att.

FREMUND (St) M. A.C. May 11
9th cent. An Anglo-Saxon hermit, who seems to have been killed by the Danes and to have been honoured as a martyr. His remains were enshrined at Dunstable.
Cf. Holw.

FRIARDUS (St) H. A.C. Aug. 1
d. c.577. Hermit on the isle of Vindomitte, near Nantes.
Cf. Zimm. — Holw. — Baud.

FRICOR (ADRIAN) (St) H. A.C. Apr. 1
See Caides and Fricor.

FRIDESWIDE (FREDESWINDA) (St) V. O.S.B. R.M. Oct. 19
d. c.735. The daughter of Didan, prince (*subregulus*) of a district bordering the Upper Thames. She was the abbess-foundress of the nunnery of St Mary's under the rule of St Benedict on the site of what is now Oxford. It is said that from her childhood she took for her maxim: "Whatsoever is not God is nothing." She is the patroness of the city and university of Oxford.
Cf. Mab. — Att. — Baud. — Chev.

FRIGIDAND (St) Ab. O.S.B.
A.C. July 17
Otherwise Fredegand, q.v.

FRIDOLIN (St) Ab. O.S.B. A.C. March 6
d. c.650. Monk of Luxeuil (or of Grandval), he became the abbot-founder of Säckingen towards the middle of the 7th cent. He is venerated as the apostle of the Upper Rhine.
Cf. Zimm. — Holw. — Att.

FRIGIDIAN (FRIDAN, FINNIAN) (St) Bp. R.M. March 18
Otherwise Frediano, q.v.

FRITHBERT (FRIDEBERT, FRITHU-BEORHT) (St) Bp. O.S.B. A.C. Dec. 23
d. 766. The successor of St Acca in the bishopric of Hexham, which church he ruled for thirty-four years.
Cf. Zimm. — Holw.

FRITHESTAN (St) Bp. O.S.B.
A.C. Sept. 10
d. 933. A disciple of St Grimbald consecrated bishop of Winchester by St Plegmund. He ruled the see for twenty-three years.
Cf. Zimm. — Stanton — Holw.

FRODOBERT (St) Ab. O.S.B.
A.C. Jan. 8
d. c.673. A monk of Luxeuil under the third abbot St Waldebert. Abbot-founder of Moutier-la-Celle, near Troyes, where he led a life of continuous prayer and great austerities.
Cf. Zimm. — Att. — P. de U. — Chev. — Holw.

FRODULPHUS (FROU) (St) H. O.S.B.
A.C. Apr. 21
d. c.750. A disciple of St Medericus (Morry), he became a monk at St Martin's, Autun, whence he was driven by the Saracen invasion and settled at Barjon, Côte d'Or, where he died.
Cf. Zimm. — Baud. — Holw.

FROILAN (St) Bp. O.S.B. R.M. Oct. 3
d. 1006. A native of Lugo in Galicia, at the age of eighteen he undertook, together with his companion Attilanus (q.v.), the reorganization of monastic observance at Moreruela, on the river Esla in Old Castile. After a very successful career as abbot he was consecrated bishop of Leon. He and St Attilanus were the great restorers of Benedictine monasticism in W. Spain.
Cf. P. de U. — Zimm. — Att. — Chev.

FROMUNDUS (St) Bp. O.S.B. Oct. 24
d. p. 690. Monk and abbot, and then bishop of Coutances.
Cf. Zimm. — Duch. Fast. Episc. — Baud.

FRONTO (St) H. R.M. Apr. 14
? 2nd cent. A solitary in the desert of Nitria in Egypt.
Cf. Holw.

FRONTO (St) M. R.M. Apr. 16
See Saragossa (Martyrs of)

FRONTO and GEORGE (SS) Bps.
R.M. Oct. 25
? Apostles of Périgueux in France at some early period. Worthless legends have completely obscured their true story.
Cf. Att. — Baud. — Duch. Fast. Episc.

FROWIN (Bl) Ab. O.S.B. Cist.
P.C. Feb. 17
d. 1165. A Cistercian of Bellevaux in Savoy and the abbot-founder of Salom in the diocese of Constance. He was a companion of St Bernard when the latter was preaching his crusade.
Cf. Chev. — Holw.

FROWIN II of ENGELBERG (Bl) Ab. O.S.B. A.C. March 7
d. 1178. A Benedictine of St Blasien in the Black Forest who was made abbot of Engelberg in Switzerland (1143). He founded the monastic school at Engelberg, a library, etc., and was himself the chronicler of the abbey and an ascetical writer of distinction.
Cf. Zimm. — Baud. — Holw. — Chev.

FRUCTULUS (St) M. R.M. Feb. 18
See Lucius, Sylvanus, etc.

FRUCTUOSA (St) M. R.M. Aug. 23
See Restitutus, Donatus, etc.

FRUCTUOSUS, AUGURIUS and EULOGIUS (SS) MM. R.M. Jan. 21
d. 259. Fructuosus, bishop of Tarragona in Spain, with his two deacons, Augurius and Eulogius, were burnt at the stake under Valerian. When the fire had burnt through their bonds, they stretched out their arms in the form of a cross and thus expired. The account of their official examination is still extant and thoroughly authentic.
Cf. P. de U. — Att. — Baud. — Holw.

FRUCTUOSUS (St) Ab. Bp.
R.M. Apr. 16
d. 665. Born in Spain, the son of a military officer belonging to the royal house of the Visigoths. He became a monk, and then a hermit in the Vierzo Mts, whither he was followed by crowds of disciples. Whole families embraced his rule, which was based on the rule of St Benedict. Fructuosus was eventually forced to ac-

cept the bishopric of Dumium and later became archbishop of Braga.
Cf. P. de U. — Baud. — Chev.

FRUCTUS (FRUTOS), VALENTINE and ENGRATIA (SS) HH. A.C. Oct. 25
d. c.715. Two brothers and their sister who were living at Sepúlveda in Old Castile at the time of one of the Saracen raids. Valentine and Engratia were killed by the Moors, but Frutos escaped and died a hermit. They are now venerated as the patron saints of Segovia where their relics are enshrined.
Cf. P. de U. — Holw.

FRUGENTIUS (St) M. O.S.B.
A.C. Sept. 3
d. 675. A Benedictine of Fleury, killed with St Aigulphus, abbot of Lérins, q.v.

FRUMENTIUS and another FRUMENTIUS (SS) MM. R.M. March 23
See Victorian, etc.

FRUMENTIUS (St) Bp. R.M. Oct. 27
d. c.380. A native of Tyre, who in the course of a voyage on the Red Sea, was wrecked on the Ethiopian coast with another young man — perhaps his brother — St Aedesius. Both were taken to the king's palace at Aksum, and attained high offices at court. Eventually Frumentius applied to St Athanasius for the appointment of a bishop for Ethiopia. St Athanasius complied by consecrating Frumentius. Frumentius and Aedesius preached the gospel with signal success and are for this reason venerated as the apostles of Ethiopia.
Cf. Att. — Baud. — Holw.

FUGATIUS and DAMIAN (SS)
A.C. Jan. 3 (R.M. May 26)
? 2nd cent. The alleged missionaries sent by Pope St Eleutherius to Britain. Their names are also written, Phaganus and Diruvianus, Fagan and Deruvian, Ffager and Dyfan.
See Dyfan.

FULBERT (St) Bp. A.C. Apr. 10
d. 1029. The glory of his century. He was an Italian by birth, who became a student at the Benedictine abbey of Reims, under Gerbert (Pope Silvester II). He himself directed as headmaster the cathedral school of Chartres, of which city he was made bishop. A poet and scholar he

identified himself whole-heartedly with the Cluniac movement of reform.
Cf. Att. — Baud. — Zimm.

FULCRAN (St) Bp. A.C. Feb. 13
d. 1006. A bishop of Lodève in France, who ruled his diocese for over half a century.
Cf. Baud. — Holw.

FULGENTIUS (St) Bp. R.M. Jan. 1
468-533. An African, belonging to a family of senatorial rank. Early in life he embraced the monastic life and was elected abbot of his monastery; but he had to flee owing to the Vandal persecution. In 508 he was chosen bishop of Ruspe; but was again exiled by the Vandals. He spent his exile in Sardinia where he wrote his numerous works, which are still of the greatest importance for the history of the Arian persecutions. In 523 he returned to Africa and died ten years later.
Cf. Att. — Baud. — Holw.

FULGENTIUS (St) Bp. A.C. Jan. 16
d. c.633. Brother of SS Isidore and Leander of Seville and of St Florentina. He was bishop of Ecija, in Andalusia, and one of the leaders of the Spanish church of that time. He is often confused with St Fulgentius of Ruspe (see Jan. 1).
Cf. P. de U. — Holw.

FULGENTIUS (Bl) Ab. O.S.B.
P.C. Dec. 10
d. 1122. A Walloon by birth, he was professed a Benedictine at the abbey of St Airy, Verdun. The community of this monastery had to disband, owing to the struggle between Gregory VII and Henry IV. Fulgentius repaired to the abbey of Afflighem in Belgium, where later he was elected abbot.
Cf. Holw. — P. de U. — Chev.

FULK (FOULQUES, FULCO) (Bl) C.
A.C. March 2
d. 1201. Parish priest of Neuilly-sur-Marne in France, commissioned by Innocent III to preach the third crusade, in which Richard Coeur de Lion took part. He died before setting out for the Holy Land.
Cf. Att. — Holw.

FULK (St) C. R.M. May 22
d. p. 600. A pilgrim to Rome who gave his life in the service of the plague-

stricken at Santopadre or Castrofutli, near Arpino, in S. Italy. He is venerated as the patron saint of that district. Cult approved in 1572.
Cf. Holw.

FULK (St) Ab. O.S.B. P.C. Oct. 10
d. 845. The twenty-first abbot of Fontenelle in Normandy.
Cf. Holw.

FULK (St) Bp. R.M. Oct. 26
1164-1229. Born at Piacenza of Scottish parents, he was appointed to a canonry there. Then, after his studies in Paris, he became archpriest and bishop of Piacenza. Six years later he was transferred by Honorius III to the see of Pavia, which he occupied for thirteen years.
Cf. Holw. — Baud.

FULK (FOLQUET) (Bl) Bp.
P.C. Dec. 25
c.1155-1231. A Genoese by birth, and a minstrel by profession, he entered the Cistercian abbey of Thoronet, of which he became abbot in 1200. In 1206 he was raised to the see of Toulouse and greatly helped St Dominic in the founding of the Friars Preachers. He was known as "the Minstrel Bishop." He is venerated by the Cistercians.
Cf. Holw. — Gams — Chev.

FULRAD (St) Ab. O.S.B. A.C. July 16
d. 784. An Alsatian by origin, he became a Benedictine at the abbey of St Denis near Paris, and in 750 was elected its abbot. From this time his life is identified with that of the Carolingian court, at which he held offices: viz. councillor, court chaplain, grand-almoner, ambassador to the pope, etc. His was a crowded life in the service of the Church and of the Holy Roman Empire, as represented by Charlemagne.
Cf. Att. — Zimm. — Mab. — Chev.

FURSEY (St) Ab. O.S.B. R.M. Jan. 16
d. c.648. An Irish monk, who established a monastery at Rathmat, whence he passed over to England and founded another at Burgh-Castle, near Yarmouth, in East Anglia. He finally crossed over to France and became the abbot-founder of Lagny, near Paris. His life is also famous for his remarkable ecstasies, of which St Bede and others write.
Cf. Att. — Baud. — Holw.

FUSCA V. and MAURA (SS) MM.
R.M. Feb. 13
d. c.250. Two martyrs of Ravenna under Decius. Fusca was a young girl and Maura her nurse.
Cf. Baud. — Holw. — Menzies.

FUSCIAN (St) M. R.M. Dec. 11
See Victoricus, Fuscian and Gentian.

FUSCULUS (St) Bp. M. R.M. Sept. 6
See Donatian, Praesidius, etc.

FYMBERT (St) Bp. A.C. Sept. 25
7th cent. A bishop in the W. of Scotland, said to have been consecrated by St Gregory the Great.
Cf. Holw.

FYNCANA and FYNDOCA (SS) VV. MM.
A.C. Oct. 13
? Two martyrs listed in the Aberdeen breviary, of whom nothing is known.

G

GABDELAS (St) M. R.M. Sept. 29
See Dadas, Casdoe and Gabdelas.

GABINUS (St) M. R.M. Feb. 19
d. 295 (or 296). A Roman Christian, related to the emperor Diocletian, brother of Pope St Caius and father of the martyr St Susanna. Late in life he was ordained priest, and died in prison or by the sword, about the same time as his brother the pope. His Acts, however, are quite untrustworthy.
Cf. Baud. — Holw. — Menzies.

GABINUS and CRISPULUS (SS) MM.
R.M. May 30
d. c.130. The proto-martyrs of Sardinia. They suffered at Torres, where they had preached the gospel, under Hadrian.
Cf. Holw. — Baud.

GABRIEL of OUR LADY of SORROWS (St) C.P. R.M. Feb. 27
1838-1862. Francis Possenti was born at Assisi and educated at Spoleto under the Jesuit Fathers. He was a typical schoolboy, careless and fond of pleasure. After two serious illnesses he suddenly developed a religious vocation and joined the Passionist Fathers at Morovalle, near Macerata (1856). Six years later (1862) he died of consumption at Isola, in the

Abruzzi. He attained perfection by heroic self-denial in small things. Canonized in 1920.
Cf. Att. — Baud. — Holw. — Ricci.

GABRIEL the ARCHANGEL (St)
R.M. March 24
One of the three angels whose names are mentioned both in the Bible and in the Liturgy — Michael, Gabriel, Raphael. St Gabriel is mentioned in the Book of Daniel (VIII, 16; IX, 21) and was the angel sent to Zachary (Luke I, 11-19) and especially to our Lady, to tell her that she was chosen to be the Mother of God (Luke I, 26 sqq). He is for this reason called "The Angel of the Annunciation." His feast was added to the general calendar of the Western Church in 1921.

GABRIEL MARY (Bl) C. A.C. Aug. 27
1463-1532. Gabriel's baptismal name was Gilbert Nicolas, and he was born near Clermont. He was refused admission to several houses of the Franciscan Observants, but finally was received at Notre-Dame-de-la-Font, near Rochelle. He cooperated with St Jane of Valois, whose confessor he was, in the foundation of the order of the Annonciades (1532). On account of his favourite devotion Pope Alexander VI nick-named him "Gabriel of the Ave Maria." Cult approved in 1647.
Cf. Att. — Baud. •

GABRIEL of ST MAGDALEN (St) M.
O.F.M. A.C. Sept. 3
d. 1632. A native of Fonseca in New Castile, and a Franciscan lay-brother. In 1612 he was sent to Manila, where he studied medicine, and in 1622 passed over to Japan and ministered to the sick during the persecutions, at the risk of his own life. He was at last captured and burnt alive at Nagasaki. Beatified in 1867.
Cf. Holw.

GABRIEL PERBOYRE (Bl) M.
A.C. Sept. 11
1802-1840. Born at Puech, in the diocese of Montauban, he joined the Vincentians in 1818, and after his ordination (1825) taught theology at Saint-Flaur (1825-1835). Here he received the news of the death of his brother, a missionary in China, and offered himself to replace him. He arrived in China in 1836 and worked in the mission of Honan. In 1840, after a

long incarceration and many tortures, he was strangled at the cross. Beatified in 1889.
Cf. Holw. — Baud.

GABRIEL JOHN TAUTIN DUFRESSE
(Bl) M. A.C. Sept. 14
1751-1815. Born at Ville-de-Lezoux, diocese of Clermont, he entered the seminary for foreign missions in 1774, and arrived in China in 1777. In 1800 he was consecrated titular bishop of Tabraca and after fifteen years of continual danger was betrayed by a native Christian and beheaded. Beatified in 1900.
Cf. Holw. •

GABRIEL FERRETTI (Bl) C. O.F.M.
A.C. Nov. 12
1385-1456. A native of Ancona, and a scion of the family of the counts Ferretti. He became a Friar Minor at Ancona, and eventually provincial of Piceno (Marches). Cult confirmed in 1753.
Cf. Att. — Baud. — Menzies — Holw.

GABRIELLE BOURLA (Bl) M.
A.C. Oct. 17
1746-1794. Her name in religion was Marie-Ursule, and she belonged to the group of Ursuline martyrs of Valenciennes, q.v.
Cf. Baud.

GAIUS (St) (several)
Otherwise Caius, q.v.

GALATA (St) M. R.M. Apr. 19
See Hermogenes, Caius, etc.

GALATION (GALACTEON) and EPISTEMIS (SS) MM. R.M. Nov. 5
d. 252. According to the legend, Galation, already a Christian, converted his wife, upon which each retired to a monastery. They were martyred under Decius at Emessa in Phoenicia. It is now generally agreed that these two martyrs never existed: they are simply the hero and heroine in what may be described as the Christian continuation of the romance of Clitophon and Leucippe.
Cf. Att. — Holw.

GALDINUS (St) Bp. R.M. Apr. 18
1100-1176. A native of Milan and a member of the Della Scala family. After his ordination he was chancellor and arch-

deacon of the archdiocese. In 1161 he fled on the approach of the emperor Barbarossa; but, though absent, was elected archbishop of Milan and created cardinal (1165). He returned to Milan and was instrumental in rebuilding the city, razed to the ground by Barbarossa. He died immediately after having preached a sermon in his cathedral. The Milanese always invoke him after SS Ambrose and Charles Borromeo.
Cf. Att. — Holw. — Baud.

GALGANUS (St) C.   R.M. Dec. 3
d. 1181. A native of Siena who at first led a worldly life, but was converted to better ways and became a hermit at Monte Siepe in Tuscany, where he died. He was canonized by Alexander III. In 1196 a church was built on the site of his hermitage which was handed over to the Cistercians in 1201. It is probably for this reason that the Cistercians have always claimed him as one of their own.
Cf. Zimm. — Chev. — Prop. Cist. — Holw. — Menzies.

GALL (GALLUS) (St) Bp.   R.M. July 1
c. 489-c. 554. A native of Auvergne who became a monk but after being ordained deacon by St Quinctianus, bishop of Clermont, was sent to represent him at the court of King Thierry. In 527 he succeeded St Quinctianus. He was uncle and teacher of St Gregory of Tours.
Cf. Holw. — Baud. — Att.

GALL (St) Ab.   R.M. Oct. 16
d. c.640. An Irishman and a monk of Bangor who accompanied St Columbanus to England and France, where he helped in the foundation of Luxeuil. He was banished, together with St Columbanus, and settled in Switzerland, at a place on the Steinach, where the great abbey and town of Saint-Gall sprang up at a later period, and is venerated as one of the apostles of Switzerland.
Cf. Att. — Baud. — Holw.

GALLA (St) W.   R.M. Oct. 5
d. c.550. A Roman lady, daughter of Symmachus the younger and sister-in-law of Boethius. After her husband's death she led the life of a recluse in a small cottage on the Vatican Hill, where she died of cancer of the breast. Her life and

death are briefly described by St Gregory the Great.
Cf. Att. — Menzies — Holw.

GALLGO (St) Ab.   A.C. Nov. 27
6th cent. A Welsh saint, founder of Llanallgo in Anglesey.
Cf. Baring-Gould.

GALLICANUS (St) M.   R.M. June 25
d. c.362. Described as a high officer in the army of Constantine and consul at Rome, who in the year 330, retired to Ostia, where he founded a hospital and ministered to the sick. The R.M. makes him a martyr at Alexandria under Julian the Apostate; but both his banishment to Alexandria and his martyrdom are denied by historians.
Cf. Att. — Holw. — Baud.

GALLICANUS (St) Bp.   A.C. June 25
d. p. 541. The fifth bishop of Embrun, in France.
Cf. Baud. — Duch. Fast. Episc.

GALLUS (St)   R.M. July 1
Otherwise Gall, q.v.

GALMIER (St)   R.M. Feb. 27
The French form of Baldomerus, q.v.

GALNUTIUS (St) Ab.   A.C. March 3
Otherwise Winwaloe, q.v.

GAMALIEL (St)   R.M. Aug. 3
1st cent. The Jewish doctor of the Law, at whose feet St Paul sat (Acts XXII, 3) and whose counsel saved Peter and John (ib. V, 34-39). Tradition makes him a convert to Christianity. The R.M. commemorates the finding of his body, together with those of SS Stephen, protomartyr, Nicodemus and Abibo (415).
Cf. Holw. — Baud.

GAMELBERT (St) C.   A.C. Jan. 27
c.800. A Bavarian by birth and a soldier under King Pepin. Later he was raised to the priesthood and laboured for over fifty years as parish priest of Michaelsbuch. Cult approved in 1909.
Cf. Holw. — Baud.

GAMO (St) Ab.   A.C. May 30
See Hugbert and Gamo.

GANDULPHUS of BINASCO (Bl) C.
O.F.M.   A.C. Apr. 3
d. 1260. Born at Binasco, near Milan, he

became a Friar Minor during the life-time of St Francis, and spent all his life praying and preaching in Sicily.
Cf. Att. — Baud. — Holw. — Menzies.

GANGULPHUS (St) M.   R.M. May 11
d. 760. A Burgundian and a courtier, who retired from public life to lead the life of a recluse and was killed by his wife's paramour.
Cf. Holw. — Baud.

GARBH (St) V.   A.C. Jan. 1
Otherwise Fanchea, q.v.

GARBHAN (St) Ab.   A.C. March 26
7th cent. The Irish saint who appears to have left his name to Dungarvan. Nothing certain is known about him.
Cf. O'Hanlon.

GARCIA GONZALEZ (St) M. O.F.M.
   R.M. Feb. 5
d. 1597. A Spanish Franciscan and missionary in Japan, crucified at Nagasaki. Beatified in 1627, and canonized in 1862.
Cf. Baud. — Holw.

GARCIA (St) Ab. O.S.B.   A.C. Sept. 29
d. c.1073. A native of Quintanilla, near Burgos, in Old Castile. He became monk and abbot (1039) of Artanza, in Old Castile, and was the counsellor and companion of King Ferdinand I of Castile, whom he more than once followed into battle.
Cf. P. de U. — Zimm. — Chev.

GARDINER, GERMAN (Bl) M.
   A.C. March 7
See German Gardiner.

GAREMBERT (St) Ab.   A.C. Dec. 31
Otherwise Walembert, q.v.

GARIBALDUS (St) Bp.   A.C. Jan. 8
d. 762. A bishop in Bavaria, who was consecrated by St Boniface c.740.
Cf. Att. — Holw. — Baud.

GARMIER (GERMIER) (St)
   R.M. Feb. 27
Otherwise Baldomerus, q.v.

GARMON (St) Bp.   R.M. July 31
A French form of the name of St Germanus of Auxerre, q.v.

GARNAT (St)   A.C. Nov. 8
Otherwise Gervadius, q.v.

GASPAR (*several*)
Otherwise Caspar, q.v.

GASTON (St) Bp.   R.M. Feb. 6
A French form of Vedastus, q.v.

GATIAN (St) Bp.   R.M. Dec. 18
d. ? c.337. Venerated as one of the disciples of St Dionysius of Paris and the founder and first bishop of the diocese of Tours, in France.
Cf. Att. — Baud. — Holw.

GAUCHERIUS (GAULTIER, WALTER) (St) Ab.   A.C. Apr. 9
d. 1140. The abbot-founder of the monastery of St John at Aureil in the Limousin, for Augustinian canons regular. He was also a great benefactor of St Stephen of Gramont at Muret.
Cf. Att. — Baud. — Holw.

GAUDENTIA and Comp. (SS) VV. MM.
   R.M. Aug. 30
? St Gaudentia, a Roman maiden, is said to have suffered with three other Christians; but the more ancient martyrologies do not rank her among the martyrs.
Cf. Holw. — Baud.

GAUDENTIUS of GNESEN (St) Bp. O.S.B.   A.C. Jan. 5
d. c.1004. Younger brother of St Adalbert of Prague and his fellow-monk at the Benedictine abbey of Sant' Alessio, on the Aventine, Rome, and again his companion on his mission to Prussia. He escaped the massacre in which his brother was martyred and in 1000 was appointed first archbishop of Gnesen by Otto III.
Cf. Holw.

GAUDENTIUS of NOVARA (St) Bp.
   R.M. Jan. 22
d. c.418. A priest of Ivrea, near Turin, who was befriended first by St Laurence of Novara and then by St Eusebius of Vercelli. He succeeded the former as bishop of Novara, and governed the diocese twenty years.
Cf. Menzies — Holw. — Baud.

GAUDENTIUS of VERONA (St) Bp.
   R.M. Feb. 12
d. c.465. Bishop of Verona. His relics are enshrined at Verona in the ancient basilica of St Stephen.
Cf. Menzies — Holw. — Baud.

GAUDENTIUS of OSSERO (St) Bp. O.S.B. A.C. June 1

d. 1044. Bishop of Ossero in Istria. He was appointed to that see in 1030. Two years later he journeyed to Rome to appeal against his persecutors. On his way back he fell ill at Ancona, and, on his recovery, resigned his see (1042) and became a Benedictine under St Peter Damian.
Cf. Zimm. — P. de U. — Gams — Holw.

GAUDENTIUS and CULMATIUS (SS) MM. R.M. June 19

d. 364. Gaudentius, a bishop, and Culmatius, his deacon, are stated in the R.M. to have been martyred at Arezzo in Tuscany under Valentinian I. With them suffered Andrew, a layman, with his wife and children and a group of fifty-three companions.
Cf. Holw. — Menzies — Baud.

GAUDENTIUS of RIMINI (St) Bp. M. R.M. Oct. 14

d. c.360. An Asiatic, who joined the Roman clergy (332) and in 346 became bishop of Rimini. He suffered much at the hands of the Arians, who dominated the council of 357, and was by them done to death.
Cf. Baud. — Holw.

GAUDENTIUS of BRESCIA (St) Bp. R.M. Oct. 25

d. c.410. A pupil of St Philastrius, bishop of Brescia, he became a monk at Caesarea in Cappadocia, but was recalled to Brescia to succeed St Philastrius as bishop and was consecrated by St Ambrose (c.387). In 405 he was sent to the East to defend the cause of St John Chrysostom and was imprisoned near Thrace. He died shortly after.
Cf. Att. — Menzies — Holw.

GAUDIOSUS of BRESCIA (St) Bp. R.M. March 7

d. 445. (?) Bishop of Brescia where his relics are venerated.
Cf. Holw. — Menzies — Baud.

GAUDIOSUS of SALERNO (St) Bp. R.M. Oct. 26

7th cent. A bishop of Salerno, whose relics are venerated at Naples.
Cf. Menzies — Holw. — Baud.

GAUDIOSUS of NAPLES (St) Bp. R.M. Oct. 27

d. c.455. Surnamed "the African." He was in fact a bishop of Abitina in N. Africa, exiled by the Arian Vandal king Genseric (440). He took refuge at Naples where he founded a monastery, of which, later, St Agnellus became abbot.
Cf. Holw. — Baud.

GAUDIOSUS of TARAZONA (St) Bp. A.C. Nov. 3

d. c.585. A monk of Asan in the Aragonese Pyrenees, near Benasque, under St Victorian. About the year 565 he was made bishop of Tarazona (*not* Tarragona) in the province of Saragossa.
Cf. P. de U. — Gams — Baud. — Holw.

GAUFRIDUS (Bl) Ab. O.S.B. A.C. Sept. 9

d. 1139. A disciple of Bl Vitalis, and his successor as abbot of Savigny (1122-1139). Under him the new Benedictine congregation of Savigny spread to Normandy, England, Ireland and numbered some twenty-nine houses.
Cf. Zimm. — Holw.

GAUGERICUS (GAU, GÉRY) (St) Bp. R.M. Aug. 11

d. c.625. Gaugericus was born in the diocese of Tréves and was ordained priest by the bishop of that diocese, and later was made bishop of the united dioceses of Cambrai and Arras, which he governed for over thirty-nine years.
Cf. Att. — Baud. — Holw. — Gams.

GAUSMARUS (Bl) Ab. O.S.B. A.C. June 3

d. 984. Abbot of St Martin of Savigny (954-984).
Cf. Zimm.

GEBETRUDE (GERTRUDE) Abs. O.S.B. A.C. Nov. 7

d. c.675. Third abbess of Remiremont (Habend). Her relics were elevated and her cult approved by Leo IX in 1051.
Cf. Holw. — P.B.

GEBHARD (St) Bp. A.C. Aug. 27

d. 995. Bishop of Constance (979-995). He founded the great Benedictine abbey of Petershausen, near Constance (983), where he was buried.
Cf. Zimm. — Mab. — Chev. — Holw.

GEBIZO (St) Mk. O.S.B. A.C. Oct. 21

d. c.1087. A native of Cologne, he became a monk of Montecassino under Abbot St Desiderius (Pope Victor III) in

1076. He was sent to Croatia by Pope St Gregory VII, to crown King Zwoinimir.
Cf. Zimm. — Holw. — Chev. — Menzies.

GEBUINUS (St) Bp.　　　**A.C. Apr. 18**
d. 1080. Archbishop of Lyons. He is patron of the cathedral-chapter of Langres.
Cf. Baud. — Holw.

GEDEON (St) Bp.　　　**A.C. Aug. 8**
d. c.796. The thirteenth bishop of Besançon (790-796).
Cf. Duch. Fast. Episc. — Holw. — Baud.

GEDEON (St) Judge　　**R.M. Sept. 1**
Otherwise Gideon, q.v.

GELASINUS (St) M.　　**A.C. Aug. 26**
d. 297. An actor at Heliopolis in Phoenicia who, having to burlesque the ceremony of baptism, suddenly declared himself a Christian and was stoned to death by the mob. Probably identical with St Genesius (Aug. 25).
Cf. Holw. — P.B.

GELASIUS (St) M.　　　**R.M. Feb. 4**
See Aquilinus, Geminus, etc.

GELASIUS (GIOUA-MAC-LIAG) (St) Bp.　　　　**A.C. March 27**
d. 1174. Abbot of Derry. He was consecrated archbishop of Armagh in 1137, and is said to have been the first Irish bishop to whom the pallium was sent. In 1162 he consecrated St Laurence O'Toole archbishop of Dublin.
Cf. Holw.

GELASIUS I (St) Pope.　　**R.M. Nov. 21**
d. 496. An African by descent he was raised to the papal see in 492. He showed himself a vigorous pontiff, in fact one of the greatest in that century of great popes. Although he is not the author of the Sacramentary which goes under his name, it probably contains much that is really due to his talent and research.
Cf. Att. — Baud. — Holw.

GELASIUS (St) M.　　　**R.M. Dec. 23**
See Theodulus, Saturninus, etc.

GEMELLUS (St) M.　　　**R.M. Dec. 10**
d. 362. Crucified for the Faith at Ancyra in Galatia (Asia Minor) under Julian the Apostate.
Cf. Holw. — Baud.

GEMINIAN of MODENA (St) Bp.
R.M. Jan. 31
d. 348. Deacon to the bishop of Modena and his successor in the see. He gave shelter to St Athanasius as that great bishop passed through Italy on his way to his exile in Gaul. Geminian bravely opposed Jovinianism.
Cf. Att. — Baud. — Holw. — Menzies

GEMINIAN (St) M.　　　**R.M. Sept. 16**
See Lucy and Geminian.

GEMINUS (St) M.　　　**R.M. Jan. 4**
See Aquilinus, Geminus, etc.

GEMINUS of FOSSOMBRONE (St) M.
R.M. Feb. 4
See Aquilinus, Geminus, Gelasius, etc.

GEMINUS (St) Mk.　　　**A.C. Oct. 9**
d. ? 815. A monk of Sanpaterniano de Fano, diocese of Narni, in Umbria. He is claimed both by the Basilians and the Benedictines for their respective orders. He is the patron saint of San Gemini.
Cf. Zimm. — Holw. — Chev.

GEMMA GALGANI (St) V.　**A.C. Apr. 11**
1878-1903. Born at Camigliano, near Lucca, in Tuscany. Her mother died when she was seven years old, and from that time her life was one of domestic trials and intense suffering both spiritual and physical. Through it all, however, she remained at peace and was the subject of various extraordinary supernatural phenomena — visions, ecstasies, revelations, supernatural knowledge, visible intercourse with her guardian angel, prophecy, miracles, and above all the periodically recurring stigmata between 1899 and 1901. She was directed by the Passionist fathers. Her physical infirmities prevented her becoming a Passionist nun, as she ardently desired. She died on Holy Saturday. Beatified in 1933 and canonized in 1940, in the teeth of strong opposition based on the extraordinary nature of her religious experiences.
Cf. Att.

GEMMA (Bl) V.　　　**A.C. May 12**
d. 1249. A sheperdess, and afterwards for forty-two years a recluse at Coriano Sicoli, diocese of Sulmona in the Abruzzi. Cult approved in 1890.
Cf. Att. — Holw.

**GEMMA (HEMMA, EMMA) (St) W.
O.S.B.** A.C. June 29
d. 1045. A near relative of the emperor
St Henry II. Left a widow, she became
the foundress of the double monastery of
Gurk in Carinthia, and took the veil
among the nuns.
Cf. Zimm. — Holw. — Baud.

GEMUS (St) Mk. O.S.B. A.C. March 19
? Monk, probably of Moyenmoutier in
Alsace. His relics were enshrined at
Hürbach.
Cf. Zimm.

GENEBALD of LAON (St) Bp.
A.C. Sept. 5
d. c.555. A bishop of Laon related to St
Remigius. For a fault he committed he
is said to have performed a seven years'
continuous penance.
Cf. Holw. — Baud. — Duch. Fast. Episc.

GENEBRARD (St) M. A.C. May 15
Otherwise Gerebern, q.v.

GENERALIS (St) M. R.M. Sept. 14
See Crescentian, Victor, etc.

GENEROSA (St) M. R.M. July 17
One of the Scillitan Martyrs, q.v.

GENEROSUS (St) Ab. O.S.B.
A.C. July 16
d. c.682. An abbot of Saint-Jouin-de-
Marnes in Poitou.
Cf. Holw. — Baud.

GENEROSUS (St) M. R.M. July 17
? Venerated at Tivoli, where his relics are
enshrined in the cathedral, under the high
altar; but nothing is known about him.
Cf. Menzies — Holw.

GENESIUS (St) Bp. A.C. June 3
d. 662. Bishop of Clermont in Auvergne.
He is described as learned, benevolent,
surpassingly good, beloved by old and
young, rich and poor.
Cf. Att. — Baud. — Holw.

GENESIUS the COMEDIAN (St) M.
R.M. Aug. 25
d. c.300. An actor at Rome who, while
taking part in a burlesque of Christian
baptism in the theatre during the reign of
Diocletian — other accounts say before
Diocletian — himself was suddenly converted and forthwith martyred. The

same story is told of at least three other
martyrs. (Cf. Gelasinus above.)
Cf. Att. — Baud. — Menzies — Holw.

GENESIUS (GENÈS) of ARLES (St) M.
R.M. Aug. 25
d. c.303. A notary of Arles in S. Gaul,
who having refused to put on record an
imperial decree against Christians and
declaring that he himself believed in
Christ, was martyred under Maximian
Herculius.
Cf. Att. — Baud. — Holw.

GENESIUS (St) M. R.M. Oct. 11
See Anastasius, Placid, etc.

GENESIUS (St) Bp. A.C. Nov. 1
d. c.679. From being prior at Fontenelle
he was chosen abbot-chaplain of the palace by Queen Bathildis, and in 658 raised
to the see of Lyons. He died at the nunnery of Chelles while on a visit there.
Cf. Holw. — Baud.

GENISTUS (St) M. O.S.B.
A.C. Apr. 30
c.1100. A Benedictine monk of Beaulieu,
in the Limousin, diocese of Limoges.
Killed by his nephew at Aynac-en-Quercy.
He is venerated as a martyr and as patron
saint of Aynac.
Cf. Zimm. — Chev. — Holw.

GENEVIÈVE (St) V. R.M. Jan. 3
c.422-c.500. Born at Nanterre near Paris.
In her seventh year she happened to become known to St Germanus of Auxerre,
who befriended her. When fifteen years
old she received the veil from the bishop of
Paris, and gave herself up to penance and
the exercise of charity. When Paris was
occupied by the Franks and afterwards
threatened by Attila and his Huns, St
Geneviève encouraged the people to defend the city. She has always been considered the special protectress and patroness of Paris.
Cf. Att. — Baud. — Holw.

GENGULPHUS (St) M. R.M. May 11
Otherwise Gangulphus, q.v.

GENNADIUS (St) M. R.M. May 16
See Felix and Gennadius.

GENNADIUS (St) Bp. O.S.B.
A.C. May 25
d. c.936. A monk at Argeo, near Astorga,

in Spain, abbot-restorer of San Pedro de Montes, and a zealous propagator of St Benedict's Rule throughout N.W. Spain. About the year 895 he was raised to the see of Astorga, which he resigned five years before his death, returning to live as a monk-hermit in his beloved San Pedro. *Cf. Mab. — Zimm. — P. de U. — Chev. — Att. — Holw.*

GENNARD (St) Ab. O.S.B.   A.C. Apr. 6
d. 720. Educated at the court of Clotaire III, he became a monk at Fontenelle under St Wandrille, and eventually abbot of Flay (Saint-Germer) in the diocese of Beauvais. Before his death he resigned and returned to die at Fontenelle. *Cf. Holw. — Baud.*

GENNARO (St) M.   R.M. Sept. 19
The Italian form of Januarius, q.v.

GENNYS (GENEWYS) (St) Bp.
R.M. July 26
Otherwise Germanus of Auxerre, q.v.

GENOCHUS (St) C.   A.C. Apr. 18
See Bitheus and Genochus.

GENOVEFA (St) V.   R.M. Jan. 3
Otherwise Geneviève, q.v.

GENTIAN (St) M.   R.M. Dec. 11
See Victoricus, Fuscian and Gentian.

GENTILIS (Bl) M. O.F.M.   A.C. Sept. 5
d. 1340. A native of Matelica in the Marches, Piceno, where he joined the Friars Minor. He spent some time on Mt Alvernia and then went as a missionary among the Mohammedans of Egypt and Persia. He was martyred at Toringa in Persia. Cult approved by Pius VI. *Cf. Att. — Holw. — Baud.*

GENUINUS (INGENUINUS) (St) Bp.
R.M. Feb. 5
7th cent. A bishop of the small town of Sabion (which has since disappeared) near Brixen in the Tyrol. With him is commemorated on the same day St Albinus, bishop of Brixen in the 11th century. *Cf. Baud. — Gams.*

GENULFUS (GENOU) and GENITUS (SS)   A.C. Jan. 17
? 3rd. cent. There are said to have been two holy monks so named who lived at Celles-sur-Naton in France. Another St Genulfus is honoured at Cahors as the first bishop of that see. *Cf. Holw. — Baud.*

GEOFFREY (GODFREY) (St) Ab.
A.C. June 21
Otherwise Agofredus, q.v.

GEOFFREY (St) Ab.   A.C. Sept. 25
The Norman form of the Saxon name Ceolfrid, q.v.

GEOFFREY (St) Bp.   R.M. Nov. 8
Otherwise Godfrey, q.v.

GEORGE of LODÈVE (St) Bp. O.S.B.
A.C. Feb. 19
d. c.884. Born near Rodez and a Benedictine at Sainte-Foi-de-Conques in Rouergue. After the destruction of the monastery by the Norsemen (862) he became a monk at Vabres, diocese of Rodez. When quite old he was elected to the see of Lodève. *Cf. Holw. — Baud. — P.B.*

GEORGE of AMASTRIS (St) Bp.
A.C. Feb. 21
d. c.825. A native of Kromna, near Amastris, on the Black Sea. He was first a hermit on Mt Sirik, then a monk of Bonyssa, and lastly bishop of Amastris. He deserved well of his people during the Saracen attacks, against which he successfully defended his episcopal city. *Cf. Att. — Baud. — Holw.*

GEORGE the YOUNGER (St) Bp.
A.C. Apr. 7
d. c.816. Bishop of Mitylene, the capital of Lesbos. He is called "the Younger" because two of his predecessors in the see and of that century, also named George, are venerated as saints. *Cf. Att. — Baud. — Holw.*

GEORGE GERVASE (Bl) M. O.S.B.
A.C. Apr. 11
d. 1608. A native of Bosham, Sussex. In his youth he had a very adventurous career under Drake in the W. Indies. He was educated for the priesthood at Douai and ordained priest in 1603. At Douai, too, he was received into the Benedictine Order. Sent to the English mission he was condemned for his priesthood and suffered at Tyburn. Beatified in 1929. *Cf. Newdigate — Camm.*

GEORGE of ANTIOCH (St) Bp. M.
R.M. Apr. 19
d. 814. A monk, who became bishop of
Antioch in Pisidia. He was one of the
Fathers of the second council of Nicea
(787) against the Iconoclasts. Banished
by the emperor Leo V. the Armenian, he
died in exile.
Cf. Holw. — Baud.

GEORGE the GREAT (St) M.
R.M. Apr. 23
d. c.300. It is now almost universally
agreed that St George was a martyr who
suffered at Diospolis (Lydda, Ludd) in
Palestine, probably under Diocletian.
All the other legends which have grown up
around his name may safely be regarded
as fictitious, including the story of the
dragon, which seems to have originated in
Italy at a comparatively recent period.
The Crusaders certainly gave great im-
petus to devotion to St George in the West,
though he was venerated there long before.
He is venerated in the East as one of the
fourteen Holy Helpers and, universally, as
the model of knighthood and avenger of
women. He is the acknowledged patron
saint of England, Aragon, Portugal and
Germany, also of Genoa and Venice, and
protector of Ferrara. In the East he is
especially honoured as the patron of soldiers. His veneration as protector of
England was officially approved by Pope
Benedict XIV.
Cf. Att. — Menzies — Holw. — Baud.

GEORGE SWALLOWELL (Bl) M.
A.C. July 26
d. 1594. Born near Durham, he became
a Protestant minister and schoolmaster.
He was condemned to death for being
reconciled to the Church, and executed at
Darlington. Beatified in 1929.
Cf. Newdigate.

**GEORGE, AURELIUS and NATALIA,
FELIX and LILIOSA (SS) MM.**
R.M. July 27 (Oct. 20)
d. c.852. Martyrs who suffered at Cordova in Spain under the Caliph Abderrahman II. Aurelius and Felix, with
their wives, Natalia and Liliosa, were
Spaniards; but the deacon George was a
monk from Palestine, who, though offered
pardon as a foreigner, preferred to throw in
his lot with the others.
Cf. Baud. — Holw.

GEORGE LIMNIOTES (St) M.
R.M. Aug. 24
d. c.730. A hermit of Mt Olympus in
Asia Minor, who had reached the age,
it is said, of ninety-five, when he was
martyred under Leo the Isaurian for defending the worship of sacred images.
Cf. Holw. — Baud.

GEORGE and AURELIUS (SS) MM.
R.M. Oct. 20
See George, Aurelius, etc., July 27. The
relics of SS Aurelius and George were
translated to the abbey church of St
Germain at Paris. The anniversary of
this translation is celebrated on Oct. 20.

GEORGE of PÉRIGUEUX (St) Bp.
R.M. Oct. 25
See Fronto and George.

GEORGE of VIENNE (St) Bp.
R.M. Nov. 2
? A bishop of Vienne in France, who
flourished probably at the beginning of
the eighth century, though some put
Nov. 2, 699 as the date of his death.
Canonized in 1251.
Cf. Holw. — Baud.

GEORGE NAPPER (Bl) M. A.C. Nov. 9
d. 1610. Born at Holywell Manor, Oxford,
and educated at Corpus Christi College,
Oxford. He studied for the priesthood at
Douai where he was ordained in 1596.
Sent to the English mission he laboured in
Oxfordshire and was finally condemned
for his priesthood and executed at Ox-
ford. Beatified in 1929.
Cf. Newdigate — Att.

GEORGIA (St) V.
R.M. Feb. 15
d. c.500. A maiden who became a recluse
near Clermont in Auvergne, France. It
is said that a flight of white doves coming,
no one knew whence, accompanied her
body to the tomb, and long hovered over
her resting place.
Cf. Holw. — Baud.

GERALD (St) Bp. O.S.B.
A.C. Feb. 6
d. 1077. From being prior at Cluny
Gerald was raised by Pope Alexander II
to the see of Ostia as successor to St Peter
Damian. He was papal legate to France,
Spain and Germany, and was arrested and
imprisoned by the German emperor,

Henry V. He is the principal patron saint of Velletri.

Cf. Holw. — P.B.

GERALD (St) Ab. A.C. March 13
d. 732. A Northumbrian monk who followed St Colman from Lindisfarne to Ireland and became his successor in the English house built at Mayo for the English monastic colony. He lived to an old age and must have witnessed the introduction of the Roman observances into his abbey.

Cf. Att. — Baud. — Holw.

GERALD of SAUVE-MAJEURE (St) Ab. O.S.B. A.C. Apr. 5
d. 1095. A native of Corbie, he was educated and became a monk and cellarer at the famous abbey of his native town. He suffered from acute headaches. He was taken by his abbot to Rome and Montecassino, and at Rome Pope Leo IX ordained him priest. On his return to Corbie, he was cured by St Adalard; then he went to Palestine. Next, he was chosen abbot of St Vincent's at Laon and of St Medard at Soissons; but, being expelled by a usurper, he founded Sauve-Majeure, which became the centre of a powerful Benedictine congregation. Canonized in 1197.

Cf. Att. — Zimm. — Holw.

GERALD (St) Bp. O.S.B. A.C. May 29
d. 927. A monk of Brou. He became bishop of Mâcon but after some forty years in the episcopate he returned to his old abbey to die.

Cf. Zimm. — Baud. — Duch. Fast. Episc. — Holw.

GERALD of AURILLAC (St) C. A.C. Oct. 13
855-909. Gerald, count of Aurillac, led a life of great virtue at a period when it was difficult for one of his rank to do so. He founded a Benedictine abbey on his estate and endowed it in princely fashion. He is the patron saint of Upper Auvergne.

Cf. Att. — Baud. — Holw.

GERALD (Bl) Ab. O.S.B. Cist. A.C. Oct. 16
d. 1177. A native of Lombardy and professed at the Cistercian monastery at Fossanuova in the Roman Campagna, being eventually chosen abbot. He was

later promoted to the abbacy of Clairvaux (1170) and was killed by an unruly monk while on a canonical visitation to Igny.

Cf. Prop. Cist. — Chev. — Holw.

GERALD of BEZIERS (St) Bp. A.C. Nov. 5
d. 1123. A canon regular who became bishop of Beziers in S. France. He spent all his revenues in relieving the distress of the poor of the diocese.

Cf. Holw.

GERALD (St) Bp. O.S.B. P.C. Dec. 5
d. 1109. Born near Cahors in Gascony, he took the Benedictine habit at Moissac. He accompanied Archbishop Bernard of Toledo to Spain, and was eventually made archbishop of Braga in Portugal (1100).

Cf. Chev. — Holw.

GERARD (Bl) C. O.S.B. Cist. A.C. Jan. 30
d. 1138. The second and favourite brother at St Bernard of Clairvaux. He was not of the party of thirty who accompanied St Bernard to Cîteaux. He was then soldiering and, on being wounded, made up his mind to become a monk. He entered Cîteaux and followed his brother to Clairvaux where he excelled as a cellarer. St Bernard mourned him deeply when he died.

Cf. Att. — Zimm. — P. de U. — Prop. Cist.

GERARD (Bl) C. O.S.B. Cam. A.C. Apr. 1
1280-1367. At the age of nine Gerard received the Camaldolese habit at the abbey of the Holy Cross, at Sassoferrato. After his ordination he was entrusted with the care of the parish, which he served with untiring zeal. He died on Nov. 18; but his feast is kept by the Camaldolese on Apr. 1.

Cf. Prop. Camald. — Holw. — Baud. — Chev.

GERARD of ORCHIMONT (Bl) Ab. O.S.B. A.C. Apr. 23
d. 1138. A Benedictine monk and afterwards abbot, of Florennes (1126-c.1136).

Cf. Chev. — Zimm.

GERARD of TOUL (St) Bp. R.M. Apr. 23
d. 994. A native of Cologne, who became

bishop of Toul in 963. He rebuilt the cathedral and established religious houses in which teaching was given by Greek and Irish monks to the great furtherance of religion and learning in the diocese. He was canonized by Pope Leo IX, his successor in the see.
Cf. Att. — Baud. — Holw.

GERARD (St) C.   A.C. Apr. 28
? One of four English pilgrims — the other three were Ardwine, Bernard and Hugh — who died at Galinaro in S. Italy while on a visit to the shrine of St Michael on Monte Gargano. Many scholars doubt of their very existence.
Cf. Att. — Baud. — Holw. — Menzies.

GERARD of BOURGOGNE (Bl) Ab. O.S.B. Cist.   P.C. Apr. 28
d. 1172. The successor of St Fastred as abbot of the Cistercian monastery of Cambron.
Cf. Holw. — Baud.

**GERARD of VILLAMAGNA (Bl) C.
          A.C. May 13**
1174-1242. A native of Tuscany who, as esquire to a knight, took part in the crusades and was taken prisoner. On being ransomed, he returned to Italy, joined the third order of St Francis and lived as a recluse for the rest of his life. Cult approved in 1833.
Cf. Menzies — Att. — Baud. — Holw.

GERARD de LUNEL (St) C. A.C. May 24
1275-1298. Said to have been a French pilgrim, belonging to the third order of St Francis, who died at Monte Santo, near Ancona, on his return from Palestine. His cult was approved by Benedict XIV and Pius VI, and he is now honoured as the patron saint of Monte Santo.
Cf. Menzies — Holw. — Baud. — Att. (under Gerius).

**GERARD TINTORIO (Bl) C.
          A.C. June 6**
d. 1207. A young citizen of Monza in Lombardy, belonging to the upper middle class, who expended his wealth in founding a hospital, where he served the sick, especially lepers. Cult approved in 1582.
Cf. Att. — Menzies — Ricci — Holw.

**GERARD SAGREDO (St) Bp. M. O.S.B.
          R.M. Sept. 24**
d. 1046. Apostle of Hungary, where he is

venerated as St Collert. He was a Venetian by birth and a Benedictine monk and abbot of San Giorgio Maggiore in his native city. On a pilgrimage to Palestine he was stopped when passing through Hungary by King St Stephen and persuaded to work among the Magyars. He became the tutor of Prince St Emeric and, in 1035, first bishop of Csanad. He worked most zealously, but during the pagan reaction after St Stephen's death Gerard was martyred at Buda, and his body cast into the Danube.
Cf. Att. — Zimm. — Holw. — P. de U.

**GERARD of BROGNE (St) Ab. O.S.B.
          R.M. Oct. 3**
d. 959. Born in the county of Namur, and trained for the army, as a page of the count of Namur he was sent on a special mission to the French court (918). He stayed in France and joined the Benedictines of St Denis. After some eleven years he was ordained priest, and left for Belgium in order to found a new abbey on his own estate of Brogne. He was its abbot for twenty-two years and during that period was instrumental in introducing St Benedict's Rule into numerous houses in Flanders, Lorraine and Champagne. He was noted for his engaging sweetness of temper.
Cf. Zimm. — Att. — Chev.

**GERARD MAJELLA (St) C.SS.R.
          R.M. Oct. 16**
1725-1755. A native of Muro in S. Italy, he was apprenticed to a tailor before asking to be received by the Redemptorists as a lay-brother. He continued his trade in the monastery, where he soon attracted the attention of St Alphonsus de Liguori, who shortened his novitiate. His wonderful and well authenticated life was a series of supernatural phenomena — bilocations, reading of consciences, prophecies, multiplying of food, etc. Canonized in 1904.
Cf. Att. — Holw. — Baud. — Menzies.

**GERARD of POTENZA (St) Bp.
          R.M. Oct. 30**
d. 1119. A native of Piacenza, who was enrolled among the clergy of Potenza, in S. Italy, and elected bishop there at an advanced age. Canonized by Pope Callistus II.
Cf. Menzies — Baud. — Holw.

GERARD de BAZONCHES (St) Mk.
O.S.B. A.C. Nov. 4
d. 1123. A Benedictine monk-priest of
St Aubin, at Angers.
Cf. Chev. — Holw.

GERARD (St) Ab. O.S.B. A.C. Dec. 6
d. 1109. First prior of the Cluniac house
of La-Charité-sur-Loire, in the diocese of
Namur. He founded several more Cluniac houses in France and elsewhere and
finally governed the abbey of Soigny, but
resigned and returned to La-Charité to
end his days as a simple religious.
Cf. Baud. — Holw. — P.B.

GERARD CAGNOLI (Bl) C. O.F.M.
A.C. Dec. 30
d. 1345. The son of noble parents, until
the age of forty he led a wandering life in
Sicily. He then joined the Franciscans as
a lay-brother. He was noted for his true
Franciscan spirit of child-like simplicity.
Cult confirmed in 1908.
Cf. Att. — Holw. — Baud.

GERARDESCA (Bl) W. O.S.B. Cam.
A.C. May 29
d. c.1260. A native of Pisa, who married a
citizen of that city. After some years of
married life she induced her husband to
become a Camaldolese monk at San
Salvio, while she lived nearby as a recluse,
under the obedience of the abbey. Cult
confirmed in 1856.
Cf. Holw. — P. de U. — Baud.

GERASIMUS (St) Ab. R.M. March 5
d. c.475. A monk first in Lycia, Asia
Minor, and afterwards in Palestine.
Eventually he himself founded a *laura* on
the banks of the Jordan, near Jericho,
which grew to be second only to that of
St Sabas.
Cf. Att. — Baud. — Holw.

GERSALD (Bl) M. C.S.B. A.C. May 25
See Norard, Winebald, etc.

GERBOLD (St) Bp. O.S.B. A.C. Dec. 5
d. c.690. Monk of Ebriciacum under Abbot
Alnobert, and afterwards abbot-founder
of the abbey of Livray (*Liberiacum*).
Eventually he became bishop of Bayeux.
Cf. Zimm. — Baud. — Chev.

GERBRAND (Bl) Ab. O.S.B. Cist.
P.C. Oct. 13
d. 1218. Second abbot of the Cistercian

monastery of Klaarkamp in Frisia, and
founder of Bloemkamp (1191). He died
at Foigny, in the Laonnais, when returning from a general chapter, and has been
venerated there ever since.
Cf. Chev. — Baud. — Holw. — Zimm.

GEREBALD (St) Bp. A.C. June 12
d. 885. Bishop of Châlons-sur-Seine
(864-885).
Cf. Duch. Fast. Episc. — Holw. — Baud.

GEREBERN (GEREBRAND) (St) M.
A.C. May 15
7th cent. The aged Irish priest who accompanied St Dympna to Belgium and
shared in her martyrdom (q.v.). He is
the patron saint of a village in the Rhineland, where his relics are enshrined.
Cf. Holw. — Baud.

GEREMARUS (GERMER) (St) Ab.
O.S.B. R.M. Sept. 24
d. c.658. A native of Beauvais, attached
to the court of Dagobert I. With the
consent of his saintly wife he retired to the
abbey of Pentale on the Seine, near Brionne, of which he eventually became
abbot. He was over-severe, with the result that some of his monks made an attempt on his life, whereupon he resigned
and retired to a cave near the abbey to
live as a hermit. In 655 he founded Flay
abbey, between Beauvais and Rouen,
which was afterwards called Saint-Germer.
Cf. Att. — Baud. — Chev.

GEREON and Comp. (SS) MM.
R.M. Oct. 10
? These martyrs represent a band of
Christians — said to have been three hun-
dred and nineteen in number — who suf-
fered at Cologne, where their tomb was
shown in the fifth century. They have
been wrongly associated with the Theban
Legion.
Cf. Att. — Baud. — Holw.

GERINUS (GARINUS, WERINUS) (St)
M. R.M. Oct. 2
d. 676. Brother of St Leodegaruis
(Leger) and, like him, persecuted by
Ebroin, mayor of the palace. He was
stoned to death near Arras.
Cf. Baud. — Holw.

GERIUS (St) C. A.C. May 24
Otherwise Gerard de Lunel, q.v.

GERLAC (St) H.   **A.C. Jan. 5**
d. c.1170. A Dutch soldier of licentious life, who after the death of his wife, experienced a moral conversion and led thenceforth a life of most austere penance: he lived in a hollow tree near Valkenberg, his native place. It is said that neighbouring monasteries were scandalized by his eccentricities.
Cf. Att. — Baud. — Holw.

GERLAND (St) Bp.   **A.C. Feb. 25**
d. 1104. Said to have been born at Besançon in France, and to have been related to the Norman conqueror of Sicily, Robert Guiscard. He was certainly consecrated bishop of Girgenti, in Sicily, by Urban II.
Cf. Att. — Holw. — Menzies — Baud.

GERLAND (St) C.   **A.C. June 18**
13th cent. A knight — either a Templar or a Hospitaller — whose relics are venerated at Caltagirone in Sicily.
Cf. Att. — Baud. — Holw.

GERMAN GARDINER (Bl) M.
                       C.A. March 7
Otherwise Jermyn Gardiner, q.v.

GERMANA (St) M.   **R.M. Jan. 19**
See Paul, Gerontius, etc.

GERMANA (French: GERMAINE) COUSIN (St) V.   **R.M. June 15**
c.1579-1601. Born at Pibrac, near Toulouse, daughter of a poor farmer. She suffered from scrofula, was neglected by her father and treated with much harshness by her step-mother. She was sent to tend the sheep, and spent her short life in the fields, communing with God in prayer, and practising charity towards others poorer than herself. She died all alone on her straw bed at the age of twenty-two. Canonized in 1867.
Cf. Att. — Baud. — Holw.

GERMANICUS (St) M.   **R.M. Jan. 19**
d. 156. A youth of Smyrna thrown to the wild beasts in the amphitheatre at the public games. The letter describing his martyrdom — together with that of St Polycarp — is one of the most authentic documents of early ecclesiastical history.
Cf. Att. — Baud. — Holw.

GERMANUS and RANDCALD (SS) MM. O.S.B.   **A.C. Feb. 21**
d. c.677. Germanus was born at Trèves,

and became a monk at Remiremont. Thence he migrated to Luxeuil under its third abbot St Walbert, who introduced the Benedictine rule into the abbey. At a later date he was made abbot of Granfel. He and his prior St Randcald, were put to death by the duke of that district while interceding with him on behalf of the poor.
Cf. Att. — Zimm. — Chev. — Baud. — Holw.

GERMANUS (St) M.   **R.M. May 2**
See Saturninus, Neopolus, etc.

GERMANUS (St) Bp. M.   **A.C. May 2**
d. c.460. Of Irish or Scottish origin, he was converted by St Germanus of Auxerre whose name he took. He was martyred in Normandy.
Cf. Baud. — Holw.

GERMANUS of CONSTANTINOPLE (St) Bp.   **R.M. May 12**
d. 732. A churchman of senatorial rank, who, from being bishop of Cyzieus, was made patriarch of Constantinople (715). He bravely opposed the iconoclast emperor, Leo III, the Isaurian and was forced to resign (732). He died in exile. Several of his writings are still extant.
Cf. Att. — Baud. — Holw.

GERMANUS of PARIS (St) Bp.
                       R.M. May 28
496-576. Born near Autun, he was ordained priest and became abbot of a monastery. In 554 he was promoted to the see of Paris. By him King Childebert I was cured in the body and converted from a licentious life. The king built for him the abbey of St Vincent now known as Saint-Germain-des-Prés. St Germanus is one of those bishops to whom history has given the title of "father of the poor."
Cf. Att. — Baud. — Holw.

GERMANUS (St) Bp.   **A.C. July 3**
d. c.474. Said to have been a nephew of St Patrick and a missionary monk in Ireland, Wales and Brittany. Eventually he was sent as a bishop to the Isle of Man, where his memory is still preserved in several place-names under the forms "Gremain" and "Jarman."
Cf. Att.

GERMANUS (St) M.   **R.M. July 7**
See Peregrinus, Lucian, etc.

GERMANUS of AUXERRE (St) Bp.
R.M. July 31
c.378-448. A native of Auxerre, he studied civil law in Rome, and embarked upon a secular career. In 418 he received priest's orders and shortly after became bishop of Auxerre. He had relations with the church in Britain, whither he came twice (in 429, in 447) and where he succeeded in completely stamping out Pelagianism. He led the Britons to their great "Alleluia" victory over the Saxons. He died at Ravenna in Italy on a mission which he undertook on behalf of his people.
Cf. Att. — Baud. — Menzies — Holw.

GERMANUS (St) Bp. M.   R.M. Sept. 6
See Donatian, Praesidius, etc.

GERMANUS of BESANÇON (St) Bp. M.
R.M. Oct. 11
d. c.390. Successor of St Desideratus in the see of Besançon. He is said to have been martyred by the Arians.
Cf. Holw. — Baud.

GERMANUS (St) M.   R.M. Oct. 23
See Servandus and Germanus.

GERMANUS of CAPUA (St) Bp.
R.M. Oct. 30
d. c.545. Bishop of Capua, and a great friend of St Benedict. He seems to have been sent to Constantinople as papal legate to heal the Acacian schism and to have met with ill-treatment at the hands of the schismatics. St Benedict saw his soul being carried to heaven.
Cf. Att. — Baud. — Menzies.

GERMANUS of MONTFORT (St) Mk.
O.S.B.   A.C. Nov. 1
c.906-c.1000. Born at Montfort, he studied at Paris and was ordained priest. Afterwards he entered the abbey of Savigny and was made prior of Talloires. He ended his life as a recluse. His relics were elevated by St Francis of Sales in 1621.
Cf. Chev. — Holw. — Baud.

GERMANUS, THEOPHILUS, CAESARIUS and VITALIS (SS) MM.
R.M. Nov. 3
d. 250. Martyrs of Caesarea in Cappadocia under Decius.

GERMANUS (St) M.   R.M. Nov. 13
See Antoninus, Zebinas, etc.

GERMANY (Martyrs of) (SS)
R.M. Oct. 15
d. 303. This is the same group of martyrs as that listed under St Gereon, twice commemorated in the R.M. on Oct. 10 (318 martyrs) and on Oct 15 (300 martyrs).

GERMERIUS (St) Bp.   A.C. May 16
d. ? 560. Bishop of Toulouse for fifty years. His cult is very ancient.
Cf. Att. — Baud. — Holw.

GERMOC (St) C.   A.C. June 24
6th cent. An Irish chieftain, brother of St Breaca, who settled in Cornwall, near Mount's Bay.
Cf. Holw.

GEROLD (St) H.   A.C. Apr. 19
d. 978. A member of the Rhetian family of the counts of Saxony. He bestowed his lands upon the abbey of Einsiedeln where his two sons, Cuno and Ulrich, were monks, and retired to live as a hermit, under the obedience of the abbot of Einsiedeln, in a village near Mitternach. After his death his hermitage was occupied by his two sons. It is now a place of pilgrimage.
Cf. Att. — Mab. — Zimm. — Baud. — Holw.

GEROLD (St) Bp. O.S.B.   A.C. June 14
d. 806. One of Charlemagne's courtiers who became a monk of Fontenelle and in 787 was made bishop of Evreux. At a later period he resigned and returned to Fontenelle, where he died.
Cf. Holw. — P.B. — Baud. — Chev.

GEROLD (Bl) M.   A.C. Oct. 7
13th cent. A pilgrim from Cologne killed by robbers near Cremona and honoured as a martyr at Cremona and at Cologne.
Cf. Holw.

GERONTIUS (St) M.   R.M. Jan. 19
See Paul, Gerontius, etc.

GERONTIUS (St) Bp. M.   R.M. May 9
a. 501. A bishop of Cervia, near Ravenna, who was murdered at Cagli on the Flaminian Way, under circumstances which led to his being honoured as a martyr.
Cf. Att. — Menzies — Holw.

GERONTIUS (GERAINT) (St) King M.
A.C. Aug. 10
d. ? 508. Son of Erbin and king of

Damnonia (Devon). He fell in battle against the Saxons. He and his wife Enid have been the subject of much romantic legend. Another St Gerontius, king of Cornwall, died in 596. St Gerrans in Cornwall and St Géran in Brittany have one or the other of these for patron saint.
Cf. Holw. — Baring-Gould.

GERTRUDE van OOSTEN (Bl) V.
A.C. Jan. 6

d. 1358. Gertrude began life as a servant girl at Delft in Holland. Having been jilted by her lover, she entered the *béguinage* in her native town. In her new life she rapidly advanced in the way of perfection and was rewarded with the stigmata. "Van Oosten" is said to be a nickname she earned by her frequent repetition of the hymn *"Het daghet in den Oosten."* "The day breaks in the East."
Cf. Att. — Holw.

GERTRUDE of NIVELLES (St) Abs.
O.S.B. R.M. March 17

626-659. Younger daughter of Pepin of Landen and of Bl. Ita. Ita founded the nunnery of Nivelles for herself and her daughter, but insisted on Gertrude being the first abbess. Though then only twenty years of age, Gertrude performed her duties admirably. At the age of thirty she resigned in favour of her niece Wulfetrudis. She befriended the Irish saints SS Foillan and Ultan.
Cf. Att. — Holw. — Baud.

GERTRUDE of ALTENBERG (Bl) Abs.
O.Praem. A.C. Aug. 13

d. 1297. Daughter of Louis IV, landgrave of Thuringia and of St Elisabeth of Hungary. She was educated and became a nun at the nunnery of Altenberg. She was chosen abbess very young and ruled the house for half a century. Cult authorised by Clement VI.
Cf. Att. — Holw. — Baud.

GERTRUDE of REMIREMONT (St)
Abs. O.S.B. A.C. Nov. 7

d. c.690. Sister of St Adolphus and granddaughter of St Romaricus, she was educated at the nunnery of Saint-Mont, near Remiremont, where she took the veil, and was abbess after her aunt St Clare (c.654). Cult authorized by St Leo IX (1051).
Cf. Baud. — Chev.

GERTRUDE the GREAT (St) N. O.S.B.
R.M. Nov. 16, 17

c.1256-c.1302. "The Prophetess of devotion to the Sacred Heart." She was born at Eisleben in Germany, and as a child of five years old was offered to God at Helfta in Saxony, a Black Benedictine nunnery which in its early days had for political reasons been fictitiously designated Cistercian. Gertrude had her first mystical experience in 1281, and from that year her life was a continuous familiar communing with Christ, whose Heart she learned to love and worship. Her mystical writings have done much to spread devotion to the Sacred Heart. Her feast was extended to the whole Church in 1677. St Teresa of Avila had a great devotion to her. St Gertrude is patroness of the W. Indies.
Cf. Att. — Zimm. — P. de U. — Baud. — Holw.

GERTRUDE the ELDER (St) W. O.S.B.
A.C. Dec. 6

d. 649. A widow, who founded and was the first abbess of the nunnery of Hamaye (Hamay, Hamage) near Douai.
Cf. Chev. — Baud.

GERULPH (St) M.
A.C. Sept. 21

d. c.746. A Flemish youth, heir to a vast estate who was treacherously murdered by a relative who hoped to succeed to his inheritance. At the time of his death Gerulph was returning home after having received confirmation. He died with words of pardon on his lips.
Cf. Holw. — P.B.

GERUNTIUS of MILAN (St) Bp.
R.M. May 5

d. c.470. Successor of St Eusebius in the see of Milan (c.465-c.470).
Cf. Menzies — Holw. — Baud.

GERUNTIUS of ITALICA (St) Bp. M.
R.M. Aug. 25

d. c.100. A missionary in Spain in the apostolic age, said to have been bishop of Talco (Italica, near Seville) and a martyr. A special hymn in the old Mozarabic breviary commemorates him.
Cf. Baud. — Holw.

GERVADIUS (GERNARD, GARNET)
(St) C. A.C. Nov. 8

10th cent. An Irish saint, who crossed over

to Moray and afterwards became a recluse near Elgin.
Cf. Holw.

GERVASE and PROTASE (SS) MM.
R.M. June 19
? 2nd cent. In 386, during the episcopate of St Ambrose, there were discovered at Milan the relics of SS Gervase and Protase, whom the saintly bishop styles the proto-martyrs of the city. Even then next to nothing was remembered about them, ex-cept their names and the fact of their martyrdom in one of the early persecu-tions. Their supposed *Acta* have no his-torical value.
Cf. Att. — Menzies — Baud. — Holw.

GERVINUS (St) Ab. O.S.B.
A.C. March 3
d. 1075. Born near Reims, and educated at the episcopal school, Gervinus became a canon of that city. Subsequently he entered the Benedictine abbey of St Vannes at Verdun, and eventually became abbot of Saint-Riquier. As such he vis-ited England where the abbey owned lands, and where too he enjoyed the friendship of St Edward the Confessor. He is described as great in his devotion to the Divine Office, great in preaching, and great in collecting Greek and Latin MSS. This last was, after the service of God, the great passion of his life.
Cf. Att. — Zimm. — Chev. — Baud. — Holw.

GERVINUS (Bl) Ab. O.S.B.
A.C. Apr. 17
d. 1117. A monk of Saint-Winnoc, and then a hermit at Munster in Aldenburg, he was finally chosen abbot (1095) of Aldenburg (Oudenburg) in Flanders.
Cf. Zimm. — Chev. — Baud. — Holw.

GERY (St) Bp.
R.M. Aug. 11
Otherwise Gaugericus, q.v.

GETULIUS, CAEREALIS, AMANTIUS and PRIMITIVUS (SS) MM.
R.M. June 10
d. c.120. Getulius, a Roman, is said to have been the husband of St Symphorosa. He and his brother Amantius, and the two officers sent to capture him, and con-verted by him, were clubbed to death at Tivoli under Hadrian.
Cf. Att. — Baud. — Holw.

GIBARDUS (St) Ab. O.S.B.
A.C. Apr. 7
d. c.888. Abbot of Luxeuil at the time of the invasion of the Huns. He and his monks fled from the abbey. The bar-barians found them and put them to death. St Gibardus is venerated at Martinville in the Vosges.
Cf. Chev. — Baud. — Holw.

GIBITRUDIS (St) N. O.S.B.
A.C. Oct. 26
d. c.655. A nun at Faremoutiers under St Fara.
Cf. Chev. — Baud. — Holw.

GIBRIAN (St) C.
A.C. May 8
d. ? c.515. An Irish hermit, the eldest of five brothers and three sisters, all alleged to have migrated to Brittany and to have become saints there. Their names are given as Tressan, Helan, Ger-manus, Abran, Petran, Franca, Promptia, Possenna.
Cf. Att. — Baud. — Holw.

GIDEON (GEDEON) (St)
R.M. Sept. 1
14th cent B.C. The Judge of Israel (Judges VI, VII), commemorated with Josua by the Greek and Latin Churches on Sept 1. The Copts keep his feast on Dec. 16; and the Armenians on the second Saturday of August.
Cf. Baud. — Holw.

GILBERT of SEMPRINGHAM (St) C. Founder.
R.M. Feb. 4
1083-1189. A native of Sempringham in Lincolnshire, who became parish priest of that village in 1123. A group of seven ladies of his parish wishing to live in com-munity he drew for them a set of rules. This developed into the Gilbertine Order, which came to comprise monks under the Augustinian Rule as well as nuns under that of St Benedict. He was their first master-general until he became blind. Canonized in 1202.
Cf. Att. — Baud. — Holw. — Zimm. — Stanton.

GILBERT (St) Bp.
A.C. Apr. 1
d. 1245. For twenty years bishop of Caithness, of which diocese he built the cathedral. He was a valued servant of the Scottish kings, and a zealous opponent of Scottish independence against the arch-bishop of York.
Cf. Att. — Baud. — Holw.

GILBERT (Bl) Ab. O. PRAEM.
A.C. June 6
d. 1152. The abbot-founder of the Premonstratensian monastery of Neuffons (Neufontaines).
Cf. Holw. — P.B.

GILBERT (Bl) Ab. O.S.B.   A.C. Aug. 21
d. 1185. A monk at Saint-Crespin-en-Chaie, Soissons, and then the second abbot of the monastery of St John the Baptist at Valenciennes. He suffered persecution at the hands of the count of Hainault.
Cf. Holw. — P.B.

GILBERT of HEXHAM (St) Bp.
A.C. Sept. 7
Otherwise Tilbert, q.v.

GILBERT (Bl) Ab. O.S.B. Cist.
A.C. Oct. 17
d. 1167. An Englishman by birth who became a Cistercian, probably at Ourscamp, of which he was made abbot in 1147. In 1163 he was promoted abbot of Cîteaux. The Cistercian writers surname him "the Great," or "the Theologian."
Cf. Zimm.

GILDARD (GODARD) (St) Bp.
R.M. June 8
d. c.514. Bishop of Rouen for about fifteen years. The R.M. unfortunately reechoes a later fable, according to which Gildard was a brother of St Medard of Soissons "born on the same day, consecrated bishops on the same day, and on the same day withdrawn from this life." In fact Gildard had been dead at least five years when St Medard was consecrated.
Cf. Att. — Baud. — Holw.

GILDAS the WISE (St) Bp.
R.M. Jan. 29
d. c.570. Often called Badonicus, because born in the year the Britons defeated the Saxons at Bath. He was trained by St Illtyd, and towards the end of his life, crossing over to Brittany, lived as a hermit on the island of Rhuys. St Gildas is famous for a Latin work on the miseries of his fatherland *De excidiis Britanniae*; his authorship of part of it, however, is doubtful.
Cf. Att. — Baud. — Holw.

GILES (*several*)
Note. Giles is the English form of the Latin name Aegidius. It was a very common name in the Middle Ages. The other Western European variants are as follows: Italian, Egido; French, Gilles; Spanish and Portuguese, Gil.

GILES of LORENZANA (Bl) C. O.F.M.
A.C. Jan. 28
c.1443-1518. A native of Lorenzana, in the kingdom of Naples, who began life as a farm-hand. Later he became a Franciscan lay-brother and was allowed to live as a hermit in the garden of the friary. He is famous for his love of animals. Cult approved in 1880.
Cf. Att. — Baud. — Holw.

GILES MARY of ST JOSEPH (Bl) C. O.F.M.   A.C. Feb. 7
d. 1812. Born at Taranto in S. Italy, and a rope-maker by trade. He joined the Alcantarine Franciscans at Naples. He spent the rest of his life as porter of the Neapolitan friary. Beatified in 1888.
Cf. Baud. — Holw. — Att.

GILES of ASSISI (Bl) C. O.F.M.
A.C. Apr. 23
d. 1262. The third follower of St Francis of Assisi and one of the most delightful figures of the *Fioretti*. He went to preach to the Mohammedans in Tunis, but his mission was a failure. The rest of his life he spent in Italy, being eagerly consulted by all sorts of people on spiritual matters. He died at Perugia.
Cf. Att. — Baud. — Holw. — P. de U.

GILES of SAUMUR (Bl) Bp. A.C. Apr. 23
d. 1266. Chaplain to St Louis, king of France, with whom he went on crusade. In 1243 he became bishop of Damietta, and in 1245 archbishop of Tyre. He died at Dinant in Belgium.
Cf. Holw. — Baud.

GILES of SANTAREM (Bl) C. O.P.
A.C. May 14
1185-1265. A native of Vaozela in Portugal, who became a medical student, and, it is said, practised necromancy. After his conversion, he joined the Dominicans at Palencia, resided a long time at Santarem, and was made provincial for Spain.
Cf. Holw. — Att. — Chev. — Baud.

GILES (St) Ab. O.S.B.   R.M. Sept. 1
d. c.712. If we discard the legends which have been woven round the memory of this saint, the historical residue is as

follows: Giles was probably a Provencal by birth, and abbot of a monastery on the Rhone, where the city of Saint-Gilles now stands. He became one of the most "popular" saints of the Middle Ages, and his shrine a much frequented place of pilgrimage. Over one hundred and sixty churches were dedicated in his name in England alone. He is venerated as the patron saint of cripples, beggars, and blacksmiths.
Cf. Att. — Baud. — Chev. — Holw.

GILES and ARCANUS (SS) O.S.B.
                                   P.C. Sept. 1
d. c.1050. Giles was of Spanish birth, and together with the Italian St Arcano, founded an abbey under the Benedictine rule, to enshrine the relics which they had brought from Palestine. This grew into the present day Borgo San Sepolcro in central Italy.
Cf. Zimm. — Bolw.

GILES of CASTAÑEDA (Bl) Ab. O.S.B. Cist.   **A.C. Sept. 1**
d. c.1203. Cistercian abbot of the monastery of Castañeda in the Asturias. He was renowned as a confessor. He is now greatly venerated in the diocese of Astorga, in Spain.
Cf. Zimm. — Butler-Thurston (Sept. 3) — Chev. — Baud. — Holw.

GIRALD (GIRARD, GIRAUD) (St) Ab. O.S.B.   **A.C. Dec. 29**
d. 1031. A Benedictine monk at Lagny and afterwards abbot of Saint-Arnoul. Richard IV, duke of Normandy, enlisted his services as abbot of Fontenelle, where he was murdered by an unruly monk.
Cf. Holw. — Baud. — P.B.

GISLENUS (GHISLAIN, GUISLAIN) (St) Ab. O.S.B.   **R.M. Oct. 9**
d. c.680. A Frankish recluse, living in a forest in Hainault, whither he was followed by numerous disciples. He built for them the abbey of SS Peter and Paul now Saint-Ghislain near Mons, which he governed for thirty years.
Cf. Att. — Baud. — Holw.

GISTILIAN (St) C.   **A.C. March 4**
5th-6th cent. The uncle of St David and a monk of Menevia, or St Davids.
Cf. Holw.

GLADYS (St) W.   **A.C. March 29**
5th cent. A Welsh saint, daughter of Brychan of Brecknock. She became the wife of St Gundleus and mother of St Cadoc.
Cf. Holw.

GLAPHYRA (St) V.   **R.M. Jan. 13**
d. c.324. A female slave in the service of Constantia, wife of the emperor Licinius, who, in order to safeguard her chastity, fled to St Basil, bishop of Amasea in Pontus. She was recaptured and condemned to death. She died on the way to martyrdom.
Cf. Holw. — Baud.

GLASTIAN (St) Bp.   **A.C. Jan. 28**
d. 830. The patron saint of Kinglassie in Fife. As mediator between the Picts and Scots, he did much to alleviate the lot of the former when subjugated by their foes.
Cf. Holw. — Baud.

GLEB (St)   **A.C. July 24**
See Romanus and David.

GLODESIND (Bl) Abs. O.S.B.
                                   A.C. June 30
c.635-714. Daughter of St Adalbert of Douai and St Rictrude. With her mother she retired to the nunnery of Marchiennes, where she succeeded her mother as abbess.
Cf. Chev. — Holw.

GLODESIND (St) Abs.   **A.C. July 25**
d. c.608. Betrothed to a courtier who was arrested on their wedding day and afterwards executed. She took the veil in a nunnery at Metz, of which she became abbess.
Cf. Holw. — Chev. — Baud.

GLUNSHALLAICH (St) C.   A.C. June 3
7th cent. An Irish penitent, converted by St Kevin and buried in the same grave with him at Glendalough.
Cf. Holw.

GLUVIAS (GLYWYS) (St) C.
                                   A.C. May 2
6th cent. Brother of St Cadoc of Llancarfan, and possibly sent by him into Cornwall, where he made a monastic foundation. A parish in Cornwall perpetuates his name.
Cf. Holw.

GYLCERIA (St) V.M.   R.M. May 13
d. c.177. A Roman maiden, living with her father at Trajanopolis in Greece, who was martyred at Heraclea in the Propontis.
Cf. Att. — Baud. — Holw.

GLYCERIUS (St) Bp.   A.C. Sept. 20
d. c.438. Archbishop of Milan.
Cf. Menzies — Baud.

GLYCERIUS (St) M.   R.M. Dec. 21
d. 303. A priest of Nicomedia in Asia Minor, burnt at the stake under Diocletian.
Cf. Holw. — Baud.

GLYWYS (St) C.   A.C. May 2
Otherwise Gluvias, q.v.

GOAR (St) C.   R.M. July 6
d. c.575. A secular priest of Aquitaine, who led the life of a hermit near Oberwesel on the Rhine. His extant life is most untrustworthy. Charlemagne built a stately church over St Goar's hermitage.
Cf. Att. — Baud. — Holw.

GOBAN GOBHNENA (St) C.
A.C. May 23
6th or 7th cent. Supposed to be the Goban mentioned in the life of St Laserian as governing the monastery of Old-Leighlin, from which he migrated to Tascaffin, in the present Co Limerick.
Cf. Holw.

GOBAN (GOBAIN) M. O.S.B.
A.C. June 20
d. c.670. An Irishman by birth, and a disciple of his countryman St Fursey, under whom he became a monk at Burgh Castle in Suffolk. He followed his abbot to France and both took to the solitary life in the great forest near the Oise. He was murdered by barbarian marauders at the place now called Saint-Gobain.
Cf. Att. — Chev. — Baud. — Holw.

GOBERT (Bl) Mk. O.S.B.   A.C. Aug. 20
d. 1263. Count of Apremont. After fighting as a crusader in Palestine he became a Cistercian at Villiers in Brabant.
Cf. Holw. — Chev. — Baud.

GOBNATA (GOBNET) (St) V.
A.C. Feb. 11
? 6th cent. St Abban is said to have founded a convent in Ballyvourney, Co

Cork, and to have placed St Gobnet over it as abbess. A well still exists there called after her.
Cf. Holw.

GOBRIAN (St) Bp.   A.C. Nov. 16
d. 725. A Breton monk who became bishop of Vannes, and at the age of eighty-seven resigned his see to retire to a hermit's cell, where he died.
Cf. Baud. — Chev. — Holw.

GODARD (St) Bp. O.S.B.   R.M. May 4
Otherwise Godehard, q.v.

GODARD (St) Bp.   R.M. June 8
Otherwise Gildard, q.v.

GODEBERTHA (St) Abs.   A.C. Apr. 11
d. c.700. Born in the diocese of Amiens. In 567 she received the veil from St Eligius, bishop of Noyon, who also composed a rule for her nunnery at Noyon. She was the first abbess.
Cf. Att. — Baud. — Holw.

GODEHARD (GODARD, GOTHARD)
(St) Bp. O.S.B.   R.M. May 4
d. 1038. A Bavarian, whose father was employed in the service of the canons of Niederaltaich. Godehard joined them and became their provost. He was instrumental in re-introducing the Benedictine Rule at Niederaltaich and was commissioned by the emperor St Henry to revive the Benedictine observance in several German dioceses. Tegernsee, Hersfeld and Kremsmünster received abbots from Niederaltaich. In 1022 the saint was made bishop of Hildesheim and did much to foster religion and culture. Canonized in 1131.
Cf. Att. — Baud. — Holw. — Chev. — Zimm.

GODELEVA (GODLIVA) (St) M.
A.C. July 6
d. 1070. Married very young to Bertulf of Ghistelles, who after ill-treating her for two years, had her strangled. She has been venerated as a martyr ever since.
Cf. Holw. — Baud. — Att.

GODFREY (several)
Note. This name, in Latin, Godefridus, is variously spelt in English: Godefrid, Geoffrey, Gotfrid, Goffry, etc. In other languages the spelling is: Gottfried,

Geoffroy, Gioffredo, Gaufrid, Geofroi, Goffredo, Gofrido, etc.

GODFREY of CAPPENBERG (Bl) C. O. Praem. A.C. Jan. 13
1097-1127. Born at Cappenberg Castle in Westphalia, where, besides being a count, he owned large estates. He made the acquaintance of St Norbert and in the teeth of violent opposition from his relatives, made over his lands to the holy founder, turned his castle into a Premonstratensian abbey and himself joined the order with his brother, while his wife and two sisters took the veil in a nunnery which he founded for them. He died at the age of thirty and not yet a priest.
Cf. Att. — Holw. — Baud.

GODFREY of DUYNEN and GODFREY of MERVILLE (SS) MM. R.M. July 9
d. 1572. The former was a secular priest and at one time rector of a school in Paris; the latter was custos of the Franciscan house at Gorkum, Holland, and a painter. Both were hanged with others by the Calvinists at Briel. The group is known as the martyrs of Gorkum, q.v.
Cf. Holw. — Baud.

GODFREY (St) Bp. O.S.B. R.M. Nov. 8
c.1066-1115. Born in the province of Soissons and placed at the age of five at the abbey of Mont-Saint-Quentin, where in due course he was professed and ordained. In 1096 he was promoted abbot of Nogent-sous-Coucy in Champagne and in 1104 bishop of Amiens. He was rigidly austere, both with himself and with others. In spite of this when he wished to resign and become a Carthusian his people would not allow it. He was a lifelong opponent of simony and incontinency.
Cf. Att. — Zimm. — Holw. — Chev.

GODO (GAON) (St) Ab. O.S.B.
A.C. July 24
d. c.690. A native of Verdun, and a nephew of St Wandrille, under whom he was professed at Fontenelle. Afterwards he was the abbot-founder of Oye Abbey, near Sezanne-en-Brie.
Cf. Mab. — Chev. — Baud. — Holw.

GODRIC (St) H. O.S.B. A.C. May 21
d. 1170. A native of Walpole in Norfolk, after years of adventurous seafaring and of many pilgrimages he became a hermit

at Finchale in Co Durham, under the obedience of the prior of Durham. There he lived for sixty years, remarkable for his austerities, his supernatural gifts and also for his familiarity with wild animals.
Cf. Att. — Baud. — Holw. — Chev.

GODWIN (St) Ab. O.S.B. A.C. Oct. 28
d. c.690. Abbot of the great Belgian monastery of Stavelot-Malmédy.
Cf. Zimm. — Holw. — Chev.

GOERIC (St) Bp. A.C. Sept. 19
d. 647. Also called Abbo. The successor of St Arnulphus in the bishopric of Metz.
Cf. Att. — Baud. — Holw.

GOEZNOVEUS (St) Bp. A.C. Oct. 25
d. 675. A Cornish saint, brother of St Maughan, who crossed into Brittany and became bishop of Léon.
Cf. Holw. — Baud.

GOFOR (St) C. A.C. May 9
? A Welsh saint, patron of Llanover in Monmouthshire.
Cf. Baring-Gould.

GOHARDUS (St) Bp. M. A.C. June 25
d. 843. Bishop of Nantes, slain by raiding Normans while celebrating Mass; many monks and priests were killed with him.
Cf. Att. — Holw.

GOLLEN (COLLEN, COLAN) (St) C.
A.C. May 21
? 7th cent. A saint who has given his name to Llangollen in Denbighshire. His name is connected in legend with Wales, Glastonbury and Rome.
Cf. Holw. — Baring-Gould (Collen).

GOLVINUS (GOLWEN) (St) Bp.
A.C. July 9
? 7th cent. A Breton saint, but of British origin, where fame for sanctity led to his promotion to the see of St Pol-de-Léon. He died at Rennes where his relics are still enshrined.
Cf. Holw. — Baud.

GOMER (St) R.M. Oct. 11
Otherwise Gummarus, q.v.

GOMIDAS (Bl) M. A.C. Nov. 5
c.1656-1707. Gomides Keumurjian, an Armenian by descent, was born at Constantinople, married at the age of twenty and was ordained a priest of the dissident

Armenian Church. In 1696, he and his family made their submission to Rome. This angered the dissidents, who unjustly accused Gomides to the Turkish authorities as an agent of hostile Western powers. Consequently he was beheaded at Parmark-Kapu, on the outskirts of Constantinople. Beatified in 1929.
Cf. Att.

GONERI (St) C.　　　　**A.C. July 18**
6th cent. An exile from Britain to Brittany, where he led an eremitical life near Tréguier.
Cf. Holw.

GONSALVO of AMARANTHA (Bl) C.
　　　　　　　　　　　　A.C. Jan. 16
Otherwise Gundisalvus, q.v.

GONTRAM (St) King　R. M. March 28
Otherwise Gunthramnus, q.v.

GOOD THIEF, THE (St)
　　　　　　　　　　R.M. March 25
1st cent. The repentant thief, to whom the dying Saviour promised paradise. The name of Dismas has been given him by tradition, and a number of legends have grown up around his name; but except for the episode recorded in the gospel, nothing is known about him.
Cf. Att. — Baud. — Holw.

GORAN (WORANUS) (St) C.
　　　　　　　　　　　　A.C. Apr. 7
6th cent. Several Cornish churches are dedicated in his honour. He was a friend of St Patrick.
Cf. Holw.

GORDIAN and EPIMACHUS (SS) MM.
　　　　　　　　　　R.M. May 10
d. 362 and 250. Epimachus was martyred at Alexandria under Decius, and his relics were taken to Rome. Gordian suffered at a later date, very probably under Julian the Apostate, and was buried in the same tomb. Their *Acta* are not trustworthy.
Cf. Att. — Baud. — Holw.

GORDIAN (St) M.　　　　**R.M. Sept. 17**
See Valerian, Macrinus and Gordian.

GORDIUS (St) M.　　　　**R.M. Jan. 3**
d. 304. A soldier of Caesarea in Cappadocia, dismissed from the army on account of his religion. He retired to the desert,

but during the persecution under Diocletian gave himself up and was beheaded.
Cf. Att. — Baud. — Holw.

GORGONIA (St) M.　　　　**R.M. Dec. 9**
d. c.375. Daughter of St Gregory Nazianzen senior and of St Nonna, and sister of St Gregory Nazianzen junior, the great Greek theologian. She married and was a model Christian matron.
Cf. Att. — Baud. — Holw.

GORGONIUS and FIRMUS (or FIRMINUS) (SS) MM.　　**R.M. March 11**
3rd cent. Martyrs, either of Nicaea in Bithynia, or of Antioch in Syria.
Cf. however Holw. who identifies this Gorgonius with the next (Sept. 9).

GORGONIUS (St) M.　　　　**R.M. Sept. 9**
See Dorotheus and Gorgonius.

GORKUM (Martyrs of) (SS)
　　　　　　　　　　　　R.M. July 9
d. 1572. A group of nineteen martyrs, ten Franciscans, two Premonstratensians, a Dominican, a canon regular, four secular priests and a layman — put to death with unspeakable cruelty by the Calvinists at Gorkum, near Dordrecht in Holland. Each receives a separate notice in this book. Canonized in 1867.
Cf. Att. — Baud. — Holw.

GORMAN (St) Bp. O.S.B.　A.C. Aug. 28
d. 965. A Benedictine of Reichenan, who went to preach the gospel in the North and became bishop of Sleswig in Denmark.
Cf. Baud.

GORMCAL (St) Ab.　　　　**A.C. Aug. 5**
d. 1016. An Irish abbot of the monastery of Ardoilen in Galway.
Cf. Holw.

GOSBERT (St) Bp. O.S.B.　A.C. Feb. 13
d. c.859. The fourth bishop of Osnabruck and a disciple of St Ansgar. His was a particularly laborious episcopate.
Cf. Holw. — Baud.

GOSCELINUS (GOSLIN, GOZZELINUS) (St) Ab. O.S.B.　A.C. Feb. 12
d. 1153. Second abbot of San Solutore, near Turin (1147-1153). The solemn translation of his relics took place in 1472.
Cf. Zimm. — Baud. — Holw.

GOSWIN (St) Ab. O.S.B.   A.C. Oct. 9
d. 1165. A native of Douai and a student
at Paris, he first taught theology in his
native city where he held a canonry;
then he professed the Benedictine Rule
at Anchin (1113), where he eventually became abbot (c.1130): one of the greatest
abbots of that great abbey.
Cf. Chev. — Holw. — Baud.

GOSWIN (Bl) O.S.B. Cist.   A.C. Oct. 27
d. 1203. A Cistercian monk, first at
Clairvaux and then at Chemnion.
Cf. Zimm.

GOTHARD (St) Bp.   R.M. May 4
Otherwise Godehard, q.v.

GOTTESCHALK (St) M.   A.C. June 7
d. 1066. A Wendish prince who renounced
Christianity because his father had been
murdered by Christian Saxons. As the
husband of Canute's grandniece he came
to England and returned to the Faith,
which he henceforth fostered with great
zeal. He was murdered at Lenzen by
assassins in the service of his brother-in-
law. Many doubt whether he has a true
claim to the title of either saint or martyr.
Cf. Att. — Holw.

**GOWAN (GOVAN, GOVEN, COFEN)
(St) Matron.**   A.C. Dec. 28
5th cent. The wife of King Tewdrig of
Glamorgan. The parish of Llangoven in
Monmouthshire takes its name from her,
and a chapel in Pembrokeshire is likewise
dedicated in her honour.
Cf. Holw.

GRACE and PROBUS (SS)   A.C. July 5
? Two Cornish saints, said to have been
husband and wife. They are patron
saints of the parish of Probus in Cornwall.
Cf. Holw.

**GRACILIAN and FELICISSIMA (SS)
MM.**   R.M. Aug. 12
d. c.304. Gracilian, a Christian of Faleria,
while in prison awaiting martyrdom, restored the sight of a blind girl and converted her to Christ. They were beheaded on the same day.
Cf. Holw. — Baud.

GRATA (St) W.   R.M. May 1
4th (or 8th) cent. A holy woman of
Bergamo, zealous in securing Christian
burial for the bodies of the martyrs. The
evidence regarding her life is very conflicting.
Cf. Att. — Baud. — Holw.

GRATIA of CATTARO (Bl) C. O.S.A.
   A.C. Nov. 16
1438-1509. A native of Cattaro in Dalmatia. For thirty years he was a fisherman in the Adriatic and then professed the
Augustinian Rule as a lay-brother. He
was famous for the gift of infused knowledge. Cult approved in 1889.
Cf. Att. — Baud. — Holw.

GRATIAN (St) Bp.   R.M. Dec. 18
Otherwise Gatian. q.v.

GRATINIAN (GRATIAN) (St) M.
   R.M. June 1
See Felinus and Gratianus.

GRATUS (St) Bp.   A.C. Sept. 7
d. c.470. Bishop of Aosta. He is now its
patron saint.
Cf. Baud. — Holw.

GRATUS (St) Bp.   A.C. Oct. 8
d. c.652. A French bishop of Châlons-
sur-Saône.
Cf. Duch. Fast. Episc. — Holw.

GRATUS (St) Bp.   A.C. Oct. 11
d. c.506. The first bishop of the ancient
see, long suppressed, of Oloron, in S.
France.
*Cf. Duch. Fast. Episc. — Gams — Baud.—
Holw.*

GRATUS (St) M.   R.M. Dec. 5
See Julius, Potamia, etc.

GREDIFAEL (St) C.   A.C. Nov. 13
7th cent. A Breton or Welsh saint who
accompanied St Padarn from Brittany to
Wales. He is said to have been abbot of
Whitland in Pembrokeshire.
Cf. Holw.

**GREGORY NAZIANZEN the ELDER
(St) Bp. C.**   A.C. Jan. 1
c.276-374. A native of Nazianzos in
Cappadocia, Asia Minor, a state function-
ary and a pagan, he was converted (325)
by his wife, St Nonna. They had three
children — all saints: Gregory Nazianzen,
junior, the Great Father of the Church,
Caesarius and Gorgonia. Gregory senior
became bishop of his native city (c.328)
and attached himself to some heretical

sect; but was converted to orthodoxy (361) by his more gifted son, Gregory, who, in 372, became his coadjutor. He died when nearly one hundred years of age. *Cf. Holw. — Baud.*

GREGORY of LANGRES (St) Bp.
R.M. Jan. 4

d. 539. A leading citizen (*comes*) of the district round Autun and the civil governor of the city, firm and severe. Later in life he lost his wife, was ordained priest and became bishop of Autun, and as such gained a reputation for gentleness and understanding. He was instrumental in consolidating the Christian religion in his diocese. He was the father of St Tetricus, who succeeded him in the see, and the great-grand-father of St Gregory of Tours. *Cf. Att. — Baud. — Duch. Fast. Episc.*

GREGORY X (Bl) Pope. R.M. Jan. 10

d. 1276. Theobald Visconti was a native of Piacenza in Italy, who became archdeacon of Liége, in Belgium. While holding this office he was entrusted with the preaching of the last crusade. He himself accompanied the crusaders to Palestine, and he was still there when elected pope in 1271. He was not yet a priest. The outstanding event of his pontificate was the holding of the council of Lyons, at which the Eastern orthodox became reconciled, unhappily for only a short time, to the Catholic Church. His name was inserted in the R. M. by Benedict XIV. *Cf. Att. — Baud. — Holw.*

GREGORY II (St) Pope. R.M. Feb. 11

d. 731. Roman born and educated at the Lateran, he held the offices of Librarian and Archivist of the Roman Church, when he was elected pope in 715. He devoted much of his time to the affairs of the Eastern Church, and his pontificate is also famous for the spreading of the gospel among the Teuton races, to whom he sent as missionaries St Boniface and St Corbinian. He fostered Benedictine life everywhere, and restored several Italian abbeys, notably Montecassino. An old tradition makes him in fact a Benedictine monk, and his office figured for centuries in several Benedictine *Propria*. He opposed Iconoclasm and checked the advancing Lombards. He is one of the great popes. *Cf. Att. — Baud. — Holw. — Menzies.*

GREGORY of NYSSA (St) Bp.
R.M. March 9

d. c.395. A younger brother of St Basil the Great. After his marriage he practised as a professor of rhetoric but abandoned this profession for the priesthood. In 372 his brother Basil nominated him bishop of Nyssa, a small township in Lower Armenia. It was a somewhat unfortunate choice, as Gregory was not a man of affairs, and the Arians were predominant in the diocese. He returned home and after his brother's death was the mainstay of orthodoxy throughout Cappadocia. His writings are remarkable for depth of thought and lucidity of expression. Of the three "great Cappadocians" — Basil, Gregory Nazianzen, Gregory of Nyssa — he is the least prolific but the most profound. *Cf. Att. — Holw. — Baud.*

GREGORY the GREAT (St) Pope, Dr. O.S.B. R.M. March 12 and Sept. 3

c.540-604. The R.M. (Sept. 3) aptly surnames him *Vir incomparabilis* — an incomparable man. Born in Rome of patrician parents — his mother was St Sylvia — he became before he was thirty years of age the prefect — *praetor*, mayor — of the city. He soon resigned the office, turned his ancestral home on the Caelian Hill into a Benedictine abbey and became a monk there. Next he was sent to Constantinople as *apocrisarius* — papal nuncio. On his return he was chosen pope (590), and what he achieved in his fourteen years pontificate makes him one of the most commanding figures in world history. First in importance was his mission to England, whither he sent St Augustine and some forty of his Benedictines from the Caelian Hill; this was important not only on account of the conversion of England itself, but also because of the spreading of the Benedictine Rule among the new races of W. Europe. He promoted likewise the conversion of the Lombards in Italy and of the Goths in Spain; upheld the rights of the Roman see against Constantinople; embellished the Liturgy in its sacramentary and in its chant; defended and befriended monachism; and cared for the poor in Rome, at Ravenna and on his estates in Sicily. He was moreover a prolific writer; his dialogues, comprising the only extant life

of St Benedict, and his *Regula Pastoralis* are classics in ascetical literature.
Cf. Att. — Menzies. — Zimm. — Mab.

GREGORY MAKAR (St) Bp.
A.C. March 16

d. c.1000. He is described as an Armenian, who became a monk and was elected bishop of Nicopolis in Armenia. He is said to have fled to France and settled as a hermit at Pithiviers in the diocese of Orleans.
Cf. Holw. — Att. — Baud.

GREGORY of ELVIRA (St) Bp.
R.M. Apr. 24

d. c.400. Bishop of Elvira, in S. Spain — a see which has since been-translated to Granada. He was one of the champions of the Faith against Arianism, and one of the few bishops who at Rimini (359) consistently refused to compromise with the heretics. In all good faith he sided with the party of Lucifer of Cagliari, but never left the communion of the Roman see.
Cf. P. de U. — Holw. — Baud.

GREGORY of BESIANS (Bl) C.O.P.
A.C. Apr. 26

See Dominic and Gregory.

GREGORY CELLI of VERUCCHIO (Bl) C.O.S.A.
A.C. May 4

d. 1343. A native of Verucchio, in the diocese of Rimini. His mother founded a monastery for the Augustinians in his native town, and Gregory took the habit there. After a time he was dismissed for some unjust reason, but was charitably received by the Franciscans of Monte Carnerio, near Rieti, where he died. Cult confirmed in 1769.
Cf. Att. — Baud. — Menzies.

GREGORY NAZIANZEN (St) Bp. Dr.
R.M. May 9

c.329-390. A native of Arianzos in Cappadocia and eldest son of St Gregory Nazianzen the Elder (q.v.). He read law for ten years at Athens and then joined his friend St Basil in his monastic solitude in Pontus. In 361 he was ordained priest and in 372 consecrated bishop of the small township of Sasima. This see he refused to accept, acting instead as coadjutor to his father at Nazianzos, until, in 380, he was prevailed upon to accept the see of Constantinople. He was there only one month: after which he resigned and re-tired to Arianzos where he died in 390. The tragedy of his life was his promotion to the rank of bishop, since his character was not fitted for a life of action. On the other hand, as a writer he stands far above most other Greek Doctors, in fact, he is surnamed by the Greeks "the Divine" — *'o Theologos.* He is venerated in East and West as a Doctor of the Church.
Cf. Att. — Baud. — Holw.

GREGORY of OSTIA (St) Bp. O.S.B.
A.C. May 9

d. c.1044. A Benedictine cardinal, bishop of Ostia, who exercised legatine powers in the old kingdoms of Spanish Navarre and Old Castile. He died at Logroño. He is still greatly venerated throughout Navarre and Rioja. His life, however, as handed down to us, is full of conflicting statements.
Cf. Gams — P. de U. — Zimm. — Chev. — Holw.

GREGORY VII (St) Pope, O.S.B.
R.M. May 25

c.1020-1085. A native of Soana, in Tuscany. His baptismal name was Hildebrand. He was sent very young to Rome, where his uncle was superior of the Cluniac abbey of St Mary on the Aventine, and there Hildebrand professed the Benedictine Rule. He accompanied the deposed Pope Gregory VI to Germany, but returned to Rome with St Leo IX, and became abbot of St Paul-outside-the-Walls (1059). From this date begins his close association with the popes, five of whom he served as archdeacon. In 1073 he himself became supreme pontiff and continued his life-long struggle against lay investiture, simony and clerical concubinage. He succeeded in imposing his will on his persistent and childishly cunning enemy the emperor Henry IV of Germany, but nevertheless a few years later he was driven into exile at Salerno where he died. Few men have been so admired by their friends and reviled by their foes. Canonized in 1728.
Cf. Mab. — Zimm. — Att. — Holw. — Chev.

GREGORY, DEMETRIUS and CALOGERUS (SS) CC.
A.C. June 18

d. 5th cent. Respectively a bishop, an archdeacon and an abbot, in N. Africa, whence they were driven by Arian Vandals. They settled down at Fragalata, near Messina, in Sicily, and preached the

gospel there. They are now honoured as the patron saints of Fragalata.
Cf. Menzies — Holw.

GREGORY BARBADIGO (Bl) Bp.
A.C. June 18
1625-1697. Venetian-born, he was first bishop of Bergamo and then of Padua, and was created cardinal in 1660. He was equally distinguished as a churchman and as a statesman. His charities were on a princely scale, and his benefactions to Padua numerous and lasting. He was an earnest worker for the reconciliation of the dissident Greeks. Beatified in 1761.
Cf. Att. — Menzies — Holw.

GREGORY ESCRIVANO (Bl) M. S.J.
A.C. July 15
d. 1570. Born at Logroño, in Old Castile, he was a Jesuit coadjutor, and a companion of Bl Ignatius de Azevedo q.v.
Cf. Holw.

GREGORY LOPEZ (Bl) H. P.C. July 20
1542-1596. A native of Madrid, where he served as page to Philip II. In 1562 he migrated to Mexico and lived as a hermit among the Indians near Zacatecas and later near the capital. His cult spread all over Mexico, but the process of his beatification, begun in 1752, fails to make progress in Rome.
Cf. Holw. — Att. — P. de U.

GREGORY of NONANTULA (Bl) Ab. O.S.B.
A.C. Aug. 3
d. 933. A Benedictine abbot of the great Italian abbey of Nonantula, near Modena.
Cf. Chev. — Menzies — Holw.

GREGORY of UTRECHT (St) Ab. O.S.B.
R.M. Aug. 25
703-c.776. A native of Trèves. When a child he met St Boniface, under whom he became a monk. The old apostle loved him as a son and made him abbot of St Martin's at Utrecht. Without relinquishing his office of abbot, St Gregory administered the diocese as well for twenty-two years. During his abbacy St Martin's became a great missionary centre and a nursery of saints.
Cf. Mab. — Zimm. — Att. — Chev. — Holw.

GREGORY the ILLUMINATOR (St) Bp.
R.M. Sept. 30
d. c.330. Also surnamed "the apostle of Armenia." Unfortunately his life, as given by tradition, is not well authenticated. The following main facts seem certain: he began to preach to the Armenians and converted their king Tiridates, had himself consecrated bishop and set up his see at Ashtishat, whence his apostolate spread far and wide. Armenian legends, obviously fictitious, about St Gregory run to several volumes.
Cf. Att. — Baud. — Holw.

GREGORY of BURTSCHEID (St) Ab. O.S.B.
A.C. Nov. 4
d. 999. A Basilian monk at Cerchiara, in Calabria, who fled from the Saracens and met the emperor Otto III in Rome. The emperor befriended him, invited him to Germany and built for him the abbey of Burtscheid, near Aix-la-Chapelle, under the Benedictine Rule.
Cf. Zimm. — Chev. — Holw.

GREGORY of EINSIEDELN (St) Ab. O.S.B.
A.C. Nov. 8
d. 996. An Anglo-Saxon by birth, who on a pilgrimage to Rome received the Benedictine cowl on the Caelian Hill at Rome. On his way home he stayed at the Swiss abbey of Einsiedeln, and joined the community (949). He was elected abbot and his rule coincided with the period of the greatest monastic splendour of the abbey.
Cf. Mab. — Zimm. — P. de U. — Chev.

GREGORY THAUMATURGUS (St) Bp.
R.M. Nov. 17
c.213-c.270. A native of Pontus and a disciple of Origen. He was made bishop of Neocaesarea in 240. It is related that on his accession to the see he found just seventeen Christians, and that when he died he left only seventeen pagans. His title of "the Wonder-Worker" explains itself. He is also an ecclesiastical writer.
Cf. Att. — Holw. — Baud.

GREGORY of TOURS (St) Bp.
R.M. Nov. 17
539-596. This saint was born in Auvergne, and was baptized George Florentius, but took the name Gregory when he was raised to the see of Tours in 573. He was a great bishop much revered by St Gregory the Great. He excelled, however, as a historian, and his writings are now the best historical source of the Merovingian period.
Cf. Att. — Duch. Fast. Episc. — Chev. — Baud.

GREGORY DECAPOLITES (St) C.
R.M. Nov. 20
9th cent. So-called from his birthplace in Asia Minor. He opposed the Iconoclasts zealously and suffered much at their hands.
Cf. Holw. — Baud.

GREGORY of GIRGENTI (St) Bp.
R.M. Nov. 23
d. c.638. A Sicilian of the Byzantine rite, who, after a protracted sojourn in the Eastern *lauras*, was nominated by St George the Great bishop of Girgenti (*Agrigentum*) his native town. His interesting commentary on the book of Ecclesiastes is still extant.
Cf. Menzies — Att. — Holw.

GREGORY III (St) Pope. R.M. Dec. 10
d. 741. A Syrian by birth who reigned as pope from 731 to 741. His was a very stormy pontificate, troubled in the beginning by the foolish excesses of the Iconoclasts and at the end by the incursions of the Lombards. Gregory sought the aid of Charles Martel against the latter, thus establishing a connection with the Franks which was to prove of historic importance.
Cf. Menzies — Baud. — Att. — Holw.

GREGORY of TERRACINA (St) C.
O.S.B. **A.C. Dec. 12**
See Speciosus and Gregory.

GREGORY of AUXERRE (St) Bp.
R.M. Dec. 19
d. c.540. The twelfth bishop of Auxerre. He governed the see thirteen years, and died aged eighty-five.
Cf. Baud. — Duch. Fast. Episc.

GREGORY of SPOLETO (St) M.
R.M. Dec. 24
A priest said to have been martyred under Maximinian Herculius. His *Acta* are not reliable; and doubt has been thrown on his very existence.
Cf. Att. — Menzies — Baud.

GRIGNON de MONTFORT (Bl) C.
A.C. Aug. 19
See Louis-Mary Grignon de Montfort.

GRIMBALD (St) Ab. O.S.B. A.C. July 8
d. 903. A Benedictine monk, and prior of Saint-Bertin. In 885 King Alfred, then on his way to Rome, invited him to Eng-land. Grimbald came, but declined the see of Canterbury offered to him by the king. Eventually he was made abbot of the New Minister at Winchester. He was a restorer of learning in England.
Cf. Att. — Chev. — Zimm. — Holw. — Baud.

GRIMOALDUS (St) C. **R.M. Sept. 29**
d. p. 1137. Archpriest of Pontecorvo, near Aquino, in S. Italy. Some writers state that he was an Englishman.
Cf. Menzies — Holw. — Baud.

GRIMONIA (GERMANA) (St) V.M.
A.C. Sept. 7
4th cent. Said to have been an Irish maiden, martyred in Picardy in defence of her virtue.
Cf. Att. — Baud. — Holw.

GRWST (St) C. **A.C. Dec. 1**
7th cent. The Welsh saint whose memory is perpetuated by the place-name Llanrwst, Denbighshire.
Cf. Holw.

GUALA (Bl) C. O.P. **A.C. Sept. 3**
d. 1244. One of the first disciples of St Dominic in Italy and the first Dominican prior of Brescia and Bologna. In 1228 he was made bishop of Brescia, but resigned in 1242 on account of civil strife and retired to the Vallumbrosans of San Sepolcro d'Astino, where he died. Cult approved in 1866.
Cf. Att. — Zimm. — Holw.

GUALFARDUS (WOLFHARD) (St) H.
O.S.B. **A.C. May 11**
d. 1127. A native of Augsburg and a saddler, who plied his trade in Verona, till the people began to look upon him as a saint. Then he retired to live as a monk-hermit in the Camaldolese priory of San Salvatore, near Verona.
Cf. Prop. Camald. — Zimm. — Att. — Holw.

GUALTERUS (*several*)
Otherwise Walter, q.v.

GUARINUS (St) Bp. O.S.B. Cist.
A.C. Jan. 6
d. 1150. Originally a monk of Molesmes, he was made abbot of Aulps, near Geneva. At his request his community was affiliated

to Clairvaux. Afterwards he was raised to the see of Sion in the Valais.
Cf. Att. — Gams — Baud. — Holw.

GUARINUS (St) Bp. O.S.A. R.M. Feb. 6
d. 1159. A native of Bologne, who joined the Augustinian canons regular. After forty years of religious life he was elected bishop of Pavia; but nothing could induce him to accept the post. However, Lucius II created him cardinal bishop of Palestrina. Canonized by Alexander III.
Cf. Att. — Menzies — Holw.

GUASACHT (St) Bp. A.C. Jan. 24
4th cent. Son of Maelchu, the master under whom St Patrick worked as a slave in Ireland. Guasacht was converted by Patrick, whom he helped, as bishop of Granard (Longford), in the evangelization of Ireland.
Cf. Holw.

GUDELIA (St) M. R.M. Sept. 29
d. c.340. A maiden martyred in Persia under Shapur II.
Cf. Holw.

GUDULA (GOULE) (St) V. A.C. Jan. 8
d. 712. Daughter of St Amalberga, she was trained by St Gertrude at Nivelles, and afterwards lived at home a life of great holiness. She is the patroness of Brussels. In art she is often shown with a lantern.
Cf. Att. — Baud. — Holw.

GOUDWALL (CURVAL) (St) Bp.
A.C. June 6
7th cent. A Welsh bishop who founded monasteries in Devon and Cornwall. By many he is supposed to be the Gurval who succeeded St Malo at Aleth in Brittany. His relics are venerated at Ghent.
Cf. Holw. — Baud.

GUENHAEL (St) Ab. A.C. Nov. 3
d. c.550. Guenhael means "white Angel." He was born in Brittany and educated at Landevenec under St Winwaloë, where in due course he became abbot.
Cf. Holw. — Baud.

GUENNINUS (St) Bp. A.C. Aug. 19
7th cent. A bishop of Vannes in Brittany, whose relics are enshrined in the cathedral.
Cf. Holw. — Duch. Fast. Episc.

GUEREMBALDUS (St) Mk. O.S.B.
A.C. Nov. 10
d. 965. A Monk of Hirschau, who, through humility, renounced the bishopric of Spire.
Cf. Baud. — P. de U. — Zimm.

GUERRICUS (Bl) Ab. O.S.B. Cist.
A.C. Aug. 19
d. c.1157. Born at Tournai, he studied there and became canon and headmaster of the cathedral school. He visited Clairvaux to see St Bernard, and stayed there. In 1138 St Bernard sent him as first abbot of Igny, in the diocese of Reims. He was a prolific ascetical writer; some of his writings indeed have been attributed to St Bernard.
Cf. Baud. — P. de U. — Zimm.

GUESNOVEUS (GOUERNOU) (St) Bp.
A.C. Oct. 25
d. 675. A bishop of Quimper in Brittany and founder of a monastery near Brest, where he died.
Cf. Holw. — Baud.

GUETHENOC (GWENTHENOC) (St)
A.C. Feb. 6
See Jacut and Guethenoc.

GUEVROCK (GUEROC, KERRIC) (St) Ab. A.C. Feb. 17
6th cent. A Briton who followed St Tugduald to Brittany, and became the advisor and helper of St Paul of Léon.
Cf. Holw. — Baud.

GUIBERTUS (St) Mk. O.S.B.
A.C. May 23
d. 962. A noble of Lorraine who served with distinction in several campaigns. He then lived the life of a hermit on his own estate of Gembloux, in Brabant, but eventually he turned it into a monastery and retired himself to the Benedictine abbey of Gorze. Several times, however, he had to leave the peace of Gorze in order to defend the rights of his foundation at Gembloux. He died at Gorze.
Cf. Att. — Baud. — Zimm. — Chev.

GUIDO (*several*)
Otherwise Guy, q.v.

GUINGAR (St) M. A.C. Dec. 14
Otherwise Fingar, q.v.

GUINGALOC (GUIGNOLE, GUINVA-LOEUS) A.C. March 3
Otherwise Winwaloë, q.v.

GUINIZO (St) Mk. O.S.B. A.C. May 26
d. c.1050. A native of Spain who professed the Benedictine Rule at Montecassino, and remained as a hermit on the holy mountain after one of the destructions of the abbey.
Cf. Zimm. — Chev. — Holw.

GUINOC (St) Bp. A.C. Apr. 13
d. c.838. A Bishop in Scotland, commemorated in the Aberdeen breviary.
Cf. Holw.

GUISLAIN (St) Ab. R.M. Oct. 9
Otherwise Gislenus, q.v.

GUITMARUS (St) Ab. O.S.B.
A.C. Dec. 10
d. c.765. Fourth abbot of Saint-Riquier (Centula) in France.
Cf. Chev. — Baud.

GULSTAN (GUSTAN, CONSTANS) (St)
Mk. O.S.B. A.C. Nov. 29
d. c.1010. A Benedictine of the abbey of St Gildas of Rhuys, in Brittany, under St Felix.
Cf. Zimm. — Chev. — Baud. — Holw.

GUMESINDUS and SERVUSDEI (SS)
MM. R.M. Jan. 13
d. 850. Two Spanish martyrs, one a parish-priest, the other a monk, who suffered at Cordova under Abderrahman II.
Cf. P. de U. — Holw. — Baud.

GUMMARUS (GOMER) (St) H.
R.M. Oct. 11
717-c.774. A courtier of King Pepin who married a wife of extravagant and tiresome disposition. After long and patient endurance of her perversity he was at last obliged to separate from her and died a recluse. The present Flemish town of Lierre (Lier) has grown up around his hermitage.
Cf. Att. — Holw.

GUNDEBERT (GUMBERT, GONDEL-BERT) (St) Bp. O.S.B. A.C. Feb. 21
d. c.676. A Frankish bishop (of Sens) who resigned and retired into the Vosges, where he founded the abbey of Senones (c.660).
Cf. Zimm. — P. de U. — Holw. — Baud.

GUNDEBERT (St) M. A.C. Apr. 29
8th cent. Tradition describes this saint as a Frankish monk, brother to St Niard, bishop of Reims, who crossed over to Ireland and was killed there by heathen marauders.
Cf. Att. — Baud. — Holw.

GUNDECHAR (KUNDEKAR) (St) M.
O.S.B. R.M. June 5
d. 754. A German Benedictine monk, not in priest's orders, who suffered martyrdom with St Boniface at Dokkum, in Frisia.
Cf. Holw. — Zimm.

GUNDELINDIS (GUENDELINDIS) V.
O.S.B. A.C. March 28
d. c.750. A daughter of the duke of Alsace, and a niece of St Ottilia, whom she succeeded as abbess in the nunnery of Niedermünster.
Cf. P. de U. — Holw. — Baud.

GUNDENIS (St) V.M. R.M. July 18
d. 203. A maiden martyred at Carthage, under Septimius Severus.
Cf. Holw.

GUNDISALVUS (Bl) C. O.P.
A.C. Jan. 16
d. ? 1259. A native of Vizella in the diocese of Braga, in Portugal. After his ordination to the priesthood he led the life of a solitary at Amarante, and later entered the Dominican order. Cult approved in 1560.
Cf. Att. — Baud. — Holw.

GUNDISALVUS GARCIA (St) M. O.F.M.
A.C. Feb. 5
1556-1597. Born in the East Indies of Portuguese parents, he first served the Jesuits as a catechist, then opened a flourishing business in Japan, and finally (1591) joined the Franciscans at Manila as a lay-brother. He returned to Japan as an interpreter to St Peter Baptist, with whom he was crucified at Nagasaki. Canonized in 1862.
Cf. Holw.

GUNDISALVUS (Bl) Ab. O.S.B. Cist.
A.C. June 6
d. 1466. Cistercian abbot of Azebeyro, in Spanish Galicia.
Cf. Zimm.

GUNDISALVUS HENRIQUEZ (Bl) M. S.J. A.C. July 15
d. 1570. A Portuguese deacon and a Jesuit scholastic, companion of Bl Ignatius de Azevedo, q.v.
Cf. Holw.

GUNDISALVUS FUSAI (Bl) M. S.J.
A.C. Sept. 10
1582-1622. A Japanese who held a high office at court but, after baptism, attached himself to the Jesuit missionaries. He was put in gaol at Omura, and there received into the Society of Jesus by Bl. Charles Spinola, with whom he was burnt alive at Nagasaki. Beatified in 1867.
Cf. Holw.

GUNDISALVUS (St) O.S.B. Cist.
A.C. Oct. 10
d. c.1135. First abbot, or prior, of the Cistercian abbey of Las Juniás, in Portugal, founded from Osera in 1135.
Cf. Zimm.

GUNDISALVUS of LAGOS (Bl) C. O.S.A.
A.C. Oct. 21
d. 1422. A native of Lagos in Portugal. He became an Augustinian, and excelled as a preacher. Cult approved in 1778.
Cf. Holw.

GUNDISALVUS (GONZALO) (Bl) Mk. O.S.B. A.C. Dec. 20
d. c.1073. Monk of the Benedictine abbey of Silos, in Old Castile, under its great abbot St Dominic.
Cf. Zimm.

GUNDLEUS (St) H. A.C. March 29
d. c.500. Gundleus is the latinized form of the Welsh Gwynllyn, anglicized as Woollos. He is said to have been the husband of St Gladys and the father of St Cadoc, and to have ended his life as a hermit in Wales. There is a church dedicated to him at Newport.
Cf. Att. — Holw.

GUNDULPHUS (St) Bp. R.M. June 17
6th cent. A bishop somewhere in Gaul, who is said to have died at Bourges.
Cf. Holw.

GUNIFORT (St) M. R.M. Aug. 8
? Said to have been a Northerner — Irish, Scottish or English — martyred at Pavia. The similarity of his legend with the history of St Richard and his children Winebald, Willibald and Walburga suggests some confusion of sources.
Cf. Menzies — Holw.

GUNTHER (Bl) Mk. O.S.B. A.C. Oct. 9
955-1045. A cousin of St Stephen of Hungary. He began life full of worldly ambition, but was brought to better ways by St Gothard of Hildesheim, and became a monk at Niederaltaich in Bavaria. But his ambitious nature asserted itself once more and he had himself made abbot of Göllingen, but proved a failure. Made wise by experience, he resigned and asked to live as a recluse for the rest of his life, thus amply compensating for his past restlessness.
Cf. Att. — Zimm. — Chev. — Holw.

GUNTHIERN (St) C. A.C. July 3
d. c.500. A Welsh prince who adopted the solitary life in Brittany.
Cf. Holw.

GUNTHILDIS (St) V. O.S.B.
A.C. Dec. 8
d. c.748. An English nun of Wimborne, who, at the request of St Boniface, passed over to Germany, and was abbess of a nunnery in Thuringia, and inspector of all the schools founded by the English nuns in the Germanies.
Cf. Baud. — Holw.

GUNTHRAMMUS (GONTRAM) (St) King R.M. March 28
d. 592. King of Burgundy. Having divorced his wife and over-hastily ordered the execution of his physician, he was overcome with remorse and lamented these sins for the rest of his life. On his death he was at once proclaimed a saint.
Cf. Att. — Baud. — Holw.

GURIAS amd SAMONAS (SS) MM.
R.M. Nov. 15
d. 306. Martyrs beheaded at Edessa in Syria under Diocletian.
Cf. Att. — Baud. — Holw.

GURLOËS (St) Ab. O.S.B. A.C. Aug. 25
d. 1057. A Benedictine monk, prior of Redon Abbey, who in 1029 became abbot of Sainte-Croix of Quimperlé in Brittany.
Cf. Zimm. — Chev.

GURVAL (St) Bp. A.C. June 6
Otherwise Gudwall, q.v.

GUTHAGON (St) C. A.C. July 3
8th cent. An Irishman who crossed over into Belgium, where he became a recluse.
Cf. Holw. — Baud.

GUTHLAC (St) H. O.S.B. A.C. Apr. 12
667-714. From being a warrior in the army of Ethelred, king of Mercia, Guthlac entered the Benedictine abbey of Repton, a double house under the abbess Elfrida where he was duly professed. Afterwards he asked to leave to become a recluse in the heart of the Lincolnshire fens: here he spent the last fifteen years of his life. At a later period the abbey of Croyland was erected on the site of his cell.
Cf. Att. — Zimm. — Mab. — Holw.

GUY
Note. This is the English form of the Latin Vitus and also of Guido. Variants in other languages are: — Gui, Gwin, Guidone, Viton, Wido, Witen, Wit, Wye, Wyden.

GUY (GUIDO) (St) Ab. O.S.B.
A.C. March 31
d. 1046. Born near Ravenna, Guy became a Benedictine at the abbey of St Severus in that city, of which he was chosen abbot. Afterwards he was promoted to the abbey of Pomposa, near Ferrara. He loved sacred learning, and at his request, St Peter Damian delivered lectures on the scriptures to his monks for two years. Towards the end of his life he was fiercely, though unjustly, persecuted by the bishop of Ravenna.
Cf. Att. — Zimm. — Chev. — Baud. — Holw.

GUY of VICOGNE (Bl) P. Praem.
A.C. March 31
d. 1147. Founder of the Premonstratensian abbey of Vicogne, in the diocese of Arras, whither he retired and was professed a member of the community.
Cf. Baud. — Holw.

GUY DE GHERARDESCA (Bl) H.
A.C. May 20
d. 1099. A native of Pisa, who led the life of a solitary at Campo in the diocese of Massa Maritima, in Italy.
Cf. Baud. — Holw.

GUY of ACQUI (Bl) Bp. A.C. June 2
d. 1070. Bishop of Acqui in Monferrato, Piedmont, from 1034 till 1070. Cult confirmed in 1853.
Cf. Baud.

GUY VIGNOTELLI (Bl) C. Tert. O.F.M.
A.C. June 16
1185-c.1245. A rich citizen of Cortona who gave up his wealth on hearing a sermon by St Francis of Assisi. He was received into the third order of St Francis by the holy Founder himself. Ordained a priest, he lived the rest of his life as a recluse near Cortona.
Cf. Att. — Baud. — Holw.

GUY (St) Ab. O.S.B. A.C. June 18
d. p. 940. The successor of Bl Berno in the abbey of Baume. About the year 940 he resigned and retired to a hermitage near Fay-en-Bresse.
Cf. Zimm.

GUY MARAMALDI (Bl) C. O.P.
A.C. June 25
d. 1391. A native of Naples who became a Dominican, taught philosophy and theology, established a friary at Ragusa, and died as the General Inquisitor for the kingdom of Naples. Cult confirmed in 1612.
Cf. Att. — Holw.

GUY (St) C. R.M. Sept. 12
d. c.1012. Surnamed "the Poor Man of Anderlecht." He was a native of Brabant and the sacristan of Our Lady of Laken, and afterwards for seven years a pilgrim in the Holy Land. On his return he was admitted to the public hospital at Anderlecht, near Brussels, where he died.
Cf. Att. — Baud. — Holw.

GUY of DURNES (Bl) Ab. O.S.B. Cist.
A.C. Sept. 23
d. c.1157. A monk of Clairvaux, and one of St Bernard's most beloved disciples. He was sent to be abbot-founder of Our Lady of Cherlieu, in the diocese of Besançon. At the request of St Bernard he revised the Cistercian liturgical chant, which was approved in the general chapter of 1150.
Cf. Butler-Thurston (Sept. 23) — Baud. — P. de U.

GUY of CASAURIA (Bl) Ab. O.S.B.
A.C. Nov. 23
d. 1045. A Benedictine of Farfa, who was promoted abbot of Casauria, near Chieti.
Cf. Chev. — Holw.

GWEN (BLANCA, BLANCHE) (St)
A.C. July 5
See Fragan and Gwen.

GWEN (St) W. A.C. Oct. 18
5th cent. Said to have been the sister of
St Nonna and therefore aunt to St David
of Wales. She is alleged to have been the
mother of SS Cyby and Cadfan.
Cf. Att. — Holw.

GWEN (CANDIDA, BLANCHE) (St)
W.M. A.C. Oct. 18
d. c.492. Reputed to have been a
daughter of Brychan of Brecknock,
murdered by the heathen Saxons at Tal-
garth.
Cf. Att. — Holw.

GWENDOLINE (St) V. O.S.B.
A.C. March 28
Otherwise Gundelindis, q.v.

GWENDOLINE (St) V. A.C. Oct. 18
See Brothen and Gwendolen.

GWENHAEL (St) Ab. A.C. Nov. 3
Otherwise Guenhael, q.v.

GWERIR (St) H. A.C. Apr. 4
? A hermit near Liskeard in Cornwall, at
whose grave King Alfred is said to have
been cured of a serious malady. St
Gwerir's cell was after his death occupied
by St Neot.
Cf. Holw.

GWINOC (St) C. A.C. Oct. 26
See Aneurin and Gwinoc.

H

Note. Names beginning with a vowel to
which by some an aspirate is prefixed,
by others not, will be found either under
the letter H or under the initial vowel,
according as the one or the other form may
appear the more usual or the more authentic.

HABACUC (HABAKKUK) (St) Prophet.
R.M. Jan. 15
6th cent. B.C. One of the twelve lesser
prophets. He prophesied in Judaea during the time of captivity. The reason why
his name has been inserted in the R.M. is
the alleged finding of his relics by bishop
Zebenus of Eleutheropolis under Theodosius the Great (379-383). Churches
have been dedicated to him in the Holy
Land.
Cf. Baud. — Holw.

HABAKUK (St) M. R.M. Jan. 19
Otherwise Abachum. See Marius, Matha,
etc.

HABENTIUS (St) M. R.M. June 7
See Peter, Wallabonsus, etc.

HABERILLA (HABRILIA) (Bl) V. O.S.B.
A.C. Jan. 30
d. c.1100. A virgin who became a recluse
under the obedience of the abbot of
Mehrerau, in Switzerland. Mehrerau at
that time was a Black Benedictine monastery.
Cf. Zimm. — P. de U. — Baud. — Holw.

HABET-DEUS (St) Bp. M. A.C. Feb. 17
d. c.500. Bishop of Luna in Tuscany, an
ancient city now in ruins. He was martyred by the Arian Vandals (?), and is now
venerated at Sarzana.
Cf. Holw. — Baud. — P.B.

HADELIN (St) Ab. O.S.B. A.C. Feb. 3
d. c.690. A native of Gascony who followed St Remaclus first to Solignac and
then to Maestricht and Stavelot. He became the founder of Celles, in the diocese
of Liége. He lived as a hermit near
Dinant on the Meuse.
Cf. Zimm. — Baud. — Holw.

HADELIN (St) Ab. O.S.B. A.C. June 27
d. c.700. A monk under St Landelinus,
who appointed him abbot of Crespin in
Hainault.
Cf. Zimm. — Baud. — Chev. — Holw.

HADELIN (ADELHEIM) (St) Bp. O.S.B.
A.C. Nov. 10
d. c.910. Monk and abbot of Saint-
Calais, and then bishop of Séez from
c.884 till 910.
Cf. Zimm. — Holw.

HADELOGA (St) V. O.S.B. A.C. Feb. 2
Otherwise Adeloga, q.v.

HADRIAN (*several*)
See Adrian.

HADUIN (HARDUIN) (St) Bp.
A.C. Aug. 20
d. c.662. A bishop of Le Mans, founder of the monastery of Notre-Dame-d'Evron.
Cf. Duch. Fast. Episc. — *Baud.* — *Holw.*

HADULPH (St) Bp. O.S.B. A.C. May 19
d. c.728. A prelate who simultaneously held the offices of abbot of Saint-Vaast and bishop of Arras-Cambrai.
Cf. Mab. — *Zimm.* — *Holw.* — *Baud.* — *Chev.* — *Duch. Fast. Episc.*

HADULPH (St) M. O.S.B.
R.M. June 5
d. 754. One of the Benedictine monks who shared St Boniface's martyrdom at Dokkum.
Cf. Zimm. — *Holw.*

HALWARD (HALLVARD) (St) M.
A.C. May 14
d. c.1043. A scion of the royal family of Norway. He is said to have met his death while defending from ill-usage a woman who had appealed to him for help. He is the patron saint of Oslo.
Cf. Att. — *Baud.* — *Holw.*

HARDOIN (St) Bp.   A.C. Nov. 29
7th cent. Bishop of St Pol-de-Léon in Brittany. The name is variously written: Ouardon, Wardon, Hoarzon, Huardo, etc.

HARDUIN (Bl) Mk. O.S.B. A.C. Apr. 20
d. 811. Born in the diocese of Rouen he became a Benedictine at Fontenelle (749). After a time he asked leave to live as a recluse near the abbey, and spent his leisure time copying the writings of the Fathers.
Cf. Baud. — *Holw.* — *P. de U.*

HARDULPH (St)   A.C. Aug. 21
? The church at Breedon-on-the-Hill in Leicestershire was dedicated to this saint, of whom nothing is known. He may be identical with the hermit of Bredon or Breedon mentioned in the life of St Modwenna, q.v.
Cf. Stanton.

HARMON (St) Bp.   R.M. July 31
Otherwise Germanus of Auxerre, q.v.

HAROLD (St) M.   A.C. March 25
d. 1168. A child said to have been put to death by Jews in Gloucester.
Cf. Stanton — *Holw.*

HARTMANN (Bl) Bp.   A.C. Dec. 23
d. 1164. A native of Polling in Austria, who was educated by the Augustinians of Passau, and became dean of the cathedral at Salzburg (1122) and eventually bishop of Brixen. He was highly respected by emperors and popes as well as by the poor people of his diocese. He did much for the canons regular, but was also a great benefactor of other religious, notably of the Benedictines. Cult confirmed in 1784.
Cf. Att. — *Baud.* — *Holw.*

HARTWIG (Bl) Bp.   A.C. June 14
d. 1023. Twenty-first archbishop of Salzburg (991-1023).
Cf. Baud. — *Holw.*

HARUCH (St) Bp. O.S.B.   A.C. July 15
d. c.830. Abbot and regionary bishop in the territory of Werden.
Cf. Zimm. — *Chev.* — *Holw.*

HATEBRAND (St) Ab. O.S.B.
A.C. July 30
d. 1198. A native of Frisia, who professed the Benedictine Rule at St Paul's, in Utrecht. In 1183 he became abbot of Olden-Klooster in his native land, and as such he revived the Benedictine life throughout Frisia.
Cf. Chev. — *Holw.* — *Baud.*

HATTO (Bl) Mk. O.S.B.   A.C. July 4
d. 985. Born of a noble Swabian family, he left all his property to the Benedictine abbey of Ottobeuren, and became a monk therein. Afterwards he lived as a recluse; but the abbot thought that he was showing too much attachment to his old property, and recalled him back to community life — a call which he at once obeyed.
Cf. Att. — *Zimm.* — *Holw.*

HEBEDJESUS (St)   R.M. Apr. 22
Otherwise Abdiesus, q.v.

HEDDA and Comp. MM. O.S.B.
A.C. Apr. 9
d. c.870. Hedda was the abbot of Peterborough (Medehampstead). He and eighty-four monks of his community were slain by the Danes, and thenceforward venerated as martyrs.
Cf. Holw. — *Stanton.*

HEDDA (St) Bp. O.S.B.   R.M. July 7
d. 705. An Anglo-Saxon monk and ab-

bot, probably of Whitby, who in 676 was made bishop of the divided diocese of Wessex. He resided first at Dorchester, near Oxford, whence he removed to the see of Winchester. He was a great benefactor of Malmesbury and King Ina's chief adviser. He ruled the diocese for about forty years.

Cf. Mab. — Att. — Baud. — Holw. — Stanton.

HEDWIG (Bl) Queen. **P.C. Feb. 28**
1371-1399. She succeeded her father Louis on the throne of Poland at the age of thirteen. She was married to Jagiello of Lithuania, but she made it a condition that he should become a Christian, which he did. Afterwards she was instrumental in bringing to the Faith many Lithuanians. She is venerated throughout Poland with a popular cult.

Cf. Att. — Baud.

HEDWIG (HADWIGIS) (Bl) Abs. O.S.B.
A.C. Sept. 13
d. c.887. A niece of Bl Warinus of Corvey. She became a Benedictine nun and abbot of Herford (*Herivordien*) in Westphalia.

Cf. Zimm. — Chev. — Holw.

HEDWIG (JADWIGA) (St) W. O.S.B.
Cist. **R.M. Oct. 16**
c. 1174-1243. Born at Andechs in Bavaria, but of Moravian descent, she was the daughter of the duke of Croatia and Dalmatia, and the aunt of St Elisabeth of Hungary. She was educated by the Benedictine nuns of Hitzingen in Franconia, and at the age of twelve was married to the duke of Silesia, head of the Polish royal family. She bore him seven children, who were in after-life the cause of great anxiety to their parents. The king and the queen were at one in fostering the religious life in their kingdom. Among other houses, they founded the Cistercian nunnery of Trebnitz, whither Hedwig retired in her widowhood. She was canonized in 1266.

Cf. Att. — Zimm. — Chev. — Baud. — Holw. — Prop. Cist.

HEGESIPPUS (St) C. **R.M. Apr. 7**
d. c.180. A Jew and a native of Jerusalem who spent twenty years of his life in Rome. He is considered the father of ecclesiastical history and the first to trace the succession of popes from St Peter to his own day. Only a few chapters of his work remain. It was warmly commended by Eusebius and by St Jerome, who knew it well and made use of it.

Cf. Att. — Holw. — Baud.

HEIMRAD (St) Mk. O.S.B.
P.C. June 28
d. 1019. A priest of Baden, who, after many pilgrimages, lived as a monk at Hersfeld, and then as a hermit at Hasungen in Westphalia. In his wanderings throughout Europe he was often taken for a lunatic rather than a pilgrim. His cult has never been officially confirmed.

Cf. Att. — Holw.

HELDRAD (ELDRAD) (St) Ab. O.S.B.
A.C. March 13
d. 842. A native of Provence who spent his large fortune in good works, and then set out on a pilgrimage to Rome. He heard from other pilgrims of the Benedictine abbey of Novalese, at the foot of the Alps, and joined that community. After a time he was made abbot and ruled the house for thirty years. The library was his special care. He was moreover a great builder, and had a hospice erected at the highest point of Mt Cenis pass. Cult approved in 1904.

Cf. Att. — Baud. — Chev. — Zimm.

HELANUS (St) H. **R.M. Oct. 7**
6th cent. An Irishman who crossed over to France, it is said, with six brothers and three sisters, and settled near Reims. He was ordained priest and ministered to the people of the neighbourhood.

Cf. Baud. — Holw.

HELEN of POLAND (Bl) W.
A.C. March 6
d. 1298. Daughter of Bela IV of Hungary. In 1256 she married Boleslas V of Poland, after whose death (1279) she lived as a Poor Clare at Gnesen. Cult approved in 1827.

Cf. Holw.

HELEN VALENTINI (Bl) W.
A.C. Apr. 23
d. 1458. A lady of Udine noted by her contemporaries both for her devotion to the duties of married life for twenty-five years and for her charity and austerities as an Augustinian tertiary after her husband's death. Cult confirmed in 1848.

Cf. Att. — Menzies.

HELEN (St) V.   **R.M. May 22**
d. p. 418. A maiden mentioned in the Acts of St Amator of Auxerre as assisting him on his deathbed.
Cf. Baud. — Holw.

HELEN (HELENA) (St) V. M.
                          A.C. June 24
Otherwise Alena, q.v.

HELEN of SKÖFDE (St) W. M.
                          A.C. July 31
d. c.1160. A noble Swedish lady, who, left a widow, spent her fortune in the service of the poor and the church. She was barbarously put to death in a family feud. Canonized in 1164.
Cf. Att. — Baud. — Holw.

HELEN (St) M.   **R.M. Aug. 13**
See Centolla and Helen.

HELEN (St) Empress.   **R.M. Aug. 18**
c. 250-c. 330. An Asiatic by birth, probably a native of Bithynia (certainly not of Britain), who became the wife of Constantius Chlorus, to whom she bore a child who became Constantine the Great. Helen became a Christian after the Edict of Milan (313), and spent the rest of her life in the East and in Rome. She helped in the building of several Roman basilicas and many churches in the Holy Land. Her name is chiefly associated with the discovery of the True Cross in a rock-cistern near Mt Calvary.
Cf. Att. — Baud. — Holw. — Menzies.

HELEN DUGLIOLI (Bl) W.
                          A.C. Sept. 23
1472-1520. A native of Bologna, who, to please her mother, married against her own inclinations, and lived a happy married life for thirty years. After her husband's death she devoted herself completely to works of charity. Already revered as a saint during her life, she was venerated as such after her death. Cult confirmed in 1828.
Cf. Att. — Baud. — Holw.

HELEN ENSELMINI (Bl) V. Poor Clare.
                          A.C. Nov. 4
d. 1242. A native of Padua, who at the age of twelve received the veil of the Poor Clares from St Francis himself at Arcella, near her native city. It is narrated of her that her only food for months was the Blessed Eucharist. Before her death she became blind and dumb. Cult approved in 1695.
Cf. Menzies — Holw. — Att. — Baud.

HELIA (HELIADA) (St) Abs. O.S.B.
                          A.C. June 20
d. c.750. A Benedictine abbess of the nunnery of Öhren (*Horreum*) at Trèves.
Cf. Zimm.

HELICONIS (St) M.   **R.M. May 28**
d ? 250. A woman of Thessalonica, who was arrested at Corinth and beheaded, during the persecution of Decius.
Cf. Holw.

HELIER (HELEROUS) (St) M.
                          A.C. July 16
6th cent. A native of Tongres (Limburg), who lived as a hermit in the island of Jersey and was murdered by a heathen whom he was endeavouring to convert.
Cf. Att. — Baud. — Holw.

HELIMENAS (St) M.   **R.M. Apr. 22**
See Parmenius, Helimenas, etc.

HELINAND (ELINANDUS) (Bl or St) C. O.S.B. Cist.   **A.C. Feb. 3**
d. 1237. A native of Pronleroy (Oise) in the diocese of Beauvais, who from being a court singer, was converted and became a Cistercian at Froidmont. The Cistercians venerate him as a saint.
Cf. Baud. — Holw. — P.B.

HELIODORUS, VENUSTUS and Comp. (SS) MM.   **R.M. May 6**
3rd cent. A group of seventy-seven martyrs who suffered under Diocletian. Heliodorus and seven others seem to have been martyred in Africa; St Ambrose claims the greater part of the rest for Milan.
Cf. Holw. — Baud.

HELIODORUS (St) Bp.   **R.M. July 3**
c. 332-c. 390. A Dalmatian who, early in life, became an intimate friend of St Jerome, whom he followed to Palestine and helped financially and otherwise, in the preparation of the Vulgate. Later he settled in Aquileia and was made bishop of Altinum, a small town, since destroyed, near Venice. He was a great bishop, and a brave opponent of Arianism.
Cf. Att. — Baud. — Menzies — Holw.

HELIODORUS (St) M.   **R.M. Sept. 28**
See Mark, Alphius, etc.

HELIODORUS and Comp. (SS) MM.
                 R.M. Nov. 21
d. c.270. A group of martyrs, who suffered under Aurelian in Pamphylia. *Cf. Holw. — Baud.*

HELLADIUS (St) M.   **R.M. Jan. 8**
See Theophilus and Helladius.

HELLADIUS of TOLEDO (St) Bp.
                 R.M. Feb. 18
d. 632. A native of Toledo, and a minister of the court of the Visigothic kings. He loved to pay frequent visits to the abbey of Agali (Agallia) near Toledo on the banks of the Tagus, until one day he joined the community and eventually was made its abbot (605). In 615 he was promoted archbishop of Toledo.
Cf. Att. — P. de U. — Baud. — Holw.

HELLADIUS of AUXERRE (St) Bp.
                 R.M. May 8
d. 387. Bishop of Auxerre in France for thirty years. He converted his own successor St Amator to a devout life.
Cf. Duch. Fast. Episc. — Gams — Chev. — Baud. — Holw.

HELLADIUS (St) M.   **R.M. May 28**
See Crescens, Dioscoorides, etc.

HELWISA (Bl) H. O.S.B.   **A.C. Feb. 11**
d. p. 1066. A recluse under the obedience of the Benedictine abbey of Coulombs in Normandy.
Cf. Zimm.

HEMITERIUS and CHELEDONIUS (SS) MM.   **R.M. March 3**
? 4th cent. Two Spanish martyrs, believed to have been soldiers, who suffered at Calahorra in Old Castile. Their Acts have been lost; but both Prudentius and St Gregory of Tours have handed down to us the few details we have of them.
Cf. P. de U. — Holw. — Baud.

HEMMA (*several*)
Otherwise Gemma, q.v.

HENEDINA (St) M.   **R.M. May 14**
See Justa, Justina and Henedina.

HENRY
Note. A Teuton name latinized into Henricus. The most common variants in other languages are — German, Heinrich; French, Henri; Danish, Eric; Spanish and Portuguese, Enrique; Hungarian, Emeric; Italian, Enrico (Arrigo, Amerigo — whence America) etc.

HENRY (St) H. O.S.B.   **A.C. Jan. 16**
d. 1127. A Dane by birth, he lived as a recluse on Cocket Island, off the coast of Northumberland, under the obedience of the monks of Tynemouth to whom the island belonged. Tynemouth itself was a daughter-house of St Alban's. He was buried at Tynemouth.
Cf. Att. — Holw. — Baud. — Zimm. — Stanton.

HENRY of UPSALA (St) Bp. M.
                 A.C. Jan. 19
d. c.1156. An Englishman who accompanied King St Eric to Sweden as bishop of Upsala (1152), and then to Finland as a member of an expedition led by the same king. He was murdered by a Finn whom he had excommunicated. He was canonized in 1158 and is venerated as a martyr and as the patron saint of Finland.
Cf. Att. — Baud. — Holw.

HENRY MORSE (Bl) M. S.J.
                 A.C. Feb. 1
d. 1645. A native of Norfolk (or Suffolk?) and a convert, who after being a member of the Inns Court, studied for the priesthood at Douai in Rome. He entered the Society of Jesus in 1625 and worked in London. He was martyred for his priesthood at Tyburn. Beatified in 1929.
Cf. Newdigate.

HENRY SUSO (Bl) C. O.P.
                 A.C. March 2
c.1295-1365. A native of Bihlmeyer, near Constance, who joined the Friars Preachers at an early age, was prior in several houses of the order, and excelled as a director of souls. He is one of the greatest Dominican mystics and his *Book of the Eternal Wisdom* is still one of the most widely read classics on Christian mysticism. Cult approved in 1381.
Cf. Prop. O.P. — Att. — Holw.

HENRY of GHEEST (Bl) C. O.S.B. Cist.
                 A.C. Apr. 4
d. c.1190. A Cistercian monk at Villiers, in the diocese of Namur. His relics were solemnly raised in 1599.
Cf. Zimm. — Holw.

HENRY WALPOLE (Bl) M. S.J.
A.C. Apr. 7
d. 1595. A native of Docking, Norfolk, who was educated at Norwich, Cambridge (Peterhouse) and Gray's Inn. He was reconciled to the Church, and studied for the priesthood at the English College, Rome, there entering the Society of Jesus (1584). Ordained in 1588, he worked at York. Here also he was martyred for his priesthood. Beatified in 1929.
Cf. Att. — Newdigate.

HENRY the SHOEMAKER (Bl) C.
? P.C. June 9
d. 1666. Henry Michael Buche — "der gute Heinrich" — was a native of Luxemburg, and a shoemaker by trade. In 1645 he settled at Paris and, with the help of Baron de Renti, founded the confraternity of SS Crispinus and Crispinianus (Frères Cordonniers), for his fellow-craftsmen, He is usually called "saint" or "blessed" but there is no evidence of cult.
Cf. Att. — Holw.

HENRY of TREVISO (Bl) C. A.C. June 10
d. 1315. Usually called in Italy, San Rigo (a diminutive form of Arrigo). He was born at Bolzano in the Tyrol, but lived at Treviso, earning his daily bread as a hired labourer (*facchino*). In his old age he lived on alms. Cult approved by Benedict XIV.
Cf. Att. — Baud. — Holw.

HENRY (HERIC) (Bl) C. O.S.B.
A.C. June 24
d. c.880. A native of Hery (Yonne), who became a Benedictine, and the headmaster of the monastic school, at Saint-Germain d'Auxerre. He was also a hagiographer.
Cf. Zimm. — Chev.

HENRY ZDIK (Bl) Bp. O. Praem.
P.C. June 25
d. 1150. A son of King Wratislas I of Bohemia who was elected bishop of Olmütz in 1126. In 1137 he went to Palestine and donned the Premonstratensian habit at Jerusalem. On his return to his diocese he introduced the Premonstratensians in many places and founded for them the abbey of Strahov.
Cf. Att. — Holw.

HENRY of ALBANO (Bl) Bp. O.S.B. Cist.
A.C. July 4
d. 1188. Usually surnamed "Henricus Gallus." He was a French Cistercian who became cardinal bishop of Albano in 1179, and died at Arras.
Cf. Gams.

HENRY ABBOT (Bl) M. **A.C. July 4**
d. 1597. A native of Howden, in Yorkshire. He was a layman and a convert, and was, for this reason, hanged at York. Beatified in 1929.
Cf. Newdigate.

HENRY II (St) Emperor. **R.M. July 15**
972-1024. Henry the Good was born in Bavaria and was educated by St Wolfgang of Ratisbon. From being duke of Bavaria he was raised to the imperial throne in 1002. He, with his wife St Cunegundis, were providentially raised up to protect the Church in that troublous period. Henry, though very much a political and temporal ruler, had always at heart the welfare of religion, and readily co-operated with the Benedictine abbeys of that time — Cluny, Montecassino, Camaldoli, Eiasiedeln, St Emmeran, Verdun, Gorsch — in the restoration of ecclesiastical and social discipline. He himself tried to become a Benedictine, and was for this reason officially declared by Pius X the patron saint of the Benedictine Oblates. Canonized in 1146.
Cf. Zimm.—Chev.—Att.—Baud.—Holw.

HENRY of COLOGNE (Bl) C. O.P.
P.C. Oct. 23
d. 1225. One of the first Dominicans recruited from among the students of the university of Paris, who became the first prior of the friary at Cologne. He was a friend of Bl. Jordan.
Cf. Holw.

HENRY of ZWIEFALTEN (Bl) C. O.S.B.
P.C. Nov. 4
d. p. 1250. A Benedictine monk of the abbey of Zwiefalten, who became prior of Ochsenhausen. Both monasteries were in Swabia.
Cf. Chev. — Holw.

HERACLAS (St) Bp. **R.M. July 14**
d. 247. An Egyptian, brother of St Plutarch the martyr. He was at first a pupil and afterwards the successor of Origen as head of the catechetical school of Alexandria. He was raised to the pastoriarchal see in 231.
Cf. Holw. — Baud.

HERACLEA (St) M. R.M. Sept. 29
See Eutychius, Plautus and Heraclea.

HERACLIDES (St) M. R.M. June 28
See Plutarch, Serenus, etc.

HERACLIUS (St) M. R.M. March 2
See Paul, Heraclius, etc.

HERACLIUS and ZOSIMUS (SS) MM.
  R.M. March 11
d. c.263. African martyrs who suffered at
Carthage under Valerian and Gallienus.
Cf. Holw. — Baud.

HERACLIUS (St) M. R.M. May 26
See Felicissimus, Heraclius and Paulinus.

HERACLIUS of SENS (St) Bp.
  R.M. June 8
d. c.515. The fourteenth bishop of Sens.
He was present in the cathedral of Reims
at the baptism of Clovis (25 Dec. 496).
He built the abbey of St John the Evan-
gelist at Sens, where he was buried.
Cf. Duch. Fast. Episc. — Gams — Baud.

HERACLIUS (St) M. R.M. Sept. 1
See Priscus, Castrensis, etc.

HERACLIUS (St) M. R.M. Oct. 22
See Alexander, Heraclius and Comp.

**HERADIUS, PAUL, AQUILINUS and
Comp. (SS) MM.** R.M. May 17
d. 303. Five martyrs put to death at
Nyon (*Noviodunum*) on the lake of
Geneva, under Diocletian.
Cf. Holw. — Baud.

HERAIS (St) V. M. R.M. Sept. 22
Otherwise Irais, q.v.

HERBERT (St) H. A.C. March 20
d. 687. A priest, friend of St Cuthbert,
who lived as a solitary on the island named
after him on Lake Derwentwater. The
two saints were granted their prayer to die
on the same day.
*Cf. Att. — Baud. — Holw. — Zimm. —
Stanton.*

HERBERT HOSCAM (St) Bp.
  A.C. Aug. 20
d. 1180. An Englishman by birth, who
became archbishop of Conza, in the
Basilicata, Italy. He is venerated as the
principal patron saint of Conza.
Cf. Holw. — Baud. — Menzies.

**HERBERT (HABERNE, HERBERN) (St)
Bp. O.S.B.** A.C. Oct. 30
? Abbot of Marmoutier, and afterwards
archbishop of Tours.
Cf. Baud. — Holw.

**HERCULANUS of PIEGARE (Bl) C.
O.F.M.** A.C. June 1
d. 1541. A native of Piegare, near Perugia,
he joined the Franciscans, and became one
of their foremost preachers. Beatified in
1860.
Cf. Att. — Baud. — Holw.

HERCULANUS of BRESCIA (St) Bp.
  R.M. Aug. 12
d. c.550. A bishop of Brescia in Lombardy.
Cf. Menzies — Holw. — Baud.

HERCULANUS (St) M. R.M. Sept. 5
d. ? c.180. A martyr who suffered at
Porto, near Rome, probably under Marcus
Aurelius.
Cf. Menzies — Baud. — Holw.

HERCULANUS (St) M. R.M. Sept. 25
2nd cent. A Roman soldier, mentioned
in the untrustworthy Acts of St Alexander I as having been converted by the
pontiff and martyred shortly afterwards.
Cf. Holw. — Baud.

HERCULANUS (St) Bp. R.M. Nov. 7
d. 549. A bishop of Perugia, beheaded by
the soldiers of Totila, the marauding
leader of the Ostro-Goths.
Cf. Ricci — Menzies — Att. — Holw.

HEREBALD (HERBAND) (St) C.
  A.C. June 11
8th cent. A native of Britain who embraced the solitary life in Brittany, where
a church is dedicated to him.
Cf. Stanton — Holw.

HERENA (St) M. R.M. Feb. 25
See Donatus, Justus, etc.

HERENIA (St) M. R.M. March 8
See Cyril, Rogatus, etc.

HERESWITHA (St) W. O.S.B.
  A.C. Sept. 3
d. c.690. A Northumbrian princess, sister
of St Hilda and mother of SS Sexburga,
Withburga and Ethelburga. She spent
the closing years of her life as a nun at
Chelles in France.
Cf. Stanton — Chev. — Holw. — Zimm.

HERIBALDUS (St) Bp. O.S.B. A.C. Apr. 25
d. c.857. A Benedictine monk and abbot
of the monastery of St Germanus, at
Auxerre, who was promoted bishop of the
same city.
*Cf. Duch. Fast. Episc. — Gams — Att. —
Holw. — Baud.*

HERIBERT (St) Bp. R.M. March 16
d. 1022. Born at Worms, and educated
by the Benedictines of Gorze, he became
chancellor to the emperor Otto III and
(998) archbishop of Cologne. He was an
outstanding churchman, learned, zealous
and enterprising. He built the Benedictine abbey of Deutz on the Rhine where he
was buried.
Cf. Holw. — Att. — Baud.

**HERLINDIS and RELINDIS (SS) Abs.
O.S.B. A.C. Oct. 12**
d. c.745. Daughters of Count Adelard,
who built for them the nunnery of
Maaseyk, on the Meuse, of which they
became respectively first and second
abbesses. They were friends of SS Willibrord and Boniface.
Cf. Chev. — Baud. — Holw.

HERLUIN (Bl) Ab. O.S.B. P.C. Aug. 26
d. 1078. A native of Normandy who was
bred to the profession of arms and served
as a knight at the court of the count of
Brionne. He left it to found a monastery
on his own estate at Bonneville, of which
he became abbot. In 1040 the community moved to a new site on the banks
of the little river Bec. One of the first
novices was Bl Lanfranc; shortly afterwards came St Anselm. Under these
three great men Bec became the foremost
school of Christendom. Herluin has
always been given the title of *Beatus.*
Cf. Att. — Zimm. — Holw. — Baud.

**HERMAGORAS and FORTUNATUS
(SS) MM. R.M. July 12**
d. c.66. According to tradition, St Herma-
goras was a disciple of St Mark, by whom
he was appointed first bishop of Aquileia.
After a fruitful apostolate he and his deacon
Fortunatus were beheaded under Nero.
Cf. Menzies — Baud. — Holw. — Att.

**HERMAN of ZÄHRINGEN (Bl) Mk.
O.S.B. A.C. March 25**
d. 1074. Margrave of Zähringen, who
became a monk at Cluny.
Cf. Holw. — P.B.

**HERMAN JOSEPH (Bl) C. O. Praem.
A.C. Apr. 7**
c.1150-1241. A native of Cologne, who, at
an early age, began to have mystical
experiences which made him famous
throughout the Germanies. He joined
the Premonstratensians at Steinfeld and
has left some remarkable mystical writings. He had a special devotion to St
Irsula.
Cf. Att. — Baud. — Holw.

**HERMAN of HEIDELBERG (Bl) H.
O.S.B. P.C. Sept. 3**
d. c.1326. A Benedictine monk professed
at Niederaltaich in Bavaria in 1320, who
lived as a hermit. An altar is dedicated
to him in the parish church of Rinchnach.
Cf. Holw.

**HERMAN the CRIPPLE (CONTRAC-
TUS) (Bl) Mk. O.S.B. P.C. Sept. 25**
d. 1054. His nickname "the Cripple"
describes his physical condition. He was
offered as a child of seven to the abbey of
Reichenau on the Rhine, and became the
most famous religious poet of his age. He
has always been given the title of *Beatus.*
Cf. Mab. — Zimm.

**HERMAN (Bl) Ab. O. Praem.
A.C. Dec. 23**
d. c.1200. A Jew, born in Cologne, who
became a Christian and joined the
Premonstratensians. He was elected first
abbot of Scheda in the archdiocese of
Cologne.
Cf. Holw.

HERMAS (St) Bp. R.M. May 9
1st cent. A Roman, whom St Paul mentions in his Epistle to the Romans (XVI,
14). A Greek tradition makes him bishop
of Philippi and a martyr.
Cf. Holw. — Baud.

**HERMAS, SERAPION and POLY-
AENUS (SS) MM. R.M. Aug. 18**
? Roman martyrs who were dragged by
their feet over rough ground till they expired; they were the victims of the infuriated mob.
Cf. Holw. — Baud.

HERMAS (St) M. R.M. Nov. 4
See Nicander and Hermas.

HERMELLUS (St) M. R.M. Aug. 3
? An Eastern solitary, venerated at Con-

stantinople from the earliest times, about whom, however, nothing is known.
Cf. Holw. — Baud.

HERMENEGILD (St) M. R.M. Apr. 13
d. 585. Son of the Visigothic king of Spain Leovigild, and brought up an Arian at the court of Seville. He became a Catholic on his marriage to the daughter of Sigebert of Austrasia. His father disinherited him on account of his change of religion, whereupon he rose in arms, was defeated and captured and, on refusing to give up the Catholic faith, was put to death at the instigation of his stepmother.
Cf. Att. — Holw. — P. de U.

HERMENEGILD (St) Mk. O.S.B.
A.C. Nov. 5
d. 953. A Spanish Benedictine of Salcedo in the diocese of Tuy, in Spanish Galicia — one of those who helped in the spreading of Benedictinism throughout N. W. Spain under St Rudesind.
Cf. Chev. — Holw.

HERMENGAUDIUS (ARMENGOL) (St) Bp. R.M. Nov. 3
d. 1035. Bishop of Urgell, in the Spanish Pyrenees, from 1010 till 1035. He built the cathedral and gave its canons a rule of life based on that of St Augustine.
Cf. Holw. — Baud. — P. de U.

HERMENLAND (HERMELAND, HERBLAND, ERBLON) R.M. March 25
d. c.720. A native of the diocese of Noyon, he served in his youth as royal cup-bearer. Then he withdrew to Fontenelle and became a monk under St Lambert. He was ordained priest and sent, with a band of twelve monks, to establish a new abbey on the island of Aindre, in in the estuary of the Loire.
Cf. Zimm. — Mab. — Chev. — Att.

HERMES, AGGAEUS and CAIUS (SS) MM. R.M. Jan. 4
d. c.300. There is some uncertainty as to where these martyrs suffered. The R.M. says at Bologna, under Maximian; but it is now thought that Bononia on the Danube was the scene of their martyrdom. A feast celebrated in their honour at Bologna was abolished in 1914.
Cf. Holw. — Baud.

HERMES and ADRIAN (SS) MM.
R.M. March 1
d. c.290. Martyrs who suffered under Maximian Herculius. The R.M. says "at Marseilles" but most writers now identify this group of martyrs — Hermes and Adrian are only the first in a list of twenty-six — with "the Massylitan martyrs on whose birthday St Augustine delivered a discourse" (see R.M. Apr. 9). The original reading of the martyrology was *Massylis* (Marula) in Numidia, the spelling of which is very similar to the Latin *Massilia* (Marseilles).
Cf. Holw. — Baud.

HERMES and Comp. (SS) MM.
R.M. Aug. 28
d. c.120. Roman martyrs who perished under the judge Aurelian, and are mentioned in the Acts of Pope St Alexander.
Cf. Att. — Baud. — Holw. — Menzies.

HERMES (St) M. R.M. Oct. 22
See Philip, Severus, etc.

HERMES (St) M. R.M. Nov. 2
See Publius, Victor, etc.

HERMES (St) M. R.M. Dec. 31
d. c.270. A cleric, of the rank of exorcist, who is believed to have suffered under Aurelian. He may be the same as the martyr commemorated on Jan. 4.
Cf. Holw. — Baud.

HERMIAS (St) M. R.M. May 31
d. 170. A veteran soldier, martyred at Comana in Cappadocia — not in Pontus, as Baronius thought. He has a prominent place in the Greek liturgy.
Cf. Holw. — Baud.

HERMIONE (St) V. A.C. Sept. 4
d. c.117. One of the daughters of Philip the Deacon, mentioned in the Acts of the Apostles (XXI, 9) as a prophetess. She is said to have died a martyr at Ephesus.
Cf. Holw. — Baud.

HERMIPPUS (St) M. R.M. July 27
See Hermolaus, Hermippis and Hermocrates.

HERMOCRATES (St) M. R.M. July 27
See Hermolaus, Hermippus and Hermocrates.

HERMOGENES (St) M. R.M. Apr. 17
See Peter and Hermogenes.

HERMOGENES, CAIUS, EXPEDITUS, ARISTONICUS, RUFUS and GALATA (SS) MM. R.M. Apr. 19
? Armenian martyrs who are believed to have suffered at Melitene.
Cf. Baud. — Holw.

HERMOGENES (St) M. R.M. Apr. 25
See Evodius, Hermogenes and Callistus.

HERMOGENES (St) M. R.M. Dec. 10
See Mennas, Hermogenes and Eugraphus.

HERMOGENES, DONATUS and Comp. (SS) MM. R.M. Dec. 12
? Twenty-four martyrs, said to have been driven into a marsh and there left to perish of cold and exhaustion.
Cf. Holw. — Baud.

HERMOGIUS (St) Bp. O.S.B.
A.C. June 26
d. c.942. A native of Tuy and founder of the abbey of Labrugia (915) in Spanish Galicia. He was taken captive by the Moors and brought to Cordova, but was subsequently given his freedom; his nephew, the boy St Pelagius, being retained there as a hostage. St Hermogius resigned his see and retired to Ribas del Sil.
Cf. P. de U.

HERMOLAUS, HERMIPPUS and HERMOCRATES (SS) MM.
R.M. July 27
d. c.300. St Hermolaus, an aged priest of Nicomedia, having succeeded in converting St Pantaleon, the imperial physician, was martyred with him and with the two brothers Hermippus and Hermogenes.
Cf. Holw. — Baud.

HERMYLUS and STRATONICUS (SS) MM. R.M. Jan. 13
d. 315. Hermylus, a deacon of *Singidunum* (Belgrade) and Stratonicus his servant, were drowned in the Danube under Licinius.
Cf. Holw. — Baud.

HERNAN (St) C. A.C. Sept. 15
6th cent. A native of Britain, who took refuge in Brittany at the time of the Anglo-Saxon conquest. He lived as a solitary at a place called after him Loc-Harn, and he is the patron saint of that village.
Cf. Holw.

HERODION, ASYNCRITUS and PHLEGON (SS) MM. R.M. Apr. 8
1st cent. Herodion, whom St Paul styles his kinsman (Rom XVI, 11), with Asyncritus and Phlegon, likewise mentioned by the Apostle, are said to have become bishops, Herodion of Patras, Asyncritus of Marathon and Phlegon of Hyrcania, and to have been done to death at the instigation of the Jews.
Cf. Holw. — Att.

HERON (St) M. R.M. June 28
See Plutarch, Serenus, etc.

HERON (St) Bp. M. R.M. Oct. 17
d. c.136. The disciple, and successor of St Ignatius in the see of Antioch, which he governed for twenty years (c.116-c.136). He died a martyr.
Cf. Holw. — Baud.

HERON, ARSENIUS, ISIDORE and DIOSCORUS (SS) MM. R.M. Dec. 14
d. 250. The three first named were burnt to death at Alexandria in Egypt under Decius. Dioscorus, a boy, was whipped and then dismissed.
Cf. Holw. — Baud.

HEROS (St) M. R.M. June 24
See Orentius, Heros, etc.

HERULPH (HARIOLFUS) (St) Bp. O.S.B. A.C. Aug. 13
d. 785. A son of the count of Ellwangen. He became a Benedictine at St Gall and afterwards founded the abbey of Ellwangen (764) in the diocese of Augsburg. He was later raised to the see of Langres.
Cf. Chev. — Holw. — Baud.

HERUNDO (St) V. R.M. July 23
See Romula, Redempta and Herundo.

HERVEUS (HERVÉ) (St) Ab.
A.C. June 1
d. c.575. A Welsh saint and singer, blind from his childhood. He was taken very young to Brittany, where he grew up to become a teacher and minstrel. Though blind he became abbot of Plouvien, whence he migrated with part of his community to Lanhouarneau. He is still a most popular saint in Brittany. In art he is represented as blind, and led about by a wolf.
Cf. Att. — Baud. — Holw.

HERVEUS (Bl) H.   A.C. July 18
d. 1130. A native of the British Isles, he
led the life of an anchorite on the island of
Chalonnes, in Anjou.
Cf. Zimm. — Baud. — Holw.

HESPERIUS (St) M.   R.M. May 2
Otherwise Exuperius, q.v.

HESSO (ESSO) (Bl) Ab. O.S.B.
          A.C. Dec. 27
d. 1133. Benedictine monk and procurator of Hirschau under St William. He was
sent to Beinwil in Switzerland as its first
abbot (1085).
Cf. Prop. Beinwil. — Holw.

HESYCHIUS (St) Bp.   R.M. May 15
See Torquatus, Ctesiphon, etc.

HESYCHIUS (St) M.   R.M. June 15
d. c.302. A Roman soldier martyred at
Dorestorum (Sillistria) in Maesia, together with the veteran St Julius.
Cf. Holw. — Baud.

HESYCHIUS (St) M.   R.M. July 7
See Diomedes, Julian, Lucian, etc.

HESYCHIUS (St) M.   R.M. Sept. 2
See Diomedes.

HESYCHIUS (St) H.   R.M. Oct. 3
d. c.380. A disciple of St Hilarion, under
whom he became a monk at Majuma,
near Gaza, in Palestine. He followed his
master from solitude to solitude, and
when St Hilarion fled to Sicily, St Hesychius spent three years searching for him.
At St Hilarion's death (371) he conveyed
the remains back to Majuma, where he
lived until his own death.
Cf. Att. — Baud. — Holw.

HESYCHIUS (St) M.   R.M. Nov. 7
See Hieron, Nicander, etc.

HESYCHIUS of ANTIOCH (St) M.
          R.M. Nov. 18
d. c.303. A Roman soldier who cast away
his military belt (the *cingulum militare*)
proclaiming himself a Christian. As a
punishment for this he was drowned in the
river Orontes.
Cf. Holw. — Baud.

HESYCHIUS (St) Bp. M.   R.M. Nov. 26
See Faustus, Didius, etc.

HEWALD (SS) MM.   R.M. Oct. 3
Otherwise Ewald, q.v.

HIA (IA, IVES) (St) V.   A.C. Feb. 3
Otherwise Ia, q.v.

HIDULPHUS (St) Mk. O.S.B.
          A.C. June 23
d. c.707. Count of Hainault and a courtier at the royal palace of Austrasia. He
married St Aye, but by mutual consent
they became religious, Hidulphus entering
the abbey of Lobbes, which he had helped
to found.
Cf. Chev. — Holw. — Baud.

HIDULPHUS (St) Bp. O.S.B.
          A.C. July 11
d. 707. A native of Ratisbon who became a monk of the abbey of Maximinus,
at Trèves. At a later date he was consecrated a regionary bishop; but about
the year 676 he resigned, and founded the
Benedictine abbey of Moyenmoutier.
When he died he was abbot both of
Moyenmoutier and Bonmoutier (Galilaea,
afterwards called Saint-Dié).
*Cf. Mab. — Zimm. — Baud. — Att. —
Chev.*

HIERLATH (St) Bp.   A.C. Feb. 1
Otherwise Jarlath, q.v.

HIERO (IERO) (St) M.   A.C. Aug. 17
d. 885. An Irish missionary in Holland,
where he died a martyr.
Cf. O' Hanlon.

**HIERON, NICANDER, HESYCHIUS
and Comp. (SS) MM.**   R.M. Nov. 7
d. c.300. A group of thirty-three Armenian martyrs, who suffered at Mitilene
under Diocletian.
Cf. Holw. — Baud.

**HIERONIDES, LEONTIUS, SERAPION,
(SELESIUS) SELEUCUS, VALERIAN
and STRATON (SS) MM. R.M. Sept. 12**
d. c.300. Martyrs, cast into the sea at
Alexandria in Egypt under Diocletian.
Hieronides was a deacon far advanced in
years; Leontius and Serapion were
brothers. The name Selesius should be
Seleucus.
Cf. Holw. — Baud.

HIEROTHEUS (St) Bp.   R.M. Oct. 4
? The alleged teacher and friend of St

Dionysius the Areopagite. Modern writers either deny his existence or post-date him to the fourth or fifth century.
Cf. Holw. — Baud.

HIEU (St) V. A.C. Sept. 2
d. c.657. A Northumbrian maiden who received the veil from St Aidan, by whom she was made abbess of Tadcaster in Yorkshire. By some St Hieu is thought to be one and the same with St Bega or Bee.
Cf. Holw. — Baud.

HILARIA, DIGNA, EUPREPIA, EUNOMIA, QUIRIACUS, LARGIO, CRESCENTIAN, NIMMIA, JULIANA and Comp. (SS) MM. R.M. Aug. 12
d. c.304. A group of twenty-nine martyrs put to death at Augsburg under Diocletian. Hilaria is the alleged mother of St Afra, q.v. She and her three maids were seized while burying St Alfa and burnt alive. All these names and details are very doubtful.
Cf. Holw. — Baud.

HILARIA (St) M. R.M. Dec. 3
See Claudius, Hilaris, etc.

HILARIA (St) M. R.M. Dec. 31
See Donata, Paulina, etc.

HILARINUS (St) R.M. Aug. 7
See Donatus and Hilary.

HILARINUS (St) M. A.C. Aug. 23
See Altigianus and Hilarinus.

HILARION (St) M. R.M. July 12
See Proclus and Hilarion.

HILARION (St) Ab. R.M. Oct. 21
c.291-c.371. A native of Gaza in Palestine, Hilarion became a Christian while studying at Alexandria, and took St Antony the Great as his model. On his return to Gaza, he introduced there the eremitical life. Disciples soon flocked around him and he founded several monasteries in Palestine. The latter part of his life is the story of his escapes from the crowds who followed him on account of his miracles. He lived on Mt Sinai, in Egypt, Sicily, Dalmatia, Paphos and Cyprus, where he died at the age of eighty.
Cf. Att. — Menzies — Holw.

HILARUS (St) Pope. R.M. Feb. 28
d. 468. A Sardinian by birth, promoted to

high office in the Roman curia by St Leo the Great, who sent him as his legate to the "Robber Synod of Ephesus" from which he escaped with difficulty (449). He was made pope in 461 and worked energetically against the Nestorians and Eutychians, as well as in consolidating the Church in Spain, Africa and Gaul.
Cf. Att. — Menzies — Holw. — Baud.

HILARY (St) Bp. and Dr. R.M. Jan. 14
d. 368. Born at Poitiers of pagan patrician parents, he studied rhetoric and philosophy and married early in life. Shortly after he became a Christian and in 353 was elected bishop of Poitiers. At once he began his masterly campaign against Arianism, and for this reason was exiled to Phrygia by the Arian emperor Constantius. But in Phrygia he was even more objectionable to the Arians, who clamoured for his recall. He returned to Poitiers in 360. Hilary is the Doctor of the Divinity of Christ. He was officially declared a Doctor of the Church in 1851.
Cf. Att. — Baud. — Duch. Fast. Episc.

HILARY, TATIAN, FELIX, LARGUS and DENIS (SS) MM. R.M. March 16
d. c.284. Hilary was a bishop of Aquileia, Tatian his deacon, and the rest laymen. All were beheaded under Numerian.
Cf. Holw. — Baud.

HILARY (St) M. R.M. Apr. 9
See Demetrius, Concessus, etc.

HILARY (St) Bp. R.M. May 5
c.400-449. Born in Lorraine, while still a pagan he gained high office in the local administration. His relative and friend, St Honoratus, invited him to the monastery recently founded at Lerins, and Hilary received baptism there, and joined the community. When St Honoratus became bishop of Arles he took Hilary as his secretary. St Hilary succeeded to the see and showed himself a zealous prelate, though not always prudent. In fact, he was twice reproved by the Holy See. His sanctity, however, won for him popular veneration in life and after death.
Cf. Duch. Fast. Episc. — Att. — Gams — Baud.

HILARY (St) Ab. A.C. May 15
d. 558. A hermit near the river Ronco in Italy. Joined by others he built the monastery called Galeata, afterwards known as

Sant'Ilaro, which at a later period was handed over to the Camaldolese.
Cf. Att. — Holw.

HILARY (St) Bp. A.C. May 16
d. 376. Bishop of Pavia. One of the prelates of N. Italy who fought Arianism.
Cf. Menzies — Holw.

HILARY (St) Bp. A.C. May 20
4th cent. Bishop of Toulouse.
Cf. Duch. Fast. Episc. — Baud. — Holw.

HILARY (St) Bp. A.C. June 3
? 4th cent. Bishop of Carcassonne.
Cf. Duch. Fast. Episc. — Baud.

HILARY (St) M. R.M. Sept. 27
See Florentinus and Hilary.

HILARY of MENDE (St) Bp.
R.M. Oct. 25
d. 535. Born at Mende, the ancient *Gavallus*, in S. France, he received baptism on coming to man's estate, became a hermit on the banks of the Tarn, monk of Lérins, and finally bishop of Mende.
Cf. Holw. — Baud. — Duch. Fast. Episc.

HILARY of VITERBO (St) M.
R.M. Nov. 3
See Valentine and Hilary.

HILARY (St) Ab. O.S.B. P.C. Nov. 21
d. c.1045. A native of Matera in S. Italy, he became abbot of San Vincenzo at Volturno (1011-1045). He revived the ancient glory of his monastery.
Cf. Zimm.

HILDA (St) Abs. O.S.B. A.C. Nov. 17
617-680. A native of Northumbria and a kinswoman of King St Edwin. She was baptized when a child by St Paulinus (631) and at the age of thirty-three joined the nuns of Hartlepool, by the river Wear in Northumberland, of whom soon after she became the abbess. Later on, she migrated also as abbess to the double monastery of Whitby at Streaneshalch. Her influence was certainly one of the decisive factors in securing unity in the English church. Although she and her double community had professed and favoured the Celtic rule and observances, they gave them up after the council of Whitby convened by St Hilda herself in 664, when the Roman observances, including the Roman monastic Rule of St Benedict, were definitely adopted throughout England. Five of her monks, including St Wilfrid of York and St John of Beverley, became bishops. Hilda is one of the greatest Englishwomen of all time.
Cf. Mab. — Zimm. — Chev. — Att. — Holw. — Stanton.

HILDEBERT (St) Ab. M. O.S.B.
A.C. Apr. 4
d. 752. Abbot of the Benedictine monastery of St Peter at Ghent. He was killed by some fanatics for his defence of holy images, and was venerated as a martyr.
Cf. Chev. — Baud. — Holw.

HILDEBRAND (Bl) M. A.C. Apr. 11
See Stephen and Hildebrand.

HILDEBRAND (St) Pope O.S.B.
R.M. May 25
Otherwise Gregory VII, q.v.

HILDEGARD (Bl) Empress A.C. Apr. 30
d. 783. A daughter of the duke of Swabia. In 771 she was married to Charlemagne, who had just repudiated Queen Hermengard. Hildegard bore him eight children during the twelve years of their married life. She befriended monks and nuns, among whom she had a special predilection for St Lioba. She is considered as the foundress of Kempten Abbey, where she was buried.
Baud. — Holw.

HILDEGARD (St) Abs. O.S.B.
R.M. Sept. 17
1098-1179. Surnamed "the Sibyl of the Rhine." Born at Bockelheim, she joined the Benedictines at Diessenberg when she was only eight years old, and in early womanhood was chosen abbess of the place. She removed the community to Mt St Rupert, near Bingen (c.1147), and founded another daughter house in the neighbourhood. Her claim to fame, however, rests on her amazing writings. "Hildegard was the first of the great German mystics, a poetess and a prophetess, a physician and a political moralist, who rebuked popes and princes, bishops and lay-folk, with complete fearlessness and unerring justice" (Attwater). Accused by her numerous enemies, she was defended by St Bernard and by his pope-disciple Bl Eugene III. "Hildegard's mys-

tical writings have provoked comparison with Dante and William Blake . . . she was alike one of the greatest figures of the 12th century, of the followers of St Benedict, and of the women of all time" (Attwater).
Cf. Zimm. — Mab. — P. de U. — Chev.

HILDEGRIN (St) Bp. A.C. June 19
d. c.827. Younger brother of St Ludger, q.v., and his fellow-worker in the evangelization of the Saxons. At a later period (802?) he was promoted bishop of Châlons-sur-Marne. It is usually stated that towards the end of his life he became a monk, and abbot of the Benedictine monastery of Werden.
Cf. Duch. Fast. Episc. — Baud. — Zimm.

HILDEGUND (St) W. O. Praem.
A.C. Feb. 6
d. 1183. Wife of Count Lothair. In her widowhood she turned her castle of Meer, near Cologne, into a Premonstratensiam nunnery and entered there with her daughter, in the teeth of fierce family opposition. Hildegund became the prioress of the new foundation.
Cf. Att. — Holw. — Baud.

HILDEGUND, or Joseph (Bl) N. O.S.B. Cist. P.C. Apr. 20
d. 1188. The Cistercian menology states: "Hildegund, died a novice at the abbey of Schönau, disguised in male apparel and calling herself Brother Joseph. She died most holily and is famous for her miracles." Hers is a romantic story. She was born in the Rhineland and posing as a boy went to the Holy Land; on her return she joined the Cistercian monks at Schönau; her sex was discovered after death. Of the several women of whom similar stories are related, Hildegund is almost the only one in whose story there seems to be a measure of truth. Her cult is, however, only a popular one.
Cf. Att. — Chev. — Baud. — Holw.

HILDELID (HILDILID, HILDELTHA) (St) Abs. O.S.B. A.C. March 24
d. c.717. A young Anglo-Saxon princess who took the veil either at Chelles or at Faremoutiers, in France. She was recalled to England by St Erconwald to train her sister Ethelburga of Berking. When the latter became abbess Hildelid stayed on as one of her nuns, and eventually succeeded her as abbess. She won

the admiration of SS Aldhelm, Bede and Boniface.
Cf. Mab. — Zimm. — Att. — Chev. — Holw.

HILDEMAR (Bl) M. O.S.A. A.C. Jan. 13
d. 1097(8). A hermit at Arrouaise in Artois. He was joined by many disciples for whom he founded the monastery of Arrouaise under the Augustinian rule of canons regular. He was killed by a cleric who posed as a novice.
Cf. Chev. — Baud.

HILDEMAR (St) Bp. O.S.B. A.C. Dec. 10
d. p. 844. A monk of Corbie who was appointed bishop of Beauvais in 821.
Cf. Duch. Fast. Episc. — Holw. — Baud.

HILDEMARCA (St) Abs. O.S.B.
A.C. Oct. 25
d. c.670. A nun of St Eulalia at Bordeaux, who was invited by St Wandrille to govern his new monastery at Fécamp.
Cf. Baud. — Holw. — P.B.

HILDUARD (HILWARD, GARIBALD) (St) Bp. O.S.B. A.C. Sept. 7
d. c.750. A missionary bishop in Flanders, founder of St Peter's abbey at Dickelvenne, between Ghent and Audenarde, in the Schelde.
Cf. Zimm. — Holw. — Baud.

HILLONIUS (St) C. A.C. Jan. 7
Otherwise Thillo, q.v.

HILSINDIS (Bl) Abs. O.S.B. A.C. May 4
d. 1028. Of the family of the dukes of Lorraine. In her widowhood she was the abbess-foundress of the nunnery of Thorn, on the Marne.
Cf. Holw. — Baud.

HILTRUDE (St) V. O.S.B.
R.M. Sept. 27
d. c.790. A recluse in a cell near the abbey of Liessies, under the obedience of its abbot, who was her own brother, Gundrad.
Cf. Holw. — Baud.

HILTUTUS (St) Ab. A.C. July 7
Otherwise Illtyd, q.v.

HIMELIN (St) C. A.C. March 10
d. c.750. An Irish, or Scottish, priest, who died at Vissenaeken, near Tirlemont, in Belgium, on his return from a Roman pil-

grimage. He is still venerated at Vissenaeken.
Cf. Att. — Holw. — Baud.

HIMERIUS (St) Bp. R.M. June 17
d. c.560. A native of Calabria, who from
being a monk, was raised to the see of
Amelia (*Ameria*) in Umbria. He is
described as a very austere man, first with
himself and then with others. In 995 his
relics were translated to Cremona, where
he is venerated as one of its principal
patron saints.
Cf. Menzies.

HIMERIUS (IMIER) (St) Ab.
A.C. Nov. 12
d. c.610. A monk-hermit and a missionary
in the district of the Swiss Jura, now called
after him Immertal, Val-Saint-Imier.
Cf. Holw. — Baud. — Zimm.

HIPPOLYTUS (St) M. R.M. Jan. 30
d. c.250. A Syrian priest, converted from
the errors of Novatus, and martyred at
Antioch.
Cf. Holw. — Baud.

HIPPOLYTUS (St) M. R.M. Feb. 3
See Felix, Symphronius, etc.

HIPPOLYTUS GALANTINI (Bl) C.
A.C. March 20
1565-1619. A native of Florence, and a
silk-weaver by trade. From his twelfth
year he assisted the priests in teaching
Christian doctrine to the children. This
practice was imitated by others, whom Bl
Hippolytus formed into the congregation
of Italian Doctrinarians. It soon spread
throughout Italy. Beatified in 1825.
Cf. Att. — Baud. — Menzies.

HIPPOLYTUS, CONCORDIA and Comp.
(SS) MM. R.M. Aug. 13
d. c.236. A native of Rome who became a
member of the Roman clergy, among
whom he was known for his rigoristic
leanings. He began by censuring Pope St
Callistus I, causing himself to be elected
antipope. He was exiled to Sardinia and
there reconciled to the church before his
martyrdom. He is one of the most important ecclesiastical writers of his time.
Unfortunately in the liturgy he is confused
with the Hippolytus of the unreliable *Acta*
of St Laurence. See also with Pontian,
Oct. 30.
Cf. Att. — Baud. — Menzies — Holw.

HIPPOLYTUS of PORTO (St) Bp. M.
R.M. Aug. 22
? The R.M. confuses this Hippolytus
with his namesake of Aug. 13. He was
bishop of Porto and was martyred there by
drowning under the emperor Alexander.
Cf. Menzies — Att. — Baud.

HIPPOLYTUS (St) M. R.M. Oct. 30
See Pontian and Hippolytus.

HIPPOLYTUS (St) Bp. O.S.B.
A.C. Nov. 28
d. c.775. Abbot-bishop of Saint-Claude,
in France.
Cf. Zimm. — Chev.

HIPPOLYTUS (St) M. R.M. Dec. 2
See Eusebius, Marcellus, etc.

HIRENARCHUS, ACACIUS and Comp.
(SS) MM. R.M. Nov. 27
d. c.305. Martyrs of Sebaste in Armenia.
They include Acacius, a priest, seven
women, and Hirenarchus, converted on
witnessing the courage of the other
martyrs.
Cf. Holw. — Baud.

HOMOBONUS (St) C. R.M. Nov. 13
d. 1197. A merchant of Cremona, who
throughout his life practised the most
scrupulous honesty and was conspicuous
for his charity to the poor. One day,
during the celebration of Mass, at which
he assisted every day, he fell prostrate on
the ground and was picked up dead.
Two years after his death his fellow-citizens petitioned the Holy See for his canonization and their petition was granted
at once (1199).
Cf. Att. — Baud. — Chev. — Holw.

HONESTUS (St) M. A.C. Feb. 16
d. 270. A native of Nîmes, who was ordained priest and sent into Spain by St
Saturninus to preach the gospel, which he
did with much fruit. He appears to have
been martyred at Pampeluna in Spanish
Navarre.
Cf. Baud. — Holw.

HONORATA (St) V. R.M. Jan. 11
d. c.500. The sister of St Epiphanius,
bishop of Pavia. She was a nun at Pavia,
when Odoacer, the king of the Heruli,
dragged her into captivity. She was ransomed by her brother and returned to Pavia.
Cf. Holw. — Menzies — Baud.

HONORATUS of ARLES (St) Bp.
R.M. Jan. 16
d. 429. Born probably in Lorraine of a Roman consular family, he renounced paganism in his youth and went to the East to study monasticism. Returning to France, he founded on the Mediterranean islet of Lérins, the abbey of that name. In 426 he was forced to accept the archbishopric of Arles; but died only three years later.
Cf. Att. — Duch. Fast. Episc. — Gams — Holw.

HONORATUS of FONDI (St) Ab.
R.M. Jan. 16
6th cent. The abbot-founder of the monastery of Fondi on the confines of Latium and Campania. St Gregory the Great gives a pleasing, though all too short, account of his life.
Cf. Menzies — Holw. — Baud.

HONORATUS of MILAN (St) Bp.
R.M. Feb. 8
d. 570. Appointed bishop of Milan in 567, at a time when much trouble was being caused by the Arian disputes and by the Lombard invasion. He himself was driven from his see by these barbarians, and died in exile.
Cf. Menzies — Holw. — Baud.

HONORATUS of AMIENS (St) Bp.
R.M. May 16
d. c.600. A native of Ponthieu who became bishop of Amiens. The church and thoroughfare of Saint-Honoré, in Paris, take their name from him.
Cf. Chev. — Gams. — Duch. Fast. Episc. — Holw. — Baud.

HONORATUS, FORTUNATUS, ARONTIUS (ORONTIUS), SABINIAN (SAVINIAN) (SS) MM.
R.M. Aug. 27 and Sept. 1
d. 303. Martyrs beheaded at Potenza under Maximian. They are one of the groups associated under the title of "the Twelve Brothers," q.v.
Cf. Builer-Thurston (Sept. 1)

HONORATUS of VERCELLI (St) Bp.
R.M. Oct. 28
c.330-415. A native of Vercelli who was trained in the monastic and the ecclesiastical life by St Eusebius. He accompanied his master into his exile at Scythopolis (355), and in his wanderings through Cappadocia, Egypt and Illyricum. In 396 he was elected bishop on the recommendation of St Ambrose, to whom he administered holy viaticum.
Cf. Menzies — Holw. — Baud.

HONORATUS of TOULOUSE (St) Bp.
A.C. Dec. 21
d. 3rd cent. Born in Spanish Navarre, he succeeded St Saturninus in the see of Toulouse. He consecrated St Firminus bishop of Amiens.
Cf. Duch. Fast. Episc. — Gams — Holw. — Baud.

HONORATUS (St) M.
R.M. Dec. 22
See Demetrius, Honoratus and Florus.

HONORATUS (St) M.
R.M. Dec. 29
See Dominic, Victor, etc.

HONORÉ (St) Bp.
R.M. May 16
Otherwise Honoratus of Amiens, q.v.

HONORINA (St) V.M.
A.C. Feb. 27
? One of the early martyrs of Gaul. Her Acts have been lost.
Cf. Holw.

HONORIUS of BUZANCAIS (St or Bl) M.
A.C. Jan. 9
d. 1250 (?) Born at Buzancais in Berry, France, Honorius was a rich trader in cattle and sheep. On his return from a voyage, he found out that he had been robbed by his servants and remonstrated with them. He was killed for this reason, at Parthenay in Poitou and venerated as a martyr. Canonized in 1444.
Cf. Baud. — Att.

HONORIUS of BRESCIA (St) Bp.
R.M. Apr. 24
d. c.586. A hermit near Brescia, who was chosen bishop of that city (c.577).
Cf. Holw. — Baud.

HONORIUS of CANTERBURY (St) Bp.
O.S.B.
R.M. Sept. 30
d. 653. A Roman by birth and a Benedictine by profession, he succeeded St Justus as archbishop of Canterbury (627). He was consecrated at Lincoln by St Paulinus, and himself consecrated bishops St Felix for the East Angles and St Ithamar, the first English born bishop, for Rochester.
Cf. Att. — Zimm. — Mab. — Chev.

HONORIUS (St) M. R.M. Nov. 21
See Demetrius and Honorius.

HONORIUS, EUTYCHIUS and STEPHEN (SS) MM. R.M. Nov. 21
d. c.300. Spanish martyrs, who suffered at Asta, in Andalusia, under Diocletian.
Cf. Holw. — Baud. .

HONORIUS (St) M. R.M. Dec. 30
See Mansuetus, Severus, etc.

HOPE (St) V.M. R.M. Aug. 1
See Faith, Hope, and Charity.

HORMISDAS (St) Pope. R.M. Aug. 6
d. 523. Born at Frosinone in Latium, he succeeded St Symmachus in 514. He is best remembered for the confession of faith called the Formula of Hormisdas, which was accepted in the East (519) and thus ended the Monophysite schism of Acacius. His son, St Sylverius, became pope in 536.
Cf. Holw. — Att. — Menzies.

HORMISDAS (St) M. R.M. Aug. 8
d. 420. A noble Persian youth, who refused to apostatize, and was degraded by King Varannes to the rank of an army camel-driver.
Cf. Att. — Baud. — Holw.

HORRES (St) M. R.M. March 13
See Theusetas, Horres, etc.

HORTULANUS (St) Bp. M.
R.M. Nov. 28
See Valerian, Urban, etc.

HOSANNA of CATTARO (Bl) V. Tert. O.P. A.C. Apr. 27
d. 1565. Her baptismal name was Catherine Cosie, and she was the daughter of dissident orthodox parents in Montenegro. She abjured the schism at Cattaro, and became a Dominican tertiary, taking the new name of Hosanna. Cult confirmed in 1928.
Cf. Att. — Prop. O.P.

HOSANNA of MANTUA (Bl) V. Tert. O.P. A.C. June 18
1449-1505. A native of Mantua, daughter of the patrician, Andreasio. She spent her large fortune in the service of the poor as a Dominican tertiary. Cult confirmed by Leo X and Innocent XII.
Cf. Holw. — Prop. O.P.

HOSPITIUS (St) H. R.M. May 21
d. c.580. A hermit at the place now called after him Cap-Saint-Hospice, between Villefrance and Banlieu. His relics were translated to Lérins on May 21, the day on which his feast is now celebrated.
Cf. Att. — Baud. — Holw.

HROZNATA (Bl) M. O. Praem.
A.C. July 19
1160-1217. A member of a noble family of Bohemia, who married and lost by sudden death his wife and only child. He now founded the Premonstratensian abbey of Tepl in Bavaria, and was himself professed therein. He died of starvation in a dungeon, into which he had been thrown by robbers. Cult approved in 1897.
Cf. Att. — Baud. — Holw.

HUBERT (St) Bp. R.M. Nov. 3
d. 727. A courtier of Pepin of Heristal who, having lost his wife, entered the ecclesiastical state. According to a late legend his conversion happened while he was hunting, in circumstances similar to those narrated of St Eustace and others. He is also said by some writers to have joined the community of Stavelot. Eventually he succeeded St Lambert as bishop of Maestricht (c.706) whence he transferred the see to Liége. He is venerated as the patron saint of hunters.
Cf. Chev. — Baud. — Att. — Ricci.

HUBERT (HUGBERT) of BRETIGNY (St) C. O.S.B. A.C. May 30
d. c.714. At the age of twelve he entered, in spite of much opposition from his family, the abbey of Brétigny, near Noyon. There his life was an uninterrupted series of portentous happenings.
Cf. Zimm. — Baud. — Holw. — P. de U. — Chev.

HUGH of FOSSE (Bl) O. Praem.
A.C. Feb. 10
1164. Born at Fosse near Namur in Belgium, he was ordained priest and in 1119 joined St Norbert the founder of the premonstratensians, whose companion and assistant he became, and whom he succeeded as abbot of Prémontré and superior general of the order. Cult confirmed in 1927.
Cf. Att.

HUGH dei LIPPI-UGUCCIONI (St) C. O.S.M. R.M. Feb. 12 and May 3
d. 1282. A Florentine by birth. One of

the Seven Founders of the Servite Order. He accompanied St Philip Benizi to France and Germany and was vicar-general of the order in Germany for eight years. He died on Mt Senario.
Cf. Holw.

HUGH of VAUCELLES (Bl) O.S.B. Cist.
A.C. March 29
d. 1239. From being dean of the church at Cambrai he became a monk at the Cistercian abbey of Vaucelles.
Cf. Holw.

HUGH of GRENOBLE (St) Bp. O.S.B.
R.M. Apr. 1
1053-1132. A native of Dauphiné, who, although a layman, was at the age of twenty-five already a canon of Valence. He was appointed bishop of Grenoble in 1080. Convinced of his own inefficiency, he retired to the austere abbey of Chaise-Dieu and received the Benedictine habit. Pope Gregory VII, however, ordered him back to Grenoble. He gave to St Bruno the land of La Grande Chartreuse. He was canonized in 1134, two years after his death.
Cf. Att. — Baud. — Holw. — Chev.

HUGH of BONNEVAUX (Bl or St) Ab.
O.S.B. Cist. **A.C. Apr. 1**
d. 1194. A nephew of St Hugh of Grenoble who became a Cistercian at Mezières. In 1163 he was made abbot of Léoncel, and in 1169 promoted to Bonnevaux. He was possessed of singular powers of divination and exorcism, but he is chiefly remembered as the mediator between Alexander III and Barbarossa (1177).
Cf. Prop. Cist. — Zimm. — Att.

HUGH of ROUEN (St) Bp. O.S.B.
R.M. Apr. 9
d. 730. At a very early age he became a monk, either at Fontenelle or Jumièges. Then he was called to be *primicerius* of Metz and shortly after was made bishop of Rouen (722) as well as of Paris, being at the same time abbot of Fontenelle and Jumièges. He made use of all these offices to foster piety and learning. Before his death, however, he resigned them all and died at Jumièges as a simple monk.
Cf. Att. — Chev. — Baud. — Holw.

HUGH of ANZY-LE DUC (St) C. O.S.B.
A.C. Apr. 20
d. c.930. A native of Poitiers, he was trained from infancy at the Benedictine abbey of Saint-Savin, Poitou, where he became a monk. Later he was sent to several houses to revive monastic observance, the last of which was the newly founded abbey of Cluny where he helped Bl Berno. His relics were elevated in 1001.
Cf. Att. — Chev. — Baud. — Holw.

HUGH the GREAT of CLUNY (St) Ab.
O.S.B. **R.M. Apr. 29**
1024-1109. Born at Samur, he made his Benedictine profession at Cluny at the age of 15 (1039), was ordained priest at twenty, chosen prior shortly after, and elected abbot at twenty-five. He was abbot from 1049 till 1109, and during this period he was the adviser of nine popes, consulted and revered by all the sovereigns of Europe, and the rulers of over 200 monasteries. He and his Cluniac monk St Gregory VII were instrumental in promoting the powerful revival of spiritual life throughout W. Europe which characterizes the 11th century. He founded a hospital at Marcigny in which he loved to wait upon the lepers with his own hands. Few men have been so universally esteemed. He is one of the greatest glories of Benedictine monachism. Canonized in 1120.
Cf. Zimm. — P. de U. — Baud. — Chev. — Att. — Holw.

HUGH of MARCHIENNES (Bl) Ab.
O.S.B. **P.C. June 11**
d. 1158. Born at Tournai and educated at Reims, he became a Benedictine at St Martin, Tournai, and abbot of Marchiennes in 1148.
Cf. Holw. — P.B.

HUGH of MONTAIGU (Bl) Bp. O.S.B.
A.C. Aug. 10
d. 1136. A nephew of St Hugh of Cluny, under whom he was educated and professed a Benedictine at Cluny. In 1096 he was made bishop of Auxerre.
Cf. Holw. — P.B.

HUGH (LITTLE) (St) M. **A.C. Aug. 18**
d. 1255. A boy of Lincoln, aged nine, who was put to death by Jews. King Henry III conducted the judicial investigations which resulted in eighteen Jews being hanged for their crime. That the child was tortured to death for being a Christian is a historical fact, thoroughly established.
Cf. Att. — Baud. — Holw.

HUGH GREEN (Bl) M.   A.C. Aug. 19
d. 1642. A Londoner, educated at Peterhouse, Cambridge. After his conversion he studied for the priesthood at Douai, and was ordained there in 1612. He worked in Dorset, and was hanged for his priesthood at Dorchester.
Cf. Newdigate.

HUGH MORE (Bl) M.   A.C. Aug. 28
d. 1588. Born at Grantham in Lincolnshire, he was educated at Oxford (Broadgates Hall) and Gray's Inn. He became a convert at Reims and was hanged for this at Lincoln's Inn Fields. Beatified in 1929.
Cf. Newdigate.

HUGH of SASSOFERRATO (Bl) C.
O.S.B. Silv.   A.C. Sept. 19
d. c.1290. Born at Serra San Quirico in the diocese of Camerino, he studied at Bologna. He received the monastic habit from St Silvester, of whom he was a devoted disciple. He died at Sassoferrato. Cult approved in 1747.
Cf. Chev. — Baud. — Holw.

HUGH CANEFRO (St or Bl) C.
      A.C. Oct. 8
1168-1230. Priest and chaplain of the knights of St John of Jerusalem at Genoa.
Cf. Menzies — Holw. — P.B.

HUGH of MÂCON (Bl) Bp. O.S.B. Cist.
      P.C. Oct. 10
d. 1151. A Cistercian under St Stephen, and then abbot of Pontigny (1114). In 1137 he was elected bishop of Auxerre, the first Cistercian to be raised to the episcopate.
Cf. Gams — Chev. — Holw.

HUGH of AMBRONAY (St) Ab. O.S.B.
      A.C. Oct. 21
9th-10th cent. Third abbot of the Benedictine monastery of Ambronay in the diocese of Belley.
Cf. Chev. — Bolland. — Zimm. — Holw.

HUGH FARINGDON (Bl) Ab. M. O.S.B.
      A.C. Nov. 15
d. 1539. Hugh Faringdon (*vere* Cook) became abbot of Reading in 1520. He was an intimate friend of Henry VIII, but at the dissolution he refused to surrender his abbey. He was martyred at Reading with two prebendaries of the abbey (doubtless monks).
Cf. Att. — Holw. — Baud.

HUGH of NOARA (St) Ab. O.S.B. Cist.
      A.C. Nov. 17
d. c.1172. First abbot of the Cistercian abbey of Noara in Sicily, founded in 1172 by the community of Sambucina.
Cf. Zimm.

HUGH of LINCOLN (St) Bp. O.Cart.
      R.M. Nov. 17
1140-1200. A native of Burgundy and a canon regular, who at the age of twenty joined the Carthusians. In 1175 he was invited by King Henry II to found the first English Charterhouse at Witham in Somerset, which he did in the face of obstacles of all kinds. In 1181 he was raised to the see of Lincoln, and governed it zealously and wisely; the present cathedral of Lincoln was built during his episcopate. He died, aged sixty, deeply lamented by all, especially by the Jews, whom he had always defended and befriended. At his magnificent funeral the kings of England and Scotland helped to carry the bier. Canonized in 1220.
Cf. Att. — Baud. — Holw.

HUGOLINUS of GUALDO (Bl) C. O.S.A.
      A.C. Jan. 1
d. 1260. A hermit of St Augustine who ruled as prior a monastery of that order at Gualdo, in Umbria. Cult approved in 1919.
Cf. Att. — Holw. — Baud.

HUGOLINUS ZEFFERINI (Bl) C. O.S.A.
      A.C. March 22
d. c.1470(?). An Augustinian friar who lived at Cortona (or perhaps Mantua). Cult confirmed in 1804.
Cf. Att. — Holw.

HUGOLINUS (St) M. O.F.M.
      R.M. Oct. 13
See Daniel, Samuel, etc.

HUGOLINUS MAGALOTTI (Bl) C.
O.F.M.   A.C. Dec. 11
d. 1373. A native of Camerino who lived as a hermit after having joined the third order of the Friars Minor. Cult confirmed in 1856.
Cf. Att. — Baud. — Holw.

HUMBELINE (St) Abs. O.S.B.
      A.C. Feb. 12
1092-1141. A younger sister of St Bernard of Clairvaux. She married a rich

man and was leading a worldly life when a visit to her brother in Clairvaux resulted in her spiritual conversion. She asked and obtained her husband's consent to become a nun, and entered the Black Benedictine nunnery of Jully-les-Nonnais, near Troyes, of which she became abbess. She founded Tart nunnery for the Cistercians, but she herself remained a Black Benedictine at Jully, where she died in St Bernard's arms. Cult approved in 1763.
Cf. Prop. Cist. — Zimm. — Holw. — Att. — Baud.

HUMBERT of SAVOY (Bl) C.
A.C. March 4
1136-1188. Humbert III was king of Savoy, and was three, perhaps four times married. Ever just and pious, in his old age he retired to the Cistercian abbey of Haute Combe, where he died in the Cistercian habit. Cult confirmed in 1838. He was an ancestor of the Italian royal house.
Cf. Att. — Zimm. — Baud.

HUMBERT (St) Ab. O.S.B.
A.C. March 25
d. c.680. A disciple of St Amandus who became the joint founder and first abbot of the abbey of Marolles in Flanders.
Cf. Chev. — Baud. — Holw.

HUMBERT of ROMANS (Bl) C. O.P.
P.C. July 14
d. 1277. The fifth master general of the Dominicans. He was particularly successful in the development of the foreign missions, and in the definitive planning of the studies among the Friars Preachers. Cult not yet confirmed.
Cf. Att.

HUMBERT (Bl) C. O.S.B.   A.C. Oct. 26
d. 7th or 8th cent. Monk of Fritzlar in Hesse and prior of Buraburg.
Cf. Zimm. — Holw. — Baud.

HUMBERT (Bl) Ab. O.S.B. Cist.
P.C. Dec. 7
d. 1148. A monk of Chaise-Dieu who went over to Clairvaux in 1117. St Bernard made him prior and then sent him as abbot to Igny (1127). Humbert sought to return to Clairvaux, but St Bernard ordered him back to Igny under pain of monastic excommunication. On Humbert's death St Bernard delivered a

most touching homily to his brethren at Clairvaux.
Cf. Zimm. — Chev.

HUMILIANA de'CERCHI (Bl) Tert. O.F.M.   A.C. May 19
1220-1246. Daughter of a Florentine family, she married at the age of sixteen. After the early death of her husband she became the first cloistered Franciscan tertiary at Florence. Cult approved by Innocent XII.
Cf. Holw.

HUMILIS of BISIGNANO (Bl) C. O.F.M.
A.C. Nov. 27
1582-1637. A native of Bisignano in Calabria, and a Franciscan lay-brother. He became so widely known for his sanctity that he was called to Rome, where both Gregory XV and Urban VIII consulted him. Beatified in 1882.
Cf. Att. — Holw.

HUMILITAS (or ROSANNA) (St) Abs. O.S.B. Vall.   A.C. May 22
1226-1310. Born at Faenza, in the Romagna, at fifteen years of age she was compelled to marry a frivolous young man named Ugoletto. After nine years of married life he became seriously ill, and on his recovery consented to become a religious and allowed Humilitas to receive the veil. She first lived as a recluse near the Vallumbrosan church of St Apollinaris where her husband was a monk, and later, persuaded by the general of the Vallumbrosans, founded and ruled two houses for Vallumbrosan nuns.
Cf. Att. — Chev. — Zimm.

HUMPHREY (several)
Otherwise Onuphrius, q.v.

HUMPHREY (HUNFRID) (St) Bp. O.S.B.   A.C. March 8
d. 871. A monk of the Benedictine abbey of Prüm, in the Ardennes, at the time of its greatest splendour. He became bishop of Therouanne and ruled at the same time the abbey of St Bertin. He was a source of strength and comfort to the people during the Norman invasion.
Cf. Att. — Zimm. — Holw. — Chev.

HUMPHREY MIDDLEMORE (Bl) M. O.Cart.   A.C. June 19
d. 1535. A Carthusian monk, belonging

to the London Charterhouse, who was
hanged at. Tyburn with two others of his
brethren. Beatified in 1886.
Cf. Newdigate — Camm.

HUNA (St) C. O.S.B.   **A.C. Feb. 13**
d. c.690. A monk-priest at Ely under St
Etheldreda, whom he assisted in her last
moments, afterwards retiring to a hermitage in the Fens where he died.
Cf. Holw.

HUNEGUND (St) N. O.S.B.
                           A.C. Aug. 25
d. c.690. Compelled to marry against her
wish, she prevailed on her bridegroom to
accompany her to Rome, where she received the veil at the hands of Pope St
Vitalian. They returned to their country
and Hunegund entered the nunnery of
Homblières, while her former betrothed
served there as chaplain.
Cf. Chev. — Holw. — Baud.

HUNGER (St) Bp.   **A.C. Dec. 22**
d. 866. Bishop of Utrecht from 856.
During the Norman invasion he fled to
Prüm, where he died.
Cf. Holw. —Zimm.

HUNNA (St) W.   **A.C. Apr. 15**
d. 679. The wife of an Alsatian nobleman. Her neighbours called her "the
holy washerwoman," because she was wont
to help them all in that capacity. Canonized in 1520.
Cf. Att.

HYACINTH (St) M.   **R.M. Feb. 10**
See Zoticus, Irenaeus, etc.

HYACINTH (St) M.   **R.M. July 3**
d. c.120. A chamberlain of the emperor
Trajan at Caesarea in Cappadocia. He
was imprisoned and offered as sustenance
only meat consecrated to idols. This he
constantly refused and died in consequence
of starvation.
Cf. Holw. — Baud.

HYACINTH (St) M.   **R.M. July 17**
? A martyr of Amastris in Paphlagonia,
put to death for having cut down a tree
consecrated to an idol.
Cf. Holw. — Baud.

HYACINTH (St) M.   **R.M. July 26**
d. ? c.110. A martyr under Trajan. His

existence is certain, but his acts are
thoroughly untrustworthy.
Cf. Baud. — Holw.

HYACINTH (St) C. O.P.   R.M. Aug. 17
1185-1257. Surnamed "the Apostle of
the North." Polish by birth, and a canon
of Cracow, he received the Dominican
habit from St Dominic himself. In three
apostolic journeys he is said to have travelled through Poland, Pomerania, Denmark, Sweden, Norway, Russia, and as far
as Tibet and China. However, the details of his life are very uncertain. He
died at Cracow and was canonized in 1594.
Cf. Prop. O.P. — Att. — Holw.

**HYACINTH, ALEXANDER and TI-
BURTIUS (SS) MM.   R.M. Sept. 9**
? Martyrs who are said to have suffered
at some place in the Sabine country, about
thirty miles from Rome.
Cf. Holw. — Baud.

HYACINTH ORFANEL (Bl) M. O.P.
                           A.C. Sept. 10
1578-1622. A native of Llana, Valencia,
Spain. He joined the Dominicans at
Barcelona and was sent to the missions of
Japan. He was burnt alive at Nagasaki,
after many years of apostolic labours.
Beatified in 1867.
Cf. Holw.

HYACINTH (St) M.   R.M. Sept. 11
See Protus and Hyacinth.

**HYACINTH, QUINCTUS, FELICIAN
and LUCIUS (SS) MM.   R.M. Oct. 29**
? Martyrs of Lucania in S. Italy.
Cf. Baud. — Holw.

HYACINTH CASTAÑEDA (Bl) M. O.P.
                           A.C. Nov. 7
d. 1773. Born at Sétavo in the diocese of
Valencia, Spain. After his profession as a
Friar Preacher and his ordination to the
priesthood, he was sent to the mission,
first to China, then to Tonkin, where he
was beheaded. Beatified in 1906.
Cf. Holw.

**HYACINTH of MARISCOTTI (St) Tert.
V. O.F.M.   R.M. Jan. 30**
1585-1640. A lady of Viterbo, who, at the
age of twenty, was passed over by the
Marquis Cassizucchi in favour of her
younger sister, whom he married. Hya-

cinth became so very troublesome that her family almost forced her into the convent of Franciscan tertiaries at Viterbo. Here, she began by scandalously ignoring or transgressing the Rule, was then converted to better ways, but relapsed, and finally, during twenty-four years, gave herself up to a life of heroic humility, prayer, patience and penance. Beatified in 1276, and canonized in 1807.
Cf. Att. — Holw. — Baud.

HYDROC (St) C.   A.C. May 5
5th cent. The patron saint of Lanhydroc in Cornwall.
Cf. Holw.

HYGBALD (HUGBALD, HIGBALD, HY-BALD) (St) H. O.S.B.   A.C. Sept. 18
d. c.690. An abbot in Lincolnshire to whom several churches are dedicated.
Cf. Zimm. — Holw.

HYGINUS (St) Pope M.   R.M. Jan. 11
d. c.142. The probable dates of his pontificate are 138 to 142; but even this much is not certain. It is also doubtful whether he died a martyr. His pontificate was occupied with the struggle against Gnosticism.
Cf. Att. — Menzies.

HYPATIUS (St) M.   R.M. June 3
See Lucillian, Claudius, etc.

HYPATIUS (St) C.   R.M. June 17
d. c.450. Born in Phrygia, at the age of nineteen he embraced the solitary life, first in Thrace, and then at Chalcedon in Bithynia, where he became abbot of a flourishing *laura*. He was a determined opponent of Nestorianism.
Cf. Att. — Baud. — Holw.

HYPATIUS (St) M.   R.M. June 18
See Leontius, Hypatius and Theodulus.

HYPATIUS and ANDREW (SS) MM.
R.M. Aug. 29
d. 735. Natives of Lydia. Hypatius was a deacon, and Andrew a priest. They were martyred at Constantinople under Leo the Isaurian for their defence of the veneration of sacred images.
Cf. Holw. — Baud.

HYPATIUS (St) Bp. M.   R.M. Nov. 14
d. c.325. A bishop of Gangra in Paphlagonia, who attended the council of Nicaea

and was a prominent defender of the divinity of Christ. While on his return from Nicaea, he was attacked by a band of heretics and stoned to death.
Cf. Holw. — Baud.

HYWYN (St) C.   A.C. Jan. 6
d. p. 516. Probably a companion of St Cadfan on his return journey (516) from Brittany to Cornwall and Wales. He is said to have been the founder of Aberdaron in Carnarvonshire. Several churches in W. England known as St Owen's or St Ewen's possibly have him for their titular saint.
Cf. Holw.

I

IA (HIA, IVES) (St) V. M.   A.C. Feb. 3
d. 450. An Irish maiden, sister of St Ercus, who crossed into Cornwall, with SS Fingar, Piala, and other missionaries, and there suffered martyrdom at the mouth of the Hayle river. She has left her name to St Ives in Cornwall.
Cf. Att. — Holw.

IA and Comp. (SS) MM.   R.M. Aug. 4
d. 360. A Greek slave, who suffered martyrdom in Persia with many other Christians (the figure usually given is nine thousand) during the persecution of King Shapur II.
Cf. Att. — Holw.

IAGO (St) Apostle   R.M. July 25
Note. An antiquated Spanish form of the name of St James. Iago is now always used with the prefixed hagiological title of Sant (Saint) in this way: Santiago.

IBERIUS (IBAR, IVOR) (St) C.
A.C. Apr. 23
5th cent. One of the missionaries — SS Kiaran, Ailbe, Declan, etc. — who evangelized Ireland at the time of, or as some writers hold, shortly before, St Patrick. St Ibar preached chiefly in Leinster and in Meath.
Cf. Holw. — Baud.

IDA of ARGENSOLLES (Bl) Abs. O.S.B. Cist.   A.C. Jan. 13
d. 1226. A Black Benedictine nun of St Leonard's, Liége, who was elected abbess of the Cistercian nunnery of Argensolles, in the diocese of Soissons.
Cf. Holw. — Baud.

IDA of HOHENFELS (Bl) **N. O.S.B.**
A.C. Feb. 24
d. c.1195. Wife of Eberhard, count of Spanheim, and, after his death, a Benedictine nun at Bingen.
Cf. Chev.

IDA of BOULOGNE (Bl) **W.**
A.C. Apr. 13
1040-1113. A daughter of Godfrey IV, duke of Lorraine, descended from Charlemagne. She was the mother of Godfrey and Baldwin de Bouillon. After the death of her husband she endowed several monasteries in Picardy, herself living as a Benedictine oblate under the obedience of the abbot of St Vaast.
Cf. Att. — Baud. — Holw.

IDA of LOUVAIN (Bl) **N. O.S.B. Cist.**
P.C. Apr. 13
d. c.1300. A native of Louvain. She joined the Cistercians at the nunnery of Rossendael (*Vallis Rosarum-Rosenthal*), near Malines, where she was favoured by God with a life-long series of amazing supernatural charismata. Her cult has survived to this day in Louvain and among the Cistercians.
Cf. Prop. Cist. — Att. — Holw. — Chev.— Zimm.

IDA of NIVELLES (Bl) **N. O.S.B.**
A.C. May 8
d. 652. She is also named Itta or Iduberga. She was the wife of Pepin of Nanden, after whose death (640) she became a Benedictine at Nivelles under her own daughter St Gertrude.
Cf. Zimm. — Baud. — Chev. — Holw.

IDA of HERZFELD (St) **W. A.C. Sept. 4**
d. c.813. Great-granddaughter of Charles Martel. She married and was very happy in her married life; but lost her husband very young. She then founded the nunnery of Herzfeld in Westphalia, devoted herself to good works, and died at the convent.
Cf. Att. — Baud. — Holw.

IDA of TOGGENBURG (Bl) **N. O.S.B.**
A.C. Nov. 3
1156-1226. She married a Count Henry of Toggenburg, to whom she bore no child, and from whom she suffered much persecution. She escaped, and at last succeeded in obtaining her husband's consent to her becoming a nun in the Benedictine convent of Fieshingen.
Cf. Att. — Holw.

IDABERGA (St) **V.** A.C. June 20
Otherwise Edburga, q.v.

IDESBALD (Bl) **Ab. O.S.B. Cist.**
A.C. Apr. 18
1100-1167. Born in Flanders, he spent his youth at the court of the count of Flanders. In 1135 he was made canon of Furnes, but resigned his office to become a Cistercian at the abbey of our Lady of the Dunes on the sand-hills between Dunkirk and Nieuport. He became the third abbot and ruled for twelve years. Cult confirmed in 1894.
Cf. Att. — Baud. — Chev.

IDUS (St) **Bp.** A.C. July 14
5th cent. A disciple of St Patrick by whom he was baptized and appointed bishop of Alt-Fadha in Leinster.
Cf. Holw.

IGNATIUS of ANTIOCH (St) **Bp. M.**
R.M. Feb. 1
d. c.107. Surnamed Theophorus (the God-bearer). Bishop of Antioch in Syria for forty years. Under Trajan he was carried to Rome, where he was thrown to the wild beasts in the amphitheatre during the public games. On his way to Rome he wrote seven epistles, which are still extant, and which show the whole system of Christianity — doctrinal, sacramental and hierarchical — as perfect then as it is today. His relics are kept at St Peter's, Rome, and his name is mentioned in the canon of the Roman Mass.
Cf. Att. — Holw. — Baud. — Menzies.

IGNATIUS of AFRICA (St) **M.**
R.M. Feb. 3
See Laurentinus, Ignatius and Celerina.

IGNATIUS DELGADO (Bl) **Bp. M. O.P.**
A.C. July 11
d. 1838. A Spaniard by birth, Ignatius Delgado y Cebrián professed the Dominican rule and was sent to the missions in Tonkin. He laboured for nearly fifty years and was appointed vicar apostolic of E. Tonkin and consecrated bishop. He died in his cage at Annam from hunger and exposure. Beatified in 1900.
Cf. Prop. O.P. — Att. — Holw.

IGNATIUS de AZEVEDO and Comp. (BB) MM. S.J. A.C. July 15

d. 1570. A band of forty Portuguese and Spanish Jesuit missionaries, who were put to death by the Huguenot skipper, Jacques Sourie, near the Canary Islands, while on their way to the West Indies. Ignatius was the superior and leader of the band. He was born at Coimbra, where he joined the Society of Jesus in 1548. He was a religious of outstanding ability, highly revered by his superiors. Cult officially confirmed in 1854.
Cf. Prop. S.J. — Att. — Baud. — Holw.

IGNATIUS of LOYOLA (St) Founder.
R.M. July 31

1491-1556. Iñigo de Recalde de Loyola was born on the estate of his family at Loyola in the Basque province of Guipuzcoa (Spain) and, after some time as a page at court, joined the army and was grievously wounded at the siege of Pampeluna in 1521. On his recovery he turned his mind to the service of the militant church. He prepared himself by a retreat at Montserrat and Manresa, where he wrote his epoch-making classic, *The Book of Spiritual Exercises*. At Paris he gathered nine companions and together they took their first vows at the church of Montmartre. Ignatius's aim was simply this: to work for the greater glory of God under the obedience of the pope. In 1537 he called his little band the Society of Jesus and in April, 1541, all took their final vows in the Benedictine basilica of St Paul-outside-the-Walls, Rome. Ignatius was naturally elected the first general and ruled the Society until his death. Before this time the original band had already become a veritable army scattered throughout the world — from Japan in the Far East to the furthermost West Indies. Ignatius was canonized in 1622.
Cf. Prop. S.J.—Att.—Menzies—Holw.

IGNATIUS JORJES (Bl) M. A.C. Sept. 10

d. 1622. The four-year-old son of Dominic Jorges and Isabel Fernandez. He was beheaded with his mother at Nagasaki (see Charles Spinola).
Cf. Holw.

IGNATIUS of CONSTANTINOPLE (St) Bp. R.M. Oct. 23

c.799-877. Son of the Byzantine emperor Michael, he was successively monk, priest, abbot, and patriarch (842) of his native Constantinople. He stood firm against intrigue and corruption, even in high places, and openly refused holy communion to Bardas Caesar on account of his public incest. Ignatius was driven from the see, and the scheming Photius intruded. After nine years Ignatius was recalled and governed the see till his death.
Cf. Att. — Holw. — Baud.

IGNATIUS of LACONI (Bl) O.F.M. Cap.
An Italian Capuchin lay-brother. Beatified in 1940.

ILDEPHONSUS (St) Bp. R.M. Jan. 23

607-667. Nephew of St Eugene of Toledo. He was born also at Toledo, studied at Seville under St Isidore, became monk and abbot of Agli (Agalia), on the Tagus near Toledo, and was made archbishop of that city in 657. He was responsible for the unification of the Spanish liturgy and excelled as a writer, chiefly on Mariology. It is said that our Lady appeared to him and gave him a chasuble. In Spain he is honoured liturgically as a Doctor of the church.
Cf. Zimm. — P. de U. — Att.

ILLADAN (ILLATHAN, IOLLADHAN) (St) Bp. A.C. June 10

6th cent. Bishop of Rathliphthen (now Rathlihen) in Offaly, Ireland.
Cf. O'Hanlon.

ILLIDIUS (ALLYRE) (St) Bp.
R.M. July 7

d. 385. The fourth bishop of Clermont, France. St Gregory of Tours had a great veneration for him.
Cf. Holw. — Baud. — Duch. Fast. Episc.

ILLOG (St) C. A.C. Aug. 8
Otherwise Ellidius, q.v.

ILLTYD (ILLTUT) (St) Ab. A.C. July 7

d. c.505. One of the most celebrated of the Welsh saints, but unfortunately the details of his life have not reached us in trustworthy form. From being a courtier and minister, he embraced the monastic life under St Cadoc, and later founded the great abbey of Llan-Illtut, or Llantwit, whence issued most of the Welsh saints of that period. According to some the original foundation was on Caldey Island. He is said to have died in Brittany.
Cf. Att. — Holw. — Baud.

ILLUMINATA (St) V.   R.M. Nov. 29
d. c.320. A maiden of Todi, in Italy, where she is still held in great veneration.
Cf. Baud. — Holw.

ILLUMINATUS (St) Mk. O.S.B.
R.M. May 11
d. c.1000. A Benedictine monk of the abbey of San Mariano, in his native township of Sanseverino in the Marches of Ancona.
Cf. Zimm. — Menzies — Holw.

ILLUMINATUS (St) C. O.F.M.
A.C. May 11
d. c.1230. Said to have been a disciple of St Francis of Assisi. He is often confused with his homonym of Sanseverino.
Cf. Menzies — Baud.

IMANA of LOSS (IMAINA, HIM-MANNA, IMAINE) (Bl) Abs. O.S.B.
P.C. Oct. 21
d. 1270. Cistercian abbess of Salzinnes, near Namur, and afterwards of Flines, in the diocese of Cambrai.
Cf. Baud. — Holw.

IMELDA LAMBERTINI (Bl) V. O.P.
A.C. May 12
d. 1333. Daughter of Count Egano Lambertini of Bologna, she was a pupil at the Dominican convent of that city, and "is stated to have received her first holy communion miraculously at the age of eleven, and to have died immediately after." (Attwater). Cult confirmed in 1826.
Cf. Prop. O.P. — Att. — Holw. — Baud. — Menzies.

IMELIN (St) Ab.   A.C. March 10
Otherwise Emilian, q.v.

IMMA (IMMINA) (St) Abs. O.S.B.
A.C. Nov. 25
c.700-c.752. A native of Würzburg and abbess of a nunnery at Karlburg in Franconia.
Cf. Zimm. — Holw.

INA and ETHELBURGA (SS)
P.C. Sept. 8
d. 727. Ina was king of Wessex from 688 till 726. As such he is best remembered as the restorer of Glastonbury. About the year 726 he resigned and, with his wife Ethelburga, journeyed to Rome, where he ended his days in practices of piety and penance. They have never been formally recognized as saints.
Cf. Stanton — Holw. — Zimm.

INAN (St) H.   A.C. Aug. 18
Otherwise Evan, q.v.

INDALETIUS (St) Bp.   R.M. May 15
See Torquatus, Ctesiphon, etc.

INDES, DOMNA, AGAPES and THEO-PHILA (SS) MM.   R.M. Dec. 28
d. 303. A group of martyrs, who suffered at Nicomedia under Diocletian.
Cf. Holw. — Baud.

INDRACT (St) M.   A.C. Feb. 5
d. c.710. An old legend makes him an Irish chieftain, who, on his return from a Roman pilgrimage, was put to death, with his sister St Dominica (Drusa) and others, by heathen Saxons, near Glastonbury, where their relics were enshrined. A still later legend has made them contemporaries of St Patrick.
Cf. Att. — Baud. — Holw.

INES de BENIGANIM (Bl) V. O.S.A.
A.C. Jan. 21
1625-1696. Born near Valencia, in Spain, she entered the nunnery of Augustinian hermitesses at Beniganim with the new name of Josepha Maria. In Spain she was usually called by her baptismal name as above. Beatified in 1888.
Cf. Att. — Holw.

INÉS, INEZ (*several*)
Note. The Spanish and Portuguese forms respectively of the name Agnes, q.v.

IÑGEN (St) M.   R.M. Dec. 20
See Ammon, Zeno, etc.

INGENUINUS (St) Bp.   R.M. Feb. 5
Otherwise Genuinus, q.v.

IÑIGO (St) Ab. O.S.B.   R.M. June 1
Otherwise Eneco, q.v.

INJURIOSUS and SCHOLASTICA (SS)
A.C. May 25
d. c.550. A married couple of Auvergne, who lived the whole of their married life as brother and sister, "*Les Deux Amants.*"
Cf. Holw. — Baud.

INNOCENT of TORTONA (St) Bp.
R.M. Apr. 17
d. c.350. He was a confessor under Diocletian, being scourged and just escaping death. After Constantine's peace, he was ordained a priest and consecrated bishop of Tortona in Italy (c.326).
Cf. Att. — Menzies — Holw.

INNOCENT (St) M.　　　R.M. June 17
See Isaurus, Innocent, etc.

INNOCENT (St) Bp.　　　A.C. June 19
d. 559. Bishop of Le Mans, in France, for over forty years.
Cf. Duch. Fast. Episc. — Gams — Baud.

INNOCENT V. (Bl) Pope O.P.
R.M. June 22
1245-1277. Born at Tarentaise in Burgundy, he entered the Dominican order and acquired great fame as a theologian and as a preacher. In 1272 he was made archbishop of Lyons, and during his episcopate the general council was held in that city, in which he took a prominent part. Created cardinal of Ostia, he was made pope in 1276, but died only a few months later.
Cf. Menzies — Prop. O.P. — Att.

INNOCENT, SEBASTIA (SABBATIA) and Comp. (SS) MM.　　　R.M. July 4
? A group of thirty-two martyrs who suffered at Sirmium, now Mitrovica, in the Balkans.
Cf. Holw. — Baud.

INNOCENT I (St) Pope　　　R.M. July 28
d. 417. A native of Albano, near Rome, St Innocent was pope from 402 till 417. The outstanding event in his pontificate was the sack of Rome by the Goth Alaric in 410. He firmly maintained the supremacy of the Roman see, both in the West, in the case of the African synods against Pelagianism, and in the East, witness the appeal of St John Chrysostom.
Cf. Menzies — Att. — Baud.

INNOCENT (St) M.　　　R.M. Sept. 22
See Maurice and Comp.

INNOCENTS, The Holy (SS) MM.
R.M. Dec. 28
1st cent. From a very early date "the men children that were in Bethlehem and in all the borders thereof" (Matt. II, 16),
murdered by Herod, have been liturgically venerated as martyrs. Prudentius most fittingly styles them *Flores Martyrum.* Their number is not known, and this has led to the multiplication of their relics in many churches.
Cf. Menzies — Att. — Baud.

IPHIGENIA (St) V.　　　R.M. Sept. 21
1st cent. An alleged maiden of Ethiopia converted by St Matthew the apostle and evangelist.
Cf. Baud. — Holw.

IRAIS (HERAIS, RHAIS) (St) V. M.
R.M. Sept. 22
d. c.300. An Egyptian maiden of Alexandria, or of Antinoë, beheaded under Diocletian.
Cf. Holw. — Baud.

IRCHARD (St) Bp.　　　A.C. Aug. 24
7th cent. An apostle of the Picts and disciple of St Ternan, born in Kincardineshire, and said to have been consecrated bishop in Rome by St Gregory the Great.
Cf. Holw. — Baud.

IRENAEUS (St) M.　　　R.M. Feb. 10
See Zoticus, Irenaeus, etc.

IRENAEUS of SIRMIUM (St) Bp. M.
R.M. March 25
d. 304. A bishop in Pannonia (Hungary), who suffered martyrdom under Diocletian at Sirmium (Mitrovica). His Acts are authentic and most touching.
Cf. Holw. — Baud.

IRENAEUS (St) M.　　　R.M. March 26
See Theodore, Irenaeus, etc.

IRENAEUS (St) M.　　　R.M. Apr. 1
See Quinctian and Irenaeus.

IRENAEUS, PEREGRINUS and IRENE (SS) MM.　　　R.M. May 5
d. c.300. Martyrs of Thessalonica, burnt at the stake under Diocletian.
Cf. Holw. — Baud.

IRENAEUS of LYONS (St) Bp. M.
R.M. June 28
c.125-c.202. A native of Asia Minor and a disciple of St Polycarp, who was a pupil of St John the Apostle. He migrated to Gaul, and became bishop of Lyons (c.177). Tradition adds that he was a martyr, but

of this we have no proof. St Irenaeus is the first great ecclesiastical writer of the West. His work against Gnosticism is a witness to the apostolic tradition, derived from St John: in it we find already a testimony to the primacy of the Roman see.
Cf. Att. — Baud. — Duch. Fast. Episc.

IRENAEUS and MUSTIOLA (SS) MM.
R.M. July 3
d. 273. Irenaeus, a deacon, and Mustiola, a noble lady, were martyred at Chiusi in Tuscany under Aurelian for having ministered to other martyrs and buried their bodies.
Cf. Menzies — Att. — Baud. — Holw.

IRENAEUS and ABUNDIUS (SS) MM.
R.M. Aug. 26
d. c.258. Roman martyrs, who were drowned in the public sewers during the persecution of Valerian.
Cf. Holw. — Baud.

IRENAEUS, ANTONY, THEODORE, SATURNINUS, VICTOR and Comp. (SS) MM. R.M. Dec. 15
d. c.258. A group of twenty-two martyrs, who suffered under Valerian.
Cf. Holw. — Baud.

IRENE (St) V. M. R.M. Apr. 5
d. 304. The sister of SS Agape and Chionia, q.v.

IRENE (St) M. R.M. May 5
See Irenaeus, Peregrinus, etc.

IRENE (St) M. R.M. Sept. 18
See Sophia and Irene.

IRENE (St) V. M. R.M. Oct. 20
d. c.653. A Portuguese nun who suffered death in defence of her chastity. Her shrine is at Santarem (*Sancta Irenes*) the ancient Scalabris. The legend as handed down to us is full of fiction, but the essential facts are certain.
Cf. P. de U. — Baud. — Holw.

IRENION (St) Bp. R.M. Dec. 16
d. 389. A bishop of Gaza in Palestine in the time of Theodosius the Great.
Cf. Holw. — Baud.

IRMENGARD (Bl) Abs. O.S.B.
A.C. July 16
d. 866. Daughter of King Louis the German, grandson of Charlemagne. By

her father she was appointed abbess, first of Buchau and then of Chiemsee. Cult confirmed in 1928.
Cf. Att. — Zimm. — Holw.

IRMINA (St) Abs. O.S.B. R.M. Dec. 24
d. 708. Daughter of Dagobert II. At the age of fifteen she was given in marriage but on the day of her wedding her betrothed died. She then persuaded her father to build for her the nunnery of Oehren (Horreum) near Trèves, under the Benedictine Rule. She was a generous benefactress of both Celtic and Saxon monks; and built Echternach for St Willibrord (698). She died at the monastery of Weissenburg, another foundation of her father's.
Cf. Zimm. — Att. — Chev. — Holw.

ISAAC JOGUES (St) M. S.J.
A.C. March 16
d. 1646 (Oct. 18). A Jesuit missionary who arrived in Canada in 1636, and after several heroic adventures, was tomahawked by the Mohawks in an Iroquois village. Canonized in 1930.
Cf. Att.

ISAAC (St) H. R.M. Apr. 11
d. c.550. A Syrian monk, who fled from the Monophysite persecution and founded a *laura* at Monteluco, near Spoleto, in Umbria. He was one of the restorers of eremitical life in 6th-century Italy.
Cf. Menzies — Att. — Holw. — Chev.

ISAAC (ISACIUS) (St) M. R.M. Apr. 21
See Apollo, Isacius and Codratus.

ISAAC (St) Ab. A.C. May 30
d. c.410. A brave defender of the Catholic faith against the Arian emperor Valens, whom he publicly denounced. He narrowly escaped death, and became a monk, and eventually abbot, of a large monastery at Constantinople.
Cf. Att. — Holw.

ISAAC (St) M. R.M. June 3
d. 852. Born at Cordova, in Spain, he became very proficient in Arabic and was made a notary under the Moorish government. He resigned this office to embrace the monastic life at Tabanos, about seven miles from Cordova. In a public debate at Cordova he denounced Mohammed and was put to death at the age of 27.
Cf. P. de U. — Att. — Holw. — Chev.

ISAAC the GREAT (St) Bp.
                               A.C. Sept. 9
d. c.440. Son of the Armenian patriarch
(or katholikos) St Nerses the Great, to
whose office he succeeded. He is the real
founder of the Armenian church. He
translated a large part of the Bible,
founded monasteries, and was practically
the only ruler — ecclesiastical and civil —
of the Armenians. He died a centenarian.
Cf. Holw. — Att.

ISAAC (ISACIUS) (St) Bp. M.
                              R.M. Sept. 21
? An Eastern martyr, honoured chiefly in
Cyprus.
Cf. Holw.

ISAAC (St) M. O.S.B.   **R.M. Nov. 12**
See Benedict, John, etc.

ISABEL FERNANDEZ (Bl) M.
                              A.C. Sept. 10
d. 1622. A Spanish lady, widow of Dominic Jorjes, beheaded with her son Ignatius
at Nagasaki, for having given shelter to
Bl Charles Spinola, q.v. Beatified in
1867.
Cf. Holw.

ISABELLA (St) Queen.   **R.M. July 8**
Otherwise Elisabeth, q.v.

**ISABELLE of FRANCE (Bl) V. Poor
Clare.**   **A.C. Feb. 26**
d. 1270. The only sister of St Louis of
France. She declined marriage with the
emperor of Germany, and after the death
of her mother, Blanche of Castile, founded
the convent of Poor Clares at Longchamps,
near Paris, where she lived as a nun, without, however, taking vows. Beatified in
1520.
Cf. Att. — Holw. — Baud.

ISAIAS, SABAS and Comp. (SS) MM.
                              R.M. Jan. 14
d. 309. Thirty-eight monks on Mt Sinai,
massacred by pagan Arabs. This massacre was followed by several others in the
neighbourhood of the Red Sea.
Cf. Holw. — Baud.

ISAIAS BONER (Bl) C. O.S.A.
                              A.C. Feb. 8
d. 1471. Born at Cracow, where also he
studied theology. He joined the Augustinians and was employed chiefly in teach-

ing Scripture, which he did with extraordinary zeal and success.
Cf. Att. — Holw.

ISAIAS of CORDOVA (St) M.
                              R.M. Feb. 16
See Elias, Jeremias, etc.

ISAIAS (ISAIAH) (St) Prophet.
                              R.M. July 6
d. c.681. One of the four greater prophets
of the O.T. Tradition tells us that he was
sawn in two by order of King Manasses of
Juda, and buried under an oak tree. His
tomb was still venerated in the fifth century of our era.
Cf. Holw. — Baud.

**ISARNUS (YSARN) of TOULOUSE (St)
Ab. O.S.B.**   **A.C. Sept. 24**
d. 1048. Born at Marseilles, he was educated, and became a monk and abbot, at
St Victor's, Marseilles. He was famous
for his charity, chiefly towards criminals.
Cf. Mab. — Chev. — Holw. — Baud.

**ISAURUS, INNOCENT, FELIX, JERE-
MIAS and PEREGRINUS (SS) MM.**
                              R.M. June 17
? Athenians who during one of the perse-
cutions concealed themselves in a cave at
Apollonia in Macedonia. On being dis-
covered they were beheaded.
Cf. Holw. — Baud.

ISBERGA (ITISBERGA) (St) V. O.S.B.
                              A.C. May 21
d. c.800. A supposed sister of Charlemagne. She was a nun at Aire (*Aria*) in
the Artois. She is venerated as the patroness of Artois.
Cf. Zimm. — Holw. — Baud.

ISCHYRION and Comp. (SS) MM.
                        R.M. June 1 and Dec. 22
d. 250. Ischyrion was an Egyptian official who was impaled for the Faith under
Decius. The Ischyrion commemorated in
the R.M. on June 1 is identical with the
one mentioned on Dec. 22.
Cf. Att. — Holw. — Bolland.

ISIDORA (St) V.   **A.C. May 1**
c. 365. A nun in an Egyptian monastery
who, to escape being honoured in the
cloister, fled to a desert hermitage where
she died.
Cf. Holw. — Baud.

ISIDORE of ANTIOCH (St) Bp. M.
R.M. Jan. 2
4th cent. An Eastern bishop martyred at
Antioch by the Arians.
Cf. Holw. — Baud.

ISIDORE of NITRIA (St) Bp.
R.M. Jan. 2
4th cent. Mentioned by St Jerome as
"a holy venerable bishop" who had welcomed him to Egypt. Some think that he
is identical with St Isidore of Pelusium
(Feb. 4).
Cf. Holw. — Baud.

ISIDORE the EGYPTIAN (St) C.
R.M. Jan. 15
d. 404. An Egyptian priest, who was in
charge of the hospice for pilgrims at Alexandria. He defended St Athanasius and
had much to suffer at the hands of the
Arians. Accused of Origenism by St
Jerome, Isidore went to Constantinople
where he was befriended by St John
Chrysostom.
Cf. Att. — Holw. — Baud.

ISIDORE of PELUSIUM (St) C.
R.M. Feb. 4
d. c.540. An Egyptian abbot of a monastery at Pelusium. He was much esteemed by St Cyril of Alexandria. A
great number of his letters are still extant.
Cf. Att. — Baud. — Holw.

ISIDORE (St) M. **R.M. Feb. 5**
A duplicate of Isidore of Chios (May 15)
q.v.

ISIDORE of SEVILLE (St) Bp. and Dr.
R.M. Apr. 4
c.560-636. A native of Cartagena, in
Spain, and brother to SS Leander, Fulgentius and Florentina. He was educated
by St Leander whom he succeeded in the
see of Seville in 600. He presided over
several synods, reorganized the Spanish
church, encouraged monastic life, completed the Mozarabic liturgical rite, was
responsible for the decree of the council of
Toledo in 633 that there should be a
school in every diocese where the liberal
arts, Hebrew and Greek should be taught,
and was himself an encyclopaedical writer
on theology, scripture, biography, history,
geography, astronomy and grammar. He
is often called "the schoolmaster of the
Middle Ages." The Englishman St Bede,

was much indebted to St Isidore, of whom
he was an ardent admirer. Declared
Doctor of the Church by Benedict XIV.
Cf. P. de U. — Chev. — Att. — Holw.

ISIDORE (St) M. **R.M. Apr. 17**
See Elias, Paul and Isidore.

ISIDORE the FARMER (St) C.
R.M. May 10
d. 1170. A native of Madrid, he spent his
whole life working in the fields on an estate just outside the city. He was married to St Mary de la Cabeza. Canonized
in 1622 and venerated as the patron saint
of Madrid.
Cf. P. de U. — Holw. — Att. — Baud.

ISIDORE of CHIOS (St) M. R.M. May 15
d. ? 251. A martyr of Chios under
Decius.
Cf. Att. — Baud. — Holw.

ISIDORE (St) M. **R.M. Dec. 14**
See Heron, Arsenius, etc.

ISMAEL (St) Bp. **A.C. June 16**
6th cent. A disciple of St Teilo, and by
him consecrated bishop. Several Welsh
churches are dedicated to him.
Cf. — Holw. — Baud.

ISMAEL (St) M. **R.M. June 17**
See Manuel, Sabel and Ismael.

ISNARD de CHIAMPO (Bl) C. O.P.
A.C. March 22
d. 1244. A native of Chiampo, diocese of
Vicenza, he received the Dominican habit
at the hands of St Dominic himself (1219)
and was the founder and first prior of the
friary at Pavia. It is narrated of him
that, in spite of his mortified life, "he
was excessively fat and people used to
ridicule him about it when he was preaching." (Attwater h. 1). Cult confirmed
in 1919.
Cf. Prop. O.P. — Holw. — Att.

ISSELL (ISSEY) (St) Bp. **A.C. Feb. 9**
Otherwise Teilo, q.v.

ISSERNINUS (St) Bp. **A.C. Dec. 6**
See Auxilius, Issernimus and Secundinus.

ISSEY (St) Ab. **A.C. Feb. 9**
Otherwise Teilo, q.v. Perhaps also a
Cornish variant of Ita.

ITA (YTHA, MEDA) (St) V. A.C. Jan. 15
d. c.570. Surnamed "the second St Bridget" or the "St Bridget of Munster." In popular veneration among the Irish she is second only to St Bridget. She was a native of Drum in Co Waterford. She founded the nunnery of Hy Conaill, in Co Limerick and soon attracted thither large numbers of maidens. Her life is full of incredible anecdotes.
Cf. Att. — Holw. — Baud.

ITHAMAR (St) Bp. A.C. June 10
d. c.656. A native of Kent, and the first Anglo-Saxon to be appointed bishop, being promoted to the see of Rochester after St Paulinus.
Cf. Zimm. — Stanton — Att. — Holw.

ITTA (IDUBERGA) (Bl) N. O.S.B.
A.C. May 8
Otherwise Ida of Nivelles, q.v.

IVAN (St) H. A.C. June 24
d. 845. A hermit in Bohemia, who had renounced a brilliant position at court. He was buried by St Ludmilla, duchess of Bohemia.
Cf. Holw. — Baud.

IVE (IVES) (St) V. M. A.C. Feb. 3
Otherwise Ia, q.v.

IVES (St) Bp. A.C. Apr. 24
Otherwise Ive, q.v.

IVETTA (JUTTA) (Bl) W. A.C. Jan. 13
d. 1228. A Dutch mystic who was left a widow and the mother of three children at the age of eighteen. Consecrating her widowhood to God, she undertook the care of lepers, till she took to the solitary life, in which she spent more than forty years famous for her discernment of spirits and gift of council.
Cf. Holw.

IVO (St) Bp. A.C. Apr. 24
? According to the medieval legend he was a Persian bishop, who became a hermit in Huntingdonshire. The town of St Ives in Huntingdonshire takes its name from him (but not that in Cornwall).
Cf. Att. — Stanton — Holw.

IVO (YVO) HÉLORY (St) C.
R.M. May 19
1253-1303. A native of Brittany, born near Tréguier. He studied at Paris and Orleans and he practised law in his native city, both in the ecclesiastical and in the civil courts. He defended the poor and unprotected as well as the rich and was called "the Advocate of the Poor." Canonized in 1347, and venerated by lawyers as their patron saint.
Cf. Holw. — Baud. — Att.

IVO of CHARTRES (St) Bp. O.S.A.
A.C. May 23
d. 1115. The provost of the Augustinian canons regular of Saint-Quentin, who in 1091 was made bishop of Chartres. He was renowned for his knowledge of canon law, and was consulted by King Philip of France on difficult canonical questions. Upright and just, Ivo opposed the rapacity of ecclesiastical dignitaries. He wrote much on canon law.
Cf. Att. — Holw. — Baud.

IVOR (St) Bp. A.C. Apr. 23
Otherwise Iberius, q.v.

J

JACOBINUS de' CANEPACI (Bl) C. O.C.
A.C. March 3
1438-1508. A native of the diocese of Vercelli, in Piedmont, and a Carmelite lay-brother there. Cult approved in 1845.
Cf. Att. — Baud. — Holw.

JACOPONE da TODI (Bl) C. O.F.M
P.C. Dec. 25
d. 1306. Jacopone Benedetti was a native of Todi, who read law at Bologna, married, and lived in easy circumstances. In 1268 he lost his wife and his sorrow knew no bounds. He became a "fool for Christ's sake" and eventually joined the Friars Minor. Unfortunately his tempestuous temperament led him to join the party of the Franciscan Spirituals; he wrote against the pope and was put in prison. He is the alleged author of the *Stabat Mater*, etc. Cult never confirmed.
Cf. Att. — Baud.

JACUT and GUETHENOC (SS) CC.
A.C. Feb. 6
5th cent. Sons of SS Fragan and Gwen, and brothers of the more celebrated St Gwenaloe or Winwaloë. They became disciples of St Budoc, and like him were driven from Britain by the invading Saxons.
Cf. Holw. — Baring-Gould.

JADER (St) Bp. M. R.M. Sept. 10
See Nemesian, Felix, etc.

JADWIGA (*several*)
Otherwise Hedwig, q.v.

JAMBERT (St) Bp. O.S.B. A.C. Aug. 12
d. 790. Abbot of St Augustine's, Canterbury, chosen to succeed St Bregwin as archbishop in that see (766).
Cf. Stanton — Holw.

JAMES (*several*)
Note. James is the English form of the Hebrew Jacob, latinized into Jacobus. Hence the modern variants in different languages: in Italian, Giacomo; in French, Jacques; in Spanish, Santiago, Iago, Jaime, Diego; in Portuguese, Iago, Diogo; in Catalan, Jaume.

JAMES of TARENTAISE (St) Bp.
A.C. Jan. 16
d. ? 429. A disciple of St Honoratus at Lérins and venerated at Chambéry as an apostle of Savoy and the first bishop of Tarentaise.
Cf. Baud. — Holw. — Att.

JAMES the HERMIT (St) C.
R.M. Jan. 28
6th cent. The R.M. says: "In Palestine the memory of St James the Hermit, who, after a lapse from the faith, lay hid long in a tomb for penance, and, renowned for miracles, passed to the Lord." A later legend changes the "lapse from the faith" into one of adultery and homicide, committed under most romantic circumstances.
Cf. Holw. — Baud.

JAMES the ALMSGIVER (Bl) C. or M.
A.C. Jan. 28
d. 1304. Born near Chiusi in Lombardy, Bl James studied law, but on attaining manhood became a priest and restored a ruined hospital, where he tended the sick and gave legal advice gratuitously. Having discovered that the former revenues of this hospital had been unjustly appropriated, he found it necessary to sue the bishop of Chiusi in the courts and won his case. The bishop retaliated by hiring assassins who murdered the saint.
Cf. Att. — Holw.

JAMES KISAI (St) M. S.J. R.M. Feb. 5
d. 1597. A native of Japan, temporal

coadjutor of the Society of Jesus, and catechist at Ozaka. He was crucified at Nagasaki at the age of sixty-four. Canonized in 1862.
Cf. Prop. S.J. — Holw.

JAMES SALÈS and WILLIAM SAULTEMOUCHE (BB) MM. S.J. A.C. Feb. 7
d. 1593. James Salès was born in 1556, the son of a manservant, and joined the Society of Jesus. In 1592, in company with William Saultemouche, a temporal coadjutor, he was sent to preach the Advent course at Aubenas in the Cévennes. His sermons, in which he attacked the teaching of the Protestants, were a great success, and the town being then without a parish priest, Bl James was begged to remain till Easter. Early in February, 1593, a band of Huguenot raiders dragged the Jesuits before an improvised court of Calvinist ministers. After a heated theological discussion Salès was dragged from the hall and shot, while Saultemouche, who refused to make his escape, was stabbed to death. Both were beatified in 1926.
Cf. Prop. S.J. — Att. — Baud.

JAMES FENN (Bl) M. A.C. Feb. 12
d. 1584. A native of Montacute, near Yeovil, Somerset, he was educated at Oxford (Corpus Christi College and Gloucester Hall), became a schoolmaster and married. On his wife's death he studied at Reims and was ordained priest (1580). Four years later he was martyred at Tyburn. Beatified in 1929.
Cf. Newdigate.

JAMES CARVALHO (Bl) M. S.J.
A.C. Feb. 25
d. 1624. A Portuguese Jesuit who laboured as a missionary in the Far East. Together with other Christians he was slowly martyred by exposure to cold at Sendai in Japan.
Cf. Prop. S.J.

JAMES CAPOCCI (Bl) Bp. O.S.A.
A.C. March 14
d. 1308. Born at Viterbo. From being an Augustinian friar he was promoted (1302) to the see of Benevento and in 1303 transferred to Naples. Cult approved in 1911.
Cf. Att. — Holw. — Baud.

JAMES BIRD (Bl) M. A.C. March 25
d. 1593. A native of Winchester who, at

the age of nineteen, was hanged in that city for being reconciled to the Church. Beatified in 1929.
Cf. Newdigate — Att.

JAMES of PADUA (Bl) M. O.F.M.
                              A.C. Apr. 9
d. 1322. A Franciscan missionary martyred in the East Indies, a companion of St Thomas of Tolentino, q.v. Cult approved in 1809.
Cf. Baud. — Holw.

JAMES of CERTALDO (Bl) C. O.S.B. Cam.   **A.C. Apr. 13**
d. 1392. James Guidi was born at Certaldo, the son of a knight of Volterra. He joined the Camaldolese Benedictines at the abbey of SS Clement and Justus at Volterra. He spent there sixty years, during forty of which he acted as parish priest of the abbey church. His father and his brother joined the abbey as lay-brothers. Twice he refused the abbacy.
Cf. Zimm. — Chev. — Att. — Holw. — Baud.

JAMES of CERQUETO (Bl) C. O.S.A.
                              A.C. Apr. 17
d. 1367. A native of Cerqueto, near Perugia. He joined the Augustinian friars in the latter city. Cult approved in 1895.
Cf. Att. — Baud. — Holw.

JAMES of OLDO (Bl) C. Tert. O.F.M.
                              A.C. Apr. 19
d. 1404. A native of Lodi who married and for a time gave himself up to pleasure and good living. He was converted to higher things during a time of pestilence, became, with his wife, a Franciscan tertiary, turned his house into a church, and eventually was ordained priest.
Cf. Att. — Holw.

JAMES DUCKETT (Bl) M. A.C. Apr. 19
d. 1602. A native of Gilfortrigs, Skelsmergh, Westmorland, who became a convert and settled as a bookseller in London. After several terms of imprisonment, amounting to altogether nine years, for printing and selling Catholic books, he was hanged at Tyburn for the same reason. Beatified in 1929.
Cf. Newdigate — Att.

JAMES BELL (Bl) M.   A.C. Apr. 20
d. 1584. A native of Warrington, Lancs,

and educated at Oxford. He was ordained priest under Queen Mary, conformed to the state Church under Elizabeth, repented and was reconciled to the true Church. On this account he was hanged at Lancaster in his sixty-fourth year. Beatified in 1929.
Cf. Newdigate — Att.

JAMES of PERSIA (St) M. R.M. Apr. 22
See Persian Martyrs.

JAMES of BITETTO (Bl) C. O.F.M.
                              A.C. Apr. 27
d. c.1485. Surnamed also "of Sclavonia," or "of Illyricum," or "of Zara," or "of Dalmatia." He was a native of Sebenico in Dalmatia, and donned the Franciscan habit as a lay-brother at Zara; but spent most of his life at the friary of Bitetto, near Bari, in S. Italy. Cult approved by Innocent XII.
Cf. Att. — Baud. — Holw.

JAMES of NUMIDIA (St) M.
                              R.M. Apr. 30
See Marianus, James, etc.

JAMES the LESS (St) Apostle.
                              R.M. May 1
d. c.62. James the Less (*Jacobus Minor*) or "the Younger," surnamed also "the Just," was a cousin of our Lord, and one of the twelve. After the Resurrection he became the first bishop of Jerusalem. He is the author of one of the canonical epistles. He was martyred at Jerusalem by being thrown from a pinnacle of the temple and then stoned to death.
Cf. Att. — Baud. — Holw.

JAMES WALWORTH (Bl) M. O.Cart.
                              A.C. May 11
d. 1537. A monk of the London Charterhouse, hanged in chains at York under Henry VIII. Beatified in 1886.
Cf. Newdigate — Camm.

JAMES of NOCERA (Bl) C. O.S.B.
                              A.C. May 27
d. 1300. A native of Nocera in Umbria, and a monk of Santa Croce di'Fontavellana.
Cf. Holw. — Chev.

JAMES BERTONI (Bl) C. O.S.M.
                              A.C. May 30
c.1444-1483. A native of Faenza. At the age of nine he joined the Servites, whom he served as procurator of the friary from

the time of his ordination till his death. Cult confirmed in 1766.
Cf. Att. — Holw. — Prop. O.S.M.

JAMES SALOMONE (Bl) C. O.P.
A.C. May 31
1231-1314. A native of Venice who joined the Dominicans at Santa Maria Celeste, in that city, and held office in several houses of the Order until he died of cancer at Forlí. Cult approved in 1526.
Cf. Prop. O.P. — Att. — Baud. — Holw.

JAMES of STREPAR (Bl) Bp. O.F.M.
A.C. June 1
1392-1411. Of Polish birth, he joined the Franciscans and worked very successfully as vicar-general of the Franciscan missions among the schismatics and pagans of W. Russia. In 1392 he was appointed archbishop of Halicz in Gallicia. Cult approved in 1791.
Cf. Holw. — Att. — Baud.

JAMES BUZABALIAO (Bl) M.
A.C. June 3
d. 1886. A soldier to King Mwanga of Uganda. He was baptized in 1885 and burnt alive at Namuyongo in the following year. Beatified in 1912.
Cf. Holw.

JAMES of TOUL (St) Bp. A.C. June 23
d. 769. Born probably at Bertigny in Haute Marne. It is commonly asserted that he was a monk of Hornbach in the diocese of Metz, before he was raised to the see of Toul (756). He was a great benefactor of the Benedictines. He died at Dijon, praying before the tomb of St Benignus, while on his return from a pilgrimage to Rome.
Cf. Holw. — Baud.

JAMES LACOP (St) M. O. Praem.
R.M. July 9
d. 1572. A native of Oudenarden, Flanders. He was a Norbertine at Middelburg, and in 1566 he apostatized, wrote and preached against the Church; then he repented, returned to his abbey and was martyred by the Calvinists with the group of Gorkum martyrs, q.v. Canonized in 1867.
Cf. Holw.

JAMES of VORAGINE (Bl) Bp. O.P.
A.C. July 13
c.1230-c.1298. A native of Varezze (Vora-gine), in the diocese of Savona, he took the Dominican habit (1244), was provincial of Lombardy (1267-1286), and finally was consecrated archbishop of Genoa at Rome (1292). His highest title to fame is the compilation of the Legenda Aurea Sanctorum, a classic now known everywhere as The Golden Legend. Beatified in 1816.
Cf. Prop. O.P. — Att. — Menzies — Holw.

JAMES of NISIBIS (St) Bp.
R.M. July 15
d. c.340. A Syrian who became a monk and eventually was promoted bishop of Nisibis in Mesopotamia. We have very few authentic facts concerning him, but he will always be remembered as an ecclesiastical writer; indeed, among the Syrian Fathers, second only to St Ephrem.
Cf. Holw. — Att. — Baud.

JAMES ANDRADE (Bl) M. S.J.
A.C. July 15
d. 1570. Born at Pedrogao in the diocese of Coimbra, Portugal. He was a Jesuit priest and a companion of Bl Ignatius de Azevedo, whose martyrdom he shared. Beatified in 1854.
Cf. Holw. — Prop. S.J.

JAMES the GREATER (St) Apostle
R.M. July 25
d. 43. The son of Zebedee and Salome and brother of St John the Evangelist, called with him to the apostolate by our Lord. He was the first of the Twelve to be martyred (Acts XII, 2) under King Herod Agrippa. A 9th-century legend makes him apostle of Spain and points to Compostella as the place where his body is enshrined; the legend grew, under Cluniac influence, and spread throughout W. Europe, so that Compostella became, after Jerusalem and Rome, the most famous place of pilgrimage in Christendom. St James is the patron saint of Spain.
Cf. Att.

JAMES GERIUS (Bl) C. O.S.B. Cam.
A.C. Aug. 5
d. 1345. A Camaldolese monk of Florence who died aged thirty-three. His great devotion was the "Sacred Will of God."
Cf. Zimm.

JAMES the SYRIAN (St) C. R.M. Aug. 6
d. p. 500. A Syrian by birth, who led a

solitary life in the environs of Amida (Diarbekir) in Mesopotamia.
Cf. Holw. — Baud.

JAMES NAM (Bl) M. A.C. Aug. 12
d. 1838. A native Tonkin priest, attached to the Society of Foreign Missions of Paris. Martyred in Tonkin. Beatified in 1900.
Cf. Holw.

JAMES the DEACON (St) C. O.S.B.
A.C. Aug. 17
7th cent. An Italian monk and deacon, companion of St Paulinus in his mission to Northumbria, where he remained in spite of the pagan reaction which set in after the death of St Edwin.
Cf. Stanton — Holw.

JAMES GUENGORO (Bl) M.
A.C. Aug. 18
d. 1620. A native Japanese child, aged two, son of BB. Thomas and Mary Guengoro, with whom he was crucified at Cocura. Beatified in 1867.
Cf. Holw.

JAMES DENXI (Bl) M. A.C. Aug. 19
d. 1622. A Japanese sailor on board the ship of Bl Joachim Firaiama, q.v. He was beheaded at Nagasaki. Beatified in 1867.
Cf. Holw.

JAMES of MEVANIA (Bl) C. O.P.
A.C. Aug. 23
d. 1301. James Bianconi was a native of Mevania — now Bevagna — in the diocese of Spoleto, and the founder and first prior of the Dominican friary in his native city. Cult approved in 1400 and again in 1674.
Cf. Att. — Holw. — Prop. O.P.

JAMES CLAXTON (Bl) M. A.C. Aug. 28
d. 1588. Born in Yorkshire and educated at Reims, where he was ordained in 1582. He was hanged for his priesthood at Isleworth. Beatified in 1929.
Cf. Newdigate.

JAMES FAYAXIDA (Bl) M. Tert. O.P.
A.C. Sept. 8
d. 1628. A Japanese who became a Dominican tertiary and was beheaded at Nagasaki. Beatified in 1867.
Cf. Holw.

JAMES GRIESINGER (Bl) C. O.P.
A.C. Oct. 11
1407-1491. Born at Ulm in Swabia, he joined the army, but abandoned this profession to take the Dominican habit as a lay-brother at Bologna (1441). For the rest of his life he was employed in painting on glass, in which art he excelled. Beatified in 1825.
Cf. Prop. O.P. — Att. — Holw. — Menzies.

JAMES the PERSIAN (St) M.
R.M. Nov. 1
See John and James.

JAMES of SASSEAU (St) C. O.S.B.
A.C. Nov. 19
d. c.865. A native of Constantinople and an army officer, after many travels he came to Gaul, was ordained priest at Clermont and joined the Benedictines near Bourges, whence at a later date he retired to the solitude of Sasseau (Saxiacum).
Cf. Zimm. — Holw.

JAMES BENFATTI (Bl) Bp. O.P.
A.C. Nov. 26
d. 1338. A native of Mantua and a Friar Preacher. He was a master in theology and in 1303 was chosen bishop of Mantua, in which office he merited the title of "Father of the Poor." Cult confirmed in 1859.
Cf. Prop. O.P. — Att. — Holw.

JAMES INTERCISUS (St) M.
R.M. Nov. 27
d. 421. A Persian officer of high rank who apostatized to keep the favour of King Yezdegird; but repented, and, under King Varanes V, was martyred by being cut into twenty-eight parts. Hence his surname of *Intercisus* (cut into pieces). The R.M. adds that many other Christians suffered with him.
Cf. Att. — Baud. — Holw.

JAMES della MARCA (St) C. O.F.M.
R.M. Nov. 28
1391-1475. James Gangala was born in the March of Ancona (the ancient Picenum). He studied law, but abandoned that career to join the Friars Minor. He became a fellow-missionary of St John Capistran, and for forty years he never

let a day pass without preaching the Word of God.

Cf. Att. — Holw. — Baud.

JAMES THOMPSON (alias HUDSON) (Bl) M. A.C. Nov. 28

d. 1582. Born at York and educated for the priesthood at Reims, he was ordained in 1581, and hanged the following year at York for his priesthood. Beatified in 1895.

Cf. Att. — Newdigate.

JANE (*several*)

The English feminine form of John. The variants in other modern languages are numerous. In hagiology, however, the principal are: In Italian, Giovanna; in French, Jeanne;. in Spanish, Juana; in Portuguese and Catalan, Joana. Another English form is Joan.

JANE of BAGNO (Bl) V. O.S.B. Cam. A.C. Jan. 16

d. 1105. Born at Fontechiuso in Tuscany, she became a Camaldolese lay-sister at Santa Lucia, near Bagno, in Tuscany. Cult approved in 1823.

Cf. Prop. Camal. — Chev. — Att. — Zimm.

JANE de LESTONNAC (Bl) Foundress A.C. Feb. 2

1556-1640. She was born at Bordeaux, the daughter of a Calvinist mother, and a niece of Montaigne. After the death of her husband, the baron de Montferrand, to whom she bore four children, and in her forty-seventh year, she entered the Cistercian novitiate which she had to leave on account of ill-health. She now felt called to found a new religious institute for the education of girls with the object of stemming the tide of Calvinism. Her scheme was approved by Paul V in 1607 and the first house was opened at Bordeaux. The Order spread rapidly, some thirty houses being established, and she ruled them all as superioress general. But as the result of a calumny and intrigue on the part of one of the sisters she was deposed, and spent her last years in peaceful, though very humiliating, seclusion. Her character was completely vindicated only one year before she died. Beatified in 1891.

Cf. Att. — Baud. — Zimm.

JANE of VALOIS (Bl) Foundress A.C. Feb. 4

1461-1504. The daughter of Louis XI of France, who married her to the duke of Orleans, afterwards King Louis XII. Her husband obtained a decree of nullity of marriage, and she retired to Bourges, where, together with the Franciscan Bl Gabriel Mary, she founded the order of nuns of the Annunciation — known as *Les Annonciades*. Cult confirmed in 1738.

Cf. Baud. — Att. — Holw.

JANE MARY BONOMO (Bl) V. O.S.B. A.C. March 1

1606-1670. Born at Asiago, diocese of Vicenza, in N. Italy and educated by the Poor Clares at Trent. She became a Benedictine at Bassano in 1622 and fell into ecstasy for the first time at the ceremony of profession. She held the offices of novice mistress, abbess (three times) and prioress. She was bitterly persecuted by some members of her own community. Beatified in 1783.

Cf. Zimm. — P. de U. — Baud. — Prop. O.S.B. (*Italy*).

JANE MARY de MAILLÉ (Bl) V. Tert. O.F.M. A.C. March 29

1331-1414. The daughter of the Baron de Maillé, she married the Baron de Silly, with whom she lived in virginity for sixteen years. After his death (1362) she joined the Franciscan tertiaries and retired to Tours, where she spent the rest of her life in much poverty and privation due to the persecution of her husband's relatives. Cult confirmed in 1871.

Cf. Att. — Baud. — Holw.

JANE of TOULOUSE (Bl) V. Tert. O.C. A.C. March 31

d. 1286. A native of Toulouse, she was affiliated to the Carmelite Order, as a tertiary, by St Simon Stock, and is for this reason venerated as the foundress of the Carmelite third order. She spent her time and substance in training young boy-candidates for the Carmelite Friars. Cult confirmed in 1895.

Cf. Att. — Holw. — Baud.

JANE of PORTUGAL (Bl) V. O.P. A.C. May 12

1452-1490. Born at Lisbon, a daughter of King Alphonsus V of Portugal. In 1473 she entered the Dominican convent at Aveiro, but her family would not allow her to take her vows until 1485, when the Portuguese succession was secured. She

had to suffer much annoyance on this account. Cult confirmed in 1693.
Cf. Prop. O.P. — Att. — Baud. — Holw.

JANE of ARC (St) V.   R.M. May 30
Otherwise Joan of Arc, q.v.

JANE GERARD (Bl) M.   A.C. June 26
d. 1794. One of the Sisters of Charity of Arras in France, who were arrested in 1792, and guillotined at Cambrai. Beatified in 1920.
Cf. Holw. — Baud.

JANE SCOPELLI (Bl) V. O.C.
A.C. July 9
c.1428-1491. A native of Reggio d'Emilia, Italy. She was the foundress and first prioress of the Carmelite nunnery at Reggio, for which she refused all endowments except those freely given to the nuns as alms. Cult confirmed in 1771.
Cf. Att. — Baud. — Holw.

JANE of ORVIETO (Bl) Tert. O.P.
A.C. July 23
d. 1306. Usually called Vanna, an Italian derivative of Giovanna (Jane). She was born at Carnajola, near Orvieto, where also she took the Dominican habit of the third order. Cult approved in 1754.
Cf. Prop. O.P. — Att. — Holw.

JANE of AZA (Bl) W. O.P.   A.C. Aug. 8
d. c.1190. Born at the family castle of Aza, near Aranda, in Old Castile, she married Felix de Guzman, to whom she bore two sons and a daughter and finally — in answer to prayer before the shrine of St Dominic of Silos — the Dominic who became the founder of the friars preachers. Cult approved in 1828.
Cf. Prop. O.P. — P. de U. — Att. — Holw.

JANE FRANCES FRÉMIOT de CHANTAL (St) W. Foundress   R.M. Aug. 21
1572-1641 (Dec. 13). Jane Frances Frémiot was born at Dijon, in Burgundy, and in 1592 married the Baron de Chantal. They spent together eight years of happy married life and had four children; then the Baron died as the result of a hunting accident. St Jane now found her spiritual father and friend in St Francis de Sales, under whose guidance, she founded the new Order of the Visitation, chiefly for widows and ladies who could not stand the austerities of the older orders. Sixty-six convents were established during her lifetime. Her last years were a period of intense suffering in body and mind. St Francis described her as "the perfect woman." She died at Moulins, but her remains rest at Annecy in Savoy.
Cf. Att. — Menzies — Baud.

JANE ANTIDE THOURET (Bl) V. Foundress   A.C. Aug. 25
1765-1828. Born near Besançon, the daughter of a tanner. In 1787 she joined the Sisters of Charity of St Vincent de Paul, but on the outbreak of the Revolution she was forced to return home. She now (1798) started at Besançon, a school of her own for poor girls. Soon her helpers in this and in other works of charity were so numerous as to lead her to found a new Institute of Daughters of Charity which was approved by the Holy See before the Foundress's death. Beatified in 1926.
Cf. Att. — Baud. — Holw.

JANE SODERINI (Bl) V. Tert. O.S.M.
A.C. Sept. 1
1301-1367. Born at Florence and educated by St Juliana Falconieri, under whom she became a Servite tertiary. Beatified in 1827.
Cf. Att. — Baud. — Holw.

JANE-LOUISE BARRÉ and JANE-REINÉ PRIN (BB) MM.   A.C. Oct. 17
d. 1794. Two Ursuline nuns, called in religion, respectively, Sister Cordula and Sister Laurentina, guillotined at Valenciennes. They formed part of a group of martyrs, listed in this book under the title Ursuline Nuns, MM., q.v.
Cf. Baud. — Holw.

JANE of SEGNA (Bl) V.   A.C. Nov. 17
d. 1307. Born at Segna, near Florence, she tended sheep. Both the Vallumbrosans and the Franciscans claim her as one of their tertiaries. Cult approved in 1798.
Cf. Att. — Baud. — Holw. — Chev.

JANE of CÁCERES (Bl) Abs. O.S.B. Cist.
P.C. Dec. 8
d. 1383. Cistercian abbess of the nunnery of St Benedict, at Castro, near Cáceres, in W. Spain. She was killed by marauding soldiers.
Cf. Chev. — Holw.

JANUARIA (St) M.   R.M. March 2
See Paul, Heraclius, etc.

JANUARIA (St) M.   R.M. July 17
See Scillitan Martyrs.

JANUARIUS (St) M.   R.M. Jan. 7
See Felix and Januarius.

JANUARIUS (St) M.   R.M. Jan. 19
See Paul, Gerontius, etc.

JANUARIUS, MAXIMA and MACARIA
(SS) MM.   R.M. Apr. 8
? African martyrs of whom nothing
further is known.

JANUARIUS (St) M.   R.M. July 10
See Seven Holy Brothers.

JANUARIUS, MARINUS, NABOR and
FELIX (SS) MM.   R.M. July 10
? African martyrs, of whom nothing
further is known.

JANUARIUS and PELAGIA (SS) MM.
      R.M. July 11
d. 320. Martyrs beheaded at Nicopolis
in Lesser Armenia under Licinius.
Cf. Holw. — Baud.

JANUARIUS (St) M.   R.M. July 15
See Catulinus, Januarius, etc.

JANUARIUS (St) M.   R.M. Aug. 6
See Sixtus and Comp.

JANUARIUS and Comp. MM.
      R.M. Sept. 19
d. 304. Januarius, bishop of Benevento,
Festus, his deacon, Desiderius, lector or
reader, Sosius, deacon of the church of
Misenum, Proculus, deacon of Pozzuoli,
and two other Christians, were beheaded
at Pozzuoli, under Diocletian. The body
of St Januarius (Gennaro) was eventually
enshrined at Naples, of which city he has
become the patron saint. The yearly
liquefaction of some of his blood preserved
in a phial is a well known phenomenon,
of which there are records for the past
four hundred years. No natural explanation has been found, although many have
been advanced.
Cf. Menzies — Att. — Holw. — Baud.

JANUARIUS (St) M.   R.M. Oct. 13
See Faustus, Januarius and Martial.

JANUARIUS (St) M.   R.M. Oct. 24
See Felix (Africanus), Audactus, etc.

JANUARIUS (St) M.   R.M. Oct. 25
See Protus and Januarius.

JANUARIUS (St) M.   R.M. Dec. 2
See Severus, Securus, etc.

JANUARIUS (St) M.   R.M. Dec. 15
See Faustinus, Lucius, etc.

JAPAN (Martyrs of) (SS and BB) MM.
      R.M. Feb. 5 (and A.C. several dates)
d. 1597 and 1614 and following years.
There are two main groups of Japanese
martyrs: the first comprises six Franciscans, three Jesuits and nineteen lay people.
The friars were Spanish or Portuguese
with one Mexican; the rest were Japanese.
All were crucified near Nagasaki in 1597.
They were canonized by Pius IX in 1862.
The second group is formed of thirty-six
Jesuits, twenty-six Franciscans, twenty-
one Dominicans, and five Augustinians,
and one hundred seven lay victims. They
were martyred between 1614 and 1644,
and were beatified by Pius IX and Leo
XIII at different dates. Most of the religious were Spanish; most of the lay
people native Japanese. Each is given a
special notice in this book.
Cf. Att. — Holw. — and the Propria of
the various Orders.

JARLATH (HIERLATH) (St) Bp.
      A.C. Feb. 1
d. c. 480. One of St Patrick's disciples,
who succeeded St Benignus in the see of
Armagh.
Cf. Holw.

JARLATH (St) Bp.   A.C. June 6
d. c.550. The founder and first abbot-
bishop of Tuam, in Connaught, Ireland,
where he established a monastic school
which became famous. St Brendan of
Clonfert and St Colman of Cloyne were
pupils there.
Cf. Att. — Holw. — Baud.

JARMAN (St) Bp.   A.C. July 3
Otherwise Germanus, q.v.

JASON (St)   R.M. July 12
1st cent. The Acts of the Apostles
(XVII, 5) say that St Paul stayed at
Jason's house in Thessalonica. St Paul

mentions him in his Epistle to the Romans (XVI, 21). In the Greek legend he is described as a bishop of Tarsus in Cilicia, going to Corfu, evangelizing that island, and dying there. The R.M. wrongly identifies him with the Mnason mentioned in the Acts (XXI, 6) "a Cyprian, an old disciple," with whom St Paul was staying in Jerusalem and whom tradition makes bishop of Tamasus in Cyprus.
Cf. Att.

JASON (St) M.   R.M. Dec. 3
See Claudius, Hilaria, etc.

JEREMIAS (St) M.   R.M. Feb. 16
See Elias, Jeremias, etc.

JEREMIAS (St) Prophet   R.M. May 1
c.590 B.C. The second of the greater prophets. The tradition concerning him is that at the age of fifty-five he was stoned to death in Egypt by the Jews who shared his captivity. His feast is observed chiefly at Venice, where some of his alleged relics are enshrined.
Cf. Holw. — Baud.

JEREMIAS (St) M.   R.M. June 7
See Peter, Wallabonsus, etc.

JEREMIAS (St) M.   R.M. June 17
See Isaurus, Innocent, etc.

JEREMIAS (St) M.   R.M. Sept. 15
See Emilias and Jeremias.

**JERMYN (GERMAN) GARDINER (Bl)
M.**   A.C. March 7
d. 1544. Educated at Cambridge, he became secretary to Stephen Gardiner, bishop of Winchester, and was executed at Tyburn with BB John Larke and John Ireland. Beatified in 1886.
Cf. Att. — Newdigate.

JEROME LU (Bl) M.   A.C. Jan. 28
c.1810-1858. Born at Mao-Cheu in China. He worked as a native catechist and was beheaded in his native town. Beatified in 1909.
Cf. Holw.

**JEROME of VALLUMBROSA (Bl) C.
O.S.B. Vall.**   A.C. June 18
d. 1135. A Vallumbrosan monk who retired to the hermitage of the abbey, called *Masso delle celle*, where he spent thirty-

five years, living all the time, it is said, only on bread and water.
Cf. Il Faggio Vallomb, XV, n. 6.

**JEROME of WERDEN (St) M. O.F.M.
R.M. July 9**
1522-1572. A native of Werden in Holland, who spent several years in Palestine as a Franciscan missionary. He was a powerful preacher against Calvinism. At the time of his martyrdom he was the vicar of the friary at Gorkum under St Nicholas Piek (see Gorkum, Martyrs of).
Cf. Holw. — Baud.

JEROME of PAVIA (St) Bp. A.C. July 19
d. 787. Bishop of Pavia, 778-787.
Cf. Menzies — Holw.

JEROME EMILIANI (St) C.
R.M. July 20
1481-1537. A Venetian who in his youth served in the army of the Republic. Being taken prisoner he was miraculously set free after praying to our Lady. He took holy orders and devoted himself to charitable works. In 1542 he founded a congregation of clerks regular vowed to the care of orphans. They were called *Somaschi*, from the little town in Lombardy — Somasca — where they started. Jerome died of a contagious malady caught while tending the sick. Canonized in 1767, and in 1928 declared the patron saint of orphans and abandoned children.
Cf. Att. — Baud. — Holw.

**JEROME of the CROSS de TORRES M.
Tert. O.F.M.**   A.C. Sept. 3
d. 1632. A Japanese secular priest, educated in the seminary of Arima and ordained at Manila. He returned to Japan (1628), was arrested (1631) and burnt alive at Nagasaki. Beatified in 1867.
Cf. Holw.

JEROME (St) C. Dr.   R.M. Sept. 30
c.342-420. Eusebius Hieronymus Sophronius was born at Stridonium in Dalmatia. He studied in Rome, particularly the classics for which he developed a lifelong passion. He then travelled extensively in Italy and Gaul, lived as a hermit in Palestine, returned to Rome, where, after his ordination to the priesthood, he joined the Roman clergy and acted as secretary to the pope, and finally, having come to be on bad terms with those who

surrounded him, went back to Palestine and settled at Bethlehem. He spent the rest of his life translating, and commenting, the Bible, and became the most learned biblical scholar of his day. He himself was the first to appreciate this fact and was apt to resent any opposition to his way of thinking. However, he acknowledged his own shortcomings, particularly his shortness of temper, with a rather tempestuous but virile humility. His place as an exponent of Catholic dogma is still the highest ever alloted to a biblical scholar. He died at Bethlehem and is officially venerated as a Doctor of the Church.
Cf. Att. — Holw. — Baud.

JEROME HERMOSILLA (Bl) M. O.P.
A.C. Nov. 1
d. 1861. A native of La Calzada, in Old Castile, who after his profession in the Dominican Order, was sent to Manila, where he was ordained priest and in 1828 appointed to the mission of E. Tonkin. He succeeded Bl Ignatius Delgado as vicar-apostolic and was consecrated bishop. Like his predecessor he was beheaded. Beatified in 1908.
Cf. Att. — Holw. — Prop. O.P.

JEROME de ANGELIS (Bl) M. S.J.
A.C. Dec. 5
d. 1623. A native of Castrogiovanni in Sicily, who became a Jesuit at Messina and was sent to the missions of the Far East. He worked for twenty-two years in various parts of Japan and finally, betrayed to the persecutors, was martyred by burning at Tokyo, together with BB Simon Yempo and Peter Gálvez. Beatified in 1867.
Cf. Att. — Holw. — Prop. S.J.

JEROME RANUZZI (Bl) C. O.S.M.
A.C. Dec. 12
d. 1455. Born at Sant' Angelo in Vado (Urbino), he took his religious vows as a Servite and eventually became the personal adviser of Duke Frederick of Montefeltro, of Urbino. On this account he was surnamed "the Angel of Good Counsel." Cult approved in 1775.
Cf. Holw. — Att. — Menzies.

JOACHIM SACCACHIBARA (St) M. Tert. O.F.M.
R.M. Feb. 5
d. 1597. A native of Japan, catechist of the Franciscan Fathers. He was crucified at Nagasaki with twenty-four companions. Beatified in 1627. Canonized in 1862.
Cf. Holw.

JOACHIM of FIORE (de FLORIS) (Bl) Ab. O.S.B. Cist.
P.C. March 30
c.1130-1202. Born at Celico in Calabria, after a pilgrimage to Palestine, he joined the Cistercians at Sambucina and in 1176 was made abbot of Corazzo, about the year 1190 he inaugurated at Fiore a new Cistercian Congregation. He was a prolific ascetical and biblical writer, and his commentary on the Apocalypse gave him the title of "the Prophet" by which he is described by Dante: "the Calabrian abbot Joachim, endowed with prophetic spirit" (Paradiso, XII). Unfortunately, after his death the Franciscan Spirituals made use of his books to uphold their heretical tendencies. The holy abbot, however, has always been given the title of *Beatus*.
Cf. Menzies. — Chev. — Holw. — Baud.

JOACHIM PICCOLOMINI (Bl) C. O.S.M.
R.M. Apr. 16
d. 1305. A member of the illustrious Piccolomini family of Siena, he joined the Servites as a lay-brother under St Philip Benizi. Beatified by Paul V.
Cf. Holw. — Baud.

JOACHIM (St) Patriarch R.M. Aug. 16
1st cent. B.C. Joachim is now the usual name given to the father of our Lady. Other names attributed to him are: Heli, Cleopas, Eliacim, Jonachir, Sadoc. Nothing is known about him. Liturgically, he has been honoured in the East from time immemorial; in the West only since the 16th cent. The traditions concerning him rest only on the apocryphal Gospel of James.
Cf. Att. — Holw.

JOACHIM FIRAIAMA-DIAZ (Bl) M.
A.C. Aug. 19
d. 1622. A Japanese captain of a ship at Manila. When bringing Bl Peter Zuñiga and Louis Flores to Japan his ship was captured by Dutch Protestant pirates, and brought to Firando. He and his crew, all members of the Confraternity of the Holy Rosary, were beheaded at Nagasaki. Beatified in 1867.
Cf. Holw.

JOACHIM ROYO (Bl) M. O.P.
A.C. Oct. 28
d. 1848. A Spanish missionary of the Dominican Order, who was sent to China to work under Bl Peter Sanz, and was ordained there. He was strangled in prison at Fu-tshen. Beatified in 1893.
Cf. Prop. O.P. — Holw.

JOACHIM HO (Bl) M.   **A.C. Nov. 24**
d. 1839. A Chinese, martyred at Kouei-Tcheou. Beatified in 1900.
Cf. Holw.

JOAN of ARC (St) V.   **R.M. May 30**
1412-1431. Called "the Maid of Orleans" — *La Pucelle.* She was born at Domrémy in Lorraine, the daughter of a peasant. When she was seventeen, while minding her father's sheep, she heard supernatural voices commanding her to take up arms and lead the French army against the English invaders of France. Accordingly, Charles VII entrusted her with an armed force, and Joan's rapid successes enabled him to be crowned at Reims. However, as Joan herself had predicted, she was captured by the Burgundians and handed over to the English. She was tried by an ecclesiastical court presided over by the bishop of Beauvais, a tool of the English, and condemned to be burnt alive at the stake as a heretic. The sentence was executed at Rouen, May 31, 1431. In 1456 the case was re-tried and Joan was declared innocent. After centuries of popular veneration she was beatified in 1909 and canonized in 1920. In 1922 she was declared the patroness of France.
Cf. Att. — Baud. — Holw.

JOANNA (St) W.   **R.M. May 24**
1st cent. The wife of Chuza, steward of Herod Antipas, tetrarch of Galilee. She is mentioned by St Luke in his gospel as one of the holy women who ministered to our Lord.
Cf. Luke VIII, 3 and XXIV, 10.

JOANNICIUS (St) H.   **R.M. Nov. 4**
750-846. A native of Bithynia who, after serving as a soldier, retired at the age of forty to lead a solitary life near Mt Olympus. Popular veneration however, drove him from solitude to solitude. He was a strenuous opponent of Iconoclasm.

His memory is held in high honour among the Greeks.
Cf. Att. — Baud. — Holw.

JOANNINUS de SAN JUAN (Bl) M.
A.C. July 15
d. 1570. A nephew of the captain of the ship which carried Bl Ignatius de Azevedo and his companions (q.v.). He voluntarily joined the martyrs and was thrown into the sea by the French Calvinist pirates.
Cf. Holw.

JOAQUINA VEDRUNA de MAS (Bl)
Foundress   A.C. May 19
1783-1854. A Spanish lady, wife of Theodore de Gas, of the Spanish nobility, who died in the Napoleonic wars. Joaquina then retired to Vich, where she founded the Institute of the Carmelite Sisters of Charity, now spread throughout Spain and S. America. She died at Barcelona during a cholera epidemic. Beatified in 1940.

JOAVAN (St) Bp.   **A.C. March 2**
d. c.576. An Irishman who passed over to Brittany to live under his uncle St Paul of Léon, whom he succeeded in the see.
Cf. Att. — Holw. — Baud.

JOB (St) Patriarch   **R.M. May 10**
? 1500 B.C. The man "simple and upright and fearing God and avoiding evil," whose patience forms the subject matter of a canonical book of Scripture. (See also James V, 11). His liturgical cult obtains chiefly in the East.
Cf. Holw.

JODOC (JUDOCUS, JOSSE, JOST) (St)
C.   R.M. Dec. 13
Otherwise Judocus, q.v.

JOEL (Bl or St) Ab. O.S.B. A.C. Jan. 25
d. 1185. A disciple of St John of Matera, founder of the Benedictine Congregation of Pulsano. St Joel was its third general.
Cf. Zimm.

JOEL (St) Prophet   **R.M. July 13**
8th cent. B.C. One of the twelve minor prophets. His body is said to be enshrined under the high altar of the cathedral of Zara in Dalmatia.
Cf. Holw. — Baud.

JOHN

Note. This is the most popular proper name in Christendom. The original Hebrew form has been Hellenized and Latinized into Joannes, whence the numerous variants in all languages. For hagiological purposes we mention only the following: Italian, Giovanni; French, Jean; Spanish, Juan; Portuguese, Xuan; Catalan, Jean; Dutch, Jan; German, Johann; Russian, Iwan, Ivan. There are also numerous diminutive forms, e.g., Italian, Giovannino, Nanino; Spanish, Juanito; French, Jeannin; Old English, Johnikin, etc. Moreover, especially in the Latin countries, the name is very often used in combination with others, as follows: Gianpier, Gianluigi, Jean-Benoît, Jean-François, Juan-José, Juan-Maria, etc. No less than seventy-three of the post-Reformation English martyrs — one canonized, forty-eight *Beati*, nineteen *Venerabiles*, five *dilati* — were called John.

JOHN de RIVERA (Bl) Bp.   A.C. Jan. 6
1532-1611. A native of Seville, and the son of the duke of Alcalá, viceroy of Naples. He was educated at the university of Salamanca and ordained priest in 1557. He remained at Salamanca as professor of theology, gifts became widely known and gained him the esteem of Pope Pius V, and of Philip II of Spain. He was appointed bishop of Badajoz, but transferred shortly after to the archbishopric of Valencia, with the added dignity of viceroy of that province. While all may not regard him as an enlightened statesman, one cannot but admire his conscientious devotion to duty and his heroic patience in bearing the responsibilities of his office. Beatified in 1796.
Cf. Holw. — Att. — Baud. — P. de U.

JOHN CAMILLUS BONUS (St) Bp.
R.M. Jan. 10
d. c.600. Bishop of Milan. The Lombard invasion forced the bishops of Milan to live away from that city eighty years. With John Camillus the line of resident bishops recommenced. He worked successfully against Arianism and the Monothelitism.
Cf. Menzies — Holw. — Att.

JOHN of RAVENNA (St) Bp.
R.M. Jan. 12
d. 494. Bishop of Ravenna from 452 to 494. He is said to have saved his flock from the fury of Attila the Hun, and mitigated its sad lot when the city was taken by Theodoric, king of the Ostro-Goths.
Cf. Menzies — Holw. — Baud.

JOHN CALABYTES (St) H.
R.M. Jan. 15
d. c.450. Born at Constantinople, he became at the age of twelve a monk at Gomon on the Bosphorus, and after some years returned home so changed in appearance that his parents did not recognize him. He lived on their charity in a small hut — Calybe in Greek, whence *Kalabytes* — near their home until his death, so runs the legend, which is remarkably reminiscent of that of St Alexis of Rome and other saints.
Cf. Att. — Holw. — Baud.

JOHN of ROME (St) C. O.S.B.
R.M. Jan. 17
See Antony, Merulus and John.

JOHN the ALMONER (St) Bp.
R.M. Jan. 23
d. ? 616. A Cypriot, who became patriarch of Alexandria (c.608). He set himself to redress social evils by means of almsgiving. He compiled a list of the 7,500 poor of the diocese, and one of his first episcopal acts was the distribution of 80,000 pieces of gold to hospitals and monasteries. He followed this policy systematically till his death.
Cf. Holw. — Att. — Baud.

JOHN GROVE (Bl) M.   A.C. Jan. 24
d. 1679. A layman, servant of Bl William Ireland, S.J., with whom he was martyred at Tyburn for alleged complicity in the Oates Plot. Beatified in 1929.
Cf. Newdigate.

JOHN CHRYSOSTOM (St) Bp. Dr.
R.M. Jan. 27
c.344-407(Sept. 14). Surnamed *Chrysostom* ("Golden Mouthed") on account of his great eloquence, and also "the Doctor of the Eucharist." He was born at Antioch, tried the monastic life in his youth and ruined his health, and was then ordained priest. It was as a priest at Antioch that he delivered that series of sermons which made him famous throughout the East. In 398, much against his own will, he was raised to the see of Constantinople, where his ardent zeal, which

knew no compromise, brought down upon him the imperial wrath. In 403, at a gathering of bishops known as the Synod of the Oak, he was deposed and banished, but public opinion was so strongly in his favour that the court was unable to prevent his triumphant return. Two months later, however, on account of another of his outspoken denunciations of vice, he was exiled again to Armenia, in defiance of the pope who strenuously espoused the saint's cause. John died in exile on Sept. 14. Besides being the most prolific of the Greek Doctors, St John was famous for his revision of the Greek Liturgy.
Cf. Att. — Baud. — Holw.

JOHN of WARNETON (Bl) Bp.
A.C. Jan. 27

d. 1130. Born at Warneton, in French Flanders, he became a monk at Mont-Saint-Eloi, near Arras, under St Ivo of Chartres, and was eventually raised to the see of Thérouanne, which he accepted only under a papal order. He was a great founder of monasteries. Though he had a reputation for strictness, he showed himself extremely gentle when dealing with certain individuals who had conspired against his life.
Cf. Att. — Baud. — Holw.

JOHN MARY MZEC (Bl) M.
A.C. Jan. 27

d. 1887. A negro of Uganda who baptized many in the hour of death. Beheaded in January, 1887. Beatified in 1912.
Cf. Holw.

JOHN of REOMAY (St) Ab.
R.M. Jan. 28

425-c.544. Born at Dijon, he was first a solitary at Reomay (Réôme), then for a time a monk at Lérins. Here he learnt the monastic traditions of St Macarius of Egypt which afterwards he handed on to his own monks at Reomay. This abbey became at a later period a great Benedictine centre, known as Moutier-Saint-Jean.
Cf. Holw. — Att.

JOHN (St) M.
R.M. Jan. 31
See Cyrus and John.

JOHN ANGELUS (Bl) C. O.S.B.
A.C. Jan. 31

d. c.1050. A native of Venice and a Bene-
dictine at Pomposa in the diocese of Ferrara, under St Guy, q.v.
Cf. Holw.

JOHN BOSCO (St) Founder.
R.M. Jan. 31

1815-1888. Born at Becchi, Castelnuovo d'Asti, in Piedmont, son of a peasant. After his ordination to the priesthood in 1841 he began at once his life-long work of educating boys. From the first he had a clear programme of education in his mind — viz., to educate through love, to compel the boys to love their teachers, their studies, and all the conditions which surround their education. A group of willing helpers offered themselves to Don Bosco and in 1860 the new Institute was approved by the Holy See. St John placed it under the protection of our Lady Help of Christians and of St Francis of Sales — *Salesians*. It grew rapidly and spread throughout Europe and the foreign missions. He also formed on the same lines a new sisterhood, the Daughters of Mary Auxiliatrix, for the education of girls. The happy mixture of play, prayer, study and manual work in John Bosco's system of education is one of the greatest achievements of the Church in modern times. Beatified in 1929 and canonized in 1934.
Cf. Att.

JOHN of the GRATING (St) Bp. O.S.B. Cist.
A.C. Feb. 1

d. c.1170. Surnamed *de Craticula* "of the Grating," from the metal railings that surrounded his shrine. He was a Breton who entered Clairvaux and was professed under St Bernard. He returned to Brittany as abbot-founder of Buzay and Bégard and finally was promoted to the bishopric of Aleth, which see he transferred to Saint-Malo.
Cf. Att. — Baud. — Holw.

JOHN NELSON (Bl) M. S.J.
A.C. Feb. 3

d. 1578. A native of Skelton, near York. He began his studies for the priesthood at Douai at the age of forty and was ordained in 1575. He was sent to London, but was soon arrested and subsequently executed at Tyburn. He became a Jesuit shortly before his death.
Cf. Newdigate — Att.

JOHN SPEED (Bl) M.
A.C. Feb. 4

d. 1594. *Alias* Spence. A layman, born

at Durham, and martyred also at Durham for befriending priests. Beatified in 1929.
Cf. Newdigate.

JOHN de BRITTO (Bl) M. S.J.
A.C. Feb. 4

1647-1693. A native of Lisbon, he joined the Society of Jesus in 1662 and was soon after sent to the missions of the Far East. He worked in Malabar, Tanjore, Marava and Madura, first as a simple religious and afterwards as superior. He joined the Brahmin caste in an endeavour to reach the nobility, and his methods were in many other respects unconventional and enlightened. He was captured and tortured and ordered to leave the country; but he refused and was martyred at Oreiour in India. Beatified in 1853.
Cf. Holw. — Baud. — Att.

JOHN MOROSINI (Bl) Ab. O.S.B.
Feb. 5

d. 1012. A native of Venice who became a Benedictine at Cuxá in the Catalonian Pyrenees. At a later period he returned to Venice where he founded and was the first abbot of San Giorgio Maggiore (c.982). Most writers call him beatus, although there is no evidence of cult.
Cf. Zimm.

JOHN SOAN de GOTO (St) M. S.J.
R.M. Feb. 5

d. 1597. A Japanese temporal-coadjutor of the Society of Jesus, and catechist at Ozaka. Crucified at Nagasaki in his nineteenth year, with many companions. Canonized in 1862.
Cf. Holw.

JOHN KISAKA (or KIMOIA) (St) M.
Tert. O.F.M.
R.M. Feb. 5

d. 1597. A Japanese silk-weaver, born at Meaco. He was baptized and received into the third order of St Francis shortly before his crucifixion at Nagasaki with some fellow-Christians.
Cf. Holw.

JOHN of MATHA (St) Founder.
R.M. Feb. 8

1160-1213 (Dec. 17). A native of Faucon in Provence, who studied at Paris and later founded the order of Trinitarians for the redemption of captives, which was approved by Pope Innocent III. It is said that John himself ransomed many captives at Tunis, but of this and many

other episodes of his life there are no trustworthy records. He died at Rome.
Cf. P. de U. — Att. — Holw.

JOHN CHARLES CORNEY (Bl) M.
A.C. Feb. 8

1809-1837. Born at Loudon, in the diocese of Poitiers, France. He belonged to the Paris Society of Foreign Missions and worked in Annam. He was seized at Ban-no, Tonkin, kept in a cage for three months being put often in irons and brutally beaten. He was finally beheaded (Sept. 20). Beatified in 1900.
Cf. Holw. — Att. — Baud.

JOHN NUTTER and JOHN MUNDEN (BB) MM.
A.C. Feb. 12

d. 1584. John Nutter was born near Burnley, Lancs, and was a fellow of St John's College, Cambridge. He studied for the priesthood at Reims, and was ordained in 1581. Bl John Munden, a native of Coltley, S. Maperton, Dorset, studied at New College, Oxford, became a schoolmaster, went to Reims and to Rome for his ecclesiastical training and was ordained in 1582. They were martyred at Tyburn with three other priests. Beatified in 1929.
Cf. Newdigate.

JOHN LANTRUA of TRIORA (Bl) M. O.F.M.
A.C. Feb. 13

1760-1816. A native of Triora in Liguria, who at the age of seventeen joined the Friars Minor. After having been guardian of Velletri, near Rome, he volunteered for the Chinese missions, where at that time a fierce persecution was raging. He arrived there in 1799 and worked with great success in spite of many obstacles. At length he was seized and martyred by strangulation at Ch'angsha Fu. Beatified in 1900.
Cf. Att. — Baud. — Holw.

JOHN BAPTIST of the CONCEPTION (Bl) C.
A.C. Feb. 14

1561-1613. A native of Almodovar, Toledo, Spain. After entering the Trinitarian order at Toledo, he began to interest himself in the question of reviving the ancient observance of that order, and he inaugurated such a revival at his own foundation of Valdepeñas in 1597. The reform, called the Discalced Trinitarians, was approved by Rome and John had to endure on this account the bitter

though not unnatural opposition of the "unreformed." At the time of his death thirty-four houses had adopted the reform. Beatified in 1819.
Cf. Att. — Baud. — Holw.

JOHN PIBUSH (Bl) M. A.C. Feb. 18
d. 1601. Born at Thirsk, Yorks, and educated at Reims. Ordained in 1587, he was sent to the English Mission, where he spent his time mostly in prison and was finally executed at Southwark, solely for his priesthood. Beatified in 1929.
Cf. Newdigate.

JOHN PETER NÉEL (Bl) A.C. Feb. 18
1832-1862. A French missionary priest working in Kuy-tsheu, China, who was arrested, tied to a horse's tail by his hair, and beheaded at Kuy-tsheu. Beatified in 1919.
Cf. Holw.

JOHN the SAXON (Bl) M. A.C. Feb. 22
d. 895. Apparently a native of Old Saxony and a monk in some French abbey who was invited by King Alfred to restore religion and learning in the English abbeys after the devastation of the Danes. The king appointed him abbot of Athelingay. John worked zealously in furthering the king's wishes. Two French monks of his own community murdered him one night in church.
Cf. Holw.

JOHN THERISTUS (St) Mk.
R.M. Feb. 24
d. 1129. Of Calabrian parentage, he was born in Sicily, whither his mother had been carried as a slave by the Saracens. He contrived to escape to Calabria while still a child, and there he became a Benedictine.
Cf. Menzies — Holw. — Baud.

JOHN of GORZE (St) Ab. O.S.B.
A.C. Feb. 27
d. c.975. Born at Vandières, between Metz and Toul, in Lorraine. After an excellent education and some years spent in administering his large estates, he made a pilgrimage to Rome, and on his return restored, and entered, the abbey of Gorze (933). The emperor Otto I sent him as his ambassador to the khalif Abd-er-Rahman of Cordova, where he stayed for two years. In 960 he was made abbot of Gorze, and the wise reforms which he introduced spread even to distant Benedictine abbeys. The saint is said to have been gifted with a prodigious memory.
Cf. Zimm. — P. de U. — Att. — Chev. — Holw.

JOHN-JOSEPH of the CROSS (St) C. O.F.M. R.M. March 5
1654-1734. Carlo Gaetano was born on the island of Ischia, off the coast of Naples. In 1670 he joined the Franciscan-Alcantarines and was given the new name of Gianguiseppe (John-Joseph). He held various offices in the Order and finally that of superior of the new Italian branch of the Alcantarines. Canonized in 1839.
Cf. Menzies — Att. — Holw. — Baud.

JOHN LARKE and JOHN IRELAND (BB) MM. A.C. March 7
d. 1544. Both were secular priests. John Larke was rector of St Ethelburga's Bishopsgate, then of Woodford, Essex, and finally of Chelsea, to which he was nominated by St Thomas More. John Ireland, after being chaplain to the same saint, was made rector of Eltham, Kent. Both were martyred at Tyburn, with Bl Jermyn Gardiner. John Larke was beatified in 1886 and John Ireland in 1929.
Cf. Att. — Newdigate.

JOHN of GOD (St) Founder.
R.M. March 8
1495-1550. Born at Montemoro Novo, diocese of Evora, in Portugal, John followed various vocations for the first forty years of his life — shepherd, soldier, peddler, superintendent of slaves in Morocco, vendor of religious books in the district near Gibraltar, etc. He was led to a more perfect life by a sermon of Bl John of Avila, but the fervour of his conversion produced in him such extravagant behaviour that he was taken for a madman. Finally, in 1540, he settled at Granada and founded a hospital where he tended the sick. This was the beginning of the new Order of Brothers Hospitallers (Brothers of St John of God), which still exists, chiefly in the Latin countries. In Italy indeed they are called the *Fatebene-Fratelli* — "Do good brethren." St John was canonized in 1690 and declared patron of the sick and of hospitals in 1886.
Cf. Menzies — Holw. — Att.

JOHN of VALLUMBROSA (Bl) C. O.S.B. Vall. A.C. March 10

d. c.1380. A Florentine monk of the Holy Trinity in his native city. As a result of poring over forbidden books night and day, he took secretly to the practice of the Black Art and became a necromancer, and a slave to vice and depravity. On being found out, he was summoned before the abbot-general of Vallumbrosa and, after first denying ultimately confessed his guilt and was imprisoned in a pestilential gaol. This proved his salvation: he became truly penitent and by voluntary fasting reduced himself to a skeleton, so that his fellow monks implored him to return to community life. He, however, preferred to remain in prison till his death, living as a hermit to a very old age and attaining to great sanctity. He was an elegant writer, and a great friend of St Catherine of Siena, who often appeared to him.
Cf. Zimm. — Att. — Baud. — Chev. — Holw.

JOHN OGILVIE (Bl) M. S.J. A.C. March 10

d. 1615. Born at Drum-na-Keith, Banffshire, and brought up a Calvinist, he was received into the Church at Louvain (1596), at the age of seventeen. He joined the Society of Jesus (1599) and worked in Austria and in France till 1613. He then returned to his native Scotland where he was beginning to make converts when he was betrayed and imprisoned. For eight days and nights on end he was forcibly kept from sleep so that he should reveal the names of other Catholics. The attempt was unsuccessful. He was hanged at Glasgow. Beatified in 1929.
Cf. Newdigate — Att.

JOHN RIGHI of FABRIANO (Bl) C. O.F.M. A.C. March 11

1469-1539. John Baptist Righi was a native of Fabriano, province of Ancona, who professed the Franciscan rule and lived a hermit's life at Massaccio. Cult approved in 1903.
Cf. Holw. — Baud. — Att.

JOHN SORDI, or CACCIAFRONTE (Bl) Bp. M. O.S.B. A.C. March 16

d. 1183. A native of Cremona who, at the age of fifteen, was already a canon. At sixteen he joined the Benedictines of the abbey of St Laurence in his native city.

Eight years later he was made prior of another house, but in 1155 he was recalled to St Laurence as abbot. He is described as most loyal to, and gentle with his monks. He sided with the pope against the emperor Barbarossa, by whom he was banished from his abbey. He lived as a hermit near Mantua, and, in 1174, the bishop of this city being deposed by the pope, Bl John was raised to the see. But, some three years afterwards, the former bishop repented and Bl John asked permission to resign in his favour, being himself transferred to Vicenza (1177). Here he was killed by a man whom he had rebuked for embezzling episcopal revenues.
Cf. Gams — Chev. — Zimm. — Att.

JOHN AMIAS (or ANNE) (Bl) M. A.C. March 16

d. 1589. Born near Wakefield, he began life as a clothier and married, but on his wife's death, studied for the priesthood at Reims and was ordained in 1581. He was executed for his priesthood at York, together with Bl Robert Dalby. Beatified in 1929.
Cf. Newdigate — Att.

JOHN BRÉBEUF and JOHN de la LANDE (SS) MM. S.J. A.C. March 16

d. 1649 and 1646. Two Jesuit martyrs, belonging to the group of the North American Martyrs (q.v.). John Brébeuf, born at Condé in 1596, was a priest who landed at Quebec in 1615 and worked chiefly among the Hurons for thirty-four years. He was martyred by the Iroquois in 1646. John de la Lande, a native of Dieppe was a coadjutor, and was martyred in 1646. Both were canonized, with four companions, in 1930.
Cf. Att.

JOHN SARKANDER (Bl) M. A.C. March 17

1576-1620. Born in Austrian Silesia, he became a parish priest of Holleschau in Moravia. He converted many Hussites and Bohemian Brethren, but as a result, he was unjustly accused by the heretics of conspiring to bring Polish troops into the country, and was ordered to reveal what he had heard in confession from his penitent the baron of Moravia. On refusing he was cruelly racked and left to die in prison. Beatified in 1859.
Cf. Att. — Holw.

JOHN the SYRIAN of PINNA (St) H.
R.M. March 19

6th cent. According to the R.M. he was a Syrian monk who settled at Pinna, near Spoleto, where for forty-four years he was abbot of a large monastic colony. It is probable that he was a refugee from Monophysite persecution.
Cf. Att. — Baud. — Holw.

JOHN BAPTIST SPAGNUOLO (Bl) C. O.C.
A.C. March 20

1448-1516. Usually called *Baptista Mantuanus.* His family name *Spagnuolo* denotes his Spanish origin. He was, however, born at Mantua, studied at Padua, joined the Carmelites (1464) and in 1513 became their prior-general. He is famous as a Latin poet — he wrote over 50,000 lines of Latin verse — and he is considered one of the most eminent representatives of Christian Humanism in Italy. Beatified in 1885.
Cf. Att. — Baud. — Holw.

JOHN of PARMA (Bl) C. O.F.M.
A.C. March 20

1209-1289. A native of Parma, who after his profession in the Franciscan Order and his ordination, taught theology at Bologna and Naples. In 1247 he was elected seventh minister general of the Franciscans and held the office until 1257. He visited the Franciscan provinces of different countries, including England. He was sent to Constantinople as papal legate. His final years he lived in retirement at Greccio. Cult approved in 1777.
Cf. Att. — Holw.

JOHN, SERGIUS and Comp. (SS) MM.
A.C. March 20

d. 796. A group of twenty monks of the *laura* of St Sabas, near Jerusalem, who were killed in one of the anti-Christian Arab raids. Many more were wounded, and a few escaped. One of the last category, Stephen the poet, has left a detailed account of the event.
Cf. Holw. — Att. — Baud.

JOHN del BASTONE (Bl) C. O.S.B. Silv.
A.C. March 24

d. 1290. One of the first disciples of St Silvester at Monte Fano.
Cf. Propr. Camald. — Chev. — Holw.

JOHN of LYCOPOLIS (St) H.
R.M. March 27

c.305-394. Surnamed "the Egyptian" or "the Prophet of the Thebaid." He was born near Assiut, in Egypt, and was a carpenter by trade. At the age of twenty-five he journeyed to a mountain near Lycopolis and lived there for forty years as a recluse. He was consulted by the emperor Theodosius and greatly admired by his contemporaries SS. Jerome, Augustine, Cassian, Palladius, etc. He was remarkable for his gift of prophecy.
Cf. Att. — Holw. — Baud.

JOHN DAMASCENE (St) C. Dr.
R.M. March 27

c.676-c.749. A native of Damascus, where his father was the caliph's vizier. He was educated by Cosmos, a Greek monk who had been brought into Syria as a slave. After succeeding his father as vizier, he retired to the *laura* of St Sabas at Jerusalem and embraced there the monastic life. He boldly resisted the Inconoclast emperor, Leo the Isaurian, but he is best remembered as a theologian. He was the author of the first real *Summa Theologica*, as well as of numerous liturgical hymns. He was the last of the Greek fathers and the first of the Christian Aristotelians. Leo XIII proclaimed him Doctor of the Church in 1890.
Cf. Att. — Baud. — Holw.

JOHN of CAPISTRANO (St) C. O.F.M.
R.M. March 28

1386-1456 (Oct. 23). A native of Capistrano in the Abruzzi, he began life as a lawyer, and was made governor of Perugia in the Papal States. When he was thirty he was left a widower and became a Franciscan and a life-long friend of St Bernardinus of Siena. His whole religious life was spent as papal legate to various states, Palestine, Milan, France, Sicily, Austria, Bavaria, Poland, Bohemia, and Silesia. The most important was that to Bohemia, where his conduct in connection with the Hussite movement has been adversely criticized. St John was also instrumental in the heroic resistance of the Hungarians to the Turks. Canonized in 1724.
Cf. Menzies — Att. — Holw.

JOHN CLIMACUS (St) Ab.
R.M. March 30

c.525-605. Called *"Climacus"* from the title of his book *The Climax,* or *Ladder of Perfection,* which is a classic in ascetical literature. He was born in Palestine and, at the age of sixteen, became a monk on Mt Sinai and afterwards a solitary in different places in the Arabian Desert. He was already seventy-five when he was made abbot of Sinai, but four years later he resigned and died as a hermit. *Cf. Att. — Holw.*

JOHN PAYNE (Bl) M. A.C. Apr. 2
d. 1582. Born in the diocese of Peterborough, he was educated for the priesthood at Douai, where he was ordained in 1576. He worked on the English mission at Ingatestone in Essex until his martyrdom at Chelmsford. Beatified in 1886. *Cf. Newdigate — Att.*

JOHN of PENNA (Bl) C. O.F.M.
A.C. Apr. 3
d. 1271. A native of Penna San Giovanni in the diocese of Fermo who, after being ordained priest, joined the Franciscans at Recanati and founded several houses in Provence, where he lived for twenty-five years. (See his life in ch. 45 of the *Little Flowers of St Francis*). Cult approved by Pius VII. *Cf. Holw. — Att.*

JOHN of VESPIGNANO (Bl) C.
A.C. Apr. 9
d. 1331. Born at Vespignano in the diocese of Florence. During the civil wars he devoted himself to works of charity among the refugees who flocked to Florence. Cult approved by Pius VII. *Cf. Holw.*

JOHN of CUPRAMONTANA (Bl) C. O.S.B. Cam. A.C. Apr. 11
d. 1303. A Camaldolese monk-hermit who lived many years in the cave of Cupramontana, on Mt Massaccio. *Cf. Zimm.*

JOHN LOCKWOOD (Bl) M.
A.C. Apr. 13
d. 1642. John Lockwood, *alias* Lascelles, was born at Sowerby, Yorks, and studied for the priesthood at Rome. Ordained in 1597, he was sent to the English mission, where he worked from 1598 till 1642. At the age of eighty-one he was hanged, drawn and quartered for his priesthood at York. Beatified in 1929. *Cf. Att. — Newdigate.*

JOHN of VILNA (St) M. A.C. Apr. 14
See SS Antony, John and Eustace.

JOHN of GRACE-DIEU (Bl) Ab. O.S.B. Cist. P.C. Apr. 20
d, 1280. A Benedictine monk of St Denis, who passed over to the Cistercians and became successively abbot of Igny, of Clairvaux (1257) and of Grace-Dieu (c.1262). *Cf. Chev. — Baud. — Holw.*

JOHN FINCH (Bl) M. A.C. Apr. 20
d. 1584. A yeoman farmer of Eccleston in Lancashire, who suffered at Lancaster for being reconciled to the Church and for harbouring priests. Beatified in 1929. *Cf. Newdigate — Att.*

JOHN of VALENCE (Bl) Bp. O.S.B. Cist.
A.C. Apr. 26
d. 1146. A native of Lyons, he was a canon of that city, and after a pilgrimage to Compostella, entered Clairvaux under St Bernard. In 1117 he was sent to found Bonneval (*Bona Vallis*) on the Loire, and proved to be an excellent abbot. In 1141 he was raised to the see of Valence, but had to be carried by main force to the altar to be consecrated. Cult approved in 1901. *Cf. Holw. — Att. — Baud. — Chev.*

JOHN of CONSTANTINOPLE (St) Ab.
R.M. Apr. 27
d. 813. Abbot of the monastery called *Cathares* at Constantinople, a staunch opponent of the Iconoclast emperors Leo the Isaurian and Leo the Armenian. *Cf. Holw. — Baud.*

JOHN BAPTIST THAUH (Bl) M.
A.C. Apr. 28
d. 1840. A native catechist in Tonkin, attached to the Society of Foreign Missions. He was beheaded with Bl Peter Hieu, q.v. *Cf. Holw.*

JOHN-LOUIS BONNARD (Bl) M.
A.C. May 1
d. 1852. A missionary priest, a native of France, who belonged to the Paris Society of Foreign Missions and was beheaded in Annam. Beatified in 1900. *Cf. Holw. — Att.*

JOHN HOUGHTON (Bl) M. O.Cart.
A.C. May 4
d. 1535. A native of Essex and prior of the London Charterhouse. As such, he was the first to oppose Henry VIII's Acts

of Succession and Supremacy, giving to his monks and the whole of England a magnificent example of fidelity to the Catholic faith, for which he was martyred at Tyburn, with four companions. He is the proto-martyr of the post-reformation English martyrs. Beatified in 1886.
Cf. Newdigate — Att. — Camm.

JOHN HAILE (Bl) M. A.C. May 5
d. 1535. A secular priest, vicar of Isleworth, Middlesex. He was martyred at Tyburn with Bl John Houghton, q.v.
Cf. Newdigate — Att.

JOHN of BEVERLEY (St) Bp. O.S.B.
R.M. May 7
d. 721. He was born at Harpham in Yorkshire and studied at Canterbury under SS Adrian and Theodore; then he became a monk at Whitby. Eventually he was consecrated bishop of Hexham, whence he was transferred to York as metropolitan. As such he ordained St Bede to the priesthood. He was the founder of Beverley Abbey, to which he retired in his old age.
Cf. Att. — Zimm. — Chev. — Holw.

JOHN of CHÂLON (St) Bp. A.C. May 9
d. c.475. The third bishop of Châlon-sur-Saone. He was consecrated by St Patiens of Lyons.
Cf. Holw. — Baud.

JOHN of AVILA (Bl) C. A.C. May 10
d. 1569. Born at Almodovar, in New Castile, he studied law at Salamanca and theology at Alcalá (*Complutum*). After his ordination he was preparing to sail for the missions of the West Indies and Mexico, but was detained by the archbishop of Seville. He spent the forty years of his priestly career evangelizing Andalusia — preaching, writing, directing souls (among others those of SS Teresa, Francis Borgia, John of God, Louis of Granada) and converting sinners. His ascetical writings, chiefly his letters, rank high among the Spanish classics. He is usually called "the Apostle of Andalusia." Beatified in 1894.
Cf. P. de U. — Att. — Holw.

JOHN ROCHESTER (Bl) M. O.Cart.
A.C. May 11
d. 1537. He was born at Terling, Essex, and a professed Carthusian of the London Charterhouse. He was martyred at York, with Bl James Walworth. Beatified in 1886.
Cf. Newdigate — Camm.

JOHN STONE (Bl) M. O.S.A.
A.C. May 12
d. 1538. An Augustinian friar at Canterbury, martyred in that place for denying the royal supremacy.
Cf. Newdigate — Camm. — Att.

JOHN the SILENT (St) Bp. R.M. May 13
454-558. Born at Nicopolis in Armenia, before his twentieth year he had already founded a monastery and become a monk in his native city. At the age of twenty-eight he was chosen bishop of Colonia (Taxara). He resigned after nine or ten years, and hiding his episcopal dignity, entered the *laura* of St Sabbas near Jerusalem. Here he spent the rest of his life, part of it as a "walled-up" recluse.
Cf. Holw. — Att. — Baud.

JOHN BAPTIST de la SALLE (Bl)
Founder. R.M. May 15
1654-1719. A native of Reims and a canon of the cathedral chapter (1667), before he was ordained a priest (1678). His life-work was the foundation, on new, original and revolutionary educational principles, of the congregation of the Brothers of the Christian Schools. In the teeth of extreme opposition, he succeeded in establishing his system and his new Institute on solid foundations. He died in retirement at Saint-Yon. Canonized in 1900.
Cf. Att. — Holw.

JOHN NEPOMUCEN (St) M.
R.M. May 16
c.1345-1393. A native of Nepomuk, in Bohemia, he became canon of Prague and eventually court chaplain and confessor to Queen Sophie, second wife of the dissolute Wenceslaus IV. He was of a retiring disposition, and repeatedly refused bishoprics which were offered to him. In 1383 he was, by order of Wenceslaus, thrown into the river Moldau and drowned. A tradition, still widely credited in Central Europe, attributes his martyrdom to his refusal to reveal to the king what he had heard from the queen in sacramental confession. Canonized in 1729.
Cf. Holw. — Att. — Baud.

JOHN of PARMA (St) Ab. O.S.B.
A.C. May 22
d. c.982. He was born at Parma and early in life was made canon of the cathedral in that city. He is said to have made six pilgrimages to Jerusalem and to have taken the Benedictine habit there. He was abbot of St John's, at Parma (973-c.982) then under the Cluniac observance. He is a minor patron of Parma.
Cf. Prop. O.S.B. (*Ital.*) — *Chev.* — *Holw.*

JOHN of CETINA and PETER de DUEÑAS (BB) MM. O.F.M. A.C. May 22
d. 1397. Two Spanish Franciscans who were commissioned to evangelize the Moors at Granada and were martyred in the attempt.
Cf. Att. — *Holw.*

JOHN FOREST (Bl) M. O.F.M.
A.C. May 22
d. 1538. Born in all probability at Oxford, where, after his profession as a Friar Minor, he was also educated in the Franciscan college. He was stationed at Greenwich when he became confessor to Queen Catherine of Aragon. He opposed the queen's divorce and the king's supremacy in matters spiritual, and was for this cause burnt to death at Smithfield under conditions of most revolting cruelty. Beatified in 1886.
Cf. Newdigate — *Att.*

JOHN BAPTIST MACHADO (Bl) M. S.J. A.C. May 22
1580-1617. Born at Terceira, in the Azores, he became a Jesuit at Coimbra, and in 1609 was dispatched to the Japanese missions. He was beheaded at Nagasaki with two companions. Beatified in 1867.
Cf. Att. — *Holw.*

JOHN BAPTIST de ROSSI (St) C.
R.M. May 23
1698-1764. Born at Voltaggio, diocese of Genoa, he studied at the Roman College and, after his ordination in 1721, remained in Rome as a member of the Roman clergy. In 1737 he was made canon of Santa Maria in Cosmedin at the foot of the Aventine. His main work as as missioner and catechist was among the teamsters, farmers and herdsmen of the Campagna, and among the sick and prisoners. Canonized in 1881.
Cf. Att. — *Holw.* — *Baud.*

JOHN of MONTFORT (Bl) Knight O.S.B. A.C. May 24
d. 1177(8). A Knight Templar of Jerusalem. Wounded in a battle against the Saracens he was taken to Cyprus, where he died at Nikosia. His feast was for a long time celebrated at Cyprus on May 25.
Cf. Zimm.

JOHN del PRADO (St) M. O.F.M.
R.M. May 24
d. 1636. Born at Morgobresio, León, Spain. While following his theological course at Salamanca he joined the barefooted Franciscans of the Strict Observance. Eventually he was sent to Morocco with special ecclesiastical powers, and was martyred there with two other Spanish friars.
Cf. Att. — *Holw.*

JOHN HOAN (Bl) M. A.C. May 26
c.1789-1861. Born at Kim-long, in Cochin-China, he was ordained priest, and worked zealously until his martyrdom by beheading under King Yu-Duc, near Dougl Hoi. Beatified in 1909.
Cf. Holw.

JOHN I (St) Pope M. R.M. May 27
d. 526. A Tuscan, who was ordained for the Roman clergy, became archdeacon and finally pope (523). In 526 he went to Constantinople on an embassy from Theodoric the Arian king of the Ostrogoths. On his return Theodoric cast the pope into prison on suspicion of having conspired with the emperor Justin. The pope died therein of want and hardship. Some modern writers contest his claim to martyrdom.
Cf. Att. — *Menzies* — *Holw.*

JOHN SHERT (Bl) M. A.C. May 28
d. 1582. Born at Shert Hall, near Macclesfield, Cheshire and educated at Brasenose College, Oxford. After his conversion he studied at Douai and Rome and was ordained in 1576. In 1579 he began his work on the English mission. He suffered at Tyburn with BB. Thomas Ford and Robert Johnstone. Beatified in 1886.
Cf. Newdigate — *Camm.*

JOHN de ATARÉS (St) H. A.C. May 29
d. c.750. A hermit in the diocese of Jaca, in the Aragonese Pyrenees, whose cell was situated under a huge rock, where at a

later time the Benedictine abbey of St John de la Peña (of the Rock) was built. The saint and the place are famous in Spanish history, since the abbey of La Peña became the cradle of the Christian kingdoms of Navarre and Aragon.
Cf. P. de U. — Holw.

JOHN PELINGOTTO (Bl) C. Tert. O.F.M.   A.C. June 1
1240-1304. A native of Urbino, the son of a merchant. He was received into the Franciscan third order, and devoted his whole life to prayer and works of charity. Cult approved in 1918.
Cf. Att. — Holw. — Baud.

JOHN STOREY (Bl) M.   A.C. June 1
d. 1571. He was born in N. England and educated at Oxford, where he received the degree of Doctor of Law and subsequently was appointed president of Broadgate Hall and first Regius Professor of civil law. He married (after 1547), became a member of parliament, and opposed several laws against the Catholic faith, enacted under Edward VI and Elisabeth. He was imprisoned and managed to escape abroad, but was followed by Elisabeth's secret agents, kidnapped, brought back to England and martyred at Tyburn for alleged treason.
Cf. Newdigate — Att.

JOHN de ORTEGA (St) H. A.C. June 2
d. c.1150. A priest of the diocese of Burgos, in Spain, who after sundry pilgrimages to Palestine, Rome, and Compostella, became a hermit in a small village near Burgos, and helped St Dominic de la Calzada (q.v.) in the work of building bridges and hospices, opening roads, etc. His feast is liturgically observed in the diocese of Burgos.
Cf. P. de U. — Holw.

JOHN GRANDE (Bl) C.   A.C. June 3
1546-1600. Born at Carmona in Andalusia, Spain, he worked in the linen trade but abandoned that occupation to become a hermit at Marcena. From this time up to his death, punning on his Spanish surname — *Grande* i.e. Great — he always called himself *Juan Grande Pecador* — John the Great Sinner. He left his cell to work in the prisons and hospitals at Xeres, where a recently opened hospital was entrusted to his care. This he handed over to St John of God, taking the habit of the latter's new order at Granada. He died at Xeres while still caring for the prisoners and the sick. Beatified in 1853.
Cf. Holw. — Att. — Baud.

JOHN of VERONA (St) Bp.
R.M. June 6
4th cent. The successor of St Maurus in the see of Verona, in N. Italy.
Cf. Baud. — Holw.

JOHN DAVY (Bl) M. O.Cart.
A.C. June 6
d. 1537. A Carthusian monk, professed at the London Charterhouse, starved to death at Newgate, where he was imprisoned for resisting Henry VIII's spiritual supremacy. He suffered with a group of six other Carthusians. Beatified in 1886.
Cf. Newdigate — Camm.

JOHN RAINUZZI (Bl) C. O.S.B.
A.C. June 8
d. ? 1330. A Benedictine monk of St Margaret's monastery, at Todi. His charity earned for him the title of "John the Almsgiver," by which he is often called.
Cf. Att. — Baud. — Chev. — Holw.

JOHN DOMINIC (Bl) Bp. O.P.
A.C. June 10
1376-1419. Born at Florence, he entered the Dominican Order, in which he distinguished himself as one of the leaders in the restoration of discipline. In 1408 he was named archbishop of Ragusa and created cardinal. He was one of those who worked most successfully for the healing of the Great Schism of the West, and, as papal legate for Hungary and Bohemia, converted many Hussites. Cult confirmed in 1832.
Cf. Prop. O.P. — Att. — Holw.

JOHN of SAHAGUN (of ST FACUNDO) (St) C. O.S.A.   R.M. June 12
1419-1479. Born at Sahagún, province of León, in Spain, and educated by the Benedictines at the great abbey of his native town, and then at Salamanca and Burgos. While still quite young he held several benefices in the diocese of Burgos, but eventually he surrendered all but one. In 1463 this too he gave up to become an Augustinian at Salamanca, where he held the offices of novice-master and prior. By

his fearless preaching he effected a great change in the social life of Salamanca. Canonized in 1690.
Cf. P. de U. — Att. — Holw. — Baud.

JOHN of PULSANO (of MATERA) (St) Ab. O.S.B. A.C. June 20
d. 1139. A native of Matera in the Basilicata, who early in life entered a Benedictine monastery, where his austerity was not looked upon with much favour. He next joined the monks of Montevergine under St William the founder, but left him to become a popular preacher at Bari. Finally he settled at Pulsano, near Monte Gargano, where he established an abbey, the first of a series of foundations which coalesced into a new Benedictine congregation. He died at Pulsano. He is often called, from his birthplace, St John of Matera.
Cf. Chev.—Zimm.—Baud.—Holw.—Att.

JOHN BAPTIST ZOLA (Bl) M. S.J. A.C. June 20
1576-1626. Born at Brescia in Italy, he became a Jesuit (1595) and was sent to India (1602) and thence to Japan (1606). He settled at Tacacu; but in 1614 was banished to China. On his return to Japan he was captured and burnt alive at Nagasaki. Beatified in 1867.
Cf. Prop. S.J. — Holw.

JOHN KINSACO (Bl) M. S.J. A.C. June 20
d. 1626. A native of Ocinozu in Japan, who became a Jesuit novice, and was arrested and burnt alive at Nagasaki. Beatified in 1867.
Cf. Prop. S.J. — Holw.

JOHN FENWICK and JOHN GAVAN (BB) MM. S.J. A.C. June 20
d. 1679. John Fenwick was born at Durham and educated at Saint-Omer. He became a Jesuit in 1656. John Gavan, a Londoner by birth, was also educated at Saint-Omer and received into the Society of Jesus in 1660. Both were martyred at Tyburn, with three other Jesuits, for alleged complicity in the Oates Plot. Beatified in 1929.
Cf. Newdigate.

JOHN RIGBY (Bl) M. A.C. June 21
d. 1600. A layman, born at Harrock Hall, near Wigan, Lancs, who was condemned for being reconciled to the Catholic Church and executed at Southwark. Beatified in 1929.
Cf. Newdigate — Att.

JOHN I of NAPLES (St) Bp. R.M. June 22
5th cent. The bishop of Naples who translated the body of St Januarius from Puteoli to Naples, "whom blessed Paulinus bishop of Nola, called to the heavenly kingdoms" (R.M.).
Cf. Menzies — Baud. — Holw.

JOHN IV of Naples (St) Bp. A.C. June 22
d. 835. Locally known as *San Giovanni d'Acquarola*, or "the Peacemaker." Bishop of Naples, where he is now venerated as one of the patron saints of the city.
Cf. Menzies — Holw. — Baud.

JOHN (St) M. R.M. June 23
d. 362. A Roman priest beheaded under Julian the Apostate. The relic venerated as the head of John the Baptist at San Silvestro in Capite, the English church in Rome, is supposed to be in reality the head of this martyred priest.
Cf. Baring-Gould — Holw.

JOHN the BAPTIST (St) Prophet. M. R.M. June 24
1st cent. "The man sent from God," the voice crying in the wilderness: "Prepare ye the way of the Lord," of whom Christ said "among those that are born of women there is not a greater prophet." His career as a forerunner of the Messiah is fully described in the four Gospels. Patristic tradition maintains that St John was freed from original sin and sanctified in his mother's womb: hence from the earliest time the Church has liturgically celebrated the nativity of St John. His martyrdom under Herod is also commemorated (August 29). St John has always been, and still is, one of the most popular of saints. Liturgically, he even ranks above St Joseph, the foster-father of our Lord.
Cf. Att. — Holw. — Baud. — Menzies.

JOHN of TUY (St) H. A.C. June 24
9th cent. A native of Spanish Galicia, who lived as a hermit near Tuy. His body is now enshrined in the Dominican church at Tuy.
Cf. P. de U. — Holw.

JOHN the SPANIARD (Bl) C. O.Cart.
A.C. June 25

1123-1160. A native of Almanza in Spain, who, when still a boy, travelled to France and studied at Arles. He became a Carthusian at Montrieu, was transferred to the Grande Chartreuse under St Anthelmus and finally sent as founder and first prior of the charterhouse of Reposoir, near lake Geneva. He was the first to draw up constitutions for the Carthusian nuns. Cult approved in 1864.
Cf. Holw. — Att.

JOHN and PAUL (SS) MM.
R.M. June 26

d. 362. Roman martyrs who suffered at Rome, probably under Julian the Apostate. Their names occur in the canon of the Mass, and there is a stately basilica erected in their name on the Coelian Hill. Their Acts, however, are held by most scholars to be merely a pious fiction.
Cf. Menzies — Att. — Holw.

JOHN of the GOTHS (St) Bp.
A.C. June 26

d. c.800. A bishop of the Goths in S. Russia, noted for his defence of the veneration of images. He was driven from his see by the invading Khazars, and died in exile.
Cf. Holw. — Baud. — Att.

JOHN of CHINON (St) H.
R.M. June 27

6th cent. A native of Brittany who became a hermit at Chinon in Touraine, where he was the spiritual adviser of Queen St Radegund.
Cf. Holw. — Baud. — Att.

JOHN SOUTHWORTH (Bl) M.
A.C. June 28

d. 1654. A Lancashire man who became a student at Douai. He was ordained in 1619 and sent to the English mission, where his ministrations during the plague of 1636 were specially noteworthy. He was arrested and imprisoned as early as 1627, but was subsequently released. He was executed at Tyburn for his priesthood under the commonwealth. Beatified in 1929.
Cf. Newdigate — Att.

JOHN CORNELIUS S.J. and **JOHN CAREY** (BB) MM.
A.C. July 4

d. 1594. Bl John Cornelius was born at Bodmin of Irish parents. He became a fellow of Exeter College, Oxford, and a student at Reims and then at Rome, where he was ordained priest in 1583. He worked for ten years on the English mission at Lanherne and became a Jesuit only in 1594. He was condemned for the priesthood. Bl John Carey was a layman, an Irish servant of Bl Thomas Bosgrave and a fellow-servant of Bl Patrick Salmon. The four were martyred at Dorchester. Beatified in 1929.
Cf. Newdigate.

JOHN FISHER (St) Card. Bp. M.
A.C. July 9

1469-1535 (June 22). Born at Beverley in Yorkshire, the son of a draper. He was educated at Cambridge and ever afterwards was connected with the life of the university, of which he eventually became chancellor. As such he did much to further the growth and progress of his Alma Mater, of which he may justly be considered the second founder. In 1504 he was appointed bishop of Rochester and proved to be the most faithful of the English bishops of that period: he upheld the cause of the queen against her adulterous husband, Henry VIII, and refused to take the oath of supremacy. He was for this reason beheaded on Tower Hill. Shortly before his death he had been created cardinal by the pope. He died with the words *Te Deum* on his lips. Canonized in 1935.
Cf. Newdigate — Att. — Holw.

JOHN of COLOGNE (St) M. O.P.
R.M. July 9

d. 1572. A native of Cologne who became a Dominican and parish priest of Horner, Holland. He was hanged with the other Gorkum martyrs, q.v. They were canonized in 1867.
Cf. Holw.

JOHN of OSTERWICK (St) M. O.S.A.
R.M. July 9

d. 1572. A native of Holland who joined the Augustinians at Briel and was director and confessor of a community of Augustinian nuns at Gorkum when the town was taken by the Calvinists. He suffered with the group of the Gorkum Martyrs, q.v.
Cf. Holw.

JOHN of BERGAMO (St) Bp.
R.M. July 11
d. c.690. A bishop of Bergamo (c.656 to c.690) renowned for his learning and great success in combating Arianism. The letters B.M. appended to his name, instead of being read *Bonae Memoriae* — "of good memory," were wrongly taken for *Beati Martyris* — "of the Blessed Martyr," — and he was in consequence formerly considered to have been a martyr.
Cf. Att. — Holw.

JOHN the Georgian (St) Ab.
A.C. July 12
d. c.1002. This John is usually surnamed "the Iberian," i.e., the Georgian, and also "the Hagiorite." With his wife's consent, he and his son St Euthymius became monks on Mt Olympus in Bithynia. Thence they migrated to Mt Athos in Macedonia, where they founded the monastery of Iviron (Iweron — the Iberian), which still exists.
Cf. Holw. — Att.

JOHN GUALBERT (St) Ab. O.S.B. Vall.
R.M. July 12
d. 1073. A Florentine by birth, of the noble family of the Visdomini. As a young man he spent his time in worldly amusements, until one Good Friday, having pardoned his brother's murderer, he saw the image of the crucifix miraculously bow its head in acknowledgement of Gualbert's good action. Thereupon John became a Benedictine at San Miniato del Monte, at Florence. When it seemed likely that he would be appointed abbot he left the abbey for a more secluded spot and founded the monastery of Vallumbrosa — *Vallis Umbrosa* — near Fiesole, under St Benedict's Rule. His foundation soon grew into a powerful Congregation spread chiefly through Tuscany and Lombardy. St John died at Passignano, one of his own foundations, and was canonized in 1193.
Cf. Zimm. — Att. — Menzies — Chev. — Holw.

JOHN JONES (Bl) M. O.F.M.
A.C. July 12
d. 1598. John Jones, alias Buckley, was born at Clynog Fawr, Carnarvon. He became a Franciscan Observant at Rome and worked on the London mission from 1592 till 1597. He was martyred for his priesthood at Southwark. Beatified in 1929.
Cf. Newdigate — Att.

JOHN NAISEN (Bl) M.   A.C. July 12
d. 1626. A wealthy Japanese layman from Arima. When the persecutors threatened him with the prostitution of his wife, his constancy gave way for a time, but he repented and was burnt alive at Nagasaki. Beatified in 1867.
Cf. Holw.

JOHN TANACA (Bl) M.   A.C. July 12
d. 1626. A Japanese layman who gave shelter to Bl Balthassar Torres. After a long imprisonment at Omura he was burnt alive at Nagasaki. Beatified in 1867.
Cf. Holw.

JOHN FERNANDEZ, born at Lisbon.

JOHN of SAN MARTIN, born at Toledo.

JOHN de BAEZA, a Spaniard by birth.

JOHN de ZAFRA, born at Toledo.

JOHN de MAVORGA, born in Aragon.

JOHN FERNANDEZ (BB) MM. S.J.
A.C. July 15
d. 1570. Born at Braga, Portugal.
All belonged to the Society of Jesus; the first two were clerics and the rest temporal-coadjutors. All suffered martyrdom with Bl Ignatius de Azevedo and comp., q.v.

JOHN PLESINGTON (Bl) M.
A.C. July 19
d. 1679. Born at Dimples, near Garstang, Lancs, and educated at Valladolid, he worked on the mission in Cheshire, and was hanged for his priesthood at Chester. Beatified in 1929.
Cf. Newdigate — Att

JOHN of EDESSA (St) H. R.M. July 21
6th cent. A Syrian monk of Edessa and an associate of St Simeon Stylites, q.v.

JOHN and BENIGNUS (SS) O.S.B.
A.C. July 21
d. 707. Said to have been twin brothers and monks of Moyenmoutier under St Hidulphus.
Cf. Chev. — Holw. — P.B.

JOHN LLOYD (Bl) M. A.C. July 22
d. 1679. A native of Brecknockshire who received his priestly education at Valladolid and then served the Welsh mission. He was executed for his priesthood at Cardiff with Bl Philip Evans, S.J. Beatified in 1929.
Cf. Newdigate — Att.

JOHN CASSIAN (St) Ab. A.C. July 23
c.360-c.433. An Eastern monk who received his monastic training in Egypt, and afterwards established himself at Marseilles, where he founded the abbey of St Victor and a nunnery, and ruled both from Lérins. His *Conferences* and his *Institutes* were commended by St Benedict as authoritative treatises on the training of monks, and in consequence have exerted a lasting influence in the Christian world.
Cf. P. de U. — Att. — Holw. — Baud.

JOHN of TOSSIGNANO (Bl) C.
A.C. July 24
d. 1446. John Tavalli was born at Tossignano, near Imola, and, after his studies at the university of Bologna, joined the order of the Gesuati. In 1431 he was raised to the see of Ferrara. He is best remembered as the translator of the Bible into Italian. Cult confirmed by Benedict XIV.
Cf. Att. — Holw.

JOHN BOSTE (Bl) M. A.C. July 24
d. 1594. Born at Dufton in Westmorland and educated at Queen's College, Oxford, and after his conversion, at Reims. He was ordained in 1581 and laboured in the northern counties for twelve years until his martyrdom for the priesthood at Durham. Beatified in 1929.
Cf. Newdigate.

JOHN INGRAM (Bl) M. A.C. July 26
d. 1594. Born at Stoke Edith, Herefordshire. He became a convert, studied at New College, Oxford, and afterwards at Reims and Rome. After his ordination in 1589, he worked in Scotland. He was condemned for his priesthood, and suffered at Gateshead.
Cf. Newdigate.

JOHN of EPHESUS (St) M. R.M. July 27
See Seven Sleepers.

JOHN BAPTIST LO (Bl) M. A.C. July 29
1825-1861. A Chinese servant beheaded at Tsin-gai. Beatified in 1909.
Cf. Holw.

JOHN SORETH (Bl) C. O.C.
A.C. July 30
c.1420-1471. A native of Caen in Normandy. He joined the Carmelites and was their prior general from 1451 to 1471. He was a forerunner of St Teresa in his efforts to return to the primitive observance and to admit nunneries into the order. Cult approved in 1865.
Cf. Holw. — Baud. — Att.

JOHN COLOMBINI (Bl) Founder.
R.M. July 31
c.1300-1367. A native of Siena, who became a prominent citizen, held the office of *Gonfalionere* (first magistrate), and is described as an ambitious, avaricious and bad-tempered man. While reading the story of the conversion of St Mary of Egypt, he was suddenly converted and eventually formed a small society of lay persons devoted to penance and deeds of charity. They were called *Gesuati* and were approved in 1367. Bl John was beatified by Gregory XIII.
Cf. Menzies — Att. — Holw.

JOHN FELTON (Bl) M. A.C. Aug. 8
d. 1570. Born at Bermondsey, of a Norfolk family. He was living at Southwark when the bull of Pope St Pius V excommunicating Queen Elizabeth reached London, and he bravely affixed a copy to the door of the Bishop of London's house. For this he was martyred in St Paul's churchyard. Beatified in 1886.
Cf. Newdigate — Att.

JOHN of SALERNO (Bl) C. O.P.
A.C. Aug. 9
c.1190-1242. A native of Salerno, who received the religious habit from St Dominic and eventually became the founder of the Dominican friary of Santa Maria Novella at Florence (1221). Cult approved in 1783.
Cf. Holw. — Att. — Baud. — Prop. O.P.

JOHN of ALVERNIA (Bl) C. O.F.M.
A.C. Aug. 9
1259-1322. Born at Fermo, he joined the Friars Minor in 1272, and thereafter lived a semi-eremitical life on Mt Alvernia, whence he evangelized the surrounding district. He was famous for his gift of infused knowledge. Cult approved in 1880.
Cf. Holw. — Att. — Baud.

JOHN of RIETI (Bl) C. O.S.A.
A.C. Aug. 9
d. c.1530. John Bufalari was a native of Castel Porziano, near Rome, and an Augustinian friar-hermit at Rieti. Cult approved in 1832.
Cf. Att. — Holw.

JOHN BAPTIST VIANNEY (St) C.
R.M. Aug. 9
1786-1859. More often called "the Curé d'Ars." Born at Dardilly, near Lyons, he was a farm-hand and already nineteen when he began his studies for the priesthood, which he completed only with considerable difficulty. He was, however, ordained in 1815 and three years after was appointed parish priest of Ars, a small village near Lyons, where he worked for the rest of his life, and for which he won world-wide fame. His chief work was the direction of souls: his confessional was thronged with all classes of persons, who flocked to him from far and wide, and during the last ten years of his life he spent in it sixteen to eighteen hours a day. His characteristics were zeal, amiability, humility and patience. He was gifted with discernment of spirits, prophecy and hidden knowledge, and was often tormented by evil spirits. Before his death he was made honorary canon of Lyons by his bishop and a knight of the Legion of Honour by the French government. Canonized in 1925 and declared patron saint of parish-priests in 1929.
Cf. Att. — Holw.

JOHN and PETER BECCHETTI (BB) CC. O.S.A.
A.C. Aug. 11
13th cent. Descendants of the family of St Thomas Becket (Becchetti) from a branch that settled in Fabriano, in Italy. Both belonged to the Augustinian hermits, and Bl John is said to have taught at Oxford. Cult approved in 1835.
Cf. Holw.

JOHN BERCHMANS (St) C. S.J.
R.M. Aug. 13
1599-1621. Born at Diest in Brabant, the son of a master-shoemaker. He studied at Malines and there also he entered the Society of Jesus at the age of seventeen and was sent to Rome for his novitiate. His short life of twenty-two years was remarkable for the heroic fidelity with which he kept the minutest points of regular observance. He was canonized in

1888, and is venerated as patron of young mass-servers.
Cf. Holw. — Att. — Baud.

JOHN of MARTHA (Bl) M. O.F.M.
A.C. Aug. 16
1578-1618. Born at Prados, near Tarragona, in Spain, after his ordination (1606) he was sent to Japan, where he is said to have gained a perfect mastery of the language. Arrested at Maeco in 1615, he was beheaded after a three years' imprisonment. Beatified in 1867.
Cf. Holw.

JOHN of MONTE MARANO (St) Bp. O.S.B.
A.C. Aug. 17
d. 1094. A Benedictine monk, probably of Monte Cassino. He was nominated bishop of Monte Marano by Gregory VII (1074) while that pope was in exile at Salerno. His cult was approved in 1906, and he is venerated as the principal patron saint of Monte Marano.
Cf. Zimm. — Gams — Chev. — Holw.

JOHN and CRISPUS (SS) MM.
R.M. Aug. 18
d. c.303. Roman priests who devoted themselves to recovering and burying the bodies of the martyrs, for which they themselves suffered martyrdom under Diocletian.
Cf. Menzies — Holw. — Baud.

JOHN MANGATA, JOHN YAGO and JOHN FOIAMON (BB) MM.
A.C. Aug. 19
d. 1622. The two first named were sailors in the ship on which Bl Joachim Firaiama (q.v.) was a traveller, and the last named was a scribe on the same ship. They were beheaded at Nagasaki. Beatified in 1867.
Cf. Holw.

JOHN EUDES (St) Founder.
R.M. Aug. 19
1601-1680. A native of Ri, France, who after his ordination (1625) entered the French Oratory and devoted himself wholeheartedly to the "home-mission," twice risking his life in attending victims of the plague. In 1641 he founded the Sisterhood of our Lady of Charity of the Refuge to care of women of ill repute and in 1643 the Society of Jesus and Mary — *Eudists* — for the education of priests. He was moreover the originator of the

liturgical cult of the Sacred Heart. He died at Caen, and was canonized in 1925.
Cf. Att. — Holw. — Baud.

JOHN KEMBLE (Bl) M.   A.C. Aug. 22
d. 1679. A native of Herefordshire. After his studies and ordination at Douai, he served the missions of Monmouthshire and Herefordshire for fifty-three years (1625-1679). In his 81st year he was hanged, drawn and quartered at Hereford for being a priest. Beatified in 1929.
Cf. Newdigate — Att.

JOHN WALL (Bl) M. O.F.M.
                              A.C. Aug. 22
d. 1679. Born near Preston, in Lancs, he was educated at Douai and in Rome. Here he joined the Friars Minor with the new name of Fr. Joachim of St Anne (1651). In 1656 he joined the Worcester mission which he served until the year of his martyrdom for his priesthood at Worcester. Beatified in 1929.
Cf. Newdigate — Att.

JOHN of CARAMOLA (Bl) C. O.S.B.
Cist.   **P.C. Aug. 26**
d. 1339. A native of Toulouse who became a hermit on Mt Caramola in the Basilicata, Italy, and afterwards a Cistercian lay-brother at the abbey of Sagittario, near Chiaramonte, Naples.
Cf. Chev. — Holw.

JOHN BASSAND (Bl) C. O.S.B. Cel.
                              A.C. Aug. 26
1360-1445. A native of Besançon, where he joined the Canons Regular of St Paul. Shortly after, however, he passed over to the Celestine Benedictines at Paris. He held important offices in the congregation, and was spiritual director of St Colette. He made great efforts to establish his congregation in England and Aragon.
Cf. Zimm. — P. de U. — Chev. — Holw.

JOHN (St) M.   R.M. Aug. 27
See Marcellinus, Mannea etc.

JOHN (St) Bp.   R.M. Aug. 27
d. 813. Bishop of Pavia, in Lombardy, 801-813.
Cf. Bolland — Gams.

JOHN ROCHE (Bl) M.   A.C. Aug. 30
d. 1588. John Roche (*alias* Neale) was an Irish waterman who was condemned to death for rescuing a priest. He suffered

at Tyburn with five companions: BB. Richard Leigh, etc. Beatified in 1929.
Cf. Newdigate.

JOHN du LAU (Bl) Bp. M. A.C. Sept. 2
d. 1792. Archbishop of Arles. During the French Revolution he was imprisoned in the Carmelite church in the rue de Rennes at Paris, and later martyred, by the mob, with the approval of the Legislative Assembly, for refusing the oath and constitution of the clergy which had been condemned by the Holy See. He forms part of the group Carmes (Martyrs of) q.v.

JOHN of PERUGIA and PETER of SASSOFERRATO (BB) MM. O.F.M.
                              A.C. Sept. 3
d. 1231. These two Franciscan friars, priest and lay-brother respectively, were sent by St Francis of Assisi in 1216 to preach to the Mohammedans in Spain. They worked in the district between Teruel and Valencia. Having been seized in a mosque at Valencia and refusing to apostatize they were beheaded. Cult approved in 1783.
Cf. Att. — Holw.

JOHN of NICOMEDIA (St) M.
                              R.M. Sept. 7
d. 303. A Christian of rank, who, when the edict of persecution against the Christians was first published at Nicomedia, removed it and tore it to pieces. He was burnt alive.
Cf. Holw. — Baud. — Att.

JOHN of LODI (St) Bp. O.S.B.
                              A.C. Sept. 7
d. 1106. A native of Lodi Vecchio in Lombardy, who, after being a hermit for some years, entered the abbey of Fontavellana, where he professed the Benedictine Rule under St Peter Damian. In 1072 he was chosen prior of the abbey and in 1105 bishop of Gubbio. He wrote the life of St Peter Damian.
Cf. Gams — Chev. — Prop. Camald. — Butler-Thurston (Feb. 23) — Baud.

JOHN MAKI (Bl) M.   A.C. Sept. 7
d. 1627. An adopted son of Bl Louis Maki. He was burnt alive at Nagasaki. Beatified in 1867.
Cf. Holw.

JOHN DUCKETT (Bl) M.   A.C. Sept. 7
d. 1644. A kinsman of Bl James Duckett,

the bookseller (q.v.). He was born at Underwinder, near Sedbergh, Yorks, educated for the priesthood at Douai and ordained in 1639. He ministered to the Catholics at Durham. Martyred for his priesthood at Tyburn with Bl Ralph Corby. Beatified in 1929.
Cf. Att. — Newdigate.

JOHN TOMAKI and JOHN INAMURA (BB) MM. Tert. O.P.   A.C. Sept. 8
d. 1628. Japanese laymen and Dominican tertiaries, beheaded at Nagasaki for helping the missionaries. Bl John Tomaki was a very active Christian and the proud father of four martyr sons. Beatified in 1867.
Cf. Holw.

JOHN KINGOCU (Bl) M. S.J.
A.C. Sept. 10
d. 1622. Born at Amanguchi in Japan, he was a catechist of Bl Charles Spinola, by whom he was received into the Society of Jesus in the prison at Omura. He was beheaded at Nagasaki. Beatified in 1867.
Cf. Holw.

JOHN of COREA (Bl) M.   A.C. Sept. 10
d. 1622. A boy of twelve, son of Bl Antony of Corea and his wife Mary, beheaded at Nagasaki. Beatified in 1867.
Cf. Holw.

JOHN-GABRIEL PERBOYRE (Bl) M.
A.C. Sept. 11
See Gabriel Perboyre.

JOHN the DWARF (St) H. A.C. Sept. 15
d. c.540. John, nicknamed *Kolobos*, "the Dwarf," was a native of Basta in Lower Egypt. He became a disciple of St Poemen in the desert of Skete, and is described as short-tempered and conceited by nature, but gentle and humble by grace. He was also famous for his absentmindedness. In obedience to orders he watered a walking stick, and when it sprouted, it was called "the tree of obedience."
Cf. Holw. — Att. — Baud.

JOHN (St) M.   R.M. Sept. 16
See Abundius, Abundantius, etc.

JOHN de MASSIAS (Bl) C. O.P.
A.C. Sept. 18
1585-1645. A native of Ribera, in Estremadura, Spain, who crossed over to S. America and worked on a cattle ranch before becoming a Dominican lay-brother at Lima. He was employed as the doorkeeper of the friary to the end of his life. Beatified in 1837.
Cf. Prop. O.P. — Holw. — Att.

JOHN EUSTACE (Bl) Ab. O.S.B. Cist.
P.C. Sept. 20
d. 1481. A canon regular at Mons who became a Cistercian and eventually was made first abbot of Jardinet, in the diocese of Namur. He was deputed to restore discipline in several other houses.
Cf. Holw. — Zimm.

JOHN (St) M.   R.M. Sept. 23
See Andrew, John, etc.

JOHN of MEDA (St) Ab. O.S.B.
A.C. Sept. 26
d. 1159 (?). A native of Meda, and a member of the clergy of Milan, who about the year 1134 joined the *Humiliati* and advised them to adopt St Benedict's Rule, which they did, although they continued to call themselves canons. Canonized by Alexander III.
Cf. Att. — Baud. — Chev. — Holw.

JOHN MARK (St) Bp.   R.M. Sept. 27
1st cent. The R.M. makes this John Mark (see Acts XII, 25) a bishop of Byblos in Phoenicia. Nowadays most biblical scholars identify him with St Mark the evangelist, first bishop of Alexandria.
Cf. Att. — Holw. — Baud.

JOHN of CORDOVA (St) M.
R.M. Sept. 27
See Adolphus and John.

JOHN COCHUMBUCO (Bl) M.
A.C. Sept. 28
d. 1630. A tertiary of St Augustine and a native catechist to Bl Bartholomew Gutierrez. Beheaded at Nagasaki, and beatified in 1867.
Cf. Holw.

JOHN de MONTMIRAIL (Bl) C. O.S.B. Cist.   A.C. Sept. 29
1165-1217. Besides other titles of nobility he was Seigneur de Montmirail on the Marne. He was bred to arms and married and had several children, but as soon as he could win his wife's consent, he became a Cistercian at Longpont, where he died. He is venerated liturgically by

the Cistercians and in several French dioceses.
Cf. Baud. — Chev. — Holw.

JOHN of GENT (Bl) C. O.S.B.
P.C. Sept. 29
d. 1439. A Benedictine of the abbey of Sainte-Claude on the Jura Mountains. A collaborator with St Joan of Arc, known as "the Hermit of St Claude."
Cf. Zimm. — Holw.

JOHN of DUKLA (Bl) C. O.F.M.
A.C. Oct. 1
d. 1484. A native of Dukla in Polish Galicia, who became a Franciscan conventual at Lemberg, and at the instigation of St John of Capistrano passed over to the Observants, and worked successfully among the Ruthenian schismatics. Cult approved in 1739.
Cf. Holw. — Att.

JOHN ROBINSON (Bl) M. A.C. Oct. 1
d. 1588. Born at Ferrensby, Yorks. Having become a widower he went to Reims to study for the priesthood and was ordained there in 1585. He was executed for his priesthood at Ipswich. Beatified in 1929.
Cf. Newdigate.

JOHN HEWETT (Bl) M. A.C. Oct. 5
d. 1588. *Alias* Weldon and Savell. A native of Yorkshire, he was educated at Caius College, Cambridge and studied for the priesthood at Reims. He was ordained in 1586 and hanged for his priesthood at Mile End Green. Beatified in 1929.
Cf. Newdigate.

JOHN LEONARDI (Bl) Founder.
R.M. Oct. 9
c.1550-1609. A native of Diecimo in the diocese of Lucca. While serving as an apprentice to a pharmacist at Lucca he studied for the priesthood and was ordained in 1571. He worked with great zeal among the prisoners and in hospitals and, with the help of two laymen and some priests, founded the Institute of Clerks Regular of the Mother of God, approved in 1593. He is reckoned one of the founders also of the College of Propaganda Fide in Rome, and was appointed visitor of the Vallombrosans and Monteverginians. Beatified in 1861.
Cf. Att. — Menzies — Holw.

JOHN of BRIDLINGTON (St) C. O.S.A.
A.C. Oct. 11
d. 1379. John Thwing, a student at the university of Oxford, joined the community of Augustinian canons at Bridlington and in due course ruled it as prior for seventeen years. Canonized in 1403. Nothing else is known about him.
Cf. Att. — Baud. — Holw.

JOHN CANTIUS (St) C. R.M. Oct. 20
c.1395-1473 (Dec. 24). Born at Kenty in Silesia, he graduated at the university of Cracow, and was appointed there to the chair of Sacred Scripture. For some time he took charge of a parish but, fearing the responsibility of the care of souls, returned to his biblical teaching, which he carried on until his death. He made a practice of sharing his earnings with the poor. Canonized in 1767.
Cf. Holw. — Att. — Baud.

JOHN of SYRACUSE (St) Bp. O.S.B.
A.C. Oct. 23
d. c.609. Bishop of Syracuse from 595 till c.609.
Cf. Gams — Menzies.

JOHN BUONI (Bl) C. O.S.B.
R.M. Oct. 23
d. 1249. A native of Mantua who in early life was a licentious jester at various Italian courts. In 1208, after a severe illness, he changed his life completely and retired to do penance as a hermit near Cesena, whither a number of disciples followed him. They were given the Augustinian rule (*Boniti*) by Innocent IV, and soon they coalesced with similar hermits to form the order of Augustinian hermit friars. Cult approved in 1483.
Cf. Menzies — Holw. — Att.

JOHN ANGELO PORRO (Bl) C. O.S.M.
A.C. Oct. 24
d. 1504. A native of Milan who joined the Servites, and after a time spent at Monte Senario, returned to Milan where he worked to the end of his life. Cult approved in 1737.
Cf. Holw. — Menzies — Att.

JOHN DAT (Bl) M. A.C. Oct. 28
1764-1798. A native of W. Tonkin, ordained to the priesthood in 1798. After three months' captivity he was beheaded in the same year. Beatified in 1900.
Cf. Holw.

JOHN of AUTUN (St) Bp. R.M. Oct. 29
? A bishop-saint venerated at Autun, of whom no particulars are extant.
Cf. Baud. — Holw.

JOHN SLADE (Bl) M.   A.C. Oct. 30
d. 1583. A native of Manston, Dorset (?) and a student at New College, Oxford. He became a schoolmaster, and was martyred at Winchester for denying the royal supremacy in spiritual matters. Beatified in 1929.
Cf. Newdigate — Att.

JOHN and JAMES (SS) MM.
R.M. Nov. 1
d. c.344. Persian martyrs who suffered under King Shapur II. John is described as a bishop.
Cf. Baud. — Holw.

JOHN BODEY (Bl) M.   A.C. Nov. 2
d. 1583. Born at Wells, Somerset, and a fellow of New College, Oxford. He became a convert and studied law at Douai. He returned to England and became a schoolmaster. He was condemned for repudiating the royal supremacy in spiritual matters and was hanged at Andover. Beatified in 1929.
Cf. Newdigate — Att.

JOHN ZEDAZNELI (St) Ab. A.C. Nov. 4
6th cent. The leader of the group of Syrian monks, who evangelized Georgia (Iberia) and introduced the monastic life there.
Cf. Att. — Holw.

JOHN BAPTIST COU (Bl) M.
A.C. Nov. 7
d. 1840. A native of Tonkin, a layman and married, who was beheaded for the faith. Beatified in 1900.
Cf. Holw.

JOHN of RATZEBURG (St) Bp. M.
A.C. Nov. 10
d. 1066. A native of Scotland, who became a missionary in Germany. He was appointed bishop of Ratzeburg and evangelized the Baltic coastal region, where he was martyred.
Cf. Holw.

JOHN of POLAND (St) M. O.S.B.
R.M. Nov. 12
See Benedict and Comp.

JOHN CINI "della PACE" (Bl) C. Tert.
O.F.M.   A.C. Nov. 12
d. 1433. Surnamed "the Soldier," or "Stipendario," or from his domicile, *"de Porta pacis," "della pace."* He was a native of Pisa, bred to arms, who in 1396, became a Franciscan tertiary and founded several charitable organizations and a confraternity of flagellants. Cult approved in 1856.
Cf. Holw. — Att.

JOHN LICCI (Bl) C. O.P. A.C. Nov. 14
1400-1511. Born at Caccamo in the diocese of Palermo, in Sicily. He joined the Dominican Order and died at the age of 111. Cult confirmed in 1753.
Cf. Prop. O.P. — Att. — Holw.

JOHN THORNE (Bl) M. O.S.B.
A.C. Nov. 15
d. 1539. A Benedictine at Glastonbury and treasurer of the abbey at the time of the dissolution. He was executed at Glastonbury with his abbot, Bl Richard Whiting and a brother-monk, Bl Roger James. The charge against John Thorne was that of *sacrilege*, the sacrilege consisting in his having hidden various treasures of the abbey church to save them from the rapacious hands of the king. Beatified in 1895.
Cf. Camm — Newdigate.

JOHN EYNON and JOHN RUGG (BB)
MM. O.S.B.   A.C. Nov. 15
d. 1539. John Eynon was priest in charge of St Giles, at Reading, and John Rugg a prebendary of Chichester living at Reading Abbey. Both were executed at Reading with the abbot Bl Hugh Faringdon. They are generally considered to have been monks of the abbey. Beatified in 1895.
Cf. Camm — Newdigate — Att.

JOHN XOUN (Bl) M.   A.C. Nov. 18
d. 1619. A Japanese layman, born at Meaco and baptized by the Jesuits at Nagasaki. He was a member of the confraternity of the Holy Rosary. Burnt alive at Nagasaki. Beatified in 1867.
Cf. Holw.

JOHN of the CROSS (St) Dr. O.C.
R.M. Nov. 24
1542-1591. Juan de Yepes was born at Fontiberos in Old Castile, the son of a weaver. He joined the Carmelites at

Medina (1562) and from 1564 to 1567 was a student of theology at Salamanca. He now fell under the influence of St Teresa and was her first "half-friar" of the first house of the reform, founded for men, at Durnelo. From 1572 to 1577 he was the confessor of St Teresa at Avila. There followed a most trying period of ill-treatment, calumny and imprisonment at Toledo, until, in 1578 the Discalced were definitely separated from the Calced Carmelites. St John was now made prior successively of several houses, and in 1585 visitor of Andalusia. The last years of his life were again a period of intense humiliation, misunderstanding and physical suffering. He died in obscurity at Ubeda. St John's highest title to fame are his mystical writings (*The Ascent of Mount Carmel, The Dark Night of the Soul, The Spiritual Canticle, etc*) which, besides being superb masterpieces of Spanish literature, contain a thorough exposition of Catholic mysticism. St John was canonized in 1726 and declared a Doctor of the Church in 1926.
Cf. Holw. — Att.

JOHN ANGELOPTES (St) Bp.
                              A.C. Nov. 27
d. 433. Bishop of Ravenna, 430-433. He was appointed by the pope metropolitan of Aemilia and Flaminia. The nickname *Angeloptes* means "the man who saw an angel": it was given him because, according to the legend, an angel visible to him alone once came and assisted him in the celebration of mass.
Cf. Menzies — Holw.

JOHN IVANANGO and JOHN MONTAJANA (BB) MM.   **A.C. Nov. 27**
d. 1619. Japanese laymen, both belonging to the royal family of Firando. They were beheaded at Nagasaki with eight companions. Beatified in 1867.
Cf. Holw.

JOHN of VERCELLI (Bl) C. O.P.
                              A.C. Dec. 1
d. 1283. Born at Mosso Santa Maria, near Vercelli, he studied at Paris and taught law at Paris and Vercelli. He then joined the Friars Preachers, among whom he held several offices ending with that of master-general (1264-1283). He was commissioned by the pope to draw up the

Schema for the second ecumenical council of Lyons. Cult approved in 1903.
Cf. Prop. O.P. — Att. — Holw.

JOHN BECHE (Bl) Ab. M. O.S.B.
                              A.C. Dec. 1
d. 1539. As a young Benedictine Beche took his D.D. at Oxford (1515) and eventually became abbot of St Werburgh at Chester, whence in 1533 he was promoted to the abbacy of Colchester. He was a great friend of SS John Fisher and Thomas More, and opposed Henry VIII's ecclesiastical policy. He took the oath of supremacy, but when in 1538 his abbey was dissolved, he openly denied the king's right to do this. Within the year he was charged with treason and executed at Colchester. Beatified in 1895.
Cf. Camm — Att. — Newdigate.

JOHN RUYSBROECK (Bl) C. O.S.A.
                              A.C. Dec. 2
1293-1381. A native of Ruysbroeck, near Brussels, who after his ordination was appointed to a canonry at Sainte-Gudule. In 1343 he founded, and ruled as first prior, the monastery of Groenendael, for Augustinian canons. It was here that he composed his numerous ascetical works, which have entitled him to a prominent place among medieval mystical writers. Cult confirmed in 1908.
Cf. Holw. — Att. — Baud.

JOHN ARMERO (Bl) C. O.P.
                              P.C. Dec. 2
d. 1566. A Dominican lay-brother at Baeza, Spain, who was directed by his superiors to take Holy Orders. His two great interests in life were study and prayer before the Blessed Sacrament. He is the object of a popular cultus.
Cf. Holw. — P. de U.

JOHN (St) M.   **R.M. Dec. 3**
See Claudius, Crispin, etc.

John the WONDER-WORKER (St) Bp.
                              R.M. Dec. 5
d. p. 750. Bishop of Polybotum in Phrygia, one of the most strenuous champions of orthodoxy against the emperor Leo, the Image-Breaker. Such was his fame as a wonder-worker that the emperor did not dare to interfere with him.
Cf. Holw. — Baud.

JOHN GRADENIGO (Bl) H. O.S.B.
A.C. Dec. 5

d. 1025. A Venetian nobleman, who was professed as a Benedictine at Cuxa, in the Catalonian Pyrenees, together with his friend St Peter Urseolo. After a life of manifold vicissitudes, he died as a hermit near Montecassino.
Cf. Zimm. — Chev.

JOHN ALMOND (Bl) M. A.C. Dec. 5

d. 1612. A native of Allerton, near Liverpool, and educated at Much Woolton, Reims, and Rome. Ordained in 1598 he worked on the English mission from 1602 till 1612. He was put to death for his priesthood at Tyburn. Beatified in 1929.
Cf. Newdigate — Att.

JOHN MASON (Bl) M. A.C. Dec. 10

d. 1591. A native of Kendal, Westmorland. He was a layman and was hanged at Tyburn for relieving priests. He suffered with four companions. Beatified in 1929.
Cf. Newdigate.

JOHN ROBERTS (Bl) M. O.S.B.
A.C. Dec. 10

1577-1610. Born at Trawfynydd in Merionethshire, he was brought up nominally a Protestant, but was always a Catholic at heart. At the age of nineteen he went up to St John's College Oxford, and in 1598 was entered at the Inns of Court as a student of law. This same year travelling on the Continent on holiday, he was received into the Church at Notre Dame, Paris, and went to Valladolid in October for his ecclesiastical course. While there he joined the Benedictines at San Benito el Real (1599), and was professed the following year at Compostella. In December, 1602, after his ordination, he set out for the English mission. His resourcefulness and courage made him an outstanding figure even among the priests of the English mission. Six or seven times he was imprisoned and released; during the plague of 1603 his services to the sick in London made his name known throughout the land. Meanwhile, he was the chief assistant of Dom Augustine Bradshaw in the founding of St Gregory's, at Douai (now Downside Abbey). He was captured in his priestly vestments while saying Mass and executed for his priesthood at Tyburn. Beatified in 1929.
Cf. Zimm. — Camm — Att.

JOHN MARINONI (Bl) C. A.C. Dec. 13

1490-1562. A Venetian, canon of St Mark's cathedral, who gave up his canonry to join (1530) St Cajetan, the founder of the Theatines. He was a ubiquitous preacher, the exclusive theme of his sermons being Christ crucified. He refused the archbishopric of Naples, the city in which he died. Cult approved in 1762.
Cf. Att. — Holw. — Baud.

JOHN BREAD-and-WATER (Bl) C.
O.S.B. Cist. A.C. Dec. 14

d. p. 1150. A Cistercian lay-brother of the abbey of Sagramenia (*Sacra Moenia*) in Spain, founded in 1142. On account of Bl John's life-long fasting on bread and water the people nicknamed him Brother John Bread-and-Water. (*Pan y Agua*).
Cf. Zimm. — Men. Cist.

JOHN and FESTUS (SS) MM.
R.M. Dec. 21

? Martyrs honoured in Tuscany.

JOHN VINCENT (St) Bp. O.S.B.
A.C. Dec. 21

d. 1012. A native of Ravenna, who became a Benedictine at St Michael of Chiusa, and then a hermit on Monte Caprario; finally he was made bishop of a diocese in the neighbourhood.
Cf. Zimm.

JOHN CIRITA (Bl) H. O.S.B.
P.C. Dec. 23

d. c.1164. A Spanish Benedictine who was first a hermit in Galicia and then a monk at Toronca in Portugal. He was instrumental in handing over the abbey to the Cistercians, and is said to have written the rule of the Knights of Avis.
Cf. Chev. — Holw.

JOHN (St) Apostle and Evang.
R.M. Dec. 27

d. c.100. Often surnamed in English the Divine i.e. the theologian. A Galilean, the son of Zebedee and brother of St James the Greater, John was a fisherman by profession until called by Christ to be an apostle. He became in fact "the Disciple whom Jesus loved," whom our Lord, dying on the Cross, made the guardian of his mother. He wrote the fourth Gospel, chiefly to prove Christ's Divinity, three canonical epistles and the Apocalypse (Revelation). After the resurrection he spent most of his time at Ephesus. A very ancient tradition holds that he was cast into a cauldron of boiling oil at Rome under Domitian, but was preserved unhurt and banished to Patmos. This fact is liturgically commemorated in the Western Church on May 6 — St John before the Latin Gate, *ante Portam Latinam.* St John died at Ephesus at a great age. *Cf. Att. — Holw. — Menzies.*

JOHN ALCOBER (Bl) M. O.P.
                                   A.C. Dec. 30
1694-1748. Born at Gerona, in Spain, after his profession in the Dominican order, he was sent to China (1728) and for sixteen years he worked in the province of Fo-kien. Arrested in 1746, he was strangled in the prison at Fu-tsheu. Beatified in 1893.
Cf. Holw.

JOHN-FRANCIS REGIS (St) C. S.J.
                                   R.M. Dec. 31
1597-1640. Born at Font-Couverte in the diocese of Narbonne, in Languedoc. At the age of eighteen he entered the Society of Jesus at Béziers, was ordained in 1631, and from that moment knew no rest, spending himself in preaching the gospel to unlettered farming folk of Languedoc and Auvergne, providing for prisoners and fallen women, establishing confraternities of the Bl Sacrament, and effecting everywhere numerous conversions among the Huguenots. He died while preaching a mission (Dec. 30) and was canonized in 1737.
Cf. Att. — Holw.

Note. There are some two hundred or more other saints, named John — e.g. John Thauler, John Gelibert, John Wagner, John Duns Scotus, John of Jesus-Mary, John of Lerida etc. — who are usually called *Beati* in their respective orders or nations, but there is no evidence of their being the object of any cult, whether official or popular.

JOLENTA of HUNGARY (Bl) W. Poor Clare.   A.C. March 6
Otherwise Helen of Poland, q.v.

JONAS (St) H.   R.M. Feb. 11
4th cent. A monk of Demeskenyanos in Egypt under St Pachomius. He was the gardener of the community for eighty-five years, working in this capacity during the day, and at night plaiting ropes and singing psalms.
Cf. Baud. — Holw.

JONAS, BARACHISIUS and Comp. (SS) MM.   R.M. March 29
d. 327. Jonas and Barachisius were brothers, born at Beth-Asa in Persia. They suffered martyrdom under Shapur II. We have an eye-witness's account of their passion: the brutal inventiveness of the persecutors in devising new tortures was only surpassed by the quiet heroism of the martyrs. Some nine companions suffered at the same time.
Cf. Att. — Holw. — Baud.

JONAS (JONAH) (St) Prophet.
                                   R.M. Sept. 21
d. c.761. One of the twelve minor Prophets and the subject of a canonical book of the Bible. It is said that, after preaching in Niniveh, he returned to Palestine. In the time of St Jerome his supposed tomb was shown at Diospolis.
Cf. Holw. — Baud.

JONAS (YON) (St) M.   R.M. Sept. 22
? A companion or disciple of St Dionysius of Paris, who preached in the neighbourhood of that city, and was martyred.
Cf. Holw. — Baud.

JONATUS (St) Ab. O.S.B.   A.C. Aug. 1
d. c.695. A monk of Elnone under St Amandus. He was abbot first of Marchiennes (c.643-c.652). and then of Elnone (c.652-c.659).
Cf. Mab. — Chev. — Holw. — Baud.

JORANDUS (St) H. O.S.B.   A.C. Nov. 2
d. 1340. A monk-hermit at Kergrist and later Saint-Juhec in Pédernec.
Cf. Zimm.

JORDAN of SAXONY (Bl) C. O.P.
                                   A.C. Feb. 15
d. 1237. Jordan joined the Dominican order under St Dominic himself in 1220, and while yet a novice, attended the first general chapter of the order at Bologna. He was later elected second master-general and under him the new order advanced apace, spread throughout Germany and reached Denmark. He was a powerful preacher and one of his sermons won St Albert the Great for the order. He was shipwrecked and drowned when on a voy-

age to the Holy Land. Cult confirmed in 1828.
Cf. Prop. O.P. — Att. — Holw.

JORDAN of PISA (Bl) C. O.P.
A.C. March 6
d. 1131. Bl Jordan received the Dominican habit at Pisa in 1280. After having studied at Paris he returned to Italy and he became a preacher of very great renown at Florence. It was he who began to make use of the Italian vernacular, instead of Latin, in his sermons, and he is reckoned as one of the creators of the Italian language. Cult approved in 1833.
Cf. Prop. O.P. — Att. — Holw.

JORDAN FORZATEI (Bl) Ab. O.S.B.
A.C. Aug. 7
1158-1248. A native of Padua, where he became a monk and then abbot of the Benedictine abbey of St Justina. He was entrusted with the government of the city by Frederick II. The tyrant Count Ezzelino cast him into prison where he remained for three years. He died at Venice. His feast is observed at Padua, Treviso, Praglia, etc.
Cf. Prop. O.S.B. (Italy) — Chev. — Holw.

JORDAN of PULSANO (Bl) Ab. O.S.B.
A.C. Sept. 5
d. 1152. A monk of Pulsano under the founder St John of Pulsano, whom he succeeded as abbot general of the congregation (1139-1152).
Cf. Chev. — Holw.

JOSAPHAT (St) Bp. M. R.M. Nov. 12
1584-1623. A native of Vladimir in Poland, who, at the age of twenty, became a monk of the Byzantine rite and abbot of Vilna. He devoted himself unsparingly to the work of reuniting schismatics with the Holy See. In his thirty-ninth year he was consecrated archbishop of Polotsk in Lithuania, where he continued his labours, refusing to be dragged into politics. He was martyred by a mob of schismatics. He was the first of the Orientals to be formally canonized in Rome (1867).
Cf. Att. — Holw.

JOSAPHAT (St) M. R.M. Nov. 27
See Barlaam and Josaphat.

JOSCIUS (JOSBERT, VALBEBERTUS) (Bl) C. O.S.B. A.C. Nov. 30
d. 1186. A Benedictine monk of Saint-Bertin (Saint-Omer) in the diocese of Arras, renowned for his devotion to the *Ave Maria*. The legend adds, that after his death, a rose tree grew out of his mouth and that the name of Mary was written on the leaves of one of the roses!
Cf. Baud. — Holw. — P.B.

JOSEPH (*several*)
Note. The spelling is the same in most modern languages, excepting the Italian: Giuseppe, and the Spanish: José. In both Italy and Spain the name is frequently joined to that of our Lady, viz. Giuseppe Maria, José Maria. The feminine form takes the following variants: Italian: Giuseppa, Giuseppina; Spanish: Josefa, Josefina, French: Josephine.

JOSEPH MARY TOMMASI (Bl) Card.
A.C. Jan. 1
1649-1713. A son of the duke of Palermo. He joined the Theatines and was stationed in Rome, where he devoted his great natural gifts to the methodical study of the Liturgy and produced several very valuable works on this subject. He was the confessor of Cardinal Albani, who, on being elected pope (Clement XI), was ordered by Bl Joseph to accept the papacy under pain of mortal sin. The pope retaliated by appointing Bl Joseph cardinal. He was wont to teach the catechism to the children in his titular church. Beatified in 1803.
Cf. Att. — Holw. — Menzies.

JOSEPH of FREISING (Bl) Bp. O.S.B.
A.C. Jan. 17
d. 764. A Benedictine of Freising, who in 764 became third bishop of that Bavarian see. In 752 he founded the monastery of St Zeno at Isen. His relics are at Isen.
Cf. Holw.

JOSEPH CAFASSO (Bl) C. A.C. Jan. 23
1811-1860. Born at Castelnuova d' Asti, he was ordained priest in 1833, and three years later was appointed professor of moral theology at the ecclesiastical college at Turin. Ten years later he was appointed superior of the college, and he remained in that position till his death. He led a very penitential life and was renowned for his devotion to the Bl Sacrament and as a confessor. Beatified in 1925.
Cf. A.A.S.

JOSEPH of LEONISSA (St) C. O.F.M. Cap. R.M. Feb. 4
1556-1612. A native of Leonissa, in the States of the Church, who became a Capuchin (1574). He was sent as a missionary to Turkey, chiefly to care for the Christian galley-slaves. During his stay at Constantinople he suffered both imprisonment and torture. He returned to Italy and died after an operation for cancer. Canonized in 1745.
Cf. Att. — Menzies — Holw.

JOSEPH (JOSIPPUS) of ANTIOCH (St) M. R.M. Feb. 15
? A deacon who, with seven others, is stated to have suffered martyrdom at Antioch.
Cf. Holw. — Baud.

JOSEPH TSHANG-TA-PONG (Bl) M.
A.C. March 12
c.1754-1815. A Chinese catechist martyr. Beatified in 1909.
Cf. Holw.

JOSEPH of ARIMATHAEA (St) C.
R.M. March 17
1st cent. "The noble counsellor" (Mark, XV, 43), mentioned in the gospels in connection with our Lord's burial. Later legends concerning him are numerous: in the sacristy of San Lorenzo, Genoa, is the *Sacro Catino*, in which Joseph is said to have caught the blood of Christ at the crucifixion; in England there is the well-known story which connects St Joseph with Glastonbury. None of these legends have any evidence to support them.
Cf. Att. — Holw.

JOSEPH (St) Patriarch R.M. March 19
1st cent. Spouse of our Lady and foster-father of our Lord. All that we know of him is to be found in Matt. I-II and Luke I-II. He is described with the all-embracing phrase "a just man." (Matt. I, 9). From the circumstance of his not being mentioned in the history of the Passion, it is believed that he was then already dead. Devotion to him as a saint, widespread in the East from early ages, has, since the 14th century, grown in the West to such an extent that Pope Pius IX formally constituted him the patron of the universal Church. Besides the feast of his *Transitus* on March 19, he is liturgically honoured as patron of the universal

Church with the feast and octave of the Solemnity of St Joseph the third Wednesday after Easter.
Cf. Holw. — Baud. — Att.

JOSEPH (St) M. R.M. March 20
See Photina, Joseph, etc.

JOSEPH ORIOL (St) C. R.M. March 23
1650-1702. The son of humble parents, citizens of Barcelona, Joseph Oriol succeeded in his ambition to become a priest, took the degree of doctor of theology, and was appointed canon of Santa Maria del Pino in his native city. He lived on bread and water for twenty-six years, carrying on at the same time a very active apostolate, being particularly successful with soldiers and children. Canonized in 1909.
Cf. Holw. — Att. — Baud.

JOSEPH of PERSIA (St) M.
R.M. Apr. 22
See Persian Martyrs.

JOSEPH BENEDICT COTTOLENGO (St) C. A.C. Apr. 30
1786-1842. Born at Bra, near Turin, where after his ordination he became canon of the church of *Corpus Domini*. In 1827 he opened a small house near this church for the sick and derelict which in 1832 was transferred to Valdocco, and called the Little House of Divine Providence. All this he achieved exclusively on voluntary alms. The *Piccola Casa* soon grew into a veritable township, comprising asylums, orphanages, hospitals, schools, workshops, almshouses of all descriptions, and catering for all needs. To meet the large daily expenditure required to keep up all these institutions the saint continued to depend almost entirely on alms: he kept no books of accounts and made no investments and his trust in Divine Providence never once failed him. From his time to this the Piccola Casa has cared for a daily average of from 8,000 to 9,000 inmates. The several branches of the institution are under the direction of different communities, founded by St Joseph Benedict. Throughout his life he was first and foremost a man of prayer. Canonized in 1934.
Cf. Att. — Baud. — Holw.

JOSEPH LUU (Bl) M. A.C. May 2
c.1790-1854. A native catechist, born at

Cai-nhum, Cochin-China, who died in prison at Vinh-long. Beatified in 1909.
Cf. Holw.

JOSEPH the HYMNOGRAPHER (St) Bp. A.C. June 14
d. c.845. Bishop of Salonica, brother of St Theodore Studites. He bravely opposed the Iconoclast emperor, Theophilus. He is one of the great liturgical poets of the Byzantine Church.
Cf. Holw.

JOSEPH HEIU (YUEN) (Bl) M. O.P. A.C. June 27
d. 1840. A native Dominican priest of Annam, who was starved to death in prison. Beatified in 1900.
Cf. Holw.

JOSEPH PETER VYEN (Bl) M. Tert. O.P. A.C. July 3
1773-1838. A native catechist, born in E. Tonkin, who died in prison. Beatified in 1910.
Cf. Holw.

JOSEPH BARSABAS (St) Disciple. R.M. July 20
1st cent. Surnamed "the Just," (Acts, I, 23). He was the competitor of St Matthias for the twelfth place among the apostles left vacant by Judas Iscariot.
Cf. Holw. — Baud. — Att.

JOSEPH of PALESTINE (St) C. R.M. July 22
d. c.356. A Jew belonging to the Biblical school of Tiberias. After prolonged interior resistance he became a Christian and was much favoured by the emperor Constantine, who bestowed on him the title of *Comes* (count). He devoted himself to building churches and spreading the Gospel in the Holy Land. He was the host of St Eusebius of Vercelli, St Epiphanius and others.
Cf. Holw. — Att.

JOSEPH FERNANDEZ (Bl) M. A.C. July 24
1774-1838. A Spaniard and a professed friar of the Dominican order. He was sent to Tonkin in 1805, and having been ordained priest, was appointed provincial vicar in Tonkin, where later he was beheaded. Beatified in 1900.
Cf. Holw.

JOSEPH TSHANG (Bl) M. A.C. July 29
c.1832-1861. A young native seminarian, born in the province of Su-tchuen China. He was beheaded at Tsin-gai with three companions. Beatified in 1909.
Cf. Holw.

JOSEPH NIEN (VIEN) (Bl) M. A.C. Aug. 21
d. 1838. A priest in Tonkin, beheaded at Tien-Chu. Beatified in 1900.
Cf. Holw.

JOSEPH CALASANCTIUS (St) Founder. R.M. Aug. 27
1556-1648. Joseph Calasanz was born at Peralta, near Barbastro, in Aragon and educated in Lérida, Valencia and Alcalá. Ordained priest in 1583, he was engaged in pastoral work until in a vision he learned that he was to go to Rome. He did so in 1592 and at once joined the Confraternity of Christian Doctrine for the free schooling of neglected children. He gradually organized it into a religious order, called *Le Scuole Pie* (Religious Schools), whose members were, and are still, known as *Scolopi*, or Piarists (in Spain Escolapios). The new congregation had to pass through a period of violent persecution, mainly from other religious engaged in similar work. In his old age Joseph himself was unjustly accused, brought before the Holy Office and removed from control of the Congregation. Later, however, he was restored. His patience through it all earned him the title of a "second Job." Canonized in 1767.
Cf. Holw. — Baud. — Att.

JOSEPH CANH (Bl) M. Tert. O.P. A.C. Sept. 5
d. 1838. A native physician of Tonkin, and a Dominican tertiary, beheaded in 1838. Beatified in 1900.
Cf. Holw.

JOSEPH of ST HYACINTH (Bl) M. O.P. A.C. Sept. 10
d. 1622. A native of Villareal in the Spanish Mancha. He was provincial vicar of the Dominican missions in Japan and spoke Japanese perfectly. He was burnt alive at Nagasaki. Beatified in 1867
Cf. Holw. — Prop. O.P.

JOSEPH ABIBOS (St) Ab. A.C. Sept. 15
d. c.590. Abbot of Alaverdi in Georgia;

one of the thirteen Syriac disciples of St John Zedadzneli.

Cf. Holw.

JOSEPH of CUPERTINO (St) C. O.F.M. R.M. Sept. 18

1602-1663. Joseph Desa was born at Cupertino, near Brindisi. He tried his vocation in several places, but was summarily dismissed on account of his "poor intelligence." Finally he was received by the Conventual Franciscans of Grotella as a stable-hand and a lay tertiary. On account, however, of the rare spiritual gifts which now began to be manifest in him, he was professed as a friar and duly ordained priest. From this time on his life is an amazing, and perfectly authenticated, succession of preternatural phenomena. The most remarkable of these was his power of levitation: he would fly straight from the church door to the altar over the heads of the worshippers; once he flew to an olive tree and remained kneeling on a branch for half an hour. Happenings like these were almost every day occurrences, witnessed by hundreds of persons. Withal he was a simple, gentle, humble follower of St Francis. His brethren, however, resented so much publicity, and on this account the saint had much to suffer from them. Canonized in 1767.

Cf. Att. — Holw. — Menzies.

JOSEPH THI (Bl) M.   A.C. Oct. 24

d. 1860. A native captain in the army of King Tu-duc of Cochin-China. He was garroted at An-hoa. Beatified in 1909.

Cf. Holw.

JOSEPH NGHI (Bl) M.   A.C. Nov. 8

d. 1840. A native priest of Tonkin, attached to the Society of Foreign missions of Paris. He was beheaded. Beatified in 1900.

Cf. Holw.

JOSEPH PIGNATELLI (Bl) C. S.J. A.C. Nov. 11

1737-1811. A native of Saragossa and a scion of one of the noblest Aragonese families, who at the age of fifteen joined the Jesuits at Tarragona. After his profession he taught at Manresa, Bilbao and Saragossa. After the banishment of the Jesuits from Spain he went to Corsica, and thence to Ferrara, in charge of the young Jesuits. Finally, after the suppression of the Society in 1773, he resided at Bologna for twenty years, contributing to the temporal support of his religious brethren, and strengthening their courage with brotherly advice. At the same time he worked hard for the restoration of his beloved Institute. In 1799 he was allowed to open a quasi-novitiate, and in 1804 he became the first Italian provincial of the restored Order — "the link between the old and the new Society." Pius XI described him as a priest of "manly and vigorous holiness." Beatified in 1933.

Cf. Prop. S.J. — Att.

JOSEPH MKASA (Bl) M.   A.C. Nov. 16

d. 1885. A Negro, prefect of the royal pages of Uganda, baptized in 1881 and beheaded in 1885. Beatified in 1912.

Cf. Holw.

JOSEPH MARCHAND (Bl) M. A.C. Nov. 30

d. 1835. Born at Passavant in the diocese of Besançon, in France. He joined the Missionary Seminary of Paris, and was sent to Annam, where he died while the flesh was being torn from his body with red-hot tongs. Beatified in 1900.

Cf. Holw.

JOSEPH KHANG (Bl) M. Tert. O.P. A.C. Dec. 6

1832-1861. Born at Tra-vi, province of Nam-Dinh, Tonkin, he was a servant of Bl Jerome Hermosilla, whom he tried to deliver from prison. Caught in the attempt, he was punished with one hundred and twenty lashes and after other most cruel tortures, was beheaded. Beatified in 1906.

Cf. Holw.

JOSEPH-MARIA of ST AGNES (Bl) V. O.S.A.   A.C. Jan. 21

Otherwise Bl Ines de Beniganim, q.v.

JOSEPHINE (ANN-JOSEPH) LEROUX (Bl) V.M.   A.C. Oct. 23

1747-1794. Born at Cambrai, she became an Ursuline nun at Valenciennes under the name of Josephine. When the convents were closed by the French Revolution she retired to Mons in Hainault, but returned to Valenciennes in 1793. The following year she was captured and guillotined with ten other Ursulines. Beatified in 1920.

Cf. Holw.

JOSHUA (JOSUE) (St) Patriarch.
R.M. Sept. 1
15th cent. B.C. The leader of the Is-
raelites into the land of Chanaan. All
that we know of him is to be found in the
Pentateuch and in the canonical book
which bears his name. He figures, with
Gideon, in both the Eastern and Western
martyrologies.

JOSSE (JOST, JODER) (St)
R.M. Dec. 13
Otherwise Judocus, q.v.

JOVINIAN (St) M. R.M. May 5
d. c.300. A fellow missioner with St
Peregrinus of Auxerre, whom he served as
reader (*lector*). He is believed to have
survived his bishop, and to have died a
martyr.
Cf. Holw. — Baud.

JOVINUS and BASILEUS (SS) MM.
R.M. March 2
d. c.258. Two martyrs, who suffered in
Rome under Gallienus and Valerian, and
were buried on the Latin Way.
Cf. Holw. — Baud.

JOVINUS (St) M. R.M. March 26
See Peter, Marcian, etc.

JOVITA (St) M. R.M. Feb. 15
See Faustinus and Jovita.

JUCUNDA (St) M. R.M. July 27
See Felix, Julia and Jucunda.

JUCUNDA (St) V. R.M. Nov. 25
d. 466. A virgin of Reggio in Aemilia,
Italy, a spiritual daughter of St Prosper,
bishop of that city.
Cf. Holw. — Baud.

JUCUNDIAN (St) M. R.M. July 4
? An African, who was martyred by being
cast into the sea.
Cf. Holw. — Baud.

JUCUNDINUS (St) M. R.M. July 21
See Claudius, Justus, etc.

JUCUNDUS (St) M. R.M. Jan. 9
See Epictetus, Jucundus, etc.

JUCUNDUS of BOLOGNA (St) Bp.
R.M. Nov. 14
d. 485. A bishop of Bologna who flourished in the fifth or sixth century.
Cf. Baud. — Holw. — Menzies.

JUDE THADDAEUS (St) Apostle.
R.M. Oct. 28
1st cent. One of the Twelve, brother of
St James the Less and therefore related by
blood to our Lord. He is the writer of one
of the canonical epistles. The tradition is
that he preached in Mesopotamia, and
afterwards, together with St Simon, in
Persia, where he was martyred.
Cf. Holw. — Baud. — Att.

JUDGOENOC (JUDGANOC, JOUVEN)
(St) R.M. Dec. 13
Otherwise Judocus, q.v.

JUDICAËL (St) King. A.C. Dec. 17
d. 658. King of Brittany, much beloved
by his people. After a victorious reign
he abdicated and spent the last twenty
years of his life in the monastery of Gaël,
near Vannes.
Cf. Mab. — Holw. — Att. — Baud.

JUDOCUS (JUDGANOC, JOSSE, etc.)
(St) H. R.M. Dec. 13
d. 668. A priest, brother of King Judicaël of Brittany, and on the abdication
of the latter for some months occupant of
the throne. After a pilgrimage to Rome,
he left Brittany and retired to Villiers-
Saint-Josse, near Saint-Josse-sur-Mer,
where he ended his life as a solitary.
Cf. Holw. — Att. — Baud. — Zimm.

JULIA of CERTALDO (Bl) V. O.S.A.
A.C. Feb. 15
d. 1367. Julia began life as a domestic
servant, but in her nineteenth year she
joined the third order of St Augustine at
Florence. Returning to her native city
of Certaldo, she lived as an anchoress beside the church of SS Michael and James.
She died aged forty-eight, on Jan. 9. Cult
confirmed in 1819.
Cf. Att. — Holw.

JULIA BILLIART (Bl) V. Foundress.
A.C. Apr. 8
1751-1816. Marie Rose Julia Billiart was
born at Cuvilly in Picardy, the daughter of
a peasant farmer. At the age of fourteen
she took a vow of chastity, and gave herself up to the service and instruction of the
poor. Soon her health completely broke
down, and she remained a helpless cripple
until miraculously cured in 1804. During the French Revolution (1794-1804)
pious friends gathered round her couch
seeking to give a permanent shape to

their works of charity. These activities finally developed into the Institute of Notre Dame, for the Christian education of girls, which was definitely established at Amiens in 1804. In the teeth of much opposition the Institute grew apace, spreading to Ghent, Namur and Tournai. The conduct of a young priest confessor of the sisters at Amiens, caused much misunderstanding; and Mother Julia, though fully vindicated, thought it wiser to move the mother house to Namur (1809). Thence it spread over the whole world. Beatified in 1906.
Cf. Att. — Baud. — Holw.

JULIA of SARAGOSSA (St) M.
R.M. Apr. 16
See Saragossa (Martyrs of)

JULIA (St) V.M. R.M. May 22
5th cent. A noble maiden of Carthage sold into slavery by the Vandal conquerors. The ship on which she was being taken to Gaul touched at Corsica. A heathen festival was just being observed by the islanders, and when Julia refused to join in it, she was forthwith nailed to a cross.
Cf. Menzies — Att. — Holw.

JULIA (St) M. R.M. July 15
See Catulinus, Januarius, etc.

JULIA LOUISE of JESUS (Bl) M. O.C.
A.C. July 17
Otherwise Rose Chrétien, q.v.

JULIA of TROYES (St) V.M.
R.M. July 21
d. p. 272. A maiden of Troyes, France, seized by the soldiers of the emperor Aurelian after his victory over the usurper Tetricus. Committed to the charge of Claudius, an officer of the army, she succeeded in converting him to Christ, and both were beheaded at Troyes under the same Aurelian.
Cf. Baud. — Holw.

JULIA of NICOMEDIA (St) M.
R.M. July 27
See Felix, Julia and Jucunda.

JULIA of LISBON (St) M. R.M. Oct. 1
See Verissimus, Maxima and Julia.

JULIA (St) V.M. R.M. Oct. 7
d. c.300. A martyr, either in Egypt or in Syria, under Diocletian.
Cf. Holw. — Baud.

JULIA of MÉRIDA (St) V.M.
R.M. Dec. 10
d. c.303. A fellow-sufferer with St Eulalia at Mérida in Spain, under Diocletian.
Cf. Holw. — Baud.

JULIA (Bl) V. O.S.B. Cam.
A.C. Dec. 15
? A Camaldolese nun in St Benedict's convent, at Arezzo, Italy.
Cf. Zimm.

JULIAN of CAGLIARI (St) M.
R.M. Jan. 7
? A martyr honoured at Cagliari in Sardinia, whose relics were discovered and enshrined in 1615. Locally he is often styled *Comes* (Count), but nothing is now known of his history.
Cf. Holw. — Baud.

JULIAN (St) M. R.M. Jan. 8
See Lucian, Maximian and Julian.

JULIAN, BASILISSA, ANTONY, ANASTASIUS, CELSUS, MARCIONILLA and Comp. (SS) MM. R.M. Jan. 9
d. c.304. Julian and Basilissa, a married couple, turned their house into a hospital: for this reason they are often confused with St Julian the hospitaller (Feb. 12). Antony was a priest; Anastasius a new convert; Marcionilla a married woman and Celsus her little son. All except Basilissa, were put to death at Antioch — which Antioch it is not known — under Diocletian. The very existence, however, of Julian and Basilissa is questioned.
Cf. Att. — Baud. — Holw.

JULIAN SABAS the ELDER (St) C.
R.M. Jan. 17 and Oct. 18
d. 377. A Mesopotamian solitary who did much to encourage the Christians when persecuted by Julian the Apostate, and the Catholics in their conflict with the Arians. St John Chrysostom and Theodoret have left us an account of his life.
Cf. Baud. — Holw.

JULIAN (St) M. R.M. Jan. 27
See Datius, Julian, etc.

JULIAN of SORA (St) M. R.M. Jan. 27
d. c.150. A Dalmatian, arrested, put to the torture and beheaded at Sora in Campania, under Antoninus Pius (138-161).
Cf. Baud. — Holw.

JULIAN of LE MANS (St) Bp.
R.M. Jan. 27
? 3rd cent. Honoured as the first bishop
of Le Mans in France. Various English
churches and places dating from Norman
and Plantagenet times have this Julian
for their titular.
Cf. Att. — Duch. Fast. Episc. — Baud.

JULIAN of CUENCA (St) Bp.
R.M. Jan. 28
1127-1208. A native of Burgos in Spain
who, on the recapture of Cuenca in New
Castile from the Moors by King Alphonsus
IX, was appointed bishop of that city.
In his longing to help the poor he is said to
have spent all his spare time in earning
money for them by the work of his hands.
He is the principal patron saint of the dio-
cese of Cuenca.
Cf. P. de U. — Baud. — Holw.

JULIAN (St) M. R.M. Feb. 12
See Modestus and Julian.

JULIAN the HOSPITALLER (St) C.
A.C. Feb. 12
? Also surnamed "the Poor." The legend,
very popular in the Middle Ages, runs as
follows: Julian in error slew his own parents; in penance he and his wife went to
Rome to obtain absolution and, on their
return home, built a hospice by the side of
a river, where they tended the poor and
the sick and rowed travellers across the
river. Julian is for this reason venerated
as patron saint of boatmen, innkeepers and
travellers. Probably the whole story is
fictitious. This St Julian is often confused with other saints of the name, especially with the saint venerated on Jan. 9
(q.v).
Cf. Holw. — Att. — Baud.

JULIAN of LYONS (St) M.
R.M. Feb. 13
? A martyr registered in the R.M. as hav-
ing suffered at Lyons in France, though
many maintain that he was martyred at
Nicomedia.
Cf. Holw. — Baud.

JULIAN of EGYPT and Comp.
R.M. Feb. 16
? It is said that this saint Julian was the
leader of 5,000 martyrs who suffered in
Egypt. Nothing, however, is known of
him and his fellow-sufferers.
Cf. Holw. — Baud.

JULIAN of CAESAREA (St) M.
R.M. Feb. 17
d. 308. According to Eusebius, this St
Julian was a native of Cappadocia who
happened to be present at Caesarea in
Palestine at the martyrdom of St Pamphilus and ten companions. He instantly
offered himself to the executioners to make
up the number of twelve and was roasted
to death at a slow fire.
Cf. Holw. — Baud.

JULIAN (St) M. R.M. Feb. 19
See Publius, Julian, etc.

JULIAN (St) M. R.M. Feb. 24
See Montanus, Lucius, etc.

**JULIAN, CRONION (surnamed EUNUS)
and BESAS (SS) MM.**
R.M. Feb. 27 and Oct. 30
d. 250. Martyrs at Alexandria in Egypt
under Decius. Julian, too infirm to walk,
was carried to the court by his two slaves,
both Christians. One apostatised through
fear, the other, Eunus, bravely shared his
master's lot. They were carried on cam-
els through Alexandria, scourged, and finally, burnt to death. Besas, a sympathetic
soldier, was killed by the mob for having
sought to shield them. We have these
particulars from St Dionysius of Alexandria, a contemporary and their own
bishop.
Cf. Att. — Holw. — Ruinart.

JULIAN of TOLEDO (St) Bp.
R.M. March 8
d. 690. Monk of Agali under St Eugene,
whom he succeeded first as abbot in the
same monastery and then (680) as archbishop of Toledo. He was the first bishop
to exercise the primacy over the whole
Iberian Peninsula. Besides presiding over
several national councils and revising and
developing the Mozarabic liturgy, he was
a voluminous writer. He was an outstanding churchman in the Spain of his
day.
Cf. P. de U. — Att. — Holw. — Baud.

JULIAN of ANAZARBUS (St) M.
R.M. March 16
d. c.302. A Christian of senatorial rank
of Anazarbus in Cilicia who suffered under
Diocletian. After being tortured he was
taken to the coast, sewn up in a sack half-
filled with scorpions and vipers and cast
into the sea. His body was recovered and

enshrined at Antioch, where St John
Chrysostom delivered a sermon in his
praise.
Cf. Att. — Baud. — Holw.

JULIAN (St) M.   R.M. March 23
? The R.M. styles him a confessor but it
appears certain that he was also a martyr.
Nothing more is known about him.
Cf. Baud. — Holw.

JULIAN of ST AUGUSTINE (Bl) C.
O.F.M.   A.C. Apr. 8
d. 1606. Born at Medinaceli in the diocese of Segovia, in Castile. After being
twice rejected he was finally admitted to
the Dominican Order as a lay-brother at
Santorcaz. He accompanied the Franciscan preachers on their missions and it
was his custom to ring the bell through
the streets to summon people to the sermon. Beatified in 1825.
Cf. P. de U. — Att. — Holw.

JULIAN CESARELLO de VALLE (Bl) C.
O.F.M.   A.C. May 11
? Born and died at Valle in Istria where
his tomb is venerated. Cult approved in
1910.
Cf. Prop. O.F.M. — Holw.

JULIAN (St) M.   R.M. May 23
See Quinctian, Lucius and Julian.

JULIAN of PERUGIA (St) M.
**   R.M. June 5**
See Florentius, Julian, etc.

JULIAN (St) C.   R.M. June 9
d. c.370. A captive from the West who
was sold into slavery in Syria. On regaining his freedom he entered a monastery in Mesopotamia under St Ephrem.
Cf. Holw. — Baud.

JULIAN (St) M.   R.M. July 18
One of the alleged sons of St Symphorosa,
q.v.

JULIAN (St) M.   R.M. July 20
See Sabinus, Julian, etc.

JULIAN (St) M.   R.M. Aug. 7
See Peter, Julian, etc.

JULIAN, MARCIAN and Comp. (SS)
MM.   R.M. Aug. 9
d. 730. Ten Catholics of Constantinople
(among them a patrician lady, named

Mary) who opposed by force the attempts
of the Iconoclasts to deface the picture of
our Lord set up over the Brazen Gate of
the city. They were put to death by
order of Leo the Isaurian.
Cf. Holw. — Baud.

JULIAN (St) M.   R.M. Aug. 12
See Macarius and Julian.

JULIAN (St) M.   R.M. Aug. 25
? Baronius describes him as a Syrian
priest, but nothing certain is known about
him.

JULIAN of AUVERGNE (St) M.
**   R.M. Aug. 28**
d. 304. A native of Vienne in France, an
officer in the imperial army, and secretly
a Christian. On returning from military
service, he withdrew into Auvergne, where
he was eventually martyred near Brioude.
Cf. Att. — Baud. — Holw.

JULIAN (St) M.   R.M. Sept. 2
See Diomedes, Julian, etc.

JULIAN (RENATUS) MASSEY (Bl) M.
O.S.B.   A.C. Sept. 2
d. 1792. Julian (his baptismal name was
René) Massey was a Benedictine monk of
St Melania of Rennes, of the Congrega-
tion of St Maur. He was martyred at
Paris with the martyrs of September
(Carmes), q.v. Beatified in 1926.
Cf. Zimm.

JULIAN (St) M.   R.M. Sept. 4
See Theodore, Oceanus, etc.

JULIAN (St) M.   R.M. Sept. 13
See Macrobius and Julian.

JULIAN MAJALI (Bl) Ab. O.S.B.
**   A.C. Oct. 4**
d. 1470. A Benedictine of San Martino
delle Scale in Sicily. He was held in high
esteem by popes and kings. Six years before his death he became a recluse.
Cf. Zimm.

JULIAN, EUNUS, MACARIUS and
Comp. (SS) MM.   R.M. Oct. 30
d. c.250. Martyrs of Alexandria in Egypt.
St Julian and St Eunus are identical with
the martyrs of that name commemorated
on Feb. 27; St Macarius is again mentioned on Dec. 8. The duplication has
been caused by the inserting in the R.M.

of another group of sixteen martyrs, which includes the above-mentioned. This larger group is commemorated in the Greek calender on this day.
Cf. Holw. — Baud.

JULIAN (St) M. R.M. Nov. 1
See Caesarius and Julian.

JULIAN of APAMAEA (St) Bp.
R.M. Dec. 9
3rd cent. Bishop of Apamaea in Syria. He distinguished himself in the controversies with the Montanist and Kata-Phrygian heretics.
Cf. Holw. — Baud.

JULIANA of BOLOGNA (St) W.
R.M. Feb. 7
d. 435. A matron of Bologna in Italy whose piety and charity are extolled by St Ambrose of Milan. Her husband, having with her consent left her to become a priest, she devoted herself to bringing up her four children and to the service of the church and the poor.
Cf. Holw. — Baud.

JULIANA (St) V.M. R.M. Feb. 16
d. 305. The R.M. describes this virgin martyr as having suffered at Nicomedia in Asia Minor, but it is more probable that she was martyred in the neighbourhood at Naples, perhaps at Cumae, where her relics are supposed to be enshrined.
Cf. Att. — Baud. — Holw.

JULIANA (St) V.M. R.M. March 20
See Alexandra, Claudia, etc.

JULIANA of CORNILLON (Bl) V. O.S.A.
A.C. Apr. 6
1192-1258. Born at Retinnes near Liége and educated by the Augustinians at Mt Cornillon, where she herself became an Augustinian and eventually prioress. As such she promoted the institution of the feast of Corpus Christi. On this account she was reviled as a visionary and driven from Cornillon. Recalled by the bishop of Liége, she was expelled definitely from her convent in 1248. She took refuge at the Cistercian nunnery of Salzinnes, and when this place was burnt down, she retired to Fosses, where she lived as a recluse. She was interred at her own wish at the Cistercian abbey of Villers as one of their own. Her great achievement was the institution of the feast of Corpus

Christi, which, having received papal sanction, was by 1312 already obligatory throughout the Western Church. Cult confirmed in 1869.
Cf. Mart. Cist. — Att. — Baud.

JULIANA of NORWICH (Bl) H. O.S.B.
May 13
d. c.1423. Dame Juliana of Norwich is one of the most celebrated of English mystics. She was a recluse at Norwich and was under the spiritual direction of the Benedictines of that city. "The book in which she narrates her visions *Revelations of Divine Love,* is the tenderest and most beautiful exposition in the English language of God's loving dealings with men." (Attwater, h.l.) She has never been beatified.
Cf. Att. — Baud.

JULIANA FALCONIERI (St) V. O.S.M
R.M. June 19
1270-1340. A lady of Florence who, at the age of sixteen embraced the Rule of the Servite Friars, of whom her uncle St Alexis Falconieri, was a co-founder. In 1304 the community of Servite Tertiaries, known as the "Mantellate" of which she was the first superior was formally established and admitted into the Order by St Philip Benizi. She received Holy Viaticum miraculously on her death-bed. Canonized in 1737.
Cf. Att. — Baud. — Holw. — Menzies.

JULIANA (St) M. R.M. Aug. 12
See Hilaria, Digna, etc.

JULIANA PURICELLI (Bl) V. O.S.A.
A.C. Aug. 14
1427-1501. A native of Busto-Arizio in upper Italy, who, as an Augustinian nun, was the first companion of Bl Catherine da Pallanza at the Sacro Monte sopra Varese, where she died. Cult approved in 1769.
Cf. Baud. — Holw.

JULIANA (St) V. M. R.M. Aug. 17
See Paul and Juliana.

JULIANA (St) M. R.M. Aug. 18
See Leo and Juliana.

JULIANA of COLLALTO (Bl) V. O.S.B.
A.C. Sept. 1
d. 1262. Born near Treviso of the noble Collalto family. At the age of ten she be-

came a Benedictine at Salarola, whence, in 1222, she migrated with Bl Beatrix of Este, to Gemmola. In 1226 she became the abbess-foundress of SS Biagio and Cataldo at Venice. Cult approved by Gregory XVI.
Cf. Chev. — Holw. — Bolland. — (Bib. Hag. Lat. 1899, p. 971.)

JULIANA of PAVILLY (St) Abs. O.S.B.
A.C. Oct. 11
d. c.750. A servant girl, who became a nun at Pavilly in Normandy under St Benedicta, and finally abbess of the same nunnery. She is called "the Little Sister of Jesus."
Cf. Chev. — Holw. — Baud.

JULIANA (St) M. **R.M. Nov. 1**
See Cyrenia and Juliana.

JULIE BILLIART (Bl) V. **A.C. Apr. 8**
French form for Julia Billiart, q.v.

JULIETTE VEROLOT (Bl) M. O.C.
A.C. July 17
d. 1794. Called in religion Sister St Francis Xavier. She was born in the diocese of Troyes and became a Carmelite nun at Compiègne, the last Carmelite to be professed there (Jan. 12, 1789) before the outbreak of the French Revolution. She was guillotined with her community at Compiègne. Beatified in 1906.
Cf. Baud. — Holw.

JULIOT (St) M. **R.M. June 16**
See Quiricus and Julitta. (The Cornish form of the name).

JULITTA (St) V.M. **R.M. May 18**
See Theodotus, Thecusa, etc.

JULITTA (St) M. **R.M. June 16**
See Quiricus and Julitta.

JULITTA (St) M. **R.M. July 30**
d. 303. A rich lady of Caesarea in Cappadocia, who, after losing her property, was condemned to be burnt at the stake.
Cf. Att. — Baud. — Holw.

JULIUS (St) M. **R.M. Jan. 19**
See Paul, Gerontius, etc.

JULIUS of NOVARA (St) C. **R.M. Jan. 31**
d.p. 390. Julius was a priest and his brother Julian a deacon. They were authorized by the emperor Thedosius, to devote themselves to converting the heathen temples into Christian churches, one of which was on an island in the Lago Maggiore. St Julius died at Novara in Piedmont.
Cf. Holw. — Baud.

JULIUS I (St) Pope. **R.M. Apr. 12**
d. 352. A Roman; he ruled the church from 337 to 352. He received the appeal of St Athanasius, whom he defended against his Arian accusers. The letter he wrote to the East on this occasion is one of the most momentous pronouncements of the Roman see. He built several churches in Rome, and ranks as one of the most distinguished occupants of the Holy See.
Cf. Att. — Baud.

JULIUS of DOROSTORUM (St) M.
R.M. May 27
d. c.302. A veteran soldier of the Roman army put to death at Dorostorum on the Danube (now Silistra in Rumania) under Diocletian. Other soldiers of his legion were martyred about the same time.
Cf. Att. — Holw. — Baud.

JULIUS and AARON with others (SS) MM. **R.M. July 1**
d. c.305. According to tradition these martyrs met their death at Caerleon-upon-Usk under Diocletian.
Cf. Att. — Baud. — Holw.

JULIUS (St) M. **R.M. Aug. 19**
d. c.190. A Roman senator, one of the few martyrs during the respite from persecution under the emperor Commodus (180-193). He was scourged to death.
Cf. Holw. — Baud.

JULIUS (St) M. **R.M. Dec. 3**
See Ambicus, Victor and Julius.

JULIUS, POTAMIA, CRISPIN, FELIX, GRATUS and Comp. (SS) MM.
R.M. Dec. 5
d. 302. Twelve African martyrs, who suffered at Thagura in Numidia under Diocletian.
Cf. Holw. — Baud.

JULIUS (St) M. **R.M. Dec. 20**
? A martyr registered in the martyrologies as having suffered at Gelduba (Gildoba) in Thrace.
Cf. Holw. — Baud.

JUNIAN (St) Ab. A.C. Aug. 13
d. 587. Founder and first abbot of Mairé
(*Mariacum*) in Poitou, France, and then a
recluse at Chaulnay.
Cf. Holw. — Baud.

JUNIAN (St) H. A.C. Oct. 16
5th cent. A hermit at Commodoliacus —
now Saint-Junien (Haute Vienne), in the
diocese of Limoges, France.
Cf. Baud. — Holw.

JUNIAS A.C. May 17
See Adronicus and Junias.

JURMIN (St) C. A.C. Feb. 23
7th cent. An E. Anglian prince, son, or
more probably, nephew of King Anna.
His relics were eventually enshrined at
Bury St Edmunds.
Cf. Holw.

JUST (St)
The titular saint of a parish in Cornwall.
He may be identical with Justus (or
Justin), a boy-martyr commemorated on
Oct. 18, or with the Justus commemorated
on Aug. 12.
Cf. Holw.

**JUSTA, JUSTINA and HENEDINA (SS)
MM.** R.M. May 14
d. c.130. Saints, said to have been venerated in Sardinia, where they were martyred under Hadrian (117-138), either at
Cagliari or at Sassari.
Cf. Holw. — Baud.

JUSTA (St) M. R.M. July 15
See Catulinus, Januarius, etc.

JUSTA and RUFINA (SS) VV. MM.
R.M. July 19
d. 287. Two sisters of Seville, in Spain,
potters by trade, who suffered under Diocletian. They are greatly honoured in
the Mozarabic liturgy and are now venerated as principal patron saints of Seville.
It is to be noted that in the early MSS.
Justa is given as Justus.
Cf. Att. — Holw. — Baud.

JUSTIN of CHIETI (St) C. R.M. Jan. 1
d. c.? 540. This saint has been from time
immemorial venerated at Chieti. Some
writers describe him as a bishop of that
city.
Cf. Holw. — Baud.

**JUSTIN the PHILOSOPHER or JUSTIN
MARTYR (St) M.** R.M. Apr. 13 and 14
c.100-c.165. Born at Nablus in Palestine
of pagan parents. He was converted to
Christ when about thirty years of age by
reading the Scriptures and witnessing
the heroism of the martyrs. His two
Apologies for the Christian Religion and
his *Dialogue with the Jew Tryphon* are
among the most instructive second-cen-
tury writings which we possess. He was
beheaded in Rome with other Christians.
Cf. Att. — Holw. — Baud.

JUSTIN (St) M. R.M. July 18
One of the alleged sons of St Symphorosa,
q.v.

JUSTIN (St) M. R.M. Aug. 1
d. c.290. A child said to have been martyred at Louvre, near Paris. He may be
identical with Justus, the boy-martyr of
Beauvais, commemorated on Oct. 18. At
any rate his story appears to have been
taken from the same source.
Cf. Holw. — Baud.

JUSTIN (St) M. R.M. Sept. 17
d. 259. A priest who devoted himself to
burying the bodies of martyrs, and was
eventually martyred himself. His relics
were transferred to Frisingen in Germany.
Cf. Holw. — Baud.

JUSTIN (St) M. R.M. Dec. 12
See Maxentius, Constantius, etc.

JUSTINA BEZZOLI (Bl) N. O.S.B.
A.C. March 12
d. 1319. Francuccia (in religion Justina)
Bezzoli, was born at Arezzo, and at the
age of thirteen entered the Benedictine
convent of St Mark in her native city,
whence she migrated to that of All Saints,
also Benedictine, at Arezzo. Later she
lived as a recluse at Civitella, and finally
returned to community life at All Saints.
Cult confirmed in 1890.
Cf. Att. — Zimm. — Holw.

JUSTINA (St) M. R.M. May 14
See Justa, Justina and Henedina.

JUSTINA (St) M. R.M. June 16
See Aureus, Justina, etc.

JUSTINA (St) V. M. R.M. Sept. 26
See Cyprian and Justina.

JUSTINA (St) V. M. R.M. Oct. 7
d. c.300. A virgin-martyr of Padua under Diocletian. A medieval forgery associates her with St Prosdocimus "a disciple of blessed Peter." Her cult spread throughout Italy on account of the Benedictine abbey dedicated in her name at Padua, which became the cradle of the Cassinese Congregation of St Justina.
Cf. Att. — Baud. — Holw.

JUSTINA (St) V. M. R.M. Nov. 30
? A maiden martyred at Constantinople.

JUSTINIAN (STINAN) (St) M.
P.C. Dec. 5
6th cent. A hermit, a native of Brittany, who became a recluse off the coast of S. Wales, where he was murdered by evildoers and was thenceforward venerated as a martyr.
Cf. Holw. — Baring-Gould.

JUSTUS (St) M. R.M. Feb. 25
See Donatus, Justus, etc.

JUSTUS (St) M. R.M. Feb. 28
See Macarius, Rufinus, etc.

JUSTUS of URGELL (St) Bp.
R.M. May 28
d. p. 527. The first recorded bishop of Urgell in Spanish Catalonia. He is numbered by St Isidore among the "viri illustres," of whom he wrote the lives. St Justus has left us a very interesting commentary on the *Song of Songs.*
Cf. Att. — P. de U. — Holw.

JUSTUS (St) M. R.M. July 2
See Ariston, Crescentian, etc.

JUSTUS of POLAND (St) H. O.S.B.
A.C. July 9
d. 1008. One of the four Polish Brethren — viz. SS Benedict, Andrew, Barnabas and Justus. (See Benedict, July 9).

JUSTUS (St) M. R.M. July 14
? A Roman soldier in the imperial army martyred at Rome (or perhaps at New Rome, i.e. Constantinople).
Cf. Holw. — Baud.

JUSTUS (St) M. R.M. July 21
See Claudius, Justus, etc.

JUSTUS and PASTOR (SS) MM.
R.M. Aug. 6
d. c.304. Two brothers, aged respectively

thirteen and nine years, who were scourged and beheaded at Alcalá under Diocletian. Prudentius numbers them among the most glorious martyrs of Spain.
Cf. P. de U. — Att. — Holw.

JUSTUS (St) A.C. Aug. 12
Otherwise Ust, q.v.

JUSTUS of LYONS (St) Bp.
R.M. Sept. 2 and Oct. 14
d. 390. A deacon of Vienne who was bishop of Lyons in 350. In 381 he attended the council of Aquileia and then instead of returning to his see, repaired to Egypt, where, in spite of remonstrances, he lived as a hermit till his death.
Cf. Holw. — Att. — Baud.

JUSTUS of BEAUVAIS (St) M.
R.M. Oct. 18
d 287. A child-martyr, aged nine, who is alleged to have suffered at Beauvais. He is probably identical with some other saint of this name, and certainly his Acts, as we now possess them, are pure fiction.
Cf. Att. — Baud. — Holw.

JUSTUS of TRIESTE (St) M.
R.M. Nov. 2
d. 303. A citizen of Trieste martyred under Diocletian by being cast into the sea. He is still much honoured at Trieste.
Cf. Baud. — Holw.

JUSTUS of CANTERBURY (St) Bp.
O.S.B. R.M. Nov. 10
d. 627. A Roman Benedictine, one of those sent by St Gregory the Great in 601 to reinforce the mission to the Anglo-Saxons. In 604 St Augustine of Canterbury consecrated him bishop of Rochester, and in 624 he succeeded St Mellitus at Canterbury itself. Pope Boniface V, in sending Justus the *Pallium,* writes to him in words of high appreciation.
Cf. Att. — Zimm. — Mab. — Chev.

JUSTUS and ABUNDIUS (SS) MM.
R.M. Dec. 14
d. 283. Spanish martyrs who suffered under Numerian. After a futile attempt to burn them at the stake, they were beheaded. The Mozarabic liturgy has a solemn office in their honour.
Cf. P. de U. — Holw. — Baud.

JUTHWARE (St) V. A.C. July 1
7th cent. Sister of St Sidwell. They were

probably of British lineage and appear to have lived in Devonshire before the Anglo-Saxons of Wessex penetrated into that county.
Cf. Holw.

JUTTA (Bl) W.   **A.C. Jan. 13**
Otherwise Bl Ivetta, q.v.

JUTTA (St) W.   **A.C. May 5**
d. 1250. A Thuringian of noble family whose husband lost his life crusading in the Holy Land, and who, after providing for her children, became a recluse near Kulmsee in Prussia. She is venerated as patroness of Prussia.
Cf. Att. — Holw.

JUTTA (JULITTA) (Bl) Abs. O.S.B. Cist.
    A.C. Nov. 29
d. c.1250. Foundress and first abbess (1234-c.1250) of the Cistercian nunnery of Heiligenthal.
Cf. Zimm.

JUTTA (JUDITH) (Bl) Abs. O.S.B.
    A.C. Dec. 22
d. 1136. Sister of the count Palatine of Spanheim, she became a recluse in a cell near the monastery-church of Dissienberg (Disibodi Mons). Here she was entrusted with the education of St Hildegarde. Other disciples gathered round her and she formed them into a Benedictine community, which she ruled for twenty years.
Cf. Zimm. — Att. — Chev. — Baud.

JUVENAL of NARNI (St) Bp.
    R.M. May 3
d. 369. First bishop of Narni, in central Italy, ordained, it is said by Pope St Damasus. His biographers have confused him with other saints of the same name, with the result that we have no certainty as to the details of his career.
Cf. Holw. — Baud.

JUVENAL of BENEVENTO (St) Bp.
    R.M. May 7
d. c.132. A saint of Narni. His reputed shrine is at Benevento.
Cf. Holw. — Baud.

JUVENAL ANCINA (Bl) Bp.
    A.C. Sept. 12
1545-1604. Born at Fossano in Piedmont, he became professor of medicine at the university of Turin and as such he accompanied the ambassador of Savoy to Rome as his private physician (1575). At Rome he came under the influence of St Philip Neri and joined the Oratory in 1575. He was duly ordained and sent to Naples to open a new oratory there. He was noted especially for his work for the poor. Finally in 1602 he was made bishop of Saluzzo and at once set out on his first episcopal visitation. On his return he was poisoned by a friar whose evil life he had rebuked. Beatified in 1869.
Cf. Att. — Baud. — Holw.

JUVENTINUS and MAXIMUS (SS) MM.
    R.M. Jan. 25
d. 363. Officers in the army of Julian the Apostate. For criticizing the laws against Christians and refusing to sacrifice to idols, they were degraded, imprisoned, scourged and finally beheaded at Antioch in Syria.
Cf. Att. — Holw. — Baud.

JUVENTIUS of PAVIA (St) Bp.
    R.M. Feb. 8 and Sept. 12
1st cent.(?). The tradition is that St Hermagoras, bishop of Aquileia, the disciple of St Mark, despatched SS Syrus and Juventius to evangelize Pavia (*Ticinum*), of which city the latter became the first bishop. The R.M. commemorates him a second time with St Syrus on Sept. 12.
Cf. Menzies — Baud. — Holw.

JUVENTIUS (St) M.   **R.M. June 1**
? A Roman martyr, whose relics were translated in the 16th century to the Benedictine abbey of Chaise-Dieu, Evreux, France.
Cf. Holw. — Baud.

K

Note. For Katherine and similar names sometimes written with an initial K, see also C and CH.

KANTEN (CANNEN) (St) C. A.C. Nov. 5
8th cent. A Welsh saint. Founder of Llanganten Abbey (Brecknock).

KARANTOC (St)   **Jan. 16**
Probably identical with St Carantog of May 16, q.v.

KEA (KAY, KENAN) (St) Bp. A.C. Nov. 5
6th cent. A British saint who has left his name to Landkey in Devon. He passed

some of his life in Brittany, where he is venerated as St Quay. The details of his life are very uncertain.
Cf. Baring-Gould.

KEBIUS (St) Bp.   **A.C. Nov. 8**
Otherwise Cuby (Cyby), q.v.

KELLACH (St) Bp.   **A.C. May 1**
Otherwise Ceallach, q.v.

KENAN (CIANAN) (St) Bp. A.C. Nov. 24
d. c.500. An Irish bishop. He was with St Patrick a disciple of St Martin of Tours. He was the first bishop in Ireland to build his cathedral (Damleag or Duleek, in Meath) of stone.
Cf. Holw. — Att.

KENELM (St) King M.   A.C. July 17
d. 821. Said to have been a Mercian prince, who at the age of seven succeeded to the throne of his father, King Kenulph. He was murdered in the forest of Clent by order of his sister Cynefrith. In medieval England he was universally venerated as a saint and martyr.
Cf. Att. — Holw.

KENNERA (St) V. M.   A.C. Oct. 29
5th cent. A recluse at Kirk-Kinner, Galloway, Scotland. She had been educated with St Ursula and also with St Regulus of Patras.
Cf. Holw.

KENNETH (St) H.   A.C. Aug. 1
6th cent. A Welsh hermit, the son of a chieftain. He made his cell among the rocks in the peninsula of Gower.
Cf. Bolland — Baring-Gould.

KENNETH (St) Ab.   R.M. Oct. 11
Otherwise Canice or Canicus, q.v.

KENNOCHA (KYLE, ENOCH) (St) V.
A.C. March 25
d. 1007. A Scottish nun belonging to a convent in Fife. Formerly she was held in great veneration in Scotland, especially in the district round Glasgow.
Cf. Holw.

KENNY (St) Ab.   R.M. Oct. 11
Otherwise Canice, q.v.

KENTIGERN MUNGO (St) Bp.
A.C. Jan. 14
d. 603. The surname *Mungo* means "darling." He began his missionary labours at Cathures, on the Clyde, on the site of the present city of Glasgow, and was consecrated first bishop of the Strathclyde Britons. Driven into exile, he preached around Carlisle and then went to Wales, and he is said to have stayed with St David at Menevia. Tradition credits him with having founded the monastery of Llanelwy (St Asaph), but it is now thought that he was not the founder, but merely the abbot of that monastery for a time. Returning to Scotland, he continued his missionary labours, making Glasgow his centre. He died while taking a bath. He is venerated as the apostle of N.W. England and S.W. Scotland.
Cf. Att. — Holw. — Baud.

KENTIGERNA (St) W.   A.C. Jan. 7
d. 734. The mother of St Foelan. After her husband's death she led the life of a recluse on the island of Inchebroida, in Loch Lomond, where a church is dedicated in her name.
Cf. Holw. — Att.

KERIC (St) Ab.   A.C. Feb. 17
Otherwise Guevrock, q.v.

KERRIER (St)
A.C. March 5.   R.M. Sept. 9
A variant of the name Kieran, Pyran, Queranus, q.v.

KESSOG (MACKESSOG) (St) Bp.
A.C. March 10
d. c.560. Born at Cashel. Even as a child he is said to have worked miracles. He became a missionary and laboured in Scotland, where he was consecrated bishop. It is not certain where he died: according to one tradition he was martyred at Bandry. He is the patron of Lennox.
Cf. Att. — Holw.

KESTER (St) M.   R.M. July 25
Otherwise Christopher, q.v.

KEVERNE (St)   Nov. 18
6th cent. A Cornish saint, friend of St Kieran or Pyran, with whom indeed some identify him.
Cf. Baring-Gould.

KEVIN (COEMGEN, CAOIMHGHIN) (St) Ab.   A.C. June 3
d. c.618. The name has been Latinized as Coemgenus. A native of Leinster, he

was educated by St Petroc of Cornwall who was then in Ireland. He is best remembered as the abbot-founder of Glendalough, one of the most famous names in Irish history. His extant biographies abound in romantic but untrustworthy legends, which, however, may be based on actual facts. He is one of the patron saints of Dublin.
Cf. Holw. — Att. — Baud.

KEVOCA (KENNOTHA, QUIVOCA) (St)
A.C. May 1
7th cent. She is honoured at Kyle in Scotland.
Cf. Holw.

KEWE (KWYA, CIWA) (St) A.C. Feb. 8
Otherwise Kigwe, q.v.

KEYNA (KEYNE, KEAN) (St) V.
A.C. Oct. 8
5th cent. A Welsh saint, an alleged daughter of Brychan of Brecknock. She lived as a recluse in Somersetshire — at Keynsham, so called after her — but she returned to Wales to die. Many churches were dedicated in her honour.
Cf. Att. — Holw.

KIARA (CHIER) (St) V.
A.C. Jan. 5 (Oct. 16)
d. c.680. An Irish maiden, directed in the religious life by St Fintan Munnu. She lived near Nenagh, Co Tipperary, at a place now called after her Kilkeary.
Cf. O'Hanlon.

KIERAN (KIERNAN, KYRAN, CIARAN) (St) Bp. A.C. March 5
5th cent. Styled "the first-born of the saints of Ireland." A native of Ossory, he was probably consecrated bishop by St Patrick. He has certainly been venerated from time immemorial as the first bishop of Ossory and as founder of the monastery of Saighir. He is wrongly identified with St Pyran of Cornwall.
Cf. Holw. — Att.

KIERAN (KYRAN, Latin: QUERANUS) (St) Ab. R.M. Sept. 9
d. c.556. (?). Surnamed "The Younger." He was born in Connacht, and was trained in the monastic life by St Finian of Clonard, where he was one of the "Twelve Apostles of Ireland." At a later date he became the abbot-founder of Clonmacnois in West Meath, on the Shannon, and gave

his monks an extremely austere monastic rule, known as "the Law of Kieran."
Cf. Att. — Baud. — Holw.

KIGWE (KEWE) (St) V. A.C. Feb. 8
? She is probably the same as St Ciwa, a 6th or 7th-century saint venerated in Monmouthshire. The name is also spelt: Ciwg, Cwick, Kigwoe, etc.
Cf. Baring-Gould.

KILDA (St)
An unidentified saint whose name has been given to an Island off the Scottish coast, in which there is a well known as St Kilder's or St Kilda's Well.

KILIAN (CHILIANUS), COLMAN and TOTNAN (SS) MM. R.M. July 8
d. c.689. Irish missionary monks who were commissioned by Pope John V to evangelize Franconia and East Thuringia, where they were martyred after a successful apostolate.
Cf. Holw. — Att.

KILIAN (St) Ab. A.C. July 29
7th cent. An Irish abbot of a monastery in the island of Inishcaltra, and author of a life of St Brigid.
Cf. Holw.

KILIAN (St) C. A.C. Nov. 13
Otherwise Chillien, q.v.

KINGA (St) V. A.C. July 24
13th cent. A niece of St Elizabeth of Hungary and great-niece of St Hedwig. She shared with her husband, King Boleslaus of Poland, the sufferings to which the Tartar invasion subjected that land. She died a Franciscan tertiary in the nunnery she had founded at Sandiez. Her name is also given as Cunegunde, Kioga, Zinga, etc.
Cf. Att. — Baud. — Holw.

KINGSMARK (CYNFARCH) (St) C.
A.C. Sept. 8
5th cent. Said to have been a Scottish chieftain who lived in Wales, where some churches are dedicated to him.
Cf. Holw.

KINNIA (St) V. A.C. Feb. 1
5th cent. An Irish maiden, baptized by St Patrick, and by him also consecrated to God. She is greatly venerated in Co Louth.
Cf. Holw.

KITT (St) M. R.M. July 25
Otherwise Christopher, q.v.

"KLAUS" (St) R.M. Dec. 6
A corrupt form of the name Nicholas
(Niklaus), q.v.

KYBI (St) Bp. A.C. Nov. 8
Otherwise Cuby, q.v.

**KYNEBURGA, KYNESWIDE and TIBBA
(SS) O.S.B.** A.C. March 6
d. c.680. Kyneburga and Kyneswide
were daughters of Penda of Mercia, famous for his fierce opposition to Christianity. The former became the abbess-
foundress of Dormancaster, now Castor,
in Northamptonshire, and was succeeded
by her sister as abbess. Tibba was their
kinswoman, who joined them at the convent. Their relics were enshrined at
Peterborough Abbey.
Cf. Att. — Baud. — Holw.

KYRAN (St) Ab. R.M. Sept. 9
Otherwise Kieran, q.v.

KYRIN (KYRSTIN) (St) Bp.
A.C. March 14 or 16
d. 660. A Scottish saint, bishop of Ross,
also known as Boniface, q.v.

KYNESWIDE (St) V. O.S.B.
A.C. March 6
See SS. Kyneburga, Kyneswide and Tibba.

L

LACTAN (LACTINUS) Ab.
A.C. March 19
d. 672. Born near Cork, in Ireland, he
was educated at Beuchor under SS Comgall and Molna. Eventually St Comgall
sent him to be abbot-founder of Achadh-
Ur, now Freshford in Kilkenny.
Cf. Holw. — Baud.

LADISLAS (LANCELOT) (St) King.
R.M. June 27
1040-1095. Son of Bela, king of Hungary,
to which kingdom, after his accession in
1077, he added Dalmatia and Croatia.
His enlightened government, with regard
both to church and state affairs, makes
him one of the great national heroes of
Hungary. He fought just and successful
wars against the Poles, Russians and
Tartars. He died while preparing to take

part, as commander-in-chief, in the first
crusade. Canonized in 1192. The Hungarians call him Laszlo.
Cf. Holw. — Att. — Baud.

LADISLAS of GIELNIOW (Bl) C. O.F.M.
A.C. Sept. 25
1440-1505 (May 4). A Pole by birth, he
joined the Observant Franciscans at Warsaw and eventually became their minister
provincial. As such he sent Franciscan
missionaries to Lithuania. He himself
was an untiring preacher and travelled
the whole length and breadth of Poland
evangelizing the country. Beatified in
1586.
Cf. Att. — Baud. — Holw.

LAETANTIUS (St) M. R.M. July 17
See Scillitan Martyrs.

LAETUS (St) M. R.M. Sept. 1
See Vincent and Laetus.

LAETUS (St) Bp. M. R.M. Sept. 6
See Donatian, Praesidius, etc.

LAETUS (St) Priest. R.M. Nov. 5
d. 533. Honoured in the diocese of Orleans, his relics being enshrined in the village of St Lié in that diocese. He is said
to have embraced the monastic state at
the age of twelve years.
Cf. Holw.

LAICIN (St) Ab. A.C. Jan. 20
Otherwise Molagga, q.v.

LAMALISSE (St) H. A.C. March 3
7th cent. A Scottish hermit who has left
his name to an islet (Lamlash) off the
coast of the isle of Arran.
Cf. Holw.

LAMBERT of LYONS (St) Bp. O.S.B.
R.M. Apr. 14
d. 688. Born in N. France and reared at
the court of Clotaire III, he became a
monk at Fontenelle under St Wandrille
whom he succeeded as abbot in 666. In
678 he was raised to the see of Lyons.
*Cf. Gams — Duch. Fast. Episc. — Mab. —
Att. — Holw.*

LAMBERT of SARAGOSSA (St) M.
R.M. Apr. 16
d. c.900. A servant, killed near Saragossa in Spain, by his Saracen master

during the Moorish occupation. His cult was promoted by Pope Hadrian VI.
Cf. Holw. — Baud.

LAMBERT PÉLOGUIN (St) Bp. O.S.B.
A.C. May 26
c.1080-1154. He was born in the diocese of Riez, France, and became a Benedictine at Lérins. In 1114 he was made bishop of Vence in Provence, and ruled his diocese for forty years. His relics are still enshrined at Vence.
Cf. Att. — Baud. — Holw. — Gams — Zimm.

LAMBERT (Bl) Ab. O.S.B.
A.C. June 22
d. 1125. From childhood he was trained in the monastic life at the Benedictine abbey of Saint-Bertin, of which he eventually became the fortieth abbot. He finished the abbey church and introduced the Cluniac observances.
Cf. Holw. — Baud.

LAMBERT (Bl) Ab. O.S.B. Cist.
A.C. July 12
d. 1163. He became a Cistercian monk at Morimond and afterwards ruled successively as abbot Clairfontaine, Morimond and Cîteaux (1155-1161). The last two years of his life he spent in retirement at Morimond, where he died.
Cf. Baud. — Holw. — P.B.

LAMBERT (Bl) Ab. O.S.B. Cist.
A.C. Aug. 22
d. 1151. A brother of St Peter of Tarentaise, and, like him, a Cistercian monk at Bonnevaux. In 1140 he was sent to preside as abbot-founder over the new Abbey of Chézery, in the diocese of Belley, France.
Cf. Baud. — Holw. — P.B.

LAMBERT (St) Bp. M. O.S.B.
R.M. Sept. 17
d. 709. Born at Maestricht, he became bishop of that city in 668, but in 674 he was driven from his see by the tyrant Ebroin. He now lived for seven years at the Benedictine abbey of Stavelot as a simple monk. He was recalled to his see by Pepin of Heristal, and did much to foster the apostolate of St Willibrord. He was murdered in the then village of Liége, and has ever since been venerated as a martyr.
Cf. Holw. — Baud. — Att. — Zimm.

LAMBERT and VALERIUS (BELLÈRE, BERLHER) (SS) CC. O.S.B. A.C. Oct. 9
d. c.680. Disciples of St Ghislenus, and his fellow-workers in preaching the Gospel.
Cf. Zimm. — Holw.

LANDELINUS (St) Ab. O.S.B.
R.M. June 15
c.625-c.686. Born near Bapaume, in N. France, Landelinus, though carefully brought up by St Aubert of Cambrai, was for a time led astray and turned robber, but repented and became a monk. Afterwards he was ordained priest and founded the abbeys of Lobbes (*Lanbacum*) in 654, Aulne (656), Walers (657) and Crespin (Crepy, *Crespiacum*) in 670, which he governed till his death.
Cf. Mab. — Zimm. — Att. — Holw.

LANDERICUS (LANDRY) (St) Bp. O.S.B. A.C. Apr. 17
7th cent. The eldest son of SS Vincent-Maldegarus and Wandru. From 641 to 650 he was bishop of Meaux, but on the death of his father, the abbot of Soignies, Landericus resigned his see in order to undertake the government of that abbey.
Cf. Mab. — Zimm. — Att. — Holw.

LANDERICUS (St) Bp. A.C. June 10
d. c.661. Bishop of Paris from 650 to his death. He is best remembered as the founder of the first hospital — *Hôtel-Dieu* — in Paris.
Cf. Duch. Fast. Episc. — Att. — Baud. — Holw.

LANDERICUS (St) M. O.S.B.
A.C. June 10
d. 1050(?). A Benedictine monk of Novalese in Savoy, drowned in the R. Arc by some malefactors whom he had reprimanded.
Cf. Holw. — Zimm.

LANDOALD and AMANTIUS (SS) CC.
R.M. March 19
d. c.668. Said to have been a Roman priest and his deacon, sent by the pope to evangelize what is now Belgium and N.E. France. They founded the church at Wintershoven.
Cf. Holw. — Baud. — Att.

LANDRADA (St) V. O.S.B. A.C. July 8
d. c.690. Foundress and first abbess of

the nunnery of Münsterbilsen, in Belgic Luxemburg.
Cf. Zimm. — Baud. — Holw.

LANDULF VARIGLIA (St) Bp. O.S.B.
A.C. June 7
1070-1134. Born at Asti in Piedmont, he took the Benedictine habit at San Michele in Ciel d'Oro at Pavia and became bishop of Asti in 1103.
Cf. Holw. — Gams — Chev.

LANFRANC of CANTERBURY (Bl) Bp. O.S.B.
P.C. May 28
c.1005-1089. Born of a family of senatorial rank at Pavia, he studied at Bologna, taught civil law at Pavia, and in 1042 became a Benedictine at Bec in Normandy, where he founded the school which was to become famous throughout Christendom. He left Bec to be the first abbot of St Stephen's at Caen and in 1070 was raised to the see of Canterbury. Both as a zealous churchman and as a theological writer he left his mark on the ecclesiastical as well as on the civil history of his time. He has always been given the title of *Beatus*, although he does not seem to have been honoured with a public cult.
Cf. Mab. — P. de U. — Baud.

LANFRANC BECCARIA (Bl) Bp. O.S.B. Vall.
A.C. June 23
d. 1194. He was born near Pavia, and in 1178 was made bishop of that city. During his episcopate he was troubled much by heretics and rapacious civil magistrates. He left the city and joined the monks of S. Sepolcro, but was recalled. At the time of his death he had definitely determined to become a Vallumbrosan.
Cf. Att. — Holw.

LANTFRID, WALTRAM and ELILANTUS (BB or SS) O.S.B.
A.C. July 10
d. p. 770. Three brothers who became founders of Benediktbeuren in Bavaria and succeeded one another as abbots of the monastery. St Lantfrid, the first to be abbot, was still alive in 770.
Cf. Zimm.

LANUINUS (Bl) C. O.Cart.
A.C. Apr. 14
d. 1120. A disciple of St Bruno, who accompanied the saint to Calabria, where he succeeded him as prior of the charterhouse which he founded at Torre in the diocese of Squillace. He was also appointed visitor apostolic of all the monastic houses in Calabria. Cult confirmed in 1893.
Cf. Holw. — Att.

LARGIO (St) M.
R.M. Aug. 12
See Hilaria, Digna, etc.

LARGUS of AQUILEIA (St) M.
R.M. March 16
See Hilary, Tatian, etc.

LARGUS of ROME (St) M. R.M. Aug. 8
See Cyriacus, Largus, etc.

LASAR (LASSAR, LASSERA) (St) V.
A.C. March 29
6th cent. An Irish nun, niece of St Forchera. She was in early life placed under the care of SS Finnian and Kiernan at Clonard. Her name means "Flame."
Cf. Holw.

LASERIAN (St) Bp.
A.C. Apr. 18
d. 639. Otherwise Molaisse, and (probably) Lamliss. He was an Irishman by birth and the founder of the monastery and bishopric of Leighlin. He was appointed by Pope Honorius I apostolic legate to Ireland, where he strenuously upheld the Roman observance. He was prominent at the synod of Whitefield (635).
Cf. Att. — Holw.

LASZLO (St) King.
R.M. June 27
Magyar form of Ladislas, q.v.

LATINUS of BRESCIA (St) Bp.
R.M. March 24
d. 115. Flavius Latinus, disciple and successor of St Viator, third bishop of Brescia, is believed to have been imprisoned and put to the torture with other Christians under Domitian, to have escaped with his life, and to have governed the diocese of Brescia from 84 to 115.
Cf. Menzies — Holw.

LAUDO (St) Bp.
R.M. Sept. 22
Otherwise Lauto, q.v.

LAURA (St) Abs. M.
A.C. Oct. 19
d. 864. A native of Cordova in Spain. In her widowhood she became a nun at Cuteclara. Condemned as a Christian by the Moorish conquerors she was thrown into a cauldron of molten lead.
Cf. P. de U. — Baud.

LAURENCE GIUSTINIANI (St) Bp.
R.M. Jan. 8
1381-1455. A scion of the noble Venetian
family of the Giustiniani, who at the age
of nineteen joined the canons regular of
San Giorgio in Alga, of whom in due time
he became the general. In 1433 he was
forced to accept the see of Castello, and
in 1451 was translated to that of Grado
which carried with it the title of patriarch.
The see itself with its patriarchal title was
transferred at the same time from Grado
to Venice. His writings on mystical contemplation are sublime in their simplicity.
Canonized in 1690.
Cf. Att. — Holw. — Baud.

LAURENCE WANG (Bl) M. A.C. Jan. 28
1811-1858. A Chinese catechist, born at
Kuy-yang and beheaded at Mao-Ken.
Beatified in 1909.
Cf. Holw.

LAURENCE of CANTERBURY (St) Bp.
O.S.B. R.M. Feb. 2
d. 619. One of the Benedictines sent by
Pope St Gregory the Great to convert
England. St Augustine sent him back to
Rome to report to St Gregory on the
progress of the English mission and to
bring back reinforcements for the work.
Succeeding to the archbishopric of Canterbury in 604, he had much to suffer during
the pagan reaction in Kent under Eadbald
and thought of escaping to France, but
was forcibly rebuked by St Peter in a
dream, and in the end succeeded in converting Eadbald. The Irish Stowe Missal
commemorates him by name in the canon
of the Mass.
Cf. Att. — Holw. — Baud. —Zimm.

LAURENCE the ILLUMINATOR (St)
Bp. A.C. Feb. 3
d. 576. A Syrian Catholic, driven by the
Monophysite persecution to Italy, where
he was ordained and founded a monastery
near Spoleto. Chosen bishop of that city,
he held the see for twenty years: he then
resigned and founded the famous abbey of
Farfa in the Sabine hills near Rome. St
Laurence was renowned as a peacemaker,
and his title, it is said, derives from his gift
of healing blindness, both spiritual and
physical.
Cf. Att. — Baud. — Holw.

LAURENCE of SIPONTO (St) Bp.
A.C. Feb. 7
d. c.546. Surnamed Majoranus. Bishop
of Siponto from 492 to his death. He is
said to have built the sanctuary of St
Michael on Mt Gargano.
Cf. Menzies — Holw.

LAURENCE HUNG (Bl) M. A.C. Apr. 27
c.1802-1856. A native priest of Tonkin,
beheaded near Ninh-biuh, in W. Tonkin.
Beatified in 1909.
Cf. Holw.

LAURENCE of NOVARA and Comp.
(SS) MM. R.M. Apr. 30
d. c.397. Said to have come from the
West (Spain or France?) and to have attached himself to St Gaudentius, bishop
of Novara in Piedmont. He was put to
death with a group of children whom he
was instructing.
Cf. Menzies — Holw.

LAURENCE RICHARDSON (vere JOHN-
SON) (Bl) M. A.C. May 30
d. 1582. A native of Great Crosby in
Lancashire, he was educated at Brasenose
College, Oxford, and after his conversion,
studied for the priesthood at Douai. He
was ordained in 1577 and was sent to the
English mission, where he worked in Lan-
cashire. He was martyred at Tyburn.
Beatified in 1886.
Cf. Holw. — Newdigate.

LAURENCE of VILLAMAGNA (Bl) C.
O.F.M. A.C. June 6
1476-1535. Born at Villamagna, in the
Abruzzi, of the noble family dei Mascoli,
he joined the Franciscan order and he became a most powerful and successful
preacher. Cult approved in 1923.
Cf. Holw. — Att.

LAURENCE HUMPHREY (Bl) M.
A.C. July 7
1571-1591. A native of Hampshire and a
convert, he was only twenty years of age
when he was hanged, drawn and quartered
at Winchester for his conversion to the
Catholic faith. Beatified in 1929.
Cf. Newdigate.

LAURENCE of BRINDISI (St) C. O.F.M.
Cap. R.M. July 22
1559-1619. A native of Brindisi who
joined the Capuchins and was sent to
Germany as one of the pioneers of the
Capuchin Order in that country. He
preached throughout Central Europe, and
was appointed chaplain to the forces of the

Archduke Matthias fighting against the Turks. He contributed to the success of the Christian army by his prayers and shrewd military advice. He died at Lisbon during one of his diplomatic missions. Canonized in 1881.
Cf. Att. — Holw. — Baud.

LAURENCE of ROME (St) M.
R.M. Aug. 10

d. 258. According to a very early tradition Laurence was born at Huesca, Aragon, Spain, and with his family migrated to Rome, where he joined the clergy as one of the seven deacons of the city, under Pope St Sixtus II. Three days after the martyrdom of that pope Laurence himself was put to death, the legend says, by being roasted alive on a gridiron. Whatever may be said of the authenticity of his Acts the fact remains that Laurence has always been venerated, both in the West and in the East, as the most celebrated of the numerous Roman martyrs — witness the writings of SS Ambrose, Leo the Great, Augustine and the Spanish poet Prudentius. His martyrdom must have deeply impressed the Roman Christians. His death, says Prudentius, was the death of idolatry in Rome, which from that time began to decline. He was buried on the Via Tiburtina, at the *Campus Veranus*, where his basilica now stands, and his name is mentioned in the canon of the Mass.
Cf. Holw. — Baud. — Att.

LAURENCE NERUCCI, AUGUSTINE CENNINI, BATHOLOMEW SONATI, and JOHN BAPTIST PETRUCCI (BB) MM. O.S.M.
A.C. Aug. 11

d. 1420. Four Servite friars sent from Siena to Bohemia by Pope Martin V to combat the Hussite heresy. With sixty other Servites they were burnt in their own church at Prague while singing the *Te Deum*. Cult approved in 1918.
Cf. Holw.

LAURENCE LORICATUS (Bl) H. O.S.B.
A.C. Aug. 16

d. 1243. Born at Fanello, near Siponto, he was bred to arms and, having accidentally killed a man, undertook a pilgrimage to Compostella. On his return in 1209 he joined the Benedictines at Subiaco and obtained leave to live as a recluse in the ruins of one of the twelve monasteries founded there by St Benedict. His name Lori-

catus was given to him on account of a coat of mail which he wore next his skin. His relics are enshrined at the Sagro Speco, Subiaco. Cult approved in 1778.
Cf. Att. — Holw.

LAURENCE RUKEIMON (Bl) M.
A.C. Aug. 19

d. 1622. A Japanese sailor on the ship of Bl Joachim Firaiama. He was beheaded at Nagasaki. Beatified in 1867.
Cf. Holw.

LAURENCE JAMADA (Bl) M.
A.C. Sept. 8

d. 1628. Son of Bl Michael Jamada, and a Dominican tertiary. He was beheaded at Nagasaki. Beatified in 1867.
Cf. Holw.

LAURENCE IMBERT, Bp. PETER MAUBANT, JAMES CHASTAN, ANDREW KIM and Comp. (BB) MM. A.C. Sept. 22

d. 1839-1846. These martyrs perished in the persecution of the Christians which raged in Corea from 1839 till 1846. Imbert, a native of Aix-en-Provence, was a member of the Paris Society of Missions. He worked first as a missionary priest in China and then as a bishop in Corea. With Maubant and Chastan, missionary priests of the same society, he was exiled and cruelly tortured to death in 1839. Andrew Kim, a native priest, suffered the same fate shortly afterwards, and in the course of the next few years seventy-five other native converts, of both sexes and including many catechumens, suffered martyrdom with heroic constancy. Beatified in 1925.
Cf. Att.

LAURENCE of AFRICA (St) M.
R.M. Sept. 28

See Martial, Laurence, etc.

LAURENCE of RIPPAFRATTA (Bl) C. O.P.
A.C. Sept. 28

d. 1457. Born at Rippafratta in Tuscany, he joined the Friars Preachers at Pisa under Bl John Dominic, and was made novice-master at Cortona. St Antoninus and BB Benedict of Mugello and Fra Angelico were his novices. Cult approved in 1851.
Cf. Holw. — Att. — Baud.

LAURENCE XIZO (Bl) M. A.C. Sept. 28

d. 1630. A native of Japan and a tertiary

of St Augustine. He was condemned to death for having sheltered the Augustinian fathers and was beheaded at Nagasaki. Beatified in 1867.
Cf. Holw.

LAURENCE O'TOOLE (St) Bp. O.S.A.
R.M. Nov. 14
1128-1180. Lorcan O'Tuathail was born in Leinster, and at the age of twelve became an Augustinian canon at Glendalough of which he was made abbot at the age of twenty-five. Eight years later he was promoted to the archbishopric of Dublin. In 1179 he attended the Lateran Council at Rome and was made papal legate in Ireland. He carried out many reforms in his diocese and was much engaged in negotiating on behalf of the Irish with King Henry II of England. It was while on an embassy to the latter that he died at the Augustinian abbey of Eu in Normandy. Canonized in 1226.
Cf. Att. — Baud. — Holw.

LAURENCE PE-MAN (Bl) M.
A.C. Nov. 24
d. 1856. A Japanese labourer martyred as a Christian.
Cf. Holw.

LAURENTIA (St) M. **R.M. Oct. 8**
See Palatias and Laurentia.

LAURENTINUS, IGNATIUS and CELERINA (SS) MM. **R.M. Feb. 3**
3rd cent. African martyrs, of whom St Cyprian writes movingly in one of his epistles. SS Laurentinus and Ignatius were uncles, and St Celerina, an aunt, of the deacon St Celerinus, who is commemorated on the same day.
Cf. Holw. — Baud.

LAURENTINUS SOSSIUS (Bl) M.
A.C. Apr. 15
d. 485. A boy aged five, said to have been killed by the Jews on Good Friday at Valrovina in the diocese of Vicenza, in Italy. Cult approved in 1867.
Cf. Holw.

LAURENTINUS (St) M. **R.M. June 3**
See Pergentinus and Laurentinus.

LAURIANUS (St) M. **R.M. July 4**
d. ? c.544. Said to have been a Hungarian by birth, ordained deacon in Milan, and later appointed archbishop of Seville.

The place of his supposed martyrdom is given as Bourges in France. All these details are open to grave doubt.
Cf. Holw. — P. de U.

LAURUS (St) M. **R.M. Aug. 18**
See Florus, Laurus, etc.

LAURUS (LÉRY) (St) Ab. **A.C. Sept. 30**
7th cent. A native of Wales, who crossed over to Brittany and became the abbot-founder of the monastery afterwards called after him Saint-Léry, on the R. Doneff.
Cf. Holw. — Baud.

LAUTO (LAUDO, LAUDUS, LÔ) (St) Bp.
R.M. Sept. 22
d. 568. Bishop of Coutances in Normandy for forty years (528-568). He appears to have been one of the most energetic prelates of that period. His family estate has become the village of Saint-Lô.
Cf. Holw. — Baud. — Duch. Fast. Episc.

LAWDOG (St) **A.C. Jan. 21**
6th cent. Titular of four churches in the diocese of St David's, and perhaps identical with St Lleuddad (Laudatus), abbot of Bardsey.
Cf. Stanton.

LAZARUS of MILAN (St) Bp.
R.M. Feb. 11
d. c.450 (March 14). An archbishop of Milan who was the support of his flock during the invasion of the Ostrogoths. His feast was translated to Feb. 11, in deference to the Milanese custom of not keeping saints' days in Lent.
Cf. Att. — Holw. — Baud.

LAZARUS (St) C. **R.M. Feb. 23**
d. c.867. Surnamed Zographos (the Painter). He was a monk of Constantinople, and a skilled painter, who in the time of Theophilus (829-842), one of the iconoclast emperors, busied himself in restoring the sacred pictures, defaced by the heretics.
Cf. Holw. — Baud.

LAZARUS (St) M. **R.M. March 27**
See Zanitas, Lazarus, etc.

LAZARUS (St) **A.C. June 21**
The poor man in our Lord's parable (Luke XVI). The military Order of St Lazarus, founded during the crusades, one of whose

duties was to take care of lepers, was named after him. Hence also the words *Lazaretto*, for a hospital, *Lazarone*, for a poor man of the street etc. The Abyssinians keep his feast on June 21.
Cf. Holw.

LAZARUS (St) Bp.   **R.M. Dec. 17**
1st cent. The disciple and friend of our Lord raised by Him from the dead. (John XI). The Greek tradition states that he died bishop of Kition in Cyprus. The French legend which connects him with Marseilles is first heard of in the 11th century, and has no historical foundation whatever: it is probably due to confusion with an early bishop of Aix, called Lazarus.
Cf. Att. — Holw. — Baud.

LEA (St) W.   **R.M. March 22**
d. 384. A Roman lady who, after the death of her husband, joined the community of St Marcella, where she spent her life serving the nuns.
Cf. Holw. — Baud.

LEAFWINE (St) C. O.S.B.   A.C. Nov. 12
Otherwise Lebuin, q.v.

LEANDER (St) Bp.   **R.M. Feb. 27**
d. 596. The elder brother of SS Fulgentius, Isidore and Florentina. He entered a monastery in his early youth and was later sent to Constantinople on a diplomatic mission. There he met St Gregory the Great, whose close friend he became and whose *Moralia* was published at his permission. On his return to Spain Leander was appointed archbishop of Seville. He proved himself a great prelate: revised and unified the Spanish liturgy, converted St Hermenegild, was instrumental in winning the Visigoths from Arianism and was responsible for the holding of two national synods at Toledo (589 and 590). Not the least of his achievements were the education of his younger brother St Isidore, who succeeded him in the see of Seville and the foundation of the episcopal school of that city. In Spain he is liturgically honoured as a Doctor.
Cf. Mab. — Att. — Baud. — P. de U.

LEBUIN (LEAFWINE) (St) C. O.S.B.
A.C. Nov. 12
d. c.773. A Benedictine of Ripon who crossed over to Holland and took part in the missionary work inaugurated by St

Boniface. He worked with St Marchalm under St Gregory of Utrecht and founded the church at Deventer. From there he went forth to preach to the Saxons and Frisians.
Cf. Att. — Holw.

LEBUINUS (St) Bp. M.   **R.M. Nov. 12**
Otherwise Livinus, q.v.

LEGER (St) Bp. M.   **R.M. Oct. 2**
Otherwise Leodegarius, q.v.

LELIA (St) V.   **A.C. Aug. 11**
? An Irish maiden, who seems to have lived at a very early period and to have been connected with the dioceses of Limerick and Kerry. Several place-names in Ireland perpetuate her memory.
Cf. Holw.

LEO CARASUMA (St) M.   **R.M. Feb. 5**
d. 1597. A native of Corea, who after being a pagan priest was converted to the Faith and was the first to be received into the third order of St Francis in Japan. As a catechist of the Franciscans, he was crucified at Nagasaki. Beatified in 1627 and canonized in 1862.
Cf. Holw.

LEO and PAREGORIUS (SS) MM.
A.C. Feb. 18
d. c.260. Martyrs of Patara in Lycia, greatly venerated in the East. Their alleged Acts may be merely a pious romance.
Cf. Att. — Holw.

LEO of CATANIA (St) Bp.   R.M. Feb. 20
703-787. Known in Sicily as St Leo *"il Maraviglioso,"* the wonder-worker. He was a priest of Ravenna who became bishop of Catania in Sicily. He was highly esteemed for his learning. The story of his life has been embellished with many delightful, though unreliable, *"Fioretti."*
Cf. Menzies — Holw. — Baud.

LEO of SAINT-BERTIN (Bl) Ab. O.S.B.
A.C. Feb. 26
d. 1163. Of noble Flemish birth, Leo left the court of Flanders to become a Benedictine at Auchin. He was soon appointed abbot of Lobbes where he succeeded in making good the ravages of war. In 1138 he was given charge of the great abbey of Saint-Bertin, which he ruled for twenty-five years. In 1146 he joined the

second crusade and reached Jerusalem and on his return brought with him the alleged relic of our Lord's Blood which ever since has been worshipped at Bruges. The abbey of St Bertin was destroyed by fire in 1152, but Bl Leo was energetic in its rebuilding. Some time before his death he was afflicted with blindness. Two of St Bernard's letters are addressed to him.
Cf. Att. — Holw. — Baud.

LEO, DONATUS, ABUNDANTIUS, NICEPHORUS and Comp. (SS) MM.
R.M. March 1
? A group of thirteen martyrs, believed to have laid down their lives for Christ in Africa.
Cf. Holw. — Baud.

LEO of ROUEN (St) Bp. M. A.C. March 1
c.856-c.900. Born at Carentan in Normandy, he is said to have been bishop of Rouen, and afterwards to have resigned in order to preach the gospel in Navarre and the Basque provinces — both French and Spanish — devastated by the Saracen invasion. Pirates beheaded him near Bayonne, of which city he is now the patron saint. The whole story is untrustworthy.
Cf. Baud. — Holw.

LEO (St) Bp. M. R.M. March 14
? The R.M. has the following entry: "At Rome, in the Agro Verano, St Leo, bishop and martyr." This is all that is known about him.
Cf. Holw. — Baud.

LEO the GREAT (St) Pope and Dr.
R.M. Apr. 11
d. 461. He shares the title of "the Great," with only two other popes, viz., Gregory I and Nicholas I. Born probably in Tuscany and joining the Roman clergy, he became archdeacon under Celestine I and Sixtus III, and was raised to the papal throne in 440. Ever conscious of his supreme jurisdiction and responsibility as the successor of St Peter, he combated Pelagians, Manicheans, Priscillianists, and, especially, the Eutychians and Nestorians. His celebrated *Tomos*, or Dogmatic Letter, addressed to Flavian, patriarch of Constantinople, in which he defined the exact Catholic belief on the twofold nature and one person in Christ, marks an epoch in Catholic theology. It was acclaimed as the teaching of the Church at the council

of Chalcedon (451). To the Latinist, as well as to the theologian, his works will always be a delight on account of the purity of his diction and the limpidity of his style. He was officially declared a Doctor of the Church in 1754.
Cf. Att. — Menzies — Ricci.

LEO IX (St) Pope. R.M. Apr. 19
1002-1054. A cousin of the emperor Conrad the Salic, born in Alsace, and in baptism named Bruno. He was made bishop of Toul in 1026 and constrained to accept the papal office in 1048. He took with him to Rome, as his spiritual adviser, Hildebrand, the future Gregory VII, and the reform of the Roman curia now began in earnest. Leo combated simony, condemned Berengarius, and strove to prevent the schism between the Eastern and the Western churches then being engineered by the emperor Michael Coerularius. While at Benevento, a city belonging to the Holy See, he was taken prisoner by the Normans. He was released, but shortly after died before the high altar in St Peter's.
Cf. Att. — Holw. — Baud.

LEO of SENS (St) Bp. R.M. Apr. 22
d. 541. Bishop of Sens for twenty-three years. He defended the rights of his own see against the pretensions of King Childebert.
Cf. Baud. — Holw. — Att.

LEO of TROYES (St) Ab. R.M. May 25
d. c.550. A monk who succeeded St Romanus in the government of the monastery of Mantenay, near Troyes.
Cf. Baud. — Holw.

LEO TANACA (Bl) M. A.C. June 1
d. 1617. A Japanese catechist to the Jesuit Fathers. Beheaded at Nagasaki, and beatified in 1867.
Cf. Holw.

LEO III (St) Pope. R.M. June 12
d. 816. A Roman by birth, who became pope in 795. While attempting to suppress the unruly factions of Rome he was himself seized and put to the torture. He then called to his help Charlemagne, who re-established order in Rome, and who was by Pope Leo crowned emperor of the West in St Peter's (800). Leo refused to add the "filioque" to the Nicene creed.
Cf. Att. — Baud. — Holw.

LEO (St) M.   **R.M. June 30**
See Caius and Leo.

LEO II (St) Pope.   **R.M. July 3**
d. 683. A Sicilian who became pope in
681. He governed the church only two
years and the outstanding event of his
pontificate was the condemnation of Pope
Honorius I for having been remiss in
formally denouncing the Monothelites.
Cf. Att. — Baud. — Holw.

LEO of LUCCA (St) Ab. O.S.B.
     A.C. July 12
d. 1079. Born at Lucca in Tuscany, he
entered the Benedictine abbey of La
Cava, near Naples, under its founder St
Alpherius, whom he succeeded as abbot in
1050. He stood in great favour with Duke
Gisuff II of Salerno. Cult approved —
as a saint in 1579 and again in 1893.
Cf. Zimm. — Holw. — Baud.

LEO IV (St) Pope O.S.B. R.M. July 17
d. 855. A Roman and a monk of the
Benedictine abbey of San Martino, he
was chosen pope in 847. He enclosed the
whole Vatican city with a wall (the Leo-
nine city), and through his prayers and
exhortations to the soldiers, the Saracens
from Calabria were utterly routed at
Ostia. His benefactions to churches take
up twenty-eight pages in the *Liber
Pontificalis*. The English king Alfred
visited Rome during his pontificate (853)
and Leo stood godfather for him at his
confirmation.
*Cf. Holw. — Att. — Zimm. — Mab. —
Chev.*

LEO and JULIANA (SS) MM.
     R.M. Aug. 18
? Leo was martyred at Myra, in Lycia,
and Juliana at Strobylum.
Cf. Holw.

LEO SUCHEIEMON (Bl) M. A.C. Aug. 19
d. 1622. A native Japanese, pilot of the
ship of Bl Joachim Firaiama. Beheaded
at Nagasaki. Beatified in 1867.
Cf. Holw.

LEO II of CAVA (Bl) Ab. O.S.B.
     A.C. Aug. 19
d. 1295. The fifteenth abbot of the Benedictine abbey of La Cava, near Naples.
He ruled from 1268 to 1295. Cult approved in 1929.
Cf. Zimm. — Holw.

LEO COMBIOGE (Bl) M. A.C. Sept. 8
d. 1628. A Japanese catechist, member
of the third order of St Dominic. Beheaded at Nagasaki. Beatified in 1867.
Cf. Holw.

LEO SATZUMA (Bl) M. A.C. Sept. 10
d. 1622. A Japanese catechist, and a
Franciscan tertiary. He was burnt alive
at Nagasaki on the day of the great
martyrdom.
Cf. Holw.

LEO (St) M. O.F.M.   **R.M. Oct. 10**
See Daniel and Comp.

LEO of MELUN (St) C. R.M. Nov. 10
? A saint held in veneration from time
immemorial at Melun, near Paris. He
is now identified by scholars with St Leo
the Great, who died on Nov. 10.
Cf. Holw. — Baud.

LEO of NONANTULA (St) Ab. O.S.B.
     A.C. Nov. 20
d. 1000. Monk and abbot of the Benedictine monastery of Nonantula, near
Modena.
Cf. Holw. — Chev.

LEO NACANIXI (Bl) M. A.C. Nov. 27
d. 1619. A Japanese layman, born at
Amangucchi, of the royal family of
Firando. He was beheaded with ten
companions at Nagasaki. Beatified in
1867.
Cf. Holw.

LEOBALD (LIEUBAULT) (St) Ab. O.S.B.
     A.C. Aug. 8
d. 650. Abbot-founder of Fleury, afterwards called Saint-Benoît-sur-Loire, in the
diocese of Orleans. He had been a monk
at Saint-Aignan, in the same diocese.
Cf. Holw.

LEOBARD (LIBERD) (St) C.
     R.M. Jan. 18
d. 593. A recluse at Tours who shut himself up in a cell near the abbey of Marmoutiers and lived there for twenty-two
years under the direction of St Gregory of
Tours.
Cf. Holw. — Baud.

LEOBINUS (LUBIN) (St) Bp.
     R.M. Sept. 15
d. c.556. Born near Poitiers, the son of a
peasant family. Early in life he became

a hermit, then a priest, abbot of Brou, and, finally bishop of Chartres — one of the most distinguished occupants of that important see.
Cf. Att.

LEOCADIA (St) V. M. R.M. Dec. 9
d. c.303. According to the R.M. she was a maiden of Toledo, who died in prison, after having been condemned to death, under Diocletian. Her cult at Toledo dates from the 5th century, at the latest. In Flanders she is known as St Locaie.
Cf. P. de U. — Att. — Baud. — Holw.

LEOCRITIA (LUCRETIA) (St) V. M.
R.M. March 15
d. 859. A maiden of Cordova, Spain, born of Moorish parents, but early converted to Christianity and in consequence driven from her home. She was sheltered by St Eulogius, and both were flogged and beheaded.
Cf. Holw. — Att. — P. de U.

LEODEGARIUS (St) Bp. M. O.S.B.
R.M. Oct. 2
c.616-678. Nephew of the bishop of Poitiers by whom he was educated. In 653 he was made abbot of the monastery of St Maxentius, where he introduced the Benedictine rule. On the death of King Clovis II he assisted St Bathildis, the queen regent during the minority of her son, Clotaire III. In 659 he became bishop of Autun, in which capacity he reformed church discipline and imposed on all the monasteries the observance of the Rule of St Benedict. His connection with the court brought upon him the full fury of the tyrant Ebroin, mayor of the palace, who had the saint, degraded, imprisoned, blinded and finally murdered. He is widely venerated in France as St Leger.
Cf. Zimm. — Mab. — Att. — Holw.

LEOMENES (St) M. R.M. Dec. 23
See Theodulus, Saturninus, etc.

LEONARD (Bl) H. O.S.B. Cam.
A.C. May 15
d. c.1250. Monk-hermit at Camaldoli.
Cf. Chev. — Zimm.

LEONARD WEGEL (WICHEL, VECHEL) (St) M. R.M. July 9
d. 1572. Born at Bois-le-duc, in Holland, he studied for the priesthood at Louvain, and was appointed parish priest of Gor-

kum, where he was noted for his opposition to Calvinism. He was one of the group of the Gorkum martyrs, q.v. Canonized in 1867.
Cf. Holw.

LEONARD of CAVA (Bl) Ab. O.S.B.
A.C. Aug. 18
d. 1255. Eleventh abbot of La Cava, in S. Italy. Beatified in 1929.
Cf. Chev. — Zimm.

LEONARD of VANDOEUVRE (St) Ab.
A.C. Oct. 15
d. c.570. A hermit, who eventually became the abbot-founder of Vandoeuvre, now Saint-Leonard-aux-Bois, near Le Mans.
Cf. Att. — Baud. — Holw.

LEONARD of NOBLAC (St) Ab.
R.M. Nov. 6
d. c.559. A French courtier converted by St Remigius of Reims. On the advice of that saint, St Leonard retired to the abbey of Micy near Orleans, and later became a hermit in a neighbouring forest, now called Noblac. His cult was widespread in the west during the Middle Ages.
Cf. Att. — Holw. — Baud.

LEONARD of RERESBY (St) C.
P.C. Nov. 6
13th cent. A native of Thryberg in Yorkshire. According to local tradition, he was a crusader, who, taken prisoner by the Saracens, was miraculously set free and returned safely home.
Cf. Stanton — Holw.

LEONARD CHIMURA and Comp. (BB) MM. A.C. Nov. 18
d. 1619. A Japanese nobleman, who, after his conversion, became a temporal coadjutor in the Society of Jesus, and with others of his countrymen was burnt to death at Nagasaki.
Cf. Att. — Holw. — Baud. — Prop. S.J. (Nov. 27).

LEONARD of PORT MAURICE (St) C. O.F.M. R.M. Nov. 26
1676-1751. Born at Porto Maurizio, on the Italian Riviera, he studied in the Roman College and became a Franciscan of the Strictest Observance in the convent of St Bonaventure on the Palatine. Soon after his ordination he began his career as a missionary, spreading everywhere devo-

tion to the Blessed Sacrament, to the Sacred Heart, to the Immaculate Conception and to the Stations of the Cross: he is said to have established the Way of the Cross in five hundred seventy-two places including the Colosseum in Rome. He was a prolific ascetical writer, his works filling thirteen volumes. In 1744 he was sent to restore discipline in Corsica. In 1751 he was called to Rome by Benedict XIV but died on the night after his arrival at his old friary of St Bonaventure. Canonized in 1867.
Cf. Att. — Baud. — Prop. O.F.M.

LEONIANUS (St) C. A.C. Nov. 6
d. c.570. A Pannonian by birth, he was taken as a captive to Gaul, and, on regaining his freedom, lived as a recluse near Autun. Later he embraced the monastic life at the abbey of St Symphorianus, also at Autun. Cult approved in 1907.
Cf. Holw. — Baud.

LEONIDAS and Comp. (SS) MM.
R.M. Jan. 28
d. 304. Egyptian martyrs, associated with SS Apollonius and Philemon. All suffered under Diocletian.
Cf. Baud. — Holw.

LEONIDAS (St) M. R.M. Apr. 22
d. 202. The father of Origen, and himself a distinguished philosopher. He was martyred at Alexandria, his native city, under Septimius Severus.
Cf. Att. — Holw. — Baud.

LEONIDES (St) M. R.M. Aug. 8
See Eleutherius and Leonides.

LEONIDES (St) M. R.M. Sept. 2
See Diomedes, Julian, etc.

LEONILLA (St) M. R.M. Jan. 17
See Speusippus, Eleusippus, etc.

LEONIS (St) V. M. R.M. June 15
See Lybe, Leonis and Eutropia.

LEONORIUS (LUNAIRE) (St) Ab. Bp.
A.C. July 1
d. c.570. A son of Hoel, king of Brittany, but born in Wales, educated by St Illtyd, and consecrated bishop by St Dubritius of Caerleon. Crossing to Brittany, then ruled by his brother Hoel II, he founded

the monastery of Pontual, near Saint Malo.
Cf. Att. — Baud. — Holw.

LEONTIA (St) Bp. R.M. Dec. 6
See Dionysia, Dativa, etc.

LEONTIUS of CAESAREA (St) Bp.
R.M. Jan. 13
d. 337. Bishop of Caesarea in Cappadocia and one of the fathers of the council of Nicaea (325). He is specially praised by St Athanasius and described as "an angel of peace" by the Greeks.
Cf. Holw. — Baud.

LEONTIUS (St) Bp. R.M. March 19
See Apollonius and Leontius.

LEONTIUS (St) Bp. A.C. March 19
d. 640. Bishop of Saintes. A friend of St Malo, whom he received into his diocese when he was exiled from Brittany.
Cf. Holw. — Baud. — Duch. Fast. Episc.

LEONTIUS (St) M. R.M. Apr. 24
See Eusebius, Neon, etc.

LEONTIUS, HYPATIUS and THEO-DULUS (SS) MM. R.M. June 18
d. ? 135. Greeks martyred at Tripoli in Phoenicia at an early date.
Cf. Holw. — Baud.

LEONTIUS, MAURICE, DANIEL and Comp. (SS) MM. R.M. July 10
d. c.329. A band of forty-five martyrs who suffered together at Nicopolis in Armenia under the emperor Licinius and were among the last martyrs of the great persecution.
Cf. Holw. — Baud.

LEONTIUS the YOUNGER (St) Bp.
A.C. July 11
c.510-c.565. A soldier who served against the Visigoths. He married and went to reside at Bordeaux; he was forced to accept the see and government of that city, his wife taking the veil.
Cf. Duch. Fast. Episc. — Holw. — Baud.

LEONTIUS, ATTIUS, ALEXANDER and Comp. R.M. Aug. 1
d. c.300. Three Christians of Perge in Pamphylia, who, together with six farm labourers, were martyred under Diocletian for having destroyed the altar of Artemis.
Cf. Holw. — Baud.

LEONTIUS the ELDER (St) Bp.
A.C. Aug. 21
d. c.541. Bishop of Bordeaux, the immediate predecessor of St Leontius the Younger (v. July 11).
Cf. Duch. Fast. Episc. — Holw. — Baud.

LEONTIUS (St) M. **R.M. Sept. 12**
See Hieronides, Leontius, etc.

LEONTIUS (St) M. **R.M. Sept. 27**
See Cosmas and Damian.

LEONTIUS (St) Bp. **A.C. Dec. 1**
d. c.432. Bishop of Fréjus in France from c.419 to c.432. He was a great friend of Cassian, who dedicated to him his first ten conferences.
Cf. Duch. Fast. Episc. — Holw. — Baud.

LEOPARDINUS (St) Ab. M.
A.C. Nov. 24
d. 7th cent. Monk and abbot of the monastery of St Symphorianus of Vivaris in the province of Berry, France. He perished at the hands of assassins and was forthwith venerated as a martyr.
Cf. Holw. — Baud.

LEOPARDUS (St) M. **R.M. Sept. 30**
d. 362. A servant, or slave, in the household of Julian the Apostate. His execution probably took place in Rome.
Cf. Holw. — Baud.

LEOPOLD of GAICHE (Bl) C. O.F.M.
A.C. Apr. 2
1732-1815 (Apr. 15). A native of Gaiche, in the diocese of Perugia, he joined the Franciscans, and after his ordination was professor of philosophy and theology, and apostolic missionary for the Papal States. During the Napoleonic invasion he was compelled to put off his habit and became parish priest, although then seventy-seven years of age. Beatified in 1893.
Cf. Att. — Holw.

LEOPOLD the GOOD (St) C.
R.M. Nov. 15
1073-1136. Born at Melk in Austria, a grandson of the emperor Henry III. In 1096 he succeeded his father as fourth margrave of Austria. He married Agnes, daughter of Henry IV, by whom he had eighteen children. He ruled firmly and successfully for forty years, and was especially interested in the spread of religious institutions. He was the founder of

Mariazell (Benedictine), Heiligenkreuz (Cistercian) and Klosternenburg (Augustinian). He was buried in the last mentioned monastery.
Cf. Att. — Baud. — Holw.

LEOTHADIUS (LÉOTHADE) (St) Ab.
O.S.B. **A.C. Oct. 23**
d. 718. Of noble Frankish family, Léothade became a monk and shortly after abbot of Moissac, in S. France. Later he was raised to the see of Auch.
Cf. Duch. Fast. Episc. — Baud.

LEOVIGILD and CHRISTOPHER (SS)
MM. **R.M. Aug. 20**
d. 852. Leovigild was a monk of SS Justus and Pastor of Cordova, and Christopher of the monastery of St Martin de La Rojana, near Cordova. They were beheaded at Cordova under Abderrahman II.
Cf. P. de U. — Holw. — Baud.

LESBOS (Martyrs of) **R.M. Apr. 5**
? Five maidens venerated by the Greeks as having suffered martyrdom in the island of Lesbos.
Cf. Holw. — Baud.

LESMES (St) Ab. O.S.B. **A.C. Jan. 30**
The Spanish form of Adelelmus, q.v.

LETARD (St) Bp. **A.C. May 7**
Otherwise Liudhard, q.v.

LEU (St) Bp. **R.M. Sept. 1**
French form for Lupus of Sens, q.v.

LEUCHTELDIS (LIUTHILD) (St) V.
A.C. Jan. 23
Otherwise Lufthild, q.v.

LEUCIUS (St) M. **R.M. Jan. 11**
See SS Peter, Severus and Leucius.

LEUCIUS of BRINDISI (St) Bp.
R.M. Jan. 11
d. c.180. Venerated as the first bishop of Brindisi whither he is said to have come as a missionary from Alexandria. Another saint of the same name, likewise bishop of Brindisi, who flourished at the beginning of the 5th century, is mentioned by St Gregory the Great.
Cf. Att. — Baud.

LEUCIUS (St) M. **R.M. Jan. 28**
See Thyrsus, Leucius and Callinicus.

LEUDOMER (LOMER) (St) Bp.
A.C. Oct. 2
d. c.585. A French bishop of Chartres.
Cf. Holw.

LEUTFRID (LEUFROI) Ab. O.S.B.
R.M. June 21
d. 738. Abbot-founder of the monastery La-Croix-Saint-Ouen (afterwards Saint-Leufroy), near Evreux, which he governed for nearly fifty years. In art he is represented surrounded by a group of the poor children it was his delight to befriend.
Cf. Mab. — Zimm. — Holw. — Baud.

LEVAN (St) C.
A.C. June 8
6th cent. An Irish saint who came over to Cornwall and who has given his name (spelt also Levin — possibly an abbreviated form of Silvanus) to a parish in that county.
Cf. Holw.

LEWINA (St) V. M.
A.C. July 24
5th cent. The first surviving record of this saint dates from 1058, when her relics were translated from Seaford in Sussex where she is said to have been venerated, to Berg in Flanders. She is supposed to have been a British maiden martyred by the Saxon invaders.
Cf. Att. — Holw. — Baud.

LEZIN (St) Bp.
A.C. Feb. 13
Otherwise Lucinius, q.v.

LIBENTIUS (LIÄWIZO) (St or Bl) Bp.
O.S.B.
A.C. Jan. 4
d. 1013. Born in S. Swabia, he became bishop of Hamburg in 988, professing at the same time the Benedictine Rule at the cathedral abbey of Hamburg. He is venerated as one of the apostles of the Slavs.
Cf. Zimm. — Baud. — Mab.

LIBERALIS (St) C.
A.C. Apr. 27
d. c.400. A priest of the district round Ancona, who worked zealously for the conversion of the Arians and suffered much at their hands. His relics are enshrined at Treviso.
Cf. Holw. — Baud.

LIBERATA (St) V.
R.M. Jan. 18
d. c. A maiden of Como, at which city she, with her sister St Faustina, founded the nunnery of Santa Margarita.
Cf. Holw.

LIBERATA (St) V.
R.M. July 20
Otherwise Wilgefortis, q.v.

LIBERATUS, BONIFACE, SERVUS, RUSTICUS, ROGATUS, SEPTIMUS and MAXIMUS (SS) MM.
R.M. Aug. 17
d. 483. Liberatus was abbot of a nunnery in Africa, the rest were his monks: Boniface, a deacon; Servus and Rusticus, subdeacons; Rogatus and Septimus, simple monks; Maximus, a child educated in the monastery. All were martyred by the Arian king Hunneric.
Cf. Att. — Baud. — Holw.

LIBERATUS da LORO (Bl) C. O.F.M.
A.C. Sept. 6
d. 1258. Born at San Liberato, in Piceno, of the Brumforti family, he joined the Franciscans, among whom at a later date he introduced the initial austerity of the Order, aided by BB Humilis and Pacificus. His cult was forbidden in 1730, but restored in 1731 and again approved in 1868.
Cf. Holw. — Baud. — Att.

LIBERATUS and BAJULUS (SS) MM.
R.M. Dec. 20
? Martyrs venerated at Rome, of whom nothing certain is known.

LIBERIUS (St) Bp.
R.M. Dec. 30
d. c.200. A bishop of Ravenna, venerated as one of the founders of that see.
Cf. Menzies — Holw.

LIBERT (LIEBERT) (St) Bp.
A.C. June 23
d. 1076. Bishop of Cambrai from 1051 till his death. He went on a pilgrimage to Palestine, but failing to reach the Holy Places, he built instead, on his return to his diocese, the abbey of the Holy Sepulchre. He excommunicated the lord of Cambrai and was on that account brutally persecuted.
Cf. Att. — Holw. — Baud.

LISBERT (St) M. O.S.B.
A.C. July 14
d. 783. Born at Malines, baptized and educated by St Rumoldus, from whom he received the Benedictine habit. Afterwards he migrated to the abbey of Saint-Trond, where he was put to death by invading barbarians.
Cf. Holw. — Baud. — Zimm.

LIBORIUS (St) Bp.
R.M. July 23
d. 390. Bishop of Le Mans from 348 to

390. He is the patron saint of Paderborn, whither his relics were translated in 836.
Cf. Duch. Fast. Episc. — Holw. — Baud. — Att.

LICERIUS (LIZIER) (St) Bp.
R.M. Aug. 27
d. c.548. Born in Spain, probably at Lérida (Ilerda). He went to France and in 506 was chosen bishop of Conserans (now in the diocese of Pamiers). The R.M. wrongly makes him bishop of Lérida.
Cf. Holw. — Baud.

LICINIUS (St) M.
R.M. Aug. 7
See Carpophorus, Exanthus, etc.

LICINIUS (LESIN) (St) Bp.
R.M. Nov. 1
d. c.616. Count of Anjou under King Chilperic. He became a monk and afterwards was chosen bishop of Angers (586), and consecrated by St Gregory of Tours. He wished to resign, but his people would on no account allow him to do so.
Cf. Holw. — Att.

LIDANUS (St) Ab. O.S.B. A.C. July 2
1026-1118. A native of Antina in the Abruzzi who became the abbot-founder of the Benedictine abbey of Sezze in the Papal States. He deserves well of humanity for his work in draining the Pontine Marshes. In his old age he retired to Montecassino. He is the patron saint of Sezze.
Cf. Holw. — Baud. — Menzies.

LIDWINA (St) V.
A.C. Apr. 14
Otherwise Lydwina of Schiedam, q.v.

LIÉ, of LYÉ (several)
French forms of Laetus and Leo, q.v.

LIEPHARD (St) Bp. M.
A.C. Feb. 4
d. 640. An Englishman by birth and perhaps a bishop, said to have been the companion of King Cadwalla on the latter's pilgrimage to Rome. While on his way back to England, Liephard was done to death near Cambrai.
Cf. Holw. — Baud.

LIGORIUS (St) M.
R.M. Sept. 13
? An eastern saint who met his death at the hands of a pagan mob. His relics are enshrined at Venice.
Cf. Holw.

LILIOSA (St) M.
R.M. July 27
See George, Aurelius, etc.

LIMBANIA (St) V. O.S.B. A.C. Aug. 15
d. 1294. A Cyprian by birth who became a Benedictine nun at Genoa, and then lived as a recluse in a cave below the church of St Thomas in that city. Cult approved by Paul V. (*Note.* In 1509 the church of St Thomas was handed over to the Augustinians and this is the reason why Limbania is often described as an Augustinian.)
Cf. Holw. — Menzies — Baud.

LIMNAEUS (St) H.
A.C. Feb. 22
See Thalassius and Limnaeus.

LINUS (St) Pope M.
R.M. Sept. 23
d. c.79. The immediate successor of St Peter in the see of Rome, which he ruled for twelve years (67-79). He is traditionally venerated as a martyr, but there is no evidence for his martyrdom. His name is mentioned in the Canon of the Mass.
Cf. Holw. — Menzies — Att. — Baud.

LIOBA (St) Abs. O.S.B.
R.M. Sept. 28
d. c.779. An Anglo-Saxon by birth and a kinswoman of St Boniface, St Lioba professed the Benedictine Rule at Wimborne. In 748, at the request of St Boniface, she, with a band of missionary nuns, left England for the German mission and was at once appointed abbess of Bischoffsheim and was given the general supervision of all the daughter-houses founded from that nunnery. "Lioba ruled her home in the very spirit of St Benedict's moderation and gentleness, and insisted equally on manual work and studies for all her nuns" (Attwater). She was greatly loved by her nuns and a close friend of the empress St Hildegard, Charlemagne's wife, while the tender affection which subsisted between herself and St Boniface forms one of the most charming episodes in church history. St Lioba's convents were one of the most powerful factors in the conversion of Germany by the Benedictines.
Cf. Zimm. — Mab. — Att. — Holw.

LIPHARDUS (LIFARD) (St) Ab.
R.M. June 3
d. c.550. A prominent lawyer of Orleans who at the age of fifty embraced the solitary life and eventually became the abbot-

founder of the monastery of Meung-sur-Loire.
Cf. Att. — Holw.

LITTEUS (St) M. R.M. Sept. 10
See Nemesian, Felix, etc.

LIUDHARD (St) Bp. A.C. Feb. 4
d. c.600. Frankish chaplain to Queen Bertha of Kent. He is said to have been a bishop and to have played an important part in the conversion of King Ethelbert, q.v. He was buried in the abbey of SS Peter and Paul, at Canterbury.
Cf. Att. — Stanton — Holw.

LIUTWIN (St) Bp. O.S.B. A.C. Sept. 29
d. c.713. Founder and monk of Mettlach, and then bishop of Trèves.
Cf. Zimm.

LIVINUS (LEBWIN) (St) Bp. M.
R.M. Nov. 12
d. c.650. An Irishman by birth, he was ordained priest by St Augustine of Canterbury, and crossed over to Flanders, where for some years he preached the gospel with great success. At some time during this period he is said to have been consecrated bishop in Ireland. He was martyred near Alost in Brabant. He is perhaps to be identified with St Lebuinus.
Cf. Att. — Baud. — Holw.

LIZIER (St) Bp. R.M. Aug. 27
Otherwise Licerius, q.v.

LLEUDADD (LAUDATUS) (St) Ab.
A.C. Jan. 15
6th cent. A Welsh saint, abbot of Bardsey (Carnarvon), who accompanied St Cadfan to Brittany. By some scholars he is thought to be no other than St Lô of Coutances.
Cf. Holw. — Baud.

LLEWELLYN (LLYWELYN) and GWRNERTH (SS) CC. A.C. Apr. 7
6th cent. Welsh monks at Welshpool and afterwards at Bardsey.
Cf. Baring-Gould.

LLIBIO (St) C. A.C. Feb. 28
6th cent. The patron saint of Llanllibio in the isle of Anglesey.
Cf. Baring-Gould.

LÔ (St) Bp. R.M. Sept. 22
Otherwise Lauto, q.v.

LOARN (St) C. A.C. Aug. 30
5th cent. A native of W. Ireland and a disciple of St Patrick. Some writers describe him as a regionary bishop of Downpatrick.
Cf. Holw.

LOCAIE (St) V.M. R.M. Dec. 9
Otherwise Leocadia, q.v.

LOLANUS (St) C. A.C. Sept. 2
d. c.?1034. A Scottish bishop. The legend which makes him a native of Galilee who preached the gospel in Scotland during the 5th century deserves no credence.
Cf. Holw.

LOMAN (LUMAN) (St) Bp.
A.C. Feb. 17
d. c.450. Said to have been a nephew of St Patrick and the first bishop of Trim in Meath.
Cf. Att. — Holw.

LOMBARDS (Martyrs under the) (SS)
R.M. March 2
d. c.579. A group of eighty martyrs slain by the Lombards in Campania for refusing "to adore the head of a goat" (R.M.). They are also mentioned by St Gregory the Great.
Cf. Att. — Holw.

LOMER (LAUDOMARUS) (St) Ab.
A.C. Jan. 19
d. 593. A French priest who became the abbot-founder of the monastery of Corbion, near Chartres. His name is also spelled Launomar, Laumer, etc.
Cf. Holw. — Att. — Baud.

LONDON (Martyrs of)
Three main groups of post-Reformation martyrs may be listed under the above heading, namely: (I) those of 1582, executed for being concerned in a spurious plot called the conspiracy of Reims and Rome; (II) those of 1588, following on the defeat of the Armada; (III) those of 1591, following on a stricter enforcement of the laws against Catholics. Each martyr receives in this book a special notice.

LONGINUS (St) M. R.M. March 15
1st cent. This is the name given by tradition to the soldier who pierced the side of our Lord hanging on the Cross (John XIX, 34). The centurion who acknowledged

Christ to be the son of God, after the crucifixion, is also called Longinus. (Matt. XXVII, 54). He is said to have died a martyr in Cappadocia, his alleged native country.
Cf. Att. — Holw.

LONGINUS (St) M. R.M. Apr. 24
See Eusebius, Neon, etc.

LONGINUS (St) Bp. M. R.M. May 2
See Vindemnialis, Eugene and Longinus.

LONGINUS (St) M. R.M. June 24
See Orentius, Heros, etc.

LONGINUS (St) M. R.M. July 21
See Victor, Alexander, etc.

LORGIUS (St) M. R.M. March 2
See Lucius, Absalom and Lorgius.

LOTHARIUS (St) Bp. O.S.B.
A.C. June 14
c.756. Founder of a monastery in the forest of Argentan, which was later called after him. Saint-Loyer-des-Champs. Afterwards he was raised to the see of Séez, which he ruled for thirty-two years.
Cf. Zimm.

LOUIS (*several*)
Otherwise Aloysius, q.v.

LOUIS IBARCHI (St) M. R.M. Feb. 5
1585-1597. A Japanese boy of twelve who served Mass for the Franciscan missionaries in Japan. He was crucified at Nagasaki with twenty-five companions. Canonized in 1867.
Cf. Holw.

LOUIS MARY GRIGNON de MONT FORT (Bl) C. A.C. Apr. 28
1673-1716. Born in Brittany of poor parents. Some charitable persons having defrayed the cost of his education, he was ordained priest in 1700. He became chaplain to a hospital at Nantes, where he founded the institute of Sisters of the Divine Wisdom. He now began his missionary activities throughout France, and in order to train helpers in his forceful methods of preaching, he formed, shortly before his death, the Society of Priests of the Holy Ghost. His writings, especially his little treatise on "True Devotion to our Lady" are of great doctrinal value

He was a Dominican tertiary, but never a professed member of that order. Beatified in 1888.
Cf. Att. — Holw. — Baud.

LOUIS of CORDOVA (St) M.
R.M. Apr. 30
See Amator, Peter and Louis.

LOUIS (LUDWIG) von BRUCK (St) M.
A.C. Apr. 30
d. 1429. A boy born of Swiss parents at Ravensburg in Swabia, who was murdered by the Jews at Easter.
Cf. Holw.

LOUIS NAISEN (Bl) M. A.C. July 12
1619-1626. A Japanese boy of seven years, son of BB John and Monica Naisen. He was beheaded at Nagasaki. Beatified in 1867.
Cf. Holw.

LOUIS CORREA (Bl) M. S.J.
A.C. July 15
d. 1570. A Jesuit cleric, born at Evora in Portugal. A companion of Bl Ignatius de Azevedo, q.v.

LOUIS BERTRÁN (Bl) M. O.P.
A.C. July 29
d. 1629. Born at Barcelona a kinsman of St Louis Bertrán, the apostle of Colombia. After his profession in the Dominican Order, he was sent to the Philippine Islands in 1618 and then to Japan, where he worked until his martyrdom. He was burnt alive at Omura. Beatified in 1867.
Cf. Holw. — Prox. O.P.

LOUIS MATZUO (Bl) M. A.C. Aug. 17
d. 1627. A Japanese layman, of the third order of St Francis, beheaded at Nagasaki. Beatified in 1867.
Cf. Holw.

LOUIS of TOULOUSE (St) Bp. O.F.M.
R.M. Aug. 19
1274-1297. Son of Charles II of Anjou, king of Naples, great-nephew of St Louis of France and of St Elisabeth of Hungary. He was born in Provence and spent 7 years in prison, as a hostage for his father, at Barcelona. At the age of twenty-three he was ordained and joined the Friars Minor. Reluctantly he accepted the see of Toulouse, but died only six months later. Canonized in 1297.
Cf. Att. — Holw. — Baud.

LOUIS FLORES (Bl) M. O.P.
A.C. Aug. 19

1570-1622. Born of Spanish parents at Antwerp, he went with his parents to Mexico, where he joined the Dominicans. After serving as novice-master, he was sent in 1602 to the Philippine Islands. In 1620, while on a journey, he was captured by the Dutch, handed over to the Japanese, tortured, and imprisoned for two years, and finally burnt alive at the Mount of Martyrs at Nagasaki. Beatified in 1867.
Cf. Holw.

LOUIS IX (St) King.
R.M. Aug. 25

1215-1270. Born at Poissy, near Paris, he succeeded to the throne under the regency of his mother Blanche of Castile in 1226. He reigned for forty-four years. In his private life he was more austere and more prayerful than a religious, as a ruler he was energetic but considerate to his people, especially to the poor, and he was a brave warrior who knew how to lead his armies to victory, as when he defeated King Henry III of England at Taillebourg in 1242. He was the father of eleven children and a devoted husband. He led the two crusades: in the first he was made prisoner in Egypt, and during the second he died of dysentery before Tunis. He was canonized, with the universal approbation of Western Christendom, in 1297.
Cf. Att. — Holw. — Baud. — Chev.

LOUIS SOTELO (Bl) M. O.F.M.
A.C. Aug. 25

d. 1624. Born of a noble family at Seville, in Spain, he became a Franciscan at Salamanca. After his ordination he was sent to Manila (1601) and then to Japan (1603). He was arrested and shipped back to Spain (1613), but after a visit to Rome, he returned to Japan (1622). Again arrested at Nagasaki, he was burnt alive at Ximabura. Beatified in 1867.
Cf. Holw. — Prop. O.F.M.

LOUISE SASANDA (Bl) M. O.F.M.
A.C. Aug. 25

d. 1624. Son of Bl Michael Sasanda, a martyr at Yeddo, Japan. In 1613, he accompanied Bl Louis Sotelo to Mexico, where he became a Franciscan. In 1622 he was ordained at Manila. Two years later he was burnt alive at Ximabura,

with Bl Louis Sotelo and comp. Beatified in 1867.
Cf. Holw.

LOUIS BABA (Bl) M. O.F.M.
A.C. Aug. 25

d. 1624. A Japanese catechist. He accompanied Bl Louis Sotelo to Europe. On his return to Japan he was arrested, received the Franciscan habit in prison at Omura, and was burnt alive at Ximabura. Beatified in 1867.
Cf. Holw.

LOUIS BARREAU de la TOUCHE (Bl) M. O.S.B.
A.C. Sept. 2

d. 1792. A French Benedictine of the congregation of St Maur, monk of Saint-Florent-de-Saumur, and nephew of Bl Augustine Chevreux, with whom he was massacred at Paris (see September, Martyrs of).
Cf. Zimm. — P. de U.

LOUIS MAKI (Bl) M.
A.C. Sept. 7

d. 1627. A Japanese layman, burnt alive at Nagasaki for having allowed Bl Thomas Tzugi to say Mass in his house. Beatified in 1867.
Cf. Holw.

LOUIS NIFAKI (Bl) M.
A. C. Sept. 8

d. 1628. A Japanese Dominican tertiary, beheaded at Nagasaki with his two sons, Francis and Dominic, for having sheltered the missionaries. Beatified in 1867.
Cf. Holw.

LOUIS CAVARA (Bl) M. S.J.
A.C. Sept. 10

d. 1622. A page at the court of Arima, Japan, who was later exiled by the apostate prince, Michael. Received into the Society of Jesus by Bl Charles Spinola, he was burnt alive at Nagasaki. Beatified in 1867.
Cf. Holw. — Prop. S.J.

LOUIS (LUDWIG) (Bl) C.
P.C. Sept. 11

1200-1227. Landgrave of Thuringia and husband of St Elizabeth of Hungary. An able ruler and brave warrior, he died at Otranto while following the emperor Frederick II to the crusade. His cult has never been confirmed, but is certainly well deserved.
Cf. Att. — Holw.

LOUIS GABRIEL TAURIN DUFRESSE (Bl) Bp. M. A.C. Sept. 14
d. 1815. A missionary priest in China for nearly forty years. In 1801 he was appointed vicar apostolic and titular bishop of Tabraca. He was beheaded at Ch'in-Tu for being a "foreign preacher." Beatified in 1900.
Cf. Att.

LOUIS ALLEMAND (Bl) Bp. Card.
A.C. Sept. 16
d. 1450. Appointed archbishop of Arles in 1423 and cardinal shortly after, Louis was one of the leaders of the "Council party" during the troubled period of the Western Schism. He was one of those who elected and remained faithful to the antipope Felix V. On this account he was deprived of the cardinalate and excommunicated by Eugenius IV. Pope Nicholas V restored him, and from this time till his death Louis attended exclusively to the government of his diocese. In his private life, he was always a model of virtue.
Cf. Holw. — Att.

LOUIS CHAKICHI (Bl) M. A.C. Oct. 2
d. 1622. A Japanese layman who released Bl Louis Flores from prison at Firando. He was burnt alive at Nagasaki. His wife and children were beheaded. Beatified in 1867.
Cf. Holw.

LOUIS BERTRÁN (St) C. O.P.
R.M. Oct. 9
1526-1581. A native of Valencia, in Spain, and a blood relation of St Vincent Ferrer; like him he was a Dominican. After filling very successfully the office of novice-master, he was in 1562 sent to evangelize S. America, and for 7 years worked in what are now Colombia, Panama and some of the West Indian islands. Under obedience he returned to Spain, and served as prior in several houses. Canonized in 1671.
Cf. Att. — P. de U. — Holw.

LOUIS MORBIOLI (Bl) C. A.C. Nov. 16
1439-1495. A native of Bologna, who as a young man was notorious for his loose living, even after he had contracted marriage. He was converted by sickness, became a Carmelite tertiary, and went about teaching Christian doctrine to the young, and begging alms which he gave to the poor. Cult confirmed in 1842.
Cf. Holw. — Att.

LOUISE degli ALBERTONI (Bl) W.
R.M. Jan. 31
1474-1533. A Roman born, she married James de Citara to whom she bore three children. After his death she put on the habit of the third order of St Francis and spent her life in works of charity. Cult approved in 1671.
Cf. Holw. — Baud. — Menzies.

LOUISE de MARILLAC (St) Foundress.
A.C. March 15
1591-1660. Born in Paris. She wished to become a nun, but on the advice of her confessor, married Antony Le Gras. After his death (1625), Louise spent the remainder of her life in co-operating with St Vincent de Paul in the establishment of the Sisters of Charity. The sisters took their vows for the first time in 1638, and Louise remained their superioress till her death. Beatified in 1920, canonized in 1934.
Cf. Att. — Baud. — Holw.

LOUISE of SAVOY (Bl) W. Poor Clare.
A.C. July 24
1462-1503. Daughter of Bl Amadeus IX, duke of Savoy, and cousin of Bl Joan of Valois. In 1479 she was married to Hugh of Châlons, who left her a widow when she was only twenty-seven. She now joined the Poor Clares at Orbe and was employed in collecting food for the community, which she did most graciously and cheerfully. Cult approved in 1839.
Cf. Att. — Holw. — Baud.

LOUISE of OMURA (Bl) M.
A.C. Sept. 8
d. 1628. A Japanese woman martyred at Omura.
Cf. Holw.

LOUP (St) Bp. R.M. July 29
Otherwise Lupus of Troyes, q.v.

LOUTHIERN (St) Bp. A.C. Oct. 17
6th cent. An Irish saint, patron of St Ludgran in Cornwall, possibly identical with St Luchtighern, abbot of Ennistymon, associated with St Ita.
Cf. Baring-Gould — O'Hanlon (Apr. 28).

LUANUS (LUGID, MOLUA) (St) Ab.
A.C. Aug. 4
d. 622. A disciple of St Comgall and founder of many monasteries (the number is given as 120). His rule was most austere. *Cf. Holw.*

LUBIN (St) Bp. R.M. Sept. 15
Otherwise Leobinus, q.v.

LUCANUS (St) M. R.M. Oct. 30
5th cent. A martyr who is believed to have suffered at Lagny, near Paris, where his relics were enshrined.
Cf. Baud. — Holw.

LUCERIUS (St) Ab. O.S.B. A.C. Dec. 10
d. 739. While still a child he joined the Benedictines of Farfa near Rome under its restorer, St Thomas of Maurienne, whom he eventually succeeded as abbot.
Cf. Zimm.

LUCHESIUS (Bl) C. A.C. Apr. 28
d. 1260. Born near Poggibonsi, in Umbria, he married Bl Bonadonna and was in business as a grocer, money changer and corn merchant. About the year 1221 he and his wife gave themselves to a life of alms-deeds and penance as Franciscan tertiaries. They are venerated as the first to have become tertiaries, but this is not quite established.
Cf. Att. — Holw. — Baud.

LUCHTIGHERN (St) Ab. A.C. Apr.28
See under Louthiern.

LUCIAN of ANTIOCH (St) M.
R.M. Jan. 7
d. 312. A native of Edessa, where he distinguished himself as a scriptural scholar. He travelled to Antioch and then to Nicomedia, where he was martyred after nine years in prison. He is highly praised by SS John Chrysostom and Jerome.
Cf. Att. — Holw.

LUCIAN, MAXIMIAN and JULIAN (SS) MM. R.M. Jan. 8
d. c.290. Alleged to have been missionaries from Rome martyred at Beauvais.
Cf. Att. — Baud. — Holw.

LUCIAN (St) M. R.M. May 28
See Emilius, Felix, etc.

LUCIAN (St) M. R.M. June 13
See Fortunatus and Lucian.

LUCIAN (St) M. R.M. July 7
See Peregrinus, Lucian, etc.

LUCIAN, FLORIUS and Comp. (SS) MM. R.M. Oct. 26
d. c.250. A group of martyrs who suffered at Nicomedia under Decius. Their Acts were fancifully embellished at a later date.
Cf. Att. — Baud. — Holw.

LUCIAN, METROBIUS, PAUL, ZENOBIUS, THEOTIMUS and DRUSUS (SS) MM. R.M. Dec. 24
? African martyrs who suffered at Tripoli.

LUCIDIUS (St) Bp. R.M. Apr. 26
? A bishop of Verona, famous for his life of prayer and study.
Cf. Menzies — Holw.

LUCIDUS (St) H. O.S.B. A.C. July 28
d. ? 938. Benedictine monk of St Peter's, near Aquara in S. Italy. He died as a recluse in the cell of Santa Maria del Piano. Some writers identify him with St Lyutius, a monk of Montecassino who died as a hermit at Cava (c. 1038).
Cf. Zimm.

LUCILLA, FLORA VV., EUGENE, ANTONY, THEODORE and Comp (SS) MM. R.M. July 29
d. c.260. A band of twenty-three martyrs who suffered under Gallienus. It seems that this group should be identified with the three groups commemorated on the following days: June 24 (SS Faustus, etc.), June 25 (SS Lucy and Comp.), July 6 (SS Lucy, Antoninus, etc.).
Cf. Bolland.

LUCILLA (St) V.M. R.M. Aug. 25
See Nemesius and Lucilla.

LUCILLIAN, CLAUDIUS, HYPATIUS, PAUL and DIONYSIUS (SS) MM.
R.M. June 3
d. 273. Lucillian is said to have become a Christian in his old age. He was crucified at Byzantium, and on the same occasion the four youths, mentioned above, were beheaded. Another version of the story states that Lucillian was the father, the four youths his sons, and Paula, a lady commemorated on the same day, their respective wife and mother.
Cf. Att. — Holw. — Baud.

LUCINA (three of the same name) (St)
R.M. June 30
Some modern writers affirm that there
were three Roman saints of this name.
(I) St Lucina of apostolic times, mentioned
in the (spurious) Acts of SS Processus and
Martinianus. (II) St Lucina who minis-
tered to the martyrs under Decius (250).
(III) St Lucina, connected with St Sebas-
tian and other martyrs under Diocletian.
The first is commemorated on June 30.
Cf. Holw. — Baud.

LUCINUS (LEZIN) (St) Bp. A.C. Feb. 13
d. c.618. A courtier who eventually became bishop of Angers, which see he ruled
for many years.
Cf. Duch. Fast. Episc. — Baud. — Holw.

LUCIOLUS (St) M. R.M. March 3
See Felix, Luciolus, etc.

LUCIUS (St) M. R.M. Feb. 8
See Paul, Lucius and Cyriacus, etc.

LUCIUS and Comp. (SS) MM.
R.M. Feb. 11
d. 350. Lucius, bishop of Adrianople,
played a leading part in the council of
Sardica (347). Under the protection of
Pope St Julius I, he returned to Adrianople, but refused to be in communion
with the Arian bishops condemned at
Sardica. On this account he was martyred with a group of his faithful Catholics
by order of the emperor Constantius.
Cf. Att. — Holw.

LUCIUS (St) M. R.M. Feb. 15
See Saturninus, Castulus, etc.

**LUCIUS, SILVANUS, RUTULUS, CLAS-
SICUS, SECUNDINUS, FRUCTULUS
and MAXIMUS** (SS) MM.
R.M. Feb. 18
? African martyrs, whose names Baronius
inserted in the R.M. on the authority, he
states, of reliable MSS.

LUCIUS (St) M. R.M. Feb. 24
See Montanus, Lucius, etc.

LUCIUS, ABSALOM and LORGIUS MM.
R.M. March 2
? Martyrs of Cappadocia. The spelling
of their names varies: Lucius becomes
Lucus; Lorgius, Largus; and Absalom,
Absolucius.
Cf. Holw.)

LUCIUS I (St) Pope M. R.M. March 4
d. c.254. He was pope for only eight
months. Modern hagiographers reject
the story of his martyrdom.
Cf. Att. — Holw. — Baud.

LUCIUS (St) M. R.M. Apr. 22
See Apelles, Lucius and Clement.

LUCIUS of CYRENE (St) Bp.
R.M. May 6
1st cent. One of the "prophets and doctors" mentioned as being in the church at
Antioch when Paul and Barnabas were
set apart for their apostolate (Acts XIII,
1). He is stated to have been "of Cyrene," whence the tradition that he was
the first bishop of that city in the Ptolemais (Africa).
Cf. Holw.

LUCIUS (St) M. R.M. May 23
See Quintian, Lucius and Julian.

LUCIUS and Comp. (SS) MM.
R.M. Aug. 20
d. 311. A group of martyrs who suffered
at Cyprus under Diocletian. There has
been a confusion between this Lucius and
Lucius of Cyrene (May 6).
Cf. Holw.

LUCIUS (St) Bp. M. R.M. Sept. 10
See Nemesian, Felix, etc.

LUCIUS (St) M. R.M. Oct. 4
See Caius, Faustus, etc.

LUCIUS (St) M. R.M. Oct. 19
See Ptolemy, Lucius, etc.

LUCIUS (St) M. R.M. Oct. 25
See Theodosius, Lucius, etc.

LUCIUS (St) M. R.M. Oct. 29
See Hyacinth, Quintus, etc.

**LUCIUS, ROGATUS, CASSIAN and
CANDIDA** (SS) MM. R.M. Dec. 1
? Roman martyrs.

LUCIUS (St) King. R.M. Dec. 3
d. c.200. King of Britain. According to
a tradition, first heard of in the sixth century, he asked Pope St Eleutherius
(d. c.189) to send missionaries into Britain, where he founded the dioceses of
London and Llandaff and whence he eventually set out as a missionary to the Gri-

sons in Switzerland. Present-day scholars incline to regard the whole story as fictitious.
Cf. Att. — Baud. — Holw.

LUCIUS (St) M. R.M. Dec. 15
See Faustinus, Lucius, etc.

LUCRETIA (St) V.M. R.M. March 15
Otherwise Leocritia, q.v.

LUCRETIA (St) V.M. R.M. Nov. 23
d. 306. A Spanish maiden, martyred at Mérida (Emerita) in W. Spain, under Diocletian.
Cf. P. de U. — Holw. — Baud.

LUCY (Bl) V.M. A.C. Feb. 19
1813-1862. A Chinese school-teacher beheaded at Kuy-tszheu. Beatified in 1909.
Cf. Holw.

LUCY (LUCIA) FILIPPINI (St) V.
A.C. March 25
1672-1732. Born in Tuscany, she joined Rosa Verini at Montefiascone and helped her in the work of training school-mistresses. This was the origin of the flourishing Italian institute of the *Maestre Pie*, or Filippine, of which St Lucy is venerated as the co-foundress. Canonized in 1930.
Cf. Att.

LUCY and 20 Comp. (SS) MM.
R.M. June 25
See the notice of SS Lucilla, etc., of July 29.

LUCY, ANTONINUS, SEVERINUS, DIODORUS, DION and Comp. (SS) MM.
R.M. July 6
See the notice of SS. Lucilla, etc., of July 29.

LUCY BUFALARI (Bl) V. O.S.A.
A.C. July 27
d. 1350. Born at Castel Ponziano, near Rome, a sister of Bl John of Rieti, she took the veil in the Augustinian convent of Amelia where she became prioress. She is venerated as patroness against diabolical possession. Cult confirmed in 1832.
Cf. Holw. — Att.

LUCY de FREITAS (Bl) M.
A.C. Sept. 10
d. 1622. Of Japanese birth, but married to a Portuguese, Philip de Freitas. For having given shelter to the missionaries she was burnt alive at Nagasaki on the day of the great martyrdom. Beatified in 1867.
Cf. Holw.

LUCY and GEMINIAN (SS) MM.
R.M. Sept. 16
d. c.300. A Roman widow (said to have been 75 years old) and a neophyte, who were martyred together under Diocletian. Their Acts are untrustworthy.
Cf. Holw. — Baud.

LUCY of CALTAGIRONE (Bl) V. O.F.M.
A.C. Sept. 26
d. ? 1304. Born at Caltagirone in Sicily, she became a Poor Clare at Salerno. Cult approved in 1514.
Cf. Holw. — Baud.

LUCY CHAKICHI (Bl) M. A.C. Oct. 2
d. 1622. The wife of Bl Louis Chakichi, q.v. She was beheaded with her two boys at Nagasaki. Beatified in 1867.
Cf. Holw.

LUCY of SETTEFONTI (Bl) V. O.S.B. Cam.
A.C. Nov. 7
d. 12th cent. Born at Bologna, she took the Camaldolese habit in the convent of St Christina, at Settefonti, diocese of Bologna. The Camaldolese venerate her as the foundress of their sisterhoods.
Cf. Prop. Camald. — Holw.

LUCY BROCOLELLI (Bl) V. O.P.
A.C. Nov. 15
1476-1544. Born at Narni in Umbria, after three years of virginal wedlock she was allowed by her husband to become a Dominican regular tertiary at Viterbo, where she received the *Stigmata*. In 1499 she was sent as the first prioress of the convent of Ferrara, but she proved a very incapable superior, and was deposed, treated with un-Christian cruelty by her successor, and forgotten by all. Thus she lived thirty-nine years without ever complaining. Cult confirmed in 1710.
Cf. Holw. — Att.

LUCY of SYRACUSE (St) V.M.
R.M. Dec. 13
d. 304. A Sicilian maiden who suffered at Syracuse under Diocletian. She is one of the most famous of the Western virginmartyrs, and is still daily commemorated in the canon of the Mass. Her *Acta*, however, though written before the 6th

century, are unfortunately not trustworthy.
Cf. Att. — Holw. — Baud. — Menzies.

LUDAN (LUDEN, LOUDAIN) (St) C.
A.C. Feb. 12
d. c.1202. The saint of this name honoured at Scherkirchen in Alsace is said to have been a Scottish or Irish pilgrim who died in that country on his way back from Jerusalem.
Cf. Att. — Holw.

LUDGER (St) Bp. O.S.B. R.M. March 26
d. 809. A Frisian by birth, educated under St Gregory in the abbey school of Utrecht and under Bl Alcuin in England. Returning to his fatherland as a missionary, he worked chiefly in Westphalia, of which he is the apostle. His gentleness did more to attract the Saxons to Christ than all the armies of Charlemagne. He lived for a time at Montecassino, learning the genuine Benedictine observance. He was the founder and the first bishop of Münster.
Cf. Att. — Holw. — Zimm.

LUDMILLA (St) M. A.C. Sept. 16
d. 921. Duchess of Bohemia entrusted with the education of the young prince St Wenceslaus. She fell a victim to the jealousy of her mother-in-law, by whose orders she was strangled by hired assassins at Tetin.
Cf. Att. — Baud. — Holw.

LUDOLPHUS (St) Bp. O.Praem.
A.C. March 29
d. 1250. A Premonstratensian canon who became bishop of Ratzeburg and had to endure much persecution at the hands of the Duke Albert of Sachsen-Lauenberg.
Cf. Holw. — Att. — Baud.

LUDOLPHUS (St) Ab. O.S.B.
A.C. Aug. 13
d. 983. Abbot of New Corvey in Westphalia from 971 to 983. During his abbacy there was a marked revival of the monastic school and studies.
Cf. Holw. — Baud.

LUDWIN (LEODWIN, etc.) (St) Bp. O.S.B. A.C. Sept. 29
d. 713. Born in Austrasia and educated under St Basinus, he married early in life. Left a widower, he founded the abbey of Mettlach (*Mediolacus*) and became a monk there. Later he was raised to the see of Trèves.
Cf. Holw. — Baud.

LUFTHILD (St) V. A.C. Jan. 23
d. ? 850. A saint honoured in the neighbourhood of Cologne. She is said to have lived as an anchoress in that locality.
Cf. Att. — Holw.

LUKE the YOUNGER A.C. Feb. 7
d. c.946. A Greek farm labourer who was admitted as a novice to a monastery at Athens, and eventually became a solitary on Mt Joannitza, near Corinth. He worked so many miracles in this place that it was known as *Soterion* (place of healing) and he himself as the Thaumaturgus (the wonder-worker).
Cf. Att. — Holw.

LUKE BELLUDI (Bl) C. O.F.M.
A.C. Feb. 17
1200-1285. He received the Franciscan habit from St Francis himself at Padua and became the intimate associate of St Antony of Padua, at whose death he assisted. On his own death he was laid in the empty tomb from which the body of St Antony had been taken. Cult confirmed in 1927.
Cf. Att. — Holw.

LUKE (St) M. R.M. Apr. 22
See Parmenius, Helimenes, etc.

LUKE KIRBY (Bl) M. A.C. May 30
d. 1582. Born in N. England and educated, probably, at Cambridge. After his conversion he studied for the priesthood at Rome and Douai. On his return to England as a priest (1580) he was arrested and subjected in the Tower to the terrible torture known as the "scavenger's daughter." He was finally martyred at Tyburn.
Cf. Newdigate — Holw.

LUKE BANABAKIUTU (Bl) M.
A.C. June 3
d. 1886. A Negro, baptized in 1881 and burnt alive at Namuyongo in Uganda. Beatified in 1912.
Cf. Holw.

LUKE LOAN (Bl) M. A.C. June 4
1760-1840. An old priest, native of Tonkin, beheaded for his priesthood.
Cf. Holw.

LUKE KIEMON (Bl) M.　　**A.C. Aug. 17**
d. 1627. A native of Japan, and a Franciscan tertiary, beheaded at Nagasaki. Beatified in 1867.
Cf. Holw.

LUKE MELLINI (Bl) Ab. O.S.B. Cel.
A.C. Aug. 24
d. c.1460. A Benedictine monk of the Celestine congregation. Pope Nicholas V appointed him general of the Celestines.
Cf. Zimm.

LUKE (St) M.　　**R.M. Sept. 10**
See Apelles, Luke and Clement, etc.

LUKE (St) Evangelist.　　**R.M. Oct. 18**
1st cent. A Greek of Antioch, and a physician by profession, who became the fellow worker of St Paul and remained with him till the great apostle's martyrdom. He wrote the third gospel — "St Paul's Gospel" — and the Acts of the Apostles. The later tradition that he was a painter seems to be based on the picturesque style of his narrative. There is no evidence that he died a martyr.
Cf. Att. — Holw. — Baud.

LULLUS (St) Bp. O.S.B.　　**R.M. Oct. 16**
d. 787. An Anglo-Saxon monk of Malmesbury, and a kinsman of St Boniface, whom he joined in Germany, becoming his archdeacon and chief assistant. In 751 he was sent to Rome, and on his return Boniface consecrated him regionary bishop and his coadjutor in the see of Mainz, which he ruled after his master's martyrdom.
Cf. Att. — Baud. — Holw. — Zimm.

LUNAIRE (St) Bp.　　**A.C. July 1**
Otherwise Leonorius, q.v.

LUPERCUS (St) M.　　**R.M. Apr. 16**
See Saragossa (Martyrs of).

LUPERCUS (St) M.　　**R.M. Oct. 30**
See Claudius, Lupercus and Victorius.

LUPERIUS (St) Bp.　　**R.M. Nov. 15**
6th (or 8th) cent. A bishop of Verona, of whom nothing further is known.
Cf. Holw. — Menzies.

LUPICINUS and FELIX (SS) Bps.
R.M. Feb. 3
5th cent. Described in the Martyrologies as bishops of Lyons. To St Lupicinus is

usually assigned the date 486. Nothing else is known of either saint.
Cf. Holw.

LUPICINUS (St) Ab.　　**R.M. March 21**
d. c.480. Brother of St Romanus (Feb. 28), with whom he founded the abbeys of St Claud in the Jura and Lauconne.
Cf. Att. — Holw.

LUPICINUS (St) Bp.　　**R.M. May 31**
5th cent. Bishop of Verona, described as "the most holy, the best of bishops."
Cf. Holw. — Menzies.

LUPUS (St) M.　　**R.M. Aug. 23**
? A slave who gave his life for Christ.

LUPUS of CHÂLONS (St) Bp.
A.C. Jan. 27
d. c.610. Bishop of Châlons-sur-Saône. We have a letter of St Gregory the Great addressed to him 601.
Cf. Duch. Fast. Episc. — Holw. — Baud.

LUPUS of TROYES (St) Bp.
R.M. July 29
384-478. A native of Toul who married the sister of St Hilary. After seven years husband and wife separated by mutual consent, Lupus becoming a monk at Lérins. In 426 he was made bishop of Troyes. In the course of his episcopate he accompanied St Germanus of Auxerre to Britain to rid the country of Pelagianism, and in 453 he succeeded in saving Troyes from being sacked by Attila. He died at the age of ninety-six.
Cf. Att. — Holw. — Duch. Fast. Episc.

LUPUS of Sens (St) Bp.　　**R.M. Sept. 1**
d. 623. A monk of Lérins who became bishop of Sens in 609. He was slandered and banished from his see under Clotaire, but was recalled by his own people and his cause fully vindicated.
Cf. Att. — Duch. Fast. Episc. — Holw.

LUPUS of LYONS (St) Bp.　　**R.M. Sept. 25**
d. 542. A monk of a monastery near Lyons who became archbishop of that see. He had much to suffer in the political troubles which followed the death of St Sigismund, king of Burgundy.
Cf. Holw. — Baud.

LUPUS (St) M.　　**R.M. Oct. 14**
See Saturninus and Lupus.

LUPUS of SOISSONS (St) Bp.
A.C. Oct. 19
d. c.540. A nephew of St Remigius of
Reims who became bishop of Soissons.
Cf. Holw. — Baud.

LUPUS of BAYEUX (St) Bp.
A.C. Oct. 25
5th cent. A bishop of Bayeux, said to
have ruled that diocese about the year
465.
Cf. Duch. Fast. Episc. — Holw. — Baud.

LUPUS of VERONA (St) Bp.
R.M. Dec. 2
? A bishop of Verona of whom nothing is
known save the bare name.

LUPERCULUS (LUPERCUS) (St) Bp. M.
A.C. March 1
300. A French, or Spanish, martyr under
Diocletian. He is venerated chiefly at
Tarbes, near Lourdes.
Cf. Holw. — Baud.

LUTGARD (St) V. O.S.B. Cist.
R.M. June 16
1182-1246. Born at Tongres in Brabant,
she became a Black Benedictine nun at
the age of twenty, and after some years,
in order to escape being made abbess, she
migrated to the Cistercian nunnery of
Aywières. Here she lived for thirty years
a wonderful life full of mystical experiences: she is an outstanding figure among
the women mystics of the Middle Ages.
She was blind for eleven years before her
death.
Cf. A.t. — Zimm. — Holw.

**LUXORIUS, CISELLUS and CAMER-
INUS (SS) MM.**
R.M. Aug. 21
d. c.303. Sardinian martyrs, beheaded
under Diocletian. Luxorius had been a
soldier in the imperial army; the other
two were boys whom he encouraged to
brave martyrdom.
Cf. Holw. — Menzies.

**LYBE, LEONIS and EUTROPIA (SS)
VV. MM.**
R.M. June 15
d. 303. Martyrs under Diocletian, at
Palmyra in Syria. Lybe was beheaded;
Leonis, her sister, died at the stake; and
Eutropia, a girl of twelve, was, by order
of the judge, used as a target for the sol-
diers to shoot at.
Cf. Holw. — Baud.

LYBOSUS (St) M.
R.M. Dec. 29
See Dominic, Victor, etc.

LYCARION (St) M.
R.M. June 7
? A martyr who suffered in Egypt.
Cf. Holw.

LYDIA (St) M.
R.M. March 27
See Philetus, Lydia, etc.

LYDIA PURPURARIA (St) Matron.
R.M. Aug. 3
1st cent. A native of Thyatira (now Ak-
Hissar), a city in Asia Minor famous for
its dye-works, whence Lydia's trade —
purpuraria, purple seller. She was at
Philippi in Macedonia when she became
St Paul's first convert in Europe and after-
wards his hostess (Acts XVI, 14-15).
Cf. Holw. — Baud.

LYDWINA of SCHIEDAM (Bl) V.
A.C. Apr. 14
1380-1433. In the words of her proper
office she was "a prodigy of human suffering and heroic patience." The daughter
of a labourer, at the age of sixteen she met
with an accident and became completely
bedridden. The disease increased in viru-
lence up to the moment of her death.
Through it all she was favoured by God
with mystical experiences. During the
last seven years of her life her greatest
suffering was from insomnia.
Cf. Att. — Holw. — Baud.

LYÉ (several)
Note. Both St Leo of Troyes (May 25)
and St Leo of Melun (Nov. 10) are frequently called Lié or Lyé, which is also a
French form of Laetus.

LYONS and VIENNE (Martyrs of).
R.M. June 2
See Photinus (Pothinus) and Comp.

LYTHAN (LLYTHAOTHAW) (St)
A.C. Sept. 1
? Titular saint of two Welsh churches in
the Llandaff diocese.
Cf. Holw.

LYUTIUS (St) H. O.S.B.
? A.C. July 28
See under Lucidus.

M

MABYN (St)   A.C. Sept. 21
6th cent. Welsh and Cornish saints, Mabyn, Mabon, Mabenna, are associated with St Teilo, and have originated some place-names, but nothing definite can be stated in regard to them. One of the daughters of the chieftain Brychan of Brecknock is venerated as St Mabenna; and the place-name, Ruabon (Denbighshire) perpetuates the name of another saint of similar name.
Cj. Holw.

MACAILLE (St) Bp.   A.C. Apr. 25
d. c.489. A disciple of Mel who became bishop of Croghan, Offaly. He assisted St Mel in receiving Brigid's vows. He seems to be other than his contemporary, St Maccai, also a disciple of St Patrick, venerated in the isle of Bute.
Cf. Holw.

MACANISIUS (St) Bp.   A.C. Sept. 3
d. 514. Or *Aengus Mc Nisse.* He is said to have been baptized as an infant by St Patrick, by whom he is also alleged to have been consecrated bishop. He became the abbot-founder of a monastery, probably at Kells, which grew into the diocese of Connor.
Cf. Holw.

MACARIA (St) M.   R.M. Apr. 8
See Januarius, Maxima and Macaria, martyrs in Africa. In several martyrologies they are given as SS Januarius, Maximus and Macarius.

MACARIUS the YOUNGER (St) H.
R.M. Jan. 2
d. c.408. Surnamed also "of Alexandria." He is said to have abandoned the trade of a fruiterer to become a monk in the Thebaid in Upper Egypt, c.335. Thence passing into Lower Egypt, he took up his abode in the desert of Nitria. Lucius, the intruded Arian patriarch of Alexandria, banished him on account of his unflinching orthodoxy.
Cf. Att. — Holw. — Baud.

MACARIUS the ELDER (St) H.
R.M. Jan. 15
c.300-390. Born in Upper Egypt, in his youth he retired to a solitary hut, where he combined assiduous prayer with the tending of sheep and the plaiting of bas-

kets. To escape notice he migrated to the desert of Skete, where he was promoted to the priesthood and passed the remaining 60 years of his life. His chief duty was to say daily Mass for the several thousand members of the monastic colony. He was banished for a time for having upheld the Catholic faith against the Arians.
Cf. Att. — Holw.

MACARIUS, RUFINUS, JUSTUS and THEOPHILUS (SS) MM. R.M. Feb. 28
d. c.250. Martyrs under Decius. The R.M. claims them for Rome; other martyrologies for Alexandria. They are said to have been potters by trade.
Cf. Holw. — Menzies.

MACARIUS of JERUSALEM (St) Bp.
R.M. March 10
d. c.335. Bishop of Jerusalem from 314 till his death. It is said that during his episcopate St Helen found the True Cross and that it was he who identified it. He planned Constantine's basilica of the Holy Sepulchre and of the Resurrection, which was completed before his death.
Cf. Holw. — Att. — Baud.

MACARIUS the WONDER-WORKER (St) Ab.   R.M. Apr. 1
d. 830. Abbot of Pelecete, near Constantinople. He was singled out as the special object of their persecution by the inconoclast emperors Leo the Armenian and Michael the Stammerer. After several years in prison he died in exile.
Cf. Att. — Holw. — Baud.

MACARIUS (St) M.   R.M. Apr. 8
See Macaria, above.

MACARIUS of ANTIOCH (St) Bp.
R.M. Apr. 10
d. 1012. Said to have been a native of Antioch in Pisidia and a bishop, who travelled westward as a pilgrim and was received by the Benedictines of St Bavo, Ghent, in whose hospice he died of the plague, then raging in Belgium.
Cf. Holw. — Att. — Baud.

MACARIUS (St) Bp.   R.M. June 20
d. c.350. A bishop of Petra in Palestine. He took part in the council of Sardica against the Arians, who succeeded in securing his banishment to Africa, where he died. His name was originally Arius, but he has been renamed Macarius to dis-

tinguish him from the founder of Arianism, whom Macarius opposed throughout his life.
Cf. Holw. — Baud.

MACARIUS and JULIAN (SS) MM.
R.M. Aug. 12
? Described as martyrs of Syria.

MACARIUS (St) M. R.M. Sept. 5
? 3rd cent. A soldier put to death with several companions at Melitene in Armenia.
See Eudoxius, Zeno, etc.

MACARIUS (St) M. R.M. Sept. 6
See Faustus, Macarius and Comp.

MACARIUS and Comp. (SS) MM.
R.M. Oct. 30
They seem to be identical with the group noticed under Feb. 28.

MACARIUS (St) M. R.M. Dec. 8
This Macarius also seems to be identical with those noticed under Feb. 28 and Oct. 30.

MACARIUS the SCOT (Bl) Ab. O.S.B.
A.C. Dec. 19
d. 1153. A Benedictine monk who crossed over to Würzburg from Scotland (or Ireland) and was elected first abbot of St James's monastery, founded by Bishop Embricho (1125-1146).
Cf. Holw. — Chev.

MACARIUS (St) M. R.M. Dec. 20
See Eugene and Macarius.

MACARTIN (MACARTAN, MACCARTHEN) (St) Bp. A.C. March 24
d. c.505. An early disciple and companion of St Patrick, by whom he is said to have been consecrated bishop of Clogher. His name in Irish is Aedh mac Carthin.
Cf. Holw. — Att.

MACCABEAN MARTYRS (SS)
R.M. Aug. 1
See Machabees.

MACCALDUS (St) Bp. A.C. Dec. 28
Otherwise Maughold, q.v.

MACCALLIN (MALCALLAN) Ab. O.S.B.
A.C. Jan. 21
d. 978. An Irishman who made a pilgrimage to St Fursey's shrine at Péronne, and entered the Benedictine abbey of

Gorze. Later he became a hermit and later still abbot of St Michael's monastery at Thiérache and Waulsort (Valciodorum), near Dinant, on the R. Meuse.
Cf. Holw. — Baud. — Mab. — Zimm.

MACCALLIN (MACALLAN, MACCULIN DUS) (St) Bp. A.C. Sept. 6
d. c.497. An Irish bishop of Lusk, who is venerated also in Scotland, which country he is known to have visited.
Cf. Holw.

MACDARA (St)
The saint who has given its name to St Macdaras Island off the coast of Galway.
Cf. Holw.

MACEDO (St) M. R.M. March 27
See Philetus, Lydia, etc.

MACEDONIUS (St) H. A.C. Jan. 24
d. c.340. A Syrian hermit who wandered for forty years in Syria, Phoenicia and Cilicia, living all the time on barley; hence his surname of Kriophagos "the barley-eater."
Cf. Holw. — Att. — Baud.

MACEDONIUS, PATRICIA and MODESTA (SS) MM. R.M. March 13
d. c.304. A group of three martyrs, husband, wife and daughter, whom the R.M. assigns to Nicomedia.
Cf. Holw. — Baud.

MACEDONIUS, THEODULUS and TATIAN (SS) MM. R.M. Sept. 12
d. 362. Martyrs of Phrygia, roasted alive on gridirons at Mevos for having broken into the temple and destroyed the idols during the restoration of paganism under Julian the Apostate.
Cf. Holw. — Baud.

MACHABEES (SS) MM. R.M. Aug. 1
d. 166 B.C. These are the only saints of the Old Testament liturgically venerated in the Western Church. Prominent among them were a scribe by name Eleazar, ninety years of age, and a mother with her seven sons (II Mac. 6, 7), all Jews and probably natives of Antioch, martyred under Antiochus IV Epiphanes for refusing to eat the flesh of swine forbidden by the Jewish Torah. Their relics are said to be enshrined in the church of St Peter ad vincula in Rome.
Cf. Holw. — Att. — Baud.

MACHABEO (GILDA-MARCHAI-BEO) (St) Ab. A.C. March 31
1104-1174. An Irishman, abbot of the monastery of SS Peter and Paul at Armagh from 1134 till his death.
Cf. Holw.

MACHAI (St) Ab. A.C. Apr. 11
5th cent. A disciple of St Patrick, who founded a monastery in the isle of Bute.
Cf. Holw.

MACHAN (St) Bp. A.C. Sept. 28
? A Scottish saint trained in Ireland and consecrated bishop in Rome.
Cf. Holw.

MACHAR (MACHARIUS, MOCHUMNA) (St) Bp. A.C. Nov. 12
6th cent. An Irishman by birth, he was baptized by St Colman and became a disciple of St Columba at Iona. Afterwards he was sent with twelve disciples to convert the Picts, and fixed his episcopal residence at Old Aberdeen.
Cf. Holw. — Att.

MACHUDD (MACHELL) (St) Ab. A.C. Nov. 15
7th cent. Abbot-founder of Llanfechell (Anglesey).
Cf. Holw. — Baring-Gould.

MACHUTUS (MACLOVIUS) (St) Bp. R.M. Nov. 15
Otherwise Malo, q.v.

MACKESSOG (KEGSAG) (St) A.C. March 10
Otherwise Kessog, q.v.

MACRA (St) V.M. R.M. Jan. 6
d. 287. A maiden of Reims, martyred at Fismes in Champagne under the prefect Rictiovarus, before the outbreak of the persecution under Diocletian. In art she is usually represented with a pair of pincers in her hand, in memory of one of the fiendish tortures to which she was subjected.
Cf. Holw. — Baud.

MACRINA the ELDER (St) W. R.M. Jan. 14
d. c.340. The paternal grandmother of SS Basil and Gregory of Nyssa. In her youth she had been directed by St Gregory Thaumaturgus, and during the perse-

cution of Diocletian she and her husband were forced to remain concealed for seven years or more in a hiding place on the shores of the Black Sea. They had much to suffer later under Licinius. Nevertheless they succeeded in rearing up one of the most saintly families in Cappadocia.
Cf. Att. — Holw. — Baud.

MACRINA the YOUNGER (St) V. R.M. July 19
d. c.380. Granddaughter of St Macrina the Elder (v. Jan. 14) and eldest daughter of SS Basil and Emmelia. She was one of ten children among whom were SS Basil the Great and Gregory of Nyssa. She helped her parents in the training of her younger brothers and sisters and afterwards became a nun and abbess.
Cf. Holw. — Att. — Baud.

MACRINA (St) V.M. R.M. July 20
Otherwise Margaret, q.v.

MACRINUS (St) M. R.M. Sept. 17
See Valerian, Macrinus and Gordian.

MACROBIUS (St) M. R.M. July 20
See Sabinus, Julian, etc.

MACROBIUS and JULIAN (SS) MM. R.M. Sept. 13
d. c.321. Martyrs who seem to have suffered under Licinius — Macrobius, a Cappadocian, at Tomis on the Black Sea, and Julian, a priest, in Galatia. It appears, however, that these two martyrs have been confused with those of Sept. 17, Valerian, Macrinus (Macrobius) and Gordian (Julian).
Cf. Holw. — Baud.

MACULL (St) Bp. A.C. Apr. 25
Otherwise Maughold, q.v.

MADALBERTA (St) V. O.S.B. A.C. Sept. 7
d. 706. Daughter of SS Vincent Madelgar and Waldetrudis. She was educated by her aunt, St Aldegund, the foundress of Maubeuge, where she took the veil. About the year 697 she succeeded her aunt as abbess.
Cf. Holw. — Baud. — Chev. — Zimm.

MADELEINE (several)
French form of Magdalen. See under Mary Magdalen.

MADELGISILUS (French: **MAU-GUILLE**) (St) H. O.S.B. A.C. May 30
d. c.655. An Irish monk, disciple and trusted confident of St Fursey. After some years of monastic life at St Riquier, he, together with St Pulgan, retired to a solitude, near Monstrelet, where he died. *Cf. Holw.— Att. — Baud.— Att.—Zimm.*

MADEN (MADERN, MADRON) (St) C. A.C. May 17
d. c.545. A Breton hermit of Cornish descent, to whom many churches are dedicated, the most noted being that at St Madern's Well in Cornwall, the reputed site of his hermitage. *Cf. Att. — Holw.*

MADIR (St) M. R.M. March 3
Otherwise Hemiterius, q.v.

MADOES (MADIANUS) (St) C. A.C. ? Jan. 31
? A saint who has left his name to a place in the Carse of Gowrie. Some identify him with St Modocus or Aedan of Ferns. Another tradition makes of him a fellow missionary to Scotland with St Boniface Quiritinus or Curitan, who appears to have been sent from Rome to preach in N. Britain. It seems impossible to disentangle the facts from the legendary accretions.

MADRUN (MATERIANA) (St) W. A.C. Apr. 9
5th cent. A Welsh or Cornish saint to whom some Welsh churches are dedicated. *Cf. Baring-Gould.*

MAEDHOG (AEDHAN, MOGUE) (St) Ab. A.C. Apr. 11
6th cent. An Irish abbot, whose chief monastery was at Clonmore. He was closely associated with SS Onchu and Finan. *Cf. O'Hanlon — Holw.*

MAEDOC (MODOC, AEDAN, EDAN) (St) Bp. A.C. Jan. 31
Otherwise Edan (Aidus, Aedan, Aidan) q.v.

MAEL (MAHEL) (St) C. A.C. May 13
6th cent. A disciple of St Cadfan with whom he came from Brittany into Wales. He became one of the solitaries of the isle of Bardsey. *Cf. Holw.*

MAELMUIRE (MARIANUS) (St) C. A.C. July 3
d. p. 1167. Maelmuire O'Gorman was an abbot of Knock (Louth), and is best known as a composer in Irish verse of an Irish menology. *Cf. Holw.*

MAELRHYS (St) C. A.C. Jan. 1
6th cent. A saint of the isle of Bardsey, probably a Breton by birth, venerated in N. Wales. *Cf. Holw.*

MAELRUBIUS (MAOLRUBHA) (St) C. A.C. Apr. 31
d. 724. A member of St Comgall's community at Benchor, who migrated to Iona. He afterwards founded a church at Applecross in the isle of Skye. *Cf. Holw.*

MAETHLU (AMAETHLU) (St) C. A.C. Dec. 26
6th cent. An Anglesey saint who has given his name to Llanfaethlin. *Cf. Baring-Gould.*

MAFALDA (St) N. O.S.B. Cist. A.C. May 2
1203-1252. Daughter of King Sancho II of Portugal. At the age of twelve she was married to King Henry I of Castile, but her marriage was declared null by the Holy See on account of consanguinity. She at once entered the Cistercian nunnery of Arouca in Portugal and there professed the Benedictine Rule. Cult, as a saint, approved in 1793. *Cf. P. de U. — Att. — Baud. — Holw. — Zimm.*

MAGDALEN (*several*)
See under Mary Magdalen.

MAGDALVEUS (MADALVEUS, MAUVÉ) (St) Bp. O.S.B. A.C. Oct. 5
d. c.776. Born at Verdun, he became a monk of St Vannes, and afterwards (c.736) bishop of his native city. *Cf. Duch. Fast. Episc. — Holw. — Baud.*

MAGENULPUS (St) C. A.C. Oct. 5
Otherwise Meinuph, q.v.

MAGI (Three Holy Kings): BALTHASSAR, CASPAR (GASPAR) and **MELCHIOR** (SS) A.C. Jan. 6
1st cent. According to a very ancient,

though not altogether constant tradition the Wise Men from the East were three in number (Matt. II). The idea, traced back to the sixth century, that they were kings was almost certainly suggested by the passage in the psalm: "The kings of Tharsis and the islands shall offer presents; the kings of the Arabians and of Saba shall bring gifts." Names were attributed to them as early as the eighth century. A magnificent medieval shrine in Cologne cathedral contains their reputed bones.
Cf. Holw. — Baud. — Att.

MAGINA (St) M. R.M. Dec. 3
See Claudius, Crispinus, etc.

MAGINUS (Catalan: MAGÍ) (St) M.
R.M. Aug. 25
d. c.304. Born at Tarragona, in Spain, he evangelized the people of the *Montes Brufagani* near his native city, and was finally beheaded under Diocletian.
Cf. Holw. — Baud.

MAGLORIUS (St) Bp. R.M. Oct. 24
d. c.586. Maglorius, or Maelor, was born in S. Wales and educated under St Illtyd. He was a kinsman of St Samson, with whom he crossed over to Brittany, where they became abbots of two monasteries, St Samson of Dol and St Maglorius of Lammeur. St Samson became moreover bishop of Dol, and on his death he is said to have been succeeded by St Maglorius, who finally retired to the Channel Islands and built an abbey on Sark, where he died.
Cf. Att. — Baud. — Holw.

MAGNERICUS (St) Bp. R.M. July 25
d. 596. Of Frankish descent, he was the first of his race to be raised to the see of Trèves (c.566). He was an intimate friend of St Gregory of Tours, and one of the most illustrious of the prelates of his time.
Cf. Att. — Holw. — Baud.

MAGNOALDUS (St) Ab. A.C. Sept. 6
Otherwise Magnus, q.v.

MAGNOBODUS (MAINBOEUF) (St) Bp. A.C. Oct. 16
d. c.670. A Frank of noble birth, appointed at the demand of the people bishop of Angers.
Cf. Holw. — Baud.

MAGNUS (St) M. R.M. Jan. 1
A martyr mentioned in the R.M., of whom nothing is known.

MAGNUS (MANNUS) (St) M.
R.M. Feb. 4
See Aquilinus, Geminus, etc.

MAGNUS (St) M. R.M. Feb. 15
See Saturninus, Castulus, etc.

MAGNUS (St) M. A.C. Apr. 16
d. 1116. A native of the Orkneys, over which he was set as governor by the king of Norway, the then overlord of the islands. When his life was threatened by conspirators, he escaped to the court of Scotland, where he gave himself up to a life of penance. In the end he was murdered by his cousin Hakon for political reasons, but has nevertheless been always venerated as a martyr.
Cf. Att. — Holw.

MAGNUS (St) M. R.M. Aug. 6
See Sixtus and Comp.

MAGNUS of ANAGNI (St) Bp. M.
R.M. Aug. 19
d. c.250. In the R.M. he is described as a bishop martyred under Decius. Actually he seems to be a duplicate of St Andrew the Tribune (Aug. 19), surnamed by the Greeks "the Megalomartyr" and listed in the martyrologies as *Andreas Tribunus Magnus Martyr.* Apparently a scribe put a comma after *Tribunus,* and thus made one martyr into two.
Cf. Holw. — Baud. — Menzies.

MAGNUS (St) Bp. O.S.B. A.C. Aug. 19
d. 660. Born at Avignon, he was appointed governor of the city. After his wife's death he joined the monks of Lérins, whither his son St Agricola had preceded him. In 656 he was raised to the see of Avignon.
Cf. Holw. — Baud. — Duch. Fast. Episc. — Gams.

MAGNUS, CASTUS and MAXIMUS (SS) MM. R.M. Sept. 4
? They probably belong to the group of 17 martyrs (SS Rufinus and Comp.) put to death at Ancyra in Galatia. Their names seem to have been separated from the remainder of the group, whose entry occurs on the same day.
Cf. Holw. — Baud.

MAGNUS (MAGNOALDUS, MAGI-NOLD, MANG, etc.) (St) Ab. O.S.B.
A.C. Sept. 6
d. c.666. A fellow-missionary with the Irish saints Columbanus and Gall. He became the abbot-founder of Füssen in Bavaria.
Cf. Zimm. — Baud. — Holw.

MAGNUS (St) Bp. R.M. Oct. 6
d. c.660. A Venetian born, who became bishop of Oderzo in the province of Treviso, on the Adriatic. In 638, owing to the incursions of the Lombards, he transferred his see to Citta Nuova, then called Heraclea in honour of the emperor Heraclius.
Cf. Menzies — Baud. — Holw.

MAGNUS (St) Bp. R.M. Nov. 5
d. 525. Archbishop of Milan from c.520 to 525. Little further is known about him.
Cf. Menzies — Holw. — Baud.

MAGUIL (St) A.C. May 30
Otherwise Madelgisilus, q.v.

MAHARSAPOR (St) M. A.C. Oct. 10
d. 421. A Persian who was martyred under Varanes V. After a three years' imprisonment he was thrown into a pit and left to die of starvation.
Cf. Holw. — Att. — Baud.

MAIDOC (MADOC) (St) Bp.
A.C. Feb. 28
There are several Welsh and Irish saints of this name. Hardy gives the following variants: Aidnus, Aidan, Edan, Aldus, Edus, Eda, Maidoc, Maedoc, Modoc, Modog, Moedoc, Moeg, Mogue, Madog. The best known saints of this name are St Edan of Ferns (Jan. 31) and St Aidan of Lindisfarne (Aug. 31). The St Maidoc assigned to Feb. 28 may be the sixth century abbot-bishop after whom Llanmadog in Glarmorganshire is called.

MAIDOC (MO-MHAEDOG) (St) Ab.
A.C. March 23
5th cent. An Irish abbot of Fiddown in Kilkenny.
Cf. O' Hanlon.

MAILDULF (St) Ab. A.C. May 17
d. 673. An Irishman by birth who came to England and founded the great abbey of Malmesbury, where he had St Aldhelm among his disciples, and where he ended his days.
Cf. Holw. — Baud.

MAIMBOD (St) M. A.C. Jan. 23
d. c.880. An Irish missionary who was put to death by pagans while evangelizing the country people near Kaltenbrunn in Alsace, diocese of Besançon.
Cf. Att. — Holw. — Baud.

MAINE (MEVENUS, MEWAN, MEEN) (St) C. A.C. June 21
d. 617. A Welsh or Cornish disciple of St Samson, whom he accompanied to Brittany. He founded there the monastery since known as Saint-Méon. He died at a great age.
Cf. Holw. — Baud.

MAJOLUS (French: MAIEUL) (St) Ab. O.S.B. R.M. May 11
c.906-994. Born at Avignon, he studied at Lyons and while still very young he was chosen archdeacon of Mâcon. He was offered the see of Besançon, but he fled instead to Cluny and became a monk there, and shortly after, in 954, was made abbot-coadjutor to St Aimard. In 965 he succeeded as the head of the Cluniac congregation, which under him grew and spread throughout W. Europe. He was the friend of emperors and popes and several times refused the tiara. He died at Souvigny.
Cf. Zimm. — Att. — Holw.

MAJORICUS (St) M. R.M. Dec. 6
d. c.490. The son of St Dionysia, who encouraged him to suffer martyrdom and buried him in her own house. The martyrdom took place in Africa under the Arian Hunneric the Vandal.
Cf. Holw. — Baud.

MALACHY (St) Prophet. R.M. Jan. 14
5th cent. b. c. The last of the twelve Minor Prophets. The tradition is that he was a native of Sapha. The Jews erroneously identify him with Esdras (Ezra).
Cf. Holw. — Baud.

MALACHY O'MORE (St) Bp.
R.M. Nov. 3
1095-1148. Maolmhaodhog ua Morgair was born at Armagh and ordained priest by St Celsus. He was successively vicar general to St Celsus, abbot of Bangor,

bishop of Connor and archbishop of Armagh (1132). He worked zealously to restore ecclesiastical discipline and succeeded in superseding once and for all the Celtic liturgy by the Roman. In 1138 he resigned the primatial see and made a pilgrimage to Rome, staying for a while at Clairvaux, then at the acme of its fame under St Bernard. He wished to remain a monk there, but this was not allowed by the pope. Instead he left at Clairvaux several young Irishmen who four years later were the pioneer monks of Mellifont abbey in Ireland. He made a second pilgrimage to Rome and on his way back died at Clairvaux in St Bernard's arms. He was formally canonized in 1190. The "prophecies of the popes" attributed to him were first found in Rome in 1590 — that is, over four centuries after his death. *Cf. Zimm. — Att. — Holw.*

MALARD (St) Bp. A.C. Jan. 15
d. p. 650. A bishop of Chartres who took part in the council of Châlon-sur-Saône. (650).
Cf. Duch. Fast. Episc. — Att. — Baud. — Holw.

MALCHUS (St) M. R.M. March 28
See Priscus, Malchus and Alexander.

MALCHUS (St) Bp. O.S.B. A.C. Apr. 10
d. 1110. An Irishman who became a monk of Winchester in England and was consecrated by St Anselm first bishop of Waterford. He was one of the preceptors of St Malachy O'More. His life has been confused with those of several among his contemporaries.
Cf. Holw. — Baud. — Zimm. — Gams — Butler-Thurston (Nov. 3).

MALCHUS (St) R.M. July 27
One of the Seven Sleepers, q.v.

MALCHUS (St) H. R.M. Oct. 21
d. c.390. A Syrian monk at Chalcis near Antioch. After about twenty years of monastic life he was kidnapped by the Bedouins, who sold him for a slave. He was given an already married woman to wife, but they lived as brother and sister. After some seven years of bondage they succeeded in escaping together and Malchus returned to his monastery. St Jerome knew him there and wrote his life.
Cf. Att. — Baud. — Holw.

MALCOLDIA (Bl) H. O.S.B.
A.C. March 15
d. c.1090. Benedictine nun and then a recluse near the abbey church of St Anastasia, at Asti.
Cf. Zimm.

MALO (MACHUTIS, MACLOU) (St) Bp.
R.M. Nov. 15
d. 621. A Welshman who became a monk at Llancarfan and eventually migrated to Brittany with a band of Welsh missionaries. He settled at a place called Alethnow St Malo — of which he is recognized as the first bishop. For a time he was banished and resided at Saintes.
Cf. Holw. — Baud. — Att.

MALRUBIUS (St) M. A.C. Aug. 27
d. c.1040. An anchorite in Merns (Kincardineshire) Scotland. He was martyred by Norwegian invaders.
Cf. Holw.

MAMAS (MAMMAS, MAMANS) (St) M. R.M. Aug. 17
d. c.275. A shepherd of Caesarea in Cappadocia, martyred under Aurelian. He is greatly venerated throughout the East. His *Acta* are not reliable.
Cf. Holw. — Att. — Baud.

MAMELTA (St) M. R.M. Oct. 17
d. c.344. Said to have been a heathen priestess at Bethfarme in Persia, who, on being converted to Christ, was stoned and finally drowned in a lake.
Cf. Holw. — Baud.

MAMERTINUS (St) Bp. A.C. March 30
d. c.462. A monk, and then abbot, of St Cosmas and Damian at Auxerre in France.
Cf. Holw. — Baud.

MAMERTUS (MAMMERTUS) (St) Bp.
R.M. May 11
d. 475. Archbishop of Vienne, 461-475. He is best remembered as the originator of the Rogation Days before the Ascension, which he established in his diocese in consequence of the many calamities which afflicted his people.
Cf. Holw. — Att. — Baud. — Duch. Fast. Episc.

MAMILIAN (MAXIMILIAN) (St) M.
R.M. March 12
? A Roman martyr, of whom nothing definite is known.

MAMILIAN (St) Bp.   A.C. Sept. 15
d. 460. A bishop of Palermo in Sicily, said to have been exiled to Tuscany by the Arian king Genseric. His relics were eventually taken back to Palermo.
Cf. Menzies — Holw.

MAMILLUS (St) M.   R.M. March 8
See Cyril, Rogatus, etc.

MAMMEA (St) M.   R.M. Aug. 27
Otherwise Mannea, q.v. with Marcellinus.

MANAHEN (St) Prophet.   R.M. May 24
1st century. Mentioned in the Acts of the Apostles (XIII, 1) as the foster-brother of King Herod Antipas and as a prophet. He is supposed to have died at Antioch in Syria.
Cf. Holw. — Baud.

MANAKUS (MANACCUS) (St) Ab.
A.C. Oct. 14
6th cent. A Welshman, abbot of Holyhead, connected with St Cuby. He appears to have died in Cornwall. Manaccan (Minster), near Falmouth, is said to owe its name to him.
Cf. Baring-Gould.

MANCIUS (St)   R.M. March 15
5th (or 6th ?) cent. Of Roman origin, he appears to have been bought as a slave by Jewish traders and taken to Evora in Portugal, where he was martyred by his masters.
Cf. Holw. — Baud.

MANCIUS ARAKI (Bl) M.   A.C. July 8
d. 1626. A Japanese layman, brother of Bl Matthew Araki. For giving shelter to the missionaries he was imprisoned at Omura, where he died of consumption. His body was burnt at Nagasaki (July 12). Beatified in 1869.
Cf. Holw.

MANCIUS of the HOLY CROSS (Bl) M. O.P.   A.C. July 29
d. 1627. An aged catechist, burnt alive at Omura with Bl Louis Bertrán. Beatified in 1867.
Cf. Holw.

MANCIUS of ST THOMAS (Bl) M. O.P.   A.C. Sept. 12
d. 1622. A Japanese catechist imprisoned and burnt alive with Bl Thomas Zumárraga and companions at Omura. Beatified in 1867.
Cf. Holw.

MANCIUS XIZIZOIEMON (Bl) M.
A.C. Sept. 25
d. 1630. A native of Japan, and a tertiary of St Augustine, beheaded at Nagasaki. Beatified in 1867.
Cf. Holw.

MANCUS (St)   A.C. May 31
See Winnow, Mancus and Myrbad.

MANDAL (St) M.   R.M. June 10
See Basilides, Tripos, etc.

MANEHILDIS (MÉNÉHOULD) (St) V.
A.C. Oct. 14
d. c.490. Born at Perthois, she was the youngest of seven sisters, all of whom are honoured as saints in different parts of Champagne. She is the patroness of Sainte-Ménéhould on the R. Aisne.
Cf. Holw. — Att. — Baud.

MANETTUS (MANETIUS, MANETTO) (St) C. O.S.M.
R.M. Aug. 20 and Feb. 12
d. 1268. Benedict dell' Antella was a Florentine merchant who became one of the seven founders of the Servite Order, q.v. From provincial of Tuscany he became general of the Order. In 1246 he attended the council of Lyons, and at the request of St Louis introduced the Order into France. He resigned his generalate to St Philip Benizi and retired to Monte Senario, where he died in the following year.
Cf. Holw. — Baud.

MANEZ (MANNES, MANES) (Bl) C. O.P.   A.C. July 30
d. 1230. Manez de Guzmán, an elder brother of St Dominic, was born at Calaruega. He joined the original sixteen members of the Order of Preachers in 1216 and later was prior of St James's in Paris, and the founder of a convent for nuns at Madrid. Cult approved in 1834.
Cf. Att. — Holw. — Prop. O.P.

MANIRUS (St) Bp.   A.C. Dec. 19
? One of the apostles of N. Scotland. His work seems chiefly to have been the promoting of good feeling and union among the newly converted Highlanders.
Cf. Holw. — Baud.

MANNEA (St) M.　　**R.M. Aug. 27**
See Marcellinus, Mannea, etc.

MANNUS (St) M.　　**R.M. Feb. 4**
Otherwise Magnus, q.v.

MANSUETUS (St) Bp.　**R.M. Feb. 19**
d. c.690. A Roman by birth, he was appointed to the see of Milan (c.627) and ruled it with vigour and wisdom. He wrote a treatise against the Monothelites.
Cf. Holw. — Menzies — Baud.

MANSUETUS (MANSUY) (St) Bp.
　　　　　　　　R.M. Sept. 3
d. c.350. Bishop of Toul in France (c.338-c.350). His biography as it has come down to us is full of fictitious matter.
Cf. Holw. — Baud.

MANSUETUS (St) M.　　**R.M. Sept. 6**
See Donatian, Praesidius, etc.

MANSUETUS (St) Bp. M. R.M. Nov. 28
See Papinian and Mansuetus.

MANSUETUS, SEVERUS, APPIAN, DONATUS, HONORIUS and Comp. (SS) MM.　　　　　**R.M. Dec. 30**
d. c.483. A group of ten martyrs, who suffered at Alexandria in connection with the troubles raised by the Monophysites.
Cf. Holw. — Baud.

MANUEL (*several*)
The Spanish, Portuguese and Catalan form of Emmanuel, q.v.

MANUEL, SABEL and ISMAEL (SS) MM.　　　　　　**R.M. June 17**
d. 362. Persian magnates sent to negotiate for peace with Julian the Apostate at Chalcedon. The tradition is that Julian, finding that they were Christians, had them beheaded. Theodosius the Great dedicated a church in their honour near Byzantium.
Cf. Holw. — Baud.

MAOLRUAIN (St) Ab.　　**A.C. July 7**
d. 792. Abbot-founder of the monastery of Tallaght in Ireland and compiler of the martyrology named after that place.
Cf. Holw.

MAPPALICUS and Comp. (SS) MM.
　　　　　　　　R.M. Apr. 17
d. 250. African martyrs who suffered at Carthage under Decius. They are highly praised by St Cyprian.
Cf. Holw. — Att. — Baud.

MAPRILIS (St) M.　　**R.M. Aug. 22**
See Martial, Saturninus, etc.

MARANA and CYRA (SS) MM.
　　　　　　　　R.M. Aug. 3
5th cent. Two maidens who embraced the eremitical life near Beroea in Syria. It is recorded of them that they observed continuous silence throughout the year except on Whit Sunday.
Cf. Holw. — Baud.

MARCELLA (St) W.　　**R.M. Jan. 31**
d. 410. She belonged to the nobility of Rome, and after the early death of her husband turned her house into a sort of "retreat" for ladies of the aristocracy. St Jerome was her guest for three years and under his direction she devoted herself to the study of the Bible, to prayer and to alms-deeds. When Alaric sacked Rome, Marcella was cruelly scourged for concealing, as the Goths thought, her wealth, which she had already distributed to the poor. She died from the effects of this treatment shortly after.
Cf. Att. — Holw. — Baud. — Menzies.

MARCELLA (St) M.　　**R.M. June 28**
See Plutarch, Serenus, etc.

MARCELLIAN (St) M.　　**R.M. June 18**
See Mark and Marcellian.

MARCELLIAN (St) M.　　**R.M. Aug. 9**
See Secundian, Marcellian and Verian.

MARCELLINA (St) V.　　**R.M. July 17**
d. c.398. Born in Rome, the elder sister of St Ambrose of Milan and of St Satyrus. She received the veil of a consecrated virgin from the hands of Pope Liberius on Christmas day, 353. She outlived both her brothers. Her remains are enshrined at Milan.
Cf. Holw. — Baud. — Menzies.

MARCELLINUS (St) M.　　**R.M. Jan. 2**
See Argeus, Narcissus and Marcellinus.

MARCELLINUS of ANCONA (St)
　　　　　　　　R.M. Jan. 9
d. c.566. A native of Ancona, who was promoted to that see c.550. He is mentioned by St Gregory the Great.
Cf. Menzies — Holw.

MARCELLINUS (St) M.   R.M. Apr. 6
d. 413. Marcellinus was the imperial representative in Africa at the time of the Donatist disturbances. He and his brother the judge Agrarius endeavoured to enforce the decisions of a conference at Carthage against those heretics, but the Donatists resorted to false accusation, and the two brothers were put to death without even the formality of a trial. St Augustine was an intimate friend of Marcellinus, to whom the holy Doctor dedicated his masterpiece *"De civitate Dei"*. *Cf. Att. — Holw. — Baud.*

MARCELLINUS, VINCENT and DOMNINUS (SS)   R.M. Apr. 20
d. c.374. African missionaries who crossed over to Gaul and preached in Dauphiné. St Marcellinus was consecrated first bishop of Embrun by St Eusebius of Vercelli. The relics of the three saints are venerated at Digne, in the Alps of Savoy. *Cf. Att. — Holw. — Baud. — Duch. Fast. Episc.*

MARCELLINUS (St) Pope M.
R.M. Apr. 26 (and Oct. 25)
d. 304. A native of Rome, he was pope from 296 to his death, during the persecution under Diocletian. It seems to be the fact that Marcellinus was guilty of some personal weakness during the persecution, though the story of his lapse as told in the Roman Breviary up to the year 1883 is now discredited. He certainly died a good death, in all probability as a martyr. St Marcellinus is mentioned a second time in the R.M. on Oct. 25. *Cf. Att. — Baud. — Menzies — Holw.*

MARCELLINUS and PETER (SS) MM.
R.M. June 2
d. 304. Marcellinus was a priest and Peter probably an exorcist, both belonging to the Roman clergy. Although their extant Acts are unreliable, these two martyrs were certainly greatly venerated by the Romans, since their names occur in the canon of the Latin Mass and Constantine built a basilica over their tombs. *Cf. Att. — Holw. — Menzies.*

MARCELLINUS (St) M.   R.M. June 5
See Florentius, Julian, etc.

MARCELLINUS (or MARCELLIANUS) (St) M.   R.M. June 18
See Mark and Marcellianus.

MARCELLINUS (MARCHELM, MARCULF) (St) C.   R.M. July 14
d. c.762. An Anglo-Saxon who followed St Willibrord to Holland. Together with St Lebuin he preached the gospel to the people of Over-Yssel. In 738 he accompanied St Boniface to Rome. He died at Oldensee (Oldenzeel), but his remains were transferred to Deventer. *Cf. Holw.*

MARCELLINUS (or MARCELLUS), MANNEA, JOHN, SERAPION, PETER and Comp. (SS) MM.   R.M. Aug. 27
d. c.303. According to their authentic *Acta*, Marcellinus, a tribune, with his wife Mannea, his three sons, John, Serapion and Peter, a bishop, three clerics, eight laymen and another woman, that is the entire Christian congregation of a small place, now said to be Oxyrinchus, in Egypt, were taken to Thmuis and beheaded. Marcellinus is often known as Marcellus. *Cf. Att. — Holw.*

MARCELLINUS of RAVENNA (St) Bp.
R.M. Oct. 5
3rd cent. The second or third bishop of Ravenna, said to have occupied that see in the second half of the third century. *Cf. Holw.*

MARCELLINUS, CLAUDIUS, CYRINUS (QUIRINUS) and ANTONINUS (SS) MM.   R.M. Oct. 25
d. 304. Claudius, Cyrinus and Antoninus are named on this day as having been beheaded together with Pope St Marcellinus. See April 26.

MARCELLUS (St) Pope M.
R.M. Jan. 16
d. 309. St Marcellus was pope for one year only (308-309). He seems to have suffered much in the persecution of Diocletian, but not to have died a martyr. The story of his having been forced to work as a slave in the stables seems to be legendary. *Cf. Att. — Baud. — Holw. — Menzies.*

MARCELLUS (St) M.   R.M. Feb. 19
See Publius, Julian, etc.

MARCELLUS (St) Bp.   R.M. Apr. 9
d. 474. A native of Avignon, he was educated by his own brother St Petronius, bishop of Die (not of Saint-Dié), whom he

succeeded in the see, being consecrated by
St Mamertus, bishop of Vienne. He
suffered much from the Arians, and died
after a long episcopate.
Cf. Holw. — Baud. — Duch. Fast. Episc.

**MARCELLUS and ANASTASIUS (SS)
MM.** R.M. June 29
d. 274. Roman missionaries sent into
Gaul to preach the gospel. They were put
to death in the neighbourhood of Bourges.
Marcellus was beheaded and Anastasius
scourged to death.
Cf. Holw. — Baud.

MARCELLUS (St) Bp. M. R.M. Aug. 14
d. 389. A native of Cyprus, who from
being a conscientious civil magistrate was
elected to the see of Apamoea in Syria.
While supervising the destruction of a
pagan shrine, at Aulona, in accordance
with the edict of Theodosius the Great,
he was attacked and murdered by the mob.
Cf. Att. — Holw.

MARCELLUS (St) M. R.M. Aug. 27
Otherwise Marcellinus, q.v.

MARCELLUS (St) M. R.M. Sept. 4
d. c.178. A priest of Lyons who escaped
from prison and, being again arrested, was
buried up to the waist on the banks of the
Saône and left to die. It is said that he
survived three days.
Cf. Holw. — Att. — Baud.

MARCELLUS (St) Bp. M. R.M. Sept. 4
? A bishop of Trèves (or of Tongres) listed
in the R.M. His name seems to have been
invented in the tenth century.
Cf. Holw.

MARCELLUS (St) Mk. O.S.B.
P.C. Sept. 27
d. c.869(?) An Irishman (or Scot) by
birth, he became a monk at St Gall in
Switzerland and is best known as the tutor
of Bl Notker Balbulus.
Cf. Holw.

**MARCELLUS, CASTUS, AEMILIUS and
SATURNINUS (SS) MM. R.M. Oct. 6**
? Martyrs of Capua, of whom no par-
ticulars are extant.

MARCELLUS and APULEIUS (SS) MM.
R.M. Oct. 7
? Apocryphal saints perhaps to be identi-
fied with Niceta and Aquilina, q.v.
Cf. Holw.

MARCELLUS (St) M. R.M. Oct. 30
d. 298. A centurian of the Roman army
stationed at Tangier. During a festival
in honour of the birthday of the emperor he
refused to join in the celebrations, threw
away his arms and insignia and declared
himself a Christian. The notary, who refused to write the official report of the case
and who was in consequence martyred, was
St Cassian (v. Dec. 3). The *Acta* of St
Marcellus are quite reliable.
Cf. Att. — Holw. — Baud.

MARCELLUS (St) Bp. R.M. Nov. 1
d. c.430. A bishop of Paris, who was buried in the old Christian cemetery outside
the walls of the city, where now is the
suburb of Saint-Marceau.
Cf. Att. — Duch. Fast. Episc. — Holw.

MARCELLUS (St) M. R.M. Nov. 16
See Elpidius, Marcellus, etc.

MARCELLUS (St) M. R.M. Nov. 26
d. 349. A priest of Nicomedia, in Asia
Minor, who during the reign of the emperor Constantius was seized by the Arians and killed by being hurled from a
high rock.
Cf. Holw.

MARCELLUS (St) M. R.M. Dec. 2
See Eusebius, Marcellus, etc.

MARCELLUS (St) Ab. R.M. Dec. 29
d. c.485. Surnamed "Akimetes" the
"non-rester." A native of Apamea in
Syria, who joined the monks called *Akimetes*, because they recited the divine office
in relays throughout the day and night.
He became the third abbot of their chief
abbey at Constantinople, and under his
rule the *Akimetes* grew in number and
influence. He was present at the council
of Chalcedon.
Cf. Att. — Holw.

MARCELLUS (St) M. R.M. Dec. 30
See Sabinus, Exuperantius, etc.

MARCHELM (St) R.M. July 14
Otherwise Marcellinus, q.v.

MARCIA (St) M. R.M. March 3
See Felix, Luciolus, etc.

MARCIA (St) M. R.M. June 5
See Zenais, Cyria, etc.

MARCIA (St) M. R.M. July 2
See Ariston, Crescentian, etc.

MARCIAN (St) M. R.M. Jan. 4
See Aquilinus, Geminus, etc.

MARCIAN (St) C. R.M. Jan. 10
d. c.480. A native of Constantinople, though connected with a Roman family. He was ordained priest and appointed treasurer of the church of St Sophia. In this capacity he superintended the building of several churches, notably of that of the Anastasis. He was wrongly suspected of Novatianism and had to suffer much on this account.
Cf. Holw. — Att. — Baud.

MARCIAN (St) Bp. R.M. March 6
d. 120. Said to have been a disciple of St Barnabas and first bishop of Tortona in Piedmont, where he is alleged to have been martyred under Hadrian, after an episcopate of forty-five years.
Cf. Holw. — Baud. — Menzies.

MARCIAN (St) M. R.M. March 26
See Peter, Marcian, etc.

MARCIAN (St) M. R.M. Apr. 17
See Fortunatus and Marcian.

MARCIAN of AUXERRÉ (St) Mk.
R.M. Apr. 20
d. c.470. A native of Bourges, of humble birth, who was admitted as a lay-brother into the abbey of St Germanus at Auxerre. There he discharged menial duties and had charge of the cattle of the abbey.
Cf. Holw. — Baud.

MARCIAN of RAVENNA (St) Bp.
R.M. May 22
d. c.127. The fourth bishop of Ravenna, where he is known as San Mariano. He ruled the diocese from c.112 to c.127.
Cf. Holw. — Menzies — Baud.

MARCIAN, NICANOR, APOLLONIUS and Comp. (SS) MM. R.M. June 5
d. c.304. According to the R.M. they were a group of Egyptian martyrs who suffered under Diocletian. Their Acts are, however, quite unreliable. It is more probable that Marcian and Nicander (not Nicanor) were soldiers in the Roman army, who suffered either in Bulgaria or Rumania.
Cf. Holw. — Att.

MARCIAN of SYRACUSE (St) Bp. M.
R.M. June 14
d. c.255. Said to have been "the first bishop of the West," having been, according to the Sicilian legend, sent to Syracuse by St Peter himself. It is more likely that Marcian was sent to Sicily by a pope of the third century. He is said to have been thrown from a tower by the Jews.
Cf. Holw. — Menzies — Baud.

MARCIAN (St) M. R.M. June 17
See Nicander and Marcian (a duplicate of the martyrs listed under June 5).

MARCIAN (St) Bp. A.C. June 30
d. c.757. Bishop of Pampeluna, in Spanish Navarre. He signed the decrees of the sixth council of Toledo in 737.
Cf. Holw. — Baud.

MARCIAN (St) M. R.M. July 11
d. 243. A youth martyred at Iconium in Lycaonia. He is specially notable for his courage in confessing Christ.
Cf. Holw. — Baud.

MARCIAN (St) M. R.M. Aug. 9
See Julian, Marcian, etc.

MARCIAN of SAIGNON (St) Ab. O.S.B.
A.C. Aug. 25
d. 1010. Born at Saignon (Vaucluse) he became the abbot-founder of St Eusebius at Apt, diocese of Avignon.
Cf. Mab. — Holw. — Baud.

MARCIAN (St) M. R.M. Sept. 16
See Abundius, Abundantius, etc.

MARCIAN (St) M. R.M. Oct. 4
See Mark, Marcian, etc.

MARCIAN (St) M. R.M. Oct. 25
See Martyrius and Marcian.

MARCIAN (St) H. R.M. Nov. 2
d. 387. He left the emperor's court and gave up a brilliant military career in order to lead the solitary life in the desert of Chalcis. He had several illustrious disciples.
Cf. Holw. — Baud.

MARCIANA (St) V.M. R.M. Jan. 9
d. c.303. A maiden of Mauritania, accused of having shattered a statue of the goddess Diana and thrown to the wild beasts in the amphitheatre, where she was

gored to death by a bull. The Mozarabic office has a special hymn in her honour.
Cf. Att. — Baud. — Holw.

MARCIANA (St) M.   **R.M. May 24**
See Susanna, Marciana, etc.

MARCIANA (St) V.M.   **R.M. July 12**
d. c.303. The R.M. assigns this virgin-martyr to Toledo in Spain, but she is almost certainly identical with St Marciana of Mauretania (v. Jan. 9).
Cf. Holw. — Baud.

MARCIONILLA (St) M.   **R.M. Jan. 9**
See Julian, Basilissa, etc.

MARCIUS (MARK, MARTIN) H. O.S.B.
    R.M. Oct. 24
d. c.679. An Italian hermit at Montecassino, mentioned by St Gregory the Great in the life of St Benedict. The Cassinese tradition adds that Marcius (or Martin) became a monk at the abbey and then retired into a cave on Mount Massicus (Mondragone) where he died.
Cf. Holw. — Baud.

MARCOLINO of FORLÌ (Bl) C. O.P.
    A.C. Jan. 24
1317-1397 (Jan. 2). Marcolino Amanni was born at Forlì and became a Dominican in his early years. He was a model religious, but it was only after his death that his brethren realized his heroic sanctity. Cult confirmed in 1750.
Cf. Menzies — Holw. — Att. — Baud.

MARCULFUS (St) Ab.   **A.C. May 1**
d. 558. The abbot-founder of a monastery of hermit-monks, on the Egyptian model, at Nanteuil. His relics were in 898 enshrined at Corbigny, diocese of Laon, and thither the kings of France resorted after their coronation. After touching the relics of the saint they healed those afflicted with "the king's evil" (scrofula).
Cf. Holw. — Att. — Baud.

MARD (St) Bp.   **R.M. June 8**
Otherwise Medard, q.v.

MARDARIUS (St) M.   **R.M. Dec. 13**
See Eustratius, Auxentius, etc.

MARDONIUS, MUSONIUS, EUGENE and METELLUS (SS) MM. R.M. Jan. 24

d. ? 305. Four martyrs burnt at the stake somewhere in Asia Minor.
Cf. Holw.

MARDONIUS (St) M.   **R.M. Dec. 23**
See Migdonius and Mardonius.

MAREAS (St) Bp. M.   **R.M. Apr. 22**
d. 342. A Persian bishop martyred under King Shapur II. Together with him there suffered twenty-one other bishops, nearly two hundred and fifty clerics, many monks and nuns, and a great number of lay people. The church of Persia was brought to the verge of extinction.
Cf. Holw. — Baud.

MARGARET (*several*)
Note. The Latin, Spanish, Portuguese and Catalan form of this name is Margarita; the Italian Margherita and the French Marguerite. There are numerous dimunitives of the same name in all languages.

MARGARET of RAVENNA (Bl) V.
    P.C. Jan. 23
d. 1505. Born at Russi, near Ravenna, Margaret was from her youth almost blind and suffered much from want of sympathy on the part of those around her; nevertheless in course of time she gained many friends by her patience and humility. With the help of a priest she formed a religious association of persons living in the world, but this did not survive her. Her cult has never been officially confirmed.
Cf. Bolland. — Att. — Holw. — Menzies.

MARGARET of HUNGARY (Bl) V. O.P.
    A.C. Jan. 26
d. 1270. Daughter of Bela IV, king of Hungary. She founded a convent for Dominican nuns on an island in the Danube near Budapest and herself joined the community. The details of her life of self-crucifixion have been described very aptly as "horrifying." "There can be little doubt that Margaret shortened her life by her austerities" (Attwater). Cult confirmed in 1789.
Cf. Att. — Holw. — Baud.

MARGARET of ENGLAND (St) M.
O.S.B. Cist.   **A.C. Feb. 3**
d. 1192. Born in Hungary, probably of an English mother and related to St Thomas of Canterbury. She lost her mother in

the Holy Land, made a pilgrimage to our Lady of Montserrat in Spanish Catalonia and joined the Cistercian nuns at Sauve-Benite, in the diocese of Puy-en-Velay. She was greatly venerated in that district. *Cf. Att. — Zimm. — Baud. — Holw.*

MARGARET of CORTONA (St) O.F.M.
R.M. Feb. 22
1247-1297. Born at Laviano in Tuscany, a farmer's daughter, she was the mistress of a young nobleman for nine years. In his sudden death she saw a judgment from heaven, and publicly confessing her sins in the church of Cortona, she placed herself under the direction of the Franciscan friars. She became a tertiary herself and the foundress of a convent and a hospital where she and her nuns tended the sick. She suffered from calumny and obloquy, but God favoured her with supernatural charismata. Canonized in 1728. *Cf. Menzies — Att. — Holw.*

MARGARET CLITHEROW (Bl) M.
A.C. March 25
1556-1586. Margaret Middleton was born at York, married John Clitherow and shortly after became a Catholic. For this she was imprisoned for two years, and on her release she began to shelter priests in her house. She was again arrested, and, refusing to plead, was condemned to the horrible death of being pressed to death. The sentence was carried out at York. Beatified in 1929. *Cf. Newdigate — Att.*

MARGARET of CITTÀ-DI-CASTELLO
(Bl) V. **A.C. Apr. 13**
d. 1320. Born at Meldola, in the diocese of S. Angelo in Vado, Italy, she was left a foundling at Città-di-Castello and was brought up by several families in the city, being usually occupied in looking after children. She died at the age of thirty-three. Cult approved in 1609. *Cf. Att. — Holw.*

MARGARET of AMELIA (Bl) V. O.S.B.
P.C. Apr. 20
d. 1666. A Benedictine abbess of the nunnery of St Catherine at Amelia, possessed of mystical gifts. *Cf. Holw.*

MARGARET POLE (Bl) M. A.C. May 28
d. 1541. Margaret Plantagenet was a niece of Edward IV and Richard III. She married Sir Reginald Pole, to whom she bore five children. Left a widow she was created countess of Salisbury in her own right and appointed governess to Princess Mary, daughter of Henry VIII. When her son Cardinal Pole opposed the royal supremacy and refused to return to England, Henry revenged himself on the cardinal's mother, and lodged her in the Tower of London for two years. Finally she was condemned for high treason by Bill of Attainder and beheaded on Tower Hill at the age of seventy. Beatified in 1886. *Cf. Newdigate — Att.*

MARGARET of VAU-LE-DUC (Bl) V.
O.S.B. Cist. **P.C. June 4**
d. 1277. Daughter of Duke Henry II of Brabant, she became a Cistercian nun, and second abbess, of the convent of Vau-le-Duc in Brabant, which had been founded by her father. She has always been venerated as a *beata* by the Cistercians. *Cf. Holw. — Baud.*

MARGARET of SCOTLAND (St) W.
R.M. June 10 and Nov. 16
c.1050-1093 (Nov. 16). Granddaughter of King Edmund Ironside of England, in 1070 she married King Malcolm III Canmore of Scotland. She used her influence as queen for the good of religion and for the promotion of justice, ever having a special thought for the poor. She had six sons and two daughters, one of whom was "Good Queen Maud," wife of Henry I. Among the foundations she made was the Benedictine abbey of Dunfermline, where she was buried. Canonized in 1251. *Cf. Holw. — Att. — Baud.*

MARGARET or MARINA (St) V.M.
R.M. July 20
d. c.304. Said to have been a maiden of Antioch in Pisidia martyred under Diocletian. This much is probably true; everything else related in her *Acta* is pure legend, including, of course, the story of the fierce dragon which swallowed her before she was beheaded. Nevertheless, she is one of the most popular of maiden-martyr saints and her cult is very ancient. In the East she is known as Marina. *Cf. Menzies — Att. — Holw.*

MARGARET of FAENZA (Bl or St) Abs.
O.S.B. Vall. **A.C. Aug. 26**
d. 1330. A native of Faenza, she became

a Vallombrosan nun under St Humilitas
at the convent of St John the Evangelist,
near Florence, and eventually its second
abbess.
Cf. Menzies — Holw. — Baud.

MARGARET the BAREFOOTED (St) W.
R.M. Aug. 27
d. 1395. A poor girl of Sanseverino, near
Ancona, in Italy, who in her fifteenth year
was married to a man who ill-treated her.
She bore it all with patience for many
years.
Cf. Menzies — Att. — Baud. — Holw.

MARGARET WARD (Bl) M.
A.C. Aug. 30
d. 1588. A gentlewoman of Congleton,
Cheshire, hanged at Tyburn with the
usual barbarous accompaniments, for
rescuing a priest. Beatified in 1929.
Cf. Newdigate.

MARGARET of LOUVAIN (Bl) V.
A.C. Sept. 2
1207-1225. Surnamed in Belgium "Marguerite la Fière." Born at Louvain, she
worked as a maid-servant at an inn in the
same city. She was murdered by robbers
whom she had seen kill and rob her em-
ployers. The Cistercian Caesarius of
Heisterbach states that she was about to
become a Cistercian nun. Cult approved
in 1905.
Cf. Holw. — Baud. — Att.

MARGARET MARY ALACOQUE (St) V.
R.M. Oct. 17
1647-1690. Born at L'Hautecourt in
Burgundy in 1669, she joined the Order of
the Visitation at Paray-le-Monial. From
a revelation made to her by our Lord in
1675 she was led to enter upon her great
work, the spreading of public and liturgical devotion to the Sacred Heart. After
violent opposition, met with chiefly in
Jansenistic milieus, the devotion tri-
umphed and became extremely popular in
the Church. St Margaret was canonized
in 1920.
Cf. Att. — Holw. — Baud.

MARGARET LEROUX (Bl) V. O.S.
Ursulae A.C. Oct. 23
d. 1794. An Ursuline nun of Valenciennes,
who formed part of the group of martyrs
guillotined on Oct. 23. She was born at
Cambrai in 1747 and was professed in
1769. Her name in religion was Ann-

Joseph, or Mother Josephine. (*See Ursuline MM.*)
Cf. Baud.

MARGARET of LORRAINE (Bl) W.
O.F.M. A.C. Nov. 6
1463-1521. A daughter of Duke Frederic
of Lorraine, she married in 1488 René,
duke of Alençon, who died in 1492 leaving
her a widow with three children. She
devoted herself exclusively to their upbringing and to works of charity. When
they were of age, she founded a convent of
Poor Clares at Argentan, and entered
there in 1519. Cult confirmed in 1921.
Cf. Att. — Holw.

MARGARET of SAVOY (Bl) W. O.P.
A.C. Nov. 23
d. 1464. Born at Pinerolo, daughter of
Duke Amadeo II of Savoy. In 1403 she
married Theodore Paleologus, marquis of
Montferrat, after whose death (1418), influenced by St Vincent Ferrer, she joined
the Dominican tertiaries. In 1426 she
founded a house at Alba in Liguria, of
which she became the first Dominican
prioress. Cult confirmed in 1669.
Cf. Menzies — Att. — Holw.

MARGARET and IDA (BB) O.S.B.
A.C. Dec. 26
d. p. 1150. Two sisters who belonged to
the family of the Hohenfels and became
Benedictine nuns at Bingen under St
Hildegard, by whom Margaret was ap-
pointed prioress.
Cf. Zimm.

**MARGARET COLONNA (Bl) V. Poor
Clare.** A.C. Dec. 30
d. 1284. Daughter of Prince Odo Colonna
of Palestrina. She turned her family
castle on the mountain side above Palestrina into a convent of Poor Clares, for
whom her brother, Cardinal James Colonna, adapted a mitigated version of the
Franciscan Rule. Cult confirmed in
1847.
Cf. Att. — Holw. — Menzies.

MARIANA of JESUS (Bl) V. O.Merc.
A.C. Apr. 27
1565-1624. Surnamed "the Lily of Madrid." Mariana Navarra de Guevara was
born in Madrid and joined the community
of Discalced Mercedarians in the same
city, where she distinguished herself by

her life of penance. Beatified by Pius VI.
Cf. P. de U. — Holw.

MARIANA de PAREDES (Bl) V.
A.C. May 26

1618-1645. Known as the "Lily of Quito."
Her family name was Mariana de Paredes
y Flores, but she chose to call herself
Mariana of Jesus. She was born at Quito,
in Ecuador, and was of Spanish descent.
She tried her vocation as a religious, but
failed. After this, she lived as a solitary
in the house of her brother-in-law. During the earthquakes at Quito in 1645 she
offered herself as a victim for the city and
died shortly after. Beatified in 1854.
Cf. P. de U. — Att.

MARIANUS SCOTUS (Bl) Ab. O.S.B.
A.C. Feb. 9

d. 1088. His Irish name Muirdach Mac-
Robartaigh was latinized as Marianus.
He was born in Donegal. In 1067, setting
out with some companions on a pilgrimage
to Rome, he was, while on his way thither,
induced to become a Benedictine at Mich-
elsberg, near Bamberg, whence he migrated to Upper Minster at Ratisbon. In
1078 he founded and became the abbot of
the abbey of St Peter, also at Ratisbon,
thus originating the congregation of Scottish monasteries in S. Germany, famous in
the Benedictine annals. Throughout his
life Bl Marianus occupied his free time in
copying manuscripts: he is said to have
transcribed the whole Bible several times.
Cf. Zimm. — Att. — Holw.

MARIANUS (St) Mk. R.M. Apr. 20
Otherwise Marcian of Auxerre, q.v.

MARIANUS, JAMES and Comp. (SS)
MM. R.M. Apr. 30

d. 259. Martyrs of Lambesa, an ancient
town in Numidia (Algeria). Marianus
was a reader and James a deacon.
Cf. Holw. — Baud.

MARIANUS (St) H. R.M. Aug. 19
d. c.515. A solitary in the forest of Entreaigues, near Evaux, in Berry, France. His
life was written by St Gregory of Tours.
Cf. Holw. — Baud.

MARIANUS (St) M. R.M. Oct. 17
See Victor, Alexander and Marianus.

MARIANUS (St) M. R.M. Dec. 1
See Diodorus, Marianus, etc.

MARIANUS SCOTUS (Bl) H. O.S.B.
A.C. Dec. 22

d. 1086. Born in Ireland, his real name
was Moelbrigte, i.e., servant of Brigid.
After becoming a monk, he migrated to
Cologne (1056), then to Fulda, where for a
time he lived as a recluse, and finally
(1069) to Mainz. He wrote a "Chronicle
of the World."
Cf. Holw. — Zimm.

MARINA (several)
Note. Marina is the Latin form of the
Greek name Pelagia, a fact which has
caused a few duplicates in our martyrologies.

MARINA (St) V.M.
R.M. June 18 (and July 17)

? In the ancient martyrologies this saint
is variously named Maria, Marina, or
even Marinus. Moreover, she is simply
called *virgin*, not martyr. Some con-
found her with St Margaret (July 20);
others with the Marina who lived in a
monastery of men dressed as a boy, i.e., a
duplicate of the Greek St Pelagia (Oct. 8).
Her life served as a model for the legends
of SS Euphrosyna, Maria, Theodora, etc.
The R.M. makes her a martyr at Alexandria.
Cf. Holw. — Att. — Menzies.

MARINA of SPOLETO (Bl) V.
A.C. June 18

d. c.1300. Marina Vallarina was an Augustinian nun of Spoleto in Umbria. Her
cult at Spoleto seems to have died out.
Cf. Att.

MARINA (St) V.M. R.M. July 18
? The R.M. states that she was a martyr of
Orense in Spanish Galicia. All records
concerning her are lost. The name was
introduced into the Roman Martyrology
by Baronius (second revision).
Cf. Holw. — P. de U.

MARINUS (AMARINUS) (St) M. O.S.B.
R.M. Jan. 25

See Amarinus.

MARINUS (St) M. R.M. Jan. 29
Otherwise Maurus. See Papias and
Maurus.

MARINUS and ASTERIUS (SS) MM.
R.M. March 3

d. 262. Marinus was a Roman soldier

stationed at Caesarea in Palestine, who, when on the point of being promoted to the rank of centurion, was denounced as a Christian by a jealous rival and forthwith martyred. Asterius, or Astyrius, a senator, buried the body, and it seems, although it is not certain, that he too died a martyr.
Cf. Holw. — Att.

MARINUS, VIMIUS and ZIMIUS (SS) Cc. O.S.B. A.C. June 12
d. p. 1100. Surnamed the *"Tres Sancti Exules,"* the *"Three Holy Exiles."* They were Benedictine monks of the Scots abbey of St James at Ratisbon, who, c.1100, became hermits at Griesstetten.
Cf. Zimm.

MARINUS, THEODOTUS and SEDOPHA (SS) MM. R.M. July 5
? Martyrs who suffered at Tomi on the Black Sea.

MARINUS (St) M. R.M. July 10
See Januarius, Marinus, etc.

MARINUS (St) M. R.M. Aug. 8
d. 290. An aged man, martyred at Anazarbus in Cilicia under Diocletian.
Cf. Holw. — Baud.

MARINUS (St) Ab.-Bp. O.S.B. A.C. Aug. 19
c.800. A Benedictine abbot-bishop of the monastery of St Peter at Besalú in Spanish Catalonia.
Cf. Holw.

MARINUS (St) H. R.M. Sept. 4
? He is said to have been born on an island off the coast of Dalmatia, and to have been by profession a stone-mason, to have been ordained a deacon by Gaudentius, bishop of Rimini, and finally to have died a hermit where now stands the tiny Republic of San Marino, which is called after him.
Cf. Menzies — Holw. — Att.

MARINUS (St) M. O.S.B. A.C. Nov. 24
d. 731. Born in Italy, he became a Benedictine at Maurienne in Savoy, and afterwards a hermit near the monastery of Chandor, where he was put to death by the Saracens.
Cf. Holw.

MARINUS (Bl) Ab. O.S.B. A.C. Dec. 15
d. 1170. A Benedictine monk of La Cava in S. Italy, where he held the office of treasurer before he was elected abbot in 1146. He received the abbatial blessing at Rome from Pope Eugene III. He was a close friend both of the supreme pontiffs and of the kings of Sicily, and he acted as mediator between the two powers in 1156.
Cf. Zimm. — P. de U.

MARINUS (St) M. R.M. Dec. 26
d. 283. He is described as a Roman, the son of a senator, who was beheaded under Numerian, after having been miraculously delivered from torture chambers, wild beasts, fire, water, etc. His *Acta* are probably a pious romance.
Cf. Holw. — Baud.

MARIUS (MARIS), MARTHA, AUDIFAX and ABACHUM (SS) MM. R.M. Jan. 19
d. c.270. A Persian nobleman, who with his wife Martha and their two sons Audifax and Abachum journeyed to Rome to venerate the tombs of the Apostles. While in the holy city they busied themselves in burying the bodies of those who were then being martyred in the persecution of Claudius. They too were arrested, the three men beheaded and St Martha drowned.
Cf. Att. — Baud. — Holw.

MARIUS (St) R.M. Jan. 27
Otherwise Maurus, q.v.

MARK dei MARCONI (Bl) C. O.S.H. A.C. Feb. 24
1480-1510. Born at Milliarino, near Mantua, he joined the Hieronymites of Bl Peter of Pisa in the monastery of St Matthew of Mantua, where he spent his life. Cult approved in 1906.
Cf. Holw.

MARK BARKWORTH (Bl) M. O.S.B. A.C. Feb. 27
d. 1601. Bl Mark Barkworth (*alias* Lambert) was born in Lincolnshire and educated at Oxford. After his conversion he studied for the priesthood at Rome and Valladolid and was received into the Benedictine Order at the abbey of our Lady of Hirache, near Estella, in Spanish Navarre. He was the first to die at Ty-

burn in the Benedictine habit after the suppression of the monasteries.
Cf. Newdigate — Camm.

MARK (St) M.　　　　**R.M. March 13**
See Theusitas, Horres, etc.

MARK (St) M.　　　　**R.M. March 19**
See Quintus, Quintilla, etc.

MARK of MONTEGALLO (Bl) C. O.F.M.
A.C. March 20
1426-1497. Born at Montegallo, diocese of Ascoli Piceno, he became a physician and married. Later, by mutual consent, both he and his wife joined the Franciscans. Bl Mark was ordained priest and travelled the length and breadth of Italy preaching and establishing charitable pawnshops for the poor, known in Italy as *Monti di Pietá*.
Cf. Holw. — Att.

MARK and TIMOTHY (SS) MM.
R.M. March 24
d. c.150. Two Roman martyrs of post-apostolic times, mentioned by Pope St Pius I in a letter to the bishop of Vienne in Gaul.
Cf. Holw.

MARK OF ARETHUSA (St) M. Bp.
A.C. March 29
d. c.362. Bishop of Arethusa on Mt Lebanon. In 351 he was present at the synod of Sirmium where he produced a creed for which he was unjustly accused of Arianism by Baronius, who excluded his name from the R.M. He has since been vindicated by the Bollandists. St Mark died a martyr under Julian the Apostate.
Cf. Att. — Holw. — Baud.

MARK FANTUCCI (Bl) C. O.F.M.
A.C. Apr. 10
1405-1479. Born at Bologna, he first studied law and in 1430 became a Friar Minor. He held several offices in the order and preached throughout Italy, Istria and Dalmatia, visiting also the friars in Austria, Poland, Russia and the Levant. He died at Piacenza. Cult approved in 1868.
Cf. Holw. — Att.

MARK (St) Evangelist　　**R.M. Apr. 25**
d. 75. He is generally thought to have been the young man who ran away when our Lord was arrested (Mark XIV, 51-52)

and the "John who is surnamed Mark" of Acts XII, 25. He accompanied SS Paul and Barnabas on their first missionary journey. Afterwards he followed St Peter to Rome, where, in the words of the R.M., he was "the disciple and interpreter of St Peter", whose preaching he set down in writing in the gospel which bears his name. St Peter calls him "my son Mark" (1 Pet V, 13). According to tradition he afterwards went to Alexandria where he established the church and died a martyr. His body was in the ninth century translated to Venice. In art he is represented with a lion at his feet and with a scroll on which are inscribed the words: Peace be to thee, O Mark, my Evangelist.
Cf. Ricci — Menzies — Att. — Holw.

MARK of GALILEE (St) Bp. M.
R.M. Apr. 28
d. 92. Said to have been a Galilean by descent and the first missionary bishop and martyr in the province of the Marsi (Abruzzi) in Italy.
Cf. Holw. — Menzies.

MARK of LUCERA (St) Bp. A.C. June 14
d. c.328. A bishop in local veneration in S. Italy.
Cf. Menzies.

MARK and MARCELLIAN (SS) MM.
R.M. June 18 (and July 29)
d. c.287. Roman martyrs, twin brothers and deacons, who suffered at Rome under Maximianus Herculeus. Their basilica in the catacombs of St Balbina was rediscovered in 1902.
Cf. Holw. — Att. — Menzies.

MARK, MUCIAN, an unnamed boy, and PAUL (SS) MM.　　　　**R.M. July 3**
? The entry in the R.M. reads as follows: "The holy martyrs Mark and Mucian who were slain with the sword for Christ's sake. When a little boy called upon them with a loud voice that they should not sacrifice to idols, he was ordered to be whipped, and as he then confessed Christ more loudly, he was slain too, together with one Paul who was exhorting the martyrs."

MARK CALDEIRA (Bl) M. S.J.
A.C. July 15
d. 1570. A native of Feira, diocese of Oporto, Portugal, and a Jesuit novice.

He was martyred with Bl Igantius de Azevedo, q.v.
Cf. Holw.

MARK XINEIEMON (Bl) M.
                              A.C. Aug. 19
d. 1622. A Japanese sailor on the ship of Bl Joachim Firajama (q.v.). He was beheaded at Nagasaki. Beatified in 1867.
Cf. Holw.

MARK (St) M.   **R.M. Aug. 31**
See Robustian and Mark

MARK (St) M.   **R.M. Sept. 1**
See Priscus, Castrensis, etc.

MARK, STEPHEN and MELCHIOR (BB) MM.   **A.C. Sept. 7**
d. 1619. Bl Mark Crisin (Körösy) was a Croat and a canon, Bl Stephen Pongracz a Hungarian Jesuit and Bl Melchior Grondech a Czech Jesuit. The three were most brutally massacred by the Calvinist soldiers at Kosice in Hungary. Beatified in 1905.
Cf. Holw. — Att.

MARK of MODENA (Bl) C. O.P.
                              A.C. Sept. 23
d. 1498. Born at Modena he joined the Friars Preachers and was a very successful preacher in N. and central Italy. Cult approved in 1857.
Cf. Att. — Holw.

MARK CRIADO (Bl) M. O.S. Trin.
                              A.C. Sept. 25
1522-1569. Born at Andujar, in Andalusia, in 1536 he joined the Trinitarians. He was tortured and slain at Almeria by the Moors. Cult approved by Leo XIII.
Cf. Holw.

MARK (St) Bp.   **R.M. Sept. 27**
Otherwise John Mark, q.v.

MARK, ALPHIUS, ALEXANDER and Comp. (SS) MM.   **R.M. Sept. 28**
d. c.303. The R.M. says: "At Antioch in Pisidia, the martyrs Mark, a shepherd, Alphius, Alexander and Zosimus, his brothers, Nicon, Neon, Heliodorus, and thirty soldiers, who through the miracles of blessed Mark believed in Christ, and were crowned with martyrdom in divers manners and places."

MARK, MARCIAN and Comp. MM.
                              R.M. Oct. 4
d. 304. Egyptian martyrs under Diocletian. Mark and Marcian were brothers. The rest are described as "victims of all ages and both sexes" and their number as "innumerable." They seem, however, to be duplicates of other groups.
Cf. Holw. — Baud.

MARK (St) Pope.   **R.M. Oct. 7**
d. 336. A Roman by birth, who was chosen pope in 336 and died within the year.
Cf. Att. — Baud. — Holw.

MARK (St) Bp. M.   **R.M. Oct. 22**
d. c.156. The first bishop of Jerusalem not of Jewish extraction. He is said to have ruled that see for twenty years and to have died a martyr: both statements are mere conjectures.
Cf. Holw. — Baud.

MARK (St)   **R.M. Oct. 24**
Otherwise Marcius, q.v.

MARK (St) M.   **R.M. Oct. 25**
See Theodosius, Lucius, etc.

MARK (Bl) Ab. O.S.B.   **A.C. Nov. 13**
d. c.1280. A Benedictine abbot of Sant' Angelo di Scala, of the Congregation of Montevergine.
Cf. Zimm.

MARK (St) M.   **R.M. Nov. 16**
See Rufinus, Mark, etc.

MARK and STEPHEN (SS) MM.
                              R.M. Nov. 22
d. c.305. Mark, with another martyr by name Stephen, suffered at Antioch in Pisidia under Galerius.
Cf. Holw.

MARK (St) M.   **R.M. Dec. 15**
See Faustinus, Lucius, etc.

MARNOCK (MARNANUS, MARNAN, MARNOC) (St) Bp.   **A.C. March 1**
d. c.625. An Irish monk under St Columba at Iona, and afterwards a missionary bishop, who died at Annandale, and was much venerated in the neighbourhood of the Scottish border. He has given his name to Kilmarnock in Scotland. His feast is celebrated again on Oct. 25.
Cf. Holw.

MARO (St) Ab.   **A.C. Feb. 14**
d. c.435. A Syrian hermit, who lived on
the bank of the R. Orontes between Homs
and Apamea. He was greatly revered by
St John Chrysostom and by Theodoret.
The monastery of Beit-Marun, built
around his shrine, gave its name to the
body of Syrian Catholics called Maronites.
Cf. Holw. — Baud. — Att.

**MARO, EUTYCHES and VICTORINUS
(SS) MM.**   **R.M. Apr. 15**
d. c.99. They belonged to the entourage
of St Flavia Domitilla, whom they accompanied in her exile to the island of Ponza.
Eventually they returned to Rome and
suffered martyrdom under Trajan: Eutyches was stabbed, Victorinus was
hung head downwards over a sulphur
spring and Maro was beheaded.
Cf. Holw. — Baud.

MAROLUS (St) Bp.   **R.M. Apr. 23**
d. 423. A Syrian by origin, he was raised
to the see of Milan in 408. The Christian
poet Ennodius wrote a poem in his honour.
Cf. Att. — Holw.

MAROTAS (St) M.   **R.M. March 27**
See Zanitas, Lazarus, etc.

MAROVEUS (St) Ab. O.S.B.
          A.C. Oct. 22
d. c.650. Monk of Bobbio. Abbot-
founder of the monastery of Precipiano,
near Tortona
Cf. Zimm.

MARQUARD (St) Bp. M. O.S.B.
          A.C. Feb. 2
d. 880. A monk at New-Corbey in Saxony, he ruled the see of Hildesheim from
874 to 880 and fell in battle against the
Norsemen at Ebbeksdorff. (See Bruno
and Comp. MM. Feb. 2).
Cf. Holw. — Zimm.

MARTANA (St) M.   **R.M. Dec. 2**
See Eusebius, Marcellus, etc.

MARTHA (St) M.   **R.M. Jan. 19**
See Marius, Martha, etc.

MARTHA (St) V.M.   **R.M. Feb. 23**
d. 252. A Spanish maiden, beheaded at
Astorga under Decius. Her relics are
enshrined in the old Benedictine abbey of

Ribas de Sil and at Ters, diocese of Astorga.
Cf. Holw. — P. de U.

MARTHA (St) V.   **R.M. July 29**
d. c.80. Sister of St Lazarus and of St
Mary of Bethany (identified in the West
with St Mary Magdalen). She was the
hostess of our Lord in their house at
Bethany (Luke X 38, John XI, 2) who was
"careful and troubled about many things."
For this reason she has become the type of
the active life. The story of her subsequent journey to S. Gaul merits no
credence.
Cf. Holw.

MARTHA WANG (Bl) M.   **A.C. July 29**
d. 1861. A native woman of Tonkin who
carried letters from the imprisoned semi-
narians BB Joseph Tshang and Paul
Tcheng to their bishop. She was arrested
and beheaded with them at Tsingai.
Beatified in 1909.
Cf. Holw.

**MARTHA, SAULA and Comp. (SS) VV.
MM.**   **R.M. Oct. 20**
? The entry in the R.M. reads: "At
Cologne the passion of the holy virgins
Martha and Saula with many others."
They are now usually assigned to the
mythical cycle of St Ursula and her 11,000
virgins (21 Oct.), and it is thought that
these martyrs of Oct. 20 formed the first
nucleus of the Ursuline legend. Indeed,
it seems that the name Ursula derives from
Sa-ula.
Cf. Holw

MARTIA (St) M.   **R.M. June 21**
See Rufinus and Martia.

MARTIAL (St) M.   **R.M. Apr. 16**
See Saragossa, Martyrs of.

**MARTIAL of LIMOGES, Bp. ALPIN-
IAN AND AUSTRICLINIAN (SS)**
          R.M. June 30
d. c.250. First bishop of Limoges, the
reputed apostle of the Limousin, and,
according to St Gregory of Tours, one of
the seven missionary bishops sent from
Rome to preach the gospel in Gaul. His
memory is still held in great veneration in
the Limousin. Other legends connected
with the saint are medieval forgeries.

Alpinian and Austriclinian were priests who collaborated with him.

Cf. Att. — Holw. — Duch. Fast. Episc.

MARTIAL (St) M. R.M. July 10

See Seven Brothers.

MARTIAL, SATURNINUS, EPICTETUS, MAPRILIS, FELIX and Comp. (SS) MM. R.M. Aug. 22

d. c.300. They were martyred at Porto Romano and seem to have been pilgrims to the shrines of the apostles. They were cast into the sea on their way to or from Rome.

Cf. Holw. — Menzies — Baud.

MARTIAL, LAURENCE and Comp. (SS) MM. R.M. Sept. 28

? A group of twenty-two African martyrs, who suffered in the province now called Algeria.

Cf. Holw.

MARTIAL (St) M. R.M. Oct. 13

See Faustus, Januarius and Martial.

MARTIN of LEON (St) C. O.S.B. A.C. Jan. 12

d. 1203. Born at Leon, in Old Castile, he joined the Augustinian canons regular, first at San Marcelo and then at St Isidore in his native city. He was a prolific ascetical writer.

Cf. P. de U. — Holw.

MARTIN MANUEL (St) M. A.C. Jan. 31

d. 1156. Born at Auranca, near Coimbra, in Portugal. As archpriest of Soure he was captured by the Saracens and died of ill-treatment at their hands.

Cf. P. de U. — Holw.

MARTIN LOYNAZ of the ASCENSION (St) M. O.F.M. R.M. Feb. 5

d. 1597. Born at Vergara, near Pampeluna, in Spanish Navarre, he studied at Alcalá, and became a Franciscan in 1586. He did missionary work in Mexico, Manila, and finally Japan. He was crucified at Nagasaki with twenty-five companions. Beatified in 1627 and canonized in 1862.

Cf. Prop. O.F.M. — Holw.

MARTIN (Bl) M. A.C. Feb. 18

1815-1862. A native Chinese catechist and host of Bl John Peter Néel. He was beheaded at Kuy-Tcheu. Beatified in 1909.

Cf. Holw.

MARTIN of BRAGA (St) Bp. A.C. March 20

d. 580. Born in Pannonia, he became a monk in Palestine, and later travelled in Spanish Galicia where he preached to the pagan Suevi. He was bishop first of Mondoñedo (Dumium) and then of Braga, and introduced monasticism throughout N.W. Spain. Several of his highly interesting writings are still extant.

Cf. P. de U. — Holw. — Att.

MARTIN of TONGRES (St) Bp. R.M. June 21

d. c.350. He is said to have been the seventh bishop of Tongres and is venerated as the apostle of the Hesbaye district in Brabant.

Cf. Holw. — Duch. Fast. Episc. — Att.

MARTIN of VIENNE (St) Bp. R.M. July 1

d. p. 132. Alleged third bishop of Vienne, sent thither by Pope St Alexander.

Cf. Holw. — Duch. Fast. Episc. — Baud.

MARTIN of TRÈVES (St) Bp. M. R.M. July 19

d. c.210. Listed in the episcopal records of Trèves as the tenth bishop of that see. There is no conclusive evidence for his martyrdom.

Cf. Holw. — Duch. Fast. Episc. — Baud.

MARTIN GÓMEZ (Bl) M. Tert. O.F.M. A.C. Aug. 17

d. 1727. A native Japanese, of Portuguese descent, beheaded at Nagasaki. Beatified in 1867.

Cf. Holw.

MARTIN de HINOJOSA (St) Bp. O.S.B. Cist. A.C. Sept. 3

d. 1213. A member of the illustrious Castilian family of the Hiñojosas. He became a Cistercian and eventually founded the abbey of Huerta, by the R. Jalón, near Soria (1164), of which he was the first abbot. In 1185 he became bishop of Sigüenza, but resigned in 1192 to live again as a monk.

Cf. P. de U. — Zimm.

MARTIN III (Bl) O.S.B. Cam. A.C. Sept. 13

d. 1259. Abbot and prior general of Camaldoli (1248-1259). He is best known as the compiler of the new constitutions of the order.

Cf. Zimm. — Chev.

MARTIN CID (St) Ab. O.S.B. Cist.
A.C. Oct. 8
d. 1152. Born at Zamora, in Spain, he became the abbot-founder of the Cistercian abbey of Val-Paraiso, for which St Bernard himself supplied the pioneer community. He is still greatly venerated in the diocese of Zamora and by the Cistercians.
Cf. P. de U. — Holw.

MARTIN (St) C. **R.M. Oct. 24**
Otherwise Marcius, q.v.

MARTIN of VERTOU (St) Ab.
R.M. Oct. 24
d. 601. Abbot-founder of Vertou Abbey, near Nantes, of Saint-Jouin-de-Marnes and of other monastic establishments. The particulars of his life, as they have come down to us, are rather confused. He is venerated in the province of Poitou.
Cf. Att. — Holw. — Baud.

MARTIN PORRES (Bl) C. O.P.
A.C. Nov. 5
1569-1639. Born at Lima, in Peru, son of a Spanish knight of Alcantara and of a negro or Indian mother from Panama. Martin became a barber and studied surgery, and finally entered as a lay-brother at the Dominican friary of Lima. Here he nursed the sick and "became a friend to all the poor in the city, especially the African slaves, and including stray cats and dogs." (Attwater, h.1.) He was beatified in 1837, the first "half-caste" who has received this honour.
Cf. Prop. O.P. — Att. — Holw. — P. de U.

MARTIN TINH and MARTIN THO (BB) MM. **A.C. Nov. 8**
d. 1840. Martin Tinh was a native of Tonkin and a priest, martyred at the age of 80 with his companion, or servant, Martin Tho, also a native of Tonkin.
Cf. Holw.

MARTIN of TOURS (St) Bp.
R.M. Nov. 11 (and July 4)
c.316-397. Born in Upper Pannonia (now Hungary), the son of a Roman officer. He was educated at Pavia and at the age of fifteen enrolled in the imperial cavalry. The episode of his sharing his cloak with a poor beggar and the subsequent heavenly vision which led to his baptism has become famous. He left the army and placed himself in the hands of St Hilary, bishop of Poitiers, living for ten years as a recluse and founding a community of monk-hermits at Ligugé. In 371 he was promoted to the see of Tours, but he accepted the office with great reluctance and, establishing another great monastic centre at Marmoutier, he continued to live there privately as a monk, while publicly he devoted himself with burning zeal to the discharge of his episcopal duties. He opposed Arianism and Priscillianism, but befriended the Priscillianists when they were persecuted and condemned the practice of invoking the civil power to punish heretics. He was the greatest of the pioneers of Western monachism before St Benedict, who had a particular veneration for St Martin. His shrine at Tours was a great resort of pilgrims.
Cf. Duch. Fast. Episc. — Att. — Holw.

MARTIN I (St) Pope. M.
R.M. Nov. 12 (and Sept. 16)
d. 655. Born in Tuscany, he was raised to the papacy in 649. At once he convened a council and condemned the Monothelites, of whom the reigning emperor Constans II was one. The imperial wrath now fell upon the pontiff, who in 653 was deported by force to Naxos, in the Aegean Sea, the following year condemned to death at a mock trial at Constantinople and finally taken as prisoner to the Chersonese where he died of starvation.
Cf. Menzies — Baud. — Att. — Holw.

MARTIN of ARADES (St) C. O.S.B.
A.C. Nov. 26
d. 726. A monk of Corbie, in France, chaplain and confessor to Charles Martel.
Cf. Baud. — Holw.

MARTIN of SAUJON (St) Ab.
R.M. Dec. 7
d. c.400. A disciple of St Martin of Tours, who, in his turn, became the abbot-founder of the monastery of Saujon, near Saintes.
Cf. Holw. — Baud.

MARTINA (St) V.M. **R.M. Jan. 30**
d. 228. A Roman martyr under Alexander Severus. She has a basilica dedicated in her honour at the Roman Forum. Her "Passion" is entirely apocryphal and identical with that of SS Tatiana and Prisca (q.v.). Some writers even doubt of her existence.
Cf. Holw. — Att.

MATINIAN (MATERNIAN) (St) Bp.
R.M. Jan. 2
d. c.435. Bishop of Milan (423-c.435).
He took part in the council of Ephesus and
wrote against Nestorianism.
Cf. Holw. — Baud.

MARTINIAN (St) H. A.C. Feb. 13
d. c.400. An alleged hermit who lived
near Caesarea in Palestine. Zoe, a woman
of evil repute, tempted him to become her
paramour; instead she was converted and
persuaded to become a nun at Bethlehem.
The evidence for the existence of this saint
is questionable.
Cf. Holw. — Att.

MARTINIAN (St) M. R.M. July 2
See Processus and Martinian.

MARTINIAN (St) M. R.M. July 27
See Seven Sleepers.

**MARTINIAN, SATURIAN and Comp.
(SS) MM.** R.M. Oct. 16
d. 458. Four Afro-Roman brothers, reduced to slavery in the house of an Arian
Vandal in Mauretania. They were encouraged to suffer for Christ by their
fellow-slave, Maxima by name. The four
brothers were martyred under Genseric by
being dragged to death by horses. Maxima died in peace.
Cf. Holw. — Att. — Baud.

MARTYRIUS (MARTORY) (St) M.
R.M. Jan. 23
6th cent. A solitary in the Abruzzi
(Valeria), whom St Gregory the Great
extols in his Dialogues (*Dial.* I, II)
Cf. Holw.

MARTYRIUS (St) M. R.M. May 29
See Sisinius, Martyrius and Alexander.

MARTYRIUS and MARCIAN (SS) MM.
R.M. Oct. 25
d. 351. Martyrius, a subdeacon, and
Marcian, a chorister, were martyred at
Constantinople under the Arian patriarch
Macedonius on a trumped-up charge of
sedition.
Cf. Holw. — Baud.

MARUTHAS (St) Bp. R.M. Dec. 4
d. c.415. One of the most prominent per-
sonalities of the Syrian church. He was
bishop of Maiferkat in Mesopotamia and

devoted all his energy to the reorganization of the church in Persia and E. Syria,
as well as to the preservation of the
memory of the numerous Syrian and Persian martyrs under Shapur. He collected
their *Passiones*, and wrote liturgical hymns
in their honour. St John Chrysostom
highly valued his friendship.
Cf. Holw. — Att. — Baud.

MARY of PISA (Bl) W. O.P.
A.C. Jan. 28
d. 1431. A member of the Mancini family of Pisa. She married at the early age
of twelve and was left a widow and the
mother of two children at sixteen. She
married again, but lost her second husband
eight years later. Mary then became a
Dominican tertiary and later took charge
of a new foundation of that order, noted
for its strict observance. Cult confirmed
by Pius IX.
Cf. Prop. O.P.

MARY CHRISTINA (Bl) A.C. Jan. 31
1812-1836. Born at Cagliari in Sardinia,
daughter of Victor Emmanuel, king of
Savoy and of Mary Teresa, niece of the
emperor Joseph II. In 1832 she married
Ferdinand II, king of the two Sicilies, to
whom she bore a son before her death at
the age of twenty-three. Beatified in
1872.
Cf. Holw.

**MARY (MILEDA, MLADA) (Bl) Abs.
O.S.B.** P.C. Feb. 8
d. 994. Daughter of Boleslas I, duke of
Bohemia. She became the abbess-
foundress of the nunnery of St George, at
Prague (967). She has always been ven-
erated as a *beata*.
Cf. Zimm. — Chev.

MARY (St) V.M. R.M. Feb. 11
See Saturninus and Comp.

MARY MAMALA (Bl) V. Poor Clare.
A.C. March 31
d. 1453. A member of the Spanish family
of the dukes of Medina-Sidonia. She married Henry de Guzmán, and in her widowhood joined the Poor Clares at Seville.
Cf. P. de U.

MARY of EGYPT (St) H. R.M. Apr. 2
d. c.500. An Egyptian by birth, who became an actress and then lived as a courte-
san at Alexandria. After her conversion,

which took place, it is said, at the holy sepulchre at Jerusalem, she fled into the desert beyond the Jordan, where she spent the remainder of her life doing penance, and where she was found dead by two disciples of St Cyriacus. Her story, which was publicly read in the East during the divine office, subsequently received numerous additions.
Cf. Att. — Holw.

MARY of CLEOPHAS (St) R.M. Apr. 9
1st cent. The wife of Cleophas or Alpheus (John XIX, 25) and the mother of the apostle St James the Less. She was one of the "three Marys" who followed our Lord from Galilee and who stood at the foot of the cross on Calvary. The legends which have grown up around her name deserve no credence.
Cf. Att. — Holw.

MARY BERNARD SOUBIROUS (St) V.
A.C. Apr. 16
Otherwise Bernadette Soubirous, q.v.

MARY of the INCARNATION (Bl) W.
O.C. A.C. Apr. 18
d. 1618. Barbara Avrillot, who in her young days was styled "the beautiful Acarie," was married to Peter Acarie, a French government official. After his death in 1613, Barbara joined the Carmelites as a lay-sister and took the new name of Mary-of-the-Incarnation. She introduced into France the Discalced Carmelites of St Teresa. Beatified in 1791.
Cf. Att. — P. de U. — Holw.

MARY SAINTE-EUPHRASIE PELLETIER (St) V. A.C. Apr. 24
Otherwise Euphrasia Pelletier, q.v.

MARY-MAGDALEN ALBRIZZI (Bl) V.
O.S.A. A.C. May 15
d. 1465. Born at Como, she entered a nunnery at Brunate, near her native city, of which she became prioress. While prioress she affiliated the convent to the Augustinian friars. She was remarkable for her promotion of frequent communion among her nuns. Cult approved in 1907.
Cf. Holw. — Att.

MARY-MAGDALEN SOPHIE BARAT (St) V. Foundress. R.M. May 25
1779-1865. Madeleine Sophie Barat was a native of Joigny, in Burgundy, and

opened the first convent of her new congregation of nuns, called the Society of the Sacred Heart of Jesus, at Amiens in 1801. She was a lady of great charm and enterprise, and before her death she had established houses throughout Europe, America and Africa — one hundred and five foundations in all, during her life-time. Canonized in 1925.
Cf. Att. — Holw.

MARY-ANN de PAREDES (Bl) V.
A.C. May 26
Otherwise Mariana de Paredes, q.v.

MARY-BARTHOLOMEW BAGNESI (Bl) A.C. May 27
Otherwise Bartholomaea Bagnesi, q.v.

MARY-MAGDALEN de'PAZZI (St) V.
O.C. R.M. May 29
1566-1607 (May 25). A native of Florence, where she became a Discalced Carmelite at the age of sixteen. Throughout her life she was subject to remarkable mystical experiences and was tried with many kinds of suffering — spiritual and physical. She filled various conventual offices with remarkable ability. Canonized in 1669.
Cf. Att. — Holw. — Baud.

MARY-MAGDALEN of CARPI (Bl) V.
O.S.M. A.C. June 10
d. 1546. A Servite lay-sister at Carpi, collector of alms for her community. Her relics were elevated in 1611.
Cf. Holw.

MARY of OIGNIES (Bl) W.
A.C. June 23
d. 1213. Born at Nivelles in Belgium, she married early in life, but persuaded her husband not to consummate the marriage. They then turned their house into a leper hospital, and tended the sick there. Finally Mary became a recluse in a cell near the church of Oignies, where she was favoured with supernatural charismata.
Cf. Att. — Holw. — Baud.

MARY-MAGDALEN FONTAINE (Bl) M.
A.C. June 26
1723-1794. Born at Etrépagny (Eure), she entered the noviciate of the sisters of Charity of St Vincent de Paul in 1748, and from 1767 was the superior of the house of that Institute at Arras. She was guillotined at Cambrai during the French Revo-

lution together with three religious of her community. Beatified in 1920.
Cf. Holw. — Baud.

MARY (St) W. R.M. June 29
1st cent. Mentioned in the Acts of the Apostles (XII, 12), as the mother of John, surnamed Mark (q.v.). From the text it appears that Mary's house was a place of assembly for the apostles and the faithful generally. Subsequent traditions about her are conflicting.
Cf. Holw.

MARY ROSE (Bl) M. O.S.B.
A.C. July 6
1741-1794. Her baptismal name was Susanne-Agatha de Loye. She was born at Sérignan, near Orange, and in 1762 became a Benedictine in the nunnery of Caderousse. At the outbreak of the French Revolution she was expelled from the convent, and in May 1794 she was arrested and guillotined, the first of a band of thirty-one martyrs put to death at Orange. Beatified in 1925.
Cf. P. de U.

MARY-MAGDALEN POSTEL (St) V.
Foundress. R.M. July 16
1756-1846. Born at Barfleur. Early in life she opened a school for girls, but soon the French Revolution stopped her work. During that trying period she obtained permission to administer the Bl Sacrament to the dying. In 1805 she reopened her school at Cherbourg, and this proved to be the origin of the Sisterhood of Christian Schools, which, after severe trials, spread and flourished throughout the world. Canonized in 1925.
Cf. Att.

MARY ST-HENRY (MARGUERITE-ELÉONORE de JUSTAMOND) and MARY-MAGDALEN du ST-SACREMENT (MAGDALEN-FRANÇOISE de JUSTAMOND) (BB) MM. O.S.B. Cist.
A.C. July 16
1794. Sisters by blood and Cistercian nuns at the convent of St Catherine at Avignon. They were guillotined at Orange during the French Revolution. Beatified in 1925.
Cf. P. de U.

MARY MAGDALEN LIDOIN (In religion: Mère Thérèse de St Augustine, Prioress) MARY ANN PIEDCOURT

(Soeur de Jésus Crucifié), **MARY HANISSET (Soeur Thérèse du Coeur de Marie), MARY TRÉSEL (Soeur Thérèse de St Ignace), MARY DUFOUR (Soeur Sainte Marthe) (BB) MM. O.C.** A.C. July 17
d. 1794. They belong to the community of Carmelite nuns of Compiègne, q.v., guillotined at Paris during the French Revolution. The first four were solemnly professed choir sisters, Bl Mary Dufour a lay-sister.
Cf. Holw. — Baud.

MARY MAGDALEN (St) R.M. July 22
1st cent. Mary Magdalen is mentioned in the four gospels as one of the most devoted followers of our Lord. Chiefly under the influence of St Gregory the Great's writings, the Western liturgies have identified her with Mary the Sinner (Luke VII, 37) and Mary the sister of Martha and Lazarus (John XI). This identification is challenged by Eastern tradition and by the writings of the Eastern Fathers. The story connecting St Mary Magdalen with France is pure legend.
Cf. Att. — Holw. — Baud.

MARY-MAGDALEN MARTINEGO (Bl) V. O.F.M. Cap. A.C. July 27
1687-1737. A native of Brescia, where she entered the convent of Capuchin nuns. She filled the post of novice-mistress and prioress with marked success. Beatified in 1900.
Cf. Att. — Holw.

MARY the BLESSED VIRGIN, Mother of God (St) R.M. Aug. 15 and as below
d. ? 45. The Virgin Mother of God is venerated with a special cult, called *hyperdoulia*, by the Catholic Church, as the highest of God's creatures. The invocation of Mary pervades all Catholic devotion, public and private, and among Catholics her name is more commonly bestowed at baptism than any other. In Latin countries Mary's mysteries also are frequently taken as baptismal, or religious names, as noted below. The principal events of the life of our Lady are the object of special liturgical feasts celebrated by the universal Church and listed in the R.M. as follows: (1) Dec. 8: her Immaculate Conception, viz., the singular privilege by which God preserved her from all stain of original sin at the first moment of her conception (Italian: Immacolata;

raised in 532. He had been a monk and abbot in his native province of Auvergne. As a bishop he withstood the cruelty of the Frankish barbarians and excommunicated Kings Theudebert I and Clotaire, by whom he was exiled for a time. He restored discipline among the clergy, founded a school of clerical studies, rebuilt the cathedral and combated heresy. *Cf. Holw. — Att. — Duch. Fast. Episc.*

NICETUS (St) Bp. R.M. May 5
d. p. 449. The fifteenth bishop of Vienne in Gaul.
Cf. Holw. — Baud.

NICHOLAS STUDITES (St) Ab.
A.C. Feb. 4
d. 863. A native of Crete, who at an early age entered the monastery of the Studion at Constantinople in which he had been educated. During the iconoclastic persecution he followed his abbot into banishment, and on his return, when peace was temporarily restored, succeeded as abbot. He went again into exile under the emperor Michael, refusing to recognize the usurping patriarch Photius. He was, however, taken prisoner and sent back to his monastery which was placed under another abbot. When the emperor Basil restored St Ignatius, the lawful patriarch, Nicholas considered himself too old to resume charge and died as a simple monk.
Cf. Holw. — Att. — Baud.

NICHOLAS SAGGIO (Bl) C. O.Minim.
A.C. Feb. 12
d. 1709. Born of poor parents at Longobardi in Calabria, he became a lay-brother in the Order of Minims of St Francis of Paola. Beatified by Pius VI.
Cf. Holw.

NICHOLAS PALEA (Bl) C. O.P.
A.C. Feb. 14
1197-1255. Born at Giovinazzo, near Bari. As a young man he heard St Dominic preach at Bologna and joined the Friars Preachers. He established houses of the order at Perugia (1233) and at Trani (1254) and became provincial of the Roman province in 1230 and again in 1255. He died at Perugia. Cult confirmed in 1828.
Cf. Prop. O.P. — Holw. — Att.

NICHOLAS of VANGADIZZA (Bl) C. O.S.B. Cam. A.C. Feb. 21
d. c.1210. A Camaldolese monk and priest at the abbey of Vangadizza. A great helper of the holy souls.
Cf. Zimm.

NICHOLAS of PRUSSIA (Bl) C. O.S.B.
P.C. Feb. 23
c.1379-1456. A native of Prussia who became one of the original members of the reformed abbey of St Justina at Padua under the Ven. Ludovico Barbo, the founder of the Benedictine Cassinese congregation. Nicholas lived successively at Padua, Venice, Padolirone, and finally at the abbey of San Niccolò del Boschetto, near Genoa, where he was novice-master and prior. Cult not yet officially approved.
Cf. Zimm. — Chev. — Holw.

NICHOLAS OWEN (Bl) M. S.J.
A.C. March 12
d. 1606. A Jesuit lay-brother who, both before and after entering the Society of Jesus, was employed in making hiding-places for hunted priests. He was twice imprisoned and tortured, and when he was arrested a third time and refused to give any information concerning the Gunpowder Plot, he was tortured so mercilessly that he died therefrom, being literally torn to pieces. Beatified in 1929.
Cf. Att. — Newdigate.

NICHOLAS von FLÜE (Bl) H.
A.C. March 22
1417-1487. Born near Sachseln, Canton Obwalden, Switzerland, the son of a peasant, he married and had ten children. Besides fighting bravely in the army of his canton, he was appointed judge and councillor for Obwalden. At the age of fifty he left his family with their consent and for nineteen years lived as a hermit at Ranft without any food besides Holy Communion. His advice was much sought after, especially by civil magistrates. He is still greatly venerated in Switzerland as "Bruder Klaus." Cult confirmed in 1669.
Cf. Holw. — Att. — Baud.

NICHOLAS (Bl) C. O.S.B. Cist.
A.C. Apr. 1
d. c.1220. A Cistercian monk at Santa Maria dell' Arcu, near Neti, in Sicily.
Cf. Zimm. — Chev.

NICHOLAS ALBERGATI (Bl) Bp. O.Cart.
R.M. May 9
1375-1443. A native of Bologna who in 1394 joined the Carthusians and in 1418, much against his will, was made archbishop of his native city. In 1426 he was created cardinal. He was called in as mediator between the emperor and the pope and the latter and the French king, and was prominent at the councils of Basle and Ferrara-Florence. He was a generous patron of learned men. Cult confirmed in 1744.
Cf. Holw. — Att. — Baud.

NICHOLAS the MYSTIC (St) Bp.
A.C. May 15
d. 925. Patriarch of Constantinople. He was deposed and banished from this see by the emperor Leo the Wise, because he would not permit that monarch to marry a fourth time, this being forbidden in the Eastern Church. He is surnamed "the mystic" because he was the oldest member of the mystic, or secret, council of the Byzantine court.
Cf. Holw. — Att.

NICHOLAS (Bl) Ab. O.S.B. Cist.
A.C. May 31
d. c.1163. He and his father gave up splendid worldly prospects in order to receive the Cistercian habit from St Bernard. Nicholas became abbot of Vaucelles. He is venerated by the Cistercians.
Cf. Holw. — Baud.

NICHOLAS PEREGRINUS (St) C.
R.M. June 2
1075-1094. A Greek who journeyed to S. Italy and wandered through Apulia, carrying a cross and crying out "*Kyrie eleison.*" Crowds of people, especially children, followed him repeating the same cry. He was taken for a lunatic and treated as such, but after his death at Trani, at the age of nineteen years, so many miracles were alleged to have taken place at his tomb that he was canonized in 1098.
Cf. Holw. — Menzies — Att.

NICHOLAS PIECK and NICHOLAS POPPEL (SS) MM. **R.M. July 9**
d. 1572. Two members of the group of the martyrs of Gorkum (q.v.). Nicholas Pieck was the Franciscan guardian of the friary at Gorkum. He was a native of Holland and a student of Louvain, and had made the conversion of Calvinists his life's work. Nicholas Poppel, also a Dutchman, was curate to Leonard van Wechel, another Gorkum martyr. Canonized in 1867.
Cf. Holw. — Att.

NICHOLAS THE (Bl) M. **A.C. July 13**
d. 1838. A Tonkinese soldier who was hacked asunder for the faith. He was a companion of Bl Augustus Huy, q.v.
Cf. Holw.

NICHOLAS DINNIS (Bl) M. S.J.
A.C. July 15
d. 1570. A native of Braganza in Portugal and a Jesuit novice. Companion of Bl Ignatius de Azevedo, q.v.

NICHOLAS HERMANSSÖN (Bl) Bp.
A.C. July 24
1331-1391. Born at Skeninge in Sweden, and educated at Paris and Orleans, he was ordained priest and appointed tutor to the sons of St Brigid of Sweden. Eventually he became bishop of Linköping. He is greatly honoured in Sweden as a liturgist and poet. It is said, but cannot be proved, that he was canonized in 1414 (or 1416).
Cf. Att. — Holw.

NICHOLAS APPLEINE (Bl) C.
A.C. (?) Aug. 11
d. 1466. A canon of St-Marcel-de-Pémery, diocese of Nevers. Cult approved by the bishop of Nevers in 1731.
Cf. Holw.

NICHOLAS POLITI (Bl) H. A.C. Aug. 17
1117-1167. Born at Adernò, in Sicily. He lived for thirty years as a hermit in a cave on Mt Etna. Cult approved by Julius II.
Cf. Holw.

NICHOLAS of TOLENTINO (St) C.
O.S.A. **R.M. Sept. 10**
1245-1305. A native of Sant'Angelo, diocese of Fermo. In 1623 he joined the hermits of St Augustine. After his ordination to the priesthood he made a resolution to preach daily to the people, and this he did, first at Cingoli, and then for thirty years at Tolentino. He was also known for his work among the poor. Canonized in 1446.
Cf. Holw. — Baud. — Att. — Menzies — Ricci.

NICHOLAS of FORCA-PALENA (Bl) C.
A.C. Oct. 1
1349-1449. A native of Palena, near Sulmona, and founder of the Hermits of St Jerome (*Romitani di San Girolamo*), for whom he established houses at Naples, Rome (Sant'Onofrio) and Florence. Afterwards he amalgamated his institute with the Hieronymites, founded by Bl Peter of Pisa. Cult approved in 1771. *Cf. Holw. — Att.*

NICHOLAS (St) M. O.F.M.
R.M. Oct. 10
See Daniel, Samuel, etc.

NICHOLAS I (St) Pope. **R.M. Nov. 13**
d. 867. Surnamed "the Great," a Roman by birth and a member of the Roman clergy, he was elected pope in 858. He was remarkable for his energy and courage. Among those who were excommunicated by him were John, the recalcitrant archbishop of Ravenna, king Lothair of Lorraine for matrimonial irregularity, and Photius, the intruded patriarch of Constantinople. He also forced Archbishop Hincmar of Reims, after a struggle, to acknowledge the papal appellate jurisdiction. Nicholas was described by his contemporaries as the champion of the people. He confirmed St Anschar as papal legate in Scandinavia, and, through his missionaries, effected the conversion of Bulgaria. *Cf. Holw. — Baud. — Att. — Menzies.*

NICHOLAS GIUSTINIANI (Bl) C. O.S.B.
A.C. Nov. 21
d. p. 1180. A Venetian belonging to the noble family of the Giustiniani. He became a Benedictine in the monastery of San Niccolò del Lido. After all his brothers had been killed in battle at Constantinople the Doge obtained from the pope a dispensation for Nicholas to marry and beget heirs for the family. He accordingly married and had six sons and three daughters. In his old age Nicholas returned to the abbey. He has always been venerated at Venice. *Cf. Zimm. — Holw.*

NICHOLAS TAVIGLI (Bl) M. O.F.M.
A.C. Dec. 5
d. 1391. Born in the diocese of Sebenico in Dalmatia, he joined the Friars Minor, and was sent to the Bosnian mission, where he worked for twenty years among the paterine schismatics. Thence he travelled to Palestine to preach to the Mohammedans and was by them cut to pieces at Jerusalem. Cult confirmed by Leo XIII. *Cf. Holw. — Att.*

NICHOLAS (St) Bp. **R.M. Dec. 6**
d. c.350. One of the most popular saints in Christendom. His cult is based mainly on legend, since almost nothing is known of his life, excepting the bare facts that he was a bishop of Myra in Lycia, and that his alleged relics were stolen by Italian merchants in 1087 and now are enshrined at Bari. Legend, however, has abundantly supplied the lack of known data, as witness the life of the saint written by Simon Metaphrastes in the tenth century. To this day he is venerated as the patron saint of sailors, of captives, and especially of children. The last mentioned veneration derives from the story that he raised to life three children who had been pickled in a brine-tub. Numerous medieval observances were connected with this saint, for example, that of Santa Klaus (Sint Klaes, Sanctus Nicolaus), and the ceremony of the boy-bishop which still survives at Montserrat in Catalonia. St Nicholas is a patron saint of Russia. *Cf. Att. — Baud. — Holw. — Menzies — Ricci.*

NICHOLAS CHRYSOBERGES (St) Bp.
A.C. Dec. 16
d. 996. Patriarch of Constantinople (983-996). He was, and always remained, a staunch Catholic. *Cf. Holw.*

NICHOLAS FACTOR (St) C. O.F.M.
A.C. Dec. 23
1520-1582. Born at Valencia in Spain. He became a Franciscan in 1537 and spent his life as an itinerant preacher, pitilessly scourging himself before every sermon. He was beatified in 1786, SS Paschal Baylon and Louis Bertrand being called as witnesses in the process of beatification. *Cf. P. de U. — Holw. — Att.*

NICODEMUS (St) M. **R.M. Aug. 3**
1st cent. The faithful, though timid, disciple of Christ mentioned in the gospel of St John (ch III), styled by our Lord "a master in Israel." He shared with St Joseph of Arimathaea the privilege of

laying Christ in the tomb. One of the apocryphal gospels was circulated under his name. On Aug. 3 is kept the feast of the finding of his body with that of St Stephen and others. He has always been venerated as a martyr.
Cf. Holw. — Baud.

NICOLINO MAGALOTTI (Bl) H.
A.C. Nov. 29
d. 1370. A Franciscan tertiary who lived as a hermit near Camerino for thirty years. Cult approved in 1856.
Cf. Holw.

NICOMEDES (St) M.   R.M. Sept. 15
d. c.90. A Roman priest martyred in Rome at a very early period. Some say under Domitian. In later legends he is associated with SS Nereus, Achilleus and Petronilla.
Cf. Holw. — Baud. — Att.

NICOMEDIA, Martyrs of (SS)
The R.M. lists four anonymous groups of martyrs who suffered at Nicomedia on the Hellespont, for a time the principal residence of the Roman emperors in the East.

R.M. March 18
d. c.300. A band of 10,000 beheaded probably about that year.

R.M. June 23
d. c.303. Numerous martyrs (some suggest 20,000) who hid in the mountains and caves, and were hunted down by the persecutors.

R.M. Dec. 23
d. c.304. A group of twenty martyrs.

R.M. Dec. 25
d. 303. Many thousands (the Greeks say 20,000) burnt alive by order of Diocletian in the great basilica of Nicomedia where they had assembled to celebrate Christmas.
Probably the above figures are exaggerated. There are other difficulties in accepting the stories as they stand, e.g., Christmas was not celebrated in the East until a later period.
Cf. Holw. — Baud. — Att.

NICON and Comp. (SS) MM.
R.M. March 23
d. c.250. Nicon was a Roman soldier of distinction, who, while travelling in the East, became a Christian and a monk. Several disciples gathered around him and

when persecution threatened Palestine, they fled to Sicily where they were martyred under Decius. The R.M. wrongly assigns them to Caesarea in Palestine.
Cf. Holw. — Baud.

NICON (St) M.   R.M. Sept. 28
See Mark, Alphius, etc.

NICON (St) C.   R.M. Nov. 26
d. 998. Surnamed *Metanoite*, because penance (in Greek *metanoia*) was always the theme of his preaching. He was an Armenian monk first at Khrysopetro and then in his native country, where he carried on missionary work. This he continued later in Crete and in Greece.
Cf. Att. — Holw. — Baud.

NICOSTRATUS, ANTIOCHUS and Comp. (SS) MM.   R.M. May 21
d. 303. A cohort of Roman soldiers said to have been put to death at Caesarea Philippi, in Palestine, under Diocletian. Nicostratus was their tribune. Their story occurs in the apocryphal *Acta* of St Procopius, M.
Cf. Holw. — Baud.

NICOSTRATUS (St) M.
R.M. July 7 and Nov. 8
See Claudius, Nicostratus, etc.

NIDAN (St) C.   A.C. Sept. 30
Otherwise Midan, q.v.

NIDGER (NIDGAR, NITGAR) (Bl) Bp. O.S.B.   A.C. Apr. 15
d. c.829. Said to have been abbot of the Benedictine monastery of Ottobeuren in Bavaria. He became bishop of Augsburg in 822.
Cf. Chev. — Holw. — Zimm.

NIGHTON (St) C.   A.C. June 17
Otherwise Nectan, q.v.

NILAMMON (St) H.   R.M. June 6
d. 404. An Egyptian monk, who to avoid consecration as a bishop, barricaded his cell and died in prayer, while the consecrating prelates were waiting outside.
Cf. Holw. — Baud.

NILUS (St) M.   R.M. Feb. 20
See Tyrannio, Sylvanus, etc.

NILUS (St) M.   R.M. Sept. 19
See Peleus, Nilus, etc.

NILUS the YOUNGER (St) Ab.
R.M. Sept. 26
d. 1004. A Greek of S. Italy, who, after a careless youth, joined the Basilian monks of the abbey of St Adrian in Calabria, of which he soon after became abbot. In 981 the invading Saracens drove the community to Vellelucio in the *Terra di Lavoro*, where they lived on land given them by Montecassino. While sick at Frascati shortly before his death Nilus designated that city as the place where his community were to be definitely established and there in fact the still flourishing abbey of Grottaferrata was founded by his disciple St Bartholomew. The monks of Grottaferrata profess the Basilian rule and use the Greek rite, and they regard St Nilus as their founder and first abbot.
Cf. Att. — Baud. — Holw.

NILUS the ELDER (St) Ab.
R.M. Nov. 12
d. c.430. Surnamed "the Wise." An imperial official at Constantinople, who when already advanced in years embraced the solitary life with one of his sons on Mt Sinai. He was a staunch friend and defender of St John Chrysostom. He is now best remembered as an ascetical theological and biblical writer of some distinction.
Cf. Att. — Baud. — Holw.

NIMMIA (St) M.   R.M. Aug. 12
See Hilaria, Digna, etc.

NINIAN (St) Bp.   R.M. Sept. 16
d. ? 432. A Briton who was educated in Rome, and thence sent to evangelize his native country. He established his episcopal see at Whithorn (*Candida Casa*, the White House) in Wigtownshire, so called because the cathedral was built of white stone. There was a monastery attached to it, and it was from this centre that Ninian and his monks evangelized the northern Britons and the Picts.
Cf. Holw. — Att. — Baud.

NINO (or CHRISTIANA) (St) V.
R.M. Dec. 15
d. c.320. A native of Colastri in Cappadocia. The R.M. not knowing her local name, calls her "Christiana." As a slave or captive she was brought into Georgia (Iberia) and was the means of spreading Christianity in that country. She is venerated as the apostle of Georgia.

Substantially her story is true, but many myths and contradictory legends have been added to it.
Cf. Holw. — Att. — Baud.

NISSEN (St) Ab.   A.C. July 25
5th cent. An Irish convert of St Patrick, by whom he was set over a monastery at Montgarth (Mountgarret) in Wexford.
Cf. Holw.

NITHARD (St) M. O.S.B.   A.C. Feb. 4
d. 845. Monk of Corbie in Saxony and companion of St Anschar, whom he followed to Sweden as a missionary. He was martyred there by the pagan Swedes.
Cf. Zimm. — Holw. — Chev. — Baud.

NIVARD (Bl) Mk. O.S.B. Cist.
P.C. Feb. 7
c.1000-p. 1150. The youngest brother of St Bernard. He followed his brother to Clairvaux and eventually was appointed novice-master at Vaucelles. Our information as to his later career is rather confused. Cult not yet officially confirmed.
Cf. Holw. — Chev.

NIVARD (St) Bp.   A.C. Sept. 1
d. c.670. Archbishop of Reims. Brother-in-law of King Childeric II of Austrasia. He restored the abbey of Hautvilliers, where he was buried.
Cf. Baud. — Holw.

NIZIER (St) Bp.   R.M. Apr. 2
Otherwise Nicetius, q.v.

NOEL (*several*)
The French form of Natalis, q.v.

NOMINANDA (St) M.   R.M. Dec. 31
See Donata, Paulina, etc.

NONIUS ALVAREZ (Bl) O.C.
A.C. Nov. 6
1360-1431. Nuñez Alvarez de Pereira was born at Bomjardin in Portugal and was bred to arms. He served his king in the wars for the independence of Portugal, and, after the death of his wife, became a Carmelite lay-brother at Lisbon. Cult confirmed in 1918.
Cf. A.A.S., 1918, p. 102 — Att. — Holw.

NONNA (St) W.   R.M. Aug. 5
d. 374. Wife of St Gregory of Nazianzen the Elder, whom she converted to the

Faith. Their three children are also venerated as saints.
Cf. Holw. — Baud. — Att.

NONNITA (NONNA, NON) (St) W.
A.C. March 3
6th cent. The mother of St David of Wales. She ended her days as a nun, according to some writers in a nunnery in Brittany.
Cf. Holw. — Baud.

NONNOSUS (St) Mk. O.S.B.
R.M. Sept. 2
d. c.575. A Benedictine monk, *praepositus* in the abbey of Mt Soracte, near Rome. His wonderful deeds of faith are recorded by St Gregory the Great.
Cf. Chev. — Holw.

NONNUS (St) Bp. **R.M. Dec. 2**
d. c.458. A monk of Tabennisi in Egypt, promoted in 448 to the see of Edessa. He laboured with great success among the Arabians around Heliopolis (Baalbeck). He is connected with the conversion of St Pelagia.
Cf. Att. — Holw.

NORBERT (St) Bp. Founder.
R.M. June 6
c.1080-1134. Born of a princely family at Xanten, he led a worldly life at the German court and even received holy orders as a means to worldly advancement. In 1115 a narrow escape from death brought about his conversion. After endeavouring to reform the chapter of canons at Xanten, he became an itinerant preacher. In 1120 he was given the territory of Prémontré near Laon, and here he founded a community of canons regular under the Rule of St Augustine, since known as Norbertines or Premonstratensians. The new Order soon spread over Western Europe. Norbert himself was compelled to accept the see of Magdeburg, where he set about the reformation of his clergy, even resorting to force when it was necessary. He was a zealous exponent of the doctrine of the Real Presence and fostered the cult of the Blessed Sacrament. Canonized in 1582.
Cf. Holw. — Baud. — Att.

NORTH AMERICA (Martyrs of) (SS)
S.J. **A.C. March 16**
1642-1649. A group of six Jesuit priests and two lay-brothers martyred in N.

America at various dates between 1642 and 1649 while evangelizing the Red Indians. Their names are: John de Brébeuf, Isaac Jogues, Antony Daniel, Gabriel Lalemant, Charles Garnier and Noel Chabanel, priests; and John Lalande and René Goupil, lay-brothers. They were working among the Hurons when they met their death at the hands of the Iroquois, the mortal enemies of the Hurons. The Iroquois were animated by bitter hatred of the missionaries, whom they subjected to indescribable tortures before putting them to death. Canonized in 1930.
Cf. Prop. S.J. — Att.

NOSTRAINUS (St) Bp. **R.M. Feb. 14**
d. c.450. Bishop of Naples, a valiant opponent of Arianism and Pelagianism.
Cf. Menzies — Holw. — Baud.

NOTBURGA (St) V. **A.C. Sept. 14**
d. 1313. A Tyrolese serving-maid. She joyfully fulfilled her humble duties first in a noble household, then in that of a peasant. She made it one of her duties to help those poorer than herself. Her shrine is at Eben in the Tyrolese mountains. Cult confirmed in 1862.
Cf. Holw. — Att. — Baud.

NOTBURGA (NOITBURGIS) (St) N.
O.S.B. **A.C. Oct. 31**
d. c.714. A Benedictine nun in the convent of St Mary in the capitol, at Cologne.
Cf. Zimm. — Holw. — Baud. — Chev.

NOTHELM (St) Bp. **A.C. Oct. 17**
d. c.740. Archbishop of Canterbury, friend and collaborator of St Bede and correspondent of St Boniface.
Cf. Stanton — Att. — Baud. — Chev.

NOTKER BALBULUS (Bl) Mk. O.S.B.
A.C. Apr. 6
d. 912. Nicknamed *Balbulus*, i.e., the Stammerer. He was born at Heiligau (now Elgg) in the canton of Zurich and when still a child entered the Benedictine abbey of St Gall, where he spent his whole life, holding the offices of librarian, guestmaster and precentor. He excelled as a musician and was the originator of liturgical sequences, he himself composing both the words and the music of many of them. A description of him by one of his contemporaries is worth quoting: "weakly in body but not in mind, slow of tongue but

not of intellect, pressing forward boldly in things divine, a vessel filled with the Holy Ghost without equal in his time." Cult confirmed in 1512.
Cf. Zimm. — P. de U. — Att. — Chev. — Holw.

NOVATUS (St) R.M. June 20
d. c.151. Alleged son of Pudens, the senator, and brother of SS Praxedes and Pudentiana.
Cf. Holw. — Baud.

NOVELLONE (Bl) H. O.S.B.
A.C. July 27
Otherwise Nevolo, q.v.

NOYALA (St) V.M. A.C. July 6
? A British maiden, beheaded at Beignan in Brittany. According to the legend she walked to Pontivy holding her head in her hands. She is greatly venerated in Brittany.
Cf. Holw. — Baud.

NUMERIAN (MEMORIAN) (St) Bp. O.S.B. R.M. July 5
d. c.666. Son of a rich senator of Trèves, he first became a monk in that city under St Arnulph, and then went to reside in the abbey of Luxeuil under St Walbert. Ultimately he was appointed bishop of his native city.
Cf. Holw. — Baud. — Duch. Fast. Episc.

NUMIDICUS and Comp. (SS) MM.
R.M. Aug. 9
d. 252. A group of African martyrs burnt at the stake at Carthage under Decius (not Valerian). Numidicus is said to have been dragged still breathing out of the ashes of the funeral pyre and to have lived to be ordained priest by St Cyprian.
Cf. Holw. — Baud.

NUNCTUS (NOINT) (St) Ab. M.
A.C. Oct. 22
d. 668. Abbot of a monastery near Mérida, in W. Spain. He was killed by robbers and venerated thenceforward as a martyr.
Cf. Holw. — Baud.

NUNILO and ALODIA (SS) VV. MM.
R.M. Oct. 22
d. 851. Two sisters born at Adahuesca, in the province of Huesca, Spain. After their birth their Christian mother married

a Mohammedan, who brutally persecuted them, had them imprisoned at Alquézar, near Barastoro, and finally beheaded at Huesca during the persecution of Abderrahman II. They are still greatly venerated in Aragon.
Cf. P. de U. — Holw. — Baud. — Att.

NYMPHA (St) V.M. R.M. Nov. 10
See Tryphon, Respicius and Nympha.

NYMPHODORA (St) M. R.M. March 13
See Theusetas, Horres, etc.

NYMPHODORA (St) V.M.
R.M. Sept. 10
See Menodora, Metrodora and Nymphodora.

O

OBDULIA (St) V. R.M. Sept. 5
? A virgin venerated at Toledo, where her relics are enshrined. Nothing is known about her beyond her name and cult.
Cf. Holw. — Baud. — P. de U.

OBITIUS (St) Mk. O.S.B. A.C. Feb. 4
d. c.1204. A knight of Brescia, who narrowly escaped drowning and, terrified by a vision of hell, gave himself to a life of austere penance as a Benedictine lay-brother in the service of the Benedictine nuns of St Julia at Brescia. Cult approved in 1900.
Cf. Holw. — Baud. — Att.

OCEANUS (St) M. R.M. Sept. 4
See Theodore, Oceanus, etc.

OCTAVIAN and Comp. MM.
R.M. March 22
d. 484. Octavian, archdeacon of the church at Carthage, and several thousand companions suffered martyrdom at that city under the Arian Vandal king Hunneric.
Cf. Holw. — Baud.

OCTAVIAN (Bl) Bp. O.S.B. A.C. Aug. 6
c.1060-c.1128. Born at Quingey in the diocese of Besançon and a brother of Pope Callixtus II. Educated by the Benedictines, he became a Benedictine himself at the abbey of St Peter in *Ciel d'Oro*, at Pavia. In 1129 he was promoted to the see of Savona. Cult confirmed in 1783.
Cf. Chev. — Gams — Holw. — Baud.

OCTAVIUS, SOLUTOR and ADVENTOR (SS) MM.   **R.M. Nov. 20**
d. 297. Patron saints of Turin, where they suffered martyrdom. At a later date their story became connected with the legend of the Theban Legion.
Cf. Holw. — Baud. — Menzies.

ODA (Bl) V. O.Praem.   **P.C. Apr. 20**
d. 1158. Daughter of a noble family in Brabant, she avoided marriage with a young nobleman by disfiguring her face. She was then allowed to follow her religious vocation in the Premonstratensian nunnery of Rivroelles, of which she eventually became prioress. Her cult has never been officially confirmed.
Cf. Att. — Baud. — Holw.

ODA (St) W.   **A.C. Oct. 23**
d. c.723. A French princess married to the duke of Aquitaine. In her widowhood she devoted herself to the care of the poor and suffering. Her shrine is at Amay, near Liége.
Cf. Holw. — Baud.

ODDINO BARROTTI (Bl) C. A.C. July 21
1324-1400. A native of Fossano in Piedmont who became parish priest at the church of St John the Baptist at Fossano and a Franciscan tertiary. Later he resigned his cure of souls and turned his house into a hospital. He is still greatly venerated at Fossano. Cult approved in 1808.
Cf. Holw. — Att.

ODERISIUS (Bl) Card. O.S.B. A.C. Dec. 2
d. 1105. A son of the noble family of de' Marsi, in the diocese of Marsi, he was educated at Montecassino, where he became a Benedictine. In 1059 he was created cardinal deacon of St Agatha and shortly after cardinal priest of St Cyriacus in Termis. Finally, in 1087 he succeeded Bl Victor III as abbot of Montecassino. He was a poet and patron of scholars and the mediator between the crusaders and the Greek emperor Alexius.
Cf. Chev. — Gams — Holw.

ODGER (St) C.   **A.C. Sept. 10**
See Wiro, Plechelm and Otger.

ODHRAN (ORAN)(St) Ab.   **A.C. Oct. 27**
Otherwise Otteran, q.v.

ODILIA (St) V. O.S.B.   **R.M. Dec. 13**
Otherwise Ottilia, q.v.

ODILO (St) Ab. O.S.B.   **R.M. Jan. 1**
c.962-1049. A scion of the noble family of Mercoeur in Auvergne. About the year 990 he joined the community of Cluny, became abbot coadjutor in 992 and abbot in 994. Gentle and kind, he was known throughout Christendom for his liberality to the needy. A friend of popes and princes, he was the promotor of the Truce of God and instituted the annual commemoration of the faithful departed (1031). Under his government the Cluniac houses increased from 37 to 65. He was surnamed by his contemporaries "the Archangel of Monks" — *Archangelus Monachorum.*
Cf. Zimm. — Holw. — Att. — Baud.

ODILO (Bl) Ab. O.S.B.   **A.C. Oct. 15**
d. p. 954. A Benedictine of Gorze in Lorraine, who in 945 was elected abbot of Stavelot-Malmédy. He raised the standard of studies and discipline in the abbey.
Cf. Zimm.

ODO of NOVARA (Bl) C. O.Cart.   **A.C. Jan. 14**
c. 1105-c. 1200. A native of Novara who became a Carthusian and was made prior of Geyrach in Slavonia. However, owing to difficulties with the bishop he resigned and became chaplain to a convent at Tagliacozzo in Italy, where he died at a very advanced age. Cult confirmed in 1859.
Cf. Att. — Baud. — Holw.

ODO of BEAUVAIS (St) Bp. O.S.B.   **A.C. Jan. 28**
801-880. Born near Beauvais, he gave up his profession of arms to become a Benedictine at Corbie, where he was tutor to the sons of Charles Martel. In 1851 he succeeded St Paschasius Radbertus as abbot. In 861 he was raised to the see of Beauvais, where his reforms greatly influenced the whole church of N. France. He was the mediator between Pope Nicholas I and Hincmar of Reims. Cult approved by Pius IX.
Cf. Chev. — Baud. — Holw.

ODO of MASSAY (Bl) Ab. O.S.B.   **A.C. June 7**
d. 967. A Benedictine abbot of Massay (935-967), a house belonging to the Cluniac observance.
Cf. Zimm.

ODO of CAMBRAI (Bl) Bp. O.S.B.
A.C. June 19
1050-1113. A native of Orleans who became the headmaster (*scholasticus*) of the cathedral school at Tournai. In c.1090 he was converted to a higher life by reading St Augustine on free will, and founded a community of Benedictines in the disused abbey of St Martin at Tournai. In 1105 he was made bishop of Cambrai, but, on refusing to receive secular investiture, was exiled to the abbey of Anchin where he died. He was one of the most learned French scholars of the eleventh century. *Cf. Zimm. — Att. — Chev. — Holw.*

ODO the GOOD (St) Bp. O.S.B.
A.C. July 4
d. 959. Born in East Anglia of Danish parents, he became a bishop in Wessex and was present at the battle of Brunanburh. In 942 he was appointed to Canterbury. He tried to escape consecration by declaring that, unlike previous archbishops, he was not a monk, and he consented to accept the dignity only after he had received the Benedictine habit from the hands of the abbot of Fleury. As archbishop he took a prominent part in the legislation of Kings Edmund and Edgar and paved the way for the monastic restoration under SS Dunstan, Oswald (Odo's nephew) and Ethelwold. *Cf. Zimm. — Att. — Baud. — Holw. — Stanton.*

ODO of URGELL (St) Bp. R.M. July 7
d. 1122. A scion of the house of the counts of Barcelona who, after following the profession of arms, entered the service of the Church. He was appointed archdeacon of Urgell in the Pyrenees and in 1095 was consecrated by Pope Urban II bishop of the same town. His outstanding characteristic was love of the poor. *Cf. Holw. — Baud.*

ODO of CLUNY (St) Ab. O.S.B.
R.M. Nov. 18
c.879-942. Born in Maine, he was educated at the cathedral school of St Martin at Tours. In 909 he became a Benedictine at Baume under Bl Berno, the abbot-founder of Cluny, to the government of which latter abbey he succeeded in 927. Under his prudent and paternal rule Cluny began to exert its influence throughout France and in Italy, including Rome, where the saint was asked to restore the

observance at St Paul-outside-the-Walls. He died at Tours, by the tomb of St Martin. He was one of the great abbots who enhanced the prestige of the Benedictine Order. *Cf. Zimm. — P. de U. — Att. — Holw. — Chev. — Baud.*

ODORIC of PORDENONE (Bl) C.
O.F.M. A.C. Feb. 3
1285-1331. Odoric Mattiuzzi was born at Villanova near Pordenone in Friuli, became ●a Franciscan, and spent some years as a recluse. Then he set out on his apostolic missions, journeying through the Near and the Far East and entering China. After sixteen years of such labours he returned to Europe to report to the pope at Avignon, but died at Udine. Cult confirmed in 1775. *Cf. Baud. — Att. — Holw.*

ODRAN (St) M. A.C. Feb. 19
d. c.452. The chariot-driver of St Patrick. He gave his life for his master by taking his place when his life was sought by pagans. *Cf. Holw. — Baud.*

ODRAN (St) Ab. A.C. July 7
6th cent. Brother of St Medran and a disciple of St Kieran of Saghir. Later he became abbot of a monastery at Muskerry. *Cf. Holw.*

ODRIAN (St) Bp. A.C. May 8
? One of the early bishops of Waterford. *Cf. Holw.*

ODULPHUS (St) C. O.S.A. A.C. June 12
d. c.855. A native of Brabant, appointed canon of Utrecht by St Frederick, whom he greatly helped in the evangelization of Frisia. He founded a monastery of Augustinian canons at Stavoren. His relics are said to have been stolen in 1034 and taken to London and from there to Evesham abbey. *Cf. Holw. — Att. — Baud.*

ODUVALD (St) Ab. A.C. May 26
d. 698. A Scottish nobleman who became a monk and later abbot of Melrose. He was a contemporary of St Cuthbert. *Cf. Holw. — Baud.*

OFFA (St) Abs. O.S.B. A.C. Dec. 31
d. c.1070. A Benedictine abbess of St Peter's at Benevento. *Cf. Chev. — Mab.*

OGERIUS (OGLER) (Bl) Ab. O.S.B. Cist.
                              A.C. Sept. 10
d. 1214. A Cistercian abbot of Locedio,
in the diocese of Vercelli. He wrote a
series of sermons in defence of the doctrine
of the Immaculate Conception. Cult confirmed in 1875.
Cf. Holw. — Baud. — Chev.

OGMUND (St) Bp.   A.C. March 8
d. 1121. Bishop of Holar in Iceland. He
is venerated as one of the apostles of that
island. Canonized in 1201. ◦
Cf. Holw.

OLALLA (St) V.M.   R.M. Dec. 10
Otherwise Eulalia of Mérida, q.v.

**OLAV of NORWAY (OLAVUS, OLAF,
OLAUS, TOOLEY) (St) King M.**
                              R.M. July 29
995-1030. Son of King Harald of Norway.
His early youth was spent, after the manner of his countrymen in those days, as a
pirate. In 1010 he received baptism at
Rouen and in 1013 helped Ethelred of
England against the Danes. In 1015 he
succeeded to the throne of Norway and
at once summoned missionaries, chiefly
from England, to complete the Christiani-
zation of the country. He succeeded to
some extent, but his measures were harsh
and he was driven from his kingdom. In
an attempt to recover it he fell in battle
at Stiklestadt. He is now regarded in
Norway as the champion of national independence.
Cf. Att. — Holw. — Baud.

OLAV of SWEDEN (St) King M.
                              A.C. July 30
d. c.950. A king of Sweden, murdered by
his rebellious heathen subjects for refusing
to sacrifice to idols at the spot where
Stockholm now stands.
Cf. Holw. — Baud.

OLCAN (St) Bp.   A.C. Feb. 20
Otherwise Bolcan, q.v.

OLGA (St) W.   A.C. July 11
c. 879-969. Wife of Igor I, duke of Kiev,
whom she married in 903. After his
assassination in 945 she ruled the country
for the rest of her life. In 958 she became
a Christian and made great, though unsuccessful, efforts to introduce Christianity
into Russia, a task which was achieved by
her grandson St Vladimir.
Cf. Att. — Holw. — Baud.

OLIVA (St) V.   R.M. June 3
? A nun of Anagni, near Rome, of whose
life we have no authentic particulars.
Cf. Holw. — Baud.

OLIVA (OLIVIA, OLIVE) (St) V.M.
                              A.C. June 10
? A virgin martyr venerated both at
Palermo and at Carthage. She is, however, a fictitious person, the heroine of a
romance the scene of which is laid among
the Mohammedans of Tunis, by whom also
she is held in high veneration.
Cf. Holw. — Att. — Baud.

**OLIVER (OLIVERIUS, LIBERIUS) (St)
C. O.S.B.   A.C. Feb. 3**
d. c.1050. A Benedictine monk of Santa
Maria di Portonuovo at Ancona.
Cf. Zimm. — Baud. — Holw.

OLIVER PLUNKET (Bl) Bp. M.
                              A.C. July 11
1629-1681. Born at Loughcrew in Co
Meath, he studied for the priesthood in
Rome, where he was ordained in 1654.
He remained there as professor of theology
in the college *de Propaganda Fide* till
1669. In that year he was consecrated
archbishop of Armagh and at once threw
himself courageously into the task of restoring the Irish church, laid waste by
continuous persecution. He was arrested
on a charge of complicity in one of the
sham plots of the time and, the Irish
judges refusing to convict him of treason,
he was brought for trial to London. Here,
too, his first trial collapsed for lack of evidence, but on a second trial he was found
guilty of treason "for propagating the
Catholic religion." While in prison Bl
Oliver made his Benedictine oblation in
the hands of his fellow prisoner, Dom
Maurus Corker, the president of the
English Benedictines, to whom also he be-
queathed his body, which is now enshrined
at Downside Abbey. He was the last
Catholic to be martyred at Tyburn. He
was beatified in 1920 and his canonization
is expected to take place before very long.
Cf. Att. — Holw.

**OLLEGARIUS (OLDEGAR, OLEGARI)
(St) Bp. O.S.A.   R.M. March 6**
1060-1137. Born at Barcelona, he joined
the Augustinian canons regular and was
prior in several houses in France before
being raised to the see of Barcelona in
1115. The following year he was trans-

ferred to the archbishopric of Tarragona. That diocese he successfully raised from the condition of neglect and decay into which it had fallen during the Moorish domination. He took part in the Lateran council of 1123.
Cf. Holw. — Att. — Baud. — P. de U.

OLYMPIADES (St) M. R.M. Apr. 15
See Maximus and Olympiades.

OLYMPIADES (St) M. R.M. Dec. 1
d. 303. Said to have been a Roman of consular rank tortured to death at Almeria (now Amelia) in central Italy, under Diocletian.
Cf. Holw. — Baud. — Menzies.

OLYMPIAS (St) W. R.M. Dec. 17
d. 408. A lady of noble birth at Constantinople who married Nebridius, prefect of the city. On her husband's death soon after their marriage she devoted herself to the service of the church, becoming a deaconess and establishing a "domestic community" of virgins in her own home. She loyally supported the cause of St John Chrysostom, and on this account was herself persecuted and exiled, her house being sold and her community disbanded. She died in exile at Nicomedia.
Cf. Att. — Holw. — Baud.

OLYMPIUS (St) Bp. R.M. June 12
d. p. 343. A bishop of Aenos (now Enos) in Rumelia, a contemporary of St Athanasius. He was a staunch opponent of Arianism and was driven from his see by the Arian emperor Constantius.
Cf. Holw. — Baud.

OLYMPIUS (St) M. R.M. July 26
See Symphronius, Olympius, etc.

OMER (AUDOMARUS) (St) Bp. O.S.B.
R.M. Sept. 9
c. 595-c. 670. Born in the territory of Constance, he became a monk at Luxeuil, and after some twenty years was raised to the see of Thérouanne (which at that time embraced what is now called Pas-de-Calais and Flanders, in Belgic Gaul). The diocese sadly needed evangelization, and for this purpose St Omer secured the services of a numerous band of fellow-monks, who literally covered that district with abbeys. The saint himself was the co-founder of Sithin, over which he placed

St Bertinus. Round this abbey grew up the town now known as Saint-Omer.
Cf. Mab. — Zimm. — Chev. — Baud. — Holw. — Att.

ONCHO (ONCHUO) (St) C. A.C. Feb. 8
d. c.600. An Irish pilgrim, who was also a poet, a guardian of the Celtic traditions and a collector of holy relics. While pursuing his search for memorials of the Irish saints he died at Clonmore monastery, then governed by St Maidoc, and his body was there enshrined together with the relics he had gathered.
Cf. Holw. — Baud.

ONESIMUS (St) M. R.M. Feb. 16
d. c.90. The slave who ran away from his master Philemon, was converted by St Paul in Rome, and was the occasion of the apostle's letter to Philemon. The R.M. has confused him with another Onesimus, who was bishop of Ephesus after St Timothy.
Cf. Att. — Holw. — Baud.

ONESIMUS (St) Bp. A.C. May 13
d. c.361. Fifth bishop of Soissons.
Cf. Duch. Fast. Episc. — Holw. — Baud.

ONESIPHORUS and PORPHYRIUS (SS) MM. R.M. Sept. 6
d. c.80. Onesiphorus is mentioned by St Paul in the second epistle to Timothy (IV, 19). Tradition adds that he followed St Paul to Spain and then back to the East, where he was martyred under Domitian somewhere on the Hellespont by being tied to wild horses and so torn to pieces. Porphyrius is described as a member of his household, who shared in the work and the martyrdom of his master.
Cf. Holw. — Baud.

ONUPHRIUS (HUMPHREY) (St) H.
R.M. June 12
d. c.400. An Egyptian who lived as a hermit for seventy years in the desert of the Thebais, in Upper Egypt. He was a very popular saint in the Middle Ages, both in the East and in the West. He is the patron saint of weavers, probably because "he was dressed only in his own abundant hair and a loin-cloth of leaves."
Cf. Att. — Holw. — Baud.

OPPORTUNA (St) Abs. O.S.B.
A.C. Apr. 22
d. c.770. Born near Ayesmes in Nor-

mandy, sister of St Chrodegand, bishop of Séez. At an early age she entered the Benedictine abbey of Montreuil, of which she became abbess. She is described as "a true mother to all her nuns." Her cult has always been very flourishing in France. *Cf. Holw. — Chev. — Att. — Baud.*

OPTATIAN (St) Bp.   **R.M. July 14**
d. c.505. Bishop of Brescia c. 451-c. 505. *Cf. Menzies — Holw. — Baud.*

OPTATUS (St) M.   **R.M. Apr. 16**
See Saragossa (Martyrs of).

OPTATUS of MILEVIS (St) Bp.
                              R.M. June 4
d. c.387. Bishop of Milevis in Numidia. He was an excellent controversialist against the Donatists — resourceful and vigorous but conciliatory. He wrote six treatises against them which are praised by his contemporaries, chiefly by SS Augustine and Fulgentius of Ruspe. He is often quoted in modern controversial works against heresy and schism. *Cf. Holw. — Att. — Baud.*

OPTATUS (St) Bp.   **R.M. Aug. 31**
d. c.530. A bishop of Auxerre who died in the second year of his episcopate. *Cf. Holw. — Baud. — Duch. Fast. Episc.*

ORAN (St) Ab.   **A.C. Oct. 27**
Otherwise Otteran, q.v.

ORANGE (Martyrs of) (BB). **A.C. July 6**
d. 1794. A group of thirty-two nuns — one Benedictine, two Cistercians, thirteen religious of the Institute of Perpetual Adoration and sixteen Ursulines — imprisoned during the French Revolution in the public gaol at Orange for several months and ultimately guillotined there. They were martyred on different days during the month of July. Beatified in 1925. Each receives a special notice in this book.

ORDONIUS (ORDOÑO) (St) Bp. O.S.B.
                              A.C. Feb. 23
d. 1066. Monk of the Benedictine abbey (Cluniac observance) of Sahagún, in the province of León, Spain, and afterwards bishop of Astorga (1062-1066). *Cf. Zimm. — P. de U.*

ORENTIUS and PATIENTIA (SS) MM.
                              R.M. May 1
d. c.240. Husband and wife, who lived at Loret, near Huesca, in N. Aragon. An ancient Spanish tradition makes them the parents of St Laurence the martyr. *Cf. Holw. — P. de U.*

ORENTIUS (or ORIENTIUS) of AUCH (St) Bp.   **R.M. May 1**
d. c.439. A hermit in the Lavendan valley near Tarbes, whom the people of Auch insisted on having for their bishop. He governed that see for over forty years. *Cf. Holw. — Baud.*

ORENTIUS, HEROS, PHARNACIUS, FIRMINUS, FIRMUS, CYRIAC and LONGINUS (SS) MM. **R.M. June 24**
d. c.304. Described in the R.M. as seven brothers who, on account of their faith, were deprived of their military belt by the Emperor Maximian, taken away to various places and put to death. *Cf. Holw. — Baud.*

ORESTES (St) M.   **R.M. Nov. 9**
d. 304. A martyr of Cappadocia, tortured to death under Diocletian. *Cf. Holw. — Baud.*

ORESTES (St) M.   **R.M. Dec. 13**
See Eustratius, Auxentius, etc.

ORGONNE (St) V.   **R.M. Jan. 30**
Otherwise Aldegund, q.v.

ORIA (St) V. O.S.B.   **A.C. March 11**
Otherwise Aurea, q.v.

ORICULUS and Comp. (SS) MM.
                              R.M. Nov. 18
d. c.430. A group of martyrs, put to death by the Arian Vandals in the province of Carthage. *Cf. Holw. — Baud.*

ORINGA (or CHRISTIANA) of the CROSS (Bl) V. O.S.A. **A.C. Jan. 4**
d. 1310. A Tuscan serving maid who, in spite of the fact that she passed most of her life in domestic service, succeeded in founding a convent at Castello di Santa Croce in the valley of the Arno, to which she gave the Augustinian Rule. *Cf. Att. — Holw. — Baud.*

ORLANDO (Bl) H. O.S.B. Vall.
                              A.C. May 20
d. 1212. A Vallombrosan lay-brother who was celebrated as an exorcist. *Cf. Holw. — Chev.*

ORONTIUS (St) M.　　　**R.M. Jan. 22**
See Vincent, Orontius and Victor.

ORSISIUS (St) H.　　　**A.C. June 15**
d. c.380. A favourite disciple of St Pachomius, and his assistant in drawing up the rules for the cenobites. He succeeded Pachomius as abbot. Some twelve years before his death he was forced to resign by his monks. He is the author of an ascetical treatise which St Jerome translated into Latin.
Cf. Holw. — Att.

OSANNA (*several*)
Otherwise Hosanna, q.v.

OSBURGA (or OSBERGA) (St) Abs. O.S.B.　　　**A.C. March 28**
d. c.1016. First abbess of the nunnery founded by King Canute at Coventry. Her cult was confirmed in the fifteenth century, and her feast is still kept in the diocese of Birmingham. The above data are commonly accepted, but she may be a saint of much earlier date.
Cf. Att. — Holw. — Zimm.

OSEE (HOSEA) (St) Prophet.
　　　R.M. July 4
8th cent. B. C. A prophet among the ten tribes of Israel. He seems to have been a contemporary of Isaiah. His prophecy was directed to his compatriots of Samaria, of which kingdom he foretells the destruction.
Cf. Holw. — Baud.

OSITH (St) M. O.S.B.　　　**A.C. Oct. 7**
Otherwise Osyth, q.v.

OSMANNA (OSANNA) (St) N. O.S.B.
　　　A.C. June 18
d. c.700. A nun of the Benedictine convent of Jouarre in France.
Cf. Zimm.

OSMANNA (or ARGARIARGA) (St) V.
　　　A.V. Sept. 9
d. c.650. An Irish maiden who crossed over to Brittany and became a solitary in a hermitage near Brieuc.
Cf. Holw. — Baud.

OSMUND (St) Bp.　　　**R.M. Dec. 4**
d. 1099. A Norman noble attached to the court of William the Conqueror, with whom he came to England and by whom he was made chancellor. In 1077 he was appointed to the see of Salisbury (Old Sarum), where he finished the cathedral and instituted a chapter of secular canons. He is especially remembered as the compiler of the liturgical services for his diocese, now known as the "Sarum use." His hobby was book-binding. Canonized in 1457.
Cf. Att. — Stanton — Holw. — Baud.

OSTIANUS (St) C.　　　**R.M. June 30**
? A saint venerated at Viviers. He is said to have been a priest, but nothing is now known about him.
Cf. Holw. — Baud.

OSWALD (St) Bp. O.S.B.　　　**A.C. Feb. 28**
d. 992. Born in England of a noble Danish family, he was educated under his uncle St Odo of Canterbury and was appointed dean of Winchester. Shortly after he crossed over to France and professed the Benedictine Rule at Fleury. At the suggestion of St Dunstan he was raised to the see of Worcester (960), and heartily identified himself with St Dunstan and with St Ethelwold in their efforts to revive monastic life and ecclesiastical discipline in England. St Oswald founded the abbey of Ramsey and the monastery at Worcester which later became the cathedral priory. In 972 he was promoted to the archbishopric of York, without relinquishing the government of the diocese of Worcester. He died while still on his knees after having performed his daily practice of washing the feet of twelve poor persons.
Cf. Zimm. — Att. — Holw. — Stanton — Baud.

OSWALD (St) King M.　　　**R.M. Aug. 5**
d. 642. The successor of King Edwin on the throne of Northumbria in the time of the Heptarchy. He was baptized at Iona during a period of exile among the Scots. In 635 he defeated the Welsh King Cadwalla near Hexham and with that victory his actual reign began. One of his chief aims was the complete evangelization of his country. In 642 he fell in battle at Maserfield fighting against the champion of paganism, Penda of Mercia. He has always been venerated as a martyr.
Cf. Stanton — Holw. — Att. — Baud.

OSWIN (St) King M.　　　**A.C. Aug. 20**
d. 651. A prince of Deira, part of the kingdom of Northumbria, he was edu-

cated by St Aidan. In 642 he succeeded St Oswald as ruler of Deira, but reigned only nine years, being killed at Gilling in Yorkshire by order of his cousin Oswy. He has ever since been venerated as a martyr.
Cf. Holw. — Att. — Stanton.

OSYTH (OSITH) (St) M. O.S.B.
A.C. Oct. 7
d. c.675. She was brought up in a Benedictine nunnery the name of which is no longer known. Later she founded a nunnery herself at a place called Chich, now St Osyth, on a creek of the Colne in Essex. She was murdered there by Danish pirates.
Cf. Att. — Stanton — Holw. — Baud.

OTHMAR (OTMAR, AUDEMAR) (St) Ab. O.S.B. R.M. Nov. 16
d. 759. Of Teutonic origin and already a priest, in 720 he was appointed abbot of the then dilapidated monastery of St Gall. He introduced at once the Benedictine Rule and a new period of prosperity began for the abbey, which soon became the most important in Switzerland. He was persecuted by two neighbouring counts, unjustly calumniated and condemned by an ecclesiastical tribunal. He bore his sufferings with great patience, and died in prison.
Cf. Holw. — Chev. — Zimm. — Baud.

OTHO (St) M. O.F.M. R.M. Jan. 16
See Berardus, Peter, etc.

OTTERAN (ODHRAN) (St) Ab.
A.C. Oct. 27
c.563. An Irish abbot of Meath who crossed over to Scotland with St Columba, and was the first to die at Iona. His feast is kept throughout Ireland. He has given its name to Oronsay.
Cf. Holw. — Baud. — Att.

OTILLIA (ODILIA, OTHILIA, ADILIA) (St) Abs. O.S.B. R.M. Dec. 13
d. c.720. According to tradition St Ottilia was born blind and cast out for this reason by her family. She was adopted by a convent, where she miraculously recovered her sight. Eventually she became abbess foundress of Hohenburg (now Odilienberg) and of Niedermünster, both under the Benedictine Rule. Her life as it comes down to us abounds in extraordinary legends.
Cf. Mab. — Att. — Baud. — Holw. — Zimm.

OTTO of BAMBERG (St) Bp.
R.M. July 2
d. 1139. Born in S. Germany, he was chosen bishop of Bamberg under the emperor Henry IV, whom he endeavoured to reconcile with the Holy See. He was more successful in his missionary activities among the Pomeranians, and is honoured as their apostle. Canonized in 1189.
Cf. Holw. — Baud. — Att.

OTTO of HEIDELBERG (Bl) H. O.S.B.
A.C. Dec. 28
d. 1344. A brother of Bl Herman of Heidelberg and, like him, a monk and priest at the Benedictine abbey of Niederaltaich in Bavaria. After his brother's death in 1326, Otto exercised his priestly office at the cell where Bl Herman had died.
Cf. Zimm. — Chev. — Baud.

OUDACEUS (In Welsh: Eddogwy) (St) Ab. (?). A.C. July 2
d. c.600. Son of Budic, prince of Brittany, but brought up in Wales by his uncle St Teilo, whom perhaps he succeeded in the abbacy of Llandeilo Fawr. He is wrongly described as bishop of Llanduff.
Cf. Stanton — Holw. — Att.

OUEN (AUDOËNUS, ALDWIN, OWEN, DADO) (St) Bp. R.M. Aug. 24
610-684. Son of St Authaire (q.v.). He founded the abbey of Rebais, was consecrated bishop of Rouen in 641, attended the Synod of Châlons in 644, and died near Paris in 684.
Cf. Chev. — Holw.

OWEN (OWIN, OUINI) (St) H. O.S.B.
A.C. March 3
d. 680. After having been steward in the household of St Etheldreda, he became a monk at Lastingham under St Chad, and when the latter was appointed bishop of Mercia he settled St Owen with other monks in a house near Lichfield.
Cf. Holw. — Zimm. — Att. — Baud.

OYAND (St) Ab. R.M. Jan. 1
Otherwise Eugendus, q.v.

OYE (St) M. R.M. Dec. 11
Otherwise Eutychius, q.v.

OYS (St) C. A.C. Apr. 22
Otherwise Authaire, q.v.

P

PABIALI (St) C.   A.C. Nov. 1
5th (or 6th) cent. Son of the British
prince Brychan by his Spanish wife
Proistri: he is said to have gone to Spain.
He is patron of a chapel called Partypallai
in Wales.
Cf. Holw.

PABO (St) C.   A.C. Nov. 9
d. c.510. Surnamed "Post-Prydain," i.e.,
the prop of N. Britain. He was the son
of a chieftain on the Scottish border and
at first a soldier. Later he came to Wales
and founded the monastery called after
him Llanbabon, in Anglesey.
Cf. Holw.

PACHOMIUS (St) Ab.   **R.M. May 9**
d. 292-346. Born in the Upper Thebaid,
he followed at first the profession of arms
which he abandoned to receive baptism
(314) and three years later became a
hermit. In 318 he built his first monastery at Tabenna (Tabennisi), north of
Thebes on the east bank of the Nile, and
subsequently he established several others.
He governed them all much as a present
day superior general and wrote for them
the first known cenobitical rule, thus de-
parting from the then common type of
eremitical monachism. At the time of his
death he had seven thousand monks under
his rule. He is one of the most outstanding figures in the history of monachism.
Cf. Holw. — Baud. — Att.

PACHOMIUS (St) Bp. M. R.M. Nov. 26
See Faustus, Didius, etc.

PACIANUS (St) Bp.   **R.M. March 9**
d. c.390. Bishop of Barcelona from 365.
He wrote much on matters of ecclesiastical
discipline, but most of it is lost. His
treatise on penance is considered a classic.
In his first letter against Novatian occurs
the famous saying: "My name is Christian, my surname is Catholic."
Cf. Att. — Baud. — P. de U. — Holw.

PACIFICUS of CERANO (Bl) C. O.F.M.
                    A.C. June 8
1424-1482. Pacificus Ramota was born
at Cerano, diocese of Novara, and became
a Friar Minor in 1445. He excelled both
as a popular preacher and as a writer of
moral theology, his *Summa Pacifica* being

much used by his contemporaries. Cult
approved in 1745.
Cf. Att. — Baud. — Holw.

**PACIFICUS of SAN SEVERINO (St) C.
O.F.M.**   **R.M. Sept. 24**
1653-1721. A native of San Severino,
near Ancona, he joined the Franciscans of
the Observance and was ordained priest
in 1677. In his early years as a priest his
preaching bore much fruit, but in 1688 he
became deaf and blind and almost a
cripple. From this time his life was one
of intense suffering, blessed by God with
supernatural charismata. Canonized in
1839.
Cf. Holw. — Baud. — Att. — Menzies.

PADARN (St) Bp.   **R.M. Apr. 16**
Otherwise Paternus, q.v.

PADUINUS (PAVIN) (St) Ab. O.S.B.
                    A.C. Nov. 15
d. c.703. Monk and prior of St Vincent's
abbey, at Le Mans, and later first abbot
of St Mary's near the same city.
Cf. Zimm. — Holw.

PAGANUS (Bl) Mk. O.S.B. A.C. Feb. 10
d. 1423. An Italian who became a professed monk of the Sicilian abbey of San
Niccolò d' Arena. He lived as a hermit
near the monastery, but returned to it
before his death.
Cf. Zimm.

PAGANUS of LECCO (Bl) M. O.P.
                    A.C. Dec. 26
d. 1274. He was admitted into the Dominican Order by St Dominic himself and
lived in it for fifty years. He succeeded
St Peter of Verna as inquisitor general and,
like him, was murdered by heretics.
Cf. Baud.

PALAEMON (St) Ab.   **R.M. Jan. 11**
d. 325. One of the earliest of the Egyptian hermits. He took refuge in Upper
Egypt during the persecution under Diocletian. To him came St Pachomius to
be trained in the monastic life. He was
closely associated with Pachomius in
organizing the hermits on cenobitical lines,
and he eventually followed Pachomius to
Tabennisi and died there.
Cf. Holw. — Baud. — Att.

PALATIAS and LAURENTIA (SS) MM.
R.M. Oct. 8
d. 302. Palatias was a lady of Ancona converted to Christ by her slave Laurentia. Both were martyred at Fermo, near Ancona, under Diocletian.
Cf. Holw. — Baud.

PALATINUS (St) M.   R.M. May 30
See Sycus and Palatinus.

PALDO, TASO and TATO (SS) Abbots O.S.B.
8th cent. Three brothers, natives of Benevento, who became monks at the abbey of Farfa, in Sabina, and eventually founded the monastery of San Vincenzo at the headwaters of the Voltorno. Of this latter foundation they became successively abbots, Paldo dying c.720, Taso c.729, and Tato c.739.
Cf. Zimm. — Mab. — Holw. — Baud. — Chev.

PALESTINE, Martyrs of (SS)
There are five groups of anonymous Palestinian martyrs listed in the R.M.
R.M. Feb. 19
d. c.509. A number of monks and laymen massacred during the inroad of heathens.
R.M. May 16
d. c.614. Forty-four monks of the *laura* of St Sabbas, massacred during the war between Heraclius and Chosroas. (They are included among those listed under June 22, q.v.).
R.M. May 28
d. c.410. A number of monks martyred by Arabs and other pagans who invaded Palestine early in the reign of Theodosius the Younger.
R.M. June 22
d. c.614. A great number of martyrs (the R.M. speaks of 1480) massacred at Samaria or in its neighborhood during the war between Heraclius and Chosroas.
R.M. Aug. 16
A group of thirty-three martyrs of whom no details are known.
Cf. Holw. — Baud.

PALLADIA (St) M.   R.M. May 24
See Susanna, Marciana and Palladia.

PALLADIUS (St) H.   A.C. Jan. 28
d. c.390. A hermit near Antioch in Syria, a friend of St Simeon "the Ancient."
Cf. Holw. — Baud.

PALLADIUS (St) Bp.   A.C. Apr. 10
d. 661. An abbot of the abbey of St Germanus at Auxerre, who in 622 was appointed bishop of that city. He founded several monasteries.
Cf. Holw. — Baud. — Duch. Fast. Episc.

PALLADIUS (St) Bp.   A.C. July 7
d. 432. A deacon of the Roman church, consecrated bishop and sent (c.430) by Pope Celestine I to evangelize Ireland. He landed near Wicklow and after founding a few churches, left for Scotland where he died shortly after. His mission in Ireland seems to have been a complete failure.
Cf. Holw. — Baud. — Att.

PALLADIUS (St) Bp.   A.C. Oct. 7
d. c.690. Bishop of Saintes (570-c.590). He is liturgically honoured in several dioceses of France, but his claim to the title of saint is disputed, not without reason.
Cf. Holw. — Baud. — Duch. Fast. Episc.

PALMATIUS (St)   R.M. May 10
See Calepodius, Palmatius, etc.

PALMATIUS and Comp. (SS) MM.
R.M. Oct. 5
d. c.287. Apocryphal martyrs of Trèves alleged (only since the 11th century) to have been put to death under Maximian Herculeus.
Cf. Holw. — Baud.

PALUMBUS (Bl) H. O.S.B.   A.C. Jan. 4
d. c.1070. A monk-priest of the abbey of Subiaco, who lived for some years as a hermit near the monastery.
Cf. Zimm.

PAMBO (St) Ab.   A.C. July 18
d. c.390. A disciple of the great St Antony and one of the pioneers of the eremitical life in the Nitrian desert. In his old age he was a venerable figure, visited by a great number of persons from East and West. Among these were St Anthanasius, St Melania the Elder and Rufinus.
Cf. Holw. — Att. — Baud.

PAMMACHIUS (St) C.   R.M. Aug. 30
d. 410. A Roman senator, married to one of the daughters of St Paula. On the death of his wife in 395 Pammachius donned the monastic habit and received priest's orders, spending the rest of his life and his

immense wealth in the personal service of the sick and the poor. His great friends, SS Jerome and Paulinus of Nola, admired and encouraged him. His house became the present church of SS John and Paul (Titulus Pammachii).
Cf. Att. — Holw. — Baud.

PAMPHILUS (St) Bp. R.M. Apr. 28
d. c.700. Bishop of Sulmona (Sulmo) and Corfinium in the Abruzzi. He was accused to Pope Sergius of Arian practices, chiefly, it seems, on account of his singing Mass before daybreak on Sundays — but he completely vindicated himself.
Cf. Holw. — Att. — Baud.

PAMPHILUS and Comp. (St) MM.
R.M. June 1
d. 309. A native of Beirut (Berytus) in Phoenicia. He studied at Alexandria under Pierius, and then settled at Caesarea in Palestine, where he was ordained priest. Himself the greatest biblical scholar of his day, he fostered learning and protected all students. His household became famous for its practice of fraternal love, slaves and domestics being treated as sons and brothers. The historian Eusebius assumed the surname "Pamphili" in gratitude for favours received from St Pamphilus. After years of imprisonment and repeated tortures, he was martyred under Galerius. With him suffered his deacon and ten companions.
Cf. Holw. — Baud. — Att.

PAMPHILUS (St) Bp. R.M. Sept. 7
d. c.400. A Greek by birth, consecrated bishop of Capua by Pope Siricius. His relics were enshrined at Benevento.
Cf. Holw. — Baud.

PAMPHILUS (St) M. R.M. Sept. 21
? A Roman martyr, about whom nothing is known.
Cf. Holw. — Baud.

PANACREA (PANEXIA, PANASSIA) (St) V. A.C. May 1
1378-1383. Born at Quarona, diocese of Novara. When she was only five years old her stepmother killed her with a spindle while she was at prayer. Cult confirmed in 1867.
Cf. Menzies — Holw. — Baud.

PANCHARIUS (St) M. R.M. March 19
d. 303. A Roman senator, a favourite officer of the emperor Maximinian. At the outbreak of the persecution he denied, or at any rate concealed, his religion, but on receiving a letter from his mother and sister, he nobly confessed Christ and was beheaded at Nicomedia.
Cf. Holw. — Baud.

PANCHARIUS (St) M. A.C. July 22
d. c.356. Bishop of Besançon. He suffered much at the hands of the officials of the Arian emperor Constantius.
Cf. Holw. — Duch. Fast. Episc. — Baud.

PANCRAS (Latin: PANCRATIUS) (St) Bp. M. R.M. Apr. 3
1st cent. According to the Sicilian tradition, this St Pancras was an Antiochene by birth, whom St Peter consecrated bishop and sent to Taormina (Tauromenium) in Sicily, where he was stoned to death.
Cf. Holw. — Att. — Baud. — Menzies.

PANCRAS (St) M. R.M. May 12
d. c.304 (?). A martyr of this name was certainly buried in the cemetery of Calepodius in Rome. Other particulars are lacking. His story as given in Cardinal Wiseman's Fabiola is of course a literary creation of the novelist's imagination. In the seventh century Pope St Vitalian sent relics of the saint to one of the Anglo-Saxon kings, and St Pancras thenceforward became very popular in England.
Cf. Holw. — Att. — Baud. — Menzies.

PANDONIA (St) V. A.C. Aug. 26
Otherwise Pandwyna, q.v.

PANDWYNA (St) N. O.S.B.
A.C. Aug. 26
d. c.904. Born in Scotland or Ireland. She became a nun at Ettisley in Cambridgeshire.
Cf. Holw. — Stanton.

PANNONIA (Martyrs of) (SS)
R.M. Apr. 9
? The R.M. has this entry: "At Sirmium in Pannonia the passion of seven holy virgins and martyrs." Modern research has found no further particulars about them.
Cf. Holw. — Baud.

PANTAENUS (St) C. R.M. July 7
d. c.216. A Sicilian and a convert from Stoicism, Pantaenus became the head of

• the catechetical school of Alexandria, which under him began to be considered the intellectual centre of the Christian East. He is said to have ended his life as a missionary in India (more probably in Ethiopia).
Cf. Holw. — Baud. — Att.

PANTAGAPES (St) M.   **R.M. Sept. 2**
See Diomedes, Julian, etc.

PANTAGATHUS (St) Bp.   **R.M. Apr. 17**
475-540. A courtier in the service of King Clovis, he eventually left the court and received holy orders. He was afterwards raised to the see of Vienne.
Cf. Duch. Fast. Episc. — Holw. — Baud.

PANTALEEMON (St) M.   **R.M. July 27**
See Maurus, Pantaleemon and Sergius.

PANTALEON (St) M.   **R.M. July 27**
d. c.305. His Greek name is *Panteleemon* which means "the All-compassionate." The name may have given rise to the legend of his life, which, as we have it now, is not to be trusted. The main facts are probably true: viz., that he was a physician by profession, who practised his art without taking any fees, and who was martyred under Diocletian, perhaps at Nicomedia.
Cf. Holw. — Baud. — Att.

PANTALUS (St) Bp. M.   **A.C. Oct. 12**
? A legendary bishop of Basle connected with the story of St Ursula.
Cf. Holw. — Baud.

PAPAS (St) M.   **R.M. March 16**
d. c.300. A martyr of Lycaonia in Asia Minor under Diocletian.
Cf. Holw. — Baud.

PAPHNUTIUS (St) M.   **R.M. Apr. 19**
? A priest put to death at Jerusalem.
Cf. Holw. — Baud.

PAPHNUTIUS the GREAT (St) Bp.
R.M. Sept. 11
d. c.356. An Egyptian who suffered for the Faith under Maximinus Thrax by having one eye plucked out and one leg hamstrung. In 311 he joined St Antony as monk, but shortly after was consecrated bishop of a see in the Upper Thebaid. As such he assisted at the council of Nicaea, where he is said to have advocated the marriage of priests before ordination.

Throughout his life he was a strenuous opponent of Arianism. He was in great favour with the emperor Constantine.
Cf. Holw. — Att. — Baud.

PAPHNUTIUS and Comp. (SS) MM.
R.M. Sept. 24
d. c.303. Martyrs in Egypt under Diocletian.
Cf. Holw. — Baud.

PAPHNUTIUS (St) Ab.   **A.C. Sept. 25**
d. c.480. The alleged father of the girl-monk St Euphrosyne, q.v. He became a monk and abbot in Egypt and is held in great veneration in the East.
Cf. Baud. — Holw.

PAPIAS and MAURUS (SS) MM.
R.M. Jan. 29
d. c.303. Roman soldiers martyred at Rome under Maximian.
Cf. Baud. — Holw.

PAPIAS (St) Bp.   **R.M. Feb. 22**
d. c.120. Bishop of Hierapolis in the valley of the Lycus in Phrygia, a contemporary and friend of St Polycarp of Smyrna. He wrote much, but only a few fragments of his works are extant.
Cf. Holw. — Baud.

PAPIAS (St) M.   **R.M. Feb. 25**
See Victorinus, Victor, etc.

PAPIAS, DIODORUS, CONON and CLAUDIAN (SS) MM.   **R.M. Feb. 26**
d. c.250. Poor shepherds, natives of Pamphylia (Asia Minor), tortured and put to death under Decius.
Cf. Holw. — Baud.

PAPIAS (PAPIUS) (St) M. R.M. June 28
d. c.303. A martyr, possibly in Sicily, under Diocletian.
Cf. Baud. — Holw.

PAPIAS (PAPIUS) (St) M.   **R.M. July 7**
See Peregrinus, Lucian, etc.

PAPIAS (St) M.   **R.M. Nov. 2**
See Publius, Victor, etc.

PAPINIANUS and MANSUETUS (SS) MM.   **R.M. Nov. 28**
5th cent. Africian bishops, martyred under the Arian Vandal King Genseric, who had overrun that Roman province.
Cf. Holw. — Baud.

PAPOLENUS (St) Ab. A.C. June 26
Otherwise Babolenus, q.v.

PAPPUS (PAPIUS) (*several*)
Otherwise Papias, q.v.

PAPULUS (PAPOUL) (St) M. A.C. Nov. 3
d. c.300. A priest who worked as a missionary under St Saturninus in S. France, and who like him was martyred under Diocletian. His shrine is at Toulouse.
Cf. Holw. — Baud.

PAPYLUS (St) M. R.M. Apr. 13
See Carpus, Papylus, etc.

PARAGUAY (Martyrs of) (BB) S.J.
A.C. Nov. 17
d. 1628. Three Spanish Jesuits — Roch (Roque) Gonzalez, Alphonsus Rodriguez and John de Castillo — founders of the "reduction" of the Assumption on the Jiuhi river in Paraguay. In 1628 they established the new mission of All Saints, and it was here that they were murdered by order of the local chief.
Cf. Att. — Prop. S.J.

PARAMON and Comp. (SS) MM.
R.M. Nov. 29
d. 250. A group of three hundred and seventy-five martyrs, venerated especially by the Greeks. They are said to have suffered on the same day during the Decian persecution.
Cf. Holw. — Baud.

PARASCEVES (St) M. R.M. March 20
See Photina, Joseph, etc.

PARDULPHUS (PARDOUX) (St) Ab.
O.S.B. A.C. Oct. 6
c.658-c.738. Born at Sardent, near Guéret, diocese of Limoges, he first became a hermit, but afterwards joined the Benedictine community of Guéret, of which he became abbot. At the time of the Saracan invasion he remained alone in the abbey, which he saved by prayer.
Cf. Chev. — Zimm. — Holw. — Baud.

PARIS (St) Bp. R.M. Aug. 5
d. 346. According to the local tradition of Teano, a township near Naples, St Paris was born in Greece and became bishop of Teano. His life is embellished with the usual legendary additions of that period.
Cf. Holw. — Baud. — Menzies — Chev.

PARISIUS (St) C. O.S.B. Cam.
R.M. June 11
1152-1267. Born probably at Treviso. At the age of twelve he received the Camaldolese habit, and was ordained priest in 1190. In that same year he was appointed chaplain and spiritual director of the Camaldolese nuns of St Christina outside the walls of Treviso, and he filled that office for seventy-seven years. His body is enshrined in the cathedral of Treviso.
Cf. Att. — Zimm. — Holw. — Chev.

PARMENAS (St) M. R.M. Jan. 23
d. c.98. One of the seven deacons ordained by the Apostles (Acts VI, 5). Tradition says that after many years spent in preaching the gospel in Asia Minor, he was martyred at Philippi in Macedonia under Trajan.
Cf. Holw. — Baud.

PARMENIUS and Comp. (SS) MM.
R.M. Apr. 22
d. c.250. The priests Parmenius, Helimenas and Chrysotelus, and the deacons Luke and Mucius were beheaded near Babylon when the emperor Decius invaded Mesopotamia.
Cf. Holw. — Baud.

PARTHENIUS (St) M. R.M. May 19
See Calocerus and Parthenius.

PASCHAL I (St) Pope O.S.B.
R.M. Feb. 11
d. 824. A Roman, and abbot of the Roman Benedictine monastery of St Stephen near the Vatican, he was raised to the papal throne in 817. He defended the Greek Catholics against the barbarous persecution of the iconoclast emperors. He is perhaps best remembered for his zeal in the recovery and enshrining of the bodies of St Caecilia and other martyrs.
Cf. Zimm. — Att. — Baud. — Holw.

PASCHAL BAYLON (St) C. O.F.M.
R.M. May 17
1540-1592. Born of peasant stock at Torrehermosa in Aragon, he started life as a shepherd. Later he became a Franciscan lay-brother of the Alcantarine reform (1564). He spent his life mainly as doorkeeper in different friaries of Spain. All his life he was animated with an intense love for the Holy Eucharist, the true

doctrine of which he triumphantly defended against a Calvinist preacher in France. Beatified in 1618, canonized in 1690. In 1897 he was declared patron of all Eucharistic confraternities and congresses.
Cf. P. de U. — Att. — Baud. — Holw.

PASCHARIUS (PASQUIER) (St) Bp.
A.C. July 10
d. c.680. Bishop of Nantes. He founded the abbey of Aindre, where he placed St Hermeland of Fontenelle as first abbot.
Cf. Duch. Fast. Episc. — Chev. — Baud. — Holw.

PASCHASIA (St) V.M. A.C. Jan. 9
d. c.178 (?). A virgin martyr venerated at Dijon. Her cult is already described as ancient by St Gregory of Tours. Later legends connect her with St Benignus of Dijon.
Cf. Att. — Baud. — Holw.

PASCHASIUS (St) Bp. R.M. Feb. 22
d. c.312. The eleventh bishop of Vienne in Gaul.
Cf. Duch. Fast. Episc. — Holw. — Baud.

PASCHASIUS RADBERT (St) Ab. O.S.B.
A.C. Apr. 26
d. c.851. Born in the Soissonnais, he became a monk of Corbie under St Adalhard and was ordained deacon. For many years he held the offices of novice-master and headmaster, both at Old Corbie and at New Corvey, whither he accompanied his abbot in 822. In 844 he was made abbot of Corbie, an office which he found most uncongenial, and which he resigned about the year 850. He was prolific on biblical subjects and his most famous book is his treatise on the Holy Eucharist.
Cf. Zimm. — Chev. — Att. — Holw. — Baud.

PASCHASIUS (St) C. R.M. May 31
d. c.512. A Roman deacon who, in good faith, sided with the antipope Laurence against Pope Symmachus. He is mentioned by St Gregory the Great (Dial. IV, 40). He wrote some theological works which have been lost.
Cf. Holw. — Baud.

PASCHASIUS (St) M. R.M. Nov. 13
See Arcadius, Paschasius, etc.

PASICRATES, VALENTION and Comp. (SS) MM. R.M. May 25
d. c.302. Four soldiers, martyred at Silistria, in Moesia (Bulgaria). They belong to the group of St Julius, q.v.
Cf. Holw. — Baud.

PASTOR, VICTORINUS and Comp. (SS) MM. R.M. March 29
d. c.311. Seven martyrs who suffered at Nicomedia under Diocletian.
Cf. Holw. — Baud.

PASTOR (St) Bp. R.M. March 30
6th cent. (?). Bishop of Orleans. His name, however, does not appear in the ancient lists.
Cf. Holw. — Baud.

PASTOR (St) C. R.M. July 26
d. c.160. A Roman priest, said to have been brother to Pope St Pius I. He has left his name to the title (or parish) of St Pudentiana in Rome — *Titulus Pastoris*.
Cf. Holw. — Baud. — Menzies.

PASTOR (St) M. R.M. Aug. 6
See Justus and Pastor.

PATAPIUS (St) H. R.M. Dec. 8
7th cent. An Egyptian monk, who migrated to Constantinople and passed his life as a hermit in the suburbs of the city. He is much venerated in the East.
Cf. Holw. — Baud.

PATERIUS (St) Bp. R.M. Feb. 21
d. 606. A Roman monk, disciple and friend of St Gregory the Great. From being notary of the Roman Church, he was raised to the see of Brescia in Lombardy. He was a prolific writer on biblical subjects.
Cf. Menzies — Holw. — Baud.

PATERMUTHIUS, COPRAS and ALEXANDER (SS) MM. R.M. July 9
d. c.363. Patermuthius was a notorious robber converted by an Egyptian hermit, St Copras. Patermuthius then became a hermit also. The R.M. makes them martyrs together with Alexander, a converted soldier under Julian the Apostate; but the Acts of these alleged martyrs cannot be admitted as history.
Cf. Holw. — Baud.

PATERNIAN (St) Bp. R.M. July 12
d. c.470. Bishop of Bologna c.450-c.470.
Probably identical with the following.
Cf. Holw. — Baud.

PATERNIAN (St) Bp. A.C. Nov. 23
d. c.343. A Christian who, towards the
end of the persecution of Diocletian escaped to the mountains. Later he was
made bishop of Fano.
Cf. Holw. — Menzies.

PATERNUS (or PADARN) (St) C.
A.C. Apr. 16
5th cent. A monk from Brittany, who,
with other monks from the same country,
founded Llanbadarn Fawr (i.e., the great
monastery of Padarn) near Aberystwyth
in Wales. He preached the gospel in the
country round about.
Cf. Att. — Holw.

PATERNUS (or PERN) (St) Bp.
A.C. Apr. 15
d. c.500. Bishop of Vannes in Brittany,
consecrated c.465.
Cf. Duch. Fast. Episc. — Holw. — Baud.

PATERNUS (French: PAIR) (St) Bp.
R.M. Apr. 16 and Sept. 23
d. c.574 (or 563). Born at Poitiers, he became a monk at Ansion, and later a hermit
near Coutances. Eventually he was
raised to the see of Avranches in Normandy. He is often confused with St
Paternus (Padara) of Llanbadarn (see
Apr. 15).
Cf. Holw. — Baud. — Chev.

PATERNUS (Bl or St) H. O.S.B.
A.C. Apr. 10
d. 1058. A Scot by birth, he was one of
the first monks to enter the Benedictine
abbey of Abdinghof in Paderborn, founded
by St Meinwerk. Afterwards he became
a hermit and died in his cell, refusing to
leave it when the monastery was destroyed by fire. Bl Marianus Scotus visited the place a fortnight after the fire.
St Paternus was greatly revered by St
Peter Damian.
Cf. Att. — Zimm. — Chev. — Holw.

PATERNUS (St) M. R.M. Aug. 21
d. c.255. An Egyptian who, coming as a
pilgrim to Rome, was arrested in a neighbouring town and expired in the dungeon
into which he was thrown.
Cf. Holw. — Baud.

PATERNUS (St) Bp. A.C. Sept. 28
2nd cent. Born at Bilbao in Spain. He
was one of the earliest bishops — some
say the first — of Eauze (now Auch) in
France.
Cf. Gams — Baud.

PATERNUS (St) M. O.S.B.
R.M. Nov. 12
d. c.726. Born in Brittany, he was a
monk first at Cessier, in the diocese of
Avranches, and then at Saint-Pierre-le-
Vif, diocese of Sens. He was murdered
by malefactors whom he had admonished
to reform their lives.
Cf. Holw. — Baud. — Chev.

PATIENS (St) Bp. R.M. Jan. 8
2nd cent. Venerated as the fourth bishop
and the patron saint of Metz.
Cf. Gams — Baud. — Holw. — Att. —
Duch. Fast. Episc.

PATIENS (St) Bp. R.M. Sept. 11
d. c.491. Archbishop of Lyons, highly
praised by his contemporary St Sidonius
Apollinaris. He devoted all his revenues
to the relief of the poor.
Cf. Duch. Fast. Episc. — Gams — Baud.
— Att. — Holw.

PATIENTIA (St) M. R.M. May 1
See Orentius and Patientia.

PATRICIA (PATRITIA) (St) M.
R.M. May 13
See Macedonius, Patricia and Modesta.

PATRICIA (St) V. R.M. Aug. 25
d. c.665. According to the legend, she
was a maiden of Constantinople, related
to the imperial family. In order to escape marriage she went on a pilgrimage to
Jerusalem and then to Rome, where she
received the veil. She died at Naples, of
which city she is one of the patrons.
Cf. Att. — Baud. — Holw.

PATRICIAN (St) Bp. A.C. Oct. 10
5th cent. A Scottish bishop driven from
his see by heathen invaders. He spent
the remainder of his life in the Isle of Man.
Cf. Holw.

PATRICK (St) Bp. R.M. March 16
? Registered in the R.M. as bishop of
Auvergne, but his name is not to be found
in the lists of the sees of Auvergne. Quite
probably the copyists wrote Arvernia for

Hibernia, i.e., Ireland, and this duplicated the apostle of that country (see the following). At Malaga, in Spain, is kept on March 16 the feast of St Patrick, a native and bishop of that city, who, according to the local tradition, fled to Auvergne, and died there c.307.
Cf. Holw. — Baud.

PATRICK (St) Bp. R.M. March 17
c.389-c.461. A Romano-Briton by origin, at the age of sixteen he was taken captive to Ireland (c.405). He escaped after six years. He now pursued his education in continental monasteries. About the year 432, after having been consecrated bishop by St Germanus at Auxerre, he returned to Ireland as a missionary. Whatever may be said of the extant data supplied by his biographers, which in some instances are obviously conflicting or legendary, the fact remains that St Patrick established the Catholic Church throughout Ireland on lasting foundations: he travelled throughout the country preaching, teaching, building churches, opening schools and monasteries, converting chiefs and bards, and everywhere supporting his preaching with miracles. His writings show what solid doctrine he must have taught his hearers. He was, moreover, the first organizer of the Irish church, with the primatial see at Armagh (established c.444). He fully deserves his title of "Apostle of Ireland."
Cf. Holw. — Att. — Baud.

PATRICK, ACATIUS, MENANDER and POLYENUS (SS) MM. R.M. Apr. 28
? A group of martyrs of Prusa (Broussa) in Bithynia, of whom no reliable data are available.
Cf. Baud. — Holw.

PATRICK (St) Bp. A.C. May 24
d. c.469. The fourth bishop of Bayeux. Liturgically venerated at Bayeux on May 24.
Cf. Gams — Duch. Fast. Episc. — Baud. — Holw.

PATRICK (St) Ab. A.C. Aug. 24
d. c.450. Surnamed "Sen-Patrick" (Patrick the Elder). Several traditions mention him as a kinsman and contemporary of St Patrick of Ireland. There is also St Patrick, abbot of Nevers, France, likewise commemorated on Aug. 24. It is impossible to disentangle the conflicting

data concerning these and other saints of the same name.
Cf. Holw. — Baud.

PATROBAS (St) R.M. Nov. 4
See Philologus and Patrobas.

PATROCLUS (St) M. R.M. Jan. 21
d. c.275 (or 259). A very wealthy and exceedingly charitable Christian of Troyes, martyred in that city. His relics were (960) translated to Soest in Westphalia.
Cf. Holw. — Baud. — Att.

PATTO (St) Bp. O.S.B. A.C. March 30
d. c.788. A native of Britain who crossed over to Saxony, became abbot of a monastery there, and finally was appointed bishop of Werden.
Cf. Holw. — Baud.

PAUL
Note. A very widely used name in all Christian lands. The Latin form is Paulus, and its modern derivatives are: in Italian and Portuguese, Paolo; in English and French, Paul; in Spanish, Pablo; in Catalan, Pau.

PAUL the HERMIT (St) C.
R.M. Jan. 10 and 15
c.230-c.342. The life of this saint, written by St Jerome, tells us that he was an Egyptian of good birth and well educated. At the age of twenty-two he fled into the desert of Thebes to escape the persecution under Decius. He stayed there even after the ending of the persecutions until his death, that is, for ninety years. He was comforted in the end by a visit from St Antony. On a second visit St Antony found him dead and buried him.
Cf. Holw. — Att. — Baud. — Ricci.

PAUL, GERONTIUS, JANUARIUS, SATURNINUS, SUCCESSUS, JULIUS, CATUS, PIA and GERMANA (SS) MM.
R.M. Jan. 19
2nd cent (?). African martyrs, of the province of Numidia, about whom no particulars are given.
Cf. Holw. — Baud.

PAUL of TROIS-CHÂTEAUX (St) Bp.
R.M. Feb. 1
d. c.405. A native of Reims, who, escaping from the barbarian invasions, became a hermit near Arles, and eventually

was chosen bishop of Trois-Châteaux (*Augusta Tricastrinorum* — a diocese now extinct) in Dauphiné.
Cf. Gams — Duch. Fast. Episc. — Holw. — Baud.

PAUL MIKI (St) M. S.J. R.M. Feb. 5
1562-1597. Born at Tounucumada in Japan, son of a Japanese military chief, he was educated at the Jesuit college of Anziquiama, and in 1580 entered the Society of Jesus. He was famed as an orator and controversialist. Crucified at Nagasaki. Beatified in 1627; canonized in 1862.
Cf. Prop. S.J. — Holw.

PAUL YUANIQUI and PAUL SUSUQUI (SS) MM. R.M. Feb. 5
d. 1597. Japanese laymen, tertiaries of St Francis, interpreters and catechists to the Franciscan missionaries. Both were crucified at Nagasaki. Beatified in 1627; canonized in 1862.
Cf. Holw. — Prop. O.F.M.

PAUL, LUCIUS and CYRIACUS (SS) MM. R.M. Feb. 8
? Martyrs at Rome.
Cf. Holw. — Baud.

PAUL of VERDUN (St) Bp. O.S.B. R.M. Feb. 8
d. c.649. A courtier who retired first to Mt Voge (now Paulberg), near Trèves, as a hermit and afterwards entered the monastery of Tholey, where he was appointed headmaster of the monastic school. After some years (c.630) King Dagobert appointed him bishop of Verdun.
Cf. Gams — Duch. Fast. Episc. — Chev. — Holw. — Zimm.

PAUL LIEOU (Bl) M. A.C. Feb. 13
d. 1818. A Chinese layman who was martyred by strangulation. Beatified in 1900.
Cf. Holw.

PAUL LOC (Bl) M. A.C. Feb. 13
1831-1859. A native of An-nhon in Cochin-China, who, shortly after his ordination to the priesthood, was beheaded at Saigon. Beatified in 1909.
Cf. Holw.

PAUL, HERACLIUS, SECUNDILLA and JANUARIA (SS) MM. R.M. March 2
d. c.305. Martyrs who suffered under Diocletian at Porto Romano, at the mouth of the Tiber.
Cf. Baud. — Holw.

PAUL of PRUSA (St) Bp. R.M. March 7
d. 840. Bishop of Prusa (Plusias) in Bithynia. For his courageous resistance to the iconoclasts he was banished to Egypt where he died.
Cf. Holw. — Baud.

PAUL the SIMPLE (St) H. R.M. March 7
d. c.339. An Egyptian farmer who, at the age of sixty, discovered the adultery of his wife and forthwith left for the desert, where he placed himself under St Antony. His prompt obedience and childlike disposition were "the pride of the desert" and merited for him the surname of "the Simple." He is mentioned by Rufinus and Palladius.
Cf. Holw. — Baud. — Att.

PAUL (St) M. R.M. March 10
See Codratus, Dionysius, etc.

PAUL AURELIAN (St) Bp. A.C. March 12
d. c.575. A Romano-Briton by origin, he was born in Wales, and educated at Llantwit Major under St Iltyd, together with SS David, Samson, Gildas, etc. He dwelt for a time on Caldey Island, whence he crossed over into Brittany with twelve companions. He established a monastery at Porz-Pol on the isle of Ouessant and finally fixed his residence at Ouismor (now Saint-Pol-de-Léon), where he was consecrated bishop.
Cf. Att. — Baud. — Holw.

PAUL of CYPRUS (St) M. R.M. March 17
d. 777. A monk of Cyprus, who, in the reign of the iconoclast emperor Constantine Copronymus, refused to trample on a crucifix and was hung head downwards over a slow fire till he died.
Cf. Holw. — Baud.

PAUL, CYRIL, EUGENE and Comp. (SS) MM. R.M. March 20
? A group of seven martyrs, who suffered in Syria.
Cf. Holw. — Baud.

PAUL of NARBONNE (St) Bp. R.M. March 22
d. p. 250. St Gregory of Tours (*Hist.*

Franc. I. 30) writes that St Paul was consecrated at Rome towards the middle of the third century and sent to Gaul to preach the gospel, which he did with great success at Narbonne. A much later legend identifies him with the Roman proconsul Sergius Paulus, converted by St Paul the Apostle (Acts XIII).
Cf. Att. — Baud. — Holw. — Duch. Fast. Episc.

PAUL TINH (Bl) M. A.C. Apr. 6
d. 1857. Born at Trinh-ha, Tonkin, he became a priest, and was beheaded at Son-tay, in W. Tonkin. Beatified in 1909.
Cf. Holw.

PAUL of CORDOVA (St) M.
R.M. Apr. 17
See Elias, Paul and Isidore.

PAUL of the CROSS (St) C. Founder.
R.M. Apr. 28
1694-1775 (Oct. 18). Paolo Francesco Danei was born at Ovada in Piedmont. Inspired by a series of visions he with some companions went to live the religious life on Mt Argentaro, near Orbitello. In 1720 they received the habit of "Barefooted Clerks of the Cross and the Passion" (Passionists) from the bishop of Alessandria. In 1727 Paul was ordained priest in the Vatican basilica, and in 1747 the first general chapter of the new Congregation was held. St Paul lived to see its expansion throughout Italy. Canonized in 1867.
Cf. Att. — Baud. — Holw. — Menzies.

PAUL KHOAN (Bl) M. A.C. Apr. 28
d. 1840. A native of Tonkin, and a priest attached to the Paris Foreign Missions for forty years. He was in prison for two years before he was beheaded.
Cf. Holw.

PAUL (St) M. R.M. May 15
See Peter, Andrew, etc.

PAUL (St) M. R.M. May 17
See Heradius, Paul, etc.

PAUL (St) M. R.M. May 28
See Crescens, Dioscorides, etc.

PAUL HANH (Bl) M. A.C. May 28
d. 1859. A native layman of Chochin-China. He abandoned his Faith and joined a band of outlaws. When arrested, he professed his religion, and, after frightful tortures, was beheaded near Saigon. Beatified in 1909.
Cf. Holw.

PAUL (St) M. R.M. June 1
See Reverianus, Paul, etc.

PAUL (St) M. R.M. June 1
See Valens, Paul, etc.

PAUL (St) M. R.M. June 3
See Lucillian, Claudius, etc.

PAUL of CONSTANTINOPLE (St) Bp.
M. R.M. June 7
d. c.350. A patriarch of Constantinople, whose episcopate was largely spent in exile for the Catholic faith. Elected in 336, he was exiled to Pontus in 337, whence he returned in 338, but was exiled again by an Arian synod, this time to Trèves. He returned to his see c. 340, but in 342 was sent in chains to Mesopotamia by the emperor Constantius. Recalled in 344, he was banished for the last time to Kukusus in Armenia, where he was left without food for six days and then strangled.
Cf. Att. — Holw. — Baud.

PAUL BURALI d' AREZZO (Bl) Bp.
A.C. June 17
1511-1578. Born at Itri, diocese of Gaeta, he became a lawyer and practised his profession for ten years at Naples. In 1549 he was appointed royal counsellor, but in 1558 he joined the Theatine order and eventually was made superior at the houses of Naples and Rome. St Pius V appointed him bishop of Piacenza and created him cardinal. Finally he was promoted to the see of Naples. Beatified in 1772.
Cf. Holw. — Baud. — Menzies.

PAUL and CYRIACUS (SS) MM.
R.M. June 20
? Martyrs who suffered at Tomi on the Black Sea, in Lower Moesia.
Cf. Holw. — Baud.

PAUL XINSUKI (Bl) M. S.J.
A.C. June 20
d. 1626. A Japanese Jesuit, catechist to Bl Paul Navarro. He was burnt alive at Nagasaki. Beatified in 1867.
Cf. Holw.

PAUL (St) M.   **R.M. June 26**
See John and Paul.

PAUL I (St) Pope.   **R.M. June 28**
d. 767. A Roman, educated with his brother, the future Pope Stephen III, at the Lateran school. He succeeded his brother in the papal chair in 757. His pontificate was uneventful except for the iconoclast excesses of the Byzantine emperor Constantine Copronymus, whom the pope valiantly opposed. As some compensation for the destruction in the East, St Paul restored and beautified several Roman churches and enshrined the relics of many saints.
Cf. Att. — Baud. — Holw.

PAUL GIUSTINIANI (Bl) O.S.B. Cam.
     A.C. June 28
1476-1528. A member of the Venetian house of Giustiniani. He joined the Camaldolese Benedictines, and eventually established the new Congregation of Monte Corona. He ranks among the Camaldolese as their most prolific writer. His feast is kept by the Camaldolese.
Cf. Zimm. — Holw. — Menzies.

PAUL the APOSTLE (St) M.
     R.M. June 29 (30)
c.3-c.67. Born at Tarsus in Cilicia, a Jew of the tribe of Benjamin, a Pharisee, a Roman citizen, a tentmaker by trade, he was educated in the Sacred Law of the Jews at the feet of Gamaliel in Jerusalem. After taking an active part in the stoning of the first Christian martyr St Stephen, he placed himself whole-heartedly at the service of the Jewish authorities in their attempt to stamp out Christianity, but was miraculously converted on the road to Damascus, and received directly from Christ his mission to evangelize the Gentiles. He did so in at least four apostolic journeys, extending from Cappadocia and Galatia perhaps as far as Spain, establishing churches everywhere, and ever surrounded by dangers of all sorts — he was shipwrecked, imprisoned, flogged, stoned, banished from several cities, persecuted by the hatred of his own people. Nevertheless he was always burning for more sufferings and conquests for Christ, who recompensed him, even in this life, with the highest degree of mystical experience. His fourteen epistles, addressed mostly to the churches which he had founded, belong to the deposit of divine revelation.

He was beheaded in Rome, on the Ostian Way, where the basilica and Benedictine abbey of St Paul-outside-the-Walls now stand. Liturgically he is honoured with St Peter, on June 29, as the co-founder of the Roman church; while the feast of his conversion is celebrated on Jan. 25.
Cf. Att. — Holw.

PAUL (St) M.   **R.M. July 3**
See Mark, Mucianus and Paul.

PAUL of ST ZOILUS (St) M.   **R.M. July 20**
d. 851. A Spanish deacon of Cordova who belonged to the community of St Zoilus in the same city and was most zealous in ministering to his fellow-Christians imprisoned by the Mohammedans. He was beheaded for the Faith, and his fellow Christians succeeded in securing his remains, which they enshrined in the church of St Zoilus.
Cf. P. de U. — Holw. — Baud.

PAUL of GAZA (St) M.   **R.M. July 25**
d. 308. A martyr of Gaza in Palestine, beheaded under Maximian Galerius.
Cf. Holw. — Baud.

PAUL and JULIANA (SS) MM.
     R.M. Aug. 17
d. c.270. Brother and sister, beheaded at Ptolemais in Palestine under Aurelian.
Cf. Holw. — Baud.

PAUL SANCHIKI (Bl) M. A.C. Aug. 19
d. 1622. A Japanese sailor on board the ship of Bl Joachim Firaiama. Beheaded at Nagasaki. Beatified in 1867.
Cf. Holw.

PAUL (St) M.   **R.M. Aug. 29**
See Nicaeas and Paul.

PAUL TOMAKI and PAUL AYBARA (BB) MM.   **A.C. Sept. 8**
d. 1628. Paul Tomaki was a boy of seven, beheaded with his father, Bl John Tomaki, q.v., and his three brothers at Nagasaki. Paul Aybara was a Japanese catechist and Dominican tertiary, likewise beheaded at Nagasaki. Beatified in 1867.
Cf. Holw.

PAUL TANACA and PAUL NANGAXI (BB) MM.   **A.C. Sept. 10**
d. 1622. Japanese companions in martyrdom of Bl Charles Spinola, q.v.
Cf. Holw.

PAUL FIMONAYA (Bl) M. A.C. Sept. 16
d. 1628. Son of Bl Michael Fimonaya
(q.v.) and a Dominican tertiary. Beheaded at Nagasaki. Beatified in 1867.
Cf. Holw.

**PAUL, TATTA, SABINIAN, MAXIMUS,
RUFUS, and EUGENE (SS) MM.
R.M. Sept. 25**
? Paul and Tatta were husband and wife,
the others were their sons. All died under
torture in their native city of Damascus.
Cf. Chev. — Baud. — Hclw.

PAUL (St) M. R.M. Oct. 3
See Dionysius, Faustus, etc.

PAUL DOI BUONG (Bl) M. A.C. Oct. 22
d. 1833. A native of Cochin-China and
captain of the bodyguard of King Minh-
Menh. As a Christian he became attached to the Society of Foreign Missions
of Paris. He was arrested in 1832, degraded and beheaded. Beatified in 1900.
Cf. Holw.

**PAUL NAVARRO and Comp. (BB) MM.
A.C. Nov. 1**
d. 1622. Paul Navarro was born in 1560
at Laino, diocese of Cassano, in Italy.
He became a Jesuit in 1587 and while still
a scholastic was sent to India where he was
ordained, and thence to Japan. He
worked with great success as superior of
Amanguchi. He was burnt alive at
Ximabara. With him suffered three
Japanese laymen.
Cf. Prop. S.J. — Holw. — Att.

PAUL of LATROS (St) H. A.C. Dec. 15
d. 956. Born near Pergamos. After the
death of his parents he became a hermit
first on Mt Olympus, then in a cave on
Mt Latros in Bithynia, and finally on the
isle of Samos. He died on Mt Latros.
Cf. Att. — Baud. — Holw.

PAUL MI (Bl) M. A.C. Dec. 18
d. 1838. A native of Tonkin, attached to
the Society of Foreign Missions of Paris.
Martyred by strangulation. Beatified in
1900.
Cf. Holw.

PAUL (St) M. R.M. Dec. 19
See Darius and Comp.

PAUL (St) M. R.M. Dec. 24
See Lucian, Metrobius, etc.

PAULA (St) V. O.S.B. Cam. A.C. Jan. 5
1318-1368. Born in Tuscany, she was entrusted in childhood to the Camaldolese
nuns and remained with them all her life.
She was instrumental in bringing the feuds
between Pisa and Florence to a peaceful
settlement.
Cf. Prop. O. Camald.

PAULA (St) W. R.M. Jan. 26
347-404. A Roman lady of noble birth,
she married a patrician, to whom she bore
five children, among them St Eustochium
and St Blaesilla. Left a widow when she
was thirty-four Paula embraced the religious life, and for twenty years presided
over the sisterhood founded by her near
St Jerome's monastery at Bethlehem,
where she also established a hospital. St
Jerome became her spiritual director, and
after her death her biographer.
Cf. Att. — Baud. — Holw.

**PAULA GAMBARA-COSTA (Bl) Matron.
A.C. Jan. 31**
1473-1515. Born at Brescia, she married
at the age of twelve a young nobleman.
She had much to suffer from her husband,
who not only objected to her charities,
admittedly lavish, but was also shame-
fully unfaithful to her. By her heroic
patience she won him over to better things
and passed the remainder of an austere
life in peaceful wedlock. She died worn
out with self-imposed penances. Cult
confirmed by Gregory XVI.
Cf. Att. — Baud. — Holw.

PAULA (St) M.V. R.M. June 3
d. c.273. A maiden of Nicomedia who
ministered to the martyr St Lucillianus
and to four youths in prison, and was for
this reason arrested and tortured, and
finally sent to Byzantium, where she was
beheaded.
Cf. Holw. — Baud.

**PAULA FRASINETTI (Bl) Foundress.
A.C. June 11**
1809-1882. Born at Genoa, she lived with
her brother who was parish-priest at
Quinto, one of the suburbs of the city,
and there she began to teach poor children.
This was the beginning of the Congregation of St Dorothy, which she lived to see
flourishing throughout Italy and the New
World. Beatified in 1930.
Cf. Att.

PAULA (St) V.M. **R.M. June 18**
See Cyriacus and Paula.

PAULA (St) M. **R.M. July 20**
See Sabinus, Julian, etc.

PAULA (St) V.M. **R.M. Aug. 10**
See Bassa, Paula and Agathonica.

PAULA of MONTALDO (Bl) W. O.F.M.
A.C. Oct. 29
1443-1514. Born at Montaldo, near Mantua, at the age of fifteen she joined the Poor Clares at Santa Lucia in Mantua, where she was later elected abbess three times. She was favoured with mystical experiences. Cult approved in 1906.
Cf. Holw. — Baud. — Prop. O.F.M.

PAULILLUS (St) M. **R.M. Nov. 13**
See Arcadius, Paschasius, etc.

PAULILLUS (St) M. **R.M. Dec. 19**
See Cyriacus, Paulillus, etc.

PAULINA (Bl) W. O.S.B. A.C. March 14
d. 1107. A German princess, who, after the death of her husband, founded, with her son Werner, the double monastery at Zell (Paulinzelle). She died at Münsterschwarzach.
Cf. Holw. — Chev. — Bolland.

PAULINA (St) M. **R.M. June 6**
See Artemius, Candida and Paulina.

PAULINA (St) M. **R.M. Dec. 2**
See Eusebius, Marcellus, etc.

PAULINA (St) M. **R.M. Dec. 31**
See Donata, Paulina, etc.

PAULINUS of AQUILEIA (St) Bp.
A.C. Jan. 28
c.726-840. Born near Cividale in N. Italy he received a good education, and after the destruction of the Lombard kingdom in 774, was summoned to court by his great admirer Charlemagne, who in 784 sent him back to Italy as patriarch of Aquileia. Paulinus wrote much and competently against Adoptionism and was a firm supporter of the *Filioque*. He also carried on missionary work among the Avars.
Cf. Holw. — Menzies — Att.

PAULINUS of BRESCIA (St) Bp.
R.M. Apr. 29
d. c.545. Bishop of Brescia (c.524-545).

His relics are enshrined in the church of San Pietro in Oliveto.
Cf. Holw. — Chev. — Baud.

PAULINUS (St) M. **R.M. May 4**
? A martyr whose relics are enshrined at Cologne, but of whom otherwise nothing is known.
Cf. Holw. — Bolland.

PAULINUS of SINIGAGLIA (St) Bp.
A.C. May 4
d. 826. Bishop, and now patron saint, of Sinigaglia, in Italy. Nothing is known of his life.
Cf. Chev. — Holw. — Baud.

PAULINUS (St) M. **R.M. May 26**
See Felicissimus, Heraclius and Paulinus.

PAULINUS of NOLA (St) Bp.
R.M. June 22
c.354-431. Pontius Meropius Anicius Paulinus was born at Bordeaux, the son of a Roman patrician who at that time held the office of praetorian prefect in Gaul. Paulinus was taught by the poet Ausonius. He was appointed prefect of Rome, but after the death of his only child (390) he retired from the world and went to Spain, where the people of Barcelona compelled him to accept the priesthood. Finally he settled as a hermit near Nola in Campania and here the people (410) chose him for their bishop. He proved to be one of the best prelates of his time, and was in friendly intercourse with most of his great contemporaries: Ambrose, Jerome, Augustine, Martin of Tours, Victricius of Rouen, etc. He had much to suffer during the invasion of Campania by the Goths under Alaric. Most of his poems and a number of his letters are still extant, and they show him to have been a Christian poet of distinction as well as a fluent writer of prose.
Cf. Holw. — Baud. — Att. — Menzies.

PAULINUS of ANTIOCH and Comp. (SS)
MM. **R.M. July 12**
? This St Paulinus is venerated as the first bishop and patron saint of Lucca in Tuscany. The legend adds that he was a native of Antioch sent to Lucca by St Peter, and that he was martyred (c.67) with a priest, a deacon and a soldier. The whole story is most untrustworthy and it is probable that this saint is to be identified with the bishop Paulinus who governed the see c.355-365.
Cf. Holw. — Menzies — Baud.

PAULINUS of TRÈVES (St) Bp.
R.M. Aug. 31
d. 358. A native of Gascony who accompanied St Maximinus to Trèves and succeeded him as bishop in 349. He was a brave supporter of St Athanasius and was for this reason banished to Phrygia by the Arian emperor Constantius in 355. He died in exile, but his relics were brought back to Trèves.
Cf. Att. — Holw. — Baud.

PAULINUS of YORK (St) Bp. O.S.B.
R.M. Oct. 10
d. 644. A Roman monk sent to England with SS Mellitus and Justus (601) by Pope Gregory the Great to aid St Augustine in his labours. He spent twenty-four years in Kent, and in 625 was consecrated bishop of York and sent to evangelize Northumbria, which he did very successfully, baptizing King St Edwin at York on Easter Sunday, 627. After the king's death he was driven from his see and returned to Kent, where he administered the see of Rochester till his death.
Cf. Zimm. — Stanton — Chev. — Att. — Holw.

PAULINUS of CAPUA (St) Bp.
R.M. Oct. 10
d. 843. Said to have been a native of England, who, while on a pilgrimage to Jerusalem, made a stay at Capua and was constrained by the inhabitants to become their bishop. After an episcopate of eight years he died at Sicopolis, whither he had fled during the invasion of the Saracens.
Cf. Menzies — Holw. — Baud.

PAULINUS (POLIN, PEWLIN, PAULHEN) (St) C.
A.C. Nov. 23
d. c.505 (?). A Welsh abbot, pupil of St Iltyd, founder (?) of the monastery of Whitland (Caermarthen), where he had among his disciples St David and St Teilo.
Cf. Holw.

PAUSIDES (PAUSIS) (St) M.
R.M. March 24
See Timolaus, Dionysius, etc.

PAUSILIPPUS (St) M.   R.M. Apr. 15
See Theodore and Pausilippus.

PEBLIG (PUBLICUS) C.   A.C. July 3
Otherwise Byblig, q.v.

PEGA (St) V.   A.C. Jan. 8
d. c.719. A sister of St Guthlac of Croyland. She too lived as a recluse, but seems to have died while on a pilgrimage to Rome. The village of Peakirk in Northamptonshire preserves her name.
Cf. Holw. — Baud. — Att.

PEGASIUS (St) M.   R.M. Nov. 2
See Acindynus, Pegasius, etc.

PELAGIA (St) M.   R.M. March 23
See Domitius, Pelagia, etc.

PELAGIA (St) V.M.   R.M. May 4
d. c.300. A maiden of Tarsus in Cilicia, said to have been roasted to death for refusing to marry one of the sons of the emperor Diocletian. The story is regarded as apocryphal.
Cf. Holw. — Att. — Baud.

PELAGIA of ANTIOCH (St) V.M.
R.M. June 9
d. c.311. A girl of fifteen who was a disciple of St Lucian at Antioch. When soldiers were sent to arrest her, she threw herself from the top of her house to avoid the loss of her virginity and was killed. St John Chrysostom, who greatly praised her courage, attributes her action to divine inspiration.
Cf. Holw. — Att. — Baud.

PELAGIA (St) M.   R.M. July 11
See Januarius and Pelagia.

PELAGIA the PENITENT (St)
R.M. Oct. 8
Otherwise Marina (June 18) q.v.

PELAGIA (St) V.M.   R.M. Oct. 19
See Beronicus, Pelagia, etc.

PELAGIUS of LAODICEA (St) Bp.
R.M. March 25
d. p. 381. A bishop of Laodicea. He championed the Catholic cause against Arianism and on that account was banished by the Arian emperor Valens. Recalled by Gratian, he was present at the council of Constantinople (381). The date of his death is not known.
Cf. Holw. — Baud.

PELAGIUS (St) M.   A.C. Apr. 7
? A priest martyred at Alexandria in Egypt. Mentioned in the Martyrology of St Jerome.
Cf. Chev. — Baud.

PELAGIUS (Spanish: PELAYO) (St) M.
R.M. June 26
c.912-925. A young boy of Asturias left as a hostage with the Moors at Cordova. He was offered freedom and other rewards if he would turn Mohammedan and commit other shameful sins. These inducements were repeatedly put before him during the three years that he was kept in prison, and on his stubborn refusal he was put to the torture, which he endured for six hours, finally dying while under it. His relics were transferred to Leon in 967 and to Oviedo in 985. The Benedictine poetess Rhoswitha of Gandersheim (d. 973) wrote a long poem in his honour. He is still greatly honoured in Spain.
Cf. P. de U.—Holw.—Att.—Baud.—Chev.

PELAGIUS (St) M. R.M. Aug. 28
d. c.283. A boy martyred in Istria under Numerian. His relics were transferred to Città Nuova in Istria and part of them (c.915) to Constance on the Swiss lake of that name. He is venerated as the patron saint of Constance.
Cf. Holw. — Chev. — Baud.

PELAGIUS, ARSENIUS and SYLVANUS (SS) MM. A.C. Aug. 30
d. c.950. Hermits near Burgos in Old Castile, who, according to an old tradition, were done to death by the Saracens. Their cell was the origin of the Benedictine Abbey of Artanza. The three martyrs are still greatly venerated in the province of Burgos.
Cf. P. de U. — Zimm.

PELEUS (St) Bp. M.
R.M. Feb. 20 and Sept. 19
See Tyrannio, Sylvanus, etc.

PELEUS, NILUS, ELIAS and Comp. (SS) MM. R.M. Sept. 19
d. c.310. Three Egyptian bishops (or priests) together with many priests and laymen (some say, with only one layman), were sentenced to labour in the quarries and finally burnt alive, probably at Phunon, near Petra, for celebrating the liturgy in the place of detention. Some identify this group with that listed in the R.M. on Feb. 20 under St Tyrannio, q.v.
Cf. Holw. — Att. — Baud.

PELEUSIUS (St) M. R.M. Apr. 7
? According to the R.M., a priest of Alexandria.
Cf. Holw.

PELINUS (St) Bp. M. R.M. Dec. 5
d. 361. A martyr of Confinium, a town in Samnium now destroyed, who suffered under Julian the Apostate.
Cf. Holw. — Baud.

PEPIN of LANDEN (Bl) C. A.C. Feb. 21
d. c.648. Pepin, duke of Brabant, mayor of the palace under Kings Clotaire II, Dagobert and Sigebert, and ancestor of the Carolingian dynasty of French kings, was the husband of Bl Itta, and the father of St Gertrude of Nivelles and of St Begga. He is described as "a lover of peace and the constant defender of truth and justice." His feast was kept at Nivelles.
Cf. Holw. — Baud. — Att.

PEREGRINUS LAZIOSI (St) C. O.S.M.
R.M. May 1
1260-1345. A native of Forli who spent a very worldly youth, in the course of which during a popular revolt he struck St Philip Benizi across the face. Philip turned the other cheek and Peregrinus was converted on the spot and forthwith joined the Servites at Siena. He was afterwards sent back to Forli where he spent the rest of his long life. He was instantaneously cured of a cancer of the foot as a result of a vision, and is for that reason invoked against cancer. Canonized in 1726.
Cf. Holw. — Att. — Baud. — Menzies.

PEREGRINUS (St) M. R.M. May 5
See Irenaeus, Peregrinus and Irene.

PEREGRINUS (St) Bp. A.C. May 16
d. c.138 (?). Bishop of Terni in Umbria and founder of its cathedral.
Cf. Gams — Holw.

PEREGRINUS (St) Bp. M. R.M. May 16
d. c.304. A Roman by birth, venerated as the first bishop of Auxerre, to which see he is said to have been appointed by Pope St Xystus (Sixtus) II. He was martyred under Diocletian.
Cf. Holw. — Baud. — Duch. Fast. Episc.

PEREGRINUS I and PEREGRINUS II (BB) CC. O.S.B. Cam. A.C. June 3
d. c.1291. Peregrinus I was a Camaldolese abbot of Santa Maria dell' Isola. In 1290 he returned to Camaldoli as sacrist and prior. Peregrinus II was a simple monk who lived at Camaldoli and died about the same time as Peregrinus I.
Cf. Zimm.

PEREGRINUS (properly CETHEUS) (St) Bp. M. R.M. June 13
d. c.600. Bishop of Amiternum (now Aquila) in S. Italy. He was drowned in the river Atevno by the Arian Lombards for asking mercy for a condemned prisoner.
Cf. Holw. — Att. — Baud.

PEREGRINUS (St) M. R.M. June 17
See Isaurus, Innocent, etc.

PEREGRINUS, LUCIAN, POMPEIUS, HESYCHIUS, PAPIUS, SATURNINUS, GERMANUS, and ASTIUS (SS) MM. R.M. July 7
d. c.120. Astius was bishop of Dyrrachium (Durazzo) in Macedonia and was there crucified under Trajan. The others were Italians who had fled to Macedonia in order to escape the persecution in their own country and were seized on account of the sympathy they showed for Astius. They were loaded with chains, taken out to the sea and thrown overboard.
Cf. Holw. — Baud.

PEREGRINUS (St) H. R.M. July 28
2nd cent. (?). He seems to have been a priest of the diocese of Lyons in the time of St Irenaeus, and during the persecution under Severus to have lived as a hermit in an island in the R. Saône.
Cf. Holw. — Baud.

PEREGRINUS (St) H. A.C. Aug. 1
d. 643. An Irish, or Scottish, pilgrim, who, returning from a pilgrimage to the Holy Land, settled in a solitude near Modena where he passed the rest of his days.
Cf. Holw. — Baud.

PEREGRINUS (St) M. R.M. Aug. 25
See Eusebius, Pontian, etc.

PEREGRINUS of FALERONE (Bl) C. O.F.M. A.C. Sept. 6
d. 1240. Born at Falerone in the diocese of Fermo, he became a follower of St Francis of Assisi, and after a pilgrimage to Palestine, lived as a lay-brother at San Severino.
Cf. Holw. — Att. — Baud. — Menzies.

PERFECTUS (St) M. R.M. Apr. 18
d. 851. A Spanish priest of Cordova, martyred by the Mohammedans on Easter Sunday.
Cf. P. de U. — Baud. — Holw.

PERGENTINUS and LAURENTINUS (SS) MM. R.M. June 3
d. 251. Two brothers martyred at Arezzo under Decius. It is not certain whether they ever existed.
Cf. Holw. — Att. — Baud.

PERIS (St) C. A.C. Dec. 11
? The patron saint of Llanberis in N. Wales. No record of him exists.
Cf. Holw.

PERPETUA, FELICITAS, SATURUS, (SATYRUS), SATURNINUS, REVOCATUS and SECUNDULUS (SS) MM. R.M. March 6 and 7
d. 203. Vivia Perpetua was a young married woman of good social position and Saturus was her brother. Felicitas, also married, was a slave. The others were catechumens. All were imprisoned together at Carthage. Secundulus died in prison: the others were thrown to the wild beasts in the amphitheatre on March 7. Their feast is kept on the preceding day. Their Acts, which are of the highest value and interest, both theologically and historically, are undoubtedly authentic. They were written by Saturus, one of the martyrs, and completed by an eye-witness, perhaps Tertullian. SS Perpetua and Felicitas are mentioned in the canon of the Roman Mass.
Cf. Chev. — Att. — Holw. — Baud. — Ruinart — Ricci.

PERPETUA (St) R.M. Aug. 4
d. c.80. A Roman matron said to have been baptized by St Peter and to have converted her husband and her son St Nazarius the Martyr, q.v. Her relics are at Milan and Cremona.
Cf. Menzies — Baud. — Holw.

PERPETUUS (St) Bp. R.M. Apr. 8
d. c.490. Bishop of Tours (c.460-c.490). His alleged will is admittedly a forgery of the seventeenth century.
Cf. Holw. — Baud. — Att. — Duch. Fast. Episc.

PERREUX (St) Ab. A.C. June 4
The Breton form of Petroc, q.v.

PERSEVERANDA (PECINNA, PEZAINE) (St) V. R.M. June 26
d. c.726. Said to have been a Spanish maiden, who with her sisters Macrina and Columba, travelled to Poitiers, where

they founded a nunnery. While fleeing from the pirate Oliver, Perseveranda died of exhaustion in the place now called after her Sainte-Pezaine in Poitou.
Cf. Holw. — Baud. — Chev.

PERSIA, Martyrs of (SS)
The R.M. catalogues five anonymous groups of martyrs who suffered in Persia, as follows:

R.M. Feb. 8
? 6th cent. Martyrs slain under Cabas.

R.M. March 10
? A group of forty-two martyrs of whom all details are lost.

R.M. Apr. 6
? 345. Another group of one hundred and twenty martyrs, believed to have suffered under Shapur II.

R.M. Apr. 22
d. 380. A vast number of martyrs put to death under the same king Shapur II on Good Friday. Among them were some twenty-five bishops, two hundred and fifty priests and deacons and very many monks and nuns.

R.M. May 9
? A group of three hundred and ten martyrs of whom, again, no details are known.

Eastern menologies give other dates and other figures, but a fair estimate of the Persian martyrs put to death during the first six centuries would bring the number up to ten thousand.
Cf. Holw. — Baud. — Att.

PETER (*several*)
Note. The name Petrus is the latinized form of the Greek Petros, which means Rock. Modern variants of Petrus are as follows: Italian, Pietro (antiquated form Piero); Spanish and Portuguese, Pedro; French, Pierre; Catalan, Pere; English, Peter.

PETER APSELAMUS and PETER AB-SALON (SS) MM. **R.M. Jan. 3**
291 and 311. The R.M. seems to have confused two different martyrs of Palestine: Peter surnamed Apselamus, or Balsamus, who was crucified at Aulana, near Hebron (c.291 ?), and Peter Absalon, who was buried alive at Caesarea (311 ?).
Cf. Holw. — Baud. — Att.

PETER of CANTERBURY (St) Ab. O.S.B.
A.C. Jan. 6
d. c.606. A Benedictine monk of St

Andrew's, Rome, who was a member of the first band of missionaries sent to England by St Gregory the Great. He became first abbot of the monastery of SS Peter and Paul (afterwards St Augustine's), founded at Canterbury. While on a mission in France he was drowned at Ambleteuse, near Boulogne. Cult confirmed in 1915.
Cf. Zimm. — Chev. — Holw.

PETER of SEBASTE (St) Bp.
R.M. Jan. 9
d. c.391. A native of Cappadocia, and younger brother of St Basil and of St Gregory of Nyssa. He succeeded St Basil as abbot and in 380 was appointed bishop of Sebaste in Armenia. He took part in the general council of Constantinople (381).
Cf. Att. — Baud. — Holw.

PETER URSEOLUS (St) H. O.S.B.
R.M. Jan. 10
928-987. Born in Venice, Peter became, at the age of twenty, admiral of the Venetian fleet. In 976 he became Doge of Venice and succeeded in guiding the Republic safely through a time of dangerous political crisis. After two years, unknown to all — even to his family, he disappeared from Venice, to emerge as a monk in the Benedictine abbey of Cuxa, in the Spanish Pyrenees. He acted as sacristan of the abbey until some years later he retired to live as a hermit.
Cf. Zimm. — Holw. — Baud. — Att.

PETER, SEVERUS and LEUCIUS (SS) MM. **R.M. Jan. 11**
d. c. Egyptian martyrs, who suffered at Alexandria.
Cf. Holw. — Baud.

PETER of CASTELNAU (Bl) M. O.S.B. Cist. **A.C. Jan. 15**
d. 1208. Born near Montpellier, he became archdeacon of Maguelonne (1199) and shortly after (c.1202) a Cistercian at Fontfroide. The following year Pope Innocent III appointed him apostolic legate and inquisitor for the Albigensians — in fact the leader of the famous expedition, of which St Dominic was a member, for the conversion of those heretics. While engaged in that work he was run through the body with a lance by one of the heretics, his last words being: "May

God forgive thee, brother, as fully as I forgive thee."
Cf. Zimm. — P. de U. — Att. — Holw.

PETER (St) M. O.F.M. R.M Jan. 16
See Berardus, Peter, etc.

PETER THOMAS (St) Bp. O.C.
A.C. Jan. 25
1305-1366 (Jan. 6). A native of Breil in Gascony, Peter Thomas joined the Carmelites and eventually was sent to Avignon as procurator of his Order. There he entered the service of the papal court and was sent on diplomatic missions to Italy, Serbia, Hungary and the Near East, being appointed successively bishop of Patti and Lipari (1354), bishop of Coron in Morea (1359), archbishop of Candia (1363) and Latin patriarch of Constantinople (1364). On behalf of Pope Urban V and with the support of King Peter I of Cyprus he led a crusade against the Turks. In an unsuccessful attack on Alexandria he was severely wounded and died three months later at Cyprus. Throughout his active life he remained true to the spirit of his contemplative profession. Cult approved in 1608.
Cf. Att. — Holw. — Baud.

PETER NOLASCO (St) Founder.
R.M. Jan. 31
c.1182-1258 (Dec. 25). A native of Languedoc, who, after seeing service against the Albigenses, settled at Barcelona, where he became intimate with St Raymund of Penafort. About the year 1218 both saints, with the help of James I of Aragon, reorganized a lay confraternity for ransoming captives from the Moors, which was gradually transformed into the Order of the Mercedarians (B. V. Mariae de Mercede Redemptionis Captivorum), of which St Peter Nolasco is revered as the chief founder. He personally ransomed several hundred captives. Canonized in 1628.
Cf. Att. — Baud. — Holw.

PETER CAMBIAN (Bl) M. O.P.
A.C. Feb. 2
d. 1365. Peter Cambian de Ruffi, a Dominican of distinction, was sent in 1351 as inquisitor general to Piedmont and Lombardy. He had chiefly to deal with the Waldenses, who ultimately trapped and killed him. Cult approved in 1856.
Cf. Prop. O.P. — Holw. — Baud.

PETER BAPTIST (St) M. O.F.M.
R.M. Feb. 5
1545-1597. Born near Avila, in Spain, he joined the Friars Minor in 1567. He was sent as a missionary first to Mexico, then to the Philippine Islands (1583) and lastly (1593) to Japan. Political intrigues led to the arrest of Peter and twenty-six missionaries (six Franciscans, three Jesuits and seventeen native Franciscan tertiaries), who had never given a thought to politics. They were all crucified at Nagasaki. A notice of each of the other martyrs is given in this book. St Peter Baptist is considered as their leader. All were beatified in 1627, and canonized in 1862.
Cf. Holw. — Prop. O.F.M.

PETER XUKEXICO (St) M.
R.M. Feb. 5
d. 1597. A Japanese layman. He was a Franciscan tertiary, a catechist, and houseservant and sacristan to the Franciscan missionaries in Japan. He belongs to the group of St Peter Baptist, q.v.
Cf. Holw. — Prop. O.F.M.

PETER IGNEUS (St) Card. Bp. O.S.B. Vall.
R.M. Feb. 8
d. c.1089. He is said to have belonged to the Aldobrandini family of Florence. He took his vows at Vallombrosa under St John Gualbert. Shortly after, in order to convict the bishop of Florence of simony, Peter miraculously passed through the flames unharmed, whence his surname of Igneus, "of the fire." At a later period he was created cardinal-bishop of Albano and sent to foreign countries as legate of the Holy See.
Cf. Zimm. — Prop. O. Vall. — Att. — Holw.

PETER of TREJA (Bl) C. O.F.M.
A.C. Feb. 20
d. 1304. One of the early Franciscans associated with Bl Conrad of Offida in his apostolate. They preached with great success throughout Italy. Bl Peter died at Sirolo in Piceno. Cult approved in 1793.
Cf. Menzies — Att. — Holw.

PETER the SCRIBE (St) M.
R.M. Feb. 21
d. 743. Surnamed also Mavimenus, from the town of Majuma in Palestine where he worked as a scribe (chartularius). He was

put to death by the Arab sheik of Damascus.

Cf. Holw. — Baud.

PETER DAMIAN (St) Bp. Dr. O.S.B.
R.M. Feb. 23

1007-1072. Born at Ravenna, the youngest of many children, he was left an orphan in charge of a married brother, who ill-treated him and set him to herd swine. Another brother, Damian, archpriest of Ravenna, took pity on the child and paid for his schooling at Faenza and Parma. Peter soon joined the Benedictine community of Fontavellana, founded by Bl Rudolph twenty years before. Enthusiastically earnest in all his undertakings, Peter became a model monk, was chosen abbot and formed several saints in his school: St Dominic Loricatus, St John of Lodi, St Ralph of Gubbio, etc. In 1057 he was summoned to Rome and created cardinal-bishop of Ostia. He served successive popes in various delicate missions: as legate to Germany, to France, to Lombardy, as president, or papal representative, at sundry councils and synods; as visitor to bishoprics and abbeys. Meanwhile he wrote unceasingly, mostly theological or ascetical works, but also poetry, his Latin verse being among the very best of the Middle Ages. He died at Faenza worn out by his labours. Declared doctor of the Church in 1828.

Cf. Zimm. — P. de U. — Chev. — Att. — Holw.

PETER ROQUE (Bl) M. A.C. March 1

1758-1796. A native of Vannes in Brittany and a priest of the Congregation of the Mission (Vincentians) at Paris. He refused to take the constitutional oath during the French Revolution and was guillotined. Beatified in 1934.

Cf. Att.

PETER PAPPACARBONE (St) Bp.
O.S.B. A.C. March 4

d. 1123. A nephew of St Alpherius, the founder of Cava. He was born at Salerno, and became a monk of Cava under the second abbot St Leo I. About the year 1062 he was sent to Cluny, where he stayed some six years, inbibing the genuine Cluniac spirit of Benedictine observance. In 1079 he was made bishop of Policastro, but resigned and returned to Cava, where Leo I appointed him co-adjutor abbot. He succeeded to the abbacy in the same year (1079), but showed himself too strict, and in view of the remonstrances of the community he withdrew to another house. He was soon recalled and under his new, more paternal, regime, the abbey prospered exceedingly: he is said to have given the habit to over three thousand monks. When he died Cava numbered twenty-nine subject abbeys, ninety priories and over three hundred and forty cells. The abbey church of Cava was solemnly dedicated during his abbacy by Pope Urban II, who had been his fellow monk at Cluny.

Cf. Mab. — Gams — Zimm. — Att. — Holw.

PETER de GEREMIA (Bl) C. O.P.
A.C. March 10

1381-1452. A native of Palermo, who was a student of law at Bologna when he decided to join the Friars Preachers. He became one of the best known preachers and missionaries of his age. Cult approved in 1784.

Cf. Menzies — Prop. O.P. — Holw. — Att.

PETER the SPANIARD (St) C.
R.M. March 11

? A Spanish pilgrim to Rome who settled as a hermit at Babuco, near Veroli. He wore a coat of mail next to his skin.

Cf. Holw. — Chev. — Baud.

PETER of NICOMEDIA (St) M.
R.M. March 12

d. 303. A chamberlain (*cubicularius*) in the palace of Diocletian at Nicomedia. He was one of the first victims of the last great persecution. His flesh was torn from his bones, salt and vinegar were poured into his wounds, and finally he was roasted to death over a slow fire.

Cf. Holw. — Baud. — Att.

PETER the DEACON (St) C.
A.C. March 12

d. p. 605. The disciple, secretary and companion of St Gregory the Great, to whom the great pope dictated the four books of his Dialogues. He is venerated as the patron saint of Salassola, diocese of Biella, in Upper Italy. He is usually described as a Benedictine.

Cf. Holw. — Chev.

PETER II of CAVA (Bl) Ab. O.S.B.
                          A.C. March 13
d. 1208. The ninth abbot of Cava, near
Salerno, from 1195 to 1208. He is described as "an enemy of all litigation,"
which, for that time, is no small praise.
Beatified in 1928.
Cf. Zimm. — Holw.

PETER and APHRODISIUS (SS) MM.
                          R.M. March 14
5th cent. Martyrs under the Arian Vandals in N.W. Africa. Nothing else is
known about them.
Cf. Holw. — Baud.

PETER LIEOU (Bl) M.   A.C. March 17
d. 1834. A Chinese layman. Converted
when young, he was exiled for his faith to
Tartary (1814). In 1827 he was allowed
to return. During a fresh persecution,
he gained entry into the prison to comfort
and strengthen his sons and was strangled.
Beatified in 1900.
Cf. Holw.

PETER of GUBBIO (Bl) C. O.S.A.
                          A.C. March 23
d. c.1350 (?). Born at Gubbio in Umbria,
of the family of the Ghisleni. He became
a hermit of St Augustine, and was provincial of his congregation. His shrine is
at Gubbio. Cult confirmed by Pius IX.
Cf. Menzies — Holw. — Baud.

**PETER, MARCIAN, JOVINUS, THEC-
LA, CASSIAN, and Comp. (SS) MM.**
                          R.M. March 26
? Roman martyrs, of whom nothing cer-
tain is known. Some registers have
Theodula instead of *Thecla.*
Cf. Holw. — Baud.

PETER MARGINET (Bl) C. O.S.B. Cist.
                          A.C. March 26
d. 1435. A Cistercian monk of Poblet,
near Tarragona, in Spain, and the cellarer
of the abbey. From a life of high fervour
he lapsed into one of crime, apostatized
and became the leader of bandits. After
some years he repented, went back to the
abbey and spent the rest of his life doing
penance.
Cf. Zimm. — P. de U.

PETER REGALADO (St) C. O.F.M.
                          R.M. March 30
1390-1456. A Spaniard of noble birth of
Valladolid who entered the Franciscan

order and effected a strict reform in several friaries, notably at Aguilar del Campo
in New Castile.
*Cf. P. de U. — Holw. — Baud. — Chev.
— Att.*

PETER of POITIERS (St) Bp.
                          A.C. Apr. 4
d. 1115. Bishop of Poitiers (1087-1115).
A fearless prelate who publicly denounced
the sacrilegious tyranny and license of
King Philip I and of William VI, count of
Poitiers and duke of Aquitaine. He befriended and helped Bl Robert d'Arbriselle
in founding the abbey of Fontrevault.
Cf. Att. — Baud. — Holw.

PETER CERDAN (Bl) C. O.P.
                          A.C. Apr. 5
d. 1422. A Dominican friar, who accompanied St Vincent Ferrer in his travels
and apostolate. He died at Grans, diocese of Barbastro, Aragon.
Cf. Holw. — P. de U.

PETER of MONTEPIANO (Bl) C. O.S.B.
Vall.   **A.C. Apr. 12**
d. 1098. A Vallombrosan abbot of San
Virgilio at Brescia, who ended his life as
a hermit at Montepiano in Tuscany.
Cf. Zimm. — Chev. — Holw.

PETER GONZALEZ (or TELMO) (St)
C. O.P.   **A.C. Apr. 14**
1190-1246. Born at Astorga in Spain he
became a canon of Palencia and subsequently joined the Dominicans. He was
chosen by King St Ferdinand of Castile as
his confessor and court-chaplain, and in
that position did much to foster the crusade against the Moors and to obtain a
kindly treatment for the Moorish captives
when Cordova and Seville were taken.
He also worked among the sailors and
peasants of Galicia. Spanish sailors often
call him Telmo (Elmo-Erasmus).
Cf. Att. — Baud. — Holw.

PETER and HERMOGENES (SS) MM.
                          R.M. Apr. 17
? Peter, a deacon, and Hermogenes, his
servant, were martyred at an unknown
date, probably at Antioch.
Cf. Holw. — Baud.

PETER of BRAGA (St) Bp. M.
                          R.M. Apr. 26
? The alleged first bishop and martyr of
Braga in Portugal. The local tradition

connects him with the apostolate of St James the Great, q.v., in Spain. Beyond his name nothing authentic is known about him.
Cf. Holw. — Baud.

PETER ARMENGOL (St) M.
R.M. Apr. 27
1238-1304. He belonged to the house of the counts of Urgell, in the Spanish Eastern Pyrenees. He spent his youth in dissipation, but in 1258 joined the Mercedarians and devoted all his energies to the ransoming of captives. He offered himself as a hostage for eighteen Christian children, and was put to frightful tortures in his African captivity, being for this reason considered a martyr. He died near Tarragona.
Cf. Att. — Baud. — Holw.

PETER CANISIUS (St) C. Dr. S.J.
R.M. Apr. 27
1521-1597. A native of Nijmwegen in Holland. He was received into the Society of Jesus by Bl Peter Faber (1543). He was the leader of the Catholic counter-Reformation in German lands, being constantly engaged in preaching, teaching, writing, instructing, advising, arbitrating, in Germany, Austria, Switzerland, Bohemia, Poland. His short catechism in Latin and German had passed through two hundred editions before his death and was translated into twelve European languages. He also wrote theological, ascetical and historical treatises. He has been rightly called "the Second Apostle of Germany." Canonized and declared Doctor of the Church in 1925.
Cf. Holw. — Att. — Baud.

PETER CHANEL (Bl) M. A.C. Apr. 28
1803-1889. Peter Louis Mary Chanel was born at Cluet, diocese of Belley, in France, of a family of peasants. He was ordained priest in 1827 and appointed parish priest of Crozet. In 1831 he entered the Society of Mary (Marist Fathers) and was sent to Oceania as superior of the first missionary band. He was martyred on Fortuna Island by the native king. He is the first martyr of Oceania. Beatified in 1889.
Cf. Holw. — Baud. — Att.

PETER HIEU (Bl) M. A.C. Apr. 28
d. 1840. A native catechist of Tonkin, attached to the Society of Foreign Missions of Paris. He was beheaded with three companions. Beatified in 1900.
Cf. Holw.

PETER MARTYR (St) O.P.
R.M. Apr. 29 (and Apr. 6)
1206-1252. Born at Verona of heretical (Catharist) parents, he joined the Dominicans and was appointed inquisitor of Lombardy, then swarming with Catharists. He preached very successfully throughout northern and central Italy, until at length the Catharists succeeded in waylaying him on the road between Como and Milan. He was canonized in the following year (1253).
Cf. Att. — Baud. — Menzies — Holw. — Ricci.

PETER (St) M. R.M. Apr. 30
See Amator, Peter and Louis.

PETER of PAVIA (St) Bp. R.M. May 7
d. c.735. A bishop of Pavia during the reign of his kinsman Luitprand, king of the Lombards. His episcopate was brief.
Cf. Menzies — Holw. — Baud.

PETER of TARANTAISE (St) Bp. O.S.B. Cist.
R.M. May 8
1102-1175. Born near Vienne in Dauphiné, at the age of twelve he joined the Cistercians at Bonnevaux and before he was thirty he was sent as first abbot to the foundation of Tamié. In 1142 he was chosen archbishop of Tarantaise, but after holding this position thirteen years he disappeared and was eventually found serving his novitiate as a lay-brother in a remote Cistercian abbey in Switzerland. He was compelled to return to his diocese, where he made a name for himself as an upholder of papal rights. Canonized in 1191.
Cf. Holw. — Zimm. — Att. — Baud.

PETER, ANDREW, PAUL and DIONYSIA (SS) MM. R.M. May 15
d. 251. A young man of Lampsacus on the Hellespont, martyred at Troas with SS Paul, Andrew and Dionysia, under Decius.
Cf. Holw. — Att. — Baud.

PETER CELESTINE (St) Pope, Founder, O.S.B.
R.M. May 19
1210-1296. Born at Isernia in the Abruzzi, he became a hermit and a priest. In 1246 he received the Benedictine habit from the abbot of Faizola, but he returned to

the solitary life at Morone, near Salmona (1251) where he gathered numerous disciples and founded the new Benedictine congregation named after him. In 1294 he was elected pope and was compelled by the cardinals to accept, but he proved an utter failure and resigned the same year. His successor Boniface VIII kept him in custody till his death. Canonized in 1313.
Cf. Zimm. — Menzies — Holw.

PETER de DUEÑAS (Bl) M. O.F.M.
A.C. May 19
1378-1397. Born at Palencia, Spain, he became a Franciscan and in 1396 accompanied Bl John de Cetina to Granada to preach the gospel to the Moors. Both were beheaded in the following year.
Cf. Holw.

PETER WRIGHT (Bl) M. S.J.
A.C. May 19
d. 1651. Born at Slipton in Northamptonshire, he became a convert to the Catholic faith and studied for the priesthood at Ghent and in Rome. In 1629 he joined the Jesuits and was a chaplain to the royalist army during the Civil War. He was condemned to death for his priesthood and executed at Tyburn.
Cf. Newdigate — Att.

PETER PARENZI (St) M. A.C. May 22
d. 1199. A Roman by birth, he was sent to Orvieto (1199) as papal governor to repress the excesses of the Catharist heretics. He adopted severe measures, with the result that the heretics seized him and put him to a cruel death.
Cf. Att. — Holw. — Baud.

PETER of the ASSUMPTION (Bl) M. O.F.M. A.C. May 22
d. 1617. Born at Cuerva, archdiocese of Toledo. He went to Japan with a band of fifty Franciscan missionaries (1601) and was appointed guardian of the friary at Nagasaki. He was beheaded at Nagasaki with Bl John Machado. He is the first martyr of the second great Japanese persecution. Beatified in 1867.
Cf. Holw.

PETER VAN (Bl) M. A.C. May 25
c.1780-1857. A native catechist beheaded at Son-tay, in W. Tonkin. Beatified in 1900.
Cf. Holw.

PETER SANZ (Bl) Bp. M. O.P.
A.C. May 26
d. 1747. Born at Asco in Catalonia he joined the Dominicans (1697) and was sent to the Philippine Islands (1712) whence (1713) he proceeded to China. In 1730 he was nominated vicar apostolic of Fu-Kien and titular bishop of Mauricastro. In 1746 he was imprisoned and finally beheaded at Foochow. Beatified in 1893.
Cf. Att. — Holw. — Baud.

PETER ARNAUD (Bl) M. A.C. May 28
d. 1242. A layman, notary of the inquisition at Toulouse, put to death by the Albigenses at Avignonet with eleven inquisitors. Cult approved in 1866.
Cf. Holw.

PETER PETRONI (Bl) C. O.Cart.
A.C. May 29
1311-1361. A Sienese by birth, he became (1328) a Carthusian at Maggiano near Siena. His thoughtful charity was instrumental in the conversion of Boccaccio.
Cf. Holw. — Baud. — Att.

PETER (St) M. R.M. June 2
See Marcellinus and Peter.

PETER, WALLABONSUS, SABINIAN, WISTREMUNDUS, HABENTIUS and JEREMIAS (SS) MM. R.M. June 7
d. 851. Spaniards living at Cordova under the Moorish rule. Peter was a priest; Wallabonsus, a deacon; Sabinian and Wistremundus monks of St Zoilus at Cordova; Habentius a monk of St Christopher's; Jeremias, a very old man, had founded the monastery of Tábanos, near Cordova. For publicly reprobating Mohammed they were martyred under Abderrahman II. Jeremias was scourged to death, the others were beheaded.
Cf. P. de U. — Att. — Holw.

PETER TU (Bl) M. O.P. A.C. June 10
d. 1860. A native priest of Tonkin, strangled after two years' imprisonment.
Cf. Holw.

PETER RODRIGUEZ and Comp. (BB) MM. (?) P.C. June 11
d. 1242. A group of seven Portuguese knights of Santiago, whose leader was Bl Peter Rodriguez. All were murdered during an armistice by the Moors at

Tavira in Algabes, Portugal. Cult not yet approved.
Cf. Att. — Holw. — Baud.

PETER GAMBACORTA (Bl) Founder.
A.C. June 17
1355-1435. Born at Pisa or Lucca. After a misspent youth, he repented and retired to the solitude of Montebello, diocese of Urbino, where, it is said, he converted twelve robbers, with whom he founded the institute of the Poor Brothers of St Jerome. When his father and two brothers were murdered, Peter refused to leave his cell, and, like his sister, Bl Clare Gambacorta, fully forgave the assassins.
Cf. Menzies — Holw. — Att.

PETER RINXEI (Bl) M. S.J.
A.C. June 20
1589-1626. A Japanese who was educated at the Jesuit seminary of Arima. He became the catechist of Bl Francis Pacheco, by whom he was received into the Society while in prison. Burnt alive at Nagasaki. Beatified in 1867.
Cf. Holw.

PETER of TARANTAISE (Bl) Pope.
R.M. June 22
Otherwise Innocent V, q.v.

PETER of JUILLY (Bl or St) Mk. O.S.B.
A.C. June 23
d. 1136. An Englishman and a companion and friend of St Stephen Harding at Molesme. He was appointed chaplain and confessor to the Benedictine nuns of Juilly-les-Nonnais, subject to Molesme, where St Bernard's sister, St Humbelina, was abbess. Peter is described as a great preacher and wonder-worker. He died at Juilly.
Cf. Att. — Holw. — Baud.

PETER JAMES of PESARO (Bl) C. O.S.A.
A.C. June 23
d. c.1496. An Augustinian friar in the monastery of St Nicholas at Pesaro. Cult approved by Pius IX.
Cf. Holw.

PETER the APOSTLE (St) M.
R.M. June 29 (Jan. 18, Feb. 22, Aug. 1, Nov. 18)
d. c.67. Simon, son of Jona, was a Galilean fisherman, a married man living at Bethsaida. He was a disciple of St John the baptist before he was called, with his elder brother Andrew to be a disciple of Christ, by whom he was at once named "Rock" (Kephas, Petros, Petra, Peter). The culminating episode narrated of him in the gospel, is that of his confession of Christ as the Son of God (Matt. XVI, 15-19), to which Christ answered with the solemn promise: "Thou art Peter and upon this rock I will build my church . . . and I will give thee the keys of the kingdom of heaven." This promise was ratified by Christ after his resurrection with the three-fold injunction to feed His flock. As one of the most ancient catalogues of the popes puts it, St Peter "succeeded our Lord as bishop of Rome and of the universal church." After Christ's ascension he presided at Jerusalem, preached in Samaria, was perhaps for a time bishop of Antioch and finally fixed his permanent see in Rome, where he was martyred, head downwards according to tradition, in the circus of Nero on the Vatican Hill. Liturgically he is commemorated several times in the year, but his chief feast is that of June 29 on which day he has been honoured with St Paul at least since the beginning of the 4th century.
Cf. Holw. — Att. — Baud.

PETER of LUXEMBURG (Bl) Bp., Card.
A.C. July 4
1369-1389. Born at Ligny in Lorraine, of the family of the counts of Lützelburg. As a boy he showed an inclination to the clerical state, and, according to the abuse of the time, was forthwith given sundry canonries at Paris, Chartres and Cambrai and was made archdeacon of Dreux. At the age of fourteen he was appointed bishop of Metz. At sixteen he was created cardinal of San Giorgio in Velabro. He died at the age of eighteen. He was a youth of great promise and holiness of life. Beatified in 1527.
Cf. Holw. — Att. — Baud.

PETER the HERMIT (Bl) C. P.C. July 8
d. 1115. A soldier of European birth who became a hermit for a time in Palestine. Then he returned to Europe and preached the first Crusade throughout Italy, France and part of the Germanies. He accompanied the first expedition to the East and followed once more the profession of arms. He fought at the siege of Antioch and the capture of Jerusalem. Subsequently he founded the monastery of

Neumoutier at Huy in Flanders, where he died. He was never officially beatified.
Cf. Holw. — Att.

PETER van ASCHE (St) M. O.F.M.
R.M. July 9
d. 1572. Born at Asche near Brussels. He was a Franciscan lay-brother at Gorkum in Holland, and was hanged by the Calvinists at Briel.
Cf. Holw. — Prop. O.F.M.

PETER of PERUGIA (St) Ab. O.S.B.
A.C. July 10
d. 1007. Peter Vincioli was born near Perugia and belonged to the family of the counts of Agello. He was the abbot-founder of the monastery of St Peter at Perugia, where he has an altar dedicated to him in the abbey church.
Cf. Zimm. — Chev. — Holw.

PETER TU (Bl) M. A.C. July 10
d. 1840. A native catechist of Tonkin, beheaded at Anam. Beatified in 1900.
Cf. Holw.

PETER ARAKI-COBIOJE (Bl) M.
A.C. July 12
d. 1626. A Japanese layman burnt alive at Nagasaki for sheltering Christians. Beatified in 1867.
Cf. Holw.

PETER KHANH (Bl) M. A.C. July 12
c.1780-1842. A native priest of Tonkin, beheaded at Con-co in W. Tonkin. Beatified in 1909.
Cf. Holw.

PETER NUÑEZ and PETER FONTURA (BB) MM. S.J. A.C. July 15
d. 1570. Two Portuguese Jesuits, fellow-martyrs of Bl Ignatius de Azevedo. The former was a cleric, a native of Fronteria; the latter a lay-brother, born at Braga.
Cf. Holw. — Baud.

PETER BERNA (Bl) M. S.J.
A.C. July 15
d. 1583. Born at Ascona, on the lake of Locarno, Ticino, Switzerland, he studied at the German College in Rome and joined the Jesuits. He went to India with Bl Rudolph Acquaviva and was ordained at Goa. After some years of missionary work he was put to death with Bl Rudolph, q.v.
Cf. Holw. — Prop. S.J.

PETER TUAN (Bl) M. A.C. July 15
d. 1838. A native seminarian of Tonkin, who died in prison of wounds received for the Faith. Beatified in 1900.
Cf. Holw.

PETER of the HOLY MOTHER of GOD (Bl) M. O.P. A.C. July 29
d. 1627. A Japanese catechist and a Dominican. He was burnt alive at Omura with Bl Louis Bertram. Beatified in 1867.
Cf. Holw.

PETER of MOGLIANO (Bl) C. O.F.M.
A.C. July 30
d. 1490. Born at Mogliano, diocese of Fermo, he studied law at Perugia and joined the Observant Franciscans there. Later on he went about preaching with St James della Marca, q.v. "It is said of him that he would die laughing." (Attwater, h.1). Cult approved in 1760.
Cf. Holw. — Menzies.

PETER QUI (Bl) M. A.C. July 31
d. 1859. Born at Bung in Cochin China he was ordained priest and beheaded for that reason near Chau-doc, in W. Cochin-China. Beatified in 1909.
Cf. Holw.

PETER (St) M. R.M. Aug. 1
See Cyril, Aquila, etc.

PETER of OSMA (St) Bp. O.S.B.
A.C. Aug. 2
d. 1109. A French monk of Cluny, one of the numerous Cluniac monks who settled in Spain from c.1050 to c.1130. He first became archbishop of Toledo under the Cluniac archbishop Bernard de la Sauvetat, who in 1101 nominated him bishop of Osma in Old Castile. St Peter is venerated as the principal patron saint of the cathedral and diocese of Osma.
Cf. P. de U. — Zimm. — Chev. — Holw.

PETER of ANAGNI (St) Bp. O.S.B.
R.M. Aug. 3
d. 1105. Born at Salerno, he became a Benedictine monk in his native city. In 1062 Pope St Gregory VII appointed him to the see of Anagni. He built a new cathedral there, took part in the first crusade and was sent as papal legate to Constantinople. Canonized four years after his death.
Cf. Gams — Chev. — Holw. — Zimm.

PETER JULIAN EYMARD (Bl) Founder.
A.C. Aug. 3

1811-1868. A native of La Mure d'Isère. He was ordained in 1834 and worked for some time as a parish priest, but subsequently joined the congregation of the Marist Fathers, as a member of which he became renowned as a preacher and confessor. In 1856 he was dispensed from his vows in that Institute, and in the following year founded another of his own, the Congregation of priests of the Blessed Sacrament, with the special object of fostering devotion to the Holy Eucharist. Shortly after he established a congregation of women with similar aims. In both enterprises he was encouraged by St John Vianney. Beatified in 1925.
Cf. Att.

PETER, JULIAN, and Comp. (SS) MM.
R.M. Aug. 7

d. c.260. A band of twenty or more Roman martyrs under Valerian and Gallienus.
Cf. Holw. — Baud.

PETER BECKET (BECCHETTI) (Bl)
A.C. Aug. 11

See John and Peter Becchetti.

PETER FABER (Bl) C. S.J. A.C. Aug. 11

1506-1546. Peter Lefèvre was born at Vilardet in Savoy and was already a priest and a student at Paris when he attached himself to St Ignatius of Loyola. After the official approbation of the Society of Jesus (1540) he worked at Worms, Spires, Mainz, and especially at Cologne. He was a man of very winning manners, of great ability and of untiring energy. He died in Rome, when about to leave for the Council of Trent.
Cf. Att. — Holw. — Prop. S.J.

PETER ZUÑIGA (Bl) M. O.S.A.
A.C. Aug. 19

1585-1622. A native of Seville, he spent his youth in Mexico, where his father was the sixth viceroy. On his return to Spain he joined the Augustinians at Seville, and after being ordained priest asked to be sent to Japan. He arrived at Manila in 1610 and in Japan in 1620 and two years later was burnt alive at Nagasaki with Bl Louis Flores. Beatified in 1867.
Cf. Holw.

PETER VASZUEZ (Bl) M. O.P.
A.C. Aug. 25

d. 1624. Born at Berin, in Galicia, he joined the Dominicans in Madrid and ultimately was appointed to the missions in Japan. He was burnt alive at Ximabura with Bl Louis Sotelo and Comp. Beatified in 1867.
Cf. Prop. O.P. — Holw.

PETER (St) M. R.M. Aug. 27

See Marcellinus, Mannea, etc.

PETER of TREVI (St) C. R.M. Aug. 30

d. c.1060. Born at Carsoli in the diocese of Marsi, Italy. He was ordained to the priesthood and preached with signal success to the peasants of the districts of Tivoli, Anagni and Subiaco. He died while still young at Trevi, near Subiaco. Canonized in 1215.
Cf. Holw. — Baud. — Chev.

PETER of SASSOFERRATO (Bl) M. O.F.M. A.C. Sept. 3

See under John of Perugia.

PETER CLAVER (St) C. S.J.
R.M. Sept. 8

1581-1654. Born at Verdú, near Barcelona, in Spain, the son of a farmer, he became a Jesuit in 1609 and was stationed at Majorca, where he was inspired by St Alphonsus Rodriguez with the desire to work for souls in America. In 1610 he was sent there, and received priest's orders at Cartagena in Central America. During the following 40 years he worked chiefly at Cartagena, at that time the central slave-mart of the West Indies, dedicating his life by a special vow to the service of the outcast Negroes. He is said to have baptized, and cared for over 300,000 of them. During the last four years of his life he was a sick man and was often neglected by his brethren. He was canonized in 1888 and declared patron of all the Catholic missions among the Negroes in 1896.
Cf. Prop. S.J. — Holw. — Att.

PETER MARTINEZ (St) Bp. O.S.B.
R.M. Sept. 10

d. c. Surnamed also St Peter of Mozonzo. He was a native of Spanish Galicia, and about the year 950 became a Benedictine at the abbey of St Mary of Mozonzo. Later he was appointed abbot of St

Martin *de Antealtares*, at Compostella and finally (c.986) archbishop of that city. He is one of the heroes of the Spanish Reconquest, as also one of the supposed authors of the *Salve Regina*.
Cf. Gams — Chev. — P. de U.

PETER de AVILA (Bl) M. O.F.M.
A.C. Sept. 10
1562-1622. Born at Palomares in Castile, he was sent to Manila with Bl Louis Sotelo (1617) then to Japan. He was burnt alive at Nagasaki on the day of the Great Martyrdom. Beatified in 1867.
Cf. Holw.

PETER SAMPO (Bl) M. S.J.
A.C. Sept. 10
d. 1622. Born in the province of Ochu, in Japan. He was received into the Society of Jesus by Bl Charles Spinola in the prison of Omura. Burnt alive at Nagasaki on the day of the Great Martyrdom. Beatified in 1867.
Cf. Holw.

PETER NANGAXI, PETER SANGA, and PETER KIKIEMON (BB) MM.
A.C. Sept. 10 and 11
d. 1622. Three Japanese children martyred with their parents at Nagasaki. Peter Nangaxi, a boy of seven years, was the son of BB Paul and Thecla; Peter Sanga, a boy of three years, was the second son of BB Antony and Mary Magdalen Sanga, of Corea; Peter Kikiemon, a boy of seven years, was the son of Bl Bartholomew. The three were beheaded: the first two on the 10th, the third on the 11th of September. Beatified in 1867.
Cf. Holw.

PETER of CHAVANON (St) C. O.S.A.
A.C. Sept. 11
1003-1080. A native of Langeac, in Haute Loire, he became a secular priest and then founded an abbey of Augustinian canons regular at Pébrac in Auvergne and ruled it as its first provost.
Cf. Baud. — Holw. — Att.

PETER-PAUL of ST CLAIRE (Bl) M. O.F.M.
A.C. Sept. 12
d. 1622. Born at Saigo in Arima, Japan, he became a catechist under Bl Apollinaris Franco. He was burnt alive at Omura. Beatified in 1867.
Cf. Holw.

PETER ARBUES (St) M. O.S.A.
R.M. Sept. 17
1442-1485. Born at Epila in Aragon he studied philosophy at Huesca, and theology and canon law at Bologna. In 1478 he became an Augustinian canon regular at Saragossa, and in 1484 was made inquisitor of Aragon. What has been written about his cruelty is unhistorical and uncritical: not a single sentence of death or of torture can be traced to him; but his integrity was feared by the Crypto-Jews (the *Marranos*) who murdered him in his cathedral. Canonized in 1867.
Cf. Att. — Baud. — Holw. — P. de U.

PETER (St) M.
R.M. Sept. 23
See Andrew, John, etc.

PETER ACOTANTO (Bl) C. A.C. Sept. 23
d. c.1180. Born of a noble Venetian family, he spent his life tending the sick. Some years before his death he retired to live as a recluse in a cell near the Benedictine abbey of San Giorgio Maggiore in Venice, under the obedience of the abbot. Cult approved by Clement VIII.
Cf. Holw. — Chev.

PETER CUFIOJE (Bl) M. A.C. Sept. 28
d. 1630. A Japanese Augustinian tertiary, beheaded at Nagasaki for sheltering the Augustinian missionaries. Beatified in 1867.
Cf. Holw.

PETER (St) M.
R.M. Oct. 3
See Dionysius, Faustus, etc.

PETER of DAMASCUS (St) Bp. M.
R.M. Oct. 4
d. c.750. A bishop of Damascus who was maimed, blinded, exiled and ultimately bound to a cross and beheaded by the Arab rulers of the city for preaching against their prophet.
Cf. Holw. — Baud. — Chev.

PETER of SEVILLE (St) M. R.M. Oct. 8
? A martyr venerated at Seville, of whom only the name is known. Later legends are admitted to be fables.
Cf. Holw. — Baud. — Chev.

PETER TUY (Bl) M.
A.C. Oct. 11
d. 1833. A native Tonkinese priest beheaded under King Minh-Menh. Beatified in 1900.
Cf. Holw.

PETER of ALCÁNTARA (St) C. O.F.M.
R.M. Oct. 19
1499-1562. Born at Alcántara in Estremadura, at the age of fifteen he became a Franciscan Observant and after his ordination (1524) initiated at Pedrosa a still more severe Franciscan reform which was known as *Alcantarine* and received papal approval. St Peter is also remembered as one of the group of great Spanish mystics and his treatise on prayer was much valued, and used by St Francis of Sales. He encouraged and defended St Teresa, whose confessor and admirer he was. St Teresa held him in great esteem and speaks with awe of his austerities and penances as "incomprehensible to the human mind"; they had reduced him, she tells us to a condition in which he looked as if "he had been made of the roots of trees." Canonized in 1669.
Cf. Att. — Holw. — Baud. — P. de U.

PETER CAPUCCI (Bl) C. O.P.
A.C. Oct. 21
1390-1445. Born at Città di Castello (the ancient *Tifernum*), he joined the Dominicans and was raised to the priesthood at Cortona. He became known as "the preacher of death," because he used to preach with a skull in his hands. Cult confirmed by Pius VII.
Cf. Att. — Baud. — Holw. — Menzies.

PETER (St) M.
R.M. Oct. 25
See Theodosius, Lucius, etc.

PETER ONIZUKI (Bl) M. S.J.
A.C. Nov. 1
d. 1622. A Japanese born at Faciram, Arima. He became a Jesuit postulant and attached himself to Bl Paul Navarro, with whom he was burnt alive at Nagasaki. Beatified in 1867.
Cf. Holw. — Prop. S.J.

PETER ALMATÓ (Bl) M. O.P.
A.C. Nov. 1
d. 1861. Born at Sasserra, diocese of Vich, Spain, he became a Dominican and was sent to the Philippine Islands, and thence to Japan under Bl Jerome Hermosilla, with whom he was beheaded. Beatified in 1906.
Cf. Holw. — Prop. O.P.

PETER-FRANCIS NÉRON (Bl) M.
A.C. Nov. 3
1818-1860. Born in Bornay, in Jura, he was admitted into the seminary of Foreign Missions of Paris (1846), ordained priest (1848) and sent to Hong-Kong. He worked in W. Tonkin as director of the central seminary until his martyrdom by beheading. Beatified in 1919.
Cf. Baud. (François) — Holw.

PETER DUMOULIN-BORIE, PETER CHOA and VINCENT DIEM (BB) MM.
A.C. Nov. 24
d. 1838. Bl Peter Dumoulin was born at Cors, diocese of Tulle, France, in 1808, and entered the seminary for Foreign Missions at Paris in 1829, being sent to Tonkin after his ordination in 1832. In 1836 he was arrested and received when in prison his appointment as titular bishop and vicar apostolic of W. Tonkin. BB Peter Choa and Vincent Diem were natives of Tonkin and priests. The three were beheaded in Annam. Beatified in 1900.
Cf. Holw.

PETER of ALEXANDRIA (St) Bp. M.
R.M. Nov. 26
d. 311. An Alexandrian who as a young man, was a "confessor" during the Decian persecution. Then he became the head of the catechetical school and as such combated extreme Origenism. In 300 he was raised to the patriarchal see and in that position he figured as one of the opponents of the Meletian schism, being also one of the first to detect the dangerous teaching of Arius. He was martyred under Diocletian, "the seal and complement of martyrs" as the Copts term him, because he was the last to be put to death as a Christian by public authority at Alexandria.
Cf. Holw. — Att. — Baud.

PETER (St) M.
R.M. Nov. 28
See Stephen, Basil, etc.

PETER CHRYSOLOGUS (St) Bp. Dr.
R.M. Dec. 2 and 4
406-c.450. Born at Imola, he became deacon there, and then successive archdeacon and archbishop of Ravenna (c.433). He is chiefly famed for his assiduity and eloquence in preaching, whence the name given him of *Chrysologus*, "Golden Speech." A great number of his sermons are still extant. He was declared a Doctor of the Church in 1729.
Cf. Menzies — Att. — Gams — Holw.

PETER PASCUAL (St) Bp. M.
R.M. Dec. 6

1227-1300. Peter Pascual, or Pascualez (latinized as *Paschasius*), was born at Valencia in Spain. About the year 1250 he was ordained priest and was for some time tutor to the son of the king of Aragon. Later he was raised to the see of Jaén, which at that time was still under Moorish government. His heroic exertions in ransoming captives, and his preaching and writing against Islam were rewarded with his martyrdom at Granada. Cult confirmed in 1673.
Cf. P. de U. — Att. — Holw.

PETER, SUCCESSUS, BASSIANUS, PRIMITIVUS and Comp. (SS) MM.
R.M. Dec. 9

? Martyrs in Africa, of whom nothing is known.
Cf. Holw. — Baud.

PETER FOURIER (St) Founder.
R.M. Dec. 9

1565-1640. Born at Mirecourt in Lorraine, he joined the Augustinian canons regular, and some time after his ordination (1585) was put in charge of the neglected parish of Mattaincourt. Here he founded the Congregation of Notre Dame for the education of girls. He failed, however, in similar efforts to establish a new congregation for teaching boys. Canonized in 1897.
Cf. Baud. — Holw. — Att.

PETER TECELANO (Bl) C. O.F.M.
A.C. Dec. 10

d. 1287. Born at Campi in Tuscany, he started life as a comb-maker at Siena. On the death of his wife he joined the Franciscans as a lay-brother and carried on his trade in the friary for the remainder of his long life. He attained a high degree of mystical prayer. Cult confirmed in 1802.
Cf. Att. — Holw. — Menzies.

PETER DUONG and PETER TRUAT (BB) MM.
A.C. Dec. 18

d. 1838. Native catechists in Tonkin, martyred in Annam. Beatified in 1900.
Cf. Holw.

PETER de la CADIRETA (Bl) M. O.P.
P.C. Dec. 20

d. 1277. Born at Moya in Spain, he became a Dominican friar. He was stoned to death by heretics while preaching at Urgell. His body is venerated in the church of St Dominic at Urgell.
Cf. Holw.

PETER MASSALENUS (Bl) C. O.S.B. Cam.
A.C. Dec. 20

1375-1453. Peter de Massalenis was born at Othoca in Sardinia. After repeated pilgrimages to the Holy Land he joined the Camaldolese Benedictines at San Michele di Murano, Venice (1410). He was famed for his gift of mystical contemplation.
Cf. Holw. — Chev. — Zimm.

PETER THI (Bl) M.
A.C. Dec. 20

d. 1839. A native of Tonkin and a priest. At the age of sixty he suffered martyrdom in Annam. Beatified in 1900.
Cf. Holw.

PETER the VENERABLE (Bl) Ab. O.S.B.
A.C. Dec. 25

c.1092-1156. Peter de Montboissier was born in Auvergne, and became a monk at Cluny in 1109. At twenty he was prior of Vézelay and in 1122 succeeded to the abbacy of Cluny. He was one of the most eminent churchmen of his age, and during the thirty-four years of his reign Cluny retained its position as the greatest and most influential abbey in Christendom. Calm and serene in his charity, he was the counterpart of his tempestuous contemporary, friend, admirer, and, on some points, rival, St Bernard of Clairvaux. At Cluny he regulated the finances, raised the standard of studies (he was himself a poet and a theological writer of distinction) and received the vanquished Abelard under his roof. He died, according to his wish, on Christmas day, after having preached about the feast to his monks. His name was inserted in French martyrologies, and his feast is observed in the diocese of Arras on Dec. 29.
Cf. Zimm. — Att. — Chev. — Holw.

PETER of SUBIACO (Bl) M. O.S.B.
P.C. Dec. 31

d. 1003. The twenty-second abbot of Subiaco. For defending the rights of his abbey he was blinded by the baron of Monticello and died in prison.
Cf. Zimm. — Holw.

PETROC (PETROCK, PEDROG, PERREUX) (St) Ab.
A.C. June 4

d. c.594. Said to have been the son of a

Welsh chieftain, and to have studied in Ireland and settled in Cornwall, where he undoubtedly exercised a very active apostolate. There he founded a monastery at a place called after him, Petrocston (Padstow) and another at Bodmin where he died. In Brittany he is venerated under the name of Perreux.
Cf. Att. — Holw. — Chev.

PETRONAX (St) Ab. O.S.B. A.C. May 6
d. c.747. A native of Brescia who was induced by Pope St Gregory II in 717 to visit Montecassino, destroyed in 580 by the Lombards, with a view to restoring the cenobitical life there. He found a few hermits who elected him their abbot and Benedictine life began afresh. St Willibald, bishop of Eichstätt and St Sturmio of Fulda, were monks under him. He is surnamed "the second founder of Montecassino."
Cf. Zimm. — Chev. — Mab. — Att. — Holw.

PETRONILLA of MONCEL (Bl) Abs. P.C. A.C. May 14
d. 1355. Of the family of the counts of Troyes. She was the first abbess of the convent of Poor Clares at Moncel in Burgundy, founded by King Philip le Bel.
Cf. Holw. — Att.

PETRONILLA (St) V. M. R.M. May 31
1st cent. (?). A Roman virgin and martyr venerated from the earliest times. Later legends connect her with St Peter, to whom she is said to have ministered. The R.M. goes further and describes her as the daughter of the Apostle, which she certainly was not.
Cf. Holw. — Att. — Baud. — Menzies.

PETRONIUS (St) Bp. A.C. Jan. 10
d. c.463. The son of a senator of Avignon and bishop of Dié from c.456 to 463.
Cf. Duch. Fast. Episc. — Baud. — Holw.

PETRONIUS (St) Bp. R.M. Sept. 6
d. c.450. A bishop of Verona.

PETRONIUS (St) Bp. R.M. Oct. 4
d. c.445. Born in Byzantium, he was sent by the emperor Theodosius the Younger to report to the pope on the case of Nestorius. While in Italy he was raised to the see of Bologna. He is said to have built the monastery of St Stephen in that city, reproducing the general lines of the build-ings of the Holy Places at Jerusalem, which he had visited.
Cf. Holw. — Baud. — Att. — Menzies — Ricci.

PHAEBADIUS (St) Bp. A.C. Apr. 25
d. c.392. A bishop of Agen in S. Gaul, who, together with his friend St Hilary of Poitiers, succeeded in stamping out Arian heresy in Gaul. He was one of the best known prelates of his time and presided at several councils. St Jerome mentions him among "the illustrious men" of the Church.
Cf. Duch. Fast. Episc. — Gams — Chev. — Holw. — Baud.

PHAGANUS (FAGAN) (St) A.C. Jan. 3 (R.M. May 26)
Otherwise Fugatius, q.v.

PHAINA (St) V. M. R.M. May 18
See Theodotus, Thecusa, etc.

PHAL (PHELE) (St) R.M. May 16
Otherwise Fidolus, q.v.

PHARA (St) Abs. R.M. Dec. 7
Otherwise Burgundofara (Apr. 3) q.v.

PHARAÏLDIS (VAREIDE, VERYLDE, VEERLE) (St) V. A.C. Jan. 4
d. c.740. She seems to have been born in Ghent and was married against her will, having dedicated her virginity to God. She was maltreated by her husband, either because she insisted on living as a virgin or because he objected to her nocturnal visits to the churches. She is one of the patron saints of Ghent.
Cf. Holw. — Att. — Baud.

PHARNACIUS (St) M. R.M. June 24
See Orentius, Heros, etc.

PHARO (St) Bp. R.M. Oct. 28
Otherwise Faro, q.v.

PHELIM (FIDLEMINUS) (St) Bp. A.C. Aug. 9
6th cent. Said to have been a disciple of St Columba. The city of Kilmore sprang up round the place where his cell stood. Principal patron of Kilmore.
Cf. Holw.

PHILADELPHIUS (St) M. R.M. May 10
See Alphius, Philadelphus and Cyrinus.

PHILADELPHUS (St) M.   R.M. Sept. 2
See Diomedes, Julian, etc.

PHILAPPIAN (St) M.   R.M. Jan. 30
See Felician, Philappian, etc.

PHILASTRIUS (St) Bp.   R.M. July 18
d. c.387. A Spaniard who was appointed
bishop of Brescia at the time of the Arian
troubles. He wrote a book against the
Arians, which is still extant. St Gaudentius, his successor, praises him for his
"modesty, quietness and gentleness towards all men," and because he helped
the poor.
Cf. Menzies — Holw. — Att. — Baud.

PHILEAS and Comp. (SS) MM.
                R.M. Feb. 4 and Nov. 26
d. c.304-311. Martyrs whose passion is
related by their contemporary, the historian Eusebius. Phileas, bishop of
Thmuis, an ancient city in Lower Egypt,
was beheaded. From his prison at Alexandria he wrote a letter to his flock describing the sufferings of his fellow Christian prisoners. With him suffered a
Roman tribune named Philoromus and a
great number of people from Thmuis and
its neighbourhood. See also under Faustus, Didius, etc.
Cf. Holw. — Att. — Baud.

**PHILEMON and APOLLONIUS (SS)
MM.   R.M. March 8**
d. c.305. Philemon was an actor and
musician at Antinoe, who was converted
by the deacon Apollonius of the same city.
They were brought to Alexandria, bound
hand and foot, and cast into the sea.
They suffered under Diocletian.
Cf. Holw. — Baud. — Att.

PHILEMON and DOMNINUS (SS) MM.
                        R.M. March 21
? Romans by birth, who preached the
gospel in various parts of Italy and were
finally put to death, probably at Rome.
Cf. Holw. — Baud.

**PHILEMON and APPIA (APPHIA) (SS)
MM.   R.M. Nov. 22**
d. c.70. Philemon is the Christian of
Colossae, master of the runaway slave
Onesimus, to whom St Paul's shortest
epistle is addressed, Appia is supposed to
have been Philemon's wife. Both are
said to have been stoned to death at their
home at Colossae.
Cf. Att. — Holw. — Baud.

**PHILETUS, LYDIA, MACEDO, THEO-
PREPIUS (THEOPREPIDES), AMPHI-
LOCHIUS and CRONIDAS (SS) MM.**
                        R.M. March 27
d. c.121. Martyrs of Illyria under Ha-
drian. The R.M. describes Philetus as a
senator, Lydia as his wife, Macedo and
Theoprepius as their sons, Amphilochius
as a captain, and Cronidas as a notary.
Their *Acts* are not reliable.
Cf. Holw. — Baud.

PHILIBERT (St) Ab. O.S.B.
                        R.M. Aug. 20
c.608-684. Born in Germany and educated at the court of King Dagobert I.
At the age of 20 he became a monk at
Rébais and shortly afterwards its abbot.
He visited several old Columbanian foundations which at that time had already
adopted or were gradually adopting the
Benedictine Rule, and finally founded and
ruled the abbacy of Jumièges, not far from
Fontenelle. He opposed Ebroin, the
tyrannical mayor of the palace and was
imprisoned and exiled. Before his death
he had established two new abbeys, viz.,
Noirmoutier and Quinçay.
*Cf. Holw. — Zimm. — Chev. — Mab. —
Att.*

PHILIBERT (St) M.   R.M. Aug. 22
See Fabrician and Philibert.

PHILIP (several)
Note. Philip is the English form of the
Latin Philippus; the French is: Philippe;
the Italian, Filippo; the Spanish, Felipe.

PHILIP BERRUYER (Bl) Bp.
                        A.C. Jan. 9
d. 1260. A nephew of St William of
Bourges, and, like his uncle, archbishop
of that diocese.
Cf. Holw. — Baud.

PHILIP of VIENNE (St) Bp.
                        A.C. Feb. 3
d. c.578. Bishop of Vienne in Gaul
(c.560-c.578).
*Cf. Duch. Fast. Episc. — Gams — Holw.
— Baud.*

PHILIP of JESUS (St) M. O.F.M.
                        R.M. Feb. 5
d. 1597. Born in Mexico City of Spanish
parents, Philip became a Franciscan at
Puebla, but left the Order in 1589 and
travelled to the Philippines as a merchant.

He repented and rejoined the Franciscans at Manila (1590). On his way home to be ordained in Mexico, his ship was driven by a storm to Japan (1596) where he was arrested with St Peter Baptist and crucified at Nagasaki. Canonized in 1862.
Cf. Holw. — Baud.

PHILIP of GORTYNA (St) Bp.
R.M. Apr. 11
d. c.180. A bishop of Gortyna in Crete, author of a work, now lost, against the Marcionite Gnostics.
Cf. Holw. — Baud.

PHILIP the APOSTLE (St) R.M. May 1
d. c.80. One of the Twelve, a native of Bethsaida, he always takes the fifth place in the catalogue of the Apostles, and is mentioned three times as a confidant of our Lord in St John's gospel. After the ascension he is believed to have preached in Asia Minor and to have been martyred at Hierapolis in Phrygia. His relics are venerated in Rome.
Cf. Att. — Baud. — Holw.

PHILIP of ZELL (St) H. O.S.B.
A.C. May 3
d. c.770. An Anglo-Saxon pilgrim who settled as a hermit near Worms and became a great friend of King Pepin. Being joined by several disciples, he founded the monastery of Zell — thus called from his own original *cell* — which in subsequent times grew into the town of Zell.
Cf. Zimm. — Holw. — Baud. — Att.

PHILIP of AGIRONE (St) R.M. May 12
? A saint venerated in the little hill town of Agirone in Sicily as the first missionary sent to that country by the Holy See. The story abounds in contradictory, as well as improbable, statements.
Cf. Holw. — Baud.

PHILIP SUZANNI (Bl) C. O.S.A.
A.C. May 24
d. 1306. A native of Piacenza who joined the Augustinian Order in that city. He was famed for his spirit of prayer and compunction. Cult approved in 1756.
Cf. Att. — Holw.

PHILIP NERI (St) C. Founder.
R.M. May 26
1515-1595. A native of Florence, he worked first as an assistant to a merchant at San-Germano, at the foot of Monte-

cassino (1534-1541). Then he settled in Rome as tutor in the house of a Florentine nobleman. Meanwhile he devoted all his leisure time to the study of theology and to the silent unobtrusive service of his neighbour. He thought of going to the foreign missions, but a Benedictine of St Paul's told him that his apostolate was in Rome. In 1548 he gathered 14 companions into a congregation which ultimately received a definite shape as the Congregation of the Oratory. It was not until 1551 that he was ordained priest. During the 33 years that followed Philip and his Oratory constituted the centre of religious life in Rome. In 1583 his institute was officially approved with its mother-house at the church of La Valicella, which St Philip rebuilt on a magnificent scale. He fully deserves the title given him of "Second Apostle of Rome." Canonized in 1622.
Cf. Holw. — Att. — Menzies — Ricci.

PHILIP THE DEACON (St)
R.M. June 6
1st cent. One of the seven deacons ordained by the Apostles (Acts, VI, 5). He worked in Samaria, baptized the eunuch of Queen Candace of Ethiopia (ib. VI, 8), and was the host of St Paul at Caesarea (ib. XXI, 8). His four daughters (ib. XXI, 9) are honoured as saints with him.
Cf. Att. — Baud. — Holw.

PHILIP POWEL (Bl) M. O.S.B.
A.C. June 30
d. 1646. A native of Tralon in Brecknockshire, he was educated at Abergavenny grammar school, and joined the Benedictines at St Gregory's, Douai (now Downside) in 1614, being ordained priest in 1621. In the following year he was sent to the English mission and worked chiefly in Devon but also in Somerset and Cornwall for twenty years. Martyred at Tyburn. Beatified in 1929.
Cf. Camm — Att. — Newdigate.

PHILIP MINH (Bl) M. **A.C. July 3**
1815-1853. Born at Caimong in W. Cochin-China, he joined the Society for Foreign Missions and was ordained priest of Mac-Bac in E. Cochin-China. He was beheaded at Cong-ho. Beatified in 1900.
Cf. Holw.

PHILIP (St) M. **R.M. July 10**
One of the Seven Brothers, q.v.

PHILIP, ZENO, NARSEUS and Comp. (SS) MM. R.M. July 15
? Martyrs of Alexandria. The "companions" consisted of ten little children.
Cf. Baud. — Att. — Holw.

PHILIP EVANS (Bl) M. S.J.
A.C. July 22
1645-1679. Born in Monmouthshire and educated at Saint-Omer, he joined the Jesuits (1665) and served on the Welsh mission. Martyred for his priesthood at Cardiff in consequence of the "Oates plot." Beatified in 1929.
Cf. Newdigate — Att.

PHILIP (St) M. R.M. Aug. 17
See Straton, Philip and Eutychian.

PHILIP BENIZI (St) C. O.S.M.
R.M. Aug. 23
1233-1285. Born at Florence (Aug. 15), where, after his studies at Paris and Padua, he practised medicine. In 1253 he joined the Servite Order as a lay-brother and was made the gardener of the friary of Mt Senario, until 1259, when he was directed by his superiors to receive holy orders. Soon he was known as one of the most zealous preachers in Italy, was made superior of several friaries, and, in 1267, the fifth general of the Order. In the following year the cardinals were for putting him forward as a candidate for the papacy, but he fled by night and hid in a cave until another was elected. He established new foundations of his institute throughout Italy and the German lands, and was untiring in visiting them. Moreover he frequently acted as peacemaker in the interminable feuds between Guelphs and Ghibellines. Canonized in 1671.
Cf. Menzies — Att. — Holw. — Ricci.

PHILIP (St) M. R.M. Sept. 2
See Diomedes, Julian, etc.

PHILIP (St) M. R.M. Sept. 13
3rd. cent. The alleged father of St Eugenia, in whose household SS Protus and Hyacinth are said to have been employed. Since St Eugenia's story is thought now to be only a pious romance, the very existence of St Philip is problematical.
Cf. Holw. — Baud.

PHILIP ODERISI (Bl) Bp. O.S.B.
A.C. Sept. 18
d. 1285. From being a monk of Fon-

tavellana he was raised to the see of Nocera in Umbria, which he occupied from 1254 to 1285. He was a great friend and defender of the early Friars Minor.
Cf. Gams — Zimm.

PHILIP HOWARD (Bl) M. A.C. Oct. 19
d. 1595. Earl of Arundel and Surrey. He was converted from a life of indifference and neglect of his religion and became a fervent and conscientious Catholic. In 1585 he was committed to the Tower of London and in 1589 sentenced to death. The sentence was never carried out but he remained a prisoner until his death at the age of thirty-eight. Beatified in 1929.
Cf. Newdigate — Att.

PHILIP (St) Bp. M. R.M. Oct. 22
d. c.270. A bishop martyr of Fermo in Italy, whose relics are enshrined in his cathedral.
Cf. Holw. — Baud.

PHILIP, SEVERUS, EUSEBIUS and HERMES (SS) MM. R.M. Oct. 22
d. 304. Philip was bishop of Heraclea near Constantinople; Severus was his deacon; Eusebius and Hermes, two of the inferior clergy. During the persecution under Diocletian they were all arrested and brought to trial. It was insistently demanded of them that they should deliver up the sacred books of the church to be burnt. On their refusal they were taken to Adrianopolis and burnt at the stake. We have a copy of the legal process instituted against them, a document of undeniable authenticity. By mistake the recent editions of the R.M. register these martyrs as having suffered under Julian.
Cf. Ruinart — Att. — Holw.

PHILIPPA MARERI (Bl) V. Poor Clare
A.C. Feb. 16
d. 1236. Born at Cicoli in the Abruzzi. After having met St Francis of Assisi in her parents' home she decided to become a hermit, and did so on a mountain above Mareri. Eventually she founded and ruled as first abbess, a Franciscan nunnery at Rieti under the direction of Bl Roger of Todi.
Cf. Att. — Holw.

PHILIPPA GUIDONI (Bl) Abs. O.S.B.
A.C. Aug. 29
d. 1335. A disciple of Bl Santuccia of

Gubbio. Foundress and first abbess of the Benedictine convent of Santa Maria di Valverde at Arezzo.
Cf. Zimm.

PHILIPPA (St) M.   R.M. Sept. 20
See Theodore, Philippa, etc.

PHILIPPINE DUCHESNE (Bl) V.
A.C. Nov. 18
Otherwise Rose-Philippine Duchesne, q.v.

PHILO and AGATHOPUS (AGATHO-PODES) (SS)   R.M. Apr. 25
d. c.150. The two deacons of Antioch who (c.107) attended St Ignatius, their bishop, to his martyrdom in Rome. They took back to Antioch such relics of the saint as they were able to recover and are believed to have written the "Acts" of his trial and death.
Cf. Holw. — Baud.

PHILOGONIUS (St) Bp.   R.M. Dec. 20
d. 324. A lawyer at Antioch and a confessor under Licinius. After the death of his wife he became bishop of Antioch and was one of the first to denounce Arianism. St John Chrysostom preached a panegyric, still extant, in honour of St Philogonius.
Cf. Holw. — Att. — Baud.

PHILOLOGUS and PATROBAS (SS)
R.M. Nov. 4
1st cent. Roman Christians saluted by St Paul in his epistle to the Romans (XVI, 14-18).
Cf. Holw. — Baud.

PHILOMENA (St) V.   R.M. July 5
d. b. 500. A saint venerated at San Severino (*Septempeda*) near Ancona. Nothing is now known of her.
Cf. Holw. — Baud.

PHILOMENA (PHILUMENA) (St) V. M.
A.C. Aug. 11
? In 1802 the relics of a young woman were discovered in the catacomb of St Priscilla; near the tomb there was a broken tablet with the inscription, *Filumena, Paxtecum.* It was accordingly presumed that the body was there of an unknown martyr named Philomena. In 1805 the relics were enshrined in the church of Mugnano, diocese of Nola, and from that time the cult of St Philomena spread far and wide, patronized by popes and saints, among others by St John

Vianney. It seems, however, that the body of the real St Philomena was already enshrined in the church of St Praxedes in Rome.
Cf. Holw. — Att. — Baud. — Menzies.

PHILOMENUS (St) M.   R.M. Nov. 14
See Clementinus, Theodotus and Philomenus.

PHILOMENUS (St) M.   R.M. Nov. 29
d. 275. A martyr of Ancyra in Galatia under Aurelian.
Cf. Holw. — Baud.

PHILONILLA (St)   R.M. Oct. 11
See Zenais and Philonilla.

PHILOROMUS (St) M.   R.M. Feb. 4
See under Phileas.

PHILOTERUS (St) M.   R.M. May 19
d. 303. A nobleman of Nicomedia, martyred there under Diocletian. His supposed Acts are quite untrustworthy.
Cf. Holw. — Baud.

PHILOTHEUS (St) M.   R.M. Nov. 5
See Domninus, Theotimus, etc.

PHLEGON (St) M.   R.M. Apr. 8
See Herodion, Asyncritus and Phlegon.

PHOCAS (St) M.   R.M. March 5
d. c.320. A martyr of Antioch, suffocated in a bath. His Acts are not reliable. Often confused with St Phocas the Gardener (see July 14).
Cf. Holw. — Baud. — Att.

PHOCAS (St) Bp. M.   R.M. July 14
d. 117. Bishop of Sinope on the Black Sea, martyred under Trajan.
Cf. Holw. — Att.

PHOCAS the GARDENER (St) M.
A.C. July 23
d. c.303. A gardener near Sinope on the Black Sea martyred under Diocletian. His existence, martyrdom and ancient cult are established facts. He is still greatly venerated in the East.
Cf. Att. — Holw. — Baud.

PHOEBE (St)   R.M. Sept. 3
1st cent. A matron who worked as a deaconess at Cenchreae near Corinth, highly commended by St Paul and the bearer to Rome of his epistle to that

church (Rom. XVI, 1-3). It has been suggested, without the slightest foundation, that she was St Paul's wife.
Cf. Holw. — Baud. — Att.

PHOTINA, JOSEPH, VICTOR, SEBASTIAN, ANATOLIUS, PHOTIUS, PHOTIS (PHOTIDES), PARASCEVE and CYRIACA (SS) MM.   R.M. March 20
? This group of martyrs constitutes a historical puzzle. The Greek tradition connects them all with the apostles and with Palestine and identifies Photina with the Samaritan woman of St John's gospel (chap. IV). They are alleged to have been martyred in Rome. It seems that Cardinal Baronius listed them in the R.M. by an oversight.
Cf. Holw. — Att. — Baud.

PHOTINUS (or POTHINUS), SANCTIUS (SANCTUS), VETIUS, EPAGATHUS, MATURUS, PONTICUS, BIBLIS (BIBLIDES), ATTALUS, ALEXANDER, BLANDINA and Comp. (SS) MM.
                                    R.M. June 2
d. 177. Martyrs of Lyons, the details of whose martyrdom are given in an authentic letter written by the churches of Vienne and Lyons of those of Asia. The writer may have been St Irenaeus. The martyrs were at first set upon by the pagan mob, but afterwards they were tried and condemned on account of their religion, by the regular tribunals. Photinus, their leader, bishop of the city, an old man of ninety years, expired in his dungeon from the ill-usage he received. The others were thrown to the wild beasts in the amphitheatre at the public games. The slave-girl, Blandina, enmeshed in a net and tossed by a wild bull, and the boy, Ponticus, who was one of the last to suffer, have ever excited special admiration. The whole description is most graphic. They suffered under Marcus Aurelius.
Cf. Ruinart — Att. — Holw. — Baud.

PHOTINUS (St) M.   R.M. Aug. 12
See Anicetus, Photinus, etc.

PHOTIS (St) M.   R.M. March 20
See Photina, Joseph, etc.

PHOTIUS (St) M.   R.M. March 4
See Archelaus, Cyril and Photius.

PHOTIUS (St) M.   R.M. March 20
See Photina, Joseph, etc.

PIA (St) M.   R.M. Jan. 19
See Paul, Gerontius, etc.

PIALA (St) M.   A.C. Dec. 14
See Fingar, Phiala, etc.

PIATON (PIATO, PIAT) (St) M.
                          R.M. Oct. 1
d. c.286. Said to have been a native of Benevento in Italy, sent by the pope to evangelize the districts of Tournai and Chartres. He is thought to have died a martyr at Tournai under Maximian.
Cf. Baud. — Holw.

PIENTIA (St) V. M.   R.M. Oct. 11
See Nicasius, Quirinus, etc.

PIERIUS (St) C.   R.M. Nov. 4
d. c.310. A priest of Alexandria, writer of several philosophical and theological treatises.
Cf. Baud. — Holw. — Att.

PIGMENIUS (St) M.   R.M. March 24
d. 362. A Roman priest thrown into the Tiber under Julian the Apostate.
Cf. Holw. — Baud.

PINIANUS (St) M.   R.M. Dec. 31
See Melania and Pinianus.

PINNOCK (St)   Nov. 6
A church in Cornwall is called St Pinnocks, but it is probable that *Pinnock* is a corruption of *Winnoc* (q.v.).
Cf. Arnold-Forster: Studies in Church Dedications.

PINYTUS (St) Bp.   R.M. Oct. 10
d. p. 180. A Greek bishop in Crete numbered among distinguished ecclesiastical writers by Eusebius.
Cf. Holw. — Baud.

PIONIUS and Comp. (SS) MM.
                          R.M. Feb. 1
d. 251. A priest of Smyrna who, with fifteen companions, suffered under Decius. They were arrested while liturgically commemorating the anniversary of the martyrdom of St Polycarp. They were burnt at the stake after a long cross-examination and after having been put to severe torture. We have an eye-witness's account of their death.
Cf. Ruinart — Att. — Holw.

PIOR (St) H. A.C. Jan. 17
d. c.395. An Egyptian solitary, a disciple of St Antony.
Cf. Holw. — Baud.

PIPERION (St) M. R.M. March 11
See Candidus and Comp.

PIRAN (PYRAN) (St) C. A.C. March 5
5th or 6th cent. A hermit near Padstow in Cornwall, titular of the church of the canons regular at Truro. Many writers identify him with St Kyran (Kieran), q.v. He is venerated as the patron saint of miners.
Cf. Holw. — Baring-Gould.

PIRMIN (St) Bp. O.S.B. R.M. Nov. 3
d. 753. According to the latest researches, Pirmin was born in S. Aragon and became a monk there. The name of his monastery is not known. When the Saracens invaded Spain, he fled, and travelled as far as the Rhineland where he established several abbeys — Reichenau, Murbach, Amorbach — and restored others, notably Dissentis, introducing into them all the Benedictine Rule. He was ordained by the pope a chorepiscopus, or regionary bishop; he was never bishop of Meaux. He is one of the great Benedictine apostles in German lands.
Cf. Zimm. — P. de U. — Att. — Chev.

PISTIS (FAITH) (St) V. M.
R.M. Aug. 1
See Faith, Hope and Charity.

PIUS V (St) Pope O.P. R.M. May 5
1504-1572. Michael Ghislieri was born in Piedmont, joined the Dominicans in 1518, was ordained priest in 1540, taught philosophy and theology for sixteen years and in 1556 was nominated bishop of Sutri and inquisitor for Lombardy. In 1557 he was created cardinal and in 1559 was transferred to the see of Mondovi, finally being elected pope in 1565. Of an austere and severe disposition he was well fitted for the task of combating the loose discipline of that time in many ecclesiastical quarters, including the Roman curia. He insisted on the exact observance of the decrees of the Council of Trent, organized an expedition against the Turks which won the victory of Lepanto (1570), promoted ecclesiastical learning, reformed liturgical worship, excommunicated Queen Elizabeth of England and fought Protestantism everywhere. Canonized in 1712.
Cf. Att. — Menzies — Holw. — Baud.

PIUS I (St) Pope M. R.M. July 11
d. c.154. Pope from c.142 to c.154. He may have been a brother of Hermas, the writer of the work called The Shepherd; if so, Pius, like his brother, was born a slave. His pontificate was one of active opposition to the Gnostics, notably the Gnostic Marcion. It is not proved that he died a martyr.
Cf. Att. — Holw. — Baud.

PLACID (PLACIDUS, PLAIT) (St) Ab. O.S.B. A.C. May 7
d. c.675. Abbot in the basilica of St Symphorian at Autun.
Cf. Zimm. — Holw. — Baud.

PLACID (St) M. A.C. July 11
See Sigisbert and Placid.

PLACID (Bl) Ab. O.S.B. Cist.
A.C. June 12
d. 1248. Born at Rodi, near Amiterno in Italy, of working class parents. He became a Cistercian monk at St Nicholas in Corno, then a hermit at Ocre in the Abruzzi, and ultimately the abbot-founder of the monastery of Santo Spirito, near Val d'Ocre. It is narrated of him that he took his sleep in a standing posture for thirty-seven years.
Cf. Zimm. — Chev. — Holw. — Baud.

PLACID, EUTYCHIUS, VICTORINUS, FLAVIA, DONATUS, FIRMATUS, FAUSTUS, and Comp. (SS) MM.
R.M. Oct. 5
? A heterogeneous group of martyrs, some of whom, notably Placid, have been venerated as Sicilian martyrs since the fourth century, their names being included in the martyrology compiled by St Jerome. In the 12th century this Sicilian Placid was identified with Placid the disciple of St Benedict at Subiaco (d. c.550) who was also thought to have died a martyr. This latter Placid is the Placid now liturgically honoured in the R.M. Of him we know only what St Gregory tells us in Book II of the Dialogues, viz. that he was the son of the Roman patrician Tertullus, that he, when a mere child was offered to God at Subiaco and placed under the care of St Benedict, and that he was saved from drowning by the miraculous intervention of St Benedict and St

Maurus. The death of St Placid, St Benedict's disciple, is usually said to have taken place c.550.
Cf. Zimm. — P. de U. — Att.

PLACID (St) M.   R.M. Oct. 11
See Anastasius, Placid, etc.

PLACIDIA (St) V.   R.M. Oct. 11
d. c.460. A virgin venerated at Verona. She has been often erroneously identified with Placidia the daughter of the emperor Valentinian III.
Cf. Holw. — Baud.

PLATO (St) Ab.   R.M. Apr. 4
d. 813. A Greek monk, and abbot, first of Symboleon on Mt Olympus in Bithynia, and then Sakkudion near Constantinople. He opposed the divorce and subsequent attempted marriage of the emperor Constantine Porphyrogenitus, who retaliated by persecuting and imprisoning him.
Cf. Holw. — Att. — Baud.

PLATO (St) M.   R.M. July 22
d. c.306. A rich youth martyred at Ancyra in Galatia. He was a brother of St Antiochus (q.v.). He is held in great veneration in the East.
Cf. Holw. — Baud.

PLATONIS and Comp. (SS) MM.
R.M. Apr. 6
d. c.308. A deaconess and foundress of a nunnery at Nisibis in Mesopotamia. The R.M. wrongly calls her a martyr and ascribes her to Ascalon. Nothing is known about her companions.
Cf. Holw. — Baud.

PLAUTILLA (St) W.   R.M. May 20
d. c.67. The alleged mother of St Flavia Domitilla. She is said to have been baptized by St Peter and to have been present at the martyrdom of St Paul.
Cf. Holw. — Baud.

PLAUTUS (St) M.   R.M. Sept. 29
See Eutychius, Plautus and Heracleas.

PLECHEIM (St) Bp.   A.C. July 15
d. c.730. A Northumbrian by birth, he accompanied SS Wiro and Otger as a missionary to the Low Countries and worked chiefly in Guelderland.
Cf. Att. — Baud. — Holw.

PLEGMUND (St) Bp. O.S.B.
P.C. Aug. 2
d. 914. The tutor of King Alfred. At that monarch's request, consecrated archbishop of Canterbury by Pope Formosus.
Stanton — Baud. — Holw.

PLUTARCH, SERENUS, HERACLIDES, HERON, a second SERENUS, RHAIS, POTAMIOENA and MARCELLA (SS) MM.   R.M. June 28
d. 202. Martyrs of Alexandria under Septimius Severus. They were pupils of Origen at the catechetical school of Alexandria. The virgin Potamioena was lowered slowly into a cauldron of boiling pitch. Her mother St Marcella suffered at the same time.
Cf. Att. — Baud. — Holw.

PODIUS (St) Bp. O.S.A.   R.M. May 28
d. 1002. A son of the margrave of Tuscany who became a canon regular and eventually ruled the see of Florence from 990 to 1002.
Cf. Holw. — Baud.

POEMON (POEMEN) (St) H.
R.M. Aug. 27
d. c.450. His name is often written in its Latin form "Pastor." One of the most famous of the fathers of the Egyptian desert. He dwelt at Skete, where he became abbot of the numerous groups of hermits, who lived in the abandoned ruins of a pagan temple at Terenuth.
Cf. Att. — Holw. — Baud.

POL de LÉON (St) Bp.   A.C. March 12
Otherwise Paul Aurelian, q.v.

POLIUS (St) M.   R.M. May 21
See Timothy, Polius and Eutychius.

POLLIO (St) M.   R.M. Apr. 28
d. c.304. A lector of the church of Cybalae in Pannonia, burnt alive under Diocletian.
Cf. Att. — Holw. — Baud.

POLYAENUS (St) M.   R.M. Apr. 28
See Patrick, Acatius, etc.

POLYAENUS (St) M.   R.M. Aug. 18
See Hermas, Serapion and Polyaenus.

POLYANUS (St) M. Bp.   R.M. Sept. 10
See Nemesian, Felix, etc.

POLYCARP of SMYRNA and Comp. (SS) MM. R.M. Jan. 26 and Feb. 23
d. 156 (or 166). Converted to the Faith by St John the Evangelist c.80, Polycarp became bishop of Smyrna c.96. He with his friend St Ignatius of Antioch were the link between the Apostles and subsequent generations of Christians in Asia Minor, and, through their disciple St Irenaeus of Lyons, in Gaul. We have an authentic record of St Polycarp's martyrdom in a letter written by eyewitnesses of the church of Smyrna. His profession of faith before the proconsul is a touching example of loyal devotion to Christ. He was sixty-six years old when he was burnt alive with twelve of his own flock, under Marcus Aurelius. Polycarp's letter to the Philippians, still extant, was during at least three centuries publicly read in the churches of Asia.
Cf. Holw. — Att. — Baud. — Ruinart.

POLYCARP (St) C. R.M. Feb. 23
d. c.300. A Roman priest of whom mention is made in the Acts of the martyrs for his zeal in ministering to those detained in prison for their faith.
Cf. Holw. — Baud.

POLYCARP and THEODORE (SS) MM.
R.M. Dec. 7
? Martyrs at Antioch in Syria.
Cf. Holw. — Baud.

POLYCHRONIUS (St) Bp. M.
R.M. Feb. 17
d. 250. Bishop at Babylon. He was imprisoned with his clergy and suffered martyrdom under Decius. He was struck on the mouth until he expired.
Cf. Holw. — Baud.

POLYCHRONIUS (St) M. R.M. Dec. 6
4th cent. A priest who, in the reign of the emperor Constantius, was slain by Arians while he was celebrating Mass. He was present at the council of Nicaea (325).
Cf. Holw.

POLYDORE PLASDEN (Bl) M.
A.C. Dec. 10
d. 1591. Born in London and educated for the priesthood at Reims and in Rome, he was ordained in 1588 and martyred at Tyburn for his priesthood. Beatified in 1929.
Cf. Newdigate.

POLYEUCTUS (St) M. R.M. Feb. 13
d. c.259. A Roman officer martyred at Melitene in Armenia under Valerian. His Acts, as given by Metaphrastes, are as touching as any in early Christian literature. Corneille has used some elements of the martyr's story in his tragedy Polyeucte.
Cf. Holw. — Ruinart — Baud.

POLYEUCTUS, VICTORIUS and DONATUS (SS) MM. R.M. May 21
? Martyrs of Caesarea in Cappadocia, of whom we know no more than the names (variously spelt) registered in the martyrologies.
Cf. Holw. — Baud.

POLYXENA (St) M. R.M. Sept. 23
See Xantippa and Polyxena.

POMPEIUS (St) M. R.M. Apr. 10
See Terentius, Africanus, etc.

POMPEIUS (St) M. R.M. July 7
See Peregrinus, Lucian, etc.

POMPEIUS (St) Bp. R.M. Dec. 14
d. c.290. Bishop of Pavia.
Cf. Holw. — Baud.

POMPILIUS MARIA PIROTTI (St) C.
Sch. P. A.C. July 15
1710-1756. Born at Montecalvo, diocese of Benevento, he joined the Piarist fathers (Scolopi) at Naples in 1727 and devoted his life to teaching in the schools of his Order. He died at Lecce in Apulia. Canonized in 1936.
Cf. Holw. — Att.

POMPONIUS (St) Bp. R.M. Apr. 30
d. 536. Bishop of Naples (508-536). He was a strong opponent of Arianism, then under the patronage of the Gothic king Theodoric.
Cf. Holw. — Baud.

POMPOSA (St) V. M. R.M. Sept. 19
d. 835. A nun of Peñamelaria near Cordova. She was beheaded by the Moors at Cordova.
Cf. P. de U. — Holw. — Baud.

PONS (St) M. R.M. May 14
Otherwise Pontius, q.v.

PONTIAN (St) M. R.M. Jan. 19
d. 169. An Italian martyr who suffered

at Spoleto under Marcus Aurelius. His Acts are only substantially accurate.
Cf. Holw. — Menzies — Baud.

PONTIAN (St) M.　　　**R.M. Aug. 25**
See Eusebius, Pontian, etc.

PONTIAN (St) Pope M.　　**R.M. Nov. 19**
d. c.236. He succeeded St Urban I in the chair of Peter about the year 230. He was exiled by the emperor Maximinus to Sardinia c.235, where he is said to have succumbed to ill-treatment.
Cf. Holw. — Att. — Menzies.

PONTIAN and Comp. (SS) MM.
R.M. Dec. 2
d. c.259. A group of five Roman martyrs who suffered under Valerian.
Cf. Holw. — Baud.

PONTIAN (St) M.　　　**R.M. Dec. 11**
See Trason, Pontian and Praetextatus.

PONTIAN (St) M.　　　**R.M. Dec. 31**
See Stephen, Pontian, etc.

PONTICUS (St) M.　　　**R.M. June 2**
See Photinus (Pothinus), Sanctius, etc.

PONTIUS (St) C.　　　**R.M. March 8**
d. c.260. A deacon of the church of Carthage. He was the attendant of St Cyprian in his exile and at his trial and execution. He has left us a graphic account of the life and passion of St Cyprian.
Cf. Holw. — Att. — Baud. — Ruinart.

PONTIUS of CIMIEZ (St) M.
R.M. May 14
d. 258 (?). A martyr of Cimella (Cimiez) near Nice. His relics, translated into Languedoc, have given its name to the town of Saint-Pons.
Cf. Holw. — Att. — Baud.

PONTIUS of FAUCIGNY (Bl) Ab. O.S.A.
A.C. Nov. 26
d. 1178. Born in Savoy, at the age of twenty he joined the canons regular at Abondance in the Chablais. He founded and was abbot of the monastery of St Sixtus, whence he was promoted to the abbacy of Abondance. He was held in high veneration by St Francis of Sales. Cult confirmed in 1806.
Cf. Holw. — Att. — Baud.

PONTIUS of BALMEY (Bl) Bp. O.Cart.
P.C. Dec. 13
d. 1140. Born at Balmey, he became a canon of Lyons. Later he founded on his paternal estate the charterhouse of Meyriat and joined the Carthusians. He was appointed bishop of Belley in 1121, but resigned before his death and returned to Meyriat.
Cf. Holw. — Baud.

POPPO (St) Ab. O.S.B.　　**R.M. Jan. 25**
978-1048. Born in Flanders, he first followed a military career and led an unbridled life. He then made a penitential pilgrimage to Jerusalem and Rome and on his return became a Benedictine at St Thierry, Reims (1006). Two years later he migrated to Saint-Vannes and helped Bl Richard in the revival of monastic discipline. Shortly after he was appointed provost of St Vaast, Arras, and soon became known to the emperor St Henry, who chose him as one of his most trusted advisers. In 1021 the emperor made Poppo abbot of Stavelot-Malmédy and soon the revival spread to several of the most ancient abbeys of Lotharingia and neighbouring territories: Hautmont, Marchiennes, St Maximinus of Trèves, St Vaast at Arras, etc. Poppo ruled all these houses as a sort of superior general. He is one of the greatest monastic figures of the 11th century.
Cf. Zimm. — Chev. — Baud. — Att. — Holw.

PORCARIUS and Comp. (SS) MM.
O.S.B.　　　　　　　**R.M. Aug. 12**
d. c.732. Porcarius was the second of this name to be abbot of Lérins, an island off the coast of Provence. By the 8th century this great abbey numbered over five hundred monks, as well as novices, alumni and familiars. The abbot was warned that the island was on the point of being attacked by the Saracens. He accordingly hastened to place the alumni and thirty-six of the younger monks in safety; the others he exhorted to be ready for martyrdom. In fact, the whole community, including Porcarius, were massacred, with the exception of four who were carried off as slaves.
Cf. Zimm. — Holw. — Att. — Mab.

PORPHYRIUS and SELEUCUS (SS)
MM.　　　　　　　　**R.M. Feb. 16**
d. 309. Palestinian martyrs put to death

at Caesarea. We owe the account of their martyrdom to the historian Eusebius.
Cf. Holw. — Baud.

PORPHYRIUS (St) Bp. R.M. Feb. 26
d. 420. A wealthy Greek who became a hermit first in the desert of Skete in Egypt and then in Palestine on the banks of the Jordan. Much against his will he was raised to the see of Gaza, which he ruled with extraordinary energy, ability and success. He almost completely uprooted the remnants of paganism in his diocese. His biography written by his deacon Mark is one of the most valuable historical sources of the fifth century.
Cf. Holw. — Att. — Baud.

PORPHYRIUS (St) M. R.M. May 4
d. 250. A priest who is said to have preached in Umbria, chiefly at Camerino, and to have been beheaded under Decius. He belongs to the apocryphal legend of St Venantius, q.v.
Cf. Holw. — Baud. — Menzies.

PORPHYRIUS (St) M. R.M. Aug. 20
? Connected with the apocryphal legend of St Agapitus of Palestrina, whose story was transferred to the equally unhistorical legend of St Venantius.
Cf. Holw. — Baud.

PORPHYRIUS (St) M. R.M. Sept. 6
See Onesiphorus and Porphyrius.

PORPHYRIUS (St) M. R.M. Sept. 15
d. 362. Said to have been a horse-dealer and an actor, who, while playing before Julian the Apostate and burlesquing the baptism of Christians, suddenly declared himself a believer and was at once slain.
Cf. Holw. — Baud.

PORPHYRIUS (St) M. R.M. Nov. 4
d. 171. A martyr at Ephesus under Aurelian.
Cf. Holw. — Baud.

PORTIANUS (St) Ab. R.M. Nov. 24
d. 533. A slave who became a monk and, in course of time, abbot of Miranda in Auvergne. He fearlessly faced the Merovingian king Thierry of Austrasia and obtained from him the release of his Auvergnate prisoners.
Cf. Holw. — Baud.

POSSESSOR (St) Bp. A.C. May 11
d. c.485. A city magistrate of Verdun, who became bishop of that city in 470. He and his flock were reduced to great distress by the invasions of the barbarians — Franks, Vandals, Goths, etc.
Cf. Holw. — Baud. — Duch. Fast. Episc.

POSSIDIUS (St) Bp. R.M. May 16
d. 450. A favourite disciple, and the biographer, of St Augustine of Hippo. He became bishop of Calama in Numidia, whence he was driven by the Arian Vandals, and ended his days in Apulia. He was one of the ablest controversialists of his time.
Cf. Holw. — Att. — Baud.

POTAMIA (St) M. R.M. Dec. 5
See Julius, Potamia, etc.

POTAMIOENA the YOUNGER (St) V. M. A.C. June 7
d. c.304. A young girl put to death at Alexandria under Diocletian.
Cf. Holw. — Baud.

POTAMIOENA the ELDER (St) V. M. R.M. June 28
See Plutarch, Serenus, etc.

POTAMIUS and NEMESIUS (SS) MM. R.M. Feb. 20
Martyrs in Cyprus.
Cf. Holw.

POTAMON (St) Bp. M. R.M. May 18
d. c.340. Bishop of Heraclea in Upper Egypt. During the persecution of Maximinus Daza (310) he was sentenced to the mines, lamed in one leg and deprived of one eye. Released after Constantine's decree of toleration, he was present at the council of Nicaea. He supported his metropolitan St Athanasius and was as a result fiercely persecuted by the Arians, who ultimately compassed his death.
Cf. Att. — Holw. — Baud.

POTENTIAN (St) M. R.M. Dec. 31
See Sabinian and Potentian.

POTENTIANA (St) M. R.M. May 19
Otherwise Pudentiana, q.v.

POTHMIUS and NEMESIUS (SS) MM. R.M. Feb. 20
Otherwise Potamius and Nemesius, q.v.

POTHINUS (St) Bp. M. **R.M. June 2**
Otherwise Photinus, q.v.

POTITUS (St) M. **R.M. Jan. 13**
? Honoured as a boy-martyr in the diocese of Naples. His extant Acts are legendary.
Cf. Att. — Holw. — Baud.

PRAEJECTUS (PRIEST, PREST, PREILS, PRIX) Bp. M. **R.M. Jan. 25**
d. 676. Bishop of Clermont in Auvergne. A great fosterer of monasticism and a great politician. He was slain by an enemy at Volvic in the Vosges.
Cf. Holw. — Baud.

PRAEPEDIGNA (St) M. **R.M. Feb. 18**
See Maximus, Claudius, etc.

PRAESIDIUS (St) M. **R.M. Sept. 6**
See Donatian, Praesidius, etc.

PRAETEXTATUS (PRIX) (St) Bp. M.
R.M. Feb. 24
d. 586 (Apr. 14). Bishop of Rouen (550-586). For his courage in denouncing the crimes of the wicked queen Fredegonda he was exiled and, after his recall, put to death by her order on Easter Sunday in his own church.
Cf. Holw. — Baud. — Att. — Chev.

PRAETEXTATUS (St) M. R.M. Dec. 11
See Trason, Pontian and Praetextatus.

PRAGMATIUS (St) Bp. **R.M. Nov. 22**
d. c.520. Bishop of Autun. His diocese suffered much during the war between the sons of Clovis.
Cf. Duch. Fast. Episc. — Holw. — Baud. — Gams.

PRAXEDES (St) V. **R.M. July 21**
2nd cent. Said to have been the daughter of the Roman senator Pudens and sister of St Pudentiana. One of the most ancient churches in Rome perpetuates her memory.
Cf. Holw. — Att. — Baud. — Menzies.

PRIAMUS (St) M. **R.M. May 28**
See Emilius, Felix, etc.

PRILIDIAN (St) M. **R.M. Jan. 24**
See Babilas, Urban, etc.

PRIMAEL (St) H. **A.C. May 16**
d. c.450. A native of Britain who crossed

over to Brittany and became a hermit in the diocese of Quimper, where churches are dedicated to him.
Cf. Holw. — Baud.

PRIMIAN (St) M. **R.M. Dec. 29**
See Dominic, Victor, etc.

PRIMITIVA (St) M. **R.M. Feb. 24**
? An early martyr, probably of Rome. Some old martyrologies have "Primitivus."
Cf. Holw.

PRIMITIVA (St) V. M. **R.M. July 23**
? An early martyr, probably of Rome. Very probably identical with the Primitiva of Feb. 24. Several ancient lists write her name "Primitia"; others, "Privata."
Cf. Holw. — Baud.

PRIMITIVUS (St) M. **R.M. June 10**
See Getulius, Caerealis, etc.

PRIMITIVUS (St) M. **R.M. July 18**
See Symphorosa and her sons.

PRIMITIVUS (St) M. **R.M. Nov. 27**
See Facundus and Primitivus.

PRIMITIVUS (St) M. **R.M. Dec. 29**
See Peter, Successus, etc.

PRIMUS (St) M. **R.M. Jan. 3**
See Cyrinus, Primus and Theogenes.

PRIMUS and DONATUS (SS) MM.
R.M. Feb. 9
d. 362. Two African deacons slain by the Donatist schismatics when the latter were trying to get possession of the Catholic church at Lavallum in N.W. Africa.
Cf. Holw. — Baud.

PRIMUS and FELICIAN (SS) MM.
R.M. June 9
d. c.297. Two aged brothers, Roman citizens, beheaded under Diocletian on the Via Nomentana. Their Acts are not altogether trustworthy.
Cf. Att. — Holw. — Baud.

PRIMUS, CYRIL and SECUNDARIUS (SS) MM. **R.M. Oct. 2**
? Martyrs at Antioch in Syria in one of the early persecutions.
Cf. Holw. — Baud.

PRINCIPIA (St) V. A.C. May 11
d. c.420. A Roman virgin, a disciple of
St Marcella.
Cf. Holw.

PRINCIPIUS (St) Bp. R.M. Sept. 25
d. c.505. The elder brother of St Remigius of Reims. He became bishop of
Soissons.
Cf. Duch. Fast. Episc. — Gams — Holw. — Baud.

PRIOR (St) H. A.C. June 17
c.295-c.395. An Egyptian hermit, one of
the first disciples of St Antony.
Cf. Baud. — P.B.

PRISCA (St) V. M. R.M. Jan. 18
d. c.270 (?). A virgin martyr venerated
from ancient times in Rome, where a
church is dedicated in her honour on the
Aventine, but of whom nothing authentic
is known.
Cf. Att. — Holw. — Baud.

PRISCIAN (St) M. R.M. Oct. 12
See Evagrius, Priscian, etc.

PRISCIAN (St) M. R.M. Oct. 14
See Carponius, Evaristus and Priscian.

PRISCILLA (St) W. R.M. Jan. 16
1st cent. The wife of Manius Acilius
Glabrio and mother of the senator Pudens.
The tradition is that she was the hostess in
Rome of St Peter the Apostle, whose headquarters were at her villa, near the Roman
catacombs which to this day bear her
name.
Cf. Holw. — Baud. — Att.

PRISCILLA (St) R.M. July 8
See Aquila and Priscilla.

PRISCILLIAN (St) M. R.M. Jan. 4
See next below.

PRISCUS, PRISCILLIAN and BENEDICTA (SS) MM. R.M. Jan. 4
d. 362. A priest, a cleric and a Christian
woman martyred in Rome under Julian
the Apostate.
Cf. Holw. — Baud.

**PRISCUS, MALCHUS and ALEXANDER
(SS) MM.** R.M. March 28
d. 260. Martyrs thrown to the wild
beasts during the public games at Caesarea
in Palestine under Valerian.
Cf. Holw. — Baud.

PRISCUS and Comp. (SS) MM.
R.M. May 26
d. c.272. Priscus, a Roman military officer, several soldiers under his command,
and a number of citizens of Besançon were
martyred near Auxerre at a place where
they had concealed themselves.
Cf. Holw. — Baud. — Att.

PRISCUS (St) M. R.M. Sept. 1
d. c.66. The alleged first bishop of Capua,
whither he is supposed to have been sent
by St Peter. He is said to have been a
disciple of our Lord and to have died a
martyr under Nero.
Cf. Holw. — Baud. — Menzies — Ricci.

**PRISCUS, CASTRENSIS, TAMMARUS,
ROSIUS, HERACLIUS, SECUNDINUS,
ADJUTOR, MARK, AUGUSTUS, ELPIDIUS, CANION and VINDONIUS
(SS) CC.** R.M. Sept. 1
5th cent. Priscus, an African bishop,
with his priests, were cast adrift in a
rudderless boat by the Arian Vandals.
They reached S. Italy, where eventually
Priscus became bishop of Capua and several of the others were in time promoted to
different sees.
Cf. Holw. — Baud.

PRISCUS (St) M. R.M. Sept. 20
? A native of Phrygia, martyred by being
first stabbed with poniards and then beheaded.
Cf. Holw. — Baud.

**PRISCUS, CRESCENS and EVAGRIUS
(SS) MM.** R.M. Oct. 1
? Martyrs at Tomi on the Black Sea.
Cf. Holw. — Baud.

PRIVATUS (St) Bp. M. R.M. Aug. 21
d. 266. A bishop of Gévaudan (now
Mende) in Gaul. He was seized by invading barbarians, but was offered his life
on condition of his revealing the hiding
place of his flock; on his refusal he was
beaten to death.
Cf. Duch. Fast. Episc. — Holw. — Baud.

PRIVATUS (St) M. R.M. Sept. 20
See Dionysius and Privatus.

PRIVATUS (St) M. R.M. Sept. 28
d. 223. A Roman citizen, scourged to
death under Alexander Severus.
Cf. Holw. — Baud.

PRIX (St) M.   **R.M. Jan. 25**
Otherwise Praejectus, q.v.

PROBUS (St) Bp.   **R.M. Jan. 12**
d. p. 591. A bishop of Verona, about
whom no particulars are extant.
Cf. Gams — Holw. — Baud.

PROBUS (St) Bp.   **R.M. March 15**
d. c.571. Bishop of Rieti in central Italy.
St Gregory the Great describes the deathbed scene of St Probus, when St Juvenal
and St Eleutherius appeared to him in a
vision.
Cf. Holw. — Baud. — Menzies.

PROBUS and GRACE (SS)   A.C. Apr. 5
? Cornish saints, by tradition husband
and wife. The church of Tressilian, or
Probus, is dedicated in their honour.
Cf. Holw.

PROBUS (St) M.   **R.M. Oct. 11**
See Tharacus (Taracus), Probus and
Andronicus.

PROBUS (St) Bp.   **R.M. Nov. 10**
d. c.175. A Roman who became sixth
bishop of Ravenna. His relics are still
venerated in the cathedral of Ravenna.
Cf. Holw. — Menzies — Baud.

PROBUS (St) M.   **R.M. Nov. 13**
See Arcadius, Paschasius, etc.

**PROCESSUS and MARTINIAN (SS)
MM.**   **R.M. July 2**
? Roman martyrs greatly venerated in
Rome: their tomb and basilica were on
the Aurelian Way. Their connection
with the apostles Peter and Paul in the
Mamertine jail is mere legend.
Cf. Att. — Holw. — Baud. — Ricci.

PROCHORUS (St) Bp. M.   R.M. Apr. 9
1st cent. One of the seven deacons ordained by the apostles. The tradition is
that he afterwards became bishop of Nicomedia and was martyred at Antioch.
Cf. Holw. — Baud.

PROCLUS and HILARION (SS) MM.
R.M. July 12
d. 115. Martyrs of Ancyra in Galatia in
the reign of Trajan.
Cf. Holw. — Baud.

PROCLUS (St) Bp.   **R.M. Oct. 24**
d. 447. A disciple of St John Chrysostom.

He became patriarch of Constantinople in
434. His treatment of heretics, chiefly
Nestorians, was characterized by great
gentleness. According to tradition he instituted the singing of the Trisagion in
the liturgy in miraculous circumstances.
Cf. Att. — Holw. — Baud.

PROCOPIUS (St) C.   **R.M. Feb. 27**
See Basil and Procopius.

PROCOPIUS (St) Ab. O.S.Bas.
A.C. July 4
c.980-1053 (March 25). Born in Bohemia, he studied at Prague, where he was
ordained and became a canon. Later he
became a hermit, and finally abbot-
founder of Sazaba abbey in Prague. Cult
confirmed in 1053.
Cf. Holw. — Chev. — Baud.

PROCOPIUS (St) M.   **R.M. July 8**
d. 303. The first victim of the Diocletian
persecution in Palestine. He was a
reader in the church of Scythopolis and
was beheaded at Caesarea Maritima.
The account of his martyrdom is given by
his contemporary Eusebius the historian.
It has been much distorted by later legend.
Cf. Att. — Holw. — Baud.

**PROCULUS, EPHEBUS and APOLLON-
IUS (SS) MM.**   **R.M. Feb. 14**
d. 273. Mentioned as martyrs at Terni
in the untrustworthy Acts of St Valentine
of Terni. The Bollandists identify this
Proculus with the bishop of Terni venerated on March 10.
Cf. Holw. — Baud.

PROCULUS (St) Bp. M.   R.M. Apr. 14
d. 310. Bishop of Terni, in Italy, who
suffered martyrdom under Maxentius
Cf. Gams — Holw. — Baud.

PROCULUS (St) M.   **R.M. June 1**
d. c.304 (?). Said to have been a Roman
officer, martyred at Bologna under Diocletian. He has been held in great veneration at Bologna from very ancient times.
Cf. Att. — Baud. — Holw.

PROCULUS (St) Bp. M.   A.C. July 12
d. 542. Bishop of Bologna (540-542).
He was martyred by the Goths.
Cf. Holw. — Att. — Baud.

PROCULUS (St) M.   **R.M. Aug. 18**
See Florus, Laurus, etc.

PROCULUS (St) M.   **R.M. Sept. 19**
See Januarius, Festus, etc.

PROCULUS (St) Bp. M.   **R.M. Nov. 4**
d. p. 717. Bishop of Autun, said to have been put to death by the invading Huns.
Cf. Gams — Holw.

PROCULUS (St) Bp. M.   **R.M. Dec. 1**
d. c.542. Bishop of Narni (others say of Terni), put to death by order of Totila, king of the Goths.
Cf. Gams — Holw. — Baud.

PROCULUS (St) Bp.   **R.M. Dec. 9**
d. c.320. Bishop of Verona. He was a confessor during the persecution of Diocletian, but ultimately died in peace in his episcopal city.
Cf. Gams — Holw. — Baud.

PROJECTUS (St) M.   **R.M. Jan. 24**
See Thyrsus and Projectus.

PROJECTUS (St) Bp. M.   **R.M. Jan. 25**
Otherwise Praejectus, q.v.

PROSDOCIMUS (St) Bp.   **R.M. Nov. 7**
d. c.100. First bishop of Padua, greatly venerated in N.E. Italy. That he was sent from Antioch by St Peter is now generally denied by historians.
Cf. Menzies — Att. — Holw. — Ricci.

PROSPER of REGGIO (St) Bp.
    R.M. June 25
d. c.466. A bishop of Reggio in Emilia, venerated as principal patron of the city and diocese of Reggio.
Cf. Att. — Holw. — Baud. — Chev.

PROSPER of AQUITAINE (St) C.
    R.M. June 25
c.390-c.463. A native of Aquitaine, a layman and, probably, a married man, Prosper devoted his fine intellect to the study of theological questions and became an enthusiastic admirer of St Augustine, whose doctrine on grace he defended against the Semi-Pelagians. He worked for a time in the Roman curia. He was a prolific writer and a powerful controversialist.
Cf. Holw. — Baud. — Chev.

PROSPER of ORLEANS (St) Bp.
    R.M. July 29
d. c.453. A bishop of Orleans, who has

often been confused with St Prosper of Aquitaine and St Prosper of Reggio.
Cf. Gams — Chev. — Holw.

PROTASIUS (PROTASE). St)
    R.M. June 19
See Gervasius and Protasius.

PROTASIUS (St) M.   **R.M. Aug. 4**
? A martyr honoured at Cologne. Probably identical with the fellow-sufferer of St Gervasius (June 19).
Cf. Holw. — Baud.

PROTASIUS (St) Bp.   **R.M. Nov. 24**
d. 352. Bishop of Milan 331-352. He espoused the cause of St Athanasius against the Arians, doing so with special effect at the synod of Sardica (343).
Cf. Holw. — Baud. — Chev. — Gams.

PROTERIUS (St) Bp. M.   **A.C. Feb. 28**
d. 458. Patriarch of Alexandria. He replaced Dioscorus, who had been deposed by the council of Chalcedon, and did his utmost to counter the plots of the Eutychians, who were leading his flock astray. They, however, succeeded in compassing his death on Good Friday.
Cf. Holw. — Att. — Baud.

PROTHADIUS (PROTAGIUS) (St) Bp.
    A.C. Feb. 10
d. 624. The successor of St Nicetius in the see of Besançon.
Cf. Chev. — Gams — Holw. — Baud. — Att.

PROTOGENES (St) Bp.   **R.M. May 6**
4th cent. A bishop of Carrhae in Syria, who, while still a priest, had been banished by the Arian emperor Valens. He was recalled under Theodosius and consecrated bishop.
Cf. Holw. — Baud.

PROTOLICUS (St) M.   **R.M. Feb. 14**
See Bassus, Antony and Protolicus.

PROTUS (St)   **R.M. May 31**
See Cantius, Cantian, etc.

PROTUS and HYACINTH (SS) MM.
    R.M. Sept. 11
d. c.257. According to tradition they were Romans by birth, brothers, and servants in the house of St Basilla; and they are said to have been martyred in Rome. The relics of St Hyacinth were

beyond any doubt discovered in the cemetery of St Basilla at Rome in 1845. The Acts, however, of these martyrs, as handed down to us, are largely legendary.
Cf. Att. — Holw. — Baud.

PROTUS and JANUARIUS (SS) MM.
R.M. Oct. 25
d. 303. Protus, a priest, and Januarius, a deacon, were sent by the pope to work in Sardinia, where they were beheaded at Porto Torres, not far from Sassari, in the persecution of Diocletian.
Cf. Chev. — Holw. — Baud.

PROVINUS (St) Bp. **A.C. March 8**
d. c.420. A native of Gaul who became a disciple of St Ambrose at Milan. Later he was coadjutor to St Felix, bishop of Como, whom he succeeded in the see (391).
Cf. Chev. — Holw. — Baud.

PRUDENTIA (Bl) V. O.S.A.
P.C. May 6
d. 1492. Prudentia Castori joined the hermits of St Augustine at Milan and later became the abbess-foundress of a new convent at Como, where she died.
Cf. Att. — Holw. — Baud.

PRUDENTIUS GALINDO (St) Bp.
A.C. Apr. 6
d. 861. A Spaniard who in his youth fled from the Saracens to the court of France, where he changed his baptismal name Galindo to Prudentius. He became bishop of Troyes and played a prominent part in the controversy on predestination against Gottschalk and Scotus Erigena. His feast is still kept at Troyes.
Cf. Chev. — Gams — Holw. — Att. — Baud. — P. de U.

PRUDENTIUS (St) Bp. **R.M. Apr. 28**
d. p. 700. A native of Armentia, in the province of Alava, Spain. After having been a hermit for some years he was ordained priest and became bishop of Tarazona (not Tarragona) in Aragon. He is the patron saint of the diocese of Tarazona.
Cf. Gams — Chev. — Att. — Holw. — P. de U.

PSALMODIUS (French: PSALMET) (St) H. **A.C. June 14**
d. c.690. Of Irish or Scottish descent, and a disciple of St Brendan. He crossed

into France and lived as a hermit near Limoges. He is identical with St Sauman (or Saumay).
Cf. Holw. — Baud.

PTOLEMY (St) M. **R.M. Dec. 20**
See Ammon, Zeno, etc.

PTOLEMY (St) Bp. M. **R.M. Aug. 24**
1st cent. Said to have been a disciple of St Peter and bishop of Nepi in Tuscany and there to have suffered martyrdom.
Cf. Holw. — Baud.

PTOLEMY and LUCIUS (SS) MM.
R.M. Oct. 19
d. c.165. Roman martyrs under Antoninus Pius. Ptolemy was put to death for instructing a woman in the Christian religion. One Lucius and an unnamed man protested against the injustice of the sentence and were also martyred. We owe the account of their passion to St Justin Martyr, their contemporary.
Cf. Holw. — Att. — Baud.

PUBLIA (St) W. **R.M. Oct. 9**
d. c.370. A Syrian matron, head of a community of women at Antioch, put to death by order of Julian the Apostate. While the emperor was passing through Antioch, he overheard the community singing the verse: "The idols of the Gentiles are silver and gold, let them that fashion them be made like unto them," and interpreted the words as an insult to himself.
Cf. Holw. — Baud. — Att.

PUBLICUS (St) **A.C. July 3**
Otherwise Biblig, q.v.

PUBLIUS (St) Bp. M. **R.M. Jan. 21**
d. c.112. Tradition identifies this saint with the Publius, "chief man of the island of Malta," who befriended St Paul after his shipwreck (Acts XXVIII, 7). He is said to have become bishop of Athens and to have died a martyr under Trajan. Other sources describe him simply as the first bishop of Malta.
Cf. Holw. — Baud.

PUBLIUS (St) Ab. **A.C. Jan. 25**
d. c.380. An abbot of Zeugma in Syria, who housed his large community in two separate buildings, one for the Greeks and the other for the Syrians.
Cf. Att. — Holw. — Baud.

PUBLIUS, JULIAN, MARCELLUS and Comp. (SS) MM. R.M. Feb. 19
? Martyrs in Proconsular Africa.
Cf. Holw. — Baud.

PUBLIUS (St) M. R.M. Apr. 16
See Saragossa Martyrs.

PUBLIUS, VICTOR, HERMAS and PAPIAS (SS) MM. R.M. Nov. 2
? Martyrs in N.W. Africa.
Cf. Baud. — Holw.

PUBLIUS (St) Bp. M. R.M. Nov. 12
See Aurelius and Publius.

PUDENS (St) M. R.M. May 19
2nd cent. A Roman senator baptized by the apostles, the father of St Pudentiana. He is by many identified with the Pudens mentioned by St Paul (2 Tim. IV, 21).
Cf. Holw. — Baud. — Att.

PUDENTIANA (or POTENTIANA) (St) V. R.M. May 19
d. c.160. A Roman maiden, daughter of the senator St Pudens. She is said to have died at the age of sixteen. We know very little that is really certain about her.
Cf. Holw. — Att. — Baud. — Menzies — Ricci.

PULCHERIA AUGUSTA (St) V. R.M. Sept. 10
d. 453. Daughter of the Eastern emperor Arcadius, she was regent during the minority of her brother Theodosius II, and again after his death. She was a devoted adherent of the see of Rome and a firm opponent of Monophysitism.
Cf. Att. — Holw. — Baud. — Ricci.

PUPULUS (St) M. R.M. Feb. 28
See Caerealis, Pupulus, etc.

PUSICIUS (St) M. R.M. Apr. 21
See Simeon and Comp.

PYRAN (St) A.C. March 5
Otherwise Piran, q.v.

Q

QUADRAGESIMUS (St) C. R.M. Oct. 26
d. c.590. A shepherd and subdeacon at Policastro, who, according to the testimony of St Gregory the Great, raised a dead man to life.
Cf. Chev. — Baud. — Holw.

QUADRATUS (CODRATUS), THEODOSIUS, EMMANUEL and Comp. (SS) MM. R.M. March 26
d. c.304. A group of forty-three martyrs, under the leadership of St Quadratus, bishop in Anatolia, put to death under Diocletian.
Cf. Holw. — Baud.

QUADRATUS (St) M. R.M. May 7
d. 257. A martyr said to have been kept in prison for years at Nicomedia, Nicaea and Apamea, previous to his martyrdom at Herbipolis under Valerian.
Cf. Holw. — Baud.

QUADRATUS (St) M. R.M. May 26
? A martyr in Proconsular Africa in whose honour St Augustine preached a panegyric.
Cf. Holw. — Baud.

QUADRATUS (St) Bp. R.M. May 26
d. c.130. Bishop of Athens and the first to write an Apology for the Christian religion, which he addressed to the emperor Hadrian.
Cf. Att. — Holw. — Chev. — Baud.

QUADRATUS (St) Bp. R.M. Aug. 21
? A bishop, of whom nothing is known. Perhaps he is a duplicate of St Quadratus of Athens.
Cf. Chev. — Baud. — Holw.

QUARTILLA (St) M. R.M. March 19
See Quintus, Quintilla, etc.

QUARTUS and QUINTUS (SS) MM. R.M. May 10
? Two citizens of Capua, condemned and executed in Rome, whose remains were taken back to Capua and there enshrined.
Cf. Holw. — Baud.

QUARTUS (St) M. R.M. Aug. 6
See Sixtus and Comp.

QUARTUS (St) ? Bp. R.M. Nov. 3
1st cent. The disciple of the apostles whom St Paul (Rom. XVI, 23) mentions as "greeting the Christians of Rome." Some traditions describe Quartus as one of the seventy-two disciples (Luke X), others add that he was a bishop.
Cf. Holw. — Baud.

QUARTUS (St) M. R.M. Dec. 18
See Victurus, Victor, etc.

QUENTIN (St) M. R.M. Oct. 31
Otherwise Quintinus, q.v.

QUERANUS (St) A.C. Sept. 9
Otherwise Pyran, Kieran, Kerrier, q.v.,
"Quirinus" may be taken as one of the
Latinized forms of the names of both St
Kieran of Ossory and St Kyran of Saghir.
Another would be Queranus, as above.

QUINCT —
Note. For names in Quinct — see
Quint —

QUINIDIUS (St) Bp. R.M. Feb. 15
d. c.579. From being a hermit at Aix in
Provence he was raised to the see of
Vaison, also in Provence.
Cf. Holw. — Baud.

QUINTA (St) M. R.M. Feb. 8
Otherwise Cointha, q.v.

QUINTIAN and IRENAEUS (SS) MM.
R.M. Apr. 1
? Armenian martyrs, of whom nothing is
known.
Cf. Holw. — Baud.

**QUINTIAN, LUCIUS and JULIAN (SS)
MM.** R.M. May 23
d. ? c.430. Three of a group of African
martyrs under the Arian Vandal King
Hunneric. The group seems to have
numbered nineteen and to have included
several women.
Cf. Holw. — Baud.

QUINTIAN (St) Bp. R.M. June 14
? Bishop of an unidentified see in France.
The R.M. mistakenly ascribes him to
Rodez.
Cf. Holw.

QUINTIAN (St) Bp. R.M. Nov. 13
d. c.527. An African by birth, he fled to
Gaul to escape the Arian-Vandal persecu-
tion. Eventually he became bishop of
Rodez, but was driven thence, this time
by the Arian Visigoths, and went to
Auvergne, where St Euphrasius made him
his successor in the see of Clermont.
*Cf. Duch. Fast. Episc. — Gams — Holw.
— Baud.*

QUINTIAN (St) M. R.M. Dec. 31
See Stephen, Pontian, etc.

QUINTILIAN (St) M. R.M. Apr. 13
See Maximus, Dadas and Quintilian.

QUINTILIAN (St) M. R.M. Apr. 16
See Saragossa, Martyrs of.

QUINTILIS (St) Bp. M. R.M. March 8
? A martyr of Nicomedia. Most ancient
records mention St Capitolinus as a fellow-
martyr.
Cf. Baud. — Holw.

QUINTILLA (St) M. R.M. March 19
See Quintus, Quintilla, etc.

QUINTINUS (QUENTIN) (St) M.
R.M. Oct. 31
d. 287. According to the traditional story,
often recast and much embellished, Quentin was a Roman by birth who went as a
missionary to Gaul. He evangelized the
district round Amiens and was martyred
at the town on the Somme now called
Saint-Quentin. He is beyond doubt a
historical person.
Cf. Holw. — Att.

**QUINTIUS, ARCONTIUS and DO-
NATUS (SS) MM.** R.M. Sept. 5
? Martyrs venerated at Capua and else-
where in S. Italy.
Cf. Holw. — Baud.

QUINTIUS (QUENTIN) (St) M.
A.C. Oct. 4
d. c.570. A citizen of Tours and an offi-
cial at the court of the Frankish king.
The reigning queen, having tried in vain
to seduce him, had him assassinated at
L'Indrois, near Montresor.
Cf. Holw. — Chev. — Baud.

QUINTUS (St) M. R.M. Jan. 4
See Aquilinus, Geminus, etc.

**QUINTUS, QUINTILLA, QUARTILLA,
MARK and Comp. (SS) MM.**
R.M. March 19
? Martyrs venerated at Sorrento, near
Naples. The three first-named were
probably a brother and two sisters.
Cf. Holw. — Baud.

QUINTUS (St) M. R.M. May 10
See Quartus and Quintus.

QUINTUS (St) M. R.M. Oct. 29
See Hyacinth, Quintus, etc.

**QUINTUS, SIMPLICIUS and Comp.
(SS) MM.** R.M. Dec. 18
d. c.255. Martyrs in Proconsular Africa
under the emperors Decius and Valerian.
Cf. Holw. — Baud.

QUIRIACUS (St) Bp. M. R.M. May 4
Otherwise Cyriacus, q.v.

QUIRIACUS (St) M. R.M. Aug. 12
See Hilaria, Digna, etc.

**QUIRIACUS, MAXIMUS, ARCHE-
LAUS and Comp. (SS) MM. R.M. Aug. 23**
d. c.235 (or 250 ?). Stated to have been
bishop, priest and deacon of Ostia respectively, and to have been martyred
with a number of Christian soldiers under
Alexander Severus. Some modern writers
place the martyrdom twenty or more
years later.
Cf. Holw. — Baud.

QUIRIACUS (St) H. R.M. Sept. 29
d. c.550. A Greek who lived as a hermit
in various lauras of Palestine. He is said
to have died when long past his hundredth
year.
Cf. Holw. — Baud.

**QUIRICUS (French: CYR) and JULITTA
(SS) MM.** R.M. June 16
d. 304. Julitta was a widow of noble
birth from Iconium, and was martyred at
Tarsus. Previous to her own martyrdom
her three-year-old son Quiricus had been
brained before her eyes because he had
scratched the face of the infuriated magistrate. Modern writers regard the story
as fictitious.
Cf. Att. — Holw. — Baud.

QUIRINUS (St) M. R.M. March 25
d. c.269. A Roman martyr who suffered
under Claudius II.
Cf. Holw. — Baud.

QUIRINUS (St) M. R.M. March 30
d. c.117. The jailer of Pope St Alexander I, by whom he was converted with his
daughter St Balbina. He was martyred
shortly after under Hadrian. The story
forms part of what modern writers describe as "the Romance called the Passion
of St Alexander," q.v. (May 3).
Cf. Holw. — Baud.

QUIRINUS (St) Bp. M. R.M. June 4
d. 308. Bishop of Siscia (Sisak, or Seseg)
in Croatia. He fled from his city to escape the persecution of Diocletian, was
captured and brought back and ordered
to sacrifice to the gods. He refused, was
barbarously beaten and handed over to
the governor of Pannonia Prima at Sabaria (now Szombathely in Hungary).
There, on his continued refusal to apostatize, he was drowned in the river Raab.
Cf. Att. — Holw. — Baud.

QUIRINUS (St) M. R.M. June 4
? A martyr at Tivoli, near Rome.
Cf. Holw. — Baud.

QUIRINUS (St) M. R.M. Oct. 11
See Nicasius, Quirinus, etc.

QUITERIA (St) V. M. R.M. May 22
? A Spanish saint greatly venerated on
the borders of France and Spain, especially in Spanish and French Navarre.
Her traditional story is wholly untrustworthy.
Cf. Att. — Baud. — Holw. — P. de U.

QUIVOX (EVOX) (St) A.C. March 13
Otherwise Kevoca, q.v.

QUODVULTDEUS (St) Bp.
R.M. Feb. 19
d. c.450. A bishop of Carthage exiled by
the Arian Genseric, king of the Vandals,
after the capture of the city in 439. He
ended his days at Naples.
Cf. Holw. — Baud. — Chev.

R

RABANUS MAURUS (Bl) Bp. O.S.B.
A.C. Feb. 4
c.776-856. Born at Mainz, he was offered
as a child to the abbey Fulda, and there
he spent practically his whole life. After
receiving his early education at the abbey,
he completed it at Tours, where he studied
for two years under Alcuin. Already a
monk of Fulda, he was appointed headmaster of the abbey school in 799, ordained deacon (801) and priest (814), and
elected abbot in 822. In 847 he resigned
this office, but in the same year was appointed archbishop of Mainz. He governed his diocese with remarkable ability
and was noted for his charity to the poor,

three hundred of whom were entertained daily at his house. Rabanus was the outstanding scholar of his century and one of the most prolific writers of any age. Under Alcuin, who nicknamed him Maurus in memory of St Benedict's favourite disciple, he learned Greek, Hebrew and Syriac, and his biblical commentaries, homilies, martyrology and poetical works (he composed the *Veni Creator Spiritus*) have by no means lost their value or interest. He is usually regarded as a typical Benedictine.
Cf. Chev. — Gams — Att. — Holw.

RACHILDIS (St) H. O.S.B. P.C. Nov. 23
d. c.946. A female recluse who lived walled up in a cell near that of St Wiborada, under the obedience of the abbot of St Gall in Switzerland.
Cf. Chev. — Holw. — Baud.

RACHO (RAGNOBERT) (St) Bp.
A.C. Jan. 25
d. c.660. The first Frankish bishop of Autun.
Cf. Duch. Fast. Episc. — Holw. — Baud.

RADBOD (St) Bp. O.S.B. A.C. Nov. 29
d. 918. The great-grandson of the last pagan king of Friesland, Radbod became bishop of Utrecht in 900. He at once put on the Benedictine habit, all his predecessors having been monks, and ruled the monastic cathedral and the diocese as an exemplary abbot-bishop. At the end of his life he retired to Deventer, where he died.
Cf. Gams — Chev. — Att. — Baud. — Holw.

RADEGUND (St) Queen. R.M. Aug. 13
518-587. Daughter of the pagan king of Thuringia, whose assassination was avenged by the Frankish king Clotaire I. The latter had the child, then twelve years old, baptized and educated, and eventually married her; but much ill-usage, crowned by the king's murder of her brother, compelled Radegund to leave him. She received the veil from St Medard and founded the great nunnery of the Holy Cross at Poitiers, where she spent the last thirty years of her life.
Cf. Att. — Holw. — Chev. — Baud.

RADEGUND (St) V. P.C. Aug. 13
d. c.1300. A serving maid at the castle of Wellenburg, near Augsburg, who occupied herself much in works of charity. While on an errand of mercy to a neighbouring hospital she was set upon and torn to pieces by wolves. She at once became the object of a popular cult.
Cf. Holw. — Baud. — Chev.

RADINGUS (St) Ab. A.C. Sept. 17
Otherwise Rodingus, q.v.

RADULPHUS (RADULF) (several)
Otherwise Ralph, q.v.

RAINGARDIS (Bl) W. O.S.B.
P.C. June 24
d. 1135. Mother of St Peter the Venerable, abbot of Cluny. In her widowhood she became a Benedictine nun at Marcigny. She was venerated as a saint by the Cluniac Benedictines.
Cf. Chev. — Baud. — Holw.

RAITHU (Martyrs of) (SS)
R.M. Jan. 14
d. c.510. A large number of hermits, living in the desert of Raithu, near the Red Sea, who were massacred by savages from Ethiopia or by Saracens.
Cf. Holw. — Baud.

RALPH (several)
Note. Ralph is the English form of Radulphus, which is more common in its French form of Raoul. There are many other variants: Radulf, Raul, Radolph, Randulph, Rodolfo, Rudolf, Rodolphe, Rollon, Ruph, etc.

RALPH ASHLEY (Bl) M. S.J.
A.C. Apr. 7
d. 1606. A Jesuit lay-brother martyred at Worcester for being found in attendance upon Bl Edward Oldcorne. Beatified in 1929.
Cf. Newdigate — Att.

RALPH (Bl) Bp. O.S.B.Cist.
A.C. Apr. 14
d. 1241. Cistercian monk and abbot (1209) of Thoronet Abbey. Later, bishop of Sisteron, France (1216-1241).
Cf. Gams — Zimm.

RALPH (St) Bp. O.S.B. A.C. June 21
d. 866. In his boyhood he was entrusted to the care of the abbot of Solignac and, according to Benedictine historians, became a monk there. He later held several abbacies, including that of St Medard, Soissons. In 840 he was made bishop of

Bourges, and as such he fostered learning, founded monasteries and in general promoted the public welfare.
Cf. Holw. — Att. — Gams.

RALPH MILNER (Bl) M. A.C. July 7
d. 1591. A husbandman, born at Stackstead, Hants, martyred at Winchester for relieving Bl Roger Dickenson. Beatified in 1929.
Cf. Newdigate.

RALPH de la FUTAYE (de FLAGEIO) (Bl) Ab. O.S.B. A.C. Aug. 16
d. 1129. A Benedictine of Saint-Jouin-de-Marne, who helped Bl Robert of Arbrissel to establish a new Benedictine congregation, and then became the abbot-founder (1192) of the double monastery of Saint-Sulpice, diocese of Rennes.
Cf. Zimm. — Baud. — Chev. — Butler-Thurston (Feb. 25).

RALPH CORBY (*vere* CORBINGTON) (Bl) M. S.J. A.C. Sept. 7
d. 1644. Born in Dublin, he was educated at St Omer and then studied for the priesthood at Seville and Valladolid. In 1631 he was admitted to the Society of Jesus and ordained priest. He was sent to the English mission and ministered in Co Durham. He was martyred at Tyburn for his priesthood. Beatified in 1929.
Cf. Newdigate — Att.

RALPH CROCKETT (Bl) M. A.C. Oct. 1
d. 1588. Born at Barton-on-the-Hill in Cheshire, he was educated at Christ's College, Cambridge, and at Gloucester Hall, Oxford. He became a schoolmaster in Norfolk and Suffolk. Later he studied for the priesthood at Reims, where he was ordained in 1586. He was arrested while engaged in priestly work in England and martyred at Chichester. Beatified in 1929.
Cf. Newdigate.

RALPH SHERWIN (Bl) M. A.C. Dec. 1
d. 1581. Born at Rodsley in Derbyshire, he gained a fellowship at Oxford, where he was known as a classical scholar of distinction. After his conversion he studied for the priesthood at Douai and Rome, and was ordained in 1580. Within a few months he was in England and in prison. Queen Elizabeth offered him preferment if he would turn Protestant: on his indig-

nant refusal he was martyred at Tyburn. He is the protomartyr of the Venerable English College, Rome. Beatified in 1886.
Cf. Camm — Newdigate — Att.

RALPH of VAUCELLES (Bl) Ab. O.S.B. A.C. Dec. 30
d. 1152. An Englishman he became St Bernard's disciple at Clairvaux, by whom he was later sent to be the abbot-founder of Vaucelles, diocese of Cambrai. He has a cult among the Cistercians.
Cf. Chev. — Baud. — Holw.

RAMBERT (RAGNEBERT, RAGNOBERT) (St) M. A.C. June 13
d. c.680. A courtier of high standing and much influence at the court of Thierry III of Austrasia. Ebroin, mayor of the palace, had him exiled and then ambushed and murdered in the Jura mountains. He has always been considered a martyr.
Cf. Att. — Holw. — Chev.

RAMBOLD (RAMNOLD) (St) Ab. O.S.B. A.C. June 17
d. 1001. Monk of St Maximinus at Trèves, called to Ratisbon by St Wolfgang to be abbot of St Emmeram. He died at the age of one hundred.
Cf. Holw.

RAMIRUS and Comp. (SS) MM. A.C. March 13
d. c.554 (or 630). Prior of the monastery of St Claudius at Leon, Spain. Two days after the martyrdom of his abbot, St Vincent, he, with all the monks of the community, was massacred by the Arian Visigoths while chanting the Nicene creed in the choir of the abbey church.
Cf. P. de U. — Holw. — Baud. — Zimm.

RAMÓN (*several*)
The Spanish form of Raymund, q.v.

RANULPHUS (RAGNULF) (St) M. R.M. May 27
d. c.700. A martyr of Thélus, near Arras. He was the father of St Hadulph, bishop of Arras-Cambrai.
Cf. Bolland. — Holw.

RAPHAEL the ARCHANGEL (St) R.M. Oct. 24
One of the three angels whom the Church venerates liturgically by name. His name means "the Healer of God," and his

ministrations in favour of men are described in the book of Tobias. He is commonly identified with the angel of the sheep-pool (John V, 1-4). His feast was added to the calendar of the universal church in 1922.
Cf. Holw. — Baud. — Att.

RASSO (or RATHO) (Bl) Mk. O.S.B.
                               A.C. May 17
d. 953. Count of Andechs in Bavaria, remarkable for his great stature. He was a brave warrior, leader of the Bavarians against the invading Hungarians. In middle age he made a pilgrimage to Palestine and Rome, and on his return founded the abbey of Wörth in Bavaria (now called after him Grafrath), in which he took the Benedictine habit.
Cf. Att. — Zimm. — Chev.

RASYPHUS (St) M.   R.M. July 23
? A martyr venerated in Rome from early times. He may be identical with a St Rasius whose relics are enshrined in the Pantheon.
Cf. Holw. — Baud.

RASYPHUS and RAVENNUS (SS) MM.
                               A.C. July 23
5th cent. Said to have been natives of Britain who took refuge in N. France from the Anglo-Saxon invaders. There they became hermits and were ultimately slain for the Faith at Macé, diocese of Séez. Their relics are enshrined in Bayeux cathedral.
Cf. Holw. — Baud.

RATHARD (Bl) C.   A.C. Aug. 8
d. 815. A member of the family of the counts of Andechs in Bavaria, he became a priest and founded the Augustinian monastery of Diessen.
Cf. Holw. — Baud.

RAVERRANUS (RAVERIANUS) (St) Bp.
O.S.B.   A.C. Nov. 7
d. 682. Bishop of Séez. He resigned his see and became a Benedictine monk at Fontenelle.
Cf. Duch. Fast. Episc. — Holw. — Baud. — Chev.

RAYMUND of PEÑAFORT (St) C. O.P.
                               R.M. Jan. 23
1175-1275. A kinsman of the kings of Aragon, he was born at Villafranca in Catalonia and studied and taught at

Barcelona, where he became a priest and a dignitary of the cathedral. In 1222 he joined the Dominican Order and began to preach to the Moors and the Albigenses. Called to Rome by Gregory IX, he was appointed penitentiary and confessor to the pope and was entrusted with the task of systematizing and codifying the canon law. This he did in his five books of the decretals, finished in 1234, which remained the most authoritative codification of ecclesiastical legislation till 1917. In 1238 he was chosen master-general of his Order and in that capacity encouraged St Thomas Aquinas to write the *Contra Gentiles*. In his later years Raymund resided in Majorca. The part he took, if any, in the foundation of the Mercedarians is still open to controversy. Canonized in 1601.
Cf. Att. — Holw. — Prop. O.P. — P. de U.

RAYMUND of FITERO (St) Ab. O.S.B.
Cist.   A.C. March 15
d. 1163. A native of Aragon who became a canon of the cathedral of Tarazona and then a Cistercian at the abbey of Scala Dei in France. From there he was sent to found and govern the abbey of Fitero in Spanish Navarre. In 1158, the city of Calatrava in New Castile being abandoned by the Templars and threatened by the Moors, he founded for its defence the military Order of Calatrava under the Benedictine Rule and the Cistercian Customary. Under him this Order won for itself a glorious name in Spanish history. Raymund's cult, as a saint, was approved in 1719.
Cf. P. de U. — Zimm. — Baud. — Holw. — Att. — Prop. Cist. — Chev.

RAYMUND of BARBASTRO (St) Bp.
O.S.A.   A.C. June 21
d. 1126. Born at Durban, near Coserans, in France, he became an Augustinian canon regular at Pamiers and in 1104 second bishop of the recently recaptured city of Barbastro in Aragon. He is the principal patron of the city and diocese of Barbastro.
Cf. P. de U. — Holw.

RAYMUND LULL (Bl) M.   A.C. July 3
c. 1232-1315. Born at Palma, Majorca, he married young and led a gay life as seneschal at the court of Aragon. At the age of about thirty he was converted by a series of apparitions, became a Franciscan

tertiary and devoted his whole life to the conversion of the Moors. He was unsuccessful in his attempts to interest the Holy See and the courts of Western Europe in this enterprise. He himself learned Arabic and three times went to preach the gospel to the Moors of Tunis. Twice he was banished, and on the third occasion he was stoned to death. In the interests of his life's work he travelled extensively in Italy, France, England and Germany, wrote copiously in Latin, Arabic and Catalan, and encouraged the study of oriental religion and culture. For a time he taught Arabic metaphysics at the university of Paris. He was a theologian (*Doctor Illuminatus*), a philosopher, a poet, an alchemist and a chemist. His feast is kept by the Friars Minor.
Cf. P. de U. — Baud. — Holw. — Att.

RAYMUND of TOULOUSE (St) C.
A.C. July 8

d. 1118. A chanter in the church of St Sernin at Toulouse who, after the death of his wife, received a canonry in the same church and was noted for his generosity to the poor and for his personal austerity.
Cf. Holw. — Att. — Chev.

RAYMUND NONNATUS (St) Card. O.Merc.
R.M. Aug. 31

d. 1240. A member of the Mercedarian Order, which was instituted in Spain for the ransoming of Christian captives. He succeeded St Peter Nolasco as its second master general. Not only did he spend his whole substance in purchasing the freedom of Christian slaves, but he is said to have surrendered himself as a hostage to secure the liberation of one of their number until his Order succeeded in ransoming him in his turn. He was created cardinal by Gregory IX. Canonized in 1657.
Cf. Chev. — P. de U. — Att. — Holw.

RAYMUND of CAPUA (Bl) C. O.P.
A.C. Oct. 5

d. 1399. Raymund delle Vigne was born at Capua, joined the Dominicans and held various offices in different friaries of the Order. He became the spiritual director of St Catherine of Siena when living in that city, and with her his name will be always linked. Later he became master general of the Dominicans and restored discipline with such success that he has been called the second founder of the

Order. He wrote lives of St Catherine and of St Agnes of Montepulciano. Beatified in 1899.
Cf. Att. — Prop. O.P. — Holw. — Chev.

RAYNALD of NOCERA (St) Bp. O.S.B.
A.C. Feb. 9

d. 1225. Born of German parents near Nocera in Umbria, he took the Benedictine habit at Fontavellana and in 1222 was raised to the see of Nocera, of which city he is now venerated as the principal patron. The cathedral of Nocera is dedicated in his name.
Cf. Gams — Prop. Camald. — Holw. — Chev.

RAYNALD of RAVENNA (Bl) Bp.
A.C. Aug. 18

d. 1321. Raynald Congoreggi was born at Milan, became a canon of Lodi and was then raised to the see of Vicenza (1296). After holding various offices in the papal states he became archbishop of Ravenna (1303). He was a friend and defender of the Knights Templars. Cult approved in 1852.
Cf. Baud. — Holw.

RAYNALD de BAR (Bl) Ab. O.S.B.Cist.
P.C. Dec. 16

d. 1151. A monk of Clairvaux who was appointed abbot of Cîteaux in 1133. He is remembered chiefly as the compiler of the first collection of Cistercian statutes. He was also instrumental in bringing about the union of the Benedictine congregations of Obazine and Savigny with Cîteaux.
Cf. Chev. — Holw.

RAYNERIUS (RAYNIER) (St) Mk. O.S.B.
A.C. Feb. 22

d. c.967. Benedictine monk at Beaulieu in the neighbourhood of Limoges.
Cf. Zimm.

RAYNERIUS INCLUSUS (Bl) H.
A.C. Apr. 11

d. 1237. A hermit who lived in a cell near the cathedral of Osnabrück. He spent twenty-two years in his cell (inclusus means "shut up") wearing a coat of mail and heavy chains next his skin.
Cf. Holw. — Att. — Chev.

RAYNERIUS (RANIERO, RAINERIUS) (St) H.
R.M. June 17

d. 1160. Raniero Scacceri was a native of

Pisa. After a sinful youth he undertook several penetential pilgrimages to Jerusalem and afterwards lived as a conventual oblate in the Benedictine abbey of St Andrew at Pisa and then in that of San Vito in the same city, where he died.
Cf. Att. — Holw. — Menzies — Ricci.

RAYNERIUS of SPALATRO (St) M. Bp. O.S.B.   A.C. Aug. 4
d. 1180. A Benedictine of Fontavellana, raised to the see of Cagli in 1156 and to the archbishopric of Spalatro in 1175. He was murdered by members of his flock for his defence of ecclesiastical immunity.
Cf. Gams — Holw. — Chev.

RAYNERIUS of AREZZO (Bl) C. O.F.M.   A.C. Nov. 3
d. 1304. Raniero Mariani was a native of Arezzo. He became a Franciscan lay-brother and died at Borgo Sansepolcro. Cult confirmed in 1802.
Cf. Holw. — Att.

RAYNERIUS of TODI (Bl) C. O.F.M. Cap.   A.C. Nov. 5
d. c.1586. Born at Sansepolcro, he married to please his parents, but on the death of his wife became a Capuchin friar. He died at Todi. Cult confirmed by Pius VII.
Cf. Holw. — Baud. — Ricci.

RAYNERIUS (St) Bp.   R.M. Dec. 30
d. 1077. Bishop of Aquila (Forconium) in the Abruzzi.
Cf. Chev. — Gams.

REATRUS (RESTIUS) (St) M.   R.M. Jan. 27
See Datius, Reatrus, etc.

REDEMPTA (St) V.   R.M. July 23
See Romula, Redempta and Herundo.

REDEMPTUS (St) Bp.   R.M. Apr. 8
d. 586. Bishop of Ferentini (*in Hernicis*), a town to the south of Rome. He was a friend of St Gregory the Great, who bears witness to his sanctity.
Cf. Holw. — Baud. — Gams.

REDEMPTUS of the CROSS (Bl) M. O.C.D.   A.C. Nov. 26
d. 1638. A native of Pardes in Portugal who was a soldier in the East Indies when he applied for admission to the discalced Carmelites. He was professed as a lay-brother and accompanied Bl Dionysius of the Nativity to Sumatra, where he was martyred. Beatified in 1900.
Cf. Holw. — Baud.

REGINA (REGNIA, REINE) (St) V. M.   R.M. Sept. 7
d. c. ? 286. A virgin martyr venerated at Autun from an early date. We have no particulars of her life.
Cf. Att. — Baud. — Holw.

REGIMBALD (REGINBALD, REGIM-BAUT, REGINOBALDUS) Bp. O.S.B.   A.C. Oct. 13
d. 1039. A Benedictine monk of the abbey of SS Ulric and Afra at Augsburg. In 1015 he migrated to the abbey of Ebersberg. In 1022 he became abbot of Lorsch and later founded therefrom the daughter-abbey of Heiligenberg. In 1032 he was appointed bishop of Speyer.
Cf. Zimm. — Chev. — Baud. — Holw.

REGINALD of SAINT-GILLES (Bl) C. O.P.   A.C. Feb. 1
1183-1220. Born at Saint-Gilles in Languedoc. After having taught canon law at the university of Paris from 1206 to 1211 he was appointed dean of Saint-Agnan, Orleans. He met St Dominic in Rome and became one of his ablest disciples. He helped to establish the Dominicans at Bologna and Paris. Cult confirmed in 1885.
Cf. Holw. — Baud. — Att.

REGINALD MONTEMARTI (Bl) C. O.P.   A.C. Apr. 9
1292-1348. He was born near Orvieto and became a Dominican. He died at Piperno. Cult approved in 1877.
Cf. Holw. — Baud. — Chev.

REGINALD (Bl) H. O.S.B. A.C. July 2
d. c.1095. A Benedictine monk of Baume who lived as a hermit in the cell occupied by St Adegrin more than two centuries before.
Cf. Zimm.

REGINTRUDIS (Bl) Abs. O.S.B.   A.C. May 26
d. c.750. Fourth abbess of Nonnberg near Salzburg.
Cf. Zimm.

REGULA (St) V. M.   A.C. Sept. 11
See Felix and Regula.

REGULUS (French: RIEUL) (St) Bp.
R.M. March 30
d. c.260. Said to have been a Greek by origin. He is honoured as the first bishop of Senlis. An old tradition connects him with Arles.
Cf. Duch. Fast. Episc. — Gams — Baud.

REGULUS (RULE) (St) Ab.
A.C. March 30
? 4th cent. The legendary abbot who brought the relics of St Andrew from Greece to Scotland.
Cf. Holw.

REGULUS (St) M. **R.M. Sept. 1**
d. c.545. An African driven into exile by the Arian Vandals. He landed in Tuscany and appears to have been martyred under Totila.
Cf. Holw. — Baud.

REGULUS (French: REOL) (St) Bp. O.S.B. **A.C. Sept. 3**
d. 698. A monk of Rebais under St Philibert. He succeeded St Nivard (c. 673) as archbishop of Reims. He was the founder of the great abbey of Orbais (680).
Cf. Holw. — Baud. — Chev. — Duch. Fast. Episc.

REINE (St) V. M. **R.M. Sept. 7**
Otherwise Regina, q.v.

REINELDIS (RAINELDIS, REINALDES) V. and Comp. (SS) MM.
R.M. July 16
d. c.680. Daughter of St Amalberga and sister of St Gudula. She was a nun of Saintes in Hainault and was put to death, together with two clerics, by the Huns who were then ravaging the country.
Cf. Baud. — Chev.

REINHARD (Bl) Ab. O.S.B.
A.C. March 7
d. p. 1170. Monk and headmaster of the abbey school of Stavelot-Malmédy. About 1130 he was appointed first abbot of Reinhausen in Saxony.
Cf. Zimm. — Holw.

REINOLD (St) M. O.S.B. **A.C. Jan. 7**
d. 960. Said to have belonged to the family of Charlemagne. He was a Benedictine monk of the abbey of St Pantaleon at Cologne. He was in charge of the building operations there and was

killed by the stonemasons with their hammers and his body flung into a pool near the Rhine. It is said to have been found later by divine revelation.
Cf. Zimm. — Att. — Holw. — P. de U.

RELINDIS (RENILDIS, RENULA, RENULE) (St) Abs. O.S.B. **A.C. Feb. 6**
d. c.750. Educated with her sister Herlindis in the Benedictine nunnery of Valenciennes. She became an expert in embroidery and painting. St Boniface appointed her abbess of the convent of Eyck on the Meuse, founded by her parents.
Cf. Chev. — Holw.

REMACLUS (St) Bp. O.S.B. A.C. Sept. 3
d. c.663. A native of Aquitaine and a courtier. He became a monk and after his ordination to the priesthood was appointed first abbot of Solignac near Limoges, and then of Cougnon in Luxemburg. About the year 648 he founded the twin abbeys of Stavelot and Malmédy in the Ardennes, and in 652 he became bishop of Maestricht. After twelve years as a bishop he resigned and returned to Stavelot, where he died.
Cf. Zimm. — Chev. — Att. — Baud. — Holw.

REMBERT (St) Bp. O.S.B. R.M. Feb. 4
d. 888. Born in Flanders and a monk of Turholt. He shared with St Anschar the apostolate to Scandinavia and succeeded him in the see of Hamburg-Bremen (865). He died on June 11, but the R.M. commemorates him also on the day of his episcopal consecration. He wrote an excellent biography of St Anschar.
Cf. Att. — Zimm. — Chev. — Holw. — Baud.

REMEDIUS (St) Bp. **R.M. Feb. 3**
? A bishop of Gap in the French Alps.
Cf. Duch. Fast. Episc. — Holw. — Baud.

REMI (REMY) *several*
The French form of Remigius, q.v.

REMIGIUS (St) Bp. **A.C. Jan. 19**
d. c.772. A natural son of Charles Martel. He was bishop of Rouen from 755 till his death. He worked successfully for the introduction of the Roman rite and chant into Gaul.
Cf. Holw. — Baud. — Duch. Fast. Episc.

REMIGIUS (Bl or St) Bp. O.S.B.
A.C. March 20
d. 783. A son of Duke Hugh of Alsace and a nephew of St Ottilien. He was educated at, and became abbot of, Münster near Colmar, and in 776 was raised to the see of Strasburg. Pope Leo IX authorized his feast for the abbey of Münster.
Cf. Holw. — Baud. — Duch. Fast. Episc. — Chev.

REMIGIUS (St) Bp. **R.M. Oct. 1**
d. c.533 (Jan. 13). A Gallo-Roman by birth, he was elected in 459, while still a layman, to the see of Reims. During the seventy-four years of his episcopate he was the most influential prelate of Gaul, the culminating event in his life being the conversion and baptism of Clovis, king of the Franks, on Easter eve 496. The sources for his biography are not very trustworthy.
Cf. Chev. — Att. — Holw. — Baud. — Duch. Fast. Episc.

REMIGIUS (St) Bp. **P.C. Oct. 28**
d. 875. Royal arch-chaplain and in 852 archbishop of Lyons. He combated Gottschalk's doctrine on predestination but defended the latter's person against his metropolitan Hincmar of Reims.
Cf. Duch. Fast. Episc. — Chev. — Baud.— Holw.

REMO (St) Bp. **R.M. Oct. 13**
Remo is a corrupt form of Romulus, q.v.

RENATUS (French: RENÉ) GOUPIL (St) M. **A.C. March 16**
d. 1642. One of the martyrs of N. America, q.v. He was a layman and a surgeon and acted as assistant to the missionaries to the Red Indians. He was the first to be martyred (Sept. 29), being tomahawked for making the sign of the cross on the brow of some children.
Cf. Att.

RENATUS (French: RENÉ) (St) Bp.
A.C. Nov. 12
d. c.422. Said to have been bishop first at Angers and then at Sorrento in S. Italy. Probably this is a mistaken identification of two different persons.
Cf. Duch. Fast. Episc. — Holw. — Baud.

REOL (REOLUS) (St) Bp. **A.C. Sept. 3**
Otherwise Regulus, q.v.

REPARATA (St) V. M. **R.M. Oct. 8**
d. c.250. A virgin martyr of Caesarea in Palestine, martyred at the age of twelve under Decius. Her Acts are spurious.
Cf. Att. — Holw. — Baud.

REPOSITUS (St) M.
R.M. Aug. 29 and Sept. 1
See Vitalis, Sator and Repositus.

RESPICIUS (St) M. **R.M. Nov. 10**
See Tryphon, Respicius and Nympha.

RESTITUTA (St) V. M. **R.M. May 17**
d. 255 (or 304). An African maiden martyred at Carthage either under Valerian or Diocletian. Her relics are said to be enshrined in the cathedral of Naples.
Cf. Holw. — Baud. — Att.

RESTITUTA and Comp. (SS) MM.
R.M. May 27
d. 272. Said to have been a Roman maiden of patrician parentage who fled to Sora in Campania to escape the persecution under Aurelian and who was martyred there with several companions.
Cf. Att. — Baud. — Holw.

RESTITUTUS (St) M. **R.M. May 29**
d. c.299. A Roman martyr under Diocletian. His Acts are not trustworthy.
Cf. Holw. — Baud.

RESTITUTUS (St) M. **R.M. June 10**
See Crispulus and Restitutus.

RESTITUTUS, DONATUS, VALERIAN, FRUCTUOSA and Comp. (SS) MM.
R.M. Aug. 23
d. c. ? 305. A group of sixteen Syrian martyrs put to death at Antioch.
Cf. Holw. — Baud.

RESTITUTUS (St) Bp. M. **R.M. Dec. 9**
? Bishop of Carthage, in whose honour St Augustine preached a sermon which is now lost.
Cf. Holw. — Baud.

REVERIANUS, PAUL and Comp. (SS) MM. **R.M. June 1**
d. 272. Reverianus, a bishop, and Paul, a priest, Italians by birth, appear to have been sent as missionaries to Gaul by the Holy See. They evangelized Autun and the surrounding district and were martyred with several companions under Aurelian.
Cf. Holw. — Baud.

REVOCATA (St) M. R.M. Feb. 6
See Saturninus, Theophilus and Revocata.

REVOCATUS (St) M. R.M. Jan. 9
See Vitalis, Revocatus and Fortunatus.

REVOCATUS (St) M. R.M. March 7
See Perpetua, Felicitas, etc.

REYNE (St) V. M. R.M. Sept. 7
Otherwise Regina, q.v.

RHAIS (St) M. R.M. June 28
See Plutarch, Serenus, etc.

RHAIS (St) V. M. R.M. Sept. 22
Otherwise Irais, q.v.

RHEDIUS (RHEDIW) (St) A.C. Nov. 11
? A Welsh saint whose name is perpetuated by the dedication of a church in his honour at Llanllyfni in Carnarvonshire.
Cf. Baring-Gould.

RHETICUS (RHETICIUS, RHETICE) (St) Bp. A.C. July 20
d. 334. A Gallo-Roman raised to the see of Autun c.310. In 313 he was present at the Lateran synod which condemned the Donatists.
Cf. Duch. Fast. Episc. — Holw. — Baud.

RHIAN (RANUS, RIAN) (St) Ab.
A.C. March 8
? The saint who has left his name to Llanrhian in Pembrokeshire. He is described as an abbot, but we have no authentic details of his life.
Cf. Holw. — Baring-Gould.

RHIPSIME (RIPSIMIS), GAIANA and Comp. (SS) VV. MM. R.M. Sept. 29
d. c.290. A band of virgin martyrs venerated from early times as the first to suffer for Christ in the Armenian Church. Their existence is certainly established, but their Acts are in no way trustworthy.
Cf. Holw. — Att. — Baud.

RHODOPIANUS (St) M. R.M. May 3
See Diodorus and Rhodopianus.

RHUDDLAD (St) V. A.C. Sept. 4
? 7th cent. Patron of Llanrhyddlad, at the foot of Moel Rhyddlad in Anglesey.
Cf. Holw. — Baring-Gould.

RIBERT (St) Ab. O.S.B. A.C. Sept. 15
7th cent. Monk and abbot of Saint-Valéry-sur-Somme. He may have been also a regionary bishop in Normandy and Picardy. He is the patron of numerous parishes in the diocese of Rouen.
Cf. Baud. — Holw. — Chev.

RIBERT (RIBARIUS) (St) Ab. O.S.B.
A.C. Dec. 19
d. c.790. Seventeenth abbot of Saint-Oyend. He is much venerated in Franche-Comté.
Cf. Baud. — Chev. — Holw.

RICHARD the SACRIST (Bl) Mk. O.S.B. Cist. A.C. Jan. 28
d. p. 1142. An Englishman who became a Cistercian monk and sacristan of the abbey of Dundrennan in Kirkcudbrightshire.
Cf. Att. — Chev. — Holw.

RICHARD of VAUCELLES (St) Ab. O.S.B.Cist. A.C. Jan. 28
d. 1169. An Englishman who became a Cistercian in the abbey of Vaucelles near Cambrai, and who was eventually chosen its second abbot.
Cf. Zimm. — Baud. — Chev. — Holw.

RICHARD the KING (St) C.
R.M. Feb. 7
d. 722. According to the earlier Italian legend this saint was a prince in Wessex and father of SS Willibald, Winebald and Walburga: he died at Lucca on a pilgrimage to Rome. A later legend makes him duke of Swabia. Both legends have been proved to be quite untrustworthy.
Cf. Att. — Holw. — Chev. — Stanton.

RICHARD of CHICHESTER (St) Bp.
R.M. Apr. 3
1197-1253. Richard de Wych was born at Droitwich in Worcestershire and pursued his studies at Oxford, Paris and Bologna. Returning to England (1235), he was chosen chancellor of Oxford university. He then became the legal adviser of the archbishops of Canterbury, St Edmund Rich and St Boniface of Savoy. Having been ordained priest in France, he was raised to the see of Chichester, and in the early years of his episcopate he had to defend himself against the rapacity of Henry III. He died at Dover while engaged in preaching the crusade. Canonized in 1262.
Cf. Holw. — Stanton — Att. — Chev.

RICHARD REYNOLDS (Bl) M. Bridg.
A.C. May 4
c.1490-1535. Born at Devon, he studied at Christ's College, Cambridge, was elected a fellow of Corpus Christi College in 1510, took the degree of B.D. in 1513 and was appointed university preacher. In the same year he was professed a Bridgettine monk at Syon Abbey, Isleworth. He was one of the first band of martyrs executed at Tyburn for their opposition to the royal supremacy. Beatified in 1886.
Cf. Newdigate — Att.

RICHARD THIRKELD (THIRKILD) (Bl) M.   A.C. May 29
d. 1583. Born in Co. Durham, he was educated at Queen's College, Oxford, and when already advanced in years completed his studies for the priesthood at Douai and Reims, being ordained in 1579. He ministered to the Catholics of Yorkshire and was condemned and executed for his priesthood at York. Beatified in 1886.
Cf. Newdigate — Att.

RICHARD NEWPORT (*alias:* SMITH) (Bl) M.   A.C. May 30
d. 1612. Born at Harringworth in Northamptonshire, he was educated for the priesthood at Rome and ordained in 1597. On his return to England he worked in the London district and was executed at Tyburn for his priesthood.
Cf. Newdigate — Att.

RICHARD of ANDRIA (St) Bp.
R.M. June 9
d. p. 1196. An Englishman who became bishop of Andria in Italy. By a confusion of dates at a much later period he has been ascribed, quite erroneously, to the fifth century (453).
Cf. Holw. — Baud. — Att.

RICHARD of ST VANNES (Bl) Ab.
O.S.B.   A.C. June 14
d. 1046. Nicknamed "Gratia Dei," from a phrase frequently on his lips. From being dean of the cathedral of Reims, he became a Benedictine at St Vannes, Verdun. He was a personal friend of St Odilo of Cluny and of the emperor St Henry, who is said to have asked Richard to confer the monastic habit on him.
Cf. Chev. — Holw.

RICHARD LANGHORNE (Bl) M.
A.C. July 14
d. 1679. Born in Bedfordshire, he read law at the Inner Temple and was called to the bar in 1654. He was executed at Tyburn for alleged complicity in the "Popish Plot." Beatified in 1929.
Cf. Newdigate.

RICHARD FEATHERSTONE (Bl) M.
A.C. July 30
d. 1540. Educated at Cambridge, he became tutor to the princess Mary and archdeacon of Brecknock. As one of the chaplains to Queen Catherine of Aragon he defended her in convocation and was forthwith attainted for treason and executed at Tyburn. Beatified in 1886.
Cf. Newdigate — Att. — Holw. — Stanton.

RICHARD KIRKMAN (Bl) M.
A.C. Aug. 22
d. 1582. Born at Addingham, near Skipton in Yorkshire, he was educated at Douai and ordained in 1579. He was appointed tutor in the family of Dymoke of Scrivelsby. He was martyred at York for denying the queen's supremacy in spiritual matters. Beatified in 1886.
Cf. Newdigate — Att.

RICHARD HERST (Bl) M. A.C. Aug. 29
d. 1628. Richard Herst (also Hurst or Hayhurst) was born near Preston in Lancashire and worked there as a farmer. He was condemned ostensibly for murder but in fact because he was a Catholic recusant. He was hanged at Lancaster. Beatified in 1929.
Cf. Newdigate — Att.

RICHARD LEIGH and RICHARD MARTIN (BB) MM.   A.C. Aug. 30
d. 1588. Richard Leigh (*alias* Garth or Earth) was born in London, educated at Reims and Rome and ordained in 1586. Richard Martin was a Shropshire gentleman who was educated at Broadgates Hall, Oxford. They were martyred together at Tyburn with four others, Leigh for being a priest and Martin for sheltering priests. Beatified in 1929.
Cf. Newdigate.

RICHARD BERE (Bl) M.
A.C. Aug. 31 (?)
d. 1537. Born at Glastonbury, he was educated at Oxford and the Inns of Court. He became a Carthusian at the London

Charterhouse and was starved to death in Newgate, with others of his community, for opposing the royal "divorce."
Cf. Att. — Holw. — Camm.

RICHARD of ST ANN (Bl) M. O.F.M.
A.C. Sept. 10
1585-1622. Born of Spanish parents in Flanders, he was a tailor at Brussels when he joined the Friars Minor as a lay-brother. He was sent as a missionary to Mexico and thence (1611) to the Philippines, where he was raised to the priest-hood at Zebu. In 1613 he went to Japan, where he was martyred at Nagasaki on the day of the great martyrdom. Beatified in 1867.
Cf. Holw.

RICHARD ROLLE (Bl) C. P.C. Sept. 29
c.1300-1349. Born at Thornton in Yorkshire, he lived as a hermit at Hampole and elsewhere in that county. He is best known as one of the foremost mystical writers of his time. At one time he had a very considerable popular cult.
Cf. Att.

RICHARD GWYN (*alias* WHITE) (Bl) M.
A.C. Oct. 17
1537-1584. Born at Llanidloes, in Montgomeryshire, he was educated at St John's College, Cambridge. He renounced Protestantism, married and became a schoolmaster in Flintshire and Denbighshire. He was imprisoned for four years before he was martyred for his Catholic faith at Wrexham. In jail he wrote numerous religious poems in Welsh. He is the proto-martyr of Wales.
Cf. Newdigate — Att.

RICHARD WHITING (Bl) M. Ab.O.S.B.
A.C. Nov. 15
d. 1539. Born at Wrington in Somerset, he became a Benedictine monk at Glastonbury and was sent to Cambridge for his higher education. In 1525 he became abbot of Glastonbury. At the dissolution he refused to surrender his abbey to the Crown and was condemned to death for treason. He was hanged with the usual brutalities on the summit of Tor Hill overlooking Glastonbury. Beatified in 1895.
Cf. Newdigate — Camm — Zimm. — Att.

RICHARD LANGLEY (Bl) M.
A.C. Dec. 1
d. 1586. A Yorkshire gentleman of Ouse-

thorpe near Pocklington, hanged at York for sheltering priests in his house. Beatified in 1929.
Cf. Newdigate — Att.

RICHARDIS (St) Empress A.C. Sept. 18
d. c.895. She was married at twenty-two to the emperor Charles the Fat, and after nineteen years of married life was accused of unfaithfulness. Her innocence was established, but she ceased to cohabit with her husband and retired to the nunnery of Andlau, which she herself had founded, and lived there as a nun till her death. She is venerated as a Benedictine oblate. Her relics were elevated by order of Pope Leo IX.
Cf. Att. — Holw. — Baud. — Chev.

RICHARIUS (RIQUIER) Ab.
R.M. Apr. 26
d. c.645. Born at Centula (Celles) near Amiens, he became a priest and founded an abbey in his native place, afterwards called after him Saint-Riquier. He was the first to devote himself to the work of ransoming captives. After some years as abbot he resigned and spent the rest of his life as a hermit. On the spot where he died arose later the abbey of Foret-Moutier. The town of Abbeville derives its name from the abbey at Celles.
Cf. Holw. — Att. — Baud. — Chev.

RICHALM (Bl) Ab. O.S.B.Cist.
A.C. Dec. 2
d. 1219. Cistercian abbot of Schönthal (*Speciosa Vallis*) in Würtemberg.
Cf. Zimm. — Chev.

RICHILDIS (Bl) N. O.S.B. A.C. Aug. 23
d. c.1100. A Benedictine nun at Hohenwart in Upper Bavaria, diocese of Augsburg. After several years of community life she became an anchoress.
Cf. Zimm. — Baud. — Holw.

RICHIMIRUS (St) Ab. O.S.B.
A.C. Jan. 17
d. c.715. An abbot who, under the patronage of the bishop of Le Mans, founded a monastery in that diocese (afterwards called after him Saint-Rigomer-des-Bois) and gave it the Rule of St Benedict.
Cf. Chev. — Att. — Holw. — Baud.

RICTRUDIS (St) W. O.S.B.
A.C. May 12
d. 688. Born in Gascony, she married St

Adalbald, by whom she had four children — all saints, viz. Maurontius, Eusebia, Clotsindis and Adalsindis. After her husband's death she received the veil from St Amandus and became the abbess-foundress of Marchiennes, ruling that house for forty years.
Cf. Att. — Holw. — Baud. — Chev.

RIEUL (St) Bp. **R.M. March 30**
Otherwise Regulus, q.v.

RIGOBERT (St) Bp. O.S.B.
R.M. Jan. 4
d. c.745. Monk and abbot of Orbais. In 721 he was made archbishop of Reims, but some years later was banished by Charles Martel. He willingly returned to Orbais and resumed his monastic life. On being recalled to Reims he persuaded the intruded prelate to retain possession of the see and himself became a hermit.
Cf. Att. — Baud. — Holw. — Gams.

RINGAN, RINGEN
Variant forms of Ninian and Ninnian respectively.

RIOCH (St) Ab. **A.C. Aug. 1**
d. c.480. Described as a nephew of St Patrick and abbot of Innisboffin, Longford, Ireland.
Cf. Holw.

RIQUIER (St) Ab. **R.M. Apr. 26**
Otherwise Richarius, q.v.

RITA (MARGARITA) of CASCIA (St)
W. O.S.A. **R.M. May 22**
d. 1457. Born near Spoleto, she married a rude ill-tempered husband who died a violent death. Her two sons, who had sworn vengeance against their father's murderers, died shortly afterwards filled with the spirit of forgiveness. Rita now entered a convent of Augustinians at Cascia, where she sanctified herself under the strain of a chronic and very painful malady. She was canonized in 1900. In Spanish-speaking countries she is surnamed *La Abogada de Imposibles*, the saint of desperate cases.
Cf. Holw. — Att. — Baud.

RITBERT (St) Ab. O.S.B. **A.C. Sept. 15**
d. c.690. Monk and abbot of a small monastery at Varennes. He had previously been a disciple of St Ouen.
Cf. Zimm.

RIXIUS VARUS (RICTIOVARUS) (St)
M. **R.M. July 6**
The R.M. reads: "On the same day the holy martyr Lucy, a native of Campania, who, being tried and sharply tortured under the vicar Rixius Varus, converted him to Christ. . . . They suffered and were crowned together." Rixius Varus is notorious in the Martyrology as a persecuting prefect under whom hundreds of martyrs died. Modern scholars, however, not only reject the legend of his conversion, but even query his existence.
Cf. Holw. (Lucy).

RIZZERIO (RICHERIUS) (Bl) C. O.F.M.
A.C. Feb. 7
d. 1236. Referred to in the *Fioretti* as Rinieri. Born at Muccia in the Italian Marches. While studying at Bologna he heard St Francis preaching and at once attached himself to him. He was much beloved by Francis and was present at his death. He later became provincial of the Marches. Cult approved in 1836.
Cf. Att. — Holw. — Baud.

RO
Corruption of Maelrubius, q.v.

ROBERT of REIMS (St) Bp. O.S.B.
R.M. Jan. 4
Otherwise Rigobert, q.v.

ROBERT SOUTHWELL (Bl) M. S.J
A.C. Feb. 21
1561-1595. Born at Horsham St Faith's in Norfolk, at the age of 17 he joined the Jesuits in Rome and worked as a priest in London from 1584 to 1592. He was betrayed and kept three years in jail, being tortured thirteen times. He was martyred at Tyburn. He holds a place in English literature as a religious poet. Beatified in 1929.
Cf. Newdigate — Att.

ROBERT of ARBRISSEL (Bl) Ab. O.S.B.
P.C. Feb. 24
d. 1117. A native of Arbrissel in Brittany who became chancellor of the university of Paris and then vicar general of Rennes (1085). At Rennes his activities as preacher and reformer caused such a reaction that he had to quit Brittany. In 1099 he founded the Order of Fontevrault on the borders of Poitou and Anjou. This Order consisted of both men and women. Its members lived under the

Benedictine Rule, the abbess being in supreme command over both nuns and monks, the position of the latter being really that of chaplains to the nuns. After a stormy career Robert retired to Fontevrault and lived out the remainder of his life as a simple monk.
Cf. Zimm. — Att. — Baud. — Holw.

ROBERT DALBY (Bl) M. A.C. March 16
d. 1589. Born at Hemingbrough in Yorkshire. He was a convert from the Protestant ministry and was ordained priest at Reims in 1588. He was hanged for his priesthood at York.
Cf. Newdigate.

ROBERT of BURY ST EDMUNDS (St) M. A.C. March 25
d. 1181. A child said to have been put to death by Jews on Good Friday at Bury St Edmunds, where his relics were enshrined in the abbey church.
Cf. Holw.

ROBERT of CHAISE-DIEU (St) Ab. O.S.B. R.M. Apr. 17
d. 1067. Robert de Turlande, a native of Auvergne, was a priest and canon noted for his love of the poor, for whom he founded a hospice. After spending many years at Cluny under St Odilo and having made a pilgrimage to Rome, he retired to a solitude near Brioude in Auvergne, where he was joined by many disciples. Buildings soon arose which developed into the great abbey of *Casa Dei* or Chaise-Dieu, housing some 300 monks. To these Robert gave the Benedictine Rule, and the foundation became the motherhouse of an important Black Benedictine congregation.
Cf. Zimm. — Att. — Chev. — Holw.

ROBERT WATKINSON (Bl) M. A.C. Apr. 20
d. 1602. Born at Hemingbrough in Yorkshire, he studied for the priesthood at Douai and Rome and was ordained in 1602 at the age of twenty-three. The same year he suffered at Tyburn for his priesthood.
Cf. Newdigate — Att.

ROBERT of SYRACUSE (St) Ab. O.S.B. A.C. Apr. 25
d. b. 1000. Benedictine abbot of a monastery at Syracuse in Sicily.
Cf. Zimm. — Holw.

ROBERT ANDERTON (Bl) M. A.C. Apr. 25
d. 1586. Born at Chorley, Lancs, he was educated at Brasenose College, Oxford. After his conversion he studied for the priesthood at Reims and was ordained in 1585. The following year he was martyred in the Isle of Wight. Beatified in 1929.
Cf. Att.

ROBERT of MOLESMES (St) Ab. O.S.B. Cist. R.M. Apr. 29
1018-1110 (March 21). Born near Troyes in Champagne, he became a Benedictine monk at Moutier-la-Celle at the age of fifteen. He was made prior soon after his novitiate and then abbot of St Michael of Tonnerre. He left this monastery to become superior of some hermits who dwelt in the forest of Collan in the same diocese. In 1075 he migrated with this little community to Molesmes. As the community grew Robert felt less satisfied with the life and withdrew to a hermitage at Or. He was recalled to Molesmes but again left it, this time in the company of SS Stephen Harding and Alberic. On St Benedict's day, 21 March 1098, they founded at Cîteaux a new monastery more in consonance with their monastic ideals. However, the monks of Molesmes appealed to Rome and obtained Robert's recall (1099), and he ruled that abbey thenceforward until his death on St Benedict's day, 1110.
Cf. Zimm. — Baud. — Chev. — P. de U. — Att.

ROBERT of BRUGES (Bl) Ab. O.S.B. Cist. A.C. Apr. 29
d. 1157. Robert Gruthuysen was a native of Bruges. In 1131 he followed St Bernard to Clairvaux, and in 1139 was sent back to Belgium as abbot of Dunes. In 1153 he succeeded St Bernard as abbot of Clairvaux.
Cf. Zimm. — Baud. — Holw. — Chev.

ROBERT LAWRENCE (Bl) M. O.Cart. A.C. May 4
d. 1535. The prior of the charterhouse at Beauvale, Notts. He was one of the first group of Carthusians to be martyred at Tyburn under Henry VIII. Beatified in 1886.
Cf. Newdigate — Camm.

ROBERT BELLARMINE (St) Bp. Dr. S.J. R.M. May 13
1542-1621 (Sept. 17). Born at Monte-

pulciano, he was educated by the Jesuits and joined that Society in 1560. As a young man he held professorships of Greek, Hebrew and theology. It was at Louvain that he first made his reputation as a controversialist, and from that time onward his pen and voice were busy in defence of Catholic doctrine against its Protestant opponents. He was created cardinal in 1598 and archbishop of Capua in 1602. Recalled to Rome in 1605, he became head of the Vatican library and theological adviser to the popes. He was canonized in 1930 and declared a Doctor of the Church the following year.
Cf. Holw. — Att. — Baud.

ROBERT JOHNSON (Bl) M.
A.C. May 28
d. 1582. Born in Shropshire and educated at Rome and Douai, he was ordained in 1576. He began to minister to the Catholics in London in 1580. Two years later he was hanged at Tyburn. Beatified in 1886.
Cf. Newdigate — Camm.

ROBERT SALT (Bl) M. O.Cart.
A.C. June 6 (?)
d. 1537. A lay-brother of the London charterhouse, starved to death, with six of his brethren, at Newgate under Henry VIII. Beatified in 1886.
Cf. Newdigate — Camm.

ROBERT of NEWMINSTER (St) Ab. O.S.B.Cist.
R.M. June 7
d. 1159. A Yorkshire priest who took the Benedictine habit at Whitby and obtained permission to join some monks of York who were attempting to live according to a new interpretation of the Benedictine Rule at Fountains Abbey (1132). Fountains soon became Cistercian and one of the centres of the White Monks in N. England. Newminster Abbey was founded from it in 1137, and Robert became its first abbot. He is described as "gentle in companionship, merciful in judgment."
Cf. Zimm. — Holw. — Att. — Chev.

ROBERT of FRASSINORO (St) Ab. O.S.B.
A.C. June 8
d. p. 1070. Abbot of the Benedictine monastery of Frassinoro near Modena.
Cf. Zimm.

ROBERT of SALENTINO (Bl) Ab. O.S.B. Cel.
A.C. July 18
1272-1341. A Benedictine monk, disciple of St Peter Celestine at Murrone and founder of fourteen monasteries of the Celestine congregation.
Cf. Chev. — Holw.

ROBERT MORTON (Bl) M. A.C. Aug. 28
d. 1588. Born at Bawtry in Yorkshire, he studied for the priesthood at Reims and Rome and was ordained in 1587. He suffered for his priesthood the following year at Lincoln's Inn Fields, London. Beatified in 1929.
Cf. Newdigate.

ROBERT FLOWER (Bl) H. P.C. Sept. 24
d. 1218 (or 1235?). Born at York, he became a postulant at Newminster, but left that abbey to become a hermit, living in a cave by the river Nidd near Knaresborough. His cult has never been officially confirmed.
Cf. Att. — Holw.

ROBERT WILCOX and ROBERT WIDMERPOOL (BB) MM. A.C. Oct. 1
d. 1588. Robert Wilcox was born at Chester and educated at Reims, where he was ordained in 1585. Robert Widmerpool was a gentleman of Nottinghamshire who was educated at Oxford and followed the profession of a schoolmaster. They were martyred together at Canterbury, the former for his priesthood, the latter for sheltering a priest. Beatified in 1929.
Cf. Newdigate.

ROBERT SUTTON (Bl) M. A.C. Oct. 5
d. 1588. Born at Kegwell in Leicestershire, he was a schoolmaster in London and was hanged at Clerkenwell for having been reconciled to the Catholic Church. Beatified in 1929.
Cf. Newdigate.

ROBUSTIAN (St) M. R.M. May 24
? An early Milanese martyr, possibly one and the same with the following.
Cf. Holw.

ROBUSTIAN and MARK (SS) MM.
R.M. Aug. 31
? Martyrs venerated at Milan from early times, of whom nothing further is known.

ROCH (St) C. R.M. Aug. 16
d. 1337. A citizen of Montpellier in

France who devoted his life to the service of the plague-stricken. He is invoked as a protector against pestilence. The Latin form of his name is Rochus, the Italian Rocco, the Spanish Roque. Scottish corruptions of the name are Rollock, Rollox and Seemirookie.
Cf. Att. — Baud. — Holw.

ROCH (ROQUE) GONZALEZ (Bl) M. S.J. A.C. Nov. 17
See Paraguay, Martyrs of.

RODERICK (St) M. R.M. March 13
Otherwise Rudericus, q.v.

RODINGUS (ROUIN) (St) Ab. O.S.B. A.C. Sept. 17
d. c.690. An Irish monk and priest who preached in Germany and entered the abbey of Tholey near Trèves. Distracted by the visits of his converts, he migrated to the forest of Argonne, where he became the abbot-founder of Wasloi, afterwards called Beaulieu. His cult is very ancient.
Cf. Zimm. — Chev. — Baud. — Holw.

RODOLPH or RODULPH (several).
Otherwise Rudolph, q.v.

RODRIGO (St) M. R.M. March 13
The Spanish form of Roderick or Ruderic, q.v.

ROGATIAN (St) M. R.M. Feb. 11
See under Saturninus, Dativus and Comp.

ROGATIAN (St) M. R.M. May 24
See Donatian and Rogatian.

ROGATIAN and FELICISSIMUS (SS) MM. R.M. Oct. 26
d. 256. Rogatian, a priest, and Felicissimus, a layman, belonged to the church of Carthage. They are mentioned by St Cyprian as having "witnessed a good confession for Christ." These words are usually taken as referring to their martyrdom.
Cf. Holw. — Baud.

ROGATIAN (St) M. R.M. Dec. 28
See Castor, Victor and Rogatian.

ROGATUS (St) M. R.M. Jan. 12
See Zoticus, Rogatus, etc.

ROGATUS and ROGATUS (SS) MM. R.M. March 8
See Cyril, Rogatus, etc.

ROGATUS, SUCCESSUS and Comp. (SS) MM. R.M. March 28
? A band of eighteen martyrs put to death in proconsular Africa.
Cf. Holw. — Baud.

ROGATUS (St) M. R.M. June 10
See Aresius, Rogatus, etc.

ROGATUS (St) M. R.M. Aug. 17
See Liberatus, Boniface, etc.

ROGATUS (St) M. R.M. Dec. 1
See Lucius, Rogatus, etc.

ROGELLUS and SERVUS-DEI (SS) MM. R.M. Sept. 16
d. 852. A monk and his young disciple martyred at Cordova for publicly denouncing Mohammedanism.
Cf. P. de U. — Holw. — Baud.

ROGER of ELLANT (Bl) Ab. O.S.B.Cist. A.C. Jan. 4
d. 1160. An Englishman who joined the Cistercian Order at Lorroy, Berry, France, and in 1156 was chosen abbot of the new monastery of Ellant in the diocese of Reims.
Cf. Holw. — Baud. — Att. — Zimm.

ROGER of TODI (Bl) C. O.F.M. A.C. Jan. 28
d. 1237. Ruggiero da Todi was one of the early Franciscans, having been admitted to the Order by St Francis himself, who appointed him spiritual director of the convent of Poor Clares at Rieti. He died at Todi. Cult confirmed by Benedict XIV.
Cf. Att. — Baud. — Holw.

ROGER LEFORT (Bl) Bp. A.C. March 1
d. 1367. Son of the lord of Ternes in the Limousin. He became a jurist and while still only a subdeacon was raised to the see of Orleans (1321). In 1328 he was translated to Limoges and in 1343 to Bourges. He instituted a feast in honour of our Lady's conception. In his will he left all his property for the education of poor boys.
Cf. Att. — Baud. — Holw.

ROGER DICKENSON (Bl) M. A.C. July 7
d. 1591. Born at Lincoln and educated at Reims, where he was ordained in 1583. He was hanged at Winchester for his

priesthood together with Bl Ralph Milner, a layman, who had sheltered him. Beatified in 1929.
Cf. Newdigate — Att.

ROGER JAMES (Bl) M. O.S.B.
A.C. Nov. 15
d. 1539. At the time of his death he was the youngest monk of the Glastonbury community, where he held the offices of sacristan and treasurer. He was executed with his abbot, Bl Richard Whiting, and a fellow monk, Bl John Thorney, on Tor Hill near Glastonbury under Henry VIII. Beatified in 1895.
Cf. Camm — Newdigate — Zimm.

ROLAND de' MEDICI (Bl) H.
A.C. Sept. 15
d. 1386. A scion of the illustrious Florentine family of that name. For twenty-six years he lived without any shelter in the forests of Parma. He died at Borgone. Cult confirmed in 1852.
Cf. Holw. — Baud.

ROLLOCK, ROLLOX, SEEMI-ROOKIE (St) C.
R.M. Aug. 16
Scottish variants of Roch (in the case of the third, of Saint Roch), q.v.

ROMANA (St) V.
R.M. Feb. 23
d. 324. A Roman maiden who died at the age of eighteen while living as a solitary in a cave on the banks of the Tiber. She figures in the spurious life of Pope St Sylvester.
Cf. Holw. — Baud.

ROMANUS of CONDAT (St) Ab.
R.M. Feb. 28
d. c.460. A Gallo-Roman who, at the age of thirty-five, went to live as a hermit in the Jura mountains, whither he was followed by his brother, St Lupicinus. Many disciples soon gathered round the two brothers, who thereupon founded the abbey of Condat and Leuconne, over which they ruled jointly, and the nunnery of La Beaume (afterwards St-Romain-de-la-Roche) presided over by their sister.
Cf. Chev. — Baud. — Att. — Holw.

ROMANUS of SUBIACO (St) Ab. O.S.B.
R.M. May 22
d. c.560. The monk, living in a community near Subiaco, who discovered the hermitage of the youthful St Benedict, when the latter first fled from the world,

and bestowed on him the monastic habit and his daily food. There is no historical evidence of his having been an abbot.
Cf. Zimm. — Att. — Holw. — Baud.

ROMANUS (BORIS) and DAVID (GLEB) (SS) MM.
A.C. July 24
d. 1010. Sons of Vladimir, the first Catholic duke of Muscovy. Their zeal for the propagation of the Christian faith led to their martyrdom at the hands of their heathen fellow-countrymen. Benedict XIII approved their feast for the Russian Catholics. Romanus, called by the Russians Boris, is the patron saint of Moscow.
Cf. Holw. — Baud.

ROMANUS OSTIARIUS (St) M.
R.M. Aug. 9
d. 258. A doorkeeper (ostiarius) of the Roman church who, together with the priest Severus and the clerics Claudius and Crescentius, was martyred about the same time as St Laurence. He is described in the R.M. as a soldier.
Cf. Att. — Baud. — Holw.

ROMANUS of NEPI (St) Bp. M.
R.M. Aug. 24
1st cent. A bishop-martyr of Nepi in Tuscany, said to have been a disciple of St Peter.
Cf. Holw. — Baud.

ROMANUS AYBARA (Bl) M.
A.C. Sept. 8
d. 1628. A Japanese layman, father of Bl Paul Aybara, beheaded at Nagasaki. He was a Dominican tertiary. Beatified in 1867.
Cf. Holw.

ROMANUS the MELODIST (St) C.
A.C. Oct. 1
d. c.540. A Syrian Jew by origin, he became a deacon at Berytos and a priest at Constantinople. He is the greatest of the Greek hymnographers, about 1000 hymns being attributed to him. Some eighty of these have come down to us: they are marked by poetic inspiration, depth of feeling and purity of style.
Cf. Holw. — Att.

ROMANUS of AUXERRE (St) Bp. M.
R.M. Oct. 6
d. ? 564. An alleged bishop of Auxerre. His existence is doubtful.
Cf. Holw. — Baud. — Duc. Fast. Episc.

ROMANUS of ROUEN (St) Bp.
R.M. Oct. 23
d. 639. A courtier of Clothaire II who became bishop of Rouen c.629. He devoted himself to the care of prisoners, particularly those condemned to death.
Cf. Holw. — Att. — Baud. — Duch. Fast. Episc.

ROMANUS and BARULAS (SS) MM.
R.M. Nov. 18
d. 304. Romanus was a young deacon martyred at Antioch in Syria under Diocletian. His companion Barulas is described in the R.M. as a young boy, but we know nothing authentic about him.
Cf. Holw. — Baud. — Att.

ROMANUS of LE MANS (St) C.
R.M. Nov. 24
d. 385. A Gallo-Roman priest who converted the pagans at the mouth of the Gironde and died at Blaye. He seems to have exercised a special influence over sailors.
Cf. Holw. — Baud.

ROMANUS MATEVOCA (Bl) M.
A.C. Nov. 27
d. 1619. A Japanese layman, born at Omura of the royal family of Firando. He was beheaded at Nagasaki with ten companions. Beatified in 1867.
Cf. Holw.

ROMARICUS (St) Ab. O.S.B.
R.M. Dec. 8
d. 653. A Merovingian nobleman converted by St Amatus. He was professed a monk at Luxeuil and founded on his estate the abbey of Habendum (afterwards called Remiremont, i.e. *Romarici Mons*), of which Amatus became the first abbot and he himself the second. The *laus perennis* was performed there by relays of seven choirs.
Cf. Zimm. — Att. — Holw. — Chev.

ROME (Martyrs of) (SS)
The R.M. catalogues the following groups of martyrs who suffered at Rome:

R.M. Jan. 1
d. c.304. Thirty soldiers martyred under Diocletian.

R.M. Jan. 2
d. c.303. Many martyrs who suffered under Diocletian for refusing to give up the holy books.

R.M. Jan. 13
d. 262. Forty soldiers who suffered on the Via Lavicana under Gallienus.

R.M. March 1
d. 269. Two hundred and sixty martyrs condemned to dig sand on the Salarian Way and subsequently shot to death with arrows in the amphitheatre under Claudius.

R.M. March 2
d. 219. A large number of martyrs put to death under Alexander Severus and the prefect Ulpian.

R.M. March 4
d. 260 (?). A group of nine hundred martyrs buried in the catacombs of Callistus on the Appian Way, of whom no particulars are extant.

R.M. March 14
d. c.67. Forty-seven martyrs baptized by St Peter, according to an account which is not very trustworthy; they are said to have suffered under Nero on the same day.

R.M. March 25
? A group of two hundred and sixty-two martyrs who seem to be identical with those of March 1.

R.M. Apr. 10
d. c.115. A number of malefactors detained in the public jail and baptized by Pope St Alexander during his imprisonment there: they were taken to Ostia and put on board an old boat which was then sent out to sea and scuttled.

R.M. June 17
? A group of two hundred and sixty-two martyrs stated to have suffered under Diocletian and buried on the old Via Salaria; they seem to be identical with those of March 1 and March 25.

R.M. June 24
This group has already been catalogued in this book under the heading "Neronian Martyrs," q.v.

R.M. July 2
c.68. Three soldiers who, according to the legend, were converted at the passion of St Paul and martyred.

R.M. Aug. 5
d. 303. Twenty-three martyrs who suffered on the Salarian Way under Diocletian.

R.M. Aug. 10
d. 274. One hundred and sixty-five martyrs put to death under Aurelian.

R.M. Oct. 25
d. 269. Forty-six soldiers and one hundred and twenty-one civilians martyred under Claudius.

R.M. Dec. 22
d. c.303. A group of thirty martyrs who suffered under Diocletian and were buried on the Via Lavicana "between the two laurels."

Quite possibly there were many other similar groups. It is also likely that not all the data given in the R.M. are trustworthy. Nevertheless the R.M.'s description (June 24) of Rome as "a fruitful field of martyrs" is historically very exact.
Cf. Holw. — Baud.

ROMEO (ROMAEUS) (Bl) C. O.C.
A.C. March 4
d. 1310. A Carmelite lay-brother, the companion of St Avertanus. Having set out together from Limoges on a pilgrimage to the Holy Land, both died, apparently from plague, at Lucca.
Cf. Holw. — Att.

ROMUALD (St) Ab. O.S.B.
R.M. Feb. 7 and June 19
c.951-1027. A native of Ravenna, of the ducal family of the Onesti. In his youth he saw his father commit a murder and resolved to atone for that crime by becoming a monk at the Benedictine abbey of Classe near Ravenna. In 996 he was elected abbot of the monastery, but he resigned in 999 and from that time forward led a wandering life in central and northern Italy and the country of the Pyrenees establishing hermitages and monasteries. The best known of these latter, which remains to this day, is that of Camaldoli near Arezzo (1009). The Camaldolese Benedictines combine the eremitical life of the Eastern type with the cenobitical monachism of the West. Romuald made repeated attempts to embark upon missionary work among the Slavs. He died on June 19. Feb. 7 is the anniversary of the translation of his relics from Val di Castro, near Camaldoli, where he died, to Fabriano.
Cf. Zimm. — Att. — Baud. — Chev. — Holw.

ROMULA, REDEMPTA and HERUNDO (SS) VV.
R.M. July 23
d. c.580. Three Roman maidens who lived an austere life of retirement and prayer near the church of St Mary Major.

St Gregory the Great held them in high esteem.
Cf. Att. — Holw. — Baud.

ROMULUS (St) M.　　**R.M. Feb. 17**
See Donatus, Secundianus, etc.

ROMULUS (St) M.　　**R.M. March 24**
See Timolaus and Comp.

ROMULUS and SECUNDUS (SS) MM.
R.M. March 24
? Two brothers who suffered in proconsular Africa. In some MSS the name of Secundus appears as Secundulus.
Cf. Holw. — Baud.

ROMULUS (St) Ab. O.S.B.
A.C. March 27
d. c.730. Abbot of St Baudilius near Nîmes. About 720 he and his community fled before the invading Saracens and settled in a ruined monastery at Saissyles-Bois in the Nivernais.
Cf. Baud. — Holw. — Chev.

ROMULUS and Comp. (SS) MM.
R.M. July 6
d. c.90. Said to have been appointed by St Peter first bishop of Fiesole and to have been martyred with several companions under Domitian.
Cf. Holw. — Att. — Baud.

ROMULUS (St) M.　　**R.M. Sept. 5**
d. c.112. An official of the court of Trajan who, for remonstrating with the emperor on his cruelty to the Christians, was made to share their fate.
Cf. Holw. — Baud.

ROMULUS (St) Bp.　　**A.C. Oct. 13**
d. p. 641. A bishop of Genoa concerning whom we have no trustworthy documents. He died at Matuziano, a coast town on the Riviera, since called after him San Remo.
Cf. Holw. — Baud.

ROMULUS and CONINDRUS (SS) Bps.
A.C. Dec. 28
d. c.450. Two of the first preachers of Christianity in the Isle of Man, contemporaries of St Patrick.
Cf. Holw. — Baud.

RONALD (St) M.　　**A.C. Aug. 20**
d. 1158. A chieftain of Orkney who, in discharge of a vow, built the cathedral

of St Magnus at Kirkwall. He was murdered by rebels and is venerated as a martyr.
Cf. Holw.

RONAN (St) Bp.　　　　**A.C. June 1**
Otherwise Ruadan, q.v.
Note. There are several saints of this or a similar name venerated especially in Ireland.
Cf. O' Hanlon.

ROQUE (St) C.　　　　**R.M. Aug. 16**
The Spanish form of Roch, q.v.

ROSALIA (St) V.
　　　　　　R.M. Sept. 4 and July 15
d. ? 1160. According to the Sicilian tradition she was a girl of good family who became an anchoress in a cave on Mt Coschina, near Bivona, and later in a grotto on Mt Pellegrino, three miles from Palermo. Her alleged relics were found in 1624 and she was acclaimed the patron saint of Palermo.
Cf. Holw. — Att. — Baud.

ROSE de LOYE (Bl) M. O.S.B.
　　　　　　　　A.C. July 6
See Mary Rose.

ROSE CHRETIEN (Bl) M. O.C.
　　　　　　　　A.C. July 17
1741-1794. A native of Evreux who married very young and, on being left a widow, entered the Carmel of Compiègne, taking the name of Soeur Julie-Louise. She was guillotined at Paris with her community. See Carmelite Nuns of Compiègne.
Cf. Baud. — Att.

ROSE of LIMA (St) V. O.P.
　　　　　　　　R.M. Aug. 30
1586-1617. Born of Spanish parents at Lima in Peru. From childhood her life was an exact replica of that of St Catherine of Siena. She lived in her own home as a Dominican tertiary and, like her model, was favoured with extraordinary mystical gifts. She is the first American born to have been canonized (1671) and is venerated as the patron saint of S. America and the Philippines.
Cf. Att. — Holw.

ROSE of VITERBO (St) V. R.M. Sept. 4
1234-1252. Born at Viterbo of poor parents. She was a very spirited young girl

and used to preach in the streets against the Ghibellines and in favour of the pope. She sought admittance to the convent of Poor Clares and was repeatedly refused. After her death, however, her body was, by order of Pope Alexander IV (1258), laid to rest in that convent. Canonized in 1457.
Cf. Holw. — Baud. — Att. — Menzies.

ROSE-PHILIPPINE DUCHESNE (Bl) V.
　　　　　　　　A.C. Nov. 18
1769-1852. Born at Grenoble, she joined the Visitation nuns. When these were scattered during the Reign of Terror she stayed with her family at Grenoble and, in spite of the difficult times, gathered together a community there. In 1804, at the suggestion of St Magdalen Sophie Barat, she incorporated her community into the Society of the Sacred Heart. Her life's desire was to work in the missions, and in 1818 she landed at New Orleans and set up a missionary centre at St Charles, Missouri. In the teeth of many difficulties she founded six more mission stations and went herself to work among the Pottowatomies at Sugar Creek. Later she worked in the Rocky Mountain mission area. In her old age she returned to St Charles to die. Beatified in 1940.
Cf. A.A.S. men. Jun. 1940.

ROSE ELISABETH (St) Abs. O.S.B.
　　　　　　　　A.C. Dec. 13
See Elisabeth Rose.

ROSELINE de VILLENEUVE (Bl) V.
O.Cart.　　　　　**A.C. Jan. 17**
d. 1329. A Carthusian nun of noble family who became prioress of Celle Roubaud in Provence. She was favoured with frequent visions and other mystical phenomena. Cult confirmed in 1851.
Cf. Att. — Baud. — Holw.

ROSENDO (St) Bp. O.S.B.
　　　　　　　　A.C. March 1
The Spanish form of Rudesind, q.v.

ROSIUS (St)　　　　　**R.M. Sept. 1**
See Priscus, Castrensis, etc.

ROSULA (St) M.　　　　**R.M. Sept. 14**
See Crescentian, Victor, etc.

ROTRUDIS (St) V.　　　**A.C. June 22**
d. c.869. A saint whose relics were enshrined at the Benedictine abbey of

Saint-Bertin at Saint-Omer. According to popular belief she was a daughter, or sister, of Charlemagne.
Cf. Holw. — Att. — Baud.

ROUIN (St) Ab.   **A.C. Sept. 17**
Otherwise Rodingus, q.v.

RUADAN (RUADHAN, RODAN) (St) Ab.
A.C. Apr. 15
d. 584. One of the leading disciples of St Finian of Clonard and abbot-founder of the monastery of Lothra.
Cf. Att. — Holw.

RUADAN (RUADHAN, RUAN, RUMON, RONAN) (St)   **A.C. June 1**
5th cent. An Irish saint alleged to have been consecrated bishop by St Patrick. He worked in Cornwall and also apparently in Brittany. Our knowledge of him is very vague.
Cf. Holw. — Att. — Baud.

RUDERICUS (RODERICK) and SALOMON (SOLOMON) (SS) MM.
R.M. March 13
d. 857. Roderick was a priest at Cabra, near Cordova, who was betrayed by his Mohammedan brother and imprisoned at Cordova. In prison he met his fellow-martyr, Salomon, a layman. They were both martyred at Cordova.
Cf. P. de U. — Chev. — Holw. — Att.

RUDESIND (ROSENDO) (St) Bp. O.S.B.
A.C. March 1
907-977. Born of a noble family in Spanish Galicia, he became bishop of Mondoñedo (the ancient Dumium) at the age of eighteen. Shortly after he replaced an unworthy prelate, a cousin of his, as administrator of the see of Compostella. In this capacity he opposed with equal success the depredations of the Normans and the Saracens. Driven from Compostella by the ex-bishop, he founded the abbey of Celanova and became a monk there. With the help of his abbot Tranquila he built further monasteries, imposing on these, as well as on others already founded, the strict observance of the Rule of St Benedict. He was elected second abbot of Celanova, where he died. Canonized in 1195.
Cf. P. de U. — Gams — Att. — Holw. — Chev.

RUDOLPH ACQUAVIVA and Comp. (BB) MM. S.J.   **A.C. July 27**
d. 1583 (July 25). Rudolph was born at Atri in 1550 and was a nephew of Claudio Acquaviva, fifth general of the Jesuits. He too became a Jesuit and was sent to the Jesuit missions in the East Indies. He was martyred on the peninsula of Salsette, near Goa, with four companions. Beatified in 1893.
Cf. Prop. S.J. — Att. — Holw.

RUDOLPH of GUBBIO (St) Bp. O.S.B.
A.C. Oct. 17
d. c.1066. A monk of Fontavellana under St Peter Damian. In 1061, while still very young, he was appointed bishop of Gubbio. He is described as "a miracle of unselfishness."
Cf. Gams — Chev. — Holw. — Baud.

RUELLINUS (RUELLIN) (St) Bp.
A.C. Feb. 28
6th cent. Successor of St Tugwald in the see of Tréguier in Brittany.
Cf. Holw. — Baud.

RUFILLUS (RUFFILIUS) (St) Bp.
R.M. July 18
d. 382. The alleged first bishop of Forlimpopoli (*Forum Pompilii*) in Emilia.
Cf. Gams — Holw. — Baud.

RUFINA and SECUNDA (SS) VV. MM.
R.M. July 10
d. 257. Two Roman maidens martyred under Valerian and buried at Santa Rufina on the Aurelian Way. Their later Acts are apocryphal.
Cf. Holw. — Att. — Baud.

RUFINA (St) V. M.   **R.M. July 19**
See Justa and Rufina.

RUFINA (St) M.   **R.M. Aug. 31**
See Theodotus, Rufina and Ammia.

RUFINIAN (St) M.   **R.M. Sept. 9**
See Rufinus and Rufinian.

RUFINUS (St) M.   **R.M. Feb. 28**
See Macarius, Rufinus, etc.

RUFINUS (St) M.   **R.M. Apr. 7**
See Epiphanius, Donatus, etc.

RUFINUS (St) M.   **R.M. June 14**
See Valerius and Rufinus.

RUFINUS and MARTIA (SS) MM.
R.M. June 21
? Martyrs in one of the early persecutions at Syracuse.
Cf. Holw. — Baud.

RUFINUS (St) M. R.M. July 30
? A martyr in one of the early persecutions at Assisi.
Cf. Holw. — Baud.

RUFINUS and Comp. (SS) MM.
R.M. Aug. 11
? Rufinus is described in the R.M. as "bishop of the Marsi." Probably he is identical with St Rufinus of Assisi (July 30). Of his companions nothing is known.
Cf. Holw. — Baud.

RUFINUS (St) R.M. Aug. 19
? A saint, probably a priest, venerated at Mantua from early times.
Cf. Holw. — Baud.

RUFINUS (St) Bp. R.M. Aug. 26
5th cent. A bishop of Capua, whose relics are enshrined in the cathedral of that city.
Cf. Holw. — Baud.

RUFINUS, SILVANUS and VITALICUS (SS) MM. R.M. Sept. 4
? Three children who formed part of a large group of martyrs put to death at Ancyra in Galatia.
Cf. Holw. — Baud.

RUFINUS and RUFINIAN (SS) MM.
R.M. Sept. 9
? Two brothers martyred at a time and place unknown.
Cf. Holw. — Baud.

RUFINUS, MARK, VALERIUS and Comp. (SS) MM. R.M. Nov. 16
? African martyrs.
Cf. Holw. — Baud.

RUFUS of MELITENE (St) M.
R.M. Apr. 19
See Hermogenes, Caius, etc.

RUFUS (St) H. A.C. Apr. 2
? A hermit at Glendalough, where he was buried. Some writers call him a bishop.
Cf. Holw.

RUFUS (St) M. R.M. Aug. 1
See Cyril, Aquila, etc.

RUFUS of CAPUA (St) Bp. M.
R.M. Aug. 27
? 1st cent. Bishop and martyr of Capua. He is said to have been a disciple of St Apollinaris of Ravenna.
Cf. Holw. — Baud.

RUFUS and CARPOPHORUS (SS) MM.
R.M. Aug. 27
d. 295. Martyrs of Capua under Diocletian. According to the untrustworthy Acts Rufus was a deacon.
Cf. Holw. — Baud. — Bolland.

RUFUS (St) M. R.M. Sept. 25
See Paul, Tatta, etc.

RUFUS of METZ (St) Bp. R.M. Nov. 7
d. c.400. An early bishop of Metz. He was bishop for about twenty-nine years. He is perhaps identical with the Rufus of Metz mentioned c.386 in connection within the Priscillianist controversy.
Cf. Gams — Duch. Fast. Episc. — Holw. — Baud.

RUFUS of AVIGNON (St) Bp.
R.M. Nov. 12
d. c.200. Venerated as the first bishop of Avignon. He certainly existed, but the biographies we have of him are quite unhistorical.
Cf. Holw. — Gams — Duch. Fast. Episc.

RUFUS of ROME (St) Bp. (?)
R.M. Nov. 21
d. c.90. The disciple whom St Paul greets in Rom. XVI 13. Some identify him with the son of Simon of Cyrene mentioned in Mark XV 21. A later tradition makes him a bishop in the East.
Cf. Holw. — Baud.

RUFUS and Comp. (SS) MM.
R.M. Nov. 28
d. 304. A Roman citizen who was martyred with his entire household under Diocletian.
Cf. Holw. — Baud.

RUFUS and ZOSIMUS (SS) MM.
R.M. Dec. 18
d. c.107. Citizens of Philippi brought to Rome with St Ignatius of Antioch and thrown to the beasts in the Roman amphitheatre two days before the latter's martyrdom.
Cf. Holw. — Att. — Baud.

RULE (St) Ab.　　　　**A.C. March 30**
Otherwise Regulus, q.v.

RUMOLDUS (RUMBOLD, ROM-BAULD) (St) Bp. M. O.S.B.
　　　　　　　　　　　R.M. June 24
d. c.775. A monk, probably of an Anglo-Saxon abbey, who became a regionary bishop and worked under St Willibrord in Holland and Brabant. He was murdered near Malines. He is now the titular of Malines cathedral. The R.M. and later legends say that he was of Irish descent and bishop of Dublin.
Cf. Holw. — Att. — Baud. — Chev.

RUMON (St) Bp.　　　　**A.C. June 1**
Otherwise Ruadan, q.v.

RUMWOLD (St) C.　　　　**A.C. Aug. 28**
d. c.650. Said to have been a three-days' old infant, prince of Northumbria, who, immediately after baptism, pronounced aloud the profession of faith and then died. He was at one time honoured with a cult, chiefly in Northants and Bucks.
Cf. Att. — Baud. — Holw.

RUPERT (HRODBERT, ROBERT) (St) Bp. O.S.B.　　　　**R.M. March 27**
d. c.720. He seems to have been of French, not Irish, descent. Having been appointed bishop of Worms, he set himself to spread Christianity in S. Germany. He started operations at Ratisbon and pushed his way along the Danube. The duke of Bavaria gave him the old ruined town of Iuvavum, which Rupert rebuilt and called Salzburg. Here he founded the great Benedictine abbey of St Peter, with school and church attached, and also the nunnery of Nonnberg, over which he placed his sister Erentrude. He is venerated as the first archbishop-abbot of Salzburg and as the apostle of Bavaria and Austria.
Cf. Gams — Zimm. — Mab. — Chev. — Att. — Holw.

RUPERT and BERTHA (SS)
　　　　　　　　　　　A.C. May 15
9th cent. A hermit who lived with his mother Bertha on a hill near Bingen. The hill has been since called after him Rupertsberg. During the 12th century St Hildegard greatly fostered the cult of both saints.
Cf. Att. — Holw.

RUPERT (Bl) Ab. O.S.B.　　　**P.C. Aug. 15**
d. 1145. He was prior of St George's abbey in the Black Forest when (1102) he was asked to become abbot of Otto-beuren in Bavaria. He accepted, and during the forty-three years of his abbacy Ottobeuren attained great prosperity and influence. He introduced there the Cluny-Hirschau customary.
Cf. Zimm. — Holw.

RUSTICA (St) M.　　　　**R.M. Dec. 31**
See Donata, Paulina, etc.

RUSTICUS (Bl) Ab. O.S.B.
　　　　　　　　　　A.C. March 12
d. 1092. A monk of Vallumbrosa who was chosen third abbot general of the Congregation in 1076. His relics were elevated in 1200.
Cf. Chev. — Holw.

RUSTICUS of VERONA (St) M.
　　　　　　　　　　　R.M. Aug. 9
See Firmus and Rusticus.

RUSTICUS (St) M.　　　　**R.M. Aug. 17**
See Liberatus, Boniface, etc.

RUSTICUS (St) Bp.　　　　**R.M. Sept. 24**
d. 446. Bishop of Clermont in Auvergne 426-446.
Cf. Holw. — Baud. — Duch. Fast. Episc.

RUSTICUS (St) M.　　　　**R.M. Oct. 9**
See Dionysius, Rusticus and Eleutherius.

RUSTICUS (St) Bp.　　　　**R.M. Oct. 14**
d. 574. Bishop of Trèves. Accused of sexual impurity by St Goas, he resigned and retired to the hermitage of the same St Goas.
Cf. Holw. — Baud. — Duch. Fast. Episc. — Gams.

RUSTICUS (St) Bp.　　　　**R.M. Oct. 26**
d. c.462. A monk of Lérins who was raised to the see of Narbonne. He was present at the council of Ephesus in 431.
Cf. Duch. Fast. Episc. — Holw. — Baud. — Gams.

RUTILIUS (St) M.　　　　**R.M. Aug. 2**
d. 250. A native of Proconsular Africa. During the persecution of Decius he fled from place to place and even paid money to obtain exemption from sacrifice, but he was at last arrested and bravely confessed

Christ under frightful torture. He was ultimately burnt alive.
Cf. Holw. — Baud.

RUTILUS and Comp. (SS) MM.
R.M. June 4
? Martyrs at Sabaria in Pannonia (Sabar in modern Hungary).
Cf. Holw. — Baud.

RUTULUS (St) R.M. Feb. 18
See Lucius, Silvanus, etc.

S

SABAS (SAVA) (St) Bp. A.C. Jan. 14
1174-1237. Rastho, youngest son of Stephen Nemanya, king of Serbia, became a monk at Mt Athos, where he received the name of Sabas (in Slavonic Sava) and followed the observance till nearly seventy years of age. He was then appointed archbishop of Serbia and managed the ecclesiastical affairs of that kingdom with tact and skill. He was instrumental in securing the papal recognition of his brother Stephen II as king of Serbia. He is venerated as one of the principal patron saints of Yugoslavia.
Cf. Att. — Holw. — Baud.

SABAS (SABBAS) and Comp. (SS) MM.
R.M. Apr. 12
d. 372. A Goth who held the office of lector in a local church of what is now Rumania. He was captured by heathen Gothic soldiers, and on refusing to eat food which had been sacrificed to idols, was tortured to death and thrown into the river Mussovo at a spot near Tirgovist. Several others suffered with him. He is greatly venerated in the East.
Cf. Att. — Baud. — Holw.

SABAS and Comp. (SS) MM.
R.M. Apr. 24
d. 272. A Christian officer of Gothic descent martyred with seventy companions at Rome under Aurelian. Some writers identify him with his namesake of Apr. 12.
Cf. Holw. — Baud.

SABBAS (St) Ab. R.M. Dec. 5
439-532. A Cappadocian who, at a very early age, fled to Palestine, where for many years he lived a hermit's life in various places. He eventually founded a laura (Mar Saba, which still flourishes) in the mountainous desert of Judaea between Jerusalem and the Dead Sea. He was appointed archimandrite over all the Palestinian houses and in that capacity played a prominent part in the campaign against the Eutychian heresy. He is regarded as one of the founders of Eastern monachism.
Cf. Att. — Holw. — Baud.

SABBATIUS (St) M. R.M. Sept. 19
See Trophimus, Sabbatius, and Dorymedon.

SABEL (St) M. R.M. June 17
See Manuel, Sabel and Ismael.

SABINA (St) M. R.M. Aug. 29
d. ? 127. A martyr honoured at Rome from the earliest times. There is a church dedicated to her on the Aventine. Her extant Acts are worthless.
Cf. Holw. — Baud. — Att. — Ricci.

SABINA (St) V. R.M. Aug. 29
d. ? 275. The alleged sister of St Sabinian of Troyes, where she is venerated together with the latter.
Cf. Holw. — Att. — Baud.

SABINA (St) M. R.M. Oct. 27
See Vincent, Sabina and Christeta.

SABINIAN (French: SAVINIEN) (St) M.
R.M. Jan. 29
d. ? 275. A martyr honoured at Troyes in France as having suffered there in one of the early persecutions (under Aurelian?). The French tradition claims that he was a native of Samos, whence with his sister St Sabina he fled to Gaul.
Cf. Holw. — Baud. — Att.

SABINIAN (St) M. R.M. June 7
See Peter Wallabonsus, etc.

SABINIAN (St) M.
R.M. Aug. 27 and Sept. 1
See Honoratus, Fortunatus, etc.

SABINIAN (St) M. R.M. Sept. 25
See Paul, Tatta, etc.

SABINIAN (St) Ab. O.S.B. A.C. Nov. 22
d. c.720 (or c.770?). Third abbot of Moutiers-Saint-Chaffre (Ménat).
Cf. Zimm. — Chev. — Holw.

SABINIAN and POTENTIAN (SS) MM.
R.M. Dec. 31
d. c.300. Sabinian is honoured as the first bishop of Sens. Potentian was perhaps his successor. Both were martyred and are now venerated as the patron saints of the diocese of Sens. The legend that they were immediate disciples of St Peter is now discarded.
Cf. Holw. — Gams — Baud. — Chev.

SABINUS (St) M.
R.M. Jan. 25
See Donatus, Sabinus and Agapes.

SABINUS (St) Bp.
R.M. Feb. 9
d. c.566. Bishop of Canosa (the ancient Canusium, now destroyed) in Apulia and a friend of St Benedict. Pope St Agapitus I entrusted him with an embassy to the emperor Justinian (535-536). He is the patron saint of Bari, where his relics are now enshrined.
Cf. Att. — Holw. — Baud. — Ricci.

SABINUS (St) M.
R.M. March 13
d. 287. An Egyptian of noble birth, martyred by drowning in the Nile under Diocletian.
Cf. Holw. — Baud.

SABINUS (St)
R.M. July 11
d. 5th cent. A saint venerated in the neighbourhood of Poitiers. He is said to have been a disciple of St Germanus of Auxerre. The local tradition considers him a martyr.
Cf. Chev. — Baud. — Holw.

SABINUS (SAVINUS) and CYPRIAN (SS) MM.
R.M. July 11
? Two martyrs, brothers, venerated at Brescia in Italy, but probably the *Brixia* of the R.M. refers to La Bresse in Poitou, where these two saints are also venerated.
Cf. Holw. — Baud.

SABINUS, JULIAN, MAXIMUS, MACROBIUS, CASSIA, PAULA and ten Comp. (SS) MM.
R.M. July 20
? A group of Syrians put to death for the faith at Damascus.
Cf. Holw. — Baud.

SABINUS (French: SAVIN) (St) H.
A.C. Oct. 9
d. c. ? 820. Venerated as one of the apostles of the Lavedan, a district of the Pyrenees which includes Lourdes. He is said to have been born at Barcelona, edu-

cated at Poitiers, professed as a Benedictine at Ligugé, and finally to have become a hermit. All these statements are very doubtful.
Cf. Holw. — Att. — Baud. — P. de U.

SABINUS (St) Bp.
A.C. Oct. 15
d. c.760. Bishop of Catania in Sicily. After a few years as bishop he resigned and became a hermit.
Cf. Gams — Baud. — Holw.

SABINUS (St) Bp.
R.M. Dec. 11
d. 420. Bishop of Piacenza and a close friend of St Ambrose, who used to send him his writings for revision and approval. While still a deacon he was sent by Pope St Damasus to settle the Meletian schism at Antioch.
Cf. Holw. — Att. — Baud.

SABINUS, EXUPERANTIUS, MARCELLUS, VENUSTIAN and Comp. (SS) MM.
R.M. Dec. 30
d. 303. Sabinus is described as a bishop who was martyred near Spoleto. His see is unknown, but Faenza, Assisi, Spoleto and Chiusi each claim him. Venustian and his family were converts of Sabinian, while Exuperantius and Marcellus are said to have been his deacons.
Cf. Holw. — Baud. — Att. — Menzies.

SACER (MO-SACRA) (St) Ab.
A.C. March 3
7th cent. An Irish saint, abbot-founder of the monastery of Saggard, Dublin.
Cf. Holw.

SACERDOS (SARDOT, SADROC, SARDOU, SERDON, SERDOT) (St) Bp.
O.S.B.
R.M. May 4
670-c.720. Born in the neighbourhood of Sarlat in Périgord, he became a monk and eventually the abbot-founder of Calabre (Calabrum, Calviat). He was appointed bishop of Limoges, resigning his see shortly before his death.
Cf. Zimm. — Gams — Chev. — Baud. — Holw.

SACERDOS (St) Bp.
R.M. May 5
d. c.560. A Spanish saint venerated at Murviedro (the ancient Saguntum), and said to have been bishop of that city.
Cf. Holw. — Baud.

SACERDOS (St) Bp.
R.M. Sept. 12
d. 551. Bishop of Lyons 544-551 and ad-

viser of King Childebert. He presided at the council of Orleans in 549.
Cf. Gams — Baud. — Holw. — Duch.
Fast. Episc.

SADOC and Comp. (BB) MM. O.P.
A.C. June 2
d. 1260. Sadoc was received into the Dominican Order by St Dominic himself and sent to Hungary. Later he passed on to Poland, where he founded a house at Sandomir and became its prior. When the town was pillaged by the Tartars, Sadoc and his forty-eight friars were butchered while singing the Salve Regina.
Cf. Prop. O.P. — Holw. — Baud. — Att.

SADOTH (SADOSH, SCHADOST) and Comp. (SS) MM. R.M. Feb. 20
d. 345 (or 342). Sadoth was the metropolitan of Seleucia-Ctesiphon in Persia. He, with one hundred and twenty-eight other Christians, was arrested in the persecution of Shapur II. Most of these were martyred at once, but Sadoth, with eight companions, was detained for five months in a filthy prison at Bei-Lapat before being executed.
Cf. Att. — Holw. — Baud.

SADWEN (SADWRN) (St) C.
A.C. Nov. 29
6th cent. Brother of St Illtyd and disciple of St Cadfan. Some Welsh churches are dedicated to him. He has been confused with St Saturnin.
Cf. Holw.

SAGAR (St) Bp. M. R.M. Oct. 6
d. c.175. Bishop of Laodicea in Phrygia, put to death under Marcus Aurelius. It seems impossible to accept the tradition that he was a disciple of St Paul.
Cf. Holw. — Baud.

SAIR (St) Bp. A.C. July 1
Otherwise Servan, q.v.

SALABERGA (St) Abs. R.M. Sept. 22
d. c.665. As a child she was cured of blindness by St Eustace of Lisieux. She married very young, and her husband died after two months. Her second husband was St Blandinus, to whom she bore five children, two of whom are venerated as saints. In later years husband and wife decided to become religious. Salberga entered the nunnery of Poulangey and was subsequently the foundress of St

John the Baptist at Laon, where she died.
Cf. Chev. — Baud. — Holw. — Att.

SALAUN (SALOMON)(St) C. A.C. Nov. 1
d. 1358. A poor man of Leseven in Brittany. Content to be despised and considered "a fool for Christ's sake," he reached a high degree of contemplation. He is venerated at N.D. de Folgoet in Brittany.
Cf. Holw. — P.B.

SALLUSTIA (St) M. R.M. Sept. 14
See Caerealis and Sallustia.

SALLUSTIAN (St) R.M. June 8
? A saint honoured in Sardinia from time immemorial. In some martyrologies he is described as a martyr, in others as a hermit.
Cf. Holw. — Baud.

SALOME and JUDITH (SS) O.S.B.
A.C. June 29
9th cent. Salome is said to have been an Anglo-Saxon princess, exiled from her native country. She was befriended by a pious Bavarian widow named Judith. Both became anchoresses under the obedience of the Benedictine abbey of Oberaltaich.
Cf. Holw. — Att. — Baud. — Chev.

SALOME (St) R.M. Oct. 22
See Mary Salome.

SALOMEA (Bl) W. Poor Clare.
A.C. Nov. 17
c.1200-1268. Daughter of King Leski of Poland. At the age of three she was betrothed to prince Koloman of Hungary and was left a widow before her 23rd year. She founded the convent of Poor Clares at Zawichost, later removed to Skala, where she became a nun and ended her days. Cult confirmed by Clement X.
Cf. Holw. — Baud.

SALONIUS (St) Bp. R.M. Sept. 28
Otherwise Solomon, q.v.

SALUTARIS (St) M. R.M. July 13
See Eugene, Salutaris, etc.

SALVATOR of HORTA (St) C. O.F.M.
A.C. March 18
1520-1567. Born at Santa Columba, diocese of Gerona, Spain, he was a shoemaker by trade before he joined the Franciscans

as a lay-brother at Barcelona. He spent most of his life as cook of the friary of Horta, near Tortosa. He died at the friary of Cagliari in Sardinia. Canonized in 1940.
Cf. Holw. — Att. — P. de U.

SALVINUS (St) Bp.   **A.C. Sept. 4**
d. c.420. Third bishop of Verdun (c.383-c.420).
Cf. Duch. Fast. Episc. — Gams — Baud. — Holw.

SALVINUS (St) Bp.   **R.M. Oct. 12**
d. 562. Bishop of Verona. His relics are enshrined in the church of St Stephen in that city.
Cf. Holw. — Baud. — Menzies.

SALVIUS (SALVE, SAUVE) (St) Bp.
                              R.M. Jan. 11
d. c.625. Bishop of Amiens. One of the great wonder-workers of his age.
Cf. Duch. Fast. Episc. — Gams — Baud. — Att. — Holw.

SALVIUS (St) M.   **R.M. Jan. 11**
? A martyr in Proconsular Africa.
Cf. Holw. — Baud.

SALVIUS (Bl) Ab. O.S.B.   **P.C. Feb. 10**
d. 962. Benedictine abbot of Albelda in N. Spain. He was a prudent adviser at the courts of Navarre and Castile at the time of the Reconquest.
Cf. P. de U. — Chev. — Holw.

SALVIUS and SUPERIUS (SS) MM.
                              R.M. June 26
d. c.768. A regionary bishop in the district of Angoulême, who came to Valenciennes to evangelize the Flemish. There he, with his priest (or deacon) Superius (Super), was put to death by the count's son.
Cf. Att. — Holw. — Baud.

SALVIUS (St) Bp.   **R.M. Sept. 10**
d. 584. A lawyer who became a monk and abbot, then a hermit, and finally bishop of Albi (574-584). He died while tending the sick during an epidemic which was ravaging his diocese.
Cf. Gams — Duch. Fast. Episc. — Att. — Holw. — Baud.

SALVIUS (French: SAIRE) (St) H.
                              A.C. Oct. 28
6th cent. A hermit at the place now called

after him Saint-Saire in Normandy. Some writers identify him with St Salvius of Albi.
Cf. Baud. — Att. — Chev.

SAMONAS (St) M.   **R.M. Nov. 15**
See Gurias and Samonas.

SAMOSATA, The SEVEN MARTYRS of (SS)   **A.C. Dec. 9**
d. c.311. Their names were: Hipparchus and Philotheus, magistrates, and their converts James, Paragrus, Abibus, Romanus and Lollian. They were crucified at Samosata on the Euphrates for refusing to join in the public rejoicing, including pagan rites, after Maximinus's victory over the Persians.
Cf. Holw. — Att.

SAMSON (SAMPSON) (St) C.
                              R.M. June 27
d. c.530. Surnamed "the Hospitable" (Xenodochius). He was a distinguished citizen of Constantinople who studied medicine and was ordained priest in order to devote his life to the spiritual and physical care of the sick and destitute. He founded and equipped a magnificent hospital near St Sophia.
Cf. Att. — Baud. — Holw.

SAMSON (SAMPSON) (St) Bp.
                              R.M. July 28
d. c.565. Born in Glamorgan, Wales, he became a disciple of St Illtyd at Llanwit Major, and then for a time monk and abbot of the monastery on Caldey Island. He left Caldey and visited Ireland: then, on his return to England, he sojourned in Cornwall and was consecrated bishop by St Dyfrig. Finally he crossed over to Brittany and spent the rest of his life evangelizing that country, fixing his central residence at Dol (c.525). His name is still held in benediction throughout Brittany and Wales. He is indeed one of the greatest missionaries Britain has ever produced.
Cf. Att. — Baud. — Holw. — Chev.

SAMTHANA (St) V.   **A.C. Dec. 19**
6th cent. An Irish saint, abbess-foundress of Cluain-Bronach in Meath.
Cf. Holw.

SAMUEL (St) M.   **R.M. Feb. 16**
See Elias, Jeremias, etc.

SAMUEL (St) Prophet.   R.M. Aug. 20
11th cent. B.C.   The 1st book of Kings,
often for this reason called the 1st book
of Samuel, contains the history of the
prophet, the wonders of his birth and childhood (i, ii); his judgeship of Israel (iv-
vii); his anointing of Saul as king (viii-
x); his replacing of Saul by David (xvi);
and his death (xxv).

SAMUEL (St) M.   R.M. Oct. 10
See Daniel, Samuel, etc.

SANCHA (SANCTIA) (Bl) V. O.S.B.
A.C. March 13
c.1180-1229.   Daughter of King Sancho I
of Portugal, sister of BB Teresa and
Mafalda.   She helped the first Franciscan
and Dominican foundations in Portugal
and afterwards (1223) joined the Cistercians at Cellas.   Cult approved in 1705.
Cf. P. de U. — Holw. — Chev.

SANCHO (SANCTIUS, SANCIUS) (St)
M.   R.M. June 5
d. 851.   Born at Albi in France, he was
brought to Cordova as a prisoner of war,
educated at the Moorish court there, and
enrolled in the guards of the Emir.   He
was martyred by impalement on refusing
to embrace Mohammedanism.
Cf. P. de U. — Chev. — Baud. — Holw.

SANCTAN (St) Bp.   A.C. March 9
6th cent.   Bishop of the Irish sees of
Kill-da-Les and Kill-na-Sanctan (Dublin).   He was probably of British birth.
Cf. Holw. — Baud.

SANTES BRANCASINO (Bl) C. O.F.M.
A.C. Aug. 14
d. 1490.   Born at Monte Fabri, diocese of
Urbino, he became a Franciscan lay-
brother at Scotameto, where he spent most
of his life.   Cult approved by Clement
XIV.
Cf. Holw. — Baud. — Chev.

SANCTES of CORI (Bl) C. O.S.A.
A.C. Oct. 5
d. 1392.   A native of Cori, diocese of
Velletri, who joined the Augustinians and
became famous as a zealous missioner.
Cult approved by Leo XIII.
Cf. Holw. — Chev.

SANCTINUS (St) Bp.   R.M. Sept. 22
d. c.300.   Alleged to have been the first
bishop of Meaux and a disciple of St

Dionysius of Paris.   He is probably to be
identified with a St Sanctinus claimed by
the diocese of Verdun.
Cf. Gams — Duch. Fast. Episc. — Baud.
— Holw.

SANCTUS (St) M.   R.M. June 2
See Photinus (Pothinus), Sanctus, etc.

SANDILA (SANDALUS, SANDOLUS,
SANDULF) (St) M.   R.M. Sept. 3
d. c.855.   A Spanish martyr of Cordova
under the Moorish domination.
Cf. Holw. — P. de U.

SANDRATUS (SANDRADUS) Ab. O.S.B.
A.C. Aug. 24
d. 986.   Monk of the abbey of St Maximinus at Trèves.   In 972 he was sent by
the emperor Otto I to restore monastic
observance at St Gall.   Shortly after he
was made abbot of Gladbach, and in 981
also abbot of Weissenburg.   He died at
Gladbach.
Cf. Zimm. — Chev.

SANTUCCIA TERREBOTTI (Bl) W.
O.S.B.   A.C. March 21
d. 1305.   Born at Gubbio in Umbria, she
married and bore a daughter who died
young.   Santuccia and her husband then
decided to enter religion.   She became a
Benedictine at Gubbio and rose to be
abbess.   Under her the community migrated to Santa Maria in Via Lata, on the
Julian Way, Rome, where they continued
to live the Benedictine life, though usually
called the Servants of Mary.   The people
nicknamed them Le Santuccie.
Cf. Zimm. — Chev. — Att. — Baud.

SAPIENTIA (St) W.   R.M. Sept. 30
Otherwise Sophia, q.v.

SAPOR (SHAPUR), ISAAC and Comp.
(SS) MM.   A.C. Nov. 30
d. 339.   A band of Persian martyrs under
Shapur II.   Sapor and Isaac were bishops:
the former died in prison, the latter was
stoned to death.   SS Mahanes, Abraham
and Simeon suffered at the same time.
Cf. Holw. — Att. — Baud.

SARAGOSSA, The EIGHTEEN MAR-
TYRS of, viz. OPTATUS, LUPERCUS,
SUCCESSUS, MARTIAL, URBAN,
JULIA, QUINTILIAN, PUBLIUS,
FRONTO, FELIX, CAECILIAN, EVEN-

TIUS, PRIMITIVUS, APODEMIUS, and four named SATURNINUS (SS)
R.M. Apr. 16
d. c.304. Martyrs of Saragossa in Spain under the emperor Diocletian and the prefect Dacian. Prudentius, who lived at Saragossa a lifetime later, describes their martyrdom.
Cf. P. de U. — Holw. — Baud.

SARAGOSSA, The INNUMERABLE MARTYRS of (SS) R.M. Nov. 3
d. c.304. An exceedingly large number of martyrs (the R.M. uses the phrase *innumerabilis multitudo*) put to death at Saragossa under Diocletian by the savage prefect Dacian, who had been sent to Spain to enforce the decrees and whose residence was at Saragossa. He published an edict banishing all Christians from the city, and while they were leaving he ordered the soldiers to fall upon and massacre them. There is still great popular devotion to these martyrs at Saragossa.
Cf. P. de U. — Baud. — Holw.

SARBELIUS (SHARBEL) and BARBEA (BEBAIA) (SS) MM. R.M. Jan. 29
d. 101. Brother and sister martyred at Edessa under Trajan. Previous to their martyrdom they were tortured with redhot irons. Before his conversion Thatueles Sarbelius had been the pagan high priest of the city.
Cf. Holw. — Baud.

SARDON (St) Bp. R.M. May 4
Otherwise Sacerdos, q.v.

SARMATA (St) M. R.M. Oct. 11
d. 357. An Egyptian disciple of St Antony, murdered in his monastery by a band of marauding Bedouins and venerated as a martyr.
Cf. Holw. — Baud.

SATOR (St) M.
R.M. Aug. 29 and Sept. 1
See Vitalis, Sator and Repositus.

SATURIAN (St) M. R.M. Oct. 16
See Martinian, Saturian, etc.

SATURNINA (St) V. M. R.M. June 4
? A maiden said to have come from Germany into the neighbourhood of Arras and there to have met her death in defending herself against an assault on her virginity. The story is now held to be a romance.
Cf. Holw. — Baud.

SATURNINUS (St) M. R.M. Jan. 19
See Paul, Gerontius, etc.

SATURNINUS, THYRSUS and VICTOR (SS) MM. R.M. Jan. 31
d. c. ? 250. Egyptians martyred at Alexandria.
Cf. Holw. — Baud. — Chev.

SATURNINUS, THEOPHILUS and REVOCATA (SS) MM. R.M. Feb. 6
? A group of martyrs concerning whom neither place nor date of martyrdom is known.
Cf. Holw. — Baud.

SATURNINUS, DATIVUS, FELIX, AMPELIS and Comp. (SS) MM.
R.M. Feb. 11
d. 304. A group of forty-six martyrs of Albitina in Africa. They were arrested at Mass and sent to Carthage for examination. Saturninus was a priest, and with him suffered his four children, viz., Saturninus and Felix, lectors, Mary, a virgin, and Hilarion, a young child. Dativus and another Felix were senators. Other names from this group which have dome down to us are: Thelica, Ampelius, Emeritus, Rogatianus and Victoria, a maiden of undaunted courage. The child Hilarion, when threatened by the magistrates, while his companions were being tortured, replied: "Yes, torture me too; anyhow, I am a Christian." They all appear to have died in prison. Their Acts bear the stamp of authenticity.
Cf. Holw. — Att. — Baud. — Ruinart.

SATURNINUS, CASTULUS, MAGNUS and LUCIUS (SS) MM. R.M. Feb. 15
d. 273. These martyrs belonged to the flock of St Valentine, bishop of Terni in Italy. They were buried at Passae (Rocca San Zenone).
Cf. Holw. — Baud.

SATURNINUS (St) M. R.M. Feb. 21
See Verulus, Secundinus, etc.

SATURNINUS (St) M. R.M. March 7
See Perpetua, Felicitas, etc.

SATURNINUS and Comp. (SS) MM.
R.M. March 22
? A group of ten martyrs of N. W. Africa.
Cf. Holw. — Baud.

SATURNINUS (St) Bp.   **R.M. Apr. 7**
d. c.356. Bishop of Verona. No details
of his career are extant.
Cf. Gams — Holw. — Baud.

SATURNINUS (SS) MM. R.M. Apr. 16
Four of the same name among the group
of Saragossa Martyrs, q.v.

**SATURNINUS, NEOPOLUS, GERMAN-
US and CELESTINE (SS) MM.**
               R.M. May 2
d. 304. Saturninus was martyred at
Alexandria under Diocletian, not at Rome
as stated in the R.M. Of the others nothing is known.
Cf. Holw. — Att. — Baud.

SATURNINUS (St) M.   **R.M. July 7**
See Peregrinus, Lucian, etc.

SATURNINUS (St) M.   **R.M. Aug. 22**
See Martial, Saturninus, etc.

SATURNINUS (St) M.   **R.M. Oct. 6**
See Marcellus, Castus, etc.

SATURNINUS and LUPUS (SS) MM.
               R.M. Oct. 14
? Martyrs at Caesarea in Cappadocia.
Cf. Holw. — Baud.

**SATURNINUS, NEREUS and Comp.
(SS) MM.**   **R.M. Oct. 16**
d. c.450. A band of some three hundred
and sixty-five martyrs who suffered in
Proconsular Africa under the Vandal king
Genseric. Some authorities maintain that
this is merely a second listing of the band
of martyrs led by SS Martinian and Saturian, q.v.
Cf. Holw. — Baud. — Bolland.

SATURNINUS (St) M.   **R.M. Oct. 30**
d. 303. A martyr of Cagliari, in Sardinia,
under Diocletian. According to his untrustworthy Acts he was beheaded during
a pagan festival of Jupiter.
Cf. Holw. — Baud.

SATURNINUS (St) M.   **R.M. Nov. 27**
See Basileus, Auxilius and Saturninus.

SATURNINUS and SISINIUS (SS) MM.
               R.M. Nov. 29
d. ? 309. Saturninus was a Roman priest,
though by birth, it is said, a Carthaginian.
He and his deacon Sisinius were sentenced

to hard labour and subsequently martyred.
They were buried in the cemetery of St
Thraso on the Salarian Way. They have
no connexion with SS Cyriacus, Largus
and Smaragdus, as has been alleged.
Cf. Holw. — Baud. — Att.

**SATURNINUS (French: SERNIN) (St)
Bp. M.**   **R.M. Nov. 29**
d. c.257. A missionary from Rome who
evangelized the district round Pampeluna
in Spanish Navarre, and then the territory
and city of Toulouse. He is venerated as
the first bishop of Toulouse. He is said
to have been martyred in the persecution
of Valerian by being fastened behind a
wild bull which dragged him about until
he was dashed to pieces.
Cf. Att. — Holw. — Baud.

SATURNINUS (St) C.   **A.C. Nov. 29**
Otherwise Sadwen, q.v.

SATURNINUS (St) M.   **R.M. Dec. 15**
See Irenaeus, Antony, etc.

SATURNINUS (St) M.   **R.M. Dec. 23**
See Crete, Martyrs of.

SATURNINUS (St) M.   **R.M. Dec. 29**
See Dominic, Victor, etc.

SATURUS (St) M.   **R.M. March 29**
See Armogastes and Comp.

SATURUS (*several*)
Otherwise Satyrus, q.v.

SATYRUS (St) M.   **R.M. Jan. 12**
d. 267. An Arab by birth, who was martyred in Achaia (or at Antioch) for insult-
ing an idol. Another version says that the
idol fell to the ground when Satyrus made
the sign of the cross over it.
Cf. Holw. — Baud.

SATYRUS (St) M.   **R.M. March 7**
See Perpetua, Felicitas, etc.

SATYRUS (St) C.   **R.M. Sept. 17**
d. c.392. The elder brother of St Ambrose
of Milan. As a lawyer he undertook the
administration of the temporal affairs of
the diocese of Milan. His high sense of
justice, his integrity and his generosity are
eulogized by Ambrose in the funeral sermon "On the death of a brother."
Cf. Menzies — Holw. — Att. — Ricci.

SAULA (St) V. M. R.M. Oct. 20
See Martha, Saula and Comp.

SAUMAN (SAUMAY) (St) H.
A.C. June 14
Otherwise Psalmodius, q.v.

SAUVE (St) Bp. R.M. Sept. 10
Otherwise Salvius, q.v.

SAVINA (St) Matron. R.M. Jan. 30
d. 311. A woman of Milan who, during
the persecution of Diocletian, busied herself in ministering to the martyrs in prison
and in interring their bodies after execution. She died while praying at the tomb
of SS Nabor and Felix.
Cf. Holw. — Baud.

SAVINIAN (SAVINIEN) (*several*)
Otherwise Sabinian, q.v.

SAVINUS (*several*)
Otherwise Sabinus, q.v.

SAWL (St) C. A.C. Jan. 15
6th cent. A Welsh chieftain, father of St
Asaph. The traditions concerning him
are very obscure.
Cf. Holw.

SAZAN (St) M. A.C. Oct. 1
See Aizan and Sazan.

SCANNAL (St) C. A.C. May 3
d. p. 563. Scannal of Cell-Coleraine was
a disciple of St Columba and a celebrated
missionary.
Cf. Holw.

SCARTHIN (St) C. A.C. Jan. 6
Otherwise Schotin, q.v.

SCHADOST (St) M. R.M. Feb. 20
Otherwise Sadoth, q.v.

SCHENUTE (SINUTIUS) (St) Ab.
A.C. July 1
d. c.460. An Egyptian who became a
monk at Deir-al-Abiad in 371. He is said
to have become in the course of time superior of a very large number of monks
and nuns, the number being given as over
four thousand. It seems to have been
under him that the custom arose of religious binding themselves by public vows.
Cf. Att. — Holw.

SCHOLASTICA (St) V. O.S.B.
R.M. Feb. 10
d. c.550. Sister of St Benedict. She became a nun and lived near Montecassino
under the direction of her brother. She is
regarded as the first nun of the Benedictine
Order. St Gregory narrates that, at her
last meeting with her brother, she obtained
by prayer a sudden heavy rainstorm,
which prevented Benedict from returning
to his monastery and thus prolonged their
interview through the night: three days
later Benedict saw her soul ascend to
heaven in the semblance of a dove.
Cf. Zimm. — Chev. — Holw. — Att.

SCHOTIN (SCARTHIN) (St) C.
A.C. Jan. 6
6th cent. While still a youth Schotin left
Ireland to become a disciple of St David in
Wales. On his return to his native coun-
try he for many years led the life of an
anchorite at Mt Mairge, Leix. He is said
to have established a school for boys at
Kilkenny.
Cf. Holw. — Baud.

SCILLITAN MARTYRS (SS)
R.M. July 17
d. 180. Twelve martyrs, seven men and
five women, who suffered at Scillium in Pro-
consular Africa under Septimius Severus.
Their names are: Speratus, Narzales,
Cynthinus, Veturius, Felix, Acyllinus,
Laetantius, Januaria, Generosa, Vestina,
Donata and Secunda. The official Acts of
these martyrs are still extant.
Cf. Holw. — Baud. — Att.

SCUBICULUS (St) M. R.M. Oct. 11
See Nicasius, Quirinus, etc.

**SEACHNALL (SECHNALL, SECUN-
DINUS) (St) Bp.** A.C. Nov. 27
d. 457. A nephew and disciple of St
Patrick. In 433 he was appointed first
bishop of Dunsauglin, Meath, and later
served as assistant bishop of Armagh. He
wrote the earliest Latin poem of the Irish
church — an alphabetical hymn in honour
of St Patrick.
Cf. Holw. — Baud. — Chev.

SEBALD (St) H. O.S.B. R.M. Aug. 19
d. c.770. A missionary monk in the
Reichsbald, Bavaria, and probably a
fellow-worker of SS Winebald and Willibald. He is patron saint of Nuremberg.
Cf. Zimm. — Holw. — Baud. — Att.

SEBASTIA (St) M. R.M. July 4
See Innocent, Sebastia, etc.

SEBASTIAN (St) M. R.M. Jan. 20
d. ? 288. One of the most renowned of
the Roman martyrs. According to his
Acts, which however are not trustworthy,
he was an officer in the imperial army and
a favourite of Diocletian. Nevertheless
when it was discovered that he was a
Christian no mercy was shown to him.
Tied to a tree, his body was made a target
for the Roman archers, and he was finally
dispatched with clubs. His cult, both at
Rome and at Milan, dates from the 4th
century. In 367 Pope St Damasus built
a basilica over his tomb on the Appian
Way, and this is now one of the seven
principal churches of Rome.
*Cf. Holw. — Baud. — Att. — Menzies —
Ricci.*

SEBASTIAN VALFRÉ (Bl) Orat.
A.C. Jan. 30
1629-1710. Born at Verduno, diocese of
Alba, N. Italy, he joined the Oratorians at
Turin after his ordination to the priesthood, and there he spent the remainder of
his life. He became prefect of the Oratory
and was much in request as a spiritual director. He acquired in full measure the
spirit of St Philip Neri. Beatified in 1834.
Cf. Att. — Baud. — Holw.

SEBASTIAN (St) M. R.M. Feb. 8
See Dionysius, Aemilian and Sebastian.

SEBASTIAN APARICIO (Bl) C. O.F.M.
A.C. Feb. 25
d. 1600. Born at Gudina, diocese of
Orense in Spanish Galicia, he became a
farm labourer and then valet to a gentleman of Salamanca. He emigrated to
Mexico, where he was engaged by the government in building roads and in conduct-
ing the postal service between Mexico and
Zacateca. He married twice, and after
the death of his second wife, when he was
seventy years old, he gave all his property
to the Poor Clares and himself became a
Franciscan lay-brother at Puebla de los
Angeles. He lived for another twenty-six
years, his chief occupation being to beg
alms for the community. Beatified in
1787.
Cf. P. de U. — Holw. — Att. — Baud.

SEBASTIAN (St) M. R.M. March 20
See Photina, Joseph, etc.

SEBASTIAN NEWDIGATE (Bl) M.
O.Cart. A.C. June 19
d. 1535. Born at Harefield, Middlesex,
and educated at Cambridge, he professed
the Carthusian Rule in the London
Charterhouse. He was executed at Tyburn for denying the royal supremacy.
BB Humphrey Middlemore and William
Exmew suffered with him. Beatified in
1886.
Cf. Newdigate — Camm — Holw.

SEBASTIAN KIMURA (Bl) M. S.J.
A.C. Sept. 10
d. 1622. A grandson of the first Japanese
baptized by St Francis Xavier. At the
age of eighteen he joined the Jesuits and
worked as a catechist at Meaco. He was
the first Japanese to be ordained priest.
After two years imprisonment at Omura
he was burnt alive with Bl Charles Spinola.
Beatified in 1867.
Cf. Holw. — Prop. S.J.

SEBASTIAN MONTAÑOL (Bl) M. O.P.
P.C. Dec. 10
d. 1616. A Spanish Dominican and a missionary in Zacateca, Mexico, where he was
put to death by the Indians whom he had
rebuked for having profaned the Sacred
Host. Though he has never been officially
declared a martyr, he has always been the
object of a popular cult.
Cf. P. de U. — Baud.

SEBASTIAN MAGGI (Bl) C. O.P.
A.C. Dec. 16
d. 1494. A native of Brescia, he became
a Friar Preacher and was noted for his
zeal in enforcing religious observance.
He was twice vicar of the Lombard province and was for a time confessor of Savo-
narola. He died in Genoa. Cult confirmed in 1760.
Cf. Holw. — Baud. — Att.

SEBASTIANA (St) M. R.M. Sept. 16
1st cent. A woman converted by St Paul.
Beheaded at Heraclea in Thrace under
Domitian.
Cf. Holw. — Baud.

SEBBE (SEBBA, SEBBI) (St) C. O.S.B.
R.M. Aug. 29
d. c.694. King of the East Saxons at the
time of the Heptarchy. After a peaceful
reign of thirty years he received the monastic habit in London and died shortly after.
Cf. Att. — Zimm. — Baud. — Holw.

SECUNDA (St) V. M.   R.M. July 10
See Rufina and Secunda.

SECUNDA (St) M.   R.M. July 17
One of the Scillitan Martyrs, q.v.

SECUNDA (St) V. M.   R.M. July 30
See Maxima, Donatilla and Secunda.

SECUNDARIUS (St) M.   R.M. Oct. 2
See Primus, Cyril and Secundarius.

SECUNDIAN (St) M.   R.M. Feb. 17
See Donatus, Secundian, etc.

SECUNDIAN, MARCELLIAN and VER-
IAN (SS) MM.   R.M. Aug. 9
d. 250. Tuscan martyrs who suffered
near Civitavecchia under Decius. Secundian seems to have been a prominent government official; the others are described
as "scholastics."
Cf. Holw. — Baud.

SECUNDILLA (St) M.   R.M. March 2
See Paul, Heraclius, etc.

SECUNDINA (St) V. M.   R.M. Jan. 15
d. c.250. A Roman maiden, scourged to
death in the neighbourhood of Rome in
the persecution of Decius.
Cf. Holw. — Baud.

SECUNDINUS (St) M.   R.M. Feb. 18
See Lucius, Silvanus, etc.

SECUNDINUS (St) M.   R.M. Feb. 21
See Verulus, Secundinus, etc.

SECUNDINUS (St) Bp. M. R.M. Apr. 29
See Agapius and Comp.

SECUNDINUS (St) M.   R.M. May 21
d. c.306. A Spanish martyr at Cordova
under Diocletian.
Cf. Holw. — Baud.

SECUNDINUS (St) Bp. M.   R.M. July 1
See Castus and Secundinus.

SECUNDINUS (St) M.   R.M. Sept. 1
See Priscus, Castrensis, etc.

SECUNDINUS (St) Bp.   A.C. Dec. 6
See Auxilius, Isserninus and Secundinus.

SECUNDULUS (St) M.   R.M. March 7
See Perpetua, Felicitas, etc.

SECUNDUS (St) M.   R.M. Jan. 9
See Epictetus, Jucundus, etc.

SECUNDUS (St) M.   R.M. March 24
See Romulus and Secundus.

SECUNDUS (St) M.   R.M. March 29
d. 119. A patrician of Asti in Piedmont and
a subaltern officer in the imperial army.
He was beheaded at Asti under Hadrian.
Cf. Holw. — Baud.

SECUNDUS (St) Bp.   R.M. May 15
See Torquatus, Accitanus, etc.

SECUNDUS and Comp. (SS) MM.
          R.M. May 21
d. 357. Secundus, a priest of the church
of Alexandria, was martyred with a great
multitude of clergy and laity, including
many women, by the intruded Arian
patriarch George. The latter was supported in his occupation of the see of
Alexandria by the emperor Constantius,
the rightful patriarch, St Athanasius,
having been driven into exile.
Cf. Holw. — Baud.

SECUNDUS (St) M.   R.M. June 1
d. 304. An alleged martyr at Amelia,
drowned in the Tiber under Diocletian.
He is the patron saint of several places in
central Italy, but his historical existence
cannot be proved.
Cf. Holw. — Baud. — Att.

SECUNDUS (St) M.   R.M. July 31
See Democritus, Secundus and Dionysius

SECUNDUS (St) M.   R.M. Aug. 7
See Carpophorus, Exanthus, etc.

SECUNDUS (St) M.   R.M. Aug. 26
3rd cent. A legendary soldier, said to
have belonged to the Theban legion and to
have been martyred near Ventimiglia.
Cf. Att. — Baud. — Holw.

SECUNDUS, FIDENTIAN and VARICUS
(SS) MM.   R.M. Nov. 15
? Martyrs of Proconsular Africa, of whom
nothing is known.
Cf. Holw. — Baud.

SECUNDUS (St) M.   R.M. Dec. 19
See Darius, Zosimus, etc.

SECUNDUS (St) M.   R.M. Dec. 19
See Cyriacus, Paulillus, etc.

SECUNDUS (St) M. R.M. Dec. 29
See Dominic, Victor, etc.

SECURUS (St) M. R.M. Dec. 2
See Severus, Securus, etc.

SEDOPHA (St) M. R.M. July 5
See Marinus, Theodotus and Sedopha.

SEDUINUS (St) Bp. ? R.M. July 15
Possibly identical with St Swithin of Winchester, q.v.

SEINE (St) Ab. R.M. Sept. 19
Otherwise Sequanus, q.v.

SEIRIOL (St) C. A.C. Jan. 2
6th cent. A Welsh saint whose memory is perpetuated by the name of the island of Ynys-Seiriol.
Cf. Holw. — Baud.

SELESIUS (St) M. R.M. Sept. 12
See Hieronides, Leontius, etc.

SELEUCUS (St) M. R.M. Feb. 16
See Porphyrius and Seleucus.

SELEUCUS (St) R.M. March 24
? A Syrian saint honoured in the East and often described as a martyr. Our only record of him is in the Eastern calendars.
Cf. Holw. — Baud.

SELYF (St) M. A.C. June 25
Otherwise Solomon, q.v.

SENACH (SNACH) Bp. A.C. Aug. 3
6th cent. A disciple of St Finnian and his successor at Clonard.
Cf. Holw. — Baud.

SENAN (SENAMES) (St) Bp.
A.C. March 8
d. c.560. An Irish monk of Kilmanagh in Ossory. Having established a monastery, probably at Enniscorthy, he is said to have then visited Rome and on his way home to have stayed with St David in Wales. On his return to Ireland he founded more churches and monasteries, notably one at Inishcarra near Cork. Finally he settled on Scattery Island in the Shannon estuary, where he was buried. There are indications that he spent some time in Cornwall.
Cf. Att. — Baud. — Holw.

SENAN (St) H. A.C. Apr. 29
7th cent. Said to have been a hermit in N.

Wales. There is much confusion in the records of saints of this and similar names, and consequently it is impossible to give any precise account of them.
Cf. Holw. — Baud.

SENATOR (St) Bp. R.M. May 28
d. 480. A Milanese priest who, as a young man, attended the council of Chalcedon as a legate of Pope St Leo the Great. Afterwards he became archbishop of Milan.
Cf. Gams — Baud. — Att. — Holw.

SENATOR (St) Bp. A.C. May 28
d. 480. Bishop of Pavia.
Cf. Gams — Menzies — Holw.

SENATOR (St) R.M. Sept. 26
? A saint of Albanum, of whom nothing is known. Albanum may be Albano near Rome or Apt, the ancient Alba Helvetiorum, in S. France.
Cf. Holw. — Baud.

SENNEN (St) M. R.M. July 30
See Abdon and Sennen.

SENORINA (St) V. O.S.B. A.C. Apr. 22
d. 982. She was related to St Rudesind of Mondoñedo. Entrusted to the care of her aunt, the abbess Godina, at the convent of St John of Venaria (Vieyra), she joined the community and later became its abbess. As such she removed the community to Basto in the diocese of Braga. She is held in great veneration throughout Spanish Galicia and N. Portugal.
Cf. Zimm. — Att. — P. de U. — Holw. — Chev.

SEPTEMBER (Martyrs of) (BB)
A.C. Sept. 2-3
d. 1792. A group of one hundred and ninety-one martyrs who met their death during the French Revolution. They were imprisoned by the Legislative Assembly for refusing the oath to support the civil constitution of the clergy which had been condemned by the Holy See. They were massacred by the mob, with the connivance of the Assembly, on Sept. 2 and 3, 1792. The most prominent members of the group were: John Mary du Lau, archbishop of Arles, Francis de la Rochefoucauld, bishop of Beauvais, his brother Louis, bishop of Saintes, Augustine Ambrose Chevreux, O.S.B., last superior general of the Maurists, and Charles de la

Calmette, count of Valfons. One hundred and twenty were massacred at the Carmelite church (Les Carmes) in the rue de Rennes, Paris. Beatified in 1926. *Cf. Att.*

SEPTIMINUS, JANUARIUS and FELIX (SS) MM.   R.M. Aug. 28 and Sept. 1
A group among the Twelve Holy Brothers, q.v.

SEPTIMUS (St) M.   R.M. Aug. 17
See Liberatus, Boniface, etc.

SEPTIMUS (St) M.   R.M. Oct. 24
See Felix, Adauctus (Audactus), etc.

SEQUANUS (SEINE, SIGO) Ab.
     R.M. Sept. 19
d. c.580. Monk of Réomé and abbot-founder of a monastery at Segreste, diocese of Langres, which was later called after him Saint-Seine. *Cf. Holw. — Chev. — Att.*

SERAPHIA (St) V. M.   R.M. July 29
Otherwise Serapia, q.v.

SERAPHINA (or FINA) (St) V.
     A.C. March 12
d. 1253. Born at San Geminiano in Tuscany, she led a life of constant suffering, being the victim of repulsive diseases and continuous neglect. She was never a nun, but seems to have lived at home under the obedience of the Benedictines. She is greatly venerated at San Geminiano as Santa Fina. *Cf. Att. — Holw. — Baud.*

SERAPHINA SFORZA (Bl) V. Poor Clare.   A.C. Sept. 9
1434-1478. Born at Urbino, the daughter of Guido, count of Urbino and lord of Gubbio, she married in 1448 Alexander Sforza, duke of Pesaro, who treated her with great ignominy and expelled her from her home. She took refuge in the convent of Poor Clares and eventually professed their rule and became abbess. Beatified in 1754. *Cf. Holw. — Att. — Menzies.*

SERAPHINA (St)   R.M. July 29
d. ? c.426. The R.M. ascribes this saint to a *Civitas Mamiensis*, which some writers place in Armenia, others in Spain, others in Italy. *Cf. Holw. — Baud. — Menzies.*

SERAPHINUS (St) C. O.F.M.Cap.
     R.M. Oct. 12
1540-1604. Born at Montegranaro, he took the Capuchin habit as a lay-brother in 1556 and spent the whole of his uneventful life at the friary of Ascoli-Piceno. He is said to have been the spiritual adviser of high ecclesiastical and civil dignitaries. Canonized in 1767. *Cf. Holw. — Menzies — Att.*

SERAPIA (St) V. M.   R.M. July 29
d. 119. A slave of Syrian extraction in the household of St Sabina, whom she converted to the Faith. She was beheaded under Hadrian. *Cf. Holw. — Baud. — Menzies.*

SERAPION (St) M.   R.M. Feb. 25
See Victorinus, Victor, etc.

SERAPION (St) M.   R.M. Feb. 28
See Caerealis, Pupulus, etc.

SERAPION (St) Bp.   R.M. March 21
d. c.370. An Egyptian monk who was consecrated bishop of Thmuis in Lower Egypt and distinguished himself by his firm opposition to Arianism. He was a great friend of St Athanasius and of St Antony. He was the author of several works only one of which has survived, viz., his Euchologium, a valuable liturgical source discovered in 1899. *Cf. Att. — Holw. — Baud.*

SERAPION (St) M.   R.M. March 26
See Theodore, Irenaeus, etc.

SERAPION (St) M.   R.M. July 13
d. c.195. An oriental martyr who suffered under Septimius Severus, probably in Macedonia. *Cf. Holw. — Baud.*

SERAPION (St)   R.M. July 27
One of the Seven Sleepers, q.v.

SERAPION (St) M.   R.M. Aug. 18
See Hermas, Serapion and Polyaenus.

SERAPION (St) M.   R.M. Aug. 27
See Marcellinus, Mannaea, etc.

SERAPION (St) M.   R.M. Sept. 12
See Hieronides, Leontius, etc.

SERAPION (St) Bp.   R.M. Oct. 30
d. 199. A bishop of Antioch praised by

Eusebius and St Jerome for his theological writings, which however are no longer extant.

Cf. Att. — Baud. — Holw.

SERAPION (St) M. **R.M. Nov. 14**
d. 252. A martyr of Alexandria who perished in a riot raised against the Christians. The mob cast him down from the roof of his own house, a high building.

Cf. Baud. — Holw. — Att.

SERAPION (St) M. **R.M. Nov. 14**
d. 1240. Said to have been born in England and to have fought against the Moors in Spain under the banner of Castile. In Spain he joined the Mercedarian Order and surrendered himself as a hostage at Algiers, where he was crucified for preaching the gospel while awaiting his ransom. Cult confirmed, as a saint, in 1728.

Cf. P. de U. — Att. — Holw.

SERDOT (St) Bp. **R.M. Sept. 12**
Otherwise Sacerdos, q.v.

SERENA (St) **R.M. Aug. 16**
d. c.290. Described in the R.M. as "sometime wife of the emperor Diocletian," but this information is derived from the spurious Acts of St Cyriacus.

Cf. Holw. — Baud. — Menzies.

SERENICUS Ab. and SERENUS H. (SS) O.S.B. **A.C. May 7**
d. c.669. Two brothers belonging to a patrician family of Spoleto. They received the Benedictine habit at the tomb of the apostles, which was then in Benedictine custody. Later they settled in France as hermits near the river Sarthe. Serenus remained a hermit till the end of his life, but Serenicus became the head of a community of some one hundred and forty disciples who gathered round him. On these he imposed the Benedictine Rule and other Roman practices.

Cf. Mab. — Zimm. — Att.

SERENUS (St) M. **R.M. Feb. 23**
Otherwise Sirenus, q.v.

SERENUS (St) H. O.S.B. **A.C. May 7**
See Serenicus and Serenus.

SERENUS (St) M. **R.M. June 28**
Two of this name are registered as fellow-sufferers with St Plutarch, q.v.

SERENUS (St) Bp. **A.C. Aug. 9**
d. 606. Bishop of Marseilles. St Gregory wrote him several letters, in which he recommended to him the Roman missionaries travelling to England and twice reprimanded him for his iconoclastic tendencies.

Cf. Duch. Fast. Episc. — Gams — Holw. — Baud.

SERF (St) Bp. **A.C. July 1**
Otherwise Servan, q.v.

SERGIUS (St) M. **R.M. Feb. 24**
d. 304. A monk, perhaps a priest, in Cappadocia, martyred under Diocletian. His relics are said to have been translated to Ubeda, near Tarragona, in Spain.

Cf. Holw. — Baud.

SERGIUS (St) M. **R.M. July 27**
See Maurus and Sergius.

SERGIUS (St) Pope. **R.M. Sept. 8**
d. 701. Of Syrian parentage, but born at Palermo in Sicily and admitted to membership of the Roman clergy, Sergius governed the Church as Pope from 687 to 701. He opposed the interference of the Byzantine emperors in ecclesiastical affairs and rejected the false synod known as Trullanum. He blessed and fostered the missionary enterprise of the English monks in Friesland and Germany and defended St Wilfrid.

Cf. Baud. — Holw. — Att.

SERGIUS and BACCHUS (SS) MM. **R.M. Oct. 7**
d. 303. High officers of the Roman army in Syria. For refusing to join in pagan sacrifices they were dressed in women's clothes and led through the streets of Arabissus. Then Bacchus was beaten to death, and Sergius was beheaded a week later.

Cf. Att. — Holw. — Baud.

SERLO (Bl) Ab. O.S.B. **P.C. March 3**
d. 1104. A Norman by birth, he became a canon of Avranches and later a Benedictine monk at Mont Saint-Michel. Four years later (1074), on the recommendation of St Osmund, he was appointed abbot of Gloucester, receiving the abbatial blessing from St Wulstan. When he arrived at Gloucester the community consisted of two adult monks and eight boys: when he died he left a community of over one

hundred professed monks. He was noted for his building activities and his fearless defence of ecclesiastical rights and the moral law.
Cf. Zimm. — Att. — Chev. — Holw. — Baud.

SERLO (Bl) Ab. O.S.B.Cist.
A.C. Sept. 10
d. 1158. A Benedictine of Chérisy who became abbot of Savigny in 1140. He united the whole congregation of Savigny to the Cistercians in 1147 and was thenceforward a devoted member of the latter order.
Cf. Zimm. — Holw.

SERNIN (St) Bp. M.   R.M. Nov. 29
Otherwise Saturninus, q.v.

SEROTINA (St) M.   R.M. Dec. 31
See Donata, Paulina, etc.

SERVAN (SERF, SAIR) (St) Bp.
A.C. July 1
? Apostle of the Orkney Islands. The traditions concerning him are very contradictory and extravagant. He died and was buried at Culross.
Cf. Holw.

SERVANDUS and GERMANUS (SS) MM.   R.M. Oct. 23
d. c.305. Said to have been sons of St Marcellus of León. They were put to death at Cadiz while on their way under arrest to Tangiers. They are held in great veneration throughout S. Spain.
Cf. P. de U. — Holw. — Baud.

SERVATUS (French: SERVAIS) (St) Bp.
R.M. May 13
d. 384. Bishop of Tangres in the Low Countries. He was the host of St Athanasius when the latter was an exile in the West.
Cf. Att. — Baud. — Duch. Fast. Episc. — Gams — Holw.

SERVILIANUS (St) M.   R.M. Apr. 20
See Sulpicius and Servilianus.

SERVILIUS (St) M.   R.M. May 24
See Zoëllus, Servilius, etc.

SERVITE MARTYRS (BB) A.C. Aug. 31
d. 1420. Sixty-four Servite friars burnt to death in their church at Prague by the Hussites. The group included four friars

from Tuscany who had been sent to Bohemia to preach against the Hussite heresy. Cult confirmed in 1918.
Cf. Att. — Holw.

SERVULUS (St) M.   R.M. Feb. 21
See Verulus, Secundinus, etc.

SERVULUS (St) C.   R.M. Dec. 23
d. c.590. A cripple who begged for alms at the door of the church of St Clement in Rome, sharing what he received with other beggars. St Gregory the Great describes the beautiful scene of Servulus's death.
Cf. Att. — Baud. — Holw.

SERVUS (St) M.   R.M. Aug. 17
See Liberatus, Boniface, etc.

SERVUS (St) M.   R.M. Dec. 7
d. 483. A layman of noble birth in Proconsular Africa. He was seized and tortured to death under the Arian Vandal king Hunneric.
Cf. Holw. — Baud.

SERVUS-DEI (St) M.   R.M. Jan. 13
See Gumesindus and Servus-Dei.

SERVUS-DEI (St) M.   R.M. Sept. 16
See Rogelius and Servus-Dei.

SETHRIDA (SAETHRYTH) (St) Abs. O.S.B.   A.C. Jan. 10
d. c.660. Stepdaughter of Anna, king of the East Saxons (635-644). She became a nun at Faremoutiers-en-Brie under St Fara, whom she succeeded as abbess. She was half-sister to SS Ethelreda and Ethelburga.
Cf. Zimm. — Att. — Chev. — Baud. — Holw.

SEVEN ANGELS who stand before the throne of God.   A.C. Apr. 20
See Tob. XII 15; Apoc. VIII, 2-5. The names usually given to them are Michael, Gabriel, Raphael (these three names occur in the Bible), Uriel, Shealtiel, Jehudiel and Berachiel. A church at Palermo is dedicated to the Seven Angels, their feast being observed there on Apr. 20.
Cf. Holw.

SEVEN APOSTLES of BULGARIA (SS) CC.   A.C. July 17
The Bulgarians venerate liturgically their first seven apostles; they are, besides the well-known Cyril and Methodius, q.v., Gorazd, Nahum, Sabas, Angelarius and

Clement of Okarida. The last-named, who is the most important after Cyril and Methodius, died on July 17, 916.
Cf. Att. — Holw.

SEVEN BROTHERS (SS) MM.
R.M. July 10
d. c.150. The seven alleged sons of the Roman martyr Felicitas, q.v. Their names are: Januarius, Felix and Philip, scourged to death; Sylvanus, thrown over a precipice; Alexander, Vitalis and Martial, beheaded. They seem to have suffered at Rome under Antoninus Pius. Modern scholars deny that they were brothers: the fact that they were commemorated on the same day led to the legend of their being related by blood and the sons of Felicitas.
Cf Holw. — Att. — Baud.

SEVEN HOLY FOUNDERS (SS)
R.M. Feb. 12
Their names are: Bonfilio Monaldo, Alexis Falconieri, Benedict (Amadeus) dell' Antella, Bartholomew (Hugh) Amidei, Ricovero (Sostenes) Ugoccioni, Gherardino (Manettus) Sostegni, and John Buonagiunta. They were young Florentine members of the Confraternity of Our Lady who, on Aug. 15, 1233, in obedience to a vision of the Mother of God, withdrew to Mt Senario and laid the foundation of the Order of the Servants of Mary, known as Servites. The chief devotion of this Order is to the Seven Sorrows of Our Lady. Bonfilio was the first superior general, Buonagiunta the second, Manettus the fourth. Amadaeus was first prior of Carfaggio. Hugh and Sostenes established the order in France and Germany respectively. Alexis remained a laybrother and was the last to die (1310). They were canonized conjointly by Leo XIII in 1887, when their common feast was added to the Roman Missal for the universal Church.
Cf. Att. — Baud. — Holw.

SEVEN SAINTLY ROBBERS (SS) MM.
R.M. Apr. 29
See Corfu (Martyrs of)

SEVEN SLEEPERS (SS) MM.
R.M. July 27
250-362. The legend of the Seven Sleepers states that seven youths of Ephesus were walled up in a cave under Decius in the year 250 and were found alive there in the time of Theodosius II (362), having spent the intervening period in sleep. The R.M. gives their names as: Maximian, Malchus, Martinian, Dionysius, John, Serapion and Constantine. There are, however, three or four sets of different names and a large number of variants of the legend. One of the most ingenuous of these was written by St James of Sarug in Syriac (c.500). The origin of the legend is probably to be traced to the discovery of some forgotten relics. Baronius, although he included the *memoria* of the Seven Sleepers in the R.M., doubted the authenticity of their story.
Cf. Holw. — Att. — Baud.

SEVERA (St) V. Abs.   R.M. July 20
d. c.680. Sister of St Modoald, bishop of Trèves. First abbess of St Gemma (later Sainte-Sevère) at Villeneuve, diocese of Bourges.
Cf. Holw. — Baud.

SEVERA (St) Abs. O.S.B.   A.C. July 20
d. c.750. Benedictine abbess of the great nunnery of Oehren at Trèves.
Cf. Zimm.

SEVERIAN and AQUILA (SS) MM.
R.M. Jan. 23
? A husband and wife martyred at Julia Caesarea in Mauritania.
Cf. Holw. — Baud.

SEVERIAN (St) Bp. M.   R.M. Feb. 21
d. c.452. A bishop of Scythopolis (Bethsan) in Galilee who, on his return from the council of Chalcedon, was murdered by the Eutychian heretics with the connivance of the empress Eudoxia.
Cf. Holw. — Att. — Baud.

SEVERIAN (St) M.   R.M. Apr. 20
See Victor, Zoticus, etc.

SEVERIAN (St) M.   R.M. Sept. 9
d. 322. An Armenian senator who, having witnessed the martyrdom of the forty martyrs of Sebaste, openly professed his Christianity and was torn with iron rakes until he died. He suffered at Sebaste under Licinius.
Cf. Holw. — Baud.

SEVERIAN (St) M.   R.M. Nov. 8
One of the Four Crowned Martyrs, q.v.

SEVERINUS (St) Ab.   R.M. Jan. 8
d. 476. An Eastern hermit who undertook

the evangelization of Noricum (corresponding to modern Austria), where he established several monastic foundations, notably one on the Danube near Vienna, where he died. Six years after his death the monks were driven from the country and carried his relics to Naples, where the great Benedictine monastery of San Severino was built to enshrine them. *Cf. Holw. — Menzies — Baud. — Att.*

SEVERINUS (St) Bp.   R.M. Jan. 8
? Under this date the R.M. commemorates a St Severinus, bishop at Naples, brother of St Victorinus M. There is here apparently a confusion between the saint noticed above and St Severinus of Septempeda (June 8), brother of St Victorinus of Camerino. *Cf. Holw. — Baud. — Att.*

SEVERINUS (St) Ab.   R.M. Feb. 11
d. ? 507. A Burgundian said to have been the abbot of Agaunum in Switzerland. He is also alleged to have restored to health Clovis, first Christian king of the Franks. The historical evidence for these assertions is not good. *Cf. Holw. — Baud. — Att.*

SEVERINUS (St) Bp.   R.M. June 8
d. 550. Bishop of Septempeda, now called after him Sanseverino, in the Marches of Ancona. He and his brother Victorinus distributed their great wealth among the poor and became hermits at Montenero. They were forced by Pope Vigilius (540) to become bishops, the former of Septempeda, the latter of Camerino. Severinus died shortly before Septempeda was destroyed by Totila the Ostrogoth. *Cf. Holw. — Baud. — Att.*

SEVERINUS (St) M.   R.M. July 6
See Lucy, Antoninus, etc.

SEVERINUS (St) M.   R.M. Aug. 7
See Carpophorus, Exanthus, etc.

SEVERINUS (St) Bp.   R.M. Oct. 23
d. c.403. Said to have been born at Bordeaux. He was bishop of Cologne and a prominent opponent of Arianism. *Cf. Gams — Baud. — Holw. — Att.*

SEVERINUS (French: SEURIN) (St) Bp.   R.M. Oct. 23
d. c.420. Said to have been an oriental by birth. He was bishop of Bordeaux c.405-c.420. *Cf. Att. — Duch. Fast. Episc. — Gams — Holw.*

SEVERINUS BOËTHIUS (St) M.
A.C. Oct. 23
d. 525. Anicius Manlius Torquatus Severinus Boëthius is known to history as a Roman statesman in the service of Theodoric the Ostrogoth and as an eminent philosopher, author of *De consolatione philosophiae*. About the year 534 he fell into disfavour with the barbarian king and was beheaded at Pavia after a long imprisonment. His relics are enshrined at the cathedral of Pavia, where his feast is observed. His feast is also kept at the church of Santa Maria in Portico, Rome. Cult confirmed in 1883. *Cf. Holw. — Chev. — Att.*

SEVERINUS (St) H. O.S.B.
R.M. Nov. 1
d. c.699. A Benedictine monk who lived as a hermit at Tivoli. His relics are in the church of St Laurence at Tivoli. *Cf. Holw. — Baud. — Zimm.*

SEVERINUS, EXUPERIUS and FELICIAN (SS) MM.   R.M. Nov. 19
d. 170. Martyrs of Vienne in Gaul under Marcus Aurelius. *Cf. Baud. — Holw.*

SEVERINUS (St) H.   R.M. Nov. 27
d. c.540. A hermit who lived first at Paris and then in a cell at Novientum near Paris. *Cf. Holw. — Baud.*

SEVERINUS (St) Bp.   R.M. Dec. 21
d. c.300. Bishop of Trèves. *Cf. Holw. — Chev.*

SEVERUS (St) M.   R.M. Jan. 11
See Peter, Severus and Leucius.

SEVERUS (St) Bp.   R.M. Feb. 1
d. c.348. A native of Ravenna who became bishop of that city in 283. He accompanied the papal legate to the synod of Sardica (344). *Cf. Holw. — Menzies — Baud.*

SEVERUS (St) Bp.   A.C. Feb. 1
d. c.690. Born of poor parents in the Cotentin, he became successively priest, abbot and bishop of Avranches. Before his

death he resigned his see and returned to monastic life.
Cf. Holw. — Baud. — Chev.

SEVERUS (St) C.   **R.M. Feb. 15**
d. c.530. A parish priest of Interocrea (Androcca) in the Abruzzi. St Gregory the Great relates that one day, when he was pruning his vine, he was summoned to the death-bed of one of his parishioners. He finished his pruning before answering the call, with the result that the sick man died before he arrived. Such were the prayers and tears of Severus that the dead man came to life again and lived another seven days in which to do penance and receive the sacraments. The relics of Severus were translated to Münster-Maifeld, diocese of Trèves, in the 10th century.
Cf. Baud. — Holw. — Menzies.

SEVERUS (St) Bp.   **R.M. Apr. 29**
d. 409. Bishop of Naples and a famous wonder-worker. He raised a dead man to life in order that he should bear witness in favour of his persecuted widow.
Cf. Menzies — Baud. — Holw.

SEVERUS (St) C.   **R.M. Aug. 8**
d. p. 445. A priest who came from afar (some accounts say from India) and evangelized the district round Vienne in Gaul.
Cf. Baud. — Holw.

SEVERUS, MEMNON and Comp. (SS) MM.   **R.M. Aug. 20**
d. c.300. Severus was a priest and Memnon a centurion at Bizya in Thrace, where they were beheaded for the faith. Thirty-seven Christian soldiers from Philippopolis were at the same time thrown into a furnace.
Cf. Holw. — Baud.

SEVERUS (St) C.   **R.M. Oct. 1**
This saint seems to be identical with Severus, Feb. 15, q.v.

SEVERUS (St) Bp.   **R.M. Oct. 15**
d. c.455. Born in Gaul, he was a disciple of St Germanus of Auxerre and of St Lupus of Troyes. He accompanied Germanus to Britain to oppose the Pelagian heresy. He preached the gospel to the Germans on the lower Moselle and became bishop of Trèves (446-c.455).
Cf. Gams — Holw. — Baud.

SEVERUS (St) M.   **R.M. Oct. 22**
See Philip, Severus, etc.

SEVERUS (St) Bp. M.   **R.M. Nov. 6**
d. 633. Bishop of Barcelona, martyred under the Arian Visigoths, who put him to death by driving nails into his temples. He is a minor patron of Barcelona.
Cf. Gams — P. de U. — Holw. — Baud.

SEVERUS (St) M.   **R.M. Nov. 8**
One of the Four Crowned Martyrs, q.v.

SEVERUS, SECURUS, JANUARIUS and VICTORINUS (SS) MM.   **R.M. Dec. 2**
d. c.450. African martyrs who suffered under the Vandals.
Cf. Holw. — Baud.

SEVERUS (Bl) Bp. O.S.B.   **P.C. Dec. 9**
d. 1067. A Benedictine of Brevnov who became bishop of Prague (1031-1067) and was noted for his activities as a builder of churches. He is always styled either saint or blessed by Czech hagiographers.
Cf. Holw. — Zimm. — Gams.

SEVERUS (St) M.   **R.M. Dec. 30**
See Mansuetus, Severus, etc.

SEXBURGA (St) W. Abs. O.S.B.   **A.C. July 6**
d. c.699. Daughter of Anna, king of the East Angles, sister of SS Etheldreda, Ethelburga and Withburga, and half-sister of St Sethrida. She married Erconbert, king of Kent, by whom she became the mother of SS Ermengilda and Ermengota. As queen she founded the nunnery of Minster in Sheppey. Left a widow after twenty-four years of happy married life, she became a nun at Milton in Kent, whence she migrated to Ely, where she became abbess.
Cf. Att. — Zimm. — Stanton — Holw.

SEXTUS (St) M.   **R.M. Dec. 31**
See Stephen, Pontian, etc.

SEZIN (St) Bp.   **A.C. March 6**
d. c.529. A native of Britain who laboured in Ireland at the time of St Patrick and then crossed over to Guic-Sezni in Brittany, where he is said to have founded a monastery and where his relics are now venerated.
Cf. Chev. — Holw.

SIAGRIUS (St) (*several*).
Otherwise Syagrius, q.v.

SIARDUS (SIARD) (St) O.Praem.
                                        P.C. Nov. 13
d. 1230. Premonstratensian abbot of
Mariengaarden in Frisia (1196-1230).
Cf. Chev. — Holw. — Baud.

SIBYLLINA BISCOSSI (Bl) V. O.P.
                              A.C. March 23
1287-1367. Born at Pavia and left an
orphan, at the age of twelve she became
blind and was adopted by a community of
Dominican tertiaries. In 1302 she retired
to a cell near the Dominican friary at
Pavia, and there she lived as a recluse till
the age of eighty, doing penance and working miracles. Cult approved in 1853.
Cf. Holw. — Att. — Chev.

SIDNEY HODGSON (Bl) M.
                              A.C. Dec. 10
d. 1591. A layman and a convert hanged
at Tyburn for relieving priests. Beatified
in 1929.
Cf. Newdigate.

SIDONIUS APOLLINARIS (St) Bp.
                              R.M. Aug. 21
c.430-c.488. Caius Sollius Apollinaris
Sidonius was born at Lyons and ranks as
one of the last of the great Gallo-Romans.
He was first a soldier and married the
daughter of Avitus, emperor of the West.
Next he served the state as chief senator
and prefect of Rome. After his term of
office he retired to his country estate in
Gaul, and while there, although a married
man, he was promoted to the see of Clermont. As a bishop he saved his people
from the fury of the Gothic invaders under
Alaric, for which purpose he not only
employed skilful diplomacy but also instituted days of public prayers called
"Rogation Days." Sidonius was a man
of letters. He wrote Latin verse with
facility, but his letters are now much more
important than the twenty-four poems of
his which are still extant.
Cf. Holw. — Baud. — Att. — Chev.

SIDONIUS (French: SAËNS) (St) Ab.
O.S.B.   **A.C. Nov. 14**
d. c.690. An Irishman who became a
monk at Jumièges under St Philibert
(644). Later he was appointed by St
Ouen first abbot of a small monastery
which that bishop had founded near

Rouen: this monastery was in after ages
called Saint-Saëns.
Cf. Zimm. — Holw. — Baud. — Chev.

SIDRONIUS (St) M.   **R.M. July 11**
d. c.270. A Roman martyr under Aurelian. In the Middle Ages his relics were
translated to Flanders. Another St Sidronius is venerated at Sens in France.
The history of the two saints has been confused, and the traditions concerning them
are untrustworthy.
Cf. Holw. — Baud.

SIDWELL (SATIVOLA) (St) V. M.
                              A.C. Aug. 1
? Probably of British (not Anglo-Saxon)
lineage. She is said to have lived in the
West of England, and there are churches
dedicated to her in Devonshire, chiefly in
the neighbourhood of Exeter. Particulars of her life, and as to how she came to
be venerated as a martyr, are lacking.
Cf. Holw. — Stanton.

**SIFFRED (SIFFREIN, SYFFROY, SUF-
FREDUS) (St) Bp.**   **A.C. Nov. 27**
d. 540 (or 660 ?). A native of Albano,
near Rome, who became a monk at Lérins
and later bishop of Carpentras in Provence, where he is now venerated as the
principal patron saint of the diocese.
*Cf. Gams — Duch. Fast. Episc. — Holw.
— Baud. — Chev.*

SIGEBERT (St) King.   **A.C. Feb. 1**
d. 656. Sigebert III, son of Dagobert I,
was king of Austrasia, i.e., Eastern France.
Under the influence of Bl Pepin of Landen,
of St Cunibert of Cologne and of other
saintly persons, the young king grew up to
be a clean-living and pious man. He died
at the age of twenty-five. Though not a
very successful monarch, he was revered
as the founder of numerous hospitals,
churches and monasteries. The abbeys
of Stavelot and Malmédy were founded by
him.
Cf. Att. — Holw. — Chev. — Baud.

SIGEBERT (St) King M. O.S.B.
                              A.C. Sept. 27
d. 635. The first Christian king of East
Anglia. He was baptized in France and,
assisted by SS Felix and Fursey, he introduced Christianity into his realm. He
took the monastic habit (at Dunwich ?),
but was forcibly removed from the cloister
by his warrior subjects and fell while lead-

ing them in battle against Penda of Mercia. His opponents being pagans, he was venerated as a martyr.
Cf. Holw. — Chev. — Stanton.

SIGFRID (St) Bp. O.S.B. A.C. Feb. 15
d. c.1045. An English priest and monk, probably of Glastonbury. At the invitation of King Olaf of Norway he went to that country as a missionary and fixed his residence at Wexlow. Great success attended his efforts, one of his converts being Olaf, king of Sweden. He is said to have been canonized by Pope Adrian IV.
Cf. Zimm. — Att. — Dublin Rev., 1885, pp. 182 sqq.

SIGFRID (St) Ab. O.S.B. A.C. Aug. 22
d. 688. Monk and disciple of St Benet Biscop, by whom he was appointed abbot of Wearmouth in 686. They died in the same year.
Cf. Zimm. — Att. — Holw.

SIGFRID (Bl) Mk. O.S.B. A.C. Dec. 15
d. 1215. A Benedictine monk of Reinhardsbrunn in Thuringia. From the year 1212 he lived as a hermit at Georgenberg.
Cf. Zimm.

SIGHARDUS (Bl) Ab. O.S.B.Cist.
A.C. Apr. 5
d. 1162. Cistercian monk of Jouy. In 1141 he founded and became the first abbot of Bonlieu, or Carbon-Blanc, near Bordeaux.
Cf. Zimm.

SIGIBALD (St) Bp. A.C. Oct. 26
d. c.740. Bishop of Metz 716-c.740. He was a promoter of learning, a builder of schools and abbeys (notably Neuweiter and Saint-Avold) and an able administrator.
Cf. Gams — Holw.

SIGIRANUS (CYRAN, SIRAN, SIG-RAM) (St) Ab. O.S.B. A.C. Dec. 5
d. c.655 (or 690 ?). Born of a noble Frankish family, he was first cup-bearer at the court of Clotaire II and later archdeacon of Tours, of which city his father was bishop. Ultimately he became a monk and abbot-founder of Meobecq and of Lonrey (Longoretum). The latter was afterwards called after him Saint-Cyran.
Cf. Zimm. — Att. — Chev. — Holw.

SIGISBERT, Ab. and PLACID, M. (SS)
A.C. July 11
d. c.650 (or c.750 ?). Sigisbert was the abbot-founder of the great Benedictine abbey of Dissentis in Switzerland. He built it on land given him by St Placid, a wealthy landowner who joined the new community as a monk and was later murdered for defending the ecclesiastical rights of the abbey. Sigisbert survived him several years. Cult approved in 1905.
Cf. Zimm. — Att. — Holw. — Baud.

SIGISMUND (St) King, M. R.M. May 1
d. 523. A Vandal by extraction and disposition, he was king of the Burgundians for one year. During that period he ordered one of his sons to be strangled for rebuking his step-mother. He atoned for this sin by giving generously to the Church and the poor. Being defeated in battle he disguised himself in a monk's habit and hid in a cell near the abbey of Agaunum, which he had built. There he was found by his enemies and put to death. He is honoured as a martyr.
Cf. Att. — Baud. — Holw.

SIGOLENA (SEGOULÈME) (St) Abs. O.S.B. A.C. July 24
d. c.769. Daughter of a nobleman of Aquitaine and a widow early in life, she became a nun in the convent of Troclar on the Tarn, S. France, where she was later chosen abbess. She is co-patroness of the diocese of Albi.
Cf. Holw. — Baud. — Chev.

SIGOLINUS (SIGHELM) (St) Ab. O.S.B.
A.C. Oct. 29
d. c.670. Abbot of Stavelot and Malmédy, in Belgium.
Cf. Holw. — Chev. — Zimm.

SIGRADA (St) N. O.S.B. A.C. Aug. 8
d. c.678. Mother of SS Leodegarius and Warinus. In her widowhood she became a nun in the convent of St Marianus at Soissons. She died shortly after the martyrdom of her two sons, victims of the cruelty of Ebroin, mayor of the palace.
Cf. Zimm. — Holw. — Chev.

SILAS (or SILVANUS) (St) C.
R.M. July 13
1st cent. Silas, disciple and companion of St Paul, is mentioned both as Silas (Acts

XV 22; XVIII 5) and as Silvanus (2 Cor. I, 19; Thess. I, 1; 2 Thess. I, 1; 1 Pet. V, 12). Legend makes him the first bishop of Corinth. The Greeks distinguish Silas from Silvanus and commemorate both on July 20.
Cf. Holw. — Att. — Baud.

SILAUS (SILAVE, SILANUS) (St) Bp.
A.C. May 17
d. 1100. Said to have been an Irish bishop who died at Lucca on his way back from a pilgrimage to Rome. He is the subject of many extravagant legends.
Cf. Holw. — Baud.

SILIN (SULIAN) (St) C.   A.C. Sept. 1
6th cent. A prince of N. Wales who became a hermit on an island off the coast of Anglesey. Later he became a missionary in Brittany.
Cf. Chev. — Holw.

SILLAN (SILVANUS) (St) Ab.
A.C. Feb. 28
d. c.610. A disciple of St Congath at Bangor and his second successor as abbot of that monastery.
Cf. Holw. — Baud. — Chev.

SILVANUS, LUKE and MUCIUS (SS)
MM.   R.M. Feb. 6
d. 312. Silvanus was bishop of Emesa in Phoenicia, Luke his deacon, and Mucius his lector. After long imprisonment the three were martyred under Maximian. The R.M. identifies this Silvanus with the companion of Tyrannio, q.v., infra.
Cf. Holw. — Baud.

SILVANUS (St) Bp.   R.M. Feb. 10
? Bishop of Terracina. He is described as a "Confessor," which would mean that he had suffered for the Faith, by imprisonment, or torture, or even death.
Cf. Holw. — Baud.

SILVANUS (St) M.   R.M. Feb. 18
See Lucius, Silvanus, etc.

SILVANUS (St) Bp. M.   R.M. Feb. 20
See Tyrannio, Silvanus, etc.

SILVANUS (St) M.   R.M. March 8
See Cyril, Rogatus, etc.

SILVANUS and Comp. (SS) MM.
R.M. May 4
d. c.311. A group of forty-one martyrs

from Egypt and Palestine, of whose martyrdom an account is given by Eusebius. Silvanus was bishop of Gaza and was sentenced to the mines in Palestine, but being too old for heavy work, he was beheaded instead, together with forty others similarly incapacitated.
Cf. Holw. — Baud.

SILVANUS (St) M.   R.M. May 5
? A Roman martyr.
Cf. Holw. — Baud.

SILVANUS (St) H.   A.C. May 15
4th cent. An actor who left the world and became a monk at Tabennisi under St Pachomius. After twenty years of monastic life he became lax and was excommunicated by Pachomius. This led to a second conversion and to the beginning of a new life of sanctification. He is honoured by the Greeks.
Cf. Holw. — Chev.

SILVANUS (St) M.   R.M. May 24
See Zoellus, Servilius, etc.

SILVANUS (St) M.   R.M. July 10
One of the Seven Brothers, MM., q.v.

SILVANUS (St) M.   R.M. July 10
See Bianor and Silvanus

SILVANUS (St) M.   R.M. Sept. 4
See Rufinus, Silvanus and Vitalicus.

SILVANUS (St)   R.M. Sept. 22
? A saint venerated from ancient times at Levroux, diocese of Bourges. Legend identifies him with the Zacchaeus of the gospel.
Cf. Holw. — Chev. — Baud.

SILVANUS (St) M.   R.M. Nov. 5
See Domninus, Theotimus, etc.

SILVANUS (St) Bp.   R.M. Dec. 2
d. c.450. A monk at Constantinople. Later bishop of Troas in Phrygia.
Cf. Holw. — Baud.

SILVERIUS (St) Pope, M. R.M. June 20
d. c.537. A native of Frosinone in Campania and son of Pope St Hormisdas. He was only a sub-deacon when promoted to the Roman see. For refusing to countenance the restoration of the monophysite bishop Anthimos to the see of Constantinople he incurred the violent hatred of the

empress Theodora. He was summarily condemned on a charge of high treason, deported to the East and finally banished to an islet off Naples, where he was left to die of privation, or perhaps actually murdered.
Cf. Att. — Holw. — Baud.

SILVESTER (St) Ab.　　　**A.C. Apr. 15**
d. c.625. Second abbot of Moutier-Saint-Jean (Réome), diocese of Dijon.
Cf. Holw. — Baud. — Chev.

SILVESTER VENTURA (Bl) Mk. O.S.B.
A.C. June 9
d. 1348. A native of Florence and a carder and bleacher of wool by trade. At the age of forty he joined the Camaldolese at S. Maria degli Angeli at Florence as a lay-brother and served the community as cook. He was favoured with ecstasies and heavenly visions, and the angels were wont to come and cook for him. His spiritual advice was much sought after.
Cf. Zimm. — Att. — Baud. — Holw.

SILVESTER (St) Bp.　　　**R.M. Nov. 20**
d. c.525. Bishop of Châlons-sur-Saône from c.484 to c.525. St Gregory of Tours describes him as "the glory of confessors."
Cf. Gams — Duch. Fast. Episc. — Holw. — Baud.

SILVESTER GOZZOLINI (St) Ab. O.S.B.
R.M. Nov. 26
1177-1267. Born at Osimo, he read law at Padua and Bologna, then became a secular priest and canon at Osimo. Later he retired to live as a hermit at Monte-fano, near Fabriano. In 1231, directed by St Benedict in a vision, he instituted a new congregation of Benedictines known from the colour of their habit as the Blue Benedictines. The congregation spread rapidly, and Silvester governed it "with unbounded wisdom and gentleness" for thirty-six years. It was approved by Innocent IV in 1247. St Silvester represents the new efflorescence of Benedictinism in Italy which synchronized with the foundation of the new orders of friars. He was equivalently canonized in 1598.
Cf. Zimm. — Holw. — Att. — Chev.

SILVESTER (St) Pope.　　　**R.M. Dec. 31**
d. 335. Silvester was a Roman, and governed the Church as Pope from 314 to 335. In 313 Constantine had, by the Edict of Milan, granted toleration to Christianity, and Silvester was therefore enabled to govern the Church free from persecution. Very little that is historically certain is known about his life, though there are various legends which connect his name with that of Constantine. During his pontificate the first general council was held at Nicaea to deal with the Arian heresy, and he was represented at the council by bishop Hosius of Cordova. The major part of his remains are enshrined at San Silvestro in Capite, Rome.
Cf. Att. — Holw. — Menzies — Chev.

SILVINUS (St) Bp. O.S.B. R.M. Feb. 17
d. c.720. A courtier who became a regionary bishop and evangelized the district round Thérouanne. After some forty years of unceasing apostolate, a feature of which was the ransoming of numerous slaves, he retired to the Benedictine abbey of Auchy-les-Moines, where he lived the few remaining years of his life as a monk.
Cf. Holw. — Att. — Chev.

SILVINUS (St) Bp.　　　**R.M. Sept. 12**
d. c.550. Bishop of Verona. Nothing further is known about him.
Cf. Holw. — Menzies.

SILVINUS (St) Bp.　　　**R.M. Sept. 28**
d. 444. Bishop of Brescia. He was raised to the episcopate in extreme old age.
Cf. Menzies — Holw.

SILVIUS (St) M.　　　**R.M. Apr. 21**
See Arator, Fortunatus, etc.

SIMBERT (SIMPERT, SINTBERT) (St) Bp. O.S.B.　　　**A.C. Oct. 13**
d. c.809. Pupil, monk and abbot at the abbey of Murbach, near Colmar in Alsace. In 778 he was made bishop of Augsburg, but retained the government of Murbach. He was a remarkable prelate in every respect, but especially as a restorer of ecclesiastical discipline and studies. Canonized by Nicholas V.
Cf. Gams — Holw. — Baud.

SIMEON STYLITES the ELDER (St) H.
R.M. Jan. 5
390-459. Born at Sis in Cilicia, the son of a shepherd and a shepherd himself in his youth. He joined a community of Syrian monks but was dismissed on account of his excessive austerities. He then became a hermit attaching himself by chains to a

rock, but so many people came to see him that, in order to gain greater solitude, he took to living on a platform mounted on a pillar. He gradually raised the height of the pillar till it reached sixty-six feet, and it was on the flat summit of this, about three feet in width, that he spent the remaining thirty-seven years of his life: hence the name Stylites, which means "raised on a pillar." For forty years he passed the whole of Lent without taking any food. His pillar stood on a hill on the borders of Syria and Cilicia, and the wild tribes of the desert flocked to him for baptism and spiritual advice. The above facts are quite authentic, being based on the testimony of eye-witnesses.
Cf. Holw. — Att. — Baud.

SIMEON (St) Bp. M.   R.M. Feb. 18
d. c.107. The son of Cleophas and a kinsman of our Lord (Mat. XIII 55; Mk. VI 3; John XIX 25). He succeeded St James the Less in the see of Jerusalem and was crucified in extreme old age under Trajan.
Cf. Holw. — Att. — Baud.

SIMEON of TRENT (St) M.
R.M. March 24
d. 1475. A child living at Trent in N. Italy who is said to have been murdered by Jews at Eastertide out of hatred of Christ. The confession of the Jews was obtained under torture. The trial was reviewed and approved at Rome by Sixtus IV in 1478.
Cf. Holw. — Att. (both under "Simon").

SIMEON, ABDECHALAS, ANANIAS, USTHAZANES, PUSICIUS and Comp.
R.M. Apr. 21
d. 341. Persian martyrs under Shapur II. Simeon was bishop of Seleucia-Ctesiphon, Abdechalas and Ananias his priests, Usthazanes the king's tutor (a repentant apostate), and Pusicius the overseer of the king's workmen. They suffered with a band of over one hundred other Christians — bishops, priests and clerics of various ranks. Pusicius's virgin daughter was also martyred with them. They suffered on Good Friday.
Cf. Holw. — Att. — Baud.

SIMEON of TRÈVES (St) H. O.S.B.
R.M. June 1
d. 1035. A native of Syracuse who, after being educated at Constantinople, lived as a hermit by the Jordan. He then joined a community at Bethlehem, but migrated later to Mt Sinai and again became a hermit, first in a small cave near the Red Sea and then on the summit of Sinai. Thence he was sent by the abbot of Mt Sinai on a mission to the duke of Normandy. After a series of adventures he settled at Trèves, where he was walled up by the archbishop and lived under the obedience of the abbot of the great Benedictine monastery of St Martin. It was the abbot of this monastery who assisted Simeon at his death and wrote his life. St Simeon was the second saint to be formally canonized (1042).
Cf. Zimm. — Holw. — Att. — Baud. — Chev.

SIMEON SALUS (St) H.   R.M. July 1
d. p. 588. An Egyptian who lived as a hermit for close on thirty years in the desert of Sinai, by the Red Sea, and afterwards at Emesa in Syria. Out of humility he allowed himself to be considered an idiot: hence the nickname *Salus*, meaning a fool.
Cf. Att. — Holw. — Baud.

SIMEON of PADOLIRONE (St) Mk. O.S.B.   R.M. July 26
d. 1016. An Armenian who, after spending some time as a hermit, went on pilgrimage to Jerusalem, Rome, Compostella and St Martin of Tours. He was renowned for the miracles he worked on these journeys. Finally he settled at the Cluniac abbey of Padolirone near Padua, where he passed the rest of his life. Canonized by Benedict VIII.
Cf. Zimm. — Att. — Chev.

SIMEON STYLITES the YOUNGER (St) H.   R.M. Sept. 3
521-597. A native of Antioch who as a child joined the community of St John Stylites. As a boy he began to live on a pillar, and he continued to live thus uninterruptedly for sixty-nine years, until his death. In his earlier years he did not always remain on the same pillar, but he remained on his last pillar (on the Wonderful Mountain, near Antioch) for forty-five years. He was ordained priest and celebrated Mass at a small altar on the pillar itself. He was consulted by prelates and princes, as well as the common people.
Cf. Holw. — Att. — Baud.

SIMEON SENEX (St) R.M. Oct. 8
1st cent. The "just and devout man who awaited the consolation of Israel" (Luke II 25), who took the Infant Saviour in his arms when he was brought to the Temple and who on that occasion sang the *Nunc dimittis* (ib.).
Cf. Att. — Holw. — Baud.

SIMEON of CAVA (Bl) Ab. O.S.B.
A.C. Nov. 16
d. 1141. Abbot of the great Benedictine abbey of La Cava, in S. Italy, from 1124 to 1141. He was highly esteemed by Pope Innocent II and by Roger II of Sicily. It was during his abbacy that Cava reached the peak of its splendour. Cult confirmed in 1928.
Cf. Zimm. — Holw. — Baud. — Att.

SIMILIAN (French: SAMBIN) (St) Bp.
R.M. June 16
d. 310. Third bishop of Nantes. St Gregory of Tours testifies to his sanctity.
Cf. Holw. — Baud. — Gams.

SIMITRIUS and Comp. (SS) MM.
R.M. May 26
d. c.159. A band of twenty-three Roman martyrs, arrested while assembled for prayer in the *titulus* or church of St Praxedes and beheaded without trial.
Cf. Holw. — Baud.

SIMON FIDATI of CASCIA (Bl) C. O.S.B.
A.C. Feb. 3
d. 1348. Born at Cascia in Umbria, he joined the friar-hermits of St Augustine and was a prominent figure as a writer, preacher and adviser in the life of most of the cities of central Italy. In recent times scholars have claimed to find in his book *De Gestis Domini Salvatoris* the source of several of Luther's heretical doctrines.
Cf. Holw. — Att. — Baud.

SIMON of ST BERTIN (Bl) Ab. O.S.B.
A.C. Feb. 4
d. 1148. Successively monk of Saint-Bertin, abbot of Auchy, and abbot of Saint-Bertin (1131). His election as abbot of Saint-Bertin was contested, and he was unable to take up his office until 1138.
Cf. Zimm. — Chev.

SIMON RINALDUCCI (Bl) S. O.S.A.
A.C. Apr. 20
d. 1322. A native of Todi, he became an Austin friar, a famous preacher, and for a time provincial of Umbria. He kept silence under an unjust accusation rather than cause scandal among his brethren. Cult confirmed in 1833.
Cf. Holw. — Baud. — Att.

SIMON STOCK (St) C. O.C. A.C. May 6
d. 1265. Born at Aylesford in Kent, he joined the Carmelites and eventually (1247) became the sixth general of the order. As such he was instrumental in establishing houses at the principal university cities of Europe: Cambridge (1248), Oxford (1253), Paris (1260), Bologna (id.), and in modifying the rule so that the Carmelites became an order of mendicant friars rather than of hermits. According to a Carmelite tradition our Lady gave Simon the brown scapular with all the privileges attached to it. Though never formally canonized, Simon is venerated throughout the Church as a canonized saint. He died at Bordeaux.
Cf. Holw. — Att. — Chev. — Baud.

SIMON ACOSTA and SIMON LOPEZ (BB) MM. S.J. A.C. July 15
d. 1670. The former was born at Oporto in Portugal and became a Jesuit lay-brother; the latter was a native of Ourem, also in Portugal, and was a Jesuit cleric. Both formed part of the missionary expedition of Bl Ignatius Azevedo, q.v.
Cf. Holw. — Prop. S.J.

SIMON of LIPNICZA (Bl) C. O.F.M.
A.C. July 30
d. 1482. A native of Lipnicza in Poland who, as a result of hearing a sermon by St John Capistran, joined the Friars Minor and became a powerful preacher himself. He died while tending the sick during a plague at Cracow. Beatified in 1685.
Cf. Att. — Holw. — Baud.

SIMON KIOTA (Bl) M. A.C. Aug. 16
d. 1625. A Japanese, member of one of the old Christian families of Bungo and an officer in the royal army. He served as a catechist and at the age of sixty was crucified with his wife and three companions at Cocura. Beatified in 1867.
Cf. Holw.

SIMON of CRESPY (St) Mk. O.S.B.
A.C. Sept. 18
d. c.1080. Count of Crespy in Valois and a descendant of Charlemagne. He was

brought up at the court of William the Conqueror. The sight of his father's decomposing body led him to desire the monastic life, and with William's leave, though the latter wished him to marry, he set out for Rome. On the way thither he stopped at the Benedictine abbey of Condat in the Jura and there took the habit. After his profession he was employed by St Gregory VII and others in bringing about reconciliations between princes and potentates. It was while he was at Rome engaged in a mission of this kind that he died, being attended at his deathbed by Pope Gregory.
Cf. Zimm.—Att.—Holw.—Chev.—Baud.

SIMON of GENOA (Bl) A. O.S.B. Cam.
A.C. Sept. 18
d. 1292. A Genoese who became a hermit at Camaldoli.
Cf. Zimm.

SIMON de ROJAS (Bl) C. O.Trin.
A.C. Sept. 28
1522-1624. A native of Valladolid who became a Trinitarian, in which order he became a superior and a famous missionary. In later life he was appointed confessor at the court of Philip III and tutor to the royal family. Beatified in 1766.
Cf. P. de U. — Baud. — Att. — Holw.

SIMON (St) Apostle.   R.M. Oct. 28
1st cent. In the gospels he is surnamed "the Cananean," i.e., "the Zealot." His name occurs only in the lists of the apostles. The tradition of the West places the scene of his labours in Egypt and Mesopotamia, but there are several other different traditions among the Christians of the East, and nothing positive can be stated about his life and activities.
Cf. Holw. — Att. — Baud.

SIMON BALLACHI (Bl) C. O.P.
A.C. Nov. 3
d. 1319. Born at Sant' Arcangelo near Rimini, the son of Count Ballachi and nephew of two archbishops of Rimini. At the age of twenty-seven he became a Dominican lay-brother in his native city and was remarkable for his extraordinary austerities. Cult confirmed in 1821.
Cf. Holw. — Att. — Baud.

SIMON of AULNE (Bl) C. O.S.B.Cist.
A.C. Nov. 6
d. 1215. A Cistercian lay-brother at

Aulne renowned for his gift of mystical prayer, his visions and his ecstasies. On this account he was invited to Rome by Innocent III.
Cf. Zimm. — Holw.

SIMON YEMPO (Bl) M.   A.C. Dec. 4
d. 1623. A native of Japan who became a Buddhist monk. Having been converted to Christianity and become a lay catechist, he was burnt alive at Yeddo. Beatified in 1867.
Cf. Holw.

SIMON HOA (Bl) M.   A.C. Dec. 12
d. 1840. A native of Cochin-China, a physician and mayor of his village. He was attached to the Foreign Missions of Paris. After most cruel tortures he was beheaded for the Faith. Beatified in 1900.
Cf. Holw.

SIMPLICIAN (St) Bp.   R.M. Aug. 16
d. 400. A friend and adviser of St Ambrose, whom he succeeded in the see of Milan. He was already an old man and governed the see only three years. He played a leading part in the conversion of St Augustine, by whom he was always remembered with deep gratitude.
Cf. Att. — Baud. —Gams — Holw.

SIMPLICIAN (St) M.   R.M. Dec. 31
See Stephen, Pontian, etc.

SIMPLICIUS (St) Pope. R.M. March 10
d. 483. A native of Tivoli who was pope from 468 to 483. He upheld the decrees of the council of Chalcedon and supported the Eastern Catholics against the Monophysite heretics, who were backed by three successive Byzantine emperors.
Cf. Att. — Baud. — Holw.

SIMPLICIUS and Comp. (SS) MM.
R.M. May 10
See Calepodius, Palmatius, etc.

SIMPLICIUS (St) M.   R.M. May 15
d. 304. A martyr of Sardinia, buried alive under Diocletian.
Cf. Holw. — Baud.

SIMPLICIUS of BOURGES (St) Bp.
A.C. June 16
d. 477 (March 1). He was already married and the father of a large family when the bishops of the province raised him to

the see of Bourges. He defended the Church against the Arian Visigoths and the ambitions of lay magnates.
Cf. Holw. — Baud. — Duch. Fast. Episc.

SIMPLICIUS of AUTUN (St) Bp.
R.M. June 24
d. c.360. A married man who lived a virginal life with his wife and was raised to the see of Autun. As a bishop he worked zealously and successfully to uproot paganism.
Cf. Gams — Duch. Fast. Episc. — Holw. — Baud.

SIMPLICIUS, FAUSTINUS and BEATRIX (SS) MM. R.M. July 29
d. 303. Said to have been two brothers and their sister martyred in Rome under Diocletian. Their Acts are not trustworthy.
Cf. Holw. — Att. — Baud.

SIMPLICIUS, CONSTANTIUS and VICTORIAN (SS) MM. R.M. Aug. 26
d. c.161. A father and his two sons martyred in Rome under Marcus Aurelius. Their Acts are not trustworthy.
Cf. Holw. — Baud.

SIMPLICIUS (St) Ab. O.S.B.
A.C. Oct. 22
d. c.570. A disciple of St Benedict and third abbot of Montecassino. His relics were elevated in 1071.
Cf. Holw. — Zimm. — Chev. — Baud.

SIMPLICIUS (St) M. R.M. Nov. 8
See Claudius, Nicostratus, etc.

SIMPLICIUS of VERONA (St) Bp.
R.M. Nov. 20
d. c.535. Bishop of Verona.
Cf. Holw. — Menzies.

SIMPLICIUS (St) M. R.M. Dec. 18
See Quintus, Simplicius, etc.

SINAI (Martyrs of) (SS) R.M. Jan. 14
See under Isaias, Sabas and Comp.

SINCHEALL (St) Ab. A.C. March 26
5th cent. A disciple of St Patrick. Abbot-founder of the monastery and school at Killeigh, Offaly, Ireland, where he had one hundred and fifty monks under his direction.
Cf. Holw.

SINDULPHUS of REIMS (St) H.
R.M. Oct. 20
d. 660. A native of Gascony who lived as a hermit at Aussonce, near Reims.
Cf. Holw. — Chev. — Baud.

SINDULPHUS of VIENNE (St) Bp.
R.M. Dec. 10
d. c.669. The thirty-first bishop of Vienne in Gaul.
Cf. Holw. — Duch. Fast. Episc. — Baud.

SIRAN (St) Ab. O.S.B. A.C. Dec. 4
Otherwise Sigiranus, q.v.

SIRENUS (SERENUS, CERNEUF) (St) M. R.M. Feb. 23
d. c.303. A Greek monk who lived as a hermit at Sirmium, now Mitrovica, in the Balkans. He was martyred under Diocletian.
Cf. Holw. — Baud.

SIRICIUS (St) M. R.M. Feb. 21
See Verulus, Secundinus, etc.

SIRICIUS (St) Pope. R.M. Nov. 26
d. 399. A native of Rome who ruled the Church from 384 to 399. His episcopate is very important for the development of the Roman primacy. His letter — called the first papal decretal — to Archbishop Himerius of Tarragona marks an epoch in the history of the papal authority.
Cf. Holw. — Att. — Baud.

SIRIDION (St) Bp. R.M. Jan. 2
? Probably a scribe's error for Isidore, or for Isiridion of Antioch, mentioned by St Jerome.
Cf. Holw. — Baud.

SIRMIUM (Martyrs of) (SS)
R.M. Feb. 23 and Apr. 9
d. c.303. Two anonymous groups of martyrs are catalogued in the R.M. as having suffered under Diocletian at Sirmium, now Mitrovica in the Balkans: (i) a band of seventy-two, on Feb. 23, put to death probably in 303; and (ii) a group of seven maidens commemorated on Apr. 9 and probably martyred in the same year.
Cf. Holw. — Baud.

SISEBUTUS (St) Ab. O.S.B.
A.C. March 15
d. 1082. Abbot of the Benedictine monastery of Cardena in the diocese of Burgos, Spain. Under him the abbey became a

powerful focus of ecclesiastical and civil life. He gave shelter to the Cid (Rodrigo Diaz de Vivar), the celebrated hero of the Christian Spanish Reconquest.
Cf. P. de U. — Zimm. — Holw. — Chev.

SISENANDUS (St) M. R.M. July 16
d. 851. Born at Badajoz in Estremadura, he became a deacon in the church of St Acisclus at Cordova. He was beheaded under Abderrahman II.
Cf. P. de U. — Chev. — Holw.

SISINIUS, DIOCLETIUS and FLOR-ENTIUS (SS) MM. R.M. May 11
d. 304. Martyrs at Osimo, near Ancona, under Diocletian. They were stoned to death at the same time as the better known Roman priest, St Anthimus.
Cf. Holw. — Baud.

SISINIUS, MARTYRIUS and ALEX-ANDER (SS) MM. R.M. May 29
d. 397. Said to have been Cappadocians, received by St Vigilius of Trent on the recommendation of St Ambrose and sent to evangelize the Tyrol. They were martyred by a pagan mob who were celebrating the festival of the Ambarvalia.
Cf. Holw. — Baud. — Att.

SISINIUS (St) Bp. R.M. Nov. 23
d. p. 325. Bishop of Cyzicus and a confessor of the Faith under Diocletian. He was dragged by wild horses, but survived and was present at the council of Nicaea.
Cf. Holw. — Baud.

SISINIUS (St) M. R.M. Nov. 29
See Saturninus and Sisinius.

SISOES (St) H. A.C. July 4
d. c.429. He lived as a hermit in Egypt for sixty-two years. To some extent he resembled St Antony in the influence he exercised.
Cf. Att. — Baud. — Holw.

SITHIAN (St) Bp. A.C. July 15
Otherwise Seduinus, possibly identical with Swithun, q.v.

SIVIARD (St) Ab. O.S.B. R.M. March 1
d. c.729. Benedictine monk at Saint-Calais, on the R. Anisole. He succeeded his own father as abbot of the monastery. To him we owe an interesting life of St Calais, founder of the abbey.
Cf. Mab. — Zimm. — Holw.

SIXTUS I (XYSTUS) Pope, M. R.M. Apr. 3
d. 127. A Roman. Pope from 117 to 127. Nothing further is known about him.
Cf. Att. — Baud. — Holw.

SIXTUS II (XYSTUS) Pope, and Comp. MM. R.M. Aug. 6
d. 258. He reigned for one year: 257-258. While preaching in the catacomb of Praetextatus during the celebration of the liturgy he was seized with his deacons Felicissimus and Agapitus and martyred. His name is mentioned in the canon of the Roman Mass. The R.M. commemorates with them Januarius, Magnus, Vincent and Stephen, subdeacons, and Quartus, all as martyrs.
Cf. Holw. — Menzies — Att. — Baud.

SIXTUS III (XYSTUS) Pope. R.M. Aug. 19
d. 440. Pope from 432 to 446. A Roman by birth. As pope he is best remembered for having opposed Nestorianism and Pelagianism and for having built several Roman basilicas, among them S. Maria Maggiore.
Cf. Holw. — Att. — Menzies.

SIXTUS (XYSTUS) of REIMS (St) Bp. R.M. Sept. 1
d. c.300. First bishop of Reims, c.290-c.300. He was sent from Rome and established his see at Soissons before moving it to Reims.
Cf. Duch. Fast. Episc. — Gams — Baud. — Holw.

SLEBHENE (SLEBHINE) (St) Ab. A.C. March 2
d. 767. An Irish monk who was abbot of Iona from 752 to 767.
Cf. Holw.

SMARAGDUS (St) M. R.M. Aug. 8
See Cyriacus, Largus and Comp.

SOBEL (St) M. R.M. Aug. 5
See Cantidius, Cantidian and Sobel.

SOCRATES and DIONYSIUS (SS) MM. R.M. Apr. 19
d. 275. Martyrs of Pamphylia, stabbed to death under Aurelian.
Cf. Holw. — Baud.

SOCRATES and STEPHEN (SS) MM.
R.M. Sept. 17
d. c.304. Alleged British martyrs under Diocletian. The R.M. assigns them to Britain, but it seems certain that Socrates was martyred in Abretania, a province of Mysia in Asia Minor, and that a scribe changed the name to Britannia. Bithynia has also been suggested as the place of martyrdom.
Cf. Att. — Holw. — Baud.

SOLA (SOL, SOLUS, SUOLO) (St) H.
O.S.B. **A.C. Dec. 3**
d. 794. An Anglo-Saxon monk and priest who followed St Boniface to Germany and lived as a hermit first near Fulda under the obedience of that abbey and later near Eichstätt. Finally he settled on a piece of land bestowed on him by Charlemagne, on which he founded the abbey of Soinhofen as a dependency of Fulda.
Cf. Holw. — Zimm. — Att. — Baud.

SOLANGIA (SOLANGE) (St) V. M.
A.C. May 10
d. c.880. A poor shepherdess of the neighbourhood of Bourges, who, for resisting the attempts of the local lord on her chastity, was brutally murdered by him.
Cf. Att. — Holw. — Baud.

SOLEMNIUS (SOLEINE) (St) Bp.
R.M. Sept. 25
d. c.511. Bishop of Chartres c.490-c.511. He was present at the baptism of Clovis.
Cf. Baud. — Holw. — Gams — Duch. Fast. Episc.

SOLINA (St) V. M. **A.C. Oct. 17**
d. c.290. A Gascon maiden who escaped to Chartres to avoid marriage to a pagan. She was beheaded at Chartres.
Cf. Holw. — Baud.

SOLOCHON and Comp. (SS) MM.
R.M. May 17
d. 305. Three Egyptian soldiers in the imperial army, stationed at Chalcedon. They were clubbed to death for the Faith under Maximian.
Cf. Holw. — Baud.

SOLOMON (St) M. **R.M. March 13**
See Rudericus and Salomon.

SOLOMON I (St) M. **A.C. June 25**
d. 434. Born in Cornwall, husband of St Gwen and father of St Cuby (Cybi). He reigned as a kinglet in Brittany and was assassinated by heathen malcontents among his subjects.
Cf. Holw. — Baud. — Chev.

SOLOMON III (Breton: SELYF) (St) M.
A.C. June 25
d. 874. King of Brittany and a brave, though at times brutal, warrior against Franks, Northmen and his own rebellious subjects. The Bretons count him among their many national heroes. He did penance for the crimes of his youth, and when he was assassinated the people at once acclaimed him a martyr.
Cf. Holw. — Att. — Baud. — Chev.

SOLOMON (SALOMON, SALONIUS) (St) Bp. **R.M. Sept. 28**
d. p. 269. First bishop of Genoa. His true name was Salonius: it was changed into Salomon by a scribe's error.
Cf. Gams — Holw. — Baud.

SOLUTOR (St) M. **R.M. Nov. 13**
See Valentine, Solutor and Victor.

SOLUTOR (St) M. **R.M. Nov. 20**
See Octavius, Solutor and Adventor.

SOPATRA (St) V. **R.M. Nov. 9**
See Eustolia and Sopatra.

SOPHIA (St) V.M. **R.M. Apr. 30**
d. c.250. A maiden of Fermo in central Italy, martyred under Decius.
Cf. Menzies — Holw. — Baud.

SOPHIA and IRENE (SS) MM.
R.M. Sept. 18
d. c. ? 200. Martyrs beheaded in Egypt.
Cf. Holw. — Baud.

SOPHIA (St) W. **R.M. Sept. 30**
d. c.138. The mother of the virgin martyrs Faith, Hope and Charity, who, according to a Roman tradition, suffered at Rome under Hadrian. Three days later Sophia, while praying at their tomb, herself passed peacefully away. The story seems to have come from the East and is thought by some to be an allegorical explanation of the cult of the Divine Wisdom, from whom proceed Faith, Hope and Charity.
Cf. Holw. — Baud.

SOPHONIAS (ZEPHANIAH) (St) Prophet. **R.M. Dec. 3**
7th cent. B.C. Said to have been of the

tribe of Simeon. He prophesied in Judaea in the days of King Josiah: his most remarkable prophecy regards the ultimate conversion of the Jews. There are no trustworthy traditions concerning him.
Cf. Holw. — Baud.

SOPHRONIUS (St) Bp. R.M. March 11
d. c.639. A Syrian from Damascus who became patriarch of Jerusalem in 633. He is an ecclesiastical writer of distinction. His life's work, however, was the condemnation of Monothelism. He was engaged in this campaign when the Saracens occupied Jerusalem and drove him from his see (638). He is said to have died of grief shortly after.
Cf. Att. — Holw. — Baud.

SOPHRONIUS (St) Bp. R.M. Dec. 8
6th cent. An alleged bishop of Cyprus.
Cf. Baud. — Holw.

SOSIPATER (St) R.M. June 25
2nd cent. A kinsman and disciple of St Paul (Rom XVI 21). He accompanied the apostle on some of his journeys, and tradition connects his later life with the island of Corfu.
Cf. Holw. — Baud.

SOSIUS (St) M. R.M. Sept. 19
See Januarius and Comp.

SOSTENES (St) C. R.M. May 3
One of the Seven Founders of the Servite Order, q.v.

SOSTHENES and VICTOR (SS) MM.
R.M. Sept. 10
d. 307. Martyrs at Chalcedon under Diocletian. They were among the executioners appointed to torture St Euphemia and were converted through her prayers and the example of her fortitude.
Cf. Holw. — Baud.

SOSTHENES (St) R.M. Nov. 28
1st cent. The ruler of the synagogue at Corinth mentioned in Acts XVIII, 17. He became a disciple of St Paul and is probably the "brother" mentioned in I Cor. I, 1. Greek tradition makes him the first bishop of Colophon in Asia Minor.
Cf. Holw. — Baud.

SOTER (St) Pope. M. R.M. Apr. 22
d. 174. A native of Fondi, near Gaeta. He was pope from 166 to 174 and was an active opponent of Montanism. He is supposed to have died a martyr.
Cf. Holw. — Baud. — Att.

SOTERIS (St) V. M. R.M. Feb. 10
d. 304. A Roman maiden martyred under Diocletian. She seems to have been a sister of the great-great-grandmother of St Ambrose, by whom she is often mentioned.
Cf. Holw. — Att. — Baud.

SOZON (St) M. R.M. Sept. 7
d. c.304. A shepherd in his native Cilicia. At a pagan celebration he pulled off the golden hand of an idol, broke it up and distributed the pieces among the poor. He was forthwith burnt at the stake.
Cf. Holw. — Att. — Baud.

SPECIOSUS (St) Mk. O.S.B.
R.M. March 15
d. c.555. A wealthy landowner of Campania who, with his brother Gregory, received the habit from St Benedict at Montecassino. He was attached to the new foundation at Terracina, but died at Capua while on an errand undertaken for the benefit of his monastery.
Cf. Zimm. — Mab. — Att. — Holw. — Baud.

SPERANDEA (SPERANDIA) (St) Abs. O.S.B. A.C. Sept. 11
d. 1276. A relative of St Ubald of Gubbio. She became a Benedictine at Cingoli, in the Marches of Ancona, and eventually abbess of her nunnery. She is venerated as the patron saint of Cingoli.
Cf. Holw. — Baud.

SPERATUS (St) M. R.M. July 17
See Scillitan Martyrs.

SPES (St) Ab. R.M. March 28
d. c.513. An abbot of Campi in central Italy. He was totally blind for forty years, but fifteen days before his death his eyesight was restored.
Cf. Holw. — Att. — Baud.

SPES (HOPE, ELPIS) (St) V. M.
R.M. Aug. 1
See Faith, Hope and Charity.

SPEUSIPPUS, ELEUSIPPUS, MELEUSIPPUS and LEONILLA (SS) MM.
R.M. Jan. 17
d. 175. According to the legend, which

probably has no basis in fact, these saints were three brothers born at one birth, natives of Cappadocia, martyred with their grandmother Leonilla under Marcus Aurelius. Their alleged relics were brought to Langres, where their church bears the name of St Geome (Holy Twins). *Cf. Att. — Holw. — Baud.*

SPINULUS (SPINULA, SPIN) (St) Ab. O.S.B. A.C. Nov. 5
d. 707 (or 720). A Benedictine monk of Moyen-Moutier under St Hidulphus. Later he became the abbot-founder of the small abbey of Bégon-Celle (now Saint-Blasien).
Cf. Zimm. — Holw. — Baud.

SPIRIDION (St) Bp. R.M. Dec. 14
d. c.348. He began life as a shepherd and rose to be bishop of Tremithus in his native island of Cyprus. Under Diocletian he was condemned to lose an eye and forced to labour in the mines. He survived the persecution and was one of the venerable "confessors of the Faith" present at the council of Nicaea, where he was a strong opponent of Arianism.
Cf. Holw. — Baud. — Att.

STACHYS (St) Bp. R.M. Oct. 31
1st cent. The Christian saluted by St Paul (Rom. XVI, 9) as "my beloved." The tradition is that St Andrew consecrated him bishop of Byzantium.
Cf. Holw. — Baud.

STACTEUS (St) M. R.M. July 18
One of the alleged sons of St Symphorosa, q.v.

STACTEUS (St) M. R.M. Sept. 28
? A Roman martyr of whom no particulars are available.
Cf. Holw. — Baud.

STANISLAUS (St) Bp. M. R.M. May 7
1030-1079. Stanislaus Szczepanovsky was born near Cracow and educated at Gnesen and Paris. In 1072 he was raised to the see of Cracow. He excommunicated King Boleslaus the Cruel for his evil life, and that monarch in consequence slew the saint with his own hand while he was celebrating Mass. Pope St Gregory VII laid Poland under an interdict and Boleslaus fled the country and died a fugitive in Hungary. Stanislaus was canonized in 1253. Some Polish historians contend

that the saint was plotting to dethrone Boleslaus.
Cf. Holw. — Baud. — Att.

STANISLAUS KOSTKA (St) C. S.J. R.M. Aug. 15
1550-1568. Born at Rostkovo in Poland, the son of a senator, he was sent in 1563 to Vienna to study at the Jesuit college recently established in that city. Despite fierce opposition from his family he resolved to become a Jesuit himself. St Peter Canisius sent him to Rome, where he was received into the Jesuit noviceship by St Francis Borgia in Oct. 1567. He died within a year, but during that brief period he had gained a reputation for angelic innocence. Canonized in 1726.
Cf. Att. — Holw. — Baud.

STEPHANA de QUINZANIS (Bl) V. O.P. A.C. Jan. 2
1457-1530. She was born near Brescia and at the age of fifteen joined the Dominican tertiaries. After living at home for many years she eventually founded a convent called San Paolo, near Soncino, of which she became first abbess. She was noted for her ecstasies, which were attested by many eye-witnesses. Cult confirmed by Benedict XIV.
Cf. Holw. — Baud. — Att.

STEPHEN
Note. Stephen is the English variant of the Graeco-Latin Stephanus (crowned). Other modern variants of the same name are: Italian, Stefano; French, Etienne; Spanish, Esteban; German, Stephan; Hungarian, Istvan.

STEPHEN du BOURG (St) O.Cart. P.C. Jan. 4
d. 1118. A canon of St Rufus at Valence who became one of the first companions of St Bruno at the foundation of the Grande-Chartreuse. He was sent (1116) to found the charterhouse at Meyria, and there he died.
Cf. Baud. — Chev. — Holw.

STEPHEN of LIÉGE (Bl) Ab. O.S.B. A.C. Jan. 13
d. 1061. A canon of St Denis, Liége, who became a Benedictine monk at St Vannes, Verdun. Later he returned to Liége as abbot-founder of St Laurence.
Cf. Holw. — Chev.

STEPHEN BELLESINI (Bl) C. O.S.A.
A.C. Feb. 3
1774-1840. A native of Trent who joined
the Augustinian hermits at Bologna and
studied there and at Rome. Owing to the
disturbances following the French Revolution he retired to his home in the Trentino,
where he held the post of government inspector of schools. At the earliest opportunity, however, he returned to the religious life and was appointed novice
master in Rome and later parish priest at
the shrine of our Lady at Genazzano.
Here he died as a result of his devoted
ministrations to the victims of the cholera
epidemic. Beatified in 1904.
Cf. Att. — Baud. — Holw.

STEPHEN of GRANDMONT (St) Ab.
R.M. Feb. 8
1046-1124. Born at Thiers in Auvergne,
the son of the lord of the district, he accompanied his father at the age of twelve
to the tomb of St Nicholas of Bari. He
fell ill at Benevento and remained there,
being educated by Archbishop Milo.
On his return to France he founded at
Murat a congregation of Benedictine
monk-hermits on the model of those he had
seen in Calabria. He ruled them for
forty-six years but does not seem ever to
have become a monk himself. After his
death the large community migrated to
Grandmont, whence the name of Grand-
montines given to this new branch of the
Benedictine order. Stephen was canonized in 1189 at the request of Henry II of
England.
Cf. Holw. — Baud. — Chev. — Att.

STEPHEN CUÉNOT (Bl) Bp. M.
A.C. Feb. 8
1802-1861. Born at Beaulieu, France, he
joined the Society of Foreign Missions at
Paris and was sent to Annam. In 1833
he was appointed vicar apostolic of E.
Cochin-China, receiving episcopal consecration at Singapore. After fifteen years
more of fruitful labour he was one of the
first to be arrested on the outbreak of the
persecution of 1861. He died in prison
(perhaps from poison) on Nov. 4, shortly
before the date fixed for his execution.
Beatified in 1909.
Cf. Holw. — Att.

STEPHEN of LYONS (St) Bp.
R.M. Feb. 13
d. 512. Bishop of Lyons. He was active

in converting the Arian Burgundians to
the Catholic faith.
Cf. Holw. — Baud. — Duch. Fast. Episc.

STEPHEN of RIETI (St) Ab.
R.M. Feb. 13
d. c.590. An abbot at Rieti whom St
Gregory the Great describes as "rude of
speech but of cultured life." Possibly
he was a Benedictine.
Cf. Holw. — Att. — Baud.

STEPHEN of OBAZINE (St) Ab. O.S.B.
Cist. **A.C. March 8**
d. 1154. Stephen and another priest
withdrew into the forest of Obazine near
Tulle, France, to lead a solitary life.
When disciples wished to join them they
obtained leave of the bishop of Limoges to
build a monastery. The new abbey had
no written rule, and St Stephen arranged
for its affiliation to the Cistercian order,
he himself receiving both the Cistercian
habit and an abbot's blessing. He was
greatly esteemed by the Cistercians.
*Cf. Zimm. — Att. — Baud. — Chev. —
Holw.*

STEPHEN of PALESTRINA (Bl) Card.
Bp. O.S.B.Cist. **P.C. March 17**
d. 1144. A monk of Clairvaux who was
promoted to the cardinalate and to the see
of Palestrina (1141). By Cistercian
writers he is always called either saint or
blessed.
Cf. Gams — Zimm. — Menzies.

STEPHEN (St) M. **R.M. Apr. 1**
See Victor and Stephen.

STEPHEN and HILDERBRAND (BB)
MM. O.S.B.Cist. **P.C. Apr. 11**
d. 1209. Two Cistercians, the former an
abbot, the latter a monk, slain by the
Albigenses at Saint-Gilles in Languedoc.
They are venerated at Saint-Gilles, though
their cult has not been officially confirmed.
Cf. Holw. — Baud.

STEPHEN HARDING (St) Ab. O.S.B.
Cist. **R.M. Apr. 17**
d. 1137. An English monk of Sherborne
who, after a pilgrimage to Rome, joined
St Robert at Molesmes and with him migrated to Cîteaux. Here he became successively sub-prior under St Robert, prior
under St Alberic, and third abbot (1109).
As such he was responsible for the original
constitutions of the Cistercians, as also

for the Charter of Charity which he presented to the general chapter of Cîteaux in 1119. To him therefore, much more than to St Robert, the Cistercians owe their definite status as a new branch of the Benedictines. It was Stephen who received St Bernard and his thirty companions at Cîteaux and two years later sent him to become the abbot-founder of Clairvaux and the principal exponent of the Cistercian ideal. St Stephen was canonized in 1623.
Cf. Zimm. — Chev. — Baud. — Att. — Holw.

STEPHEN of ANTIOCH (St) Bp. M.
R.M. Apr. 25
d. 481. A patriarch of Antioch who was a special target for the fury of the Monophysite heretics. In the end they flung him into the R. Orontes and so caused his death.
Cf. Holw. — Baud.

STEPHEN (St) M.   R.M. Apr. 27
See Castor and Stephen.

STEPHEN of NARBONNE and Comp. (BB) MM.   A.C. May 28
d. 1242. Stephen was a member of the Inquisition of Toulouse: he was a Franciscan. Together with eleven companions — Benedictines, Franciscans, Dominicans, and one secular priest — he was murdered at Avignonet by the Albigensian heretics. Cult approved in 1866.
Cf. Baud. — Holw. — Chev.

STEPHEN of CORVEY (St) Bp. O.S.B.
A.C. June 2
d. ? 1075. A monk of Corvey in Saxony who was appointed regionary bishop in Sweden, where he worked as a missionary with signal success. He was the first to plant the faith on the shores of the Sound. He was martyred, probably at Nora.
Cf. Zimm. — Att. — Holw.

STEPHEN BANDELLI (Bl) C. O.P.
A.C. June 12
d. 1450. Born at Castelnuovo, diocese of Piacenza, where he became a Dominican. He was an eminent preacher and reformer. Cult approved in 1856.
Cf. Holw. — Baud. — Att.

STEPHEN of REGGIO (St) Bp. M.
A.C. July 5
1st cent. Said to have been ordained first bishop of Reggio by St Paul and to

have been martyred under Nero. It is only since the 17th century that this story has gained currency and that he has been venerated as the principal patron of Reggio.
Cf. Holw. — Menzies.

STEPHEN de ZUDAIRA (Bl) M. S.J.
A.C. July 15
d. 1570. Born at Viscaya in Spain, he became a Jesuit lay-brother and formed one of the martyr-band headed by Bl Ignatius de Azevedo, q.v.
Cf. Prop. S.J. — Holw.

STEPHEN del LUPO (St) Ab. O.S.B.
A.C. July 19
d. 1191. Benedictine monk of San Liberatore di Majella, and afterwards abbotfounder of St Peter's at Vallebona, near Manopello, in Italy. He is said to have been befriended by a wolf: hence his nickname of "del lupo."
Cf. Zimm.

STEPHEN I (St) Pope. M. R.M. Aug. 2
d. 257. A Roman of the *gens Julia*. He became pope in 254, and during his short pontificate he was occupied with the question of the re-baptizing of heretics. He invoked the apostolic tradition in favour of the Roman practice and met with stout opposition from St Cyprian. Tradition says that he was beheaded while seated in his chair during the celebration of his Mass in the catacombs.
Cf. Holw. — Baud. — Att.

STEPHEN (St) M.   R.M. Aug. 6
See Sixtus and Comp.

STEPHEN of CARDEÑA and Comp. (SS) MM. O.S.B.   R.M. Aug. 6
d. 872. Abbot of the great Castilian monastery of Cardeña, near Burgos, in which were housed over two hundred monks. The abbot and community were slain by Saracens from S. Spain during one of their inroads into Christian territory (summer of 872). The cult of these martyrs was approved in 1603 and Card. Baronius composed the proper lessons for their office.
Cf. P. de U. — Zimm. — Holw. — Baud.

STEPHEN of HUNGARY (St) King.
R.M. Sept. 2
d. 1038. On the death of his father Geza (997) Stephen succeeded as sovereign of

the Magyars of Hungary. He married Gisela, a sister of the emperor St Henry II, and they set their hands to the common task of christianizing their people. With the help of the Holy See and as a result of numerous victories over external and internal foes, Stephen gradually welded the Magyars into a national unity. He organized dioceses and founded abbeys (among them the great Benedictine abbey of Pannonhalma, which still stands), and secured the services of prominent foreign monks, notably of St Gerard Sagredo, abbot of San Giorgio Maggiore at Venice, who became the tutor of the king's son, the young St Emeric. The latter died in the prime of life, and the declining years of St Stephen were darkened by many misfortunes and difficulties. His relics were enshrined in 1083 by order of St Gregory VII. To this day the Magyars consider him their greatest national saint and hero.
Cf. Holw. — Baud. — Att. — Chev.

STEPHEN of CHATILLON (St) Bp. O.Cart. A.C. Sept. 7
d. 1208. Born at Lyons of the noble family of the Chatillons, he entered the charterhouse of Portes, where he became prior in 1196. In 1203 he was raised to the see of Dié. Cult approved in 1907.
Cf. Holw. — Chev. — Baud.

STEPHEN PONGRACZ (Bl) M. S.J. A.C. Sept. 8
1582-1619. A Croat, born at Alvinez, who became a Jesuit at Brünn and taught at the colleges of Laibach (Ljubljana) and Klagenfurt. From 1611 to 1615 he was professor of theology at Graz. He was slain by the Calvinists at Kashan in Hungary after protracted tortures, and several companions were martyred with him. He was beatified in 1905.
Cf. Holw. — Prop. S.J.

STEPHEN of PERUGIA (St) Ab. O.S.B. A.C. Sept. 16
d. 1026. Third abbot of the Benedictine monastery of St Peter at Perugia, where an altar is dedicated to him.
Cf. Zimm.

STEPHEN (St) M. R.M. Sept. 17
See Socrates and Stephen.

STEPHEN of CAJAZZO (St) Bp. O.S.B. A.C. Oct. 29
935-1023. Born at Macerata and edu-cated at Capua, he was appointed abbot of San Salvatore Maggiore and later, in 979, bishop of Cajazzo. He is now venerated as the principal patron of the city and diocese.
Cf. Gams. — Holw.

STEPHEN of APT (St) Bp. P.C. Nov. 6
975-1046. Born at Agde, he was elected bishop of Apt, S. France, in 1010. He rebuilt the cathedral.
Cf. Holw. — Baud. — Gams.

STEPHEN (St) M. R.M. Nov. 21
See Honorius, Eutychius and Stephen.

STEPHEN (St) M. R.M. Nov. 22
See Mark and Stephen.

STEPHEN, BASIL, PETER, ANDREW and Comp. (SS) MM. R.M. Nov. 28
d. 764. St Stephen, surnamed "the Younger," was born at Constantinople in 714 and became a monk and abbot of Mt St Auxentius. He firmly opposed the fanatical iconoclasm of the emperor Constantine Copronymus. When all attempts to win him over to heresy had failed, the emperor had him put to death, along with SS Basil, Peter, Andrew and a band of over three hundred monks.
Cf. Att. — Holw. — Baud.

STEPHEN (St) M. R.M. Dec. 3
See Claudius, Crispin, etc.

STEPHEN VINH (Bl) M. A.C. Dec. 19
? A peasant of Tonkin and a Dominican tertiary. Hanged at Tonkin. Beatified in 1900.
Cf. Holw.

STEPHEN the DEACON (St) Protomartyr. R.M. Dec. 26 (Aug. 3)
d. 33. The disciple chosen by the apostles, "full of faith and the Holy Ghost" as the first of the seven deacons (Acts VI 1-5). He was stoned to death by the Jews at the instigation of the Sanhedrin, thus becoming the Christian protomartyr. His dying prayer obtained the conversion of St Paul, who was actively engaged in his martyrdom. The R.M. commemorates on Aug. 3 the finding of the reputed relics of St Stephen at Kafr Gamala in 415, and on May 7 their translation to Rome.
Cf. Att. — Holw. — Baud.

STEPHEN, PONTIAN, ATTALUS, FAB-IAN, CORNELIUS, SEXTUS, FLOS, QUINTIAN, MINERVINUS and SIM-PLICIAN (SS) MM. R.M. Dec. 31
? Catalogued as martyrs of Catania in Sicily.
Cf. Holw. — Baud.

STERCATIUS (St) M. R.M. July 24
See Victor, Stercatius and Antinogenes.

STILLA (Bl) V. A.C. July 19
d. c.1141. Daughter of Count Wolfgang II of Abenberg and a sister of Archbishop Conrad I of Salzburg. She founded the church of St Peter at Abenberg, near Nuremburg, where she was buried and venerated as a saint. Cult confirmed in 1927.
Cf. Holw. — Att.

STRATON, PHILIP and EUTYCHIAN (SS) MM. R.M. Aug. 17
d. c.301. Influential citizens of Nicomedia who converted a great number of people to Christianity and effectively discouraged attendance at immoral spectacles. For this reason they were burnt at the stake. In most MSS a fourth martyr is added, by name Cyprian.
Cf. Holw. — Baud.

STRATON (St) M. R.M. Sept. 9
? A martyr who was bound to two trees bent towards each other and torn asunder by their recoil. Place and era unknown.
Cf. Holw. — Baud.

STRATON (St) M. R.M. Sept. 12
See Hieronides, Leontius, etc.

STRATONICUS (St) M. R.M. Jan. 13
See Hermylus and Stratonicus.

STURMIUS (STURMI) (St) O.S.B. R.M. Dec. 17
d. 779. The first German to become a Benedictine. As a child he was entrusted to St Boniface and educated by St Wigbert in the abbey of Fritzlar. He was ordained and sent to evangelize the Saxons. Under orders from Boniface, whose favourite disciple he was, he led an expedition to discover a suitable site for a central abbey for Germany. He chose Fulda, and the abbey of that name was founded there in 744. Sturmius was then dispatched to Montecassino to learn the true Benedic-

tine observance, and on his return he was appointed abbot of Fulda. One of his lasting achievements was the establishment of the celebrated school at Fulda. Dearly loved by his monks, Sturmius was considered as second only to Boniface as the apostle of the Germanies. Canonized in 1139.
Cf. Zimm. — Att. — Holw. — Baud.

STYLIANUS (St) H. R.M. Nov. 26
d. 390. A hermit in the vicinity of Adrianople in Paphlagonia. His life has come down to us in a naively legendary form.
Cf. Holw. — Baud.

STYRIACUS (St) R.M. Nov. 2
See Carterius, Styriacus, etc.

SUAIRLECH (St) Bp. A.C. March 27
d. c.750. First bishop of Fore, Westmeath, Ireland, from c.735 to c.750.
Cf. Holw.

SUCCESSUS (St) M. R.M. Jan. 19
See Paul, Gerontius, etc.

SUCCESSUS (St) M. R.M. March 28
See Rogatus, Successus and Comp.

SUCCESSUS (St) M. R.M. Apr. 16
See Saragossa (Martyrs of).

SUCCESSUS (St) M. R.M. Dec. 9
See Peter, Successus, etc.

SULINUS (St) Ab. A.C. Sept. 1
Otherwise Silin, q.v.

SULPICIUS (II) PIUS (St) Bp. R.M. Jan. 17
d. 647. Bishop of Bourges from 624 to 647. He devoted himself to the care and defence of the poor and persecuted, particularly those who were victims of a certain official of King Dagobert. He is the titular saint of the church and seminary of Saint-Sulpice at Paris.
Cf. Holw. — Att. — Baud.

SULPICIUS (I) (St) Bp. R.M. Jan. 29
d. 591. Bishop of Bourges from 584 to 591. Though often called Sulpicius Severus, he is not to be confused with the celebrated man of letters of that name, whose name was likewise for some centuries included in the R.M.
Cf. Holw. — Att. — Duch. Fast. Episc.

SULPICIUS and SERVILIAN (SS) MM.
R.M. Apr. 20
d. c.117. Roman martyrs whose conversion is traditionally ascribed to the prayers of St Flavia Domitilla. They were beheaded under Trajan.
Cf. Holw. — Baud.

SULPICIUS of BAYEUX (St) Bp. M.
A.C. Sept. 4
d. 843. Bishop of Bayeux from c.838 to 843. He was slain by the Normans at Livry, diocese of Versailles.
Cf. Duch. Fast. Episc. — Holw. — Baud.

SUNAMAN (St) M. O.S.B. A.C. Feb. 15
See Winaman, Unaman and Sunaman.

SUNNIVA (SUNNIFA) (St) V. A.C. July 8
10th cent. According to the legend, Sunniva was an Irish princess who fled from her country with her brother Alban and a number of other maidens. They were shipwrecked off the coast of Norway and succeeded in landing at Selje Island. Here they were slain by people from the mainland. Their alleged relics were enshrined at Bergen. The whole story seems to be a somewhat modified version of the legend of St Ursula.
Cf. Att. — Baud. — Holw.

SUPERIUS (St) M.   R.M. June 26
See Salvius and Superius.

SURANUS (St) Ab.   R.M. Jan. 24
d. c.580. Abbot of a monastery at Sora, near Caserta, who distributed all the goods of the monastery among the refugees from the Lombards. When the latter arrived and found that nothing remained in the abbey to plunder, they slew Suranus on the spot. We owe the story to St Gregory the Great (Dial. IV, 22).
Cf. Menzies — Holw. — Baud.

SUSANNA, MARCIANA, PALLADIA and Comp. (SS) MM.   R.M. May 24
2nd cent. Wives of certain soldiers belonging to the military unit commanded by St Meletius. They were put to death together with their children and other martyrs in Galatia. Their Acts are legendary.
Cf. Holw. — Baud.

SUSANNA COBIOJE (Bl) M.
A.C. July 12
d. 1628. Wife of Bl Araki Cobioje. Six months before her death she was hung naked by her hair from a tree for eight hours. She was beheaded at Nagasaki. Beatified in 1867.
Cf. Holw.

SUSANNA (St) V. M.   R.M. Aug. 11
d. 295. A Roman maiden, alleged niece of Pope St Caius, martyred under Diocletian for refusing to marry the emperor's son. The Acts of this saint are wholly untrustworthy, but there certainly was a famous Roman martyr of this name, and to her is dedicated the Roman church of St Susanna, which still stands. There is no connexion between St Susanna and the martyr St Tiburtius commemorated on the same day.
Cf. Holw. — Att. — Baud. — Menzies.

SUSANNA (St) V. M.   R.M. Sept. 19
d. 362. According to the R.M. she was the daughter of a pagan priest and a Jewess. Being converted to Christ after their death, she was made a deaconess at Eleutheropolis, where she was martyred under Julian the Apostate.
Cf. Holw. — Baud.

SUSU, HENRY (Bl) C.   A.C. Oct. 25
See Henry Suso.

SWITHBERT (St) Bp. O.S.B.
R.M. March 1
647-715. A Northumbrian Benedictine, he formed one of the group of twelve missionary monks who in 690 crossed over to Friesland under the leadership of St Willibrord. He preached the gospel with great success, mainly in Hither Friesland. In 693 he was consecrated regionary bishop by St Wilfrid at Ripon and returned to preach along the right bank of the Rhine. His work here was undone by the Saxon invaders, and he retired to the small island of Kaiserswerth in the Rhine, near Düsseldorf. Here he founded a Benedictine monastery (710) and here he died.
Cf. Att. — Baud. — Holw. — Zimm.

SWITHBERT the YOUNGER (St) Bp.
A.C. Apr. 30
d. 807. An Englishman, perhaps a Benedictine monk, who joined the missionaries in Germany and was made bishop of Werden in Westphalia.
Cf. Holw. — Baud.

SWITHUN (SWITHIN) (St) Bp.
A.C. July 15. R.M. July 2
d. 862. He was born in Wessex and spent his youth at the Old Abbey at Winchester, but it is not certain that he ever became a monk. After being ordained priest he was made chaplain to Egbert, king of the W. Saxons and tutor to the young prince Ethelwolf. In 852 he was appointed bishop of Winchester. The origin of the popular saying: "If it rains on St Swithun's day" etc., is not known.
Cf. Holw. — Baud. — Att. — Stanton.

SWITHUN WELLS (Bl) M. A.C. Dec. 10
d. 1591. A gentleman of Bambridge, Hants, executed at Gray's Inn Fields for sheltering a priest named Edmund Genings, q.v., who suffered with him. Beatified in 1929.
Cf. Newdigate.

SY
Note. Names beginning with Sy are quite as often written Si. Sometimes too the initial letters Sy stand for the Greek Su.

SYAGRIUS (SIACRE) (St) Bp. O.S.B.
A.C. May 23
d. c.787. A kinsman of Charlemagne. He became a monk of Lérins and later abbot-founder of the monastery of St Pons at Cimiez in Provence, whence he was promoted to the see of Nice (777).
Cf. Zimm. — Gams — Holw. — Baud.

SYAGRIUS (SIACRE) (St) Bp.
R.M. Aug. 27
d. 600. Bishop of Autun c.560-600. He played a prominent part in the ecclesiastical and political life of his time. He entertained St Augustine and his fellow monks on their way to England.
Cf. Holw. — Att. — Baud. — Duch. Fast. Episc.

SYCUS and PALATINUS (SS) MM.
R.M. May 30
? Martyrs of Antioch in Syria. Probably the original entry was: Hesychius Palatinus (March 2), q.v.
Cf. Holw. — Baud.

SYLVESTER (several).
Otherwise Silvester, q.v.

SYLVIA (St) W. R.M. Nov. 3
d. c.572. The mother of St Gregory the

Great. Over her former house on the Coelian Hill at Rome a chapel was built in her honour.
Cf. Holw. — Baud. — Menzies.

SYMMACHUS (St) Pope. R.M. July 19
d. 514. A Sardinian by birth, he became pope in 498. His pontificate was a troubled one owing to the activities of his enemies, who set up an antipope. He was a holy and able pope and well deserved the title "father of the poor" which was bestowed upon him.
Cf. Holw. — Baud. — Att.

SYMPHORIAN (St) M. R.M. July 7
See Claudius, Nicostratus, etc.

SYMPHORIAN (St) M. R.M. Aug. 22
d. c.180. A member of a senatorial family at Autun, put to death under Marcus Aurelius for refusing to sacrifice to the goddess Cybele. He is one of the most celebrated martyrs of France.
Cf. Holw. — Att. — Baud.

SYMPHORIAN (St) M. R.M. Nov. 8
One of the Four Crowned Martyrs, q.v.

SYMPHOROSA (St) M. R.M. July 2
See Ariston, Crescentian, etc.

SYMPHOROSA and Comp. (SS) MM.
R.M. July 18
d. c.135. A martyr of Tivoli under Hadrian, widow of the martyr St Getulius. The R.M. describes her as the mother of seven other martyrs, viz., Crescens, Julian, Nemesius, Primitivus, Justin, Stacteus and Eugene. Her Acts, however, are very untrustworthy, being a Christian adaptation of the story of the Maccabees. She was not the mother of seven martyrs, and these seven martyrs were not brothers, nor were they martyred together.
Cf. Holw. — Baud. — Att.

SYMPHRONIUS (St) M. R.M. Feb. 3
See Felix, Symphronius, etc.

SYMPHRONIUS, OLYMPIUS, THEODULUS and EXUPERIA (SS) MM.
R.M. July 26
d. 257. Symphronius was a Roman slave who brought about the conversion of the tribune Olympius, the latter's wife Exuperia and their son Theodulus. They were all burnt to death under Valerian.
Cf. Holw. — Baud.

SYNCLETICA (St) V.   R.M. Jan. 5
d. c.400. A wealthy lady of Macedonia who abandoned the world and lived as a recluse in a disused tomb till her eighty-fourth year. For a long time she suffered from temptations and spiritual desolation, and in her later years from cancer and consumption.
Cf. Holw. — Att. — Baud.

SYNDIMIUS (St) M.   R.M. Dec. 19
See Cyriacus, Paulillus, etc.

SYNESIUS and THEOPOMPUS (SS) MM.   R.M. May 21
Identical with Theopemptus and Theonas of Jan. 3, q.v., Theonas being also known as Synesius.

SYNESIUS (St) M.   R.M. Dec. 12
d. 275. A lector of the Roman church martyred under Aurelian.
Cf. Baud. — Holw.

SYNTYCHE (St)   R.M. July 22
d. 1st cent. A female member of the church of Philippi, described by St Paul as his fellow labourer in the gospel and as one whose name is in the book of life. (Philip. IV, 2-3).

SYRA (SYRIA) (St) V.   A.C. June 8
7th cent. An alleged sister of St Fiacre (Flaker) who followed her brother from Ireland to France and there lived as a recluse.
Cf. Holw. — Baud. — Chev.

SYRA (St) V. O.S.B.   A.C. Oct. 23
d. c.660. Nun of Faremoutiers, whence she was summoned by Bishop Ragne-boldus to be abbess of a convent at Châlons-sur-Marne.
Cf. Holw. — Chev.

SYRIAN MARTYRS (SS)   R.M. July 31
d. 517. A group of three hundred and fifty monks slain by the Monophysites for defending the decrees of the council of Chalcedon.
Cf. Holw. — Baud.

SYRIAN MARTYRS (SS)   R.M. Nov. 14
d. 773. A large number of women cruelly put to death at Emessa in Phoenicia by the Mohammedan conquerors of the country.
Cf. Holw. — Baud.

SYRUS of GENOA (St) Bp.   R.M. June 29
d. c.380. Bishop of Genoa from c.324 to c.380. He had been parish priest of St Romulus (now San Remo). He is the titular of the cathedral of Genoa and principal patron of the city and diocese. His feast is kept on July 7.
Cf. Gams — Holw. — Baud.

SYRUS (St) Bp. M.   R.M. Dec. 9
1st cent. (?) Alleged first bishop of Pavia and said to have been sent thither by the apostles. He probably belongs to the 3rd or 4th century. He is the principal patron of Pavia. See also under Juventius (Feb. 8).
Cf. Gams — Baud. — Holw.

SYTHA (St) V.   A.C. May 19
Otherwise Osyth, q.v.

T

TABITHA (or DORCAS) (St) W.   A.C. Oct. 25
1st cent. A widow of Joppe who believed in Christ. She was raised from the dead by St Peter (Acts IX, 36-43).
Cf. Holw.

TALARICAN (St) Bp.   A.C. Oct. 30
? 6th cent. A bishop, probably Pictish, in whose honour various Scottish churches were dedicated. Mentioned in the Aberdeen Breviary.
Cf. Holw. — Baring-Gould.

TALIDA (St) V.   A.C. Jan. 5
4th cent. Palladius relates that she was abbess of one of the twelve nunneries at Antinoë in Egypt, and that she had been eighty years at her convent when he visited her.
Cf. Holw.

TALMACH (St) C.   A.C. March 14
7th cent. A disciple of St Barr at Lough Erc, and founder of a monastery which he placed under the same saint.
Cf. Holw. — Chev.

TAMMARUS (St) C.   R.M. Sept. 1
See Priscus, Castrensis, etc.

TANCA (St) V. M.   A.C. Oct. 10
d. c.637. A young girl of the neighbourhood of Troyes in France, who lost her life

in defence of her virginity and is locally venerated as a virgin martyr.
Cf. Chev. — Baud. — Holw.

TANCO (TANCHO) (St) Bp. M. O.S.B.
A.C. Feb. 15
d. 808. An Irish monk who became abbot of the Benedictine monastery of Amalbarich in Saxony, and who was eventually promoted to the see of Werden. He died at the hands of a pagan mob whose savage customs he had denounced.
Cf. Att. — Zimm. — Holw. — Baud.

TARACUS (St) M. R.M. Oct. 11
Otherwise Tharacus, q.v.

TARAGHTA (St) V. A.C. Aug. 11
Otherwise Attracta, q.v.

TARASIUS (THARASIUS) (St) Bp.
R.M. Feb. 25
d. 806. A patrician of Constantinople, imperial secretary in the court of Constantine VI. Though a layman he was chosen patriarch, and he accepted on condition that a general council should be convened to end the iconoclastic persecution. He was accordingly consecrated (Christmas 784) and the second council of Nicaea held, the decrees of which were approved by the pope. Shortly after, however, on his refusing to countenance the emperor's bigamous marriage, he was cruelly persecuted by the empress Irene. On the other hand St Theodore and his monks of Studium accused the patriarch of being too lenient. Tarasius is highly venerated in the Orthodox Church.
Cf. Att. — Holw. — Baud.

TARBULA (TARBO, TARBA) (St) V. M.
R.M. Apr. 22
d. 345 (May 5). Sister of St Simeon, the great bishop-martyr of Persia, and a virgin consecrated to God. After her brother's death Tarbula was accused by Jews of having caused by witchcraft the sickness of King Shapur's wife, and she was put to death by being sawn in two.
Cf. Holw. — Baud.

TARKIN (St) Bp. A.C. Oct. 30
Otherwise Talarican, q.v.

TARSICIA (TARSITIA) (St) V.
A.C. Jan. 15
d. c.600. Said to have been a granddaughter of Clotaire II and sister of St Ferreol of Usèz. She lived as a recluse

near Rodez, where she is now venerated.
Cf. Holw. — Baud. — Att. — Chev.

TARSICIUS, ZOTICUS, CYRIACUS and Comp. (SS) MM. R.M. Jan. 31
? Martyrs at Alexandria.
Cf. Holw. — Baud.

TARSICIUS (St) M. R.M. Aug. 15
d. ? 255. The inscription upon his tomb, written by Pope St Damasus, informs us that Tarsicius, while carrying the Blessed Sacrament to some Christians in prison, was seized by a heathen mob and preferred to die rather than expose to profanation the Sacred Mysteries. The story was of course embellished by Cardinal Wiseman in his *Fabiola*.
Cf. Att. — Baud. — Holw.

TARSILLA (St) V. R.M. Dec. 24
d. c.581. An aunt of St Gregory the Great, sister of St Emiliana and niece of Pope St Felix. In her paternal home she led a life of seclusion and mortification.
Cf. Holw. — Baud.

TARSUS (Martyrs of) (SS) R.M. June 6
d. c.290. A group of twenty martyrs at Tarsus in Cilicia under Diocletian.
Cf. Holw. — Baud.

TASSACH (St) Bp. A.C. Apr. 14
d. c.495. One of St Patrick's earliest disciples and first bishop of Raholp (Co. Down). He was a skilful artisan and made crosses, croziers and shrines for St Patrick. It was he who administered the last sacraments to St Patrick.
Cf. Holw.

TASSILO (Bl) Mk. O.S.B. A.C. Dec. 13
d. p. 794. Duke of Bavaria and one of the greatest benefactors of the Benedictine monks. After founding many abbeys and churches he himself became a monk at Jumièges, whence he migrated to Lorsch, where he died.
Cf. Zimm.

TASSO (TASO) (St) Ab. O.S.B.
A.C. Jan. 11
d. c.739. A native of Benevento. With his two brothers, SS Paldo and Tato, he became a monk of Farfa and then the co-founder of San Vincenzo al Voltorno, where he succeeded his brothers as third abbot.
Cf. Zimm. — Holw. — Baud.

TATE (St) W. A.C. Apr. 5
Otherwise Ethelburga, q.v.

**TATHAI (TATHAN, TATHAEUS, ATH-
AEUS) (St) H.** A.C. Dec. 26
Early 6th cent. A nephew of St Samson
of Dol who settled in Glamorganshire,
where he founded a church.
Cf. Baring-Gould.

TATIAN (St) M. R.M. March 16
See Hilary, Tatian, etc.

TATIAN DULAS (St) M. R.M. June 15
Otherwise Dulas, q.v.

TATIAN (St) M. R.M. Sept. 12
See Macedonius, Theodulus and Tatian.

TATIANA (St) M. R.M. Jan. 12
d. c.230. According to the R.M., a
woman put to death in Rome under Alexander Severus. On this day the Greeks
also honour a St Tatiana together with
two others, Euthasia and Mertios, MM.
Cf. Holw. — Baud. — Att.

TATION (St) M. R.M. Aug. 24
d. c.304. A martyr beheaded at Claudip-
olis in Bithynia under Diocletian.
Cf. Holw. — Baud.

TATO (St) Ab. O.S.B. A.C. Jan. 11
d. c.729. Second abbot of San Vincenzo
al Volturno, near Benevento, and brother
of SS Paldo and Tasso, q.v.
Cf. Zimm. — Holw. — Baud.

TATTA (St) M. R.M. Sept. 25
See Paul, Tatta, etc.

TATWIN (St) Bp. O.S.B. A.C. July 30
d. 734. Monk of Bredon, or Brenton, in
Worcestershire. He succeeded St Brithwald in the see of Canterbury in 731 and
received the pallium in 733.
Cf. Zimm. — Stanton — Holw. — Baud.

TAURINUS (St) Bp. R.M. Aug. 11
d. c.412. Bishop of Evreux in Normandy.
The legend connecting him with St Denis
of Paris is now rejected by all scholars.
*Cf. Holw. — Baud. — Duch. Fast. Episc.
— Gams.*

TAURION (St) M. R.M. Nov. 7
See Auctus, Taurion and Thessalonica.

TEATH (TEATHA, EATHA) (St)
A.C. Jan. 15
Otherwise Ita, q.v.
The title-saint of the church of St Teath
in Cornwall is perhaps another of that
name, for there is believed to have been a
St Teath from Wales, one of the daughters
of Brychan of Brecknock.
Cf. Holw.

TEGLA (THECLA) (St) V. A.C. June 1
? The patron saint of the church and holy
well at Llandegla in Denbighshire.
Cf. Baring-Gould.

**TEILO (TEILIO, TEILUS, THELIAN,
TEILAN, TEILOU, TELIOU, DILLO,
DILLON, etc.) (St) Bp.** A.C. Feb. 9
d. c.580. Born at Penally, near Tenby, in
S. Wales, and educated by St Dyfrig. He
was a companion and friend of SS David
and Samson. He became the founder and
abbot-bishop of Llandaff monastery (Llandeilo Fawr) in Carmarthenshire.
Cf. Att. — Holw. — Baud.

TELEMACHUS (St) M. R.M. Jan. 1
Otherwise Almachius, q.v.

TELESPHORUS (St) Pope M.
R.M. Jan. 5
d. 136. A Calabrian Greek, he was pope
for ten years, and according to the Roman
tradition suffered martyrdom under Hadrian.
Cf. Att. — Holw. — Baud.

TENENAN (St) Bp. A.C. July 16
d. c.635. A Briton by birth who became
a hermit in Brittany and was eventually
raised to the see of Léon.
Cf. Holw. — Baud.

**TERENCE, AFRICANUS, POMPEIUS
and Comp. (SS) MM.** R.M. Apr. 10
d. 250. A band of fifty martyrs, imprisoned with a number of snakes and
scorpions, and finally beheaded at Carthage under Decius.
Cf. Holw. — Baud.

TERENCE (St) Bp. M. R.M. June 21
1st cent. Bishop of Iconium in apostolic
times. Some hagiographers conjecture
that he is identical with the Tertius mentioned as his amanuensis by St Paul in his
epistle to the Romans (XVI, 22).
Cf. Holw. — Baud.

TERENCE of TODI (St) M.
R.M. Sept. 27
See Fidentius and Terentius.

TERENCE of METZ (St) Bp.
A.C. Oct. 29
d. 520. 16th bishop of Metz.
Cf. Holw. — Duch. Fast. Episc. — Baud.

TERENTIAN (St) Bp. M.   R.M. Sept. 1
d. 118. Bishop of Todi in Umbria. He
was racked, had his tongue cut out, and
was finally beheaded under Hadrian.
Cf. Holw. — Baud.

TERESA MARGARET REDI (Bl) V.
O.C.D. A.C. March 11
1747-1770. Anna Maria, in religion Teresa Margaret, Redi became a Discalced
Carmelite nun at the convent of St Teresa
at Florence in 1765. She died at the age
of twenty-three, her short life in religion
being remarkable for penance and prayer.
Beatified 1929.
Cf. Att.

TERESA (TARASIA) (St) N. O.S.B. Cist.
A.C. June 17
d. 1250. Daughter of King Sancho I of
Portugal. She married her cousin Alphonsus IX, king of León, but the marriage was declared null by the Holy See
on the grounds of consanguinity. She returned to Portugal and entered the Cistercian convent at Lorvão, near Coimbra,
where she died. Cult confirmed, with the
title of saint, by Clement XI in 1705.
*Cf. Zimm. — P. de U. — Att. — Baud. —
Chev.*

TERESA FANTOU (Bl) V. M.
A.C. June 26
d. 1794. A Sister of Charity of Arras.
With three other Sisters she was arrested
by the French revolutionaries in 1794,
brought to Cambrai and there guillotined.
Beatified 1920.
Cf. Holw. — Baud.

TERESA SOIRON (Bl) V. M.
A.C. July 17
d. 1794. A sister of Bl Catherine Soiron.
She was a maid in the service of the Princess Lamballe. During the French Revolution she attached herself to the Carmelites of Compiègne, q.v., with whom she
was executed.
Cf. Holw. — Baud.

TERESA of LISIEUX (St) V. O.C.D.
R.M. Oct. 3
1873-1897. Marie Françoise Thérèse
Martin (her religious name was Teresa of
the Infant Jesus) was born at Alençon,
entered the Carmelite Order at Lisieux at
the age of fifteen, and such was her
progress in the spiritual life that she was
appointed novice-mistress at the age of
twenty-two. Two years later she died,
her short life having been remarkable for
its humility, simplicity and silently heroic
endurance of suffering. Since her death
she has worked innumerable miracles, and
her cult has spread throughout the world.
Pius XI declared her, together with St
Francis Xavier, patron saint of foreign
missions. Canonized 1925. In English-
speaking countries she is often known as
the Little Flower of Jesus.
Cf. Holw. — Baud. — Att.

TERESA (St) V. O.C.D.   R.M. Oct. 15
1515-1582. Teresa Cepeda de Ahumada
was born at Avila in Old Castile and at
the age of eighteen entered the Carmelite
convent in her native town. In 1562 she
founded her first reformed convent of St
Joseph at Avila, and from that year till
her death she was always on the move,
opening new houses (fifteen directly and
seventeen through others), smoothing
away difficulties for her nuns, placating
those in authority (both clerical and lay),
who often fiercely opposed her and called
her the "roving nun." All this time she
was being favoured with remarkable mystical experiences, which she described,
under obedience, in treatises which may
be regarded as veritable text-books of mystical prayer and rank as classics of Spanish
literature. She is the saint of sound
common sense, of sane good humour, of
generous ideals, "one of the greatest, most
attractive and widely appreciated women
the world has ever known." (Attwater,
h.l.). She died at Alba de Tormes.
Canonized 1622.
Cf. Holw. — Att. — P. de U. — Baud.

TERNAN (St) Bp.   A.C. June 12
? 5th cent. An early missionary bishop
among the Picts in Scotland. He is said
to have resided at Abernethy and to have
been consecrated by St Palladius. He is
the reputed founder of the abbey of Culross in Fifeshire.
Cf. Holw. — Att.

TERNATIUS (TERNISCUS) (St) Bp.
A.C. Aug. 8
d. c.680. Eleventh bishop of Besançon.
Cf. Duch. Fast. Episc. — Holw. — Baud.

TERTIUS (St) M. R.M. Dec. 6
See Dionysia, Dativa, etc.

TERTULLA (St) V. M. R.M. Apr. 29
See Agapius and Comp.

TERTULLIAN (St) Bp. R.M. Apr. 27
d. c.490. Eighth bishop of Bologna.
Cf. Gams — Holw. — Baud.

TERTULLINUS (St) M. R.M. Aug. 4
d. 257. A Roman priest, martyred under
Valerian two days after his ordination.
Cf. Holw. — Baud.

TETRICUS (St) Bp. A.C. March 20
d. 572. Son of St Gregory, bishop of
Langres, and uncle of St Gregory of Tours.
He succeeded his father in the see of
Langres about the year 540.
*Cf. Holw. — Baud. — Duch. Fast. Episc.
— Gams.*

TETRICUS (St) Bp. M. O.S.B.
A.C. Apr. 12
d. 707. Abbot of the Benedictine monastery of St Germanus at Auxerre. He was
raised to the see of Auxerre by popular
acclamation. The saint met his death at
the hand of his archdeacon Raginfred,
who slew him with a sword as he lay
asleep on a bench.
*Cf. Gams — Duch. Fast. Episc. — Holw.
— Att. — Baud.*

TETTA (St) Abs. O.S.B. A.C. Sept. 28
d. c.772. Abbess of Wimborne in Dorsetshire. She helped St Boniface by sending
him band after band of missionary nuns
from her community, among whom were
SS Lioba, Thecla, etc. She is said to have
ruled over some five hundred nuns.
Cf. Zimm. — Baud. — Holw.

TEUZZO (Bl) C. O.S.B. A.C. Aug. 9
d. c.1072. Monk of St Mary's Abbey (La
Badia) at Florence. During some fifty
years he lived as a recluse near his monastery. He supported St John Gualbert in
his campaign against simony.
Cf. Zimm.

THADDEUS (TADHG) (Bl) Bp.
A.C. Oct. 25
d. 1497. Thaddeus McCarthy (Machar)

was made bishop of Ross in 1482 but
driven from his see in 1488. The Holy
See next nominated him bishop of Cork
and Cloyne, but he was not allowed into
the diocese. Then the perplexed bishop
went to Rome to plead his cause personally, but died on his way home at Ivrea in
Piedmont. Cult approved 1910.
Cf. Holw. — Baud. — Att.

THADDEUS (St) Apostle. R.M. Oct. 28
Otherwise Jude, q.v.

THADDEUS LIEU (Bl) M. A.C. Nov. 24
d. 1823 (Nov. 30). A Chinese priest in
the province of Zyu-Thuan. He was imprisoned for two years and then strangled.
Beatified 1900.
Cf. Holw.

THAIS (St) Penitent. A.C. Oct. 8
d. c.348. A wealthy and beautiful courte-
san of Alexandria converted by St Paphnutius (other accounts say St Bessarion or
St Serapion) and walled up, for three years
in a cell. Only towards the end of her life
was she admitted to full conventual life
with the other nuns. Some modern
writers consider the story a moral tale with
no foundation of fact.
Cf. Holw. — Att. — Baud.

THALASSIUS and LIMNAEUS (SS) HH.
A.C. Feb. 22
5th cent. Two Syrian hermits who lived
in a cave near Cyrrhus. Our knowledge of
them is due to the historian Theodoret,
who knew them personally.
Cf. Att. — Holw. — Baud.

THALELAEUS (St) H. A.C. Feb. 27
d. c.450. Surnamed Epiclautos, i.e.,
weeping much. A hermit who dwelt at
Gabala in Syria, next to the shrine of an
idol, where he converted many of the
pagan pilgrims. For many years he lived
in an open barrel.
Cf. Holw. — Att. — Baud.

**THALELAEUS, ASTERIUS, ALEXAN-
DER and Comp.** R.M. May 20
d. ? 284. Thalelaeus practised medicine
and attended his patients gratis at Anazarbus in Cilicia. He suffered martyrdom
at Aegae, a town on the coast of that
province, and not at Edessa as has been
sometimes stated. The R.M. adds Asterius and Alexander, two of his executioners,
and others of the spectators, who were

converted by the constancy of the martyr.
Cf. Att. — Holw. — Baud.

THALUS (St) M. R.M. March 11
See Trophimus and Thalus.

THAMEL and Comp. (SS) MM.
  R.M. Sept. 4
d. c.125. A converted pagan priest, martyred with four or five others (one of them his own sister) somewhere in the East, under Hadrian.
Cf. Holw. — Baud.

THARACUS (TARACHUS), PROBUS and ANDRONICUS (SS) MM.
  R.M. Oct. 11
d. 304. Tarachus, aged sixty-five, was a retired officer of the Roman army, Probus a Roman citizen from Pamphilia, and Andronicus a young man of good birth from Ephesus. They were beheaded near Tarsus in Cilicia under Diocletian. The authenticity of their Acts is disputed.
Cf. Att. — Holw. — Baud.

THARASIUS (St) Bp. R.M. Feb. 25
Otherwise Tarasius, q.v.

THAW (St) A.C. Sept. 1
Otherwise Lythan, q.v.

THEA (St) M. R.M. Dec. 19
See Meuris and Thea.

THÉAU (St) A.C. Jan. 7
Otherwise Tillo, q.v.

THEBAN LEGION, The (SS) MM.
  R.M. Sept. 22
d. c.287. The story of the Theban Legion is as follows. In the army of Maximinian Herculeus there was a legion (6,600 men) consisting of Christians recruited in Upper Egypt. When the emperor marched his army across the Alps to suppress a revolt in Gaul he camped near Agaunum, in Switzerland, and prepared for the battle with public sacrifices. The Christian legion refused to attend (another version says that they refused to attack innocent people) and were in consequence twice decimated. When they still persevered in their refusal they were massacred *en masse*. Among those who suffered were Maurice, the *primicerius*, Exuperius, Candidus, Vitalis, two Victors, Alexander (at Bergamo) and Gereon (at Cologne). At Agaunum. now St-Maurice-

en-Valois, a basilica was built (c.369-391) to enshrine the relics of the martyrs. The story can therefore be accepted as substantially true, but it is almost unbelievable that the whole legion was Christian and that the whole of it was put to death. Probably a very large number of soldiers were put to death and that gave rise to the story as now told.
Cf. Att. — Baud. — Holw.

THECLA (St) M. R.M. March 26
See Peter, Marcian, etc.

THECLA (St) M. R.M. Aug. 19
See Timothy, Thecla and Agapius.

THECLA (St) M. R.M. Aug. 30
See Boniface and Thecla.

THECLA (St) V. M. R.M. Sept. 3
See Euphemia, Dorothea, etc.

THECLA NANGAXI (Bl) M.
  A.C. Sept. 10
d. 1622. A Japanese woman, wife of Bl Paul Nangaxi, beheaded at Nagasaki (see Charles Spinola).
Cf. Holw.

THECLA (St) V. M. R.M. Sept. 23
1st cent. According to the second century novel called the *Acts of Paul and Thecla*, which abounds in extravagant stories and is not quite orthodox in doctrine, Thecla was a maiden of Iconium who heard St Paul preaching while she sat at her chamber window, became a Christian and followed the apostle dressed in boy's clothes. Several times she underwent most cruel tortures for the Faith — in the prayer for the dying the Roman Ritual refers especially to "three most cruel torments" — and finally died a solitary in Seleucia. The story seems to have a foundation of fact, but it is not possible to disentangle truth from fiction.
Cf. Holw. — Baud. — Att.

THECLA (St) Abs. O.S.B. R.M. Oct. 15
d. c.790. A Benedictine nun of Wimborne under St Tetta. She was one of the party which set out for the German mission under St Lioba. She was named by St Boniface first abbess of Ochsenfürt, and then of Kitzingen on the Main, over which she ruled for many years.
Cf. Holw. — Baud. — Zimm. — Att.

THECUSA (St) V. M.   R.M. May 18
See Theodotus, Thecusa, etc.

THELIAU (St) Bp.   A.C. Feb. 8
Otherwise Teilo, q.v.

THELICA (St) M.   R.M. Feb. 11
See under Saturninus and Comp.

THEMISTOCLES (St) M.
                          R.M. Dec. 21
d. 253.   A shepherd of Myra in Lycia who
was beheaded for refusing to reveal the
hiding-place of a fellow Christian.
Cf. Holw. — Att.

**THENEVA (THENEW, THENOVA,
DWYNWEN) (St) W.   A.C. July 18**
7th cent. The mother of St Kentigern
and together with him the patron saint of
Glasgow.
Cf. Holw.

**THEOBALD (THIBAUD) of VIENNE
(St) Bp.   A.C. May 21**
d. 1001.   Archbishop of Vienne 970-1001.
Cult confirmed 1903.
Cf. Holw. — Att. — Gams.

THEOBALD ROGGERI (Bl) C.
                          A.C. June 1
d. 1150. Born at Vico in Liguria of a
good family, he left home and chose to
work as a cobbler at Alba in Piedmont.
After a pilgrimage to Compostella he
earned his living as a carrier, sharing his
wages with the poor and suffering.
Cf. Holw. — Baud. — Att.

**THEOBALD (THIBAUT) (St) H. O.S.B.
Cam.   R.M. June 30**
1017-1066. Born in Brie, the son of Count
Arnoul of Champagne, he was bred to
arms, but at the age of eighteen, filled
with a desire for greater perfection as a
result of reading the lives of the saints,
he became a pilgrim and then a hermit.
Finally he settled at Salanigo, near Vicenza, received the Camaldolese habit and
was ordained priest.   Canonized by Alexander II in 1073.
Cf. Zimm. — Att. — Baud. — Holw.

**THEOBALD of MARLY (St) Ab. O.S.B.
Cist.   A.C. July 27**
d. 1247. Born in the castle of Marly, the
son of Buchard of Montmorency, he was a
distinguished knight at the court of Philip
Augustus of France. He abandoned his

worldly prospects and entered the Cis-
tercian abbey of Vaux-de-Cernay (1220),
becoming prior in 1230 and abbot in 1235.
He was highly esteemed by St Louis of
France.
Cf. Zimm. — Holw. — Att. — Baud.

THEOCTISTE (St) V.   R.M. Nov. 10
10th cent. A nun of Lesbos who became a
solitary in the isle of Paros. The story of
her last Holy Communion seems to be an
adaptation from the life of St Mary of
Egypt.
Cf. Holw. — Baud. — Att.

THEODARD (St) Bp. O.S.B.
                          A.C. May 1
d. 893. Educated at the Benedictine
abbey of St Martin at Montauriol, he
became archbishop of Narbonne. Before
his death he returned to St Martin's,
where he was clothed with the Benedictine habit. Later the abbey was named
after him, St Audard.
Cf. Duch. Fast. Episc. — Chev. — Att. —
Holw.

THEODARD (St) Bp. M. O.S.B.
                          R.M. Sept. 10
d. c.670. A disciple of St Remaclus at
Malmédy-Stavelot and his successor as
abbot (653) and as bishop of Maestricht
(662). On a journey undertaken in defence of his church he was murdered by
robbers in the forest of Bienwald, near
Speyer.
Cf. Zimm. — Baud. — Chev. — Att. —
Holw. — Duch. Fast. Episc.

THEODEMIR (St) M.   R.M. July 25
d. 851. A monk martyred at Cordova
under Abderrahman II.
Cf. Holw. — Baud. — P. de U.

**THEODICHILDIS (TELCHILDIS) (St)
Abs. O.S.B.   A.C. June 28**
d. p. 660. A nun of Faremoutiers, she
became the first abbess of Jouarre, diocese
of Meaux.
Cf. Holw. — Baud. — Chev.

THEODORA (St) Empress. A.C. Feb. 11
d. 867. Wife of the iconoclast emperor
Theophilus. During the regency of her
son, Michael the Drunkard, she did her
utmost to restore the veneration of images.
She ended her life in a convent. Her claim
to sanctity is questionable.
Cf. Holw. — Chev. — Att.

THEODORA (St) M.   R.M. March 13
See Theusetas, Horres, etc.

THEODORA (St) M.   R.M. Apr. 1
d. 132. A woman of Rome, sister of St Hermes (Aug. 28) whom she assisted in prison and under torture. She was herself martyred some months later. Brother and sister were buried side by side.
Cf. Holw. — Baud.

THEODORA V. and DIDYMUS (SS) MM.   R.M. Apr. 28
d. 304. A maiden of Alexandria, sentenced to prostitution, but delivered from the brothel by St Didymus, who was still a pagan. This led to his conversion, and the two saints were martyred together.
Cf. Holw. — Baud.

THEODORA (St) V. M.   R.M. May 7
See Flavia Domitilla, Euphrosyna and Theodora.

THEODORA (St) Penitent.
R.M. Sept. 11
d. 491. The current story of this saint is similar to that of St Pelagia of Antioch (Oct. 8) q.v. The R.M., however, simply says: "At Alexandria, St Theodora, who fell through lack of care, but repenting of her deed, persevered in the religious habit, unknown, with wondrous abstinence and patience, until her death."
Cf. Holw. — Att. — Baud.

THEODORA (St) Matron. R.M. Sept. 17
d. c.305. A Roman lady of noble birth and great wealth, who, during the persecution of Diocletian, generously devoted herself and her riches to the service of the martyrs. She seems to have died while the persecution was still raging.
Cf. Holw. — Baud.

THEODORE of EGYPT (St) H.
R.M. Jan. 7
4th cent. A monk of Egypt, disciple of St Ammonius.
Cf. Holw. — Baud.

THEODORE STRATELATES (St) M.
R.M. Feb. 7
d. 319. A general (*stratelates*) in the army of Licinius, by whose order he was tortured and crucified at Heraclea in Thrace. He is probably identical with St Theodore Tyro of Amasea.
Cf. Att. — Holw. — Baud.

THEODORE (St) M.   R.M. March 17
See Alexander and Theodore.

THEODORE, IRENAEUS, SERAPION and AMMONIUS (SS) MM.
R.M. March 26
d. 310. Theodore, bishop of Pentapolis in Libya, Irenaeus, his deacon, and Serapion and Ammonius, his two lectors, suffered martyrdom under Gallienus by having their tongues cut out. However, they survived and died in peace, being nevertheless venerated as martyrs.
Cf. Holw. — Baud.

THEODORE and Comp. (SS) MM.
O.S.B.   A.C. Apr. 9
d. 870. Theodore was abbot of Croyland, and he and his large community were put to death by the Danes. Besides the abbot, several others are mentioned by name: Askega, prior; Swethin, sub-prior; Elfgete, deacon; Savinus, subdeacon; Egdred and Ulrick, acolytes; Grimkeld and Agamund (Argamund), both centenarians.
Cf. Stanton.

THEODORE and PAUSILIPPUS (SS) MM.   R.M. Apr. 15
d. c.130. Martyrs near Byzantium under Hadrian.
Cf. Holw. — Baud.

THEODORE TRICHINAS (St) H.
R.M. Apr. 20
d. p. 330. A hermit near his native city of Constantinople. He is surnamed *Trichinas*, "the hairy," because his only garment was a rough hair-shirt.
Cf. Holw. — Baud.

THEODORE of SIKION (St) Bp.
R.M. Apr. 22
d. 613. Born at Sikion in Galatia, the son of an innkeeper, he became a monk at Jerusalem and in after life the abbot-founder of several monasteries. About 590 he was made bishop of Anastasiopolis in Galatia. He was a great fosterer of the cult of St George.
Cf. Holw. — Baud. — Att.

THEODORE of TABENNA (St) Ab.
R.M. Apr. 27
d. c.368. Usually called "Theodore the Holy" by the Greeks. He was trained in the monastic life by St Pachomius, whom he succeeded as abbot of Tabenna. His

feast is kept in the East on May 16, but the actual date of his death was Apr. 27.
Cf. Holw. — Att. — Baud.

THEODORE of BOLOGNA (St) Bp.
R.M. May 5
d. c.550. A bishop of Bologna c.530-c.550.
Cf. Menzies — Holw.

THEODORE of PAVIA (St) Bp.
R.M. May 20
d. 778. Bishop of Pavia 743-778. He had much to endure, including repeated banishment, at the hands of the Arian Lombard kings.
Cf. Menzies — Baud. — Holw.

THEODORE of CYRENE (St) Bp. M.
R.M. July 4
d. c.310. Bishop of Cyrene in Lybia. He had great skill in copying books, and was brutally martyred under Diocletian for refusing to deliver up his manuscripts of the Holy Scriptures.
Cf. Holw. — Baud.

THEODORE (St) M. **R.M. July 29**
See Lucilla, Flora, etc.

THEODORE (St) M. **R.M. Sept. 2**
See Zeno, Concordius and Theodore.

THEODORE, OCEANUS, AMMIANUS and JULIAN (SS) MM. **R.M. Sept. 4**
d. c.310. Oriental martyrs, burnt at the stake, probably under Maximian Herculeus.
Cf. Holw. — Baud.

THEODORE (St) M. **R.M. Sept. 5**
See Urban, Theodore, etc.

THEODORE (St) M. **R.M. Sept. 15**
See Maximus, Theodore and Asclepiodus.

THEODORE of CANTERBURY (St) Bp. O.S.B. **R.M. Sept. 19**
c.602-690. Born at Tarsus in Cilicia, he spent some time at Athens and became a monk at Rome. He was sixty-six years old when Pope St Vitalian appointed him to the see of Canterbury at the suggestion of the African St Adrian. These two travelled to England together, Adrian becoming abbot of the monastery of SS Peter and Paul at Canterbury and acting as adviser to the new archbishop. Theodore is rightly called the second founder of the see of Canterbury and the first primate of the English Church. He visited all parts of the country, consolidated or re-established dioceses, promoted learning and opened schools, and held the first national council at Hertford in 673. His activities involved him in disputes on questions of jurisdiction with St Chad and St Wilfrid, but these controversies were conducted with dignity and settled in a spirit of charity. St Theodore has a claim to be considered one of the greatest figures in English history.
Cf. Zimm. — Att. — Stanton — Holw. — Chev.

THEODORE, PHILIPPA and Comp. (SS) MM. **R.M. Sept. 20**
d. 220. A group of four Christians crucified at Perge in Pamphilia under Heliogabalus. They were: Theodore and Socrates, soldiers; Dionysius, a former pagan priest; and Philippa, Theodore's mother. They expired after three days on the cross.
Cf. Holw. — Baud.

THEODORE (THEODORET) of ANTIOCH (St) M. **R.M. Oct. 23**
d. 362. A priest, treasurer of the Church of Antioch, martyred under Julian the Apostate for continuing to minister to the faithful in spite of the imperial decrees to the contrary.
Cf. Holw. — Baud.

THEODORE (THEUDAR) (St) Ab.
R.M. Oct. 29
d. c.575. A priest, disciple of St Caesarius of Arles and abbot of one of the monasteries of Vienne in Gaul. He made several ecclesiastical and monastic foundations and died as a recluse in the church of St Laurence in Vienne.
Cf. Holw. — Chev. — Baud.

THEODORE GUÉNOT (Bl) Bp. M.
A.C. Nov. 4
1802-1861. A native of Bessieux, diocese of Besançon. He joined the Society of Foreign Missions and after his ordination was sent to Cochin-China. Later he was appointed vicar apostolic of that region and titular bishop of Metellopolis. He was arrested and sentenced to death, but died in prison as a result of ill-treatment.
Cf. Baud.

THEODORE TYRO (St) M.
R.M. Nov. 9
d. c.306. Said to have been a recruit (hence his nickname of Tyro) in the Roman army, who set fire to the temple of Cybele at Euchaïta, near Amasea in Pontus, for which he paid the penalty by being burnt alive at the same place. Beyond the fact of his martyrdom nothing certain is known about him. He is greatly venerated in the East as one of the "three soldier saints," viz., SS George, Demetrius and Theodore. He is almost certainly identical with St Theodore Stratelates. *Cf. Holw. — Baud. — Att.*

THEODORE STUDITES (St) Ab.
R.M. Nov. 11
759-826. A native of Constantinople who became a monk at the monastery of the Studium (more correctly *Studios*) in that city. In 799 he became abbot, and under his rule the monastery developed into a centre from which a monastic revival spread throughout the East, its influence reaching to Mt Athos and later to Russia, Rumania and Bulgaria. Studium stood for all that is lasting in monastic observance: liturgical prayer, community life, enclosure, poverty, studies and manual work (the monks excelled in calligraphy). The community, with St Theodore at their head, uncompromisingly defended the supreme authority of the see of Rome, the veneration of images (against a series of iconoclastic emperors), and opposed Caesaropapism in every form. Theodore suffered banishment for seven years on this account. He is one of the great figures of monastic history.
Cf. Holw. — Att. — Baud.

THEODORE (St) Bp. M. R.M. Nov. 26
See Faustus, Didius, etc.

THEODORE (St) M. R.M. Dec. 7
See Polycarp and Theodore.

THEODORE (St) M. R.M. Dec. 14
See Drusus, Zosimus and Theodore.

THEODORE (St) M. R.M. Dec. 15
See Irenaeus, Antony, etc.

THEODORE the SACRISTAN (St) C.
R.M. Dec. 26
d. 6th cent. A contemporary of St Gregory the Great, from whom we derive all our information concerning his life.

Theodore was a sacristan (*mansionarius*) in the basilica of St Peter, Rome, where, while busy about his duties in the church, he engaged in visible intercourse with the angels.
Cf. Holw. — Baud.

THEODORE, M. and THEOPHANES Bp. (SS) R.M. Dec. 27
c.841 and c.845. Two brothers, monks of the *laura* of St Sabbas in Jerusalem, who were prominent in defence of the veneration of images. They were cruelly persecuted by the Byzantine emperors. Verses were cut in the flesh of their faces (for this reason they are called *Graphi*, "the Written-on"), and they were otherwise ill-treated. Theodore died in prison in consequence of his sufferings. Theophanes survived him a few years and according to the R.M. became bishop of Nicaea.
Cf. Holw. — Att. — Baud.

THEODORET (St) M. R.M. Oct. 23
Called Theodorus in the R.M. (see above, Oct. 23).

THEODORIC II of ORLEANS (St) Bp. O.S.B. A.C. Jan. 27
d. 1022. Monk of Saint-Pierre-le-Vif at Sens. He was summoned to court as counsellor and afterwards nominated bishop of Orleans. He died at Tonnerre on his way to Rome.
Cf. Mab. — Chev. — Baud. — Holw.

THEODORIC (St) Bp. M. A.C. Feb. 2
See Bruno and Comp.

THEODORIC (THIERRY, THEODERICUS) (St) Ab. R.M. July 1
d. c.533. Educated by St Remigius of Reims, by whom he was appointed abbot of Mont d'Or, near Reims.
Cf. Holw. — Att. — Baud.

THEODORIC of EMDEN (St) M. O.F.M. R.M. July 9
d. 1572. A Dutch Friar Minor, confessor to the Franciscan nuns at Gorkum. He was hanged at Briel with the group of Gorkum martyrs, q.v.
Cf. Holw. — Baud.

THEODORIC (St) Bp. A.C. Aug. 5
d. 863. Bishop of Cambrai-Arras, c.830-863.
Cf. Duch. Fast. Episc. — Holw. — Baud.

THEODORIC of ST-HUBERT (Bl) Ab. O.S.B. A.C. Oct. 25
d. 1087. Educated at Maubeuge, he became a Benedictine at Lobbes, and in 1055 abbot of St Hubert in the Ardennes. Here and at the neighbouring abbeys of Stavelot-Malmédy he introduced with great success the Cluniac observance.
Cf. Holw. — Baud. — Chev.

THEODOSIA (St) M. R.M. March 20
See Alexandra, Claudia, etc.

THEODOSIA (St) M. R.M. March 23
See Domitius, Pelagia, etc.

THEODOSIA (St) V. M. R.M. Apr. 2
d. 308. A maiden of Tyre, eighteen years old, who, on a visit to Caesarea in Palestine, seeing some martyrs on Easter Sunday on their way to execution, asked them to pray for her. Whereupon she was seized, tortured, hanged by the hair, pierced with nails, and finally cast into the sea.
Cf. Att. — Holw. — Baud.

THEODOSIA and Comp. (SS) MM.
R.M. May 29
d. c.303. Theodosia, the alleged mother of St Procopius, is said to have been martyred at Caesarea Philippi in Palestine under Diocletian. She is said to have been put to death with twelve other women. The whole story seems to be a fabrication.
Cf. Holw. — Baud.

THEODOSIA (St) V.M. A.C. May 29
d. 745. A nun of Constantinople who led a group of other nuns in an attempt to resist by force the soldiers who were sent to destroy the image of Christ over the main door of their monastery. She was tortured and put to death.
Cf. Holw. — Att. — Baud.

THEODOSIUS the CENOBIARCH (St) Ab. R.M. Jan. 11
423-529. A Cappadocian who was put in charge of the church of Our Lady situated on the road between Jerusalem and Bethlehem. He next founded a monastery in the desert of Juda by the Dead Sea, where several hundred monks were soon living under his rule. He divided them according to nationality — Greeks, Armenians and Arabs — and built a church for each group. The patriarch of Jerusalem appointed him visitor to all the cenobitical communities in Palestine — as distinct from eremitical — whence the title cenobiarch given to the saint. The Byzantine emperor tried unsuccessfully to bribe Theodosius to support Monophysitism. The saint died at the age of one hundred and five.
Cf. Holw. — Att. — Baud.

THEODOSIUS (St) Bp. A.C. Feb. 14
d. 554. Bishop of Vaison in France and predecessor of St Quinidius.
Cf. Duch. Fast. Episc. — Holw. — Baud.

THEODOSIUS (St) M. R.M. March 26
See Quadratus, Theodosius, etc.

THEODOSIUS (St) Bp. R.M. July 17
d. 516. Bishop of Auxerre c.507-516.
Cf. Gams — Duch. Fast. Episc. — Holw.

THEODOSIUS, LUCIUS, MARK and PETER (SS) MM. R.M. Oct. 25
d. 269. They belong to a group of fifty soldiers martyred at Rome under Claudius.
Cf. Holw. — Baud.

THEODOTA (St) M. R.M. July 17
d. c.735. A lady of Constantinople martyred under the iconoclastic emperor Leo the Isaurian for hiding three holy icons from the imperial officers.
Cf. Holw. — Baud. — Att.

THEODOTA and her three Sons (SS) MM. R.M. Aug. 2
d. 304. Martyrs of Nicaea. Theodota with Evodius and her other two sons were cast into a furnace and perished in the flames. Their Acts are not trustworthy.
Cf. Holw. — Att. — Baud.

THEODOTA (St) Penitent.
? A.C. Sept. 29
d. c.318. Described as a penitent harlot, martyred at Philippopolis in Thrace. According to her untrustworthy Acts her executioners exhausted their ingenuity in devising fresh tortures for her.
Cf. Holw. — Baud. — Att.

THEODOTUS (St) M. R.M. Jan. 4
See Aquilinus, Geminus, etc.

THEODOTUS (St) Bp. R.M. May 6
d. c.325. Bishop of Cyrenia in Cyprus. He suffered a long term of imprisonment under Licinius.
Cf. Holw. — Baud.

THEODOTUS, THECUSA, ALEXAN-
DRA, CLAUDIA, FAINA (PHAINA),
EUPHRASIA, MATRONA and JULITTA
(SS) MM. R.M. May 18
d. 304. According to their Acts, Theodotus was an innkeeper of Ancyra who was
martyred there under Diocletian for giving Christian burial to the bodies of the
seven virgins mentioned above, also martyrs of Ancyra. The Bollandist Father
Delehaye contends that the Acts are
merely a moral tale.
Cf. Holw. — Baud. — Att.

THEODOTUS (St) M. R.M. July 5
See Marinus, Theodotus and Sedopha.

THEODOTUS, RUFINA and AMMIA
(SS) MM. R.M. Aug. 31
d. c.270. Theodotus and Rufina were the
parents, and Ammia the foster-mother, of
St Mamas (v. Aug. 17). They also are
said to have suffered in Cappadocia under
Aurelian. The Acts are very untrustworthy.
Cf. Holw. — Baud.

THEODOTUS (St) Bp. R.M. Nov. 2
d. 334. A bishop of Laodicea at the time
of the Arian troubles and a great friend of
the Arianizing Eusebius the historian, who
is loud in his praise. Theodotus subscribed to the Nicene formula, but seems
to have sided with the Arians and the
semi-Arians up to his death.
Cf. Holw. — Baud.

THEODOTUS (St) M. R.M. Nov. 14
See Clementinus, Theodotus and Philomenus.

THEODULA (St) V. M. R.M. March 25
Otherwise Dula, q.v.

THEODULPHUS (THIOU) (St) Bp.
O.S.B. R.M. June 24
d. 776. The third abbot-bishop (*chore-
piscopus* — choir-bishop) of the great
Benedictine abbey of Lobbes, near Liége.
Cf. Zimm. — Att. — Chev. — Holw.

THEODULUS (St) M. R.M. Feb. 17
d. 308. An aged man in the household of
Firmilian, governor of Palestine, by whom
he was ordered to be crucified at Caesarea
in Palestine.
Cf. Att. — Holw. — Baud.

THEODULUS (St) C. R.M. March 23
? A priest of Antioch in Syria, of whom
nothing else is known. His name is also
given as Theodore and Theodoricus.
Cf. Holw. — Baud.

THEODULUS, ANESIUS, FELIX, COR-
NELIA and Comp. (SS) MM.
R.M. March 31
? Martyrs in Proconsular Africa.
Cf. Holw. — Baud.

THEODULUS (St) M. R.M. Apr. 4
See Agathopedes and Theodulus.

THEODULUS (St) M. R.M. May 2
See Exuperius, Zoe, etc.

THEODULUS (St) M. R.M. May 3
See Alexander, Eventius and Theodulus.

THEODULUS (St) M. R.M. June 18
See Leontius, Hypatius and Theodulus.

THEODULUS (St) M. R.M. July 26
See Symphronius, Olympius, etc.

THEODULUS of GRAMMONT (St) Bp.
O.S.B. A.C. Aug. 17
d. c.840. A native of Besançon who became a chaplain to Charlemagne. He was
promoted successively to the abbacy of
Agaunum and to the bishopric of Sion in
the Valais.
Cf. Baud.

THEODULUS (St) M. R.M. Sept. 12
See Macedonius, Theodulus and Tatian.

THEODULUS, SATURNINUS, EU-
PORUS, GELASIUS, EUNICIAN, ZETI-
CUS, CLEOMENES (LEOMENES),
AGATHOPUS, BASILIDES and EVAR-
ISTUS (SS) MM. R.M. Dec. 23
d. 250. Martyrs of Crete who suffered
under Decius.
Cf. Holw. — Att.

THEOFRID (THEOFROY) (St) Bp.
O.S.B. A.C. Jan. 26
d. c.690. A monk of Luxeuil who became
abbot of Corbie (662) and a regionary
bishop.
Cf. Holw. — Baud.

THEOFRID (THEOFROY, CHAFFRE)
(St) Ab. O.S.B. A.C. Oct. 19
d. 728. A native of Orange who became
monk and abbot of Carmery-en-Velay

(Monastier-Saint-Chaffre). He died as a consequence of ill-treatment received at the hands of the invading Saracens and has been ever since venerated as a martyr.
Cf. Chev. — Baud. — Holw. — P. de U.

THEOGENES (St) M. R.M. Jan. 3
See Cyrinus, Primus and Theogenes.

THEOGENES and Comp. (SS) MM.
R.M. Jan. 26
d. 258. According to the R.M. Theogenes was bishop of Hippona (Hippo Regius) in Africa, where he suffered with thirty-six of his flock under Valerian. A modern opinion places these martyrs at Laodicea in Phrygia.
Cf. Holw. — Baud.

THEOGER (THEOGAR, DIETHGER) (Bl) Bp. O.S.B. P.C. Apr. 29
d. 1120. A native probably of Alsace who became successively canon of Mainz, monk of Hirschau, prior of Raichenbach on the Murg, abbot of St Georgen in the Black Forest (1090) and bishop of Metz (1118). However, after his consecration at Corbie he retired to the abbey of Cluny, where he died.
Cf. Holw. — Chev.

THEOGONIUS (St) M. R.M. Aug. 21
See Bassa, Theogonius, etc.

THEONAS (St) M. R.M. Jan. 3
See Theopemptus and Theonas.

THEONAS (St) M. R.M. Apr. 20
See Victor, Zoticus, etc.

THEONAS (St) Bp. R.M. Aug. 23
d. 300. Bishop of Alexandria 281-300. He fostered sacred studies, chiefly by his care of the catechetical school of his episcopal city. He was also known as a determined opponent of Sabellianism.
Cf. Holw. — Baud.

THEONESTUS (St) Bp. M.
R.M. Oct. 30
d. 425. Said to have been bishop of Philippi in Macedonia, to have been driven from his see by the Arians, and to have been sent by the pope with several companions (among whom was St Alban of Mainz) to evangelize Germany. Arrived at Mainz, they were obliged to flee from the invading Vandals, and on their way home Theonestus was martyred at Altino

in the Veneto. Probably Theonestus is a local martyr of Altino having no connexion with the others.
Cf. Holw. — Menzies — Baud.

THEONILLA (St) M. R.M. Aug. 23
See Claudius, Asterius, etc.

THEOPEMPTUS and THEONAS (SS) MM. R.M. Jan. 3
d. 284. Theopemptus was bishop of Nicomedia and was martyred there after a series of miraculous escapes. Theonas was a magician converted by the example of Theopemptus and himself martyred. Their Acts are wholly untrustworthy, though the martyrs themselves seem to be historical personages.
Cf. Holw. — Baud.

THEOPHANES VÉNARD (Bl) M.
A.C. Feb. 2
1829-1861. A native of the diocese of Poitiers who joined the Society of Foreign Missions at Paris, was ordained in 1852 and arrived in Tonkin in 1854. After teaching in an Annamite seminary he took up work in W. Tonkin. He was barbarously put to death in a persecution which soon after broke out. Beatified 1900.
Cf. Holw. — Att. — Baud.

THEOPHANES (St) Ab. R.M. March 12
d. 818. A native of Constantinople and educated at the imperial court, he married early in life, but eventually allowed his wife to become a nun and himself joined the monks of Polychronion. Some time later he founded two monasteries and governed one of them as abbot, viz., that of Mt Sigriana, near Cyzicus. For his steadfast opposition to iconoclasm he was banished by Leo the Armenian to Samothrace, where he died from the ill-treatment he had received.
Cf. Att. — Holw. — Baud.

THEOPHANES and Comp. (SS) MM.
R.M. Dec. 4
d. c.810. Four officers of the court of Leo the Armenian, imprisoned and tortured for their opposition to iconoclasm. Theophanes died under torture; the rest survived and eventually became monks.
Cf. Holw. — Baud.

THEOPHANES (St) Bp. C.
R.M. Dec. 27
See Theodore and Theophanes.

THEOPHILA (St) V. M.   R.M. Dec. 28
See Indes, Domna, etc.

THEOPHILUS and HELLADIUS (SS)
MM.   R.M. Jan. 8
? Africans martyred in Lybia, where they
had preached the gospel. Theophilus
was a deacon, Helladius a layman. They
were tortured and thrown into a furnace.
Cf. Holw. — Baud.

THEOPHILUS the PENITENT (St)
Feb. 4
c.538. Metaphrastes is responsible for
the legend connected with this saint. He
is said to have been archdeacon of Adana
in Cilicia and, having been deposed from
his office through a calumny, to have made
a pact with the devil. He repented, and
our Lady appeared to him and returned
the pact, which was then torn up and publicly burnt. Goethe made use of this
legend in his *Faust.*
Cf. Holw. — Att.

THEOPHILUS the LAWYER (St) M.
R.M. Feb. 6
d. 304. Said to have been beheaded at
Caesarea in Cappadocia. He figures in
the legend of St Dorothy, where he is surnamed *Scholasticus*, i.e., the lawyer.
Cf. Holw.

THEOPHILUS (St) M.   R.M. Feb. 6
See Saturninus, Theophilus and Revocata.

THEOPHILUS (St) M.   R.M. Feb. 28
See Macarius, Rufinus, etc.

THEOPHILUS (St) Bp.   R.M. March 5
d. c.195. A bishop of Caesarea in Palestine and a prominent opponent of the
Quartodecimans, a sect which insisted on
keeping Easter on the Jewish Passover
day, whether it fell on a Sunday or not.
Cf. Holw. — Baud.

THEOPHILUS (St) Bp.   R.M. March 7
His real name is Theophylact, q.v.

THEOPHILUS (St) Bp.   R.M. Apr. 27
d. p. 427. Bishop of Brescia and successor
to St Gaudentius.
Cf. Holw. — Menzies — Gams.

THEOPHILUS of CORTE (St) C. O.F.M.
A.C. May 21
1676-1740. Biagio Arrighi was born at
Corte in Corsica and joined the Friars

Minor, taking the name of Theophilus
(1693). He was ordained priest at Naples
and taught theology at Civitella in the
Roman Campagna. Later he became a
famous missioner in Italy and Corsica and
a zealous worker for the revival of Franciscan observance. Canonized in 1930.
Cf. Holw. — Baud. — Att.

THEOPHILUS (St) M.   R.M. July 22
d. 789. An officer of the imperial forces
stationed in Cyprus when the Saracens
invaded the island. As admiral of the
Christian fleet he refused to flee when the
battle went against him. He was taken
prisoner and after one year's incarceration
was martyred for refusing to deny Christ.
Cf. Holw. — Baud.

THEOPHILUS (St) M.   R.M. July 23
See Trophimus and Theophilus.

THEOPHILUS (St) M.   R.M. Sept. 8
See Ammon, Theophilus, etc.

THEOPHILUS (St) Mk. O.S.B.
R.M. Oct. 2
d. c.750. A native of Bulgaria, who became a monk of a monastery in Asia
Minor, in which the community followed
the Western Rule of St Benedict. For
opposing iconoclasm he was fiercely persecuted, maltreated and finally exiled by
the emperor Leo the Isaurian.
Cf. Holw. — Baud.

THEOPHILUS (St) Bp.   R.M. Oct. 13
d. 181. An Eastern philosopher who became a Christian as a result of reading the
Scriptures with a view to attacking them.
He became bishop of Antioch. He is now
best known as one of the Apologists of the
second century.
Cf. Holw. — Baud.

THEOPHILUS (St) M.   R.M. Nov. 3
See Germanus, Theophilus, etc.

THEOPHILUS (St) M.   R.M. Dec. 20
See Ammon, Zeno, etc.

THEOPHYLACT (St) Bp. R.M. March 7
d. 845. Wrongly called Theophilus in the
R.M. An Asiatic monk who became
bishop of Nicomedia. He opposed the
iconoclastic fury of Leo the Armenian,
by whom he was banished to Caria, where
he died thirty years later.
Cf. Att. — Baud. — Holw.

THEOPISTES and THEOPISTUS (SS) MM. R.M. Sept. 20
See Eustace, Theopistes, etc.

THEOPOMPUS (St) M. R.M. May 21
See Synesius and Theopompus.

THEOPREPIS (St) M. R.M. March 27
See Philetus, Lydia, etc.

THEOROGITHA (THORDGITH, THORCTGYD) (St) N. A.C. Jan. 25
See Thordgith.

THEOTICUS (St) M. R.M. March 8
See Arian, Theoticus, etc.

THEOTIMUS (St) Bp. R.M. Apr. 20
d. 407. Bishop of Tomi on the Black Sea. He defended Origen against St Epiphanius of Salamis. He evangelized the barbarian tribes of the Lower Danube, who were then pressing into imperial territory.
Cf. Holw. — Baud.

THEOTIMUS (St) M. R.M. Nov. 5
See Domninus, Theotimus, etc.

THEOTIMUS and BASILIAN (SS) MM. R.M. Dec. 18
? Martyrs of Laodicea in Syria.
Cf. Holw. — Baud.

THEOTIMUS (St) M. R.M. Dec. 24
See Lucian, Metrobius, etc.

THEOTONIUS (St) C. O.S.A. A.C. Feb. 18
1086-1166. Born at Ganfeo, diocese of Tuy in Spain. He was educated at Coimbra in Portugal and became archpriest of Visen. He resigned that office to go on pilgrimage to the Holy Land, and on his return joined the Augustinian canons regular at Coimbra. Highly esteemed by King Alphonsus of Portugal, he was fearless in rebuking vice and exact in the performance of the divine service. Cult approved by Benedict XIV.
Cf. P. de U. — Att. — Holw.

THERESA (several).
Otherwise Teresa, q.v.

THESPESIUS (St) M. R.M. June 1
d. c.230. A Cappadocian martyred under Alexander Severus.
Cf. Holw. — Baud.

THESPESIUS (St) M. R.M. Nov. 20
See Eustace, Thespesius and Anatolius.

THESSALONICA (St) M. R.M. Nov. 7
See Auctus, Taurion, and Thessalonica.

THETHMAR (THEODEMAR) (St) C. A.C. May 17
d. 1152. A native of Bremen who became a missionary among the Wends under St Vicelinus. He was probably a Premonstratensian. He died at Neumünster.
Cf. Att. — Holw. — Chev.

THEUDERIUS (St) Ab. A.C. Oct. 29
d. c.575. A monk of Lérins who founded three monasteries near his native city of Vienne and eventually became a hermit in a walled-up cell at the church of St Laurence there. In French he is often known as St Chef.
Cf. Holw. — Att. — Chev.

THEUSITAS, HORRES, THEODORA, NYMPHODORA, MARK and ARABIA (SS) MM. R.M. March 13
? Theusitas was the parent of the young boy Horres. The whole group, which seems to have included several others, was put to death at Nicaea in Bithynia.
Cf. Holw. — Chev. (who adds other names, following Bolland.) — Baud.

THIEMO (THEODMARUS) (St) Bp. M. O.S.B. A.C. Sept. 28
d. 1102. Of the family of the counts of Meglin in Bavaria. He became a Benedictine at Niederaltaich, where he gained great celebrity as an artist in metal, a painter and a sculptor. In 1077 he was chosen abbot of St Peter's, Salzburg, and in 1090 archbishop of the same city. He was persecuted, imprisoned and exiled for his loyalty to Gregory VII. As an exile he joined the crusaders, was captured and imprisoned at Ascalon, and after long and cruel tortures was martyred at Corozain for refusing to apostatize to Islam.
Cf. Zimm. — Chev. — Holw. — Baud.

THIENTO and Comp. (BB) MM. O.S.B. A.C. Aug. 10
d. 955. An abbot of Wessobrunn in Bavaria who was martyred with six of his monks by the invading Hungarians.
Cf. Zimm. — Holw.

THIERRY (St) C. R.M. July 1
Otherwise Theodoric, q.v.

THILLO (St) Ab. O.S.B.   **A.C. Jan. 7**
Otherwise Tillo, q.v.

THIOU (St) Bp.   **R.M. June 24**
Otherwise Theodulphus, q.v.

THOMAIS (St) M.   **R.M. Apr. 14**
d. 476. An Alexandrian woman, wife of a
fisherman. Tempted to an act of impurity by her father-in-law, she refused
and was murdered by him.
Cf. Holw. — Baud.

THOMAS PLUMTREE (Bl) M.
   A.C. Jan. 4
d. 1570. A native of Lincolnshire, educated at Corpus Christi College, Oxford,
and rector of Stubton. He was chaplain
to insurgents of the North. Before being
martyred in the market-place at Durham
he was offered his life if he would turn
Protestant. Beatified 1886.
Cf. Newdigate — Camm — Stanton — Att.

THOMAS of CORI (Bl) C. O.F.M.
   A.C. Jan. 19
1655-1729. A native of Cori, diocese of
Velletri, who, after being a shepherd in
the Roman Campagna, became an Observant Franciscan (1675), and, after his
ordination to the priesthood, was stationed
ar Civitella. He spent the remainder of
his life in preaching and ministering to the
inhabitants of the mountain district
around Subiaco. Beatified 1785.
Cf. Holw. — Att. — Baud. — Menzies.

THOMAS REYNOLDS (Bl) M.
   A.C. Jan. 21
d. 1642. Thomas Reynolds, whose true
name was Green, was born at Oxford and
educated for the priesthood at Reims,
Valladolid and Seville. After his ordination is 1592 he returned to England and
worked on the English mission for nearly
fifty years. He must have been about
eighty years of age when he was hanged
for his priesthood at Tyburn, together
with Bl Bartholomew Roe, O.S.B. Beatified 1929.
Cf. Newdigate — Camm.

THOMAS XICO (St) M.   **R.M. Feb. 5**
d. 1597. A Japanese layman, Franciscan
tertiary, catechist, and interpreter to the
Franciscan missionaries in Japan. Crucified at Nagasaki with twenty-five companions. Canonized 1862.
Cf. Holw.

THOMAS COZACHI (St) M.
   R.M. Feb. 5
d. 1597. A Japanese boy of fifteen, son of
St Michael Cozachi. He served Mass for
the Franciscan missionaries and was crucified at Nagasaki with twenty-five companions, including his own father. Canonized 1862.
Cf. Holw.

THOMAS SHERWOOD (Bl) M.
   A.C. Feb. 7
1551-1578. A Londoner, who was preparing to go to Douai to study for the
priesthood when he was betrayed, imprisoned and racked in the Tower in order
to force him to disclose the place where he
had heard Mass. He was finally executed
at Tyburn on the charge of denying the
queen's ecclesiastical supremacy. Beatified 1886.
Cf. Newdigate — Att. — Holw.

THOMAS HEMERFORD (Bl) M.
   A.C. Feb. 12
d. 1584. A Dorsetshire man who was educated at St John's College and Hart Hall,
Oxford. He studied for the priesthood at
the English College, Rome, where he was
ordained in 1583. The following year,
with four priest-companions, he was
hanged at Tyburn for his priesthood.
Beatified 1929.
Cf. Newdigate.

THOMAS AQUINAS (St) Dr. O.P.
   R.M. March 7
c.1226-1274. Surnamed the "Angelic
Doctor." Born at Roccasecca, near
Aquino, Naples, and educated as an oblate
by the Benedictines at Montecassino, he
joined the then recently founded Dominicans, studied and received the doctorate
of theology at the university of Paris, and
thenceforward taught that subject at
Paris (1252-60), Orvieto (1261-4), Rome
(1265-7), Viterbo (1268), Paris (1269-71)
and Naples (1272-4). He died at Fossa-
nova, near Rome, on his way to the council
of Lyons. Canonized in 1323 and declared Doctor of the Church in 1567 and
patron saint of Catholic universities and
centres of study in 1880. St Thomas is
the acknowledged prince of Catholic
theologians, and his *Summa Theologica* is
unrivalled as an authority in that branch
of sacred learning. He was also a gifted
poet, his hymns for the feast of Corpus

Christi being still the favourites in both liturgical and extra-liturgical functions. *Cf. Menzies — Holw. — Att. — Baud. — Chev.*

THOMAS (or THOMASIUS) of COSTACCIARO (Bl) H. O.S.B. Cam.
A.C. March 25

d. 1337. Born at Costacciaro in Umbria, the son of poor peasants. He joined the Camaldolese at Sitria, then retired to Monte Cupo as a hermit, where he lived for many years. At the time of his death his existence had been almost forgotten. *Cf. Att. — Menzies — Holw. — Chev.*

THOMAS of TOLENTINO and Comp. (BB) MM. O.F.M.
A.C. Apr. 9

A native of Tolentino in Italy, who became a Franciscan and went to preach the gospel in Armenia and Persia. He was on his way to Ceylon, with a view to proceeding to China, when he was seized and beheaded by the Mohammedans. Three companions, BB James of Padua, Peter of Siena, Franciscans, and Demetrius of Tiflis, layman, suffered with him. Cult approved 1894. *Cf. Att. — Holw.*

THOMAS PICKERING (Bl) M. O.S.B.
A.C. May 9

d. 1679. A native of Westmoreland who joined the Benedictines as a lay-brother at St Gregory's, Douai (now at Downside) and took his vows in 1660. He was sent to England and attached to the small community of Benedictine chaplains who served the royal chapel. He was a victim of the "Popish Plot," being falsely accused and hanged at Tyburn. Beatified 1929. *Cf. Newdigate — Camm.*

THOMAS FORD (Bl) M.
A.C. May 28

d. 1582. A native of Devon who was educated at Trinity College, Oxford, where he was converted to the Catholic Faith. He studied for the priesthood at Douai, was ordained there in 1573, and sent on the English mission in 1576. He worked in Oxfordshire and Berkshire until his arrest and martyrdom at Tyburn with BB John Shert and Robert Johnson. Beatified 1886. *Cf. Newdigate — Holw.*

THOMAS COTTAM (Bl) M. S.J.
A.C. May 30

1549-1582. Born at Dilworth in Lancashire of Protestant parents, he graduated at Brasenose College, Oxford, and was converted to the Catholic Faith. He crossed over to Douai and then went to Rome to study for the priesthood. At Rome he was received into the Society of Jesus. He returned to England in 1580, but was arrested on landing at Dover and imprisoned in the Tower. Two years later he was hanged at Tyburn with four priest-companions. Beatified 1886. *Cf. Newdigate — Holw. — Camm.*

THOMAS DU (Bl) M.
A.C. May 31

d. 1839. A native of Tonkin who was ordained priest, became a Dominican tertiary and worked in the province of Nam-Dingh. He was tortured and beheaded. Beatified 1900. *Cf. Holw.*

THOMAS GREEN, THOMAS SCRYVEN and THOMAS REDING (BB) MM. O.Cart.
A.C. June 15

d. 1537. Thomas Green (or Greenwood) was a fellow of St John's College, Cambridge, who took monastic vows and was ordained priest at the London Charterhouse. The other two were lay-brothers of the same charterhouse. These three, with four companions, were starved to death at Newgate. Beatified 1886. *Cf. Newdigate — Camm — Stanton.*

THOMAS WOODHOUSE (Bl) M. S.J.
A.C. June 19

d. 1573. A secular priest who resided in Lincolnshire and acted also as a private tutor in Wales. In 1561 he was committed to the Fleet prison, where he was kept in custody till his death. During his imprisonment he was admitted by letter to the Society of Jesus. He was hanged at Tyburn. Beatified 1886. *Cf. Newdigate — Stanton — Holw. — Att.*

THOMAS WHITBREAD (Bl) M. S.J.
A.C. June 20

d. 1679. Thomas Whitbread, *alias* Harcourt, was a native of Essex. He was educated at St Omer and joined the Jesuits in 1635. He was provincial of the English mission and at the time of the Popish Plot was convicted with four other priests of his Order on a bogus charge of conspiring to murder Charles II. He was hanged at Tyburn. Beatified 1929. *Cf. Newdigate — Att.*

THOMAS CORSINI (Bl) **C. O.S.M.**
A.C. June 23
d. 1343. A native of Orvieto who became a Servite lay-brother and spent his life collecting alms for his friary. He is credited with many visions. Beatified 1768.
Cf. Menzies — Att. — Holw.

THOMAS GARNET (Bl) **M. S.J.**
A.C. June 23
d. 1608. Born in Southwark, a nephew of Fr Henry Garnet, S.J. Educated for the priesthood at St Omer and Valladolid. He worked first as a secular priest but in 1604 was admitted to the Society of Jesus. Hanged at Tyburn for his priesthood. Beatified 1929.
Cf. Newdigate — Att.

THOMAS TOAN (Bl) **M.** A.C. June 27
d. 1840. A native catechist of Tonkin who, having shown signs of apostatizing, repented and was in consequence cruelly scourged and exposed to the sun and insects without food or drink for twelve days until his death. Beatified 1900.
Cf. Holw.

THOMAS MAXFIELD (Bl) **M.**
A.C. July 1
d. 1616. A native of Enville, Staffs., he was educated for the priesthood at Douai and ordained in 1615. The following year he was hanged for his priesthood at Tyburn. Beatified 1929.
Cf. Newdigate.

THOMAS BOSGRAVE (Bl) **M.**
A.C. July 4
d. 1594. A gentleman, nephew of Sir J. Arundel, hanged at Dorchester with two of his servants for sheltering priests. Beatified 1929.
Cf. Newdigate.

THOMAS WARCOP (Bl) **M.**
A.C. July 4
d. 1597. A gentleman of Yorkshire, hanged with three companions at York for sheltering priests. Beatified 1929.
Cf. Newdigate.

THOMAS ALFIELD (Bl) **M.**
A.C. July 6
d. 1585. Born at Gloucester and educated at Eton and King's College, Cambridge. He was reconciled to the Catholic Church and went abroad to study for the priest-hood at Douai and Reims. After his ordination in 1581 he returned to England and was arrested while engaged in distributing copies of Dr Allen's *True and Modest Defence*. For this he was hanged at Tyburn. Beatified 1929.
Cf. Newdigate.

THOMAS MORE (St) **M.** A.C. July 9
1478-1535. A native of London, More studied at Canterbury Hall, Oxford, and read Law at the Inns of Court, being called to the bar in 1501. He married twice and was the ideal husband, devoted to wife and children, devout, cheerful and charitable. In 1516 he published his *Utopia*, which gained for him a European reputation as a scholar and humanist. From this time he was more and more in favour with Henry VIII and Cardinal Wolsey, whom in 1529 he succeeded as Lord Chancellor. Soon, however, he found himself unable to support the king on the question of the royal divorce. He resigned the chancellorship and on refusing to take the oath of supremacy, declaring the king supreme head of the Church in England, was imprisoned in the Tower. After fifteen months' incarceration he was beheaded on Tower Hill. In the decree of his canonization in 1925 Pius XI described him as the "Martyr of the Papacy."
Cf. Holw. — Att. — Stanton — Baud.

THOMAS TUNSTAL (Bl) **M. O.S.B.**
A.C. July 13
d. 1616. Thomas Tunstal, *alias* Helmes, was born at Whinfell, near Kendal, Westmoreland. He was educated for the priesthood at Douai, ordained there in 1609, sent to the English mission in 1610 and imprisoned almost at once. He spent the rest of his life in prison, and while there was received into the Benedictine Order. He was hanged for his priest-hood at Norwich. Beatified 1929.
Cf. Newdigate — Camm.

THOMAS ABEL (Bl) **M.** A.C. July 30
d. 1540. A doctor of Oxford university, chaplain to Queen Catharine of Aragon and a loyal defender of the validity of her marriage. He was kept a prisoner in the Tower of London for six years and finally executed at Smithfield for refusing to acknowledge the king's spiritual suprem-acy. Beatified 1886.
Cf. Newdigate — Camm — Att. — Holw.

THOMAS WELBOURNE (Bl) M.
A.C. Aug. 1
d. 1605. A native of Hutton Bushel in Yorkshire and a schoolmaster by profession who was hanged at York for persuading people to turn Catholic. Beatified 1929.
Cf. Newdigate.

THOMAS of DOVER (St) M. O.S.B.
A.C. Aug. 5
d. 1295. Thomas Hales was a Benedictine monk of St Martin's Priory, Dover, a cell of Christ Church, Canterbury. On Aug. 5, 1295 the French raided Dover and all the monks went into hiding except Thomas, who was too old and infirm to get away. The raiders found him in bed and ordered him to disclose the whereabouts of the church plate: he refused and was murdered. Miracles occurred at his tomb and he was forthwith venerated as a martyr. There was an altar dedicated to him in Dover Priory church in 1500, and his image figured among those of the English saints at the English College, Rome.
Cf. Att. — Stanton — Holw. — Chev.

THOMAS VO (Bl) M.
A.C. Aug. 17
d. 1627. A Japanese layman beheaded at Nagasaki for sheltering the missionary priests. Beatified 1867.
Cf. Holw.

THOMAS GUENGORO (Bl) M.
A.C. Aug. 18
d. 1620. A Japanese layman. With his wife and his little son he was crucified at Cocura for sheltering Bl Simon Kiota. Beatified 1867.
Cf. Holw.

THOMAS COIANAQUI (Bl) M.
A.C. Aug. 19
d. 1622. A Japanese sailor on the ship of Bl Joachim Firajama, beheaded at Nagasaki. Beatified 1867.
Cf. Holw.

THOMAS of HEREFORD (St) Bp.
R.M. Aug. 25
c.1218-1282. Born at Hambledon, near Great Marlow, the son of the Norman baron William of Cantalupe. He was a brilliant student at Oxford and Paris, became chaplain to Pope Innocent IV, and in 1262 chancellor of Oxford University. In 1265 he was appointed chancellor of England, but on being deprived of this office by Henry III, he returned at once to his beloved Oxford. He was raised to the bishopric of Hereford in 1275. The seven years of his episcopate were taken up with a continuous struggle in defence of the rights of his diocese and in untiring pastoral activities. He died at Montefiascone in Italy, whither he had gone to plead the cause of his see before the pope. Canonized 1320.
Cf. Att. — Holw. — Stanton — Chev.

THOMAS PERCY (Bl) M.
A.C. Aug. 26
1528-1572. Earl of Northumberland, condemned to death and executed at York for his part in the rising of the North against Elizabeth. During the period of nearly three years' imprisonment which preceded his martyrdom he was repeatedly offered his freedom on condition of his apostasy to Protestantism. Beatified 1896.
Cf. Newdigate — Camm — Stanton — Att.

THOMAS HOLFORD (Bl) M.
A.C. Aug. 28
d. 1588. Thomas Holford, *alias* Acton or Bude, was born at Aston in Cheshire of Protestant parents and became a schoolmaster in Herefordshire, where he embraced the Catholic faith. After his studies and ordination at Reims (1583) he worked in Cheshire. He was hanged for his priesthood at Clerkenwell. Beatified 1929.
Cf. Newdigate.

THOMAS FELTON (Bl) M. O.Minim.
A.C. Aug. 28
1568-88. Born at Bermondsey, son of Bl John Felton. He was educated at Reims and became a friar minim. He was hanged at Isleworth in his twentieth year. Beatified 1929.
Cf. Newdigate.

THOMAS TZUGHI (Bl) M. S.J.
A.C. Sept. 6
d. 1627. A Japanese, educated by the Jesuit fathers at Arima, whom he joined in 1589. He was noted for his gift of oratory. Exiled to Macao, he returned in disguise. He separated himself from the Society of Jesus, but only for one day; he then repented of his act and engaged himself again in missionary work with renewed zeal. He was burnt alive with

several companions at Nagasaki. Beatified 1867.
Cf. Holw.

THOMAS of ST HYACINTH (Bl) M. O.P. A.C. Sept. 8
d. 1628. A Japanese catechist attached to the Dominican missionaries, burnt alive with Bl Dominic Cartellet and companions. Beatified 1867.
Cf. Holw.

THOMAS TOMAKI (Bl) M.
A.C. Sept. 8
d. 1628. A Japanese boy, ten years old, beheaded with his father, Bl John Tomaki, and his three brothers. Beatified 1867.
Cf. Holw.

THOMAS XIQUIRO (Bl) M.
A.C. Sept. 10
d. 1622. A Japanese layman, seventy years old, highly respected by his fellow-citizens, beheaded at Nagasaki with Bl Charles Spinola. Beatified 1867.
Cf. Holw.

THOMAS of the HOLY ROSARY (Bl) M. O.P. A.C. Sept. 10
d. 1622. A Japanese catechist, attached to the Dominican missionaries, with several of whom he was beheaded at Nagasaki. Beatified 1867.
Cf. Holw.

THOMAS ZUMARRAGA (Bl) M. O.P.
A.C. Sept. 12
1575-1622. A native of Vitoria in Spain who joined the Dominicans and was sent to their missions in Japan. He was imprisoned for three years at Suzuta (Omura) and ultimately burnt alive at Omura with several companions. Beatified 1867.
Cf. Holw.

THOMAS ACAFOXI (Bl) M.
A.C. Sept. 19
d. 1622. A Japanese nobleman from Fingo who acted as catechist to Bl Leonard Kimura. Burnt alive at Nagasaki. Beatified 1867.
Cf. Holw.

THOMAS JOHNSON (Bl) M. O.Cart.
A.C. Sept. 20
d. 1537. A priest of the London charter-house imprisoned with others of his community at Newgate for opposition to Henry VIII's ecclesiastical policy. He

died in prison from starvation. Beatified 1886.
Cf. Newdigate — Camm — Stanton — Holw.

THOMAS DIEN (Bl) M. A.C. Sept. 21
d. 1838. A native catechist in Cochin-China, attached to the Foreign Missions of Paris. He was cruelly scourged and finally strangled, being eighteen years old at the time of his death. Beatified 1900.
Cf. Holw.

THOMAS of VILLANUEVA (St) Bp. O.S.A.
R.M. Sept. 22
1488-1555 (Sept. 8). Born at Fuellana, near Villanueva, Spain, the son of a miller. He studied at Alcalá and joined the Augustinians at Salamanca. After his ordination in 1520 he was appointed prior successively of the Augustinian friaries of Salamanca (where he taught moral theology in the university), Burgos and Valladolid. Later he became in turn provincial of Andalusia and Castile, court chaplain and (1544) archbishop of Valencia. As archbishop his outstanding characteristic was self-sacrifice: he was known as the grand almoner of the poor. He left a number of theological writings. Canonized 1658.
Cf. P. de U. — Gams — Att. — Holw.

THOMAS CUFIOJE (Bl) M.
A.C. Sept. 28
d. 1630. A Japanese layman, Augustinian tertiary, beheaded at Nagasaki. Beatified 1867.
Cf. Holw.

THOMAS HÉLYE (Bl) C. A.C. Oct. 19
1187-1257. Born at Biville in Normandy, he led an ascetic life in the house of his parents and devoted part of his time to teaching the catechism to the poor. He was ordained priest at the request of his bishop and became an itinerant preacher throughout Normandy. Later he was appointed almoner to the king. He died at the castle of Vauville, Manche. Cult confirmed 1859.
Cf. Holw. — Chev. — Att.

THOMAS THWING (THWENG) (Bl) M.
A.C. Oct. 23
d. 1680. Born at Heworth in Yorkshire and educated at Douai, he was ordained in 1665 and returned to England where he worked for fifteen years on the Yorkshire

mission. He was martyred at York for his alleged part in the Oates plot. Beatified 1929.
Cf. Newdigate.

THOMAS BELLACCI (Bl) C. O.F.M.
A.C. Oct. 31
1370-1447. A native of Florence who joined the Franciscan friary at Fiesole, where, though only a lay-brother, he was made novice-master. Later he worked successfully to introduce the Franciscan Observance into Corsica and S. Italy and combated the Fraticelli in Tuscany. When over seventy he went to preach in Syria and Abyssinia where, to his sorrow, he narrowly escaped martyrdom by the Mohammedans. Cult approved 1771.
Cf. Menzies — Holw. — Att.

THOMAS of WALDEN (Bl) C. O.C.
P.C. Nov. 2
c.1375-1430. Thomas Netter was born at Saffron Walden and joined the Carmelites. He was an active opponent of Lollardism and a prominent member of the Council of Constance. King Henry V chose him as his confessor and died in his arms. He died at Rouen.
Cf. Att. — Chev.

THOMAS of ANTIOCH (St) H.
R.M. Nov. 18
d. 782. A Syrian monk who dwelt in the vicinity of Antioch. He is venerated as a protector against pestilence.
Cf. Holw. — Baud.

THOMAS COTENDA and Comp. (BB) MM.
A.C. Nov. 27
d. 1619. A scion of the Japanese royal family of Firando. He was educated by the Jesuits and lived in exile at Nagasaki, where he was ultimately beheaded with ten companions. Beatified 1867.
Cf. Holw.

THOMAS SOMERS (Bl) M.
A.C. Dec. 10
d. 1610. Thomas Somers (*alias* Wilson) was born at Skelsmergh, Westmoreland, and started life as a schoolmaster. Later he went to Douai and became a priest. On returning to England he worked on the London mission. Together with Bl John Roberts, O.S.B., he was hanged at Tyburn for his priesthood. Beatified 1929.
Cf. Newdigate — Att.

THOMAS HOLLAND (Bl) M. S.J.
A.C. Dec. 12
d. 1642. Thomas Holland (*alias* Sanderson, *alias* Hammond), born at Sutton, near Prescot, Lancs., was educated at St Omer and Valladolid and became a Jesuit in 1624. He was hanged for his priesthood at Tyburn. Beatified 1929.
Cf. Newdigate.

THOMAS DE and Comp. (BB) MM.
A.C. Dec. 19
d. 1839. A native of Tonkin, a tailor by trade and a Dominican tertiary, who was strangled with several companions for giving shelter to the missionaries. Beatified 1900.
Cf. Holw.

THOMAS of FARFA (St) Ab. O.S.B.
A.C. Dec. 10
d. c.720. A native of Maurienne in Savoy. After becoming a Benedictine he went on pilgrimage to the Holy Land and on his return settled as a hermit near Farfa in Italy. With the help of his friend, the duke of Spoleto, he restored the abbey of Farfa to its former splendour.
Cf. Holw. — Zimm. — Chev. — Menzies.

THOMAS the APOSTLE (St)
R.M. Dec. 21
1st cent. Surnamed "Didymus," i.e., the twin. All we know for certain about him is derived from the gospel narrative, where the chief episode related of him concerns his unbelief and subsequent profession of faith in Christ's resurrection (John XX, 24 sqq.). According to a very ancient tradition he is said to have preached in S. India and there to have suffered martyrdom, but there is no decisive proof of this.
Cf. Holw. — Baud. — Att.

THOMAS BECKET (St) Bp. M.
R.M. Dec. 29
1118-1170. Born in London of Norman parents, he was sent to Paris to study and in 1141 entered the service of Archbishop Theobald of Canterbury, who sent him to Bologna and Auxerre to follow a course of civil and canon law and in 1154 made him his archdeacon. He soon became a bosom friend of Henry II, who in 1155 appointed him chancellor of the kingdom and in 1162 archbishop of Canterbury. Up to this time Thomas had led a rather worldly life, but he now gave himself up completely to the faithful discharge of his

pastoral duties. Being forced to oppose the king's wanton interference in ecclesiastical matters, he was brutally done to death in his cathedral by royal retainers. The whole kingdom at once proclaimed him a martyr, and the Church confirmed the title by canonizing him in 1173. His shrine became one of the most famous in Christendom.
Cf. Holw. — Att. — Stanton — Baud.

THOMASIUS (Bl) H. O.S.B. Cam.
A.C. March 25
Otherwise Thomas of Costacciaro, q.v.

THOMIAN (TOIMEN) Bp. A.C. Jan. 10
d. c.660. Archbishop of Armagh 623–c.660. He wrote a letter to the Holy See on the paschal controversy.
Cf. Holw.

THORDGITH (THORCTGYD, THEORIGITHA) N. O.S.B. A.C. Jan. 25
d. c.700. Novice-mistress at the abbey of Barking under St Ethelburga. She is described as a miracle of patience under suffering.
Cf. Zimm. — Stanton — Holw. — Chev.

THORLAC THORHALLI (St) C. O.S.A.
P.C. Dec. 23
1133-1193. Born in Iceland, he was ordained deacon before he was fifteen and priest at the age of eighteen. He was then sent to study at Paris and Lincoln. In 1177 he became bishop of Skalholt in his native island. By vigorous measures he succeeded in stamping out simony and incontinency. He was "canonized" in 1198 by the Althing, but his cult has never been officially confirmed.
Cf. Holw. — Att. — Chev.

THRACE (Martyrs of) (SS)
R.M. Aug. 20
? A group of thirty-seven martyrs put to death somewhere in Thrace. They were cast into a furnace after their hands and feet had been cut off.
Cf. Holw. — Baud.

THRASEAS (St) Bp. M. R.M. Oct. 5
d. c.170. Bishop of Eumenia in Phrygia, an opponent of the Montanists, martyred at Smyrna.
Cf. Holw. — Baud.

THRASILLA (St) V. R.M. Dec. 24
Otherwise Tarsilla, q.v.

THYRSUS and PROJECTUS (SS) MM.
R.M. Jan. 24
? Martyrs of whom we know only the names.
Cf. Holw. — Baud.

THYRSUS, LEUCIUS and CALLINICUS (SS) MM. R.M. Jan. 28
d. 251. Martyrs of Apollonia in Phrygia. Their alleged relics were brought to Constantinople and thence to Spain and France: for this reason St Thyrsus had a full office in the Mozarabic liturgy, and he is also patron of the ancient cathedral of Sisteron in the Basses Alpes, France.
Cf. Holw. — Baud.

THYRSUS (St) M. R.M. Jan. 31
See Saturninus, Thyrsus and Victor.

THYRSUS (St) M. R.M. Sept. 24
See Andochius, Thyrsus and Felix.

TIBBA (St) H. O.S.B. A.C. March 6
d. c.680. Kinswoman of SS Kyneburga and Kineswida, with whom she was a nun at Dormancaster.
Cf. Zimm. — Stanton — Holw.

TIBERIUS, MODESTUS and FLORENCE (SS) MM. R.M. Nov. 10
d. 303. Martyrs who met their death under Diocletian at Agde, diocese of Montpellier.
Cf. Holw. — Baud.

TIBURTIUS, VALERIAN and MAXIMUS (SS) MM. R.M. Apr. 14
d. ? c.190. Three names which occur in the *Acta* of St Caecilia — Valerian as her husband, Tiburtius as his brother and Maximus as an official.
Cf. Holw. — Att. — Baud.

TIBURTIUS (St) M. R.M. Aug. 11
d. c.288. A martyr beheaded at Rome. He was later connected with the soldier-martyr St Sebastian.
Cf. Holw. — Baud.

TIBURTIUS (St) M. R.M. Sept. 9
See Hyacinth, Alexander and Tibertius.

TIGERNACH (TIGERNAKE, TIERNEY, TIERRY) (St) Bp. A.C. Apr. 4
d. 549. Said to have been abbot of the monastery of Clones and to have succeeded St Macartan as bishop at Clogher.

His life, in its present form, cannot be taken as a historical document.
Cf. Holw. — Att.

TIGIDES and REMEDIUS (SS) Bps.
                                    R.M. Feb. 3
? Two bishops who succeeded one another in the see of Gap (French Alps).
Cf. Duch. Fast. Episc. — Gams — Holw.

TIGRIDIA (or TRIGIDIA) (St) Abs. O.S.B.   A.C. Nov. 22
d. c.925. A daughter of Count Sancho García, of Old Castile, who founded for her the Benedictine nunnery of Oña, near Burgos (later it became a monastery of monks). St Tigridia is greatly venerated in the province of Burgos.
Cf. P. de U. — Chev. — Holw. — Zimm.

TIGRIUS and EUTROPIUS (SS) MM.
                                    R.M. Jan. 12
d. 404. Tigrius was a priest and Eutropius a reader in the church of Constantinople; both were loyal adherents of their bishop St John Chrysostom. When the latter was banished they were falsely accused of setting fire to the cathedral and senate-house of Constantinople and were put to the torture. Eutropius died under it; Tigrius seems to have survived and to have been deported into Asia.
Cf. Holw. — Baud. — Att.

TILBERT (GILBERT) (St) Bp. O.S.B.
                                    A.C. Sept. 7
d. 789. Bishop of Hexham, 781-789. No details are known of his life.
Cf. Gams — Att. — Zimm. — Stanton.

TILLO (THILLO, THIELMAN, THÉAU, TILLOINE, TILLON, TILMAN, HILLONIUS, etc.) (St) Ab. O.S.B.
                                    A.C. Jan. 7
d. c.702. Born in Saxony, he was kidnapped by robbers and carried as a slave to the Low Countries, where he was ransomed by St Eligius of Noyon. He became a monk at Solignac, and after his ordination to the priesthood, evangelized the district round Tournai and Courtrai. He returned to Solignac, where he passed the last years of his life.
Cf. Zimm. — Att. — Holw. — Chev.

TIMOLAUS and Comp. (SS) MM.
                                    R.M. March 24
d. 303. A group of eight martyrs, beheaded at Caesarea in Palestine under

Diocletian. Eusebius gives the names of the rest: Dionysius (two), Romulus, Pausis, Alexander (two), and Agapius.
Cf. Holw. — Baud.

TIMON (St) M.   R.M. Apr. 19
1st cent. One of the first seven deacons, chosen by the Apostles (Acts VI, 5). There are only conflicting traditions as to the rest of his life.
Cf. Holw. — Baud.

TIMOTHY (St) Bp. M.   R.M. Jan. 24
d. 97. "The beloved son in faith" of St Paul, whom he accompanied on his missionary journeys and by whom he was ordained bishop of Ephesus, while yet young. The Apostle wrote to him two epistles which are among the canonical books. According to a very ancient tradition, St Timothy was stoned to death for denouncing the worship of Diana.
Cf. Holw. — Att. — Baud.

TIMOTHY (St) M.   R.M. March 24
See Mark and Timothy.

TIMOTHY and DIOGENES (SS) MM.
                                    R.M. Apr. 6
d. ? 345. Martyrs at Philippi in Macedonia, victims probably of the Arians.
Cf. Holw. — Baud.

TIMOTHY and MAURA (SS) MM.
                                    R.M. May 3
d. 298. Husband and wife, martyred at Antinoë in Egypt, by being nailed to a wall, where they lingered for nine days, consoling each other. They had been married only three weeks. Timothy, who was a reader, had been condemned for refusing to deliver the Sacred Books.
Cf. Holw. — Baud. — Att.

TIMOTHY, POLIUS and EUTYCHIUS (SS) MM.   R.M. May 21
? Three deacons in the African province of Mauretania Caesariensis, martyred under Diocletian.
Cf. Holw. — Baud.

TIMOTHY (St) M.   R.M. May 22
See Faustinus, Timothy and Venustus.

TIMOTHY (St) Bp. M.   R.M. June 10
d. 362. Bishop of Prussa in Bithynia, martyred under Julian the Apostate.
Cf. Holw. — Baud.

TIMOTHY, THECLA and AGAPIUS (SS) MM. R.M. Aug. 19
d. 304-306. Timothy, bishop of Gaza, was burnt alive in his episcopal city (304). Agapius was cast into the sea at Caesarea in Palestine (306).
Cf. Holw. — Baud. — Att.

TIMOTHY (St) M. R.M. Aug. 22
d. 311. A priest of Antioch in Syria, who joined the Roman clergy and was martyred at Rome and buried near the place where now stands the basilica of St Paul outside the walls. His relics are enshrined at the same basilica.
Cf. Holw. — Baud. — Att.

TIMOTHY and APOLLINARIS (SS) MM. R.M. Aug. 23
d. c.290. Martyrs at Reims in France.
Cf. Holw. — Baud.

TIMOTHY of MONTECCHIO (Bl) C. O.F.M. A.C. Aug. 26
1414-1504. A native of Montecchio, near Aquila, in Italy, he became a Franciscan Observant and was celebrated for his supernatural gift of infused knowledge. Cult confirmed in 1870.
Cf. Holw. — Att.

TIMOTHY and FAUSTUS (SS) MM. R.M. Sept. 8
? Martyrs at Antioch in Syria.
Cf. Holw. — Baud.

TIMOTHY (St) M. R.M. Dec. 19
d. c.250. A deacon, burnt alive in Africa under Decius.
Cf. Holw. — Baud.

TITIAN (St) Bp. R.M. Jan. 16
d. 650. For thirty years a bishop in the neighbourhood of Venice. The seat of his bishopric (Opitergium or Oderzo) has since been destroyed.
Cf. Holw. — Baud.

TITIAN (St) Bp. R.M. March 3
d. c.536. Said to have been a German by birth, who became bishop of Brescia.
Cf. Holw. — Gams — Baud.

TITUS (St) Bp. R.M. Jan. 4 and Feb. 6
d. ? c.96. One of the favourite disciples of St Paul, by whom he was consecrated first bishop of Crete. St Paul addressed to him one of the pastoral epistles. He died in Crete (at Gortyna?).
Cf. Att. — Holw. — Baud.

TITUS (St) M. R.M. Aug. 16
d. 410 (or 425?). A Roman deacon, put to death by a soldier during the sack of Rome by the Goths, while he was distributing alms to the half-starved population.
Cf. Holw. — Baud.

TOBIAS (St) M. R.M. Nov. 2
See Carterius, Styriacus, etc.

TOCHUMRA (St) V. A.C. June 11
? A virgin venerated in the diocese of Kilmore. She is invoked by women in labour.
Cf. Holw.

TOIMAN (St) Bp. A.C. Jan. 10
Otherwise Thomian, q.v.

TOLA (St) Bp. A.C. March 30
d. c.733. An Irish abbot-bishop of Disert Tola (Meath).
Cf. Holw.

TOOLEY (St) King M. R.M. July 29
A corrupt form of the name of St Olaus or Olave, q.v.

TORANNAN (St) Bp. A.C. June 12
Otherwise Ternan, q.v.

TORELLO (Bl) H. O.S.B. Vall. A.C. March 16
1201-1281. Born at Poppi in the Casentino, he was led astray by evil companions, but repented and received the habit of a recluse from the Vallombrosan abbot of San Fedele. He lived as a recluse, walled up in his cell, for sixty years. Vallombrosans and Franciscans claim him. It seems certain that he was, at any rate, a Vallombrosan oblate. Cult confirmed by Benedict XIV.
Cf. Zimm. — Att. — Holw. — Chev.

TORPES (St) M. R.M. Apr. 29
d. ? c.65. A martyr at Pisa, said to have suffered under Nero. The legends we have about him are altogether unreliable.
Cf. Holw. — Baud.

TORQUATUS, CTESIPHON, SECUNDUS, INDALETIUS, CAECILIUS, HESYCHIUS, and EUPHRASIUS (SS) MM. R.M. May 15
1st cent. According to a tradition, which, however, is not very ancient, they were disciples of the Apostles, by whom they

were sent to evangelize Spain. They worked chiefly in the South, as follows: Torquatus at Guadix, near Granada; Ctesiphon at Verga (Vierzo?); Secundus at Avila; Indaletius at Urci, near Almeria; Caecilius at Granada; Hesychius at Gibraltar; Euphrasius at Andujar. Most of them suffered martyrdom. The Mozarabic liturgy had a common feast for all seven.
Cf. P. de U. — Holw. — Att. — Baud.

TORTHRED (St) M.　　　　**A.C. Apr. 9**
Perhaps a variant of Theodore, q.v.

TOTNAN (St) M.　　　　**R.M. July 8**
See Kilian, Colman and Totnan.

TOULOUSE (Martyrs of) (BB)
　　　　　　　　　　　　A.C. May 29
d. 1228. A group of twelve martyrs — four of the secular clergy, three Dominicans, two Benedictines, two Franciscans, one layman — put to death by the Albigensians near Toulouse on the eve of the Ascension. They died singing the *Te Deum.* Cult confirmed in 1866.
Cf. Zimm.

TOUREDEC (St) M.　　　　**A.C. Apr. 9**
Otherwise Torthred, perhaps a variant of Theodore, q.v.

TRANQUILLINUS (St) M.　R.M. July 6
d. 286. A Roman martyr connected with the legend of St Sebastian, q.v.
Cf. Holw. — Baud.

TRASON, PONTIAN and PRAETEXTATUS (SS) MM.　　**R.M. Dec. 11**
d. c.302. Roman martyrs under Diocletian, put to death for ministering to the Christian prisoners awaiting martyrdom.
Cf. Holw. — Baud.

TREA (St) V.　　　　**A.C. Aug. 3**
5th cent. Converted to Christianity by St Patrick. She passed the rest of her life as a recluse at Ardtree, Derry.
Cf. Holw.

TREMORUS (St) M.　　　　**A.C. Nov. 7**
6th cent. Infant son of St Triphina. He was murdered at Carhaix in Brittany by his stepfather, Count Conmore. He is patron saint of Carhaix.
Cf. Holw. — Baud.

TRESSAN (French: TRÉSAIN) (St) C.
　　　　　　　　　　　　A.C. Feb. 7
d. 550. An Irish missionary, ordained priest by St Remigius, who worked at Mareuil on the Marne.
Cf. Holw. — Att. — Baud.

TRÈVES (Martyrs of) (SS)　R.M. Oct. 6
d. 287. The entry in the R.M. is as follows: "At Trèves, the commemoration of the almost innumerable martyrs who were slain in divers ways in the persecution of Diocletian, under the governor Rictiovarus, for the faith of Christ."
Cf. Holw. — Baud. — Chev.

TRIDUNA (TREDWALL, TRALLEN) (St) V.　　　　**A.C. Oct. 8**
8th or 4th cent? A maiden connected with the legend of St Regulus's mission to Scotland.
Cf. Holw. — Baud.

TRIEN (TRIENAN) (St) Ab.
　　　　　　　　　　　A.C. March 22
5th cent. One of St Patrick's disciples, abbot of Killelga.
Cf. Holw.

TRILLO (DRILLO, DREL) (St) C.
　　　　　　　　　　　　A.C. June 15
6th cent. The son of a Breton chieftain, who crossed over into Wales with St Cadfan. He is the patron saint of Llandrillo (Denbigh) and of Llandrillo (Monmouth).
Cf. Holw.

TRIPHINA (St) W.　　　　**A.C. Jan. 29**
6th cent. The mother of St Tremorus the infant-martyr. She passed the latter years of her life in a convent in Brittany.
Cf. Baud. — P.B. — Holw.

TRIPHINA (St) M.　　　　**R.M. July 5**
See Agatho and Triphina.

TRIPHYLLIUS (St) Bp.　　**R.M. June 13**
d. c.370. A lawyer converted to Christianity who was made bishop of Nikosia in Cyprus. He was a companion of St Spiridion and a loyal supporter of St Athanasius against the Arians, who bitterly persecuted him.
Cf. Holw. — Att. — Baud.

TRIPOS (St) M.　　　　**R.M. June 10**
See Basilides, Tripos, etc.

TRIVERIUS (St) H.   A.C. Jan. 16
d. ? 550. A saint honoured at Lyons and
in the diocese of Belley. He has given
his name to the village of Saint-Trivier.
Cf. Att. — Holw. — Baud.

TROADIUS (St) M.   R.M. Dec. 28
d. 250. A martyr of Neo-Caesarea in
Pontus, in the persecution under Decius.
Cf. Holw. — Baud.

TROJAN (French: TROYEN) (St) Bp.
   R.M. Nov. 30
d. 533. Said to have been born of a Jewish father and a Saracen mother. He became a priest at Saintes under St Vivian,
whom he succeeded in the see.
Cf. Holw. — Baud.

TRON or TROND (St) Ab. O.S.B.
   R.M. Nov. 23
Otherwise Trudo, q.v.

TROPHIMUS and THALUS (SS) MM.
   R.M. March 11
d. c.300. Martyrs at Laodicea in Syria,
crucified under Diocletian.
Cf. Holw. — Baud.

**TROPHIMUS and EUCARPIUS (SS)
MM.**   R.M. March 18
d. c.304. Two pagan soldiers told off to
hunt up Christians; they were converted
and burnt alive at Nicomedia under Diocletian.
Cf. Holw. — Baud.

**TROPHIMUS and THEOPHILUS (SS)
MM.**   R.M. July 23
d. c.302. Martyrs, beheaded at Rome
under Diocletian.
Cf. Holw. — Baud.

**TROPHIMUS, SABBATIUS and DORY-
MEDON (SS) MM.**   R.M. Sept. 19
d. c.277. Asiatic martyrs under the emperor Probus. They suffered probably
at Antioch in Syria.
Cf. Holw. — Baud.

TROPHIMUS (St) Bp.   R.M. Dec. 29
d. c.280. First bishop of Arles, sent to
Gaul from Rome c.240-260. Since 452
(Synod of Arles) the church of Provence
has identified him with St Trophimus, the
disciples of St Paul (Acts XX, 4; XXI, 29;
II Tim. IV, 20).
Cf. Holw. — Att. — Baud. — Gams.

**TRUDO (TRUDON, TRON, TROND,
TRUYEN, TRUDJEN) (St) Ab. O.S.B.**
   R.M. Nov. 23
d. c.695. A Benedictine under St Remaclus, he was ordained priest by St Clodulphus of Metz, and eventually founded
and governed an abbey on his paternal
estate (c.660), which was afterwards called
after him St Trond. It is situated between Louvain and Tongres.
Cf. Holw. — Zimm. — Att. — Chev.

TRUDPERT (St) Ab.   A.C. Apr. 26
d. c. ? 644. A solitary in Münstethal,
one of the most beautiful valleys in the
Black Forest. The Benedictine abbey of
St Trudpert arose on that site.
Cf. Holw. — Zimm. — Att. — Baud.

TRUMWIN (St) Bp. O.S.B.   A.C. Dec. 2
d. c.700. He was appointed (681) by St
Theodore and King Egfrid bishop over
the Southern Picts, and set up his see at
the monastery of Abercorn on the Firth of
Forth. In 685 King Egfrid was killed by
the Picts and St Trumwin and all his
monks had to flee South. He retired to
Whitby and there he lived an exemplary
monastic life.
Cf. Zimm. — Att. — Holw.

TRYPHAENA (TRIPHENES) (St) M.
   R.M. Jan. 31
? A matron of Cyzicus on the Hellespont
who, after having been tortured in divers
manners, was thrown to a savage bull and
gored to death.
Cf. Holw. — Baud.

TRYPHENNA and TRYPHOSA (SS)
   R.M. Nov. 10
1st cent. Two converts of St Paul from
Iconium in Lycaonia, mentioned by the
apostle in his Epistle to the Romans
(XVI, 12). Tradition represents them as
protectresses of St Thecla.
Cf. Holw. — Baud.

TRYPHON (St) M.   R.M. Jan. 4
See Aquilinus, Geminus, etc.

TRYPHON and Comp. (SS) MM.
   R.M. July 3
? A group of thirteen martyrs, who
suffered at Alexandria in Egypt.
Cf. Holw. — Baud.

TRYPHON, RESPICIUS and NYMPHA (SS) MM. R.M. Nov. 10
d. 251. Tryphon was a gooseherd at Campsada near Apamea in Syria and was martyred at Nicaea under Decius. The names of Respicius and Nympha have been joined to that of Tryphon only since the 11th century; we know nothing about either saint.
Cf. Holw. — Att. — Baud.

TRYPHONIA (St) W. R.M. Oct. 18
3rd cent. A Roman widow martyred in the Holy City. In legend she has been made wife either of the emperor Decius, or of Decius's son, Messius Decius. Her *Acta* are worthless.
Cf. Holw. — Baud.

TRYPHOSA (St) R.M. Nov. 10
See Tryphenna and Tryphosa.

TUDA (St) Bp. P.C. (?) Oct. 21
d. 664. An Irish monk who succeeded St Colman in the see of Lindisfarne, a staunch adherent of the Roman practices. He died of the pestilence within the first year of his appointment. He does not seem to have enjoyed a public cult.
Cf. Holw.

TUDE (St) Bp. M. R.M. June 17
Otherwise Antidius, q.v.

TUDINUS (St) Ab. A.C. May 9
Otherwise Tudy, q.v.

TUDNO (St) C. A.C. June 5
6th cent. The saint after whom Llandudno in Carnarvon is named. Several Welsh legends refer to him.
Cf. Holw. — Baring-Gould.

TUDWAL (TUGDUAL, TUGDUALUS) (St) Bp. A.C. Nov. 30
d. c.564. A Welsh monk who crossed over into Brittany and became bishop of Tréguier. Three places in the Lleyn Peninsular in Carnarvonshire perpetuate his memory.
Cf. Att. — Holw. — Baud.

TUDY (TUDCLYD, TYBIE) (St) V. A.C. Jan. 30
5th cent. Daughter of Brychan of Brecknock. She has left her name to Llandybie in Carmarthenshire.
Cf. Holw.

TUDY (TUDINUS, TEGWIN, THETGO) (St) Ab. A.C. May 9
5th cent. A Breton saint, disciple of St Maudez (Mawes) and fellow-worker with St Corentin. He was first a hermit and then an abbot near Landevennec in Brittany; like St Mawes, he spent some time in Cornwall, where a church and parish still bear his name.
Cf. Chev. — Baring-Gould — Holw. — Baud.

TUGDUAL (St) Bp. A.C. Nov. 30
Otherwise Tudwal, q.v.

TURIAF (TURIAV, TURIAVUS) (St) Bp. R.M. July 13
d. c.750. A Breton who succeeded St Samson as bishop of Dol.
Cf. Holw. — Att. — Baud.

TURIBIUS de MOGROBEJO (St) Bp. R.M. March 23
1538-1606. Torbibio Alfonso de Mogrobejo was born at Mayorga, prov. of León, Spain. He was professor of law at Salamanca, and, though a layman, was made president of the court of the Inquisition at Granada. Philip II appointed him to the see of Lima in Peru (1580) and the saint, fearing God but no man, with boundless zeal and untiring energy renewed the face of the Church in S. America. Canonized in 1726.
Cf. P. de U. — Att. — Holw. — Baud.

TURIBIUS of ASTORGA (St) Bp. R.M. Apr. 16
d. c.460. Bishop of Astorga in Spain, champion of Catholic doctrine against the Priscillianists.
Cf. P. de U. — Holw. — Gams — Att.

TURIBIUS of PALENCIA (St) Ab. A.C. Apr. 16 (?)
d. c.528. Probably a bishop. The abbot-founder of the great abbey of Liébana in Asturias, which eventually became a Benedictine centre.
Cf. Zimm. — P. de U. — Chev.

TURKETIL (St) Ab. O.S.B. A.C. July 11
887-975. A nephew of King Edred of England and his chancellor. In 948 he became a monk and shortly after abbot of Croyland, which he restored, attaching a cloistral school to the monastery.
Cf. Stanton — Holw.

TURNINUS (St) C. A.C. July 17
8th cent. An Irish priest who worked as a missionary with St Foillan in the Netherlands, and more particularly in the vicinity of Antwerp.
Cf. Holw. — Baud.

TUTILO (St) Mk. O.S.B. A.C. March 28
d. c.915. Monk of St Gall in Switzerland, a companion and friend of BB Notker Balbulus and Ratpert. Handsome, eloquent, quick-witted, a giant in strength and stature, poet, orator, architect, painter, sculptor, metal worker, mechanic, musician who played and taught several instruments at the abbey school, he was everywhere in request for his artistic talents and was greatly admired by the emperor Charles the Fat.
Cf. Zimm. — Att. — Chev. — Holw.

TUTO (TOTTO) (Bl) Bp. O.S.B.
A.C. May 14
d. 930. Monk and abbot of St Emmeram at Ratisbon. He became bishop of the same city and secretary to the emperor Arnold.
Cf. Gams — Mab. — Chev. — Zimm. — Holw.

TUTO (TOTTO) (Bl) Ab. O.S.B.
A.C. Nov. 19
d. 815. Abbot-founder (764) of the great Benedictine abbey of Ottobeuren in Bavaria.
Cf. Zimm. — Chev. — Holw.

TWELVE HOLY BROTHERS, The (SS) MM. R.M. Sept. 1
d. c.303 ? The relics of several groups of martyrs, who had suffered in S. Italy, were brought together and enshrined at Benevento in 760. A legend grew up according to which all these martyrs were the sons of SS Boniface and Thecla, q.v.; they were said to have been arrested in Africa and brought to Italy where they were put to death. This legend is now considered to have no historical foundation. The several groups comprised in the so-called "twelve brothers," or Martyrs of the South, are (1) Aug. 27. At Potenza in the Basilicata, Arontius or Orontius, Honoratus, Fortunatus and Sabinian. (2) Aug. 28. At Venosa in Apulia, Septiminus, Januarius and Felix. (3) Aug. 29. At Velleianum in Apulia, Vitalis, Sator (or Satyrus) and Repositus.

(4) Sept. 1. At Sentianum in Apulia, Donatus and another Felix.
Cf. Holw. — Baud. — Att.

TWYNNELL (St)
This occurs as a place-name in Pembrokeshire. It is possibly a corrupt form of the name of St Winneur, or Winoc, or Winwaloë.

TYCHICUS (St) Bp. R.M. Apr. 29
1st cent. A disciple of St Paul the Apostle and his fellow-worker (Col. IV, 7; Eph. VI, 21 sq.). He is said to have ended his days as bishop of Paphos in Cyprus.
Cf. Holw. — Baud.

TYCHON (St) Bp. R.M. June 16
d. c.450. Bishop of Amathus in Cyprus. He energetically fought against the last remnants of paganism in the island, especially the cult of Aphrodite.
Cf. Holw. — Att. — Baud.

TYDECHO (St) A.C. Dec. 17
6th cent. A Welshman, brother of St Cadfan. He and his sister dwelt in Merionethshire. Several churches are dedicated in his honour.
Cf. Holw. — Baring-Gould.

TYDFIL (St) M. A.C. Aug. 23
d. c.480. Of the clan of Brychan. She is venerated at Merthyr-Tydfil, Glamorgan, where she was slain by the marauding Picts or Saxons.
Cf. Holw. — Baring-Gould.

TYRANNIO, SILVANUS, PELEUS, NILUS and ZENOBIUS (SS) MM.
R.M. Feb. 20
d. c.304 and 310. Tyrannio was bishop of Tyre in Phoenicia: he was martyred by drowning in the Orontes. The others were martyrs of the same district, who had suffered some six years earlier.
Cf. Holw. — Baud. — Att.

TYRE (Martyrs of). R.M. Feb. 20
d. 302-310. The R.M. has this entry: "At Tyre in Phoenicia, the commemoration of blessed martyrs whose number the wisdom of God alone can tell . . ." The group of the preceding entry were among this number.
Cf. Holw. — Baud.

TYSILIO (TYSSEL, TYSSILO, SULIAU) (St) Ab. A.C. Nov. 8
d. c.640. A Welsh prince, who became

abbot of Meifod in Montgomeryshire and founded several churches in the other parts of Wales; finally (c.617) he migrated to Brittany and died at Saint-Suliac.
Cf. Att. — Baud. — Holw.

U

UBALD BALDASSINI (St) Bp.
R.M. May 16
c.1100-1160. Born at Gubbio near Ancona, he was made dean of the cathedral and introduced community life among the canons. In 1128 he became bishop of his native city. His character was remarkable for its combination of gentleness with courage, and it was by these qualities that he succeeded in disarming the tyrannical Frederick Barbarossa. Canonized 1192.
Cf. Holw. — Baud. — Att.

UBALD ADIMARI (Bl) C. O.S.M.
A.C. Apr. 9
1246-1315. He belonged to the nobility of Florence, and as a leader in the Ghibelline party he was notorious for his wild and dissolute life. In 1276 he was converted by St Philip Benizi who admitted him to the Servite institute. Ubald spent the remainder of his life on Mt Senario, a model to penitent souls. Cult confirmed 1821.
Cf. Holw. — Baud. — Att.

UBRIC (St) Bp.   R.M. July 4
Otherwise Ulric, q.v.

UDA (St) V.   A.C. Jan. 30
Otherwise Tudy, q.v.

UGANDA (Martyrs of) (BB)
A.C. June 3
1885-1887. Twenty-two negroes of Uganda, boys and young men from thirteen to thirty years of age, for the most part pages of King Mwanga. They were converts of the White Fathers and were martyred with horrible cruelty. Their heroic courage rivalled that of the early martyrs. Beatified 1920. Each has a separate entry in this book.
Cf. Holw. — Baud. — Att.

UGUCCIO (St) C.
R.M. May 3 and Feb. 12
One of the Seven Founders of the Servite Order, q.v.

UGUZO (LUCIUS) M.   A.C. Aug. 19
? A poor shepherd in the mountains of Carvagna (Italian Alps) who gave his savings to the poor and the churches. He was killed through envy by one of his former masters. His cult has flourished at Milan since 1280 and has been repeatedly approved by Rome.
Cf. Holw.

ULCHED (ULCHAD, YLCHED) (St)
A.C. Apr. 6
? The holy man who has given his name to the church of Llechulched in Anglesey.
Cf. Holw.

ULFRID (WOLFRED, WILFRID) (St) M.
A.C. Jan. 18
d. 1029. A native of England who became a missionary in Germany and Sweden. He was martyred for destroying the idol of Thor.
Cf. Holw. — Att. — Stanton.

ULMAR (St) Ab. O.S.B.   A.C. July 20
Otherwise Wulmar, q.v.

ULPHIA (WULFIA, OLFE, WULFE) (St) H.   A.C. Jan. 31
d. 995. Said to have lived as a solitary near Amiens under the direction of the aged hermit St Domitius. At a later period the convent of the Paraclete was built over her tomb.
Cf. Holw. — Baud. — Att.

ULPIAN (St) M.   R.M. Apr. 3
Otherwise Vulpian, q.v.

ULRIC (St) H.   A.C. Feb. 20
Otherwise Wulfric, q.v.

ULRIC of EINSIEDELN (Bl) C. O.S.B.
A.C. May 29
d. p. 978. Son of St Gerold. He became a monk at the Swiss abbey of Einsiedeln and was appointed treasurer. After his father's death he retired to live as a hermit in the latter's cell. His feast is observed at Einsiedeln.
Cf. Holw.

ULRIC (ULDARICUS, UDALRIC) (St) Bp.   R.M. July 4
d. 973. A native of Augsburg, at the age of seven he was sent to be educated at the Swiss Benedictine abbey of St Gall. In 923 he was nominated bishop of Augsburg and became the protector of his people

against the invading Magyars. In his old age he retired to St Gall and took one of his nephews as his coadjutor: this led to an unjust charge of nepotism. Canonized 993 (the first recorded papal canonization).
Cf. Att. — Baud. — Holw.

ULRIC of CLUNY (St) Mk. O.S.B.
A.C. July 14
c. 1018-1093. Born at Ratisbon, he became archdeacon of Freising and then went on a pilgrimage to Rome and Jerusalem. On his return he joined the Benedictines at Cluny under St Hugh (1061). He held the following offices in rapid succession: novice master (as such he wrote the famous Cluniac Customary), prior and confessor of the Cluniac nunnery of Marcigny, prior of Peterlingen, prior of Rüggersburg, and finally prior-founder of Zell in the Black Forest. Throughout life he suffered from violent headaches.
Cf. Zimm. — Att. — Chev. — Baud. — Holw.

ULTAN (St) Ab. O.S.B. A.C. May 2
d. c.686. An Irishman, brother of SS Fursey and Foillan and a monk with them at Burghcastle near Yarmouth. Thence he crossed over to Belgium, where he was warmly welcomed by St Gertrude of Nivelles. He was chaplain to her nunnery and taught chant to the nuns until he succeeded his brother St Foillan in the abbacies of Fosses and Peronne.
Cf. Zimm. — Att. — Holw.

ULTAN (St) H. O.S.B. A.C. Aug. 8
8th cent. An Irishman and monk-priest of St Peter's monastery at Craik. He excelled in the art of illumination.
Cf. Zimm.

ULTAN (St) Bp. A.C. Sept. 4
7th cent. There are a score or so of Irish saints named Ultan. Besides the two listed above the most important seems to have been a bishop of Ardbraccan, noted for his fondness for children and said to have collected the writings of St Brigid.
Cf. Att. — Holw.

ULTIUS (St) Bp. A.C. Jan. 8
Otherwise Wulsin, q.v.

UNAMAN (St) M. O.S.B. A.C. Feb. 15
See Winaman, Unaman and Sunaman.

UNI (UNNI, UNNO, HUNO) (St) Bp. O.S.B. A.C. Sept. 17
d. 936. A Benedictine of New Corbie in Saxony, who in 917 was appointed bishop of Bremen-Hamburg. He evangelized Sweden and Denmark with signal success and died at Birka in Sweden.
Cf. Gams — Holw. — Chev. — Zimm.

URBAN (St) M. R.M. Jan. 24
See Babilas, Urban, etc.

URBAN (St) M. R.M. March 8
See Cyril, Rogatus, etc.

URBAN of LANGRES (St) Bp. R.M. Apr. 2
d. c.390. Sixth bishop of Langres, nominated to that see in 374. In some parts of Burgundy and neighbouring provinces he is honoured as the patron saint of vine dressers.
Cf. Holw. — Baud. — Gams.

URBAN (St) Ab. O.S.B. A.C. Apr. 6
d. c.940. Abbot of the Benedictine monastery of Peñalba in the diocese of Astorga, Spain. He helped St Gennadius to bring about a Benedictine revival.
Cf. Zimm.

URBAN (St) M. R.M. Apr. 16
See Saragossa (Martyrs of).

URBAN I (St) Pope M. R.M. May 25
d. 230. A Roman, successor of Callistus in the papal chair (222-230). During his pontificate the Church seems to have enjoyed comparative peace. He does not appear to have died a martyr.
Cf. Att. — Holw. — Baud.

URBAN (St) M. R.M. July 2
See Ariston, Crescentian, etc.

URBAN II (Bl) Pope O.S.B. R.M. July 29
1042-1099. Odo of Lagery was born at Chatillon-sur-Marne and belonged to the family of the counts of Semur. He studied at Reims under St Bruno and became archdeacon of that church. In 1070 he joined the Benedictines of Cluny and was soon appointed grand prior under St Hugh. In 1078 he was created cardinal bishop of Ostia and in 1088 was elected pope. As prior, as cardinal and as pope he followed and fostered the Gregorian policy of ecclesiastical reform. As pope

he had as adviser St Bruno, the founder of the Carthusians. Urban is perhaps best remembered as the promoter of the first crusade at the council of Clermont, in consequence of an appeal from the Byzantine emperor Alexius I. Beatified 1881. *Cf. Zimm. — Holw. — Att. — Baud.*

URBAN, THEODORE and Comp. (SS) MM. R.M. Sept. 5
d. 370. A group of eighty priests and clerics who, in the time of the Arian emperor Valens, were deliberately left to perish in a burning ship for having appealed to the emperor against the persecution of the Catholics.
Cf. Holw. — Att. — Baud.

URBAN (St) M. R.M. Oct. 31
See Ampliatus, Urban and Narcissus.

URBAN (St) Bp. R.M. Nov. 28
See Valerian, Urban, etc.

URBAN (St) Bp. R.M. Dec. 7
d. c.356. Bishop of Teano in Campania. *Cf. Gams — Holw. — Baud.*

URBAN V (Bl) Pope O.S.B. R.M. Dec. 19
1310-1370. William of Grimoard was born in Languedoc and educated at the universities of Montpellier and Toulouse. He became a Benedictine at the priory of Chiriac and was sent to take his doctorate at Paris and Avignon. He affiliated himself to the Cluniacs and was made abbot of St Germanus at Auxerre, and then of St Victor at Marseilles. In 1361 he was sent as papal legate to Italy (the papacy then being at Avignon) and in the following year, although not yet a cardinal, was elected pope. He succeeded in transferring the papacy back to Rome, but in 1370 he was forced to retire to France, dying the same year. Cult confirmed 1870.
Cf. Zimm. — Chev. — Holw. — Baud. — Att.

URBITIUS (St) Bp. A.C. March 20
d. c.420. Bishop of Metz. He built a church in honour of St Felix of Nola which became the abbey church of the monastery of St Clement.
Cf. Holw. — Baud. — Duch. Fast. Episc.

URBITIUS (Spanish: ÚRBEZ) (St) H. O.S.B. A.C. Dec. 15
d. c.805. Said to have been born at Bordeaux, to have become a monk in France, and to have been taken prisoner by Saracens and brought to Spain. He managed to escape and settled as a hermit in the valley of Nocito, Aragonese Pyrenees, near Huesca. There is no trustworthy biography of the saint, but his cult is still very flourishing in that district.
Cf. Holw. — Chev. — Baud.

URCISCENUS (St) Bp. R.M. June 21
d. c.216. Reckoned as the seventh bishop of Pavia, c.183-c.216.
Cf. Gams — Holw.

URSACIUS (St) R.M. Aug. 16
Otherwise Arsacius, q.v.

URSICINUS (St) M. R.M. June 19
d. c.67. Said to have been a physician at Ravenna who, on being sentenced to death for being a Christian, wavered, but was encouraged by the soldier St Vitalis and accepted martyrdom. His Acts are not trustworthy.
Cf. Holw. — Menzies — Baud.

URSICINUS (St) Bp. R.M. July 24
d. c.380. Registered as the fourth bishop of Sens. An opponent of Arianism.
Cf. Holw. — Baud.

URSICINUS (St) Bp. O.S.B. A.C. Oct. 2
d. 760. Abbot of Disentis in Switzerland, who became bishop of Chur in 754. In 758 he resigned and became a hermit.
Cf. Gams — Holw.

URSICINUS (St) Bp. R.M. Dec. 1
d. p. 347. A bishop of Brescia in Lombardy who took part in the council of Sardica (347). His shrine at Brescia still exists.
Cf. Holw. — Baud.

URSICINUS (St) Bp. A.C. Dec. 20
d. c.585. Bishop of Cahors, often mentioned by the historian St Gregory of Tours.
Cf. Holw. — Baud. — Duch. Fast. Episc.

URSICINUS (St) Ab. A.C. Dec. 20
d. c.625. An Irish missionary monk, companion of St Columbanus. He became the abbot-founder of the monastery of St Ursanne, from which the Swiss town so called takes its name.
Cf. Holw. — Att. — Chev.

URSICIUS (St) M.   **R.M. Aug. 14**
d. 304. An Illyrian tribune in the imperial army beheaded at Nicomedia under Diocletian.
Cf. Holw. — Baud.

URSINUS (St) Bp.   **R.M. Nov. 9**
3rd cent. Though alleged to have been one of several disciples of Christ sent by the apostles to be bishops in Gaul, it is certain that he flourished in the 3rd century and that he was the first bishop of Bourges.
Cf. Holw. — Duch. Fast. Episc. — Chev. — Baud.

URSMAR (St) Bp. O.S.B.   **R.M. Apr. 19**
d. 713. Abbot-bishop of the great Benedictine abbey of Lobbes on the Sambre and founder of Aulne and Wallers, also in present-day Belgium. His work as regionary bishop in Flanders was of great importance.
Cf. Zimm. — Chev. — Baud. — Att.

URSULA and Comp. (SS) VV. MM.
R.M. Oct. 21
4th cent. A group of maidens martyred at Cologne, probably under Diocletian. In the fourth century a church was built at Cologne in their honour. Medieval legends greatly embellished the scanty historical facts. The number of, probably, eleven (XI MM VV, i.e., eleven martyr-virgins)· was increased to eleven thousand (XIM VV, i.e., XI Millia Virginum — 11,000 virgins) and a convenient legendary setting was found for the increased number. Pope Benedict XIV intended to delete the entry concerning them from the R.M. With the approval of the Holy See the Benedictines have already suppressed the feast in their calendar.
Cf. Att. — Holw. — Baud.

URSULINA (Bl) V.   **A.C. Apr. 7**
1375-1410. A young woman of Parma who, alleging supernatural visions, visited Clement XII at Avignon and Benedict IX at Rome with a view to putting an end to the papal schism. After a pilgrimage to the Holy Land she was refused admittance to Parma and had to retire to Bologna, where she died.
Cf. Att. — Holw. — Baud.

URSULINE NUNS (BB) MM.
A.C. Oct. 17
d. 1794. A group of eleven Ursuline nuns

guillotined at Valenciennes for having reopened their school in spite of the prohibition of the French revolutionary authorities. Each has a special entry in this book. Beatified 1920.
Cf. Baud. — Holw. — Att.

URSUS (St) Bp.   **R.M. Apr. 13**
d. 396. A bishop of Ravenna.
Cf. Att. — Holw. — Baud.

URSUS (St) Bp.   **R.M. July 30**
d. 508. A recluse at the church of St Amator of Auxerre, who was made bishop of that city when he was already seventy-five years of age.
Cf. Holw. — Baud.

URSUS (St) M.   **R.M. Sept. 30**
See Victor and Ursus.

UST (ʃUSTUS) (St)   **A.C. Aug. 12**
? He gives its title to the church of St Just a few miles from Penzance. He is described indiscriminately as a hermit, as a martyr, and as a bishop. Possibly there were several saints of this name, whose lives have been amalgamated.
Cf. Holw. —ˌBaud.

USTHAZANES (St) M.   **R.M. Apr. 21**
See Simeon, Abdechalas, etc.

UTTO (Bl) Ab. O.S.B.   **A.C. Oct. 3**
c.750-820. Abbot-founder of the Benedictine monastery of Metten in Bavaria. Cult approved 1909.
Cf. Holw. — Baud. — Chev. — Zimm.

UVAL (St) Bp.   **A.C. Nov. 20**
Otherwise Eval, q.v.

V

VAAST (St) Bp.   **R.M. Feb. 6**
Otherwise Vedast, q.v.

VALENS and Comp. (SS) MM.
R.M. May 21
? Said to have been a bishop martyred at Auxerre with three boys.
Cf. Holw. — Baud.

VALENS, PAUL and Comp. (SS) MM.
R.M. June 1
d. 309. Martyrs at Caesarea in Palestine, companions of St Pamphilus. Valens was

an aged deacon of the church of Jerusalem. They suffered under Diocletian.
Cf. Holw. — Baud.

VALENS (St) Bp.   R.M. July 26
d. 531. Bishop of Verona, 524-531.
Cf. Gams — Baud. — Holw.

VALENTINA and Comp. (SS) VV. MM.
R.M. July 25
d. 308. A group of virgin-martyrs at Caesarea in Palestine under Diocletian.
Cf. Holw. — Baud.

VALENTINE (St) Bp.   A.C. Jan. 7
d. c.470. An abbot who became a missionary bishop in Rhaetia. He died at Mais in the Tyrol. Some years later his body was translated to Trent and finally to Passau.
Cf. Holw. — Baud.

VALENTINE (St) M.   R.M. Feb. 14
d. 269. A priest and physician in Rome martyred under Claudius the Goth and buried on the Flaminian Way. In 350 a church was built over his tomb. The custom of sending "Valentines" on Feb. 14 is based on the medieval belief that birds began to pair on the 14th of February.
Cf. Holw. — Baud. — Att.

VALENTINE (St) Bp. M.   R.M. Feb. 14
d. c.269. A bishop of Terni (*Interamna*) about sixty miles from Rome, martyred under Claudius the Goth. Some writers, we believe rightly, identify this saint with the St Valentine recorded above.
Cf. Holw. — Baud. — Att.

VALENTINE (St) Bp.   A.C. May 2
d. c. Bishop of Genoa, c.295-c.307. His relics were discovered and enshrined in 985.
Cf. Gams — Baud. — Holw.

VALENTINE (St) Bp. M.   R.M. July 16
d. c.305. A bishop of Trèves (or more probably Tongres) martyred under Diocletian.
Cf. Holw. — Baud.

VALENTINE (St) Bp.   A.C. Sept. 2
4th cent. Fourth bishop of Strassburg.
Cf. Duch. Fast. Episc. — Holw. — Baud.

VALENTINE (St) Bp.   R.M. Oct. 29
See Maximilian and Valentine.

VALENTINE BERRIO-OCHOA (Bl) Bp.
M. O.P.   A.C. Nov. 1
1827-1861. Born at Ellorio, diocese of Vitoria, Spain. After his profession in the Dominican Order he was sent to the Philippine Islands and thence (1858) to Tonkin as a bishop titular and vicar apostolic. He was beheaded with Bl Jerome Hermosilla. Beatified in 1909.
Cf. Holw. — Prop. O.P.

VALENTINE and HILARY (SS) MM.
R.M. Nov. 3
d. c.304. A priest and his deacon, beheaded at Viterbo, near Rome, under Diocletian.
Cf. Holw. — Baud.

VALENTINE, FELICIAN and VICTORINUS (SS) MM.   R.M. Nov. 11
d. c.305. Martyrs at Ravenna under Diocletian.
Cf. Holw. — Baud.

VALENTINE, SOLUTOR and VICTOR (SS) MM.   R.M. Nov. 13
d. c.305. Martyrs at Ravenna under Diocletian. Probably a duplicate of Nov. 11. To both groups some martyrologies add a number of other names.
Cf. Holw. — Baud.

VALENTINE, CONCORDIUS, NAVALIS and AGRICOLA (SS) MM. R.M. Dec. 16
d. c.305. In all probability a repetition of the two preceding entries. Since St Peter Chrysologus (d. c.450) writes that St Apollinaris was the only martyr of Ravenna, it may be that St Valentine and Comp. were merely venerated in that city, and only later said to have been martyred there.
Cf. Holw. — Baud. — Menzies.

VALENTINIAN (St) Bp.   A.C. Nov. 3
d. c.500. Bishop of Salerno in S. Italy.
Cf. Menzies — Holw. — Baud.

VALENTIO (St) M.   R.M. May 25
See Pasicrates, Valentio, etc.

VALERIA (Martyrs of) (SS)
R.M. March 14
8th cent. The R.M. has this entry: "In the province of Valeria, the birthday of two holy monks, whom the Lombards slew by hanging them on a tree: and there, although dead, they were heard even by

their enemies singing psalms." The story is taken from St Gregory the Great (Dial. IV, 21).
Cf. Holw.

VALERIA (St) M. R.M. Apr. 28
? 1st cent. The alleged mother of SS Gervase and Protase and wife of St Vitalis. She seems to be a fictitious personage.
Cf. Holw. — Baud.

VALERIA (St) M. R.M. June 5
See Zenais, Cyria, etc.

VALERIA (St) V. M. R.M. Dec. 9
? This saint probably never existed. She is said to have been converted to the Faith by St Martial of Limoges, and to have been beheaded there. (Cf. Martial of Limoges).
Cf. Baud. — Holw.

VALERIAN (St) M. R.M. Apr. 14
See Tiburtius Valerian and Maximus.

VALERIAN (St) Bp. A.C. May 13
d. c.350. Third bishop of Auxerre. A champion of the Catholic Faith against Arianism.
Cf. Duch. Fast. Episc. — Holw. — Baud.

VALERIAN (St) Bp. A.C. July 23
d. c.460. A monk of Lérins who was promoted to the see of Cimiez (now united to that of Nice).
Cf. Duch. Fast. Episc. — Baud. — Holw.

VALERIAN (St) M. R.M. Aug. 23
See Restitutus, Donatus, etc.

VALERIAN (St) M. R.M. Sept. 12
See Hieronides, Leontius, etc.

VALERIAN (St) M. R.M. Sept. 15
d. 178. A companion of St Photinus (Pothinus) of Lyons. He succeeded in escaping from prison and reappeared at Tournus, near Autun, where he again preached to the people. He was captured a second time and beheaded.
Cf. Holw. — Baud.

VALERIAN, MACRINUS and GORDIAN (SS) MM. R.M. Sept. 17
? Martyrs ascribed by some to Noyon, by others to Nevers, by others to Nyon (near Berne, Switzerland), by others to a

place called Noviodunum near the mouth of the Danube in Lower Moesia.
Cf. Holw. — Baud.

VALERIAN (St) Bp. R.M. Nov. 27
d. 389. Bishop of Aquileia in N. Italy. He succeeded immediately after an Arian bishop and his pontificate, 369-389, was spent in combating that heresy.
Cf. Holw. — Baud.

VALERIAN, URBAN, CRESCENS, EUSTACE, CRESCONIUS, CRESCENTIAN, FELIX, HORTULANUS and FLORENTIAN (SS) Bps. R.M. Nov. 28
5th cent. African bishops banished from their country by the Arian king Genseric. They died in exile and were afterwards honoured as confessors of the Faith.
Cf. Holw. — Baud.

VALERIAN (St) Bp. (M). R.M. Dec. 15
d. 457. Bishop of Abbenza in Africa, who, when over eighty years of age, was left to die of exposure for refusing to give up the sacred vessels. He died under the Arian Genseric, king of the Vandals.
Cf. Holw. — Att. — Baud.

VALERIUS (St) Bp. A.C. Jan. 16
d. c.453. A hermit taken from his solitude by the people of Sorrento, who made him their bishop.
Cf. Gams — Baud. — Holw. — Menzies.

VALERIUS (St) Bp. R.M. Jan. 28
d. 315. Bishop of Saragossa in Spain, under whom St Vincent served as deacon. He was arrested, and exiled under Diocletian; but survived and died in peace in his episcopal city.
Cf. Holw. — P. de U. — Baud.

VALERIUS (St) Bp. R.M. Jan. 29
d. c.320. Legendary second bishop of Trèves and alleged disciple of St Peter. More probably he was bishop of that city at the beginning of the fourth century.
Cf. Holw. — Att. — Baud.

VALERIUS (St) Bp. A.C. Feb. 19
d. p. 450. Bishop of Antibes in S. France.
Cf. Duch. Fast. Episc. — Baud. — Holw.

VALERIUS (St) Bp. A.C. Feb. 20
? Mentioned by St Gregory of Tours as the first bishop of Conserans in France.
Cf. Duch. Fast. Episc. — Baud. — Holw.

VALERIUS (St) Ab.   A.C. Feb. 21
d. 695. A native of Astorga in Spain, who became a monk and abbot of San Pedro de Montes. He has left several ascetical writings: he is in fact the last representative of the Isidorian revival in Spain.
Cf. P. de U. — Chev.

VALERIUS and RUFINUS (SS) MM.
          R M. June 14
d. c.287. Roman missionaries in Gaul who were martyred at Soissons.
Cf. Holw. — Att. — Baud.

VALERIUS (St) M.   R.M. Nov. 16
See Rufinus, Mark, etc.

VALERY (St) Ab.   R.M. Apr. 1
Otherwise Walaricus, q.v.

VANDRILLE (St) Ab.   R.M. July 22
Otherwise Wandregisilus, q.v.

VANNE (VAUNE) (St) Bp.   A.C. Nov. 9
Otherwise Vitonus, q.v.

VARELDE (VEERLE, VERYLDE) (St) V.
          A.C. Jan. 4
Otherwise Pharaïldis, q.v.

VARICUS (St) M.   R.M. Nov. 15
See Secundus, Fidentian and Varicus.

VARUS (St) M.   R.M. Oct. 19
d. 307. A Roman soldier in Upper Egypt who, being on guard at a prison in which certain monks condemned to death were confined, on seeing one of them expire in his dungeon, insisted on taking his place and was forthwith hanged from a tree. The Acts are genuine.
Cf. Holw. — Baud.

VASIUS (French: VAISE, VAIZE) (St) M.   A.C. Apr. 16
d. c.500. A rich citizen of Saintes, in France, murdered by his relatives for distributing his property among the poor.
Cf. Holw. — Baud.

VEDAST (VAAST, VAAT, GASTON, FOSTER) (St) Bp.   R.M. Feb. 6
d. 539. A fellow-worker with St Remigius in the conversion of the Franks. For close on forty years he ruled the united sees of Arras-Cambrai.
Cf. Holw. — Att. — Baud.

VEEP (VEEPUS, VEEPY, WIMP, WENNAPA) (St) V.   A.C. July 1
6th cent. Patron saint of St Veep in Cornwall. St Veep (in Welsh, Gwenafwy) was a daughter of Caw, chief of North Britain and a sister of St Samson of York. Driven south by the Picts, she settled in Cornwall, where place-names still recall her memory.
Cf. Holw. — Baring-Gould.

VEHO (St) Bp.   A.C. June 15
Otherwise Vouga, q.v.

VELLEICUS (WILLEIC) (St) Ab. O.S.B.
          A.C. Aug. 29
8th cent. An Anglo-Saxon, who followed St Swithbert to the apostolate in Germany and became abbot of Kaiserswerth, on the Rhine.
Cf. Stanton — Holw.

VENANTIUS (St) Bp. M.   R.M. Apr. 1
d. ?c.255. A bishop in Dalmatia, whose body was brought from Spalato to the Lateran by Pope John IV in 641.
Cf. Holw. — Baud.

VENANTIUS (St) M.   R.M. May 18
d. c.250. Said to have been a boy of fifteen who died a martyr at Camerino, near Ancona, under Decius. Nothing certain is known about him: Pope Clement X, a former bishop of Camerino, raised the feast of St Venantius to the double rite and composed the proper hymns of his office.
Cf. Holw. — Att. — Baud.

VENANTIUS (St) H.   A.C. May 30
d. c.400. Elder brother of St Honoratus, the founder of Lérins. After living as hermits on an island near Cannes, both travelled to the East to study the monastic life, and Venantius died at Modon in Morea.
Cf. Holw. — Baud. — Chev.

VENANTIUS (St) Bp.   A.C. Aug. 5
d. 544. A convert from Arianism who became a monk at Viviers and afterwards bishop of the same city.
Cf. Duch. Fast. Episc. — Baud. — Holw.

VENANTIUS (St) Ab.   R.M. Oct. 13
5th cent. An abbot of the monastery of St Martin at Tours.
Cf. Holw. — Baud.

VENANTIUS FORTUNATUS (St) Bp.
A.C. Dec. 14
c.535-c.605. Born near Treviso in N.
Italy, at the age of thirty he settled at
Poitiers and was ordained priest. He became known to Queen St Radegunde who
befriended him. He was a prolific writer
and poet; the hymn *Vexilla Regis* was
composed by him. Not all his other com-
positions, however, reach the same ex-
cellence. Shortly before his death he was
made bishop of Poitiers. His feast is
celebrated in several Italian and French
dioceses.
Cf. Att. — Baud. — Holw.

VENERANDA (St) V. M. R.M. Nov. 14
2nd cent. Described by the R.M. as a
martyr and ascribed to Gaul. It seems
that Vereranda is a later corruption of
Venera (from *dies Veneris* — Friday) the
Latin counterpart of *Parasceves*, and that
she is identical with a Parasceves, at one
time venerated by the Greeks.
Cf. Holw. — Baud.

VENERANDUS (St) M. R.M. Nov. 14
d. 275. An influential citizen of Troyes in
France, martyred under Aurelian.
Cf. Holw. — Baud.

VENERANDUS (St) Bp. A.C. Dec. 24
d. 423. Born of a senatorial family of
Clermont in Auvergne, he became bishop
of the same city.
Cf. Duch. Fast. Episc. — Baud. — Holw.

VENERIUS (St) Bp. R.M. May 4
d. 409. Ordained deacon by St Ambrose,
eventually he was promoted to the see of
Milan. He is best remembered as a loyal
supporter of St John Chrysostom.
Cf. Menzies — Baud. — Holw.

VENERIUS (St) Ab. O.S.B.
R.M. Sept. 13
7th (or 9th) cent. A hermit, and then
abbot on the island of Tino in the Gulf of
Genoa. His "Life" is very untrustworthy.
Cf. Holw. — Baud. — Zimm.

VENTURA SPELLUCCI (Bl) Ab. O.S.B.
A.C. May 3
12th cent. Born at Spello near Assisi, he
joined the Italian Cruciferi, under the
Benedictine Rule, and eventually built an
abbey-hospice on his family estate which
he ruled as abbot till his death.
Cf. Att. — Baud. — Holw.

VENUSTIAN (St) M. R.M. Dec. 30
See Sabinus, Exuperantius, etc.

VENUSTUS (St) M. R.M. May 6
See Heliodorus, Venustus, etc.

VENUSTUS (St) M. R.M. May 22
See Faustinus, Timothy and Venustus.

VERANUS (St) Bp. A.C. Sept. 10
d. c.480. Son of St Eucherius of Lyons,
he became a monk at Lérins, and afterwards bishop of Vence (Alpes Maritimes)
France.
Cf. Duch. Fast. Episc. — Holw. — Baud.

VERANUS (St) Bp. R.M. Oct. 19
d. 590. Native of Vaucluse, who became
bishop of Cavaillon, in France.
Cf. Holw. — Baud.

VERANUS (St) Bp. R.M. Nov. 11
5th cent. Ascribed by the R.M. to
Lyons. Probably he is identical with St
Veranus of Vence (Sept. 10).
Cf. Holw.

VERECUNDUS (St) Bp. R.M. Oct. 22
d. 522. Bishop of Verona.
Cf. Holw. — Gams — Baud.

VEREMUNDUS (St) Ab. O.S.B.
A.C. March 8
d. 1092. A native of Navarre who, while
still a child, entered the Benedictine abbey
of Our Lady of Hirache, under his uncle,
Abbot (Bl) Munius. He eventually became abbot, and during his abbacy the
monastery was reckoned the most influential religious centre of Navarre. St
Veremundus himself was the advisor of its
kings and was surnamed by the people
"the Light of Navarre" and "the Father
of the Kingdom." He was remarkable
for his charity towards the poor and for his
zeal for the accurate recitation of the Divine Office. In the controversy concerning the use of the Mozarabic rite, which
was warmly upheld by the saint, he won
the approval even of the Roman see which
was for suppressing it.
*Cf. P. de U. — Holw. — Att. — Baud. —
Chev.*

VERENA (St) R.M. Sept. 1
3rd cent. Said to have been an Egyptian
maiden, related to a soldier of the Theban
Legion, who travelled to Switzerland in

search of him, and settled as a recluse near Zurich. Her cult is very ancient.
Cf. Holw. — Baud. — Att.

VERGILIUS (St) Bp.   R.M. Nov. 27
Otherwise Virgilius, q.v.

VERIANUS (St) M.   R.M. Aug. 9
See Secundian, Marcellian, and Verianus.

VERIDIANA (St) H. O.S.B. Vall.
R.M. Feb. 1
d. 1242. A maiden of Castelfiorentino in Tuscany, who after a pilgrimage to Compostella, was walled up as a recluse in her native town, where she lived for thirty-four years under the obedience of a Vallombrosan abbey. Cult approved in 1533.
Cf. Att. — Holw. — Prop. Vall.

VERISSIMUS, MAXIMA and JULIA (SS) MM.   R.M. Oct. 1
d. c.302. Martyrs at Lisbon under Diocletian. Full office in the Mozarabic Breviary.
Cf. Holw. — Baud. — P. de U.

VERONICA of BINASCO (Bl) V. O.S.A.
R.M. Jan. 13
d. 1497. Born at Binasco, near Milan, the daughter of poor peasants, with whom she worked in the fields. She joined the Augustinian nuns of Milan as a lay-sister and spent her life in collecting alms for the convent in the streets of the city. She experienced wonderful ecstasies and visions. Cult confirmed in 1517.
Cf. Holw. — Baud. — Att.

VERONICA GIULIANI (St) Abs. O.F.M. Cap.   R.M. July 9
1660-1727. Born at Mercatello, diocese of Urbino, in Italy, Veronica became a Capuchin nun at Città di Castello, in Umbria, where she spent the rest of her life, being novice-mistress for thirty-four years. Her mystical experiences (visions, revelations, stigmata, etc.) were accurately authenticated by eye-witnesses. Though in a state of almost continuous supernatural vision, she was in no way visionary, but a most practical and level-headed religious. Canonized in 1839.
Cf. Holw. — Baud. — Att.

VERONICA (St)   A.C. July 12
1st cent. According to tradition, when our Lord fell beneath His cross on the road to Calvary, a compassionate woman wiped His face with a towel, on which a picture of the same Holy Face remained imprinted. Numerous legends have grown up around her; the derivation of her name from the Graeco-Latin word *Vera Ikon* — true image — is only a hypothesis.
Cf. Holw. — Baud. — Att.

VERULUS, SECUNDINUS, SIRICIUS, FELIX, SERVULUS, SATURNINUS, FORTUNATUS and Comp. (SS) MM.
R.M. Feb. 21
d. c.434. Martyrs at the hands of the Arian Vandals in N. Africa.
Cf. Holw. — Baud.

VERUS (St) Bp.   R.M. Aug. 1
d. p. 314. Bishop of Vienne in France. He assisted at the synod of Arles in 314.
Cf. Gams — Holw. — Baud.

VERUS (St) Bp.   R.M. Oct. 23
4th cent. The third bishop of Salerno.
Cf. Gams — Holw. — Baud.

VESTINA (St) M.   R.M. July 17
One of the Scillitan Martyrs, q.v.

VETIUS (St) M.   R.M. June 2
See Phothinus, Sanctus, etc.

VETURIUS (St) M.   R.M. July 17
One of the Scillitan Martyrs, q.v.

VIAL (VIAU) (St)   A.C. Oct. 16
Otherwise Vitalis, q.v.

VIATOR (St) H.   R.M. Oct. 21
d. c.390. A disciple of St Justus, archbishop of Lyons, whom he accompanied into the solitude to live as a hermit.
Cf. Holw. — Baud.

VIATOR (St) Bp.   R.M. Dec. 14
d. c.378. Said to have been one of the first bishops of Brescia, and later of Bergamo, during the first century. Probably he was never bishop of Brescia, but only of Bergamo, from 344 to 378.
Cf. Holw. — Gams — Baud.

VICELINUS (St) Bp.   A.C. Dec. 12
d. 1154. A disciple of St Norbert, who worked with considerable success among the Wagrian Wends in N.E. Germany and died a bishop at Lübeck.
Cf. Holw.

VICTOR (St) M.   **R.M. Jan. 22**
See Vincent, Orontius and Victor.

VICTOR (St) M.   **R.M. Jan. 31**
See Saturninus, Thyrsus and Victor.

VICTOR (St) M.   **R.M. Feb. 25**
See Victorinus, Victor, etc.

VICTOR (Bl) Mk. O.S.B.   A.C. Feb. 25
d. 995. A Benedictine monk of St Gall
in Switzerland who became a recluse in
the Vosges, where he died.
Cf. Zimm.

VICTOR (St) H.   **R.M. Feb. 26**
7th cent. A hermit at Arcis-sur-Aube, in
Champagne. His feast was celebrated
by the Benedictines of Montiramey at
whose request St Bernard wrote hymns in
honour of the saint.
Cf. Holw. — Baud. — Att.

**VICTOR, VICTORINUS, CLAUDIAN and
BASSA (SS) MM.**   **R.M. March 6**
? A group of martyrs, natives of Bithynia,
who perished in prison at Nicomedia.
Bassa was the wife of Claudian.
Cf. Holw. — Baud.

VICTOR (St) M.   **R.M. March 10**
? Perhaps he suffered in N. Africa under
Decius. He is mentioned by St Augus-
tine. (*In Psalm* CXV, 15).
Cf. Holw. — Baud.

VICTOR (St) M.   **R.M. March 20**
See Photina, Joseph, etc.

VICTOR (St) M.   **R.M. March 30**
See Domninus, Victor, etc.

VICTOR and STEPHEN (SS) MM.
        R.M. Apr. 1
? Martyrs in Egypt.
Cf. Holw. — Baud.

VICTOR (St) M.   **R.M. Apr. 12**
d. c.300. A catechumen, martyred at
Braga in Portugal under Diocletian. He
was thus baptized in his own blood.
Cf. Holw. — Baud. — P. de U.

**VICTOR, ZOTICUS, ZENO, ACINDY-
NUS, CAESAREUS, SEVERIAN, CHRYS-
OPHORUS, THEONAS and ANTO-
NINUS (SS) MM.**   **R.M. Apr. 20**
d. c.303. Martyrs at Nicomedia. The

apocryphal *Acta* of St George connect
them with his martyrdom.
Cf. Holw. — Baud.

VICTOR the MOOR (St) M.
        R.M. May 8
d. 303. A soldier from Mauritania in
Africa, martyred at Milan under Maximian. He is associated by St Ambrose with
the martyrs SS Nabor and Felix.
Cf. Holw. — Baud. — Att.

VICTOR and CORONA (SS) MM.
        R.M. May 14
d. c.176. Husband and wife martyred, it
seems, in Syria. Their *Acta* abound in
details of an untrustworthy character.
Cf. Holw. — Baud. — Att.

VICTOR (St) M.   **R.M. May 17**
See Adrio, Victor, and Basilla.

**VICTOR, ALEXANDER, FELICIAN and
LONGINUS (SS) MM.**   **R.M. July 21**
d. 304. Victor, an army officer stationed
at Marseilles, suffered martyrdom there
with three prison-guards whom he had converted. In the 4th century St John Cassian built a monastery over their tomb,
which afterwards became a Benedictine
abbey.
Cf. Holw. — Baud. — Att.

**VICTOR, STERCATIUS and ANTINO-
GENES (SS) MM.**   **R.M. July 24**
d. 304. Said to have been three brothers,
martyred at Merida in Estremadura,
Spain. Probably, however, only Victor
belongs to Merida; the other two to the
group who suffered with St Theozonus of
Sebaste in Armenia.
Cf. Holw. — Baud.

VICTOR I (St) Pope M.   **R.M. July 28**
d. c.199. Perhaps an African by birth.
He was pope for about ten years: c.189-
c.199. The paschal controversy was then
vexing the Church, and Victor threatened
the Asiatics with excommunication in a
synod held at Rome. He is said to have
been the first to use Latin in the celebration of the liturgy. It is not certain that
he died a martyr.
Cf. Holw. — Baud. — Att.

VICTOR of VITA (St) Bp.   R.M. Aug. 23
d. c.505. A native of Carthage who was
a member of the Carthaginian clergy
when he was promoted to the see of Vita

(hence his surname *Vitensis*). His history of the persecution under Hunneric is a first-hand document in ecclesiastical literature. Probably he died in exile in Sardinia.
Cf. Holw. — Baud.

VICTOR (Spanish: VITORES) (St) M.
R.M. Aug. 26
d. c.950. A Spanish priest of Cerezo, in the province of Burgos, who preached to the Moors and was by them put to death by beheading.
Cf. P. de U. — Holw. — Baud.

VICTOR (St) Bp. M. R.M. Sept. 10
See Nemesian, Felix, etc.

VICTOR (St) M. R.M. Sept. 10
See Sosthenes and Victor.

VICTOR (St) M. R.M. Sept. 14
See Crescentian, Victor, etc.

VICTOR III (St) Pope O.S.B.
R.M. Sept. 16
c.1027-1087. A native of Benevento, the only son of the duke of that city. His secular name was Dauferius, which he changed into that of Desiderius on becoming a Benedictine at Montecassino (1047) and into that of Victor on his election to the papacy (1087). He became a monk in the teeth of family opposition: he was successively at La Cava, at St Sophia in Benevento, at a house on an island in the Adriatic, at Salerno as a student of medicine, in the Abruzzi as a hermit, back at Salerno and finally at Montecassino. He was chosen abbot in 1057 and under him the abbey attained its high level of prosperity and glory: the community rose to two hundred monks; basilica and monastery were rebuilt on a larger scale; arts, learning, sanctity flourished. In 1086 he was acclaimed pope by the cardinals at Montecassino itself. It was not a happy choice, and the abbot was persuaded to accept only after one year of delay — the year in which he died. Cult confirmed in 1727 and again (conferring the title of saint) by Leo XIII.
Cf. Zimm. — Att. — Holw. — Chev.

VICTOR (St) M. R.M. Sept. 22
See Maurice and Comp.

VICTOR and URSUS (SS) MM.
R.M. Sept. 30
d. c.286. Two soldiers connected with the Theban Legion and venerated at Soleure in Switzerland.
Cf. Holw. — Baud.

VICTOR and Comp. (SS) MM.
R.M. Oct. 10
d. c.286. A group of three hundred and thirty soldiers, connected with the Theban Legion who were martyred at Xanten on the Lower Rhine.
Cf. Holw. — Baud.

VICTOR of CAPUA (St) Bp. R.M. Oct. 17
d. 554. A bishop of Capua in S. Italy, and an ecclesiastical writer.
Cf. Menzies — Baud. — Holw.

VICTOR (St) M. R.M. Nov. 2
See Publius, Victor, etc.

VICTOR (St) M. R.M. Nov. 13
See Valentine, Solutor and Victor.

VICTOR (St) M. R.M. Dec. 3
See Ambicus, Victor and Julius.

VICTOR of PIACENZA (St) Bp.
A.C. Dec. 7
d. 375. First bishop of Piacenza, c.322-375. He was a brave champion of the Catholic faith against the Arians.

VICTOR (St) M. R.M. Dec. 15
See Irenaeus, Antony, etc.

VICTOR (St) M. R.M. Dec. 18
See Victurus, Victor, etc.

VICTOR (St) M. R.M. Dec. 28
See Castor, Victor and Rogatianus.

VICTOR (St) M. R.M. Dec. 29
See Dominic, Victor, etc.

VICTORIA (St) V. M. R.M. Feb. 11
See Saturninus and Comp.

VICTORIA (St) M. R.M. Nov. 17
See Acisclus and Victoria.

VICTORIA (and ANATOLIA) (SS) VV. MM. R.M. Dec. 23
d. 250. Two sisters, martyred at Rome, for refusing to marry pagan husbands. Their *Acta* are unfortunately worthless. Anatolia is not mentioned in the R.M.
Cf. Att. — Baud. — Holw.

VICTORIAN of ASAN (St) Ab.
A.C. Jan. 12
d. c.560. A native of Italy, who settled in France for a time, and then became the abbot-founder of Asan (now called after him San Victorian) in the Aragonese Pyrenees, diocese of Barbastro. He is highly praised by St Venantius Fortunatus.
Cf. Holw. — P. de U. — Att.

VICTORIAN, FRUMENTIUS and Comp. (SS) MM.
R.M. March 23
d. 484. Victorian, a former pro-consul in Africa, and four wealthy merchants were martyred at Adrumetum under King Hunneric, for refusing to become Arians.
Cf. Att. — Holw. — Baud.

VICTORIAN (St) M.
R.M. May 16
See Aquilinus and Victorian.

VICTORIAN (St) M.
R.M. Aug. 26
See Simplicius, Constantius and Victorian.

VICTORICUS (St) M.
R.M. Feb. 24
See Montanus, Lucius, etc.

VICTORICUS, FUSCIAN and GENTIAN (SS) MM.
R.M. Dec. 11
d. c.287. Victoricus and Fuscian are described as early missionaries in Gaul, martyred near Amiens; and Gentian as an old man killed while endeavouring to protect them when they were arrested.
Cf. Att. — Holw. — Baud.

VICTORINUS, VICTOR, NICEPHORUS, CLAUDIAN, DIOSCORUS, SERAPION AND PAPIAS (SS) MM.
R.M. Feb. 25
d. 284. Citizens of Corinth exiled to Egypt in 249 and martyred in various ways and with great brutality, under Numidian, at Diospolis in the Thebaid.
Cf. Holw. — Baud. — Att.

VICTORINUS (St) M.
R.M. March 6
See Victor, Victorinus, etc.

VICTORINUS (St) M.
R.M. March 29
See Pastor, Victorinus, etc.

VICTORINUS (St) M.
R.M. Apr. 15
See Maro, Eutyches and Victorinus.

VICTORINUS (St) M.
R.M. May 15
See Cassius, Victorinus, etc.

VICTORINUS (St) C.
R.M. June 8
d. 543. Brother of St Severino, bishop of Septempeda (now San Severino), with whom he led an eremitical life near Ancona.
Cf. Holw. — Baud.

VICTORINUS (St) M.
R.M. July 7
See Claudius, Nicostratus, etc.

VICTORINUS (St) Bp.
A.C. Sept. 5
d. 644. Bishop of Como. A great opponent of Arianism.
Cf. Gams — Holw.

VICTORINUS (St) Bp. M.
R.M. Sept. 5
2nd cent. A fellow-sufferer with St Maro (Apr. 15). Though said to have been a bishop, it is more probable that he was only a priest.
Cf. Holw. — Baud.

VICTORINUS (St) M.
R.M. Oct. 5
See Placid, Eutychius, etc.

VICTORINUS of PETTAU (St) Bp. M.
R.M. Nov. 2
d. c.303. A bishop of Pettau in Styria (Upper Pannonia), and an exegete of distinction.
Cf. Att. — Holw. — Baud.

VICTORINUS (St) M.
R.M. Nov. 8
One of the Four Crowned Martyrs, q.v.

VICTORINUS (St) M.
R.M. Nov. 11
See Valentine, Felician and Victorinus.

VICTORINUS (St) M.
R.M. Dec. 2
See Severus, Securus, etc.

VICTORINUS (St) M.
R.M. Dec. 18
See Victurus, Victor, etc.

VICTORIUS (St) M.
R.M. May 21
See Polyeuctus, Victorius and Donatus.

VICTORIUS (St) Bp.
R.M. Sept. 1
d. c.490. A disciple of St Martin of Tours who became bishop of Le Mans c.453.
Cf. Gams — Baud. — Holw.

VICTORIUS (St) M.
R.M. Oct. 30
See Claudius, Lupercus and Victorius.

VICTRICIUS (St) Bp.
R.M. Aug. 7
d. c.409. A Roman officer, who retired

from the army, because he thought the military service incompatible with the profession of Christianity. He was sentenced to death, but the sentence was not carried out. He became bishop of Rouen (380) and one of the leading prelates of Gaul.

Cf. Holw. — Baud. — Att. — Chev.

VICTURUS, VICTOR, VICTORINUS, ADJUTOR, QUARTUS and Comp.
R.M. Dec. 18
? A group of thirty-five martyrs in N.W. Africa.

Cf. Holw. — Chev. — Baud.

VIGEAN (St) Ab. A.C. Jan. 20
Otherwise Fechin, q.v.

VIGILIUS (St) Bp. M. A.C. March 11
d. 685. Successor of St Palladius (662) in the see of Auxerre. By order of the mayor of the palace, Waraton, he was killed in a forest near Compiègne.

Cf. Duch. Fast. Episc. — Holw. — Baud.

VIGILIUS (St) Bp. M. R.M. June 26
d. 405. A Roman patrician who studied at Athens, and with his family settled in the Trentino. He was made bishop of Trent and succeeded in practically uprooting paganism from his diocese. He was stoned to death in the Val di Rendena for overturning a statue of Saturn.

Cf. Holw. — Baud. — Att.

VIGILIUS (St) Bp. R.M. Sept. 26
d. p. 506. A bishop of Brescia in Lombardy.

Cf. Holw. — Gams — Baud.

VIGOR (St) Bp. R.M. Nov. 1
d. c.537. A disciple of St Vedastus, who became bishop of Bayeux.

Cf. Duch. Fast. Episc. — Holw. — Baud. — Att.

VILLANA de' BOTTI (Bl) Matron.
A.C. Feb. 28
d. c.1305-1360. Daughter of a rich Florentine merchant. In her youth she wished to enter a convent but was opposed by her father. She married and abandoned herself completely to worldliness and vanity. One day, it is said, on looking into a mirror she saw, instead of her own reflection, the figure of a demon. She completely changed her life, became a Dominican tertiary, and, in spite of much

obloquy, persevered in heroic works. Cult confirmed in 1824.

Cf. Holw. — Att. — Baud.

VILLANUS (St) Bp. O.S.B. A.C. May 7
d. 1237. A native of Gubbio who became a monk at Fontavellana, and in 1206 was raised to the see of his native city.

Cf. Gams — Chev. — Baud.

VILLICUS (St) Bp. A.C. Apr. 17
d. 568. Bishop of Metz, 543-568. He was praised for his virtues by Venantius Fortunatus.

Cf. Duch. Fast. Episc. — Gams — Holw.

VIMIN (WYNNIN, GWYNNIN) (St) Bp.
A.C. Jan. 21
6th cent. A Scottish bishop, whose history is very confused. He is said to have been the founder of the monastery of Holywood.

Cf. Att. — Holw.

VINCENT STRAMBI (Bl) Bp. C.P.
A.C. Jan. 1
1745-1824. Born at Civitavecchia, he was ordained priest in 1767 and shortly afterwards joined the Passionists. He filled almost all the offices of the Order, being at the same time an indefatigable missioner. He was created bishop of Macerata and Tolentino in 1801 and was exiled in 1808 for refusing to take the oath of allegiance to Napoleon. At the end of his life he was summoned by Leo XII to the Vatican as papal adviser. Beatified in 1925.

Cf. Baud. — Att.

VINCENT da CUNHA (Bl) M. S.J.
A.C. Jan. 12
d. 1737. A Jesuit cleric sent to Tonkin in 1736 and martyred there with Bl John Gaspard Cratz and two companions.

Cf. Baud.

VINCENT the DEACON (St) M.
R.M. Jan. 22
d. 304. A native of Huesca who became deacon to St Valerius at Saragossa and eventually was martyred at Valencia under Diocletian. He has always been widely venerated in the Western Church. St Leo and Prudentius wrote in his honour. Rome has three churches dedicated in his name, and he is mentioned in the Ambrosian canon of the Mass. In some places

he is honoured as the patron of vine-dressers.
Cf. P. de U. — Holw. — Att.

VINCENT of DIGNE (St) Bp.
A.C. Jan. 22
d. 380. An African by birth who suc-ceeded St Domninus in the see of Digne. He is the principal patron saint of the city and diocese of Digne.

VINCENT, ORONTIUS and VICTOR (SS) MM. R.M. Jan. 22
d. 305. Vincent and Orontius were brothers, natives of Cimiez, near Nice. They preached the gospel to the people of the Spanish Pyrenees and were martyred, with St Victor, at Puigcerda, in the prov-ince of Gerona. Their bodies were subse-quently brought to Embrun, France.
Cf. Holw. — Baud.

VINCENT (St) M. R.M. Jan. 27
See Dativus, Julian, etc.

VINCENT of TROYES (St) Bp.
A.C. Feb. 4
d. c.546. Bishop of Troyes, c.536-c.546.
Cf. Gams — Duch. Fast. Episc. — Holw.

VINCENT of SIENA (Bl) C. O.F.M.
A.C. Feb. 14
d. 1442. A Friar Minor for twenty-two years, the companion of St Bernardinus of Siena in his travels through Italy.
Cf. Holw. — Baud.

VINCENT KADLUBEK (Bl or St) Bp. O.S.B.Cist. A.C. March 8
d. 1223. Born in the Palatinate, he studied in France and Italy, and was ap-pointed provost at Sandomir in Poland. In 1208 he was consecrated bishop of Cracow, but resigned (1218) and became a Cistercian at Jedrzejo Abbey. He is one of the earliest Polish chroniclers. Cult approved in 1764.
Cf. Gams — Chev. — Baud. — Holw.

VINCENT FERRER (St) C. O.P.
R.M. Apr. 5
c.1350-1418. A native of Valencia in Spain, at an early age he entered the Do-minican Order and soon became the ad-viser of the king of Aragon and of the Avignon pope, with whom he sided in good faith. To heal the schism of the papacy he travelled through Spain, France, Switzerland and Italy, preaching penance,

working miracles and converting thou-sands, being endowed with the gift of tongues. When it became clear to him that the Avignon party were not in the right, he turned his efforts towards bring-ing them into obedience to the legitimate pope. It was St Vincent who, under God, was the primary cause of the cessation of the papal schism. He died at Vannes in Brittany.
Cf. P. de U. — Holw. — Att. — Chev.

VINCENT of COLLIOURE (St) M.
R.M. Apr. 19
d. c.304. A martyr at Collioure, in Languedoc, under Diocletian. His *Acta* are worthless.
Cf. Holw. — Baud.

VINCENT (St) R.M. Apr. 20
See under Marcellinus of Embrun.

VINCENT (St) Ab. O.S.B. A.C. May 9
d. c.950. Abbot of St Peter de Montes, disciple and successor of St Gennadius.
Cf. Zimm. — P. de U.

VINCENT of LÉRINS (St) C.
R.M. May 24
d. c.445. A member of a noble family of Gaul who in early life followed a military career but later abandoned it to become a monk at Lérins, where he was ordained priest. He is best known as the writer of the *Commonitorium*, in which he deals with the doctrine of exterior development in dogma and formulates the principle that only such doctrines are to be considered true as have been held "always, every-where and by all the faithful." (*Quod semper, quod ubique, quod ab omnibus*).
Cf. Holw. — Baud. — Att.

VINCENT of PORTO (St) M.
R.M. May 24
? A martyr at Porto Romano, the former port of Rome which has long since disap-peared.
Cf. Baud. — Holw.

VINCENT of BEVAGNA (St) Bp. M.
A.C. June 6
d. 303. First bishop of Bevagna in Um-bria, martyred under Diocletian.
Cf. Holw.

VINCENT of AGEN (St) M.
R.M. June 9
d ? c.292. A deacon martyred at Agen

in Gascony for having disturbed a feast of the Gallic druids.

Cf. Holw. — Att. — Baud.

VINCENT CAUN (Bl) M. S.J.
A.C. June 20

d. 1626. A native of Seul in Corea who in 1591 was carried to Japan as a prisoner of war. He became a Christian and entered the Jesuit seminary at Arima, spending thirty years as a catechist in Japan and in China. He was burnt alive at Nagasaki with Bl Francis Pacheco and companions. Beatified in 1867.

Cf. Holw. — Prop. S.J.

VINCENT YEN (Bl) M. O.P.
A.C. June 30

1765-1830. A native of Tonkin, he became a Dominican and a priest, and worked for forty years in the mission of Tonkin, always exposed to imminent death. He was at last captured and beheaded. Beatified in 1900.

Cf. Holw.

VINCENT de PAUL (St) C. R.M. July 19

1576-1660. Born either at Pouy, near Dax, in France or at Tamarite, in Aragon, Spain, he studied with distinction at Saragossa and at Toulouse and was ordained priest at the age of twenty. He fell into the hands of corsairs and was taken captive to Tunis but contrived to escape and went to Paris. Here, under the guidance of Berulle, he embarked upon his life work of active charity. No one was excluded from his ministrations: he organized relief for all: abandoned orphans, sick children, fallen women, the poor, the destitute, the blind, the insane. He began to preach missions and retreats and enlisted for this work a number of priests whom he grouped into a new religious institute: the Lazarists, or Vincentians (Priests of the Mission, *Congregatio Missionis*). In 1633 he organized the congregation of the Sisters of Charity, who have been ever since a worldwide and glorious feature of Catholic life. He was canonized in 1737 and has been declared patron saint of all societies devoted to works of charity.

Cf. P. de U. — Att. — Holw. — Baud.

VINCENT (St) M.
R.M. July 24

? A Roman, martyred outside the walls of the city on the road to Tivoli.

Cf. Holw. — Baud.

VINCENT (St) M.
R.M. Aug. 6

See Sixtus and Comp.

VINCENT of AQUILA (Bl) C. O.F.M.
A.C. Aug. 7

d. 1504. A native of Aquila, who became a Franciscan lay-brother and was famed for his mystical gifts. Cult approved in 1785.

Cf. Holw.

VINCENT (St) M.
R.M. Aug. 25

See Eusebius, Pontian, etc.

VINCENT and LAETUS (SS) MM.
R.M. Sept. 1

? 5th cent. The R.M. ascribes these martyrs to Spain, and they are actually venerated at Toledo as natives of that diocese; but it seems that they should be identified with St Vincent of Xaintes, first bishop and patron of Dax in Gascony and St Laetus, one of his deacons.

Cf. Holw. — Baud.

VINCENT CARVALHO (Bl) M. O.S.A.
A.C. Sept. 3

d. 1632. A native of Alfama near Lisbon who joined the Augustinians at Santa Maria de la Gracia, Lisbon. In 1621 he was sent to Mexico, and thence in 1623 travelled to Japan. He was burnt alive at Nagasaki. Beatified in 1867.

Cf. Holw.

VINCENT of ST JOSEPH (Bl) M. O.F.M.
A.C. Sept. 10

1596-1622. Born at Ayamonte, diocese of Seville, he migrated to Mexico, where he became a Franciscan lay-brother (1615). In 1618 he accompanied Bl Louis Sotelo to Manila and in 1619 was sent to Japan. He was arrested in 1620 and after two years of inhuman incarceration, was burnt alive at Nagasaki. Beatified in 1867.

Cf. Holw. — Prop. O.F.M.

VINCENT of LEON (St) Ab. M.
R.M. Sept. 11

d. c.554 (or 630), March 11. Abbot of St Claudius. at Leon, in Spain. He was martyred at the hands of the Arian Suevi. His prior St Ramirus and his monks were also martyred. (See Ramirus).

Cf. P. de U. — Holw.

VINCENT MADELGARUS (St) Ab. O.S.B.
A.C. Sept. 20

d. 677. Madelgarus was the husband of

St Waldetrudis, who bore him four children, all saints: Laudericus, Dentelinus, Madelberta and Aldetrudis. About the year 653 his wife became a nun and Madelgarus took the Benedictine habit with the name of Vincent in the monastery of Haumont which he founded. Later he established another abbey at Soignies, which he ruled, and where he died.
Cf. Att. — Holw. — Baud.

VINCENT, SABINA and CHRISTETA (SS) MM. R.M. Oct. 27
d. 303. Martyrs at Avila, in Spain. Their *Acta* are not trustworthy.
Cf. Holw. — P. de U. — Baud.

VINCENT LIEM (Bl) M. O.P.
A.C. Nov. 7
d. 1773. A member of a noble family in Tonkin who became a Dominican and a priest and worked under Bl Hyacinth Castañeda, O.P. He was beheaded. Beatified in 1906.
Cf. Holw.

VINCENT DIEM (Bl) M. A.C. Nov. 24
d. 1838. A Tonkinese native priest, martyred in Tonkin by beheading. Beatified in 1900.
Cf. Holw.

VINCENTIAN (French: VIANCE, VIANTS) (St) H. A.C. Jan. 2
d. c.730. A disciple of St Menelaus, who became a hermit in the diocese of Tulle (Auvergne).
Cf. Att. — Baud.

VINCENZA GEROSA (Bl) V.
A.C. June 4
1784-1847. An Italian woman, who till her fortieth year led an undistinguished domestic life. She then came to know Bl Bartolomea Capitanio, the foundress of the Italian Sisters of Charity at Lovere. When the foundress died in 1833, Bl Vincenza succeeded her and under her guidance the institute expanded in a wonderful way. Beatified in 1933.
Cf. Att.

VINDEMIALIS, EUGENE and LONGINUS (SS) MM. R.M. May 2
d. c.485. African bishops, put to death by the Arian Vandal King Hunneric who had beforehand inflicted on them most horrible tortures.
Cf. Holw. — Baud.

VINDICIAN (St) Bp. A.C. March 12
d. 712. A disciple of St Eligius, who became bishop of Arras-Cambrai, and with great courage protested against the excesses of the Merovingian kings and the all-powerful mayors of the palace. He died in retirement as a hermit.
Cf. Holw. — Baud. — Att.

VINDONIUS (St) R.M. Sept. 1
See Priscus, Castrensis, etc.

VINTILA (St) H. O.S.B. A.C. Dec. 23
d. 890. A Benedictine monk who died as a recluse at Pugino, near Orense, in Spanish Galicia.
Cf. Zimm. — Holw. — P. de U.

VIRGILIUS of ARLES (St) Bp.
A.C. March 5
d. c.610. A monk of Lérins who was promoted to the metropolitan see of Arles. Probably it was he who consecrated St Augustine bishop of Canterbury at the request of Pope St Gregory the Great.
Cf. Holw. — Att. — Baud.

VIRGILIUS (FEARGAL) (St) Bp. O.S.B.
R.M. Nov. 27
d. 784. An Irish monk, who undertook a pilgrimage to Palestine but remained in Bavaria to help St Rupert the apostle of Austria. St Virgilius was eventually made abbot of the Benedictine abbey of St Peter at Salzburg and archbishop of that city (c.765). He is venerated as the apostle of Carinthia. Canonized in 1232 by Gregory IX.
Cf. Zimm. — Att. — Chev. — Baud. — Holw.

VIRILA (St) Ab. O.S.B. A.C. Oct. 1
d. c.1000. A Benedictine abbot of the Navarrese abbey of St Saviour, Leyre. He is undoubtedly an historical personage, but his life has been overlaid with much legendary — though often very beautiful — accretion.
Cf. P. de U. — Holw.

VISSIA (St) V. M. R.M. Apr. 12
d. c.250. An Italian maiden, martyred at Fermo, near Ancona, under Decius.
Cf. Holw. — Baud.

VITALIAN (St) Pope. R.M. Jan. 27
d. 672. Pope from 657 to 672. The whole of his pontificate was troubled by an obstinate schism in the East. He con-

secrated St Theodore of Tarsus, whom he sent to England as archbishop of Canterbury.
Cf. Holw. — Att. — Baud.

VITALIAN (St) Bp.   **R.M. July 16**
? A bishop of Capua in S. Italy.
Cf. Gams — Holw. — Baud.

VITALIAN (St) Bp.   **A.C. July 16**
d. 776. Bishop of Osimo in Italy.
Cf. Gams — Holw.

VITALICUS (St) M.   **R.M. Sept. 4**
See Rufinus, Sylvanus and Vitalicus.

VITALIS, REVOCATUS and FORTUNATUS (SS) MM.   **R.M. Jan. 9**
? Vitalis appears to have been a bishop and Revocatus and Fortunatus his two deacons. They were martyred at Smyrna.
Cf. Holw. — Baud.

VITALIS (St) M.   **R.M. Jan. 9**
See Epictetus, Jucundus, etc.

VITALIS of GAZA (St) H.   **A.C. Jan. 11**
d. c.625. An aged monk of Gaza who undertook the reclamation of fallen women, and caused great scandal by the methods he employed. He was vindicated after his death.
Cf. Att.

VITALIS, FELICULA and ZENO (SS) MM.   **R.M. Feb. 14**
? Probably Roman martyrs. Nothing is known about them.
Cf. Holw. — Baud.

VITALIS (St) M.   **R.M. Apr. 21**
See Arator, Fortunatus, etc.

VITALIS of MILAN (St) M. R.M. Apr. 28
? 1st cent. The alleged father of SS Gervase and Protase and husband of St Valeria. He is described as a wealthy citizen of Milan, who was put to death at Ravenna. The Acts are probably spurious.
Cf. Att. — Holw. — Baud.

VITALIS (St) H. O.S.B.   **A.C. May 31**
d. ? 1370. Monk of Monte Subasio, near Assisi, and then for twenty years a hermit under the obedience of the abbot of Monte Subasio at Santa Maria delle Viole, also near Assisi.
Cf. Zimm.

VITALIS (St) M.   **R.M. July 2**
See Ariston, Crescentian, etc.

VITALIS (St) M.   **R.M. July 10**
One of the Seven Holy Brothers, q.v.

VITALIS, SATOR and REPOSITUS (SS) MM.   **R.M. Aug. 29 and Sept. 1**
? 3rd or 4th cent. Martyrs of Velleianum in Apulia. They belong to the group known as the Twelve Brothers, q.v.
Cf. Holw.

VITALIS of SAVIGNY (Bl) Ab. O.S.B.   **A.C. Sept. 16**
c. 1063-1122. In early life he acted as chaplain to Robert, count of Mortain half-brother of William the Conqueror; then he spent seventeen years as a hermit; finally (1112) he founded the abbey of Savigny in Normandy which soon became the mother house of numerous monasteries throughout France and England. Bl Vitalis visited the British Isles in this connection. He died while presiding in choir at the recitation of the office of Our Lady. The Bollandists give his feast on Jan. 7.
Cf. Zimm. — Holw. — Baud. — Att. — Chev.

VITALIS (St) M.   **R.M. Sept. 22**
One of the alleged martyrs of the Theban Legion, q.v.

VITALIS (VIAL) H. O.S.B.   A.C. Oct. 16
d. c.740. An Anglo-Saxon who became a Benedictine at Moirmoutier, and afterwards a hermit on Mt Scobrit, near the Loire.
Cf. Holw. — Baud. — Zimm.

VITALIS (St) Bp. O.S.B.   **A.C. Oct. 20**
d. 745. St Rupert's successor as abbot of St Peter's at Salzburg, and as archbishop of that city (717-745).
Cf. Zimm. — Holw. — Chev. — Baud.

VITALIS (St) M.   **R.M. Nov. 3**
See Germanus, Theophilus, etc.

VITALIS and AGRICOLA (SS) MM.   **R.M. Nov. 4**
d. c.304. Martyrs at Bologna under Diocletian. St Vitalis was a slave of St Agricola. The slave suffered martyrdom in the presence of his master with such courage that Agricola was inspired by his example to face a shameful death — probably crucifixion — for Christ's sake.
Cf. Holw. — Baud. — Att.

VITONUS (VANNE, VAUNE) (St) Bp.
A.C. Nov. 9
d. c.525. Bishop of Verdun, c.500-c.525.
At a later period a great Benedictine abbey
of Lorraine was dedicated to him, which
in 1600 became the centre of the Congregation of St Vannes.
Cf. Holw. — Baud. — Att.

VITUS, MODESTUS and CRESCENTIA (SS) MM.
R.M. June 15
? Martyrs from S. Italy, perhaps Sicilians,
whose cult is certainly very ancient, but
whose Acts have reached us in various
embellished versions. St Vitus (Guy) is
described as a child, St Crescentia being
his nurse and St Modestus Crescentia's
husband. St Vitus is patron against
epilepsy and the nervous disorder called
St Vitus's dance.
Cf. Holw. — Att. — Baud.

VITUS (St) Mk. O.S.B.
A.C. Sept. 5
d. c.1095. A Benedictine monk of Pontida, near Bergamo, under its founder St
Albert.
Cf. Zimm.

**VIVALDUS (UBALDO, GUALDO) (Bl)
C.**
A.C. May 11
d. 1300. Disciple and companion of Bl
Bartolo of San Geminiano. When the
latter became a leper, Vivaldus nursed him
for twenty years. He was a Franciscan
tertiary. Cult approved in 1909.
Cf. Att. — Holw.

VIVENTIOLUS (St) Bp.
R.M. July 12
d. 524. Monk of St Oyend (Condat) who
became archbishop of Lyons. A great
friend of St Avitus of Vienne.
Cf. Holw. — Baud.

VIVENTIUS (St) H.
R.M. Jan. 13
d. c.400. A Samaritan who after becoming a priest travelled to the West and attached himself to St Hilary of Poitiers.
He closed his life as a hermit.
Cf. Holw. — Baud.

VIVIAN (St) Bp.
A.C. Jan. 21
Otherwise Vimin, q.v.

VIVIAN (St) Bp.
R.M. Aug. 28
d. c.460. A bishop of Saintes in W.
France, who protected his people during
the invasion of the Visigoths.
Cf. Holw. — Baud. — Gams.

VIVIAN (St) V. M.
R.M. Dec. 2
Otherwise Bibiana, q.v.

VIVINA (St) V.
R.M. Dec. 17
Otherwise Wivina, q.v.

VLADIMIR (St) King.
A.C. July 15
956-1015. Great Prince of Kiev in Russia.
He was baptized before his marriage to
the sister of the Byzantine emperor, and
invited the Greek clergy to evangelize
Russia. His two sons, Boris and Gleb
(known in the Western Church as Romanus and David) are venerated as martyrs. St Vladimir is honoured by the
Russian Catholics as their patron saint.
Cf. Att. — Baud.

VODOALDUS (VOEL, VODALUS, VODALIS) (St) H.
A.C. Feb. 5
d. c.725. An Irish or Scottish monk who
crossed over to Gaul as a missionary and
died a recluse near Soissons.
Cf. Att. — Holw. — Mab. — Chev.

VOLCUIN (Bl) Ab. O.S.B.Cist.
A.C. Sept. 18
d. 1154. A Cistercian monk at the German abbey of Altenkamp, whence he was
sent as prior to a new foundation at Walkenried (1129) and later as abbot to a
third foundation at Sittichenbach, or
Sichem (1141) in Westphalia.
Cf. Zimm. — Chev. — Holw.

VOLKER (Bl) M. O.S.B.
A.C. March 7
d. 1132. A missionary monk of Siegburg
put to death by the Obotrites, whom he
was evangelizing.
Cf. Att. — Baud. — Holw.

VOLOC (St) Bp.
A.C. Jan. 29
d. c.724. An Irish missionary bishop who
worked in Scotland.
Cf. Holw. — Baud.

VOLUSIAN (St) Bp. M.
R.M. Jan. 18
d. 496. A senator of Tours and a married
man who was afflicted with a bad-tempered
wife. He was chosen bishop of Tours and
shortly after driven from his see by the
Arian Visigoths. He died in exile at
Toulouse. His martyrdom is not established.
Cf. Holw. — Att. — Baud.

VOTUS, FELIX and JOHN (SS) HH.
A.C. May 29
d. c.757. Votus and Felix were brothers,

natives of Saragossa, who went in search of a hermitage and found one in the fastnesses of the Aragonese Pyrenees, already inhabited by St John. The three lived together and died about the same time. The hermitage was situated beneath a huge rock (*Peña*) where shortly afterwards arose the great Benedictine abbey of St John de la Peña.
Cf. P. de U. — Holw.

VOUGA (VOUGAR, VEHO, FEOCK, FIECH) (St) Bp. A.C. June 15
6th cent. An Irish bishop who settled in Brittany and there lived as a hermit in a cell near Lesneven.
Cf. Holw.

VULCHERIUS (St) Ab. A.C. March 13
Otherwise Mochaemhog, q.v.

VULGANIUS (St) H. O.S.B.
A.C. Nov. 3
d. c.704. An Irishman or Welshman, who crossed over to France, evangelized the Atrebati, and finally lived as a hermit at Arras, under the obedience of the abbot of St Vaast.
Cf. Zimm. — Baud. — Holw.

VULGIS (St) Bp. O.S.B. A.C. Feb. 4
d. c.760. Regionary bishop (*chorepiscopus*) and abbot of the Benedictine monastery of Lobbes in Hainault.
Cf. Chev. — Holw. — Baud.

VULMAR (St) Ab. O.S.B. R.M. July 20
Otherwise Wulmar, q.v.

VULPHY (WULFLAGIUS) (St) H.
A.C. June 7
d. c.643. A parish priest at Rue, near Abbeville, who retired to the desert and died a solitary. His memory was greatly venerated at Montreuil-sur-Mer.
Cf. Att. — Holw. — Baud.

VULPIAN (St) M. R.M. Apr. 3
d. c.304. A Syrian put to death at Tyre in Phoenicia under Diocletian. He is said to have been sewn up in a leathern sack, together with a dog and a serpent, and so cast into the sea.
Cf. Holw. — Baud.

VULSIN (St) Bp. A.C. Jan. 18
Otherwise Wulfsin, q.v.

VYEVAIN (Bl) Bp. A.C. Aug. 26
d. 1285. An archbishop of York, who was honoured with a liturgical cult at Pontigny in France.
Cf. Holw. — Baud.

W

WACCAR, GUNDEKAR, ELLEHER, HATHAWULF (SS) MM. O.S.B.
R.M. June 5
d. 755. Mentioned by name and as monks among the fifty-two companions who shared St Boniface's martyrdom. It is very probable that most of the others, if not all, were Benedictines.
Cf. Zimm. — Holw. — Att.

WALBERT (VAUBERT) (St)
A.C. May 11
d. c.678. Duke of Lorraine and count of Hainault, husband of St Bertilia and father of SS Waldetrudis and Aldegundis.
Cf. Holw. — Baud.

WALBURGA (St) Abs. O.S.B.
R.M. Feb. 25
d. 779. Sister of SS Willibald and Winebald. She became a nun at Wimborne in Dorset under St Tatta and followed St Lioba to Germany at the invitation of St Boniface. She died abbess of Heidenheim, whence her relics were translated to Eichstätt. Remarkable cures are ascribed to the use of a fluid which exudes from the rock on which her shrine is placed.
Cf. Holw. — Att. — Zimm.

WALDEBERT (WALBERT, GAUBERT) (St) Ab. O.S.B. R.M. May 2
d. c.668. A Frankish noble who left the army to become a monk at Luxeuil. About the year 628 he was made abbot, and shortly afterwards (c.630) he introduced the Rule of St Benedict. Under him the monastery reached the peak of its religious and cultural influence in W. Europe. He helped St Salaberga to establish her great nunnery at Laon.
Cf. Mab. — Zimm. — Chev. — Att.

WALDERIC (Bl) Ab. O.S.B. A.C. Nov. 29
d. c.817. Abbot-founder of Murrhardt, which he built with the help of the emperor Louis the Pious.
Cf. Zimm.

WALDETRUDIS (VAUDRU) (St) W. Abs. O.S.B. R.M. Apr. 9
d. c.688. Daughter of SS Walbert and Bertilia, wife of St Vincent Madelgarus, and mother of SS Landericus, Dentelinus, Madelberta and Aldetrudis. When her husband became a monk she founded a nunnery and took the veil there. Around her nunnery there grew up the town of Mons in Belgium, where her memory has always been greatly honoured.
Cf. Holw. — Att. — Zimm. — Baud.

WALDRADA (St) Abs. A.C. May 5
d. c.620. First abbess of the nunnery of Saint-Pierre-aux-Nonnais at Metz.
Cf. Chev. — Holw. — Zimm.

WALEMBERT (GAREMBERT) (Bl) C. O.S.A. A.C. Dec. 31
1084-1141. A native of the district of Furness in Belgium who became a hermit and then built an Augustinian abbey on Mont-Saint-Martin in the diocese of Cambrai, of which he became the first superior.
Cf. Holw. — Baud.

WALERICUS (VALÉRY) (St) Ab. R.M. Apr. 1
d. c.622. A monk under St Columbanus at Luxeuil, then a missionary in N. France, where he became the abbot-founder of Lenconans (Lencone) at the mouth of the Somme. Two towns in that district are called Saint-Valéry after him.
Cf. Holw. — Att. — Baud.

WALFRID (GUALFREDO) della GHERARDESCA (St) Ab. O.S.B. A.C. Feb. 15
d. c.765. A citizen of Pisa who married and had five sons and one daughter. In middle life he joined with two other married men in founding the abbey of Palazzuolo, between Volterra and Piombino, and a nunnery nearby for their wives and Walfrid's daughter. Walfrid ruled Palazzuolo as first abbot and was succeeded as second abbot by one of his sons. Cult confirmed in 1861.
Cf. Chev. — Zimm. — Att. — Baud.

WALHERE (St) M. A.C. June 23
? A priest in the Walloon district of Belgium. On remonstrating with an ecclesiastic for his unedifying life he was murdered by the latter, and has since been venerated as a martyr, chiefly at Dinant.
Cf. Holw. — Baud.

WALLABONSUS (St) M. R.M. June 7
See Peter, Wallabonsus, etc.

WALPURGIS (St) V. R.M. Feb. 25
Otherwise Walburga, q.v.

WALSTAN (St) C. A.C. May 30
d. 1016. Born at Bawburgh in Norfolk, he spent his life as a farm labourer at Taverham and Costessey, being remarkable for his charity to all in need. His cult, although a local one, is undisputed.
Cf. Holw. — Att. — Baud.

WALTER (GUALTERIUS, GAUTIER) (Bl) C. O.S.B.Cist. A.C. Jan. 22
d. 1222. A native of Brabant who was bred to arms. On becoming a knight he was a familiar figure at tournaments until he found his way to the Cistercian abbey of Himerode. There he was appointed guest master and attracted many to the monastic life by his affability and tact. He died at Villiers.
Cf. Chev. — Holw. — Baud.

WALTER of PONTOISE (St) Ab. O.S.B. A.C. Apr. 8
d. 1099. A Picard who became a professor of philosophy and rhetoric but later joined the Benedictines of Rebais in order to escape worldly applause. Against his will he was made abbot of Pontoise. He fled from his abbey several times, once to Cluny and on the last occasion to Rome, where he placed his resignation in the hands of the pope, who however refused to accept it but gave him orders to return to Pontoise and never again to leave it. He died on Good Friday.
Cf. Zimm. — Att. — Chev. — Holw.

WALTER (St) Ab. A.C. Apr. 9
Otherwise Gaucherius, q.v.

WALTER (Bl) Ab. O.S.B. A.C. Apr. 21
d. 1158. Abbot of the Benedictine monastery of Mondsee in Upper Austria.
Cf. Zimm.

WALTER (St) Ab. O.S.A. A.C. May 11
d. 1070. An Augustinian canon and abbot of L'Esterp in the Limousin.
Cf. Att. — Chev.

WALTER (St) Ab. O.S.B. A.C. June 4
d. c.1250. A Roman who became first a hermit and afterwards the founder and

first abbot of Serviliano in the Marches of Ancona.
Cf. Baud. — Chev. — Zimm.

WALTER (St) Ab. O.S.B. A.C. ? June 4
d. 1150. An Englishman who became abbot of Fontenelle in France. He is commended for his humility, piety and zeal by Pope Innocent II.
Cf. Chev. — Holw.

WALTER PIERSON (Bl) M. O.Cart.
A.C. June 6
d. 1537. A Carthusian lay brother of the London Charterhouse left with eight companions to starve to death in prison.
Cf. Newdigate — Camm.

WALTER of AULNE (Bl) Mk. O.S.B.Cist
A.C. Nov. 26
d. c.1180. A canon of Liége who followed St Bernard to Clairvaux and then became the first prior of the abbey of Aulne in Brabant.
Cf. Zimm. — Holw.

WALTHEOF (WALTHEN, WALÈNE) (St) Ab. O.S.B.Cist. A.C. Aug. 3
d. 1160. Son of the earl of Huntingdon, he was educated at the court of the king of Scotland, where he became a great friend of St Aelred. He joined the Augustinian canons at Nostell, but later migrated to the Cistercians and eventually became abbot of Melrose, rebuilt for him by King David. His outstanding characteristics were cheerfulness and unbounded generosity to the poor.
Cf. Zimm. — Chev. — Baud. — Holw.

WALTMANN (Bl) Ab. O.Praem.
A.C. Apr. 11
d. 1138. A disciple of St Norbert, whom he accompanied to Cambrai to preach against heresy and who left him there as abbot of St Michael's.
Cf. Holw. — Baud. — Att.

WALTO (BALTO) (Bl) Ab. O.S.B.
A.C. Dec. 27
d. 1156. Abbot of Wessobrünn in Bavaria. His sanctity attracted many friends and benefactors to the abbey.
Cf. Zimm.

WANDO (VANDO) (St) Ab. O.S.B.
A.C. Apr. 17
d. c.756. Monk and abbot of Fontenelle. As a result of a false accusation he was

exiled to Troyes but reinstated after his innocence had been proved. He died at Fontenelle.
Cf. Chev. — Holw. — Baud.

WANDRILLE (WANDREGISILUS, VANDRILLE) (St) Ab. O.S.B. R.M. July 22
d. 668. Born near Verdun, he served in the king's palace, where he had among his fellow-courtiers seven or eight future saints. In spite of his desire for the monastic life he was appointed count of the palace and married. After a pilgrimage to Rome he entered (637) the abbey of Roumain-Moutier, and some ten years afterwards founded the abbey of Fontenelle, which became the great missionary centre of that district as well as a school of arts and crafts. Soon it had a community of over three hundred monks.
Cf. Zimm. — Att. — Holw. — Chev.

WANINGUS (VANENG) (St) Ab. O.S.B.
A.C. Jan. 9
d. c.686. Assisted his friend St Wandrille in the foundation of Fontenelle, and soon after he himself made another, no less celebrated and important, at Fécamp.
Cf. Zimm. — Att. — Chev.

WASTRADA (St) Matron. A.C. July 21
d. c.760. Mother of St Gregory of Utrecht. Towards the end of her life she retired to a convent and probably became a nun, though contemporary evidence of this is lacking.
Cf. Zimm. — Holw. — Baud.

WENCESLAUS (St) M. R.M. Sept. 28
d. 935. Duke of Bohemia. He received a pious upbringing from his grandmother the martyr St Ludmilla. He took over the reins of government at the time of a pagan reaction. This he tried to stem with great patience and mildness, but in the end he met his death as a result of a political conspiracy. He was murdered by his own brother Boleslav at the door of the church of Alt-Bunzlau. He is the patron of Bohemia.
Cf. Holw. — Att. — Chev.

WENDOLINUS (WENDELINUS, WENDEL) (St) C. A.C. Oct. 21
d. 607 (or 650 ?). A shepherd who became famous for his sanctity and is venerated at St Wendel on the Nahe in W. Germany. A later legend makes him an

Irish hermit and abbot of Tholey in the diocese of Trèves.
Cf. Holw. — Chev. — Baud.

WENN (St) W.   **A.C. Oct. 18**
Otherwise Gwen, q.v.

WENNAPA (St) V.   **A.C. July 1**
Otherwise Veep, q.v.

WENOG (St)   **A.C. Jan. 3**
? A Welsh saint, mentioned in various calendars, but of whose life nothing is known.
Cf. Holw.

WEONARD (St)   **A.C. Apr. 7**
Otherwise Guainerth, q.v.

WERBURG (St) V. O.S.B.   **A.C. Feb. 3**
d. c.699. Daughter of St Ermenilda and of King Wulfhere of Mercia. She became a nun of Ely under St Etheldreda and later founded the nunneries of Hanbury near Tutbury, Trentham in Staffordshire and Wedon in Northamptonshire. She died at Trentham, but her body was enshrined at Chester, of which city she is the patron saint.
Cf. Holw. — Att. — Stanton — Baud.

WERBURG (St) Matron.   **A.C. Feb. 3**
d. c.785. Wife of a Ceolred of Mercia. In her widowhood she retired to a convent (Bardney?) of which she became abbess.
Cf. Holw. — Baud. — Chev. — Stanton.

WERENFRID (St) C. O.S.B.
A.C. Aug. 14
d. c.780. An Englishman who worked with St Willibrord among the Frisians. He died at Arnheim.
Cf. Holw. — Baud. — Chev.

WERNHER (WERNER) (St) M.
A.C. Apr. 19
d. 1275. A boy in the service of a Jewish family at Oberwesel, alleged to have been martyred by that family on Maundy Thursday after he had received Holy Communion.
Cf. Holw. — Baud. — Att.

WIBORADA (GUIBORAT, WEIB-RATH) (St) M. O.S.B.   **A.C. May 2**
d. 925. She belonged to the Swabian nobility. When her brother Hatto became a Benedictine monk at St Gall, she

asked to be walled up in an anchorhold not far from the monastery, where she lived the rest of her life under the obedience of the abbey. She occupied her time in binding books and doing similar work for the abbey. She was martyred by the invading Hungarians. Canonized in 1047.
Cf. Zimm. — Att. — Holw. — Chev.

WICTERP (WIHO, WICHO) (St) Bp.
A.C. Apr. 18
d. 749. Abbot of Ellwangen. He took an active part in the foundation of the abbeys of Füssen, Wessobrünn and Kempten, all of which became famous in mediaeval Germany. St Wicterp became the tenth bishop of Augsburg.
Cf. Holw. — Gams.

WIDRADUS (French: WARÉ) (St) Ab. O.S.B.   **A.C. Oct. 3**
d. 747. Restorer of the abbey of Flavigny, diocese of Dijon, and founder of Saulieu (Sanctus Andochius — Saint-Andoche) in the diocese of Autun.
Cf. Holw. — Chev.

WIDUKIND (Bl) C.   **A.C. Jan. 7**
Otherwise Wittikund, q.v.

WIFRED (Bl) Ab. O.S.B.   **A.C. Dec. 13**
d. 1021. A Benedictine monk, prior and abbot of St Victor at Marseilles (1005-21).
Cf. Holw. — Chev.

WIGBERT (St) C.   **A.C. Apr. 12**
d. 690. An Anglo-Saxon who became a disciple of St Egbert in Ireland. He spent two years as a missionary in Friesland, but returned to Ireland to die.
Cf. Stanton — Holw.

WIGBERT (St) Ab. O.S.B. R.M. Aug. 13
d. c.746. An English monk who was invited by St Boniface to cross over into Germany. He did so, and Boniface appointed him abbot of Fritzlar, near Cassel. A few years later he was appointed to Ohrdruf in Thuringia, but before his death Boniface allowed him to return to Fritzlar.
Cf. Holw. — Baud. — Att. — Chev.

WILFETRUDIS (St) Abs. O.S.B.
A.C. Nov. 23
d. p. 670. Second abbess of the Benedictine nunnery of Nivelle in Brabant, which had been founded by her aunt St Gertrude.
Cf. Holw. — Chev. — Baud.

WILFRID the YOUNGER (St) Bp. O.S.B.
A.C. Apr. 29
d. 744. A monk and favourite disciple
of St John of Beverley at Whitby. He
was appointed abbot of the cathedral
community at York, and shortly afterwards coadjutor of St John of Beverley,
whom he succeeded in the see. Before
his death he retired to a monastery, pre-
sumably Ripon.
Cf. Holw. — Chev. — Att. — Zimm.

WILFRID (WALFRIDUS) Bp. O.S.B.
R.M. Oct. 12
d. 709. A Northumbrian who became
the champion of the Roman See in England. Born at Ripon, he became a monk
at Lindisfarne under the Celtic regime,
but he left to adopt the Roman observance
elsewhere. After a short stay at Canterbury he crossed over to Lyons (652-3) and
then went to Rome (653-657). On his
return to Northumbria he founded the
abbey of Ripon under the Roman observance. In 664 he was consecrated
bishop at Compiègne and in the same year
played a leading part in the council of
Whitby when Roman usages (date of
Easter, tonsure, Benedictine Rule, etc.)
were adopted for the whole of England.
The remainder of Wilfrid's life was occupied with long journeys, entailing lengthy
absences from his see, with appeals to
Rome (the first recorded in English history) to recover his see, which had been
filled during his absence by order of King
Egfrid and St Theodore of Canterbury,
and with missionary work among the
Frisians and South Saxons.
Cf. Zimm. — Att. — Stanton — Holw.

WILFRIDA (WULFRITHA) (St) Abs·
O.S.B. **A.C. Sept. 9**
d. c.988. Mother of St Edith of Wilton by
King Edgar. After Edith's birth Wilfrida retired to Wilton, where she took the
veil at the hands of St Ethelwold. As a
nun, and later as abbess, her edifying life
made ample amends for the irregularity
of her connection with Edgar.
Cf. Zimm. — Stanton — Holw. — Ait.

WILGEFORTIS (St) V. **R.M. July 20**
? I.e. Virgo-Fortis. She was known in
England as Uncumber, in the Low Coun-
tries as Ontkommena, in Germany as
Kümmernis, in Gascony as Livrade, in
Spain as Librada. Her story is a worth-
less romance abounding in absurdities, e.g.,

that she was one of nine sisters all born at
one birth, that she miraculously grew a
beard in order to escape marriage, etc.
Cf. Att. — Holw. (Liberata).

WILLA (Bl) H. O.S.B. **A.C. Oct. 15**
d. c.1050. A Benedictine nun at Nonnberg, near Salzburg, who died a recluse.
Cf. Zimm.

WILLEHAD of DENMARK (St) M.
O.F.M. **R.M. July 9**
1482-1572. A Danish Franciscan who, on
the introduction of Lutheranism into his
country, was sent into exile and repaired
to the Franciscan friary of Gorkum in
Holland. He was ninety years of age
when he was hanged by the Protestants
with eighteen companions at Briel.
Cf. Holw. — Baud.

WILLEHAD (St) Bp. O.S.B.
R.M. Nov. 8
d. c.790. A Northumbrian monk, probably of York or Ripon, who c.765 went to
evangelize the Frisians. Later he crossed
the Weser and preached to the Saxons, but
he had to abandon this mission and retired
to the Benedictine abbey of Echternach.
Eventually he was consecrated bishop and
fixed his see at Bremen.
Cf. Mab. — Zimm. — Att. — Holw.

WILLIAM (several)
Note. The English form of the Teutonic
WILLHELM, which has been Latinized
into GULIELMUS or GUILIELMUS,
whence the Italian GULIELMO, the
French GUILLAUME, and the Spanish
GUILLERMO.

WILLIAM of DIJON (St) Ab. O.S.B.
A.C. Jan. 1
962-1031. Son of the count of Volpiano,
William was born near Novara and educated in a monastery. He became a Benedictine at Locedio, near Vercelli, whence
he migrated to Cluny under St Majolus
(987). Sent to restore the abbey of St
Benignus at Dijon, he made this a centre
from which he extended the Cluniac observance throughout Burgundy, Normandy, Lorraine and N. Italy. Gentle
with the poor, in his dealings with the great
he showed remarkable firmness. Towards
the end of his life he founded the abbey
of Fruttuaria in Piedmont and rebuilt
that of Fécamp, where he died.
Cf. Zimm. — Holw. — Att. — Chev.

WILLIAM of BOURGES (St) Bp. O.S.B.
Cist. R.M. Jan. 10
d. 1209. William de Donjeon was born at
Nevers and shortly after his ordination
was made canon of Soissons, and later of
Paris. He joined the monks of Grandmont, whence he migrated to the Cistercians of Pontigny. He was appointed
successively abbot of Fontaine-Jean, abbot
of Châlis and bishop of Bourges (1200).
He made a great many converts among the
Albigenses. Canonized 1217.
Cf. Zimm. — Baud. — Holw. — Att.

WILLIAM PATENSON (Bl) M.
A.C. Jan. 22
d. 1592. A native of Durham, he studied
for the priesthood at Reims and was ordained there in 1587. He was condemned for his priesthood and hanged,
drawn and quartered at Tyburn. Beatified 1929.
Cf. Newdigate.

WILLIAM IRELAND (Bl) M. S.J.
A.C. Jan. 24
d. 1679. His true name was Iremonger
and he was a native of Lincolnshire. He
was educated at St Omer and received into
the Society of Jesus there in 1655. He
was martyred at Tyburn for alleged complicity in the imaginary Popish Plot.
Beatified 1929.
Cf. Newdigate.

WILLIAM SAULTEMOUCHE (Bl) M.
S.J. A.C. Feb. 7
See James Salès and William Saulte-
mouche.

WILLIAM of MALEVAL (St) H. O.S.B.
R.M. Feb. 10
d. 1157. A Frenchman by birth, after
some years of care-free military life he
went on a pilgrimage to the Holy Land
and on his return was made superior of an
abbey near Pisa. Failing to maintain
discipline there, as well as in a foundation
of his own on Monte Bruno, he embraced
the eremitical life in the solitude of Maleval near Siena (1155). He was joined by
some disciples, to whom Gregory IX gave
the Rule of St Benedict, but who were
eventually absorbed by the Augustinian
hermits. William died before this final
development.
Cf. Zimm. — Holw. — Baud. — Att.

WILLIAM RICHARDSON (Bl) M.
A.C. Feb. 17
d. 1603. William Richardson, *alias* An-
derson, was born at Wales near Sheffield
and educated for the priesthood at Valladolid and Seville, where he was ordained
in 1594. He was martyred for his priesthood at Tyburn. Beatified 1929.
Cf. Newdigate.

WILLIAM HARRINGTON (Bl) M.
A.C. Feb. 18
d. 1594. Born at Mt St John, Felixkirk,
in Yorkshire, he studied and was ordained
(1592) at Reims. He was only twenty-
seven years of age when he was hanged,
drawn and quartered for his priesthood at
Tyburn. Beatified 1929.
Cf. Newdigate.

WILLIAM HART (Bl) M. A.C. March 15
d. 1583. A native of Wells, he was educated at Lincoln College, Oxford, and on
being reconciled to the Catholic Church,
studied for the priesthood at Douai,
Reims and Rome. After his ordination
(1581) he returned to England and was
betrayed by an apostate in the house of
Bl Margaret Clitheroe. Executed at
York. Beatified 1886.
Cf. Newdigate — Camm — Att.

WILLIAM of PEÑACORADA (St) H.
O.S.B. A.C. March 20
d. c.1042. Monk of the Benedictine
(Cluniac) monastery of Satagún, province
of Leon, Spain. In 988 he fled with the
other monks from the Saracens and settled
in the solitude of Peñacorada, where he
eventually built the monastery of Santa
Maria de los Valles, later named after
him San Guillermo de Peñacorada.
Cf. Zimm.

WILLIAM of NORWICH (St) M.
A.C. March 24
d. 1144. A boy of twelve, apprentice to a
tanner at Norwich, who is alleged to have
been murdered by two Jews out of hatred
of Christianity. The case for the crime
does not seem to be established.
Cf. Holw. — Att. — Baud. — Stanton.

WILLIAM TEMPIER (Bl) Bp.
A.C. March 27
d. 1197. From being a canon regular at
Saint-Hilaire-de-la-Celle, Poitiers, he was
promoted to the see of that city and proved

a brave champion of ecclesiastical liberty.
Cf. Holw. — Att. — Baud.

WILLIAM of ESKILSOË (St) C. O.S.A.
R.M. Apr. 6
d. 1203. A Frenchman, canon regular at
the church of St Geneviève, Paris, who
was sent to Denmark to reform a community of canons regular at Eskilsoë (Ise
Fjord) and then founded the abbey of
Ebelholt, Zeeland. He worked in Denmark for thirty years. Canonized 1224.
Cf. Holw. — Baud. — Att.

WILLIAM CUFITELLA (Bl) H.
A.C. Apr. 7
d. 1411. A native of Noto in Sicily, who
for seventy years lived as a hermit at
Scicli. He was a Franciscan tertiary.
Cult approved 1537.
Cf. Holw. — Att. — Baud.

WILLIAM GNOFFI (Bl) H. A.C. Apr. 16
d. c.1317. A native of Polizzi, near
Palermo, who atoned for a sin of the flesh
by leading a very penitential life.
Cf. Holw. — Att.

WILLIAM FIRMATUS (St) H.
A.C. Apr. 24
d. 1103. A canon and medical practi-
tioner at Saint-Venance, who, in consequence of a divine warning against avarice,
gave all to the poor and spent the rest of
his life on pilgrimages and as a hermit at
Savigny and Mantilly.
Cf. Att. — Baud. — Holw.

WILLIAM MARSDEN (Bl) M.
A.C. Apr. 25
d. 1586. Born in Lancashire and educated at St Mary Hall, Oxford. He studied for the priesthood and was ordained at
Reims (1585). Shortly after, he was executed for his priesthood in the Isle of
Wight. Beatified 1929.
Cf. Newdigate — Att.

WILLIAM of PONTOISE (St) C.
A.C. May 10
d. 1192. An Englishman who lived as a
hermit at Pontoise in France. Some
writers say that he was a Benedictine of
St Martin's abbey.
Cf. Zimm. — Baud. — Chev.

WILLIAM de NAUROSE (Bl) C. O.S.B.
A.C. May 18
1297-1369. A native of Toulouse, who

joined the Augustinian hermits and was
famed as a very zealous missionary priest.
Cult confirmed 1893.
Cf. Holw. — Baud. — Att.

WILLIAM of ROCHESTER (St) M.
A.C. May 23
d. 1201. Said to have been a native of
Perth in Scotland, who was murdered at
Rochester while on a pilgrimage to Canterbury. As a result of miracles wrought
after his death he was acclaimed a martyr
by the people and his body was enshrined
in the cathedral of Rochester.
Cf. Holw. — Baud. — Att.

WILLIAM of DONGELBERG (Bl) Mk.
O.S.B.Cist   A.C. May 24
d. c.1250. A Cistercian monk at the
abbey of Villiers in Belgium.
Cf. Zimm.

WILLIAM of GELLONE (St) Mk. O.S.B.
A.C. May 28
755-812. Duke of Aquitaine and a member of Charlemagne's entourage. He
manifested the qualities of the ideal Christian knight when campaigning against the
Saracens in S. France. Afterwards he
built a monastery at Gellone, diocese of
Lodève, not far from Aniane, which he
peopled with monks from the latter abbey,
himself joining the community as a lay
brother. Later the abbey was renamed
after him Saint-Guilhem-du-Desert. Canonized 1066.
Cf. Zimm. — Att. — Baud. — Chev.

WILLIAM ARNAUD (Bl) M. O.P.
A.C. May 29
d. 1242. The inquisitor general in S.
France against the Albigensians, by whom
he was killed with eleven companions.
See Toulouse (Martyrs of).
Cf. Holw. — Baud. — Att.

WILLIAM FILBY (Bl) M.   A.C. May 30
d. 1582. Born in Oxfordshire, he was
educated at Lincoln College, Oxford, and,
after his conversion, at Reims, where he
was ordained in 1581. He was martyred
at Tyburn with three companions. Beatified 1886.
Cf. Newdigate — Att. — Holw.

WILLIAM SCOTT (Bl) M. O.S.B.
A.C. May 30
Otherwise Maurus W. Scott, q.v.

WILLIAM of YORK (St) Bp.
R.M. June 8
d. 1154. William Fitzherbert, or "of Thwayt," was a nephew of King Stephen and was appointed archbishop of York in 1142. Powerful enemies, chiefly the newly arrived White Monks supported by St Bernard of Clairvaux, contested the appointment on the ground of simony, but Pope Innocent II, St Bernard's great friend, decided in favour of William, who was consecrated and enthroned. His enemies, however, did not rest till they had him deposed from his see. William went into retirement and lived a very mortified life, giving to all a heroic example of patience and resignation, until the Holy See restored him to York, where he was received by his people with unbounded joy. Canonized 1226.
Cf. Holw. — Att. — Baud. — Chev.

WILLIAM GREENWOOD (Bl) M. O. Cart.
A.C. June 16
d. 1537. A lay brother of the London Charterhouse, starved to death at Newgate with eight companions. Beatified 1886.
Cf. Newdigate — Camm — Holw.

WILLIAM EXMEW (Bl) M. O.Cart.
A.C. June 19
d. 1535. Educated at Christ's College, Cambridge, and sub-prior of the London Charterhouse. He was martyred with BB Humphrey Middlemore and Sebastian Newdigate, q.v.
Cf. Newdigate — Camm — Holw.

WILLIAM HARCOURT (Bl) M. S.J.
A.C. June 20
d. 1679. A native of Lancashire who became a Jesuit at St Omer (1632) and worked on the English mission from 1645 to 1678, chiefly in London. He was martyred at Tyburn with five Jesuit companions for alleged complicity in the "Popish Plot." Beatified 1929.
Cf. Newdigate.

WILLIAM of MONTEVERGINE (St) Ab. Founder.
R.M. June 25
1085-1142. A native of Vercelli who, after a pilgrimage to Compostella, settled as a hermit on the summit of Monte Virgiliano, now Monte Vergine, between Nola and Benevento. Here he was joined by a band of hermit-monks to whom he gave a rule based on that of St Benedict, which

was definitively adopted by the community under William's successor. He died at the daughter house of Guleto, near Nusco.
Cf. Zimm. — Baud. — Att. — Holw.

WILLIAM ANDLEBY (Bl) M.
A.C. July 4
d. 1597. Born at Etton, near Beverley, and educated at St John's College, Cambridge. After his conversion he studied at Douai and was ordained priest in 1577. He laboured in Yorkshire for twenty years. He was condemned for his priesthood and martyred at York with three Catholic laymen. Beatified 1929.
Cf. Newdigate — Att.

WILLIAM of HIRSAU (Bl) Ab. O.S.B.
A.C. July 4
d. 1091. A monk of St Emmeram at Ratisbon, who after being named abbot of the recently restored abbey of Hirsau in Würtemberg, introduced there the observance of Cluny. He founded a monastic school, restored the *scriptorium*, attended to the instruction and well-being of the tenants and serfs of the abbey estates, supported Gregory VII against Henry IV, wrote learned treatises and founded seven new abbeys. These activities, coupled with great holiness of life, show him to have been typical of the great Benedictine abbots of his time.
Cf. Zimm. — Holw. — Att. — Baud. — Chev.

WILLIAM of BRETEUIL (St) Ab. O.S.B.
A.C. July 14
d. 1130. Abbot-restorer of the monastery of Breteuil, in the diocese of Beauvais, which had been practically destroyed during the Norman invasions.
Cf. Holw. — Baud. — Chev.

WILLIAM WARD (Bl) M. A.C. July 26
d. 1641. His true name was Webster and he was a native of Thornby in Westmoreland. He was educated at Douai and ordained there in 1608. He spent thirty-three years on the English mission, of which twenty were passed in prison. He was martyred for his priesthood at Tyburn. Beatified 1929.
Cf. Newdigate — Att.

WILLIAM of SAINT-BRIEUC (St) Bp.
R.M. July 29
d. 1234. William Pinchon was born in Brittany, and shortly after receiving holy

orders, was appointed successively canon and bishop of Saint-Brieuc (1220). During the fourteen years of his episcopate he suffered banishment to Poitiers and other penalties for maintaining the rights of the Church. Canonized 1253.
Cf. Holw. — Baud. — Chev.

WILLIAM HORNE (Bl) M. O.Cart.
A.C. Aug. 4
d. 1540. A lay brother of the London Charterhouse, martyred at Tyburn with two companions. Beatified 1886.
Cf. Newdigate — Camm.

WILLIAM FREEMAN (Bl) M.
A.C. Aug. 13
d. 1595. William Freeman, *alias* Mason, was a Yorkshire convert, who had been educated at Magdalen College, Oxford. He was ordained at Reims in 1587 and sent on the English mission. He laboured in Worcestershire and Warwickshire and was executed for his priesthood at Warwick. Beatified 1929.
Cf. Newdigate — Att.

WILLIAM LACEY (Bl) M. A.C. Aug. 22
d. 1582. Born at Horton, near Settle, in Yorkshire. He was a gentleman of means and a staunch Catholic. He was married twice, and during the fourteen years of his married life his house was a refuge for supporters of the Old Religion. After the death of his second wife he went to Reims to study for the priesthood and was ordained in Rome. On his return to England he ministered to the Catholics imprisoned in York jail. He was captured and martyred at York with Bl Richard Kirkman. Beatified 1886.
Cf. Newdigate — Camm — Att.

WILLIAM DEAN (Bl) M. A.C. Aug. 28
d. 1588. A native of Linton in Craven, Yorkshire, he was a convert minister, who was ordained at Reims in 1581. He was martyred for his priesthood at Mile End Green. Beatified 1929.
Cf. Newdigate.

WILLIAM GUNTER (Bl) M.
A.C. Aug. 28
d. 1588. Born at Raglan in Monmouthshire, and educated and ordained at Reims (1587). Condemned for his priesthood and hanged at Shoreditch. Beatified 1929.
Cf. Newdigate.

WILLIAM of ROESKILDE (St) Bp.
A.C. Sept. 2
d. 1067. An Anglo-Saxon, chaplain to King Canute. He crossed over to Denmark and was made by the same king bishop of Roeskilde. Besides being a very successful missionary, William steadfastly resisted the anti-Christian policy and crimes of King Sweyn Estridsen.
Cf. Att. — Baud. — Holw.

WILLIAM BROWNE (Bl) M. A.C. Sept. 5
d. 1605. A layman, a native of Northamptonshire, condemned and executed for the Faith at Ripon. Beatified 1929.
Cf. Newdigate.

WILLIAM WAY (Bl) M. A.C. Sept. 23
d. 1588. A native of Devon who was educated and ordained (1586) at Reims. He was martyred for his priesthood at Kingston-on-Thames. Beatified 1929.
Cf. Newdigate.

WILLIAM HARTLEY (Bl) M.
A.C. Oct. 5
d. 1588. A native of Wilne, near Derby, he was educated at St John's College, Oxford, and became an Anglican minister. After his conversion he studied at Reims, where he was ordained (1580). He was hanged for his priesthood at Shoreditch. Beatified 1929.
Cf. Newdigate.

WILLIAM of SAVIGNY (Bl) Mk. O.S.B.
A.C. Oct. 20
d. c.1122. A novice at Savigny under Bl Vitalis.
Cf. Holw. — Zimm.

WILLIAM de PAULO (Bl) Ab. O.S.B.
A.C. Nov. 30
d. 1423. Born at Catania, he professed the Benedictine Rule at San Niccolò dell' Arena, and at a later period was sent to restore monastic discipline at Maniaco.
Cf. Zimm.

WILLIAM of FENOLI (Bl) C. O.Cart.
A.C. Dec. 19
d. c.1205. A Carthusian lay brother at the charterhouse *Casularum* in Lombardy. Cult confirmed 1860.
Cf. Holw. — Att.

WILLIAM HOWARD (Bl) M.
A.C. Dec. 29
1616-1680. Grandson of Bl Philip How-

ard, and Viscount Stafford. He was accused of complicity in the "Popish Plot" and after two years' imprisonment was beheaded on Tower Hill. Beatified 1929.
Cf. Newdigate — Att.

WILLIBALD (WILLEBALD) (St) Bp'
O.S.B.   R.M. July 7
d. c.700-c.786. Born in Wessex, he was a brother of SS Winebald and Walburga and a cousin of St Boniface. At the age of five he was offered as a monk at Waltham in Hampshire. In 721 he accompanied his father and brother on a pilgrimage to Rome and the Holy Land. He visited all the holy places and many Eastern monastic lauras and stayed for two years at Constantinople. On his return to Italy he lived at Montecassino for ten years and helped in the monastic restoration under St Petronax, filling the offices of sacristan, dean and porter. While on a visit to Rome he was sent by the pope to Germany to help St Boniface in his missionary labours, and was soon after consecrated by the latter bishop of Eichstätt. With his brother St Winebald he founded the double abbey of Heidenheim, over which they placed their sister Walburga as abbess. Canonized in 938 by Leo VII.
Cf. Zimm. — Holw. — Baud. — Att. — Chev.

WILLIBRORD (St) Bp. O.S.B.
                              R.M. Nov. 7
c.658-739. A Northumbrian by birth and a Benedictine of Ripon, he crossed over to Ireland to be trained in the missionary life. Thence he went to Friesland (c.690) accompanied by eleven other English monks. Six years later he was consecrated bishop and established his see at Utrecht. His labours among the Frisians bore much fruit, but he was less successful in Heligoland and Denmark. With the help of Pepin of Heristal he founded the monastery of Echternach in Luxemburg as the centre of his missionary expeditions, and thither he retired to die.
Cf. Zimm. — Mab. — Holw. — Att. — Chev.

WILLIGIS (St) Bp.   A.C. Feb. 23
d. 1011. The son of a wheelwright of Schöningen, he became a canon of Hildesheim and as such attracted the attention of the emperor Otto III, who made him his chaplain and (971) chancellor of the Empire. About two years later he was appointed archbishop of Mainz, and Boniface VII created him vicar apostolic for Germany. Perhaps the greatest statesman of his age, Willigis was first and foremost a churchman, and ever remained humble and charitable in his dealings with others. In 1002 he consecrated the emperor St Henry II. In art he is shown with a wheel, which he chose for his arms as symbolizing his father's trade.
Cf. Holw. — Chev. — Gams.

WILLIGOD and MARTIN (SS) Abbots
O.S.B.   A.C. Sept. 28
d. ? c.690. Monks of Moyenmoutier who became co-founders and successive abbots of the monastery of Romont.
Cf. Zimm.

WILTRUDIS (St) W. O.S.B.
                              A.C. Jan. 6
d. c.986. The wife of Duke Berthold of Bavaria, who after her husband's death (c.947) founded (c.976) the nunnery of Bergen, near Neuburg on the Danube, under the Benedictine Rule, and herself became a nun and its first abbess. She was renowned for her skill in artistic handicrafts.
Cf. Att. — Holw. — Zimm.

WINAMAN, UNAMAN and SUNAMAN
(SS) MM. O.S.B.   A.C. Feb. 15
d. c.1040. Missionary monks, nephews of the English missionary St Sigfrid of Wexiow, whom they followed to the Swedish mission. They were martyred by pagans at Wexiow.
Cf. Zimm. — Holw. — Baud.

WINEBALD (VINEBAUD) (St) Ab.
O.S.B.   A.C. Apr. 6
d. c.650. At first a hermit, he afterwards took the monastic habit at Saint-Loup-de-Troyes, of which monastery he was chosen abbot.
Cf. Chev. — Holw. — Baud.

WINEBALD (St) Ab. O.S.B.
                              A.C. Dec. 18
d. 761. An Englishman, brother of SS Willibald and Walburga. When on pilgrimage to the Holy Land with his brother, Winebald was taken ill and remained at Rome, where he studied for seven years. Eventually he became a Benedictine in Rome and passed into Germany at the invitation of St Boniface. In time he became the abbot of Heiden-

heim, a double abbey built for him and his sister by their brother, now bishop of Eichstätt.
Cf. Zimm. — Holw. — Baud. — Att. — Chev.

WINEWALD (St) Ab. O.S.B. A.C. Apr. 27
d. c.731. The successor of St Bercthun as abbot of Beverley.
Cf. Holw. — Baud. — Chev.

WINEFRED (WINEFRIDE, WENE-FRIDA, GWENFREWI, GUINEVRA, etc.) V. M. R.M. Nov. 3
d. c.650. A native of Wales, she is said to have been a niece of St Beuno and to have been murdered by Caradog of Hawarden for refusing his amorous advances, a spring of water gushing forth on the spot where her head fell. This was the origin of the Holy Well, which has been a centre of pilgrimages for over a thousand years. Another version of the legend adds that she was restored to life by St Beuno and that she became a nun and abbess of Gwytherin in Denbighshire. She is evidently an historical personage, but it is equally evident that her true story can no longer be reconstructed.
Cf. Att. — Baud. — Holw.

WININ (St) Bp. A.C. Sept. 10
The Welsh form of the name of St Finnian, q.v.

WINNOW, MANCUS and MYRBAD (SS) CC. A.C. May 31
Probably 6th cent. Three Irish saints who lived in Cornwall, where they have churches dedicated in their honour.
Cf. Holw. — Baud.

WINOC (St) Ab. O.S.B. R.M. Nov. 6
d. ? 717. He was of royal blood and probably of British origin, though brought up in Brittany. He became a monk at Sithiu under St Bertinus, by whom eventually he was sent to establish a new foundation among the Morini at Wormhoult, of which he became abbot. From that centre he evangelized the whole neighbourhood.
Cf. Att. — Holw. — Baud. — Chev.

WINWALOË (GUENGALOEUS, GWEN-NO, WONNOW, WYNWALLOW, VA-LOIS, etc.) (St) Ab. A.C. March 3
d. c.532. Born in Brittany of parents exiled from England, he became a disciple of St Budoc on Isle Verte and abbot-founder of Landevennec near Brest. Several Cornish churches are dedicated to St Winwaloë, which seems to indicate that the saint had some connexion with those parts.
Cf. Holw. — Baud. — Att.

WIOMAD (WEOMADUS, WIOMAGUS) (St) Bp. O.S.B. A.C. Nov. 8
d. c.790. Monk of St Maximinus at Trèves. He became abbot of Mettlach and finally bishop of Trèves (c.750-790).
Cf. Gams — Zimm.

WIRNTO (Bl) Ab. O.S.B. A.C. Oct. 29
d. 1127. A Benedictine of Göttweig in Austria, who became abbot of Formbach in Bavaria.
Cf. Chev. — Zimm. — Holw.

WIRO, PLECHELM and OTGER (SS) MM. O.S.B. R.M. May 8
d. c.739. British missionaries in Friesland under St Willibrord (or perhaps under St Switbert). They were martyred while preaching the gospel in that country. The centre of Wiro's apostolic labours was Peterkloster, afterwards renamed Odilienberg.
Cf. Zimm. — Att. — Holw. — Baud.

WISINTO (Bl) Mk. O.S.B. A.C. Dec. 31
d. before 1250. A monk and priest of the great Austrian abbey of Kremsmünster. He has always been venerated as a saint by the Austrian Benedictines.
Information supplied by Dom Norbert Strasser, prior of Seitenstetten in Austria.

WISTAN (St) M. A.C. June 1
d. 849. Of the royal house of Mercia. He is said to have been put to death by Bertulph, king of Mercia, when the latter was regent of the kingdom during Wistan's youth. The saint's shrine was in Evesham abbey.
Cf. Att. — Holw. — Baud.

WISTREMUNDUS (St) M. R.M. June 7
See Peter, Wallabonsus, etc.

WITHBURGA (St) V. O.S.B. A.C. July 8
d. c.743 (March 17). Youngest daughter of King Anna of East Anglia. After her father had fallen in battle she took the veil and lived mostly at Dereham, a nunnery which she had founded.
Cf. Holw. — Baud. — Att.

WITTA (St) Bp. O.S.B.   **A.C. Oct. 26**
Otherwise Albinus, q.v.

WITTIKUND (Bl) C.   **A.C. Jan. 7**
d. c.804. A duke of Westphalia who resisted the arms of Charlemagne. It is related that he saw the Infant Jesus appear while communion was being distributed to the soldiers of the Christian army on Christmas night, whereupon he sought instruction and, sponsored by Charlemagne, was baptized in 785.
Cf. Att.

WIVINA (VIVINA) (St) Abs. O.S.B.
R.M. Dec. 17
d. 1170. A Flemish lady of the house of Oisy. In her twenty-third year she secretly left her father's house and became an anchoress in a wood near Brussels, called Grand-Bigard. The count of Brabant offered her the land and she built a nunnery, placing it under the direction of the Benedictines of Afflighem, near Alost. She was the first abbess.
Cf. Holw. — Att. — Zimm. — Chev.

WOLFGANG (St) Bp. O.S.B.
R.M. Oct. 31
924-994. A native of Swabia, who was educated by the Benedictines at Reichenau, and after being dean of the cathedral school at Trèves, became a Benedictine at Einsiedeln (964). He was made headmaster of the abbey school which became under him the most flourishing institution of its kind in those parts. In 971 he was raised to the priesthood and with a group of monks went as a missionary to the Magyars; but in the following year (972) he was promoted to the see of Ratisbon. He was one of those monk-bishops who have left their mark on the history of their times. He was tutor to the emperor Henry II, restored abbeys (St Emmeram at Ratisbon being one of the most important of these), raised the standard of education, reformed ecclesiastical discipline and was a great benefactor of the poor, being known as their *Eleemosynarius Major* (Great Almoner). Canonized by Leo IX in 1052.
Cf. Zimm. — Att. — Chev. — Holw.

WOLFHELM (Bl) Ab. O.S.B.
A.C. Apr. 22
d. 1091. A Rhinelander, he joined the Benedictine abbey of St Maximinus at Trèves. From there he transferred to St Pantaleon's at Cologne, and then became abbot successively of Gladbach, Siegburg and Brauweiler, at which last-named he ended his days. He is described as a great student of Holy Writ and a great lover of the Holy Rule.
Cf. Att. — Holw. — Baud. — Chev.

WOLFRID (Bl) Ab. O.S.B.   **A.C. June 21**
d. c.990. Abbot-founder (c.973) of Hohentwiel.
Cf. Zimm. — Holw.

WOOLLOS (St)   **A.C. Jan. 19**
Otherwise Gundleus, q.v.

WORONUS (St)   **A.C. Apr. 7**
Otherwise Goran, q.v.

WULFHADE and RUFFINUS (SS) MM.
A.C. July 24
d. 675. Two princes of the royal family of Mercia, baptized by a hermit and thereupon put to death by the king their father, who was as yet unconverted.
Cf. Holw. — Stanton.

WULFHILDA (St) Abs. O.S.B.
A.C. Sept. 9
d. 980. Abbess-foundress of Horton nunnery in Dorsetshire. She was later put in charge of Barking abbey on its restoration as a nunnery by King Edgar. When the king died, Queen Elfrida drove her out, but she was recalled by King Ethelred and died abbess of Barking.
Cf. Att. — Holw. — Baud. — Chev.

WULFRAM (St) Bp. O.S.B.
R.M. March 20
d. c.703. A courtier-priest who was given the see of Sens, which he occupied for only two and a half years, St Amatus being the rightful bishop. Wulfram then became a monk at the abbey of Fontenelle. From there he set out with several other monks for the Frisian mission. After spending many years among the Frisians he returned to Fontenelle, where he died.
Cf. Zim. — Baud. — Holw. — Att.

WULFRIC (St) H.   **A.C. Feb. 20**
d. 1154. A priest who, after leading a worldly life, became a hermit at Haselbury-Plucknett, near Crewkerne, in Somerset. The Cistercians lay claim to him, but he was attached to no Order.
Cf. Holw. — Att.

WULMAR (ULMAR, ULMER, VIL-MARUS, VOLMAR, VILMER, etc.) (St) Ab. O.S.B.   **A.C. July 20**
d. 689. Born near Boulogne in Picardy, he married, but was separated by force from his wife and became a Benedictine lay-brother at Haumont in Hainault. Here he was employed in keeping cattle and hewing wood for the abbey, but after a time, being considered worthy of the priesthood, he was ordained and eventually became the founder and first abbot of the monastery of Samer (Salviniacum) afterwards called after him Saint-Vulmaire, near Boulogne.
Cf. Zimm. — Att. — Holw. — Baud.

WULSIN (St) Bp. O.S.B.   **A.C. Jan. 8**
d. 1005. Described as "a loyal and trusty monk whom St Dunstan loved like a son with pure affection." When St Dunstan restored Westminster Abbey (958) he made Wulsin superior there and finally abbot (980). In 993 he was promoted to the see of Sherborne. He was a great Benedictine prelate even in that age of distinguished monks.
Cf. Zimm. — Holw. — Att.

WULSTAN (WULFSTAN, ULFSTAN, WOLSTAN) Bp. O.S.B.   **R.M. Jan. 19**
d. 1095. A native of Long Itchington in Warwickshire, he studied at the abbeys of Evesham and Peterborough. Then he became a priest and joined the Benedictines at Worcester, where he filled the offices of precentor and prior. Finally he was raised to the see of Worcester (1062), which he governed so wisely that he was the only English bishop who was allowed to retain his see after the Conquest. During his episcopate, which lasted thirty-two years, he rebuilt his cathedral. He died while engaged in his daily practice of washing the feet of twelve poor men. Canonized 1203.
Cf. Zimm. — Baud. — Holw. — Att. — Chev.

WYNNIN (St) Bp.   **A.C. Jan. 21**
Otherwise Vimin, q.v.

X

XANTIPPA and POLYXENA (SS) VV.
R.M. Sept. 23
1st cent. Described in the R.M. as "dis-

ciples of the Apostles," but we have no trustworthy information about them.
Cf. Holw. — Baud.

XYSTUS (several)
Otherwise Sixtus, q.v.

Y

YMAR (St) M. O.S.B.   **A.C. Nov. 12**
d. c.830. A monk of Reculver in Kent, martyred by the Danes.
Cf. Zimm.

YON (St) M.   **A.C. Sept. 22**
Otherwise Jonas, q.v.

YRCHARD (YARCARD) (St) Bp.
A.C. Aug. 24
5th cent. A Scottish priest, consecrated bishop by St Ternan, and like him a missionary among the Picts.
Cf. Holw.

YSARN (St) Ab. O.S.B.   **A.C. Sept. 24**
d. 1048. Born near Toulouse, he became a Benedictine monk, and then abbot of St Victor's at Marseilles. Under his government the abbey became the centre of a Benedictine congregation with houses in S. France and N.E. Spain.
Cf. Holw. — P. de U.

YTHA (St) V.   **A.C. Jan. 15**
Otherwise Ita, q.v. In Cornwall she is known as St Ide or St Syth.

YVO (St) Bp.   **R.M. May 19**
Otherwise Ivo, q.v.

YWI (YVIUS) (St) H. O.S.B. A.C. Oct. 8
d. c.690. A monk of Lindisfarne ordained deacon by St Cuthbert. His relics were translated to Wilton, near Salisbury.
Cf. Holw. — Baud.

Z

ZACCHAEUS (St) Bp.   **R.M. Aug. 23**
d. c.116. This Zacchaeus or Zacharias is reckoned by St Epiphanius and other Fathers to have been the fourth bishop of Jerusalem.
Cf. Holw. — Baud.

ZACCHAEUS (St) M.   **R.M. Nov. 17**
See Alphaeus and Zacchaeus.

ZACHARY (St) Pope. R.M. March 22
d. 752. Born at San Severino in Calabria
of a Greek family. Chosen pope in 741,
he showed himself worthy of that office:
he successfully negotiated peace between
the Lombards and the Greek empire;
sanctioned the assumption of the Frankish crown by Pepin; seconded the missionary work of St Boniface and confirmed
him as archbishop of Mainz; planned and
undertook the restoration of Montecassino under St Petronax, himself consecrating the abbey church in 748; gave the
Benedictine habit to St Ratchis, king of
the Lombards; and in many other ways
furthered the reconstruction of Europe.
He has been traditionally considered a
Benedictine; this cannot be proved, but
he is certainly one of those popes who have
done most for the Benedictine institute.
Cf. Holw. — Baud. — Att. — Chev.

ZACHARY (St) Bp. M. R.M. May 26
d. c.106. Said to have been the second
bishop of Vienne in Gaul, and to have died
a martyr under Trajan.
Cf. Gams — Holw. — Baud. — Chev.

ZACHARY (St) M. R.M. June 10
? Described by the R.M. as a martyr at
Nicomedia.
Cf. Holw. — Baud.

ZACHARY (ZECHARIAH) (St) Prophet.
R.M. Sept. 6
6th cent. B.C. A fellow-prophet of Aggaeus (Haggai). Both prophesied under
King Darius (c.B.C. 520) and exhorted the
people to rebuild the Temple.
Cf. Holw.

ZACHARY (ZACHARIAS) (St) Prophet.
R.M. Nov. 5
1st cent. Father of St John the Baptist,
known to us from Luke I. Nothing is
known of the rest of his life.
Cf. Holw. — Baud.

ZAMA (St) Bp. R.M. Jan. 24
d. c.268. The first bishop of Bologna of
whom there is any record. He is said to
have been consecrated by Pope St Dionysius c.260.
Cf. Holw. — Gams — Baud.

ZAMBDAS (St) Bp. R.M. Feb. 19
d. c.304. Said to have been the thirty-
seventh bishop of Jerusalem. He has

been connected with the legend of the
Theban legion.
Cf. Holw. — Baud.

**ZANITAS, LAZARUS, MAROTAS, NAR-
SES and Comp. (SS) MM.**
R.M. March 27
d. 344. A group of Persian martyrs who
suffered under Shapur II.
Cf. Holw. — Baud.

ZDISLAVA BERKA (Bl) Matron, O.P.
A.C. Jan. 1
d. 1252. Born in Bohemia of noble parents, she married a man of her own rank
to whom she bore four children. Her
generosity towards the poor caused difficulties with her husband, whom she con-
ciliated by her heroic patience. She died
as a Dominican tertiary in the priory of
St Lawrence, which she had founded.
Cult approved in 1907.
Cf. Holw. — Att. — Baud.

ZEBINAS (St) M. R.M. Nov. 13
See Antoninus, Zebinas, etc.

ZEBINUS (St) H. A.C. Feb. 23
5th cent. A hermit in Syria who trained
St Maro, St Polychronius and others in
the monastic life.
Cf. Holw.

**ZENAIS, CYRIA, VALERIA and MAR-
CIA (SS) MM. R.M. June 5**
? Zenais seems to have suffered at Constantinople. The other martyrs of this
group are traditionally believed to have
been contemporaries of our Lord and
among the early martyrs of the Church.
Cf. Holw.

ZENAIS and PHILONILLA (SS) MM.
R.M. Oct. 11
1st cent. Two holy women, perhaps sisters, related to St Paul the Apostle. They
were natives of Tarsus.
Cf. Holw. — Baud.

ZENAS (St) M. R.M. June 23
See Zeno and Zenas.

ZENO (St) M. R.M. Feb. 14
See Vitalis, Felicula and Zeno.

ZENO (St) M. R.M. Apr. 5
? A martyr who was burnt alive. Date
and place unknown.
Cf. Holw. — Baud.

ZENO (St) Bp.   **R.M. Apr. 12**
d. 371. Bishop of Verona, 362-371, at the time of Julian the Apostate. He is best remembered as an ecclesiastical writer of distinction, his main subject being the virgin-birth of our Lord.
Cf. Holw. — Att. — Menzies.

ZENO (St) M.   **R.M. Apr. 20**
See Victor, Zoticus, etc.

ZENO and ZENAS (SS) MM.
R.M. June 23
d. c.304. Zeno, a wealthy citizen of Philadelphia near the Dead Sea, freed all his slaves and gave his property to the poor. Zenas, a former slave, remained with him as a servant. Both were beheaded under Diocletian.
Cf. Holw. — Att. — Baud.

ZENO and Comp. (SS) MM.
R.M. July 9
d. c.300. According to the R.M. this group of martyrs numbered 10,204. The entry is in fact a record of the wholesale slaughter, ordered by Diocletian, of the Christians who had been condemned to work on the building of the baths named after him. Zeno seems to have been the chief spokesman of these martyrs.
Cf. Att. — Holw. — Baud.

ZENO (St) M.   **R.M. July 15**
See Philip, Zeno, etc.

ZENO, CONCORDIUS and THEODORE (SS) MM.   **R.M. Sept. 2**
d. 302. Zeno and his two sons were martyred at Nicomedia under Diocletian.
Cf. Holw. — Baud.

ZENO and CHARITON (SS) MM.
R.M. Sept. 3
d. c.303. Martyrs in the East under Diocletian.
Cf. Holw. — Baud.

ZENO (St) M.   **R.M. Sept. 5**
See Eudoxius, Zeno, etc.

ZENO (St) M.   **R.M. Sept. 8**
See Eusebius, Nestabus, etc.

ZENO (St) M.   **R.M. Dec. 20**
See Ammon, Zeno, etc.

ZENO (St) M.   **R.M. Dec. 22**
d. 303. A soldier at Nicomedia. As a

punishment for laughing when Diocletian was offering a sacrifice to Ceres his jaws were broken and he was beheaded.
Cf. Holw. — Baud.

ZENO (St) Bp.   **R.M. Dec. 26**
d. c.399. A cousin of the martyr-brothers Eusebius, Nestabus and Zeno, commemorated on Sept. 8. He survived Julian's persecution and was made bishop of Gaza.
Cf. Holw. — Baud.

ZENOBIA (St) M.   **R.M. Oct. 30**
See Zenobius and Zenobia.

ZENOBIUS (St) M.
R.M. Feb. 20 and Oct. 29
See Tyrannio, Sylvanus, etc.

ZENOBIUS (St) Bp.   **R.M. May 25**
d. c. ? 390. Bishop of Florence. A great friend of St Ambrose and also of St Damasus, by whom he was sent as papal representative to Constantinople in connexion with the Arian troubles.
Cf. Holw. — Att. — Baud. — Menzies — Ricci.

ZENOBIUS (St) M.   **R.M. Oct. 29**
d. 310. A priest and physician at Sidon, who was martyred at Antioch under Diocletian by being torn with iron hooks.
Cf. Holw. — Baud.

ZENOBIUS and ZENOBIA (SS) MM.
R.M. Oct. 30
d. 285-290. Bishop and physician at Aegae (now Alexandretta) on the coast of Asia Minor. He is probably identical with St Zenobius of Antioch (Oct. 29), in which case his martyrdom took place somewhat later, under Diocletian. Zenobia is said to have been his sister.
Cf. Holw. — Baud.

ZENOBIUS (St) M.   **R.M. Dec. 24**
See Lucian, Metrobius, etc.

ZEPHYRINUS (St) Pope M. R.M. Aug. 26
d. 217. Pope from 199 to 217. He does not seem to have died a martyr.
Cf. Holw. — Baud. — Att.

ZETICUS (St) M.   **R.M. Dec. 23**
See Theodulus, Saturninus, etc.

ZITA (St) V.   **R.M. Apr. 27**
1218-1278. A native of Monsagrati near

Lucca, at the age of twelve she entered the service of a family at Lucca, with whom she remained all her life. She would give her food and clothing to the poor — and sometimes her master's too. For this she was at first misunderstood and maltreated, but she ended by gaining the confidence of the whole household. She was canonized in 1696 and is greatly venerated, especially in Italy, as the patron saint of domestic servants.

ZOË (St) M. R.M. May 2
See Exuperius, Zoë, etc.

ZOË (ZOA) (St) M. R.M. July 5
d. c.286. A Roman lady, said to have been the wife of a high official of the imperial court, put to death for the Faith.
Cf. Holw. — Baud.

ZOËLLUS, SERVILIUS, FELIX, SYLVANUS and DIOCLES (SS) MM.
R.M. May 24
? Martyrs at Istria (or in Syria?).
Cf. Holw. — Baud.

ZOILUS and Comp. (SS) M.
R.M. June 27
d. c.301. A youth martyred with nineteen companions at Cordova under Diocletian. The Benedictine abbey of San Zoil de Carrión, province of Leon in N. Spain, was founded to enshrine their relics.
Cf. P. de U. — Holw. — Att. — Baud.

ZOSIMA (St) M. R.M. July 15
See Eutropius, Zosima and Bonosa.

ZOSIMUS and ATHANASIUS (SS) MM.
R.M. Jan. 3
d. 303. Martyrs in Cilicia under Diocletian. Another account says that Zosimus was put to the torture and that Athanasius, a spectator, was converted and forthwith tortured also, but that both survived and died in peace as hermits.
Cf. Holw. — Baud.

ZOSIMUS (St) M. R.M. March 11
See Heraclius and Zosimus.

ZOSIMUS (St) Bp. R.M. March 30
d. c.660. A Sicilian, placed at the age of seven in the monastery of Santa Lucia (Benedictine or Basilian) near Syracuse. After being a simple monk for thirty years, he was successively made abbot and bishop

of the city. He died at the age of ninety.
Cf. Att. — Baud. — Holw. — Chev. — Gams.

ZOSIMUS (St) H. R.M. Apr. 4
5th cent. A Palestinian anchorite who lived on the banks of the Jordan, the supposed confidant and biographer of St Mary of Egypt.
Cf. Att. — Holw. — Baud.

ZOSIMUS (St) M. R.M. June 19
d. 110. A martyr of Spoleto in Umbria under Trajan.
Cf. Holw. — Baud.

ZOSIMUS (St) M. R.M. Sept. 28
See Mark, Alphius, etc.

ZOSIMUS (St) H. R.M. Nov. 30
6th cent. A hermit in Palestine, surnamed the Wonder-Worker.
Cf. Holw. — Baud.

ZOSIMUS (St) M. R.M. Dec. 14
See Drusus, Zosimus and Theodore.

ZOSIMUS (St) M. R.M. Dec. 18
See Rufus and Zosimus.

ZOSIMUS (St) M. R.M. Dec. 19
See Darius, Zosimus, etc.

ZOSIMUS (St) Pope. R.M. Dec. 26
d. 418. A Greek, whose short pontificate was marked by the condemnation of the Pelagian heresy.
Cf. Att. — Holw. — Baud.

ZOTICUS, ROGATUS, MODESTUS, CASTULUS and Comp. (SS) MM.
R.M. Jan. 12
? A group of between forty and fifty soldiers martyred in Africa.
Cf. Holw. — Baud.

ZOTICUS (St) M. R.M. Jan. 12
Identical with St Getulius, the martyr of Tivoli (June 10), q.v.

ZOTICUS (St) M. R.M. Jan. 31
See Tarcisius, Zoticus, etc.

ZOTICUS, IRENAEUS, HYACINTH, AMANTIUS and Comp. (SS) MM.
R.M. Feb. 10
d. 120. A group of ten soldiers martyred

in Rome and buried in the Via Lavicana. *Cf. Holw. — Baud.*

ZOTICUS (St) M. R.M. Apr. 20
See Victor, Zoticus, etc.

ZOTICUS (St) M. R.M. July 21
d. 204. Bishop of Comana in Cappadocia, famous for his zeal against the Montanist heretics and for his martyrdom. *Cf. Holw. — Baud.*

ZOTICUS (St) M. R.M. Aug. 22
See Agathonicus, Zoticus, etc.

ZOTICUS (St) M. R.M. Oct. 21
See Dasius, Zoticus, etc.

ZOTICUS (St) R.M. Dec. 31
d. c.350. A Roman priest who migrated to Constantinople at the time when Constantine transferred thither the capital of the empire. Zoticus built in that city a hospital for the poor and for orphans. He was a confessor of the Faith under the Arian emperor Constantius.
Cf. Holw. — Baud. — Chev.

NOTE

In the following Calendar the Saints for each day are arranged in chronological order. The figure given in parentheses is either the actual or the approximate date of the Saint's death.

The names of Saints who are not mentioned in the Roman Martyrology are preceded by an asterisk.

The names of those Saints whose feasts are either celebrated or commemorated in accordance with the Calendar of the Universal Church are printed in italics.

A CALENDAR OF SAINTS

JANUARY 1.

The Circumcision of Our Lord Jesus Christ and the Octave Day of His Nativity.
St Concordius of Spoleto (175) M.
*SS Elvan and Mydwyn (2nd cent.).
Thirty Soldiers martyred at Rome (c.304).
St Euphrosyne (?) V. M.
St Magnus (?) M.
*St Gregory Nazianzen the Elder (374) Bp. C.
St Almachius (c.400) H. M.
*St Beoc (5th or 6th cent.) Ab.
St Eugendus (c.510) Ab.
*St Basil of Aix (521) Bp. C.
St Fulgentius of Ruspe (533) Bp. C.
St Justin of Chieti (c.540) C.
*St Fanchea (c.585) V.
*St Felix of Bourges (c.580) Bp.
*St Connat (c.590) V.
*St Maelrhys (6th cent.) C.
*St Cuan (6th cent.) Ab.
*St Clarus (c.660) Ab. O.S.B.
*St William of Dijon (1031) Ab. O.S.B.
St Odilo of Cluny (1049) Ab. O.S.B.
*Bl Adalbero of Liége (1128) Bp.
*Bl Zdislava Berka (1252) O.P.
*Bl Hugolinus of Gualdo (1260) C. O.S.A.
*Bl Bonannus (c.1320) C. O.S.B.Cel.
*Bl Joseph Mary Tommasi (1713) Card.
*Bl Vincent Strambi (1824) Bp. C.P.

JANUARY 2.

*St Abel, Patriarch.
SS Many Martyrs who suffered in Rome (c.303).

SS Argeus, Narcissus and Marcellinus (320) MM.
St Isidore of Nitria (4th cent.). Bp.
St Isidore of Antioch (4th cent.) Bp. M.
St Siridion (?) Bp.
St Macarius the Younger (c.408) H.
St Martinian of Milan (c.435) Bp.
*St Aspasius of Auch (c.560) Bp.
*St Munchin of Limerick (?) Bp.?
*St Seiriol (6th cent.) C.
*St Blidulf of Bobbio (c.630) Mk.
*St Vincentian (c.730) H.
*St Adalard of Corbie (827) Ab. O.S.B.
*St Airaldus (1160) Bp. O.Cart.
*Bl Bentivoglio de Bonis (1232) C. O.F.M.
*Bl Stephana de Quinzanis (1530) V. O.P.

JANUARY 3.

St Daniel of Padua (168) M.
St Antheros (236) Pope.
SS Theopemptus and Theonas (284) MM.
SS Peter Apselamus and Peter Absalo (291 and 311) MM.
SS Zosimus and Athanasius (303) MM.
St Gordinus of Cappadocia (304) M.
SS Cyrinus, Primus and Theogenes (320) MM.
St Florentius of Vienne (p.374) Bp. M.
St Geneviève of Paris (c.500) V.
*St Fintan of Doon (6th cent.) Ab.
*St Finlugh (6th cent.) Ab.
*St Blitmund of Bobbio (650) Ab.
*St Bertilia of Marolles (c.705) V.
*St Wenog (?)

619

JANUARY 4.

*St Titus (c.96) Bp.
St Mavilus of Adrumetum (212) M.
SS Hermes, Aggaeus and Caius (c.300) MM.
SS Priscus, Priscillian and Benedict (362) MM.
St Drafosa (?) M.
SS Aquilinus, Geminus, Eugene, Marcian, Quintus, Theodotus and Tryphon (c.484) MM.
St Gregory of Langres (539) Bp.
St Ferreolus of Uzès (581) Bp.
St Pharaïldis of Ghent (c.740) V.
St Rigobert of Reims (c.745) Bp. O.S.B.
*St Libentius of Hamburg (1013) Bp. O.S.B.
*Bl Palumbus of Subiaco (c.1070) H. O.S.B.
St Stephen du Bourg (1118) C. O. Cart.
*Bl Roger of Ellant (1160) Ab. O.S.B. Cist.
*Bl Angela of Foligno (1309) W. O.S.F.
*Bl Oringa of the Cross (1310) V. O.S.A.
*Bl Thomas Plumtree (1570) M.

JANUARY 5.

St Telesphorus (136) Pope M.
SS Martyrs of Egypt (303).
*St Talida of Antinoe (4th cent.) V.
St Syncletica (c.400) V.
St Apollinaris Syncletica (c.450) V.
St Simeon Stylites the Elder (459) H.
St Emiliana of Rome (6th cent.) V.
*St Cera of Kilkeary (7th cent.) V.
*St Conwoion of Redon (868) Ab. O.S.B.
*St Gaudentius of Gnesen (c.1004) Bp. O.S.B.
*St Gerlac of Valkenberg (c.1170) H.
*Bl Alacrinus of Casamari (1216) Bp. O.S.B.Cist.
St Paula (1368) V. O.S.B.Cam.

JANUARY 6.

The Epiphany of the Lord.
*SS Balthassar, Caspar and Melchior (1st cent.) The Magi.

SS Martyrs in Africa (c.210).
St Macra of Reims (287) V. M.
*St Hywyn of Averdaron (p.516) C.
St Melanius of Rennes (c.530) Bp.
*St Merinus (6th cent.) H.
*St Edeyrn (6th cent.) H.
*St Eigrad (6th cent.) C.
*St Schottin (6th cent.) C.
*St Peter of Canterbury (c.606) Ab. O.S.B.
*St Diman of Connor (658) Bp.
*St Wiltrudis of Bergen (c.986) W. O.S.B.
*Bl Frederick of St Vanne (1020) Mk. O.S.B.
*St Erminold of Prufenning (1121) M., Ab. O.S.B.
*St Guarinus (1150) Bp. O.S.B.Cist.
*Bl Gertrude van Oosten (1358) V.
*Bl John de Ribera (1611) Bp.
*Bl Charles of Sezze (1670) C. O.F.M.

JANUARY 7.

St Crispin of Pavia (c.250) Bp.
St Clerus of Antioch (c.300) M.
SS Felix and Januarius (?) MM.
St Julian of Cagliari (?) M.
St Lucian of Antioch (312) M.
St Theodore of Egypt (4th cent.) H.
St Nicetas of Remesiana (c.414) Bp.
St Crispin II of Pavia (p. 451) Bp.
*St Valentine (c.470) Bp.
*St Brannock (6th cent.) Ab.
*St Cedd (664) Bp. O.S.B.
*St Cronan Beg (7th cent.) Bp.
*St Tillo of Solignac (702) Ab. O.S.B.
*St Kentigerna (734) W.
*St Emilian of Saujon (767) Mk. O.S.B.
*Bl Wittikund of Westphalia (c.804) C.
*St Aldericus (856) Bp.
*St Reinold (960) M. O.S.B.
*St Anastasius of Sens (977) Bp.
St Canute Lavard (1133) M.
*Bl Edward Waterson (1593) M.

JANUARY 8.

St Apollinaris the Apologist (c.180) Bp.
*St Patiens of Metz (2nd cent.) Bp.
SS Lucian, Maximian and Julian (c.290) MM.

SS Theophilus and Helladius (?) MM.
*St Carterius (304) M.
St Eugenian of Autun (4th cent.) Bp. M.
*St Atticus of Constantinople (425) Bp.
St Severinus of Noricum (476) Ab.
St Severinus of Naples (?) Bp.
*St Ergnad of Ulster (5th cent.) V.
St Maximus of Pavia (511) Bp.
*St Frodobert (c.673) Ab. O.S.B.
St Erhard of Ratisbon (c.686) Bp.
*St Albert of Cashel (7th cent.) Bp.
*St Maurontus (c.700) Ab. O.S.B.
*St Gudula of Brussels (712) V.
*St Pega (c.719) V.
*St Garibaldus (c.762) Bp.
*St Athelm (923) Bp. O.S.B.
*St Wulsin of Sherborne (1005) Bp.
O.S.B.
St Laurence Giustiniani (1455) Bp.

JANUARY 9.

*St Paschasia of Dijon (c.178) V. M.
SS Epictetus, Jucundus, Secundus,
Vitalis, Felix and Comp. (c.250) MM.
St Marciana (c.303) V. M.
SS Julian, Basilissa, Antony, Anasta-
sius, Celsus, Marcionilla and Comp.
(c.304) MM.
SS Vitalis, Revocatus and Fortunatus
(?) MM.
St Peter of Sebaste (c.391) Bp.
St Marcellinus of Ancona (c.566) Bp.
*St Waningus of Fécamp (c.686) Ab.
O.S.B.
*St Adrian of Canterbury (710) Ab.
O.S.B.
*St Brithwald of Canterbury (731) Bp.
O.S.B.
*St Foellan (8th cent.) C.
*St Honorius of Buzancais (1250) M.
*Bl Philip Berruyer (1260) Bp.

JANUARY 10.

St Nicanor (c.76) M.
*St Petronius of Avignon (c.463) Bp.
St Marcian of Constantinople (c.480)
Bp.
St John Camillus Bonus (c.660) Bp.
*St Sethrida (c. 660) Abs. O.S.B.

*St Thomian of Armagh (c.660) Bp.
St Agatho (681) Pope.
St Peter Urseolus (987) H. O.S.B.
*St Benincasa of Cava (1194) Ab.
O.S.B.
St William of Bourges (1209) Bp.
O.S.B.Cist.
Bl Gregory X (1276) Pope.

JANUARY 11.

St Hyginus (c.142) Pope, M.
St Leucius of Brindisi (c.180) Bp.
St Alexander of Fermo (c.250) Bp. M.
SS Peter, Severus and Leucius (c.309)
MM.
St Palaemon (325) Ab.
*SS Ethenea and Fidelmia (433) VV.
*St Beandan (5th cent.) Ab.
St Honorata of Pavia (c.500) V.
St Theodosius the Cenobiarch (529)
Ab.
St Anastasius of Castel Sant'Elia
(c.570) Ab. O.S.B.
St Salvius of Amiens (c.625) Bp.
*St Boadin (?) H. O.S.B.
*St Vitalis of Gaza (c.625) H.
*SS Paldo, Taso and Tato (8th cent.)
Abbots O.S.B.

JANUARY 12.

St Tatiana of Rome (c.230) M.
St Satyrus (267) M.
St Arcadius of Mauretania (c.302) M.
SS Zoticus, Rogatus, Modestus, Castu-
lus and Comp. (?) MM.
SS Tigrius and Eutropius (404) MM.
St John of Ravenna (594) Bp.
*St Elian ap Erbin (?5th cent.) C.
*St Caesaria of Arles (c.530) V.
*St Victorian of Asan (c.560) Ab.
St Probus of Verona (p.591) Bp.
St Benedict Biscop (690) Ab. O.S.B.
SS Forty-two Martyrs of Ephesus
(c.762).
*St Aelred (1167) Ab. O.S.B.Cist.
*St Martin of Leon (1203) C. O.S.A.
*BB John Gaspard Cratz, Emmanuel d'
Abreu, Bartholomew Alvarez and
Vincent Da Cunha (1737) MM. S.J.

JANUARY 13.

*St Andrew of Trèves? (?235) Bp.?
SS Forty Soldiers martyred at Rome (262)
SS Hermylus and Stratonicus (315) MM.
St Glaphyra (c.324) V.
St Agrecius of Trèves (c.333) Bp.
St Leontius of Caesarea (337) Bp.
St Viventius (c.400) H.
St Potitus (?) M.
*St Erbin (?5th cent.) C.
*St Elian (6th cent.) H.
SS Gumersindus and Servusdei (850) MM.
*St Berno of Cluny (927) Ab. O.S.B.
*Bl Stephen of Liége (1061) Ab. O.S.B.
*Bl Hildemar of Arrouaise (1097-8) M. O.S.A.
*Bl Godfrey of Cappenberg (1127) C.O. Praem.
*Bl Ida of Argensolles (1226) Abs. O.S.B.Cist.
*Bl Ivetta (1228) W.
Bl Veronica of Binasco (1497) V. O.S.A.

JANUARY 14.

St Malachy (5th cent. B.C.) Prophet.
St Felix of Nola (c.260) M.
*St Felix of Rome (?) C.
SS Isaias, Sabas and Comp. (309) MM.
St Macrina the Elder (c.340) W.
*SS Barbasymas and Comp. (346) MM.
St Hilary of Poitiers (368) Bp. Dr.
St Euphrasius (?) Bp.
SS Martyrs of Raithu (c.510).
St Datius of Milan (552) Bp.
*St Kentigern Mungo (603) Bp.
*St Deusdedit of Canterbury (664) Bp. O.S.B.
*Bl Amadeus of Clermont (c.1150) C. O.S.B.Cist.
*Bl Odo of Novara (c.1200) C. O.Cart.
*St Sabas of Serbia (1237) Bp.

JANUARY 15.

St Micah (8th cent. B.C.) Prophet.
St Habacuc (5th cent. B.C.) Prophet.

St Secundina (c.250) V. M.
St Maximus of Nola (p. 250) Bp.
St Ephysius of Sardinia (303) M.
St Paul the Hermit (c.342) C.
St Macarius the Elder (390) H.
St Isidore the Egyptian (404) C.
*St Alexander Akimetes (430) Ab.
St John Calabytes (c.450) H.
*St Ita of Limerick (c.570) V.
St Maurus (c.580) Ab. O.S.B.
*St Sawl (6th cent.) C.
*St Lleudadd of Bardsey (6th cent.) Ab.
*St Tarsicia of Rodez (c.600) V.
*St Malard of Chartres (p.650) Bp.
St Emebert (c.710) Bp.
St Bonitus of Clermont (c.710) Bp. O.S.B.
*St Ceolwulph (764) King, Mk. O.S.B.
*St Blaithmaic of Jona (c.823) M.
*Bl Peter of Castelnau (1208) M. O.S.B.
*Bl Francis Ferdinand de Capillas(1648) M. O.P.

JANUARY 16.

St Priscilla (1st cent.) W.
St Marcellus (309) Pope M.
St Melas (c.385) Bp.
*St James of Tarentaise (c.429) Bp.
St Honoratus of Arles (429) Bp.
*St Valerius of Sorrento (c.453) Bp.
*St Triverius (c.550) H.
St Honoratus of Fondi (6th cent.) Ab.
*St Karantoc (?).
*St Fulgentius of Ecija (c.633) Bp.
St Fursey of Lagny (c.648) Ab. O.S.B.
St Titian (650) Bp.
*St Ferreolus of Grenoble (c.670) Bp.M.
*St Dunchaid O'Braoin (988) Ab.
*Bl Jane of Bagno (1105) V. O.S.B. Cam.
*St Henry (1127) H. O.S.B.
*Bl Conrad of Mondsee (1145) Ab. M. O.S.B.
SS Berardus, Peter, Otto, Accursius and Adjutus (1220) MM. O.F.M.
*Bl Gundisalvus (c.1259) C. O.P.

JANUARY 17.

SS Speusippus, Eleusippus, Meleusippus and Leonilla (175) MM.

*SS Genulfus and Genitus (3rd cent.)
St Antony (325) Ab.
St Julian Sabas the Elder (377) C.
*St Pior (c.395) H.
*SS Achillas and Amoes (4th cent.) HH.
*SS Antony, Merulus and John (c.590) Monks O.S.B.
*St Nennius (6th cent.) Ab.
*St Mildgytha (c.676) N. O.S.B.
St Sulpitius II Pius (647) Bp.
*St Richimirus (c.715) Ab. O.S.B.
*Bl Joseph of Freising (764) Bp. O.S.B.
*Bl Roseline de Villeneuve (1329) V. O.Cart.

*St Remigius of Rouen (c.772) Bp.
*St Catellus of Castellamare (9th cent.) Bp.
*St Arsenius of Corfu (959) Bp.
St Canute IV of Denmark (1086) M.
St Wulstan of Worcester (1095) Bp. O.S.B.
*St Henry of Upsala (c.1156) Bp. M.
*Bl Beatrix of Lens (p.1216) N. O.S.B. Cist.
*Bl Antony Fatati (1484) Bp.
*Bl Andrew of Peschiera (1485) C. O.P.
*Bl Bernard of Corleone (1667) C. O.F.Min.Cap.
*Bl Thomas of Cori (1729) C. O.F.M.

JANUARY 18.

SS Moseus and Ammonius (250)MM.
St Prisca of Rome (c.270?) V. M.
SS Archelais, Thecla and Susanna (293) VV. MM.
St Athenogenes (?) Bp. M.
St Volusian of Tours (496) Bp. M.
*SS Faustina and Liberata (c.580) VV.
St Leobard of Tours (593) H.
*St Diarmis (6th cent.) Ab.
St Deicola of Lure (c.625) Ab.
*St Day (?) Ab.
*St Ulfrid (1029) M.
*Bl Beatrix II of Este (1262) N. O.S.B.
*St Fazzio of Verona (1272) C.
*Bl Christina Ciccarelli (1543) V. O.S.A.

JANUARY 19.

St Germanicus of Smyrna (156) M.
St Pontian of Spoleto (169) M.
SS Paul, Gerontius, Januarius, Saturninus, Successus, Julius, Catus, Pia and Germana (2nd cent.?) MM.
SS Marius, Martha, Abachum and Audifax (c.270) MM.
*St Messalina of Foligno (3rd cent.) V. M.
St Bassian of Lodi (413) Bp.
*St Contestus of Bayeux (c.510) Bp.
*St Lomer of Corbion (593) Ab.
*St Firminus of Gabales (?) Bp.
*St Branwallader (6th cent.?) Bp.
*St Nathalan of Aberdeen (678) Bp.

JANUARY 20.

St Fabian (250) Pope M.
St Sebastian (c.288) M.
St Neophytus of Nicaea (310) M.
St Euthymius the Great (473) Ab.
*St Molagga of Fermoy (c.664) Ab.
*St Fechin of Fobhar (c.665) Ab.
St Maurus of Cesena (946) Bp. O.S.B.
*Bl Benedict Ricasoli (1107) H. O.S.B. Vall.
*Bl Desiderius of Therouanne (1194). Bp.
*Bl Daniel of Cambron (1232) Ab. O.S.B.Cist.

JANUARY 21.

St Publius of Malta (c.112) Bp. M.
SS Fructuosus, Augurius and Eulogius (259) MM.
St Patroclus of Troyes (c.275) M.
St Agnes of Rome (c.304) V. M.
St Epiphanius of Pavia (497) Bp.
*St Brigid of Kilbride (6th cent.) V.
*St Lawdog (6th cent.).
*St Vimin of Holywood (6th cent.) Bp.
St Meinrad of Einsiedeln (861) M. O.S.B.
*St Maccallin of Waulsort (978) Ab. O.S.B.
*Bl Edward Stransham (1586) M.
*BB Bartholomew Roe, O.S.B. and Thomas Reynolds (1642) MM.
*Bl Agnes de Beniganim (1696) V. O.S.A.Disc.

JANUARY 22.

St Vincent the Deacon (304) M.
SS Vincent, Orontius and Victor (305) MM.
*St Vincent of Digne (380) Bp.
*St Blaesilla of Rome (383) W.
St Gaudentius of Novara (c.418) Bp.
St Anastasius the Persian (628) M.
*St Brithwold of Sarum (1045) Bp. O.S.B.
St Dominic of Sora (1031) Ab. O.S.B.
*Bl Walter of Himmerode (1222) Mk. O.S.B.Cist.
*Bl William Patenson (1592) M.
*Bl Francis Gil (1744) M. O.P.
*Bl Matthew Alonso Leziniana (1745) M. O.P.

JANUARY 23.

St Parmenas (c.98) M.
St Asclas of Antinoe (c.287) M.
St Clement of Ancyra (303) Bp. M.
St Emerentiana (304) V. M.
St Agathangelus (c.309) M.
SS Severian and Aquila (?) MM.
*St Amasius of Teano (356) Bp.
*St Eusebius of Mount Coryphe (4th cent.) H.
St Martyrius of Valeria (6th cent.) M.
*St Ormond of Marié (6th cent.) Ab.
St John the Almoner (c.616) Bp.
St Ildephonsus of Toledo (667) Bp.
*St Colman of Lismore (c.702) Bp.
*St Barnard of Vienne (841) Bp. O.S.B.
*St Lufthild of Cologne (c.850) V.
*St Maimbod (c.880) M.
*Bl Bernard of Lippe (1217) Bp. O.S.B. Cist.
St Raymund de Peñafort (1275) C. O.P.
*Bl Margaret of Ravenna (1505) V.
*Bl Joseph Cafasso (1860) C.

JANUARY 24.

St Timothy (97) Bp. M.
SS Babilas, Urban, Prilidian and Epolonius (c.250) MM.
St Felician of Foligno (254) Bp. M.
St Zama of Bologna (c.268) Bp.

SS Mardonius, Musonius, Eugene and Metellus (c.305) MM.
*St Macedonius Kritophagos (c.340) H.
*St Artemius of Clermont (396) Bp.
SS Thyrsus and Projectus (?) MM.
*St Guasacht (4th cent.) Bp.
St Exuperantius of Cingoli (5th cent.) Bp.
*St Cadoc of Llancarvan (c.580) Bp. M.
St Suranus of Sora (c.580) Ab.
*St Bertrand of St Quentin (7th cent.) Ab. O.S.B.
*Bl Felix O'Dullany (1202) Bp. O.S.B. Cist.
*Bl Marcolino of Forli (1397) C. O.P.
*Bl William Ireland, S.J. and Bl John Grove (1679) MM.

JANUARY 25.

St Ananias of Damascus (1st cent.) M.
SS Donatus, Sabinus and Agape (?) MM.
*St Artemas of Puzzuoli (?) M.
*St Publius of Zeugma (c.380) Ab.
St Bretannion of Tomi (c.380) Bp.
SS Juventinus and Maximus (363) MM.
*St Apollo of Heliopolis (c.395) Ab.
*St Dwynwen (c.460) V.
*St Eochod (597) C.
*St Racho of Autun (c.660) Bp.
SS Praejectus of Clermont, Bp., and St Amarinus, Ab. O.S.B. (676) MM.
*St Thordgith of Barking (c.700) N. O.S.B.
St Poppo of Stavelot (1048) Ab. O.S.B.
*St Joel of Pulsano (1185) Ab. O.S.B.
*St Peter Thomas (1366) Bp. O.C.

JANUARY 26.

St Polycarp of Smyrna (c.156) Bp. M.
SS Theogenes and Comp. (258) MM.
*St Athanasius (?) Bp. of Sorrento.
St Paula of Rome (404) W.
*St Conan of Iona (c.648) Bp.
*St Theofrid of Corbie (c.690) Bp. O.S.B.
*St Alphonsus of Astorga (9th cent.) Bp. O.S.B.

St Armentarius of Pavia (c.711) Bp.

*Bl Amnichad of Fulda (1043) H. O.S.B.

*St Adelelmus of Burgos (c.1100) Ab. O.S.B.

*Bl Haberilla of Mehrerau (c.1100) V. O.S.B.

*Bl Gerard of Clairvaux (1138) C. O.S.B.Cist.

St Hyacintha of Mariscotti (1640) Tert. O.F.M.

*Bl Sebastian Velfré (1710) Orat.

JANUARY 31.

St Metranus of Alexandria (c.250) M.

SS Saturninus, Thyrsus and Victor (c.250) MM.

SS Tarcisius, Zoticus, Cyriacus and Comp. (?) MM.

St Tryphena of Cyzicus (?) Matron M.

SS Cyrus and John (c.303) MM.

St Geminian of Modena (348) Bp.

St Julius of Novara (p.390) C.

St Marcella of Rome (410) W.

*St Melangell (c.590) V.

*St Aedan of Ferns (632) Bp.

*St Madoes (?) C.

*St Adamnan of Coldinham (c.680) Mk. O.S.B.

*St Bobinus of Troyes (c.766) Bp. O.S.B.

*St Eusebius of St Gall (884) M. O.S.B.

*St Athanasius of Modon (c.885) Bp.

*St Ulphia of Amiens (995) H.

*Bl John Angelus (c.1050) C. O.S.B.

*St Martin Manuel (1156) M.

*Bl Paula Gambara-Costa (1515) Matron.

*Bl Louise degli Albertoni (1533) W.

*Bl Francis Xavier Bianchi (1815) Barn.

*Bl Mary Christina (1836) Queen.

St John Bosco (1888) Founder.

FEBRUARY 1.

St Ignatius of Antioch (c.107) Bp. M.

SS Pionius and Comp. (251) MM.

St Severus of Ravenna (c.348) Bp.

St Paul of Trois-Chateaux (c.405) Bp.

*St Jarlath of Armagh (c.480) Bp.

*St Cinnia of Ulster (5th cent.) V.

*St Crewenna (5th cent.).

St Brigid of Kildare (c.525) V. Foundress.

*St Kinnia (6th cent.) V.

*St Darlugdach of Kildare (p.525) V.

*St Sigebert III (656) King.

*St Severus of Avranches (c.690) Bp.

*St Brigid (9th cent.) V.

*St Clarus of Seligenstadt (c.1048) H. O.S.B.

*St Autbert of Landevenec (1129) Mk. O.S.B.

*St John of the Grating (c.1170) Bp. O.S.B.Cist.

*Bl Reginald of Saint-Gilles (1220) C. O.P.

St Viridiana (1242) H. O.S.B.Vall.

*Bl Antony Manzoni (1267) C.

*Bl Eustochium Calefato (1468) O.F.M.

*Bl Henry Morse (1645) M. S.J.

FEBRUARY 2.

Feast of the Purification of the Blessed Virgin Mary.

St Cornelius the Centurion (1st cent.) Bp.

St Apronian the Executioner (c.304) M.

SS Fortunatus, Felician, Firmus and Candidus (?) MM.

St Flosculus of Orléans (p.480) Bp.

*St Feock (?) V.

St Laurence of Canterbury (619) Bp. O.S.B.

*St Adalbald d'Ostrevant (652) M.

*St Adeloga of Kitzingen (c.745) V. O.S.B.

*SS Martyrs of Ebsford: Bruno, Marquard Bp. O.S.B. and Comp. (880)

*St Columbanus (959) H.

*Bl Peter Cambian (1365) M. O.P.

St Catherine dei Ricci (1590) V. O.P.

*Bl Jane de Lestonnac (1640) Foundress.

*Bl Theophanes Vénard (1861) M.

FEBRUARY 3.

St Celerinus of Carthage (p.250) M.

SS Laurentinus, Ignatius and Celerina (3rd cent.) MM.

*St Ansurius of Orense (925) Bp. O.S.B.
*St Alberic of Citeaux (1109) Ab. O.S.B. Cist.
*St Margaret of Hungary (1270) V. O.P.

JANUARY 27.

St Julian of Sora (c.150) M.
St Julian of Le Mans (3rd cent.) Bp.
*St Devota of Corsica (c.303) V. M.
St Avitus (?) M.
SS Datius, Reatrus and Comp., and SS Datius, Julian, Vincent and twenty-seven Comp. (?) MM.
St John Chrysostom (407) Bp. Dr.
St Maurus of Bodon (c.555) Ab.
*St Natalis (6th cent.) Ab.
St Lupus of Chalons (c.610) Bp.
St Vitalian (672) Pope.
*St Emerius of Banoles (8th cent.) Ab. O.S.B.
*St Candida of Banoles (8th cent.) W.
*St Gamelbert of Michaelsbuch (c.800) C.
*St Theodoric II of Orléans (1022) Bp. O.S.B.
*Bl John of Warneton (1130) Bp.
*Bl Michael Pini (1522) H. O.S.B.Cam.
*Bl John Mary Mzec (1887) M.

JANUARY 28.

SS Thyrsus, Leucius and Callinicus (251) MM.
St Flavian of Città Vecchia (c.304) M.
SS Leonidas and Comp. (304) MM.
St Valerius of Saragossa (315) Bp.
SS Martyrs of Alexandria (356).
*St Palladius of Antioch (c.390) H.
*St Cannera of Bantry (c.530) V.
St John of Reomay (c.544) Ab.
St James the Hermit (6th cent.) C.
*Bl Charlemagne (814) Emperor.
*St Antimus of Brantome (8th cent.) Ab. O.S.B.
*St Paulinus of Aquileia (804) Bp.
*St Glastian of Kinglassie (830) Bp.
*St Odo of Beauvais (880) Bp. O.S.B.
*Bl Richard the Sacrist (p. 1142) Mk. O.S.B.Cist.
*Bl Amadeus of Lausanne (1159) Bp. O.S.B.Cist.

*St Richard of Vaucelles (1169) Ab. O.S.B.Cist.
St Julian of Cuenca (1208) Bp.
*Bl Bartholomew Aiutamicristo (1224) H. O.S.B.Cam.
*Bl Roger of Todi (1237) C. O.F.M.
St Peter Nolasco (1258) Founder.
*Bl James the Almsgiver (1304) C.
*Bl Mary of Pisa (1431) W. O.P.
*Bl Antony of Amandola (1450) O.S.A.
*Bl Giles of Lorenzana (1518) O.F.M.
*BB Jerome Lu and Laurence Wang (1858) MM.

JANUARY 29.

SS Sarbellius and Barbea (101) MM.
SS Constantius and Comp. (170) MM.
St Sabinian of Troyes (c.275) M.
*St Caesarius of Angoulême (?) C.
SS Papias and Maurus (c.303) MM.
St Valerius of Trèves (c.320) Bp.
*St Blath of Kildare (523) V.
St Gildas the Wise (c.570) Bp.
St Sulpitius I Severus (591) Bp.
*St Dallan Forgaill (598) M.
*St Triphina of Brittany (6th cent.) W.
*St Aquilinus of Milan (650) M.
*St Voloc (c.724) Bp.
*Bl Charles of Sayn (1212) Ab. O.S.B. Cist.
St Francis of Sales (1622) Bp. Dr. Founder.

JANUARY 30.

St Barsimaeus (c.114) Bp. M.
St Matthias of Jerusalem (c.120) Bp.
*St Agrippinus of Alexandria (c.180) Bp.
St Martina of Rome (228) V. M.
St Hippolytus of Antioch (p. 250) M.
SS Felician, Philippian and one hundred and twenty-four Comp. (?) MM.
St Alexander (3rd cent.) M.
St Savina of Milan (311) Matron.
St Barses of Edessa (c.379) Bp.
*St Armentarius of Antibes (p. 450) Bp.
*St Tudy (5th cent.) V.
St Bathildis, Queen (680) O.S.B.
St Aldegund of Maubeuge (684) Abs. O.S.B.

St Blaise of Sebaste (c.316) Bp. M.
SS Felix, Symphronius, Hippolytus and Comp. (?) MM.
SS Tigides and Remedius (?) Bps.
*St Ia of Cornwall (450) V. M.
SS Lupicinus and Felix (5th cent.) Bps.
*St Laurence the Illuminator (576) Bp.
*St Philip of Vienne (c.578) Bp.
*St Caellainn (6th cent.) V.
*St Hadelin of Dinant (c.690) Ab. O.S.B.
*St Werburg of Chester (c.699) V. O.S.B.
*St Berlinda of Meerbeke (702) V. O.S.B.
*St Werburg of Mercia (c.785) Matron, O.S.B.
*St Deodatus of Lagny (8th cent.) C. O.S.B.
St Anschar of Hamburg (865) Bp. O.S.B.
*St Anatolius of Salins (9th cent.) Bp.
*St Oliver of Portonuovo (c.1050) C. O.S.B.
*St Margaret of England (1192) V. O.S.B.Cist.
*Bl Elinand of Froidmont (1237) C. O.S.B.Cist.
*Bl Odoric of Pordenone (1331) C. O.F.M.
*Bl Simon Fidati (1348) C. O.S.A.
*Bl Matthew of Girgenti (1450) Bp. O.F.M.
*Bl John Nelson (1578) M. S.J.
*Bl Stephen Bellesini (1840) C. O.S.A.

FEBRUARY 4.

SS Aquilinus, Geminus, Gelasius, Magnus and Donatus (3rd cent.) MM.
SS Phileas and Comp. (c.304) MM.
*St Aldate (5th cent.) C.
St Eutychius of Rome (4th cent.) M.
*St Aventinus of Chartres (c.520) Bp.
St Aventinus of Troyes (538) H.
St Theophilus the Penitent (c.538).
St Isidore of Pelusium (c.540) C.
*St Vincent of Troyes (c.546) Bp.
*St Modan (? 6th cent.) Ab.
*St Liephard (649) Bp. M.

*St Vulgis of Lobbes (c.760) Bp. O.S.B.
*St Nithard of Corbie (845) M. O.S.B.
*Bl Rabanus Maurus (856) Bp. O.S.B.
*St Nicholas Studites (863) Ab.
*Bl Simon of St-Bertin (1148) Ab. O.S.B.
St Gilbert of Sempringham (1189) C. Founder.
*St Obitius of Brescia (c.1204) C. O.S.B.
St Andrew Corsini (1373) Bp. O.C.
*Bl Jane of Valois (1504) Foundress
*Bl John Speed (1594) M.
St Joseph of Leonissa (1612) C. O.F.M.Cap.
*Bl John de Britto (1693) M. S.J.

FEBRUARY 5.

St Agatha of Catania (c.250) V. M.
*St Abraham of Arbela (c.345) Bp. M.
*St Agricola of Tongres (420) Bp.
St Avitus of Vienne (c.519) Bp.
St Genuinus of Brixen (7th cent.) Bp.
*St Bertulfus of Renty (705) Ab. O.S.B.
*St Indract of Glastonbury (c.710) M.
*St Modestus of Salzburg (c.722) Bp. O.S.B.
*St Vodoaldus (c.725) H.
*St Arcontius of Viviers (? 8th cent.) Bp. M.
*Bl John Morosini (1012) Ab. O.S.B.
*St Adelaide of Willich (c.1015) Abs. O.S.B.
*St Agatha of Carinthia (1024) W.
SS Martyrs of Japan: seven Franciscans, three Jesuits, eighteen lay people (1597).

FEBRUARY 6.

St Titus (1st cent.) Bp.
SS Martyrs of Africa (c.210).
St Antholian of Auvergne (c.267) M.
St Dorothy of Caesarea (c.300) V. M.
St Theophilus of Caesarea (c.300) M.
SS Silvanus, Luke and Mucius (312) MM.
SS Saturninus, Theophilus and Revocata (?) MM.
*St Mel of Armagh (c.490) Bp.
*SS Jacut and Guethenoc (5th cent.) CC.

*St Mun of Lough Ree (5th cent.) Bp.
St Vedast of Arras (539) Bp.
*St Amandus of Moissac (644) Ab.
O.S.B.
St Amandus of Elnone (c.676) Bp.
*St Andrew of Elnone (c.690) Ab.
O.S.B.
*St Amandus of Nantes (7th cent.) Ab.
O.S.B.
*St Relindis of Eyck (c.750) Abs. O.S.B.
*St Gerald of Ostia (1077) Bp. O.S.B.
St Guarinus of Palestrina (1159) Bp.
O.S.A.
*St Hildegund of Meer (1183) W.
O.Praem.
*St Didacus de Azevedo (1207) Bp.
O.S.B.Cist.
*Bl Angelus of Furci (1372) C. O.S.A.

FEBRUARY 7.

St Augulus (c.303) Bp. M.
St Adaucus (304) M.
St Theodore Stratelates (319) M.
St Moses (c.372) Bp.
*St Chrysolius the Armenian (4th cent.)
Bp. M.
*St Anatolius of Cahors (?) Bp.
St Juliana of Bologna (435) W.
*St Laurence of Siponto (c.546) Bp.
*St Tressan of Marauil (550) C.
*St Fidelis of Mérida (c.570) Bp.
*St Meldon of Péronne (6th cent.) Bp.
St Richard the King (722) C.
*St Amulwinus of Lobbes (c.750) Ab.-
Bp. O.S.B.
*St Luke the Younger (c.946) C.
St Romuald (1027) Founder, O.S.B.
*Bl Nivard of Vaucelles (p.1150) C.
O.S.B.Cist.
*Bl Rizzerio (1236) C. O.F.M.
*Bl Antony of Stroncone (1461) C.
O.F.M.
*Bl Thomas Sherwood (1578) M.
*BB James Sales and William Saulte-
mouche (1593) MM. S.J.
*Bl Giles Mary of St Joseph (1812) C.
O.F.M.

FEBRUARY 8.

St Juventius of Pavia (1st cent.) Bp.
St Cointha of Alexandria (249) V. M.

SS Paul, Lucius and Cyriacus (?) MM.
SS Dionysius, Aemilian and Sebastian
(?) MM.
SS Martyrs of Constantinople (485)
MM.
St Honoratus of Milan (570) Bp.
SS Martyrs in Persia (6th cent.).
*St Kigwe (?) V.
*St Oncho of Clonmore (c.600) C.
*St Nicetius of Besançon (611) Bp.
St Paul of Verdun (c.649) Bp. O.S.B.
*St Elfleda of Whitby (714) Abs. O.S.B.
*St Meingold of Huy (c.892) M.
*St Cuthman (9th cent.) H.
*Bl Mlada of Prague (994) Abs. O.S.B.
St Peter Igneus (c.1089) Card. Bp.
O.S.B.Vall.
St Stephen of Gradmont (1124) Ab.
O.S.B.
St John of Matha (1213) Founder.
*Bl Isaias Boner (1471) C. O.S.A.
*Bl John Charles Cornay (1837) M.
*Bl Stephen Guénot (1861) M. Bp.

FEBRUARY 9.

St Apollonia of Alexandria (249) V. M.
St Nicephorus of Antioch (260) M.
SS Primus and Fonatus (362) MM.
SS Ammonius and Alexander (?) MM.
SS Alexander and Comp. (?) MM.
*SS Ammon, Emilian, Lassa and Comp.
(?) MM.
St Cyril of Alexandria (444) Bp. Dr.
*St Nebridius of Egara (p. 527) Bp.
St Sabinus of Canosa (c.566) Bp.
*St Teilo of Llandaff (c.580) Bp.
*St Eingan of Llanengan (6th cent.) H.
St Ansbert of Fontenelle (c.700) Bp.
O.S.B.
*St Cuaran the Wise (p. 700) Bp.
*St Alto of Altomunster (c.760) Ab.
O.S.B.
*St Cronan the Wise (8th cent.) Bp.
*Bl Marianus Scotus (1088) Ab. O.S.B.
*Bl Erizzo (1094) Ab. O.S.B.Vall.
*St Raynald of Nocera (1225) Bp.
O.S.B.
*Bl Albaro of Cordoba (c.1430) C. O.P.

FEBRUARY 10.

*SS Andrew and Aponius (1st cent.)
MM.

SS Zoticus, Irenaeus, Hyacinth, Amantius and Comp. (120) MM.
St Soteris of Rome (304) V. M.
St Silvanus of Terracina (?) Bp.
St Scholastica (c.550) V. O.S.B.
*St Baldegundis (c.580) Abs.
*St Desideratus of Clermont (6th cent.) Bp.
*St Prothadius of Bescançon (624) Bp.
St Austreberta of Pavilly (704) Abs. O.S.B.
*St Caedmon of Whitby (7th cent.) Mk. O.S.B.
*St Erluph of Werden (830) Bp. M.
*Bl Salvius of Albelda (962) Ab. O.S.B.
St William of Maleval (1157) H. O.S.B.
*Bl Hugh of Fosse (1164) C. O.Praem.
*Bl Clare Agolanti (1346) Tert. O.F.M.
*Bl Paganus of Sicily (1423) Mk. O.S.B.
*Bl Eusebius of Murano (1501) H. O.S.B.Cam.
*Bl Alexander of Lugo (1645) M. O.P.

FEBRUARY 11.

St Calocerus of Ravenna (c.130) Bp.
SS Martyrs of Africa (c.303).
SS Saturninus, Dativus, Felix, Ampelius and Comp. (304) MM.
SS Lucius and Comp. (350) MM.
St Jonas of Demeskenyanos (4th cent.) H.
St Lazarus of Milan (c.450) Bp.
St Castrensis of Capua (5th cent.) Bp.
St Severinus of Agaunum (c.507) Ab.
*St Gobnata (? 6th cent.) V.
St Gregory II (731) Pope.
*St Benedict of Aniane (821) Ab. O.S.B.
St Paschal I (824) Pope, O.S.B.
*St Theodora (867) Empress.
*St Ardanus of Tournus (1058) Ab. O.S.B.
*Bl Helwisa of Coulombs (1066) V. O.S.B.
*St Adolphus of Osnabruck (1224) Bp. O.S.B.Cist.
*Bl Elisabeth Salviati (1519) N. O.S.B. Cam.

FEBRUARY 12.

St Eulalia of Barcelona (304) V. M.
SS Modestus and Ammonius (?) MM.

SS Modestus and Julian (?) MM.
*St Julian the Hospitaller (?) C.
St Damian (?) M.
St Meletius of Antioch (381) Bp.
St Gaudentius of Verona (p. 465) Bp.
*St Ethelwold of Lindisfarne (c.740) Bp. O.S.B.
*St Benedict Revelli (c.900) Bp. O.S.B.
St Antony Cauleas (901) Bp.
*St Humbeline (1141) Abs. O.S.B.
*St Goscelinus of Turin (1153) Ab. O.S.B.
*St Ludan of Alsace (c.1202) C.
SS Seven Holy Founders: Bonfilio Monaldi, Alexis Falconieri, Benedict (Amadeus) dell'Antella, Bartholomew (Hugh) Amidei, Ricovero (Sostenes) Ugoccioni, Gherardino (Manettus) Sostegni and John Buonagiunta (13th and 14th cent.) CC.
*BB Antony of Saxony, Gregory of Tragurio, Nicholas of Hungary, Thomas of Foligno and Ladislaus of Hungary (1369) MM. O.F.M.
*BB James Fenn, John Nutter, John Munden and Thomas Henerford (1584) MM.
*Bl Nicholas Saggio (1709) C. O.Minim.

FEBRUARY 13.

St Agabus the Prophet (1st cent.) C.
SS Fusca V. and Maura (c.250) MM.
St Polyeuctus of Melitene (c.259) M.
St Benignus of Todi (c.303) M.
St Julian of Lyons (?) M.
*St Martinian of Caesarea (c.400) H.
St Stephen of Lyons (512) Bp.
*St Modomnock O'Neil (c.550) Bp.
St Stephen of Rieti (c.590) Ab.
*St Lucinus of Angers (c.618) Bp.
*St Enogatus of Aleth (631) Bp.
*St Huna of Ely (c.690) Mk. O.S.B.
*St Dyfnog (7th cent.) C.
*St. Ermenilda of Ely (703) W. Abs. O.S.B.
*St Aimo of Meda (c.790) C.
*St Gosbert of Osnabruck (c.859) Bp. O.S.B.
*St Fulcran of Lodève (1006) Bp.
*Bl Beatrix d'Ornacieux (1309) V. O.Cart.

*Bl Christina of Spoleto (1458) Penitent.
*Bl Eustochium of Padua (1469) V. O.S.B.
*Bl Archangela Girlani (1494) V. O.C.
*Bl John Lantrua (1816) M. O.F.M.
*Bl Paul Lieou (1818) M.
*Bl Paul Loc (1859) M.

FEBRUARY 14.

St Eleuchadius of Ravenna (112) Bp.
St Valentine of Rome (269) M.
St Valentine of Terni (c.269) M. Bp.
SS Proculus, Ephebus and Apollonius (273) MM.
SS Vitalis, Felicula and Zeno (?) MM.
SS Dionysius and Ammonius (?) MM.
SS Cyrion, Bassian, Agatho and Moses (?) MM.
SS Bassus, Antony and Protolicus (?) MM.
*St Abraham of Harran (c.422) Bp.
*St Maro of Beit-Marun (c.435) Ab.
St Nostrianus of Naples (c.450) Bp.
St Auxentius of Bithynia (c.470) H.
*St Theodosius of Vaison (554) Bp.
*St Conran (?) Bp.
St Antoninus of Sorrento (830) Ab. O.S.B.
*Bl Nicholas Palea (1255) C. O.P.
*Bl Angelus of Gualdo (1325) C. O.S.B. Cam.
*Bl Vincent of Siena (1442) C. O.F.M.
*Bl John Baptist of the Conception (1613) C. Trinitarian.

FEBRUARY 15.

SS Faustinus and Jovita (c.121) MM.
St Agape of Terni (c.273) V. M.
SS Saturninus, Castulus, Magnus and Lucius (273) MM.
SS Craton and Comp. (c.273) MM.
St Joseph of Antioch (?) M.
*St Eusebius of Aschia (5th cent.) H.
*St Dochow (?).
St Georgia of Clermont (c.500) V.
St Severus of Androcca (c.530) C.
St Quinidius of Vaison (c.579) Bp.
*St Farannan (c.590) Ab.

*St Faustus of Glanfeuil (6th cent.) C. O.S.B.
*St Berach of Cluain (6th cent.) Ab.
St Decorosus of Capua (695) Bp.
*St Walfrid della Gherardesca (c.765) Ab. O.S.B.
*St Tanco of Werden (808) Bp. M. O.S.B.
*SS Winaman, Unaman and Sunaman (c.1040) Monks MM. O.S.B.
*St Sigfrid of Wexlow (c.1045) Bp. O.S.B.
*St Druthmar of Lorsch (1046) Ab. O.S.B.
*Bl Conrad of Baviera (1154) O.S.B. Cist.
*Bl Jordan of Saxony (1237) C. O.P.
*Bl Andrew Conti (1302) C. O.F.M.
*Bl Angelus of Borgo San Sepolcro (c.1306) C. O.S.A.
*Bl Julia of Certaldo (1367) V. O.S.A.
*St Euseus of Serravalle (14th cent.) H.
*Bl Claude de la Colombière (1682) C. S.J.

FEBRUARY 16.

St Onesimus (c.90) M.
*St Honestus of Nîmes (270) M.
St Juliana of Nicomedia (305) V. M.
SS Porphyrius and Seleucius (309) MM.
SS Elias, Jeremias, Isaias, Samuel and Daniel (309) MM.
St Julian of Egypt and Comp. (?) MM.
St Faustinus of Brescia (381) Bp.
*St Aganus of Airola (c.1050) Ab. O.S.B.
*Bl Philippa Mareri (1236) V. Poor Clare.
*Bl Bernard Scammacca (1486) C. O.P.

FEBRUARY 17.

St Polychronius (250) Bp. M.
SS Donatus, Secundian, Romulus and Comp. (304) MM.
St Theodulus of Caesarea (308) M.
St Julian of Caesarea (308) M.
SS Faustinus and Comp. (?) MM.
*St Loman of Trim (c.450) Bp.

*St Habet-Deus (c.500) Bp. M.
*St Guevrock (6th cent.) Ab.
*St Fortchern of Trim (6th cent.) C.
St Fintan of Clonenagh (603) Ab.
*St Finan of Jona (661) Bp.
St Silvinus of Auchy (c.720) Bp. O.S.B.
*St Benedict of Cagliari (p. 1112) Bp.
O.S.B.
*St Constabilis of Cava (1124) Ab.
O.S.B.
*Bl Frowin of Bellevaux (1165) Ab.
O.S.B.Cist.
*St Evermod of Ratzeburg (1178) Bp.
O.Praem.
*Bl Luke Belludi (1285) C. O.F.M.
*Bl William Richardson (1603) M.
*Bl Francis Regis Clet (1820) M. C.M.

FEBRUARY 18.

St Simeon of Jerusalem (c.107) Bp. M.
*SS Charalampias and Comp. (203)
MM.
*SS Leo and Paregorius (c.260) MM.
SS Maximus, Claudius, Praepedigna,
Alexander and Cutias (295) MM.
SS Lucius, Silvanus, Rutilus, Clas-
sicus, Secundinus, Fructuosus and
Maximus (?) MM.
St Flavian of Constantinople (449) Bp.
M.
St Helladius of Toledo (632) Bp.
*St Colman of Lindisfarne (676) Bp.
*St Angilbert of Centula (814) Ab.
O.S.B.
*St Theotonius of Coimbra (1166) C.
O.S.A.
*Bl William Harrington (1594) M.
*Bl John Pibush (1601) M.
*Bl Agnes De (1841) V. M.
*Bl Andrew Nam-Thung (1855) M.
*Bl Agatha Lin (1858) V. M.
*BB John Peter Néel and Martin
(1862) MM.

FEBRUARY 19.

St Auxibius of Cyprus (1st cent.) Bp.
St Gabinus of Rome (c.295) M.
St Zambdas of Jerusalem (c.304) Bp.
SS Publius, Julian, Marcellus and
Comp. (?) MM.

*St Valerius of Antibes (p.450) Bp.
*St Odran (c.452) M.
SS Martyrs of Palestine (c.509).
St Barbatus of Benevento (682) Bp.
St Mansuetus of Milan (c.690) Bp.
*St Beatus of Liébana (789) Mk. O.S.B.
*St George of Lodève (c.884) Bp. O.S.
*St Belina of Troyes (1135) V. M.
*St Boniface of Lausanne (1265) Bp.
*St Conrad of Piacenza (1354) C.
Tert. O.F.M.
*Bl Lucy (1862) V. M.

FEBRUARY 20.

SS Tyrannio, Silvanus, Peleus, Nilus
and Zenobius (c.304) MM.
SS Martyrs of Tyre (302-310).
SS Pothmius and Nemesius (?) MM.
*St Valerius of Conserans (?) Bp.
St Eleutherius of Byzantium (c.310)
Bp. M.
SS Sadoth and Comp. (c.342) MM.
*St Bolcan of Derkan (p. 480) Bp.
*St Falco of Maestricht (512) Bp.
SS Flavian and Elias (c.512) Bps.
St Eleutherius of Tournai (532) Bp.
St Eucherius of Orléans (743) Bp.
O.S.B.
St Leo of Catania (787) Bp.
*St Colgan of Clonmacnoise (c.796) Ab.
*St Wulfric (1154) H.
*St Amata of Assisi (c.1250) V. Poor
Clare.
*Bl Peter of Treja (1304) C. O.F.M.
*Bl Elisabeth Bartholomea Picenardi
(1468) V. O.S.M.

FEBRUARY 21.

St Felix of Metz (2nd cent.) Bp.
*SS Daniel and Verda (344) MM.
SS Verulus, Secundinus, Siricius, Fe-
lix, Servulus, Saturninus, Fortuna-
tus and Comp. (c.434) MM.
St Severian of Scythopolis (c.452) Bp.
M.
St Paterius of Brescia (606) Bp.
*Bl Pepin of Landen (c.646) C.
*St Gundebert of Senones (c.676) Bp.
O.S.B.

*SS Germanus and Randoald (c.677) MM. O.S.B.
*St Avitus II of Clermont (689) Bp.
*St Valerius of Astorga (695) Ab. O.S.B.
St Peter the Scribe (743) M.
*St George of Amastris (c.825) Bp.
*Bl Nicholas of Vangadizza (c.1210) C. O.S.B.Cam.
*Bl Robert Southwell (1595) M. S.J.
*Bl Noel Pinot (1794) M.

FEBRUARY 22.

St Abilius of Alexandria (c.98) Bp.
St Aristion of Salamis (1st cent.) M.
St Papias of Hierapolis (c.120) Bp.
SS Martyrs of Arabia (?).
St Paschasius of Vienne (c.312) Bp.
*St Baradates (c.460)
*SS Thalasius and Limnaeus (5th cent.) HH.
St Maximian of Ravenna (c.556) Bp.
*St Elwin (6th cent.) C.
*St Athanasius of Nicomedia (c.818) Ab.
*Bl John the Saxon (895) M. O.S.B.
*St Raynerius of Beaulieu (c.967) Mk. O.S.B.
St Margaret of Cortona (1297) O.F.M.
*Bl Angelus Portasole (1334) Bp. O.P.
*Bl Didacus Carvalho and Comp. (1624) MM. S.J.

FEBRUARY 23.

St Martha of Astorga (252) V. M.
St Polycarp of Rome (c.300) C.
St. Sirenus of Sirmium (c.303) M.
SS Martyrs of Sirmium (c.303)
St Romana of Todi (324) V.
St Florentius of Seville (c.485).
St Zebinus of Syria (5th cent.) H.
*St Dositheus of Gaza (c.530) Mk.
St Felix of Brescia (c.650) Bp.
*St Boswell of Melrose (c.664) Ab.
*St Jurmin (7th cent.).
St Milburga of Wenlock (722) Abs. O.S.B.
*St Medrald of Vendôme (c.850) Ab. O.S.B.

St Lazarus the Painter (c.867) C.
*St Willigis of Mainz (1011) Bp.
*St Ordonius of Sahagún (1066) Bp. O.S.B.
St Peter Damian (1072) Card. Bp. Dr. O.S.B.
*St Milo of Benevento (1076) Bp.
*Bl Nicholas of Prussia (1456) C. O.S.B.

FEBRUARY 24.

St Matthias (1st cent.) Apostle.
SS Montanus, Lucius, Julian, Victoricus, Flavian and Comp. (259) MM.
St Sergius of Cappadocia (304) M.
St Primitiva (?) M.
St Modestus of Trèves (489) Bp.
St Praetextatus of Rouen (586) Bp. M.
St Ethelbert of Kent (616) King.
St Betto of Auxerre (918) Bp. O.S.B.
*Bl Robert of Arbrissel (1117) Ab. O.S.B.
St John Theristus (1129) Mk.
*St Adela (1137) W. Queen.
*Bl Ida of Hohenfels (c.1195) V. O.S.B.
*Bl Mark dei Marconi (1510) C. Hierosolymite.

FEBRUARY 25.

SS Victorinus, Victor, Nicephorus, Claudian, Dioscorus, Serapion and Papias (284) MM.
St Ananias and Comp. (c.298) MM.
SS Donatus, Justus, Herena and Comp. (3rd cent.) MM.
St Caesarius of Nazianzus (369) C.
*St Aldetrudis of Maubeuge (c.696) Abs. O.S.B.
St Walburga of Eichstätt (779) Abs. O.S.B.
St Tarasius of Constantinople (806) Bp.
*St Victor of St Gall (995) C. O.S.B.
*St Gerland of Girgenti (1104) Bp.
*Bl Adelelmus of Engelberg (1131) Ab. O.S.B.
*St Avertanus of Limoges (1380) C. O.C.
*Bl Constantius of Fabriano (1481) C. O.P.
*Bl Sebastian Aparicio (1600) C. O.F.M.
*Bl James Carvalho (1624) M. S.J.

FEBRUARY 26.

SS Papias, Diodorus, Conon and Claudian (c.250) MM.
St Nestor of Perge (251) Bp. M.
*St Dionysius of Augsburg (c.303) Bp. M.
SS Fortunatus, Felix and Comp. (?) MM.
St Alexander of Alexandria (326) Bp.
St Fautinian of Bologna (4th cent.) Bp.
St Andrew of Florence (c.407) Bp.
St Porphyrius of Gaza (420) Bp.
St Quodvultdeus of Carthage (c.450) Bp.
*St Agricola of Nevers (c.594) Bp.
St Victor of Arcis-sur-Aube (7th cent.) H.
*Bl Matilda of Spanheim (1154) V. O.S.B.
*Bl Leo of Saint-Bertin (1163) Ab. O.S.B.
*Bl Isabelle of France (1270) V. Poor Clare.

FEBRUARY 27.

SS Julian, Cronion "Eunus," and Besas (250) MM.
*St Honorina (?) V. M.
SS Alexander, Abundius, Antigonus and Fortunatus (?) MM.
*St Thalelaeus Epilautos (c.450) H.
St Leander of Seville (596) Bp.
St Baldomerus of Lyons (c.650) Mk.
SS Basil and Procopius (c.750) CC.
*St John of Gorze (c.975) Ab. O.S.B.
*Bl Emmanuel of Cremona (1198) Bp.
*BB Mark Barkworth O.S.B. and Anne Linne (1601) MM.
*Bl Augustus Chapdelaine (1856) M.
St Gabriel of Our Lady of Sorrows (1862) C. C.P.

FEBRUARY 28.

SS Macarius, Rufinus, Justus and Theophilus (c.250) MM.
SS Martyrs of Alexandria (261).
SS Caerealis, Populus, Caius and Serapion (?) MM.

*St Proterius of Alexandria (458) Bp. M.
St Romanus of Condat (c.460) Ab.
St Hilarus (468) Pope.
*St Ruellinus of Tréguier (6th cent.) Bp.
*St Llibio (6th cent.) C.
*St Maidoc (?) Bp.
*St Sillan of Bangor (c.610) Ab.
*St Oswald of Worcester (992) Bp. O.S.B.
*Bl Villana de' Botti (1360) Matron, Tert. O.P.
*Bl Hedwig of Lithuania (1399) Queen.
*Bl Antonia of Florence (1472) W. O.F.M.

MARCH 1.

St Eudocia of Heliopolis (c.117) M.
SS Hermes and Adrian (c.290) MM.
*St Luperculus of Tarbes (c.300) Bp. M.
SS Leo, Abundantius, Nicephorus, Donatus and Comp. (?) MM.
St Felix III (492) Pope.
*St David of Wales (5th-6th cent.) Bp.
St Albinus of Angers (c.554) Bp.
*St Marnock of Annandale (c.625) Bp.
St Swithbert of Kaiserswerth (c.713) Bp. O.S.B.
St Siviard of St-Calais (c.729) Ab. O.S.B.
*St Monan of St Andrew's (874) M.
*St Leo of Rouen (c.900) Bp. M.
*St Rudesind of Celanova (977) Bp. O.S.B.
*Bl Roger Le Fort (1367) Bp.
*Bl Bonavita (1375) C. Tert.O.F.M.
*Bl Christopher of Milan (1484) C.O.P.
*Bl Jane Mary Bonomo V. O.S.B.
*Bl Peter Roque (1796) M. C.M.
SS Two hundred and sixty Martyrs in Rome (269).

MARCH 2.

SS Roman Martyrs (219).
SS Jovinus and Basileus (c.258) MM.
SS Paul, Heraclius, Secundilla and Januaria (c.305) MM.
SS Lucius, Absalom and Lorgius (?) MM.

*St Joavan of Leon (c.576) Bp.
*SS Martyrs of Campania (c.579).
*St Fergna the White (637) Ab.
St Chad of Lichfield (673) Bp.
*St Cynibild (7th cent.) C.
*St Slebhene (767) Ab.
*Bl Charles the Good (1127) M.
*Bl Fulk of Neuilly (1201) C.
*Bl Agnes of Bohemia (1282) V. Poor Clare.
*Bl Henry Suso (1365) C. O.P.

MARCH 3.

SS Marinus and Asterius (262) MM.
SS Cleonicus, Eutropius and Basiliscus (c.298) MM.
SS Felix, Luciolus, Fortunatus, Marcia and Comp. (?) MM.
SS Hemiterius and Cheledonius (4th cent.) MM.
*St Camilla of Auxerre (c.437) V.
*St Winwaloë of Landevennec (c.532) Ab.
St Titian of Brescia (c.536) Bp.
*St Calupan of Meallet (575) H.
*St Nonnita (6th cent.) W.
*St Foila of Galway (6th cent.) V.
*St Arthelais of Benevento (6th cent.) V.
*St Owen of Lichfield (680) H. O.S.B.
*St Sacer of Saggard (7th cent.) Ab.
*St Lamalisse of Lamlash (7th cent.) H.
*St Cele-Christ (c.728) Bp.
*St Anselm of Nonantola (803) Ab. O.S.B.
*St Cunegund (1039) Empress, O.S.B.
*St Gervinus of St-Riquier (1075) Ab. O.S.B.
*Bl Serlo of Gloucester (1104) Ab. O.S.B.
*Bl Frederick of Mariengarten (1175) Ab. O.Praem.
*Bl Jacobinus de' Canepaci (1508) C. O.C.

MARCH 4.

St Lucius I (c.254) Pope M.
SS Caius and Comp. (259) MM.
SS Nine hundred Martyrs in Rome (c.260).

SS Archelaus, Cyril and Photius (?) MM.
SS Basil, Eugene, Agathodorus, Elpidius, Aetherius, Capiton, Ephrem, Nestor, and Arcadius (4th cent.) MM.
*St Gistilian of Menevia (6th cent.) C.
*St Basinus of Treves (c.705) Bp. O.S.B.
*SS Adrian and Comp. (c.875) MM.
*St Felix of Rhuis (1038) Ab. O.S.B.
*St Peter Pappacarbone (1123) Bp. O.S.B.
*Bl Humbert of Savoy (1188) C.
*Bl Romeo of Limoges (1310) C. O.C.
*St Casimir of Poland (1483) C.
*Bl Christopher Bales (1590) M.

MARCH 5.

St Theophilus of Caesarea (c.195) Bp.
SS Adrian and Eubulus (308) MM.
SS Eusebius and Comp. (?) MM.
St Phocas of Antioch (c.320) M.
*St Eusebius of Cremona (c.423) Ab.
St Gerasimus (c.475) Ab.
*St Kieran of Ossory (5th cent.) Bp.
*St Colman of Armagh (5th cent.) C.
*St Caron of Tregaron (?) ?Bp.
*St Piran of Padstow (5th or 6th cent.) C.
*St Carthage the Elder (c.540) Bp.
*St Virgilius of Arles (c.610) Bp.
*St Clement of Syracuse (c.800) Ab. O.S.B.
*St Dionysius Fugixima (1622) M. S.J.
St John-Joseph of the Cross (1734) C. O.F.M.

MARCH 6.

St Marcian of Tortona (120) Bp.
SS Perpetua, Felicitas, Saturus, Saturninus, Revocatus and Secundulus (203) M.
St Conon of Mandona (250) M.
SS Victor, Victorinus, Claudian and Bassa (?) MM.
St Basil of Bologna (335) Bp.
St Evagrius of Constantinople (c.380) Bp.

*St Sezin of Guic-Sezni (c.529) Bp.
*St Fridolin of Säckingen (c.650) Ab.
O.S.B.
*SS Kyneburga, Kuneswide and Tibba
(c.680) VV. O.S.B.
*St Baldred of Glasgow (756) Bp.
*St Balther of Tinningham (756) C.
O.S.B.
*St Bilfrid of Lindisfarne (c.758) C.
O.S.B.
*St Chrodegang of Metz (776) Bp.
*St Cadroe of Waulsort (976) Ab. O.S.B.
*Bl Jordan of Pisa (1131) C. O.P.
St Ollegarius of Tarragona (1137) Bp.
O.S.A.
*Bl Helen of Poland (1298) W.
*St Cyril of Constantinople (1235) C.
O.C.
*St Colette (1447) V. Poor Clare.

MARCH 7.

St Eubulus of Caesarea (308) M.
St Paul the Simple (c.339) H.
St Gaudiosus of Brescia (c.445) Bp.
*St Enodoch (c.520).
*St Drausinus of Soissons (c.576) Bp.
*St Deifer of Bodfari (6th cent.) Ab.
*St Easterwine of Wearmouth (688)
Ab. O.S.B.
St Paul of Prusa (840) Bp.
*St Ardo of Aniane (843) Ab. O.S.B.
St Theophylact of Nicomedia (845) Bp.
*Bl Reinhard of Reinhausen (p. 1170)
Ab. O.S.B.
*Bl Volker of Siegburg (1132) M. O.S.B.
Bl Frowin II of Engelberg (1178) Ab.
O.S.B.
St Thomas Aquinas (1274) Dr. O.P.
*BB Jermyn Gardiner, John Larke and
John Ireland (1544) MM.

MARCH 8.

St Pontius of Carthage (c.260) C.
SS Philemon and Apollonius (c.305)
MM.
SS Arianus, Theoticus and Comp.
(c.311) MM.
St Quintilis of Nicomedia (?) Bp. M.
SS Cyril, Rogatus, Felix, another Ro-

gatus, Herenia, Felicitas, Urbanus,
Sylvanus and Mamilius (?) MM.
*St Provinus of Como (c.420) Bp.
*St Rhian (?) Ab.
*St Beoadh (c.525) Bp.
*St Senan (c.560) Bp.
St Felix of Dunwich (648) Bp.
St Julian of Toledo (690) Bp.
*St Humphrey of Prum (871) Bp. O.S.B.
*St Duthac of Ross (1065) Bp.
*St Veremundus of Hirache (1092) Ab.
O.S.B.
*St Ogmund of Holar (1121) Bp.
*St Stephen of Obazine (1154) Ab.
O.S.B.Cist.
*St Vincent Kadlubeck (1223) Bp.
O.S.B.Cist.
St John of God (1550) Founder.

MARCH 9.

SS Cyrion and Candidus (?) MM.
St Pacianus of Barcelona (c.390) Bp.
St Gregory of Nyssa (c.395) Bp.
*St Bosa of York (686) Bp. O.S.B.
*St Antony of Froidemont (10th cent.)
C. O.S.B.
St Frances of Rome (1440) W. O.S.B.
St Catherine of Bologna (1463) V.
Poor Clare.

MARCH 10.

SS Caius and Alexander (c.172) MM.
SS Codratus, Dionysius, Cyprian,
Anectus, Paul and Crescens (c.258)
MM.
SS Forty-two Martyrs of Persia (?).
St Victor (?) M.
SS Forty Armenian Martyrs (320).
St Macarius of Jerusalem (c.353) Bp.
St Simplicius (483) Pope, C.
*St Kessog of Lennox (c.560) Bp.
St Droctoveus of Paris (c.580) Ab.
*St Anastasia the Patrician (6th cent.)
V. H.
St Attalas of Bobbio (627) Ab.
*St Emilian of Lagny (675) Ab. O.S.B.
*St Himelin of Vissenaeken (c.750) C.
*St Failbhe the Little (754) Ab.
*Bl Andrew of Strumi (1097) Ab. O.S.B.
Vall.

*Bl John of Vallumbrosa (c.1380) C.
O.S.B.Vall.
*Bl Peter de Geremia (1452) C. O.P.
*Bl John Ogilvie (1615) M. S.J.

MARCH 11.

SS Candidus, Piperion and Comp.
(c.259) MM.
SS Heraclius and Zosimus (c.263)
MM.
*St Alberta of Agen (c.286) V. M.
SS Gorgonius and Firmus (3rd cent.)
MM.
SS Martyrs of Antioch (c.300).
SS Trophimus and Thalus (c.300)
MM.
St Firminus of Amiens (?) Ab.
St Constantine of Carthage (?) M.
St Constantine of Scotland (576) M.
St Sophronius of Jerusalem (c.369) Bp.
*St Vigilius of Auxerre (685) Bp. M.
St Benedict Crispus (725) Bp.
*St Aengus the Culdee (c.830) Bp.
St Euthimius of Sardis (840) Bp. M.
St Peter the Spaniard (?) C.
St Eulogius of Cordova (859) M.
*St Firmian of Fermo (c.1020) Ab.
O.S.B.
*St Aurea of San Millán (c.1069) V.
O.S.B.
*St Amunia of San Millán (c.1069) W.
O.S.B.
*Bl Christopher Macassoli (1485) C.
O.F.M.
*Bl John Righi (1539) C. O.F.M.
*Bl Teresa Margaret Redi (1770) V.
O.C.D.

MARCH 12.

SS Egdunus and Comp. (303) MM.
St Peter of Nicomedia (303) M.
St Mamilian of Rome (?) M.
*St Paul Aurelian (c.575) Bp.
St Gregory the Great (604) Pope, Dr.
O.S.B.
*St Peter the Deacon (p. 605) C. O.S.B.
*St Mura McFeredach (c.645) Ab.
*St Vindician of Cambrai (712) Bp.
St Theophanes of Mt. Sigriana (818)
Ab.

*St Elphege the Elder (951) Bp. O.S.B.
*Bl Rusticus of Vallumbrosa (1092) Ab.
O.S.B.Vall.
St Bernard of Carinola (1109) Bp.
St Seraphina of San Geminiano (1253)
V.
*Bl Justina Bezzoli (1319) V. O.S.B.
*Bl Dionysius the Carthusian (1471) C.
O.Cart.
*Bl Nicholas Owen (1606) M. S.J.
*Bl Joseph Tshang-Ta-Pong (1815) M.

MARCH 13.

St Sabinus of Egypt (287) M.
SS Theusitas, Horres, Theodora,
Nymphora, Mark and Arabia (?)
MM.
SS Macedonius, Patricia and Modesta
(c.304) MM.
St Christina of Persia (?) V. M.
St Euphrasia of Constantinople (c.420)
V.
SS Ramirus and Comp. (c.630) MM.
*St Mochoemoc of Leamokevoge (c.
656) Ab.
*St Gerald of Mayo (732) Ab.
St Nicephorus of Constantinople (828)
Bp. M.
St Ansovinus of Camerino (840) Bp.
*St Heldrad of Novalese (842) Ab.
O.S.B.
SS Rudericus and Salomon (857) MM.
*Bl Peter II of Cava (1208) Ab. O.S.B.
*Bl Sancha of Cellas (1229) V. O.S.B.
Cist.
*Bl Agnellus of Pisa (1236) C. O.F.M.
*Bl Boniface of Savoy (1270) Bp.
O.Cart.

MARCH 14.

SS Forty-seven Roman Martyrs
(c.67).
St Leo (?) Bp. M.
SS Peter and Aphrodisius (5th cent.)
MM.
SS Martyrs of Valeria (6th cent.).
St Diaconus (6th cent.) M.
St Kyrin (Boniface) (c.630) Bp.
*St Talmach (7th cent.) C.

SS Eutychius and Comp. (741) MM.
St Matilda (968) Queen, W.
*St Paulina of Zell (1107) W. O.S.B.
*Bl Arnold of Padua (1254) M. O.S.B.
*Bl James Capocci (1308) Bp. O.S.A.
*Bl Dominic Jorjes (1619) M.
*Bl Ambrose Fernández (1620) M. S.J.

MARCH 15.

St Longinus the Centurion (1st cent.) M.
St Aristobulus (1st cent.) M.
St Menignus the Dyer (251) M.
St Nicander the Physician (c.304) M.
St Matrona of Thessalonica (c.350) V. M.
St Mancius of Evora (5th cent.) M.
St Speciosus of Terracina (c.555) C. O.S.B.
St Probus of Rieti (c.571) Bp.
St Leocritia of Córdova (859) V. M.
St Sisebutus of Cardeña (1082) Ab. O.S.B.
St Malcodia of Asti (c.1090) H. O.S.B.
St Raymund of Fitero (1163) Ab. O.S.B.Cist.
*Bl William Hart (1583) M.
*St Louise de Marillac (1660) Foundress.
St Clement Mary Hofbauer (1820) C. C.SS.R.

MARCH 16.

SS Hilary, Tatian, Felix, Largus and Denis (c.284) MM.
St Papas of Lycaonia (c.300) M.
St Julian of Anazarbus (c.302) M.
St Abraham Kidunaia (c.366) C.
St Patrick of Auvergne (?) Bp.
St Agapitus of Ravenna (4th cent.) Bp.
*St Abban of Kill-Abban (5th cent.) Ab.
*St Finian Lobhar (c.560) Ab.
*St Eusebia of Hamay (c.680) Abs. O.S.B.
*St Dentlin (7th cent.) C.
*St Megingaud of Würzburg (794) Bp. O.S.B.
*St Gregory Makar (c.1000) Bp.
St Heribert of Cologne (1022) Bp.

*St John Sordi (1183) Bp. M. O.S.B.
*Bl Torello of Poppi (1281) H.
*BB Robert Dalby and John Amias (1589) MM.
*SS John de Brébeuf, Isaac Jogues, Antony Daniel, Gabriel Lalemant, Charles Garnier, Noel Chabanel, John Lalande and René Goupil (1642-49) MM. S.J.

MARCH 17.

St Joseph of Arimathaea (1st cent.) C.
St Ambrose of Alexandria (c.250) C.
SS Alexander and Theodore (?) MM.
SS Martyrs of Seramis (390).
St Patrick of Ireland (c.461) Bp.
St Agricola of Chalon (580) Bp.
St Gertrude of Nivelles (659) Abs. O.S.B.
St Paul of Cyprus (777) M.
*Bl Stephen of Palestrina (1144) Bp. O.S.B.Cist.
*Bl John Sarkander (1620) M.
*Bl Peter Lieou (1834) M.

MARCH 18.

St Alexander of Jerusalem (251) Bp. M.
SS Martyrs of Nicomedia (c.300)
SS Trophimus and Eucarpius (c.304) M.
SS Narcissus and Felix (c.307) MM.
St Cyril of Jerusalem (387) Bp. Dr.
St Frediano of Lucca (588) Bp.
St Egbert of Ripon (c.700) C. O.S.B.
St Edward the Martyr (979) King, M.
St Anselm of Lucca (1086) Bp. O.S.B.
*Bl Christianus of Mellifont (1186) Ab. O.S.B.Cist.
*Bl Fra Angelico (1455) C. O.P.
*St Salvator of Horta (1567) C. O.F.M.

MARCH 19.

St Joseph (1st cent.) Patriarch.
St Pancharius of Nicomedia (303) M.
SS Quintus, Quintilla, Quartilla, Mark and Comp. (?) MM.

SS Apollonius and Leontius (?) Bps.
MM.
St John the Syrian (6th cent.) H.
*St Leontius of Saintes (640) Bp.
*St Adrian of Maestricht (c.668) M.
SS Landoald and Amantius (c.668) CC.
*St Lactan (672) Ab.
*St Alcmund (c.800) M.
*Bl Andrew de' Gallerani (1251) C.
*St Gemus of Moyenmoutier (?) C.
O.S.B.

MARCH 20.

St Archippus of Colossi (1st cent.).
SS Alexandra, Caldia, Euphrasia, Ma-
trona, Juliana, Euphemia, Theodo-
sia, Derphuta and a sister of Der-
phuta (c.300) MM.
SS Photina, Joseph, Victor, Sebastian,
Anatolius, Photius, Photis, Para-
sceve and Cyriaca (?) MM.
SS Paul, Cyril, Eugene and Comp. (?)
MM.
St Urbitius of Metz (c.420) Bp.
St Tetricus of Langres (572) Bp.
*St Martin of Braga (580) Bp.
St Cuthbert of Lindisfarne (687) Bp.
O.S.B.
*St Herbert (687) H. O.S.B.
St Wulfram of Fontenelle (c.703) Bp.
O.S.B.
St Benignus of Flay (725) Ab. O.S.B.
St Nicetas of Bithynia (c.735) Bp.
*Bl Remigius of Strassburg (783) Bp.
O.S.B.
*SS John, Sergius and Comp. (796)
MM.
*St Anastasius of St Sabas (c.797) M.
*St William of Peñacorada (c.1042) H.
O.S.B.
*Bl Eberhard (c.1150) C. O.S.B.Cist.
*BB Evangelist and Peregrinus (c.1250)
CC. O.S.A.
*Bl Ambrose Sassedoni (1287) C. O.P.
*Bl John of Parma (1289) C. O.F.M.
*Bl Maurice Csaky (1336) C. O.P.
*Bl Mark of Montegallo (1497) C.
O.F.M.
*Bl John Baptist Spagnuolo (1516) C.
O.C.
*Bl Hippolytus Galantini (1619) C.

MARCH 21.

St Birillus of Catania (c.90) Bp.
SS Philemon and Domninus (?) MM.
SS Martyrs of Alexandria (342).
St Serapion of Thmuis (c.370) Bp.
St Lupicinus of Lauconne (c.480) Ab.
St Benedict (c.550) Founder O.S.B.
*St Enda of Arranmore (c.590) Ab.
*Bl Clementia of Oehren (1176) W.
O.S.B.
*Bl Santuccia Terrebotti (1305) W.
O.S.B.
*Bl Alphonsus de Rojas (1617) C.
O.F.M.

MARCH 22.

St Epaphroditus (1st cent.) Bp.
SS Callinica and Basilissa (250) MM.
St Paul of Narbonne (p. 250) Bp.
SS Saturninus and Comp. (?) MM.
St Basil of Ancyra (362) M.
St Lea of Rome (384) W.
St Deogratias of Carthage (457) Bp.
SS Octavianus and Comp. (484) MM.
*St Darerca (5th cent.) W.
*St Failbhe of Iona (c.680) Ab.
*St Trien of Killelga (5th cent.) Ab.
St Zachary (752) Pope.
*Bl Isnard de Chiampo (1244) C. O.P.
*Bl Benvenutus Scotivoli (1282) Bp.
O.F.M.
*Bl Hugolinus Zefferini (c.1470) C.
O.S.A.
*Bl Nicholas von Flue (1487) H.

MARCH 23.

SS Nicon and Comp. (c.250) MM.
St Fidelis (?) M.
St Julian (?) M.
St Theodolus of Antioch (?) C.
SS Domitius, Pelagia, Aquila, Epar-
chius and Theodosia (361) MM.
SS Victorian, Frumentius and Comp.
(484) MM.
*St Maidoc of Fiddown (5th cent.) Ab.
SS Felix and Comp. (5th cent.) MM.
St Benedict of Campania (c.550) H.
*St Ethelwald of Lindisfarne (699) H.
O.S.B.

*St Felix of Montecassino (c.1000) C. O.S.B.
*Bl Peter of Gubbio (c.1350) C. O.S.A.
*Bl Sibyllina Biscossi (1367) V. O.P.
St Turibius de Mogrobejo (160) Bp.
St Joseph Oriol (1702) C.

MARCH 24.

St Gabriel the Archangel.
St Latinus of Brescia (115) Bp.
SS Mark and Timothy (c. 150) MM.
St Agapitus of Synnada (3rd cent.) Bp.
St Epigmenius (c.300) M.
SS Timolaus and Comp. (303) MM.
SS Romulus and Secundus (?) MM.
St Seleucus (?) ?
St Pigmenius of Rome (362) M.
*St Domangard of Maghera (c.500) H.
*St Macartin of Clogher (c.505) Bp.
*St Cairlon of Cashel (6th cent.) Bp.
*St Caimin of Lough Derg (7th cent.) Ab.
*St Hildelid of Barking (c.717) Abs. O.S.B.
*St Aldemar the Wise (c.1080) Ab. O.S.B.
*St William of Norwich (1144) M.
*Bl Bertha of Cavriglia (1163) Abs. O.S.B.Vall.
*Bl John del Bastone (1290) C. O.S.B. Sil.
St Catherine of Sweden (1381) Bridg.
St Simeon of Trent (1475) M.
*Bl Didacus of Cádiz (1801) C. O.F.M. Cap.

MARCH 25.

Feast of the Annunciation of Our Lady.
The Good Thief.
St Quirinus of Rome (c.269) M.
St Irenaeus of Sirmium (304) Bp. M.
SS Two hundred and sixty-two Roman Martyrs (?).
St Dula the Slave (?) V. M.
St Pelagius of Laodicea (p. 381) Bp.
*St Humbert of Marolles (c.680) Ab. O.S.B.
St Hermenland of Fontenelle (c.720) Ab. O.S.B.

SS Barontius and Desiderius (c.725) Monks O.S.B.
*St Kennocha (1007) V.
*Bl Herman of Zähringen (1074) C. O.S.B.
*St Harold of Gloucester (1168) M.
*St Robert of Bury St Edmunds (1181) M.
*Bl Thomas of Costacciaro (1337) H. O.S.B.Cam.
*Bl James Bird (1593) M.
*St Lucy Filippini (1732) V.

MARCH 26.

St Castulus of Rome (288) M.
SS Quadratus, Theodosius, Emmanuel and Comp. (c.304) MM.
SS Montanus and Maxima (304) MM.
SS Peter, Marcian, Jovinus, Thecla, Cassian and Comp. (?) MM.
SS Theodore, Irenaeus, Serapion and Armonius (310) MM.
SS Eutychius of Alexandria and Comp. (356) MM.
St Felix of Trèves (c.400) Bp.
*St Sincheall of Killeigh (5th cent.) Ab.
*St Mochelloc of Kilmallock (c.639) ?
St Braulio of Saragossa (646) Bp.
*St Garbhan (7th cent.) Ab.
St Ludger of Utrecht (809) Bp. O.S.B.
*St Bertillo of Dijon (888) C. O.S.B.
*St Felicitas of Padua (9th cent.) V.
*St Basil the Younger (952) H.
*St Alfwold of Sherborne (1058) Bp. O.S.B.
*Bl Melior of Vallumbrosa (1198) H. O.S.B.Vall.
*Bl Peter Maginet (1435) C. O.S.B.Cist.

MARCH 27.

SS Philetas, Lydia, Macedo, Theoprepius, Amphilochius and Chronidas (c.121) MM.
St Alexander (3rd cent.) M.
*St Amator of Guarda (?) C.
SS Zanitas, Lazarus, Marotas, Narses and Comp. (344) MM.
St John of Lycopolis (394) H.
*St Augusta of Treviso (?) V. M.

St Rupert of Salzburg (c.720) Bp. O.S.B.

*St Romulus of Nimes (c.730) Ab. O.S.B.

St John Damascene (c.749) C. Dr.

*St Suairlech of Fore (c.750) Bp.

*St Alkeld (10th cent.) V.

*St Matthew of Beauvais (c.1098) M.

*St Gelasius of Armagh (1174) Bp.

*Bl William Tempier (1197) Bp.

MARCH 28.

SS Priscus, Malchus and Alexander (260) MM.

SS Rogatus, Successus and Comp. (?) MM.

SS Castor and Dorotheus (?) MM.

St Spes of Campi (c.513) Ab.

St Gunthrammus (592) King.

St Gundelindis of Niedermunster (c.750) V. O.S.B.

*St Tutilo of St Gall (c.915) C. O.S.B.

*St Osburga of Coventry (c.1016) Abs. O.S.B.

*St Conon of Nesi (1236) Ab.

St John of Capistrano (1456) C. O.F.M.

MARCH 29.

St Secundus of Asti (119) M.

SS Pastor, Victorinus and Comp. (c.311) MM.

SS Jonas, Barachisius and Comp. (327) MM.

*St Mark of Arethusa (c.362) Bp. M.

St Cyril of Heliopolis (c.362) M.

SS Armogastes and Comp. (p.460) MM.

*St Gladys (5th cent.) W.

*St Gundleus (c.500) H.

*St Lasar (6th cent.) V.

*St Firminus of Viviers (6th cent.) Bp.

St Eustace of Luxeuil (625) Ab.

*Bl Diemut of Wessobrunn (c.1130) H. O.S.B.

*St Berthold of Mt Carmel (c.1195) C. Foundress O.C.

*Bl Hough of Vaucelles (1239) C. O.S.B. Cist.

*St Ludolphus of Ratzeburg (1250) Bp. O.Praem.

*Bl Jane Mary de Maillé (1414) V. Tert.O.F.M.

MARCH 30.

St Quirinus the Jailer (c.117) M.

St Regulus of Senlis (c.260) Bp.

SS Domninus, Victor and Comp. (?) MM.

*St Mamertinus of Auxerre (c.462) Bp.

*St Regulus of Scotland (4th cent.) Ab.

St Pastor of Orleans (6th cent.) Bp.

*St Fergus of Downpatrick (6th cent.) Bp.

St John Climacus (605) Ab.

St Zosimus of Syracuse (c.660) Bp.

*St Tola (c.733) Bp.

*St Patto of Werden (c.788) Bp. O.S.B.

*St Forannan of Waulsort (982) Bp. O.S.B.

St Clinius of Pontecorvo (?) Ab. O.S.B.

*Bl Joachim of Fiore (1202) Ab. O.S.B. Cist.

*Bl Dodo of Asch (1231) H.

*Bl Moricus (1236) C.

St Peter Regalado (1456) C. O.F.M.

*Bl Amadeus IX of Savoy (1472) C.

MARCH 31.

St Amos (8th cent. B.C.) Prophet.

St Balbina of Rome (c.130) V.

*St Acacius Agathangelos (c.251) Bp.

SS Theodulus, Anesius, Felix, Cornelia and Comp. (?) MM.

St Benjamin the Deacon (c.421) M.

*St Aldo of Hasnon (end 8th cent.) C. O.S.B.

*St Guy of Pomposa (1046) Ab. O.S.B.

*Bl Guy of Vicogne (1147) C. O.Praem.

*St Machabeo of Armagh (1174) Ab.

*Bl Jane of Toulouse (1286) Tert.O.C.

*St Daniel of Murano (1411) H. O.S.B. Cam.

*Bl Mary Mamala (1453) W. Poor Clare.

*Bl Bonaventure Tornielli (1491) C. Servite.

APRIL 1.

St Theodora of Rome (132) M.
*St Melito of Sardis (c.180) Bp.
St Venantius of Spalato (c.255) Bp. M.
SS Victor and Stephen (?) MM.
SS Quintian and Irenaeus (?) MM.
St Walericus of Leucone (c.622) Ab.
*St Dodolinus of Vienne (7th cent.) Bp.
*SS Caidoc and Fricor (7th cent.) HH.
St Macarius the Wonder-Worker (830) Ab.
*St Cellach of Armagh (9th cent.) Bp.
St Cellagh II of Armagh (1129) Bp.
St Hugh of Grenoble (1132) Bp. O.S.B.
*St Hugh of Bonnevaux (1194) Ab. O.S.B.Cist.
*Bl Nicholas of Neti (c.1220) C. O.S.B. Cist.
*Bl Gerard of Sassoferrato (1367) C. O.S.B.Cam.
*St Catherine Tomás (1574) V. O.S.A.

APRIL 2.

St Amphianus of Lycia (c.305) M.
St Theodosia of Tyre (308) V. M.
St Urban of Langres (c.390) Bp.
St Abundius of Como (469) Bp.
St Mary of Egypt (c.500) H.
*St Bronach of Glen-Seichis (?) V.
St Nicetius of Lyons (573) Bp.
St Constantine II of Scotland (874) King M.
*Bl Drogo of Baume (10th cent.) C. O.S.B.
*Bl Meingosus of Weingarten (c.1200) Ab. O.S.B.
St Francis of Paola (1507) Founder.
*Bl John Payne (1582) M.
*Bl Margaret Clitherow (1586) M.
*Bl Leopold of Gaiche (1815) C. O.F.M.
*Bl Dominic Tuoc (1839) M.

APRIL 3.

St Pancras of Taormina (1st cent.) M.
St Sixtus I (127) Pope, M.
SS Agape, Chionia and Irene (304) VV. MM.
St Vulpian of Tyre (c.304) M.
SS Evagrius and Benignus (?) MM.
St Nicetas of Medikion (824) Ab.

St Burgundofara (657) Abs. O.S.B.
*St Attala of Taormina (c.800) Ab. O.S.B.
St Richard of Chichester (1253) Bp.
*Bl Gandulphus of Binasco (1260) C. O.F.M.
*Bl John of Penna (1271) C. O.F.M.
*Bl Alexandrina di Letto (1458) Poor Clare.

APRIL 4.

SS Agathopedes and Theodulus (303) MM.
St Zosimus of Palestine (5th cent.) H.
*St Tigernach of Clogher (549) Bp.
*St Gwerir of Liskeard (?) H.
St Isidore of Seville (636) Bp., Dr.
*St Hildebert of Ghent (752) C. O.S.B.
St Plato of Sakkudion (813) Ab.
*Bl Aleth of Dijon (1105) W.
*St Peter of Poitiers (1115) Bp.
*Bl Henry of Gheest (c.1190) O.S.B. Cist.
St Benedict the Moor (1589) C. O.F.M.

APRIL 5.

St Irene (304) V. M.
SS Martyrs of Lesbos (?).
St Zeno (?) M.
SS Martyrs of Africa (459)
*SS Probus and Grace (?).
*St Becan of Kill-Beggan (6th cent.) Ab.
*St Ethelburga of Lyminge (c.647) Abs. O.S.B.
*St Gerald of Sauve-Majeure (1095) Ab. O.S.B.
*St Albert of Montecorvino (1127) Bp.
*Bl Sighardus of Bonlieu (1162) Ab. O.S.B.Cist.
St Vincent Ferrer (1418) C. O.P.
*Bl Peter Cerdán (1422) C. O.P.
*Bl Blaise of Auvergne (14th cent.) C. O.P.
*Bl Antony Fuster (14th cent.) C. O.P.
*Bl Crescentia Höss (1744) V. Tert. O.F.M.

APRIL 6.

St Platonis and Comp. (c.308)MM.
SS Timothy and Diogenes (c.345) MM.

St Marcellinus of Carthage (413) M.
*St Ulched (?) C.
St Amandus of Bergamo (515) C.
*St Eutychius of Constantinople (582) Bp.
*St Winebald of Troyes (c.650) Ab. O.S.B.
*St Gennard of Flay (720) Ab. O.S.B.
*St Berthanc of Kirkwall (c.840) Bp.
*St Prudentius Galindo (861) Bp.
*St Notker Balbulus (912) C. O.S.B.
*St Urban of Peñalba (c.940) Ab. O.S.B.
*St Elstan of Winchester (981) Bp. O.S.B.
St William of Eskilsoe (1203) C. O.S.A.
Bl Juliana of Cornillon (1258) V. O.S.A.
*Bl Catherine of Pallanza (1478) V. O.S.A.
*Bl Paul Tinh (1857) M.

APRIL 7.

St Hegesippus (c.180) C.
St Calliopus (c.303) M.
*Bl Christian of Douai (?) C.
SS Epiphanius, Donatus, Rufinus and Comp. (?) MM.
SS Cyriacus and Comp. (?) MM.
*St Pelagius of Alexandria (?) M.
St Peleusius of Alexandria (?) M.
St Saturninus of Verona (c.356) Bp.
St Aphraates of Antioch (4th cent.) H.
*St Brynach (?5th cent.) C.
*St Villicus of Metz (568) Bp.
*SS Llewellyn and Gwrnerth (6th cent.) CC.
*St Goran (6th cent.) C.
*St Finan of Kinnitty (6th cent.) Ab.
*St George the Younger (c.816) Bp.
*St Gibardus of Luxeuil (c.888) Ab. O.S.B.
*Bl Eberhard of Schäffhausen (1078) Mk. O.S.B.
*St Aybert of Crépin (1140) C. O.S.B.
*Bl Herman Joseph (1241) C. O.Praem.
*Bl Ursulina of Bologna (1410) V.
*Bl William Cufitella (1411) H. Tert. O.F.M.
*BB Henry Walpole, S.J., and Alexander Rawlins (1595) MM.
*BB Edward Oldcorne and Ralph Ashley (1606) MM. S.J.

APRIL 8.

SS Herodion, Asyncritus and Phlegon (1st cent.) MM.
St Dionysius of Corinth (c.180) Bp.
St Concessa of Carthage (?) M.
SS Januarius, Maxima and Macaria (?) MM.
St Aedesius of Alexandria (c.306) M.
St Amantius of Como (440) Bp.
St Perpetuus of Tours (c.490) Bp.
St Redemptus of Ferentino (586) Bp.
*St Walter of Pontoise (1099) Ab. O.S.B.
*Bl Clement of St Elpidio (1291) C. O.S.A.
*Bl Julian of St Augustine (1606) C. O.F.M.
*Bl Julia Billiart (1816) V. Foundress.

APRIL 9.

St Mary Cleophas (1st cent.).
St Prochorus of Nicomedia (1st cent.) Bp. M.
SS Martyrs of Pannonia (?).
SS Demetrius, Concessus, Hilary and Comp. (?) MM.
SS Hermogenes, Caius, Expeditus, Aristonicus, Rufus and Galata (?) MM.
SS Martyrs of Sirmium (c.303).
St Eupsychius of Caesarea (362) M.
St Acacius of Amida (p. 421) Bp.
St Marcellus of Avignon (474) Bp.
*St Madrun (5th cent.) W.
*St Dotto (6th cent.) Ab.
St Waldetrudis of Mons (c.688) W. Abs. O.S.B.
St Hugh of Rouen (730) Bp. O.S.B.
*St Theodore and Comp. (c.870) MM. O.S.B.
*St Hedda and Comp. (c.870) MM. O.S.B.
*St Casilda of Briviesca (c.1050) V.
*St Gaucherius of Aureil (1140) Ab. O.S.A.
*Bl Ubald Adimari (1315) C. O.S.M.
*BB Thomas of Tolentino and Comp. (1321) MM. O.F.M.
*Bl John of Vespignano (1331) C.

*Bl Reginald Montemarti (1348) C.
O.P.
*Bl Antony Pavoni (1374) M. O.P.

APRIL 10.

St Ezechiel (6th cent. B.C.) Prophet.
SS Martyrs of Rome (c.115)
SS Terence, Africanus, Pompeius and
Comp. (250) MM.
St Apollonius of Alexandria (?) M.
*St Bademus of Perisa (c.380) Ab. M.
*St Palladius of Auxerre (661) Bp.
*SS Beocca, Ethor and Comp. (c.870)
MM. O.S.B.
*St Bede the Younger (883) Mk. O.S.B.
St Macarius of Antioch (1012) C.
*St Fulbert of Chartres (1029) Bp.
*St Paternus of Abdinghof (1058) H.
O.S.B.
*St Malchus of Waterford (1110) Bp.
O.S.B.
*Bl Mark Fantucci (1479) C. O.F.M.
*Bl Antony Neyrot (1460) M. O.P.
St Michael of the Saints (1625) C.
O.Trin.

APRIL 11.

St Antipas of Pergamus (c.90) Bp. M.
St Philip of Gortyna (c.180) Bp.
St Eustorgius of Nicomedia (c.300) M.
SS Domnio and Comp. (?) MM.
St Leo I the Great (461) Pope and Dr.
*St Machai of Bute (5th cent.) Ab.
*St Aid of Achad-Finglas (?) Ab.
St Bassanuphius of Gaza (c.540) H.
St Isaac of Monteluco (c.550) H.
*St Maedhog-Aedhan (6th cent.) Ab.
*St Agericus of Tours (c.680) Ab.
O.S.B.
St Godeberta of Noyon (c.700) Abs.
*Bl Waltmann of Cambrai (1138) Ab.
O.Praem.
*BB Stephen and Hildebrand (1209)
MM. O.S.B.Cist.
*Bl Raynerius Inclusus (1237) H.
*Bl John of Cuppramontana (1303) C.
O.S.B.Cam.
*Bl George Gervase (1608) M. O.S.B.
*St Gemma Galgani (1903) V.

APRIL 12.

St Vissia of Fermo (c.250) V. M.
St Victor of Braga (c.300) M.
St Julius I (352) Pope.
St Zeno of Verona (371) Bp.
SS Sabas and Comp. (372) MM.
St Constantine of Gap (529) Bp.
*St Wigbert of Friesland (690) C.
*St Tetricus of Auxerre (707) Bp. M.
O.S.B.
St Damian of Pavia (710) Bp.
*St Guthlac of Croyland (714) H. O.S.B.
*St Erkemboden of Thérouanne (714)
Bp. O.S.B.
*St Alferius of Cava (1050) Ab. O.S.B.
*Bl Peter of Montepiano (1098) C.
O.S.B.Vall.
*Bl Meinhard of Yxkill (1196) Bp.
O.S.A.
*Bl Andrew of Montereale (1480) C.
O.S.A.
*Bl Angelus Carletti (1495) C. O.F.M.

APRIL 13.

SS Carpus, Papylus, Agathonica, Aga-
thodorus and Comp. (150 or 250)
MM.
SS Maximus, Dadas and Quintilianus
(303) MM.
St Ursus of Ravenna (396) Bp.
St Hermenegild (583) King, M.
St Guinoc of Scotland (c.838) Bp.
*Bl Ida of Boulogne (1113) W.
*St Caradoc of Llandaff (1124) Ab.
*Bl Ida of Louvain (c.1300) V. O.S.B.
Cist.
*Bl Margaret of Città di Castello (1320)
V.
*Bl James of Certaldo (1392) C. O.S.B.
Cam.
*BB John Lockwood and Edward Ca-
therick (1642) MM.

APRIL 14.

St Justin the Philosopher (c.165) M.
SS Tiburtius, Valerian and Maximus
(c.190) MM.
St Fronto of Nitria (2nd cent.) H.
SS Domnina and Another (?) VV.
MM.

St Ardalion the Actor (c.300) M.
St Proculus of Terni (310) Bp. M.
St Thomais of Alexandria (476) M.
*St Tassach of Raholp (c.495) Bp.
St Abundius the Sacristan (c.564) C.
St Lambert of Lyons (688) Bp. O.S.B.
*St Bernard of Thiron (1117) Ab.
O.S.B.
*Bl Lanuinus of Torre (1120) C. O.Cart.
*St Benedict the Bridge-Builder (1184)
C.
*Bl Conrad of Hildesheim (c.1235) C.
O.F.M.
*Bl Ralph of Sisteron (1241) Bp. O.S.B.
Cist.
*St Peter González (1246) C. O.P.
*SS Antony, John and Eustace (1342)
MM.
*Bl Lydwina of Schiedam (1433) V.

APRIL 15.

SS Basilissa and Anastasia (c.62) MM.
SS Maro, Eutyches and Victorinus
(c.99) MM.
SS Theodore and Pausilippus (c.130)
MM.
SS Maximus and Olympiades (251)
MM.
St Crescens of Myra (?) M.
St Eutychius of Ferentino (?) M.
*Bl Laurentinus Sossius (485) M.
*St Paternus of Vannes (c.500) Bp.
*St Ruadan of Lothra (584) Ab.
*St Silvester of Réome (c.625) Ab.
*St Hunna of Alsace (679) W.
*Bl Nidger of Augsburg (c.829) Bp.
O.S.B.
*St Mundus of Argyle (c.962) Ab.

APRIL 16.

SS Callistus, Charisius and Comp. (?)
MM.
SS Eighteen Martyrs of Saragossa
(c.304).
SS Caius and Crementius (304) MM.
St Encratia of Saragossa (c.304) V. M.
St Turibius of Astorga (c.460) Bp.
*St Vasius of Saintes (c.500) M.
*St Turibius of Palencia (c.528) Ab.

*St Paternus of Wales (5th cent.) C.
St Paternus of Avranches (c.574) Bp.
St Paternus of Coutances (c.574) Bp.
M.
St Fructuosus of Braga (665) Ab. Bp.
St Lambert of Saragossa (c.900) M.
*Bl Elias of Cologne (1042) Ab. O.S.B.
*St Magnus (1116) M.
St Drogo of Sebourg (1186) H.
*St Contardo of Este (1249) C.
*Bl Joachim Piccolomini (1305) C.
O.S.M.
*Bl William Gnoffi (c.1317) H.
*Bl Archangelus Canetuli (1513) C.
O.S.A.
St Benedict Joseph Labre (1783) C.
*St Bernardette Soubirous (1879) V.

APRIL 17.

St Anicetus (160) Pope M.
SS Mappalicus and Comp. (250) MM.
SS Fortunatus and Marcian (?) MM.
SS Peter and Hermogenes (?) MM.
St Innocent of Tortona (c.350) Bp.
St Pantagathus of Vienne (540) Bp.
SS Donnan and Comp. (c.616) MM.
*St Landericus of Soignies (c.730) Bp.
O.S.B.
*St Wando of Fontenelle (c.756) Ab.
O.S.B.
SS Elias Paul and Isidore (856) MM.
St Robert of Chaise-Dieu (1067) Ab.
O.S.B.
*Bl Gervinus of Oudenburg (1117) Ab.
O.S.B.
St Stephen Harding (1134) Ab. O.S.B.
Cist.
*Bl Eberhard of Marchtal (1178) C. O.
Praem.
*Bl James of Cerqueto (1367) C. O.S.A.
*Bl Clare Gambacorta (1419) W. O.P.

APRIL 18.

SS Eleutherius and Anthia (c.117)
MM.
St Corebus of Messina (c.117) M.
St Apollonius the Apologist (c.190) M.
St Calocerus of Brescia (?) M.
*SS Bitheus and Genocus (6th cent.)
CC.

*St Laserian of Leighlin (639) Bp.
*St Agia of Mons (c.714) W. O.S.B.
*St Wicterp of Augsburg (749) Bp.
*St Cogitosus of Kildare (8th cent.) C.
St Perfectus of Córdova (851) M.
*St Gebuinus of Lyons (1080) Bp.
*Bl Idesbald of Dunes (1167) Ab.
O.S.B.Cist.
St Galdinus of Milan (1176) Bp.
*Bl Andrew Hibernón (1602) C. O.F.M.
*Bl Mary of the Incarnation (1618) W.
O.C.D.

APRIL 19.

St Timon the Deacon (1st cent.) M.
SS Socrates and Dionysius (275) MM.
St Vincent of Collioure (c.304) M.
St Paphnutius of Jerusalem (?) M.
St Crescentius of Florence (c.396) C.
St Ursmar of Lobbes (713) Bp. O.S.B.
St George of Antioch (814) Bp. M.
*St Gerold of Einsiedeln (978) H.
O.S.B.
St Elphege the Martyr (1012) Bp.
O.S.B.
St Leo IX (1054) Pope.
*Bl Burchard of Bellevaux Ab. O.S.B.
Cist.
*Bl Bernard the Penitent (1182) Mk.
O.S.B.
*St Wernher (1275) M.
*Bl Conrad Miliani of Ascoli (1289) C.
O.F.M.
*Bl James of Oldo (1404) C. Tert.
O.F.M.
*Bl James Duckett (1602) M.

APRIL 20.

*The Seven Angels who stand before
the throne of God: Michael, Ga-
briel, Raphael, Shealtiel, Uriel,
Jehudiel and Berachiel.
SS Sulpicius and Servilian (c.117)
MM.
SS Victor, Zoticus, Zeno, Acindynus,
Caesareus, Severian, Chrysophorus,
Theonas and Antoninus (c.303) MM.
St Theodore Trichinas (p. 330) H.
SS Marcellinus, Vincent and Dom-
ninus (c.374) CC.

St Theotimus of Tomi (407) Bp.
St Marcian of Auxerre (c.470) C.
*St Ceadwalla (689) King.
*Bl Harduin of Fontenelle (811) Mk.
O.S.B.
*St Hugh of Anzy-le-Duc (c.930) C.
O.S.B.
*Bl Hildegund, or Joseph (1188) V.
O.S.B.Cist.
*Bl Oda of Rivroelles (1158) V.
O.Praem.
*Bl Dominic Vernagalli (1218) C.
O.S.B.Cam.
*Bl John of Grace-Dieu (1280) Ab.
O.S.B.Cist.
St Agnes of Montepulciano (1317) V.
O.P.
*Bl Simon Rinalducci (1322) C. O.S.A.
*BB James Bell and John Finch (1584)
MM.
*BB Francis Page S.J. and Robert Wat-
kinson (1602) MM.
*Bl Margaret of Amelia (1666) V.
O.S.B.

APRIL 21.

SS Apollo, Isacius and Crotates (c.302)
MM.
SS Arator, Fortunatus, Felix, Silvius,
and Vitalis (?) MM.
SS Simeon, Abdechalas, Ananias, Us-
thazanes, Pusicius and Comp. (341)
MM.
*St Cyprian of Brescia (582) Bp.
*St Anastasius I of Antioch (599)
Patriarch.
*St Beuno of Wales (c.630) Ab.
St Anastasius the Sinaite (c.678) C.
*St Frodulphus of Barjon (c.750) H.
O.S.B.
St Anselm of Canterbury (1109) Abp.
Dr. O.S.B.
*Bl Walter of Mondsee (1158) Ab.
O.S.B.
*Bl Fastred of Cambron (1163) Ab.
O.S.B.Cist.
*Bl Bartholomew of Cervere (1466) M.
O.P.
*St Conrad of Parzham (1894) C.
O.F.M.Cap.

APRIL 22.

St Soter (174) Pope.
SS Epipodius and Alexander (178)
  MM.
St Leonidas of Alexandria (202) M.
SS Parmenius and Comp. (c.250) MM.
St Caius (c.296) Pope M.
SS Azadanes and Azades (342) MM.
SS Mareas and Comp. (342) MM.
*St Abrosimus of Persia (342) M.
St Tarbula of Persia (345) V. M.
St Acepsimas of Hnaita (376) Bp.
  M.
St Abdiesus the Deacon (4th cent.) M.
St Aithalas of Persia (4th cent.) M.
St Leo of Sens (541) Bp.
*St Rufus of Glendalough (?) H.
St Theodore of Sikion (613) Bp.
*SS Arwald and Arwald (686) MM.
*St Opportuna of Montreuil (c.770) Abs.
  O.S.B.
*St Senorina of Basto (982) V. O.S.B.
*Bl Wolfhelm of Brauweiler (1091) Ab.
  O.S.B.
*Bl Francis Venimbene of Fabriano
  (1322) C. O.F.M.

APRIL 23.

SS Felix, Fortunatus and Achilleus
  (212) MM.
St George the Great (c.300) M.
St Marolus of Milan (423) Bp.
*St Iberius of Meath (5th cent.) C.
St Gerald of Toul (994) Bp.
St Adalbert of Prague (997) Abp. M.
  O.S.B.
*Bl Gerard of Orchimont (1138) Ab.
  O.S.B.
*Bl Giles of Assisi (1262) C. O.F.M.
*Bl Giles of Saumur (1266) Bp.
*Bl Helen Valentini (1458) W.

APRIL 24.

SS Alexander and Comp. (177) MM.
SS Sabas and Comp. (272) MM.
SS Eusebius, Neon, Leontius, Longi-
  nus and Comp. (?) MM.
St Gregory of Elvira (c.400) Bp.

*St Dyfnan (5th cent.) C.
*St Deodatus of Blois (c.525) Ab.
St Honorius of Brescia (c.586) Bp.
*St Ivo of Huntingdonshire (?) Bp. H.
*St Musa of Rome (6th cent.) V.
St Mellitus of Canterbury (624) Bp.
  O.S.B.
SS Bova and Doda (c.680) VV. O.S.B.
*St Authaire of La Ferté (7th cent.) C.
St Egbert of Rathelmigisi (729) C.
  O.S.B.
*Bl Corona of Elche (?) V. O.S.B.
*St William Firmatus (1103) H.
*Bl Francis Colmenario (1590) C.
*St Fidelis of Sigmaringen (1622) M.
  O.F.M.Cap.
*St Euphrasia Pelletier (1868) V.
  Foundress.

APRIL 25.

St Mark the Evangelist (75).
St Anianus of Alexandria (1st cent.)
  Bp.
SS Philo and Agathopodes (c.150).
SS Evodius, Hermogenes and Cal-
  listus (?) MM.
*St Phebadius of Agen (c.392) Bp.
St Stephen of Antioch (481) Bp. M.
*St Macaille of Croghan (c.489) Bp.
St Erminus of Lobbes (737) Bp. O.S.B.
*St Mella of Doire-Melle (c.780) W.
  Abs.
*St Heribaldus of Auxerre (c.857) Bp.
  O.S.B.
*St Robert of Syracuse (c.1000) Ab.
  O.S.B.
*Bl Boniface of Valperga (1243) Bp.
*BB Robert Anderton and William
  Marsden (1586) MM.

APRIL 26.

St Cletus (c.91) Pope, M.
St Peter of Braga (?) Bp. M.
St Marcellinus (304) Pope, M.
St Lucidius of Verona (?) Bp.
St Exuperantia of Troyes (?) V.
St Basileus of Amasea (319) Bp. M.
St Clarentius of Vienne (c.620) Bp.
*St Trudpert of Munstethal (c.644) Ab.

St Richarius of Centula (c.645) Ab.
*St Paschasius Radbert (c.851) Ab. O.S.B.
*Bl John of Valence (1146) Bp. O.S.B. Cist.
*St Franca Visalta (1218) Abs. O.S.B. Cist.
*SS Dominic and Gregory (1300) CC. O.P.
*Bl Alda of Siena (1309) W. O.S.B.Vall.

APRIL 27.

St Anthimus of Nicomedia (303) Bp. M.
SS Castor and Stephen (?) MM.
St Theodore of Tabenna (c.368) Ab.
*St Liberalis of Ancona (c.400) C.
St Theophilus of Brescia (p. 427) Bp.
St Tertullian of Bologna (c.490) Bp.
*St Asicus of Elphin (c.490) Bp.
*St Enoder (6th cent.) Ab.
*St Winebald of Beverley (c.731) Ab. O.S.B.
*St Floribert of Liége (746) Bp.
St John of Constantinople (813) Ab.
*St Adelelmus of Flanders (1152) H.
St Zita of Lucca (1278) V.
St Peter Armengol (1304) M.
*Bl Antony de' Patrizi (1311) C. O.S.A.
*Bl James of Bitetto (c.1485) C. O.F.M.
*Bl Hosanna of Cattaro (1565) V. Tert.O.P.
St Peter Canisius (1597) C. Dr. S.J.
*Bl Mariana of Jesus (1624) V. O.Merc.
*Bl Laurence Hung (1856) M.

APRIL 28.

St Mark of Galilee (92) Bp. M.
SS Aphrodisius, Caralippus, Agapitus and Eusebius (1st cent.) MM.
St Vitalis of Milan (?1st cent.) M.
St Valeria of Milan (?1st cent.) M.
SS Patrick, Acatius, Menander and Polyenus (?) MM.
St Pollio of Pannonia (c.304) M.
SS Theodora V and Didymus (304) MM.
*St Artemius of Sens (609) Bp.
*St Cronan of Roscrea (c.626) Ab.

St Pamphilus of Sulmona (c.700) Bp.
St Prudentius of Tarazona (p. 700) Bp.
*St Gerard the Pilgrim (?) C.
*Bl Adalbero of Augsburg (909) Bp. O.S.B.
*Bl Gerard of Bourgogne (1172) Ab. O.S.B.Cist.
*Bl Luchesius of Umbria (1260) C.
*Bl Louis Mary Grignon de Montfort (1716) C.
St Paul of the Cross (1775) C. Founder.
*BB Paul Khoan, Peter Hieu and John Baptist Thauh (1840) MM.
*Bl Peter Chanel (1889) M.

APRIL 29.

St Torpes of Pisa (c.65) M.
SS Martyrs of Corfu (1st cent.).
St Tychicus of Paphos (1st cent.) Bp.
SS Agapius and Comp. (c.259) MM.
St Severus of Naples (409) Bp.
*St Dichu of Ulster (5th cent.) C.
St Paulinus of Brescia (c.545) Bp.
*St Senan of North Wales (7th cent.) H.
*St Fiachan of Lismore (7th cent.) C.
*St Wilfrid the Younger (744) Bp. O.S.B.
*St Gundebert (8th cent.) M.
*St Ava of Dinant (p. 845) Abs. O.S.B.
*St Daniel of Gerona (9th cent.) M.
St Hugh the Great of Cluny (1109) Ab. O.S.B.
St Robert of Molesmes (1110) Ab. O.S.B.Cist.
*Bl Theoger of Metz (1120) Bp. O.S.B.
*Bl Robert of Bruges (1157) Ab. O.S.B. Cist.
St Peter Martyr (1252) O.P.

APRIL 30.

St Eutropius of Saintes (?) Bp. M.
SS Aphrodisius and Comp. (?) MM.
St Sophia of Fermo (c.250) V. M.
St Maximus of Ephesus (c.251) M.
SS Marianus, James and Comp. (259) MM.
SS Laurence of Novara and Comp. (c.397) MM.
St Donatus of Euraea (late 4th cent.) Bp.

St Pomponius of Naples (536) Bp.
*St Desideratus of Gourdon (c.569) H.
*St Cynwl of Wales (6th cent.) H.
St Erconwald of London (c.686) Bp.
O.S.B.
*St Hildegard (783) Empress.
*St Swithbert the Younger (807) Bp.
SS Amator, Peter and Louis (855)
MM.
*St Genistus of Beaulieu (c.1100) M.
O.S.B.
*St Adjutor of Vernon (1131) H. O.S.B.
*St Aimo of Savigny (1173) C. O.S.B.
St Catherine of Siena (1380) V. Tert.
O.P.
*St Louis von Bruck (1429) M.
*BB Francis Dickenson and Miles Ge-
rard (1590) MM.
*Bl Benedict of Urbino (1625) C.
O.F.M.Cap.
*St Joseph Benedict-Cottolengo (1842)
C.

MAY 1.

St Jeremias (c.590 B.C.) Prophet.
SS Philip (c.80) and James the Less
(c.62), Apostles.
St. Andeolus of Smyrna (208) M.
SS Orentius and Patientia (c.240)
MM.
*SS Acius and Aceolus (c.303) MM.
*St Isidora of Egypt (c.365) V.
St Grata of Bergamo (4th or 8th cent.)
W.
St Amator of Auxerre (418) Bp.
St Orentius of Auch (c.439) Bp.
*St Brieuc (c.510) Bp.
St Sigismund of Burgundy (523) King
M.
*St Marculfus of Nanteuil (558) Ab.
*St Ceallach of Killala (6th cent.) Bp.
M.
St Asaph of Wales (c.600) Bp.
*St Bertha of Avenay (p. 680) Abs.
M. O.S.B.
*St Kevoca of Kyle (7th cent.) V.
*St Evermarus of Tongres (c.700) M.
*St Theodard of Narbonne (893) Bp.
O.S.B.
*St Aldebrandus of Fossombrone
(1219) Bp.

St Peregrinus Laziosi (1345) C. O.S.M.
*St Panacea of Quarona (1383) V.
*BB Augustine Schoffler and John-
Louis Bonnard (1851) MM.

MAY 2

SS Exuperius, Zoe, Cyriacus and The-
odulus (140) MM.
*St Felix of Seville (?) M.
SS Saturninus, Neopolus, Germanus
and Celestine (304) MM.
*St Valentine of Genoa (c.307) Bp.
St Athanasius of Alexandria (373) Bp.
Dr.
*St Germanus of Normandy (c.460) Bp.
M.
SS Vindemialis, Eugene and Longinus
(c.485) MM.
*St Neachtain (5th cent.) C.
*St Gluvias (6th cent.) C.
*St Waldebert of Luxeuil (c.668) Ab.
O.S.B.
*St Ultan of Peronne (c.686) Ab. O.S.B.
*St Bertinus the Younger (c.699) C.
O.S.B.
*St Wiborada of St Gall (925) M.
O.S.B.
*Bl Conrad of Seldenburen (1126) M.
O.S.B.
*St Mafalda of Portugal (1252) Queen,
O.S.B.Cist.
*Bl Joseph Luu (1854) M.

MAY 3.

St Alexander I (c.113) Pope.
SS Alexander, Eventius and Theodulus
(c.113) MM.
SS Timothy and Maura (298) MM.
SS Alexander and Antonina (313).
MM.
St Juvenal of Narni (369) Bp.
SS Diodorus and Rhodopianus (early
5th cent.) MM.
*St Conleth of Kildare (c.519) Bp.
*St Scannal (p. 563) C.
*St Adalsindis of Bèze (c.680) Abs.
*St Philip of Zell (c.770) H. O.S.B.
*St Ethelwin of Lindsey (8th cent.) Bp.
*St Ansfridus of Utrecht (1010) Bp.
O.S.B.

*Bl Ventura Spellucci (12th cent.) Abs.
O.S.B.
*Bl Alexander of Foigny (1229) C.
O.S.B.Cist.
*Bl Alexander Vincioli (1363) Bp.
O.F.M.

MAY 4.

St Porphyrius of Camerino (250) M.
St Curcodomus of Auxerre (3rd cent.)
C.
St Pelagia of Tarsus (c.300) V. M.
St Florian of Austria (304) M.
St Cyriacus of Ancona (?) Bp. M.
St Paulinus of Cologne (?) M.
SS Silvanus and Comp. (c.311) MM.
St Monica of Carthage (387) W.
*St Nepotian of Attino (395) C.
St Venerius of Milan (409) Bp.
*St Antony du Rocher (6th cent.) Ab.
O.S.B.
*St Ethelred of Bardney (716) King,
O.S.B.
St Sacerdos of Limoges (c.720) Bp.
O.S.B.
*St Paulinus of Sinigaglia (826) Bp.
*Bl Hilsindis (1028) Abs. O.S.B.
St Godehard of Hildesheim (1038) Bp.
O.S.B.
*St Cunegund (p.1052) V. O.S.B.
*Bl Gregory Celli of Verucchio (1343)
C. O.S.A.
*Bl Catherine of Parc-aux-Dames (13th
cent.) V. O.S.B.Cist.
*Bl Michael Gedroye (1485) C. O.S.A.
*BB Carthusian Martyrs (1535-40).
*BB Martyrs of England (1535-1681.)

MAY 5.

SS Irenaeus, Peregrinus and Irene
(c.300) MM.
*St Jovinian of Auxerre (p. 300) M.
St Euthymius of Alexandria (?) M.
St Silvanus of Rome (?) M.
St Maximus of Jerusalem (c.350) Bp.
*St Nectarius of Vienne (375) Bp.
St Eulogius of Edessa (p. 381) Bp.
*St Brito of Trèves (386) Bp.
St Hilary of Arles (449) Bp.
St Nicetus of Vienne (p. 449) Bp.
St Geruntius of Milan (c.470) Bp.

St Crescentiana (5th cent.) M.
*St Hydroc (5th cent.) C.
*St Gibrian (c.515) C.
St Theodore of Bologna (c.550) Bp.
St Sacerdos of Saguntum (c.560) Bp.
*St Waldrada of Metz (c.620) Abs.
*St Maurontus of Douai (701) Ab.
O.S.B.
*St Echa of Crayk (767) H .O.S.B.
St Angelus of Jerusalem (1220) M.
O.C.
*St Jutta of Kulmsee (1250) W.
*Bl John Haile (1535) M.
St Pius V (1572) Pope O.P.
St Mary Magdalen Sophia Barat
(1865) V. Foundress.

MAY 6.

St Evodius of Antioch (c.67) Bp. M.
St Lucius of Cyrene (1st cent.) Bp.
SS Heliodorus, Venustus and Comp.
(3rd cent.) MM.
St Theodotus of Cyprus (c.325) Bp.
St Protogenes of Syria (4th cent.) Bp.
St Benedicta of Rome (6th cent.) V.
St Eadbert of Lindisfarne (698) Bp.
O.S.B.
*St Petronax of Monte Cassino (c.747)
Ab. O.S.B.
*Bl Bonizella Piccolomini (1300) W.
*Bl Prudentia Castori (1492) V. O.S.A.
*BB Antony Middleton and Edward
Jones (1590) MM.

MAY 7.

St Juvenal of Beneventum (c.132) M.
SS Flavia Domitilla, Euphrosyna and
Theodora (2nd cent.) VV. MM.
St Quadratus of Herbipolis (c.257) M.
SS Flavius, Augustus and Augustine
(c.300) MM.
*St Domitian of Huy (c.560) Bp.
*St Michael Ulumbijski (6th cent.) C.
*St Liudhard of Canterbury (c.600) Bp.
*SS Serenicus and Serenus (c.669) CC.
O.S.B.
*St Placid of Autun (c.675) Ab. O.S.B.
St John of Beverley (721) Bp. O.S.B.
St Peter of Pavia (c.735) Bp.
*Bl Frederick of Hirsau (c.1070) Ab.
O.S.B.

St Stanislaus of Cracow (1079) Bp. M.
*St Villanus of Gubbio (1237) Bp. O.S.B.

MAY 8.

St Dionysius of Vienne (p. 193) Bp.
St Acacius of Byzantium (c.303) M.
St Victor the Moor (303) M.
St Helladius of Auxerre (387) Bp.
*St Odrian of Waterford (?) Bp.
*St Desideratus of Bourges (6th cent.) Bp.
St Boniface IV (615) Pope.
*St Ida of Nivelles (652) V. O.S.B.
St Benedict II (685) Pope.
SS Wiro, Plechelm and Otger (c.739) MM. O.S.B.
St Peter of Tarantaise (1175) Bp. O.S.B.Cist.
*Bl Amatus Ronconi (1292) C. O.S.B.
*Bl Angelus of Masaccio (1458) C. O.S.B.Cam.

MAY 9.

St Hermas of Rome (1st cent.) Bp.
St Pachomius of Tabenna (346) Ab.
St Gregory Nazianzen (390) Bp. Dr.
*St John of Chalon (c.475) Bp.
St Beatus of Beatenberg (?) C.
*St Gofor of Llanover (?) C.
*St Tudy of Landevennec (5th cent.) Ab.
St Gerontius of Cervia (501) Bp. M.
*St Sanctan of Kill-da-Les (6th cent.) Bp.
*St Vincent of Montes (c.950) Ab. O.S.B.
*St Gregory of Ostia (c.1044) Bp. O.S.B.
*St Brynoth of Scara (1317) Bp.
*Bl Nicholas Albergati (1443) Bp. O.Cart.
*Bl Thomas Pickering (1679) M. O.S.B.

MAY 10

St Job (1500 B.C.?) Patriarch.
St Aurelian of Limoges (1st or 3rd cent.) Bp.
SS Calepodius, Palmatius, Simplicius, Felix, Blanda and Comp. (232) MM.

SS Gordian (c.362) and Epimachus (c.250) MM.
SS Alphius, Philadelphius and Cyrinus (251) MM.
St Dioscorides of Smyrna (?) M.
SS Quartus and Quintus (?) MM.
*St Comgall of Bangor (601) Ab.
St Cataldus of Taranto (7th cent.) Bp.
*St Solangia of Bourges (c.880) V. M.
St Isidore the Farmer (1170) C.
*St William of Pontoise (1192) C.
*Bl Beatrix d'Este I (1226) V. O.S.B.
St Antoninus of Florence (1459) Bp. O.P.
*Bl John of Avila (1569) C.

MAY 11.

St Evellius of Pisa (c.66) M.
SS Anastasius and Comp. (251) MM.
St Anastasius of Lérida (?) C.
St Anthimus of Rome (303) M.
SS Maximus, Bassus and Fabius (304) MM.
SS Sisinius, Diocletius and Florentius (304) MM.
*St Principia of Rome (c.420) V.
St Mamertus of Vienne (475) Bp.
*St Possessor of Verdun (c.485) Bp.
*St Walbert of Hainault (c.678) C.
St Gangulphus of Burgundy (760) M.
*St Fremund of Dunstable (9th cent.) M.
St Majolus of Cluny (994) Ab. O.S.B.
St Illuminatus of Sanseverino (c.1000) C. O.S.B.
*St Walter of L'Esterp (1070) Ab. O.S.A.
*St Gualfardus of Verona (1127) H. O.S.B.Cam.
*St Illuminatus (c.1230) C. O.F.M.
*Bl Julian Cesarello de Valle (?) C. O.F.M.
*Bl Albert of Bergamo (1279) Tert. O.P.
*Bl Vivaldus (1300) C. Tert. O.F.M.
*Bl Benincasa of Montechiello (1426) C. O.S.M.
*Bl Aloysius Rabata (1490) C. O.C.
*BB James Walworth and John Rochester (1537) MM. O.Cart.
St Francis de Geronimo (1716) C. S.J.

MAY 12.

SS *Nereus and Achilleus* (c.100) *MM.*
St Philip of Arirone (?) ?
St Dionysius of Asia (304) M.
St Epiphanius of Salamis (403) Bp.
St Pancras of Rome (c.304) *M.*
*St Diomma of Kildimo (5th cent.).
St Modoald of Trèves (640) Bp.
*St Rictrudis of Marchiennes (688) W. O.S.B.
St Germanus of Constantinople (732) Bp.
*St Ethelhard of Canterbury (803) Bp.
St Dominic de la Calzada (c.1109) H.
*Bl Gemma of Goriano (1249) V.
*Bl Francis Patrizi (1328) C. O.S.M.
*Bl Imelda Lambertini (1333) V. O.P.
*Bl Jane of Portugal (1490) V. O.P.
*Bl John Stone (1538) M. O.S.A.

MAY 13.

St Glyceria of Trajanopolis (c.177) V. M.
St Mucius of Byzantium (304) M.
*St Valerian of Auxerre (p. 350) Bp.
*St Onesimus of Soissons (c.361) Bp.
SS Martyrs of Alexandria (372).
St Servatius of Tongres (384) Bp.
St John the Silent (558) Bp.
St Hermenegild (585) King.
*St Agnes of Poitiers (588) Abs.
*St Mael of Bardsey (6th cent.) C.
*St Natalis of Milan (751) Bp.
*St Anno of Verona (780) Bp.
*St Merewenna of Rumsey (c.970) Abs. O.S.B.
*Bl Fortis Gabrielli (1040) H. O.S.B.
*Bl Gerard of Villamagna (1242) C.
*Bl Juliana of Norwich (c.1423) H. O.S.B.
St Robert Bellarmine (1621) Card. Bp. Dr. S.J.
St Andrew Fournet (1834) C. Founder.

MAY 14.

SS Justa, Justina and Henedina (c. 130) MM.
SS Victor and Corona (c.176) MM.

*St Dyfan (2nd cent.) M.
St Pontius of Cimiez (c.258) M.
St Boniface of Tarsus (c.307) *M.*
St Boniface of Ferentino (6th cent.) Bp.
*St Carthage the Younger (c.637) Bp.
*St Erembert of Toulouse (c.672) Bp. O.S.B.
*Bl Tuto of Ratisbon (930) Bp. O.S.B.
*St Halward of Oslo (c.1043) M.
*Bl Giles of Santarem (1265) C. O.P.
*Bl Petronilla of Moncel (1355) Abs. Poor Clare.
*Bl Michael Garicoits (1863) Founder.

MAY 15.

SS Torquatus, Ctesiphon, Secundus, Indaletius, Caecilius, Hesychius, and Euphrasius (1st cent.) MM.
St Isidore of Chios (c.250) M.
SS Peter, Paul, Andrew and Dionysia (251) MM.
SS Cassius, Victorinus, Maximus, and Comp. (260) MM.
*St Caesarea (?) V.
St Simplicius of Sardinia (304) M.
*St Achilles of Thessaly (c.330) Bp.
*St Silvanus of Tabennisi (4th cent.) H.
St Dympna of Gheel (?) V. M.
*St Hilary of Galeata (558) Ab.
*St Colman McO'Laoighse (6th cent.) Ab.
*St Gerebern (7th cent.) M.
*St Britwin of Beverley (c.733) Ab. O.S.B.
*SS Rupert and Bertha (9th cent.).
*St Nicholas the Mystic (925) Bp.
*Bl Leonard of Camaldoli (c.1250) H. O.S.B.Cam.
*Bl Andrew Abellón (1450) C. O.P.
*Bl Mary Magdalen Albrizzi (1465) V. O.S.A.
St John Baptist de la Salle (1719) Founder.

MAY 16.

*St Fort of Bordeaux (? 1st cent.) Bp. M.
*St Peregrinus of Terni (c.138) Bp.
St Peregrinus of Auxerre (c.304) Bp. M.

SS Aquilinus and Victorian (?) MM.
SS Felix and Gennadius (?) MM.
St Maxima of Fréjus (?) V.
*St Hilary of Pavia (376) Bp.
St Audas of Persia (420) Bp. M.
St Possidius of Calama (450) Bp.
*St Primael of Quimper (c.450) H.
*St Carantac of Wales (5th cent.) C.
St Fidolus of Aumont (c.540) Ab.
*St Germerius of Toulouse (c.560) Bp.
*St Domnolus of Le Mans (581) Bp.
St Brendan the Voyager (c.583) Ab.
*St Carantock (6th cent.) Ab.
St Honoratus of Amiens (c.600) Bp.
*St Annobert of Séez (p. 689) Bp.
O.S.B.
*St Francoveus (7th cent.) C.
St Ubald Baldassini (1160) Bp.
*St Adam of Fermo (p. 1212) Ab. O.S.B.
*St Simon Stock (1265) C. O.C.
St John Nepomucen (1393) M.

MAY 17.

SS Andronicus and Junias (1st cent.)
MM.
St Restituta of Carthage (255 or 304)
V. M.
SS Adrio, Victor and Basilla (?) MM.
SS Heradius, Paul, Aquilinus and
Comp. (303) MM.
SS Solochon and Comp. (305) MM.
*St Maden of Cornwall (c.545) H.
*St Cathan (6th or 7th cent.) Bp.
*St Maildulf of Malmesbury (673) Ab.
*Bl Rasso of Grafrath (953) C. O.S.B.
*St Silaus of Lucca (1100) Bp.
*St Thethmar of Neumünster (1152) C.
St Paschal Baylon (1592) C. O.F.M.

MAY 18.

St Venantius of Camerino (c.250) M.
SS Theodotus, Thecusa, Alexandra,
Claudia, Faina, Euphrasia, Matrona
and Julitta (304) MM.
St Felix of Spoleto (c.304) Bp. M.
St Dioscorus of Kynopolis (c.305) M.
St Potamon of Heraclea (c.340) Bp. M.
*St Merililaun (8th cent.) M.
*St Feredarius of Iona (p.863) Ab.

*St Elgiva of Shaftesbury (971) W.
O.S.B.
St Eric of Sweden (1160) King M.
*Bl William de Naurose (1369) C.
O.S.A.
*Bl Camilla Gentili (1486) V.
St Felix of Cantalice (1587) C. O.F.M.
Cap.

MAY 19.

St Pudentiana of Rome (c.160) V.
St Pudens of Rome (2nd cent.) M.
SS Calocerus and Parthenius (250)
MM.
St Philoterus of Nicomedia (303) M.
SS Cyriaca and Comp. (307) VV. MM.
*St Cyril of Trèves (5th cent.) Bp.
*St Hadulph of Saint-Vaast (c.728) Bp.
O.S.B.
*Bl Alcuin of York (804) Ab. O.S.B.
St Dunstan of Canterbury (988) Bp.
O.S.B.
*BB Bellatanus and Savinus (?) HH.
O.S.B.Cam.
*Bl Humiliana de' Cerchi (1246) Tert.
O.F.M.
St Peter Celestine (1296) Pope O.S.B.
St Ivo Hélory (1303) C.
*Bl Augustine Novello (1309) C. O.S.A.
*Bl Peter de Dueñas (1397) M. O.F.M.
*Bl Peter Wright (1651) M. S.J.
*Bl Joaquina Vedruna de Mas (1854)
Foundress.

MAY 20.

St Plautilla of Rome (c.67) W.
SS Thalelaeus, Asterius, Alexander
and Comp. (c.284) MM.
St Basilla of Rome (304) V. M.
St Aquila of Egypt (311) M.
St Baudelius of Nîmes (2nd or 3rd
cent.) M.
*St Hilary of Toulouse (4th cent.) Bp.
St Anastasius of Brescia (610) Bp.
St Austregisilus of Bourges (624) Bp.
St Theodore of Pavia (778) Bp.
*St Ethelbert of East Anglia (793) M.
*Bl Guy de Gherardescha (1099) H.
*Bl Orlando of Vallumbrosa (1242) H.
O.S.B.Vall.

*Bl Albert of Bologna (1245) Ab.
O.S.B.Vall.
St Bernardine of Siena (1444) C. O.F.M.
*Bl Columba of Rieti (1501) V. Tert.
O.P.

MAY 21.

SS Nicostratus, Antiochus and Comp.
(303) MM.
St Secundinus of Córdova (c.306) M.
SS Polyeuctus, Victorius and Donatus
(?) MM.
SS Timothy, Polius and Eutychius (?)
MM.
SS Valens and Comp. (?) MM.
SS Secundus and Comp. (357) MM.
St Hospitius of Cap-Saint-Hospice
(c.580) H.
*St Barrfoin of Killbarron (6th cent.) H.
*St Gollen of Denbighshire (7th cent.)
C.
*St Isberga of Aire (c.800) V. O.S.B.
*St Ageranus of Bèze (888) M. O.S.B.
*St Theobald of Vienne (1001) Bp.
*St Godric of Finchale (1170) H. O.S.B.
*Bl Benvenutus of Recanati (1289) C.
O.F.M.
*Bl Catherine of Cardona (1577) V.
*St Theophilus of Corte (1740) C.
O.F.M.

MAY 22.

*St Ausonius of Angoulême (1st or 3rd
cent.) Bp. M.
St Marcian of Ravenna (c.127) Bp.
SS Castus and Aemilius (c.250) MM.
St Quiteria (?) V. M.
St Basiliscus of Comana (312) M.
SS Faustinus, Timothy and Venustus
(c.362) MM.
St Helen of Auxerre (p. 418) V.
St Julia of Corsica (5th cent.) V. M.
St Romanus of Subiaco (c.560) Ab.
O.S.B
St Fulk of Castrofurli (p. 600) C.
*St Conall of Inniscoel (7th cent.) Ab.
*St Boethian of Pierrepont (7th cent.)
M. O.S.B.
*St Aigulphus of Bourges (p. 835) Bp.

*St John of Parma (c.982) Ab. O.S.B.
*St Bobo of Provence (c.985) H.
St Atto of Pistoia (1153) Bp. O.S.B.
Vall.
*St Peter Parenzi (1199) M.
*St Humilitas of Faenza (1310) Abs.
O.S.B.Vall.
*BB John of Cetina and Peter de
Dueñas (1397) MM. O.F.M.
St Rita of Cascia (1457) W. O.S.A.
*Bl John Forest (1538) M. O.F.M.
*BB Peter of the Assumption O.F.M.
and John Baptist Machado S.J.
(1617) MM.
*Bl Matthias of Arima (1622) M.
*Bl Michael Ho-Dinh-Hy (1857) M.

MAY 23.

SS Epitacius and Basileus (1st cent.)
MM.
St Euphebius of Naples (?) Bp.
St Desiderius of Langres (?) Bp. M.
SS Martyrs of Cappadocia (303).
SS Martyrs of Mesopotamia (c.307).
St Mercurialis of Forlì (c.406) Bp.
SS Quintian, Lucius and Julian (c.430)
MM.
SS Eutychius and Florentius (6th
cent.) CC.
*St Goban of Old-Leighlin (6th or 7th
cent.) C.
St Desiderius of Vienne (608) Bp. M.
*St Syagrius of Nice (c.787) Bp. O.S.B.
St Michael of Synnada (c.820) Bp.
*St Guibertus of Gembloux (962) Ab.
O.S.B.
*St Ivo of Chartres (1115) Bp. O.S.A.
*St William of Rochester (1201) M.
*Bl Bartholomew Pucci-Franceschi
(1330) C. O.F.M.
*St Andrew Bobola (1657) M. S.J.
*Bl Crispin of Viterbo (1750) C. O.F.M
Cap.
*St John Baptist de Rossi (1764) C.

MAY 24.

St Joanna (1st cent.) W.
St Manahen (1st cent.) Prophet.
SS Susanna, Marciana, Palladia and
Comp. (2nd cent.) MM.

SS Donatian and Rogatian (299) MM.
St Afra of Brescia (?) V. M.
St Meletius (?) M.
St Robustian of Milan (?) M.
SS Zoellus, Servilius, Felix, Sylvanus and Diocles (?) MM.
St Vincent of Porto (?) M.
St Vincent of Lérins (c.445) C.
*St Patrick of Bayeux (c.469) Bp.
*Bl John of Montfort (1177) Knight O.S.B.
*Bl William of Dongelberg (c.1250) C. O.S.B.Cist.
*St Gerard de Lunel (1298) C.
*Bl Philip Suzanni (1306) C. O.S.A.
*Bl John del Prado (1636) M. O.F.M.

MAY 25.

St Zachary of Vienne (c.106) Bp. M.
St Urban I (230) Pope M.
SS Pasicrates, Valention and Comp. (c.302) MM.
St Dionysius of Milan (c.359) Bp.
SS Maximus and Venerandus (c.384) MM.
St Zenobius of Florence (c.390) Bp.
St Leo of Troyes (c.550) Ab.
*SS Injuriosus and Scholastica (c.550).
St Aldhelm of Sherborne (709) Bp. O.S.B.
*St Dunchadh of Iona (717) Ab.
*St Egilhard of Cornelimünster (881) M. O.S.B.
*St Gennadius of Astorga (c.936) Bp. O.S.B.
St Gregory VII (1085) Pope O.S.B.
*Bl Claritus Voglia (1348) C.
*Bl Peter Van (1857) M.

MAY 26.

*St Alphaeus (1st cent.) C.
St Quadratus the Apologist (c.130) Bp.
SS Simitrius and Comp. (c.159) MM.
St Eleutherius (189) Pope M.
*SS Fugatius and Damian (2nd cent.)
SS Priscus and Comp. (c.272) MM.
SS Felicissimus, Heraclius and Paulinus (303) MM.
St Quadratus of Africa (?) M.

*St Becan of Cork (6th cent.) C.
St Augustine of Canterbury (604) Bp. O.S.B. (feast on the 28th).
*St Odulvald of Melrose (698) Ab.
*Bl Regintrudis of Nonnberg (c.750) Abs. O.S.B.
*St Guinizo of Montecassino (c.1050) C. O.S.B.
*St Lambert Péloguin (1154) Bp. O.S.B.
*St Berengarius of St Papoul (1093) C. O.S.B.
*Bl Eva of Liége (c.1266) V.
St Philip Neri (1595) C. Founder.
*Bl Mariana de Paredes (1645) V.
*Bl Peter Sanz (1747) Bp. M. O.P.
*BB John Hoan and Matthew Phung (1861) MM.

MAY 27.

SS Restituta and Comp. (272) MM.
St Julius of Dorostorum (c.302) M.
St Eutropius of Orange (p.475) Bp.
St John I (526) Pope M.
St Ranulphus of Arras (c.700) M.
St Bede the Venerable (735) Dr. O.S.B.
St Bruno of Würzburg (1045) Bp.
*St Frederick of Liége (1121) Bp.
*Bl James of Nocera (1300) C. O.S.B.
*Bl Bartholomaea Bagnesi (1577) V. O.P.
*Bl Matthew Gam (1847) M.

MAY 28.

SS Crescens, Dioscorides, Paul and Helladius (c.244) MM.
St Heliconis of Thessalonica (c.250) V. M.
SS Emilius, Felix, Priamus and Lucian (?) MM.
St Senator of Milan (480) Bp.
*St Senator of Pavia (480) Bp.
St Caraunus of Chartres (5th cent.) M.
St Justus of Urgell (p. 527) Bp.
St Germanus of Paris (576) Bp.
*St William of Gellone (812) C. O.S.B.
St Podius of Florence (1002) Bp. O.S.A.
St Bernard of Menthon (c.1081) C. O.S.A.

*Bl Lanfranc of Canterbury (1089) Bp.
O.S.B.
*BB Stephen of Narbonne and Comp.
(1242) MM.
*Bl Margaret Pole (1541) M.
*BB John Shert, Thomas Ford and
Robert Johnson (1582) MM.
*Bl Paul Hanh (1859) M.

MAY 29.

*St Cyril of Caesarea (c.251) M.
SS Conon, Father and Son (275) MM.
St Restitutus of Rome (c.299) M.
St Maximus of Verona (6th cent.) Bp.
SS Theodosia and Comp. (c.303) MM.
St Maximinus of Trèves (c.349) Bp.
SS Sisinius, Martyrius and Alexander
(397) MM.
St Eleutherius of Rocca d'Arce (?) C.
*St Venantius of Lérins (c.400) H.
*St Theodosia of Constantinople (745)
V. M.
*St John de Atarés (c.750) H.
*SS Votus, Felix and John (c.750) HH.
*St Gerald of Macon (927) Bp. O.S.B.
*Bl Ulric of Einsiedeln (p. 978) C.
O.S.B.
*Bl Gerardesca of Pisa (c.1260) W.
O.S.B.Cam.
*Bl Peter Petroni (1361) C. O.Cart.
*Bl Richard Thirkeld (1583) M.
St Mary Magdalen de' Pazzi (1607) V.
O.C.

MAY 30.

SS Gabinus and Crispulus (c.130)
MM.
St Felix I (274) Pope M.
SS Sycus and Palatinus (?) MM.
SS Basil and Emmelia (c.370).
*St Isaac of Constantinople (c.410) Ab.
St Exuperantius of Ravenna (418) Bp.
*St Madelgisilus of Monstrelet (c.655)
H. O.S.B.
St Anastasius of Pavia (680) Bp.
*St Hubert of Brétigny (c.714) C. O.S.B.
*St Walstan of Norfolk (1016) C.
St Ferdinand III (1252) King.
*Bl Andrew Franchi (1401) Bp. O.P.

St Joan of Arc (1431) V.
*Bl James Bertoni (1483) C. O.S.M.
*BB Laurence Richardson, Luke Kirby,
Thomas Cottam S.J. and William
Filby (1582) MM.
*BB Maurus William Scott O.S.B. and
Richard Newport (1612) MM.

MAY 31.

St Petronilla of Rome (1st cent.) V. M.
St Crescentian of Sassari (c.130) M.
St Hermias of Cappadocia (170) M.
SS Cantius, Cantian, Cantianilla and
Protus (c.304) MM.
St Lupicinus of Verona (5th cent.) Bp.
St Paschasius of Rome (c.512) C.
*SS Winnow, Mancus and Myrbad (6th
cent.) CC.
*St Mechtildis of Diessen (1160) Abs.
O.S.B.
*Bl Nicholas of Vaucelles (c.1163) Ab.
O.S.B.Cist.
*Bl James Salomone (1314) C. O.P.
*St Vitalis of Monte Subasio (1370) H.
O.S.B.
*Bl Camilla Varani (1527) Abs. Poor
Clare.
St Angela de' Merici (1540) V. Found-
ress.
*Bl Thomas Du (1839) M.

JUNE 1.

St Thespesius of Cappadocia (c.230) M.
SS Ischirion and Comp. (250) MM.
SS Felinus and Gratian (250) MM.
SS Reverianus, Paul and Comp. (272)
MM.
St Crescentian of Saldo (c.287) M.
St Firmus (c.290) M.
St Secundus of Amelia (304) M.
St Proculus of Bologna (c.304) M.
SS Pamphilus and Comp. (309) MM.
*St Tegla of Denbighshire (?) V.
St Juventius (?) M.
*St Clarus of Aquitaine (?) Bp. M.
St Fortunatus of Spoleto (c.400) C.
St Caprasius of Lérins (c.430) Ab.
*St Ruadan of Cornwall (5th cent.) Bp.
*St Herveus of Brittany (c.575) Ab.

*St Wistan of Evesham (849) M.
St Simeon of Trèves (1035) H. O.S.B.
*St Gaudentius of Ossero (1044) Bp.
O.S.B.
*St Atto of Oca (c.1044) Bp. O.S.B.
St Eneco of Oña (1057) Ab. O.S.B.
*St Conrad of Trèves (1066) Bp. M.
*Bl Ermengardis (c.1147) W. O.S.B.
Cist.
*Bl Theobald Roggeri (1150) C.
*BB Bernard, Mary and Gracia (c.1180)
O.S.B.Cist.
*Bl Conrad of Hessen (13th cent.) Ab.
O.S.B.Cist.
Bl John Pelingotto (1304) C. O.F.M.
Tert.
*Bl James of Strepar (1411) Bp. O.F.M.
*Bl Herculanus of Piegare (1541) C.
O.F.M.
*Bl John Storey (1571) M.
*BB Alphonsus Navarrete, O.P. and
Ferdinand of St Joseph Ayala and
Comp. (1617) MM.
*Bl Felix of Nicosia (1787) C. O.F.M.
Cap.

JUNE 2.

SS Photinus, Sanctus, Vetius, Epaga-
thus, Maturus, Ponticus, Biblides,
Attalus, Alexander, Blandina and
Comp. (177) MM.
St Erasmus of Formiae (303) Bp. M.
SS Marcellinus and Peter (304) MM.
St Eugene I (657) Pope.
*St Adalgis (c.686) C.
*St Bodfan (7th cent.) C.
*Bl Guy of Acqui (1070) Bp.
*St Stephen of Corvey (c.1075) Bp.
O.S.B.
St Nicholas Peregrinus (1094) C.
*St John de Ortega (c.1150) H.
*BB Sadoc and Comp. (1260) MM.

JUNE 3.

SS Pergentinus and Laurentinus (251)
MM.
SS Lucillian, Claudius, Hypatius, Paul
and Dionysius (273) MM.
St Paula of Nicomedia (c.273) V. M.

St Caecilius of Carthage (3rd cent.) C.
*St Hilary of Carcassonne (4th cent.)
Bp.
St Clotilde of France (545) Queen.
St Liphardus of Orleans (c.550) Ab.
St Oliva of Anagni (?) V.
*St Cronan the Tanner (617) C.
*St Kevin of Glendalough (c.618) Ab.
St Genesius of Clermont (662) Bp.
*St Glunshallaich (7th cent.) C.
St Isaac of Córdova (852) M.
*Bl Gausmarus of Savigny (984) Ab.
O.S.B.
St Davinus of Lucca (1051) C.
*St Albert of Como (c.1092) Bp. O.S.B.
*St Morandus of Cluny (c.1115) C.
O.S.B.
*St Conus of Lucania (c.1200) C. O.S.B.
*Bl Andrew Caccioli (c.1264) C. O.F.M.
*BB Peregrinus I and Peregrinus II
(c.1291) CC. O.S.B.Cam.
*Bl John Grande (1600) C.
*BB Martyrs of Uganda (1887).

JUNE 4.

St Clateus of Brescia (c.64) Bp.
SS Aretius and Dacian (?) MM.
St Quirinus of Tivoli (?) M.
SS Rutilus and Comp. (?) MM.
St Saturnina of Arras (?) V. M.
St Quirinus of Croatia (308) Bp. M.
St Metrophanes of Byzantium (325)
Bp.
St Optatus of Milevis (c.387) Bp.
*St Nennoc (c.467) V.
*St Petroc of Cornwall (c.594) Ab.
*St Breaca of Cornwall (5th-6thcent.) V.
*St Buriana of Cornwall (6th cent.) V.
*SS Croidan, Medan and Degan (6th
cent.) CC.
St Alexander of Verona (8th cent.) Bp.
*St Adegrin of Baume (939) C. O.S.B.
*St Elsiar of Lavedan (c.1050) C. O.S.B.
*St Walter of Fontenelle (1150) Ab.
O.S.B.
*St Cornelius McConchailleach (1176)
Bp. O.S.A.
*St Walter of Serviliano (c.1250) Ab.
O.S.B.
*Bl Margaret of Vau-le-Duc (1277) V.
O.S.B.Cist.

*Bl Boniface of Villiers (c.1280) C. O.S.B.Cist.

*Bl Francis Ronci (1294) C. O.S.B.Cel.

*St Francis Caracciolo (1608) C.

*Bl Luke Loan (1840) M.

*Bl Vincenza Gerosa (1846) V.

JUNE 5.

SS Florentius, Julian, Cyriacus, Marcellinus and Faustinus (250) MM.

SS Marcian, Nicanor, Apollonius and Comp. (c.304) MM.

SS Zenais, Cyria, Valeria and Marcia (?) MM.

St Dorotheus of Tyre (c.362) M.

*St Tudno of Caernarvon (6th cent.) C.

*St Dorotheus the Archimandrite (c. 640) Ab.

St Boniface and Comp. (755) MM. O.S.B.

*St Felix of Fritzlar (c.790) M. O.S.B.

St Sancho of Córdova (851) M.

*Bl Meinwerk of Paderborn (1036) Bp.

*St Dorotheus the Younger (11th cent.) Ab.

*St Franco of Asserigo (c.1275) H. O.S.B.

*Bl Ferdinand of Portugal (1443) M.

JUNE 6.

St Philip the Deacon (1st cent.).

SS Martyrs of Tarsus (c.290).

SS Arthemius, Candida and Paulina (302) MM.

SS Amantius, Alexander and Comp. (?) MM.

St John of Verona (4th cent.) Bp.

St Nilamnon of Egypt (404) H.

*St Ceratus of Grenoble (c.455) Bp.

St Eustorgius II of Milan (518) Bp.

*St Jarlath of Tuam (c.550) Bp.

St Alexander of Fiesole (590) M.

*St Cocca of Kilcock (?) V.

St Claudius of Besançon (c.699) Bp. O.S.B.

*St Gudwall of Wales (7th cent.) Bp.

*St Agobard of Lyons (840) Bp.

St Norbert (1134) Bp. Founder.

*Bl Falco of Cava (1146) Ab. O.S.B.

*Bl Gilbert of Neuffons (1152) Ab. O.Praem.

*Bl Gerard Tintorio (1207) C.

*St Bertrand of Aquileia (1350) Bp. M.

*Bl Gundisalvus of Azebeyro (1466) Ab. O.S.B.Cist.

*Bl Laurence of Villamagna (1535) C. O.F.M.

*BB John Davy, Robert Salt and Walter Pierson (1537) MM. O.Cart.

*Bl Felicia de Montmorency (1666) V. O.Visit.

JUNE 7.

St Potamioena the Younger (c.304) V.M.

St Lycarion of Egypt (?) M.

St Paul of Constantinople (c.350) Bp. M.

*St Colman of Dromore (6th cent.) Bp.

*St Vulphy of Abbeville (c.643) H.

*St Meriadec of Vannes (c.688) Bp.

*St Aventinus of Bagnères (732) M.

*St Deochar (847) Ab. O.S.B.

SS Peter, Wallabonso, Sabinianus, Wistremundus, Habentius and Jeremias (851) MM.

*Bl Odo of Massay (967) Ab. O.S.B.

*St Gotteschalk (1066) M.

*St Landulf Variglia (1134) Bp. O.S.B.

St Robert of Newminster (1159) Ab. O.S.B.Cist.

*St Meriadec II of Vannes (1302) Bp.

*Bl Anne of St Bartholomew (1626) V. O.C.D.

*Bl Antony Mary Gianelli (1846) Bp.

JUNE 8.

St Maximinus of Aix (1st cent.) Bp.

St Calliope (c.250) M.

St Sallustian of Sardinia (?).

*St Melania the Elder (c.400) W.

*St Bron of Cassel (c.511) Bp.

St Gildard of Rouen (c.514) Bp.

St Heraclius of Sens (c.515) Bp.

St Victorinus (543) Bp.

St Severinus of Sanseverino (550) Bp.

St Medard of Noyon (c.558) Bp.

*St Levan (6th cent.) C.

*St Eustadiola of Moyen-Moutier (690) Abs. O.S.B.

St Clodulphus of Metz (696) Bp.

*St Muirchu (7th cent.) C.

*St Syra of Troyes (7th cent.) V.

*St Robert of Frassinoro (p.1070) Ab. O.S.B.

St William of York (1154) Bp.

*Bl John Rainuzzi (c.1330) C. O.S.B.

*Bl Pacificus of Cerano (1482) C. O.F.M.

JUNE 9.

St Vincent of Agen (c.292) M.

SS Primus and Felician (c.297) MM.

St Pelagia of Antioch (c.311) V. M.

St Julian of Syria (c.370) C.

St Maximian of Syracuse (594) Bp. O.S.B.

St Columba of Iona (597) Ab.

*St Baithin of Iona (c.598) Ab.

*St Cumian of Bobbio (1st half of 8th cent.) Bp. O.S.B.

St Richard of Andria (p. 1196) Bp.

*BB Diana, Caecilia and Amiata (13th cent.) VV. O.P.

*Bl Silvester Ventura (1348) C. O.S.B. Cam.

*Bl Henry the Shoemaker (1666) C.

*Bl Anne Mary Taigi (1837) Matron.

JUNE 10.

SS Crispulus and Restitutus (1st cent.) MM.

SS Getulius, Caerealis, Amantius and Primitivus (c.120) MM.

SS Basilides, Tripos, Mandal and Comp. (275) MM.

SS Aresius, Rogatus and Comp. (?) MM.

St Oliva of Palermo (?) V. M.

St Zachary of Nicomedia (?) M.

St Asterius of Petra (p. 362) Bp.

St Timothy of Prussa (362) Bp. M

St Maximus of Naples (4th cent.). Bp .M.

St Censurius of Auxerre (486) Bp.

St Maurinus of Cologne (?) Ab. M.

*St Illadan of Rathlihen (6th cent.) Bp.

*St Ithamar of Rochester (c.656) Bp.

*St Landericus of Paris (c.661) Bp.

*St Evermund of Fontenay (c.720) Ab. O.S.B.

*St Landericus of Novalese (1050) M. O.S.B.

*St Bardo of Mainz (1053) Bp. O.S.B.

St Margaret of Scotland (1093) Queen.

*St Bogumilus of Gnesen (1182) Bp. O.S.B.Cam.

*Bl Amata of San Sisto (1270) V. O.P.

*Bl Henry of Treviso (1315) C.

*Bl Bonaventure Baduario (1386) C. O.Erem.S.A.

*Bl John Dominici (1419) Bp. O.P.

*Bl Mary Magdalen of Carpi (1546) V. O.S.M.

JUNE 11.

St Barnabas (1st cent.) Apostle M.

SS Felix and Fortunatus (296) MM.

*St Tochumra of Kilmore (?) V.

*St Blitharius of Seganne (7th cent.) C.

*St Herebald of Brittany (8th cent.) C.

*Bl Hugh of Marchiennes (1158) Ab. O.S.B.

*BB Peter Rodríguez, Damian Vaz and Comp. (1242) MM.

St Parisius of Treviso (1267) C. O.S.B. Cam.

*Bl Flora of Beaulieu (1347) V.

*Bl Paula Frasinetti (1882) Foundress.

JUNE 12.

St Antonia (c.304) V. M.

SS Basilides, Cyrinus, Nabor and Nazarius (?) MM.

St Amphion of Cilicia (p.325) Bp.

St Olympius of Enos (p.343) Bp.

St Onuphrius of Egypt (c.400) H.

*St Ternan of Culross (5th cent.) Bp.

*St Cunera (?) V.

St Leo III (816) Pope.

*St Odulphus of Stavoren (c.855) C. O.S.A.

*St Gerebald of Châlons-sur-Seine (885) Bp.

*SS Marinus, Vimius and Zimius (p.1100) CC. O.S.B.

*St Christian of Clogher (1138) Bp.
*Bl Placid of Val d'Ocre (1248) Ab.
O.S.B.Cist.
*Bl Stephen Bandelli (1450) C. O.P.
St John of Sahagún (1479) C. O.S.A.
*Bl Louis Naisen (1626) M.

JUNE 13.

St Felicula of Rome (c.90) V. M.
St Aquilina of Syria (293) V. M.
SS Fortunatus and Lucian (?) MM.
St Triphyllius of Cyprus (c.370) Bp.
*St Damhnade (?) V.
*St Peregrinus of Aquila (c.600) Bp.
*St Rambert (c.680) M.
St Fandilas of Peñamelaria (853) M.
*St Eskill of Sweden (c.1080) Bp. M.
St Antony of Padua (1231) C. O.F.M.

JUNE 14.

St Eliseus (8th cent. B.C.) Prophet.
St Marcian of Syracuse (c.255) Bp. M.
SS Valerius and Rufinus (c.287) MM.
*St Mark of Lucera (c.328) Bp.
St Basil the Great (379) Bp. Dr.
St Quintian (?) Bp.
*St Dogmael of Wales (5th-6th cent.) C.
St Etherius of Vienne (c.675) Bp. C.
*St Psalmodius of Limoges (c.690) H.
*St Nennus of Arran (7th cent.) Ab.
*St Lotharius of Séez (c.756) Bp. O.S.B.
*St Gerold of Fontenelle (806) Bp.
O.S.B.
*St Joseph the Hymnographer (c.845)
Bp.
St Methodius the Confessor (847) Bp.
SS Anastasius, Felix and Digna (853)
MM. O.S.B.
*St Cearan the Devout (870) Ab.
*Bl Hartwig of Salzburg (1023) Bp.
*Bl Richard of St Vannes (1046) Ab.
O.S.B.
*St Elgar of Bardsey (c.1100) H.
*Bl Castora Gabrielli (1391) W. Tert.
O.F.M.

JUNE 15.

St Dulas of Cilicia (300) M.
St Hesychius of Dorostorum (c.302) M.

SS Lybe, Leonis and Eutropia (303)
MM.
SS Vitus, Modestus and Crescentia (?)
MM.
*St Orsisius the Cenobite (c.380) H.
St Abraham of Saint-Cyrgues (c.480)
Ab.
*St Melan of Viviers (p. 549) Bp.
*St Vouga of Lesneven (6th cent.) Bp.
*St Trillo of Wales (6th cent.) C.
St Landelinus of Lobbes (c.686) Ab.
O.S.B.
*SS Domitian and Hadelinus of Lobbes
(c.686) CC. O.S.B.
*St Constantine of Beauvais (c.706) Bp.
*St Edburga of Winchester (960) Abs.
O.S.B.
*St Adelaide of La Cambre (1250) V.
O.S.B.Cist.
*BB Thomas Green, Thomas Scryven
and Thomas Reding (1537) MM.
O.Cart.
St Germana Cousin (1601) V.

JUNE 16.

SS Ferreolus and Ferrutio (c.212)
MM.
SS Quiricus and Julitta (304) MM.
St Similian of Nantes (310) Bp.
*SS Actinea and Graecina (4th cent.)
VV. MM.
St Tychon of Cyprus (c.450) Bp.
*St Simplicius of Bourges (477) Bp.
*St Cettin (5th cent.) Bp.
*St Berthaldus (c.540) H.
St Aurelian of Arles (c.550) Bp.
*St Colman McRoi (6th cent.) Ab.
*St Curig of Wales (6th cent.) Bp.
*St Ismael (6th cent.) Bp.
*SS Felix and Maurus (6th cent.) CC.
SS Aureus, Justina and Comp. (?)
MM.
St Benno of Meissen (1106) Bp.
*Bl Guy Vignotelli (c.1245) C. Tert.
O.F.M.
St Lutgardis of Aywières (1246) V.
O.S.B.Cist.

JUNE 17.

SS Nicander and Marcian (173 or
303?) MM.

St Antidius of Besançon (c.265) Bp.M.
St Montanus of Gaeta (c.300) M.
SS Isaurus, Innocent, Felix, Jeremias and Peregrinus (?) MM.
SS Manuel, Sabel and Ismael (362) MM.
*St Prior of Egypt (c.395) H.
*St Bessarion of Egypt (c.400) H.
St Hypatius of Bithynia (c.450) C.
St Avitus of Micy (c.530) Ab.
St Himerius of Cremona (c.560) Bp.
*St Briavel (?) H.
*St Gundulphus of Bourges (6th cent.) Bp.
*St Nectan of Hartland (6th cent.) M.
*St Agrippinus of Como (615) Bp.
*SS Botulph and Adulph (c.680) CC. O.S.B.
*St Molling of Wexford (697) Bp.
*St Rambold of Ratisbon (1001) Ab. O.S.B.
St Raynerius of Pisa (1160) H. O.S.B. Ol.
*Bl Euphemia of Andechs (1180) Abs. O.S.B.
*St Teresa of Portugal (1250) Queen, O.S.B.Cist.
*Bl Peter Gambacorta (1435) Founder.
*Bl Paul Burali d'Arezzo (1578) Bp.

JUNE 18.

SS Leontius, Hypatius and Theodulus (135?) MM.
SS Mark and Marcellian (c.287) MM.
St Etherius of Nicomedia (c.303) M.
St Marina (?) V. M.
SS Cyriacus and Paula (305) MM.
St Ephrem the Syrian (c.379) Dr.
St Amandus of Bordeaux (c.431) Bp.
St Calogerus the Anchoret (c.486) H.
*SS Gregory, Demetrius and Calogerus (5th cent.) CC.
*St Fortunatus the Philosopher (c.569) C.
*St Osmanna of Jouarre (c.700) V. O.S.B.
*St Guy of Baume (p. 940) Ab. O.S.B.
*Bl Jerome of Vallumbrosa (1135) C. O.S.B.Vall.
St Elisabeth of Schönau (1164) V. O.S.B.

*St Gerland of Caltagirone (13th cent.) C.
*Bl Marina of Spoleto (c.1300) V.
*Bl Hosanna of Mantua (1505) V. Tert. O.P.
*Bl Gregory Barbadigo (1697) Bp.

JUNE 19.

St Ursicinus of Ravenna (c.67) M.
St Zosimus of Spoleto (110) M.
SS Gervase and Protase (?2nd cent.) MM.
SS Gaudentius and Culmatius (364) MM.
St Innocent of Le Mans (559) Bp.
*St Deodatus of Nevers (679) Bp.
*St Deodatus of Jointures (c.680) Bp. O.S.B.
*St Hildegrin of Châlons-sur-Marne (c.827) Bp.
St Bruno-Boniface (1009) M. O.S.B. Cam.
*Bl Odo of Cambrai (1113) Bp. O.S.B.
St Juliana Falconieri (1340) V. O.S.M.
*Bl Thomas Woodhouse (1573) M. S.J.

JUNE 20.

St Novatus of Rome (c.151).
SS Paul and Cyriacus (?) MM.
St Macarius of Petra (c.350) Bp.
St Silverius (c.537) Pope M.
St Florentina of Carthagena (c.636) Abs.
*St Goban (c.670) M. O.S.B.
*St Edburga of Caistor (late 7th cent.) V. O.S.B.
*St Bain of Calais (c.710) Bp. O.S.B.
*St Helia of Öhren (c.750) Abs. O.S.B.
*St Adalbert of Magdeburg (981) Bp. O.S.B.
*St John of Pulsano (1139) Ab. O.S.B.
*St Benignus of Breslau (13th cent.) M. O.S.B.Cist.
*Bl Michelina of Pesaro (1356) W.
*BB Francis Pacheco and Comp. (1626) MM. S.J.
*BB Thomas Whitbread and Comp. (1679) MM. S.J.

JUNE 21.

St Lazarus (1st cent.)
St Terence of Iconium (1st cent.) Bp. M.
St Urciscenus of Pavia (c.216) Bp.
SS Cyriacus and Apollinaris (?) MM.
SS Rufinus and Martia (?) MM.
St Martin of Tongres (c.350) Bp.
St Demetria (363) V. M.
St Eusebius of Samosata (c.379) Bp. M.
St Alban of Mainz (c.400) M.
*St Corbmac of Durrow (6th cent.) Ab.
*St Maine of Brittany (617) C.
St Leutfrid of Saint-Leufroy (738) Ab. O.S.B.
*St Agofredus of Saint-Leufroy (p. 738) Ab. O.S.B.
*St Engelmund of Vebsen (c.739) Ab. O.S.B.
*St Dominic of Comacchio (p. 820) C. O.S.B.
*St Ralph of Bourges (866) Bp. O.S.B.
*Bl Wolfrid of Hohentwiel (c.990) Ab. O.S.B.
*St Raymund of Barbastro (1126) Bp. O.S.A.
St Aloysius Gonzaga (1591) C. S.J.
*Bl John Rigby (1600) M.

JUNE 22.

St Flavius Clemens (c.96) M.
SS Acacius and Comp. (?) MM.
St Alban of Great Britain (3rd or 4th cent.) M.
St Nicaeas (c.414) Bp.
St Paulinus of Nola (431) Bp.
St John I of Naples (5th cent.) Bp.
*St Aaron of Brittany (p.552) Ab.
St Consortia (?570) V.
*St Rotrudis of Saint-Omer (c.869) V.
*St John IV of Naples (835) Bp.
*Bl Lambert of Saint-Bertin (1125) Ab. O.S.B.
*St Eberhard of Salzburg (1164) Bp. O.S.B.
*Bl Innocent V (1277) Pope O.P.

JUNE 23.

St Felix of Sutri (257) M.
St Agrippina of Rome (c.262) V. M.

SS Zeno and Zenas (c.304) MM.
St John of Rome (362) M.
*St Moeliai of Nendrum (c.493) Ab.
St Etheldreda of Ely (679) Abs. O.S.B.
*St Walhere of Dinant (?) M.
*St Hidulphus of Lobbes (c.707) C. O.S.B.
*St James of Toul (769) Bp.
*St Libert of Cambrai (1076) Bp.
*Bl Felix of Citeaux (1113) C. O.S.B. Cist.
*St Peter of Juilly (1136) C. O.S.B.
*Bl Lanfranc Beccaria (1194) Bp. O.S.B.Vall.
*Bl Mary of Oignies (1213) W.
*Bl Thomas Corsini (1343) C. O.S.M.
*Bl Peter James of Pesaro (c.1496) C. O.S.A.
*Bl Thomas Garnet (1608) M. S.J.

JUNE 24.

St John the Baptist (1st cent.) Prophet.
SS Roman Martyrs under Nero (64).
SS Faustus and Comp. (?) MM.
*St Amphibalus of Verulam (c.304) M.
SS Orentius, Heros, Pharnacius, Firminus, Firmus, Cyriac and Longinus (c.304) MM.
St Simplicius of Autun (c. 360)Bp.
*St Alena of Brussels (c.640) V. M.
SS Agoard, Aglibert and Others (5th-7th cent.) MM.
St Rumoldus of Malines (c.775) Bp. M. O.S.B.
St Theodulphus of Lobbes (776) Bp. O.S.B.
*St Ivan of Bohemia (845) H.
*St Henry of Auxerre (c.880) C. O.S.B.
*St John of Tuy (9th cent.) H.
*Bl Erembert I of Kremsmünster (p.1050) Ab. O.S.B.
*Bl Raingardis of Marcingy (1135) W. O.S.B.
*St Bartholomew of Durham (c.1193) H. O.S.B.

JUNE 25.

St Sosipater (2nd cent.).
St Febronia of Nisibis (304) V. M.

St Gallicanus of Ostia (c.362) M.
*St Solomon of Brittany (434) M.
St Prosper of Aquitaine (c.463) C.
St Prosper of Reggio (c.466) Bp.
St Maximus of Turin (c.470) Bp.
*St Gallicanus of Embrun (p.541) Bp.
*St Moloc of Mortlach (c.572) Bp.
*St Molonachus of Lismore (7th cent.) Bp.
*St Eurosia of Jaca (714) V. M.
St Adalbert of Egmont (c.740) C. O.S.B.
*St Gohardus of Nantes (843) Bp. M.
*St Solomon III (874) M.
*St William of Montevergine (1142) Ab. Founder.
*Bl Burchard of Mallersdorf (1122) Ab. O.S.B.
*Bl Henry Zdik (1150) Bp. O.Praem.
*Bl. John the Spaniard (1160) C. O.Cart.
*Bl Guy Maramaldi (1391) C. O.P.
*BB Dominic Henares O.P. and Francis Chien (1838) MM.

JUNE 26.

SS John and Paul (362) MM.
St Vigilius of Trent (405) Bp. M.
St Maxentius of Poitou (c.515) Ab.
St David of Thessalonica (5th cent.) H.
*St Babolenus of Fosses (c.677) Ab.
St Perseveranda of Poitiers (c.726) V.
SS Salvius and Superius (c.768) MM.
*St Corbican (8th cent.) C.
*St John of the Goths (c.800) Bp.
St Pelagius of Oviedo (925) M.
*St Hermogius of Tuy (c.942) Bp. O.S.B.
*Bl Bartholomew de Vir (1157) Bp. O.S.B.Cist.
St Anthelmus of Belley (1178) Bp. O.Cart.
*BB Mary Magdalen Fontaine, Jane Gerard, Frances Lanel, and Teresa Fantou (1794) VV. MM. Sisters of Charity.

JUNE 27.

St Crescens (2nd cent.) Bp. M.
SS Zoilus and Comp. (c.301) MM.

St Anectus (303) M.
*St Deodatus of Nola (473) Bp.
St Samson Xenodochius (c.530) C.
St John of Chinon (6th cent.) H.
*St Hadelin of Crespin (c.700) Ab. O.S.B.
*St Arialdus of Milan (1066) M.
St Ladislas (1095) King.
*Bl Eppo of Mallersdorf (1143) Ab. O.S.B.
*Bl Benvenutus of Gubbio (1232) C. O.F.M.
*St Ferdinand of Aragón (13th cent.) Bp.
*BB Joseph Heiu O.P. and Thomas Toan (1840) MM.

JUNE 28.

St Irenaeus of Lyons (c.202) Bp. M.
SS Plutarch, Serenus, Heraclides, Heron, a second Serenus, Rhais, Potamioena and Marcella (202) MM.
St Papias of Sicily (c.303) M.
*St Crummine of Lackan (5th cent.) Bp.
*St Austell of Cornwall (6th cent.) C.
St Benignus of Utrecht (6th cent.) Bp. M.
*St Theodichildis of Jouarre (p. 660) Abs. O.S.B.
St Paul I (767) Pope.
St Argymirus of Cordova (858) M.
*St Egilo of Prüm (871) Ab. O.S.B.
*St Heimrad of Hersfeld (1019) C. O.S.B.
*Bl Ekhard of Huysburg (1084) Ab. O.S.B.
*St Almus of Balmerino (1270) Ab. O.S.B.Cist.
*Bl Paul Giustiniani (1528) O.S.B.Cam.
*Bl John Southworth (1654) M.

JUNE 29.

SS Peter and Paul (c.67) Apostles MM.
St Mary (1st cent.) W.
SS Marcellus and Anastasius (274) MM.
St Syrus of Genoa (c.380) Bp.

St Benedicta of Sens (?) V. M.
St Cassius of Narni (558) Bp.
*St Cocha of Ross-Benchuir (6th cent.) V.
*SS Salome and Judith (9th cent.) VV. O.S.B.
*St Gemma (1045) W. O.S.B.

JUNE 30.

St Lucina of Rome (1st cent.) V.
St Astriclinian of Limoges (1st or 3rd cent.) C.
St Basilides of Egypt (205) M.
St Martial of Limoges (c.250) Bp.
SS Caius and Leo (?) MM.
St Ostianus of Viviers (?) C.
St Emiliana of Rome (?) M.
*St Eurgain of Glamorgan (6th cent.) V.
*St Bertrand of Le Mans (623) Bp.
*St Clotsindis (c.700) Abs. O.S.B.
*St Erentrudis of Nonnberg (c.718) Abs. O.S.B.
*St Marcian of Pampeluna (c.757) Bp.
*St Theobald of Salanigo (1066) H. O.S.B.Cam.
*St Alrick (11th cent.) H.
*Bl Arnulf Cornibout (1228) C. O.S.B. Cist.
*Bl Philip Powel (1646) M. O.S.B.
*Bl Vincent Yen (1830) M. O.P.

JULY 1.

St Aaron (15th cent. B.C.) First High Priest.
SS Castus and Secundinus (c.305) Bps.
SS Julius and Aaron with others (c.305) MM.
St Domitian of Bebron (c.440) Ab.
*St Schenute of Egypt (c.460) Ab.
St Theodoric of Mont d'Or (c.533) Ab.
*St Carilefus of Anisole (c.536) Ab.
St Gall of Clermont (c.554) Bp.
*St Leonorius of Pontual (c.570) Ab. Bp.
St Eparchius of Angoulême (581) Ab.
St Simeon Salus (p.588) H.
*St Cewydd of Anglesey (6th cent.).
*St Veep of Cornwall (6th cent.) V.
*St Servan of Culross (?) Bp.

*St Juthware (7th cent.) V.
*St Arnulf of Mainz (1160) Bp. M.
*Bl Thomas Maxfield (1616) M.

JULY 2.

Feast of the Visitation of the Blessed Virgin Mary.
*St Acestes (1st cent.) M.
SS Processus and Martinian (?) MM.
SS Ariston, Crescentian, Eutychian, Urban, Vitalis, Justus, Felicissimus, Felix, Marcia and Symphorosa (c.285) MM.
St Monegundis (570) W.
*St Oudaceus of Wales (c.600) Ab.?
*Bl Reginald of Baume (c.1095) H. O.S.B.
*St Lidanus of Sezze (1118) Ab. O.S.B.
St Otto of Bamberg (1139) Bp.

JULY 3.

St Hyacinth of Cappadocia (c.120) M.
St Dathus of Ravenna (190) Bp.
SS Irenaeus and Mustiola (273) MM.
St Anatolius of Alexandria (c.283) Bp.
SS Mark, Mucian, an un-named boy and Paul (?) MM.
SS Tryphon and Comp. (?) MM.
SS Eulogius and Comp. (364-370) MM.
St Heliodorus of Altinum (c.390) Bp.
*St Anatolius of Constantinople (458) Bp.
*St Germanus of the Isle of Man (c.474) Bp.
*St Gunthiern of Brittany (c.500) C.
*St Byblig of Wales (?).
*St Bladus of the Isle of Man (?) Bp.
St Leo II (683) Pope.
*St Cillene of Iona (c.752) Ab.
*St Guthagon (8th cent.) C.
*St Maelmuire O'Gorman (p.1167) C.
*Bl Raymund Lull (1315) M.
*Bl Bernardinus Realini (1616) C. S.J.
*Bl Joseph Peter Vyen (1838) M. O.P.
*Bl Philip Minh (1853) M.

JULY 4.

St Osee (8th cent. B.C.) Prophet.
St Aggaeus (c.516 B.C.) Prophet.

SS Namphanion and Comp. (c.180) MM.

SS Innocent, Sebastia and Comp. (?) MM.

St Jucundian of Africa (?) M.

St Theodore of Cyrene (c.310) Bp. M.

St Sisoes of Egypt (c.429) H.

St Laurian of Seville (c.544) M.

*St Finbar of Wexford (6th cent.) Ab.

*St Bertha of Blangy (c.725) W. O.S.B.

*St Andrew of Crete (740) Bp.

*St Aurelian of Lyons (895) Bp. O.S.B.

*St Odo the Good (959) Bp. O.S.B.

St Ulric of Augsburg (973) Bp.

*Bl Hatto of Ottobeuren (985) C. O.S.B.

*St Procopius of Sazaba (1053) Ab. O.S.Bas.

*Bl William of Hirsau (1091) Ab. O.S.B.

*St Albert Quadrelli (1179) Bp.

*Bl Henry of Albano (1188) Bp. O.S.B. Cist.

*Bl Peter of Luxemburg (1387) Card. Bp.

*BB John Cornelius S.J., Thomas Bosgrave and John Carey (1594) MM.

*BB William Andleby, Edward Fulthrop, Thomas Warcop and Henry Abbot (1597) MM.

JULY 5.

St Stephen of Reggio (1st cent.) Bp. M.

St Zöe of Rome (c.286) M.

St Cyrilla of Cyrene (c.300) M.

SS Agatho and Triphina (306) MM.

SS Marinus, Theodotus and Sedolpha (?) MM.

St Domitius of Phrygia (362) M.

St Athanasius of Jerusalem (452) M.

*SS Fragan and Gwen (5th cent.).

*St Edana of West Ireland (?) V.

*St Erfyl (?) V.

*SS Grace and Probus of Cornwall (?).

St Philomena of Sanseverino (c.500) V.

St Numerian of Trèves (c.666) Bp. O.S.B.

*St Modwenna of Whitby (c.695) V.

*St Modwenna of Polesworth (c.900) V.

*St Athanasius the Athonite (920-1003) Ab.

*Bl Elias of Bourdeilles (1484) Bp. O.F.M.

St Antony Mary Zaccaria (1539) C. Founder.

JULY 6.

St Isaias (c.681 B.C.) Prophet.

SS Romulus and Comp. (c.90) MM.

St Tranquillinus of Rome (286) M.

St Dominica of Campania (?) V. M.

St Rixius Varus (?) M.

*St Noyala of Brittany (?) V. M.

*St Moninne (518) V.

St Goar of Aquitaine (c.575) C.

*St Sexburga of Ely (c.699) W. Abs. O.S.B.

*St Godeleva of Ghistelles (1070) M.

*Bl Thomas Alfield (1585) M.

*BB Thirty-two Martyrs of Orange (1794).

*Bl Mary Rose (1797) M. O.S.B.

JULY 7.

SS Peregrinus, Lucian, Pompeius, Hesychius, Papius, Saturninus, Germanus and Astius (c.120) MM.

St Pantaenus of Alexandria (c.216) C.

SS Claudius, Nicostratus, Castorius, Victorinus and Symphorina (c.288) MM.

St Apollonius of Brescia (?) Bp.

St Illidius of Clermont (385) Bp.

*St Palladius of Ireland (432) Bp.

*St Illtyd of Wales (c.505) Ab.

*St Bonitus of Monte Cassino (c.582) Ab. O.S.B.

*St Felix of Nantes (584) Bp.

*SS Medran and Odran (6th cent.) CC.

*St Ercongotha of Faremoutiers (660) O.S.B.

*St Ethelburga of Faremoutiers (c.664) Abs.O.S.B.

*St Ampelius of Milan (c.672) Bp.

St Hedda of Winchester (705) Bp. O.S.B.

St Willibald of Eichstätt (c.786) Bp. O.S.B.

*St Maolruain of Tallagh (792) Ab.

*St Angelelmus of Auxerre (828) Bp. (O.S.B.?)

SS Cyril and Methodius (869 and 885)
CC.
St Odo of Urgell (1122) Bp.
Bl Benedict XI (1304) Pope O.P.
*BB Roger Dickenson and Ralph Milner (1591) MM.
*Bl Laurence Humphrey (c.1591) M.

JULY 8.

SS Aquila and Priscilla (1st cent.).
St Auspicius of Trèves (p.130) Bp.
St Procopius of Scythopolis (303) M.
St Apollonius of Benevento (p.326) Bp.
*St Auspicius of Toul (c.475) Bp.
*St Morwenna of Cornwall (5th cent.) V.
*St Landrada of Munsterbilsen (c.690) V. O.S.B.
SS Kilian, Colman and Totnan (c.689) MM.
*St Withburga of Dereham (c.743) V. O.S.B.
*St Arnold of Julich (p. 800) C.
SS Abrahamite Monks (830-840) MM.
St Adrian III (885) Pope.
*St Grimbald of Winchester (903) Ab. O.S.B.
*St Edgar the Peaceful (975) King.
*St Sunniva of Bergen (10th cent.) V.
*Bl Peter the Hermit (1115) C.
*St Raymund of Toulouse (1118) C.
Bl Eugene III (1153) Pope O.S.B.Cist.
*St Albert of Genoa (1239) C. O.S.B. Cist.
*Bl Benedict d'Alignan (1268) Bp. O.F.M.
St Elisabeth of Portugal (1336) Queen Tert.O.F.M.
*Bl Mancius Araki (1626) M.

JULY 9.

SS Anatolia and Audax (c.250) MM.
St Cyril of Crete (250) Bp. M.
SS Zeno and Comp. (c.300) MM.
St Brictius of Martola (c.312) Bp.
SS Patermuthius, Copras and Alexander (c.363) MM.
† Agrippinus of Autun (538) Bp.

*St Golvinus of Rennes (? 7th cent.) Bp.
*St Everildis of Everingham (late 7th cent.) Abs. O.S.B.
*St Agilulph of Cologne (p. 720) M. Bp. O.S.B.
*SS Benedict, Andrew, Barnabas and Justus (1008) HH. O.S.B.
*Bl Jane Scopelli (1491) V. O.C.
SS John Fisher Bp. and Thomas More (1535) MM.
*Bl Adrian Fortescue (1539) M.
SS Nineteen Martyrs of Gorkum (1572) MM.
St Veronica Giuliani (1727) Abs. O.F.M.Cap.

JULY 10.

SS Seven Brothers (c.150) MM.
SS Rufina and Secunda (257) VV. MM.
SS Januarius, Marinus, Nabor and Felix (?) MM.
SS Leontius, Maurice, Daniel and Comp. (c.329) MM.
St Apollonius of Sardis (early 4th cent.) M.
SS Bianor and Sylvanus (4th cent.) MM.
*St Etto of Fescau (c.670) Bp. O.S.B.
*St Paschasius of Nantes (c.680) Bp.
*St Amelberga of Maubeuge (c.690) W. O.S.B.
St Amelberga of Munsterbilsen (c.770) V. O.S.B.
*SS Lantfrid, Waltram and Elilantus (p.770) CC. O.S.B.
*St Peter of Perugia (1007) Ab. O.S.B.
*Bl Peter Tu (1840) M.
*BB Emmanuel Ruiz and Comp. (1860) MM.

JULY 11.

St Pius I (c.154) Pope M.
St Marcian of Iconium (243) M.
St Sidronius of Rome (c.270) M.
St Cindeus of Pamphilia (c.300) M.
SS Sabinus and Cyprian (?) MM.
SS Januarius and Pelagia (320) MM.
St Sabinus of Poitiers (5th cent.).

*St Leontius the Younger (c.565) Bp.
*St Drostan of Deer (c.610) Ab.
*SS Sigisbert and Placid (c.650 or 750?).
*St Amabilis of Rouen (p. 684) V.
*St John of Bergamo (c.690) Bp.
*St Hydulphus of Moyenmoutier (707) Bp. O.S.B.
St Abundius of Cordova (854) M.
*St Olga of Russia (969) W.
*St Turketil of Croyland (975) Ab. O.S.B.
*Bl Oliver Plunkett (1681) Bp. M.
*Bl Ignatius Delgado (1838) Bp. M. O.P.

JULY 12.

St Jason (1st cent.).
*St Veronica (1st cent.).
SS Hermagoras and Fortunatus (c.66) MM.
SS Proclus and Hilarion (115) MM.
St Epiphana (?) M.
SS Paulinus of Antioch and Comp. (?) MM.
St Marciana of Toledo (c.303) V. M.
SS Nabor and Felix (c.304) MM.
St Paternian of Bologna (c.470) Bp.
St Viventiolus of Lyons (524) Bp.
*St Proculus of Bologna (542) Bp. M.
*St Menulphus of Quimper (7th cent.) Bp.
*St Ansbald of Prüm (886) Ab. O.S.B.
*St John the Georgian (c.1002) Ab.
St John Gualbert (1073) Ab. O.S.B.Vall.
*St Leo I of Cava (1079) Ab. O.S.B.
*Bl Benno of Osnabruck (1088) Bp. O.S.B.
*Bl Lambert of Morimond (1163) Ab. O.S.B.Cist.
*Bl Andrew of Rinn (1462) M.
*Bl David Gonson (1541) M.
*Bl John Jones (1598) M. O.F.M.
*BB Japanese Martyrs (1626).
*Bl Peter Khanh (1842) M.

JULY 13.

St Joel (8th cent. B.C.) Prophet.
St Esdras (5th cent. B.C.) Prophet.
St Silas (1st cent.) C.

St Anacletus (1st cent.) Pope M.
St Serapion of Macedonia (c.195) M.
St Myrope of Chios (c.251) M.
*SS Brigid and Maura (5th cent.).
*St Dofgan of Wales (5th cent.) M.
SS Eugene, Salutaris, Muritta and Comp. (505) MM.
*St Mildred of Thanet (c.700) Abs. O.S.B.
St Turiaf of Dol (c.750) Bp.
*Bl Berthold of Scheda (c.1214) C. O.Praem.
*Bl James of Voragine (c.1298) Bp. O.P.
*Bl Thomas Tunstal (1616) M. O.S.B.
*Bl Nicholas The (1838) M.

JULY 14.

St Phocas of Sinope (117) Bp. M.
St Heraclias of Alexandria (247) Bp.
St Cyrus of Carthage (?) Bp.
St Justus of Rome (?) M.
St Felix of Como (c.390) Bp.
*St Idus of Leinster (5th cent.) Bp.
St Optatian of Brescia (c.505) Bp.
St Marcellinus of Oldensee (c.762) C.
*St Libert of Saint-Trond (783) M. O.S.B.
*St Ulric of Cluny (1093) C. O.S.B.
*St William of Breteuil (1130) Ab. O.S.B.
St Bonaventure (1274) Card. Bp. Dr. O.F.M.
*Bl Humbert of Romans (1277) C. O.P.
*Bl Caspar de Bono (1604) O.Minim.
St Francis Solano (1610) C. O.F.M.
*Bl Richard Langhorne (1679) M.

JULY 15.

SS Eutropius, Zosima and Nonosa (c.273) MM.
SS Catulinus, Januarius, Florentius, Julia and Justa (?) MM.
St Felix of Pavia (?) Bp. M.
SS Philip, Zeno, Narseus and Comp. (?) MM.
SS Antiochus and Cyriacus (3rd cent.) MM.
St James of Nisibis (c.340) Bp.
St Abudimus of Tenedos (4th cen* M.

*St Apronia of Troyes (5th or 6th cent.)
V.

*St Eternus of Evreux (p. 660) Bp.

*St Plechelm of Guelderland (c.730)
Bp.

*St Donald of Ogilvy (8th cent.) C.

*St Benedict of Angers (c.820) Bp.

*St Adalard the Younger (c.824) C.
O.S.B.

*St Haruch of Werden (c.830) Bp.
O.S.B.

St Benildis of Cordova (853) M.

St Swithun of Winchester (862) Bp.
O.S.B.

St Athanasius of Naples (872) Bp.

*St Edith of Polesworth (?925) W.
O.S.B.

*St Vladimir of Russia (1015) King.

St Henry II (1024) Emperor Ob.O.S.B.

*St David of Sweden (c.1080) Bp.
O.S.B.

*St Egino of Augsburg (1122) Ab.
O.S.B.

*St Baldwin of Rieti (1140) Ab. O.S.B.
Cist.

*Bl Angelina of Marsciano (1435) W.
Tert.O.F.M.

*Bl Bernard of Baden (1458) C.

*BB Ignatius de Azevedo and Comp.
(1570) MM. S.J.

*St Pompilius Mary Pirotti (1756) C.
Sc.P.

*Bl Peter Tuan (1838) M.

JULY 16.

Feast of Our Lady of Mount Carmel.
St Faustus (250) M.

St Domnio of Bergamo (c.295) M.

St Vitalian of Capua (?) Bp.

St Valentine of Trèves (c.305) Bp. M.

St Eustace of Antioch (c.335) Bp.

*St Helier of Tongres (6th cent.) M.

*St Tenenan of Léon (c.635) Bp.

St Reneldis and Comp. (c.680) MM.

*St Generosus of Poitou (c.682) Ab.
O.S.B.

*St Vitalian of Osimo (776) Bp.

*St Fulrad of St-Denis (784) Ab. O.S.B.

St Sisenandus of Cordova (851) M.

*Bl Irmengard of Chiemsee (866) Abs.
O.S.B.

*Bl Milo of Selincourt (1159) Bp. O.
Praem.

*BB Mary St-Henry and Mary Magda-
len Justamond (1794) MM. O.S.B.
Cist.

St Mary Magdalen Postel (1846) V.
Foundress.

JULY 17.

SS Scillitan Martyrs (180).

St Generosus of Tivoli (?) M.

St Hyacinth of Paphlagonia (?) M.

St Marcellina of Rome (c.398) V.

St Alexius of Rome (early 5th cent.) C.

*St Cynllo of Wales (5th cent.).

St Theodosius of Auxerre (516) Bp.

St Ennodius of Pavia (521) Bp.

St Theodota of Constantinople (c.735)
M.

*St Fredegand of Kerkelodor (c.740)
Ab. O.S.B.

*St Turninus of Antwerp (8th cent.) C.

*St Kenelm (821) King M.

St Leo IV (855) Pope O.S.B.

*SS Seven Apostles of Bulgaria (7th-
8th cent.) CC.

*SS Andrew and Benedict (c.1020)
MM. O.S.B.Cam.

*SS Ansuerus and Comp. (p.1066) MM.
O.S.B.

*St Nerses Lambronazzi (1198) Bp.

*Bl Benignus Visdomini (1236) Ab.
O.S.B.Vall.

*Bl Ceslas of Poland (1242) C. O.P.

*BB Carmelite Nuns of Compiègne
(1794) MM.

JULY 18.

SS Symphorosa and Comp. (c.135) MM.

St Gundenis of Carthage (203) V. M.

St Marina of Orense (?) V. M.

St Maternus of Milan (c.307) Bp.

St Emilian of Bulgaria (362) M.

St Rufilius of Forlimpopoli (382) Bp.

St Philastrius of Brescia (c.387) Bp.

St Pambo of the Nitrian Desert (c.390)
Ab.

*St Goneri of Brittany (6th cent.) C.

St Arnulf of Metz (640) Bp.

*SS Edburga and Edith (c.650) VV. O.S.B.

*St Theneva of Glasgow (7th cent.) W.

St Frederick of Utrecht (838) Bp. M.

*St Minnborinus of Cologne (986) Ab. O.S.B.

St Bruno of Segni (1123) Bp. O.S.B.

*St Herveus of Anjou (1130) H.

*Bl Bertha of Marbais (1247) W. O.S.B. Cist.

*Bl Alanus of Sassovivo (1313) H. O.S.B.

*Bl Robert of Salentino (1341) Ab. O.S.B.Cel.

St Camillus de Lellis (1614) Founder.

*Bl Dominic Nicholas Dat (1838) M.

JULY 19.

St Epaphras (1st cent.) Bp. M.

St Martin of Trèves (c.210) Bp. M.

SS Justa and Rufina (287) VV. MM.

St Felix of Verona (?) Bp.

St Macrina the Younger (c.380) V.

St Arsenius the Great (c.449) H.

St Symmachus (514) Pope.

*St Ambrose Autpertus (c.778) Ab. O.S.B.

*St Jerome of Pavia (787) Bp.

St Aurea of Cordova (856) W. M.

*Bl Bernard of Rodez (1079) Card. O.S.B.

*Bl Stilla of Abenberg (c.1141) V.

*St Stephen del Lupo (1191) Ab. O.S.B.

*Bl Hroznata of Bohemia (1217) M. O.Praem.

St Vincent de Paul (1660) C. Founder.

*Bl John Plesington (1679) M.

JULY 20.

St Elias (8th cent. B.C.) Prophet.

St Joseph Barsabas (1st cent.) Disciple.

St Margaret of Antioch (c.304) V. M.

SS Sabinus, Julian, Maximus, Macrobius, Cassia, Paula and ten Comp. (?) MM.

St Wilgefortis (?) V.

*St Rheticus of Autun (334) Bp.

*St Barhadbesciabas (355) M.

*St Aurelius of Carthage (429) Bp.

St Severa of Villeneuve (c.680) Abs.

*St Wulmar of Samer (689) Ab. O.S.B.

*St Severa of Öhren (c.750) Abs. O.S.B.

*St Ansegisus of Fontenelle (833) Ab. O.S.B.

St Paul of Cordova (851) M.

*St Etheldwitha of Winchester (903) W. O.S.B.

St Jerome Emiliani (1537) C. Founder.

*Bl Gregory López (1596) H.

JULY 21.

St Daniel (5th cent. B.C.) Prophet.

St Praxedes of Rome (2nd cent.) V.

St Zoticus of Cappadocia (204) Bp. M.

St Julia of Troyes (p. 272) V. M.

SS Claudius, Justus, Jucundinus and Comp. (273) MM.

SS Victor, Alexander, Felician and Longinus (304) MM.

*St Constantine of Montecassino (c.560) Ab. O.S.B.

St John of Edessa (6th cent.) H.

St Arbogast of Strassburg (c.678) Bp.

*SS John and Benignus (707) CC. O.S.B.

*St Wastrada of Utrecht (c.670) Matron.

*Bl Oddino Barrotti (1400) C. Tert. O.F.M.

JULY 22.

St Mary Magdalen (1st cent.).

St Syntyche of Philippi (1st cent.).

St Cyril of Antioch (c.300) Bp.

St Plato of Ancyra (c.306) M.

St Joseph of Palestine (c.356) C.

*St Pancharius of Besançon (c.356) M.

*St Movean of Inis-Coosery (?) Ab.

*St Dabius of Scotland (?) C.

St Wandrille of Fontenelle (668) Ab. O.S.B.

St Meneleus (c.720) of Ménat. Ab. O.S.B.

St Theophilus of Cyprus (789) M.

*Bl Augustine Fangi (1493) C. O.P.

St Laurence of Brindisi (1619) C. O.F.M.Cap.

*BB Philip Evans S.J. and John Lloyd (1679) MM.

JULY 23.

St Apollinaris of Ravenna (1st cent.) Bp. M.
SS Trophimus and Theophilus (c.302) MM.
*St Phocas the Gardener (c.303) M.
SS Apollonius and Eugene (?) MM.
St Rasyphus of Rome (?) M.
St Primitiva of Rome (?) V. M.
St Liborius of Le Mans (390) Bp.
*St John Cassian (c.433) Ab.
*St Valerian of Cimiez (c.460) Bp.
*SS Rasyphus and Ravennus (5th cent.) MM.
SS Romula, Redempta and Herundo (c.580) VV.
SS Martyrs of Bulgaria (9th cent.).
*St Anne of Constantinople (c.918) V. H.
*Bl Jane of Orvieto (1306) V. Tert.O.P.

JULY 24.

SS Victor, Stercatius and Antinogenes (304) MM.
SS Meneus and Capito (?) MM.
SS Niceta and Aquilina (?) MM.
St Christina of Tuscany (?) V. M.
St Vincent of Rome (?) M.
St Ursicinus of Sens (c.380) Bp.
*St Dictinus of Astorga (420) Bp.
*St Declan of Ardmore (5th cent.) Bp.
*St Lewina of Berg (5th cent.) V. M.
*St Menefrida of Cornwall (5th cent.) V.
*St Germoc of Cornwall (6th cent.) C.
*SS Wulfhade and Ruffinus (675) MM.
*St Godo of Oye (c.690) Ab. O.S.B.
*St Christiana of Termonde (7th cent.) V.
*St Sigolena of Troclar (c.769) Abs. O.S.B.
*St Aliprandus of Ciel d'Oro (8th cent.) Ab. O.S.B.
*SS Romanus and David (1010) MM.
*Bl Christina the Astonishing (1224) V.
*St Kinga of Poland (13th cent.) V. Tert.O.F.M.

*Bl Nicholas Hermansson (1391) Bp.
*Bl John of Tossignano (1446) C.
*Bl Louise of Savoy (1503) W. Poor Clare.
*Bl John Boste (1594) M.
*Bl Antony Turriani (1694) C. O.S.A.
*Bl Joseph Fernández (1838) M. O.P.

JULY 25.

St James the Greater (c.43) Apostle.
St Christopher (?) M.
SS Florentius and Felix (235) MM.
St Cucufas of Barcelona (304) M.
St Paul of Gaza (308) M.
SS Valentina and Comp. (308) VV. MM.
*St Nissen of Wexford (5th cent.) Ab.
St Magnericus of Trèves (596) Bp.
*St Ebrulfus of Beauvais (c.600) Ab.
*St Glodesind of Metz (c.608) Abs.
St Theodemir of Cordova (851) M.
*St Fagildus of Compostella (1086) Ab. O.S.B.

JULY 26.

St Anne (1st cent.).
St Erastus of Corinth (1st cent.) Bp. M.
St Hyacinth (c.110) M.
St Pastor of Rome (c.160) C.
*BB George Swallowell and John Ingram (1594) MM.
*Bl William Ward (1641) M.
*Bl Bartholomaea Capitanio (1833) V. Foundress.

JULY 27.

SS Maurus, Pantaleemon and Sergius (c.117) MM.
SS Felix, Julia and Jucunda (?) MM.
SS Hermolaus, Hermippus and Hermocrates (c.300) MM.
St Pantaleon the Physician (c.305) M.
SS Seven Sleepers (250-362) MM.
St Celestine I (432) Pope.
*St Ecclesius of Ravenna (532) Bp.
St Etherius of Auxerre (573) Bp. C.

St Anthusa of Constantinople (8th cent.) V.

SS George, Aurelius, Natalia, Felix and Liliosa (c.852) MM.

*Bl Berthold of Garsten (1142) Ab. O.S.B.

*Bl Conrad of Ottobeuren (1227) Ab. O.S.B.

*St Theobald of Marly (1247) Ab. O.S.B.Cist.

*Bl Nevolo of Faenza (1280) H. O.S.B. Cam.

*Bl Lucy Bufalari (1350) V. O.S.A.

*BB Rudolph Acquaviva and four Comp. (1583) MM. S.J.

*Bl Mary Magdalen Martinengo (1737) V. O.F.M.Cap.

JULY 28.

SS Nazarius and Celsus (c.68) MM.

St Victor I (c.199) Pope.

St Peregrinus of Lyons (2nd cent.) H.

St Eustace of Galatia (?) M.

St Acacius of Miletus (c.310) M.

St Innocent I (417) Pope.

*St Camelian (c.525) Bp.

*St Samson of Brittany (c.565) Bp.

*St Arduinus of Ceprano (7th cent.) C.

*St Lucidus of Aquara (c.938) H. O.S.B.

*St Botwid of Sweden (1100) M.

*Bl Antony della Chiesa (1459) C. O.P.

JULY 29.

St Martha (c.80) V.

St Serapia of Syria (119) V. M.

SS Lucilla, Flora VV., Eugene, Antony, Theodore and Comp. (c.260) MM.

St Callinicus of Paphlagonia (3rd cent.) M.

SS Simplicius, Faustinus and Beatrix (303) MM.

St Felix II (366) Pope M.

St Faustinus of Spello (4th cent.) C.

St Seraphina (c.426).

St Prosper of Orléans (c.453) Bp.

St Lupus of Troyes (478) Bp.

*St Kilian (7th cent.) Ab.

St Olav of Norway (1030) King M.

Bl Urban II (1099) Pope O.S.B.

St William of Saint-Brieuc (1234) Bp.

*Bl Beatrix of Valfleury (1268) V. O.S.B.Cist.

*BB Louis Bertrán and two Comp. (1629) MM. O.P.

*BB Joseph Tshang, Hohn Baptist Lo and Martha Wang (1861) MM.

JULY 30.

SS Abdon and Sennen (3rd or 4th cent.) MM.

St Julitta of Caesarea (303) M.

SS Maxima, Donatilla and Secunda (304) VV. MM.

St Rufinus of Assisi (?) M.

St Ursus of Auxerre (508) Bp.

*St Ermengytha of Thanet (c.680) V. O.S.B.

*St Tatwin of Canterbury (734) Bp. O.S.B.

*St Olav of Sweden (c.950) King M.

*St Hatebrand of Olden-Klooster (1198) Ab. O.S.B.

*Bl Manes de Guzman (1230) C. O.P.

*Bl John Soreth (1471) C. O.C.

*Bl Archangelus of Calafatimi (1460) C. O.F.M.

*Bl Simon of Lipnicza (1482) C. O.F.M.

*Bl Peter of Mogliano (1490) C. O.F.M.

*BB Edward Powell, Richard Featherstone and Thomas Abel (1540) MM.

*Bl Everard Hanse (1581) M.

JULY 31.

St Calimerius of Milan (c.190) Bp. M.

St Fabius of Mauritania (300) M.

SS Democritus, Secundus and Dionysius (?) MM.

St Firmus of Tagaste (?) Bp.

St Germanus of Auxerre (448) Bp.

*St Neot of Cornwall (c.880) H. O.S.B.

*St Helen of Sköfde (c.1160) W. M.

*Bl John Colombini (1367) Founder.

St Ignatius of Loyola (1556) Founder.

*BB Emmanuel Phung and Peter Qui (1859) MM.

AUGUST 1.

SS Machabees (166 B.C.) MM.

SS Faith, Hope and Charity (c.120) VV. MM.

SS Bonus, Faustus, Maurus and Comp. (257) MM.

St Justin of Paris (c.290) M.

SS Leontius, Attius, Alexander and Comp. (c.300) MM.

St Felix of Gerona (303) M.

SS Cyril, Aquila, Peter, Domitian, Rufus and Menander (?) MM.

St Nemesius of Lisieux (?).

St Verus of Vienne (p. 314) Bp.

*St Rioch of Innisboffin (c.480) Ab.

*St Sidwell (?) V. M.

*St Friardus of Nantes (c.577) H.

*St Kenneth of Wales (6th cent.) H.

*St Peregrinus of Modena (643) H.

*St Jonatus of Elnone (c.695) Ab. O.S.B.

*St Almedha of Brecknock (9th cent.) V. M.

St Ethelwold of Winchester (984) Bp. O.S.B.

*Bl Albert of Vallumbrosa (end 11th cent.) C. O.S.B.Vall.

*Bl Emeric of Aosta (1318) Bp.

*Bl Thomas Welbourne (1605) M.

*BB Bernard Due and Dominic Dien O.P. (1838) MM.

AUGUST 2.

St Maximus of Padua (c.195) Bp.

St Rutilius of Africa (250) M.

St Stephen I (257) Pope M.

St Theodota and her three Sons (304) MM.

*St Boetharius of Chartres (7th cent.) Bp.

*St Etheldritha of Croyland (834) V. O.S.B.

*St Plegmund of Canterbury (914) Bp. O.S.B.

*St Peter of Osma (1109) Bp. O.S.B.

St Alphonsus Mary Liguori (1787) Bp. Dr. Founder.

AUGUST 3.

St Nicodemus (1st cent.) M.

St Gamaliel (1st cent.).

St Abibas (1st cent.) C.

St Aspren of Naples (1st cent.) Bp.

St Lydia Purpuraria (1st cent.) Matron.

St Hermellus of Constantinople (?) M.

SS Marana and Cyra (5th cent.) MM.

St Euphronius of Autun (p. 475) Bp.

*St Trea of Ardtree (5th cent.) V.

*St Senach of Clonard (6th cent.) Bp.

*Bl Gregory of Nonantula (933) Ab. O.S.B.

*Bl Benno of Metz (940) Bp. O.S.B.

St Peter of Anagni (1105) Bp. O.S.B.

*St Waltheof of Melrose (1160) Ab. O.S.B.Cist.

*Bl Augustine Gazotich (1323) Bp. O.P.

*Bl Peter Julian Eymard (1868) Founder.

AUGUST 4.

St Perpetua of Rome (c.80).

St Aristarchus of Salonika (1st cent.) Bp. M.

St Agabius of Verona (c.250) Bp.

St Tertullinus of Rome (257) M.

St Protasius of Cologne (?) M.

St Eleutherius of Constantinople (before 310) M.

SS Ia and Comp. (360) MM.

St Euphronius of Tours (573) Bp.

*St Luanus (622) Ab.

*St Raynerius of Spalatro (1180) M. Bp. O.S.B.

St Dominic of Guzman (1221) Founder O.P.

*Bl Cicco of Pesaro (1350) C. Tert. O.F.M.

*BB William Horne and Comp. (1540) MM. O.Cart.

AUGUST 5.

Dedication of the Church of Our Lady of the Snow.

SS Addai and Mari (1st cent.?) Bps.

SS Cantidius, Cantidian and Sobel (?) MM.

St Memmius of Chalons-sur-Marne (c.300) Bp.

St Emygdius of Ascoli (c.303) Bp. M.

St Afra of Augsburg (c.304) V. M.

St Paris of Teano (346) Bp.

St Cassian of Autun (c.350) Bp.

St Eusignius of Antioch (362) M.
St Nonna of Nazianzen (374) W.
*St Venantius of Viviers (544) Bp.
St Oswald of Northumbria (642) King M.
*St Abel of Reims (c.571) Bp. O.S.B.
*St Theodore of Cambrai (863) Bp.
*St Gormgal of Ardoilen (1016) Ab.
*St Thomas of Dover (1295) M. O.S.B.
*Bl James Gerius (1345) C. O.S.B.Cam.

AUGUST 6.

Transfiguration of Our Lord Jesus Christ.
St Sixtus II Pope and Comp. (258) MM.
SS Justus and Pastor (c.304) MM.
St James the Syrian (p. 500) C.
St Hormisdas (523) Pope.
SS Stephen of Cardeña and Comp. (872) MM. O.S.B.
*Bl Octavianus of Savona (c.1128) Bp. O.S.B.

AUGUST 7.

St Claudia (1st cent.) W.
St Fautus of Milan (c.190) M.
SS Peter, Julian and Comp. (c.260) MM.
SS Carpophorus, Exanthus, Cassius, Severinus, Secundus and Licinius (c.290) MM.
St Donatian of Chalons-sur-Marne (?) Bp.
SS Donatus and Hilary (361) MM.
SS Domitius and Comp. (4th cent.) MM.
St Victricius of Rouen (c.409) Bp.
*St Donatus of Besançon (before 660) Bp. O.S.B.
*Bl Jordan Forzatei (1248) Ab. O.S.B.
St Albert of Trapani (1306) C. O.C.
*Bl Vincent of Aquila (1504) C. O.F.M.
*St Cajetan of Tienne (1547) C. Founder.
*BB Agathangelus and Cassian (1638) MM. O.F.M.Cap.

AUGUST 8.

SS Fourteen Holy Helpers.
St Marinus of Cilicia (290) M.

SS Eleutherius and Leonides (?) MM.
SS Cyriacus, Largus and Comp. (304) MM.
St Myron the Wonder-Worker (c.350) Bp.
St Hormisdas of Persia (420) M.
St Severus of Gaul (p. 445) C.
St Gunifort of Pavia (?) M.
*St Leobald of Fleury (650) Ab. O.S.B.
*St Mummolus of Fleury (c.678) Ab. O.S.B.
*St Sigrada of Soissons (c.678) W. O.S.B.
*St Ternatius of Besançon (c.680) Bp.
*St Agilberta of Jouarre (c.680) Abs. O.S.B.
*St Ellidius of Hirnant (7th cent.) C.
*St Gedeon of Besançon (c.796) Bp.
*St Ultan of Craik (8th cent.) H. O.S.B.
*Bl Rathard of Andechs (815) C.
St Emilian of Cyzicus (c.820) Bp.
*St Altman of Passau (1091) Bp.
*St Famianus of Gallese (1150) H. O.S.B.Cist.
*Bl Jane of Aza (c.1190) W. O.P.
*Bl John Felton (1570) M.

AUGUST 9.

SS Secundian, Marcellian and Verian (250) MM.
St Numidicus and Comp. (252) MM.
St Romanus Ostiarius (258) M.
SS Firmus and Rusticus (c.290) MM.
*St Amor of Burgundy (?) M.
St Domitian of Chalons-sur-Marne (?) Bp.
*St Autor of Metz (5th cent.) Bp.
*St Bandaridus of Soissons (566) Bp.
*St Phelim of Kilmore (6th cent.) Bp.
*St Serenus of Marseilles (606) Bp.
*St Nathy of Achonry (c.610) Bp.
SS Julian, Marcian and Comp. (730) MM.
*St Maurilius of Rouen (1067) Bp. O.S.B.
*Bl Teuzzo of Florence (c.1072) C. O.S.B.
*Bl John of Salerno (1242) C. O.P.
*Bl John of Alvernia (1322) C. O.F.M
*Bl Falco of Palena (1440) H.
*Bl John of Rieti (c.1530) C. O.S.A.
St John Baptist Vianney (1859) C.

AUGUST 10.

St Laurence of Rome (258) M.
SS Martyrs of Alexandria (260-267).
SS Bassa, Paula and Agathonica (?) VV. MM.
St Asteria of Bergamo (c.307) V. M.
*St Gerontius (?508) King M.
*St Blane of Scotland (6th cent.) Bp.
St Deusdedit of Rome (6th cent.) C.
*SS Thiento and Comp. (955) MM. O.S.B.
*Bl Hugh de Montaigu (1136) Bp. O.S.B.
*Bl Conrad Nantwin (1268) M.
*Bl Amadeus of Portugal (1482) C. O.F.M.

AUGUST 11.

St Alexander Carbonarius (250) Bp. M.
St Tiburtius of Rome (c.288) M.
St Susanna of Rome (295) V. M.
*St Chomatius of Rome (3rd cent.) C.
SS Rufinus and Comp. (?) MM.
*St Philomena of Mugnano (?) V. M.
St Digna of Todi (4th cent.) V.
St Taurinus of Evreux (c.412) Bp.
*St Attracta of Drum (5th cent.) V.
*St Lelia of Limerick (?) V.
St Equitius of Valeria (c.540) Ab.
St Gaugericus of Cambrai (c.625) Bp.
*BB John and Peter Becchetti (13th cent.) CC. O.S.A.
*BB Laurence Nerucci, Augustine Cennini, Bartholomew Sonati and John Baptist Petrucci (1420) MM. O.S.M.
*Bl Nicholas Appleine (1466) C.
*Bl Peter Faber (1546) C. S.J.

AUGUST 12.

St Antoninus of Rome (186) M.
St Euplius of Catania (304) M.
SS Gracilian and Felicissima (c.304) MM.
SS Hilaria, Digna, Euprepia, Eunomia, Quiriacus, Largio, Crescentian, Nimmia, Juliana and Comp. (c.304) MM.
SS Anicetus, Photinus and Comp. (c.305) MM.
SS Macarius and Julian (?) MM.

St Merewenna (?) V.
*St Ust of Penzance (?).
*St Cassian of Benevento (c.340) Bp.
St Eusebius of Milan (465) Bp.
SS Porcarius and Comp. (c.732) MM. O.S.B.
*St Jambert of Canterbury (790) Bp. O.S.B.
St Clare of Assisi (1253) V. Foundress.
*BB Michael Mi, James Nam and Antony Dich (1838) MM.

AUGUST 13.

SS Hippolytus, Concordia and Comp. (c.236) MM.
SS Centolla and Helen (c.304) MM.
St Cassian of Imola (?) M.
St Cassian of Todi (4th cent.) Bp. M.
*St Muredach of Killala (c.455) Bp.
St Herculanus of Brescia (c.550) Bp.
St Radegund of Poitiers (587) Queen.
*St Junian of Chaulnay (587) Ab.
SS Maximus Homologetes and Comp. (662) CC.
St Wigbert of Fritzlar (c.746) Ab. O.S.B.
*St Herulph of Langres (785) Bp. O.S.B.
*St Ludolphus of New Corvey (983) Ab. O.S.B.
*St Nerses Glaietsi (1173) Bp.
*Bl Gertrude of Altenberg (1297) Abs. O.Praem.
*St Radegund of Augsburg (before 1300) V.
*Bl Francis of Pesaro (1530) C. O.F.M. Tert.
*Bl William Freeman (1595) M.
St John Berchmans (1621) C. S.J.

AUGUST 14.

*St Eusebius of Palestine (3rd cent.) M.
St Demetrius of Africa (?) M.
St Ursicius of Nicomedia (304) M.
St Eusebius of Rome (c.357) C.
St Marcellus of Apamaea (389) Bp. M.
St Callistus of Todi (528) Bp. M.
*St Fachanan of Ross (late 6th cent.) Bp.
*St Werenfrid of Arnheim (c.780) C. O.S.B.

*St Athanasia of Constantinople (860) W.

*Bl Eberhard of Einsiedeln (958) Ab. O.S.B.

*BB Antony Primaldi and Comp. (1480) MM.

*Bl Sanctes Brancasino (1490) C. O.F.M.

*Bl Juliana Puricelli (1501) V. O.S.A.

AUGUST 15.

Feast of the Assumption of Our Lady.
St Tarcisius of Rome (c.255) M.
St Napoleon of Alexandria (c.300) M.
St Alipius of Tagaste (c.430) Bp.
*St Altfrid of Hildesheim (874) Bp. O.S.B.
*St Arduinus of Rimini (1009) H. O.S.B.
St Arnulf of Soissons (1087) Bp. O.S.B.
*St Rupert of Ottobeuren (1145) Ab. O.S.B.
*St Limbania of Genoa (1294) V. O.S.B.
St Stanislaus Kostka (1568) C. S.J.

AUGUST 16.

St Joachim (1st cent. B.C.) Patriarch.
St Serena of Rome (c.290).
St Diomedes of Tarsus (300) M.
St Ambrose of Ferentino (c.303) M.
St Arsacius of Nicomedia (358) C.
St Simplician of Milan (400) Bp.
St Titus of Rome (c.410) M.
St Eleutherius of Auxerre (561) Bp.
*St Armagillus of Brittany (c.570) C.
*St Uguzo of Carvagna (?) M.
*Bl Ralph de la Futaye (1129) Ab. O.S.B.
*Bl Laurence Loricatus (1243) H. O.S.B.
St Roch of Montpellier (1337) C.
*Bl Angelus Agostini Mazzinghi (1438) C. O.C.

AUGUST 17.

St Myron of Cyzicus (c.250) M.
SS Paul and Juliana (c.270) MM.
St Mamas of Cappadocia (c.275) M.
SS Straton, Philip and Eutychian (c.301) MM.
St Eusebius (310) Pope.
SS Liberatus, Boniface, Servus, Rusti-

cus, Rogatus, Septimus and Maximus (483) MM.

St Anastasius of Terni (653) Bp.

*St James the Deacon (7th cent.) C. O.S.B.

*St Drithelm of Melrose (c.700) H.

*Bl Carloman of Austrasia (755) King O.S.B.

*St Amor of Amorbach (c.767) Ab. O.S.B.

*St Theodulus of Grammont (c.840) Bp. O.S.B.

*St Hiero of Holland (885) M.

*SS Benedicta and Caecilia (10th cent.) Abs. O.S.B.

*St John of Monte Marano (1094) Bp. O.S.B.

*Bl Nicholas Politi (1167) H.

*St Donatus of Ripacandida (1198) C. O.S.B.

St Hyacinth of Cracow (1257) C. O.P.

*St Clare of Montefalco (1308) V. O.S.A.

AUGUST 18.

SS Floridus, Laurus, Proculus and Maximus (2nd cent.) MM.

St Agapitus of Palestrina (c.274) M.

SS Hermas, Serapion and Polyaenus (?) MM.

SS Leo and Juliana (?) MM.

SS John and Crispus (c.303) MM.

St Firminus of Metz (496) Bp.

*St Dagaeus of Iniskin (c.560) Bp.

*Bl Milo of Fontenelle (c.730) H. O.S.B.

*St Evan of Ayrshire (9th cent.) H.

*Bl Leonard of Cava (1255) Ab. O.S.B.

*St Hugh of Lincoln (1255) M.

*Bl Raynald of Ravenna (1321) Bp.

*Bl Beatrix da Silva (1490) Abs. O.S.B. Cist.

Bl Aimo Taparelli (1495) C. O.P.

AUGUST 19.

St Julius of Rome (c.190) M.
St Magnus of Anagni (c.250) Bp. M.
St Rufinus of Mantua (?).
SS Andrew the Tribune and Comp. (c.303) MM.

SS Timothy, Thecla and Agapius (304-306) MM.

St Sixtus III (440) Pope.

St Marianus of Entreaigues (c.515) H.

*St Mochta of Louth (c.534) Bp.

St Donatus of Sisteron (c.535) C.

*St Elaphius of Chalons-sur-Marne (580) Bp.

*St Bertulfus of Bobbio (640) Ab.

*St Magnus of Avignon (660) Bp. O.S.B.

*St Calminius of Villars (c.690) H.

*St Guenninus of Vannes (7th cent.) Bp.

*St Namadia of Marsat (c.700) V. O.S.B.

St Sebald of Nuremberg (c.770) H. O.S.B.

*St Credan of Evesham (c.780) Ab. O.S.B.

*St Marinus of Besalú (c.800) Bp. O.S.B.

*St Badulfus of Ainay (c.850) Ab. O.S.B.

*Bl Guerricus of Igny (c.1157) Ab. O.S.B.Cist.

*Bl Leo II of Cava (1295) Ab. O.S.B.

St Louis of Toulouse (1297) Bp. O.F.M.

*Bl Angelus of Acquapagana (1313) C. O.S.B.Cam.

*Bl Emily Bicchieri (1314) V. O.P.

*BB Louis Flores O.P., Francis of St Mary O.F.M., Peter Zúniga O.S.A., Joachim Firaiama-Diaz and Comp. (1622) MM.

*Bl Hugh Green (1642) M.

St John Eudes (1680) Founder.

AUGUST 20.

St Samuel (11th cent. B.C.) Prophet.

SS Severus, Mennon and Comp. (c. 300) MM.

St Porphyrius of Palestrina (?) M.

SS Martyrs of Thrace (?).

St Amator of Rocamadour (?) C.

SS Lucius and Comp. (311) MM.

*St Oswin (651) King M.

St Haduin of Le Mans (c.662) Bp.

St Philibert of Jumièges (684) Ab. O.S.B.

*St Edbert of York (768) King O.S.B.

SS Leovigild and Christopher (852) MM.

*Bl Burchard of Worms (1026) Bp. O.S.B.

St Bernard of Clairvaux (1153) Ab. Dr. O.S.B.Cist.

*St Bernard of Valdeiglesias (p. 1155) C. O.S.B.Cist.

*St Ronald of Orkney (1158) M.

*St Herbert Hoscam (1180) Bp.

*Bl Gobert of Villiers (1263) C. O.S.B. Cist.

St Manettus (1268) C. O.S.M.

AUGUST 21.

St Euprepius of Verona (1st cent.) Bp.

St Cyriaca of Rome (249) W.

St Paternus of Egypt (c.255) M.

St Privatus of Mende (266) Bp. M.

St Anastasius Cornicularius (274) M.

SS Luxorius, Cisellus and Camerinus (c.303) MM.

SS Bassa, Theogonius, Agapius and Fidelis (304) MM.

St Quadratus (?) Bp.

SS Bonosus and Maximian (362) MM.

St Sidonius Apollinaris (c.488) Bp.

*St Hardulph (?).

*St Leontius the Elder (c.541) Bp.

*St Avitus I of Clermont (c.600) Bp.

*SS Mary and Gratia (c.1180) VV. MM.

*Bl Gilbert of Valenciennes (1185) Ab. O.S.B.

Bl Bernard Tolomeo (1348) Founder, O.S.B.

*BB Ambrose Piccolomini and Patrick de'Patrizi (c.1348) CC. O.S.B.Oliv.

St Jane Frances Fémiol de Chantal (1641) W. Foundress.

*Bl Joseph Nien (1838) M.

AUGUST 22.

St Symphorian of Autun (c.180) M.

SS Athanasius, Anthusa and Comp. (c.257) MM.

SS Agathonicus, Zoticus and Comp. (end 3rd cent.) MM.

SS Fabrician and Philibert (?) MM.
St Hippolytus of Porto (?) *Bp. M.*
SS Maurus and Comp. (?) MM.
SS Martial, Saturninus, Epictetus, Maprilis, Felix and Comp. (c.300) MM.
St Neophytus of Nicaea (310) M.
St Timothy of Rome (311) M.
*St Sigfrid of Wearmouth (688) Ab. O.S.B.
*St Ethelgitha of Northumbria (c.720) Abs. O.S.B.
*St Arnulf of Eynesbury (9th cent.) H.
*St Andrew of Tuscany (c.880) Ab. O.S.B.
*Bl Lambert of Chézery (1151) Ab. O.S.B.Cist.
*BB William Lacey and Richard Kirkman (1582) MM.
*BB John Wall O.F.M. and John Kemble (1679) MM.
*Bl Bernard of Offida (1694) C. O.F.M. Cap.

AUGUST 23.

St Zaccheus of Jerusalem (c.116) Bp.
SS Quiriacus, Maximus, Archelaus and Comp. (c.235) MM.
SS Timothy and Apollinaris (c.290) MM.
SS Minervus, Eleazar and Comp. (3rd cent.) MM.
St Theonas of Alexandria (300) Bp.
SS Claudius, Asterius, Neon, Donvina and Theonilla (303) MM.
St Lupus (?) M.
SS Restitutus, Donatus, Valerian, Fructuosa and Comp. (c.305) MM.
St Maximus of Chinon (c.470) Ab.
*St Tydfil of Glamorgan (c.480) M.
St Victor of Vita (c.505) Bp.
*St Eugene of Tyrone (618) Bp.
*St Flavian of Autun (7th cent.) Bp.
*SS Altigianus and Hilarinus (731) MM. O.S.B.
*St Ebba the Younger and Comp. (c. 870) VV. MM. O.S.B.
*Bl Richildis of Hohenwart (c.1100) V. O.S.B.
St Philip Benizi (1285) C. O.S.M.
*Bl James of Mevania (1301) C. O.P.

AUGUST 24.

St Bartholomew (1st cent.) Apostle M.
St Romanus of Nepi (1st cent.) Bp. M.
St Eutychius of Phrygia (1st cent.).
St Ptolomy of Nepi (1st cent.) Bp. M.
SS Massa Candida (c.260) MM.
St Aurea of Ostia (c.260) V. M.
St Tation of Cladiopolis (c.304) M.
*St Patrick the Elder (c.450) Ab.
*St Yrchard of Scotland (5th cent.) Bp.
St George Limniotes (c.730) M.
*Bl Sandratus of Gladbach (986) Ab. O.S.B.
*Bl Alice Rich (c.1270) V. O.S.B.
*Bl Luke Mellini (c.1460) Ab. O.S.B. Cel.

AUGUST 25.

St Geruntius of Italica (c.100) Bp. M.
SS Eusebius, Pontian, Vincent and Peregrinus (192) MM.
SS Nemesius and Lucilla (c.260) MM.
St Genesius the Comedian (c.300) M.
St Genesius of Arles (c.303) M.
St Maginus of Tarragona (c.304) M.
St Julian the Syrian (?) M.
St Mennas of Constantinople (552) Bp.
*St Aredius of Atane (591) Ab.
St Patritia of Naples (c.665) V.
*St Ebba the Elder (683) Abs. O.S.B.
*St Hunegund of Homblieres (c.690) V. O.S.B.
St Gregory of Utrecht (c.776) Ab. O.S.B.
*St Marcian of Saignon (1010) Ab. O.S.B.
*St Gurloës of Quimperlé (1057) Ab. O.S.B.
St Louis IX (1270) King.
St Thomas of Hereford (1282) Bp.
*BB Louis Sotelo O.F.M., Michael Carvalho S.J. and Comp. (1627) MM.
*Bl Jane Antide Thouret (1828) V. Foundress.
*St Mary Michaela (1865) V. Foundress.

AUGUST 26.

SS Simplicius, Constantius and Victorian (c.161) MM.

St Zephyrinus (217) Pope M.
SS Irenaeus and Abundius (c.258) MM.
St Gelasinus of Heliopolis (297) M.
St Alexander of Bergamo (297) M.
St Secundus of Ventimiglia (3rd cent.) M.
St Adrian of Nicomedia (?) M.
St Rufinus of Capua (5th cent.) Bp.
*St Elias of Syracuse (660) Bp. O.S.B.
*St Bregwin of Canterbury (765) Bp. O.S.B.
St Felix of Pistoia (9th cent.) H.
*St Pandwina of Ettisley (c.904) V. O.S.B.
St Victor of Cerezo (c.950) M.
*Bl Herluin of Bec (1078) Ab. O.S.B.
*Bl Vyevain of York (1285) Bp.
*St Margaret of Faenza (1330) Abs. O.S.B.Vall.
*Bl John of Caramola (1339) C. O.S.B. Cist.
*Bl John Bassano (1445) C. O.S.B.Cel.
*Bl Timothy of Montecchio (1504) C. O.F.M.
*Bl Thomas Percy (1572) M.

AUGUST 27.

St Narnus of Bergamo (c.75) Bp.
St Rufus of Capua (1st cent.) Bp. M.
St Rufus and Carpophorus (295) MM.
St Anthusa the Younger (?) V. M.
St Euthalia of Lentini (?) V. M.
SS Honoratus, Fortunatus, Arontius, Sabinian (c.303) MM.
SS Marcellinus, Mannea, John, Serapion, Peter and Comp. (c.303) MM.
St Poemon of Skete (c.450) H.
St Caesarius of Arles (542) Bp.
St Licerius of Conserans (c.548) Bp.
St Syagrius of Autun (600) Bp.
*St Etherius of Lyons (602) Bp.
*St Decuman of Wales (716) M.
*St Ebbo of Sens (740) Bp. O.S.B.
St John of Pavia (813) Bp.
*Bl Agilo of Sithiu (957) Ab. O.S.B.
*St Gebhard of Constance (995) Bp.
*St Malrubius of Scotland (c.1040) M.
*Bl Ebbo of Hamberg (1162) Ab. O.S.B.
*Bl Angelus of Foligno (1312) C. O.S.A.
*Bl Margaret the Barefooted (1395) W.

*Bl Gabriel Mary (1532) C.
St Joseph Calasanctius (1648) Founder.
*Bl David Lewis (1679) M. S.J.

AUGUST 28.

SS Hermes and Comp. (c.120) MM.
St Pelagius of Istria (c.283) M.
SS Fortunatus, Caius and Anthes (303) MM.
St Julian of Auvergne (304) M.
St Helen (c.330) Empress.
St Alexander of Constantinople (340) Bp.
St Moses the Black (c.395) M.
St Augustine of Hippo (430) Bp. Dr. Founder.
St Vivian of Saintes (c.460) Bp.
*St Ambrose of Saintes (p.475) Bp.
*St Facundinus of Taino (c.620) Bp.
*St Rumbold of Northumbria (c.650) C.
*Bl Adelindis of Buchau (c.930) W. O.S.B.
*St Gorman of Sleswig (965) Bp. O.S.B.
*Bl Adelina of Poulangy (1170) V. O.S.B.Cist.
*BB Hugh More, James Claxton, Robert Morton, Thomas Holford, Thomas Felton, William Dean and William Gunter (1588) MM.
*Bl Edmund Arrowsmith (1628) M. S.J.

AUGUST 29.

St Sabina of Rome (c.127) M.
St Sabina of Troyes (c.275) V.
St Basilla of Smyrna (?) V.
St Candida of Rome (?) V. M.
SS Nicaeas and Paul (?) MM.
SS Vitalis, Sator and Repositus (3rd or 4th cent.) MM.
St Euthymius of Perugia (4th cent.) C.
St Adelphius of Metz (5th cent.) Bp.
St Sebbe (c.694) King O.S.B.
St Medericus of Autun (c.700) Ab. O.S.B.
SS Hypatius and Andrew (735) MM.
*St Velleicus of Kaiserswerth (8th cent.) Ab. O.S.B.

*Bl Alberic of Ocri (c.1050) H. O.S.B.
Cam.
*Bl Philippa Guidoni (1335) Abs. O.S.B.
*Bl Richard Herst (1628) M.

AUGUST 30.

SS Boniface and Thecla (c.250) MM.
SS Felix and Adauctus (c.304) MM.
St Gaudentia and Comp. (?) VV. MM.
St Pammachius the Senator (410) C.
*St Loarn of Downpatrick (5th cent.) C.
*St Agilus of Rebais (650) Ab.
St Fiacre of Breuil (c.670) Ab.
*SS Pelagius, Arsenius and Silvanus
(c.950) MM.
St Fantinus of Calabria (p.980) Ab.
St Bononius of Locedio (1026) Ab.
O.S.B.Cam.
St Peter of Trevi (c.1060) C.
*Bl Bronislava of Poland (1259) V.
O.Praem.
*BB John Roche, Edward Shelley,
Richard Leigh, Richard Martin and
Margaret Ward (1588) MM.
St Rose of Lima (1617) V. O.P.

AUGUST 31.

St Aristides the Athenian (c.133).
SS Theodotus, Rufina and Amnia
(c.270) MM.
SS Caesidius and Comp. (3rd cent.)
MM.
SS Robustian and Mark (?) MM.
St Paulinus of Trèves (358) Bp.
St Optatus of Auxerre (c.530) Bp.
St Babolenus of Bobbio (c.640) Ab.
O.S.B.
St Aidan of Lindisfarne (651) Bp.
St Cuthburga of Wimborne (c.725)
Abs. O.S.B.
St Amatus of Nusco (1093 or 1193) Bp.
O.S.B.
St Raymund Nonnatus (1240) Card.
O.Merc.
*St Dominic del Val (1250) M.
*St Albertinus of Fonteavellana (1294)
C. O.S.B.
*BB Servite Martyrs (1420)
*Bl Richard Bere (1537) M.

SEPTEMBER 1.

St Joshua (15th cent. B.C.) Patriarch.
St Gideon (14th cent. B.C.).
St Anna the Prophetess (1st cent.) W.
St Priscus of Capua (c.66) M.
St Terentian of Todi (118) Bp. M.
St Verena of Zurich (3rd cent.) V.
St Sixtus of Reims (c.300) Bp.
St Ammon and Comp. (c.322) MM.
St Victorius of Le Mans (c.490) Bp.
SS Vincent and Laetus (5th cent.)
MM.
SS Priscus, Castrensis, Tammarus,
Rosius, Secundus, Heraclius, Adju-
tor, Mark, Augustus, Elpidius, Ca-
nion and Vindonius (5th cent.) CC.
*St Lythan of Wales (?).
St Constantius of Aquino (c.520) Bp.
St Regulus of Tuscany (c.545) M.
*St Silin of Brittany (6th cent.) C.
*St Agia of Sens (6th cent.) W.
St Lupus of Sens (c.623) Bp.
*St Nivard of Reims (c.670) Bp.
St Giles of Provence (c.712) Ab. O.S.B.
*SS Giles and Arcanus (c.1050) CC.
O.S.B.
*Bl Agnes of Venosa (c.1144) V. O.S.B.
Mont.
*Bl Giles of Castañeda (c.1203) Ab.
O.S.B.Cist.
*Bl Juliana of Collalto (1262) V. O.S.B.
*Bl Jane Soderini (1367) V. Tert.
O.S.M.
*Bl Michael Ghebre (1855) M. C.M.

SEPTEMBER 2.

SS Diomedes, Julian, Philip, Euty-
chian, Hesychius, Leonides, Phila-
delphus, Menalippus and Pantagapes
(?) MM.
St Antoninus (?) M.
St Maxima of Rome (304) M.
St Justus of Lyons (390) Bp.
*St Valentine of Strassburg (4th cent.)
Bp.
St Elpidius the Cappadocian (4th cent.)
Ab.
*St Castor of Apt (c.420) Bp.
St Elpidius of Lyons (422) Bp.
St Nonnosus of Mount Soracte (c.570)
C. O.S.B.

*St Heiu of Tadcaster (c.657) V.
St Agricola of Avignon (700) Bp.
*St Lolanus of Scotland (c.1034) C.
St Stephen of Hungary (1038) King.
*St William of Roeskilde (1067) Bp.
*Bl Margaret of Louvain (1225) V.
*St Brocard of Mount Carmel (1231) C.
O.C.
*BB Martyrs of September (1792) .

SEPTEMBER 3.

SS Euphemia, Dorothy, Thecla and
Erasma (1st cent.) VV. MM.
St Phoebe of Cenchreae (1st cent.).
SS Zeno, Concordius and Theodore
(302) MM.
SS Zeno and Chariton (c.303) MM.
St Basilissa of Nicomedia (c.303) V.
M.
SS Aristaeus and Antoninus (?) MM.
St Mansuetus of Toul (c.350) Bp.
*St Ambrose of Sens (c.355) Bp.
*St Macanisius (514) Bp.
St Auxanus of Milan (568) Bp.
*St Maurilius of Cahors (580) Bp.
St Simeon Stylites the Younger (598)
H.
*St Natalis of Casale (6th cent.) C.
*St Remaclus of Maestricht (c.663) Bp.
O.S.B.
St Aigulphus of Lérins (676) Ab. M.
O.S.B.
*St Frugentius of Fleury (676) M.
O.S.B.
*St Hereswitha of Chelles (c.690) W.
O.S.B.
*St Regulus of Reims (698) Bp. O.S.B.
*St Balin of Techsaxon (7th cent.) C.
St Sandila of Córdova (c.855) M.
*St Martin of Hinokosa (1213) Bp.
O.S.B.Cist.
*BB John of Perugia and Peter of Sas-
soferrato (1231) MM. O.F.M.
*Bl Guala of Brescia (1244) C. O.P.
*Bl Andrew Dotti (1315) C. O.S.M.
*Bl Herman of Heidelberg (c.1326) H.
O.S.B.
*Bl Degenhard of Niederaltaich (1374)
H. O.S.B.
*BB Antony Ixida and Comp. (1632)
MM.

SEPTEMBER 4.

St Moses (12th cent. B.C.) Prophet.
St Candida the Elder (c.78) V. M.
St Hermione of Ephesus (c.117) V.
SS Thamel and Comp. (c.125) MM.
SS Marcellus of Lyons (c.178) M.
SS Marinus, Castus and Maximus (?)
MM.
SS Rufinus, Silvanus and Vitalicus (?)
MM.
St Marinus of San Marino (?) H.
St Marcellus of Trèves (?) Bp.
SS Theodore, Oceanus, Ammianus
and Julian (c.310) MM.
St Silvinus of Verdun (c.420) Bp.
St Boniface I (423) Pope.
*St Monessa of Ireland (456) V.
*St Caletricus of Chartres (c.580) Bp.
*St Ultan (7th cent.) Bp.
*St Rhuddlad (7th cent.) V.
*Bl Ida of Herzfeld (c.813) W.
*St Sulpitius of Bayeux (843) Bp. M.
*Bl Agnes of Bagno (c.1105) V. O.S.B.
Cam.
St Rosalia of Palermo (1160) V.
St Rose of Viterbo (1252) V.
*Bl Catherine Mattei (1574) V. Tert.
O.P.

SEPTEMBER 5.

St Romulus the Courtier (c.112) M.
St Herculanus of Porto (c.180) M.
SS Eudoxius, Zeno, Macarius and
Comp. (2nd cent.) MM.
St Victorinus (2nd cent.) Bp. M.
SS Quintius, Arcontius and Donatus
(?) MM.
St Obdulia of Toledo (?) V.
St Macarius of Melitene (?) M.
SS Urban, Theodore and Comp. (370)
MM.
*St Genebald of Laon (c.555) Bp.
*St Victorinus of Como (644) Bp.
St Bertinus of Sithiu (c.709) Ab.
O.S.B.
*St Albert of Butrio (1073) Ab. O.S.B.
*St Alvitus of Leon (c.1073) Bp. O.S.B.
*Bl Albert of Pontida (1095) Ab. O.S.B.
*St Vitus of Pontida (c.1095) C. O.S.B.
*Bl Jordan of Pulsano (1152) Ab.
O.S.B.

*Bl Gentilis of Matelica (1340) M.
O.F.M.
St Laurence Justinian (1455) Bp.
*Bl William Browne (1605) M.
*Bl Joseph Canh (1838) M. Tert.O.P.

SEPTEMBER 6.

St Zachary (6th cent. B.C.) Prophet.
SS Onesiphorus and Porphyrius (c.80)
MM.
SS Faustus, Macarius and Comp.
(250) MM.
SS Augustine, Sanctian and Beata
(273) MM.
SS Cottidus, Eugene and Comp. (?)
MM.
St Petronius of Verona (c.450) Bp.
*St Arator of Verdun (c.460) Bp.
*St Maccallin of Lusk (c.497) Bp.
SS Donatian, Praesidius, Mansuetus,
Germanus, Fusculus and Laetus
(5th cent.) MM.
St Eleutherius of Spoleto (c.590) Ab.
O.S.B.
*St Faustus of Syracuse (c.607) Ab.
*St Chainoaldus (633) Bp.
*St Magnus of Füssen (c.666) Ab.
*SS Felix and Augebert (7th cent.)
MM.
*Bl Bertrand of Garrigue (1230) C. O.P.
*Bl Peregrinus of Falerone (1240) C.
O.F.M.
*Bl Liberatus da Loro (1258) C. O.F.M.

SEPTEMBER 7.

St Eupsychius of Caesarea (c.130)
St Regina of Autun (c.286) V. M.
St John of Nicomedia (303) M.
St Anastasius the Fuller (304) M.
St Sozon of Cilicia (c.304) M.
St Evortius of Orléans (c.340) Bp.
*St Grimonia of Picardy (4th cent.)
V. M.
St Pamphilus of Capua (c.400) Bp.
St Augustalis of Gaul (c.450) Bp.
SS Memorius and Comp. (451) MM.
*St Gratus of Aosta (c.470) Bp.
*St Carissima of Albi (5th cent.) V.
St Clodoaldus of Nogent (c.560) Ab.

*St Madalberta of ·Maubeuge (706) V.
O.S.B.
*St Hilduard of Dickelvenne (c.750) Bp.
O.S.B.
*St Alcmund of Hexham (781) Bp.
O.S.B.
*St Tilbert of Hexham (789) Bp. O.S.B.
*St Faciolus of Poitiers (c.950) C.
O.S.B.
*St John of Lodi (1106) Bp. O.S.B.
*St Stephen of Chatillon (1208) Bp.
O.Cart.
*St Eustace of Flay (1211) Ab. O.S.B.
Cist.
*BB Mark, Stephen S.J. and Melchior
(1619) MM.
*BB John Duckett and Ralph Corby
S.J. (1644) MM.

SEPTEMBER 8.

Feast of the Nativity of Our Lady.
SS Ammon, Theophilus, Neoterius and
Comp. (?) MM.
SS Timothy and Faustus (?) MM.
SS Adrian and Natalia (c.304) MM.
SS Eusebius, Nestabus, Zeno and
Nestor (362) MM.
St Nestor of Gaza (362) M.
*St Kingsmark of Wales (5th cent.) C.
*St Disibod of Bingen (c.700) Bp.
O.S.B.
St Sergius I (701) Pope.
*SS Ina and Ethelburga (727).
St Corbinian of Freising (730) Bp.
*St Adela of Messines (1071) W. O.S.B.
*Bl Alanus de Rupe (1475) C. O.P.
St Peter Claver (1654) C. S.J.

SEPTEMBER 9.

SS Dorotheus and Gorgonius (303)
MM.
SS Rufinus and Rufinian (?) MM.
SS Hyacinth, Alexander and Tiburtius
(?) MM.
St Straton (?) M.
St Severian of Sebaste (322) M.
St Isaac the Great (c.440) Bp.
St Kieran the Younger (c.556) Ab.
*St Ciarin of Clonmacnoise (c.556) Ab.

*St Osmanna of Brieuc (c.650) V.

St Omer of Thérouanne (c.670) Bp. O.S.B.

*St Bettelin of Croyland (8th cent.) H. O.S.B.

*St Wulfhilda of Barking (980) Abs. O.S.B.

*St Wilfrida of Wilton (c.988) Abs. O.S.B.

*Bl Gaufridus of Savigny (1139) Ab. O.S.B.

*Bl Mary de la Cabeza (c.1175) W.

*Bl Seraphina Sforza (1478) V. Poor Clare.

SEPTEMBER 10.

SS Apelles, Lucius and Clement (1st cent.) MM.

St Barypsebas of Dalmatia (1st cent.) M.

SS Nemesian, Felix, Lucius, Another Felix, Litteus, Polyanus, Victor, Jader, Dativus and Comp. (257) Bps. MM.

SS Menodora, Metrodora and Nymphodora (306) VV. MM.

SS Sosthenes and Victor (307) MM.

St Agapius of Novara (c.420) Bp.

St Veranus of Bence (c.480) Bp.

St Pulcheria Augusta (453) V.

*St Finian of Moville (c.575) Bp.

St Salvius of Albi (584) Bp.

St Candida the Younger (c.586).

St Theodard of Maestricht (c.670) Bp. M. O.S.B.

*St Autbert of Avranches (p. 709) Bp.

*St Frithestan of Winchester (933) Bp. O.S.B.

St Peter de Mozonzo (c.1000) Bp. O.S.B.

*St Cosmas of Aphrodisia (1160) Bp. M.

*Bl Serlo of Savigny (1158) Ab. O.S.B. Cist.

*Bl Ogerius of Locedio (1214) Ab. O.S.B.Cist.

St Nicholas of Tolentino (1305) C. O.S.A.

*BB Apollinaris Franco O.F.M. and Comp. (1622) MM.

*Bl Ambrose Edward Barlow (1641) M. O.S.B.

SEPTEMBER 11.

SS Protus and Hyacinth (c.257) MM.

*SS Felix and Regula (3rd cent.) MM.

SS Diodorus, Diomedes and Didymus (?) MM.

St Paphnutius the Great (c.356) Bp.

St Theodora of Alexandria (491) Penitent.

St Patiens of Lyons (c.491) Bp.

St Emilian of Vercelli (520) Bp.

*St Daniel of Bangor (545) Bp.

St Vincent of León (c.554) Ab. M.

*St Almirus of Gréez (c.560) Ab.

*St Adelphius of Rémiremont (c.670) Ab. O.S.B.

*St Bodo of Toul (p. 670) Bp. O.S.B.

*St Peter of Chavanon (1080) C. O.S.A.

*Bl Louis of Thuringia (1227) C.

*St Sperandea of Cingoli (1276) Abs. O.S.B.

*Bl Matthew of Mount Massaccio (1303) H. O.S.B.Cam.

*BB Charles Spinola and Comp. (1622) MM. S.J.

*Bl Bonaventure Grau (1684) C. O.F.M.

*Bl Gabriel Perboyre (1840) M.

SEPTEMBER 12.

Feast of the Most Holy Name of Mary.

St Curonotus of Iconium (c.258) Bp. M.

SS Hieronides, Leontius, Serapion, Seleucus, Valerian and Straton (c.300) MM.

St Autonomus of Bithynia (c.300) Bp. M.

SS Macedonius, Theodulus and Tatian (362) MM.

St Sacerdos of Lyons (551) Bp.

St Silvinus of Verona (c.550) Bp.

*St Ailbe of Emly (6th cent.) Bp.

St Eanswida of Folkestone (c.640) Abs. O.S.B.

*St Guy of Laken (c.1012) C.

*Bl Miro of Vich (1161) C. O.S.A.

*Bl Juvenal Ancina (1604) Bp. Cong. Orat.

*Bl Mary Victoria Fornari-Strata (1617) Foundress.

*BB Thomas Zumárraga and Mancius of St Thomas (1622) MM. O.P.

SEPTEMBER 13.

St Philip (3rd cent.) M.
St Ligorius (?) M.
SS Macrobius and Julian (c.321) MM.
St Maurilius of Angers (c.430) Bp.
*St Nectarius of Autun (c.550) Bp.
St Eulogius of Alexandria (607) Bp.
St Amatus of Rémiremont (c.630) Ab.
  O.S.B.
*St Columbinus of Lure (c.680) Ab.
  O.S.B.
St Amatus of Sion in Valais (690) Bp.
  O.S.B.
*St Barsenorius of Fécamp (7th cent.)
  Ab. O.S.B.
*St Venerius of Tino Island (7th or 9th
  cent.) Ab. O.S.B.
*Bl Hedwig of Herford (c.887) Abs.
  O.S.B.
*Bl Martin III of Camaldoli (1259)
  O.S.B.Cam.
*Bl Francis of Calderola (1407) C.
  O.F.M.

SEPTEMBER 14

SS Caerealis and Sallustia (251) MM.
SS Crescentian, Victor, Rosula and
  Generalis (c.258) MM.
St Crescentius of Perugia (c.300) M.
St Maternus of Cologne (c.325) Bp.
*St Cormac of Cashel (908) Bp.
*St Notburga of Tyrol (1313) V.
*Bl Gabriel-John Tautin Dufresse
  (1815) M.

SEPTEMBER 15.

Feast of the Seven Sorrows of the B. V.
  Mary.
St Nicomedes of Rome (c.90) M.
St Melitina of Marcianopolis (middle
  of 2nd cent.) M.
St Valerian of Lyons (178) M.
SS Maximus, Theodore and Scelpiodo-
  tus (c.310) MM.
St Porphyrius the Actor (362) M.
St Nicetas the Goth (c.378) M.
St Albinus of Lyons (c.390) Bp.
St Mamilian of Palermo (460) Bp.

St Eutropia of Auvergne (5th cent.) W.
St Aprus of Toul (507) Bp.
*St John the Dwarf (c.540) H.
St Leobinus of Chartres (c.556) Bp.
*St Joseph Abibos (c.590) Ab.
*St Hernan of Brittany (6th cent.) C.
*St Merinus of Benchor (c.620) Bp.
St Aichardus of Jumièges (c.687) Ab.
  O.S.B.
*St Ritbert of Varennes (c.690) Ab.
  O.S.B.
*St Ribert of Saint-Valéry (7th cent.)
  Ab. O.S.B.
SS Emilas and Jeremias (852) MM.
*Bl Aichardus of Clairvaux (c.1170) C.
  O.S.B.Cist.
*Bl Roland de' Medici (1386) H.
St Catherine of Genoa (1510) W.

SEPTEMBER 16.

St Sebastiana of Heraclea (1st cent.)
  M.
St Cornelius (253) Pope M.
St Cyprian of Carthage (258) Bp. M.
*St Dulcissima of Sutri (?) V. M.
SS Lucy and Geminianus (c.300) MM.
SS Abundius, Abundantius, Marcian
  and John (c.303) MM.
St Euphemia of Chalcedon (307) V. M.
St Ninian of Whithorn (c.432) Bp.
*St Cunibert of Maroilles (c.680) Ab.
  O.S.B.
*St Eugenia of Hohenburg (735) Abs.
  O.S.B.
SS Rogelius and Servus-Dei (852)
  MM.
*St Ludmilla of Bohemia (921) M.
St Edith of Wilton (984) V. O.S.B.
*St Stephen of Perugia (1026) Ab.
  O.S.B.
St Victor III (1087) Pope O.S.B.
*Bl Vitalis of Savigny (1122) Ab. O.S.B.
*Bl Louis Allemand (1450) Card. Bp.
*Bl Francis of Camporosso (1866) C.
  O.F.M.Cap.

SEPTEMBER 17.

St Ariadne of Phrygia (c.130) M.
St Flocellus of Autun (2nd cent.) M.

St Justin (259) M.
SS Narcissus and Crescentio (c.260) MM.
SS Valerian, Macrinus and Gordian (?) MM.
St Agathoclia (?) V. M.
SS Socrates and Stephen (c.304) MM.
St Theodora of Rome (c.305) Matron.
St Satyrus of Milan (c.392) C.
*St Rodingus of Beaulieu (c.690) Ab. O.S.B.
St Lambert of Liége (709) Bp. M. O.S.B.
St Columba of Córdova (853) M. V.
*St Uni of Birka (936) Bp. O.S.B.
St Hildegard of Bingen (1179) Abs. O.S.B.
St Peter Arbués (1485) M. O.S.A.
*Bl Emmanuel Trieu (1797) M.

SEPTEMBER 18.

SS Sophia and Irene (c.200) MM.
St Eumenes of Crete (3rd cent.) Bp.
St Ferreolus of Vienne (304) M.
St Methodius of Olympus (311) Bp. M.
St Eustorgius of Milan (p. 331) Bp. M.
*St Ferreolus of Limoges (4th cent.) Bp.
St Eustochius of Tours (461) Bp.
*St Hygbald (c.690) H. O.S.B.
*St Richardis (c.895) Empress.
*St Simon of Crespy (c.1080) C. O.S.B.
*Bl Volcuin of Schem (1154) Ab. O.S.B. Cist.
*Bl Philip Oderisi (1285) Bp. O.S.B.
*Bl Simon of Genoa (1292) H. O.S.B. Cam.
*Bl John de Massias (1645) C. O.P.
St Joseph of Cupertino (1663) C. O.F.M.
*Bl Dominic Trach (1843) M.

SEPTEMBER 19.

SS Felix and Constantia (1st cent.) MM.
SS Trophimus, Sabbatius and Dorymendon (c.277) MM.
St Januarius and Comp. (304) MM.
SS Peleus, Nilus, Elias and Comp. (c.310) MM.
St Susanna (662) V. M.

St Sequanus of Saint-Seine (c.580) Ab.
*St Goeric of Metz (647) Bp.
St Theodore of Canterbury (690) Bp. O.S.B.
St Pomposa of Córdova (853) V. M.
*St Arnulfus of Gap (1070) Bp. O.S.B.
St Mary de Cervellon (1290) V.
*Bl Hugh of Sassoferrato (c.1290) C. O.S.B.Silv.
*Bl Alphonsus de Orozco (1591) C. O.S.A.
*Bl Emily de Rodat (1852) Foundress.

SEPTEMBER 20.

SS Eustace, Theopistes, Agapitus and Theopistus (118) MM.
SS Theodore, Philippa and Comp. (220) MM.
SS Digna and Emerita (259) VV. MM.
St Candida of Carthage (c.300) V. M.
St Priscus of Phrygia (?) M.
SS Dionysius and Privatus (?) MM.
SS Fausta and Evilasius (303) MM.
*St Glycerius of Milan (c.438) Bp.
St Agapitus I (536) Pope.
*St Vincent Madelgarus (677) Ab. O.S.B.
*St Eusebia of Marseilles and Comp. (c.731) Abs. MM. O.S.B.
*Bl John Eustace (1481) Ab. O.S.B. Cist.
*Bl Thomas Johnson (1537) M. O.Cart.
*Bl Francis de Posadas (1713) C. O.P.

SEPTEMBER 21.

St Jonas (c.761 B.C.) Prophet.
St Matthew (1st cent.) Apostle.
St Iphigenia (1st cent.) V.
St Alexander of Rome (2nd cent.) Bp. M.
St Eusebius of Phoenicia (?) M.
St Isaac of Cyprus (?) Bp. M.
St Meletius of Cyprus (?) Bp.
St Pamphilus of Rome (?) M.
*St Mabyn (6th cent.).
*St Gerulph of Flanders (c.746) M.
*St Maura of Troyes (850) V.
*BB Francis Jaccard and Comp. (1838) MM.
*BB Martyrs of Corea (1839-1846) MM.

SEPTEMBER 22.

The Theban Legion (c.287) MM.
St Sanctinus of Meaux (c.300) Bp.
St Irais of Alexandria (c.300) V. M.
St Silvanus of Levroux (?).
St Jonas of Paris (?) M.
St Florentius of Mt Glonne (5th cent.)
  C.
St Felix III (530) Pope.
St Lauto of Coutances (568) Bp.
St Salaberga of Poulangey (c.665) Abs.
St Emmeramus of Ratisbon (c.690) Bp.
  M. O.S.B.
*St Thomas of Villanueva (1555) Bp.
O.S.A.*

SEPTEMBER 23.

St Linus (c.79) Pope M.
SS Xantippa and Polyxena (1st cent.)
  VV.
St Thecla of Iconium (1st cent.) V. M.
St Constantius of Ancona (6th cent.)
  C.
*St Cissa of Northumbria (late 7th
  cent.) H. O.S.B.
*St Adamnan of Iona (704) Ab.
SS Andrew, John, Peter and Antony
  (c.900) MM.
*Bl Guy of Durnes (c.1157) Ab. O.S.B.
  Cist.
*Bl Peter Acotanto (c.1180) C., O.S.B.
*Bl Mark of Modena (1498) C. O.P.
*Bl Helen Duglioli (1520) W.
*Bl William Way (1588) M.

SEPTEMBER 24.

Our Lady of Ransom.
St Anathalon of Milan (1st cent.) Bp.
SS Andochius, Thyrsus and Felix
  (2nd cent.) MM.
St Paphnutius and Comp. (c.303) MM.
SS Martyrs of Chalcedon (304).
St Rusticus of Clermont (446) Bp.
St Geremarus of Flay (c.658) Ab.
  O.S.B.
SS Cuniald and Gislar (7th cent.) CC.
*St Berchtun of Beverley (733) Ab.
  O.S.B.

St Gerard Sagredo (1046) Bp. M. O.S.B.
*St Ysarn of Marseilles (1048) Ab. O.S.B.
*Bl Robert Flower (1218) H.
St Pacificus of Sanseverino (1721) C.
  O.F.M.

SEPTEMBER 25.

St Cleophas (1st cent.) Disciple M.
St Herculanus (2nd cent.) M.
St Firminus of Amiens (2nd cent.) Bp.
SS Bardomian, Eucarpus and Comp.
  (?) MM.
SS Paul, Tatta, Sabinian, Maximus,
  Rufus and Eugene (?) MM.
SS Aurelia and Neomisia (?) VV.
St Paphnutius of Egypt (c.480) Ab.
St Caian (5th cent.).
St Mewrog (?).
St Principius of Soissons (c.505) Bp.
St Solemnius of Chartres (c.511) Bp.
St Lupus of Lyons (542) Bp.
*St Barr of Cork (6th cent.) Bp.
St Anacharius of Auxerre (604) Bp.
*St Fymbert of Scotland (7th cent.) Bp.
*St Ermenfridus of Cusance (c.670) Ab.
  O.S.B.
*St Ceolfrid of Wearmouth (716) Ab.
  O.S.B.
*St Egelred of Croyland (c.870) M.
  O.S.B.
*Bl Herman the Cripple (1054) C.
  O.S.B.
*St Austindus of Auch (1068) Bp.
  O.S.B.
*St Albert of Jerusalem (1214) Bp. M.
*St Christopher of Guardia (c.1490) M.
*Bl Ladislas of Gielniow (1505) C.
  O.F.M.
*Bl Mark Criado (1569) M. O.S.Trin.

SEPTEMBER 26.

SS Callistratus and Comp. (c.300)
  MM.
SS Cyprian and Justina (?) MM.
St Senator of Albanum (?).
St Eusebius of Bologna (c.400) Bp.
St Vigilius of Brescia (p. 506) Bp.
*St Meugant of Cornwall (6th cent.).
St Amantius of Città di Castello (c.600)
  C.

*St Colman Elo (c.610) Ab.
St Nilus the Younger (1004) Ab.
*Bl Meginhard of Hersfeld (1059) Ab.
O.S.B.
*St John of Meda (1159) Ab. O.S.B.
*Bl Dalmatius Moner (1341) C. O.P.
*Bl Lucy of Caltagirone (1304) V.
O.F.M.

SEPTEMBER 27.

St John Mark (1st cent.) Bp.
St Caius of Milan (1st cent.) Bp.
St Adheritus of Ravenna (2nd or 3rd
cent.) Bp.
St Epicharis of Byzantium (c.300) M.
SS Cosmas and Damian (c.303) MM.
St Anthimus (c.303) M.
St Euprepius (c.303) M.
SS Florentinus and Hilary (?) MM.
SS Fidentius and Terentius (?) MM.
*St Deodatus of Sora (?).
*St Ceraunus of Paris (p. 614) Bp.
*St Sigebert of East Anglia (635) King
M. O.S.B.
*St Barrog of Wales (7th cent.) H.
*St Hiltrude of Liessies (c.790) V.
O.S.B.
SS Adolphus and John (c.850) MM.
*St Marcellus of St Gall (c.869) C.
O.S.B.
*St Bonfilius of Foligno (1125) Bp.
O.S.B.
*St Elzear of Provence (1323) C.

SEPTEMBER 28.

St Privatus of Rome (223) M.
St Solomon of Genoa (p. 269) Bp.
St Paternus of Auch (3rd cent.) Bp.
SS Mark, Alphius, Alexander and
Comp. (c.303) MM.
SS Martial, Laurence and Comp. (?)
MM.
St Stacteus (?) M.
St Maximus (?) M.
*St Machan of Scotland (?) Bp.
St Exuperius of Toulouse (411) Bp.
St Eustochium of Rome (419) V.
St Silvinus of Brescia (444) Bp.
*St Faustus of Riez (c.493) Bp.
*St Conwall of Scotland (c.630) C.
*St Annemundus of Lyons (657) Bp. M.

*SS Willigod and Martin (7th cent.)
Abb. O.S.B.
*St Tetta of Wimborne (c.772) Abs.
O.S.B.
St Lioba of Bischoffsheim (c.779) Abs.
O.S.B.
St Wenceslaus of Bohemia (935) M.
*St Thiemo of Salzburg (1102) Bp. M.
O.S.B.
*Bl Laurence of Rippafratta (1457) C.
O.P.
*Bl Bernardinus of Feltre (1494) C.
O.F.M.
*Bl Simon de Rojas (1624) C. O.S.Trin.
*BB Bartholomew Gutiérrez and Comp.
(1630) MM. O.S.A.

SEPTEMBER 29.

St Michael the Archangel.
SS Ripsime, Gaiana and Comp. (c.290)
VV. MM.
SS Eutychius, Plautus and Heracleas
(?) MM.
*St Theodota of Philippopolis (c.318)
Penitent.
St Gudelia of Persia (c.340) M.
SS Dadas, Casdoë and Gaboelas (368)
MM.
St Fraternus of Auxerre (c.450) Bp. M.
St Quiriacus of Palestine (c.550) H.
*St Ludwin of Mettlach (713) Bp.
O.S.B.
*SS Catholdus, Anno and Diethardus
(late 8th cent.) CC. O.S.B.
*St Alaricus of Uffnan (975) H. O.S.B.
*St Garcia of Arlanza (c.1073) Ab.
O.S.B.
St Grimoaldus of Pontecorvo (p. 1137)
C.
*Bl John of Montmirail (1217) C.
O.S.B.Cist.
*Bl Richard Rolle (1349) C.
*Bl Charles of Blois (1364) C.
*Bl John of Ghent (1439) C. O.S.B.

SEPTEMBER 30.

St Sophia of Rome (c.138) W.
SS Victor and Ursus (c.286) MM.
St Antoninus of Piacenza (3rd cent.)
M.
St Gregory the Illuminator (c.330) Bp.

St Leopardus of Rome (362) M.
St Jerome of Rome (420) C. Dr.
St Midan (c.610).
St Honorius of Canterbury (653) Bp.
O.S.B.
*St Laurus of Brittany (7th cent.) Ab.
*St Enghenedl of Wales (7th cent.).
*Bl Conrad of Zähringen (1227) Card.
Bp. O.S.B.Cist.

OCTOBER 1.

St Platon of Tournai (c.286) M.
SS Verissimus, Maxima and Julia
(c.302) MM.
SS Priscus, Crescens and Evagrius (?)
MM.
SS Aretas and Comp. (?) MM.
*SS Aizan and Sazan (c.400) MM.
*St Albaud of Toul (c.520) Bp.
St Remigius of Reims (c.533) Bp.
*St Romanus the Melodist (c.540) C.
*St Melorius of Cornwall (c.540) M.
St Bavo of Ghent (654) H. O.S.B.
*St Dodo of Wallers (c.750) Ab. O.S.B.
*St Fidharleus of Rathin (762) Ab.
*St Virila of Leyre (c.1000) Ab. O.S.B.
*Bl Nicholas of Forca-Palena (1449) C.
*Bl John of Dukla (1484) C. O.F.M.
*BB Edward Campion, Christopher
Buxton, Robert Wilcox, Robert
Widmerpool, Edward James, Ralph
Crockett and John Robinson (1588)
MM.

OCTOBER 2.

Feast of the Guardian Angels.
SS Primus, Cyril and Secundarius (?)
MM.
SS Eleutherius and Comp. (c.303)
MM.
St Modestus of Sardinia (c.304) M.
*St Leudomer of Chartres (c.585) Bp.
*St Beregisus of St-Hubert (p.725) C.
St Gerinus of Arras (676) M.
St Leodegarius (678) Bp. M. O.S.B.
St Theophilus of Bulgaria (c.750) C.
O.S.B.
*St Ursicinus II of Chur (760) Bp.
O.S.B.

OCTOBER 3.

SS Dionysius, Faustus, Caius, Peter,
Paul and Comp. (257) MM.
St Candidus of Rome (?) M.
St Hesychius of Gaza (c.380) H.
*St Menna of Lorraine (c.395) V.
St Maximian of Numidia (404) Bp.
*St Cyprian of Toulon (6th cent.) Bp.
SS Ewald the Fair and Ewald the
Dark (c.695) CC. O.S.B.
*St Widradus of Saulieu (747) Ab.
O.S.B.
*Bl Utto of Metten (820) Ab. O.S.B.
St Gerard of Brogne (959) Ab. O.S.B.
St Froilan of León (1006) Bp. O.S.B.
*St Ebontius of Barbastro (1104) Bp.
O.S.B.
*St Adalgott of Chur (1165) Bp. O.S.B.
Cist.
*Bl Dominic Spadafora (1521) C. O.P.
St Teresa of Lisieux (1897) V. O.C.D.

OCTOBER 4.

SS Crispus and Caius (1st cent.) MM.
St Hierotheus of Athens (?) Bp.
SS Caius, Faustus, Eusebius, Chaere-
mon, Lucius and Comp. (3rd cent.)
MM.
SS Domnina, Berenice and Prosdoce
(303-310) MM.
SS Mark, Marcian and Comp. (304)
MM.
*SS Adauctus and Callisthene (c.312)
MM.
*St Ammon the Great (c.350) Ab.
St Petronius of Bologna (c.445) Bp.
*St Quintus of Tours (c.570) M.
St Aurea of Paris (666) Abs.
St Peter of Damascus (c.750) Bp. M.
St Francis of Assisi (1226) Founder.
*Bl Julian Majali (1470) Ab. O.S.B.
*Bl Francis Titelmans (1537) C. O.F.M.
Cap.

OCTOBER 5.

St Thraseas of Eumenia (c.170) Bp.
M.
SS Palmatius and Comp. (c.287) MM.

St Marcellinus of Ravenna (3rd cent.) Bp.

*St Alexander of Trèves (3rd cent.) M.

SS Firmatus and Flaviana (?) MM.

SS *Placid, Eutychius, Victorinus, Flavia, Donatus, Firmatus, Faustus and Comp.* (?) *MM.*

St Charitina (c.304) V. M.

St Apollinaris of Valence (c.520) Bp.

St Galla of Rome (c.550) W.

*St Magdalveus of Verdun (c.776) Bp. O.S.B.

*St Aurea of Amiens (8th cent.) Abs.

*St Meinulf of Bödeken (c.859) C.

*Bl Aymard of Cluny (965) Ab. O.S.B.

St Attilanus of Zamora (1009) Bp. O.S.B.

*Bl Sanctes of Cori (1392) C. O.S.A.

*Bl Raymund of Capua (1399) C. O.P.

*Bl Felicia Meda (1444) V. Poor Clare.

*BB John Hewett, William Hartley and Robert Sutton (1588) MM.

OCTOBER 6.

St Sagar of Laodicea (c.175) Bp. M.

SS Martyrs of Trèves (287).

SS Marcellus, Castus, Aemilius and Saturninus (?) MM.

St Faith of Agen (?) V. M.

St Erotis of Greece (4th cent.) M.

St Romanus of Auxerre (c.564) Bp. M.

St Magnus of Città Nuova (c.660) Bp.

*St Cumine the White (669) Ab.

St Ceollach (7th cent.) Bp.

*St Pardulphus of Guéret (c.738) Ab. O.S.B.

*St Epiphania of Pavia (c.800) V. O.S.B.

*St Nicetas of Constantinople (c.838) C.

*St Adalbero of Würzburg (1090) Bp.

St Bruno (1101) Founder.

St Mary Frances (1791) V.

*Bl Francis Trung (1858) M.

OCTOBER 7.

St Justina of Padua (c.300) V. M.

St Julia of Egypt (c.300) V. M.

SS *Sergius and Bacchus (303) MM.*

St Mark (336) Pope.*

*St Canog of Wales (c.492) M.

*St Dubtach of Armagh (c.513) Bp.

*St Palladius of Saintes (c.590) Bp.

*St Helanus of Reims (6th cent.) H.

St Augustus of Bourges (6th cent.) C.

*St Osyth of Chich (c.675) M. O.S.B.

*St Adalgis of Novara (c.850) Bp.

*Bl Artaldus of Belley (1206) Bp. O.Cart.

*Bl Gerold of Cologne (13th cent.) M.

*Bl Matthew Carreri (1471) C. O.P.

OCTOBER 8.

St Simeon Senex (1st cent.).

St Reparata of Palestine (c.250) V. M.

St Peter of Seville (?) M.

St Benedicta of Laon (?) V. M.

SS Palatias and Laurentia (302) MM.

St Nestor of Thessalonica (c.304) M.

St Artemon of Laodicea (c.305) M.

St Thais of Alexandria (c.348) Penitent.

St Demetrius the Megalomartyr (early 4th cent.) M.

*St Triduana (4th or 8th cent.) V.

*St Keyna of Wales (5th cent.) V.

St Evodius of Rouen (5th cent.) Bp.

*St Gratus of Chalons - sur - Saone (c.652) Bp.

*St Ywi of Lindisfarne (c.690) H. O.S.B.

*St Badilo of Leuze (c.870) Ab. O.S.B.

*St Amor of Aquitaine (9th cent.) H.

*St Martin Cid (1152) Ab. O.S.B.Cist.

*Bl Companius (12th cent.) Ab. O.S.B. Cam.

*St Hugh Canefro (1230) C.

*Bl Mechtildis of Magdeburg (1282) V. O.S.B.

St Brigid of Sweden (1373) W. Foundress.

OCTOBER 9.

St Abraham (20th cent. B.C.) Patriarch.

St Dionysius the Areopagite (1st cent.) Bp. M.

St Demetrius of Alexandria (231) Bp.

SS *Dionysius, Rusticus and Eleutherius (3rd cent.) MM.*

St Domninus of Parma (304) M.

St Publia of Antioch (c.370) W.

SS Andronicus and Athanasia (5th cent.) HH.

St Gislenus of St-Ghislain (c.680) Ab. O.S.B.

SS Lambert and Valerius (c.680) CC. O.S.B.

St Geminus of Sanpaterniano (c.815) C.

*St Savinus of Lavedan (c.820) H.

St Deusdedit of Monte Cassino (836) Ab. O.S.B.

*St Gunther of Niederaltaich (1045) C. O.S.B.

*Bl Aaron of Cracoa (1059) Bp. O.S.B.

*St Alfanus of Salerno (1085) Bp. O.S.B.

*St Goswin of Anchin (1165) Ab. O.S.B.

St Louis Bertran (1581) C. O.P.

Bl John Leonardi (1609) Founder.

OCTOBER 10.

St Pinytus of Crete (p. 180) Bp.

SS Victor and Comp. (c.286) MM.

SS Gereon and Comp. (?) MM.

St Clarus of Nantes (?) Bp.

SS Cassius, Florentius and Comp. (303) MM.

SS Eulampius, Eulampia and Comp. (c.310) MM.

St Cerbonius of Verona (c.400) Bp.

*St Maharsapor of Persia (421) M.

*St Patrician of Scotland (5th cent.) Bp.

St Cerbonius of Piombino (c.580) Bp.

*St Tranca of Troyes (c.637) V. M.

St Paulinus of York (644) Bp. O.S.B.

*St Aldericus of Sens (841) Bp. O.S.B.

St Paulinus of Capua (843) Bp.

*St Fulk of Fontenelle (845) Ab. O.S.B.

*St Gundisalvus of Las Junias (p. 1135) C. O.S.B.Cist.

*Bl Hugh of Mâcon (1151) Bp. O.S.B. Cist.

SS Daniel, Samuel, Angelus, Domnus, Leo, Nicholas and Hugolinus (1221) MM. O.F.M.

St Francis Borgia (1572) C. S.J.

OCTOBER 11.

SS Zenais and Philonilla (1st cent.) MM.

SS Nicasius, Quirinus, Scubiculus and Pientia V. (c.285) MM.

St Emilian of Rennes (?) C.

SS Anastasius, Placid, Genesius and Comp. (?) MM.

SS Tharacus, Probus and Andronicus (304) MM.

St Sarmata the Hermit (357) M.

St Germanus of Besançon (c.390) Bp. M.

*St Nectarius of Constantinople (397) Bp.

St Placidia of Verona (c.460) V.

*St Gratus of Oloron (p. 506) Bp.

St Firminus of Uzes (553) Bp.

St Canice of Kilkenny (599) Ab.

*St Ethelburga (c.678) Abs. O.S.B.

*St Agilbert of Paris (c.685) Bp. O.S.B.

*St Eufridus of Alba (7th cent.) C. O.S.B.

*St Ansilio of Lagny (late 7th cent.) C. O.S.B.

*St Juliana of Pavilly (c.750) Abs. O.S.B.

St Gummarus of Lier (c.774) H.

*St Bruno the Great (965) Bp.

*St John of Bridlington (1379) C. O.S.A.

*Bl James Griesinger (1491) C. O.P.

St Alexander Sauli (1593) Bp.

*Bl Peter Tuy (1833) M.

OCTOBER 12.

St Monas of Milan (249) Bp.

St Maximilian of Lorch (284) Bp. M.

SS Evagrius, Priscian and Comp. (?) MM.

St Eustace (?).

*St Pantalus of Basle (?) Bp. M.

St Edistius of Ravenna (c.303) M.

St Domnina of Anazarbus (303) M.

SS Felix and Cyprian (c.484) Bps. MM.

*St Fiace (5th cent.) Bp.

St Salvinus of Verona (562) Bp.

*St Edwin (633) King M.

St Wilfrid of York (709) Bp. O.S.B.

*SS Herlindis and Relindis (c.745) Abs. O.S.B.

*SS Amicus and Amelius (773) MM.

St Seraphinus of Ascoli-Piceno (1604) C. O.F.M.Cap.

*Bl Camillus Costanzi (1622) M. S.J.

OCTOBER 13.

St Theophilus of Antioch (181) Bp.
St Carpus of Troas (1st cent.).
SS Fyncana and Fyndoca (?) VV. MM.
SS Faustus, Januarius and Martial (304) MM.
St Florentius of Thessalonica (312) M.
St Venantius of Tours (5th cent.) Ab.
*St Romulus of Genoa (p.641) Bp.
*St Berthold of Cambrai (7th cent.) Bp.
*St Comgan of Scotland (8th cent.) Ab.
*St Simbert of Augsburg (c.809) Bp. O.S.B.
*St Gerald of Aurillac (909) C.
St Colman of Stockerau (1012) M.
*St Regimbald of Speyer (1039) Bp. O.S.B.
St Edward the Confessor (1066) King.
St Chelidonia of Subiaco (1152) V. O.S.B.
*St Maurice of Carnoet (1191) Ab. O.S.B.Cist.
*Bl Gerbrand of Bloemkamp (1218) Ab. O.S.B.Cist.
*Bl Mary Magdalen dei Panattieri (1503) V. O.P.

OCTOBER 14.

St Callistus I (c.222) Pope.
SS Saturninus and Lupus (?) MM.
St Fortunata of Caesarea (303) V. M.
SS Carponius, Evaristus and Priscian (303) MM.
St Gaudentius of Rimini (c.360) Bp. M.
St Donatian of Reims (390) Bp.
*St Manehildis of Champagne (c.490) V.
St Fortunatus of Todi (537) Bp.
St Rusticus of Trèves (574) Bp.
*St Manakus of Wales (6th cent.) Ab.
*St Angadresima of Beauvais (c.695) Abs. O.S.B.
St Burchard of Würzburg (c.754) Bp. O.S.B.
St Bernard of Arce (9th cent.) C.
St Dominic Loricatus (1060) H. O.S.B.

OCTOBER 15.

St Agileus of Carthage (c.300) M.
SS Martyrs of Germany (303).

St Severus of Trèves (c.455) Bp.
*St Cannatus of Marseilles (5th cent.) Bp.
St Antiochus of Lyons (5th cent.) Bp.
*St Leonard of Vandoeuvre (c.570) Ab.
*St Sabinus of Catania (c.760) Bp.
St Thecla of Kitzingen (c.790) Abs. O.S.B.
*St Euthymius the Thessalonian (886) Ab.
*Bl Odilo of Stavelot (p.954) Ab. O.S.B.
*St Callistus of Huesca (1003) M.
*St Aurelia of Strassburg (1027) V. O.S.B.
*Bl Willa of Nonnberg (c.1050) H. O.S.B.
St Teresa of Avila (1582) V. O.C.D.

OCTOBER 16.

St Eliphius of Toul (362) M.
*St Bolonia (362) V. M.
St Florentinus of Trèves (4th cent.) Bp.
SS Saturninus, Nereus and Comp. (c.450) MM.
*St Dulcidius of Agen (c.450) Bp.
SS Martinian, Saturian and Comp. (458) MM.
*St Conogan of Quimper (460) Bp.
*St Junian (5th cent.) H.
St Gall (c.640) Ab.
*St Magnobodus of Angers (c.670) Bp.
*St Baldwin of Laon (c.680) M.
*St Kiara of Kilkeary (c.680) V.
*St Mummolinus of Noyon (c.686) Bp. O.S.B.
St Bercharius of Moutier-en-Der (696) Ab. M. O.S.B.
*St Balderic of Montfaucon (7th cent.) C.
*St Eremberta of Wierre (late 7th cent.) Abs. O.S.B.
*St Vitalis of Noirmoutier (c.740) H. O.S.B.
St Ambrose of Cahors (p.772) Bp.
St Lullus of Mainz (787) Bp. O.S.B.
*St Anastasius of Cluny (1085) C. O.S.B.
*St Bertrand of Comminges (1123) Bp.
*St Gerald of Clairvaux (1177) Ab. O.S.B.Cist.
St Hedwig (1243) Queen O.S.B.Cist.
St Gerard Majella (1755) C. C.SS.R.

OCTOBER 17.

St Heron of Antioch (c.136) Bp. M.
*St Solina of Gascony (c.290) V. M.
St Mamelta of Persia (c.344) M.
St Florentius of Orange (c.526) Bp.
St Victor of Capua (554) Bp.
*St Louthiern of Cornwall (6th cent.) Bp.
*St Colman of Kilroot (6th cent.) Bp.
SS Ethelbert and Ethelred (670) MM.
*St Berarius I of Le Mans (c.680) Bp.
*St Anstrudis of Laon (688) V. O.S.B.
*St Nothelm of Canterbury (c.740) Bp.
*St Rudolph of Gubbio (c.1066) Bp. O.S.B.
*Bl Gilbert the Theologian (1167) Ab. O.S.B.Cist.
*Bl Balthassar of Chiavari (1492) C. O.F.M.
*Bl Richard Gwyn (1584) M.
St Margaret Mary Alacoque (1690) V.
*BB Ursuline Nuns (1794) MM.
*Bl Francis Isidore Gagelin (1833) M.

OCTOBER 18.

St Luke (1st cent.) Evangelist.
St Asclepiades of Antioch (217) Bp. M.
St Athenodorus of Pontus (c.269) Bp. M.
St Justus of Beauvais (287) M.
St Tryphonia of Rome (3rd cent.) W. M.
*St Gwen of Wales (c.492) W. M.
*St Gwen (5th cent.) W.
*SS Brothen and Gwendolen (6th cent.).
*St Monon of Scotland (c.645) M.

OCTOBER 19.

*St Altinus of Orleans (1st or 4th cent.) Bp. M.
SS Ptolemy and Lucius (c.165) MM.
SS Veronicus, Pelagia and Comp. (?) MM.
St Varus of Upper Egypt (307) M.
*St Cleopatra of Syria (319) W.
St Eusterius of Salerno (5th cent.) Bp.
*St Lupus of Soissons (c.540) Bp.
St Veranus of Cavaillon (590) Bp.
St Ethbin of Kildare (c.600) Ab.
St Aquilinus of Evreux (695) Bp.

*St Desiderius of Lonrey (c.705) C. O.S.B.
*St Theofrid of Carmery (728) Ab. O.S.B.
St Frideswide of Oxford (c.735) V. O.S.B.
*St Laura of Córdova (864) Abs. M.
*St Eadnot of Dorchester (1016) Bp. O.S.B.
*Bl Thomas Hélye (1257) C.
St Peter of Alcántara (1562) C. O.F.M.
*Bl Philip Howard (1595) M.

OCTOBER 20.

St Maximus of Aquila (c.250) M.
SS Martha, Saula and Comp. (?) VV. MM.
St Caprasius of Agen (303) M.
*SS Barsabas and Comp. (c.342) MM.
St Artemius (363) M.
*SS Bradan and Orora (?).
St Irene of Santarem (c.653) V. M.
St Sindulphus of Reims (660) H.
*St Acca of Hexham (742) Bp. O.S.B.
*St Vitalis of Salzburg (745) Bp. O.S.B.
St Andrew the Calabyte (766) M.
*St Aidan of Mayo (768) Bp.
*St Bernard of Bagnorea (p. 800) Bp.
*St Aderald of Troyes (1004) C.
*Bl William of Savigny (c.1122) C. O.S.B.
*St Adelina of Moriton (1125) V. O.S.B.
St John Cantius (1473) C.
*BB Francis Serrano and Francis Diaz (1648) MM. O.P.

OCTOBER 21.

St Asterius of Ostia (c.223) M.
SS Dasius, Zoticus, Caius and Comp. (c.303) MM.
St Hilarion of Gaza (c.371) Ab.
St Viator of Lyons (c.390) H.
St Malchus of Chalcis (c.390) H.
SS Ursula and Comp. (before 4th cent.) VV. MM.
*St Agatho of Egypt (4th cent.) Ab.
St Cilinia of Laon (p. 458) Matron.
*St Wendelinus (c.607) C.
*St Finian of Taghmon (c.635) Ab.
*St Tuda of Lindisfarne (664) Bp.

*St Condedus of Fontenelle (c.690) H. O.S.B.

*St Maurontus of Marseilles (c.804) Bp. O.S.B.

*St Hugh of Ambronay (9th or 10th cent.) Ab. O.S.B.

*St Gebizo of Monte Cassino (c.1087) C. O.S.B.

*St Berthold of Parma (1111) C. O.S.B.

*Bl Imana of Loss (1270) Abs. O.S.B. Cist.

*Bl Gundisalvus of Lagos (1422) C. O.S.A.

*Bl Peter Capucci (1445) C. O.P.

OCTOBER 22.

St Mary Salome (1st cent.).
St Mark of Jerusalem (c.156) Bp. M.
St Abercius of Hierapolis (c.167) Bp.
St Philip of Fermo (c.270) Bp. M.
SS Alexander, Heraclius and Comp. (?) MM.
SS Philip, Severus, Eusebius and Hermes (304) MM.
St Mellonius of Rouen (314) Bp.
*St Nepotian of Clermont (c.388) Bp.
St Cordula (c.453) V. M.
St Verecundus of Verona (522) Bp.
*St Simplicius of Monte Cassino (c.570) Ab. O.S.B.
*St Maroveus of Precipiano (c.650) Ab. O.S.B.
*St Nunctus of Mérida (668) Ab. M.
*St Moderan of Berceto (c.730) Bp. O.S.B.
*St Benedict of Macerac (845) Ab.
SS Nunilo and Alodia (851) VV. MM.
St Donatus of Fiesole (874) Bp.
*St Bertharius of Monte Cassino (c.884) Ab. M. O.S.B.
*Bl Paul Doi Buong (1833) M.

OCTOBER 23.

SS Servandus and Germanus (c.305) MM.
St Theodore of Antioch (362) M.
St Verus of Salerno (4th cent.) Bp.
*St Amo of Toul (4th cent.) Bp.
*St Severinus of Cologne (c.403) Bp.
St Severinus of Bordeaux (c.420) Bp.
*St Clether of Wales (c.520).

*St Severinus Boëthius (525) M.
*St John of Syracuse (c.609) Bp. O.S.B.
St Romanus of Rouen (639) Bp.
St Benedict of Sebaste (c.654) Bp.
St Syra of Faremoutiers (c.660) V. O.S.B.
*St Leothadius of Moissac (718) Ab. O.S.B.
*St Oda of Amay (c.723) W.
St Domitius of Amiens (8th cent.) C.
St Ignatius of Constantinople (877) Bp.
*St Elfleda of Glastonbury (c.936) V. O.S.B.
*St Allucio of Pescia (1134) C.
*Bl Bertrand of Grandselve (1149) Ab. O.S.B.Cist.
*Bl Henry of Cologne (1225) C. O.P.
*Bl John Buoni (1249) C. O.S.A.
*Bl Bartholomew of Braganza (1271) Bp. O.P.
*Bl Thomas Thwing (1680) M.

OCTOBER 24.

St Raphael the Archangel.
SS Felix, Audactus, Januarius, Fortunatus and Septimus (303) MM.
St Proclus of Constantinople (447) Bp.
St Evergislus of Cologne (5th cent.) Bp. M.
SS Martyrs of Nagran (523).
St Maglorius of Wales (c.586) Bp.
*St Cadfarch of Wales (6th cent.).
St Martin of Vertou (601) Ab.
St Marcius of Mt Massico (c.679) H. O.S.B.
*St Fromundus of Coutances (p.690) Bp. O.S.B.
*St Bernard Calvô (1243) Bp. O.S.B. Cist.
*Bl John Angelo Porro (1504) C. O.S.A.
*Bl Joseph Thi (1860) M.
*Bl Antony Mary Claret (1870) Bp. Founder.

OCTOBER 25.

*St Tabitha or Dorcas (1st cent.) W.
St Minias of Florence (c.250) M.
SS Theodosius, Lucius, Mark and Peter (269) MM.

SS *Chrysanthus and Daria* (*283*) *MM*.
SS Crispin and Crispinian (c.287) MM.
St Cyrinus of Rome (3rd cent.) M.
SS Marcellinus, Claudius, Cyrinus and Antoninus (3rd cent.) MM.
SS Fronto and George (?) Bps.
SS Protus and Januarius (303) MM.
SS Martyrius and Marcian (351) MM.
St Gaudentius of Brescia (c.410) Bp.
*St Lupus of Bayeux (5th cent.) Bp.
St Hilary of Mende (535) Bp.
*St Dulcardus of Micy (584) H.
St Hildemarca of Fécamp (c.670) Abs. O.S.B.
*St Goeznoveus of Leon (675) Bp.
*St Guesnoveus of Quimper (675) Bp.
*SS Fructus, Valentine and Engratia (c.715) HH.
*Bl Theodoric of St-Hubert (1087) Ab. O.S.B.
*Bl Albert of Sassoferrato (1330) C. O.S.B.Cam.
*Bl Thaddeus McCarthy (1497) Bp.

OCTOBER 26.

St *Evaristus* (*c.197*) *Pope M*.
SS Lucian, Florius and Comp. (c.250) MM.
SS Rogatian and Felicissimus (256) MM.
St Rusticus of Narbonne (c.462) Bp.
SS Alanus and Aldrus (5th cent.) Bps.
St Quadragesimus of Policastro (c.590) C.
*SS Aneurin and Gwinoc (6th cent.) CC.
*St Gibitrudis of Faremoutiers (c.655) V. O.S.B.
*St Eadfrid of Leominster (c.675) C. O.S.B.
*St Eata of Hexham (c.686) Bp. O.S.B.
St Gaudiosus of Salerno (7th cent.) Bp.
*St Humbert of Fritzlar (7th or 8th cent.) C. O.S.B.
*St Sigibald of Metz (c.740) Bp.
*St Cuthbert of Canterbury (758) Bp. O.S.B.
*St Albinus of Buraburg (p.760) Bp. O.S.B.
*St Bean of Aberdeen (p. 1012) Bp.

*Bl Adalgott of Dissentis (1031) Ab. O.S.B.
St Fulk of Pavia (1229) Bp.
*Bl Damian dei Fulcheri (1484) C. O.P.
*Bl Bonaventure of Potenza (1711) C. O.F.M.
*Bl Dominic Doan (1839) M. O.P.

OCTOBER 27.

St Florentius of Burgundy (3rd cent.) M.
SS Vincent, Sabina and Christeta (303) MM.
SS Capitolina and Erotheis (304) MM.
*St Abraham the Child (367) H.
St Frumentius of Ethiopia (c.380) Bp.
St Gaudiosus of Naples (c.455) Bp.
*St Namatius of Clermont (p.462) Bp.
St Elesbaan (c.555) King.
*St Otteran of Iona (c.563) Ab.
*St Abban of Wexford (6th cent.) Ab.
*St Cyriacus of Constantinople (606) Bp.
*St Desiderius of Auxerre (c.625) Bp.
*St Colman of Senboth-Fola (c.632) Ab.
*Bl Goswin of Chemnion (1203) C. O.S.B.Cist.
*Bl Antonia of Brescia (1507) V. O.P.

OCTOBER 28.

SS *Simon the Zealot and Jude Thaddaeus* (*1st cent.*) *Apostles*.
SS Anastasia and Cyril (c.253) MM.
St Cyrilla of Rome (c.270) V. M.
St Ferrutius of Mainz (?) M.
St Fidelis of Como (c.304) M.
St Honoratus of Vercelli (c.410) Bp.
*St Salvius of Normandy (6th cent.) H.
*St Abraham of Ephesus (6th cent.) Bp.
St Faro of Meaux (c.675) Bp.
*St Godwin of Stavelot (c.690) Ab. O.S.B.
*St Dorbhene of Iona (713) Ab.
*St Anglinus of Stavelot (c.768) Ab. O.S.B.
*St Alberic of Stavelot (779) Ab. O.S.B.
*St Remigius of Lyons (875) Bp.
*St Eadsin of Canterbury (1050) Bp.
*Bl John Dat (1798) M.
*Bl Joachim Royo (1848) M. O.P.

OCTOBER 29.

St Narcissus of Jerusalem (c.222) Bp.
St Maximilian of Lorch (284) Bp. M.
St Eusebia of Bergamo (late 3rd cent.)
V. M.
St Donatus of Corfù (?) C.
SS Hyacinth, Quintus, Felician and
Lucius (?) MM.
St John of Autun (?) Bp.
St Zenobius of Antioch (310) M.
*St Kennera of Scotland (5th cent.)
V. M.
*St Terence of Metz (520) Bp.
*St Theuderius of Vienne (c.575) Ab.
*St Ermelinda of Meldaert (c.595) V.
*St Colman of Kilmacduagh (632) Bp.
*St Sigolinus of Stavelot (670) Ab.
O.S.B.
*St Bond of Sens (7th cent.) H.
*St Anne, or Euphemian (820) W. H.
*St Elfleda of Ramsey (c.1000) Abs.
O.S.B.
*St Stephen of Caiazzo (1023) Bp.
O.S.B.
*Bl Berengarius of Formbach (1108)
Ab. O.S.B.
*Bl Wirnto of Göttweig (1127) Ab.
O.S.B.
*Bl Paula of Montaldo (1514) W.
O.F.M.
*BB Martyrs of Douai (16th and 17th
cent.).

OCTOBER 30.

*St Artemas of Lystra (1st cent.) Bp.
St Serapion of Antioch (199) Bp.
St Eutropia of Africa (c.253) M.
SS Zenobius and Zenobia (285-290)
MM.
St Marcellus of Tangier (298) M.
SS Julian, Eunus, Macarius and Comp.
(?) MM.
SS Claudius, Lupercus and Victorius
(c.300) MM.
St Saturninus of Cagliari (303) M.
St Maximus of Cumae (304) M.
St Asterius of Amasea (c.400) Bp.
St Theonestus of Altino (425) Bp. M.
St Lucanus of Lagny (5th cent.) M.
St Germanus of Capua (c.545) Bp.

*St Talarica of Scotland (6th cent.) Bp.
*St Arilda of Gloucestershire (?) V. M.
*St Herbert of Tours (?) Bp. O.S.B.
*St Egelnoth the Good (1038) Bp.
O.S.B.
*St Nanterius of St-Mihiel (c.1044) Ab.
O.S.B.
St Gerard of Potenza (1119) Bp.
*Bl Bernard de la Tour (1258) C.
O.Cart.
*Bl Benvenuta Bojani (1292) V. Tert.
O.P.
*St Dorothy of Montau (1394) W.
*Bl John Slade (1583) M.
*Bl Angelus of Acri (1739) C. O.F.M.
Cap.

OCTOBER 31.

SS Ampliatus, Urban and Narcissus
(1st cent.) MM.
St Stachys of Byzantium (1st cent.)
Bp.
St Quintinus of Amiens (287) M.
*St Erth of Cornwall (6th cent.).
*St Foillan of Fosses (c.655) Ab. O.S.B.
St Antoninus Fontana (660) Bp.
*St Bega (681) V.
*St Notburga of Cologne (c.714) V.
O.S.B.
*St Arnulfus of Novalese (p.840) M.
O.S.B.
St Wolfgang of Ratisbon (994) Bp.
O.S.B.
*Bl Christopher of Romagnola (1272)
C. O.F.M.
*Bl Thomas Bellaci (1447) C. O.F.M.
St Alphonsus Rodríguez (1617) C.
S.J.

NOVEMBER 1.

Feast of All Saints.
St Austremonius of Clermont (1st or
3rd cent.) Bp.
St Benignus of Dijon (3rd cent.) M.
SS Caesarius and Julian (?) MM.
SS Caesarius, Decius and Comp. MM.
St Mary the Slave (c.300) V. M.
SS Cyrenia and Juliana (306) MM.
SS John and James (c.344) MM.
St Mathurin of Sens (388) C.
St Marcellus of Paris (c.430) Bp.

*St Amabilis of Auvergne (475) C.
*St Dingad of Wales (5th cent.) C.
*St Cledwyn of Wales (5th cent.) C.
*St Pabiali of Wales (5th or 6th cent.) C.
St Vigor of Bayeux (c.537) Bp.
*St Cadfan of Wales (early 6th cent.) Ab.
*St Ceitho of Wales (6th cent.) C.
St Licinius of Angers (c.616) Bp.
*St Caesarius of Clermont (p.627) Bp.
*St Floribert of Ghent (c.660) Ab. O.S.B.
*St Genesius of Fontenelle (c.679) Bp. O.S.B.
St Severinus of Tiboli (c.699) H. O.S.B.
*St Germanus of Montfort (c.1000) C. O.S.B.
*St Salaun of Brittany (1358) C.
*Bl Conradin of Brescia (1429) C. O.P.
*BB Paul Navarro and Comp. (1622) MM. S.J.
*BB Jerome Hermosilla, Peter Almató and Valentine Berrio-Ochoa (1861) MM. O.P.

NOVEMBER 2.

Commemoration of All the Souls of the Faithful Departed.
SS Publius, Victor, Hermas and Papias (?) MM.
St George of Vienne (?) Bp.
St Victorinus of Pettau (c.303) Bp. M.
St Justus of Trieste (303) M.
SS Carterius, Styriacus, Tobias, Eudoxius, Aagpius and Comp. (c.315) MM.
St Theodotus of Laodicea (334) Bp.
SS Acindynus, Pegasius, Aphthonius, Elpidephorus and Anempodistus (345) MM.
St Eustochium of Tarsus (362) V. M.
St Marcian of Chalcis (387) H.
St Ambrose of Agaune (523) Ab.
*St Cumgar of Devon (6th or 8th cent.) C.
*SS Baya and Maura (10th cent.) VV.
*St Amicus of Monte Cassino (c.1045) C. O.S.B.
*St Jorandus of Kergrist (1340) H. O.S.B.

*Bl Thomas of Walden (1430) C. O.C.
*Bl John Bodey (1583) M.

NOVEMBER 3.

St Quartus (1st cent.).
SS Germanus, Theophilus, Caesareus and Vitalis (250) MM.
*St Papulus of Toulouse (c.300) M.
SS Innumerable Martyrs of Saragossa (c.304).
SS Valentine and Hilary (c.304) MM.
*St Florus of Lodeve (389) Bp.
*St Acepsimas of Cyrrhus (5th cent.) H.
*St Valentinian of Salerno (c.500) Bp.
St Domnus of Vienne (527) Bp.
*St Guenhael of Landevenec (c.550) Ab.
St Sylvia of Rome (c.572) W.
*St Gaudiosus of Tarazona (c.585) Bp.
*St Elerius of Wales (6th cent.) C.
St Winifred of Wales (c.680) V. M.
*St Cristiolus of Wales (7th cent.).
*St Vulganius of Arras (c.704) H. O.S.B.
St Hubert of Liége (727) Bp.
St Pirminius of Reichenau (753) Bp. O.S.B.
*SS Acheric and William (p.860) CC. O.S.B.
*St Englatius of Scotland (966) Bp.
St Hermengaudius of Urgell (1035) Bp.
St Malachy O'More (1148) Bp.
*Bl Berthold of Engelberg (1197) Ab. O.S.B.
*Bl Alpais of Cudot (1211) V.
*Bl Ida of Toggenburg (1226) O.S.B.
*Bl Raynerius of Arezzo (1304) C. O.F.M.
*Bl Simon Ballachi (1319) C. O.P.
*Bl Peter-Francis Neron (1860) M.

NOVEMBER 4.

SS Philologus and Patrobas (1st cent.).
St Porphyrius of Ephesus (171) M.
SS Nicander and Hermas (?) MM.
SS Vitalis and Agricola (c.304) MM.
St Pierius of Alexandria (c.310) C.
*St John Zedazneli (6th cent.) Ab.
*St Modesta of Öhren (c.680) Abs. O.S.B.

St Proculus of Autun (p.717) Bp. M.
St Joannicius of Mt Olympus (846) H.
St Clarus of Rouen (c.875) M. O.S.B.
*St Birnstan of Winchester (c.934) Bp. O.S.B.
*St Gregory of Burtscheid (999) Ab. O.S.B.
St Emeric of Hungary (1031) Prince.
*St Gerard of Bazonches (1123) C. O.S.B.
*Bl Helen Enselmini (1242) V. Poor Clare.
*Bl Henry of Zwiefalten (p.1250) C. O.S.B.
Bl Frances d'Amboise (1485) C. O.C.
St Charles Borromeo (1584) Bp.
*Bl Theodore Guenot (1861) M.

NOVEMBER 5.

St Zachary (1st cent.) Prophet.
St Elisabeth (1st cent.) W.
SS Felix and Eusebius (1st cent.) MM.
SS Galation and Epistemis (252) MM.
SS Domninus, Theotimus, Philotheus, Sylvanus and Comp. (?) MM.
*St Domninus of Grenoble (4th cent.) Bp.
St Dominator of Brescia (c.495) Bp.
St Fibitius of Trèves (c.500) Bp.
St Magnus of Milan (525) Bp.
St Laetus of Orleans (533) C.
*St Kanten of Wales (6th cent.) C.
*St Kea (6th cent.) Bp.
*SS Augustine and Paulinus (6th cent.) CC. O.S.B.
*St Bertilla of Chelles (c.705) V. O.S.B.
*St Spinulus of Moyen-moutier (707) Ab. O.S.B.
St Hermenegild of Salcedo (953) C. O.S.B.
*St Gerald of Beziers (1123) Bp.
*Bl Raynerius of Todi (c.1586) C. O.F.M.Cap.
*Bl Martin Porres (1639) C. O.P.
*Bl Gomidas Keumurjian (1707) M.

NOVEMBER 6.

St Felix of Thynissa (?) M.
St Atticus of Phrygia (?) M.

*St Pinnock (?).
St Leonard of Noblac (c.559) Ab.
*St Leonianus of Autun (c.570) C.
St Felix of Fondi (6th cent.) C. O.S.B.
St Severus of Barcelona (633) Bp. M.
SS Ten Martyrs of Antioch (637).
*St Edwen of Anglesey (7th cent.) V.
*St Efflam of Brittany (a.700) C.
St Winoc of Wormhoult (717) Ab. O.S.B.
*St Appian of Commachio (c.800) C. O.S.B.
*St Erlafrid of Hirsau (p.830) Ab. O.S.B.
*St Demetrian of Cyprus (c.912) Bp.
*St Stephen of Apt (1046) Bp.
*Bl Simon of Aulne (1215) C. O.S.B. Cist.
*St Leonard of Reresby (13th cent.) C.
*Bl Christina of Stommeln (1312) V.
Bl Nonius Alvarez (1431) C. C.
*Bl Margaret of Lorraine (1521) W. O.F.M.

NOVEMBER 7.

St Prosdocimus of Padua (c.100) Bp.
St Amaranthus of Albi (3rd cent.) M.
SS Hieron, Nicander, Hesychius and Comp. (c.300) MM.
SS Auctus, Taurion and Thessalonica (?) MM.
St Achillas of Alexandria (313) Bp.
SS Melasippus, Antony and Carina (360) MM.
St Rufus of Metz (c.400) Bp.
St Herculanus of Perugia (549) Bp.
*St Tremorus of Brittany (6th cent.) M.
*St Raverannus of Séez (682) Bp. O.S.B.
*St Gertrude of Remiremont (c.690) Abs. O.S.B.
St Florentius of Strassburg (c.693) Bp.
*St Amarand of Albi (p.700) Bp. O.S.B.
St Willibrord of Echternach (739) Bp. O.S.B.
*St Blinlivet of Quimperlé (9th cent.) Bp.
*St Ernest of Zwiefalten (1148) Ab. O.S.B.
*Bl Lucy of Settefonti (12th cent.) V. O.S.B.Cam.

St Engelbert of Cologne (1225) Bp. M.
*Bl Antony Baldinucci (1717) C. S.J.
*BB Hyacinth Castañeda and Comp. (1773) MM. O.P.
*Bl John Baptist Cou (1840) M.

NOVEMBER 8.

SS Four Crowned Martyrs (c.305).
St Maurus of Verdun (383) Bp.
St Clarus of Marmoutier (397) H.
*St Cuby of Caernarvon (6th cent.) Bp.
St Deusdedit I (618) Pope.
*St Tysilio of Wales (c.640) Ab.
St Willehad of Bremen (c.790) Bp. O.S.B.
*St Wiomad of Trèves (c.790) Bp. O.S.B.
*St Moroc of Scotland (9th cent.) Bp.
*St Gregory of Einsiedeln (996) Ab. O.S.B.
*St Gervadius of Elgin (10th cent.) C.
St Godfrey of Amiens (1115) Bp. O.S.B.
*Bl Columbus of Toulouse (1229) C. O.P.
*BB Joseph Nghi, Martin Tinh and Martin Tho (1840) MM.

NOVEMBER 9.

St Agrippinus of Naples (2nd or 3rd cent.) Bp.
St Ursinus of Bourges (3rd cent.) Bp.
St Orestes of Cappadocia (304) M.
St Theodore Tyro (c.306) M.
St Alexander of Salonica (4th cent.) M.
*St Benignus of Ireland (c.468) Bp.
*St Pabo of Brittany (c.510) C.
*St Vitonus of Verdun (c.525) Bp.
SS Eustiola and Sopatra (7th cent.) VV.
*Bl George Napper (1610) M.

NOVEMBER 10.

SS Tryphena and Tryphosa (1st cent.).
St Probus of Ravenna (c.175) Bp.
SS Tryphon, Respicius and Nympha (251) MM.

SS Demetrius, Anianus, Eustosius and Comp. (?) MM.
St Leo of Melun (?) C.
St Tiberius, Modestus and Florence (303) MM.
St Monitor of Orleans (c.490) Bp.
St Justus of Canterbury (627) Bp. O.S.B.
*St Elaeth of Anglesey (6th cent.) King.
*St Aedh McBricc (6th cent.) Bp.
*St Hadelin of Séez (c.910) Bp. O.S.B.
*St Guerembaldus of Hirsau (965) C. O.S.B.
St Theoctiste of Lesbos (10th cent.) V.
*St John of Ratzeburg (1066) Bp. M.
*Bl Andrew of Baudiment (1142) Ab. O.S.B.Cist.
*Bl Andrew Avellino (1608) C. Theatine

NOVEMBER 11.

St Mennas of Egypt (c.295) M.
St Athenodorus of Mesopotamia (c.304) M.
SS Valentine, Felician and Victorinus (c.305) MM.
St Martin of Tours (397) Bp.
*St Cynfran of Wales (5th cent.) C.
St Veranus of Lyons (5th cent.) Bp.
*St Rhedius of Wales (?).
St Mennas of Santomena (6th cent.) H.
*St Bertuin of Malonne (c.698) Bp. O.S.B.
St Theodore Studites (826) Ab.
St Bartholomew of Rossano (1065) Ab.
*Bl Bartholomew of Marmoutier (1067) Bp. O.S.B.
*Bl Alradus of Isenhagen (c.1250) C. O.S.B.Cist.
*Bl Agnes of Bavaria (1532) V. Poor Clare.
*Bl Joseph Pignatelli (1811) C. S.J.

NOVEMBER 12.

SS Aurelius and Publius (2nd cent.) Bps. MM.
St Rufus of Avignon (c.200) Bp.
St Renatus of Angers (c.422) Bp.

St Nilus the Elder (c.430) Ab.
St Evodius of Le Puy (p.560) Bp.
St Aemilian of La Cogolla (574) Ab.
St Machar of Iona (6th cent.) Bp.
St Imerius of Immertal (c.610) Ab.
St Cunibert of Trèves (c.633) Bp.
St Livinus of Alsot (c.650) Bp. M.
St Martin I (655) Pope M.
St Cumian Fada (662) Ab.
St Cadwallador of Wales (c.662) King.
St Paternus of St-Pierre-le-Vif (c.729) M. O.S.B.
*St Lebuin of Deventer (c.773) C. O.S.B.
*St Namphasius of Marcillac (c.800) H. O.S.B.
*St Yvar of Reculver (c.830) M. O.S.B.
SS Benedict, John, Matthew, Isaac and Christinus (1005) MM. O.S.B.
*St Anastasius of Pannonhalma (c.1030) Bp. O.S.B.
*Bl John Cini "della Pace" (1433) C. O.F.M.
*Bl Gabriel Ferretti (1456) C. O.F.M.
St Didacus of Alcalá (1463) C. O.F.M. (*Feast on the 13th*).
*Bl Christopher of Portugal (c.1500) M.
St Josaphat of Poland (1623) Bp. M. (*Feast on the 14th.*)

NOVEMBER 13.

SS Antoninus, Zebinas, Germanus and Ennatha (297) MM.
SS Valentine, Solutor and Victor (c.305) MM.
St Mitrius of Aix (314) M.
SS Arcadius, Paschasius, Probus, Eutychian and Paulillus (437) MM.
St Brice of Tours (444) Bp.
St Quintian of Rodez (c.527) Bp.
*St Dalmatius of Rodez (580) Bp.
*St Devinicus of Caithness (6th cent.) Bp.
*St Columba of Cornwall (?) V. M.
St Eugene II of Toledo (657) Bp.
*St Maxellendis of Caudry (c.670) V. M.
*St Gredifael of Wales (7th cent.) C.
*St Chillien of Aubigny (7th cent.) C.
*St Caillin of Ferns (7th cent.) Bp.
St Nicholas the Great (867) Pope.

*St Abbo of Fleury (1004) Ab. M. O.S.B.
St Homobonus of Cremona (1197) C.
*St Siardus of Mariengaarden (1230) C. O.Praem.
*Bl Mark of Scala (c.1280) Ab. O.S.B.

NOVEMBER 14.

St Veneranda of Gaul (2nd cent.) V. M.
St Serapion of Alexandria (252) M.
St Venerandus of Troyes (275) M.
SS Clementinus, Theodotus and Philomenus (?) MM.
St Hypatius of Gangra (p.325) Bp. M.
St Jucundus of Bologna (c.485) Bp.
*St Modanic of Aberdeen (?) Bp.
*St Dubricius of Wales (c.545) Bp.
*St Sidonius of St-Saens (c.690) Ab. O.S.B.
*St Alberic of Utrecht (784) Bp. O.S.B.
St Laurence O'Toole (1180) Bp. O.S.A.
St Serapion of Algiers (1240) M. O.Merc.
*Bl John Licci (1511) C. O.P.

NOVEMBER 15.

St Felix of Nola (287) Bp.
SS Secundus, Fidentian and Varicus (?) MM.
St Eugene (?) Bp. M.
SS Gurias and Samonas (306) MM.
St Abibus of Edessa (322) M.
St Luperius of Verona (6th or 8th cent.) Bp.
St Malo of Brittany (621) Bp.
*St Desiderius of Cahors (655) Bp.
*St Machudd of Llanfechell (7th cent.) Ab.
*St Paduinus of Le Mans (c.703) Ab. O.S.B.
*St Arnulfus of Toul (871) Bp.
*St Findan of Rheinau (879) H. O.S.B.
St Albert the Great (1280) Bp. Dr. O.P.
St Leopold the Good (1136) C.
*BB Richard Whiting, Roger James and John Thorne (1539) MM. O.S.B.
*BB Hugh Faringdon, John Eynon and John Rugg (1539) MM. O.S.B.

*Bl Lucy Brocolelli (1544) V. O.P.
*Bl Caius of Corea (1624) M.

· NOVEMBER 16.

SS Rufinus, Mark and Valerius and
Comp. (?) MM.
St Fidentius of Padua (?) Bp.
SS Elpidius, Marcellus, Eustochius
and Comp. (362) MM.
St Eucherius of Lyons (450) Bp.
*St Afan of Wales (6th cent.) Bp.
*St Gobrian of Vannes (725) Bp.
St Othmar of St-Gall (759) Ab. O.S.B.
*St Africus of Comminges (7th cent.) C.
*St Alfrick of Canterbury (1006) Bp.
O.S.B.
*Bl Simeon of Cava (1141) Ab. O.S.B.
St Edmund Rich (1242) Bp.
*St Agnes of Assisi (1253) V. Poor
Clare.
St Gertrude the Great (c.1302) V.
O.S.B.
*Bl Louis Morbioli (1495) C.
*Bl Gratia of Cattaro (1509) C. O.S.A.

NOVEMBER 17.

St Dionysius of Alexandria (265) Bp.
St Gregory Thaumaturgus (c.270) Bp.
SS Alphaeus and Zacchaeus (303)
MM.
SS Acisclus and Victoria (304) MM.
St Eugene of Florence (422) C.
St Anianus of Orleans (453) Bp.
*St Namasius of Vienne (c.559) Bp.
St Gregory of Tours (596) Bp.
*St Hilda of Whitby (680) Abs. O.S.B.
*St Hugh of Noara (p.1172) Ab. O.S.B.
Cist.
St Hugh of Lincoln (1200) Bp. O.Cart.
*Bl Salomea of Poland (1268) W. Poor
Clare.
*Bl Jane of Segna (1307) V.
*BB Martyrs of Paraguay (1628) S.J.

NOVEMBER 18.

St Hesychius of Antioch (c.303) M.
SS Romanus and Barulas (304) MM.

St Maximus of Mainz (378) Bp.
SS Oriculus and Comp. (c.430) MM.
St Nazarius of Lérins (c.450) Ab.
*St Mawes (6th cent.) Ab.
*St Keverne (6th cent.).
*St Mummolus of Lagny (c.690) Ab.
O.S.B.
*SS Amandus and Anselm (8th cent.)
Abbots O.S.B.
*St Fergus (p.721) Bp.
*St Constant (777) M.
St Thomas of Antioch (782) H.
St Odo of Cluny (942) Ab. O.S.B.
*SS Burginus and Guilminus (p.1065)
CC. O.S.B.
*Bl Andrew Trong (1835) M.
*Bl Rose-Philippine Duchesne (1852)
V. I.S.H.

NOVEMBER 19.

St Abdias (9th cent. B.C.) Prophet.
SS Exuperius, Severinus and Felician
(170) MM.
St Pontian (c.236) Pope M.
St Maximus of Rome (c.255) M.
St Barlaam of Caesarea (c.304) M.
SS Azas and Comp. (c.304) MM.
*St Nerses the Great (373) Bp. M.
St Crispin of Ecoja (4th cent.) Bp. M.
St Faustus of Alexandria (4th cent.)
M.
St Anastasius II (498) Pope.
*St Ermenburga of Thanet (c.650) W.
O.S.B.
*St Medana of Galloway (8th cent.) V.
*Bl Tuto of Ottobeuren (815) Ab.
O.S.B.
*St James of Sasseau (c.865) C. O.S.B.
*St Atto of Tordino (p.1010) Ab. O.S.B.
St Elisabeth of Hungary (1231) Queen,
Tert.O.F.M.
*St Mechtildis of Hackeborn (1298) V.
O.S.B.
*BB Martyrs of Annam (1754-1861,
1820-1841).

NOVEMBER 20.

SS Eustace, Thespesius and Anatolius
(235) MM.

SS Octavius, Solutor and Adventor (297) MM.
SS Bassius, Dionysius, Agapitus and Comp. (?) MM.
SS Ampelius and Caius (c.302) MM.
St Dasius of Dorostorum (c.303) M.
St Agapius of Caesarea (c.306) M.
SS Nerses and Comp. (343) MM.
St Benignus of Milan (c.477) Bp.
*St Maxentia of Beauvais (?) V. M.
St Silvester of Chalons-sur-Saone (c.525) Bp.
St Simplicius of Verona (c.535) Bp.
*St Eval of Cornwall (6th cent.) Bp.
*St Autbodus of Laon (690) C.
*St Eudo of Cormery (c.760) Ab. O.S.B.
St Edmund (870) King, M.
*St Gregory Decapolites (9th cent.) C.
*St Leo of Nonantula (1000) Ab. O.S.B.
St Bernward of Hildesheim (1022) Bp. O.S.B.
St Felix of Valois (1212) C. Founder.
*Bl Ambrose Traversari (1439) Ab. O.S.B.Cam.
*Bl Francis Xavier Can (1837) M.

NOVEMBER 21.

Feast of the Presentation of the B. V. Mary.
St Rufus of Rome (c.90) Bp.?
SS Heliodorus and Comp. (c.270) MM.
SS Demetrius and Honorius (?) MM.
SS Celsus and Clement (?) MM.
SS Honorius, Eutychius and Stephen (c.300) MM.
St Gelasius I (496) Pope.
*St Digain of Cornwall (5th cent.) C.
St Columbanus of Luxeuil (615) Ab.
*St Columbanus Junior (p.616) M.
St Maurus of Verona (c.600) Bp.
*St Amelberga of Susteren (p.900) Abs. O.S.B.
*St Hilary of Volturno (c.1045) Ab. O.S.B.
*Bl Nicholas Giustiniani (p.1180) C. O.S.B.

NOVEMBER 22.

SS Philemon and Appia (c.70) MM.
St Caecilia of Rome (2nd-3rd cent.) V. M.

St Maurus of Africa (c.284) M.
St Mark of Antioch (c.305) M.
St Pragmatius of Autun (c.520) Bp.
*St Dayniol the Younger (621).
*St Savinian of Menat (c.720) Ab. O.S.B.
*Bl Christian of Auxerre (c.873) Bp.
*St Trigidia of Oña (c.925) Abs. O.S.B.
*Bl Eugenia of Matera (c.1093) Abs. O.S.B.
*Bl Benedict de Ponte (13th cent.) C. O.P.

NOVEMBER 23.

St Clement of Rome (c.100) Pope, M.
St Felicitas of Rome (165) M.
*St Clement of Metz (?) Bp.
St Lucretia of Merida (306) V. M.
St Sisinius of Cyzicus (p.325) Bp.
*St Paternian of Fermo (c.343) Bp.
St Amphilochius of Iconium (p.392) Bp.
*St Paulinus of Wales (c.505) C.
St Gregory of Girgenti (c.638) Bp.
*St Wilfretudis of Nivelle (p.670) Abs. O.S.B.
*St Trudo of St-Trond (c.695) Ab. O.S.B.
*St Rachildis of St-Gall (c.946) H. O.S.B.
*Bl Margaret of Savoy (1464) W. O.P.

NOVEMBER 24.

St Firmina of Amelia (c.303) V. M.
St Felicissimus of Perugia (c.303) M.
St Chrysogonus of Aquileia (c.304) M.
St Crescentian of Rome (309) M.
St Protasius of Milan (352) Bp.
St Alexander of Corinth (361) M.
St Romanus of Le Mans (385) C.
*St Kenan of Damleag (c.500) Bp.
St Portianus of Miranda (533) Ab.
*St Colman of Cloyne (c.600) Bp.
*St Leopardinus of Vivaris (7th cent.) Ab. M.
*St Bieuzy of Brittany (7th cent.) M.
*St Eanfleda of Whitby (c.700) W. O.S.B.
*St Marinus of Maurienne (731) M. O.S.B.

SS Flora and Mary (856) VV. MM.
*Bl Balsamus of Cava (1232) Ab. O.S.B.
*Bl Conrad of Frisach (1239) C. O.P.
St John of the Cross (1591) C. O.C.D.
*BB Peter Dumoulin-Borie and Comp.
(1838) MM.
*BB Martyrs of China and Cochin-
China (1823-1856).

NOVEMBER 25.

St Moses of Rome (c.250) M.
St Mercurius of Caesarea (c.250) M.
St Erasmus of Antioch (?) M.
St Catherine of Alexandria (c.310) V.
M.
St Mesrob the Teacher (441) C.
St Jucunda of Reggio (466) V.
*St Lavanus of Gascony (7th cent.) Ab.
O.S.B.
*St Alnoth of Stowe (c.700) M.
*St Imma of Karlburg (c.752) Abs.
O.S.B.
*SS Adalbert and Guido of Casauria
(c.1045) CC. O.S.B.
*Bl Bernold of Ottobeuren (c.1050) C.
O.S.B.
*Bl Ekbert of Münsterschwarzach
(1075) Ab. O.S.B.
*Bl Conrad of Heisterbach (c.1200) C.
O.S.B.Cist.
*Bl Elisabeth the Good (1420) V. Tert.
O.F.M.

NOVEMBER 26.

St Amator of Autun (3rd cent.) Bp.
St Peter of Alexandria (311) Bp. M.
SS Faustus, Didius, Ammonius, Phi-
leas, Hesychius, Pachomius, Theo-
dore and Comp. (c.311) MM.
St Marcellus of Nicomedia (349) M.
St Stylianus of Adrianopolis (390) H.
St Siricius (399) Pope.
St Basolus of Verzy (c.620) H.
*St Egelwine of Athelney (7th cent.) C.
*St Martin of Arades (726) C. O.S.B.
*St Conrad of Constance (975) Bp.
St Nicon Metanoite (998) C.
St Bellinus of Padua (1151) Bp. M.
*Bl Pontius of Faucigny (1178) Ab.
O.S.B.

*Bl Walter of Aulnes (c.1180) C. O.S.B.
Cist.
St Silvester Gozzolini (1267) Ab. O.S.B.
*Bl Albert of Haigerloch (1311) C.
O.S.B.
*Bl James Benfatti (1338) Bp. O.P.
*Bl Redemptus of the Cross (1638) M.
O.C.D.
St Leonard of Port Maurice (1751) C.
O.F.M.

NOVEMBER 27.

SS Basileus, Auxilius and Saturninus
(?) MM.
SS Barlaam and Josaphat (?).
SS Facundus and Primitivus (c.300)
MM.
SS Hirenarchus, Acacius and Comp.
(c.305) MM.
St Valerian of Aquileia (389) Bp.
St James Intercisus (421) M.
St John Angeloptes (433) Bp.
*St Seachnall of Dunshauglin (457) Bp.
St Maximus of Riez (460) Bp.
St Severinus of Paris (c.540) H.
*St Siffred of Carpentras (540) Bp.
*St Gallgo of Wales (6th cent.) Ab.
*St Acharius of Noyon (640) Bp.
*St Bilhild of Altenmünster (c.710) W.
O.S.B.
St Virgilius of Salzburg (784) Bp.
O.S.B.
*St Apollinaris of Monte Cassino (828)
Ab. O.S.B.
*St Edwold of Cerne (9th cent.) C.
St Albert of Louvain (1192) Bp. M.
*Bl Angelus Sinesio (c.1386) Ab. O.S.B.
*Bl Bernardinus of Fossa (1503) C.
O.F.M.
*BB Antony Kimura and Comp. (1619)
MM.
*Bl Humilis of Bisignano (1637) C.
O.F.M.

NOVEMBER 28.

St Sosthenes (1st cent.).
SS Rufus and Comp. (304) MM.
SS Valerian, Urban, Crescens, Eustace, Cresconius, Crescentian, Felix, Hortulanus and Florentian (5th
cent.) Bps.

SS Papinianus and Mansuetus (5th cent.) MM.

*St Fionnchu of Bangor (6th cent.) Ab.

SS Stephen, Basil, Peter, Andrew and Comp. (764) MM.

*St Hippolytus of St-Claude (c.775) Bp. O.S.B.

St James della Marca (1475) C. O.F.M.

*Bl Calimerius of Montechiaro (1521) C. O.P.

*Bl James Thompson (1582) M.

NOVEMBER 29.

SS Paramon and Comp. (250) MM.

St Saturninus of Toulouse (c.257) Bp. M.

St Philomenus of Ancyra (275) M.

SS Blaise and Demetrius (?) MM.

SS Saturninus and Sisinius (c.309) MM.

St Illuminata of Todi (c.320) V.

*St Brendan of Birr (c.562) Ab.

*St Sadwen of Wales (6th cent.) C.

*St Hardoin of Brittany (7th cent.) Bp.

*St Walderic of Murrhardt (p. 817) Ab. O.S.B.

*St Radbod of Utrecht (918) Bp. O.S.B.

*St Gulstan of Rhuys (c.1010) C. O.S.B.

*Bl Jutta of Heiligenthal (c.1250) Abs. O.S.B.Cist.

*Bl Frederick of Ratisbon (1329) C. O.S.A.

*Bl Nicolino Magalotti (1370) H. Tert. O.F.M.

*Bl Cuthbert Mayne (1577) M.

*BB Dionysius and Redemptus (1638) MM. O.C.D.

NOVEMBER 30

St Andrew (1st cent.) Apostle M.

St Maura of Constantinople (?) V. M.

St Justina of Constantinople (?) V. M.

SS Castulus and Euprepis (?) MM.

SS Sapor, Isaac and Comp. (339) MM.

St Constantius of Rome (5th cent.) C.

St Trojan of Saintes (533) Bp.

*St Truwal of Treguier (c.564) Bp.

St Zosimus the Wonder-Worker (6th cent.) H.

*St Arnold of Gemblours (1155) Ab. O.S.B.

*Bl Joscius of St-Bertin (1186) C. O.S.B.

*Bl Andrew of Antioch (1348) C. O.S.A.

*Bl William de Paulo (1423) Ab. O.S.B.

*Bl Joseph Marchand (1835) M.

DECEMBER 1.

St Nahum (c.660 B.C.) Prophet.

St Castritian of Milan (137) Bp.

SS Diodorus, Marianus and Comp. (283) MM.

SS Lucius, Rogatus, Cassian and Candida (?) MM.

St Ananias of Arbela (?) M.

St Olympiades of Rome (303) M.

St Ansanus the Baptizer (304) M.

St Natalia of Nicomedia (c.311).

St Ursicinus of Brescia (347) Bp.

St Evasius of Asti (c.362) Bp. M.

*St Leontius of Fréjus (c.432) Bp.

*St Candres of Maestricht (5th cent.) Bp.

St Proculus of Narni (c.542) Bp. M.

*St Constantian of Javron (570) Ab.

St Agericus of Verdun (591) Bp.

St Eligius of Noyon (660) Bp.

*St Grwst of Wales (7th cent.) C.

*Bl John of Vercelli (1283) C. O.P.

*Bl Christian of Perugia (13th cent.) C. O.P.

*Bl Antony Bonfadini (1482) C. O.F.M.

Bl John Beche (1539) Ab. M. O.S.B.

*BB Alexander Briant S.J. and Ralph Sherwin (1581) MM.

*Bl Richard Langley (1586) M.

DECEMBER 2.

SS Pontian and Comp. (c.259) MM.

SS Eusebius, Marcellus, Hippolytus, Maximus, Adria, Paulina, Neon, Mary, Martana and Aurelia (254-259) MM.

St Lupus of Verona (?) Bp.

St Evasius of Brescia (?) Bp.

St Bibiana of Rome (?) V. M.

St Chromatius of Aquileia (c.406)Bp.

SS Severus, Securus, Januarius and Victorinus (c.450) MM.

St Silvanus of Troas (c.450) Bp.
St Nonnus of Edessa (c.458) Bp.
*St Trumwin of Whitby (c.700) Bp. O.S.B.
*Bl Oderisius of Monte Cassino (1105) Card. O.S.B.
*Bl Richard of Schonthal (1219) Ab. O.S.B.Cist.
*Bl John Ruysbroeck (1231) C. O.S.A.
*Bl John Armero (1566) C. O.P.

DECEMBER 3.

St Sophonias (7th cent. B.C.) Prophet.
St Lucius (c.200) King.
SS Claudius, Hilaria, Jason, Maurus and Comp. (c.283) MM.
St Cassian of Tangier (298) M.
SS Claudius, Crispin, Magna, John and Stephen (?) MM.
St Agricola of Hungary (?) M.
St Ethernan of Scotland (?) Bp.
St Mirocles of Milan (318) Bp.
SS Ambicus, Victor and Julius (4th cent.) MM.
St Birinus of Dorchester (c.650) Bp.
*St Attalia of Strassburg (741) Abs. O.S.B.
*St Sola of Solnhofen (794) H. O.S.B.
*St Abbo of Auxerre (c.860) Bp. O.S.B.
St Galganus of Monte Siepe (1181) C.
*Bl Bernard of Toulouse (1320) M. O.P.
St Francis Xavier (1552) C. S.J.
*Bl Edward Coleman (1678) M.

DECEMBER 4.

St Clement of Alexandria (c.217) C.
St Meletius of Pontus (c.295) Bp.
St Barbara of Nicomedia (?) V. M.
St Maruthas of Mesopotamia (c.415) Bp.
St Felix of Bologna (429) Bp.
St Peter Chrysologus (c.450) Bp. Dr.
*St Bertoara (p. 614) Abs.
*St Ada of Le Mans (late 7th cent.) Abs.
SS Theophanes and Comp. (c.810) MM.
*St Maurus of Pecs (c.1070) Bp. O.S.B.

St Annon of Cologne (1075) Bp.
St Osmund of Salisbury (1099) Bp.
St Bernard degli Uberti (1133) Card. Bp. O.S.B.Val.
*Bl Mary of St Martin (1240) V. O.S.B. Cam.
*Bl Christian of Prussia (1245) Bp. O.S.B.Cist.
*Bl Francis Gálvez (1623) M. O.F.M.

DECEMBER 5.

St Bassus of Nice (c.257) Bp. M.
St Anastasius (?) M.
SS Julius, Potamin, Crispin, Felix, Gratus and Comp. (302) MM.
St Dalmatius of Pavia (304) Bp. M.
St Crispina of Numidia (304) V. M.
St Pelinus of Corfinium (361) Bp. M.
St Sabbas of Palestine (532) Ab.
*St Cawrdaf of Wales (c.560).
St Nicetius of Trèves (566) Bp.
*St Justinian of S. Wales (6th cent.) M.
*St Firminus of Verdun (6th cent.) Bp.
*St Sigiranus of Lonrey (c.655) Ab. O.S.B.
*St Gerbold of Bayeux (c.690) Bp. O.S.B.
St John the Wonder-Worker (p.750) Bp.
*St Basilissa of Oehren (c.780) Abs. O.S.B.
*Bl John Gradenigo (1025) H. O.S.B.
*St Gerald of Braga (1109) Bp. O.S.B.
*Bl Nicholas Tavigli (1391) M. O.F.M.
*Bl Bartholomew Fanti (1495) C. O.C.
*Bl John Almond (1612) M.
*BB Jerome de Angelis S.J. and Comp. (1623) MM.

DECEMBER 6.

St Nicholas of Myra (c.350) Bp.
St Polychronius (4th cent.) M.
St Asella of Rome (c.406) V.
SS Dionysia, Dativa, Leontia, Tertius, Aemilian, Boniface and Comp. (484) MM.
St Majoricus of Africa (c.490) M.
SS Auxilius, Isserninus and Secundinus (5th cent.) Bps.

*St Abraham of Kratia (c.558) Bp.
*St Gertrude the Elder (649) W. O.S.B.
*St Gerard of Joigny (1109) Ab. O.S.B.
St Peter Pascual (1300) Bp. M.
*Bl Joseph Khang (1861) M. O.P. Tert.

DECEMBER 7.

St Agatho (250) M.
St Eutychian (283) Pope M.
SS Polycarp and Theodore (?) MM.
St Urban of Teano (c.356) Bp.
*St Victor of Piacenza (375) Bp.
St Ambrose of Milan (397) Bp. Dr.
St Martin of Saujon (c.400) Ab.
St Servus of Africa (483) M.
*St Anianus of Chartres (5th cent.) Bp.
*St Buithe of Scotland (521) C.
*St Humbert of Igny (1148) Ab. O.S.B. Cist.

DECEMBER 8.

Feast of the Immaculate Conception of the Blessed Virgin Mary.
St Eucharius of Trèves (1st cent.) Bp.
St Sophronius of Cyprus (6th cent.) Bp.
St Romaricus of Remiremont (653) Ab. O.S.B.
St Patapius of Constantinople (7th cent.) H.
*St Gunthildis of Wimborne (c.748) V. O.S.B.
*Bl Jane of Cáceres (1383) Abs. O.S.B. Cist.

DECEMBER 9.

St Syrus of Pavia (1st cent.) Bp. M.
St Julian of Apamaea (3rd cent.) Bp.
St Restitutus of Carthage (?) Bp. M.
St Valeria of Limoges (?) V. M.
SS Peter, Successus, Bassianus, Primitivus and Comp. (?) MM.
St Leocadia of Toledo (c.303) V. M.
SS Seven Martyrs of Samosata (c.311).

St Proculus of Verona (c.320) Bp.
St Gorgonia of Cappadocia (c.375) Matron.
St Cyprian of Perigeux (586) Ab.
*St Budoc of Dol (7th cent.) Bp.
*St Balda of Jouarre (late 7th cent.) Abs. O.S.B.
*St Ethelgiva of Shaftesbury (896) Abs. O.S.B.
*Bl Enguerrammus the Wise (1045) Ab. O.S.B.
*Bl Severus of Prague (1067) Bp. O.S.B.
*Bl Delphina of Languedoc (1358) V. Tert.O.F.M.
St Peter Fourier (1640) Founder.

DECEMBER 10.

SS Carpophorus and Abundius (290-300) MM.
St Nercurius and Comp. (c.300) MM.
St Eulalia of Merida (304) V. M.
St Julia of Merida (304) V. M.
SS Mennas, Hermogenes and Eugraphus (c.312) MM.
St Miltiades (314) Pope.
St Gemellus of Ancyra (362) M.
St Sindulphus of Vienne (c.669) Bp.
St Deusdedit of Brescia (c.700) Bp.
*St Thomas of Farfa (c.720) Ab. O.S.B.
*St Lucerius of Farfa (739) Ab. O.S.B.
St Gregory III (741) Pope.
*St Guitmarus of Centula (p.756) Ab. O.S.B.
*St Hildemar of Beauvais (p.844) Bp. O.S.B.
*Bl Albert of Sassovivom (p.1102) Ab. O.S.B.
*Bl Fulgentius of Afflighem (1122) Ab. O.S.B.
*St Florentius of Carracedo (1156) Ab. O.S.B.
*Bl Peter Tecelano (1287) C. O.F.M.
*Bl Edmund Campion (1581) M. S.J.
*BB Eustace White and Comp. (1591) MM.
*BB Edmund Gennings and Swithun Wells (1591) MM.
*BB Thomas Somers and John Roberts, O.S.B. (1610) MM.
*Bl Sebastian Montañol (1616) M. O.P.

DECEMBER 11.

SS Victoricus, Fuscian and Gentian (c.287) MM.
SS Trason, Pontian and Praetextatus (c.302) MM.
St Barsabas of Persia (c.342) M.
St Damasus (384) Pope.
St Eutychius of Cádiz (4th cent.) M.
St Sabinus of Piacenza (420) Bp.
St Daniel the Stylite (493) M.
*St Peris of Wales (?) C.
*St Cian of Wales (6th cent.) C.
*St Fidweten of Redon (c.888) C. O.S.B.
*Bl David of Himmerode (1179) Ab. O.S.B.Cist.
*Bl Franco Lippi (1291) C. O.C.
*Bl Hugolinus Magalotti (1373) C. O.F.M.

DECEMBER 12.

SS Ammonaria, Mercuria, Dionysia and a second Ammonaria (c.250) MM.
St Synesius of Rome (725) M.
SS Maxentius, Constantius, Crescentius, Justin and Comp. (c.287) MM.
SS Hermogenes, Donatus and Comp. (?) MM.
*St Abra of Poitiers (c.360) V.
*St Cury of Cornwall (401) C.
*St Corentinus of Quimper (c.490) Bp.
St Columba of Tyrdaglas (548) Ab.
*St Finian of Clonard (c.552) Bp.
*St Cormac (6th cent.) Ab.
*St Colman of Glendalough (659) Ab.
*St Edburga of Thanet (751) Abs. O.S.B.
*St Agatha of Wimborne (c.790) V. O.S.B.
*St Vicelinus of Lübeck (1154) Bp.
*Bl Jerome Ranuzzi (1455) C. O.S.M.
*Bl Thomas Holland (1642) M. S.J.
*Bl Simon Hoa (1840) M.

DECEMBER 13.

St Antiochus of Sardinia (c.110) M.
SS Eustratius, Auxentius, Eugene, Mardarius and Orestes (c.302) MM.

St Lucy of Syracuse (304) V. M.
St Jodocus of Brittany (668) H.
St Autbert of Cambrai (c.669) Bp.
*St Edburga of Lyminge (7th cent.) V. O.S.B.
St Ottilia of Hohenburg (c.720) Abs. O.S.B.
*Bl Tassilo of Bavaria (p.794) C. O.S.B.
*BB Einhildis and Roswinda (8th cent.) VV. O.S.B.
*Bl Wifred of Marseilles (1021) Ab. O.S.B.
*St Elisabeth-Rose (1130) Abs. O.S.B.
*Bl Pontius of Balmey (1140) Bp. O.Cart.
*Bl John Marinoni (1562) C.
*Bl Antoni Grassi (1671) C. C.Orat.

DECEMBER 14.

SS Heron, Arsenius, Isidore and Dioscorus (250) MM.
SS Justus and Abundius (283) MM.
St Pompeius of Pavia (c.290) Bp.
St Matronianus of Milan (?) H.
SS Drusus, Zosimus and Theodore (?) MM.
St Spiridion of Cyprus (c.348) Bp.
St Viator of Bergamo (c.378) Bp.
SS Nicasius, Eutropia and Comp. (c.407) MM.
*SS Fingar, Phiala and Comp. (5th cent.) MM.
St Agnellus of Naples (c.596) Ab. O.S.B.
*St Venantius Fortunatus (c.605) Bp.
*Bl John Bread-and-Water (p.1150) C. O.S.B.Cist.
*Bl Bartholomew Buonpedoni (1300) C.
*Bl Conrad of Offida (1306) C. O.F.M.
*Bl Bonaventure Buonacorsi (1313) C. O.S.M.

DECEMBER 15.

SS Irenaeus, Antony, Theodore, Saturninus, Victor and Comp. (c.258) MM.
SS Faustinus, Lucius, Candidus, Caelian, Mark, Januarius and Fortunatus (?) MM.
St Nino of Georgia (c.320) V.

St Valerian of Abbenza (457) Bp. M.
St Maximinus of Micy (c.520) Ab.
*St Florentius of Bangor (7th cent.) Ab.
*St Urbitius of Nocito (c.805) H. O.S.B.
*St Paul of Latros (956) H.
*Bl Adalbero of Metz (1005) Bp.
*Bl Julia of Arezzo (?) V. O.S.B.Cam.
*Bl Marinus of Cava (1170) Ab. O.S.B.
*Bl Sigfrid of Georgenberg (1215) C. O.S.B.

DECEMBER 16.

SS Ananias, Azarias and Misael (7th cent. B.C.).
St Albina of Gaeta (250) V. M.
SS Valentine, Concordius, Navalis and Agricola (c.305) MM.
St Eusebius of Vercelli (c.370) Bp. M.
St Irenion of Gaza (389) Bp.
*St Bean of Leinster (?) Bp.
St Ado of Vienne (875) Bp. O.S.B.
*St Nicholas Chrysoberges (996) Bp.
*St Adelaide (999) W. Empress.
*Bl Raynald de Bar (1151) Ab. O.S.B. Cist.
*Bl Sebastian Maggi (1494) C. O.P.
*Bl Mary of the Angels (1717) V. O.C.D.

DECEMBER 17.

St Lazarus (1st cent.) Bp.
St Olympias of Constantinople (408) W.
*St Maxentiolus of Cunault (5th cent.) Ab.
*St Tydecho of Wales (6th cent.).
*St Briach of Guingamp (c.627) Ab.
SS Florian, Calanicus and Comp. (c.637) MM.
*St Judicael (658) King.
*St Begga of Andenne (698) W. Abs. O.S.B.
St Sturmius of Fulda (779) Ab. O.S.B.
*St Eigil of Fulda (822) Ab. O.S.B.
St Wivina of Alost (c.1170) Abs. O.S.B.
*Bl Cherubinus Testa (1479) C. O.S.A.

DECEMBER 18.

SS Rufus and Zosimus (c.107) MM.
St Moses of Africa (c.250) M.

SS Quintus, Simplicius and Comp. (c.255) MM.
SS Theotimus and Basilian (?) MM.
SS Victurus, Victor, Victorinus, Adjutor, Quartus and Comp. (?) MM.
St Auxentius of Mopsuestia (p.321) Bp.
St Gatian of Tours (c.337) Bp.
*St Bodagisil (588) Ab.
*St Flannan of Killaloe (7th cent.) Bp.
*St Desideratus of Fontenelle (c.700) C. O.S.B.
*St Winebald of Heidenheim (761) Ab. O.S.B.
*BB Augustine Moi, Peter Duong, Peter Truat and Paul Mi (1838) MM.

DECEMBER 19.

St Nemesius of Alexandria (250) M.
St Timothy of Africa (c.250) M.
St Fausta of Sirmium (3rd cent.) W.
SS Darius, Zosimus, Paul and Secundus (?) MM.
St Avitus of Micy (?) Ab.
*St Manirus of Scotland (?) Bp.
SS Cyriacus, Paulillus, Secundus, Anastasius, Syndimius and Comp. (303) MM.
SS Meuris and Thaea (c.307) MM.
St Anastasius I (401) Pope.
St Gregory of Auxerre (c.540) Bp.
*St Samthana of Meath (6th cent.) V.
*St Ribert of St-Oyend (c.790) Ab. O.S.B.
*St Bernard Paleara (1122) Bp. O.S.B.
*Bl Macarius the Scot (1153) Ab. O.S.B.
*Bl William of Fenoli (c.1205) C. O.Cart.
Bl Urban V (1370) Pope O.S.B.
*Bl Caecilia of Ferrara (1511) V. O.P.
*BB Thomas De and Comp. (1839) MM. Tert.O.P.

DECEMBER 20.

SS Ammon, Zeno, Ptolemy, Ingen and Theophilus (249) MM.
St Julius of Gelduba (?) M.
SS Liberatus and Bajulus (?) MM.
St Philogonius of Antioch (324) Bp.
SS Eugene and Macarius (362) MM.

*St Ursicinus of Cahors (c.535) Bp.
St Dominic of Brescia (c.612) Bp.
*St Ursicinus of St-Ursanne (c.625) Ab.
St Dominic of Silos (1073) Ab. O.S.B.
*Bl Gundisalvus of Silos (c.1073) C.
O.S.B.
*Bl Peter de la Cadireta (1277) M.
O.P.
*Bl Peter Massalenus (1453) C. O.S.B.
Cam.
*Bl Peter Thi (1839) M.

DECEMBER 21.

St Thomas (1st cent.) Apostle, M.
St Themistocles of Lycia (253) M.
*St Honoratus of Toulouse (3rd cent.)
Bp.
SS John and Festus (?) MM.
St Severinus of Trèves (c.300) Bp.
St Glycerius of Nicomedia (303) M.
St Anastasius II the Younger (609)
Bp. M.
*St Baudacarius of Bobbio (650) C.
O.S.B.
*St John Vincent (1012) Bp. O.S.B.
*Bl Adrian of Dalmatia (13th cent.) M.
O.P.

DECEMBER 22.

SS Chaeremon and Comp. (p.250)
MM.
SS Demetrius, Honoratus and Florus
(?) MM.
St Zeno of Nicomedia (303) M.
St Flavian of Acquapendente (362) M.
*St Amaethlu of Wales (6th cent.) C.
*St Hunger of Utrecht (866) Bp.
*St Amaswinthus of Malaga (982) Ab.
*Bl Marianus Scotus (1086) H. O.S.B.
*Bl Jutta of Dissibodenberg (1136)
Abs. O.S.B.
*Bl Adam of Saxony (c.1210) C. O.S.B.
Cist.
*St Frances Xavier Cabrini (1917) V.
Foundress.

DECEMBER 23.

SS Victoria (and Anatolia) (250) VV.
MM.

SS Theodulus, Saturninus, Euporus,
Gelasius, Eunician, Zeticus, Cleo-
menes, Agathopus, Basilides and
Evaristus (250) MM.
SS Martyrs of Crete (?).
SS Migdonius and Mardonius (303)
MM.
St Servulus of Rome (c.590) C.
*St Dagobert II (679) King M.
*St Frithbert of Hexham (766) Bp.
O.S.B.
*St Mazota of Abernethy (8th cent.) V.
*St Vintila of Orense (890) H. O.S.B.
*Bl Hartmann of Brixen (1164) Bp.
*Bl John Cirita (c.1164) H. O.S.B.
*St Thorlac Thornalli (1193) C. O.S.A.
*Bl Hermann of Scheda (c.1200) Ab.
O.Praem.
*St Nicholas Factor (1583) C. O.F.M.

DECEMBER 24.

SS Adam and Eve.
SS Forty Maidens martyred at Anti-
och (250).
SS Lucian, Metrobius, Paul, Zenobius,
Theotimus and Drusus (?) MM.
St Euthymius of Nicomedia (303) M.
St Gregory of Spoleto (c.304) M.
St Delphinus of Bordeaux (404) Bp.
St Venerandus of Clermont (423) Bp.
St Tarsilla of Rome (c.581) V.
*St Caranus of Scotland (7th cent.) Bp.
St Irmina of Oehren (708) Abs. O.S.B.
*St Adela of Pfalzel (c.730) W. Abs.
O.S.B.
*St Alberic of Gladbach (10th cent.)
C. O.S.B.
*St Bruno of Ottobeuren (c.1050) C.
O.S.B.

DECEMBER 25.

Christmas Day.
St Eugenia of Rome (c.257) V. M.
St Anastasia of Sirmium (c.304) M.
*St Adalsindis of Hamay (c.715) V.
O.S.B.
*St Alburga of Wilton (c.800) W. O.S.B.
*Bl Matthew of Albano (1134) Card.
Bp. O.S.B.

*St Peter the Venerable (1156) Ab.
O.S.B.
*Bl Fulk of Toulouse (1231) Bp. O.S.B.
Cist.
*Bl Jacopone da Todi (1306) C. O.F.M.

DECEMBER 26.

*St Stephen the Deacon (33) Proto-
martyr.*
St Dionysius (269) Pope.
St Archelaus of Mesopotamia (c.278)
Bp.
St Marinus of Rome (283) M.
St Zeno of Gaza (p.399) Bp.
St Zosimus (418) Pope.
*St Tathai of Wales (5th cent.) H.
St Theodore the Sacristan (6th cent.)
C.
*St Maethlu of Anglesey (6th cent.) C.
*BB Margaret and Ida (p.1150) VV.
O.S.B.
*St Christina of Markgate (1160) H.
O.S.B.
*Bl Daniel of Villiers (late 12th cent.)
C. O.S.B.Cist.
*Bl Paganus of Lecco (1274) M. O.P.
*Bl Andrew Dung (1839) M.

DECEMBER 27.

St John (c.100) Apostle and Evangelist.
St Maximus of Alexandria (282) Bp.
*St Fabiola of Rome (c.400) W.
St Nicarete of Constantinople (c.405) V.
SS Theodore M. and Theophanes Bp.
(c.841 and c.845).
*Bl Hesso of Beinwil (1133) Ab. O.S.B.
*Bl Walto of Wessobrunn (1156) Ab.
O.S.B.
*Bl Adelheidis of Tennenbach (1273) V.
O.S.B.Cist.
*Bl Bonaventure Tolomei (1348) C.
O.P.

DECEMBER 28.

The Holy Innocents (1st cent.) MM.
St Troadius of Pontus (250) M.
SS Eutychius and Domitian (?) MM.

SS Castor, Victor and Rogatian (?)
MM.
SS Indes, Domna, Agapes and Theo-
phila (303) MM.
St Caesarius of Armenia (309) M.
St Domnio of Rome (4th cent.) C.
*SS Romulus and Conindrus (c.450)
Bps.
*St Maughold of Ireland (c.488) Bp.
*St Gowan of Wales (5th cent.) Matron.
St Antony of Lérins (c.520) H.
*Bl Otto of Heidelberg (1344) H. O.S.B.
*Bl Caspar del Bufalo (1837) Founder.

DECEMBER 29.

St David (10th cent. B.C.) King and
Prophet.
St Trophimus of Arles (c.280) Bp.
SS Dominic, Victor, Primian, Lybosus,
Saturninus, Crescentius, Secundus
and Honoratus (?) MM.
SS Callistus, Felix and Boniface (?)
MM.
St Marcellus Akimetes (c.485) Ab.
St Ebrulfus of Ouche (596) Ab.
*St Albert of Gambron (7th cent.) Ab.
O.S.B.
*St Girald of Fontenelle (1031) Ab.
O.S.B.
St Thomas Becket (1170) Bp. M.
*Bl William Howard (1680) M.

DECEMBER 30.

St Liberius of Ravenna (c.200) Bp.
St Eugene of Milan (?) Bp.
SS Sabinus, Exuperantius, Marcellus,
Venustian and Comp. (303) MM.
St Anysia of Salonika (304) M.
St Anysius of Salonika (c.407) Bp.
SS Mansuetus, Severus, Appian,
Donatus, Honorius and Comp.
(c.483) MM.
*St Egwin of Worcester (717) Bp.
O.S.B.
St Raynerius of Aquila (1077) Bp.
*Bl Ralph of Vaucelles (1152) Ab.
O.S.B.Cist.
*Bl Mattia dei Nazarei (1213) Abs.
O.S.B.

*Bl Margaret Colonna (1284) V. Poor Clare.
*Bl Gerard Cagnoli (1345) C. O.F.M.
*Bl John Alcober (1748) M. O.P.

DECEMBER 31.

St Hermes of Rome (c.270) M.
St Columba of Sens (273) V. M.
SS Stephen, Pontian, Attalus, Fabian, Cornelius, Sextus, Flos, Quintian, Minervinus and Simplician (?) MM.
SS Donata, Paulina, Rustica, Nominanda, Serotina, Hilaria and Comp. (?) MM.

SS Sabinian and Potentian (c.300) MM.
St Silvester I (335) Pope.
St Zoticus of Constantinople (c.350) C.
SS Melania the Younger and Pinian (5th cent.).
St Barbatian of Ravenna (5th cent.) C.
*Bl Peter of Subiaco (1003) M. O.S.B.
*St Offa of Benevento (c.1070) Abs. O.S.B.
*Bl Walembert of Cambrai (1141) C. O.S.A.
*Bl Wisinto of Kremsmünster (a.1250) C. O.S.B.
St John Francis Régis (1640) C. S.J.
*Bl Catherine Labouré (1876) V.